SHOWCASE PRESENTS

SUPERMAN

VOLUME THREE

SUPERMAN CREATED BY JERRY SIEGEL AND JOE SHUSTER

Dan DiDio Senior VP-Executive Editor

Mort Weisinger Editor-original series

Bob Harras Editor-collected edition

Robbin Brosterman Senior Art Director

Paul Levitz President & Publisher

Georg Brewer VP-Design & DC Direct Creative

Richard Bruning Senior VP-Creative Director

Patrick Caldon Executive VP-Finance & Operations

Chris Caramalis VP-Finance

John Cunningham VP-Marketing

Terri Cunningham VP-Managing Editor

Alison Gill VP-Manufacturing

Hank Kanalz VP-General Manager, WildStorm

Jim Lee Editorial Director-WildStorm

Paula Lowitt Senior VP-Business & Legal Affairs

MaryEllen McLaughlin VP-Advertising & Custom Publishing

John Nee VP-Business Development

Gregory Noveck Senior VP-Creative Affairs

Sue Pohja VP-Book Trade Sales

Cheryl Rubin Senior VP-Brand Management

Jeff Trojan VP-Business Development, DC Direct

Bob Wayne VP-Sales

Cover illustration by Curt Swan
Cover color by Alex Sinclair
Black-and-white cover reconstruction by Pacific Rim Graphics
Special thanks to Mark Waid for loan of source material

SHOWCASE PRESENTS SUPERMAN VOL. THREE

Published by DC Comics. Cover and compilation copyright © 2007 DC Comics.
All Rights Reserved.

Originally published in single magazine form in ACTION COMICS 279-292,
SUPERMAN ANNUAL 3-4 and SUPERMAN 146-156 ©1961, 1962 DC Comics.
All Rights Reserved. All characters, their distinctive likenesses and related
elements featured in this publication are trademarks of DC Comics.

The stories, characters and incidents featured in this publication are entirely fictional.

DC Comics, 1700 Broadway, New York, NY 10019
A Warner Bros. Entertainment Company
Printed in Canada. First Printing.
ISBN: 1-4012-1271-9
ISBN 13: 978-1-4012-1271-1

TABLE OF CONTENTS

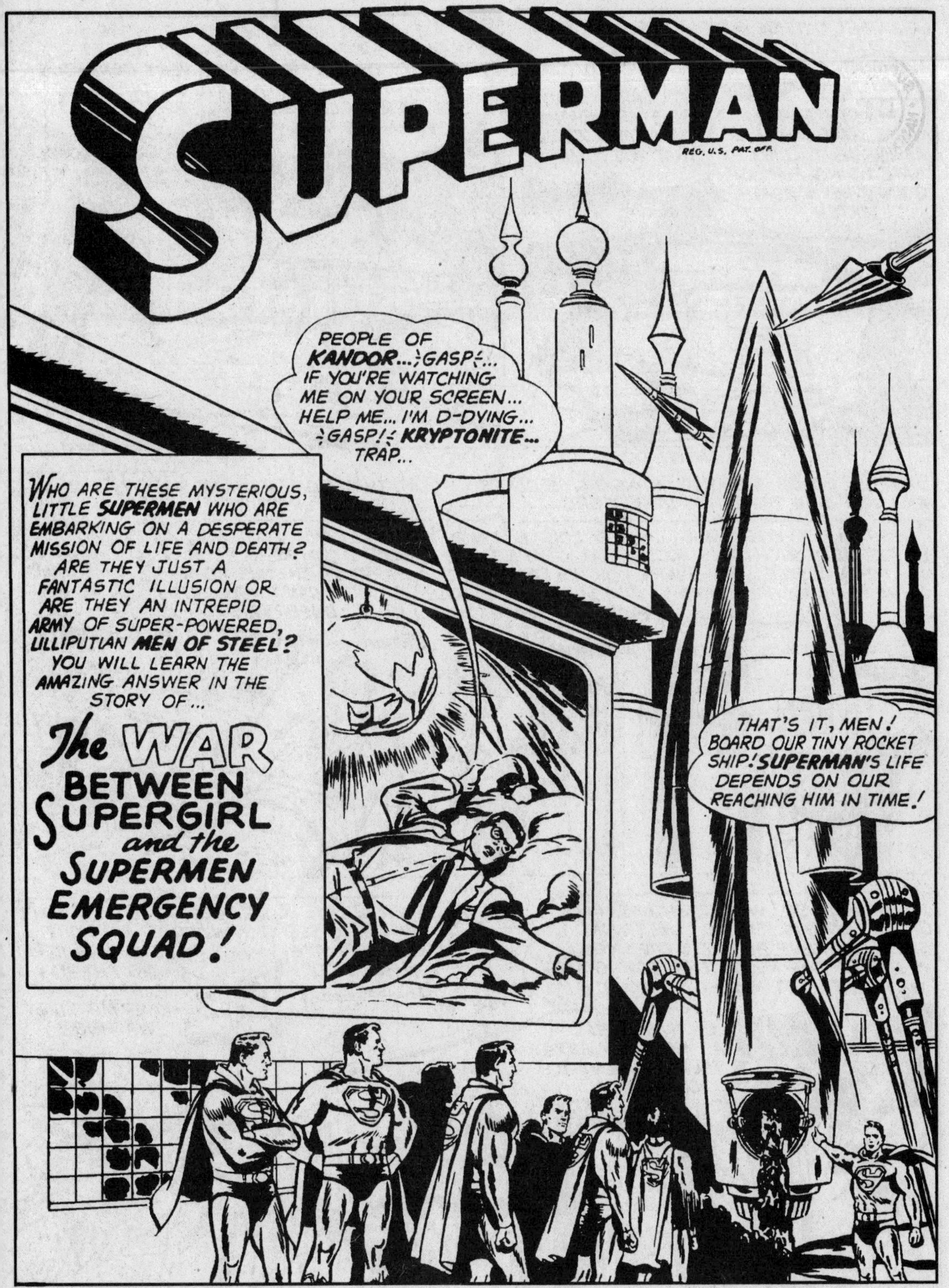
SUPERMAN
REG. U.S. PAT. OFF.
WHO ARE THESE MYSTERIOUS, LITTLE SUPERMEN WHO ARE EMBARKING ON A DESPERATE MISSION OF LIFE AND DEATH? ARE THEY JUST A FANTASTIC ILLUSION OR ARE THEY AN INTREPID ARMY OF SUPER-POWERED, LILLIPUTIAN MEN OF STEEL? YOU WILL LEARN THE AMAZING ANSWER IN THE STORY OF...
The WAR BETWEEN SUPERGIRL and the SUPERMEN EMERGENCY SQUAD!
PEOPLE OF KANDOR... GASP... IF YOU'RE WATCHING ME ON YOUR SCREEN... HELP ME... I'M D-DYING... GASP! KRYPTONITE... TRAP...
THAT'S IT, MEN! BOARD OUR TINY ROCKET SHIP! SUPERMAN'S LIFE DEPENDS ON OUR REACHING HIM IN TIME!

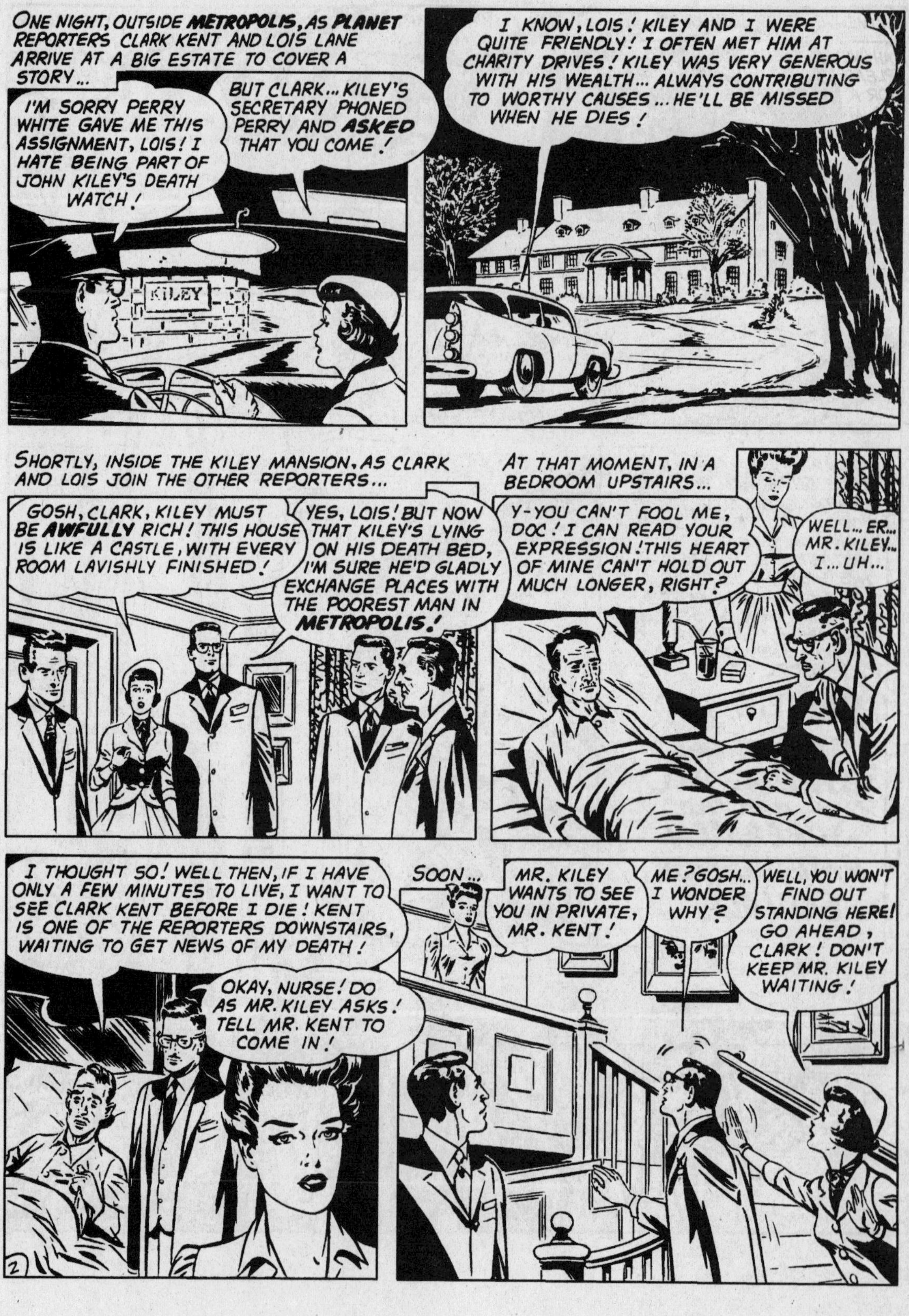
ONE NIGHT, OUTSIDE METROPOLIS, AS PLANET REPORTERS CLARK KENT AND LOIS LANE ARRIVE AT A BIG ESTATE TO COVER A STORY...
I'M SORRY PERRY WHITE GAVE ME THIS ASSIGNMENT, LOIS! I HATE BEING PART OF JOHN KILEY'S DEATH WATCH!
BUT CLARK... KILEY'S SECRETARY PHONED PERRY AND ASKED THAT YOU COME!
KILEY
I KNOW, LOIS! KILEY AND I WERE QUITE FRIENDLY! I OFTEN MET HIM AT CHARITY DRIVES! KILEY WAS VERY GENEROUS WITH HIS WEALTH... ALWAYS CONTRIBUTING TO WORTHY CAUSES... HE'LL BE MISSED WHEN HE DIES!
SHORTLY, INSIDE THE KILEY MANSION, AS CLARK AND LOIS JOIN THE OTHER REPORTERS...
GOSH, CLARK, KILEY MUST BE AWFULLY RICH! THIS HOUSE IS LIKE A CASTLE, WITH EVERY ROOM LAVISHLY FINISHED!
YES, LOIS! BUT NOW THAT KILEY'S LYING ON HIS DEATH BED, I'M SURE HE'D GLADLY EXCHANGE PLACES WITH THE POOREST MAN IN METROPOLIS!
AT THAT MOMENT, IN A BEDROOM UPSTAIRS...
Y-YOU CAN'T FOOL ME, DOC! I CAN READ YOUR EXPRESSION! THIS HEART OF MINE CAN'T HOLD OUT MUCH LONGER, RIGHT?
WELL... ER... MR. KILEY... I... UH...
I THOUGHT SO! WELL THEN, IF I HAVE ONLY A FEW MINUTES TO LIVE, I WANT TO SEE CLARK KENT BEFORE I DIE! KENT IS ONE OF THE REPORTERS DOWNSTAIRS, WAITING TO GET NEWS OF MY DEATH!
OKAY, NURSE! DO AS MR. KILEY ASKS! TELL MR. KENT TO COME IN!
2
SOON...
MR. KILEY WANTS TO SEE YOU IN PRIVATE, MR. KENT!
ME? GOSH... I WONDER WHY?
WELL, YOU WON'T FIND OUT STANDING HERE! GO AHEAD, CLARK! DON'T KEEP MR. KILEY WAITING!

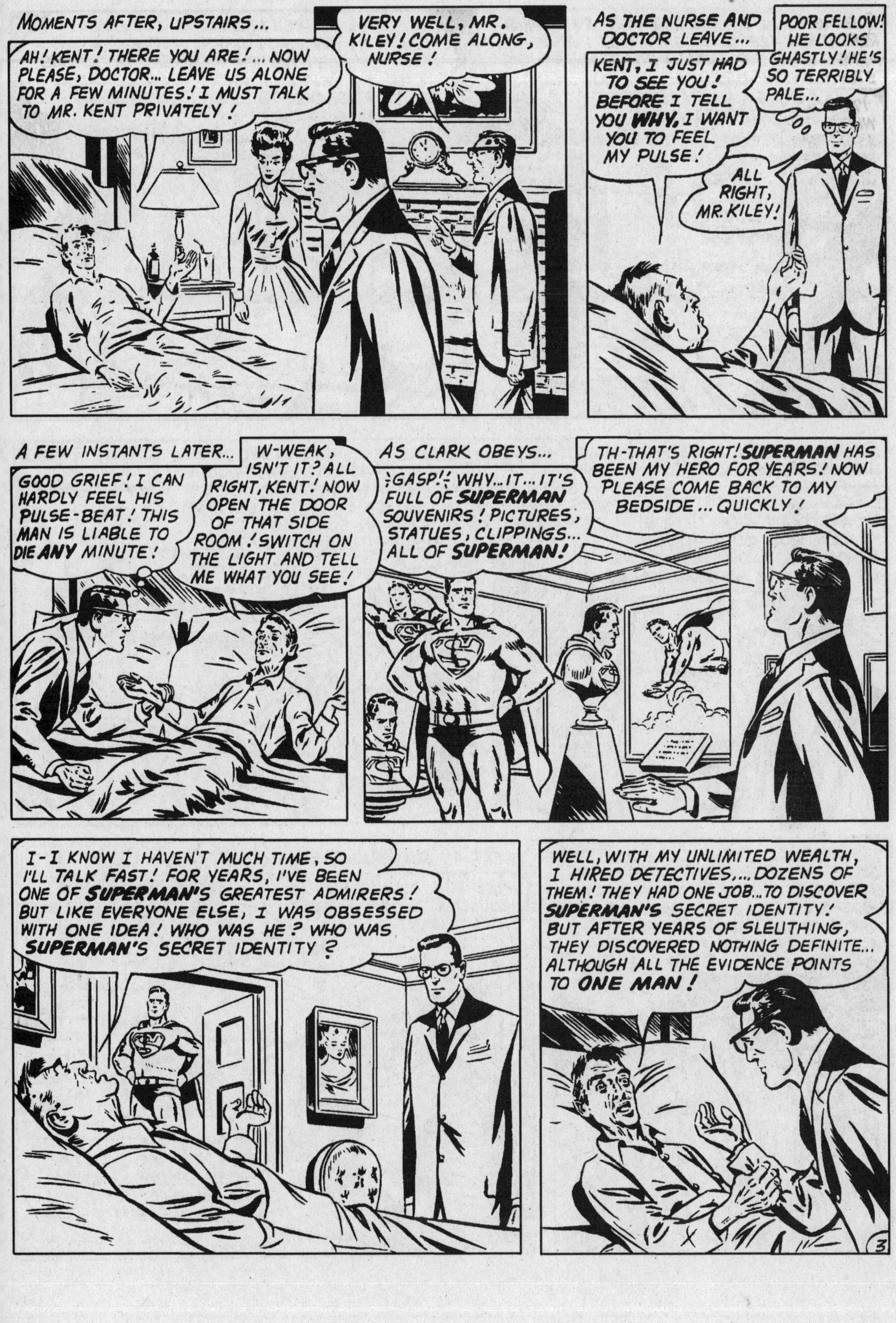

MOMENTS AFTER, UPSTAIRS...
AH! KENT! THERE YOU ARE!... NOW PLEASE, DOCTOR... LEAVE US ALONE FOR A FEW MINUTES! I MUST TALK TO MR. KENT PRIVATELY!
VERY WELL, MR. KILEY! COME ALONG, NURSE!
AS THE NURSE AND DOCTOR LEAVE...
KENT, I JUST HAD TO SEE YOU! BEFORE I TELL YOU WHY, I WANT YOU TO FEEL MY PULSE!
POOR FELLOW! HE LOOKS GHASTLY! HE'S SO TERRIBLY PALE...
ALL RIGHT, MR. KILEY!
A FEW INSTANTS LATER...
GOOD GRIEF! I CAN HARDLY FEEL HIS PULSE-BEAT! THIS MAN IS LIABLE TO DIE ANY MINUTE!
W-WEAK, ISN'T IT? ALL RIGHT, KENT! NOW OPEN THE DOOR OF THAT SIDE ROOM! SWITCH ON THE LIGHT AND TELL ME WHAT YOU SEE!
AS CLARK OBEYS...
¡GASP!¡ WHY... IT... IT'S FULL OF SUPERMAN SOUVENIRS! PICTURES, STATUES, CLIPPINGS... ALL OF SUPERMAN!
TH-THAT'S RIGHT! SUPERMAN HAS BEEN MY HERO FOR YEARS! NOW PLEASE COME BACK TO MY BEDSIDE... QUICKLY!
I-I KNOW I HAVEN'T MUCH TIME, SO I'LL TALK FAST! FOR YEARS, I'VE BEEN ONE OF SUPERMAN'S GREATEST ADMIRERS! BUT LIKE EVERYONE ELSE, I WAS OBSESSED WITH ONE IDEA! WHO WAS HE? WHO WAS SUPERMAN'S SECRET IDENTITY?
WELL, WITH MY UNLIMITED WEALTH, I HIRED DETECTIVES,... DOZENS OF THEM! THEY HAD ONE JOB... TO DISCOVER SUPERMAN'S SECRET IDENTITY! BUT AFTER YEARS OF SLEUTHING, THEY DISCOVERED NOTHING DEFINITE... ALTHOUGH ALL THE EVIDENCE POINTS TO ONE MAN!
3

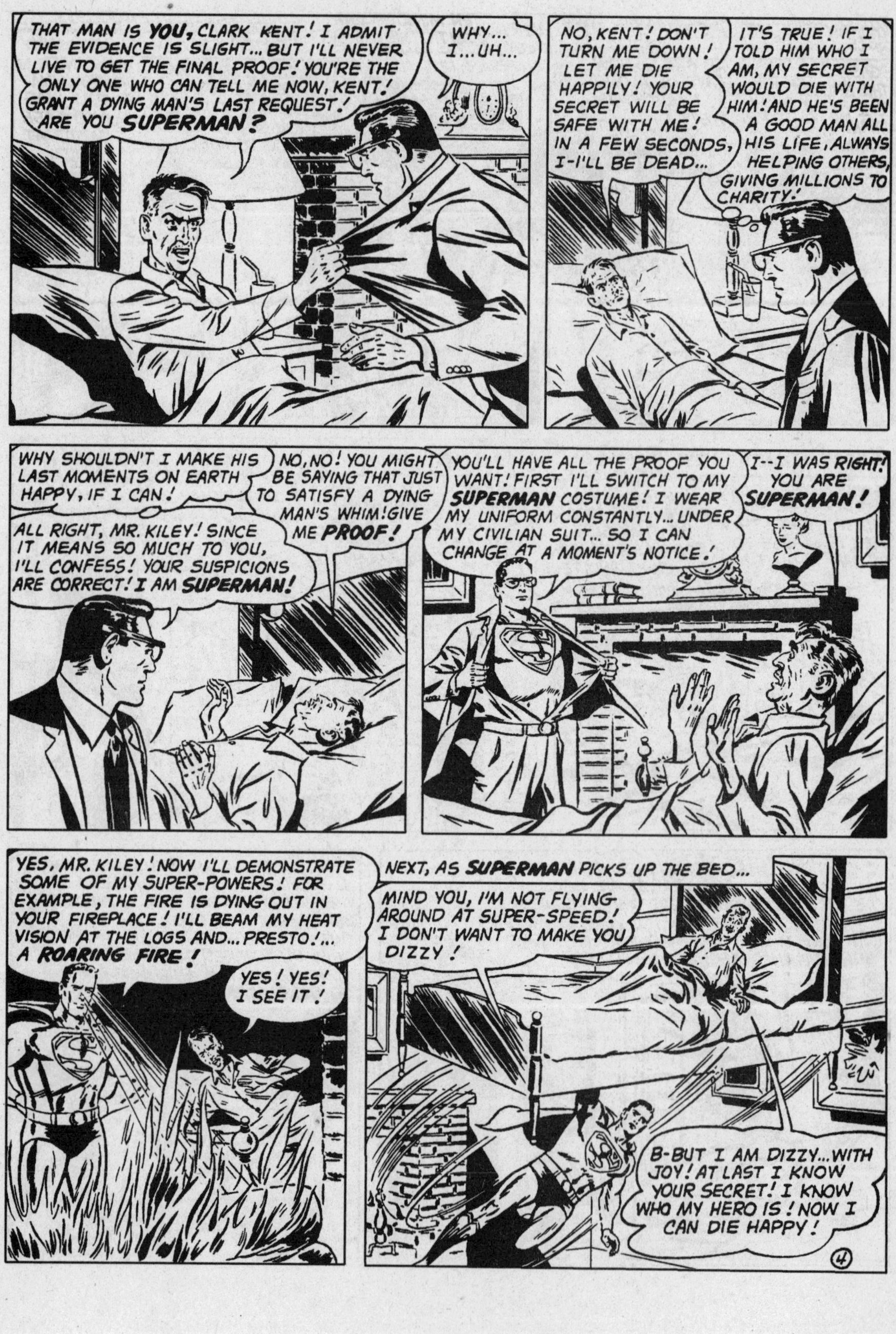
THAT MAN IS YOU, CLARK KENT! I ADMIT THE EVIDENCE IS SLIGHT... BUT I'LL NEVER LIVE TO GET THE FINAL PROOF! YOU'RE THE ONLY ONE WHO CAN TELL ME NOW, KENT! GRANT A DYING MAN'S LAST REQUEST! ARE YOU SUPERMAN?
WHY... I...UH...
NO, KENT! DON'T TURN ME DOWN! LET ME DIE HAPPILY! YOUR SECRET WILL BE SAFE WITH ME! IN A FEW SECONDS, I-I'LL BE DEAD...
IT'S TRUE! IF I TOLD HIM WHO I AM, MY SECRET WOULD DIE WITH HIM! AND HE'S BEEN A GOOD MAN ALL HIS LIFE, ALWAYS HELPING OTHERS, GIVING MILLIONS TO CHARITY!
WHY SHOULDN'T I MAKE HIS LAST MOMENTS ON EARTH HAPPY, IF I CAN!
ALL RIGHT, MR. KILEY! SINCE IT MEANS SO MUCH TO YOU, I'LL CONFESS! YOUR SUSPICIONS ARE CORRECT! I AM SUPERMAN!
NO, NO! YOU MIGHT BE SAYING THAT JUST TO SATISFY A DYING MAN'S WHIM! GIVE ME PROOF!
YOU'LL HAVE ALL THE PROOF YOU WANT! FIRST I'LL SWITCH TO MY SUPERMAN COSTUME! I WEAR MY UNIFORM CONSTANTLY... UNDER MY CIVILIAN SUIT... SO I CAN CHANGE AT A MOMENT'S NOTICE!
I--I WAS RIGHT! YOU ARE SUPERMAN!
YES, MR. KILEY! NOW I'LL DEMONSTRATE SOME OF MY SUPER-POWERS! FOR EXAMPLE, THE FIRE IS DYING OUT IN YOUR FIREPLACE! I'LL BEAM MY HEAT VISION AT THE LOGS AND... PRESTO!... A ROARING FIRE!
YES! YES! I SEE IT!
NEXT, AS SUPERMAN PICKS UP THE BED...
MIND YOU, I'M NOT FLYING AROUND AT SUPER-SPEED! I DON'T WANT TO MAKE YOU DIZZY!
B-BUT I AM DIZZY... WITH JOY! AT LAST I KNOW YOUR SECRET! I KNOW WHO MY HERO IS! NOW I CAN DIE HAPPY!
4

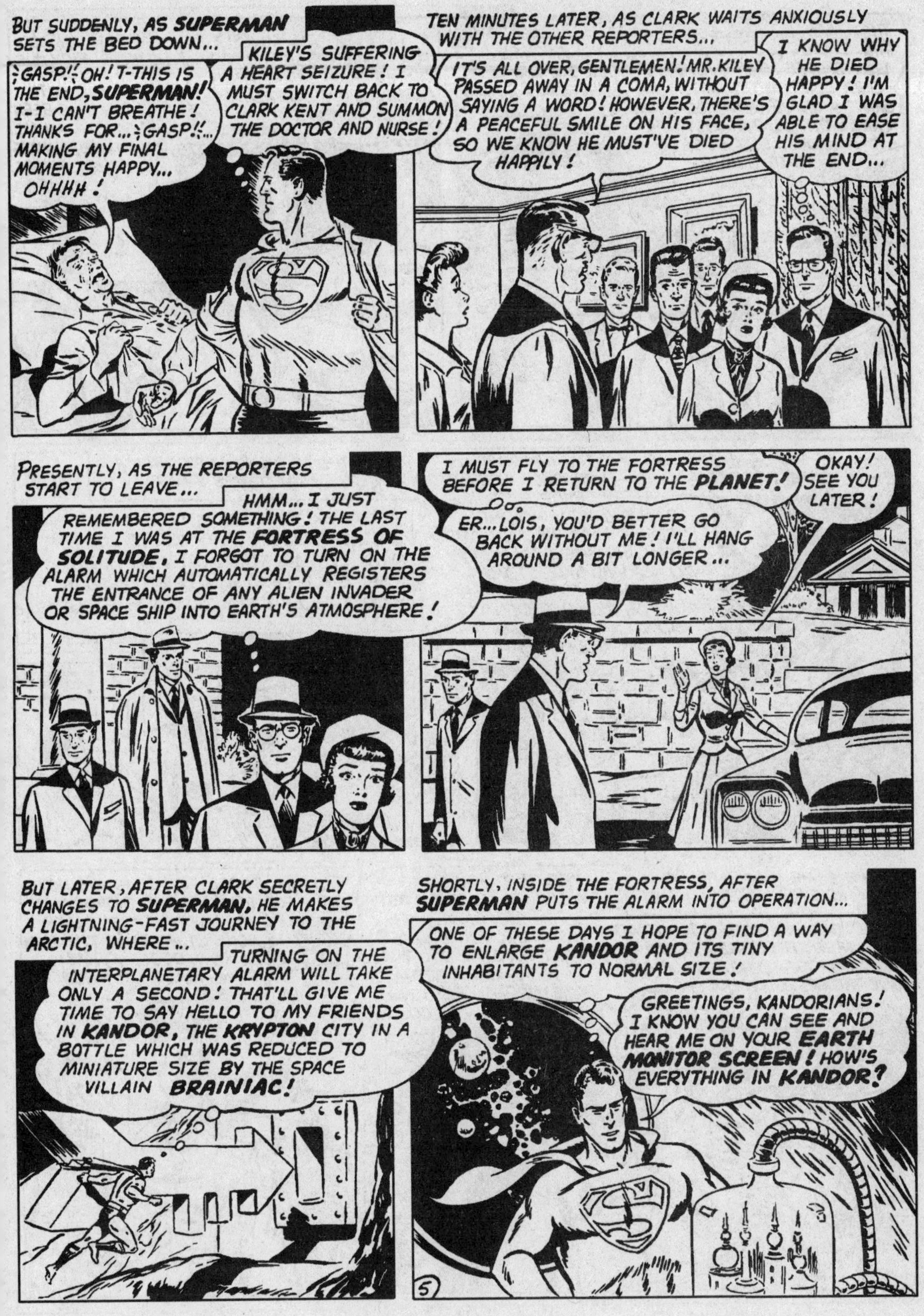
BUT SUDDENLY, AS SUPERMAN SETS THE BED DOWN...
;GASP!; OH! T-THIS IS THE END, SUPERMAN! I-I CAN'T BREATHE! THANKS FOR...;GASP!;... MAKING MY FINAL MOMENTS HAPPY... OHHHH!
KILEY'S SUFFERING A HEART SEIZURE! I MUST SWITCH BACK TO CLARK KENT AND SUMMON THE DOCTOR AND NURSE!
TEN MINUTES LATER, AS CLARK WAITS ANXIOUSLY WITH THE OTHER REPORTERS...
IT'S ALL OVER, GENTLEMEN! MR. KILEY PASSED AWAY IN A COMA, WITHOUT SAYING A WORD! HOWEVER, THERE'S A PEACEFUL SMILE ON HIS FACE, SO WE KNOW HE MUST'VE DIED HAPPILY!
I KNOW WHY HE DIED HAPPY! I'M GLAD I WAS ABLE TO EASE HIS MIND AT THE END...
PRESENTLY, AS THE REPORTERS START TO LEAVE...
HMM... I JUST REMEMBERED SOMETHING! THE LAST TIME I WAS AT THE FORTRESS OF SOLITUDE, I FORGOT TO TURN ON THE ALARM WHICH AUTOMATICALLY REGISTERS THE ENTRANCE OF ANY ALIEN INVADER OR SPACE SHIP INTO EARTH'S ATMOSPHERE!
I MUST FLY TO THE FORTRESS BEFORE I RETURN TO THE PLANET!
ER... LOIS, YOU'D BETTER GO BACK WITHOUT ME! I'LL HANG AROUND A BIT LONGER...
OKAY! SEE YOU LATER!
BUT LATER, AFTER CLARK SECRETLY CHANGES TO SUPERMAN, HE MAKES A LIGHTNING-FAST JOURNEY TO THE ARCTIC, WHERE...
TURNING ON THE INTERPLANETARY ALARM WILL TAKE ONLY A SECOND! THAT'LL GIVE ME TIME TO SAY HELLO TO MY FRIENDS IN KANDOR, THE KRYPTON CITY IN A BOTTLE WHICH WAS REDUCED TO MINIATURE SIZE BY THE SPACE VILLAIN BRAINIAC!
SHORTLY, INSIDE THE FORTRESS, AFTER SUPERMAN PUTS THE ALARM INTO OPERATION...
ONE OF THESE DAYS I HOPE TO FIND A WAY TO ENLARGE KANDOR AND ITS TINY INHABITANTS TO NORMAL SIZE!
GREETINGS, KANDORIANS! I KNOW YOU CAN SEE AND HEAR ME ON YOUR EARTH MONITOR SCREEN! HOW'S EVERYTHING IN KANDOR?
5

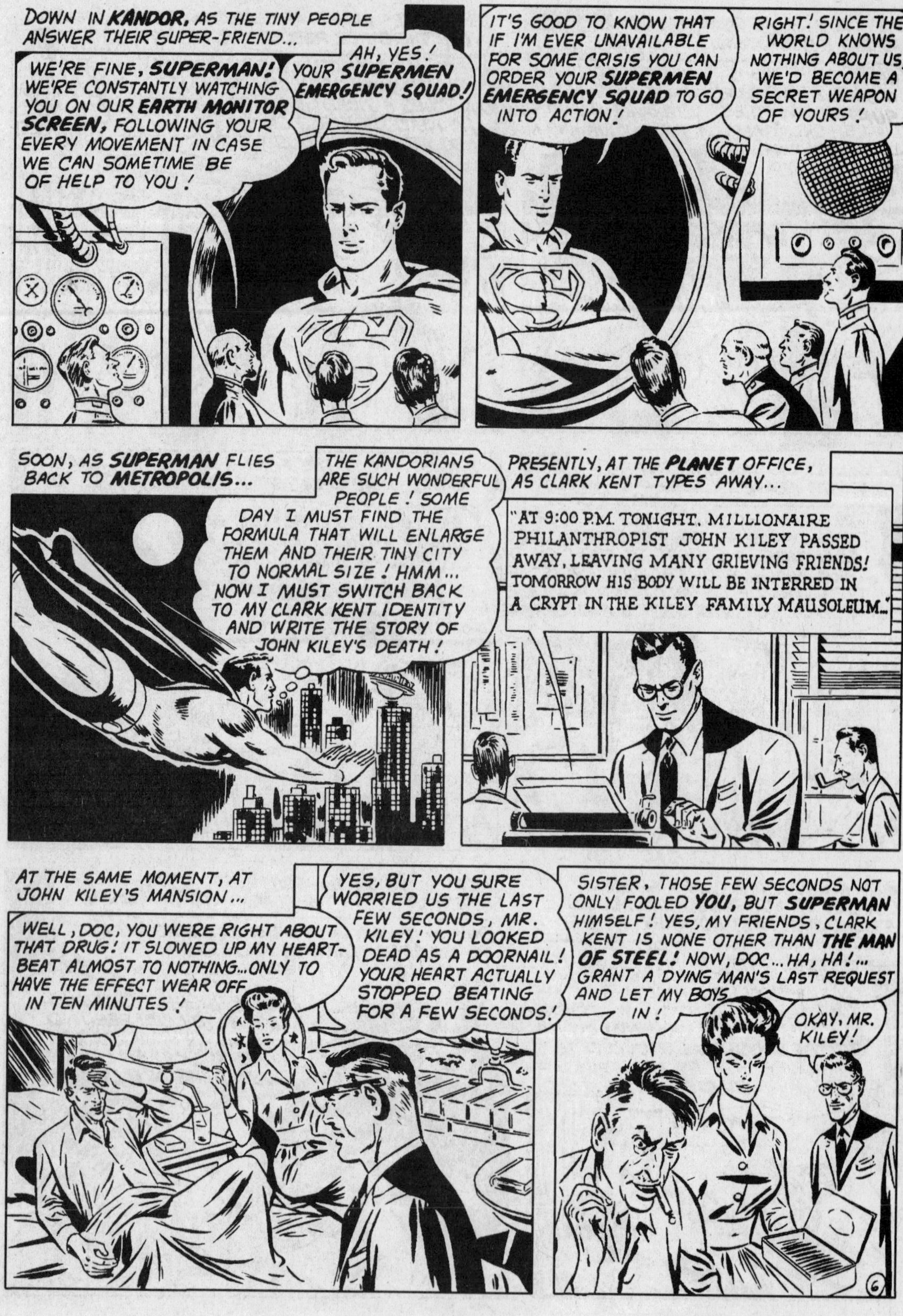
DOWN IN KANDOR, AS THE TINY PEOPLE ANSWER THEIR SUPER-FRIEND...
WE'RE FINE, SUPERMAN! WE'RE CONSTANTLY WATCHING YOU ON OUR EARTH MONITOR SCREEN, FOLLOWING YOUR EVERY MOVEMENT IN CASE WE CAN SOMETIME BE OF HELP TO YOU!
AH, YES! YOUR SUPERMEN EMERGENCY SQUAD!
IT'S GOOD TO KNOW THAT IF I'M EVER UNAVAILABLE FOR SOME CRISIS YOU CAN ORDER YOUR SUPERMEN EMERGENCY SQUAD TO GO INTO ACTION!
RIGHT! SINCE THE WORLD KNOWS NOTHING ABOUT US, WE'D BECOME A SECRET WEAPON OF YOURS!
SOON, AS SUPERMAN FLIES BACK TO METROPOLIS...
THE KANDORIANS ARE SUCH WONDERFUL PEOPLE! SOME DAY I MUST FIND THE FORMULA THAT WILL ENLARGE THEM AND THEIR TINY CITY TO NORMAL SIZE! HMM... NOW I MUST SWITCH BACK TO MY CLARK KENT IDENTITY AND WRITE THE STORY OF JOHN KILEY'S DEATH!
PRESENTLY, AT THE PLANET OFFICE, AS CLARK KENT TYPES AWAY...
"AT 9:00 P.M. TONIGHT, MILLIONAIRE PHILANTHROPIST JOHN KILEY PASSED AWAY, LEAVING MANY GRIEVING FRIENDS! TOMORROW HIS BODY WILL BE INTERRED IN A CRYPT IN THE KILEY FAMILY MAUSOLEUM..."
AT THE SAME MOMENT, AT JOHN KILEY'S MANSION...
WELL, DOC, YOU WERE RIGHT ABOUT THAT DRUG! IT SLOWED UP MY HEART-BEAT ALMOST TO NOTHING...ONLY TO HAVE THE EFFECT WEAR OFF IN TEN MINUTES!
YES, BUT YOU SURE WORRIED US THE LAST FEW SECONDS, MR. KILEY! YOU LOOKED DEAD AS A DOORNAIL! YOUR HEART ACTUALLY STOPPED BEATING FOR A FEW SECONDS!
SISTER, THOSE FEW SECONDS NOT ONLY FOOLED YOU, BUT SUPERMAN HIMSELF! YES, MY FRIENDS, CLARK KENT IS NONE OTHER THAN THE MAN OF STEEL! NOW, DOC... HA, HA!... GRANT A DYING MAN'S LAST REQUEST AND LET MY BOYS IN!
OKAY, MR. KILEY!
6

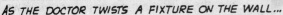

AS THE DOCTOR TWISTS A FIXTURE ON THE WALL...

WELL, BOSS? HOW'D IT GO? IS KENT *SUPERMAN*?

HE SURE *IS!* MY DEATH-BED ACT FOOLED KENT COMPLETELY! HE WAS SO SURE I WAS DYING THAT HE FIGURED HE WAS IN NO DANGER IF HE ADMITTED HE WAS *SUPERMAN!*

THE FOOL NEVER REALIZED THAT HIS ACT OF KINDNESS WAS ONLY DIGGING HIS *OWN* GRAVE! YOU SHOULD'VE SEEN THIS SUPER-SAP IN ACTION! SWITCHING TO HIS *SUPERMAN* COSTUME! FLYING AROUND THE ROOM! WHAT A PERFORMANCE!

DON'T BE SURE, MR. KILEY! MAYBE IT WAS AN HALLUCINATION!

I WARNED YOU ABOUT THIS DRUG! WHEN YOU INHALE ITS FUMES, IT NOT ONLY CAUSES SYMPTOMS THAT CAN FOOL PEOPLE INTO THINKING YOU'RE DYING, BUT IT ALSO PRODUCES *ILLUSIONS* AND *HALLUCINATIONS!*

BAH! THIS WAS NO HALLUCINATION!

CLARK KENT IS *SUPERMAN*...OR I'M NOT THE SECRET HEAD OF THE *ANTI-SUPERMAN GANG!* NOW...I KNOW WHAT I'M TALKING ABOUT! FOR YEARS, I'VE FOOLED EVERYBODY, INCLUDING *SUPERMAN*, THAT I'M A GOOD GUY WHO GIVES MONEY TO CHARITY!

WELL, TONIGHT I "DIED" TO KILL *SUPERMAN*... BY LEARNING HIS SECRET IDENTITY! TOMORROW YOU'LL SEE WHETHER I HAD AN HALLUCINATION... WHEN YOU WATCH CLARK KENT DIE IN A *KRYPTONITE* TRAP!

THE NEXT DAY, AT JOHN KILEY'S FUNERAL...

WHAT A HOAX! *METROPOLIS'* FINEST CITIZENS HAVE COME TO PAY THEIR RESPECTS TO THE DEAD! IF THEY ONLY KNEW THERE'S A DUMMY IN THAT COFFIN! AND THAT AFTER HE KILLS *SUPERMAN*, KILEY WILL START A NEW LIFE AS A SOUTH AMERICAN MILLIONAIRE!

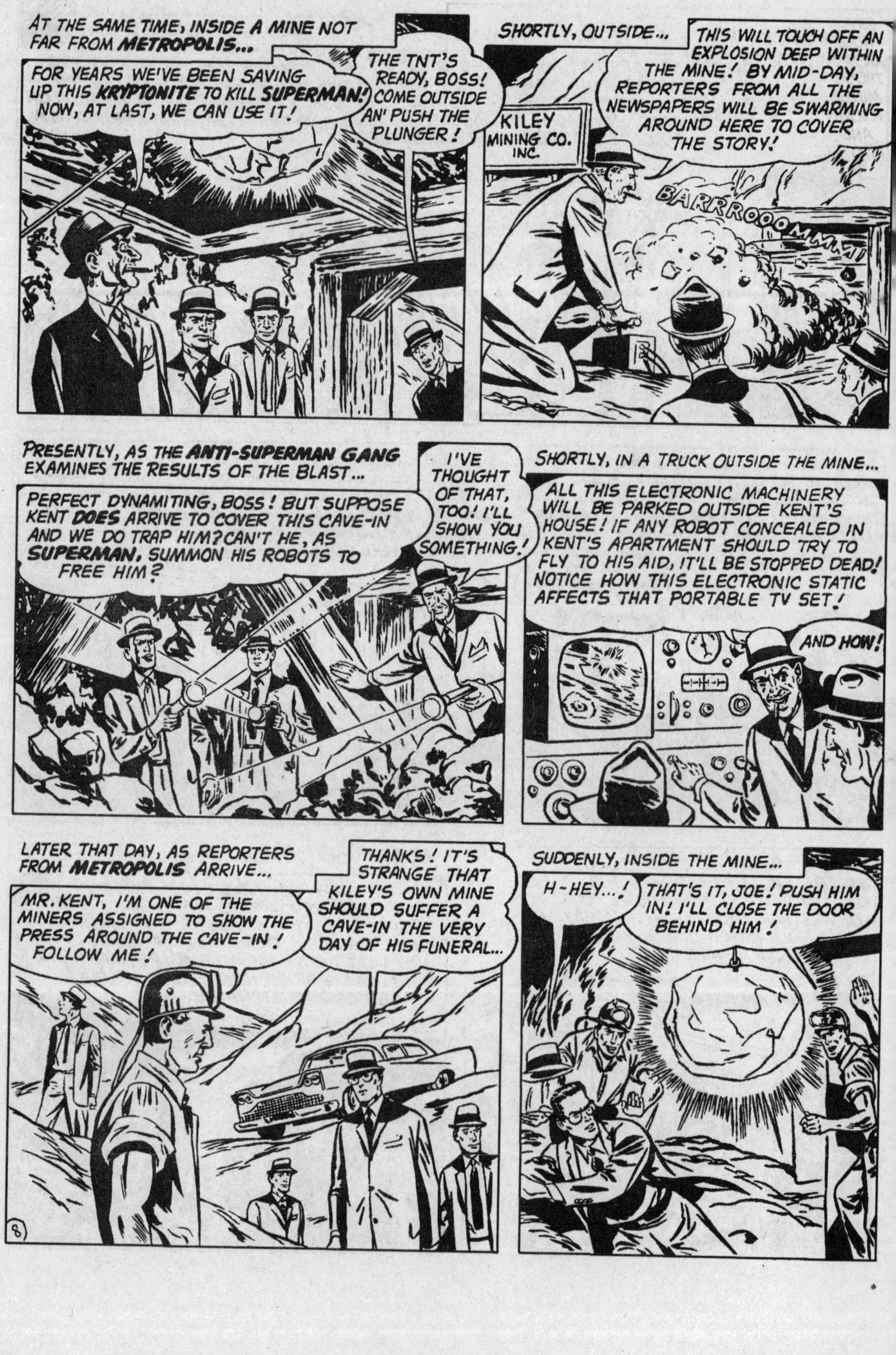
AT THE SAME TIME, INSIDE A MINE NOT FAR FROM METROPOLIS...
FOR YEARS WE'VE BEEN SAVING UP THIS KRYPTONITE TO KILL SUPERMAN! NOW, AT LAST, WE CAN USE IT!
THE TNT'S READY, BOSS! COME OUTSIDE AN' PUSH THE PLUNGER!
SHORTLY, OUTSIDE...
THIS WILL TOUCH OFF AN EXPLOSION DEEP WITHIN THE MINE! BY MID-DAY, REPORTERS FROM ALL THE NEWSPAPERS WILL BE SWARMING AROUND HERE TO COVER THE STORY!
KILEY MINING CO. INC.
BARRROOOMMM!
PRESENTLY, AS THE ANTI-SUPERMAN GANG EXAMINES THE RESULTS OF THE BLAST...
PERFECT DYNAMITING, BOSS! BUT SUPPOSE KENT DOES ARRIVE TO COVER THIS CAVE-IN AND WE DO TRAP HIM? CAN'T HE, AS SUPERMAN, SUMMON HIS ROBOTS TO FREE HIM?
I'VE THOUGHT OF THAT, TOO! I'LL SHOW YOU SOMETHING!
SHORTLY, IN A TRUCK OUTSIDE THE MINE...
ALL THIS ELECTRONIC MACHINERY WILL BE PARKED OUTSIDE KENT'S HOUSE! IF ANY ROBOT CONCEALED IN KENT'S APARTMENT SHOULD TRY TO FLY TO HIS AID, IT'LL BE STOPPED DEAD! NOTICE HOW THIS ELECTRONIC STATIC AFFECTS THAT PORTABLE TV SET!
AND HOW!
LATER THAT DAY, AS REPORTERS FROM METROPOLIS ARRIVE...
MR. KENT, I'M ONE OF THE MINERS ASSIGNED TO SHOW THE PRESS AROUND THE CAVE-IN! FOLLOW ME!
THANKS! IT'S STRANGE THAT KILEY'S OWN MINE SHOULD SUFFER A CAVE-IN THE VERY DAY OF HIS FUNERAL...
8
SUDDENLY, INSIDE THE MINE...
H-HEY...!
THAT'S IT, JOE! PUSH HIM IN! I'LL CLOSE THE DOOR BEHIND HIM!

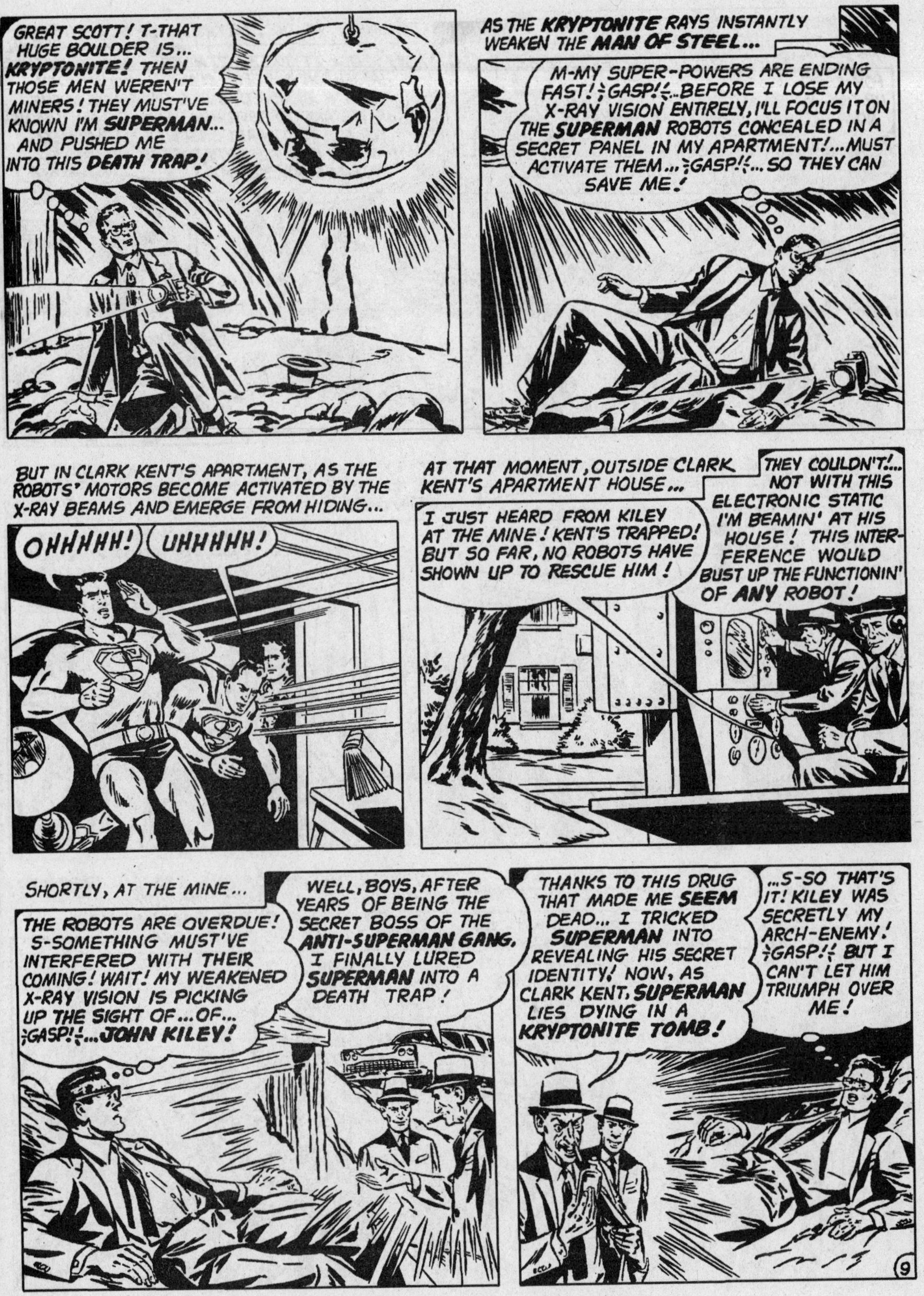
GREAT SCOTT! T-THAT HUGE BOULDER IS... KRYPTONITE! THEN THOSE MEN WEREN'T MINERS! THEY MUST'VE KNOWN I'M SUPERMAN... AND PUSHED ME INTO THIS DEATH TRAP!
AS THE KRYPTONITE RAYS INSTANTLY WEAKEN THE MAN OF STEEL...
M-MY SUPER-POWERS ARE ENDING FAST! GASP! ..BEFORE I LOSE MY X-RAY VISION ENTIRELY, I'LL FOCUS IT ON THE SUPERMAN ROBOTS CONCEALED IN A SECRET PANEL IN MY APARTMENT!...MUST ACTIVATE THEM... GASP!... SO THEY CAN SAVE ME!
BUT IN CLARK KENT'S APARTMENT, AS THE ROBOTS' MOTORS BECOME ACTIVATED BY THE X-RAY BEAMS AND EMERGE FROM HIDING...
OHHHHH!
UHHHHH!
AT THAT MOMENT, OUTSIDE CLARK KENT'S APARTMENT HOUSE...
I JUST HEARD FROM KILEY AT THE MINE! KENT'S TRAPPED! BUT SO FAR, NO ROBOTS HAVE SHOWN UP TO RESCUE HIM!
THEY COULDN'T!... NOT WITH THIS ELECTRONIC STATIC I'M BEAMIN' AT HIS HOUSE! THIS INTERFERENCE WOULD BUST UP THE FUNCTIONIN' OF ANY ROBOT!
SHORTLY, AT THE MINE...
THE ROBOTS ARE OVERDUE! S-SOMETHING MUST'VE INTERFERED WITH THEIR COMING! WAIT! MY WEAKENED X-RAY VISION IS PICKING UP THE SIGHT OF...OF... GASP!...JOHN KILEY!
WELL, BOYS, AFTER YEARS OF BEING THE SECRET BOSS OF THE ANTI-SUPERMAN GANG, I FINALLY LURED SUPERMAN INTO A DEATH TRAP!
THANKS TO THIS DRUG THAT MADE ME SEEM DEAD... I TRICKED SUPERMAN INTO REVEALING HIS SECRET IDENTITY! NOW, AS CLARK KENT, SUPERMAN LIES DYING IN A KRYPTONITE TOMB!
...S-SO THAT'S IT! KILEY WAS SECRETLY MY ARCH-ENEMY! GASP! BUT I CAN'T LET HIM TRIUMPH OVER ME!
9

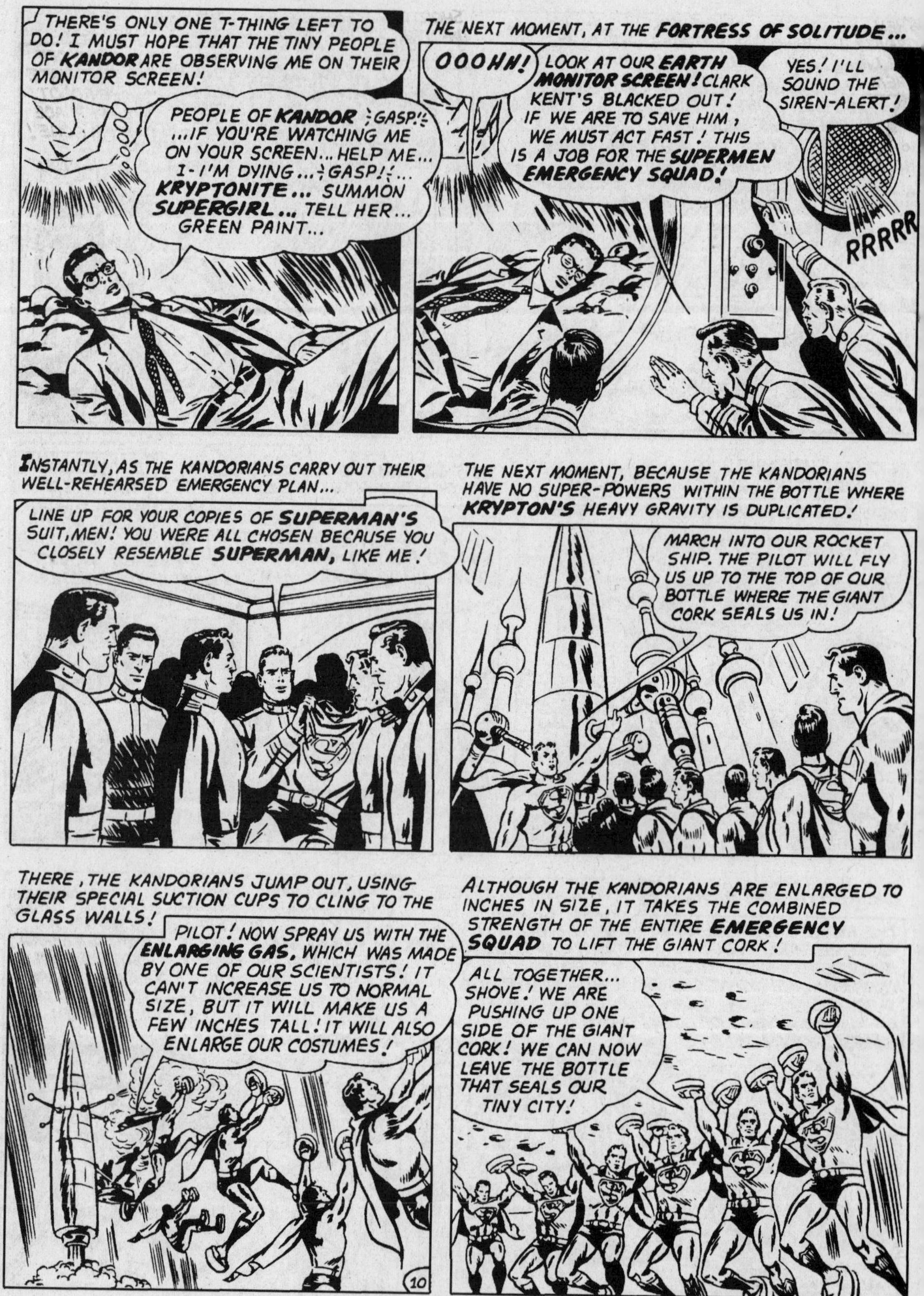
THERE'S ONLY ONE T-THING LEFT TO DO! I MUST HOPE THAT THE TINY PEOPLE OF KANDOR ARE OBSERVING ME ON THEIR MONITOR SCREEN!
PEOPLE OF KANDOR ...GASP!... ...IF YOU'RE WATCHING ME ON YOUR SCREEN... HELP ME... I-I'M DYING... GASP!... KRYPTONITE... SUMMON SUPERGIRL... TELL HER... GREEN PAINT...
THE NEXT MOMENT, AT THE FORTRESS OF SOLITUDE...
OOOHH!
LOOK AT OUR EARTH MONITOR SCREEN! CLARK KENT'S BLACKED OUT! IF WE ARE TO SAVE HIM, WE MUST ACT FAST! THIS IS A JOB FOR THE SUPERMEN EMERGENCY SQUAD!
YES! I'LL SOUND THE SIREN-ALERT!
RRRRR
INSTANTLY, AS THE KANDORIANS CARRY OUT THEIR WELL-REHEARSED EMERGENCY PLAN...
LINE UP FOR YOUR COPIES OF SUPERMAN'S SUIT, MEN! YOU WERE ALL CHOSEN BECAUSE YOU CLOSELY RESEMBLE SUPERMAN, LIKE ME!
THE NEXT MOMENT, BECAUSE THE KANDORIANS HAVE NO SUPER-POWERS WITHIN THE BOTTLE WHERE KRYPTON'S HEAVY GRAVITY IS DUPLICATED!
MARCH INTO OUR ROCKET SHIP. THE PILOT WILL FLY US UP TO THE TOP OF OUR BOTTLE WHERE THE GIANT CORK SEALS US IN!
THERE, THE KANDORIANS JUMP OUT, USING THEIR SPECIAL SUCTION CUPS TO CLING TO THE GLASS WALLS!
PILOT! NOW SPRAY US WITH THE ENLARGING GAS, WHICH WAS MADE BY ONE OF OUR SCIENTISTS! IT CAN'T INCREASE US TO NORMAL SIZE, BUT IT WILL MAKE US A FEW INCHES TALL! IT WILL ALSO ENLARGE OUR COSTUMES!
10
ALTHOUGH THE KANDORIANS ARE ENLARGED TO INCHES IN SIZE, IT TAKES THE COMBINED STRENGTH OF THE ENTIRE EMERGENCY SQUAD TO LIFT THE GIANT CORK!
ALL TOGETHER... SHOVE! WE ARE PUSHING UP ONE SIDE OF THE GIANT CORK! WE CAN NOW LEAVE THE BOTTLE THAT SEALS OUR TINY CITY!

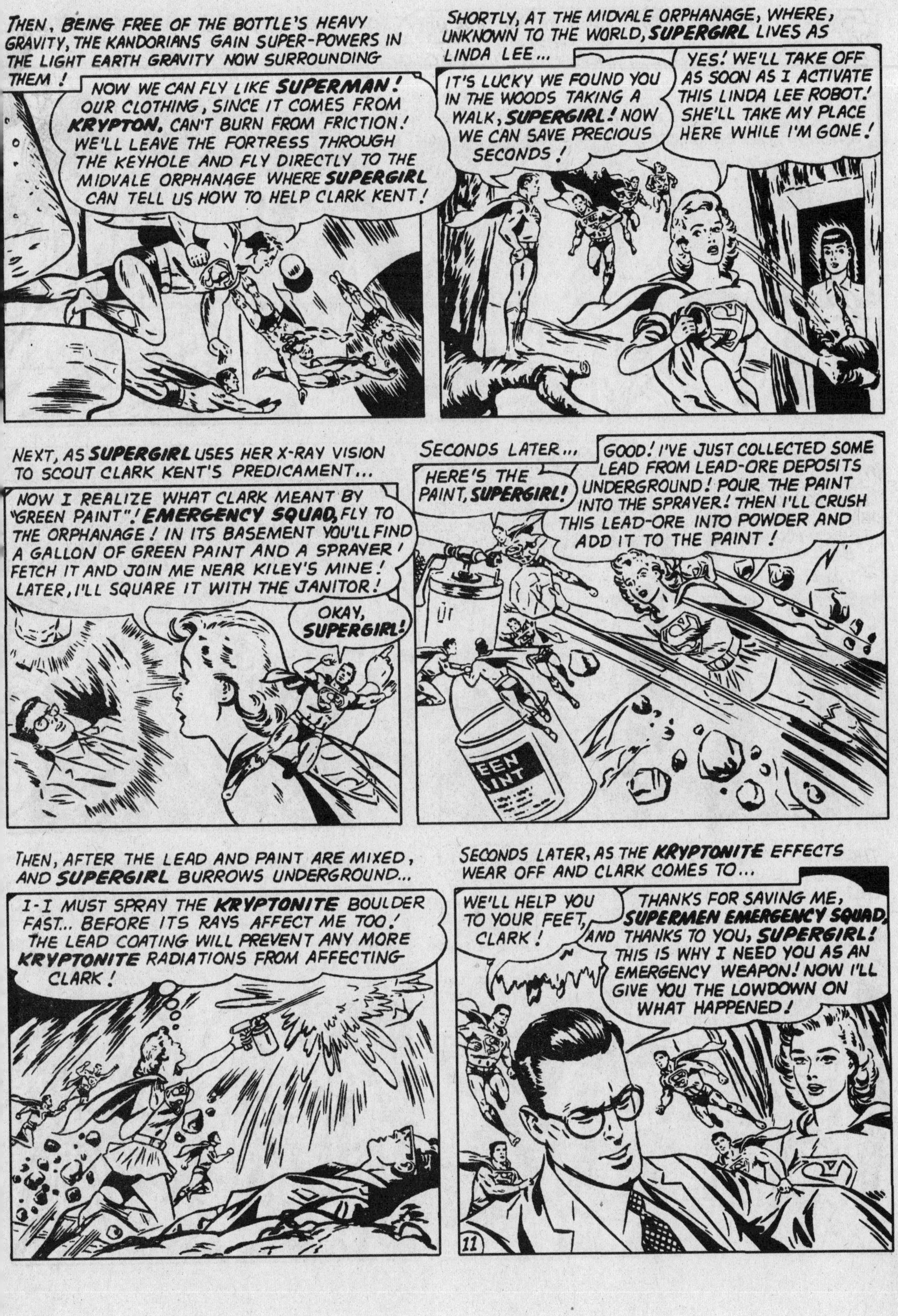
THEN, BEING FREE OF THE BOTTLE'S HEAVY GRAVITY, THE KANDORIANS GAIN SUPER-POWERS IN THE LIGHT EARTH GRAVITY NOW SURROUNDING THEM!
NOW WE CAN FLY LIKE SUPERMAN! OUR CLOTHING, SINCE IT COMES FROM KRYPTON, CAN'T BURN FROM FRICTION! WE'LL LEAVE THE FORTRESS THROUGH THE KEYHOLE AND FLY DIRECTLY TO THE MIDVALE ORPHANAGE WHERE SUPERGIRL CAN TELL US HOW TO HELP CLARK KENT!
SHORTLY, AT THE MIDVALE ORPHANAGE, WHERE, UNKNOWN TO THE WORLD, SUPERGIRL LIVES AS LINDA LEE...
IT'S LUCKY WE FOUND YOU IN THE WOODS TAKING A WALK, SUPERGIRL! NOW WE CAN SAVE PRECIOUS SECONDS!
YES! WE'LL TAKE OFF AS SOON AS I ACTIVATE THIS LINDA LEE ROBOT! SHE'LL TAKE MY PLACE HERE WHILE I'M GONE!
NEXT, AS SUPERGIRL USES HER X-RAY VISION TO SCOUT CLARK KENT'S PREDICAMENT...
NOW I REALIZE WHAT CLARK MEANT BY "GREEN PAINT"! EMERGENCY SQUAD, FLY TO THE ORPHANAGE! IN ITS BASEMENT YOU'LL FIND A GALLON OF GREEN PAINT AND A SPRAYER! FETCH IT AND JOIN ME NEAR KILEY'S MINE! LATER, I'LL SQUARE IT WITH THE JANITOR!
OKAY, SUPERGIRL!
SECONDS LATER...
HERE'S THE PAINT, SUPERGIRL!
GOOD! I'VE JUST COLLECTED SOME LEAD FROM LEAD-ORE DEPOSITS UNDERGROUND! POUR THE PAINT INTO THE SPRAYER! THEN I'LL CRUSH THIS LEAD-ORE INTO POWDER AND ADD IT TO THE PAINT!
THEN, AFTER THE LEAD AND PAINT ARE MIXED, AND SUPERGIRL BURROWS UNDERGROUND...
I-I MUST SPRAY THE KRYPTONITE BOULDER FAST... BEFORE ITS RAYS AFFECT ME TOO! THE LEAD COATING WILL PREVENT ANY MORE KRYPTONITE RADIATIONS FROM AFFECTING CLARK!
SECONDS LATER, AS THE KRYPTONITE EFFECTS WEAR OFF AND CLARK COMES TO...
WE'LL HELP YOU TO YOUR FEET, CLARK!
THANKS FOR SAVING ME, SUPERMEN EMERGENCY SQUAD, AND THANKS TO YOU, SUPERGIRL! THIS IS WHY I NEED YOU AS AN EMERGENCY WEAPON! NOW I'LL GIVE YOU THE LOWDOWN ON WHAT HAPPENED!
11

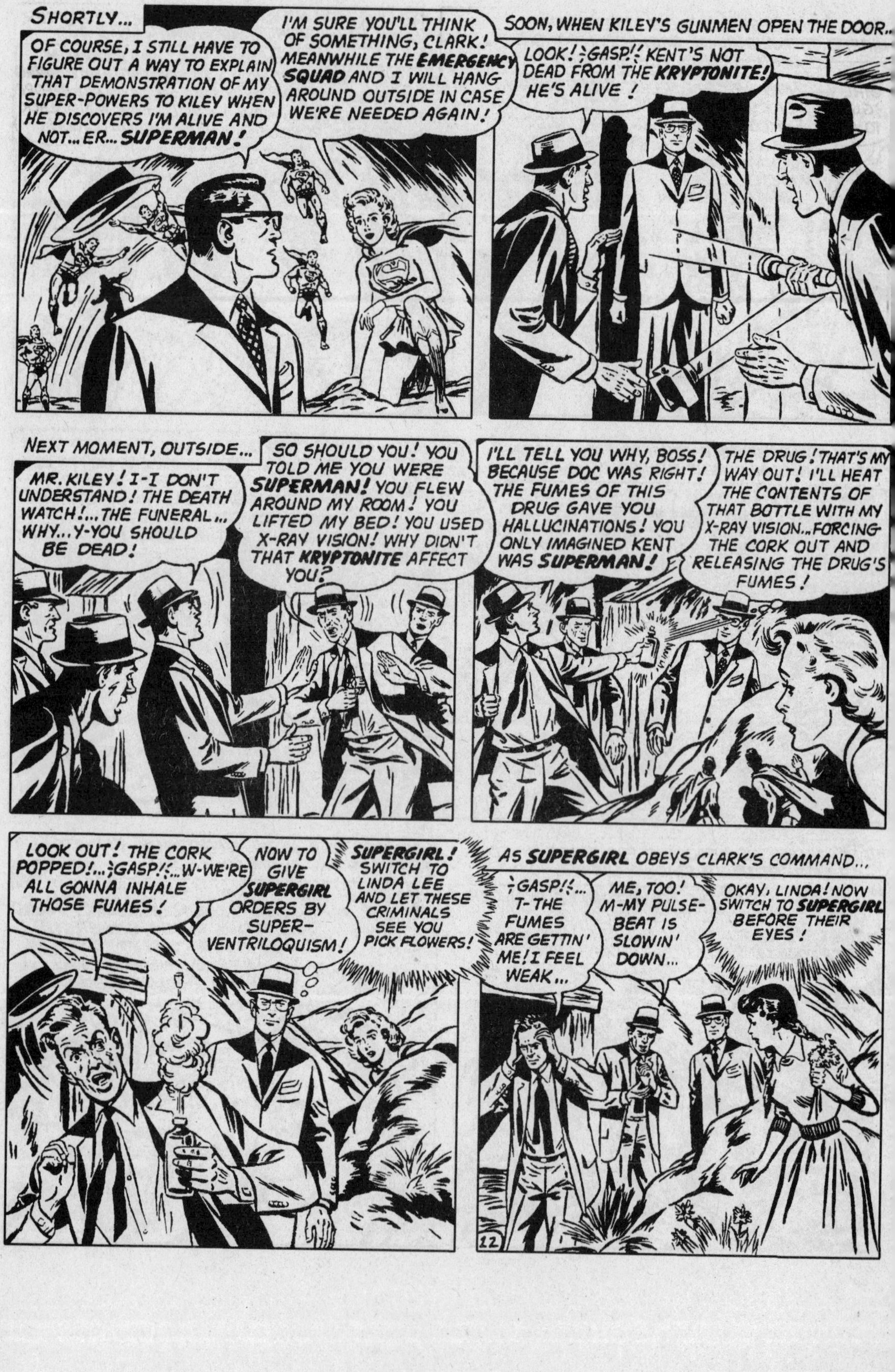
SHORTLY...
OF COURSE, I STILL HAVE TO FIGURE OUT A WAY TO EXPLAIN THAT DEMONSTRATION OF MY SUPER-POWERS TO KILEY WHEN HE DISCOVERS I'M ALIVE AND NOT... ER... SUPERMAN!
I'M SURE YOU'LL THINK OF SOMETHING, CLARK! MEANWHILE THE EMERGENCY SQUAD AND I WILL HANG AROUND OUTSIDE IN CASE WE'RE NEEDED AGAIN!
SOON, WHEN KILEY'S GUNMEN OPEN THE DOOR...
LOOK! ¿GASP!¿ KENT'S NOT DEAD FROM THE KRYPTONITE! HE'S ALIVE!
NEXT MOMENT, OUTSIDE...
MR. KILEY! I-I DON'T UNDERSTAND! THE DEATH WATCH!... THE FUNERAL... WHY... Y-YOU SHOULD BE DEAD!
SO SHOULD YOU! YOU TOLD ME YOU WERE SUPERMAN! YOU FLEW AROUND MY ROOM! YOU LIFTED MY BED! YOU USED X-RAY VISION! WHY DIDN'T THAT KRYPTONITE AFFECT YOU?
I'LL TELL YOU WHY, BOSS! BECAUSE DOC WAS RIGHT! THE FUMES OF THIS DRUG GAVE YOU HALLUCINATIONS! YOU ONLY IMAGINED KENT WAS SUPERMAN!
THE DRUG! THAT'S MY WAY OUT! I'LL HEAT THE CONTENTS OF THAT BOTTLE WITH MY X-RAY VISION... FORCING THE CORK OUT AND RELEASING THE DRUG'S FUMES!
LOOK OUT! THE CORK POPPED!... ¿GASP!¿... W-WE'RE ALL GONNA INHALE THOSE FUMES!
NOW TO GIVE SUPERGIRL ORDERS BY SUPER-VENTRILOQUISM!
SUPERGIRL! SWITCH TO LINDA LEE AND LET THESE CRIMINALS SEE YOU PICK FLOWERS!
AS SUPERGIRL OBEYS CLARK'S COMMAND...
¿GASP!¿... T-THE FUMES ARE GETTIN' ME! I FEEL WEAK...
ME, TOO! M-MY PULSE-BEAT IS SLOWIN' DOWN...
OKAY, LINDA! NOW SWITCH TO SUPERGIRL BEFORE THEIR EYES!
12

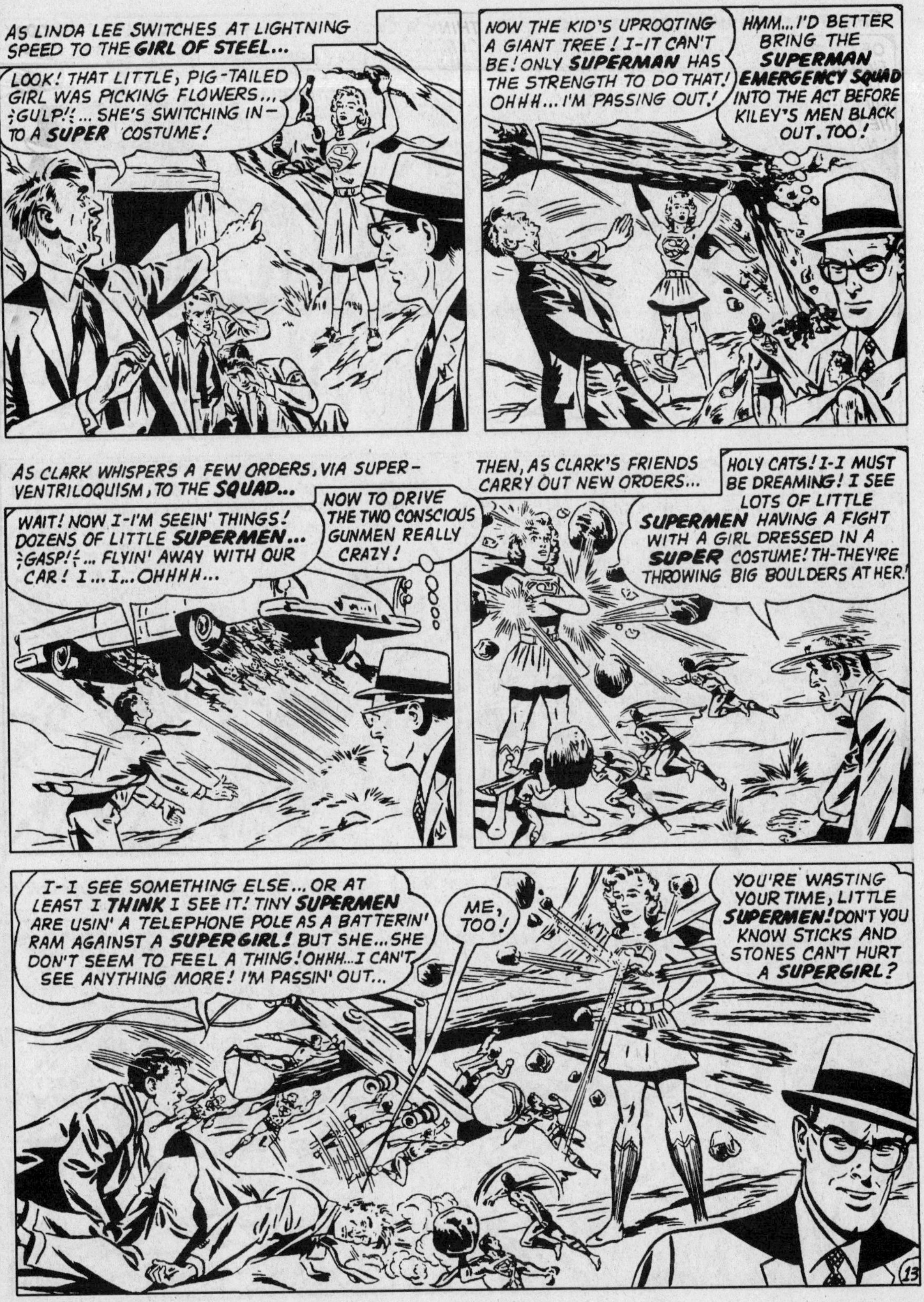
AS LINDA LEE SWITCHES AT LIGHTNING SPEED TO THE GIRL OF STEEL...
LOOK! THAT LITTLE, PIG-TAILED GIRL WAS PICKING FLOWERS... GULP! ... SHE'S SWITCHING INTO A SUPER COSTUME!
NOW THE KID'S UPROOTING A GIANT TREE! I-IT CAN'T BE! ONLY SUPERMAN HAS THE STRENGTH TO DO THAT! OHHH... I'M PASSING OUT!
HMM... I'D BETTER BRING THE SUPERMAN EMERGENCY SQUAD INTO THE ACT BEFORE KILEY'S MEN BLACK OUT, TOO!
AS CLARK WHISPERS A FEW ORDERS, VIA SUPER-VENTRILOQUISM, TO THE SQUAD...
WAIT! NOW I-I'M SEEIN' THINGS! DOZENS OF LITTLE SUPERMEN... GASP! ... FLYIN' AWAY WITH OUR CAR! I... I... OHHHH...
NOW TO DRIVE THE TWO CONSCIOUS GUNMEN REALLY CRAZY!
THEN, AS CLARK'S FRIENDS CARRY OUT NEW ORDERS...
HOLY CATS! I-I MUST BE DREAMING! I SEE LOTS OF LITTLE SUPERMEN HAVING A FIGHT WITH A GIRL DRESSED IN A SUPER COSTUME! TH-THEY'RE THROWING BIG BOULDERS AT HER!
I-I SEE SOMETHING ELSE... OR AT LEAST I THINK I SEE IT! TINY SUPERMEN ARE USIN' A TELEPHONE POLE AS A BATTERIN' RAM AGAINST A SUPERGIRL! BUT SHE... SHE DON'T SEEM TO FEEL A THING! OHHH... I CAN'T SEE ANYTHING MORE! I'M PASSIN' OUT...
ME, TOO!
YOU'RE WASTING YOUR TIME, LITTLE SUPERMEN! DON'T YOU KNOW STICKS AND STONES CAN'T HURT A SUPERGIRL?
13

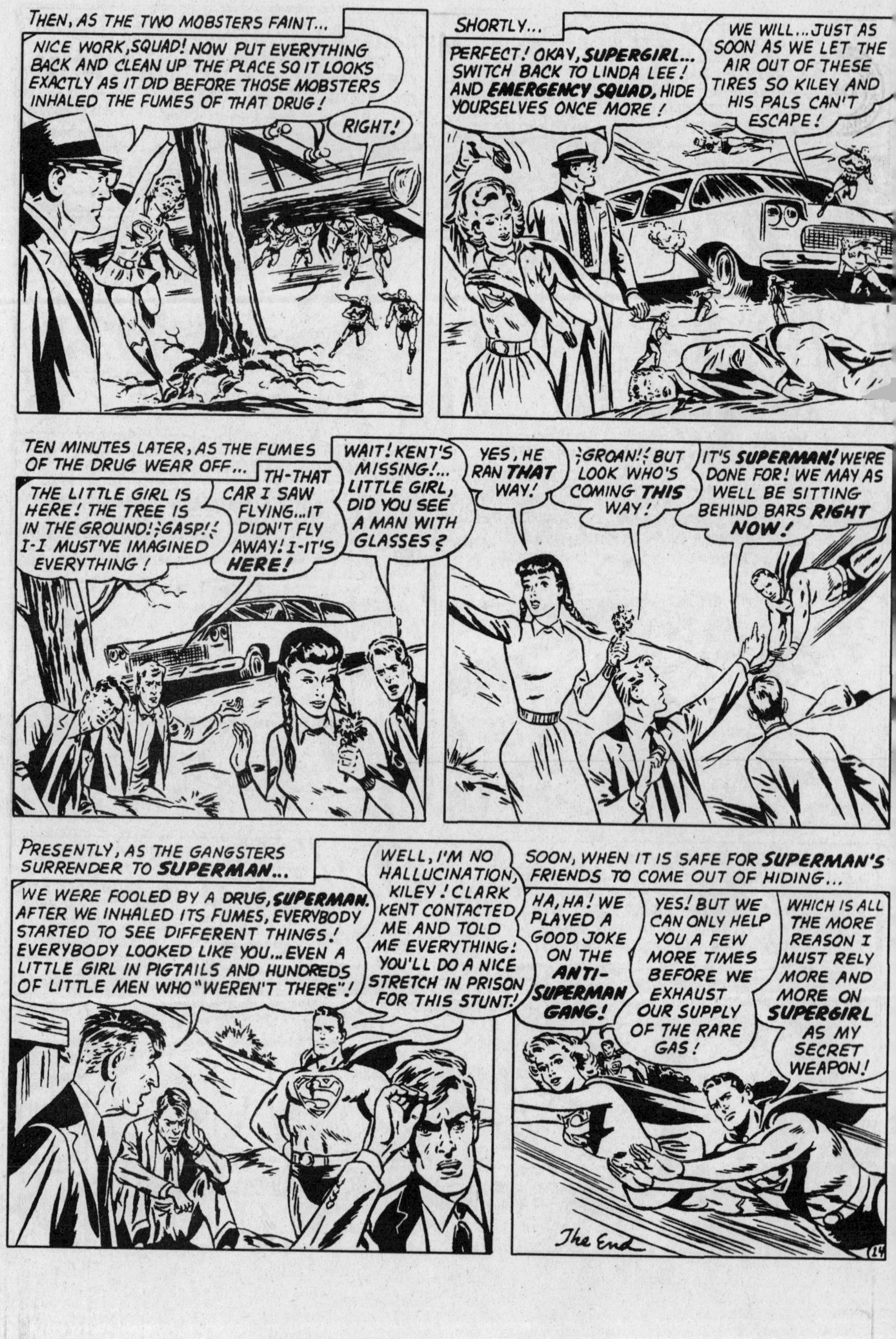
THEN, AS THE TWO MOBSTERS FAINT...
NICE WORK, SQUAD! NOW PUT EVERYTHING BACK AND CLEAN UP THE PLACE SO IT LOOKS EXACTLY AS IT DID BEFORE THOSE MOBSTERS INHALED THE FUMES OF THAT DRUG!
RIGHT!
SHORTLY...
PERFECT! OKAY, SUPERGIRL... SWITCH BACK TO LINDA LEE! AND EMERGENCY SQUAD, HIDE YOURSELVES ONCE MORE!
WE WILL... JUST AS SOON AS WE LET THE AIR OUT OF THESE TIRES SO KILEY AND HIS PALS CAN'T ESCAPE!
TEN MINUTES LATER, AS THE FUMES OF THE DRUG WEAR OFF...
THE LITTLE GIRL IS HERE! THE TREE IS IN THE GROUND! ¡GASP!¡ I-I MUST'VE IMAGINED EVERYTHING!
TH-THAT CAR I SAW FLYING... IT DIDN'T FLY AWAY! I-IT'S HERE!
WAIT! KENT'S MISSING!... LITTLE GIRL, DID YOU SEE A MAN WITH GLASSES?
YES, HE RAN THAT WAY!
¡GROAN!¡ BUT LOOK WHO'S COMING THIS WAY!
IT'S SUPERMAN! WE'RE DONE FOR! WE MAY AS WELL BE SITTING BEHIND BARS RIGHT NOW!
PRESENTLY, AS THE GANGSTERS SURRENDER TO SUPERMAN...
WE WERE FOOLED BY A DRUG, SUPERMAN. AFTER WE INHALED ITS FUMES, EVERYBODY STARTED TO SEE DIFFERENT THINGS! EVERYBODY LOOKED LIKE YOU... EVEN A LITTLE GIRL IN PIGTAILS AND HUNDREDS OF LITTLE MEN WHO "WEREN'T THERE"!
WELL, I'M NO HALLUCINATION, KILEY! CLARK KENT CONTACTED ME AND TOLD ME EVERYTHING! YOU'LL DO A NICE STRETCH IN PRISON FOR THIS STUNT!
SOON, WHEN IT IS SAFE FOR SUPERMAN'S FRIENDS TO COME OUT OF HIDING...
HA, HA! WE PLAYED A GOOD JOKE ON THE ANTI-SUPERMAN GANG!
YES! BUT WE CAN ONLY HELP YOU A FEW MORE TIMES BEFORE WE EXHAUST OUR SUPPLY OF THE RARE GAS!
WHICH IS ALL THE MORE REASON I MUST RELY MORE AND MORE ON SUPERGIRL AS MY SECRET WEAPON!
The End
14

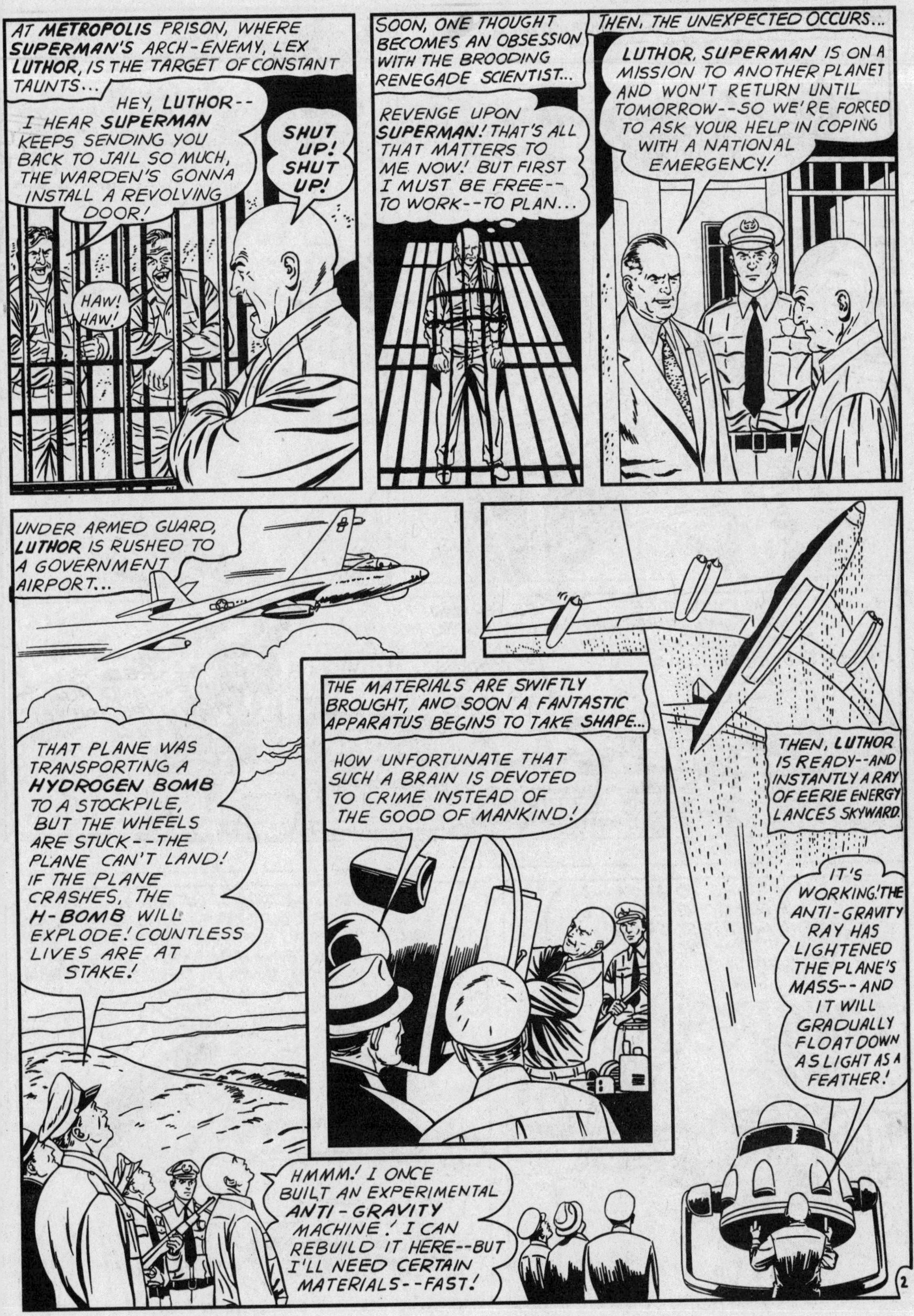
AT METROPOLIS PRISON, WHERE SUPERMAN'S ARCH-ENEMY, LEX LUTHOR, IS THE TARGET OF CONSTANT TAUNTS...
HEY, LUTHOR--I HEAR SUPERMAN KEEPS SENDING YOU BACK TO JAIL SO MUCH, THE WARDEN'S GONNA INSTALL A REVOLVING DOOR!
HAW! HAW!
SHUT UP! SHUT UP!
SOON, ONE THOUGHT BECOMES AN OBSESSION WITH THE BROODING RENEGADE SCIENTIST...
REVENGE UPON SUPERMAN! THAT'S ALL THAT MATTERS TO ME NOW! BUT FIRST I MUST BE FREE--TO WORK--TO PLAN...
THEN, THE UNEXPECTED OCCURS...
LUTHOR, SUPERMAN IS ON A MISSION TO ANOTHER PLANET AND WON'T RETURN UNTIL TOMORROW--SO WE'RE FORCED TO ASK YOUR HELP IN COPING WITH A NATIONAL EMERGENCY!
UNDER ARMED GUARD, LUTHOR IS RUSHED TO A GOVERNMENT AIRPORT...
THAT PLANE WAS TRANSPORTING A HYDROGEN BOMB TO A STOCKPILE, BUT THE WHEELS ARE STUCK--THE PLANE CAN'T LAND! IF THE PLANE CRASHES, THE H-BOMB WILL EXPLODE! COUNTLESS LIVES ARE AT STAKE!
HMMM! I ONCE BUILT AN EXPERIMENTAL ANTI-GRAVITY MACHINE! I CAN REBUILD IT HERE--BUT I'LL NEED CERTAIN MATERIALS--FAST!
THE MATERIALS ARE SWIFTLY BROUGHT, AND SOON A FANTASTIC APPARATUS BEGINS TO TAKE SHAPE...
HOW UNFORTUNATE THAT SUCH A BRAIN IS DEVOTED TO CRIME INSTEAD OF THE GOOD OF MANKIND!
THEN, LUTHOR IS READY--AND INSTANTLY A RAY OF EERIE ENERGY LANCES SKYWARD.
IT'S WORKING! THE ANTI-GRAVITY RAY HAS LIGHTENED THE PLANE'S MASS--AND IT WILL GRADUALLY FLOAT DOWN AS LIGHT AS A FEATHER!
2

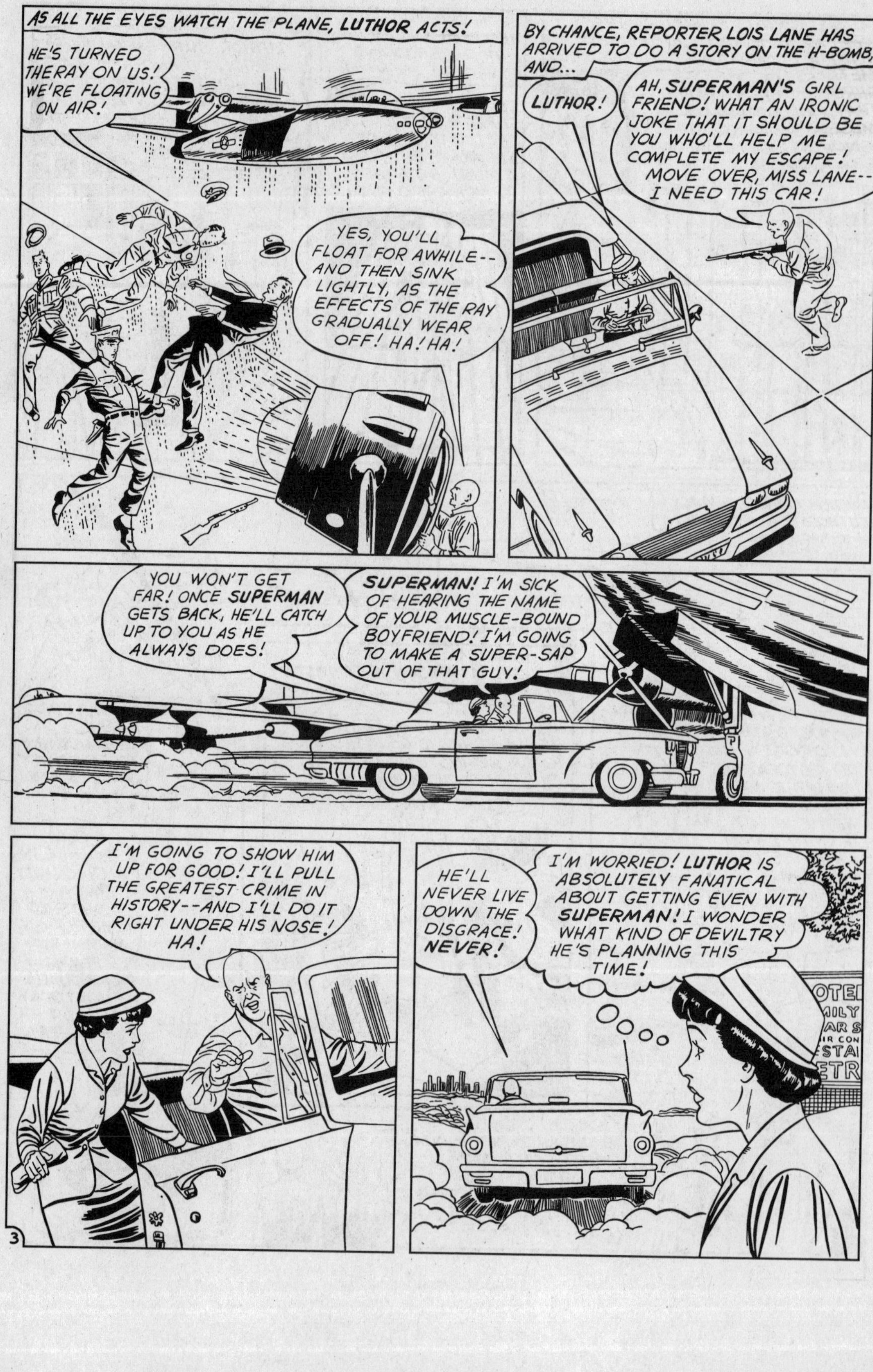
AS ALL THE EYES WATCH THE PLANE, LUTHOR ACTS!
HE'S TURNED THE RAY ON US! WE'RE FLOATING ON AIR!
YES, YOU'LL FLOAT FOR AWHILE--AND THEN SINK LIGHTLY, AS THE EFFECTS OF THE RAY GRADUALLY WEAR OFF! HA! HA!
BY CHANCE, REPORTER LOIS LANE HAS ARRIVED TO DO A STORY ON THE H-BOMB, AND...
LUTHOR!
AH, SUPERMAN'S GIRL FRIEND! WHAT AN IRONIC JOKE THAT IT SHOULD BE YOU WHO'LL HELP ME COMPLETE MY ESCAPE! MOVE OVER, MISS LANE--I NEED THIS CAR!
YOU WON'T GET FAR! ONCE SUPERMAN GETS BACK, HE'LL CATCH UP TO YOU AS HE ALWAYS DOES!
SUPERMAN! I'M SICK OF HEARING THE NAME OF YOUR MUSCLE-BOUND BOYFRIEND! I'M GOING TO MAKE A SUPER-SAP OUT OF THAT GUY!
I'M GOING TO SHOW HIM UP FOR GOOD! I'LL PULL THE GREATEST CRIME IN HISTORY--AND I'LL DO IT RIGHT UNDER HIS NOSE! HA!
3
HE'LL NEVER LIVE DOWN THE DISGRACE! NEVER!
I'M WORRIED! LUTHOR IS ABSOLUTELY FANATICAL ABOUT GETTING EVEN WITH SUPERMAN! I WONDER WHAT KIND OF DEVILTRY HE'S PLANNING THIS TIME!

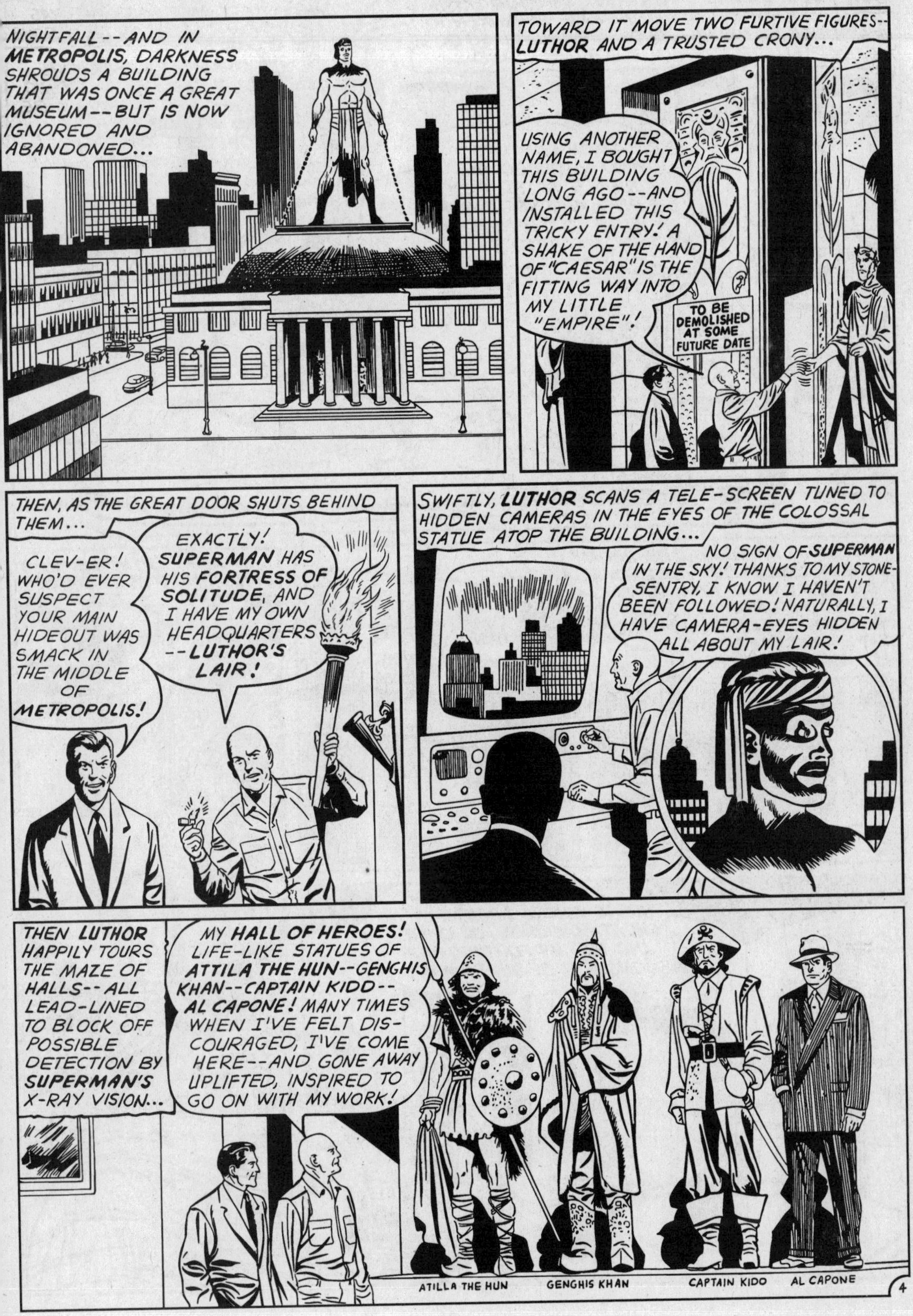
NIGHTFALL--AND IN METROPOLIS, DARKNESS SHROUDS A BUILDING THAT WAS ONCE A GREAT MUSEUM--BUT IS NOW IGNORED AND ABANDONED...
TOWARD IT MOVE TWO FURTIVE FIGURES--LUTHOR AND A TRUSTED CRONY...
USING ANOTHER NAME, I BOUGHT THIS BUILDING LONG AGO--AND INSTALLED THIS TRICKY ENTRY! A SHAKE OF THE HAND OF "CAESAR" IS THE FITTING WAY INTO MY LITTLE "EMPIRE"!
TO BE DEMOLISHED AT SOME FUTURE DATE
THEN, AS THE GREAT DOOR SHUTS BEHIND THEM...
CLEV-ER! WHO'D EVER SUSPECT YOUR MAIN HIDEOUT WAS SMACK IN THE MIDDLE OF METROPOLIS!
EXACTLY! SUPERMAN HAS HIS FORTRESS OF SOLITUDE, AND I HAVE MY OWN HEADQUARTERS--LUTHOR'S LAIR!
SWIFTLY, LUTHOR SCANS A TELE-SCREEN TUNED TO HIDDEN CAMERAS IN THE EYES OF THE COLOSSAL STATUE ATOP THE BUILDING...
NO SIGN OF SUPERMAN IN THE SKY! THANKS TO MY STONE-SENTRY, I KNOW I HAVEN'T BEEN FOLLOWED! NATURALLY, I HAVE CAMERA-EYES HIDDEN ALL ABOUT MY LAIR!
THEN LUTHOR HAPPILY TOURS THE MAZE OF HALLS--ALL LEAD-LINED TO BLOCK OFF POSSIBLE DETECTION BY SUPERMAN'S X-RAY VISION...
MY HALL OF HEROES! LIFE-LIKE STATUES OF ATTILA THE HUN--GENGHIS KHAN--CAPTAIN KIDD--AL CAPONE! MANY TIMES WHEN I'VE FELT DIS-COURAGED, I'VE COME HERE--AND GONE AWAY UPLIFTED, INSPIRED TO GO ON WITH MY WORK!
ATILLA THE HUN
GENGHIS KHAN
CAPTAIN KIDD
AL CAPONE
4

JUST AS SUPERMAN'S FORTRESS SAFEGUARDS THE BOTTLED KRYPTON CITY OF KANDOR, SHRUNKEN TO MINIATURE BY THE VILLAINOUS BRAINIAC--SO DOES LUTHOR'S LAIR CONTAIN A BOTTLED LAND...

C-CUTE'S THE WORD FOR 'EM

I ONCE CAPTURED AND REDUCED THIS JUNGLE AFTER PROBING INTO ANOTHER DIMENSION! CUTE LITTLE PETS, AREN'T THEY?

I CALL THIS MY REMINDER ROOM! THOSE CROSSED-OUT CALENDAR DAYS REMIND ME HOW MANY YEARS I'VE SPENT IN PRISON BECAUSE OF SUPERMAN--AND THAT I MUST NEVER LAG IN MY WAR AGAINST HIM!

1958
MARCH   APRIL   MAY   JUNE
AUGUST   SEPTEMBER   OCTOBER   NOVEMBER   DECEMBER
MAY   JANUARY   1959   FEBRUARY   MARCH   APRIL   MAY   JUNE
NOVEMBER   1960   AUGUST   SEPTEMBER   OCTOBER   NOVEMBER   DECEMBER

THAT NIGHT, LUTHOR SMILES IN HIS SLEEP AS HE DREAMS...

DAILY PLANET EDITORIAL OFFICE

AND HERE'S MY WORKSHOP! THIS IS WHERE I INVENT MY GREAT MACHINES FOR CRIME-- AND FOR MY FORTHCOMING CONQUEST OF SUPERMAN!

5

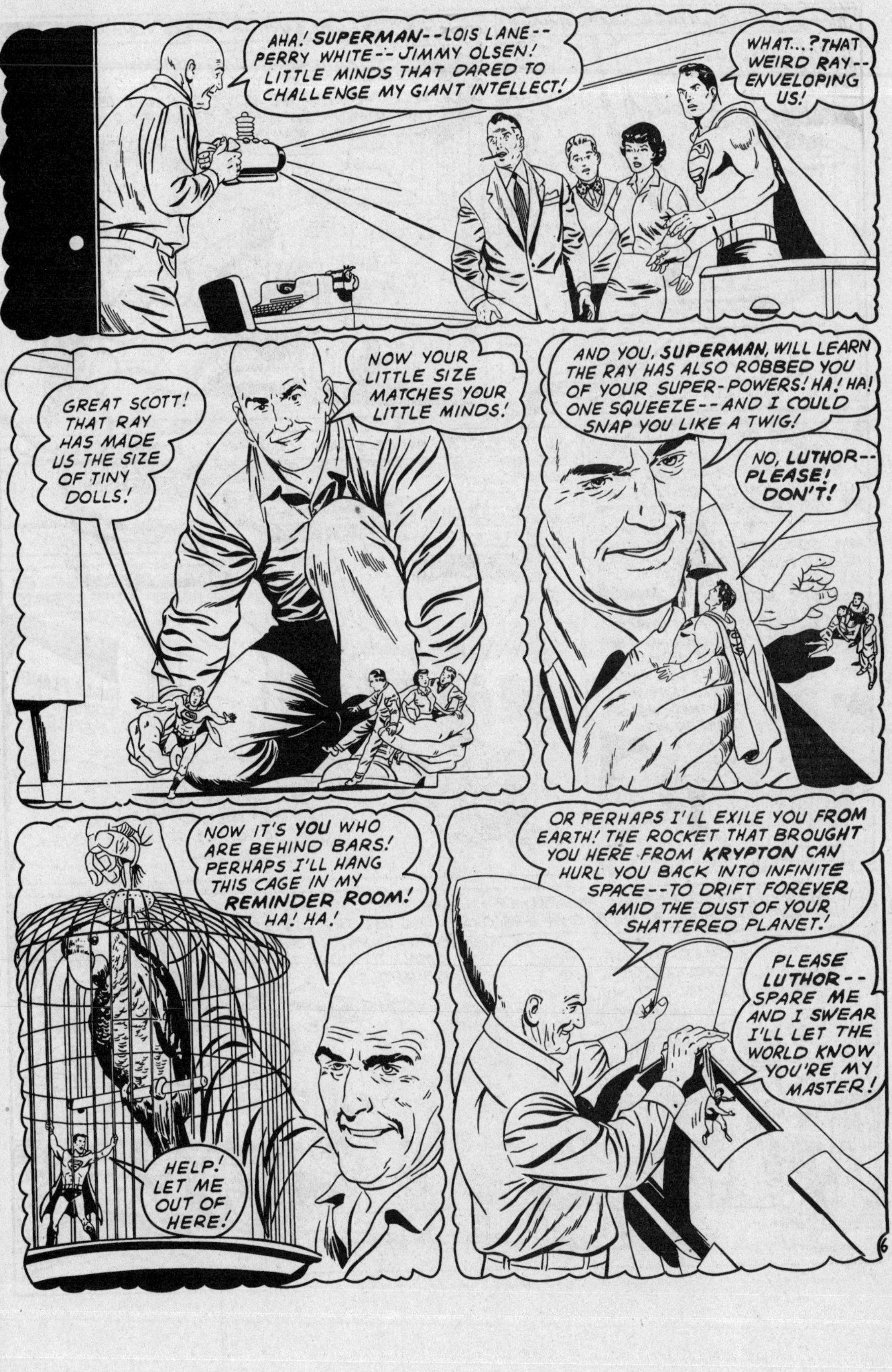
AHA! SUPERMAN--LOIS LANE--PERRY WHITE--JIMMY OLSEN! LITTLE MINDS THAT DARED TO CHALLENGE MY GIANT INTELLECT!
WHAT...? THAT WEIRD RAY--ENVELOPING US!
NOW YOUR LITTLE SIZE MATCHES YOUR LITTLE MINDS!
GREAT SCOTT! THAT RAY HAS MADE US THE SIZE OF TINY DOLLS!
AND YOU, SUPERMAN, WILL LEARN THE RAY HAS ALSO ROBBED YOU OF YOUR SUPER-POWERS! HA! HA! ONE SQUEEZE--AND I COULD SNAP YOU LIKE A TWIG!
NO, LUTHOR--PLEASE! DON'T!
NOW IT'S YOU WHO ARE BEHIND BARS! PERHAPS I'LL HANG THIS CAGE IN MY REMINDER ROOM! HA! HA!
HELP! LET ME OUT OF HERE!
OR PERHAPS I'LL EXILE YOU FROM EARTH! THE ROCKET THAT BROUGHT YOU HERE FROM KRYPTON CAN HURL YOU BACK INTO INFINITE SPACE--TO DRIFT FOREVER AMID THE DUST OF YOUR SHATTERED PLANET!
PLEASE LUTHOR--SPARE ME AND I SWEAR I'LL LET THE WORLD KNOW YOU'RE MY MASTER!
6

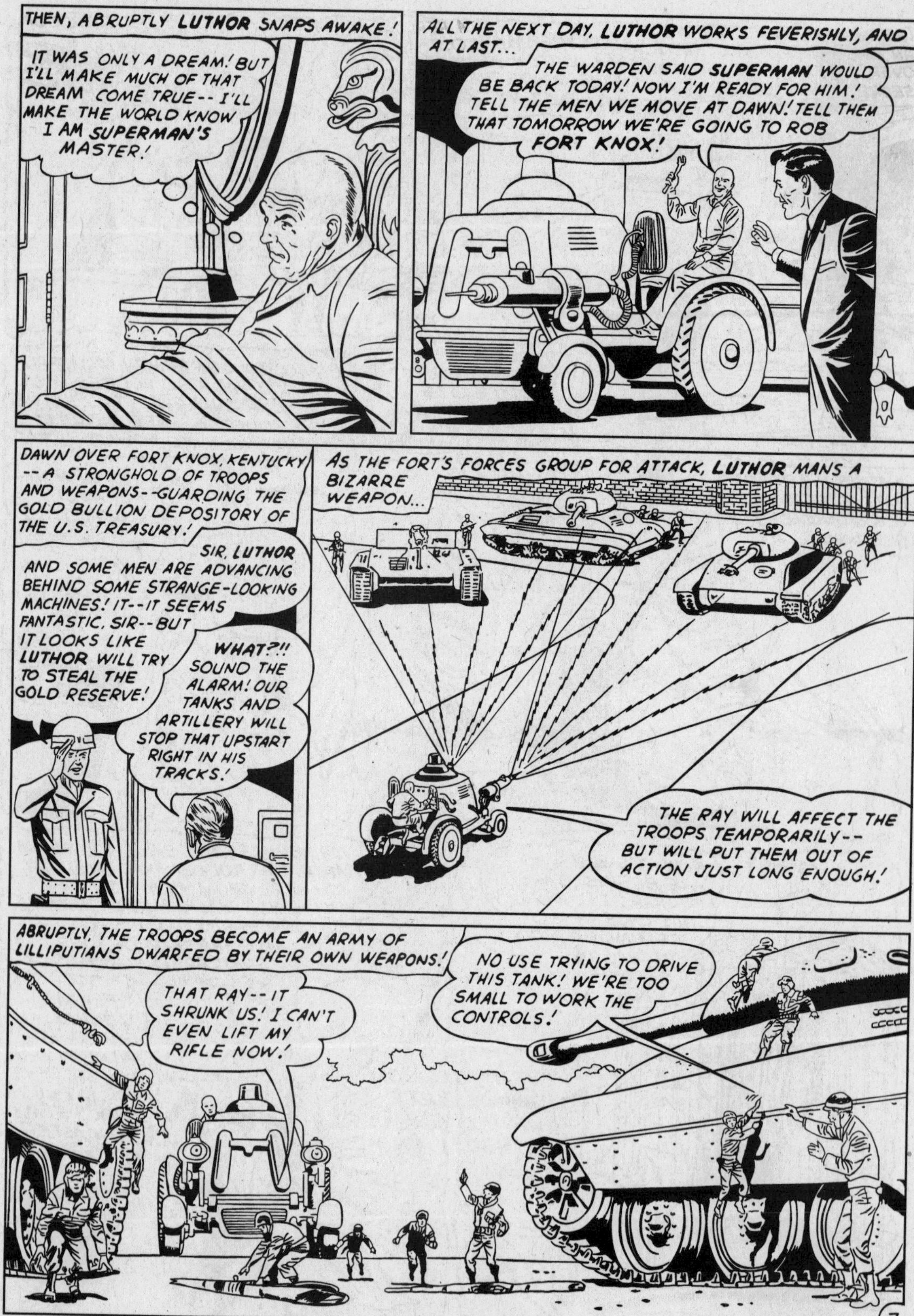
THEN, ABRUPTLY LUTHOR SNAPS AWAKE!
IT WAS ONLY A DREAM! BUT I'LL MAKE MUCH OF THAT DREAM COME TRUE-- I'LL MAKE THE WORLD KNOW I AM SUPERMAN'S MASTER!
ALL THE NEXT DAY, LUTHOR WORKS FEVERISHLY, AND AT LAST...
THE WARDEN SAID SUPERMAN WOULD BE BACK TODAY! NOW I'M READY FOR HIM! TELL THE MEN WE MOVE AT DAWN! TELL THEM THAT TOMORROW WE'RE GOING TO ROB FORT KNOX!
DAWN OVER FORT KNOX, KENTUCKY --A STRONGHOLD OF TROOPS AND WEAPONS--GUARDING THE GOLD BULLION DEPOSITORY OF THE U.S. TREASURY!
SIR, LUTHOR AND SOME MEN ARE ADVANCING BEHIND SOME STRANGE-LOOKING MACHINES! IT--IT SEEMS FANTASTIC, SIR--BUT IT LOOKS LIKE LUTHOR WILL TRY TO STEAL THE GOLD RESERVE!
WHAT?!! SOUND THE ALARM! OUR TANKS AND ARTILLERY WILL STOP THAT UPSTART RIGHT IN HIS TRACKS!
AS THE FORT'S FORCES GROUP FOR ATTACK, LUTHOR MANS A BIZARRE WEAPON...
THE RAY WILL AFFECT THE TROOPS TEMPORARILY-- BUT WILL PUT THEM OUT OF ACTION JUST LONG ENOUGH!
ABRUPTLY, THE TROOPS BECOME AN ARMY OF LILLIPUTIANS DWARFED BY THEIR OWN WEAPONS!
THAT RAY-- IT SHRUNK US! I CAN'T EVEN LIFT MY RIFLE NOW!
NO USE TRYING TO DRIVE THIS TANK! WE'RE TOO SMALL TO WORK THE CONTROLS!
7

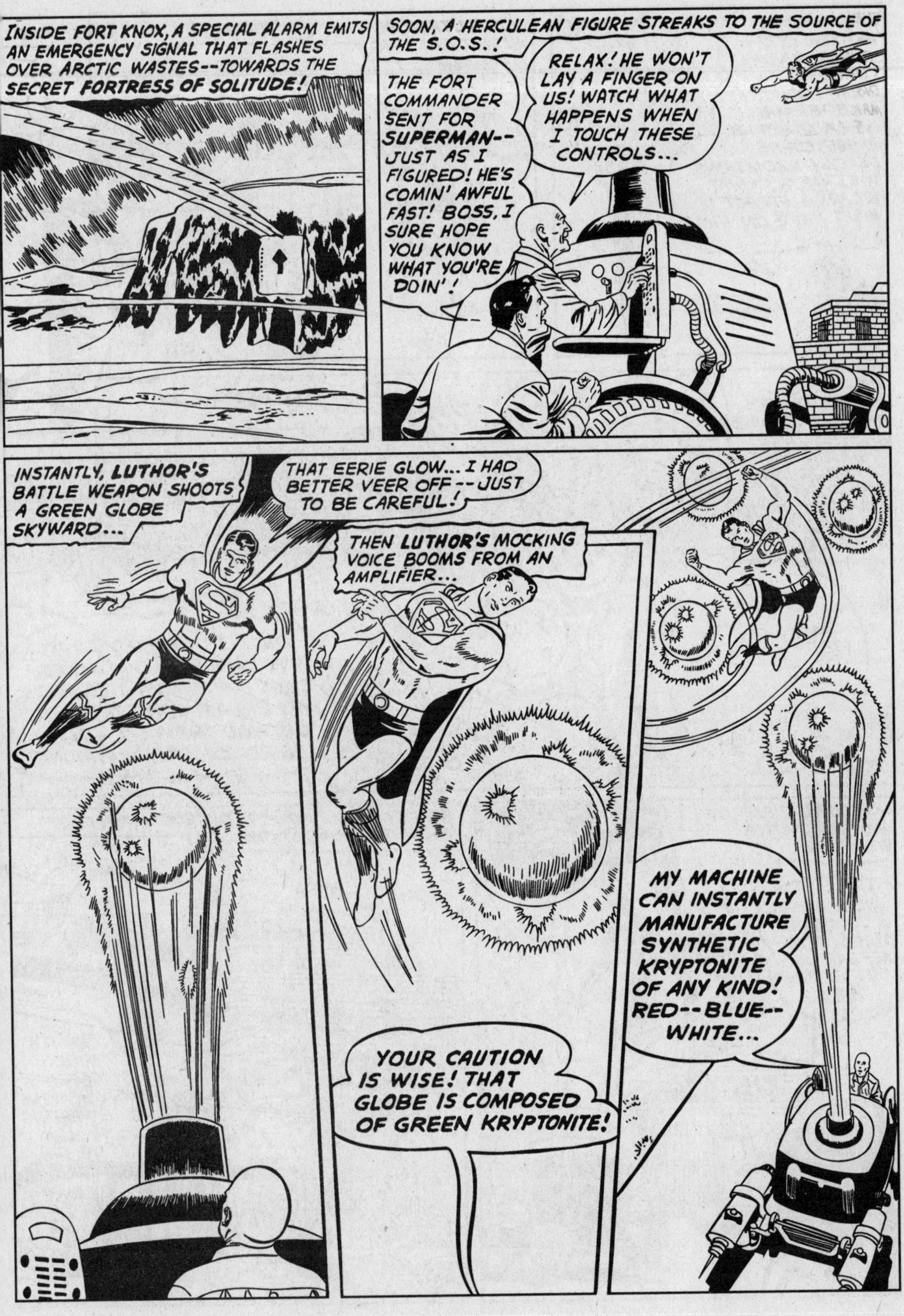
INSIDE FORT KNOX, A SPECIAL ALARM EMITS AN EMERGENCY SIGNAL THAT FLASHES OVER ARCTIC WASTES--TOWARDS THE SECRET FORTRESS OF SOLITUDE!
SOON, A HERCULEAN FIGURE STREAKS TO THE SOURCE OF THE S.O.S.!
THE FORT COMMANDER SENT FOR SUPERMAN--JUST AS I FIGURED! HE'S COMIN' AWFUL FAST! BOSS, I SURE HOPE YOU KNOW WHAT YOU'RE DOIN'!
RELAX! HE WON'T LAY A FINGER ON US! WATCH WHAT HAPPENS WHEN I TOUCH THESE CONTROLS...
INSTANTLY, LUTHOR'S BATTLE WEAPON SHOOTS A GREEN GLOBE SKYWARD...
THAT EERIE GLOW... I HAD BETTER VEER OFF--JUST TO BE CAREFUL!
THEN LUTHOR'S MOCKING VOICE BOOMS FROM AN AMPLIFIER...
YOUR CAUTION IS WISE! THAT GLOBE IS COMPOSED OF GREEN KRYPTONITE!
MY MACHINE CAN INSTANTLY MANUFACTURE SYNTHETIC KRYPTONITE OF ANY KIND! RED--BLUE--WHITE...

GREAT GUNS! ANOTHER ONE-- A NEW KIND-- YELLOW KRYPTONITE! IF SUPERMAN EVER GOT WITHIN RANGE OF ITS DEADLY RADIATIONS, WHO KNOWS WHAT BIZARRE EFFECT IT MIGHT HAVE ON HIM?

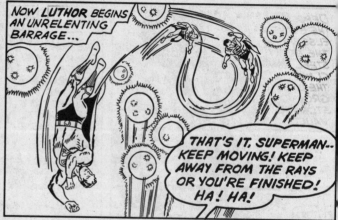

NOW LUTHOR BEGINS AN UNRELENTING BARRAGE...

THAT'S IT, SUPERMAN-- KEEP MOVING! KEEP AWAY FROM THE RAYS OR YOU'RE FINISHED! HA! HA!

THEN, FROM REMOTE CONTROL, THE GLOBES MOVE TOGETHER, LIKE A GIANT'S STRING OF BEADS, UNTIL THEY FORM A COLOSSAL, MULTI-COLORED SHAPE IN THE SKY...

ONCE I DREAMED I HAD YOU IMPRISONED IN A BIRD-CAGE--AND NOW I'VE MADE MY DREAM COME TRUE! I'VE GOT YOU TRAPPED--IN A "BIRD-CAGE" OF KRYPTONITE!

NOW LUTHOR EMPLOYS ANOTHER BATTLE WEAPON...

GREAT GUNS! A COLOSSAL STEEL ARM-- APPEARING OUT OF THIN AIR!

WITH AWESOME POWER, IT UPROOTS THE FORT FROM ITS FOUNDATIONS...

OHH! IT'S MIND-STAGGERING! THANK HEAVENS THERE WERE NO TROOPS LEFT INSIDE THE BUILDING!

9

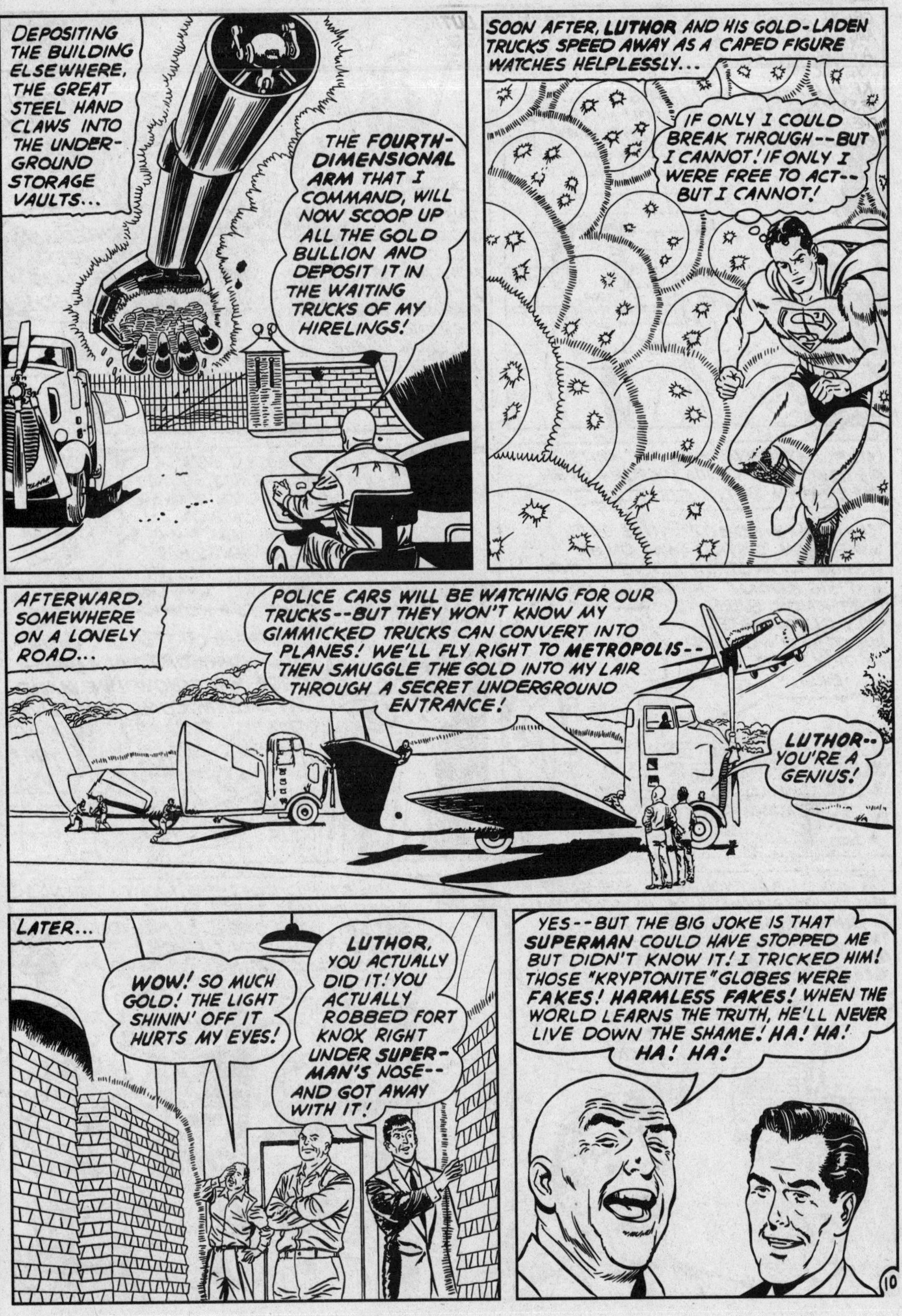
DEPOSITING THE BUILDING ELSEWHERE, THE GREAT STEEL HAND CLAWS INTO THE UNDER-GROUND STORAGE VAULTS...
THE FOURTH-DIMENSIONAL ARM THAT I COMMAND, WILL NOW SCOOP UP ALL THE GOLD BULLION AND DEPOSIT IT IN THE WAITING TRUCKS OF MY HIRELINGS!
SOON AFTER, LUTHOR AND HIS GOLD-LADEN TRUCKS SPEED AWAY AS A CAPED FIGURE WATCHES HELPLESSLY...
IF ONLY I COULD BREAK THROUGH--BUT I CANNOT! IF ONLY I WERE FREE TO ACT--BUT I CANNOT!
AFTERWARD, SOMEWHERE ON A LONELY ROAD...
POLICE CARS WILL BE WATCHING FOR OUR TRUCKS--BUT THEY WON'T KNOW MY GIMMICKED TRUCKS CAN CONVERT INTO PLANES! WE'LL FLY RIGHT TO METROPOLIS--THEN SMUGGLE THE GOLD INTO MY LAIR THROUGH A SECRET UNDERGROUND ENTRANCE!
LUTHOR--YOU'RE A GENIUS!
LATER...
WOW! SO MUCH GOLD! THE LIGHT SHININ' OFF IT HURTS MY EYES!
LUTHOR, YOU ACTUALLY DID IT! YOU ACTUALLY ROBBED FORT KNOX RIGHT UNDER SUPER-MAN'S NOSE--AND GOT AWAY WITH IT!
YES--BUT THE BIG JOKE IS THAT SUPERMAN COULD HAVE STOPPED ME BUT DIDN'T KNOW IT! I TRICKED HIM! THOSE "KRYPTONITE" GLOBES WERE FAKES! HARMLESS FAKES! WHEN THE WORLD LEARNS THE TRUTH, HE'LL NEVER LIVE DOWN THE SHAME! HA! HA! HA! HA!
10

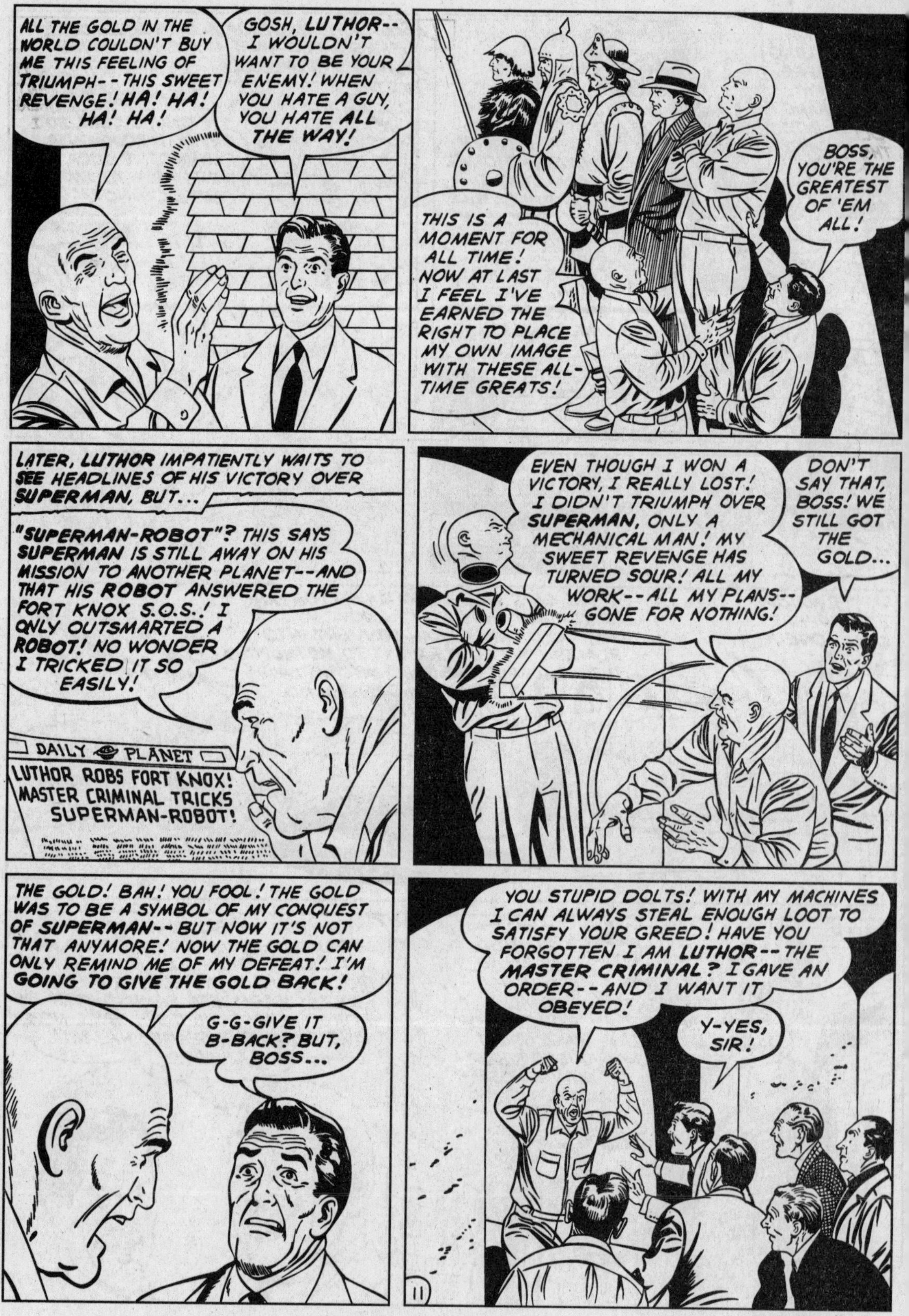
ALL THE GOLD IN THE WORLD COULDN'T BUY ME THIS FEELING OF TRIUMPH--THIS SWEET REVENGE! HA! HA! HA! HA!
GOSH, LUTHOR--I WOULDN'T WANT TO BE YOUR ENEMY! WHEN YOU HATE A GUY, YOU HATE ALL THE WAY!
THIS IS A MOMENT FOR ALL TIME! NOW AT LAST I FEEL I'VE EARNED THE RIGHT TO PLACE MY OWN IMAGE WITH THESE ALL-TIME GREATS!
BOSS, YOU'RE THE GREATEST OF 'EM ALL!
LATER, LUTHOR IMPATIENTLY WAITS TO SEE HEADLINES OF HIS VICTORY OVER SUPERMAN, BUT...
"SUPERMAN-ROBOT"? THIS SAYS SUPERMAN IS STILL AWAY ON HIS MISSION TO ANOTHER PLANET--AND THAT HIS ROBOT ANSWERED THE FORT KNOX S.O.S.! I ONLY OUTSMARTED A ROBOT! NO WONDER I TRICKED IT SO EASILY!
DAILY PLANET
LUTHOR ROBS FORT KNOX! MASTER CRIMINAL TRICKS SUPERMAN-ROBOT!
EVEN THOUGH I WON A VICTORY, I REALLY LOST! I DIDN'T TRIUMPH OVER SUPERMAN, ONLY A MECHANICAL MAN! MY SWEET REVENGE HAS TURNED SOUR! ALL MY WORK--ALL MY PLANS--GONE FOR NOTHING!
DON'T SAY THAT, BOSS! WE STILL GOT THE GOLD...
THE GOLD! BAH! YOU FOOL! THE GOLD WAS TO BE A SYMBOL OF MY CONQUEST OF SUPERMAN--BUT NOW IT'S NOT THAT ANYMORE! NOW THE GOLD CAN ONLY REMIND ME OF MY DEFEAT! I'M GOING TO GIVE THE GOLD BACK!
G-G-GIVE IT B-BACK? BUT, BOSS...
YOU STUPID DOLTS! WITH MY MACHINES I CAN ALWAYS STEAL ENOUGH LOOT TO SATISFY YOUR GREED! HAVE YOU FORGOTTEN I AM LUTHOR--THE MASTER CRIMINAL? I GAVE AN ORDER--AND I WANT IT OBEYED!
Y-YES, SIR!
11

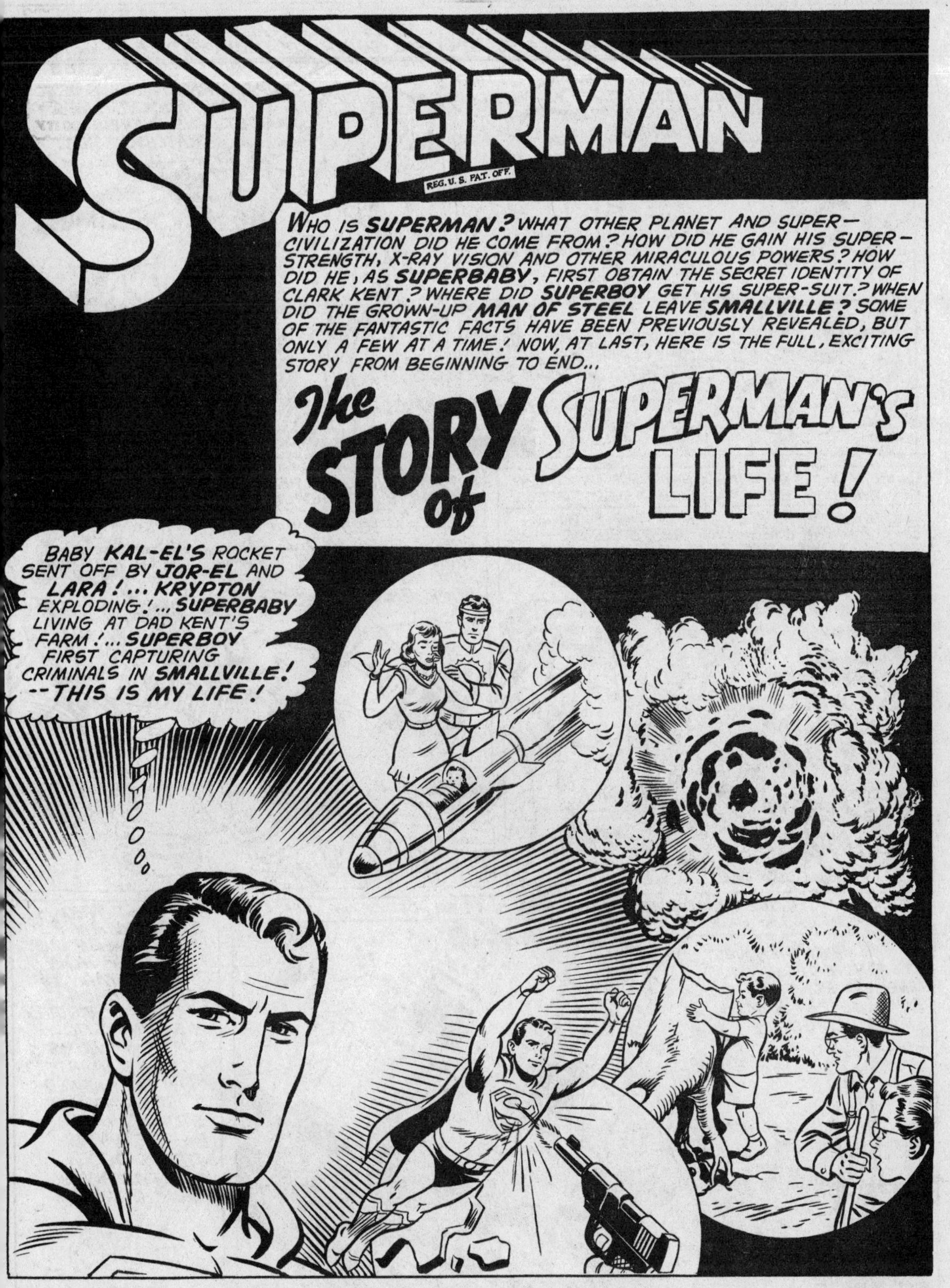
SUPERMAN
REG. U.S. PAT. OFF.
WHO IS SUPERMAN? WHAT OTHER PLANET AND SUPER-CIVILIZATION DID HE COME FROM? HOW DID HE GAIN HIS SUPER-STRENGTH, X-RAY VISION AND OTHER MIRACULOUS POWERS? HOW DID HE, AS SUPERBABY, FIRST OBTAIN THE SECRET IDENTITY OF CLARK KENT? WHERE DID SUPERBOY GET HIS SUPER-SUIT? WHEN DID THE GROWN-UP MAN OF STEEL LEAVE SMALLVILLE? SOME OF THE FANTASTIC FACTS HAVE BEEN PREVIOUSLY REVEALED, BUT ONLY A FEW AT A TIME! NOW, AT LAST, HERE IS THE FULL, EXCITING STORY FROM BEGINNING TO END...
The STORY of SUPERMAN'S LIFE!
BABY KAL-EL'S ROCKET SENT OFF BY JOR-EL AND LARA!... KRYPTON EXPLODING!... SUPERBABY LIVING AT DAD KENT'S FARM!... SUPERBOY FIRST CAPTURING CRIMINALS IN SMALLVILLE! --THIS IS MY LIFE!

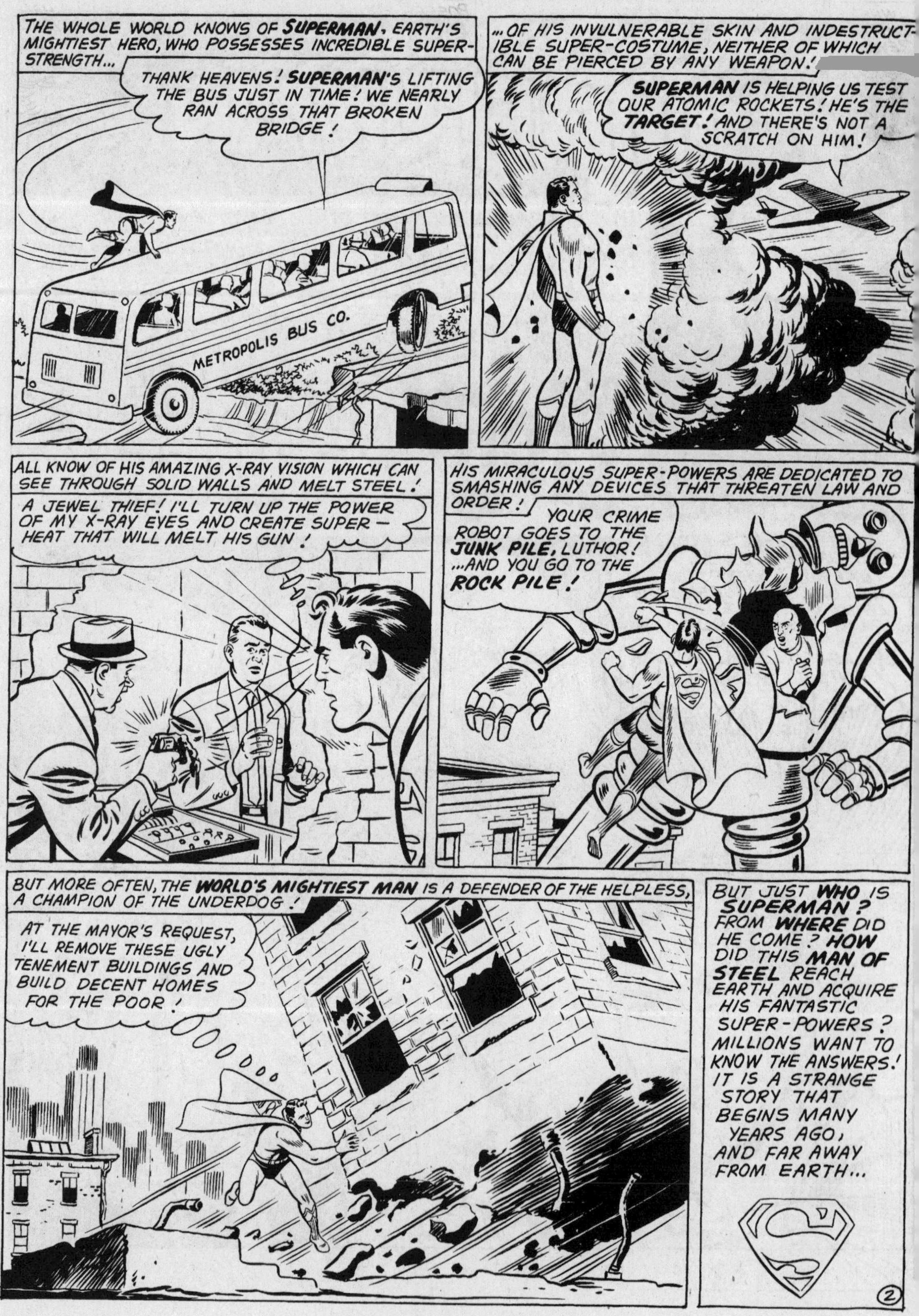

THE WHOLE WORLD KNOWS OF SUPERMAN, EARTH'S MIGHTIEST HERO, WHO POSSESSES INCREDIBLE SUPER-STRENGTH...
THANK HEAVENS! SUPERMAN'S LIFTING THE BUS JUST IN TIME! WE NEARLY RAN ACROSS THAT BROKEN BRIDGE!
METROPOLIS BUS CO.
...OF HIS INVULNERABLE SKIN AND INDESTRUCTIBLE SUPER-COSTUME, NEITHER OF WHICH CAN BE PIERCED BY ANY WEAPON!
SUPERMAN IS HELPING US TEST OUR ATOMIC ROCKETS! HE'S THE TARGET! AND THERE'S NOT A SCRATCH ON HIM!
ALL KNOW OF HIS AMAZING X-RAY VISION WHICH CAN SEE THROUGH SOLID WALLS AND MELT STEEL!
A JEWEL THIEF! I'LL TURN UP THE POWER OF MY X-RAY EYES AND CREATE SUPER-HEAT THAT WILL MELT HIS GUN!
HIS MIRACULOUS SUPER-POWERS ARE DEDICATED TO SMASHING ANY DEVICES THAT THREATEN LAW AND ORDER!
YOUR CRIME ROBOT GOES TO THE JUNK PILE, LUTHOR! ...AND YOU GO TO THE ROCK PILE!
BUT MORE OFTEN, THE WORLD'S MIGHTIEST MAN IS A DEFENDER OF THE HELPLESS, A CHAMPION OF THE UNDERDOG!
AT THE MAYOR'S REQUEST, I'LL REMOVE THESE UGLY TENEMENT BUILDINGS AND BUILD DECENT HOMES FOR THE POOR!
BUT JUST WHO IS SUPERMAN? FROM WHERE DID HE COME? HOW DID THIS MAN OF STEEL REACH EARTH AND ACQUIRE HIS FANTASTIC SUPER-POWERS? MILLIONS WANT TO KNOW THE ANSWERS! IT IS A STRANGE STORY THAT BEGINS MANY YEARS AGO, AND FAR AWAY FROM EARTH...
2

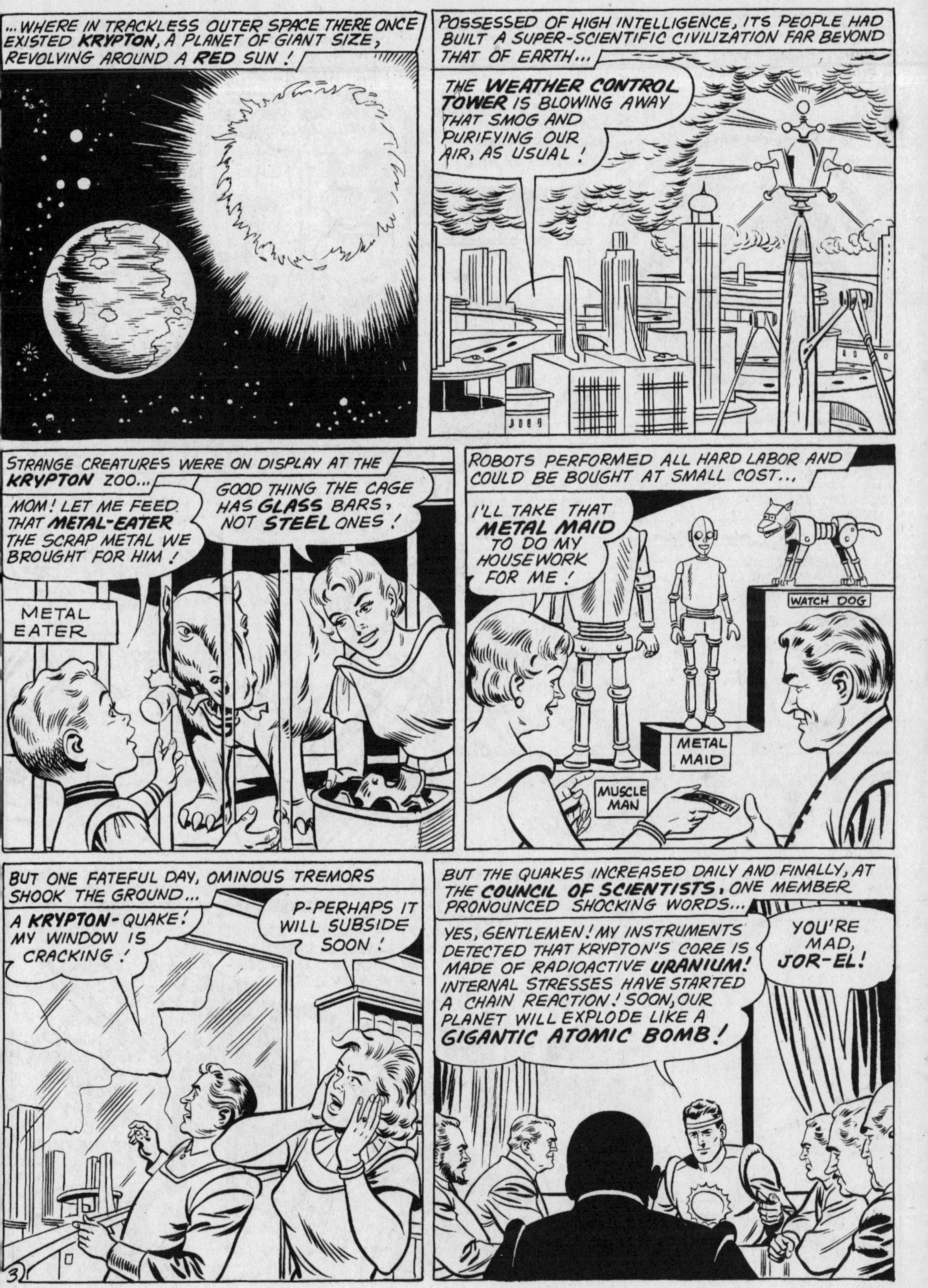

...WHERE IN TRACKLESS OUTER SPACE THERE ONCE EXISTED KRYPTON, A PLANET OF GIANT SIZE, REVOLVING AROUND A RED SUN!
POSSESSED OF HIGH INTELLIGENCE, ITS PEOPLE HAD BUILT A SUPER-SCIENTIFIC CIVILIZATION FAR BEYOND THAT OF EARTH...
THE WEATHER CONTROL TOWER IS BLOWING AWAY THAT SMOG AND PURIFYING OUR AIR, AS USUAL!
STRANGE CREATURES WERE ON DISPLAY AT THE KRYPTON ZOO...
MOM! LET ME FEED THAT METAL-EATER THE SCRAP METAL WE BROUGHT FOR HIM!
GOOD THING THE CAGE HAS GLASS BARS, NOT STEEL ONES!
METAL EATER
ROBOTS PERFORMED ALL HARD LABOR AND COULD BE BOUGHT AT SMALL COST...
I'LL TAKE THAT METAL MAID TO DO MY HOUSEWORK FOR ME!
WATCH DOG
METAL MAID
MUSCLE MAN
BUT ONE FATEFUL DAY, OMINOUS TREMORS SHOOK THE GROUND...
A KRYPTON-QUAKE! MY WINDOW IS CRACKING!
P-PERHAPS IT WILL SUBSIDE SOON!
BUT THE QUAKES INCREASED DAILY AND FINALLY, AT THE COUNCIL OF SCIENTISTS, ONE MEMBER PRONOUNCED SHOCKING WORDS...
YES, GENTLEMEN! MY INSTRUMENTS DETECTED THAT KRYPTON'S CORE IS MADE OF RADIOACTIVE URANIUM! INTERNAL STRESSES HAVE STARTED A CHAIN REACTION! SOON, OUR PLANET WILL EXPLODE LIKE A GIGANTIC ATOMIC BOMB!
YOU'RE MAD, JOR-EL!
3

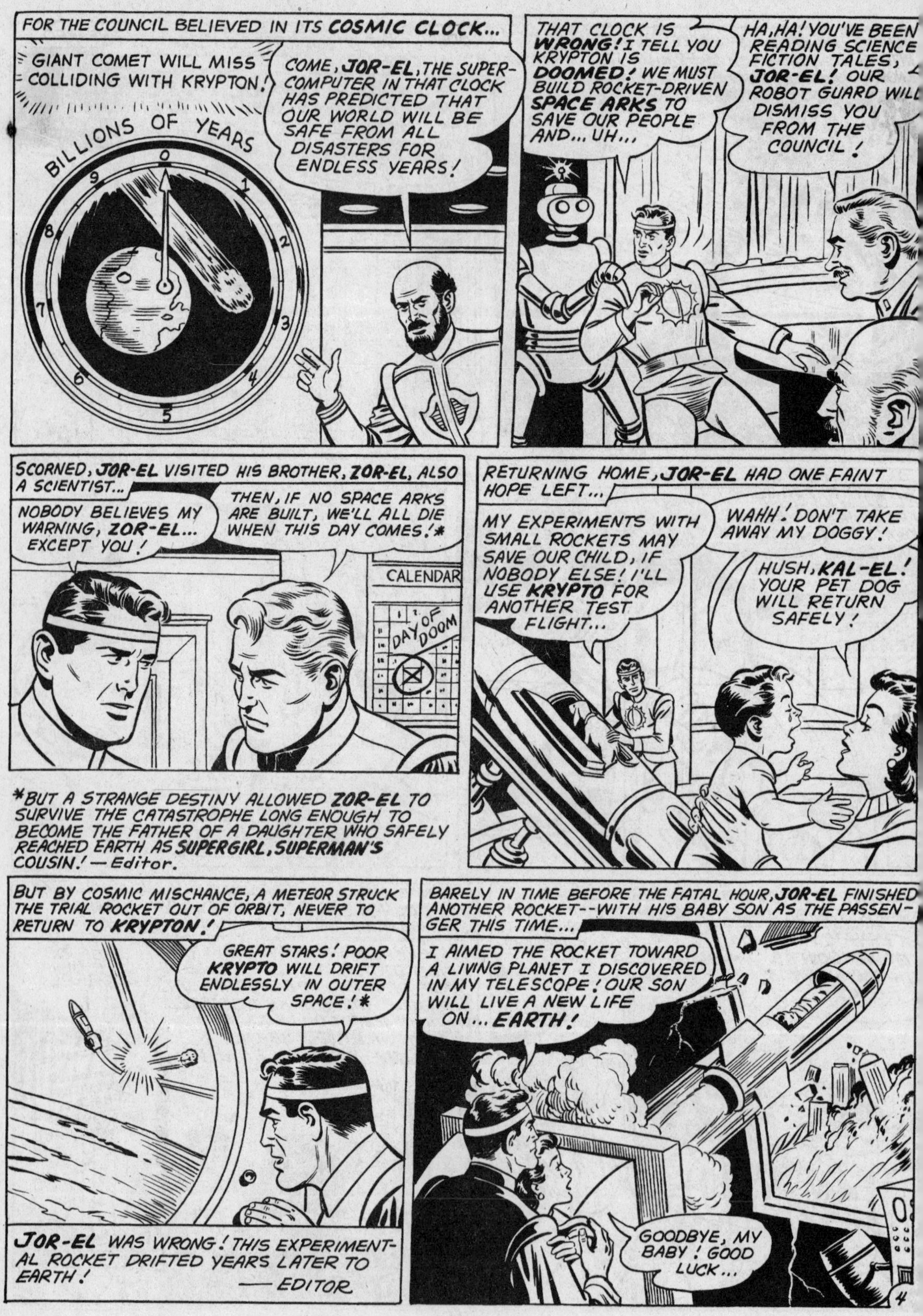
FOR THE COUNCIL BELIEVED IN ITS COSMIC CLOCK...
GIANT COMET WILL MISS COLLIDING WITH KRYPTON!
BILLIONS OF YEARS
COME, JOR-EL, THE SUPER-COMPUTER IN THAT CLOCK HAS PREDICTED THAT OUR WORLD WILL BE SAFE FROM ALL DISASTERS FOR ENDLESS YEARS!
THAT CLOCK IS WRONG! I TELL YOU KRYPTON IS DOOMED! WE MUST BUILD ROCKET-DRIVEN SPACE ARKS TO SAVE OUR PEOPLE AND... UH...
HA, HA! YOU'VE BEEN READING SCIENCE FICTION TALES, JOR-EL! OUR ROBOT GUARD WILL DISMISS YOU FROM THE COUNCIL!
SCORNED, JOR-EL VISITED HIS BROTHER, ZOR-EL, ALSO A SCIENTIST...
NOBODY BELIEVES MY WARNING, ZOR-EL... EXCEPT YOU!
THEN, IF NO SPACE ARKS ARE BUILT, WE'LL ALL DIE WHEN THIS DAY COMES! *
CALENDAR
DAY OF DOOM
*BUT A STRANGE DESTINY ALLOWED ZOR-EL TO SURVIVE THE CATASTROPHE LONG ENOUGH TO BECOME THE FATHER OF A DAUGHTER WHO SAFELY REACHED EARTH AS SUPERGIRL, SUPERMAN'S COUSIN! — Editor.
RETURNING HOME, JOR-EL HAD ONE FAINT HOPE LEFT...
MY EXPERIMENTS WITH SMALL ROCKETS MAY SAVE OUR CHILD, IF NOBODY ELSE! I'LL USE KRYPTO FOR ANOTHER TEST FLIGHT...
WAHH! DON'T TAKE AWAY MY DOGGY!
HUSH, KAL-EL! YOUR PET DOG WILL RETURN SAFELY!
BUT BY COSMIC MISCHANCE, A METEOR STRUCK THE TRIAL ROCKET OUT OF ORBIT, NEVER TO RETURN TO KRYPTON!
GREAT STARS! POOR KRYPTO WILL DRIFT ENDLESSLY IN OUTER SPACE! *
JOR-EL WAS WRONG! THIS EXPERIMENTAL ROCKET DRIFTED YEARS LATER TO EARTH! — EDITOR
BARELY IN TIME BEFORE THE FATAL HOUR, JOR-EL FINISHED ANOTHER ROCKET--WITH HIS BABY SON AS THE PASSENGER THIS TIME...
I AIMED THE ROCKET TOWARD A LIVING PLANET I DISCOVERED IN MY TELESCOPE! OUR SON WILL LIVE A NEW LIFE ON... EARTH!
GOODBYE, MY BABY! GOOD LUCK...
4

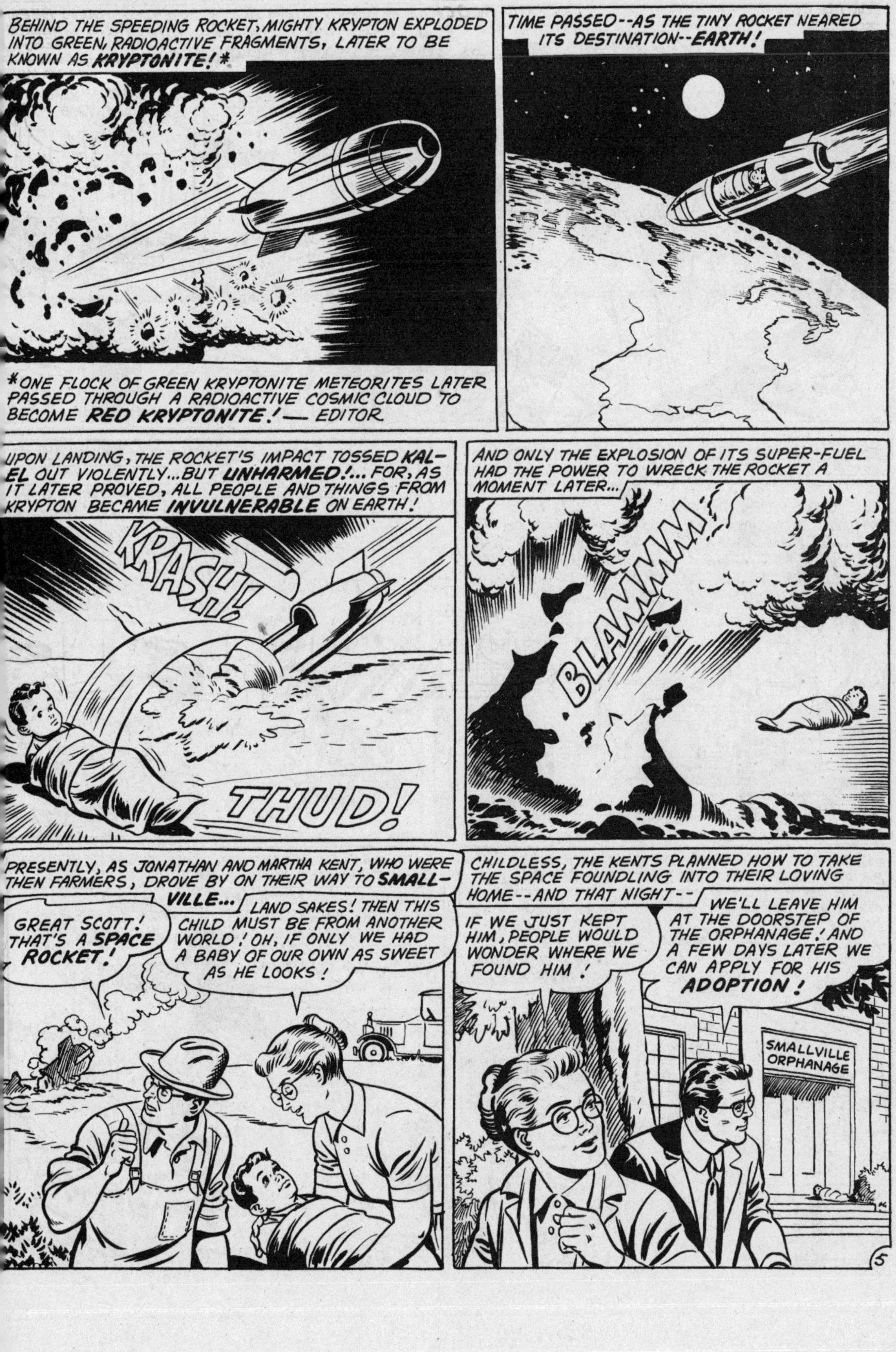
BEHIND THE SPEEDING ROCKET, MIGHTY KRYPTON EXPLODED INTO GREEN, RADIOACTIVE FRAGMENTS, LATER TO BE KNOWN AS KRYPTONITE! *
*ONE FLOCK OF GREEN KRYPTONITE METEORITES LATER PASSED THROUGH A RADIOACTIVE COSMIC CLOUD TO BECOME RED KRYPTONITE! — EDITOR
TIME PASSED--AS THE TINY ROCKET NEARED ITS DESTINATION--EARTH!
UPON LANDING, THE ROCKET'S IMPACT TOSSED KAL-EL OUT VIOLENTLY...BUT UNHARMED!... FOR, AS IT LATER PROVED, ALL PEOPLE AND THINGS FROM KRYPTON BECAME INVULNERABLE ON EARTH!
KRASH!
THUD!
AND ONLY THE EXPLOSION OF ITS SUPER-FUEL HAD THE POWER TO WRECK THE ROCKET A MOMENT LATER...
BLAMMMM
PRESENTLY, AS JONATHAN AND MARTHA KENT, WHO WERE THEN FARMERS, DROVE BY ON THEIR WAY TO SMALL-VILLE...
GREAT SCOTT! THAT'S A SPACE ROCKET!
LAND SAKES! THEN THIS CHILD MUST BE FROM ANOTHER WORLD! OH, IF ONLY WE HAD A BABY OF OUR OWN AS SWEET AS HE LOOKS!
CHILDLESS, THE KENTS PLANNED HOW TO TAKE THE SPACE FOUNDLING INTO THEIR LOVING HOME--AND THAT NIGHT--
IF WE JUST KEPT HIM, PEOPLE WOULD WONDER WHERE WE FOUND HIM!
WE'LL LEAVE HIM AT THE DOORSTEP OF THE ORPHANAGE! AND A FEW DAYS LATER WE CAN APPLY FOR HIS ADOPTION!
SMALLVILLE ORPHANAGE
5

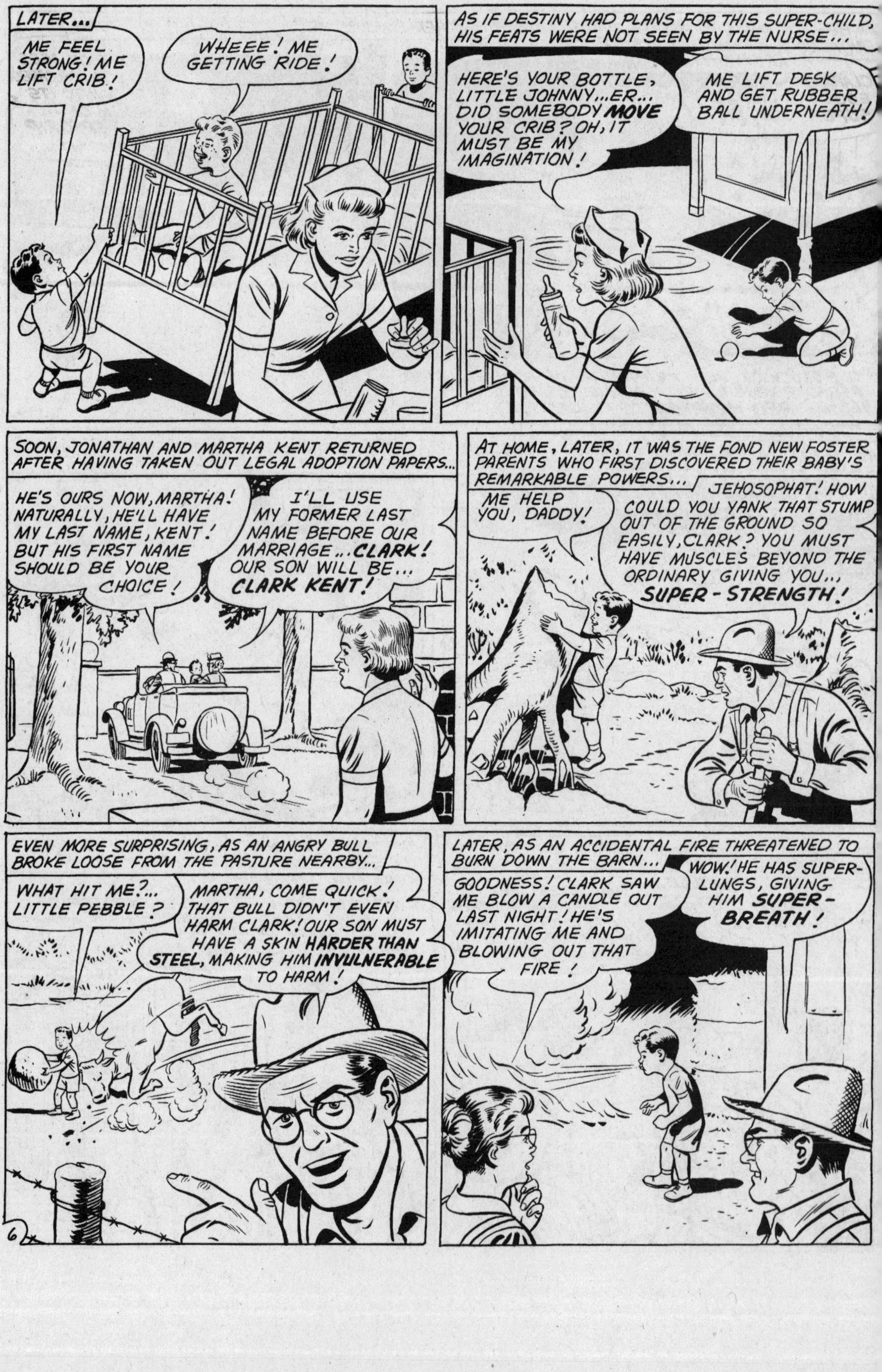
LATER...
ME FEEL STRONG! ME LIFT CRIB!
WHEEE! ME GETTING RIDE!
AS IF DESTINY HAD PLANS FOR THIS SUPER-CHILD, HIS FEATS WERE NOT SEEN BY THE NURSE...
HERE'S YOUR BOTTLE, LITTLE JOHNNY...ER... DID SOMEBODY MOVE YOUR CRIB? OH, IT MUST BE MY IMAGINATION!
ME LIFT DESK AND GET RUBBER BALL UNDERNEATH!
SOON, JONATHAN AND MARTHA KENT RETURNED AFTER HAVING TAKEN OUT LEGAL ADOPTION PAPERS...
HE'S OURS NOW, MARTHA! NATURALLY, HE'LL HAVE MY LAST NAME, KENT! BUT HIS FIRST NAME SHOULD BE YOUR CHOICE!
I'LL USE MY FORMER LAST NAME BEFORE OUR MARRIAGE... CLARK! OUR SON WILL BE... CLARK KENT!
AT HOME, LATER, IT WAS THE FOND NEW FOSTER PARENTS WHO FIRST DISCOVERED THEIR BABY'S REMARKABLE POWERS...
ME HELP YOU, DADDY!
JEHOSOPHAT! HOW COULD YOU YANK THAT STUMP OUT OF THE GROUND SO EASILY, CLARK? YOU MUST HAVE MUSCLES BEYOND THE ORDINARY GIVING YOU... SUPER-STRENGTH!
EVEN MORE SURPRISING, AS AN ANGRY BULL BROKE LOOSE FROM THE PASTURE NEARBY...
WHAT HIT ME?... LITTLE PEBBLE?
MARTHA, COME QUICK! THAT BULL DIDN'T EVEN HARM CLARK! OUR SON MUST HAVE A SKIN HARDER THAN STEEL, MAKING HIM INVULNERABLE TO HARM!
6
LATER, AS AN ACCIDENTAL FIRE THREATENED TO BURN DOWN THE BARN...
GOODNESS! CLARK SAW ME BLOW A CANDLE OUT LAST NIGHT! HE'S IMITATING ME AND BLOWING OUT THAT FIRE!
WOW! HE HAS SUPER-LUNGS, GIVING HIM SUPER-BREATH!

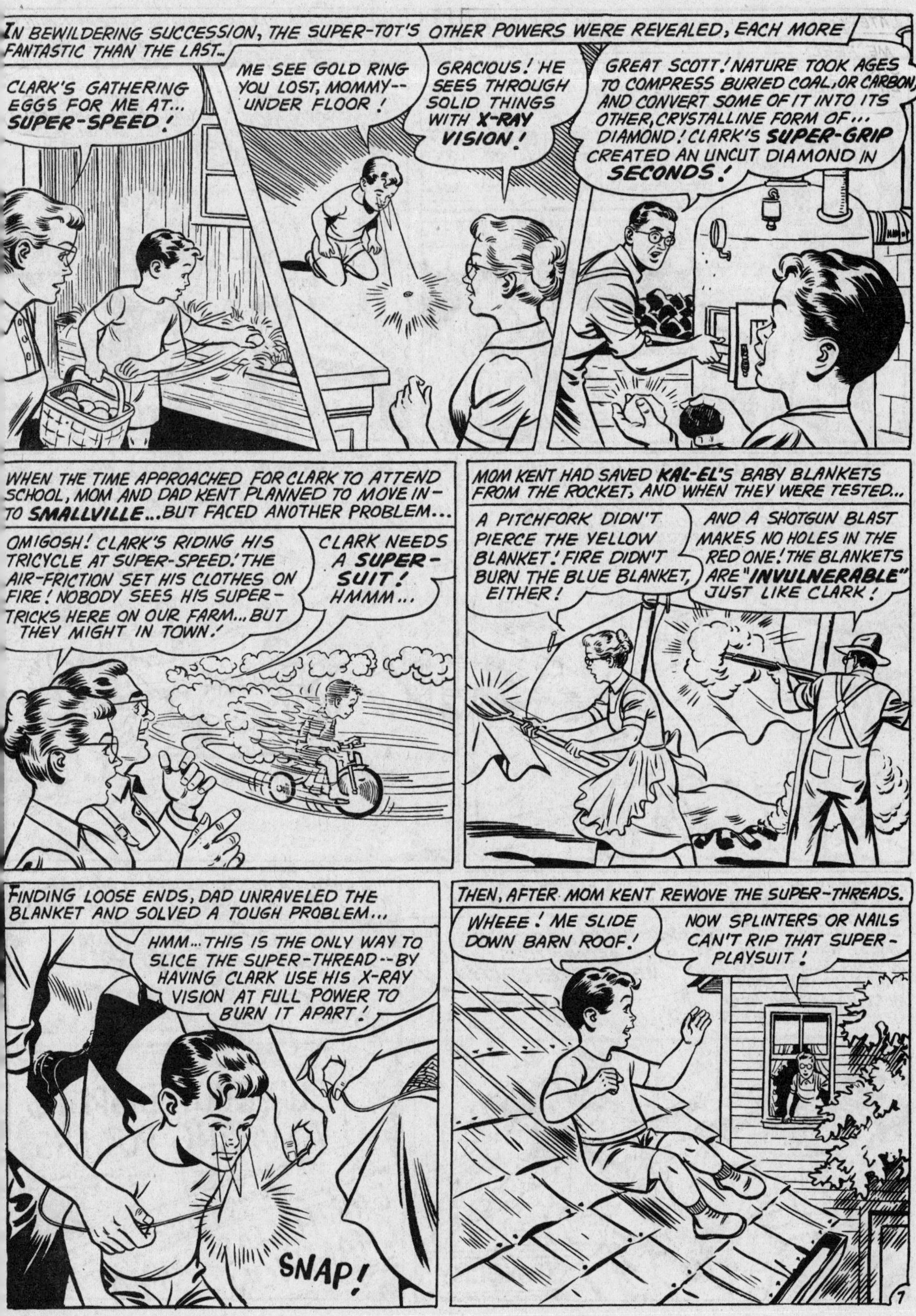
IN BEWILDERING SUCCESSION, THE SUPER-TOT'S OTHER POWERS WERE REVEALED, EACH MORE FANTASTIC THAN THE LAST...
CLARK'S GATHERING EGGS FOR ME AT... SUPER-SPEED!
ME SEE GOLD RING YOU LOST, MOMMY-- UNDER FLOOR!
GRACIOUS! HE SEES THROUGH SOLID THINGS WITH X-RAY VISION!
GREAT SCOTT! NATURE TOOK AGES TO COMPRESS BURIED COAL, OR CARBON, AND CONVERT SOME OF IT INTO ITS OTHER, CRYSTALLINE FORM OF... DIAMOND! CLARK'S SUPER-GRIP CREATED AN UNCUT DIAMOND IN SECONDS!
WHEN THE TIME APPROACHED FOR CLARK TO ATTEND SCHOOL, MOM AND DAD KENT PLANNED TO MOVE IN-TO SMALLVILLE...BUT FACED ANOTHER PROBLEM...
OMIGOSH! CLARK'S RIDING HIS TRICYCLE AT SUPER-SPEED! THE AIR-FRICTION SET HIS CLOTHES ON FIRE! NOBODY SEES HIS SUPER-TRICKS HERE ON OUR FARM... BUT THEY MIGHT IN TOWN!
CLARK NEEDS A SUPER-SUIT! HMMM...
MOM KENT HAD SAVED KAL-EL'S BABY BLANKETS FROM THE ROCKET, AND WHEN THEY WERE TESTED...
A PITCHFORK DIDN'T PIERCE THE YELLOW BLANKET! FIRE DIDN'T BURN THE BLUE BLANKET, EITHER!
AND A SHOTGUN BLAST MAKES NO HOLES IN THE RED ONE! THE BLANKETS ARE "INVULNERABLE" JUST LIKE CLARK!
FINDING LOOSE ENDS, DAD UNRAVELED THE BLANKET AND SOLVED A TOUGH PROBLEM...
HMM...THIS IS THE ONLY WAY TO SLICE THE SUPER-THREAD--BY HAVING CLARK USE HIS X-RAY VISION AT FULL POWER TO BURN IT APART!
SNAP!
THEN, AFTER MOM KENT REWOVE THE SUPER-THREADS.
WHEEE! ME SLIDE DOWN BARN ROOF!
NOW SPLINTERS OR NAILS CAN'T RIP THAT SUPER-PLAYSUIT!
7

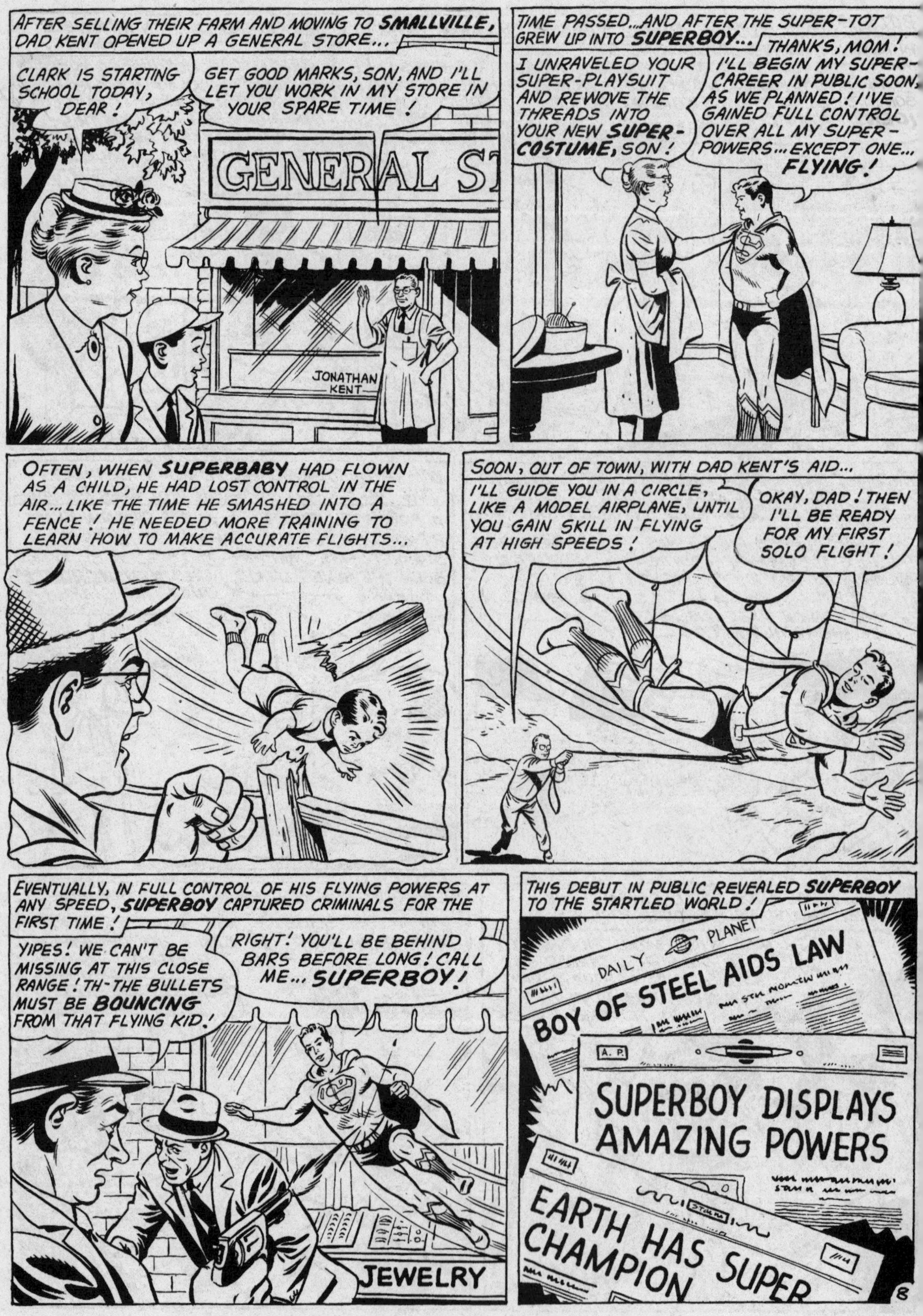

AFTER SELLING THEIR FARM AND MOVING TO SMALLVILLE, DAD KENT OPENED UP A GENERAL STORE...
CLARK IS STARTING SCHOOL TODAY, DEAR!
GET GOOD MARKS, SON, AND I'LL LET YOU WORK IN MY STORE IN YOUR SPARE TIME!
GENERAL S
JONATHAN KENT
TIME PASSED...AND AFTER THE SUPER-TOT GREW UP INTO SUPERBOY...
I UNRAVELED YOUR SUPER-PLAYSUIT AND REWOVE THE THREADS INTO YOUR NEW SUPER-COSTUME, SON!
THANKS, MOM! I'LL BEGIN MY SUPER-CAREER IN PUBLIC SOON, AS WE PLANNED! I'VE GAINED FULL CONTROL OVER ALL MY SUPER-POWERS...EXCEPT ONE... FLYING!
OFTEN, WHEN SUPERBABY HAD FLOWN AS A CHILD, HE HAD LOST CONTROL IN THE AIR...LIKE THE TIME HE SMASHED INTO A FENCE! HE NEEDED MORE TRAINING TO LEARN HOW TO MAKE ACCURATE FLIGHTS...
SOON, OUT OF TOWN, WITH DAD KENT'S AID...
I'LL GUIDE YOU IN A CIRCLE, LIKE A MODEL AIRPLANE, UNTIL YOU GAIN SKILL IN FLYING AT HIGH SPEEDS!
OKAY, DAD! THEN I'LL BE READY FOR MY FIRST SOLO FLIGHT!
EVENTUALLY, IN FULL CONTROL OF HIS FLYING POWERS AT ANY SPEED, SUPERBOY CAPTURED CRIMINALS FOR THE FIRST TIME!
YIPES! WE CAN'T BE MISSING AT THIS CLOSE RANGE! TH-THE BULLETS MUST BE BOUNCING FROM THAT FLYING KID!
RIGHT! YOU'LL BE BEHIND BARS BEFORE LONG! CALL ME... SUPERBOY!
JEWELRY
THIS DEBUT IN PUBLIC REVEALED SUPERBOY TO THE STARTLED WORLD!
DAILY PLANET
BOY OF STEEL AIDS LAW
A. P.
SUPERBOY DISPLAYS AMAZING POWERS
EARTH HAS SUPER CHAMPION
8

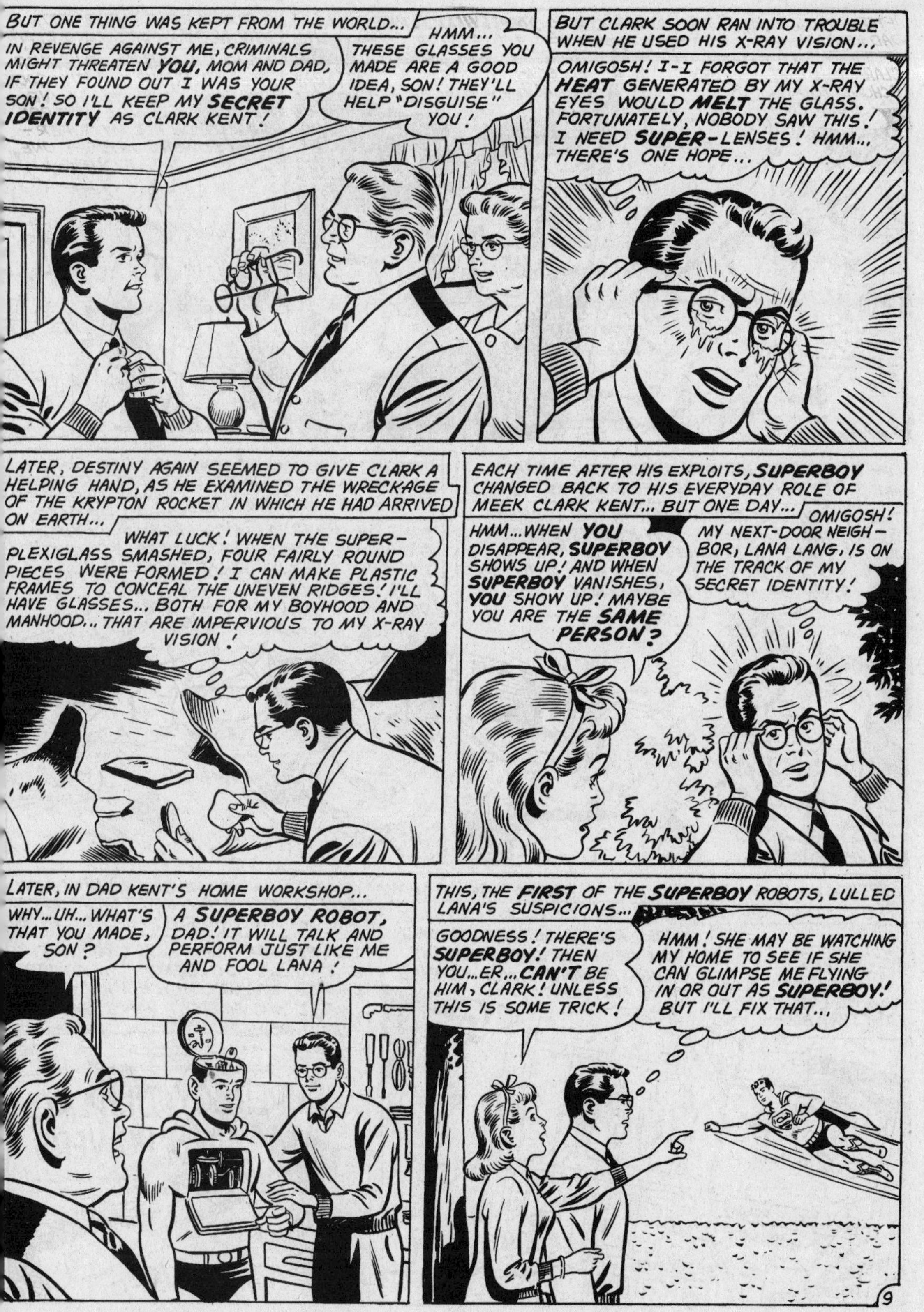
BUT ONE THING WAS KEPT FROM THE WORLD...
IN REVENGE AGAINST ME, CRIMINALS MIGHT THREATEN YOU, MOM AND DAD, IF THEY FOUND OUT I WAS YOUR SON! SO I'LL KEEP MY SECRET IDENTITY AS CLARK KENT!
HMM... THESE GLASSES YOU MADE ARE A GOOD IDEA, SON! THEY'LL HELP "DISGUISE" YOU!
BUT CLARK SOON RAN INTO TROUBLE WHEN HE USED HIS X-RAY VISION...
OMIGOSH! I-I FORGOT THAT THE HEAT GENERATED BY MY X-RAY EYES WOULD MELT THE GLASS. FORTUNATELY, NOBODY SAW THIS! I NEED SUPER-LENSES! HMM... THERE'S ONE HOPE...
LATER, DESTINY AGAIN SEEMED TO GIVE CLARK A HELPING HAND, AS HE EXAMINED THE WRECKAGE OF THE KRYPTON ROCKET IN WHICH HE HAD ARRIVED ON EARTH...
WHAT LUCK! WHEN THE SUPER-PLEXIGLASS SMASHED, FOUR FAIRLY ROUND PIECES WERE FORMED! I CAN MAKE PLASTIC FRAMES TO CONCEAL THE UNEVEN RIDGES! I'LL HAVE GLASSES... BOTH FOR MY BOYHOOD AND MANHOOD... THAT ARE IMPERVIOUS TO MY X-RAY VISION!
EACH TIME AFTER HIS EXPLOITS, SUPERBOY CHANGED BACK TO HIS EVERYDAY ROLE OF MEEK CLARK KENT... BUT ONE DAY...
HMM... WHEN YOU DISAPPEAR, SUPERBOY SHOWS UP! AND WHEN SUPERBOY VANISHES, YOU SHOW UP! MAYBE YOU ARE THE SAME PERSON?
OMIGOSH! MY NEXT-DOOR NEIGH-BOR, LANA LANG, IS ON THE TRACK OF MY SECRET IDENTITY!
LATER, IN DAD KENT'S HOME WORKSHOP...
WHY...UH...WHAT'S THAT YOU MADE, SON?
A SUPERBOY ROBOT, DAD! IT WILL TALK AND PERFORM JUST LIKE ME AND FOOL LANA!
THIS, THE FIRST OF THE SUPERBOY ROBOTS, LULLED LANA'S SUSPICIONS...
GOODNESS! THERE'S SUPERBOY! THEN YOU...ER...CAN'T BE HIM, CLARK! UNLESS THIS IS SOME TRICK!
HMM! SHE MAY BE WATCHING MY HOME TO SEE IF SHE CAN GLIMPSE ME FLYING IN OR OUT AS SUPERBOY! BUT I'LL FIX THAT...
9

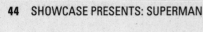

IN HIS BASEMENT, LATER, AFTER CLARK CHANGES TO SUPERBOY...

FIRST, I'LL SMASH THROUGH THE CONCRETE FLOOR AND...

...BORE MY WAY UNDER-GROUND TO FORM A PERMANENT TUNNEL...

...WITH AN EXIT OUT OF TOWN! NOW NOBODY, INCLUDING LANA, WILL EVER SEE ME ENTERING OR LEAVING THE HOUSE!

ONE JOYFUL DAY, KRYPTO APPEARED ON EARTH, AND AFTER SUPERBOY TRACKED DOWN HIS ROCKET...

THIS KRYPTONESE RECORD, PUT IN THE ROCKET BY MY FATHER, REVEALS HOW KRYPTO'S EXPERI-MENTAL ROCKET WENT ADRIFT IN SPACE...TO LAND FINALLY ON EARTH! MY PET PUP IS BACK WITH ME, GROWN UP INTO A SUPERDOG!

THEREAFTER, BETWEEN ROMPS IN OUTER SPACE, KRYPTO OFTEN RETURNED FOR SUPER-PLAY WITH HIS EARTHLY MASTER!

COME ON, KRYPTO! LET'S RACE AROUND THE WORLD! GOSH, YOU'RE THE ONLY ONE WITH WHOM I CAN PLAY SUPER-GAMES! AND YOU SURE LOOK GREAT WITH THAT CAPE I MADE YOU!

YIP, YIP, YIP!

SUPERBOY HAD ANOTHER PROBLEM AS TROPHIES OF HIS SUPER-DEEDS COLLECTED...

THERE! DAD LET ME BUILD THREE SECRET ROOMS SO THAT VISITORS WILL NEVER STUMBLE ON ANY CLUES PROVING I LIVE HERE AS "CLARK KENT"!

ATTIC ROOM
COLLECTION OF TROPHIES AND SUPER-SOUVENIRS.

BEDROOM
STOREROOM FOR SUPERBOY AND CLARK ROBOTS

BASEMENT ROOM
SUPER-WORKSHOP

HOWEVER, THERE WAS ONE MYSTERY SUPER-BOY HIMSELF COULD NEVER SOLVE UNTIL ONE DAY WHEN HE SPED FAR INTO SPACE...

I OVERTOOK LIGHT-RAYS THAT LEFT EARTH LONG AGO, BEFORE MY ROCKET LANDED! NOW I'LL WATCH MY PAST UNFOLD AND FIND OUT WHY I GAINED SUPER-POWERS!

10

ALONG WITH HIS SUPER-MEMORY OF HIS CHILDHOOD ON **KRYPTON**, THIS ALLOWED **SUPERBOY** TO GUESS THE TRUTH, AND LATER...

LOOK, DAD! BORN ON A GIANT WORLD WITH HEAVY GRAVITY, MY MUSCLES AUTOMATICALLY BECAME SUPER-STRONG IN EARTH'S LIGHT GRAVITY! I'M LIKE THE ANT WHICH, IF IT WERE MAN-SIZED, COULD CARRY A LOCOMOTIVE! GRASSHOPPERS COULD LEAP OVER BUILDINGS!

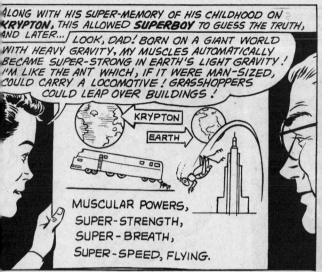

KRYPTON
EARTH

MUSCULAR POWERS,
SUPER-STRENGTH,
SUPER-BREATH,
SUPER-SPEED, FLYING.

NOW NOTICE THAT **KRYPTON** HAD A **RED** SUN, DAD! BUT ONLY THE **ULTRA SOLAR RAYS** OF EARTH'S **YELLOW** SUN CAN SUPER-ENERGIZE MY BRAIN AND FIVE SENSES TO GIVE ME THE OTHER NON-MUSCULAR SUPER-POWERS!

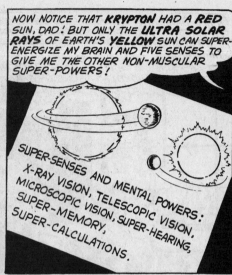

SUPER-SENSES AND MENTAL POWERS:
X-RAY VISION, TELESCOPIC VISION, MICROSCOPIC VISION, SUPER-HEARING, SUPER-MEMORY, SUPER-CALCULATIONS.

ALSO, THOSE YELLOW-SUN RAYS, WHICH ONLY **TAN** EARTH PEOPLE'S SKIN, **HARDENED** MINE LIKE STEEL! RADIUM RAYS...LIGHTNING... FIRE... **NOTHING** CAN HARM ME!

LIGHTNING
RADIUM
FIRE

YET ONE DAY, CLARK FELL MYSTERIOUSLY ILL!

WHY, HE HAS A RAGING FEVER, JONATHAN!

BUT WHAT COULD AFFECT HIS INVULNERABLE BODY? HMM...COULD IT BE THAT GREEN-GLOWING METEOR I FOUND FOR CLARK'S MINERAL COLLECTION?

A SERIES OF TESTS PROVED THE TRUTH!

LEAD **STOPS** THOSE RAYS! BUT WHY DOES THAT MINERAL HARM YOU?

HMM...WHEN KRYPTON EXPLODED, ALL THE FRAGMENTS MUST HAVE TURNED RADIOACTIVE! HARMLESS TO EARTH PEOPLE, IT'S DEADLY TO **ME**! I'LL CALL IT **KRYPTONITE**!

THUS FOREWARNED, CLARK (**SUPERBOY**) KENT AVOIDED HIS NEMESIS AND GREW TO YOUNG MANHOOD, FOLLOWED BY COLLEGE...

I COULD BE THE WORLD'S GREAT-EST FOOTBALL PLAYER...BUT I CAN'T JOIN THE TEAM AND REVEAL MY SUPER-POWERS! BESIDES, IT WOULD BE UNFAIR TO WIN THAT WAY! I'LL HAVE TO PRETEND I'M "MEEK" AND "UNATHLETIC" ALL MY LIFE!

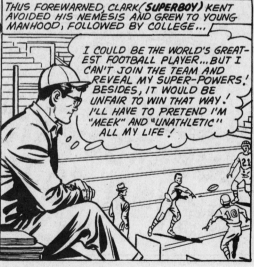

11

AFTER GRADUATION, CLARK RETURNED HOME TO MEET ONE HEARTBREAK, SOON FOLLOWED BY ANOTHER...

MOM KENT PASSED AWAY A FEW MONTHS AGO...AND NOW DAD KENT IS ON HIS DEATH BED! ¡CHOKE!¡

THERE'S NOT MUCH TIME, SON! LISTEN CAREFULLY TO MY LAST WORDS! NO ONE ON EARTH HAS YOUR AMAZING SUPER-POWERS AND...

...YOU MUST ALWAYS USE THEM TO DO GOOD! YOU MUST UPHOLD LAW AND ORDER, AID THOSE IN NEED, AND SAVE LIVES! GOOD LUCK, MY SON, AND GOODBYE...

H-HE'S GONE!

LATER, ORPHANED FOR THE SECOND TIME, CLARK IS READY TO LEAVE SMALLVILLE...

I'LL NEVER FORGET MY LOVING FOSTER PARENTS! BUT NOW I'LL GO AND LIVE IN A BIG CITY -- METROPOLIS! THEN I'LL GET SOME SORT OF JOB AS CLARK KENT, MEEK AND MILD-MANNERED AS USUAL...

JONATHAN KENT

MARTHA KENT

AS SUPERBOY PREPARED TO LEAVE SMALLVILLE, AFTER HAVING SAID GOODBYE TO LANA LANG, POLICE CHIEF PARKER, AND OTHER OFFICIALS...

I'LL RETURN SECRETLY AT NIGHT TO REMOVE MY ROBOTS AND TROPHIES FROM THE HOUSE...HUH... WHAT'S THAT CROWD BELOW?

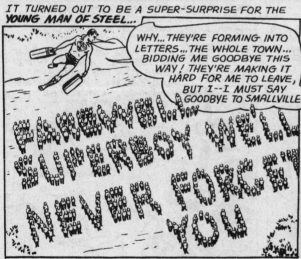

IT TURNED OUT TO BE A SUPER-SURPRISE FOR THE YOUNG MAN OF STEEL...

WHY...THEY'RE FORMING INTO LETTERS...THE WHOLE TOWN... BIDDING ME GOODBYE THIS WAY! THEY'RE MAKING IT HARD FOR ME TO LEAVE, BUT I--I MUST SAY GOODBYE TO SMALLVILLE!

FAREWELL SUPERBOY WE'LL NEVER FORGET YOU

AFTER THAT CAME A WONDERFUL FAREWELL PARTY, WHERE SUPERBOY ALSO DID HIS PART...

I KNEW I WAS COMING, SO I BAKED THIS SUPER-CAKE... ENOUGH FOR EVERYONE TO HAVE A SLICE!

12

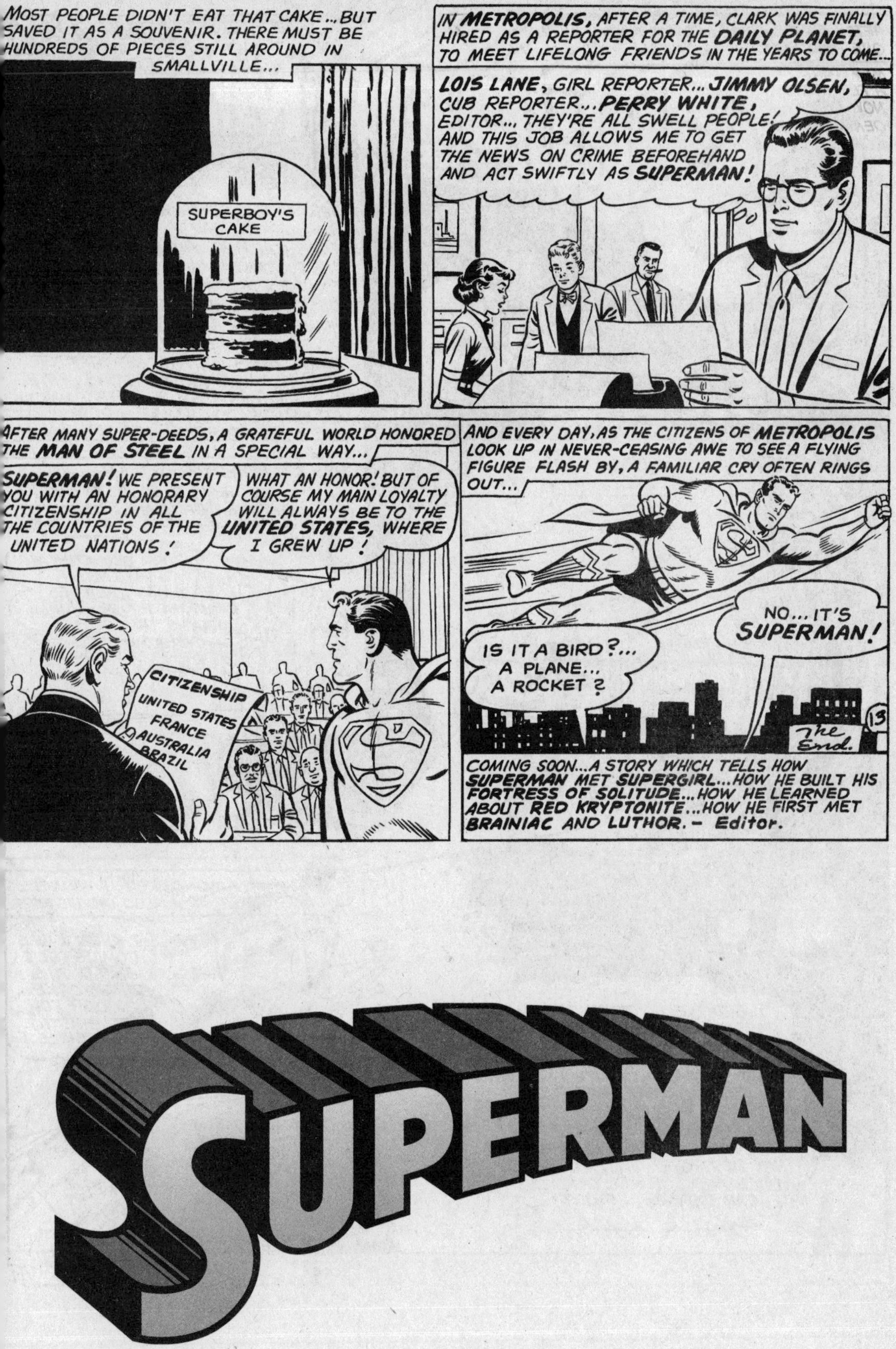
MOST PEOPLE DIDN'T EAT THAT CAKE...BUT SAVED IT AS A SOUVENIR. THERE MUST BE HUNDREDS OF PIECES STILL AROUND IN SMALLVILLE...
SUPERBOY'S CAKE
IN METROPOLIS, AFTER A TIME, CLARK WAS FINALLY HIRED AS A REPORTER FOR THE DAILY PLANET, TO MEET LIFELONG FRIENDS IN THE YEARS TO COME...
LOIS LANE, GIRL REPORTER... JIMMY OLSEN, CUB REPORTER... PERRY WHITE, EDITOR... THEY'RE ALL SWELL PEOPLE! AND THIS JOB ALLOWS ME TO GET THE NEWS ON CRIME BEFOREHAND AND ACT SWIFTLY AS SUPERMAN!
AFTER MANY SUPER-DEEDS, A GRATEFUL WORLD HONORED THE MAN OF STEEL IN A SPECIAL WAY...
SUPERMAN! WE PRESENT YOU WITH AN HONORARY CITIZENSHIP IN ALL THE COUNTRIES OF THE UNITED NATIONS!
WHAT AN HONOR! BUT OF COURSE MY MAIN LOYALTY WILL ALWAYS BE TO THE UNITED STATES, WHERE I GREW UP!
CITIZENSHIP UNITED STATES FRANCE AUSTRALIA BRAZIL
AND EVERY DAY, AS THE CITIZENS OF METROPOLIS LOOK UP IN NEVER-CEASING AWE TO SEE A FLYING FIGURE FLASH BY, A FAMILIAR CRY OFTEN RINGS OUT...
IS IT A BIRD?... A PLANE... A ROCKET?
NO... IT'S SUPERMAN!
The End
13
COMING SOON...A STORY WHICH TELLS HOW SUPERMAN MET SUPERGIRL...HOW HE BUILT HIS FORTRESS OF SOLITUDE...HOW HE LEARNED ABOUT RED KRYPTONITE...HOW HE FIRST MET BRAINIAC AND LUTHOR. - Editor.

SUPERMAN

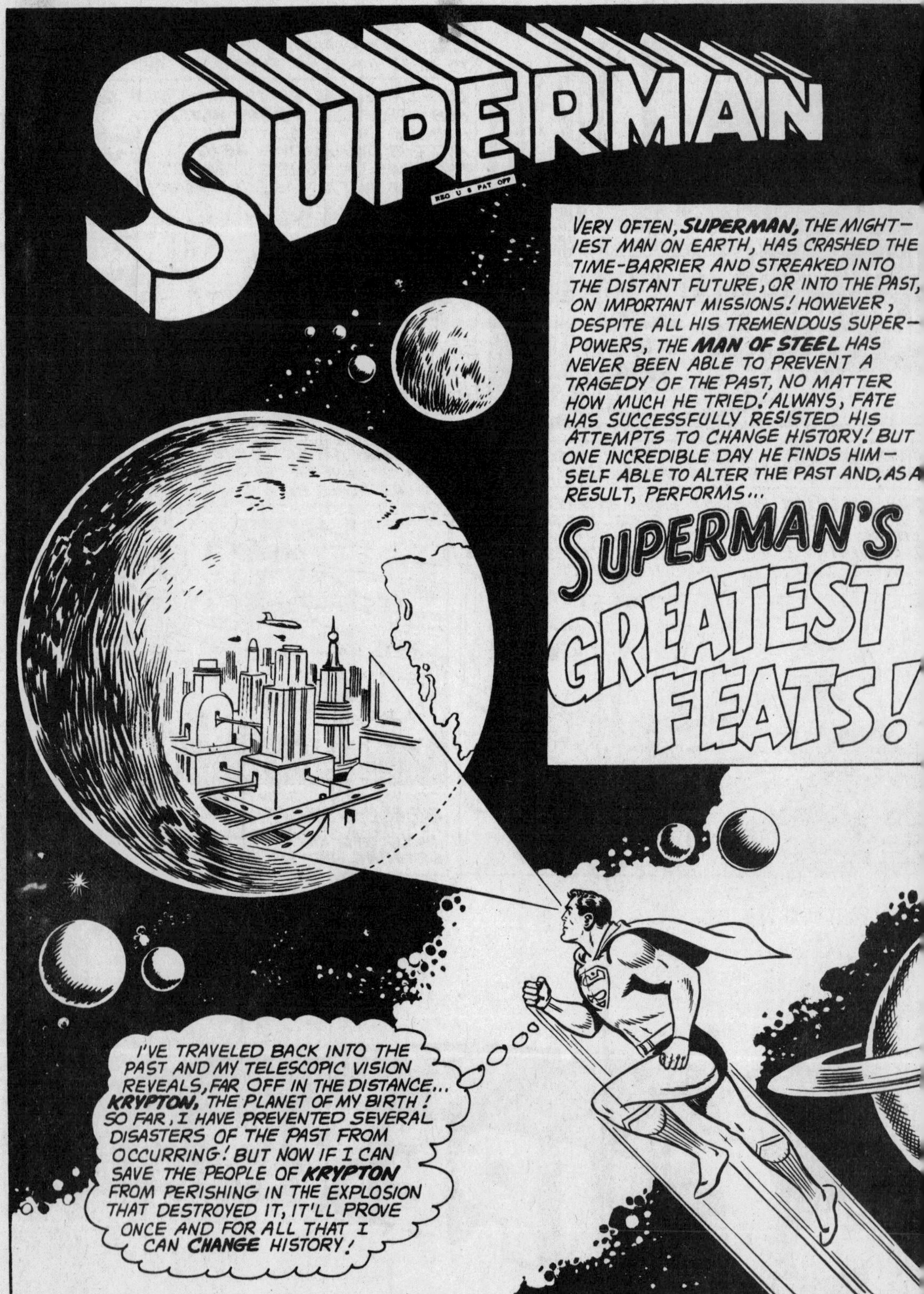
SUPERMAN
REG U S PAT OFF
VERY OFTEN, SUPERMAN, THE MIGHTIEST MAN ON EARTH, HAS CRASHED THE TIME-BARRIER AND STREAKED INTO THE DISTANT FUTURE, OR INTO THE PAST, ON IMPORTANT MISSIONS! HOWEVER, DESPITE ALL HIS TREMENDOUS SUPER-POWERS, THE MAN OF STEEL HAS NEVER BEEN ABLE TO PREVENT A TRAGEDY OF THE PAST, NO MATTER HOW MUCH HE TRIED! ALWAYS, FATE HAS SUCCESSFULLY RESISTED HIS ATTEMPTS TO CHANGE HISTORY! BUT ONE INCREDIBLE DAY HE FINDS HIMSELF ABLE TO ALTER THE PAST AND, AS A RESULT, PERFORMS...
SUPERMAN'S GREATEST FEATS!
I'VE TRAVELED BACK INTO THE PAST AND MY TELESCOPIC VISION REVEALS, FAR OFF IN THE DISTANCE... KRYPTON, THE PLANET OF MY BIRTH! SO FAR, I HAVE PREVENTED SEVERAL DISASTERS OF THE PAST FROM OCCURRING! BUT NOW IF I CAN SAVE THE PEOPLE OF KRYPTON FROM PERISHING IN THE EXPLOSION THAT DESTROYED IT, IT'LL PROVE ONCE AND FOR ALL THAT I CAN CHANGE HISTORY!

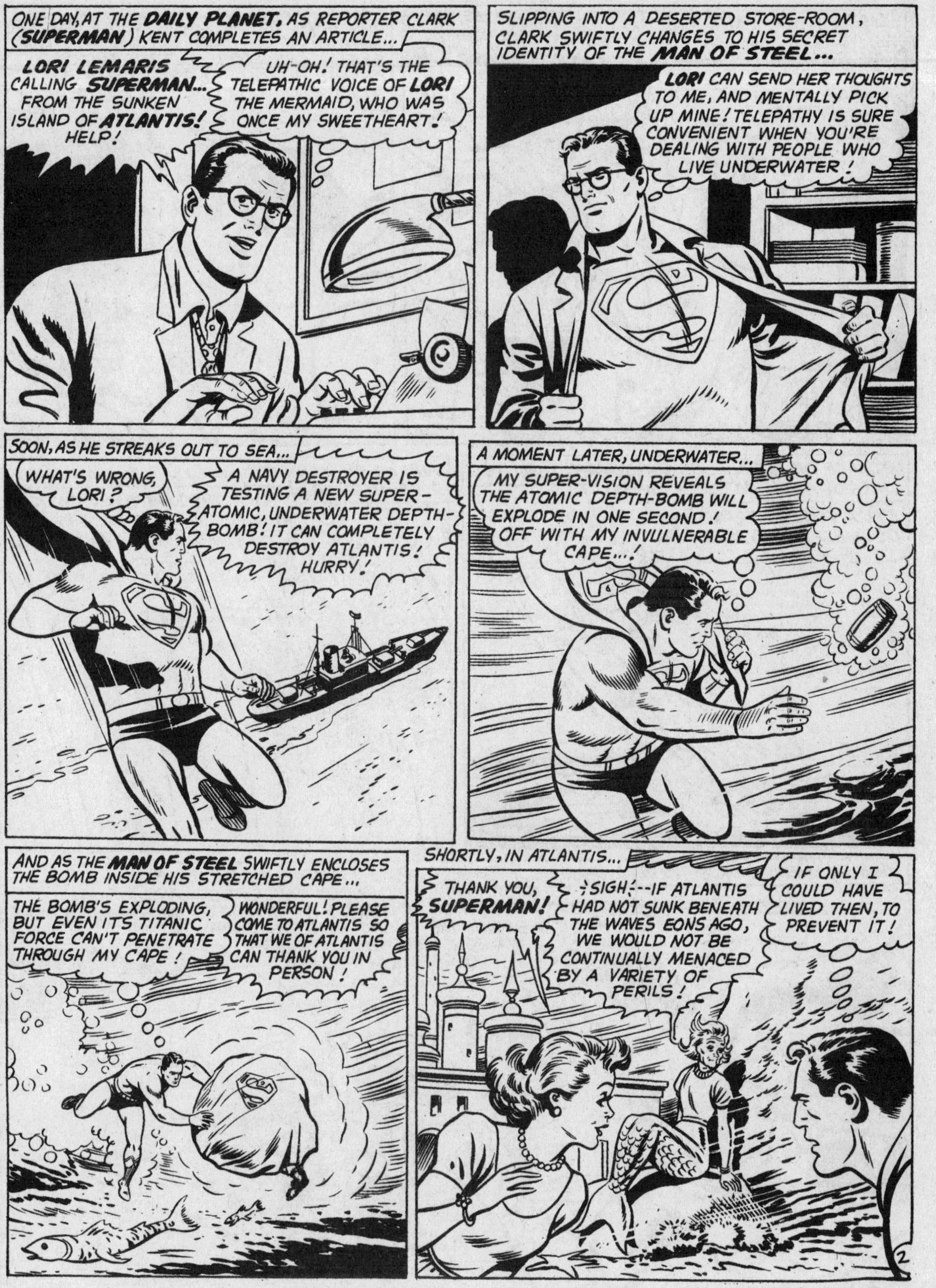
ONE DAY, AT THE DAILY PLANET, AS REPORTER CLARK (SUPERMAN) KENT COMPLETES AN ARTICLE...
LORI LEMARIS CALLING SUPERMAN... FROM THE SUNKEN ISLAND OF ATLANTIS! HELP!
UH-OH! THAT'S THE TELEPATHIC VOICE OF LORI THE MERMAID, WHO WAS ONCE MY SWEETHEART!
SLIPPING INTO A DESERTED STORE-ROOM, CLARK SWIFTLY CHANGES TO HIS SECRET IDENTITY OF THE MAN OF STEEL...
LORI CAN SEND HER THOUGHTS TO ME, AND MENTALLY PICK UP MINE! TELEPATHY IS SURE CONVENIENT WHEN YOU'RE DEALING WITH PEOPLE WHO LIVE UNDERWATER!
SOON, AS HE STREAKS OUT TO SEA...
WHAT'S WRONG, LORI?
A NAVY DESTROYER IS TESTING A NEW SUPER-ATOMIC, UNDERWATER DEPTH-BOMB! IT CAN COMPLETELY DESTROY ATLANTIS! HURRY!
A MOMENT LATER, UNDERWATER...
MY SUPER-VISION REVEALS THE ATOMIC DEPTH-BOMB WILL EXPLODE IN ONE SECOND! OFF WITH MY INVULNERABLE CAPE...!
AND AS THE MAN OF STEEL SWIFTLY ENCLOSES THE BOMB INSIDE HIS STRETCHED CAPE...
THE BOMB'S EXPLODING, BUT EVEN ITS TITANIC FORCE CAN'T PENETRATE THROUGH MY CAPE!
WONDERFUL! PLEASE COME TO ATLANTIS SO THAT WE OF ATLANTIS CAN THANK YOU IN PERSON!
SHORTLY, IN ATLANTIS...
THANK YOU, SUPERMAN!
-SIGH!- --IF ATLANTIS HAD NOT SUNK BENEATH THE WAVES EONS AGO, WE WOULD NOT BE CONTINUALLY MENACED BY A VARIETY OF PERILS!
IF ONLY I COULD HAVE LIVED THEN, TO PREVENT IT!
2

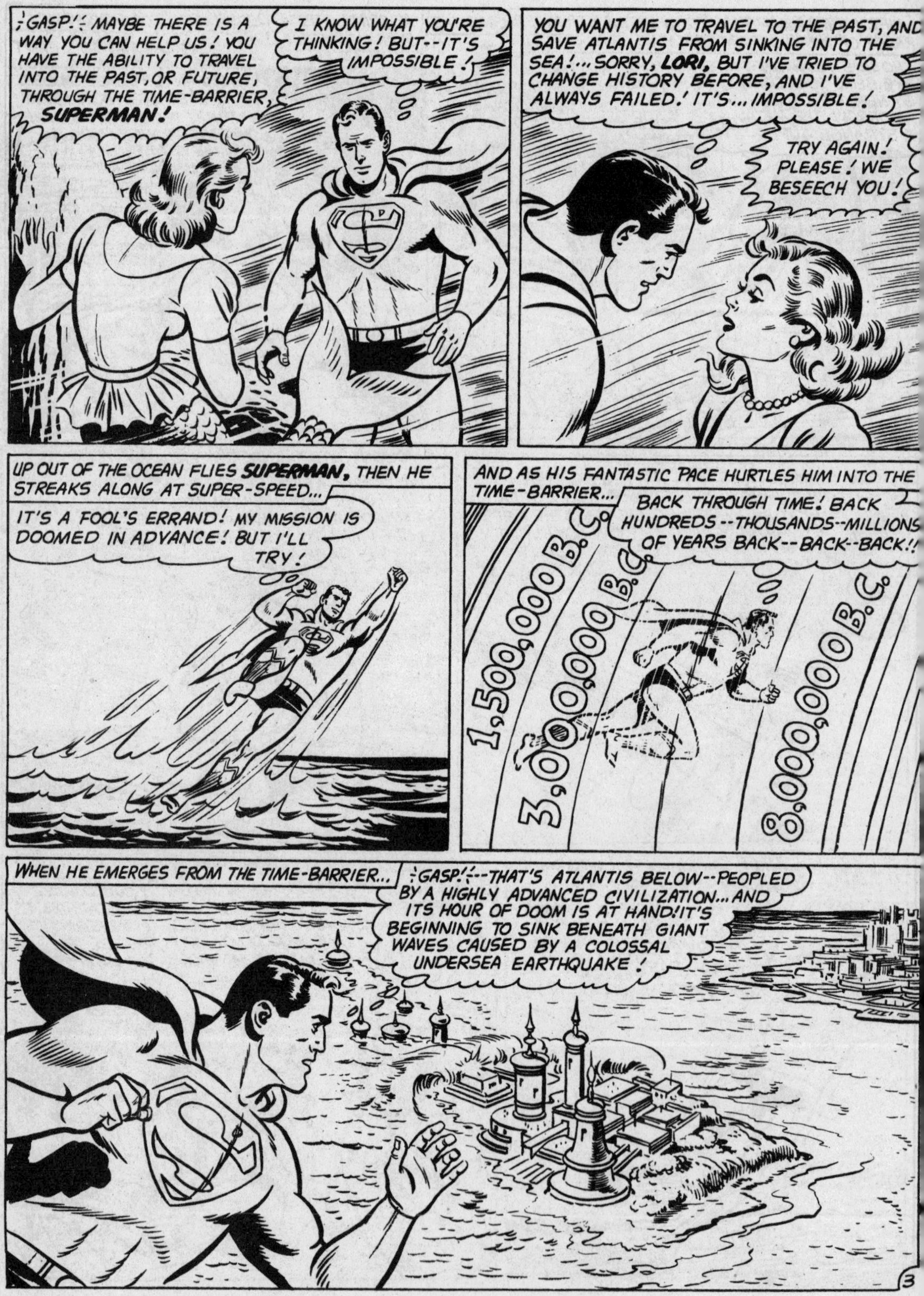
;GASP!; MAYBE THERE IS A WAY YOU CAN HELP US! YOU HAVE THE ABILITY TO TRAVEL INTO THE PAST, OR FUTURE, THROUGH THE TIME-BARRIER, SUPERMAN!
I KNOW WHAT YOU'RE THINKING! BUT--IT'S IMPOSSIBLE!
YOU WANT ME TO TRAVEL TO THE PAST, AND SAVE ATLANTIS FROM SINKING INTO THE SEA!... SORRY, LORI, BUT I'VE TRIED TO CHANGE HISTORY BEFORE, AND I'VE ALWAYS FAILED! IT'S... IMPOSSIBLE!
TRY AGAIN! PLEASE! WE BESEECH YOU!
UP OUT OF THE OCEAN FLIES SUPERMAN, THEN HE STREAKS ALONG AT SUPER-SPEED...
IT'S A FOOL'S ERRAND! MY MISSION IS DOOMED IN ADVANCE! BUT I'LL TRY!
AND AS HIS FANTASTIC PACE HURTLES HIM INTO THE TIME-BARRIER...
BACK THROUGH TIME! BACK HUNDREDS--THOUSANDS--MILLIONS OF YEARS BACK--BACK--BACK!!
1,500,000 B.C.
3,000,000 B.C.
8,000,000 B.C.
WHEN HE EMERGES FROM THE TIME-BARRIER...
;GASP!;--THAT'S ATLANTIS BELOW--PEOPLED BY A HIGHLY ADVANCED CIVILIZATION... AND ITS HOUR OF DOOM IS AT HAND! IT'S BEGINNING TO SINK BENEATH GIANT WAVES CAUSED BY A COLOSSAL UNDERSEA EARTHQUAKE!
3

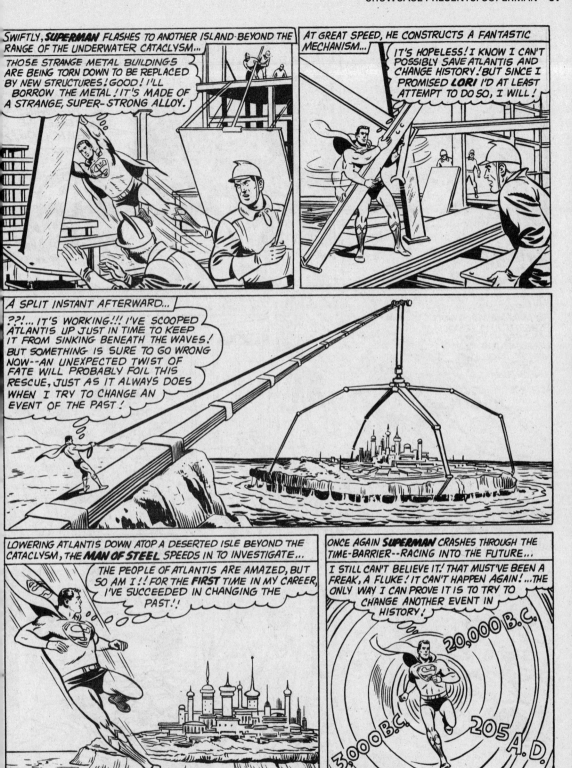

SWIFTLY, **SUPERMAN** FLASHES TO ANOTHER ISLAND-BEYOND THE RANGE OF THE UNDERWATER CATACLYSM...

THOSE STRANGE METAL BUILDINGS ARE BEING TORN DOWN TO BE REPLACED BY NEW STRUCTURES! GOOD! I'LL BORROW THE METAL! IT'S MADE OF A STRANGE, SUPER-STRONG ALLOY.

AT GREAT SPEED, HE CONSTRUCTS A FANTASTIC MECHANISM...

IT'S HOPELESS! I KNOW I CAN'T POSSIBLY SAVE ATLANTIS AND CHANGE HISTORY! BUT SINCE I PROMISED **LORI** I'D AT LEAST ATTEMPT TO DO SO, I WILL!

A SPLIT INSTANT AFTERWARD...

??!... IT'S WORKING!!! I'VE SCOOPED ATLANTIS UP JUST IN TIME TO KEEP IT FROM SINKING BENEATH THE WAVES! BUT SOMETHING IS SURE TO GO WRONG NOW-- AN UNEXPECTED TWIST OF FATE WILL PROBABLY FOIL THIS RESCUE, JUST AS IT ALWAYS DOES WHEN I TRY TO CHANGE AN EVENT OF THE PAST!

LOWERING ATLANTIS DOWN ATOP A DESERTED ISLE BEYOND THE CATACLYSM, THE **MAN OF STEEL** SPEEDS IN TO INVESTIGATE...

THE PEOPLE OF ATLANTIS ARE AMAZED, BUT SO AM I!! FOR THE **FIRST** TIME IN MY CAREER, I'VE SUCCEEDED IN CHANGING THE PAST!!

ONCE AGAIN **SUPERMAN** CRASHES THROUGH THE TIME-BARRIER-- RACING INTO THE FUTURE...

I STILL CAN'T BELIEVE IT! THAT MUST'VE BEEN A FREAK, A FLUKE! IT CAN'T HAPPEN AGAIN!...THE ONLY WAY I CAN PROVE IT IS TO TRY TO CHANGE ANOTHER EVENT IN HISTORY!

20,000 B.C.

3,000 B.C.

205 A.D.

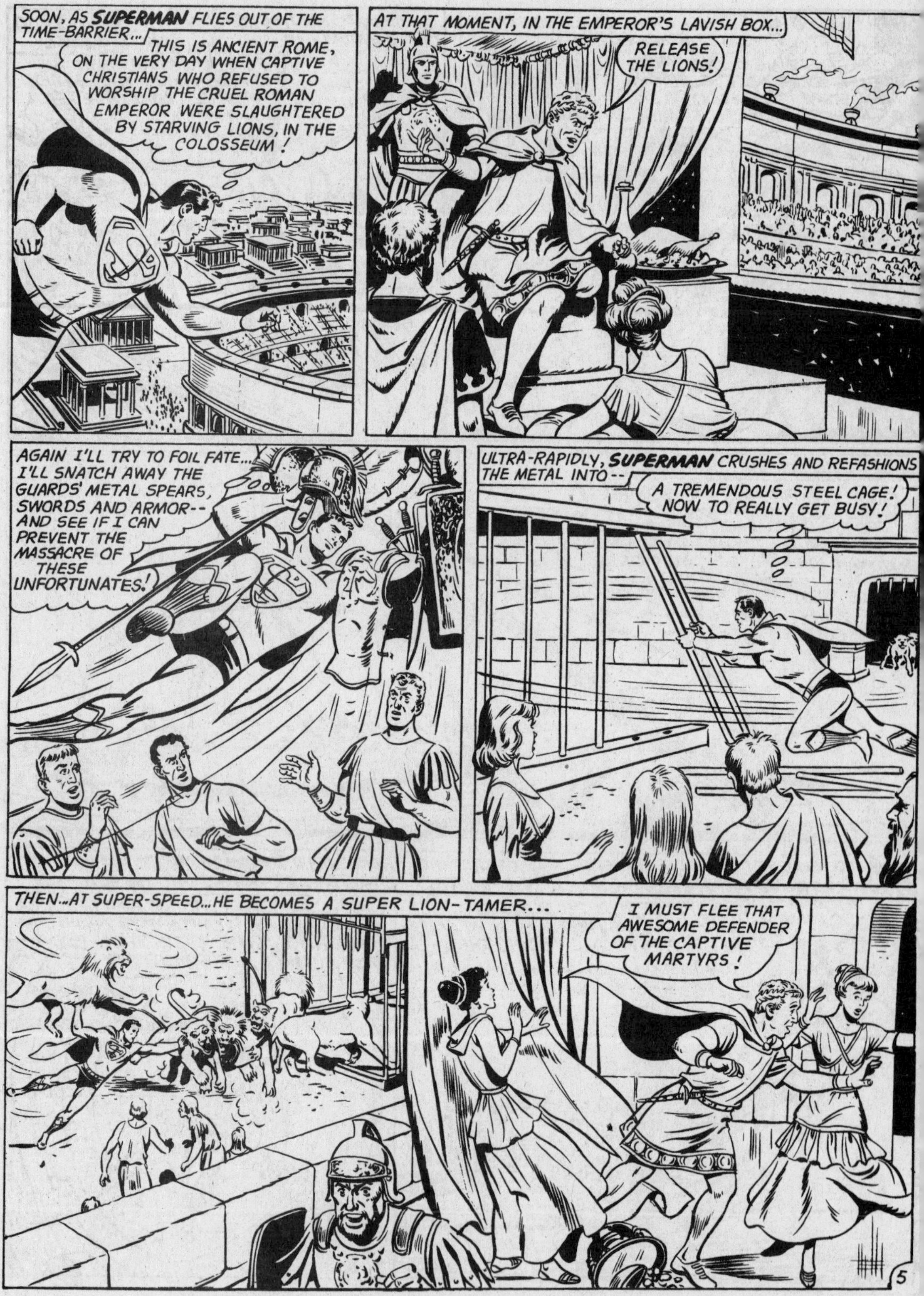
SOON, AS SUPERMAN FLIES OUT OF THE TIME-BARRIER...
THIS IS ANCIENT ROME, ON THE VERY DAY WHEN CAPTIVE CHRISTIANS WHO REFUSED TO WORSHIP THE CRUEL ROMAN EMPEROR WERE SLAUGHTERED BY STARVING LIONS, IN THE COLOSSEUM!
AT THAT MOMENT, IN THE EMPEROR'S LAVISH BOX...
RELEASE THE LIONS!
AGAIN I'LL TRY TO FOIL FATE... I'LL SNATCH AWAY THE GUARDS' METAL SPEARS, SWORDS AND ARMOR-- AND SEE IF I CAN PREVENT THE MASSACRE OF THESE UNFORTUNATES!
ULTRA-RAPIDLY, SUPERMAN CRUSHES AND REFASHIONS THE METAL INTO--
A TREMENDOUS STEEL CAGE! NOW TO REALLY GET BUSY!
THEN...AT SUPER-SPEED...HE BECOMES A SUPER LION-TAMER...
I MUST FLEE THAT AWESOME DEFENDER OF THE CAPTIVE MARTYRS!
5

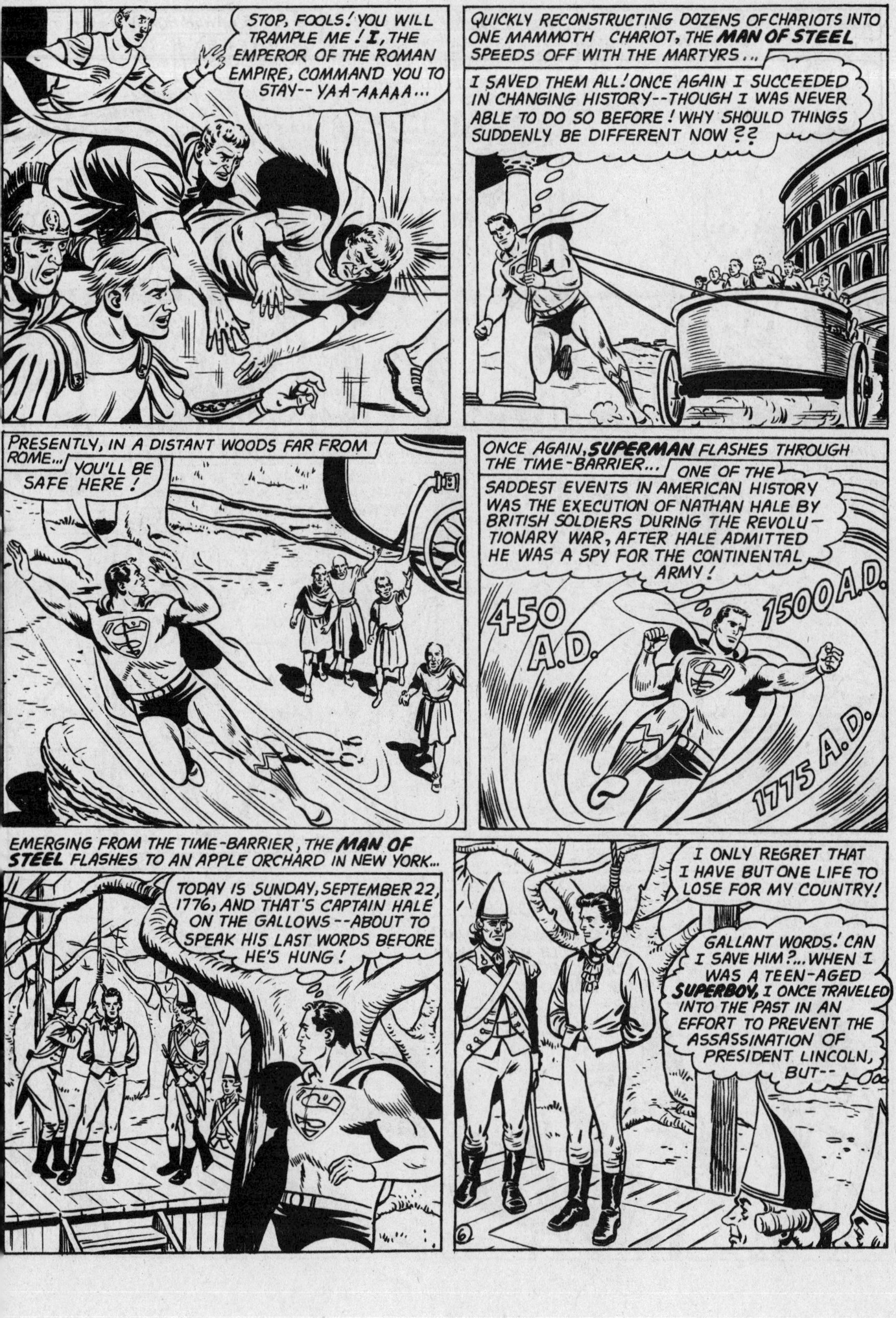
STOP, FOOLS! YOU WILL TRAMPLE ME! I, THE EMPEROR OF THE ROMAN EMPIRE, COMMAND YOU TO STAY-- YA-A-AAAAA...
QUICKLY RECONSTRUCTING DOZENS OF CHARIOTS INTO ONE MAMMOTH CHARIOT, THE MAN OF STEEL SPEEDS OFF WITH THE MARTYRS...
I SAVED THEM ALL! ONCE AGAIN I SUCCEEDED IN CHANGING HISTORY--THOUGH I WAS NEVER ABLE TO DO SO BEFORE! WHY SHOULD THINGS SUDDENLY BE DIFFERENT NOW??
PRESENTLY, IN A DISTANT WOODS FAR FROM ROME...
YOU'LL BE SAFE HERE!
ONCE AGAIN, SUPERMAN FLASHES THROUGH THE TIME-BARRIER...
ONE OF THE SADDEST EVENTS IN AMERICAN HISTORY WAS THE EXECUTION OF NATHAN HALE BY BRITISH SOLDIERS DURING THE REVOLUTIONARY WAR, AFTER HALE ADMITTED HE WAS A SPY FOR THE CONTINENTAL ARMY!
450 A.D.
1500 A.D.
1775 A.D.
EMERGING FROM THE TIME-BARRIER, THE MAN OF STEEL FLASHES TO AN APPLE ORCHARD IN NEW YORK...
TODAY IS SUNDAY, SEPTEMBER 22, 1776, AND THAT'S CAPTAIN HALE ON THE GALLOWS--ABOUT TO SPEAK HIS LAST WORDS BEFORE HE'S HUNG!
I ONLY REGRET THAT I HAVE BUT ONE LIFE TO LOSE FOR MY COUNTRY!
GALLANT WORDS! CAN I SAVE HIM?...WHEN I WAS A TEEN-AGED SUPERBOY, I ONCE TRAVELED INTO THE PAST IN AN EFFORT TO PREVENT THE ASSASSINATION OF PRESIDENT LINCOLN, BUT--
6

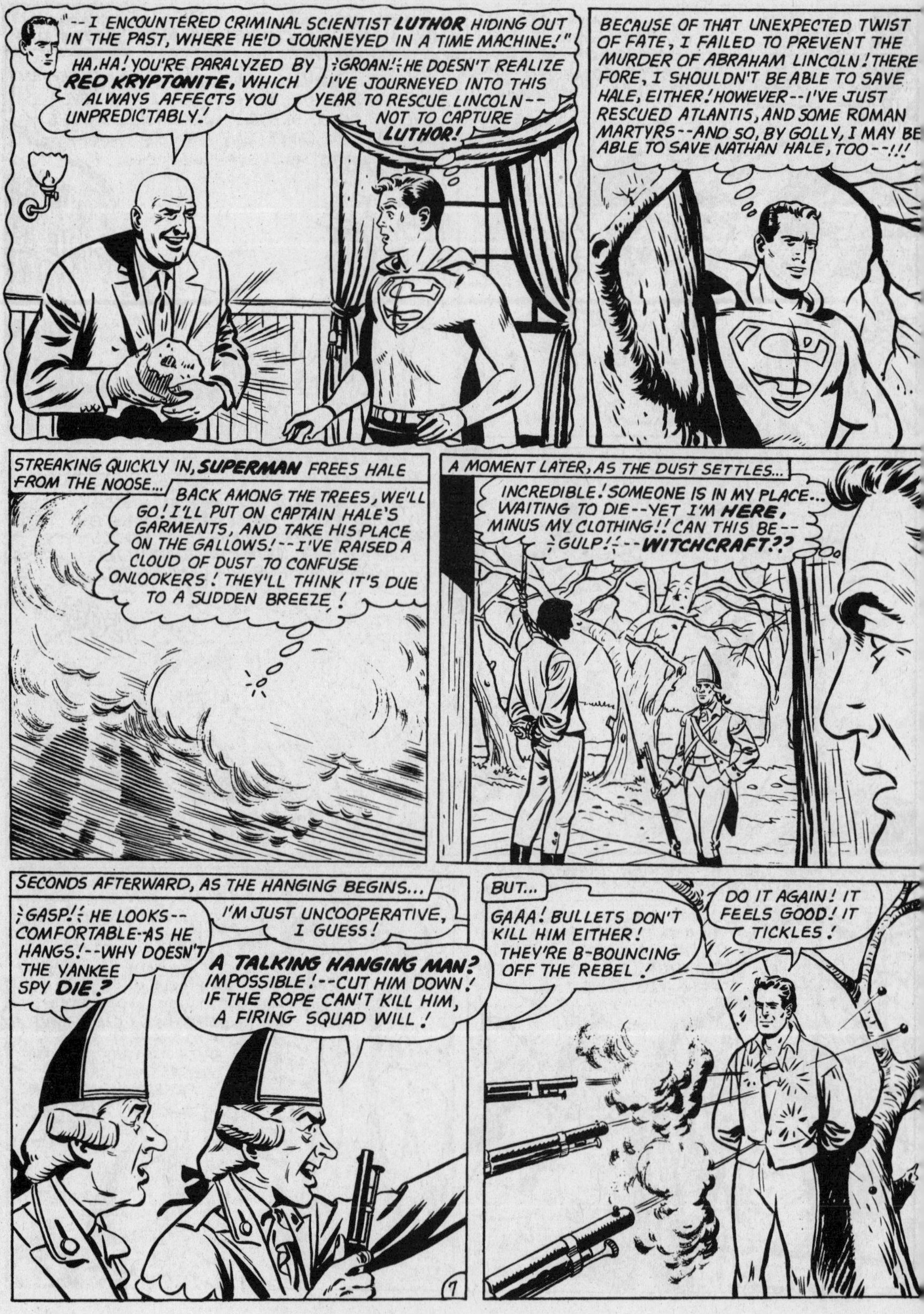
"--I ENCOUNTERED CRIMINAL SCIENTIST LUTHOR HIDING OUT IN THE PAST, WHERE HE'D JOURNEYED IN A TIME MACHINE!"
HA,HA! YOU'RE PARALYZED BY RED KRYPTONITE, WHICH ALWAYS AFFECTS YOU UNPREDICTABLY!
-GROAN!- HE DOESN'T REALIZE I'VE JOURNEYED INTO THIS YEAR TO RESCUE LINCOLN--NOT TO CAPTURE LUTHOR!
BECAUSE OF THAT UNEXPECTED TWIST OF FATE, I FAILED TO PREVENT THE MURDER OF ABRAHAM LINCOLN! THEREFORE, I SHOULDN'T BE ABLE TO SAVE HALE, EITHER! HOWEVER--I'VE JUST RESCUED ATLANTIS, AND SOME ROMAN MARTYRS--AND SO, BY GOLLY, I MAY BE ABLE TO SAVE NATHAN HALE, TOO--!!!
STREAKING QUICKLY IN, SUPERMAN FREES HALE FROM THE NOOSE...
BACK AMONG THE TREES, WE'LL GO! I'LL PUT ON CAPTAIN HALE'S GARMENTS, AND TAKE HIS PLACE ON THE GALLOWS!--I'VE RAISED A CLOUD OF DUST TO CONFUSE ONLOOKERS! THEY'LL THINK IT'S DUE TO A SUDDEN BREEZE!
A MOMENT LATER, AS THE DUST SETTLES...
INCREDIBLE! SOMEONE IS IN MY PLACE... WAITING TO DIE--YET I'M HERE, MINUS MY CLOTHING!! CAN THIS BE---GULP!--WITCHCRAFT??
SECONDS AFTERWARD, AS THE HANGING BEGINS...
-GASP!- HE LOOKS--COMFORTABLE-AS HE HANGS!--WHY DOESN'T THE YANKEE SPY DIE?
I'M JUST UNCOOPERATIVE, I GUESS!
A TALKING HANGING MAN? IMPOSSIBLE!--CUT HIM DOWN! IF THE ROPE CAN'T KILL HIM, A FIRING SQUAD WILL!
7
BUT...
GAAA! BULLETS DON'T KILL HIM EITHER! THEY'RE B-BOUNCING OFF THE REBEL!
DO IT AGAIN! IT FEELS GOOD! IT TICKLES!

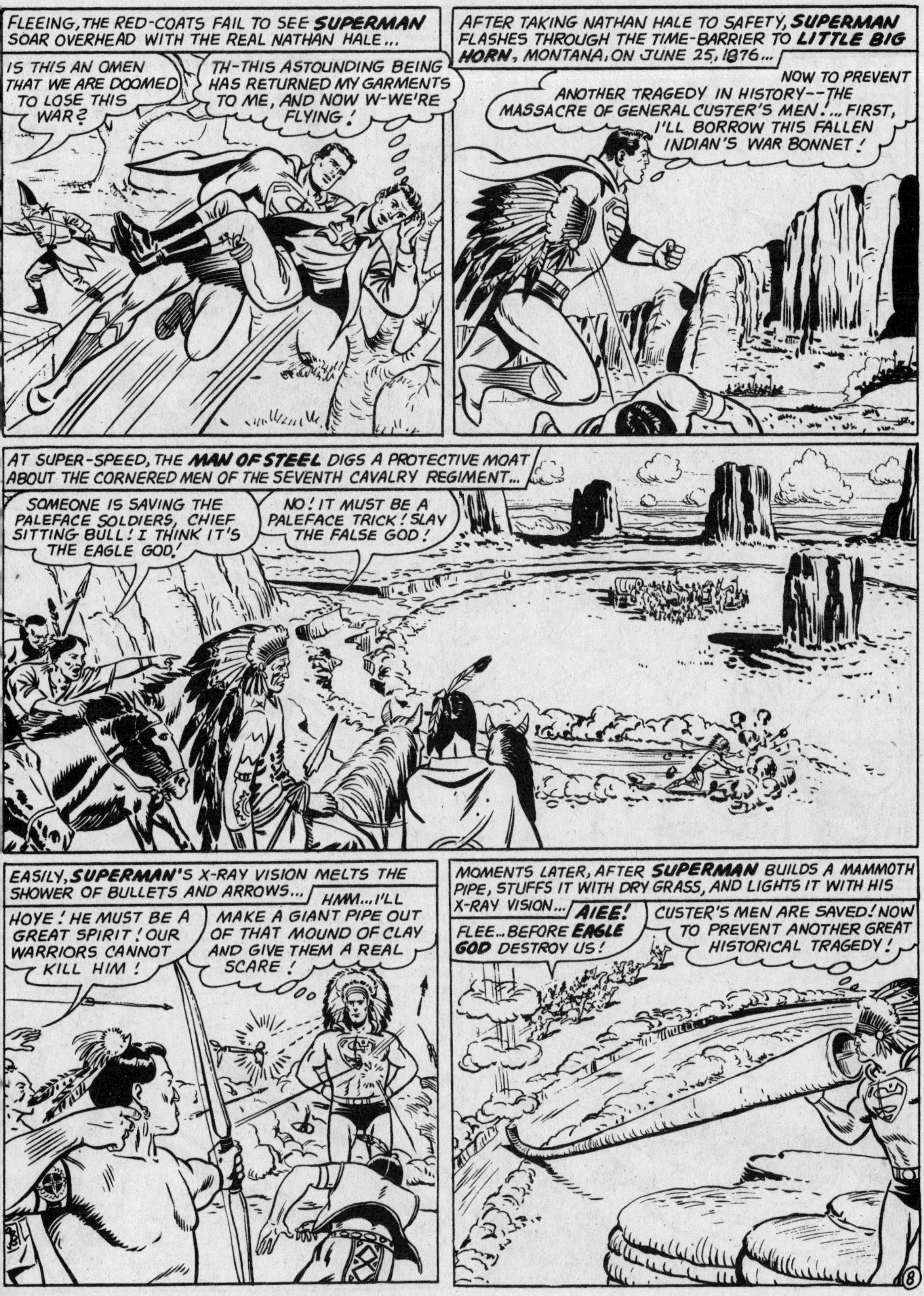
FLEEING, THE RED-COATS FAIL TO SEE SUPERMAN SOAR OVERHEAD WITH THE REAL NATHAN HALE...
IS THIS AN OMEN THAT WE ARE DOOMED TO LOSE THIS WAR?
TH-THIS ASTOUNDING BEING HAS RETURNED MY GARMENTS TO ME, AND NOW W-WE'RE FLYING!
AFTER TAKING NATHAN HALE TO SAFETY, SUPERMAN FLASHES THROUGH THE TIME-BARRIER TO LITTLE BIG HORN, MONTANA, ON JUNE 25, 1876...
NOW TO PREVENT ANOTHER TRAGEDY IN HISTORY--THE MASSACRE OF GENERAL CUSTER'S MEN!... FIRST, I'LL BORROW THIS FALLEN INDIAN'S WAR BONNET!
AT SUPER-SPEED, THE MAN OF STEEL DIGS A PROTECTIVE MOAT ABOUT THE CORNERED MEN OF THE SEVENTH CAVALRY REGIMENT...
SOMEONE IS SAVING THE PALEFACE SOLDIERS, CHIEF SITTING BULL! I THINK IT'S THE EAGLE GOD!
NO! IT MUST BE A PALEFACE TRICK! SLAY THE FALSE GOD!
EASILY, SUPERMAN'S X-RAY VISION MELTS THE SHOWER OF BULLETS AND ARROWS...
HOYE! HE MUST BE A GREAT SPIRIT! OUR WARRIORS CANNOT KILL HIM!
HMM...I'LL MAKE A GIANT PIPE OUT OF THAT MOUND OF CLAY AND GIVE THEM A REAL SCARE!
MOMENTS LATER, AFTER SUPERMAN BUILDS A MAMMOTH PIPE, STUFFS IT WITH DRY GRASS, AND LIGHTS IT WITH HIS X-RAY VISION...
AIEE! FLEE...BEFORE EAGLE GOD DESTROY US!
CUSTER'S MEN ARE SAVED! NOW TO PREVENT ANOTHER GREAT HISTORICAL TRAGEDY!
8

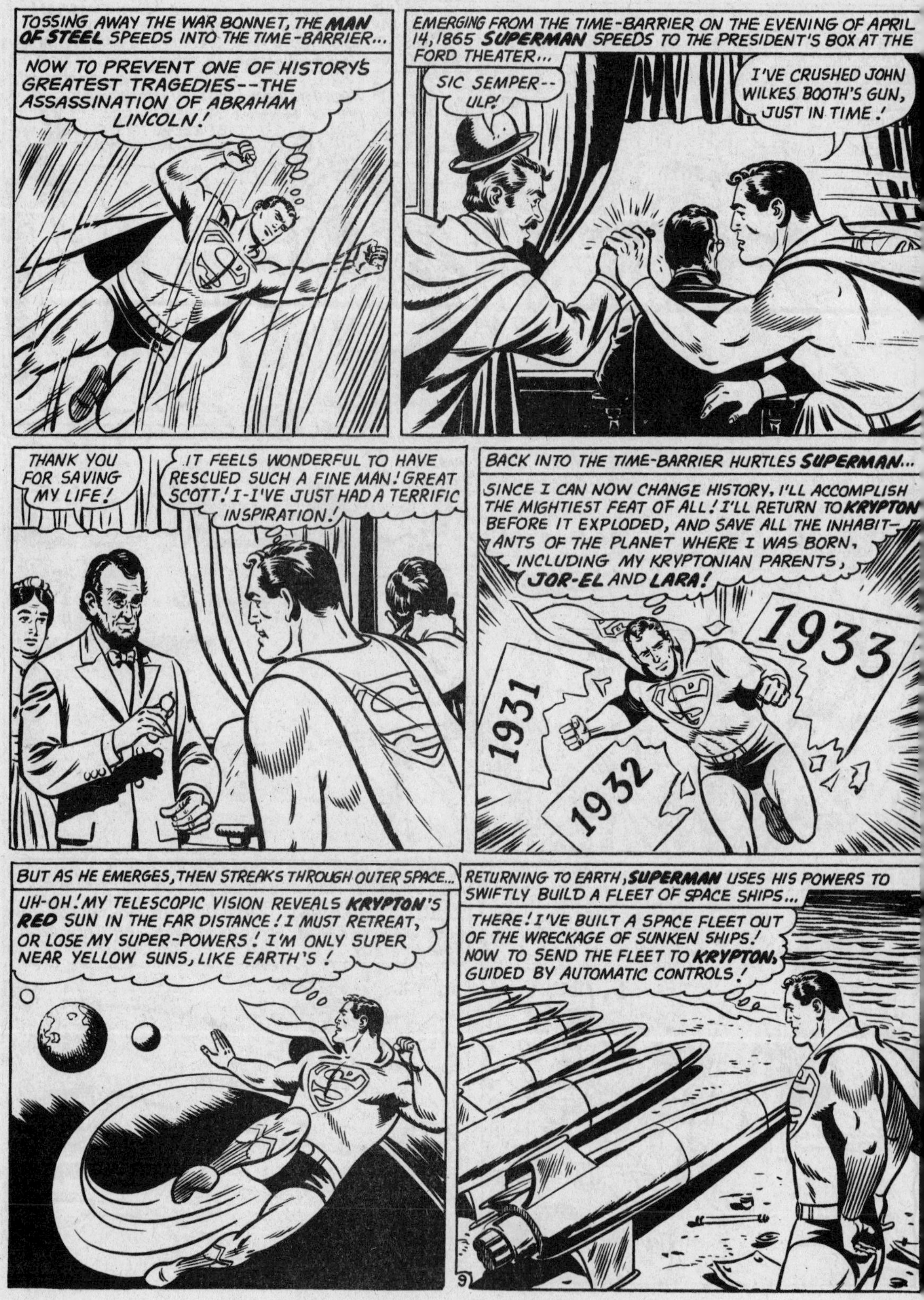
TOSSING AWAY THE WAR BONNET, THE MAN OF STEEL SPEEDS INTO THE TIME-BARRIER...
NOW TO PREVENT ONE OF HISTORY'S GREATEST TRAGEDIES--THE ASSASSINATION OF ABRAHAM LINCOLN!
EMERGING FROM THE TIME-BARRIER ON THE EVENING OF APRIL 14, 1865 SUPERMAN SPEEDS TO THE PRESIDENT'S BOX AT THE FORD THEATER...
SIC SEMPER-- ULP!
I'VE CRUSHED JOHN WILKES BOOTH'S GUN, JUST IN TIME!
THANK YOU FOR SAVING MY LIFE!
IT FEELS WONDERFUL TO HAVE RESCUED SUCH A FINE MAN! GREAT SCOTT! I-I'VE JUST HAD A TERRIFIC INSPIRATION!
BACK INTO THE TIME-BARRIER HURTLES SUPERMAN...
SINCE I CAN NOW CHANGE HISTORY, I'LL ACCOMPLISH THE MIGHTIEST FEAT OF ALL! I'LL RETURN TO KRYPTON BEFORE IT EXPLODED, AND SAVE ALL THE INHABIT-ANTS OF THE PLANET WHERE I WAS BORN, INCLUDING MY KRYPTONIAN PARENTS, JOR-EL AND LARA!
1931
1932
1933
BUT AS HE EMERGES, THEN STREAKS THROUGH OUTER SPACE...
UH-OH! MY TELESCOPIC VISION REVEALS KRYPTON'S RED SUN IN THE FAR DISTANCE! I MUST RETREAT, OR LOSE MY SUPER-POWERS! I'M ONLY SUPER NEAR YELLOW SUNS, LIKE EARTH'S!
RETURNING TO EARTH, SUPERMAN USES HIS POWERS TO SWIFTLY BUILD A FLEET OF SPACE SHIPS...
THERE! I'VE BUILT A SPACE FLEET OUT OF THE WRECKAGE OF SUNKEN SHIPS! NOW TO SEND THE FLEET TO KRYPTON, GUIDED BY AUTOMATIC CONTROLS!
9

LATER, AS THE SPACE FLEET REACHES *KRYPTON*...

THIS NOTE TO YOU WAS IN ONE OF THE EMPTY SHIPS, *ZOR-EL!* IT'S WRITTEN IN OUR *KRYPTONESE* LANGUAGE!

STRANGE! IT'S SIGNED--*SUPERMAN!* HE CLAIMS TO BE MY INFANT SON, GROWN TO ADULTHOOD...AND THAT HE SENT THESE SHIPS TO SAVE US! THE NOTE MAY BE A PRANK, BUT THE SPACESHIPS AREN'T! WE'LL FLEE DOOMED *KRYPTON* AT ONCE!

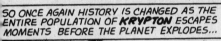

SO ONCE AGAIN HISTORY IS CHANGED AS THE ENTIRE POPULATION OF *KRYPTON* ESCAPES MOMENTS BEFORE THE PLANET EXPLODES...

AND WHEN THE SPACE FLEET LANDS ON EARTH...!

¡CHOKE¡...THE SURVIVORS OF *KRYPTON* ARE EMERGING! THERE'S *ZOR-EL* AND HIS WIFE, WHO WILL SOME DAY BECOME THE PARENTS OF *SUPERGIRL*...¡GASP!¡... AND THAT GIRL BEHIND THEM! SHE'S *LYLA!* LYLA LERROL!

"*LYLA LERROL*...A BEAUTIFUL *KRYPTONIAN* ACTRESS! ONCE, WHEN I ACCIDENTALLY RETURNED TO *KRYPTON* THROUGH THE TIME-BARRIER, WE FELL IN LOVE! BUT WE WERE TORN APART BY A CRUEL TWIST OF FATE...

SUDDENLY, A STARTLING SHOCK...

AND NOW I SEE MY PARENTS *JOR-EL* AND *LARA!* BUT GREAT GUNS! WHO'S THAT WITH THEM? OH, NO! IT CAN'T POSSIBLY BE! ¡GULP!¡--IT'S *ME*--WHEN I WAS THEIR CHILD... *BABY KAL-EL!!*

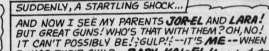

10

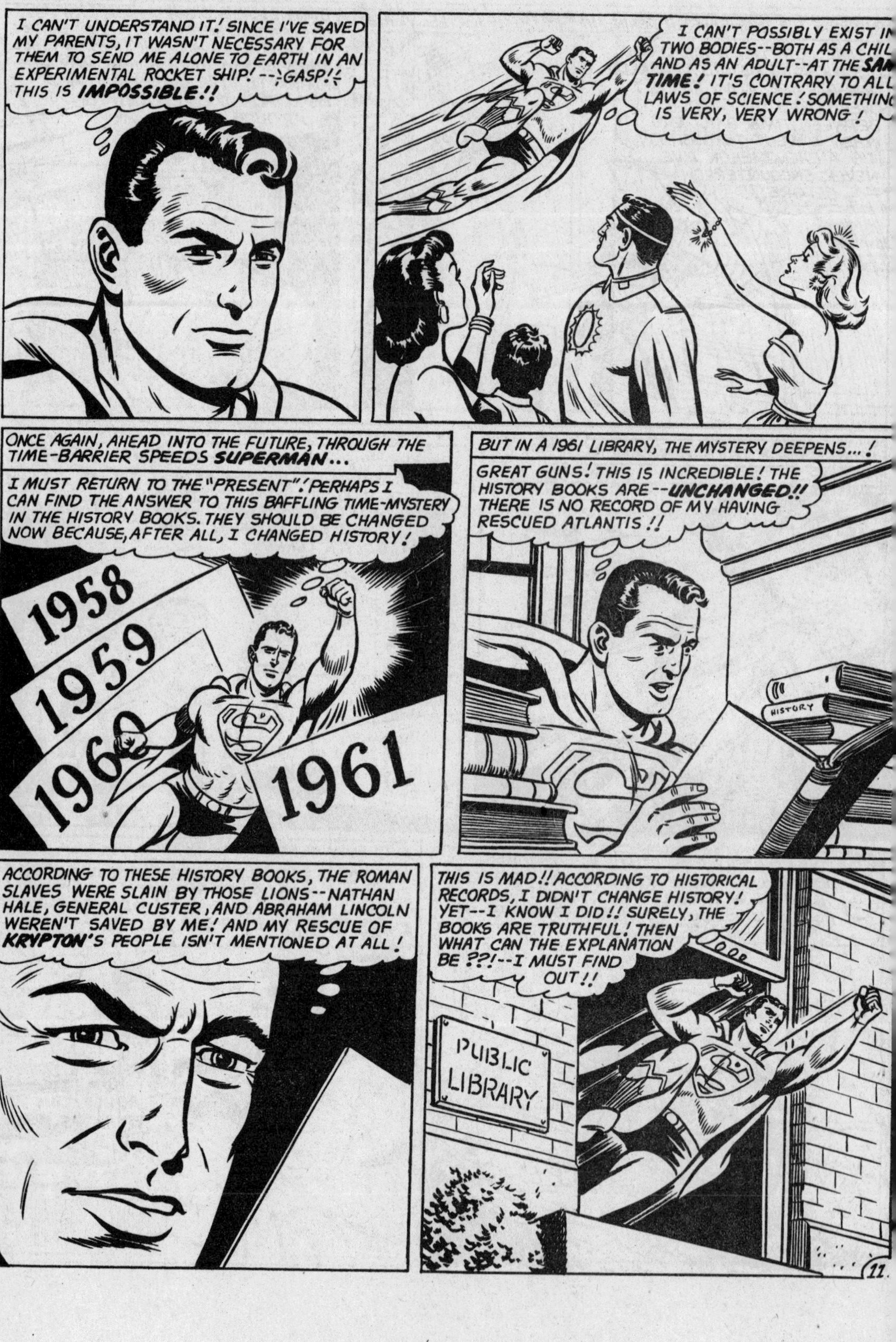
I CAN'T UNDERSTAND IT! SINCE I'VE SAVED MY PARENTS, IT WASN'T NECESSARY FOR THEM TO SEND ME ALONE TO EARTH IN AN EXPERIMENTAL ROCKET SHIP! -- GASP! -- THIS IS IMPOSSIBLE!!
I CAN'T POSSIBLY EXIST IN TWO BODIES--BOTH AS A CHILD AND AS AN ADULT--AT THE SAME TIME! IT'S CONTRARY TO ALL LAWS OF SCIENCE! SOMETHING IS VERY, VERY WRONG!
ONCE AGAIN, AHEAD INTO THE FUTURE, THROUGH THE TIME-BARRIER SPEEDS SUPERMAN...
I MUST RETURN TO THE "PRESENT"! PERHAPS I CAN FIND THE ANSWER TO THIS BAFFLING TIME-MYSTERY IN THE HISTORY BOOKS. THEY SHOULD BE CHANGED NOW BECAUSE, AFTER ALL, I CHANGED HISTORY!
1958
1959
1960
1961
BUT IN A 1961 LIBRARY, THE MYSTERY DEEPENS...!
GREAT GUNS! THIS IS INCREDIBLE! THE HISTORY BOOKS ARE--UNCHANGED!! THERE IS NO RECORD OF MY HAVING RESCUED ATLANTIS!!
HISTORY
ACCORDING TO THESE HISTORY BOOKS, THE ROMAN SLAVES WERE SLAIN BY THOSE LIONS--NATHAN HALE, GENERAL CUSTER, AND ABRAHAM LINCOLN WEREN'T SAVED BY ME! AND MY RESCUE OF KRYPTON'S PEOPLE ISN'T MENTIONED AT ALL!
THIS IS MAD!! ACCORDING TO HISTORICAL RECORDS, I DIDN'T CHANGE HISTORY! YET--I KNOW I DID!! SURELY, THE BOOKS ARE TRUTHFUL! THEN WHAT CAN THE EXPLANATION BE ??!--I MUST FIND OUT!!
PUBLIC LIBRARY
11

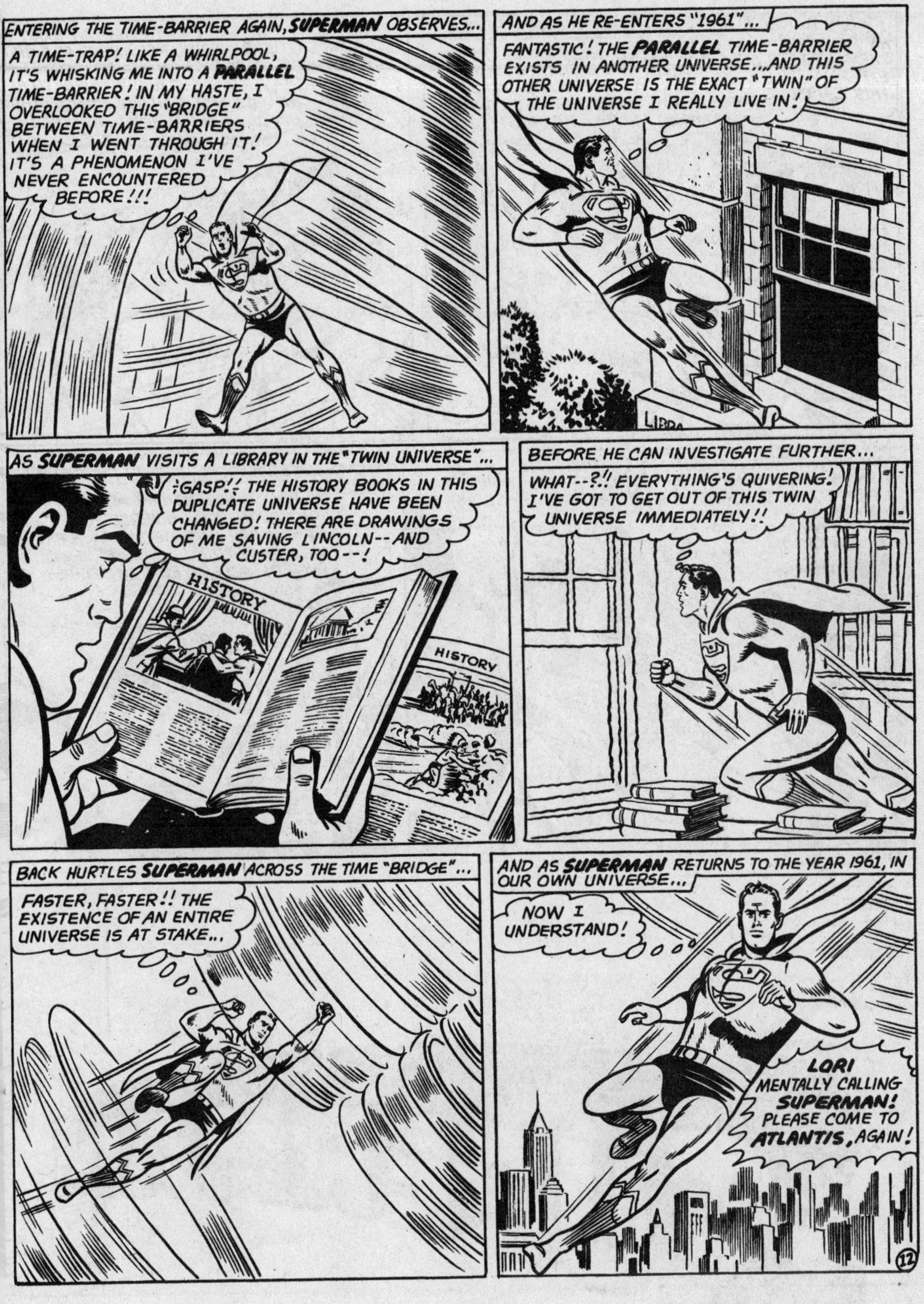
ENTERING THE TIME-BARRIER AGAIN, SUPERMAN OBSERVES...
A TIME-TRAP! LIKE A WHIRLPOOL, IT'S WHISKING ME INTO A PARALLEL TIME-BARRIER! IN MY HASTE, I OVERLOOKED THIS "BRIDGE" BETWEEN TIME-BARRIERS WHEN I WENT THROUGH IT! IT'S A PHENOMENON I'VE NEVER ENCOUNTERED BEFORE!!!
AND AS HE RE-ENTERS "1961"...
FANTASTIC! THE PARALLEL TIME-BARRIER EXISTS IN ANOTHER UNIVERSE...AND THIS OTHER UNIVERSE IS THE EXACT "TWIN" OF THE UNIVERSE I REALLY LIVE IN!
AS SUPERMAN VISITS A LIBRARY IN THE "TWIN UNIVERSE"...
¡GASP!¡ THE HISTORY BOOKS IN THIS DUPLICATE UNIVERSE HAVE BEEN CHANGED! THERE ARE DRAWINGS OF ME SAVING LINCOLN--AND CUSTER, TOO--!
HISTORY
HISTORY
BEFORE HE CAN INVESTIGATE FURTHER...
WHAT--?!! EVERYTHING'S QUIVERING! I'VE GOT TO GET OUT OF THIS TWIN UNIVERSE IMMEDIATELY!!
BACK HURTLES SUPERMAN ACROSS THE TIME "BRIDGE"...
FASTER, FASTER!! THE EXISTENCE OF AN ENTIRE UNIVERSE IS AT STAKE...
AND AS SUPERMAN RETURNS TO THE YEAR 1961, IN OUR OWN UNIVERSE...
NOW I UNDERSTAND!
LORI MENTALLY CALLING SUPERMAN! PLEASE COME TO ATLANTIS, AGAIN!
12

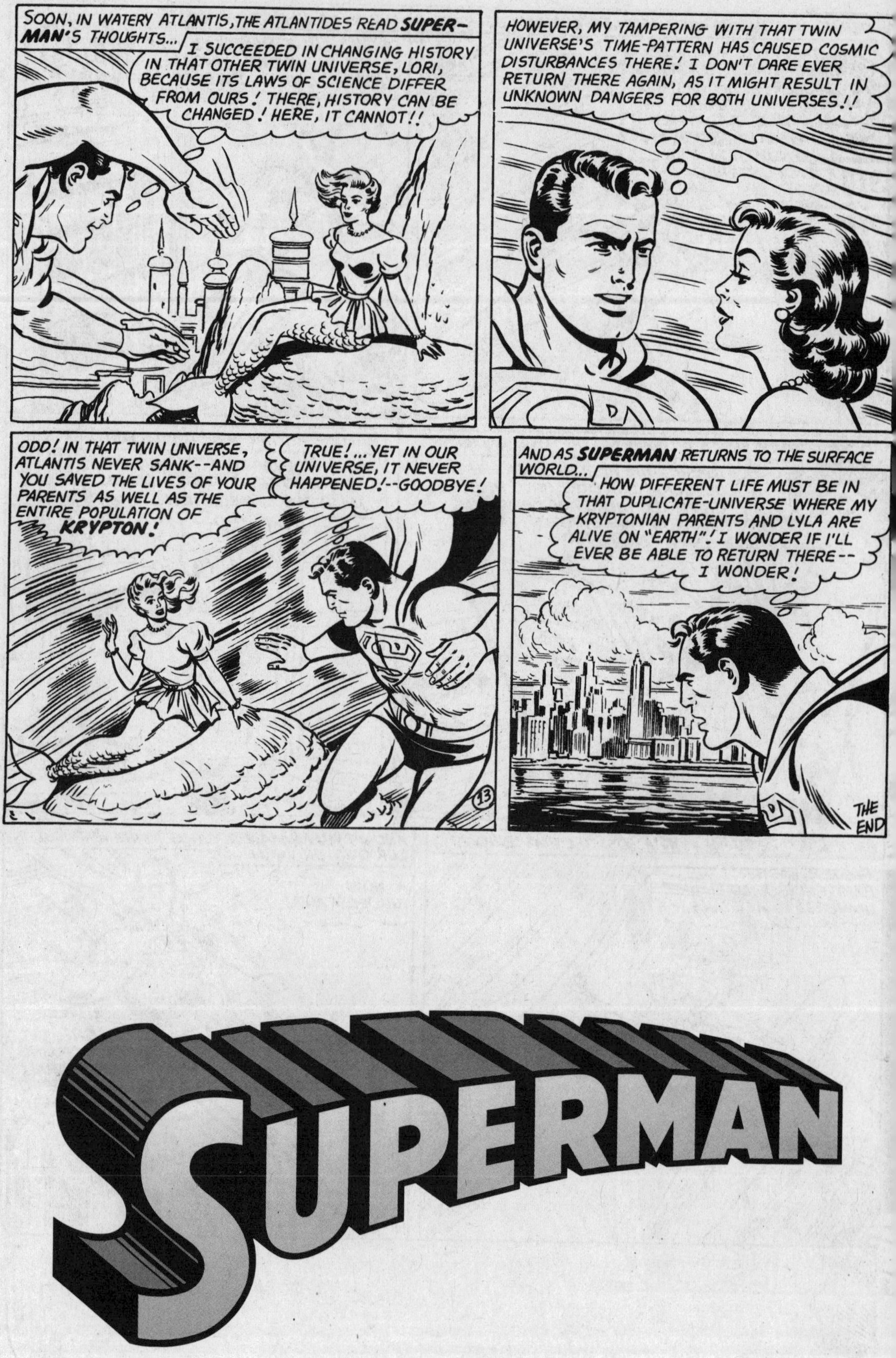
SOON, IN WATERY ATLANTIS, THE ATLANTIDES READ SUPERMAN'S THOUGHTS...
I SUCCEEDED IN CHANGING HISTORY IN THAT OTHER TWIN UNIVERSE, LORI, BECAUSE ITS LAWS OF SCIENCE DIFFER FROM OURS! THERE, HISTORY CAN BE CHANGED! HERE, IT CANNOT!!
HOWEVER, MY TAMPERING WITH THAT TWIN UNIVERSE'S TIME-PATTERN HAS CAUSED COSMIC DISTURBANCES THERE! I DON'T DARE EVER RETURN THERE AGAIN, AS IT MIGHT RESULT IN UNKNOWN DANGERS FOR BOTH UNIVERSES!!
ODD! IN THAT TWIN UNIVERSE, ATLANTIS NEVER SANK--AND YOU SAVED THE LIVES OF YOUR PARENTS AS WELL AS THE ENTIRE POPULATION OF KRYPTON!
TRUE! ...YET IN OUR UNIVERSE, IT NEVER HAPPENED!--GOODBYE!
13
AND AS SUPERMAN RETURNS TO THE SURFACE WORLD...
HOW DIFFERENT LIFE MUST BE IN THAT DUPLICATE-UNIVERSE WHERE MY KRYPTONIAN PARENTS AND LYLA ARE ALIVE ON "EARTH"! I WONDER IF I'LL EVER BE ABLE TO RETURN THERE-- I WONDER!
THE END

SUPERMAN

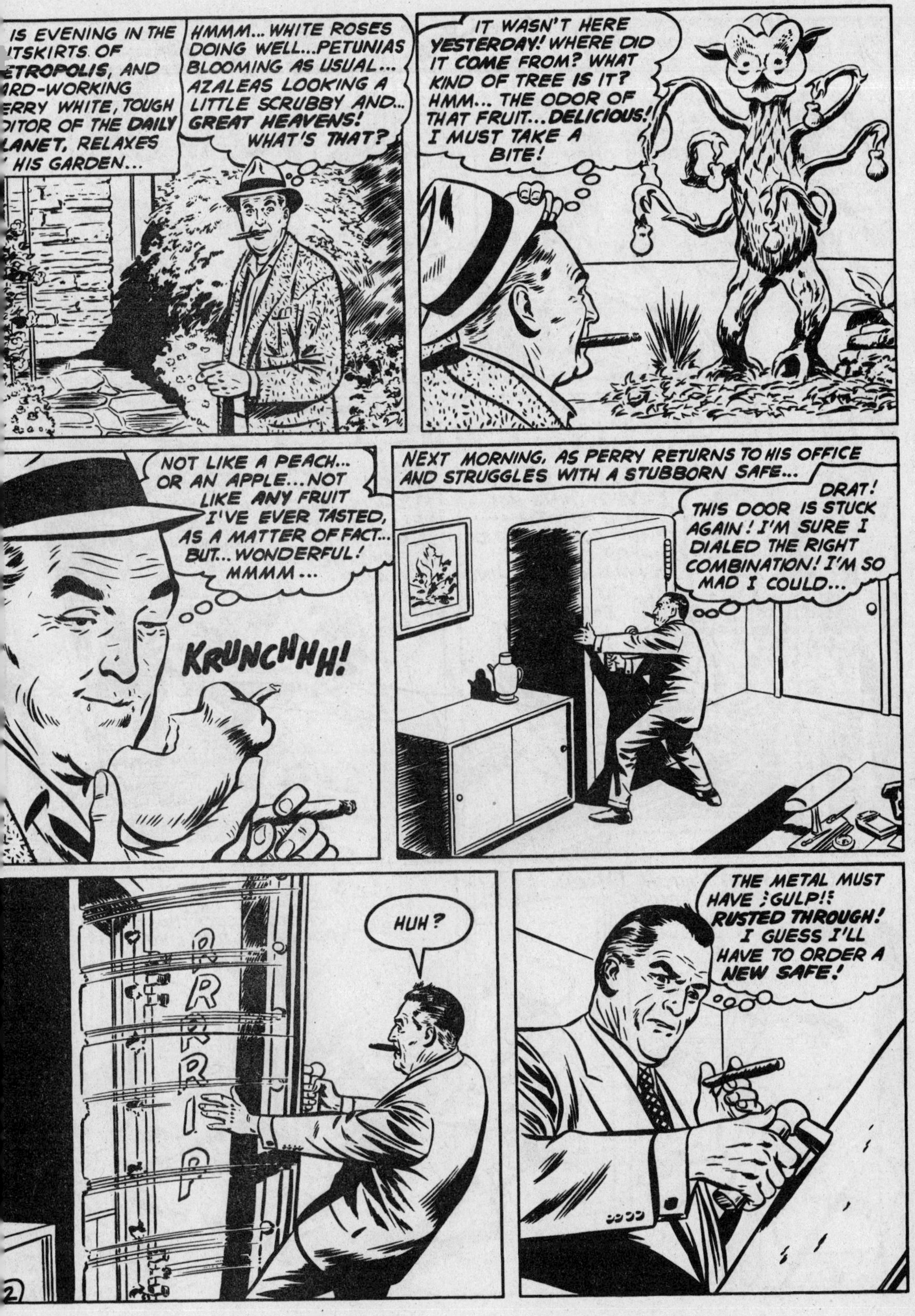
IS EVENING IN THE
ITSKIRTS OF
ETROPOLIS, AND
ARD-WORKING
ERRY WHITE, TOUGH
DITOR OF THE DAILY
LANET, RELAXES
HIS GARDEN...
HMMM... WHITE ROSES DOING WELL...PETUNIAS BLOOMING AS USUAL... AZALEAS LOOKING A LITTLE SCRUBBY AND... GREAT HEAVENS! WHAT'S THAT?
IT WASN'T HERE YESTERDAY! WHERE DID IT COME FROM? WHAT KIND OF TREE IS IT? HMM... THE ODOR OF THAT FRUIT... DELICIOUS! I MUST TAKE A BITE!
NOT LIKE A PEACH... OR AN APPLE...NOT LIKE ANY FRUIT I'VE EVER TASTED, AS A MATTER OF FACT... BUT... WONDERFUL! MMMM...
KRUNCHHH!
NEXT MORNING, AS PERRY RETURNS TO HIS OFFICE AND STRUGGLES WITH A STUBBORN SAFE...
DRAT! THIS DOOR IS STUCK AGAIN! I'M SURE I DIALED THE RIGHT COMBINATION! I'M SO MAD I COULD...
HUH?
RRRRIP
THE METAL MUST HAVE :GULP!: RUSTED THROUGH! I GUESS I'LL HAVE TO ORDER A NEW SAFE!
2

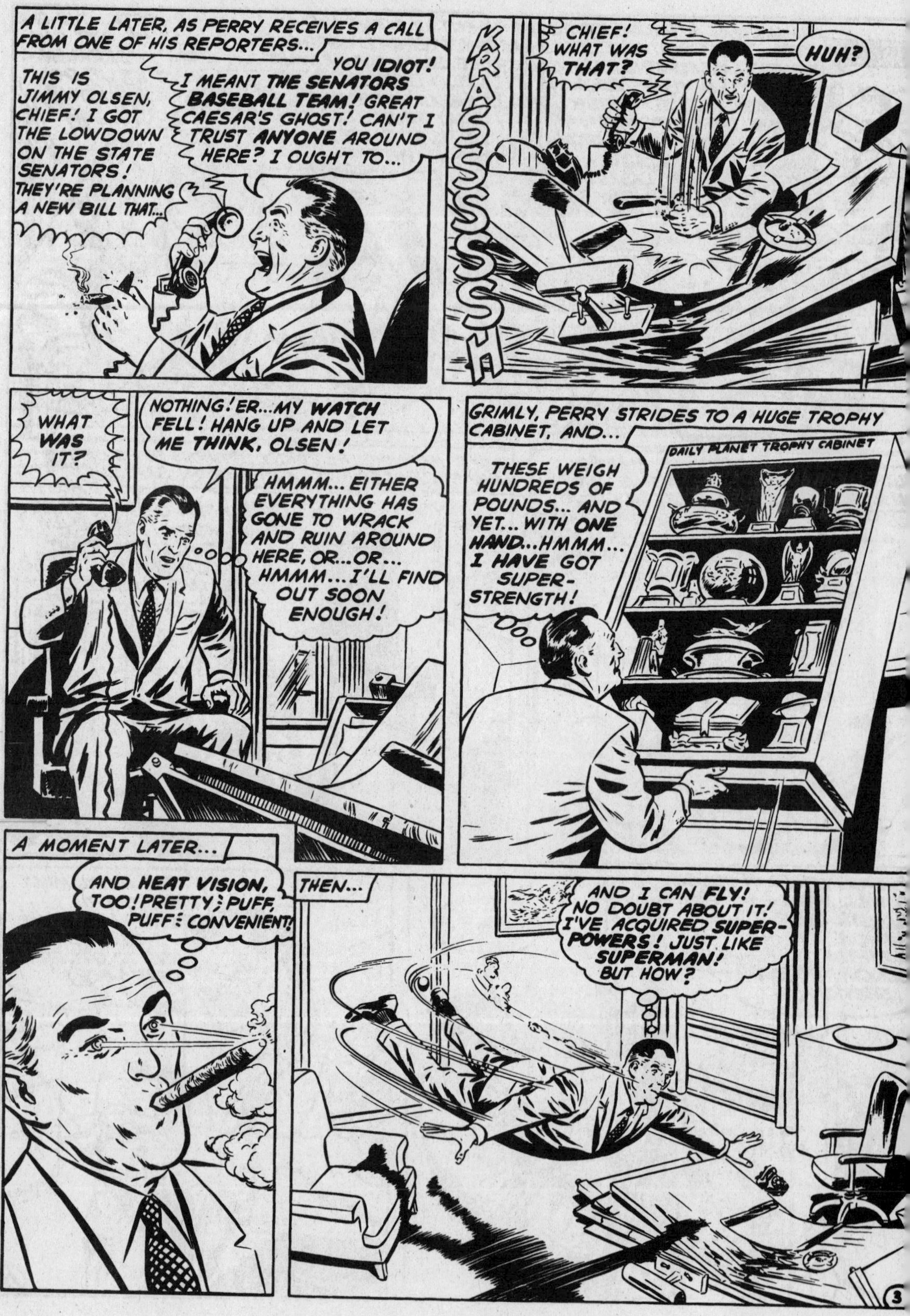
A LITTLE LATER, AS PERRY RECEIVES A CALL FROM ONE OF HIS REPORTERS...
THIS IS JIMMY OLSEN, CHIEF! I GOT THE LOWDOWN ON THE STATE SENATORS! THEY'RE PLANNING A NEW BILL THAT...
YOU IDIOT! I MEANT THE SENATORS BASEBALL TEAM! GREAT CAESAR'S GHOST! CAN'T I TRUST ANYONE AROUND HERE? I OUGHT TO...
KRASSSSH
CHIEF! WHAT WAS THAT?
HUH?
WHAT WAS IT?
NOTHING! ER...MY WATCH FELL! HANG UP AND LET ME THINK, OLSEN!
HMMM... EITHER EVERYTHING HAS GONE TO WRACK AND RUIN AROUND HERE, OR...OR... HMMM...I'LL FIND OUT SOON ENOUGH!
GRIMLY, PERRY STRIDES TO A HUGE TROPHY CABINET, AND...
DAILY PLANET TROPHY CABINET
THESE WEIGH HUNDREDS OF POUNDS... AND YET... WITH ONE HAND...HMMM... I HAVE GOT SUPER-STRENGTH!
A MOMENT LATER...
AND HEAT VISION, TOO! PRETTY; PUFF, PUFF; CONVENIENT!
THEN...
AND I CAN FLY! NO DOUBT ABOUT IT! I'VE ACQUIRED SUPER-POWERS! JUST LIKE SUPERMAN! BUT HOW?
3

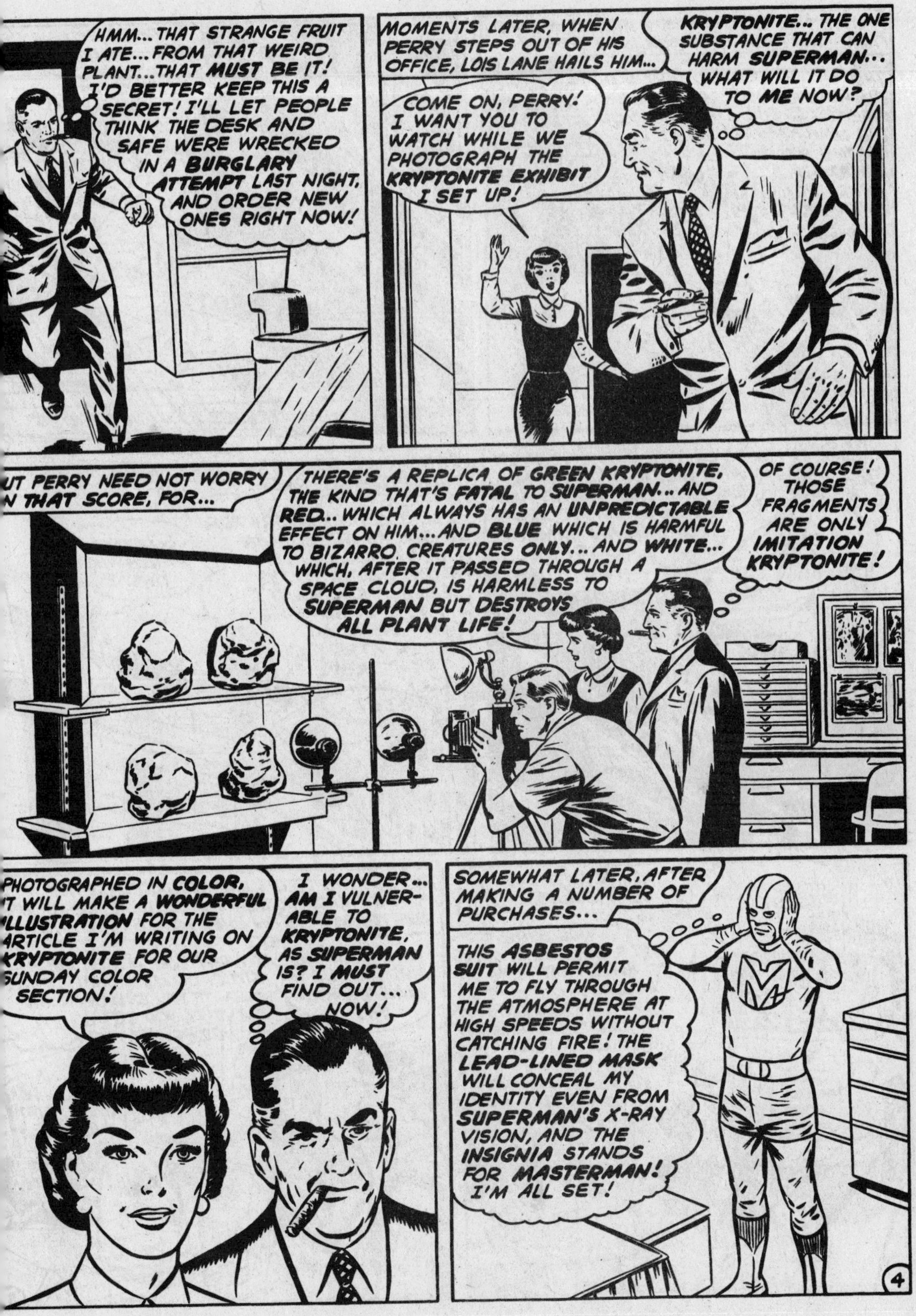
HMM... THAT STRANGE FRUIT I ATE... FROM THAT WEIRD PLANT... THAT MUST BE IT! I'D BETTER KEEP THIS A SECRET! I'LL LET PEOPLE THINK THE DESK AND SAFE WERE WRECKED IN A BURGLARY ATTEMPT LAST NIGHT, AND ORDER NEW ONES RIGHT NOW!
MOMENTS LATER, WHEN PERRY STEPS OUT OF HIS OFFICE, LOIS LANE HAILS HIM...
KRYPTONITE... THE ONE SUBSTANCE THAT CAN HARM SUPERMAN... WHAT WILL IT DO TO ME NOW?
COME ON, PERRY! I WANT YOU TO WATCH WHILE WE PHOTOGRAPH THE KRYPTONITE EXHIBIT I SET UP!
UT PERRY NEED NOT WORRY N THAT SCORE, FOR...
THERE'S A REPLICA OF GREEN KRYPTONITE, THE KIND THAT'S FATAL TO SUPERMAN... AND RED... WHICH ALWAYS HAS AN UNPREDICTABLE EFFECT ON HIM... AND BLUE WHICH IS HARMFUL TO BIZARRO CREATURES ONLY... AND WHITE... WHICH, AFTER IT PASSED THROUGH A SPACE CLOUD, IS HARMLESS TO SUPERMAN BUT DESTROYS ALL PLANT LIFE!
OF COURSE! THOSE FRAGMENTS ARE ONLY IMITATION KRYPTONITE!
PHOTOGRAPHED IN COLOR, T WILL MAKE A WONDERFUL LLUSTRATION FOR THE ARTICLE I'M WRITING ON KRYPTONITE FOR OUR SUNDAY COLOR SECTION!
I WONDER... AM I VULNERABLE TO KRYPTONITE, AS SUPERMAN IS? I MUST FIND OUT... NOW!
SOMEWHAT LATER, AFTER MAKING A NUMBER OF PURCHASES...
THIS ASBESTOS SUIT WILL PERMIT ME TO FLY THROUGH THE ATMOSPHERE AT HIGH SPEEDS WITHOUT CATCHING FIRE! THE LEAD-LINED MASK WILL CONCEAL MY IDENTITY EVEN FROM SUPERMAN'S X-RAY VISION, AND THE INSIGNIA STANDS FOR MASTERMAN! I'M ALL SET!
4

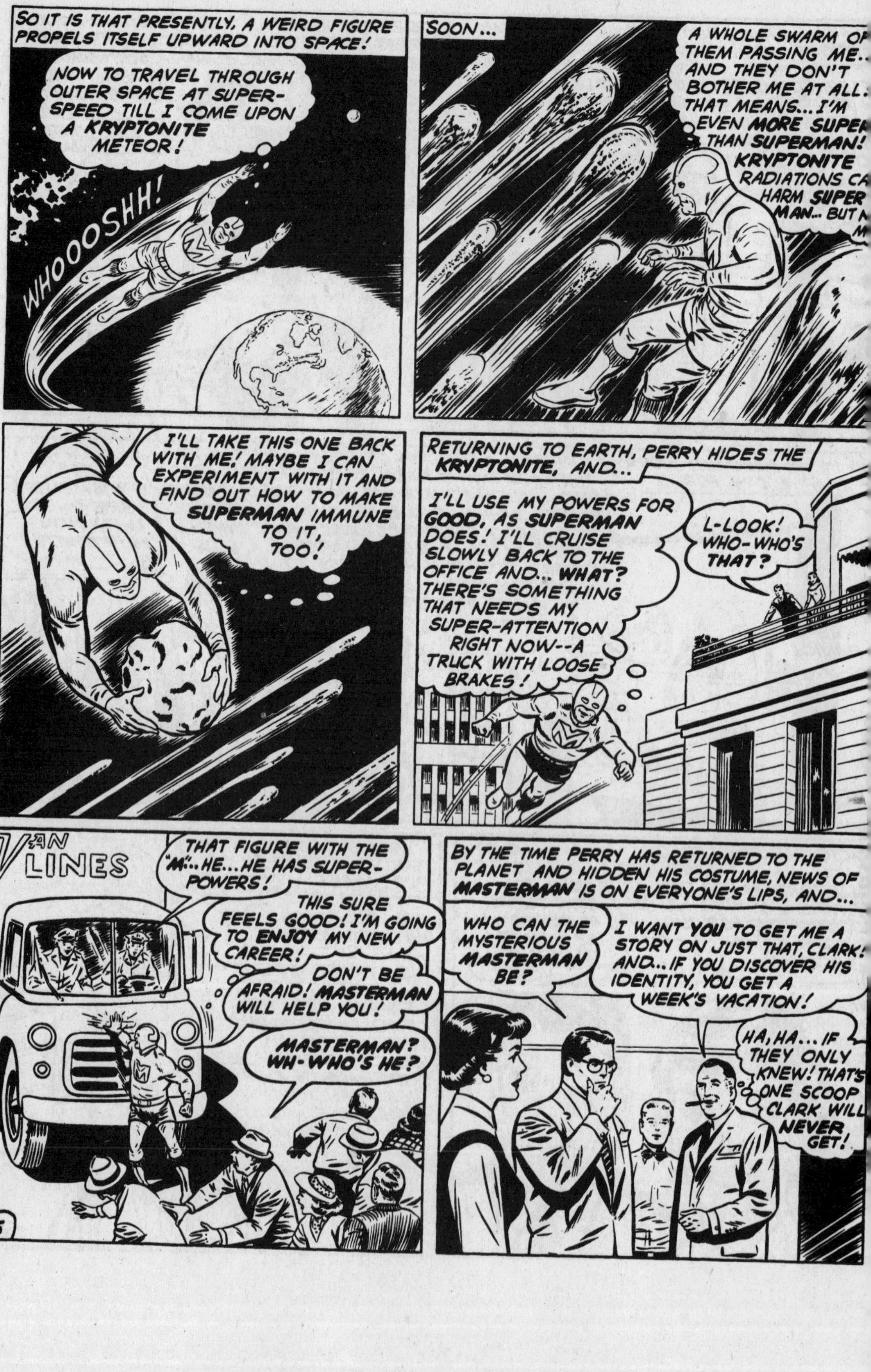
SO IT IS THAT PRESENTLY, A WEIRD FIGURE PROPELS ITSELF UPWARD INTO SPACE!
NOW TO TRAVEL THROUGH OUTER SPACE AT SUPER-SPEED TILL I COME UPON A KRYPTONITE METEOR!
WHOOOSHH!
SOON...
A WHOLE SWARM OF THEM PASSING ME... AND THEY DON'T BOTHER ME AT ALL. THAT MEANS... I'M EVEN MORE SUPER THAN SUPERMAN! KRYPTONITE RADIATIONS CA HARM SUPERMAN... BUT
I'LL TAKE THIS ONE BACK WITH ME! MAYBE I CAN EXPERIMENT WITH IT AND FIND OUT HOW TO MAKE SUPERMAN IMMUNE TO IT, TOO!
RETURNING TO EARTH, PERRY HIDES THE KRYPTONITE, AND...
I'LL USE MY POWERS FOR GOOD, AS SUPERMAN DOES! I'LL CRUISE SLOWLY BACK TO THE OFFICE AND... WHAT? THERE'S SOMETHING THAT NEEDS MY SUPER-ATTENTION RIGHT NOW--A TRUCK WITH LOOSE BRAKES!
L-LOOK! WHO-WHO'S THAT?
VAN LINES
THAT FIGURE WITH THE "M"... HE... HE HAS SUPER-POWERS!
THIS SURE FEELS GOOD! I'M GOING TO ENJOY MY NEW CAREER!
DON'T BE AFRAID! MASTERMAN WILL HELP YOU!
MASTERMAN? WH-WHO'S HE?
5
BY THE TIME PERRY HAS RETURNED TO THE PLANET AND HIDDEN HIS COSTUME, NEWS OF MASTERMAN IS ON EVERYONE'S LIPS, AND...
WHO CAN THE MYSTERIOUS MASTERMAN BE?
I WANT YOU TO GET ME A STORY ON JUST THAT, CLARK! AND... IF YOU DISCOVER HIS IDENTITY, YOU GET A WEEK'S VACATION!
HA, HA... IF THEY ONLY KNEW! THAT'S ONE SCOOP CLARK WILL NEVER GET!

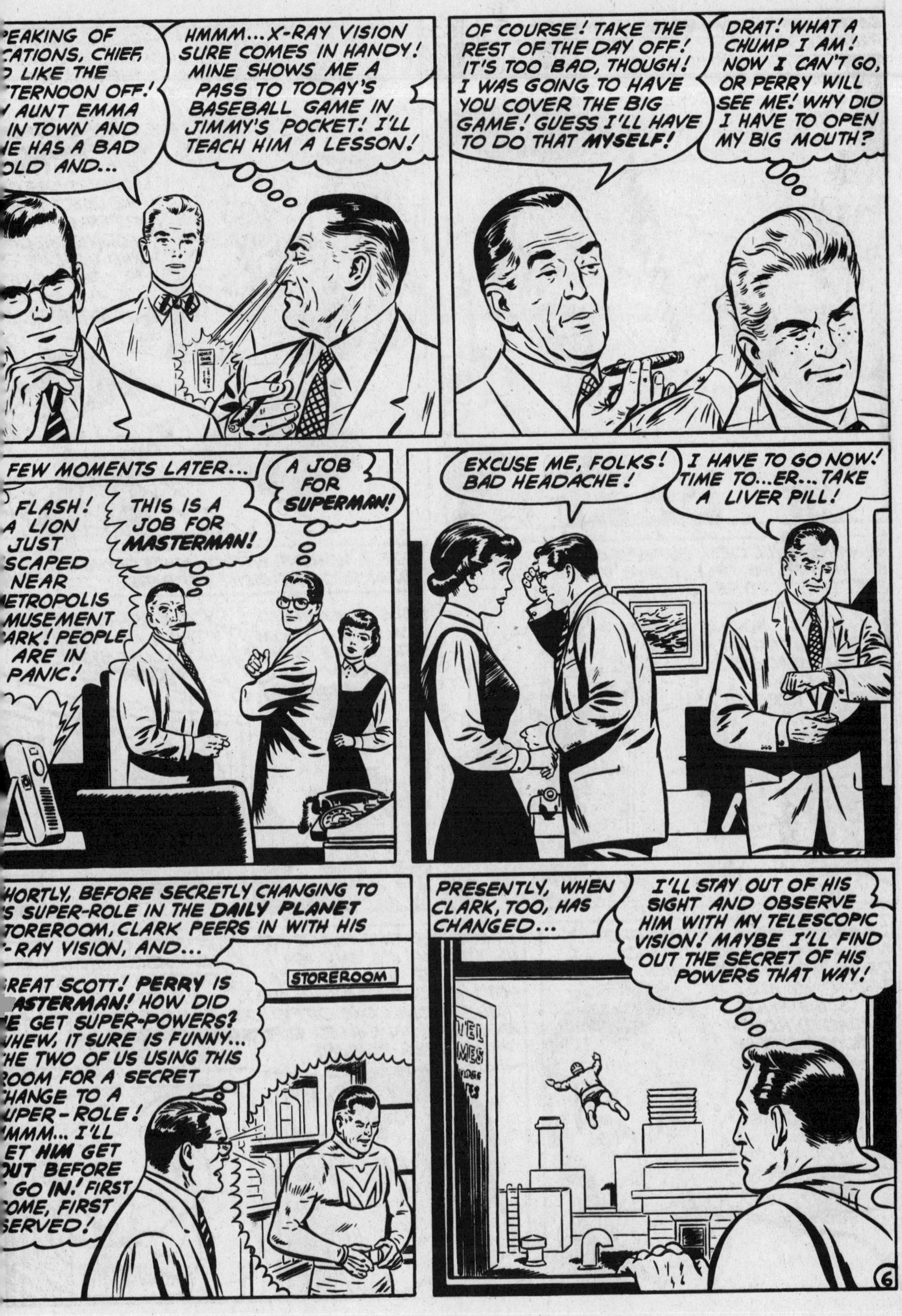
PEAKING OF CATIONS, CHIEF, D LIKE THE TERNOON OFF! Y AUNT EMMA IN TOWN AND HE HAS A BAD OLD AND...
HMMM... X-RAY VISION SURE COMES IN HANDY! MINE SHOWS ME A PASS TO TODAY'S BASEBALL GAME IN JIMMY'S POCKET! I'LL TEACH HIM A LESSON!
OF COURSE! TAKE THE REST OF THE DAY OFF! IT'S TOO BAD, THOUGH! I WAS GOING TO HAVE YOU COVER THE BIG GAME! GUESS I'LL HAVE TO DO THAT MYSELF!
DRAT! WHAT A CHUMP I AM! NOW I CAN'T GO, OR PERRY WILL SEE ME! WHY DID I HAVE TO OPEN MY BIG MOUTH?
FEW MOMENTS LATER...
FLASH! A LION JUST SCAPED NEAR ETROPOLIS MUSEMENT ARK! PEOPLE ARE IN PANIC!
THIS IS A JOB FOR MASTERMAN!
A JOB FOR SUPERMAN!
EXCUSE ME, FOLKS! BAD HEADACHE!
I HAVE TO GO NOW! TIME TO...ER...TAKE A LIVER PILL!
HORTLY, BEFORE SECRETLY CHANGING TO S SUPER-ROLE IN THE DAILY PLANET TOREROOM, CLARK PEERS IN WITH HIS -RAY VISION, AND...
REAT SCOTT! PERRY IS ASTERMAN! HOW DID E GET SUPER-POWERS? WHEW, IT SURE IS FUNNY... THE TWO OF US USING THIS ROOM FOR A SECRET CHANGE TO A UPER-ROLE! MMM... I'LL ET HIM GET UT BEFORE GO IN! FIRST OME, FIRST SERVED!
STOREROOM
PRESENTLY, WHEN CLARK, TOO, HAS CHANGED...
I'LL STAY OUT OF HIS SIGHT AND OBSERVE HIM WITH MY TELESCOPIC VISION! MAYBE I'LL FIND OUT THE SECRET OF HIS POWERS THAT WAY!
6

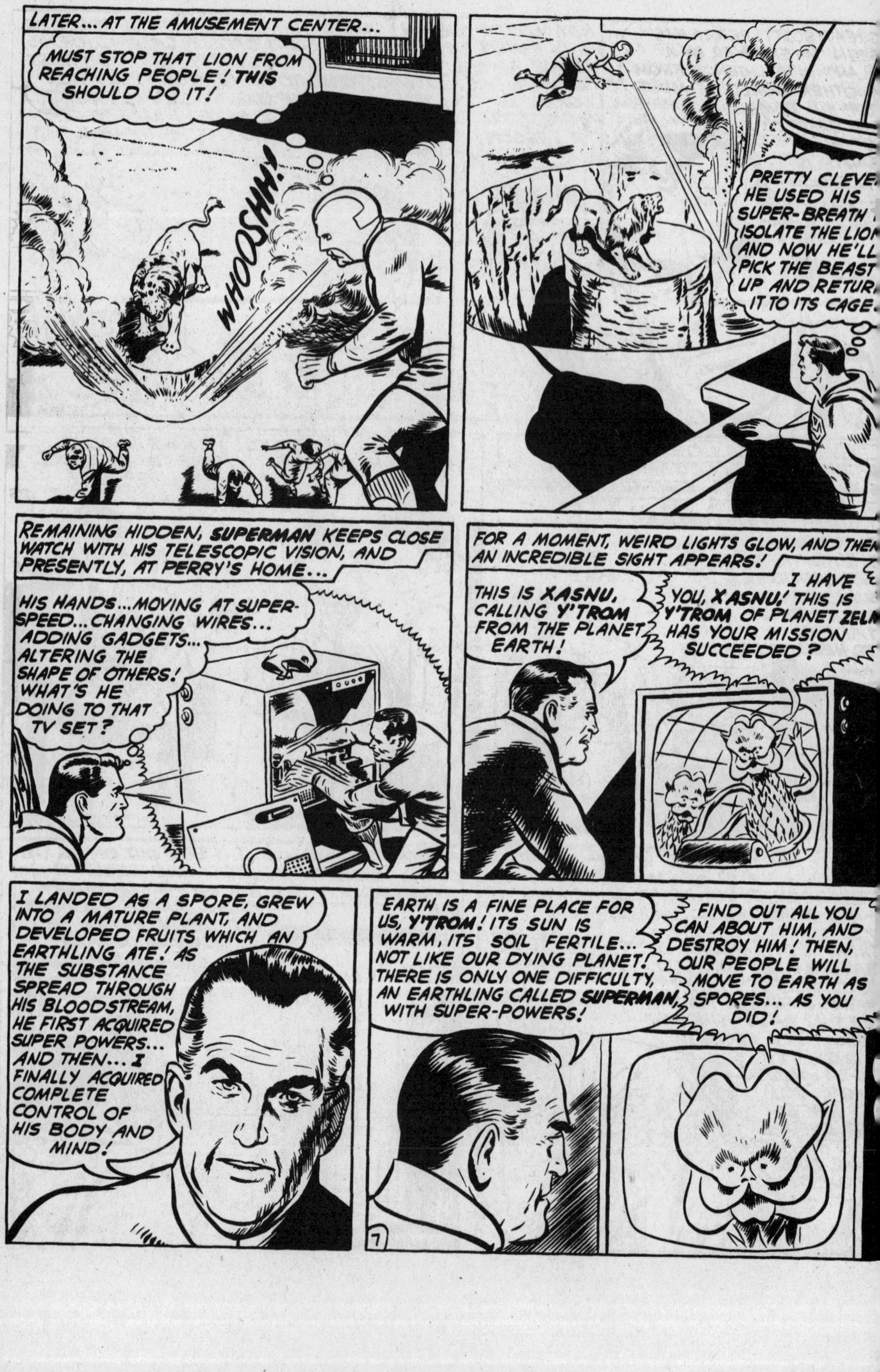
LATER... AT THE AMUSEMENT CENTER...
MUST STOP THAT LION FROM REACHING PEOPLE! THIS SHOULD DO IT!
WHOOSHH!
PRETTY CLEVE HE USED HIS SUPER-BREATH ISOLATE THE LIO AND NOW HE'LL PICK THE BEAST UP AND RETUR IT TO ITS CAGE.
REMAINING HIDDEN, SUPERMAN KEEPS CLOSE WATCH WITH HIS TELESCOPIC VISION, AND PRESENTLY, AT PERRY'S HOME...
HIS HANDS...MOVING AT SUPER-SPEED...CHANGING WIRES... ADDING GADGETS... ALTERING THE SHAPE OF OTHERS! WHAT'S HE DOING TO THAT TV SET?
FOR A MOMENT, WEIRD LIGHTS GLOW, AND THE AN INCREDIBLE SIGHT APPEARS!
THIS IS XASNU, CALLING Y'TROM FROM THE PLANET EARTH!
I HAVE YOU, XASNU! THIS IS Y'TROM OF PLANET ZEL HAS YOUR MISSION SUCCEEDED?
I LANDED AS A SPORE, GREW INTO A MATURE PLANT, AND DEVELOPED FRUITS WHICH AN EARTHLING ATE! AS THE SUBSTANCE SPREAD THROUGH HIS BLOODSTREAM, HE FIRST ACQUIRED SUPER POWERS... AND THEN... I FINALLY ACQUIRED COMPLETE CONTROL OF HIS BODY AND MIND!
EARTH IS A FINE PLACE FOR US, Y'TROM! ITS SUN IS WARM, ITS SOIL FERTILE... NOT LIKE OUR DYING PLANET! THERE IS ONLY ONE DIFFICULTY, AN EARTHLING CALLED SUPERMAN, WITH SUPER-POWERS!
FIND OUT ALL YOU CAN ABOUT HIM, AND DESTROY HIM! THEN, OUR PEOPLE WILL MOVE TO EARTH AS SPORES... AS YOU DID!
7

GREAT SCOTT! PERRY HAS BEEN TAKEN OVER BY A PLANT INTELLIGENCE FROM ANOTHER WORLD! I MUST STOP HIM SOMEHOW!... THE SAFETY OF ALL EARTH IS AT STAKE!

GRIMLY, SUPERMAN CONTINUES HIS LONG-RANGE SPYING, AND SOON...

HE'S READING EVERYTHING ABOUT ME... AT SUPER-SPEED! HE'LL USE ALL OF HIS POWERS TO DESTROY ME!' AND I MUST USE ALL MY RESOURCES TO COUNTER-ATTACK! HMMM... FIRST, I'LL CONTACT SUPERGIRL!

WHEN SUPERMAN CONVERSES WITH THE GIRL OF STEEL VIA SUPER-VENTRILOQUISM...

I WANT YOU TO KEEP US BOTH UNDER OBSERVATION! SHOULD THE ALIEN SUCCEED IN OVERCOMING ME, GET THE SUPERMAN EMERGENCY SQUAD TO COME OUT OF THE BOTTLE OF KANDOR TO HELP YOU TACKLE HIM!

I'D RATHER JOIN YOU IN FIGHTING HIM, RIGHT NOW, BUT I GUESS IT'S BETTER THAT I ONLY APPEAR IF HE DEFEATS YOU!

SHORTLY AFTERWARD...

NOW THAT I'VE ATTENDED TO THAT, THERE'S ONE PRECAUTION I MUST TAKE! IT'S KNOWN THAT IN COLONIAL DAYS, SCOUTS WHO EXPECTED TO BE TORTURED BY INDIANS HYPTONIZED EACH OTHER IN ADVANCE! THEIR POST-HYPNOTIC TRANCES MADE THEM IMMUNE TO PAIN FOR A WHILE! I MUST DO LIKEWISE!

YOU... WILL... NOT FEEL PAIN... OF KRYPTONITE! YOU... WILL... NOT... FEEL PAIN... OF KRYPTONITE!

THE VERY NEXT DAY, AT THE OFFICES OF THE DAILY PLANET...

NO ONE'S NEAR HERE NOW... SO I CAN TYPE AT SUPER-SPEED AND FINISH MY DAY'S ASSIGNMENTS IN MOMENTS. THAT WILL GIVE ME TIME TO STRENGTHEN MY DEFENSES AGAINST THE ALIEN PERRY!

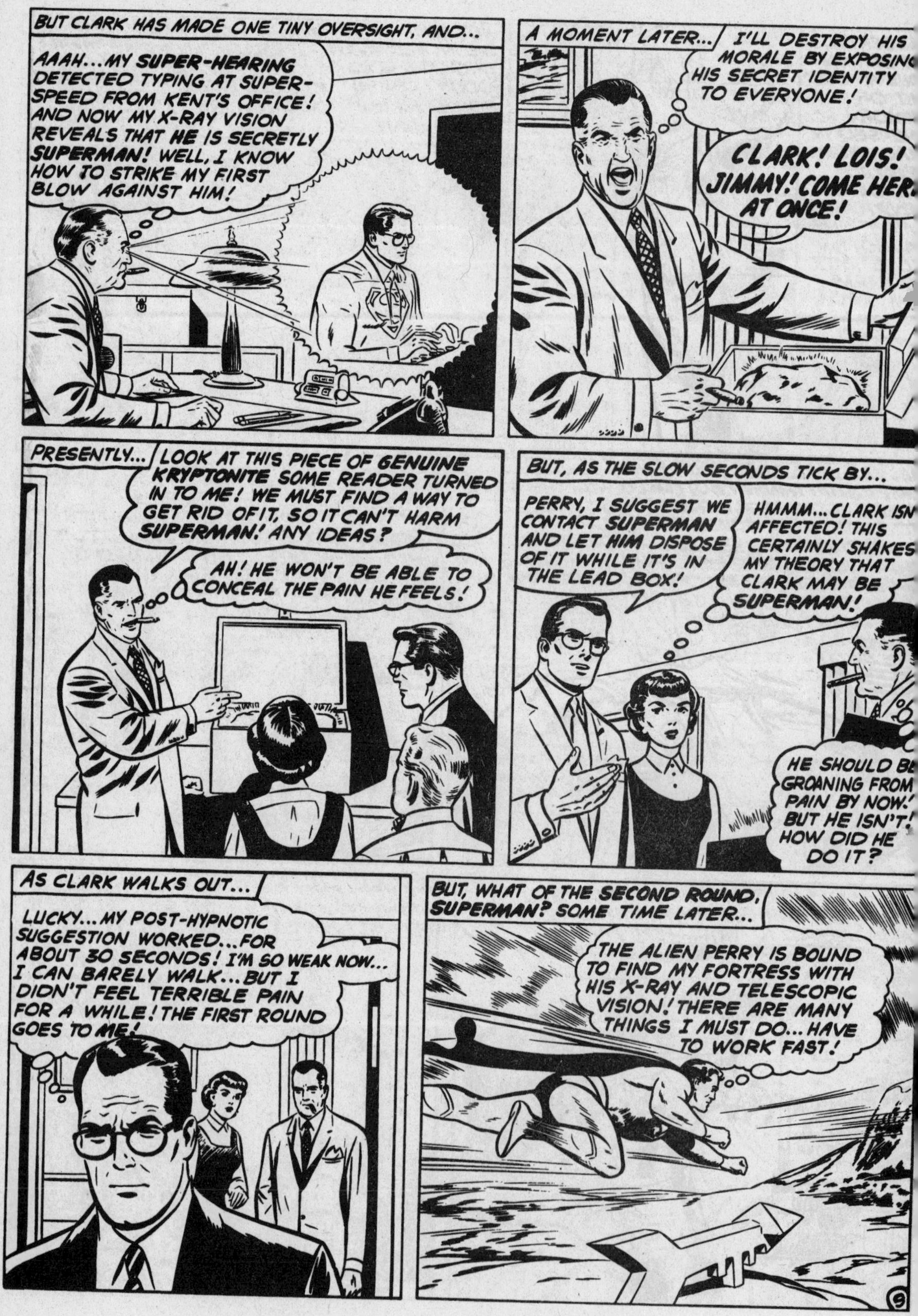
BUT CLARK HAS MADE ONE TINY OVERSIGHT, AND...
AAAH...MY SUPER-HEARING DETECTED TYPING AT SUPER-SPEED FROM KENT'S OFFICE! AND NOW MY X-RAY VISION REVEALS THAT HE IS SECRETLY SUPERMAN! WELL, I KNOW HOW TO STRIKE MY FIRST BLOW AGAINST HIM!
A MOMENT LATER...
I'LL DESTROY HIS MORALE BY EXPOSING HIS SECRET IDENTITY TO EVERYONE!
CLARK! LOIS! JIMMY! COME HERE AT ONCE!
PRESENTLY...
LOOK AT THIS PIECE OF GENUINE KRYPTONITE SOME READER TURNED IN TO ME! WE MUST FIND A WAY TO GET RID OF IT, SO IT CAN'T HARM SUPERMAN! ANY IDEAS?
AH! HE WON'T BE ABLE TO CONCEAL THE PAIN HE FEELS!
BUT, AS THE SLOW SECONDS TICK BY...
PERRY, I SUGGEST WE CONTACT SUPERMAN AND LET HIM DISPOSE OF IT WHILE IT'S IN THE LEAD BOX!
HMMM...CLARK ISN AFFECTED! THIS CERTAINLY SHAKES MY THEORY THAT CLARK MAY BE SUPERMAN!
HE SHOULD BE GROANING FROM PAIN BY NOW! BUT HE ISN'T! HOW DID HE DO IT?
AS CLARK WALKS OUT...
LUCKY...MY POST-HYPNOTIC SUGGESTION WORKED...FOR ABOUT 30 SECONDS! I'M SO WEAK NOW... I CAN BARELY WALK...BUT I DIDN'T FEEL TERRIBLE PAIN FOR A WHILE! THE FIRST ROUND GOES TO ME!
BUT, WHAT OF THE SECOND ROUND, SUPERMAN? SOME TIME LATER...
THE ALIEN PERRY IS BOUND TO FIND MY FORTRESS WITH HIS X-RAY AND TELESCOPIC VISION! THERE ARE MANY THINGS I MUST DO... HAVE TO WORK FAST!
9

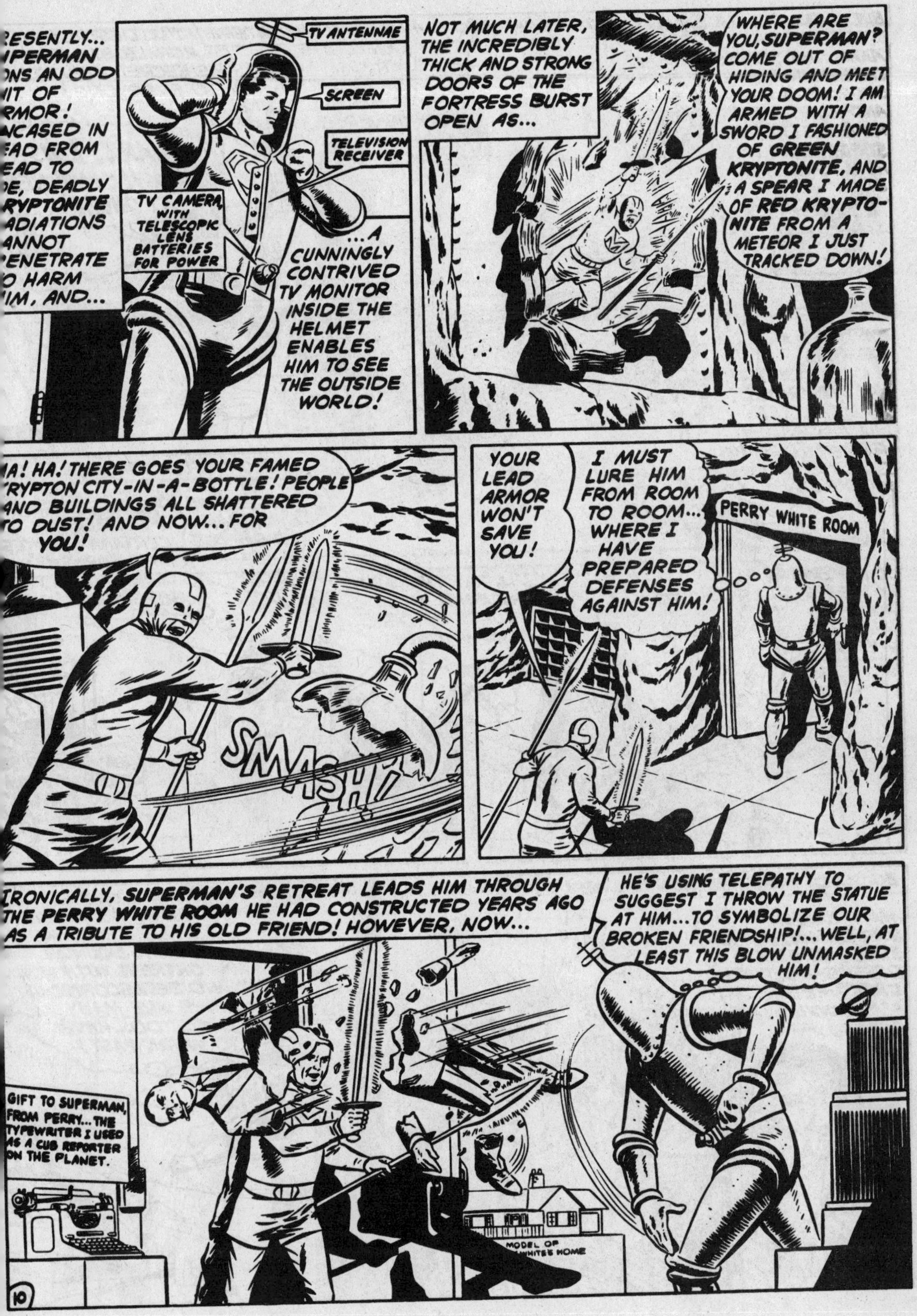

RESENTLY... UPERMAN ONS AN ODD NIT OF RMOR! NCASED IN EAD FROM EAD TO OE, DEADLY KRYPTONITE ADIATIONS ANNOT PENETRATE O HARM IM, AND...
TV ANTENNAE
SCREEN
TELEVISION RECEIVER
TV CAMERA WITH TELESCOPIC LENS
BATTERIES FOR POWER
...A CUNNINGLY CONTRIVED TV MONITOR INSIDE THE HELMET ENABLES HIM TO SEE THE OUTSIDE WORLD!
NOT MUCH LATER, THE INCREDIBLY THICK AND STRONG DOORS OF THE FORTRESS BURST OPEN AS...
WHERE ARE YOU, SUPERMAN? COME OUT OF HIDING AND MEET YOUR DOOM! I AM ARMED WITH A SWORD I FASHIONED OF GREEN KRYPTONITE, AND A SPEAR I MADE OF RED KRYPTONITE FROM A METEOR I JUST TRACKED DOWN!
A! HA! THERE GOES YOUR FAMED RYPTON CITY-IN-A-BOTTLE! PEOPLE AND BUILDINGS ALL SHATTERED TO DUST! AND NOW... FOR YOU!
SMASH!
YOUR LEAD ARMOR WON'T SAVE YOU!
I MUST LURE HIM FROM ROOM TO ROOM... WHERE I HAVE PREPARED DEFENSES AGAINST HIM!
PERRY WHITE ROOM
IRONICALLY, SUPERMAN'S RETREAT LEADS HIM THROUGH THE PERRY WHITE ROOM HE HAD CONSTRUCTED YEARS AGO AS A TRIBUTE TO HIS OLD FRIEND! HOWEVER, NOW...
HE'S USING TELEPATHY TO SUGGEST I THROW THE STATUE AT HIM...TO SYMBOLIZE OUR BROKEN FRIENDSHIP!... WELL, AT LEAST THIS BLOW UNMASKED HIM!
GIFT TO SUPERMAN, FROM PERRY... THE TYPEWRITER I USED AS A CUB REPORTER ON THE PLANET.
MODEL OF WHITE'S HOME
10

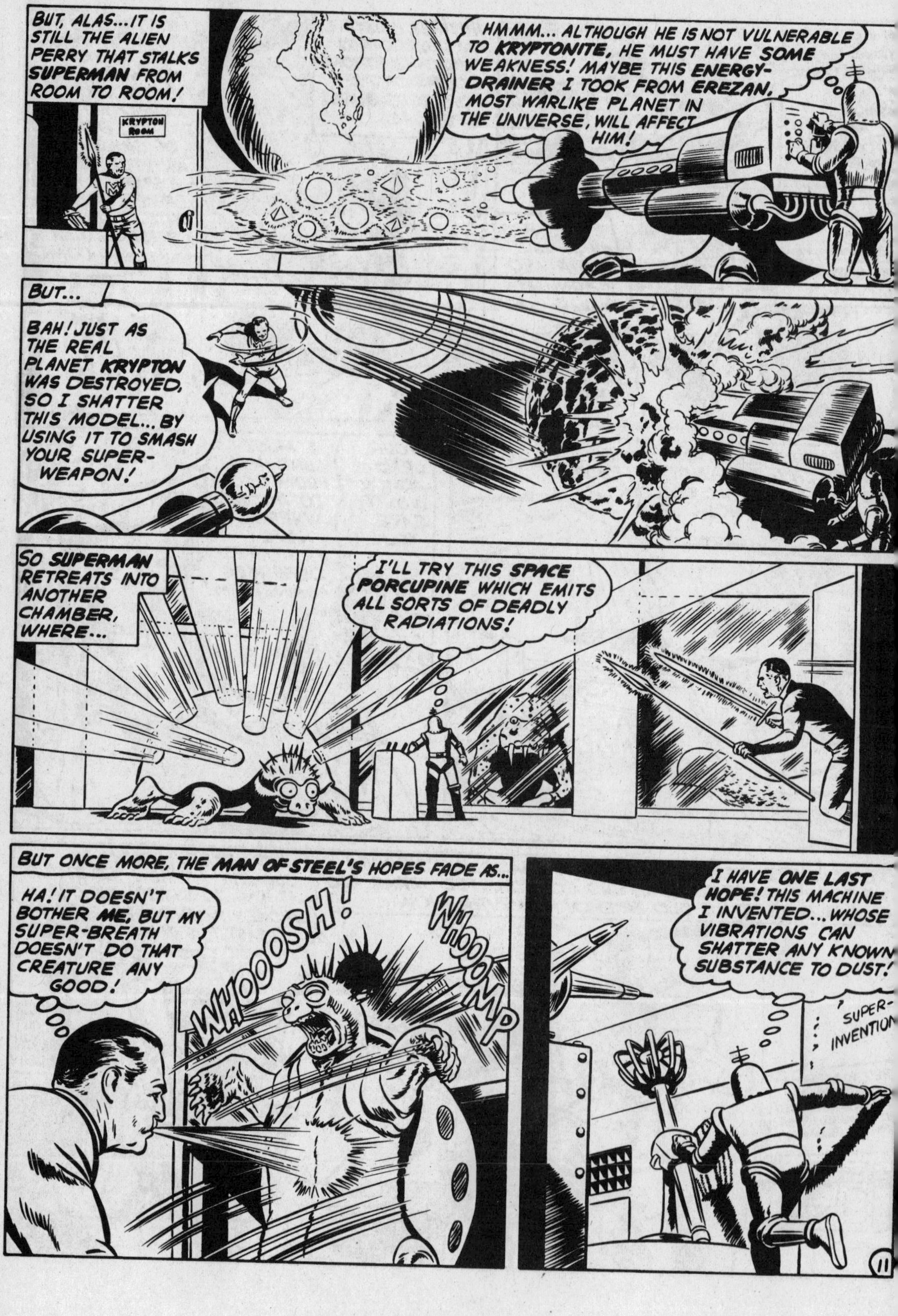
BUT, ALAS...IT IS STILL THE ALIEN PERRY THAT STALKS SUPERMAN FROM ROOM TO ROOM!
KRYPTON ROOM
HMMM... ALTHOUGH HE IS NOT VULNERABLE TO KRYPTONITE, HE MUST HAVE SOME WEAKNESS! MAYBE THIS ENERGY-DRAINER I TOOK FROM EREZAN, MOST WARLIKE PLANET IN THE UNIVERSE, WILL AFFECT HIM!
BUT...
BAH! JUST AS THE REAL PLANET KRYPTON WAS DESTROYED, SO I SHATTER THIS MODEL... BY USING IT TO SMASH YOUR SUPER-WEAPON!
SO SUPERMAN RETREATS INTO ANOTHER CHAMBER, WHERE...
I'LL TRY THIS SPACE PORCUPINE WHICH EMITS ALL SORTS OF DEADLY RADIATIONS!
BUT ONCE MORE, THE MAN OF STEEL'S HOPES FADE AS...
HA! IT DOESN'T BOTHER ME, BUT MY SUPER-BREATH DOESN'T DO THAT CREATURE ANY GOOD!
WHOOOSH!
WHOOOMP
I HAVE ONE LAST HOPE! THIS MACHINE I INVENTED... WHOSE VIBRATIONS CAN SHATTER ANY KNOWN SUBSTANCE TO DUST!
SUPER-INVENTION
11

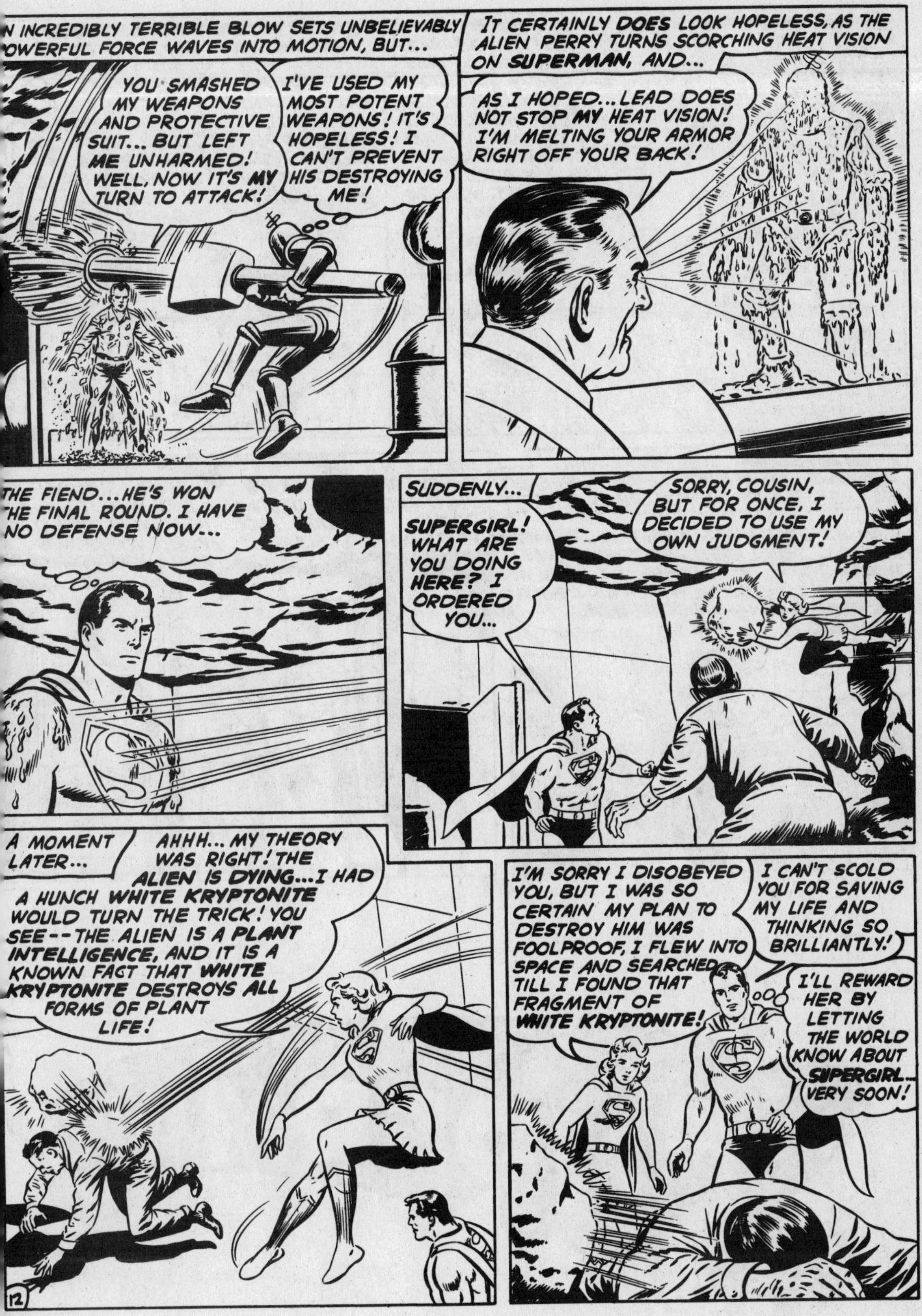
N INCREDIBLY TERRIBLE BLOW SETS UNBELIEVABLY POWERFUL FORCE WAVES INTO MOTION, BUT...
YOU SMASHED MY WEAPONS AND PROTECTIVE SUIT... BUT LEFT ME UNHARMED! WELL, NOW IT'S MY TURN TO ATTACK!
I'VE USED MY MOST POTENT WEAPONS! IT'S HOPELESS! I CAN'T PREVENT HIS DESTROYING ME!
IT CERTAINLY DOES LOOK HOPELESS, AS THE ALIEN PERRY TURNS SCORCHING HEAT VISION ON SUPERMAN, AND...
AS I HOPED... LEAD DOES NOT STOP MY HEAT VISION! I'M MELTING YOUR ARMOR RIGHT OFF YOUR BACK!
THE FIEND... HE'S WON THE FINAL ROUND. I HAVE NO DEFENSE NOW...
SUDDENLY...
SUPERGIRL! WHAT ARE YOU DOING HERE? I ORDERED YOU...
SORRY, COUSIN, BUT FOR ONCE, I DECIDED TO USE MY OWN JUDGMENT!
A MOMENT LATER...
AHHH... MY THEORY WAS RIGHT! THE ALIEN IS DYING... I HAD A HUNCH WHITE KRYPTONITE WOULD TURN THE TRICK! YOU SEE--THE ALIEN IS A PLANT INTELLIGENCE, AND IT IS A KNOWN FACT THAT WHITE KRYPTONITE DESTROYS ALL FORMS OF PLANT LIFE!
12
I'M SORRY I DISOBEYED YOU, BUT I WAS SO CERTAIN MY PLAN TO DESTROY HIM WAS FOOLPROOF, I FLEW INTO SPACE AND SEARCHED TILL I FOUND THAT FRAGMENT OF WHITE KRYPTONITE!
I CAN'T SCOLD YOU FOR SAVING MY LIFE AND THINKING SO BRILLIANTLY!
I'LL REWARD HER BY LETTING THE WORLD KNOW ABOUT SUPERGIRL... VERY SOON!

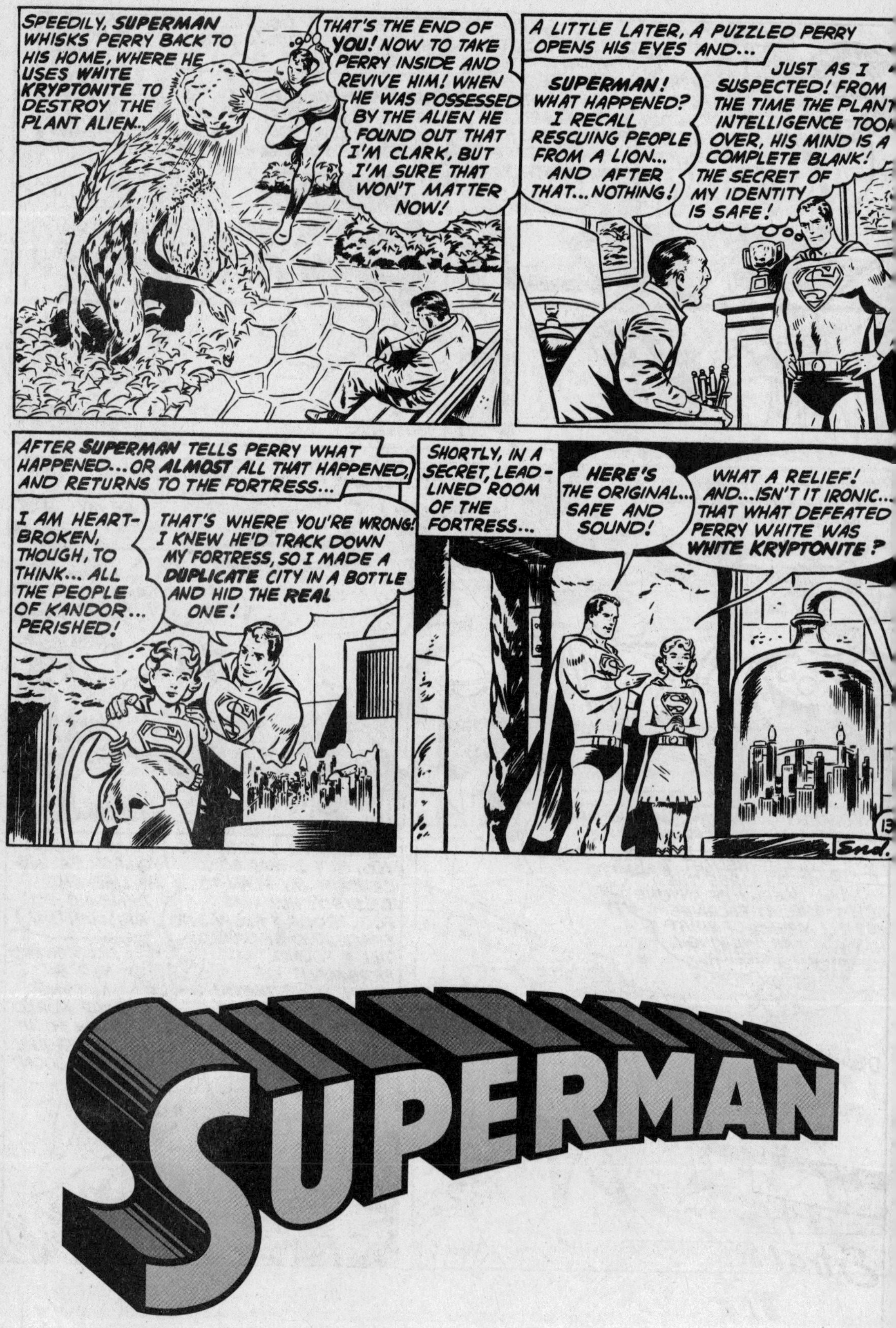
SPEEDILY, SUPERMAN WHISKS PERRY BACK TO HIS HOME, WHERE HE USES WHITE KRYPTONITE TO DESTROY THE PLANT ALIEN...
THAT'S THE END OF YOU! NOW TO TAKE PERRY INSIDE AND REVIVE HIM! WHEN HE WAS POSSESSED BY THE ALIEN HE FOUND OUT THAT I'M CLARK, BUT I'M SURE THAT WON'T MATTER NOW!
A LITTLE LATER, A PUZZLED PERRY OPENS HIS EYES AND...
SUPERMAN! WHAT HAPPENED? I RECALL RESCUING PEOPLE FROM A LION... AND AFTER THAT... NOTHING!
JUST AS I SUSPECTED! FROM THE TIME THE PLANT INTELLIGENCE TOOK OVER, HIS MIND IS A COMPLETE BLANK! THE SECRET OF MY IDENTITY IS SAFE!
AFTER SUPERMAN TELLS PERRY WHAT HAPPENED... OR ALMOST ALL THAT HAPPENED, AND RETURNS TO THE FORTRESS...
I AM HEART-BROKEN, THOUGH, TO THINK... ALL THE PEOPLE OF KANDOR... PERISHED!
THAT'S WHERE YOU'RE WRONG! I KNEW HE'D TRACK DOWN MY FORTRESS, SO I MADE A DUPLICATE CITY IN A BOTTLE AND HID THE REAL ONE!
SHORTLY, IN A SECRET, LEAD-LINED ROOM OF THE FORTRESS...
HERE'S THE ORIGINAL... SAFE AND SOUND!
WHAT A RELIEF! AND... ISN'T IT IRONIC... THAT WHAT DEFEATED PERRY WHITE WAS WHITE KRYPTONITE?
13
End.

SUPERMAN

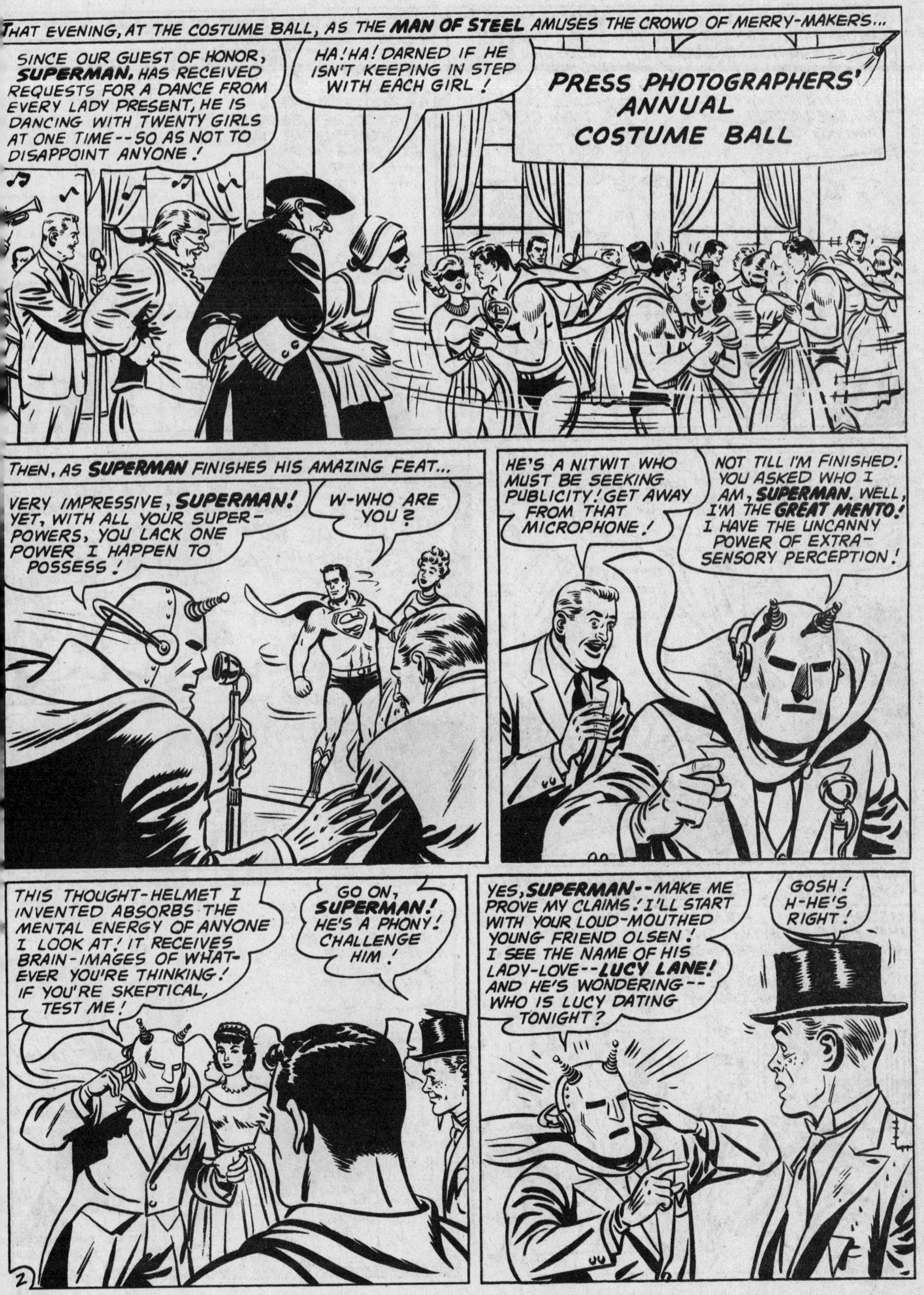
THAT EVENING, AT THE COSTUME BALL, AS THE MAN OF STEEL AMUSES THE CROWD OF MERRY-MAKERS...
SINCE OUR GUEST OF HONOR, SUPERMAN, HAS RECEIVED REQUESTS FOR A DANCE FROM EVERY LADY PRESENT, HE IS DANCING WITH TWENTY GIRLS AT ONE TIME--SO AS NOT TO DISAPPOINT ANYONE!
HA! HA! DARNED IF HE ISN'T KEEPING IN STEP WITH EACH GIRL!
PRESS PHOTOGRAPHERS' ANNUAL COSTUME BALL
THEN, AS SUPERMAN FINISHES HIS AMAZING FEAT...
VERY IMPRESSIVE, SUPERMAN! YET, WITH ALL YOUR SUPER-POWERS, YOU LACK ONE POWER I HAPPEN TO POSSESS!
W-WHO ARE YOU?
HE'S A NITWIT WHO MUST BE SEEKING PUBLICITY! GET AWAY FROM THAT MICROPHONE!
NOT TILL I'M FINISHED! YOU ASKED WHO I AM, SUPERMAN. WELL, I'M THE GREAT MENTO! I HAVE THE UNCANNY POWER OF EXTRA-SENSORY PERCEPTION!
THIS THOUGHT-HELMET I INVENTED ABSORBS THE MENTAL ENERGY OF ANYONE I LOOK AT! IT RECEIVES BRAIN-IMAGES OF WHATEVER YOU'RE THINKING! IF YOU'RE SKEPTICAL, TEST ME!
GO ON, SUPERMAN! HE'S A PHONY! CHALLENGE HIM!
2
YES, SUPERMAN--MAKE ME PROVE MY CLAIMS! I'LL START WITH YOUR LOUD-MOUTHED YOUNG FRIEND OLSEN! I SEE THE NAME OF HIS LADY-LOVE--LUCY LANE! AND HE'S WONDERING--WHO IS LUCY DATING TONIGHT?
GOSH! H-HE'S RIGHT!

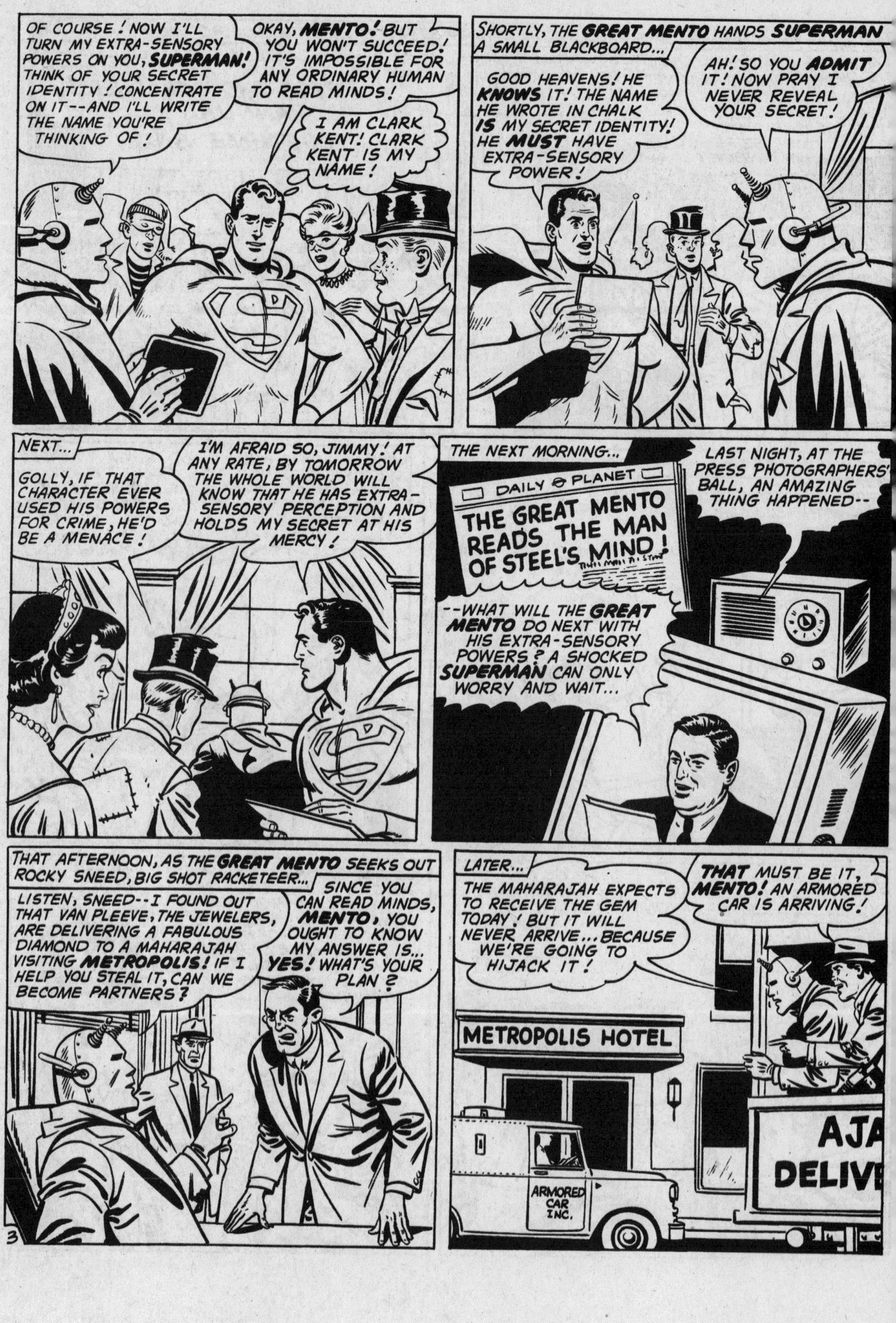
OF COURSE! NOW I'LL TURN MY EXTRA-SENSORY POWERS ON YOU, SUPERMAN! THINK OF YOUR SECRET IDENTITY! CONCENTRATE ON IT--AND I'LL WRITE THE NAME YOU'RE THINKING OF!
OKAY, MENTO! BUT YOU WON'T SUCCEED! IT'S IMPOSSIBLE FOR ANY ORDINARY HUMAN TO READ MINDS!
I AM CLARK KENT! CLARK KENT IS MY NAME!
SHORTLY, THE GREAT MENTO HANDS SUPERMAN A SMALL BLACKBOARD...
GOOD HEAVENS! HE KNOWS IT! THE NAME HE WROTE IN CHALK IS MY SECRET IDENTITY! HE MUST HAVE EXTRA-SENSORY POWER!
AH! SO YOU ADMIT IT! NOW PRAY I NEVER REVEAL YOUR SECRET!
NEXT...
GOLLY, IF THAT CHARACTER EVER USED HIS POWERS FOR CRIME, HE'D BE A MENACE!
I'M AFRAID SO, JIMMY! AT ANY RATE, BY TOMORROW THE WHOLE WORLD WILL KNOW THAT HE HAS EXTRA-SENSORY PERCEPTION AND HOLDS MY SECRET AT HIS MERCY!
THE NEXT MORNING...
DAILY PLANET
THE GREAT MENTO READS THE MAN OF STEEL'S MIND!
LAST NIGHT, AT THE PRESS PHOTOGRAPHERS' BALL, AN AMAZING THING HAPPENED--
--WHAT WILL THE GREAT MENTO DO NEXT WITH HIS EXTRA-SENSORY POWERS? A SHOCKED SUPERMAN CAN ONLY WORRY AND WAIT...
THAT AFTERNOON, AS THE GREAT MENTO SEEKS OUT ROCKY SNEED, BIG SHOT RACKETEER...
LISTEN, SNEED--I FOUND OUT THAT VAN PLEEVE, THE JEWELERS, ARE DELIVERING A FABULOUS DIAMOND TO A MAHARAJAH VISITING METROPOLIS! IF I HELP YOU STEAL IT, CAN WE BECOME PARTNERS?
SINCE YOU CAN READ MINDS, MENTO, YOU OUGHT TO KNOW MY ANSWER IS... YES! WHAT'S YOUR PLAN?
3
LATER...
THE MAHARAJAH EXPECTS TO RECEIVE THE GEM TODAY! BUT IT WILL NEVER ARRIVE... BECAUSE WE'RE GOING TO HIJACK IT!
THAT MUST BE IT, MENTO! AN ARMORED CAR IS ARRIVING!
METROPOLIS HOTEL
ARMORED CAR INC.
AJA
DELIVE

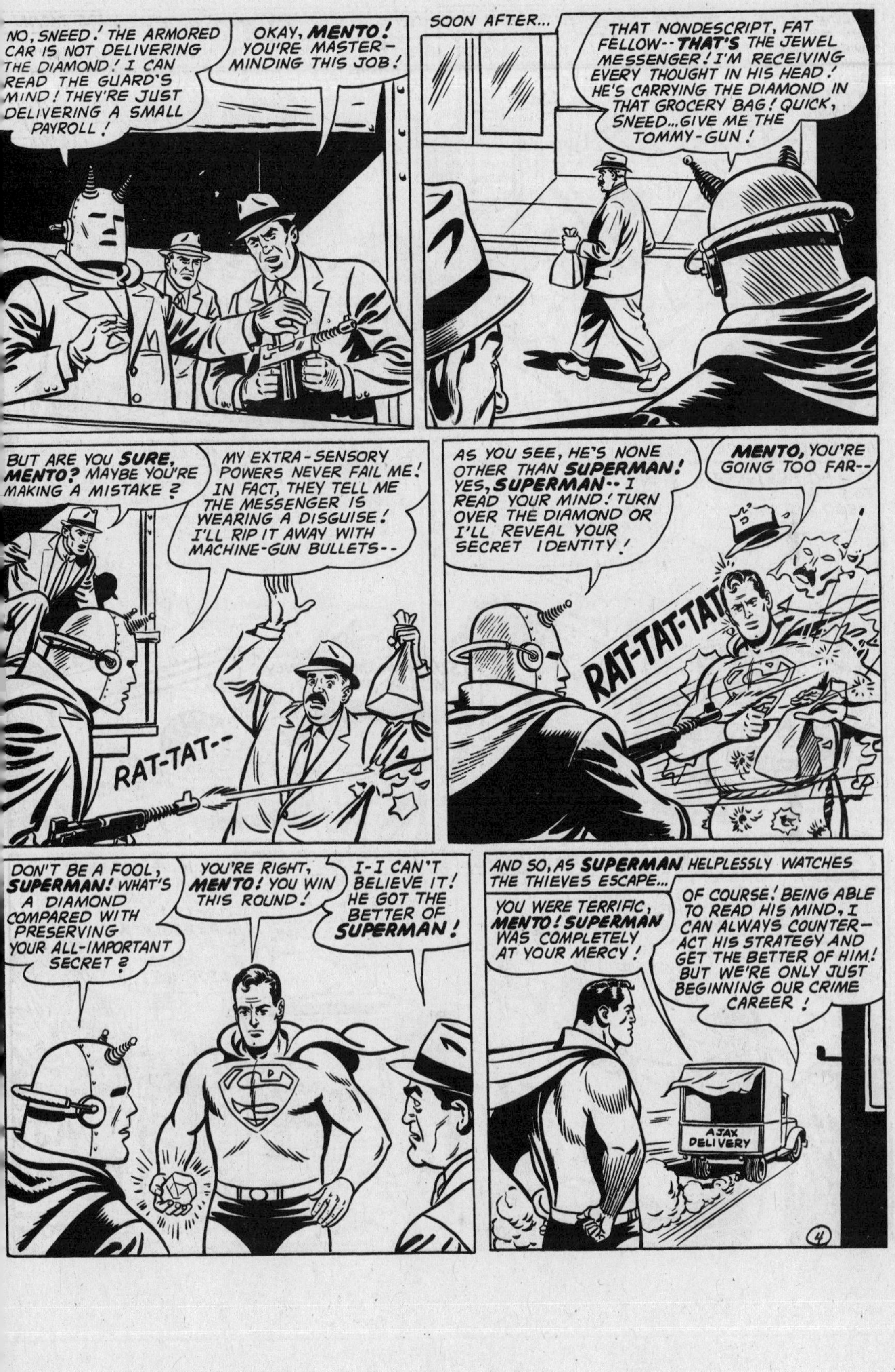
NO, SNEED! THE ARMORED CAR IS NOT DELIVERING THE DIAMOND! I CAN READ THE GUARD'S MIND! THEY'RE JUST DELIVERING A SMALL PAYROLL!
OKAY, MENTO! YOU'RE MASTER-MINDING THIS JOB!
SOON AFTER...
THAT NONDESCRIPT, FAT FELLOW--THAT'S THE JEWEL MESSENGER! I'M RECEIVING EVERY THOUGHT IN HIS HEAD! HE'S CARRYING THE DIAMOND IN THAT GROCERY BAG! QUICK, SNEED...GIVE ME THE TOMMY-GUN!
BUT ARE YOU SURE, MENTO? MAYBE YOU'RE MAKING A MISTAKE?
MY EXTRA-SENSORY POWERS NEVER FAIL ME! IN FACT, THEY TELL ME THE MESSENGER IS WEARING A DISGUISE! I'LL RIP IT AWAY WITH MACHINE-GUN BULLETS--
RAT-TAT--
AS YOU SEE, HE'S NONE OTHER THAN SUPERMAN! YES, SUPERMAN-- I READ YOUR MIND! TURN OVER THE DIAMOND OR I'LL REVEAL YOUR SECRET IDENTITY!
MENTO, YOU'RE GOING TOO FAR--
RAT-TAT-TAT
DON'T BE A FOOL, SUPERMAN! WHAT'S A DIAMOND COMPARED WITH PRESERVING YOUR ALL-IMPORTANT SECRET?
YOU'RE RIGHT, MENTO! YOU WIN THIS ROUND!
I-I CAN'T BELIEVE IT! HE GOT THE BETTER OF SUPERMAN!
AND SO, AS SUPERMAN HELPLESSLY WATCHES THE THIEVES ESCAPE...
YOU WERE TERRIFIC, MENTO! SUPERMAN WAS COMPLETELY AT YOUR MERCY!
OF COURSE! BEING ABLE TO READ HIS MIND, I CAN ALWAYS COUNTER-ACT HIS STRATEGY AND GET THE BETTER OF HIM! BUT WE'RE ONLY JUST BEGINNING OUR CRIME CAREER!
AJAX DELIVERY
4

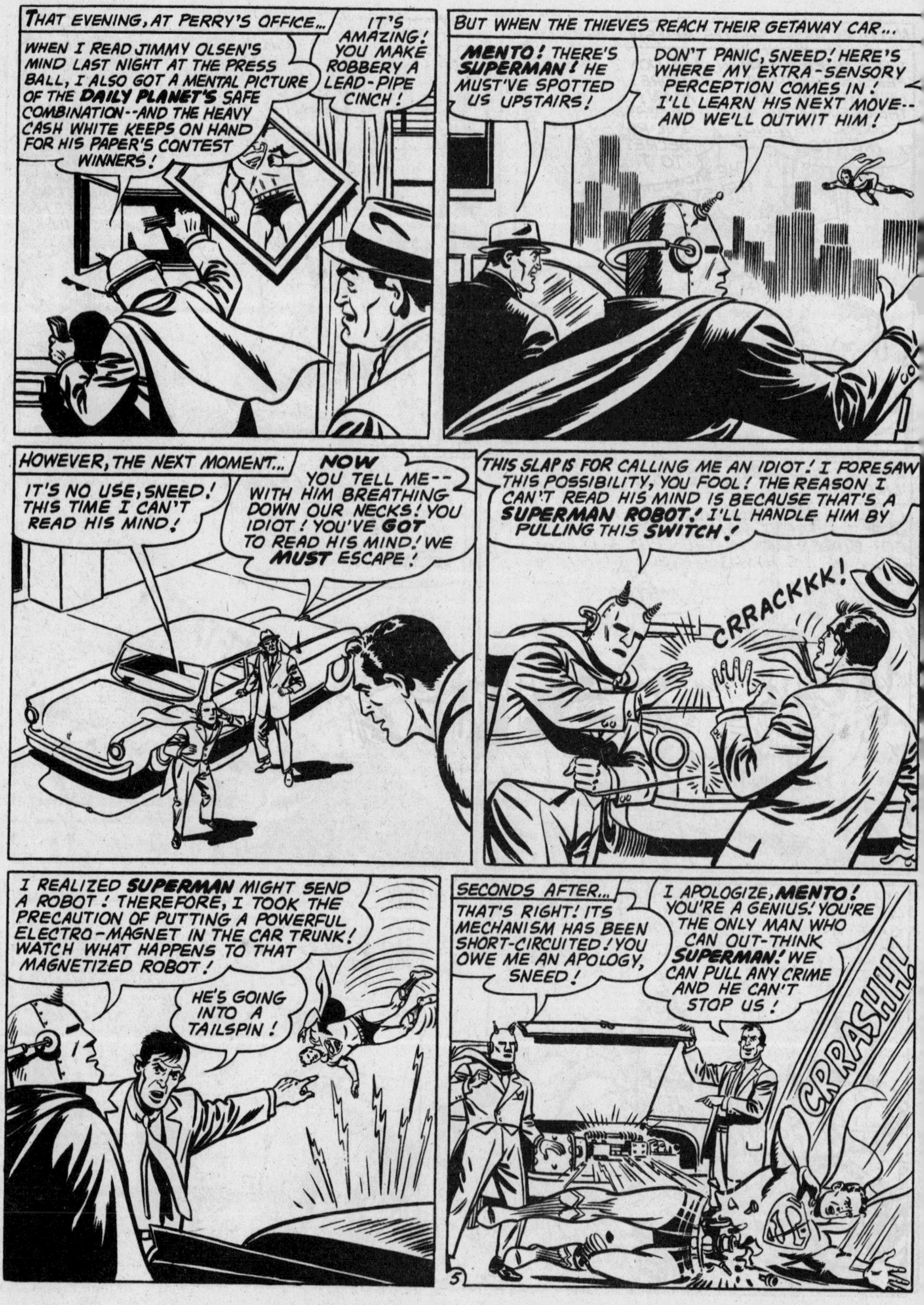
THAT EVENING, AT PERRY'S OFFICE...
WHEN I READ JIMMY OLSEN'S MIND LAST NIGHT AT THE PRESS BALL, I ALSO GOT A MENTAL PICTURE OF THE DAILY PLANET'S SAFE COMBINATION--AND THE HEAVY CASH WHITE KEEPS ON HAND FOR HIS PAPER'S CONTEST WINNERS!
IT'S AMAZING! YOU MAKE ROBBERY A LEAD-PIPE CINCH!
BUT WHEN THE THIEVES REACH THEIR GETAWAY CAR...
MENTO! THERE'S SUPERMAN! HE MUST'VE SPOTTED US UPSTAIRS!
DON'T PANIC, SNEED! HERE'S WHERE MY EXTRA-SENSORY PERCEPTION COMES IN! I'LL LEARN HIS NEXT MOVE--AND WE'LL OUTWIT HIM!
HOWEVER, THE NEXT MOMENT...
IT'S NO USE, SNEED! THIS TIME I CAN'T READ HIS MIND!
NOW YOU TELL ME--WITH HIM BREATHING DOWN OUR NECKS! YOU IDIOT! YOU'VE GOT TO READ HIS MIND! WE MUST ESCAPE!
THIS SLAP IS FOR CALLING ME AN IDIOT! I FORESAW THIS POSSIBILITY, YOU FOOL! THE REASON I CAN'T READ HIS MIND IS BECAUSE THAT'S A SUPERMAN ROBOT! I'LL HANDLE HIM BY PULLING THIS SWITCH!
CRRACKKK!
I REALIZED SUPERMAN MIGHT SEND A ROBOT! THEREFORE, I TOOK THE PRECAUTION OF PUTTING A POWERFUL ELECTRO-MAGNET IN THE CAR TRUNK! WATCH WHAT HAPPENS TO THAT MAGNETIZED ROBOT!
HE'S GOING INTO A TAILSPIN!
SECONDS AFTER...
THAT'S RIGHT! ITS MECHANISM HAS BEEN SHORT-CIRCUITED! YOU OWE ME AN APOLOGY, SNEED!
I APOLOGIZE, MENTO! YOU'RE A GENIUS! YOU'RE THE ONLY MAN WHO CAN OUT-THINK SUPERMAN! WE CAN PULL ANY CRIME AND HE CAN'T STOP US!
CRRASHH!
5

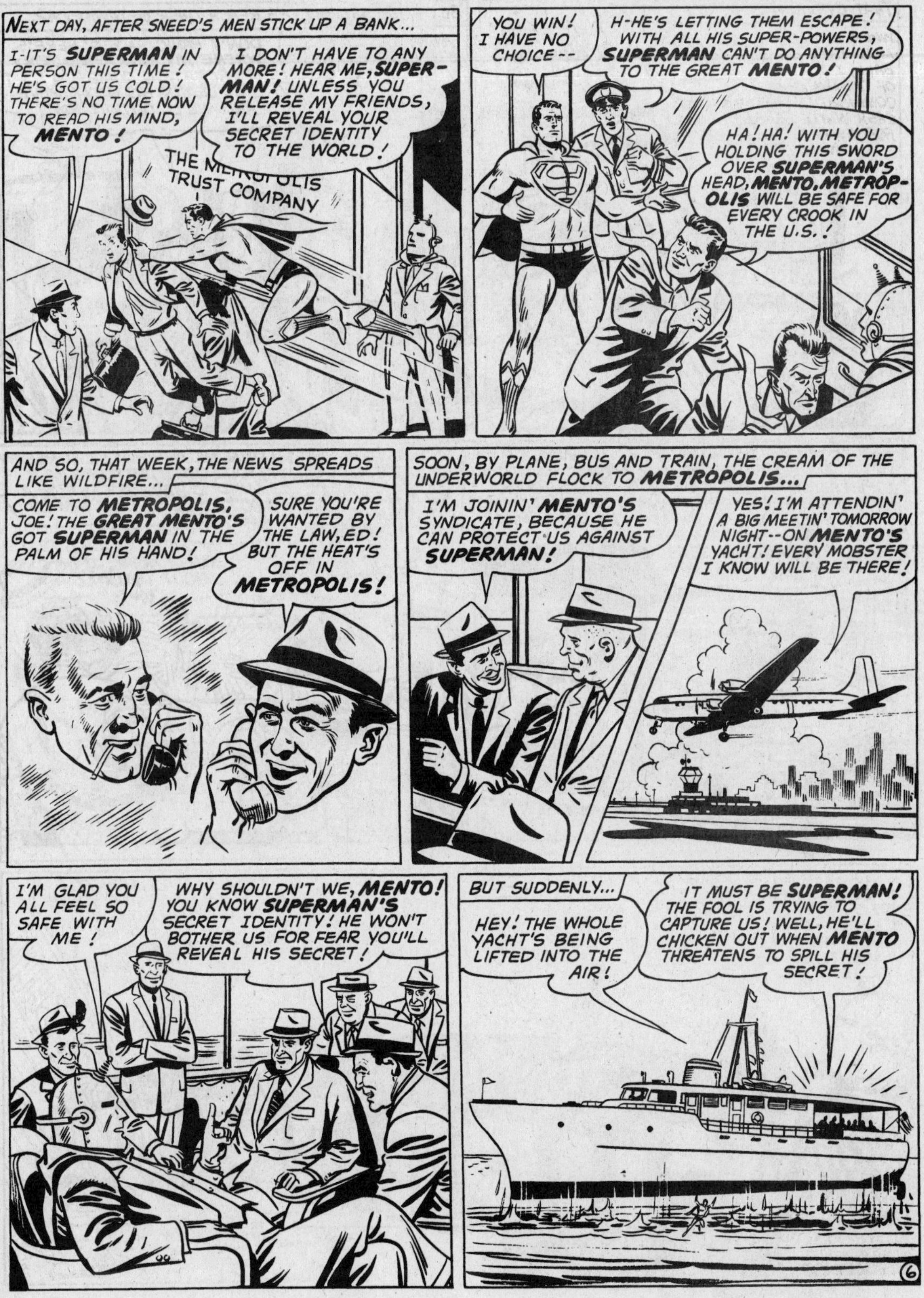
NEXT DAY, AFTER SNEED'S MEN STICK UP A BANK...
I-IT'S SUPERMAN IN PERSON THIS TIME! HE'S GOT US COLD! THERE'S NO TIME NOW TO READ HIS MIND, MENTO!
I DON'T HAVE TO ANY MORE! HEAR ME, SUPERMAN! UNLESS YOU RELEASE MY FRIENDS, I'LL REVEAL YOUR SECRET IDENTITY TO THE WORLD!
THE METROPOLIS TRUST COMPANY
YOU WIN! I HAVE NO CHOICE--
H-HE'S LETTING THEM ESCAPE! WITH ALL HIS SUPER-POWERS, SUPERMAN CAN'T DO ANYTHING TO THE GREAT MENTO!
HA! HA! WITH YOU HOLDING THIS SWORD OVER SUPERMAN'S HEAD, MENTO, METROPOLIS WILL BE SAFE FOR EVERY CROOK IN THE U.S.!
AND SO, THAT WEEK, THE NEWS SPREADS LIKE WILDFIRE...
COME TO METROPOLIS, JOE! THE GREAT MENTO'S GOT SUPERMAN IN THE PALM OF HIS HAND!
SURE YOU'RE WANTED BY THE LAW, ED! BUT THE HEAT'S OFF IN METROPOLIS!
SOON, BY PLANE, BUS AND TRAIN, THE CREAM OF THE UNDERWORLD FLOCK TO METROPOLIS...
I'M JOININ' MENTO'S SYNDICATE, BECAUSE HE CAN PROTECT US AGAINST SUPERMAN!
YES! I'M ATTENDIN' A BIG MEETIN' TOMORROW NIGHT--ON MENTO'S YACHT! EVERY MOBSTER I KNOW WILL BE THERE!
I'M GLAD YOU ALL FEEL SO SAFE WITH ME!
WHY SHOULDN'T WE, MENTO! YOU KNOW SUPERMAN'S SECRET IDENTITY! HE WON'T BOTHER US FOR FEAR YOU'LL REVEAL HIS SECRET!
BUT SUDDENLY...
HEY! THE WHOLE YACHT'S BEING LIFTED INTO THE AIR!
IT MUST BE SUPERMAN! THE FOOL IS TRYING TO CAPTURE US! WELL, HE'LL CHICKEN OUT WHEN MENTO THREATENS TO SPILL HIS SECRET!
6

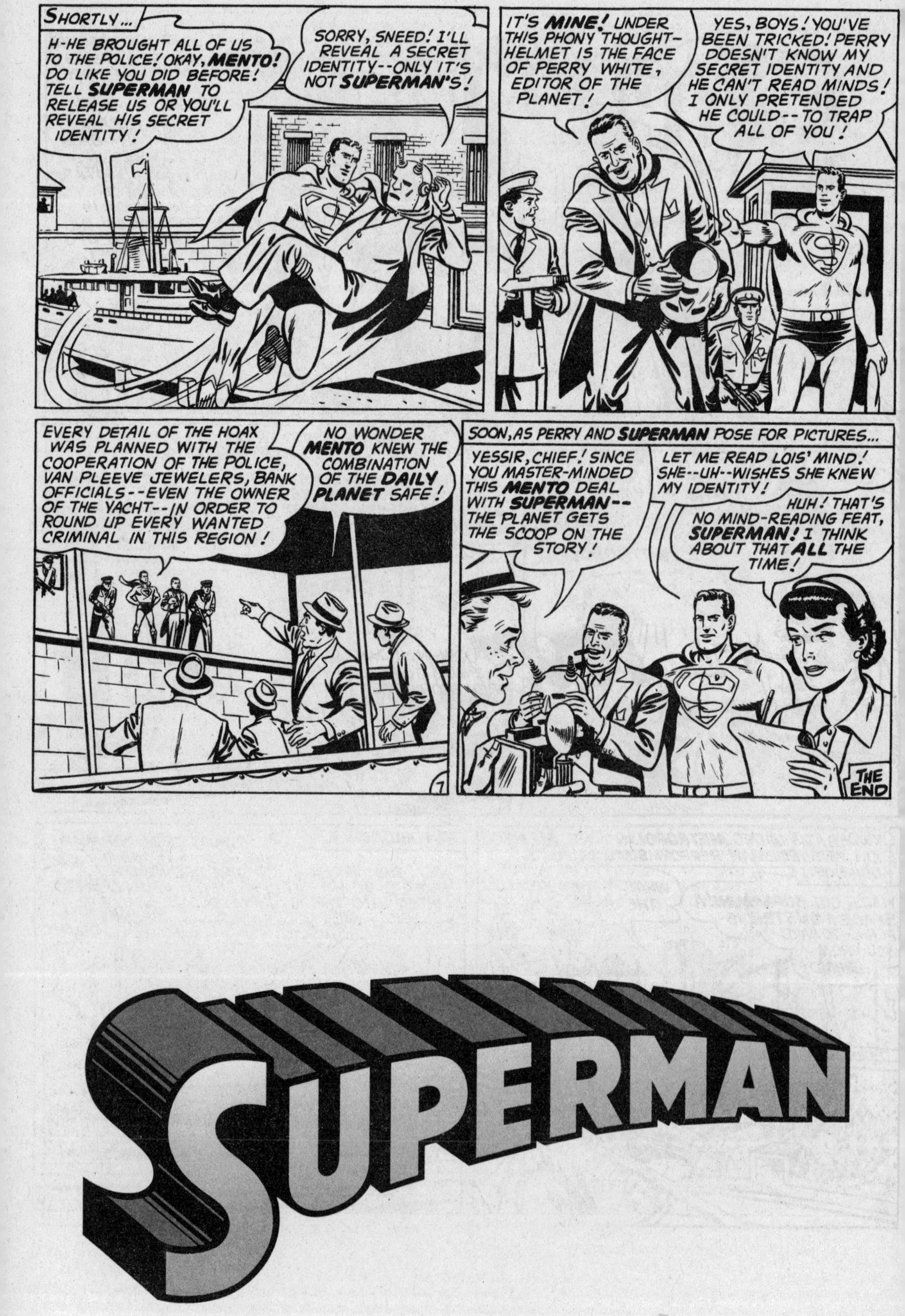
SHORTLY...
H-HE BROUGHT ALL OF US TO THE POLICE! OKAY, MENTO! DO LIKE YOU DID BEFORE! TELL SUPERMAN TO RELEASE US OR YOU'LL REVEAL HIS SECRET IDENTITY!
SORRY, SNEED! I'LL REVEAL A SECRET IDENTITY--ONLY IT'S NOT SUPERMAN'S!
IT'S MINE! UNDER THIS PHONY THOUGHT-HELMET IS THE FACE OF PERRY WHITE, EDITOR OF THE PLANET!
YES, BOYS! YOU'VE BEEN TRICKED! PERRY DOESN'T KNOW MY SECRET IDENTITY AND HE CAN'T READ MINDS! I ONLY PRETENDED HE COULD--TO TRAP ALL OF YOU!
EVERY DETAIL OF THE HOAX WAS PLANNED WITH THE COOPERATION OF THE POLICE, VAN PLEEVE JEWELERS, BANK OFFICIALS--EVEN THE OWNER OF THE YACHT--IN ORDER TO ROUND UP EVERY WANTED CRIMINAL IN THIS REGION!
NO WONDER MENTO KNEW THE COMBINATION OF THE DAILY PLANET SAFE!
7
SOON, AS PERRY AND SUPERMAN POSE FOR PICTURES...
YESSIR, CHIEF! SINCE YOU MASTER-MINDED THIS MENTO DEAL WITH SUPERMAN--THE PLANET GETS THE SCOOP ON THE STORY!
LET ME READ LOIS' MIND! SHE--UH--WISHES SHE KNEW MY IDENTITY!
HUH! THAT'S NO MIND-READING FEAT, SUPERMAN! I THINK ABOUT THAT ALL THE TIME!
THE END

SUPERMAN

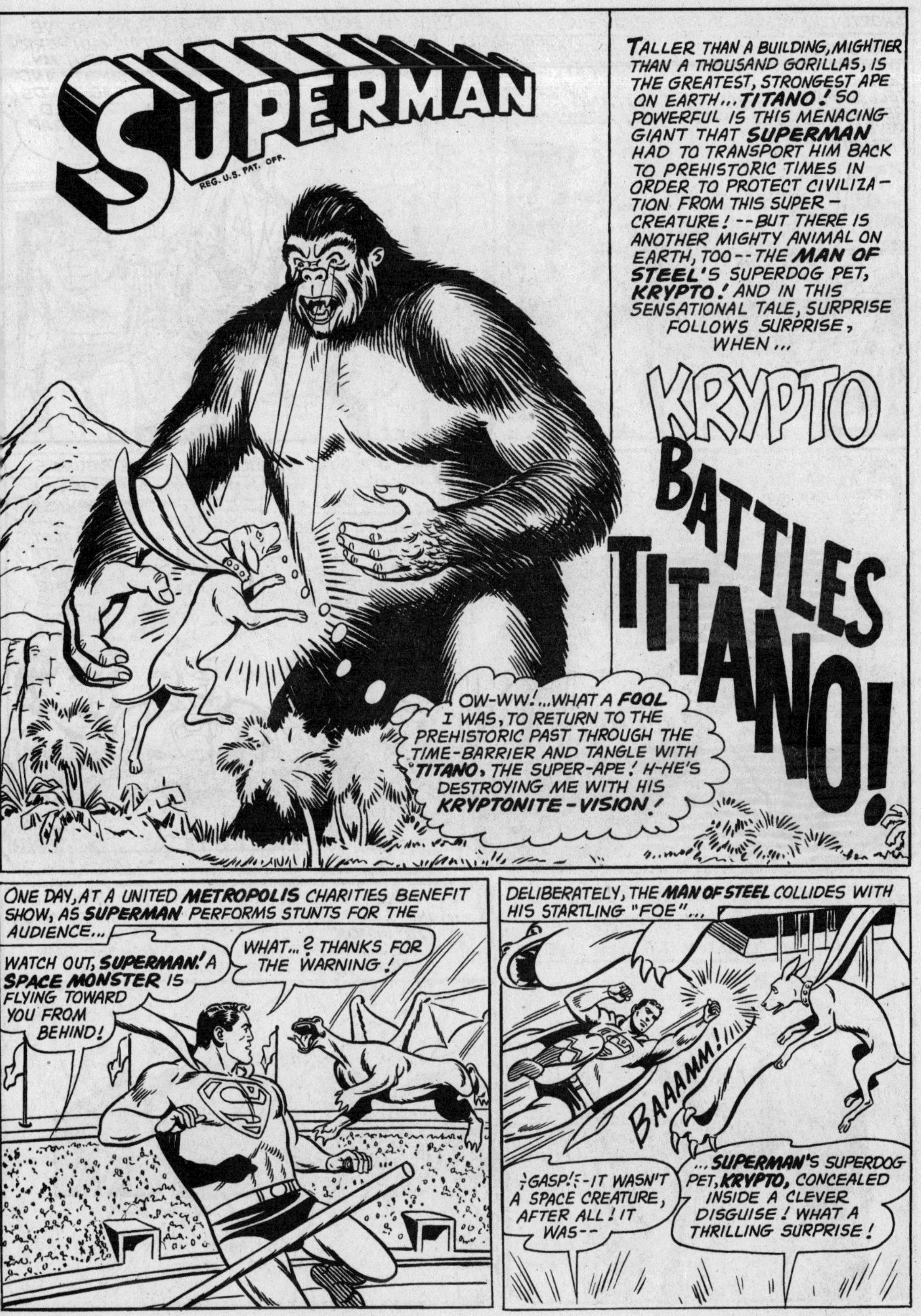
SUPERMAN
REG. U.S. PAT. OFF.
TALLER THAN A BUILDING, MIGHTIER THAN A THOUSAND GORILLAS, IS THE GREATEST, STRONGEST APE ON EARTH... TITANO! SO POWERFUL IS THIS MENACING GIANT THAT SUPERMAN HAD TO TRANSPORT HIM BACK TO PREHISTORIC TIMES IN ORDER TO PROTECT CIVILIZATION FROM THIS SUPER-CREATURE! --BUT THERE IS ANOTHER MIGHTY ANIMAL ON EARTH, TOO--THE MAN OF STEEL'S SUPERDOG PET, KRYPTO! AND IN THIS SENSATIONAL TALE, SURPRISE FOLLOWS SURPRISE, WHEN...
KRYPTO BATTLES TITANO!
OW-WW!...WHAT A FOOL I WAS, TO RETURN TO THE PREHISTORIC PAST THROUGH THE TIME-BARRIER AND TANGLE WITH TITANO, THE SUPER-APE! H-HE'S DESTROYING ME WITH HIS KRYPTONITE-VISION!
ONE DAY, AT A UNITED METROPOLIS CHARITIES BENEFIT SHOW, AS SUPERMAN PERFORMS STUNTS FOR THE AUDIENCE...
WATCH OUT, SUPERMAN! A SPACE MONSTER IS FLYING TOWARD YOU FROM BEHIND!
WHAT...? THANKS FOR THE WARNING!
DELIBERATELY, THE MAN OF STEEL COLLIDES WITH HIS STARTLING "FOE"...
BAAAMM!
...SUPERMAN'S SUPERDOG PET, KRYPTO, CONCEALED INSIDE A CLEVER DISGUISE! WHAT A THRILLING SURPRISE!
-GASP!- IT WASN'T A SPACE CREATURE, AFTER ALL! IT WAS--

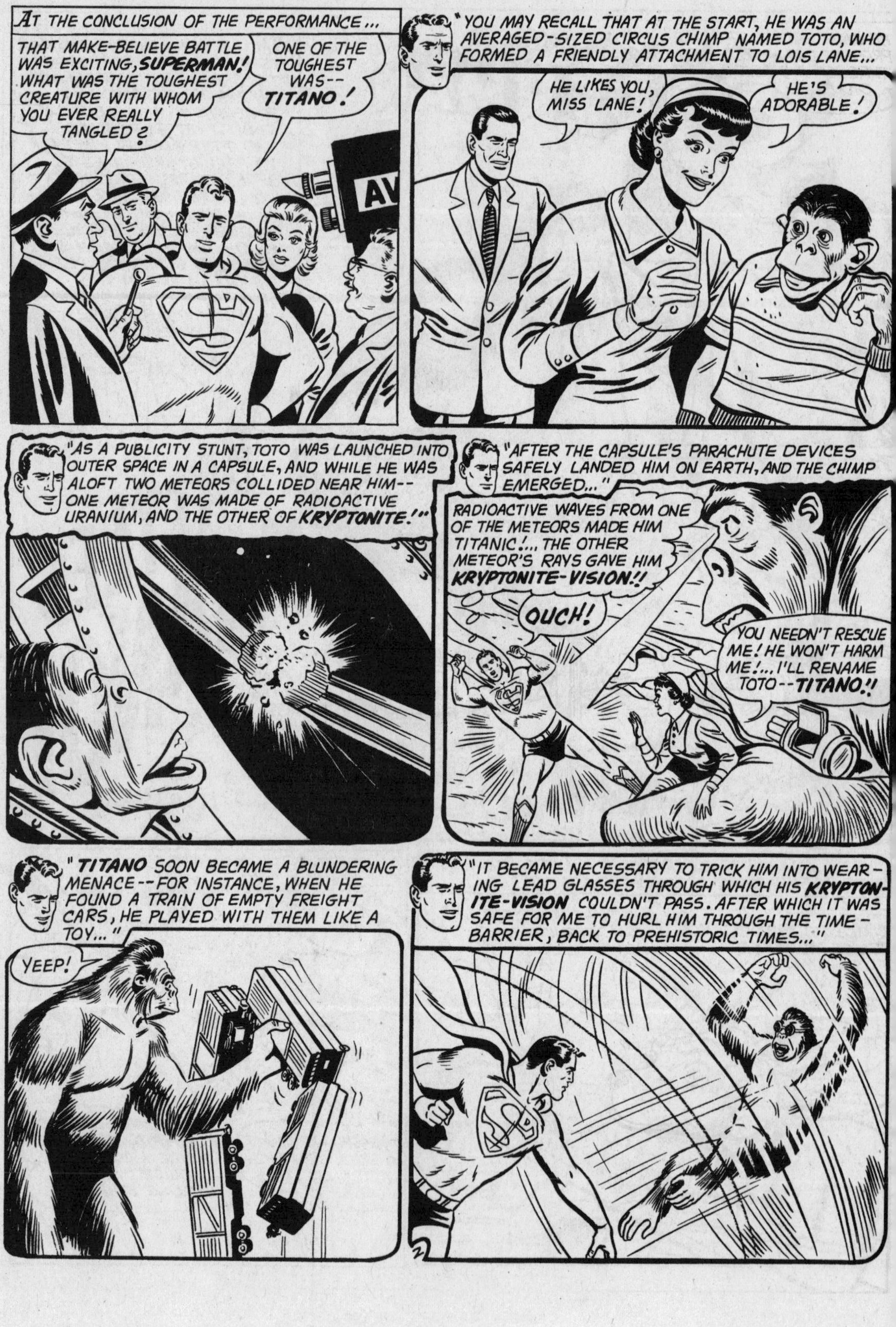
AT THE CONCLUSION OF THE PERFORMANCE...
THAT MAKE-BELIEVE BATTLE WAS EXCITING, SUPERMAN! WHAT WAS THE TOUGHEST CREATURE WITH WHOM YOU EVER REALLY TANGLED?
ONE OF THE TOUGHEST WAS-- TITANO!
AV
"YOU MAY RECALL THAT AT THE START, HE WAS AN AVERAGED-SIZED CIRCUS CHIMP NAMED TOTO, WHO FORMED A FRIENDLY ATTACHMENT TO LOIS LANE...
HE LIKES YOU, MISS LANE!
HE'S ADORABLE!
"AS A PUBLICITY STUNT, TOTO WAS LAUNCHED INTO OUTER SPACE IN A CAPSULE, AND WHILE HE WAS ALOFT TWO METEORS COLLIDED NEAR HIM-- ONE METEOR WAS MADE OF RADIOACTIVE URANIUM, AND THE OTHER OF KRYPTONITE!"
"AFTER THE CAPSULE'S PARACHUTE DEVICES SAFELY LANDED HIM ON EARTH, AND THE CHIMP EMERGED..."
RADIOACTIVE WAVES FROM ONE OF THE METEORS MADE HIM TITANIC!... THE OTHER METEOR'S RAYS GAVE HIM KRYPTONITE-VISION!!
OUCH!
YOU NEEDN'T RESCUE ME! HE WON'T HARM ME!... I'LL RENAME TOTO--TITANO!!
"TITANO SOON BECAME A BLUNDERING MENACE--FOR INSTANCE, WHEN HE FOUND A TRAIN OF EMPTY FREIGHT CARS, HE PLAYED WITH THEM LIKE A TOY..."
YEEP!
"IT BECAME NECESSARY TO TRICK HIM INTO WEARING LEAD GLASSES THROUGH WHICH HIS KRYPTONITE-VISION COULDN'T PASS. AFTER WHICH IT WAS SAFE FOR ME TO HURL HIM THROUGH THE TIME-BARRIER, BACK TO PREHISTORIC TIMES..."

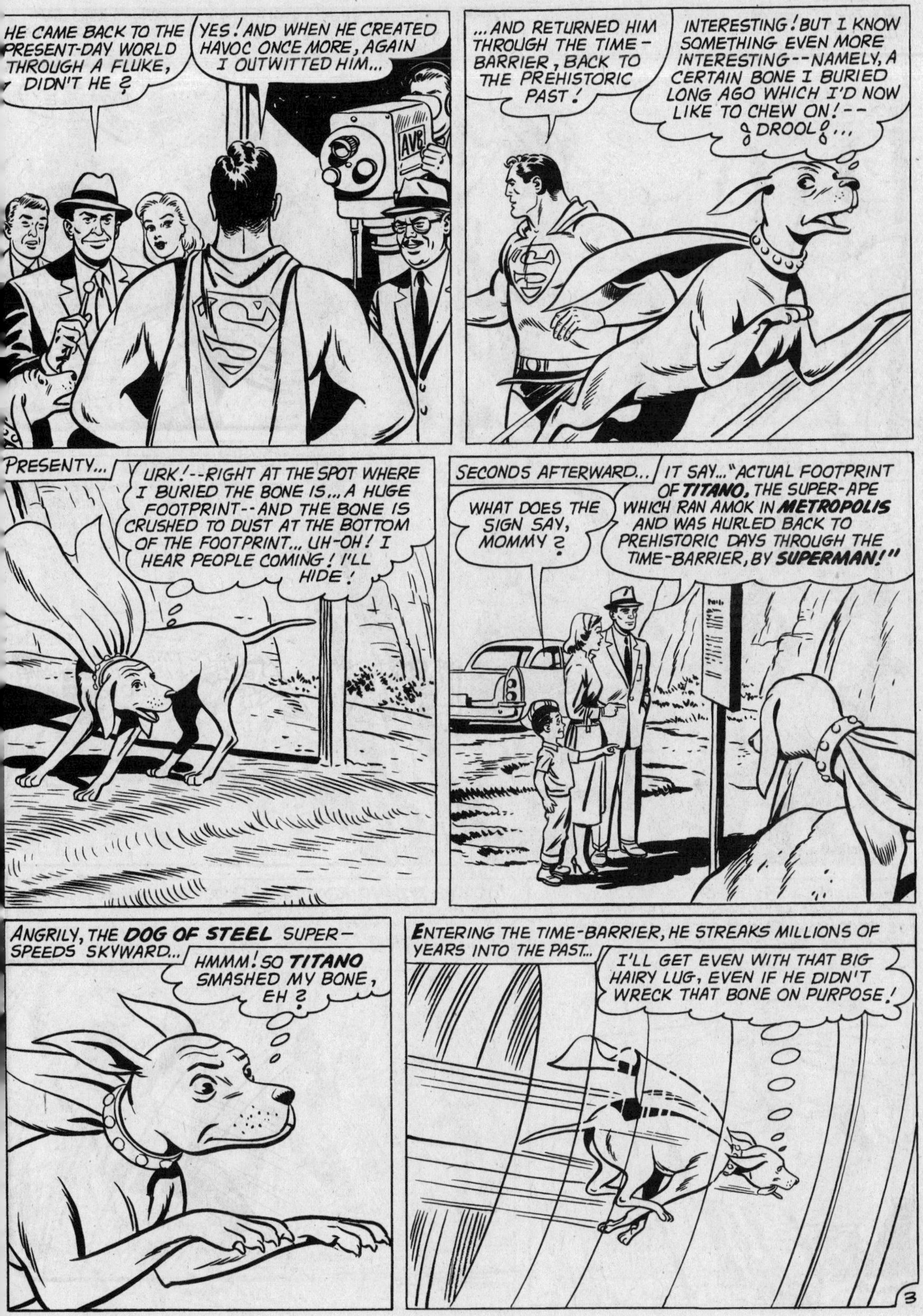
HE CAME BACK TO THE PRESENT-DAY WORLD THROUGH A FLUKE, DIDN'T HE ?
YES! AND WHEN HE CREATED HAVOC ONCE MORE, AGAIN I OUTWITTED HIM...
AVB
...AND RETURNED HIM THROUGH THE TIME-BARRIER, BACK TO THE PREHISTORIC PAST!
INTERESTING! BUT I KNOW SOMETHING EVEN MORE INTERESTING--NAMELY, A CERTAIN BONE I BURIED LONG AGO WHICH I'D NOW LIKE TO CHEW ON!-- DROOL...
PRESENTLY...
URK!--RIGHT AT THE SPOT WHERE I BURIED THE BONE IS... A HUGE FOOTPRINT--AND THE BONE IS CRUSHED TO DUST AT THE BOTTOM OF THE FOOTPRINT... UH-OH! I HEAR PEOPLE COMING! I'LL HIDE!
SECONDS AFTERWARD...
WHAT DOES THE SIGN SAY, MOMMY ?
IT SAY..."ACTUAL FOOTPRINT OF TITANO, THE SUPER-APE WHICH RAN AMOK IN METROPOLIS AND WAS HURLED BACK TO PREHISTORIC DAYS THROUGH THE TIME-BARRIER, BY SUPERMAN!"
ANGRILY, THE DOG OF STEEL SUPER-SPEEDS SKYWARD...
HMMM! SO TITANO SMASHED MY BONE, EH ?
ENTERING THE TIME-BARRIER, HE STREAKS MILLIONS OF YEARS INTO THE PAST...
I'LL GET EVEN WITH THAT BIG HAIRY LUG, EVEN IF HE DIDN'T WRECK THAT BONE ON PURPOSE!
3

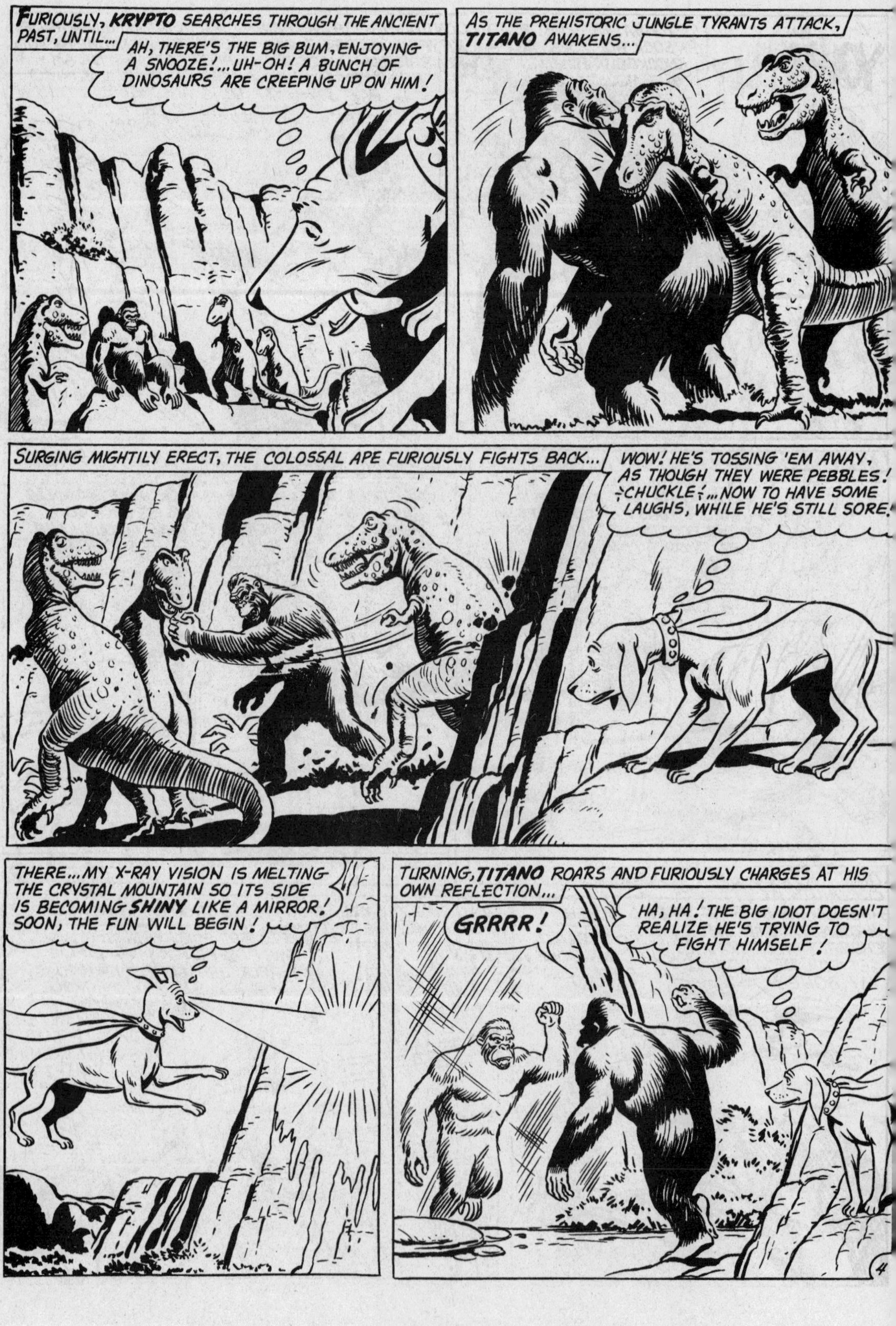
FURIOUSLY, KRYPTO SEARCHES THROUGH THE ANCIENT PAST, UNTIL...
AH, THERE'S THE BIG BUM, ENJOYING A SNOOZE!...UH-OH! A BUNCH OF DINOSAURS ARE CREEPING UP ON HIM!
AS THE PREHISTORIC JUNGLE TYRANTS ATTACK, TITANO AWAKENS...
SURGING MIGHTILY ERECT, THE COLOSSAL APE FURIOUSLY FIGHTS BACK...
WOW! HE'S TOSSING 'EM AWAY, AS THOUGH THEY WERE PEBBLES! -CHUCKLE-...NOW TO HAVE SOME LAUGHS, WHILE HE'S STILL SORE!
THERE...MY X-RAY VISION IS MELTING THE CRYSTAL MOUNTAIN SO ITS SIDE IS BECOMING SHINY LIKE A MIRROR! SOON, THE FUN WILL BEGIN!
TURNING, TITANO ROARS AND FURIOUSLY CHARGES AT HIS OWN REFLECTION...
GRRRR!
HA, HA! THE BIG IDIOT DOESN'T REALIZE HE'S TRYING TO FIGHT HIMSELF!
4

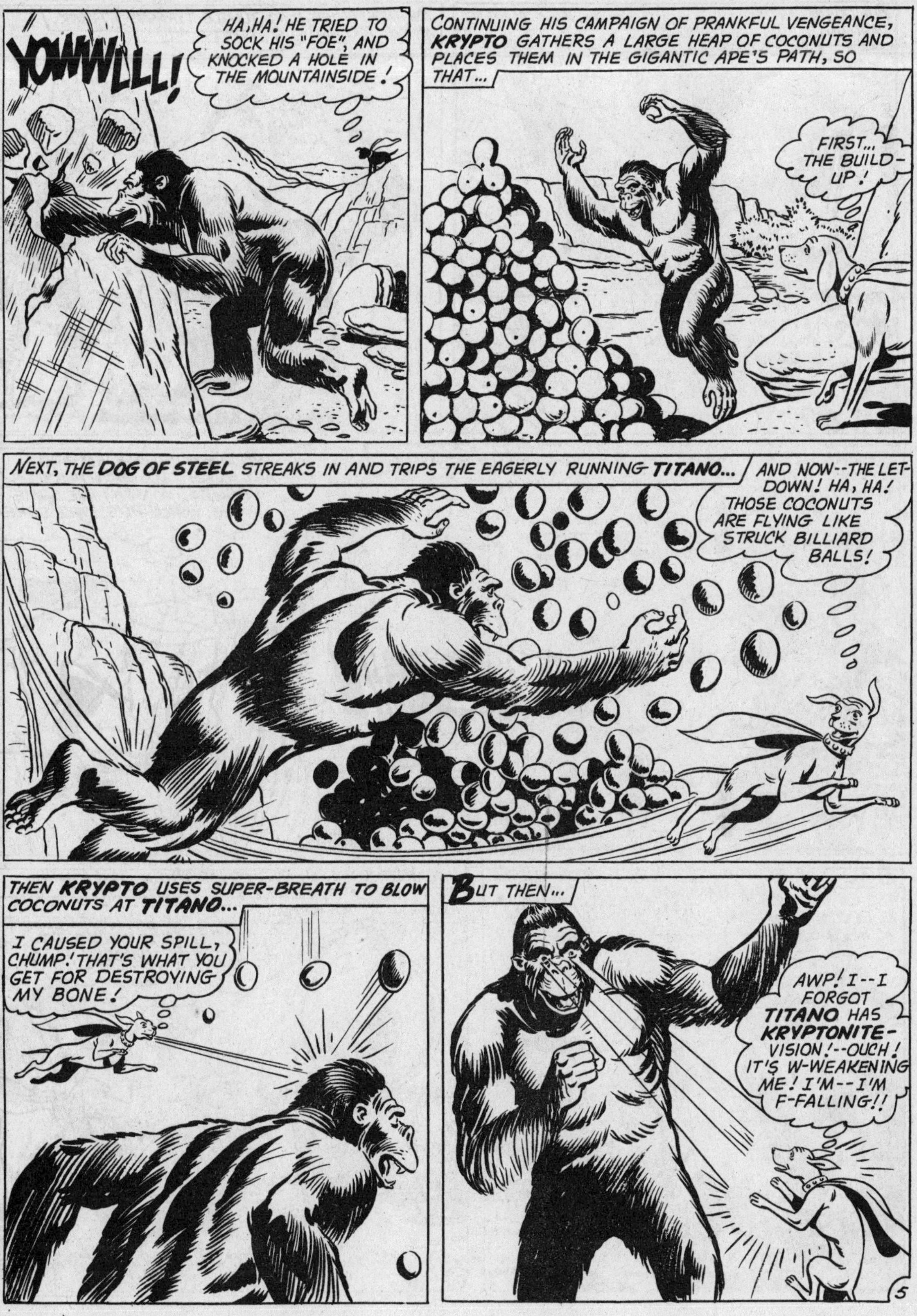
YOWWLLL!
HA,HA! HE TRIED TO SOCK HIS "FOE", AND KNOCKED A HOLE IN THE MOUNTAINSIDE!
CONTINUING HIS CAMPAIGN OF PRANKFUL VENGEANCE, KRYPTO GATHERS A LARGE HEAP OF COCONUTS AND PLACES THEM IN THE GIGANTIC APE'S PATH, SO THAT...
FIRST... THE BUILD-UP!
NEXT, THE DOG OF STEEL STREAKS IN AND TRIPS THE EAGERLY RUNNING TITANO...
AND NOW--THE LET-DOWN! HA, HA! THOSE COCONUTS ARE FLYING LIKE STRUCK BILLIARD BALLS!
THEN KRYPTO USES SUPER-BREATH TO BLOW COCONUTS AT TITANO...
I CAUSED YOUR SPILL, CHUMP! THAT'S WHAT YOU GET FOR DESTROYING MY BONE!
BUT THEN...
AWP! I--I FORGOT TITANO HAS KRYPTONITE-VISION!--OUCH! IT'S W-WEAKENING ME! I'M--I'M F-FALLING!!
5

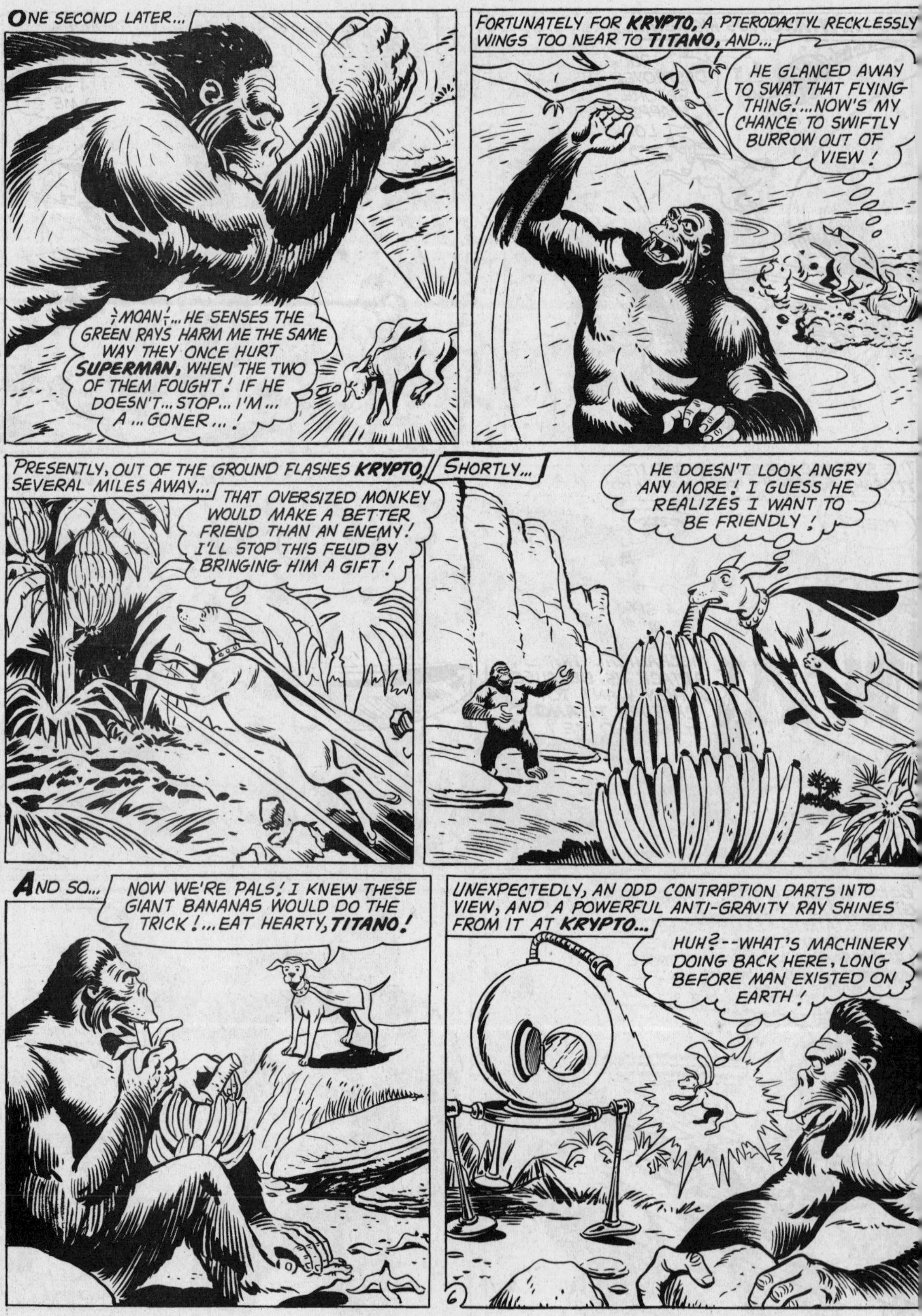
ONE SECOND LATER...
¡MOAN¡... HE SENSES THE GREEN RAYS HARM ME THE SAME WAY THEY ONCE HURT SUPERMAN, WHEN THE TWO OF THEM FOUGHT! IF HE DOESN'T... STOP... I'M... A... GONER...!
FORTUNATELY FOR KRYPTO, A PTERODACTYL RECKLESSLY WINGS TOO NEAR TO TITANO, AND...
HE GLANCED AWAY TO SWAT THAT FLYING THING!... NOW'S MY CHANCE TO SWIFTLY BURROW OUT OF VIEW!
PRESENTLY, OUT OF THE GROUND FLASHES KRYPTO, SEVERAL MILES AWAY...
THAT OVERSIZED MONKEY WOULD MAKE A BETTER FRIEND THAN AN ENEMY! I'LL STOP THIS FEUD BY BRINGING HIM A GIFT!
SHORTLY...
HE DOESN'T LOOK ANGRY ANY MORE! I GUESS HE REALIZES I WANT TO BE FRIENDLY!
AND SO...
NOW WE'RE PALS! I KNEW THESE GIANT BANANAS WOULD DO THE TRICK!... EAT HEARTY, TITANO!
UNEXPECTEDLY, AN ODD CONTRAPTION DARTS INTO VIEW, AND A POWERFUL ANTI-GRAVITY RAY SHINES FROM IT AT KRYPTO...
HUH?--WHAT'S MACHINERY DOING BACK HERE, LONG BEFORE MAN EXISTED ON EARTH!
6

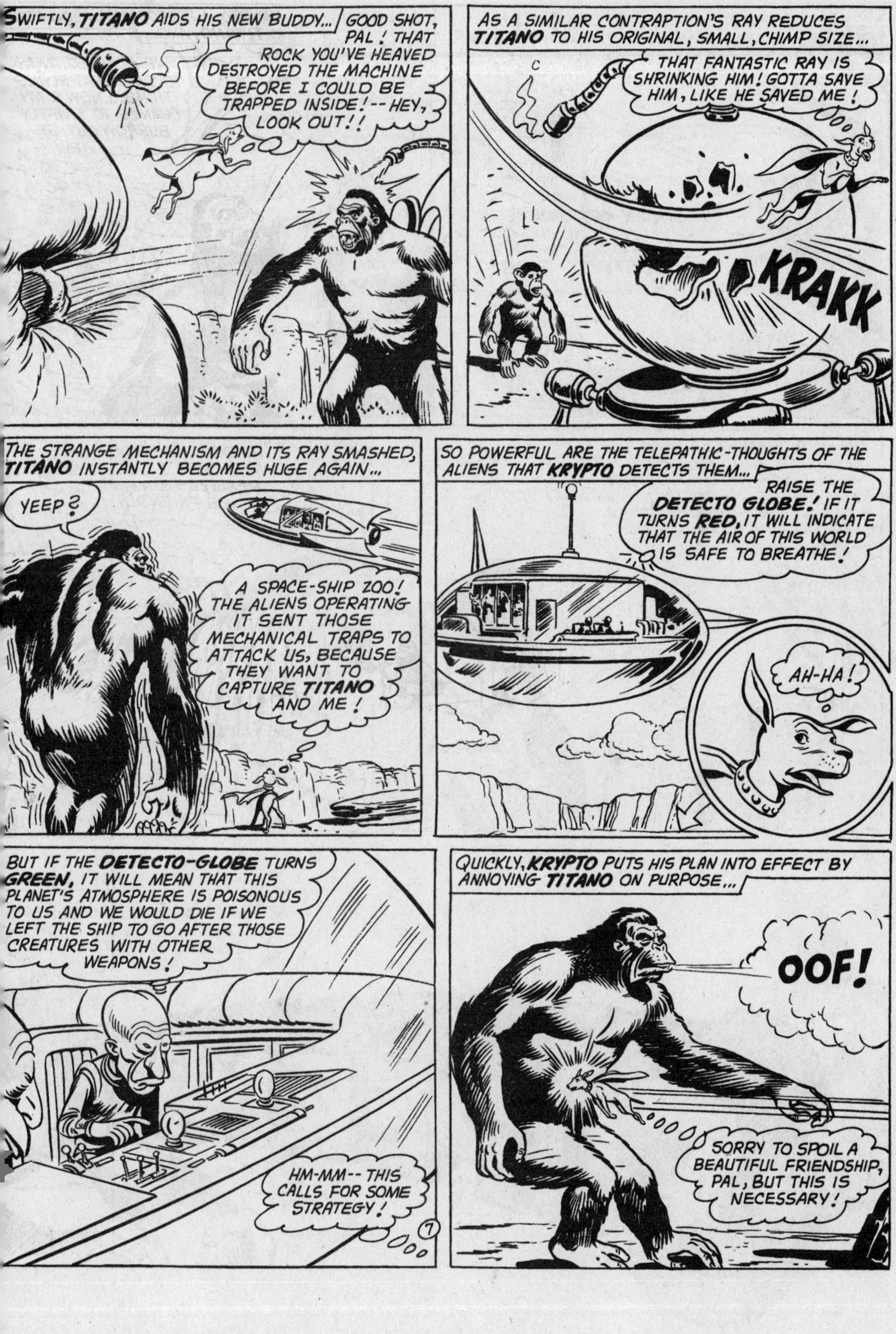
SWIFTLY, TITANO AIDS HIS NEW BUDDY...
GOOD SHOT, PAL! THAT ROCK YOU'VE HEAVED DESTROYED THE MACHINE BEFORE I COULD BE TRAPPED INSIDE! -- HEY, LOOK OUT!!
AS A SIMILAR CONTRAPTION'S RAY REDUCES TITANO TO HIS ORIGINAL, SMALL, CHIMP SIZE...
THAT FANTASTIC RAY IS SHRINKING HIM! GOTTA SAVE HIM, LIKE HE SAVED ME!
KRAKK
THE STRANGE MECHANISM AND ITS RAY SMASHED, TITANO INSTANTLY BECOMES HUGE AGAIN...
YEEP?
A SPACE-SHIP ZOO! THE ALIENS OPERATING IT SENT THOSE MECHANICAL TRAPS TO ATTACK US, BECAUSE THEY WANT TO CAPTURE TITANO AND ME!
SO POWERFUL ARE THE TELEPATHIC-THOUGHTS OF THE ALIENS THAT KRYPTO DETECTS THEM...
RAISE THE DETECTO GLOBE! IF IT TURNS RED, IT WILL INDICATE THAT THE AIR OF THIS WORLD IS SAFE TO BREATHE!
AH-HA!
BUT IF THE DETECTO-GLOBE TURNS GREEN, IT WILL MEAN THAT THIS PLANET'S ATMOSPHERE IS POISONOUS TO US AND WE WOULD DIE IF WE LEFT THE SHIP TO GO AFTER THOSE CREATURES WITH OTHER WEAPONS!
HM-MM -- THIS CALLS FOR SOME STRATEGY!
7
QUICKLY, KRYPTO PUTS HIS PLAN INTO EFFECT BY ANNOYING TITANO ON PURPOSE...
OOF!
SORRY TO SPOIL A BEAUTIFUL FRIENDSHIP, PAL, BUT THIS IS NECESSARY!

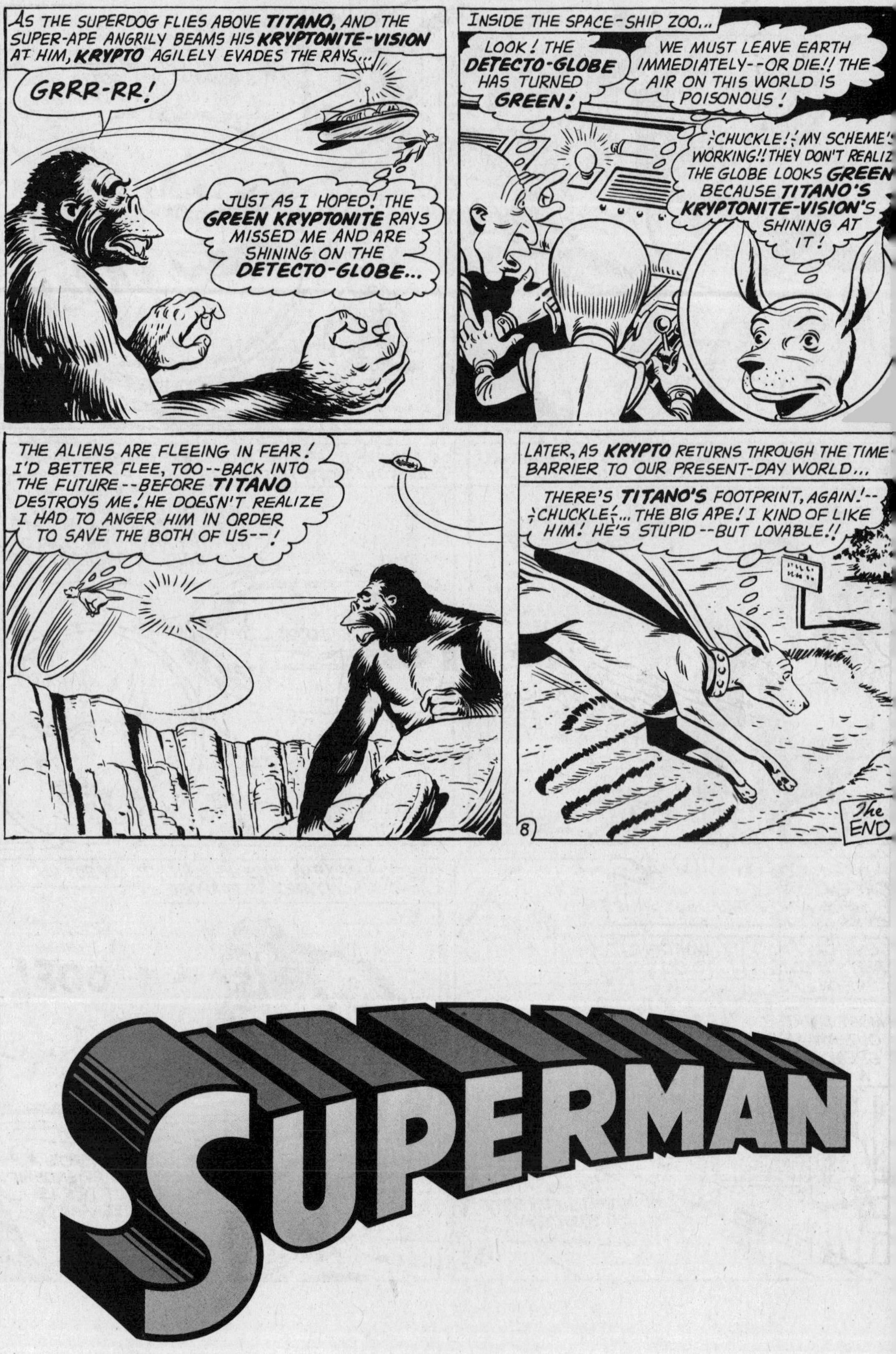
AS THE SUPERDOG FLIES ABOVE TITANO, AND THE SUPER-APE ANGRILY BEAMS HIS KRYPTONITE-VISION AT HIM, KRYPTO AGILELY EVADES THE RAYS...
GRRR-RR!
JUST AS I HOPED! THE GREEN KRYPTONITE RAYS MISSED ME AND ARE SHINING ON THE DETECTO-GLOBE...
INSIDE THE SPACE-SHIP ZOO...
LOOK! THE DETECTO-GLOBE HAS TURNED GREEN!
WE MUST LEAVE EARTH IMMEDIATELY--OR DIE!! THE AIR ON THIS WORLD IS POISONOUS!
¡CHUCKLE!¡ MY SCHEME'S WORKING!! THEY DON'T REALIZ THE GLOBE LOOKS GREEN BECAUSE TITANO'S KRYPTONITE-VISION'S SHINING AT IT!
THE ALIENS ARE FLEEING IN FEAR! I'D BETTER FLEE, TOO--BACK INTO THE FUTURE--BEFORE TITANO DESTROYS ME! HE DOESN'T REALIZE I HAD TO ANGER HIM IN ORDER TO SAVE THE BOTH OF US--!
LATER, AS KRYPTO RETURNS THROUGH THE TIME BARRIER TO OUR PRESENT-DAY WORLD...
THERE'S TITANO'S FOOTPRINT, AGAIN!--¡CHUCKLE¡... THE BIG APE! I KIND OF LIKE HIM! HE'S STUPID--BUT LOVABLE!!
8
The END

SUPERMAN

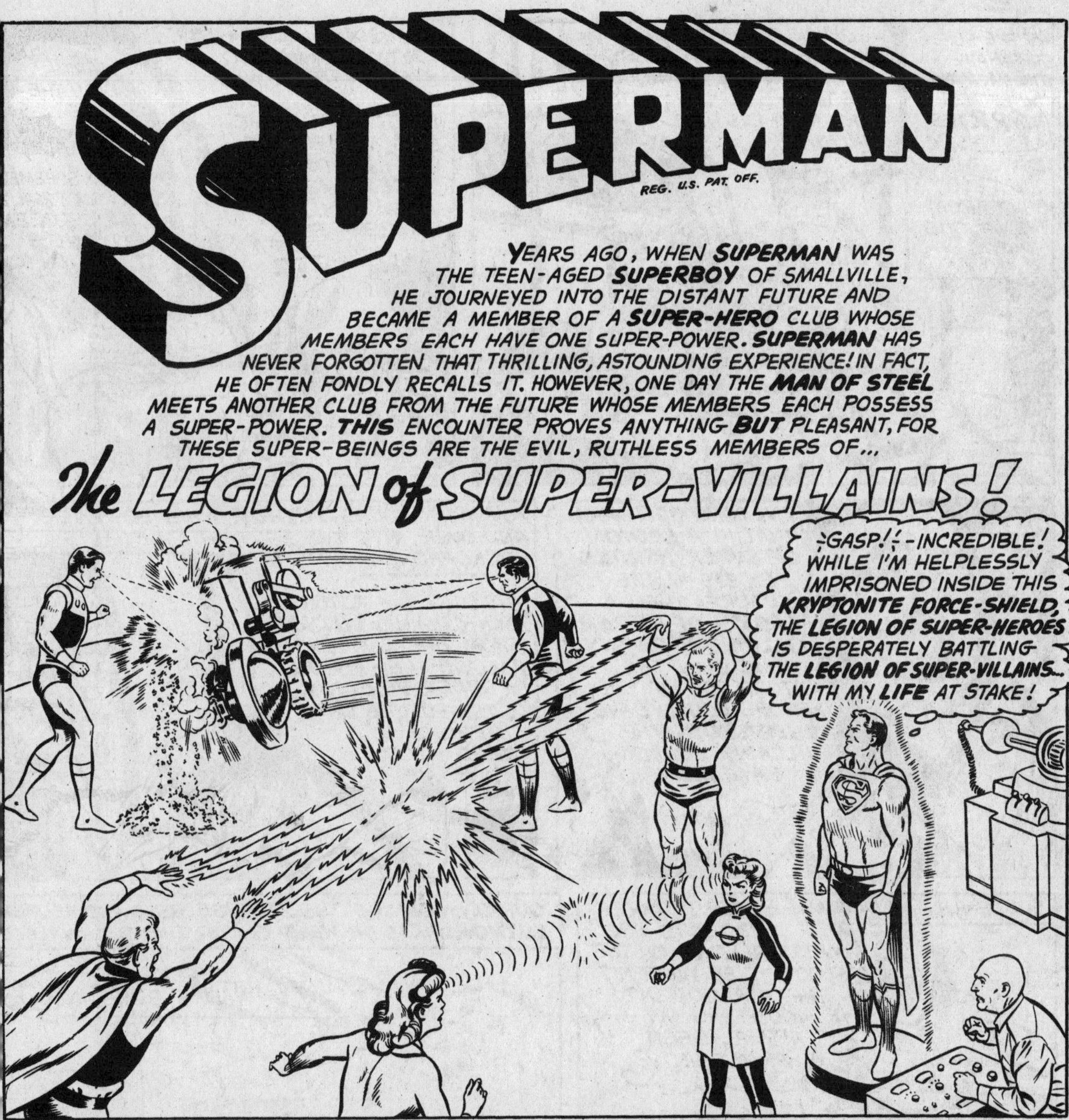
SUPERMAN
REG. U.S. PAT. OFF.
YEARS AGO, WHEN SUPERMAN WAS THE TEEN-AGED SUPERBOY OF SMALLVILLE, HE JOURNEYED INTO THE DISTANT FUTURE AND BECAME A MEMBER OF A SUPER-HERO CLUB WHOSE MEMBERS EACH HAVE ONE SUPER-POWER. SUPERMAN HAS NEVER FORGOTTEN THAT THRILLING, ASTOUNDING EXPERIENCE! IN FACT, HE OFTEN FONDLY RECALLS IT. HOWEVER, ONE DAY THE MAN OF STEEL MEETS ANOTHER CLUB FROM THE FUTURE WHOSE MEMBERS EACH POSSESS A SUPER-POWER. THIS ENCOUNTER PROVES ANYTHING BUT PLEASANT, FOR THESE SUPER-BEINGS ARE THE EVIL, RUTHLESS MEMBERS OF...
The LEGION of SUPER-VILLAINS!
¡GASP!¡ -INCREDIBLE! WHILE I'M HELPLESSLY IMPRISONED INSIDE THIS KRYPTONITE FORCE-SHIELD, THE LEGION OF SUPER-HEROES IS DESPERATELY BATTLING THE LEGION OF SUPER-VILLAINS... WITH MY LIFE AT STAKE!

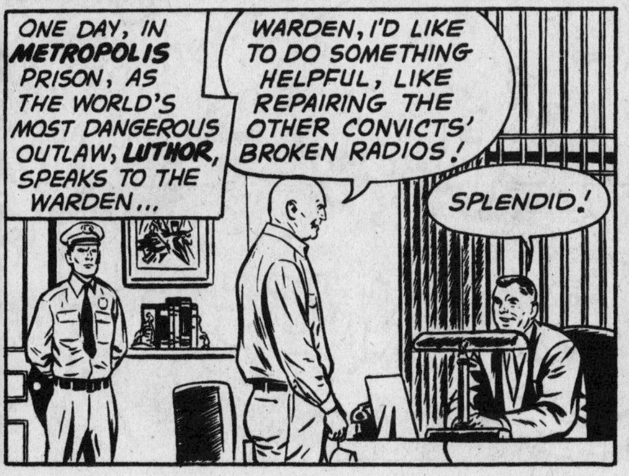
ONE DAY, IN METROPOLIS PRISON, AS THE WORLD'S MOST DANGEROUS OUTLAW, LUTHOR, SPEAKS TO THE WARDEN...
WARDEN, I'D LIKE TO DO SOMETHING HELPFUL, LIKE REPAIRING THE OTHER CONVICTS' BROKEN RADIOS!
SPLENDID!

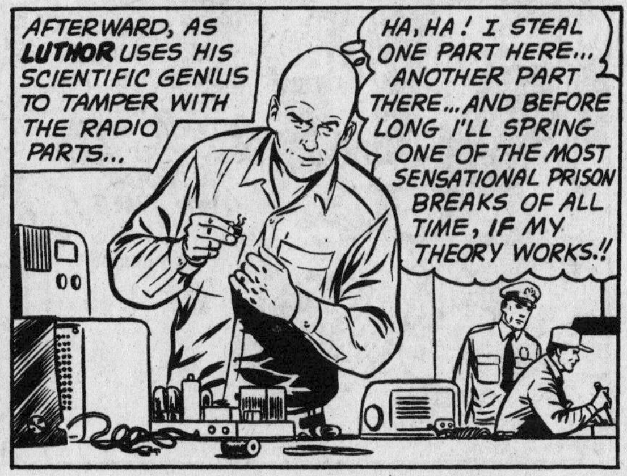
AFTERWARD, AS LUTHOR USES HIS SCIENTIFIC GENIUS TO TAMPER WITH THE RADIO PARTS...
HA, HA! I STEAL ONE PART HERE... ANOTHER PART THERE... AND BEFORE LONG I'LL SPRING ONE OF THE MOST SENSATIONAL PRISON BREAKS OF ALL TIME, IF MY THEORY WORKS!!

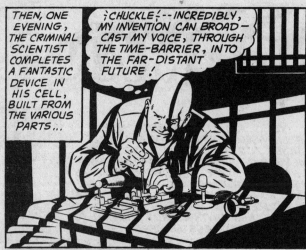

THEN, ONE EVENING, THE CRIMINAL SCIENTIST COMPLETES A FANTASTIC DEVICE IN HIS CELL, BUILT FROM THE VARIOUS PARTS...

¡CHUCKLE!--INCREDIBLY, MY INVENTION CAN BROADCAST MY VOICE, THROUGH THE TIME-BARRIER, INTO THE FAR-DISTANT FUTURE!

YEARS AGO, SUPERBOY... NOW GROWN INTO SUPERMAN... WAS SAVED FROM BEING DESTROYED BY ME, BY A MEMBER OF THE LEGION OF SUPER-HEROES FROM A FUTURE ERA!

I'VE LONG BELIEVED THAT IF A LEGION OF SUPER-HEROES EXISTS IN THE FUTURE, THEN A LEGION OF SUPER-VILLAINS PROBABLY EXISTS IN THE FUTURE TOO! IF THE HEROES COULD SAVE SUPERBOY, THE VILLAINS COULD SAVE ME!

FOR MANY HOURS, LUTHOR WHISPERS OVER AND OVER, INTO THE FANTASTIC DEVICE'S MICROPHONE...

CALLING THE FUTURE! ARCH-CRIMINAL LUTHOR FROM THE YEAR 1961 CALLING THE LEGION OF SUPER VILLAINS, IN THE FUTURE! AM IMPRISONED! NEED HELP! SAVE ME!

SUDDENLY, AT DAWN...

¡GASP!... THREE OBJECTS ARE MATERIALIZING ON THE FLOOR! THEY WEREN'T THERE A MOMENT AGO!... HAS MY APPEAL BEEN ANSWERED??

WE HEARD YOUR SUMMONS! USE THESE OBJECTS TO ESCAPE, LUTHOR! WE'LL JOIN YOU SOON IN YOUR OWN TIME!

QUICKLY, DONNING THE STRANGE BELT AND HELMET, LUTHOR FIRES THE WEIRD GUN AT THE CELL WALL...

EUREKA! THE WALL'S BURSTING OUTWARD!

SS-SSSST

BWANNNGG

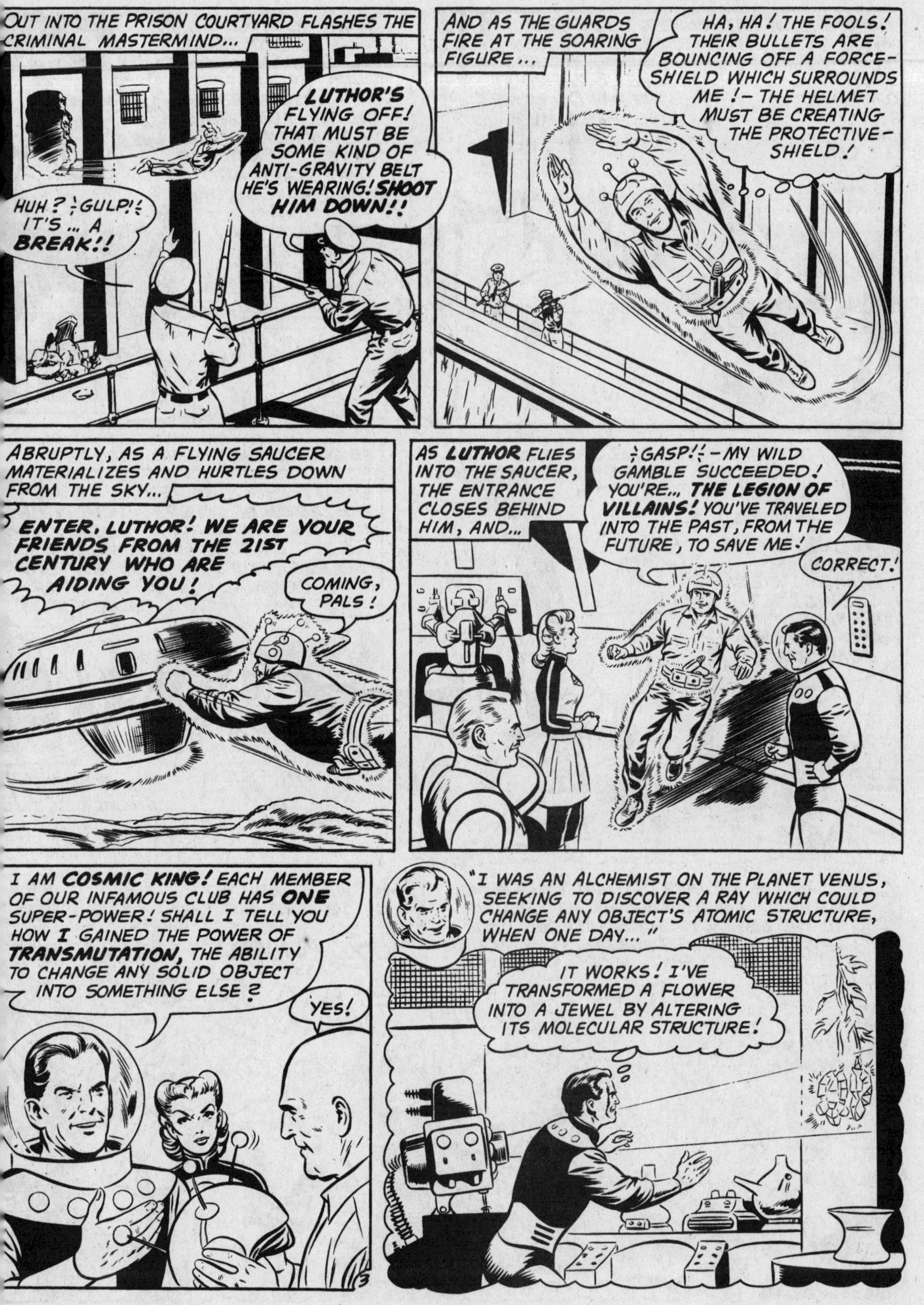
OUT INTO THE PRISON COURTYARD FLASHES THE CRIMINAL MASTERMIND...
LUTHOR'S FLYING OFF! THAT MUST BE SOME KIND OF ANTI-GRAVITY BELT HE'S WEARING! SHOOT HIM DOWN!!
HUH? -GULP!- IT'S ... A BREAK!!
AND AS THE GUARDS FIRE AT THE SOARING FIGURE...
HA, HA! THE FOOLS! THEIR BULLETS ARE BOUNCING OFF A FORCE-SHIELD WHICH SURROUNDS ME! - THE HELMET MUST BE CREATING THE PROTECTIVE-SHIELD!
ABRUPTLY, AS A FLYING SAUCER MATERIALIZES AND HURTLES DOWN FROM THE SKY...
ENTER, LUTHOR! WE ARE YOUR FRIENDS FROM THE 21ST CENTURY WHO ARE AIDING YOU!
COMING, PALS!
AS LUTHOR FLIES INTO THE SAUCER, THE ENTRANCE CLOSES BEHIND HIM, AND...
-GASP!- -MY WILD GAMBLE SUCCEEDED! YOU'RE... THE LEGION OF VILLAINS! YOU'VE TRAVELED INTO THE PAST, FROM THE FUTURE, TO SAVE ME!
CORRECT!
I AM COSMIC KING! EACH MEMBER OF OUR INFAMOUS CLUB HAS ONE SUPER-POWER! SHALL I TELL YOU HOW I GAINED THE POWER OF TRANSMUTATION, THE ABILITY TO CHANGE ANY SOLID OBJECT INTO SOMETHING ELSE?
YES!
3
"I WAS AN ALCHEMIST ON THE PLANET VENUS, SEEKING TO DISCOVER A RAY WHICH COULD CHANGE ANY OBJECT'S ATOMIC STRUCTURE, WHEN ONE DAY..."
IT WORKS! I'VE TRANSFORMED A FLOWER INTO A JEWEL BY ALTERING ITS MOLECULAR STRUCTURE!

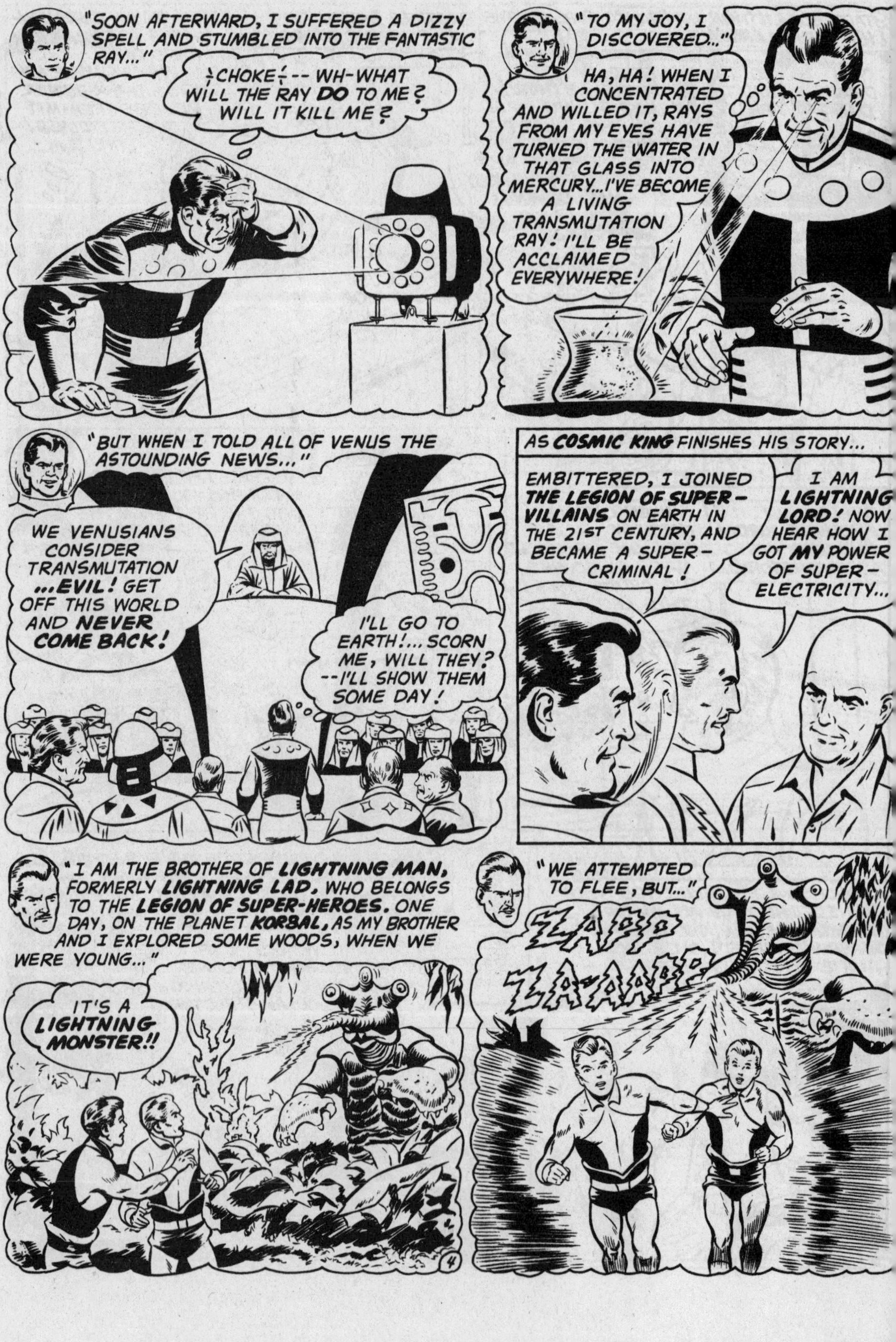

"SOON AFTERWARD, I SUFFERED A DIZZY SPELL AND STUMBLED INTO THE FANTASTIC RAY..."
CHOKE -- WH-WHAT WILL THE RAY DO TO ME? WILL IT KILL ME?
"TO MY JOY, I DISCOVERED..."
HA, HA! WHEN I CONCENTRATED AND WILLED IT, RAYS FROM MY EYES HAVE TURNED THE WATER IN THAT GLASS INTO MERCURY...I'VE BECOME A LIVING TRANSMUTATION RAY! I'LL BE ACCLAIMED EVERYWHERE!
"BUT WHEN I TOLD ALL OF VENUS THE ASTOUNDING NEWS..."
WE VENUSIANS CONSIDER TRANSMUTATION ...EVIL! GET OFF THIS WORLD AND NEVER COME BACK!
I'LL GO TO EARTH!... SCORN ME, WILL THEY? --I'LL SHOW THEM SOME DAY!
AS COSMIC KING FINISHES HIS STORY...
EMBITTERED, I JOINED THE LEGION OF SUPER-VILLAINS ON EARTH IN THE 21ST CENTURY, AND BECAME A SUPER-CRIMINAL!
I AM LIGHTNING LORD! NOW HEAR HOW I GOT MY POWER OF SUPER-ELECTRICITY...
"I AM THE BROTHER OF LIGHTNING MAN, FORMERLY LIGHTNING LAD, WHO BELONGS TO THE LEGION OF SUPER-HEROES. ONE DAY, ON THE PLANET KORBAL, AS MY BROTHER AND I EXPLORED SOME WOODS, WHEN WE WERE YOUNG..."
IT'S A LIGHTNING MONSTER!!
4
"WE ATTEMPTED TO FLEE, BUT..."
ZAPP
ZA-AAPP

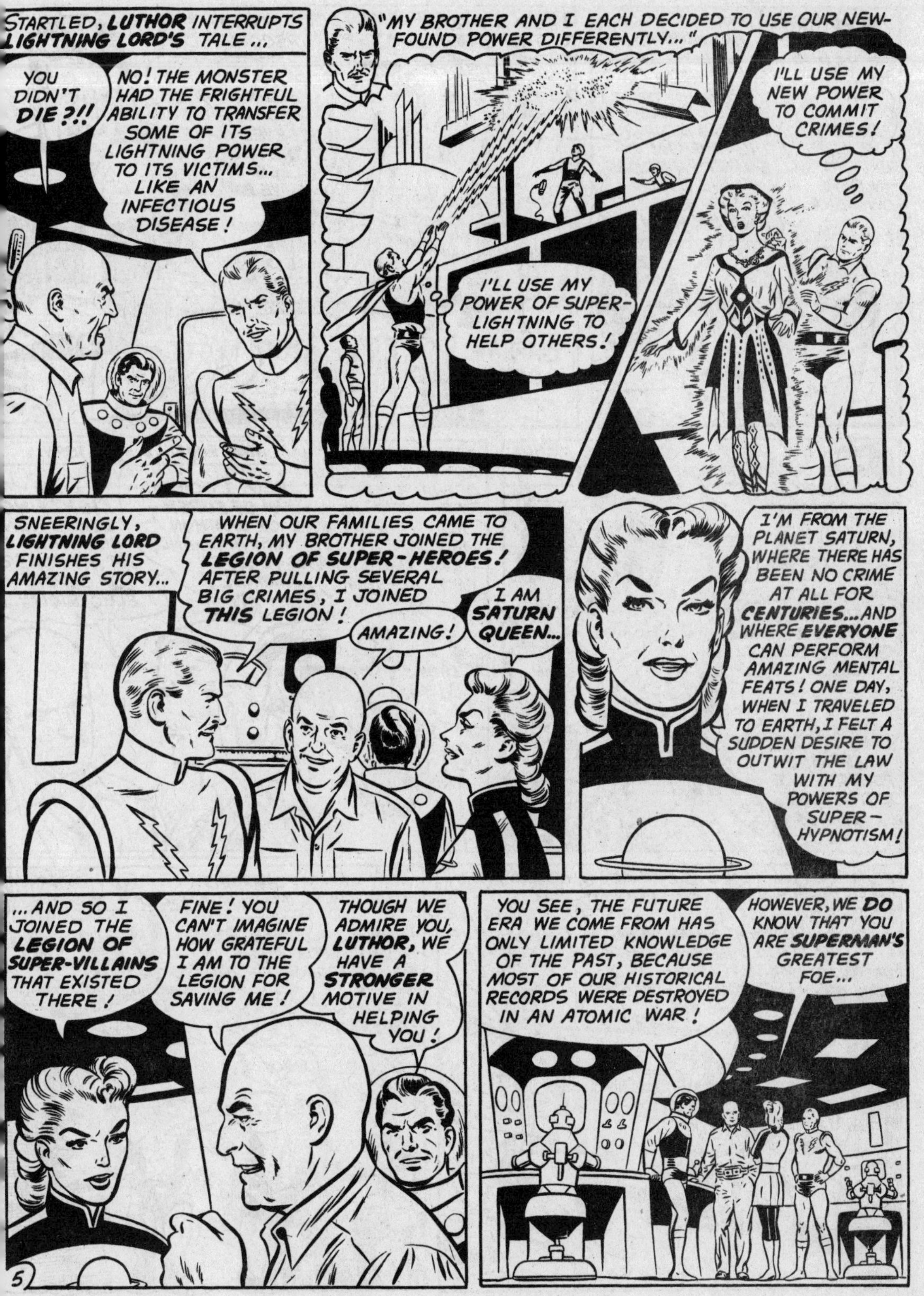
STARTLED, LUTHOR INTERRUPTS LIGHTNING LORD'S TALE...
YOU DIDN'T DIE?!!
NO! THE MONSTER HAD THE FRIGHTFUL ABILITY TO TRANSFER SOME OF ITS LIGHTNING POWER TO ITS VICTIMS... LIKE AN INFECTIOUS DISEASE!
"MY BROTHER AND I EACH DECIDED TO USE OUR NEW-FOUND POWER DIFFERENTLY..."
I'LL USE MY POWER OF SUPER-LIGHTNING TO HELP OTHERS!
I'LL USE MY NEW POWER TO COMMIT CRIMES!
SNEERINGLY, LIGHTNING LORD FINISHES HIS AMAZING STORY...
WHEN OUR FAMILIES CAME TO EARTH, MY BROTHER JOINED THE LEGION OF SUPER-HEROES! AFTER PULLING SEVERAL BIG CRIMES, I JOINED THIS LEGION!
AMAZING!
I AM SATURN QUEEN...
I'M FROM THE PLANET SATURN, WHERE THERE HAS BEEN NO CRIME AT ALL FOR CENTURIES...AND WHERE EVERYONE CAN PERFORM AMAZING MENTAL FEATS! ONE DAY, WHEN I TRAVELED TO EARTH, I FELT A SUDDEN DESIRE TO OUTWIT THE LAW WITH MY POWERS OF SUPER-HYPNOTISM!
...AND SO I JOINED THE LEGION OF SUPER-VILLAINS THAT EXISTED THERE!
FINE! YOU CAN'T IMAGINE HOW GRATEFUL I AM TO THE LEGION FOR SAVING ME!
THOUGH WE ADMIRE YOU, LUTHOR, WE HAVE A STRONGER MOTIVE IN HELPING YOU!
YOU SEE, THE FUTURE ERA WE COME FROM HAS ONLY LIMITED KNOWLEDGE OF THE PAST, BECAUSE MOST OF OUR HISTORICAL RECORDS WERE DESTROYED IN AN ATOMIC WAR!
HOWEVER, WE DO KNOW THAT YOU ARE SUPERMAN'S GREATEST FOE...
5

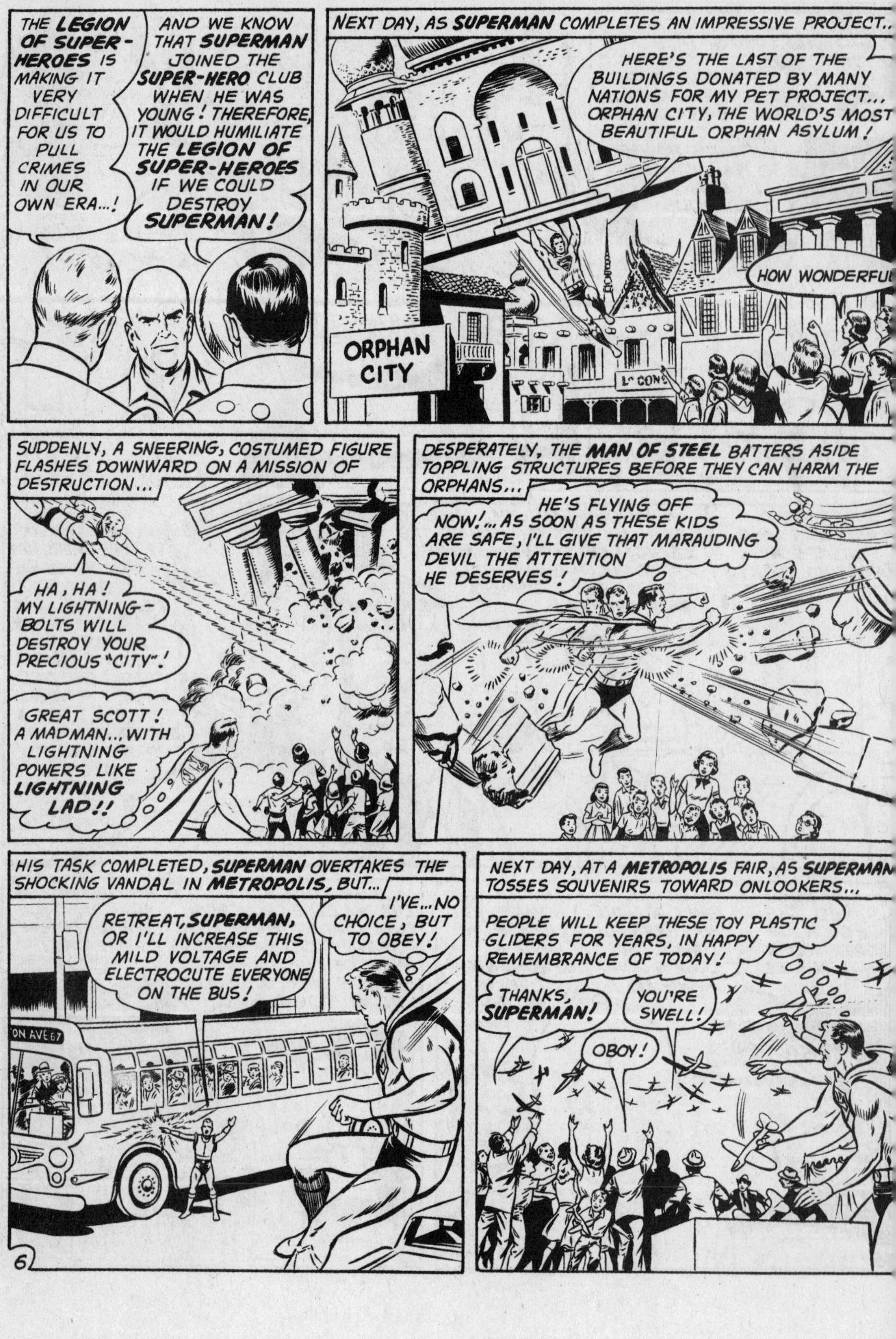
THE LEGION OF SUPER-HEROES IS MAKING IT VERY DIFFICULT FOR US TO PULL CRIMES IN OUR OWN ERA...!
AND WE KNOW THAT SUPERMAN JOINED THE SUPER-HERO CLUB WHEN HE WAS YOUNG! THEREFORE, IT WOULD HUMILIATE THE LEGION OF SUPER-HEROES IF WE COULD DESTROY SUPERMAN!
NEXT DAY, AS SUPERMAN COMPLETES AN IMPRESSIVE PROJECT...
HERE'S THE LAST OF THE BUILDINGS DONATED BY MANY NATIONS FOR MY PET PROJECT... ORPHAN CITY, THE WORLD'S MOST BEAUTIFUL ORPHAN ASYLUM!
HOW WONDERFU
ORPHAN CITY
SUDDENLY, A SNEERING, COSTUMED FIGURE FLASHES DOWNWARD ON A MISSION OF DESTRUCTION...
HA, HA! MY LIGHTNING-BOLTS WILL DESTROY YOUR PRECIOUS "CITY"!
GREAT SCOTT! A MADMAN... WITH LIGHTNING POWERS LIKE LIGHTNING LAD!!
DESPERATELY, THE MAN OF STEEL BATTERS ASIDE TOPPLING STRUCTURES BEFORE THEY CAN HARM THE ORPHANS...
HE'S FLYING OFF NOW!... AS SOON AS THESE KIDS ARE SAFE, I'LL GIVE THAT MARAUDING DEVIL THE ATTENTION HE DESERVES!
HIS TASK COMPLETED, SUPERMAN OVERTAKES THE SHOCKING VANDAL IN METROPOLIS, BUT...
RETREAT, SUPERMAN, OR I'LL INCREASE THIS MILD VOLTAGE AND ELECTROCUTE EVERYONE ON THE BUS!
I'VE... NO CHOICE, BUT TO OBEY!
ON AVE 67
6
NEXT DAY, AT A METROPOLIS FAIR, AS SUPERMAN TOSSES SOUVENIRS TOWARD ONLOOKERS...
PEOPLE WILL KEEP THESE TOY PLASTIC GLIDERS FOR YEARS, IN HAPPY REMEMBRANCE OF TODAY!
THANKS, SUPERMAN!
YOU'RE SWELL!
OBOY!

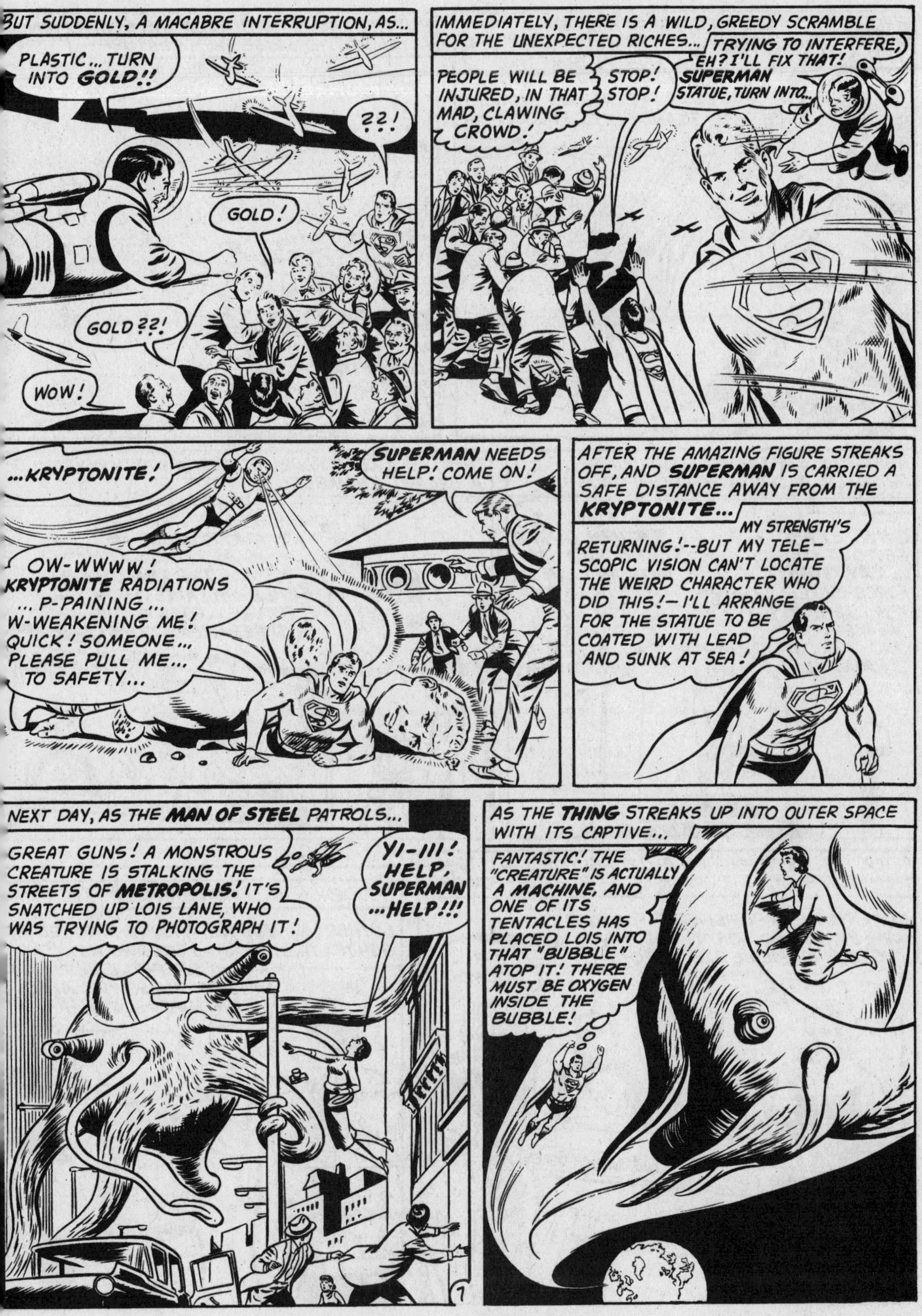
BUT SUDDENLY, A MACABRE INTERRUPTION, AS...
PLASTIC... TURN INTO GOLD!!
??!
GOLD!
GOLD??!
WOW!
IMMEDIATELY, THERE IS A WILD, GREEDY SCRAMBLE FOR THE UNEXPECTED RICHES...
PEOPLE WILL BE INJURED, IN THAT MAD, CLAWING CROWD!
STOP! STOP!
TRYING TO INTERFERE, EH? I'LL FIX THAT! SUPERMAN STATUE, TURN INTO...
...KRYPTONITE!
SUPERMAN NEEDS HELP! COME ON!
OW-WWWW! KRYPTONITE RADIATIONS ... P-PAINING ... W-WEAKENING ME! QUICK! SOMEONE... PLEASE PULL ME... TO SAFETY...
AFTER THE AMAZING FIGURE STREAKS OFF, AND SUPERMAN IS CARRIED A SAFE DISTANCE AWAY FROM THE KRYPTONITE...
MY STRENGTH'S RETURNING!--BUT MY TELE-SCOPIC VISION CAN'T LOCATE THE WEIRD CHARACTER WHO DID THIS!— I'LL ARRANGE FOR THE STATUE TO BE COATED WITH LEAD AND SUNK AT SEA!
NEXT DAY, AS THE MAN OF STEEL PATROLS...
GREAT GUNS! A MONSTROUS CREATURE IS STALKING THE STREETS OF METROPOLIS! IT'S SNATCHED UP LOIS LANE, WHO WAS TRYING TO PHOTOGRAPH IT!
YI-III! HELP, SUPERMAN ...HELP!!!
7
AS THE THING STREAKS UP INTO OUTER SPACE WITH ITS CAPTIVE...
FANTASTIC! THE "CREATURE" IS ACTUALLY A MACHINE, AND ONE OF ITS TENTACLES HAS PLACED LOIS INTO THAT "BUBBLE" ATOP IT! THERE MUST BE OXYGEN INSIDE THE BUBBLE!

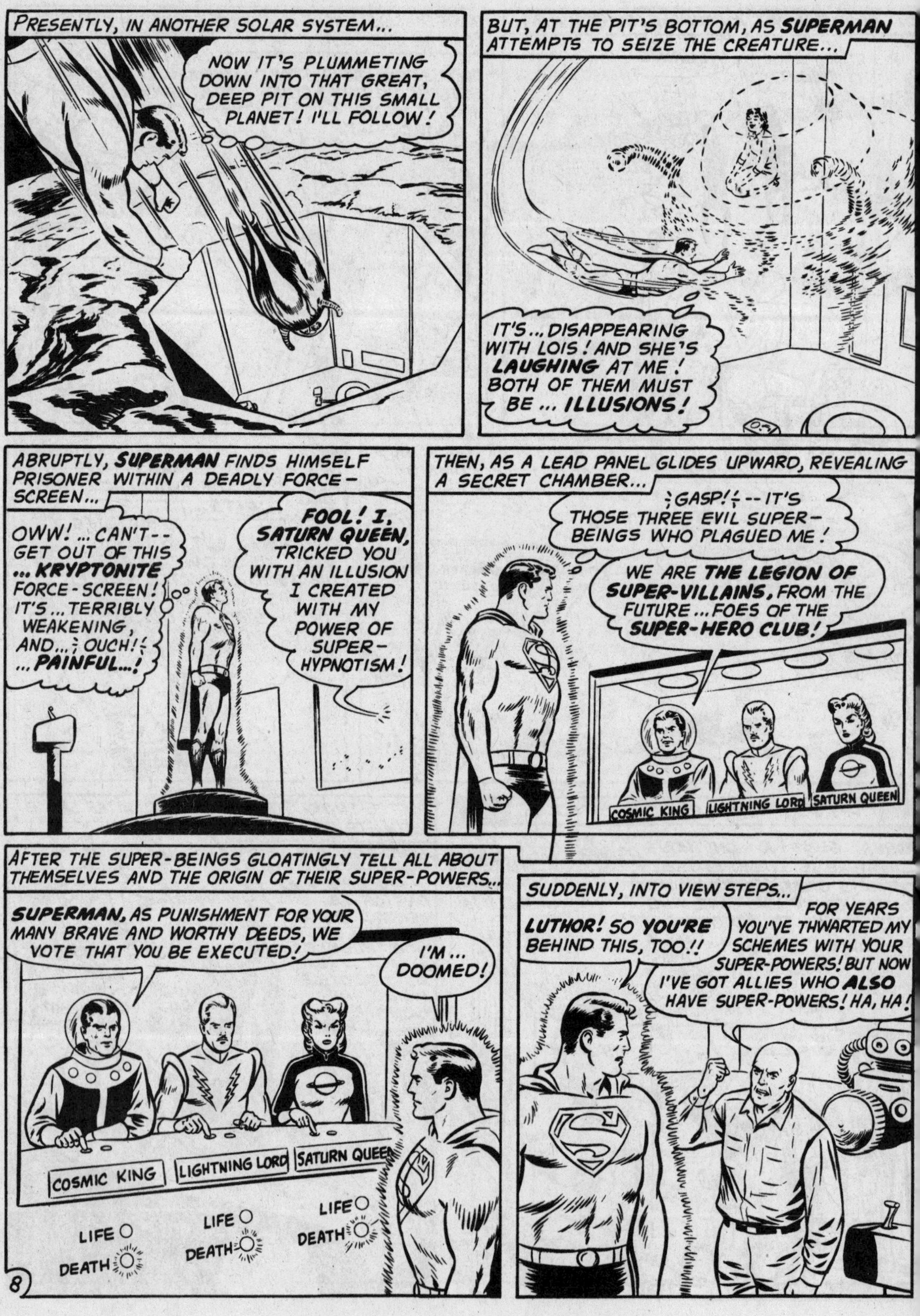
PRESENTLY, IN ANOTHER SOLAR SYSTEM...
NOW IT'S PLUMMETING DOWN INTO THAT GREAT, DEEP PIT ON THIS SMALL PLANET! I'LL FOLLOW!
BUT, AT THE PIT'S BOTTOM, AS SUPERMAN ATTEMPTS TO SEIZE THE CREATURE...
IT'S... DISAPPEARING WITH LOIS! AND SHE'S LAUGHING AT ME! BOTH OF THEM MUST BE... ILLUSIONS!
ABRUPTLY, SUPERMAN FINDS HIMSELF PRISONER WITHIN A DEADLY FORCE-SCREEN...
OWW! ... CAN'T-- GET OUT OF THIS ...KRYPTONITE FORCE-SCREEN! IT'S... TERRIBLY WEAKENING, AND... OUCH! ...PAINFUL...!
FOOL! I, SATURN QUEEN, TRICKED YOU WITH AN ILLUSION I CREATED WITH MY POWER OF SUPER-HYPNOTISM!
THEN, AS A LEAD PANEL GLIDES UPWARD, REVEALING A SECRET CHAMBER...
GASP! --IT'S THOSE THREE EVIL SUPER-BEINGS WHO PLAGUED ME!
WE ARE THE LEGION OF SUPER-VILLAINS, FROM THE FUTURE... FOES OF THE SUPER-HERO CLUB!
COSMIC KING
LIGHTNING LORD
SATURN QUEEN
AFTER THE SUPER-BEINGS GLOATINGLY TELL ALL ABOUT THEMSELVES AND THE ORIGIN OF THEIR SUPER-POWERS...
SUPERMAN, AS PUNISHMENT FOR YOUR MANY BRAVE AND WORTHY DEEDS, WE VOTE THAT YOU BE EXECUTED!
I'M ... DOOMED!
COSMIC KING
LIGHTNING LORD
SATURN QUEE
LIFE
DEATH
LIFE
DEATH
LIFE
DEATH
8
SUDDENLY, INTO VIEW STEPS...
LUTHOR! SO YOU'RE BEHIND THIS, TOO!!
FOR YEARS YOU'VE THWARTED MY SCHEMES WITH YOUR SUPER-POWERS! BUT NOW I'VE GOT ALLIES WHO ALSO HAVE SUPER-POWERS! HA, HA!

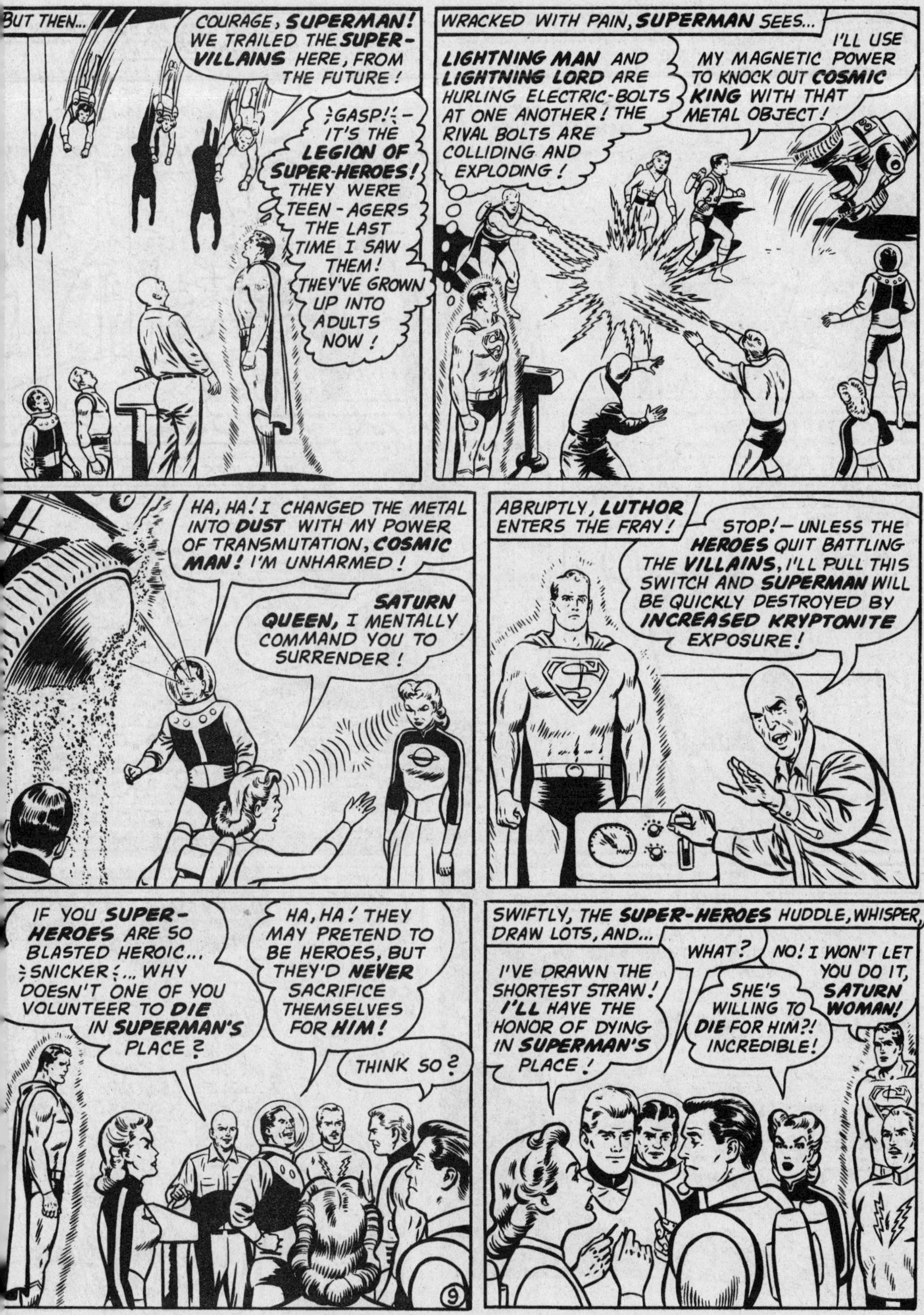
BUT THEN...
COURAGE, SUPERMAN! WE TRAILED THE SUPER-VILLAINS HERE, FROM THE FUTURE!
-GASP!- IT'S THE LEGION OF SUPER-HEROES! THEY WERE TEEN-AGERS THE LAST TIME I SAW THEM! THEY'VE GROWN UP INTO ADULTS NOW!
WRACKED WITH PAIN, SUPERMAN SEES...
LIGHTNING MAN AND LIGHTNING LORD ARE HURLING ELECTRIC-BOLTS AT ONE ANOTHER! THE RIVAL BOLTS ARE COLLIDING AND EXPLODING!
I'LL USE MY MAGNETIC POWER TO KNOCK OUT COSMIC KING WITH THAT METAL OBJECT!
HA, HA! I CHANGED THE METAL INTO DUST WITH MY POWER OF TRANSMUTATION, COSMIC MAN! I'M UNHARMED!
SATURN QUEEN, I MENTALLY COMMAND YOU TO SURRENDER!
ABRUPTLY, LUTHOR ENTERS THE FRAY!
STOP!—UNLESS THE HEROES QUIT BATTLING THE VILLAINS, I'LL PULL THIS SWITCH AND SUPERMAN WILL BE QUICKLY DESTROYED BY INCREASED KRYPTONITE EXPOSURE!
IF YOU SUPER-HEROES ARE SO BLASTED HEROIC... -SNICKER-... WHY DOESN'T ONE OF YOU VOLUNTEER TO DIE IN SUPERMAN'S PLACE?
HA, HA! THEY MAY PRETEND TO BE HEROES, BUT THEY'D NEVER SACRIFICE THEMSELVES FOR HIM!
THINK SO?
9
SWIFTLY, THE SUPER-HEROES HUDDLE, WHISPER, DRAW LOTS, AND...
I'VE DRAWN THE SHORTEST STRAW! I'LL HAVE THE HONOR OF DYING IN SUPERMAN'S PLACE!
WHAT?
SHE'S WILLING TO DIE FOR HIM?! INCREDIBLE!
NO! I WON'T LET YOU DO IT, SATURN WOMAN!

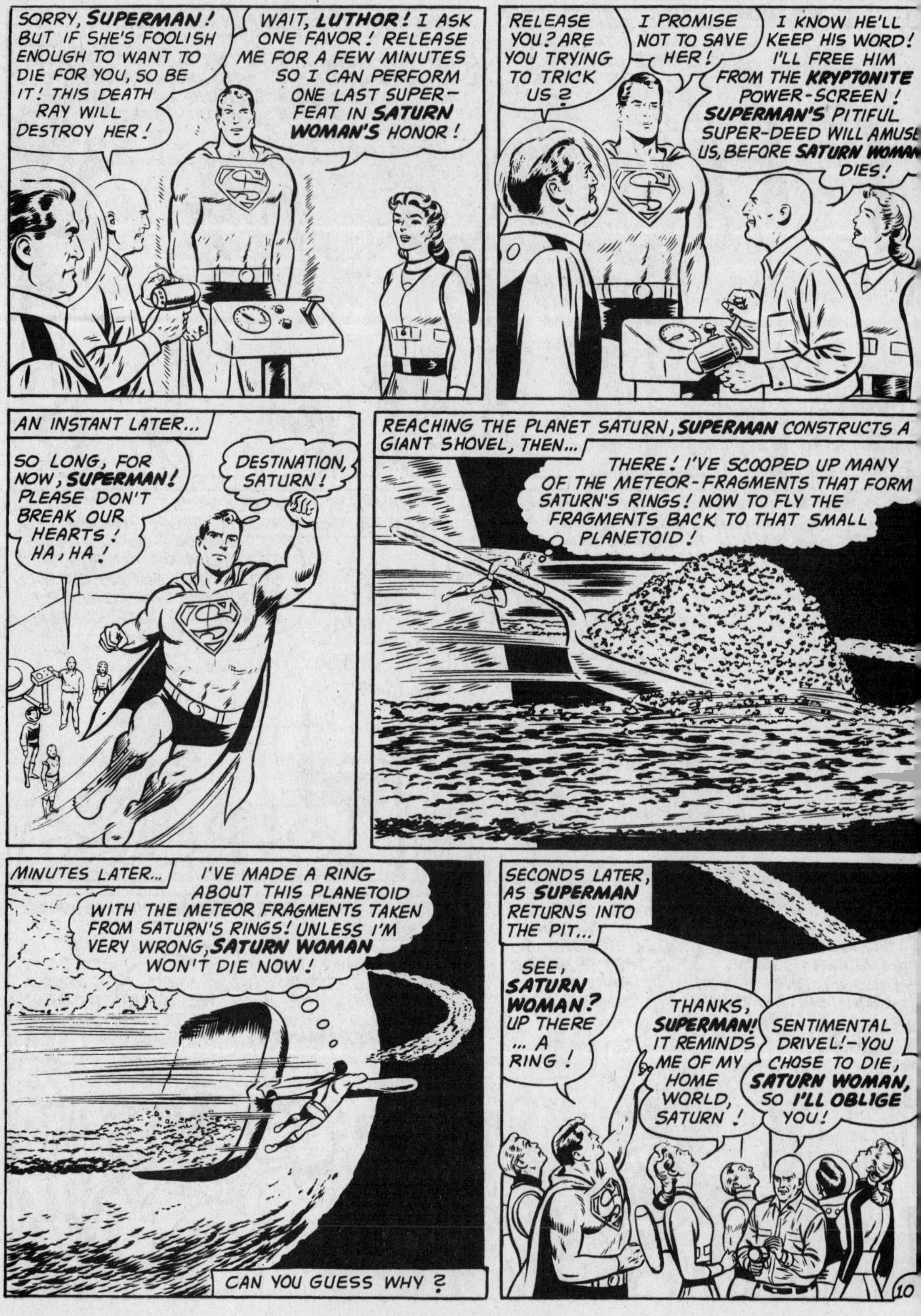
SORRY, SUPERMAN! BUT IF SHE'S FOOLISH ENOUGH TO WANT TO DIE FOR YOU, SO BE IT! THIS DEATH RAY WILL DESTROY HER!
WAIT, LUTHOR! I ASK ONE FAVOR! RELEASE ME FOR A FEW MINUTES SO I CAN PERFORM ONE LAST SUPER-FEAT IN SATURN WOMAN'S HONOR!
RELEASE YOU? ARE YOU TRYING TO TRICK US?
I PROMISE NOT TO SAVE HER!
I KNOW HE'LL KEEP HIS WORD! I'LL FREE HIM FROM THE KRYPTONITE POWER-SCREEN! SUPERMAN'S PITIFUL SUPER-DEED WILL AMUSE US, BEFORE SATURN WOMAN DIES!
AN INSTANT LATER...
SO LONG, FOR NOW, SUPERMAN! PLEASE DON'T BREAK OUR HEARTS! HA, HA!
DESTINATION, SATURN!
REACHING THE PLANET SATURN, SUPERMAN CONSTRUCTS A GIANT SHOVEL, THEN...
THERE! I'VE SCOOPED UP MANY OF THE METEOR-FRAGMENTS THAT FORM SATURN'S RINGS! NOW TO FLY THE FRAGMENTS BACK TO THAT SMALL PLANETOID!
MINUTES LATER...
I'VE MADE A RING ABOUT THIS PLANETOID WITH THE METEOR FRAGMENTS TAKEN FROM SATURN'S RINGS! UNLESS I'M VERY WRONG, SATURN WOMAN WON'T DIE NOW!
CAN YOU GUESS WHY?
SECONDS LATER, AS SUPERMAN RETURNS INTO THE PIT...
SEE, SATURN WOMAN? UP THERE ... A RING!
THANKS, SUPERMAN! IT REMINDS ME OF MY HOME WORLD, SATURN!
SENTIMENTAL DRIVEL!--YOU CHOSE TO DIE, SATURN WOMAN, SO I'LL OBLIGE YOU!
10

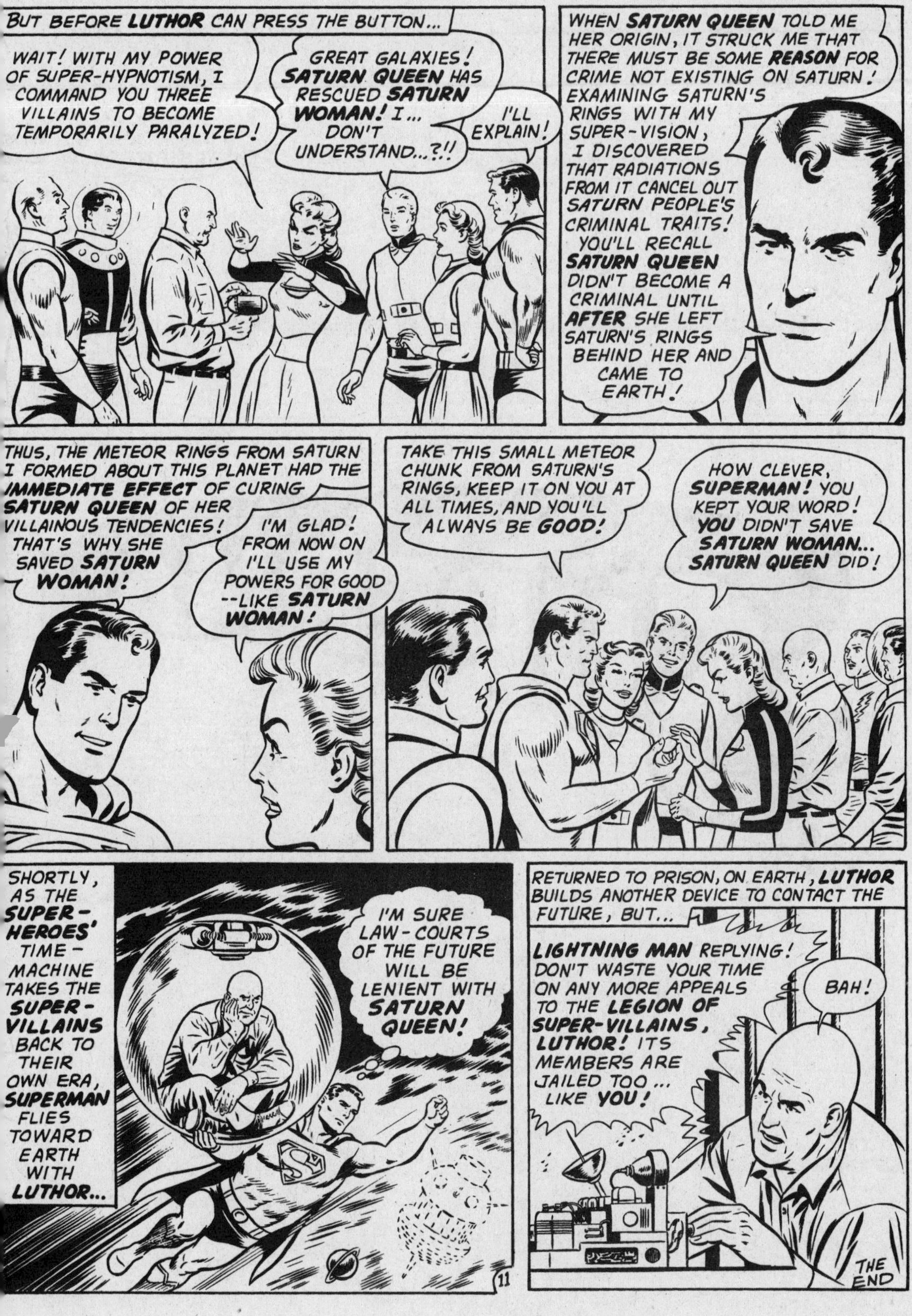
BUT BEFORE LUTHOR CAN PRESS THE BUTTON...
WAIT! WITH MY POWER OF SUPER-HYPNOTISM, I COMMAND YOU THREE VILLAINS TO BECOME TEMPORARILY PARALYZED!
GREAT GALAXIES! SATURN QUEEN HAS RESCUED SATURN WOMAN! I... DON'T UNDERSTAND...?!!
I'LL EXPLAIN!
WHEN SATURN QUEEN TOLD ME HER ORIGIN, IT STRUCK ME THAT THERE MUST BE SOME REASON FOR CRIME NOT EXISTING ON SATURN! EXAMINING SATURN'S RINGS WITH MY SUPER-VISION, I DISCOVERED THAT RADIATIONS FROM IT CANCEL OUT SATURN PEOPLE'S CRIMINAL TRAITS! YOU'LL RECALL SATURN QUEEN DIDN'T BECOME A CRIMINAL UNTIL AFTER SHE LEFT SATURN'S RINGS BEHIND HER AND CAME TO EARTH!
THUS, THE METEOR RINGS FROM SATURN I FORMED ABOUT THIS PLANET HAD THE IMMEDIATE EFFECT OF CURING SATURN QUEEN OF HER VILLAINOUS TENDENCIES! THAT'S WHY SHE SAVED SATURN WOMAN!
I'M GLAD! FROM NOW ON I'LL USE MY POWERS FOR GOOD --LIKE SATURN WOMAN!
TAKE THIS SMALL METEOR CHUNK FROM SATURN'S RINGS, KEEP IT ON YOU AT ALL TIMES, AND YOU'LL ALWAYS BE GOOD!
HOW CLEVER, SUPERMAN! YOU KEPT YOUR WORD! YOU DIDN'T SAVE SATURN WOMAN... SATURN QUEEN DID!
SHORTLY, AS THE SUPER-HEROES' TIME-MACHINE TAKES THE SUPER-VILLAINS BACK TO THEIR OWN ERA, SUPERMAN FLIES TOWARD EARTH WITH LUTHOR...
I'M SURE LAW-COURTS OF THE FUTURE WILL BE LENIENT WITH SATURN QUEEN!
11
RETURNED TO PRISON, ON EARTH, LUTHOR BUILDS ANOTHER DEVICE TO CONTACT THE FUTURE, BUT...
LIGHTNING MAN REPLYING! DON'T WASTE YOUR TIME ON ANY MORE APPEALS TO THE LEGION OF SUPER-VILLAINS, LUTHOR! ITS MEMBERS ARE JAILED TOO... LIKE YOU!
BAH!
THE END

SUPERMAN

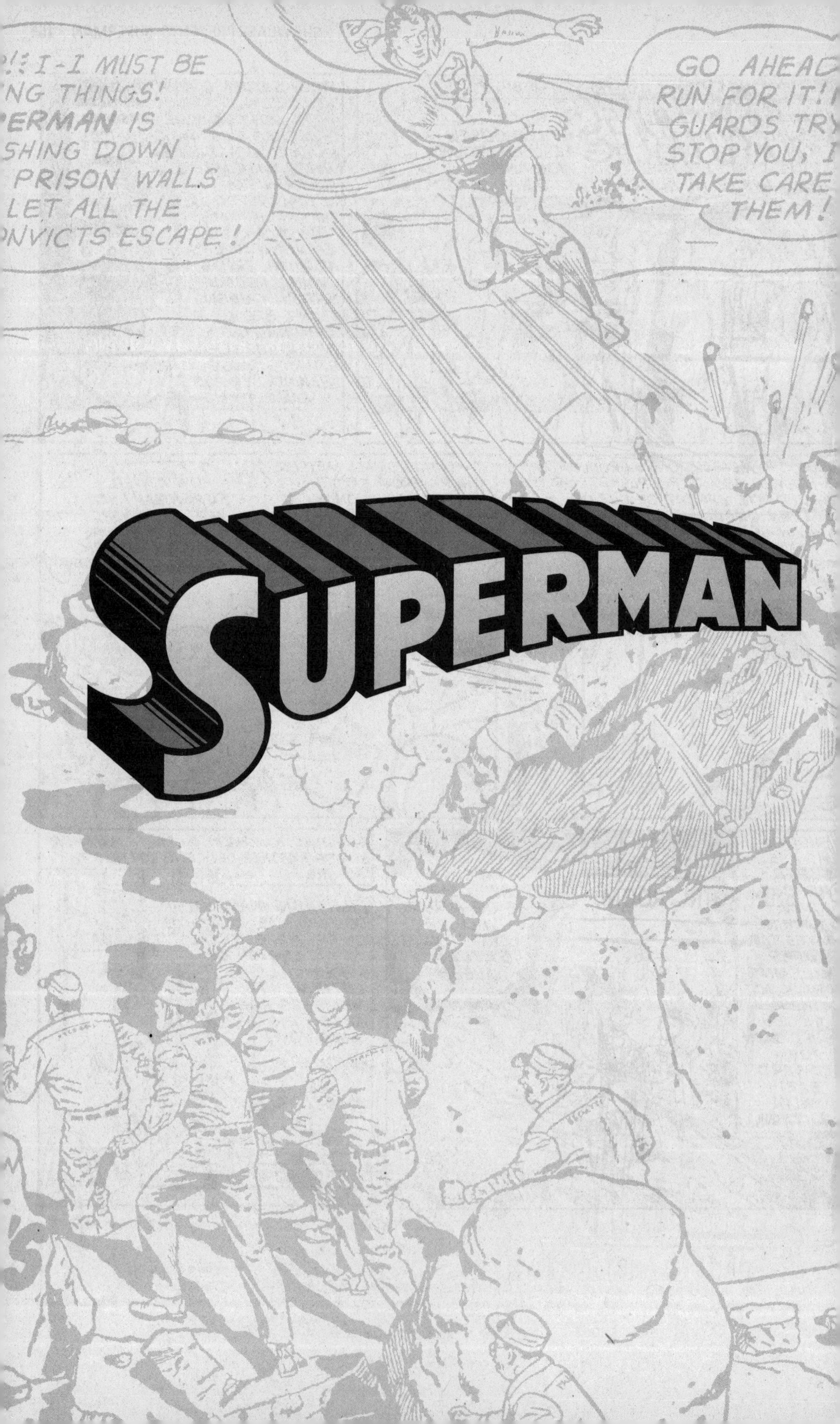
I-I MUST BE THINGS! IS DOWN PRISON WALLS LET ALL THE ESCAPE!
GO RUN FOR IT! STOP YOU, TAKE CARE THEM!

FORTRESS of SOLITUDE

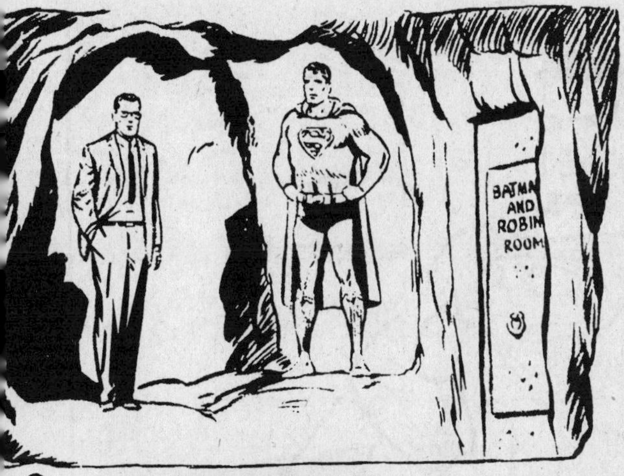
BATM
AND
ROBIN
ROOM

④ SUPERMAN ROOM

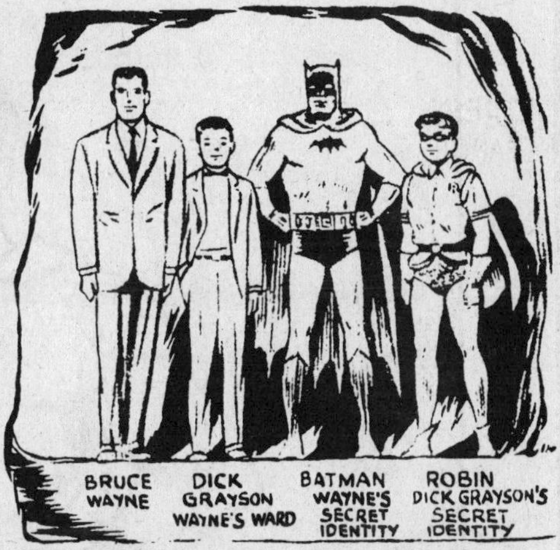
BRUCE WAYNE
DICK GRAYSON WAYNE'S WARD
BATMAN WAYNE'S SECRET IDENTITY
ROBIN DICK GRAYSON'S SECRET IDENTITY

⑤ BATMAN *and* ROBIN ROOM

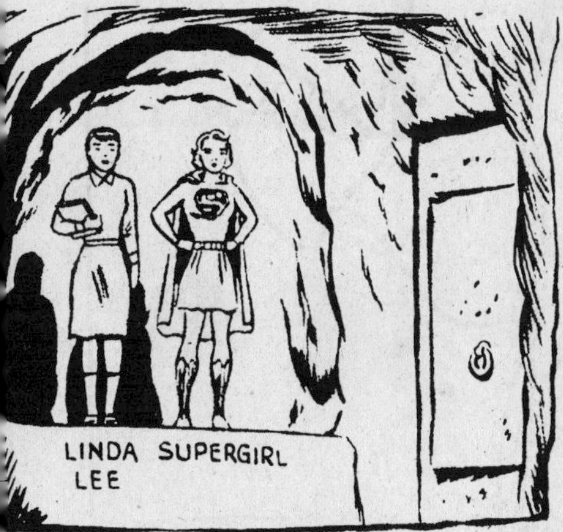
LINDA LEE
SUPERGIRL

SUPERGIRL ROOM

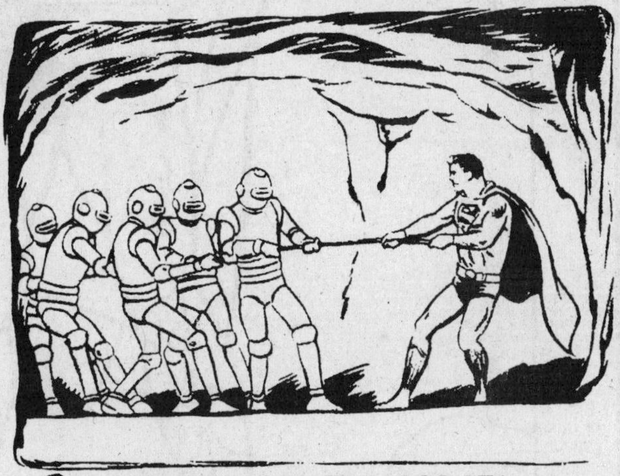

⑧ ATOMIC-POWERED ROBOTS

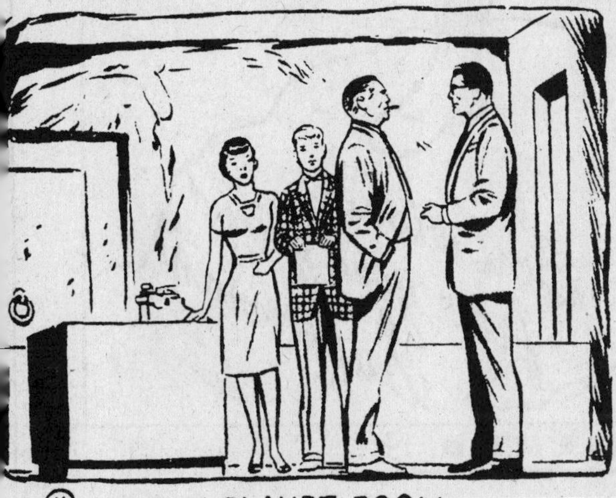

⑪ DAILY PLANET ROOM

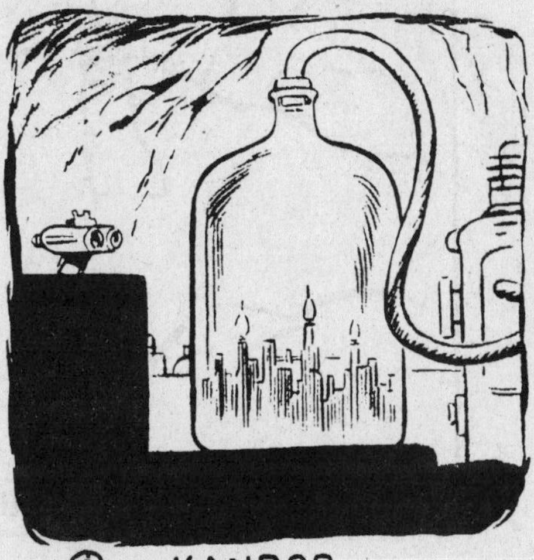

⑫ KANDOR

SEE PAGE 120 FOR FULL EXPLANATION OF THIS DIAGRAMMATIC SKETCH.

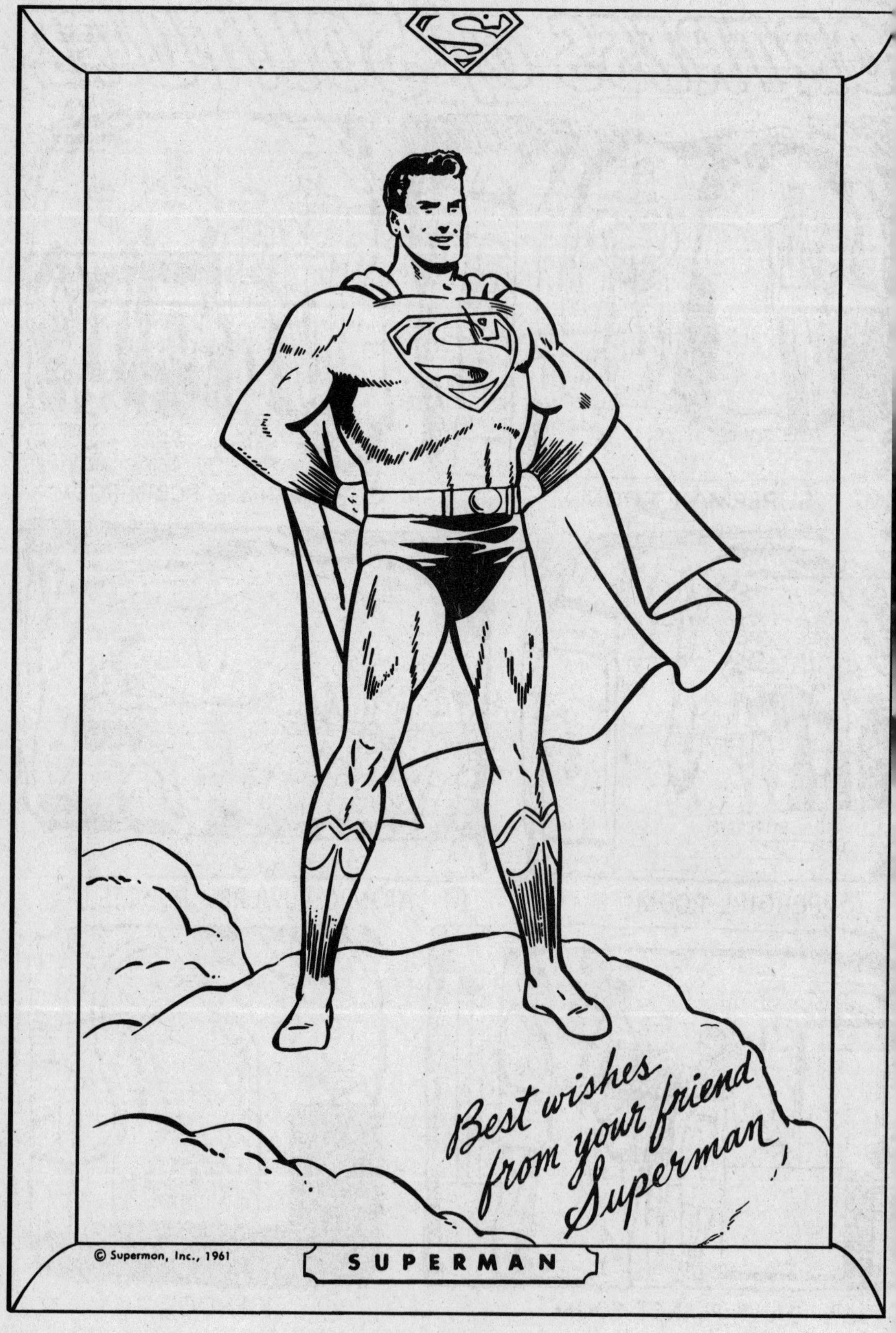
Best wishes
from your friend
Superman
© Supermon, Inc., 1961
SUPERMAN

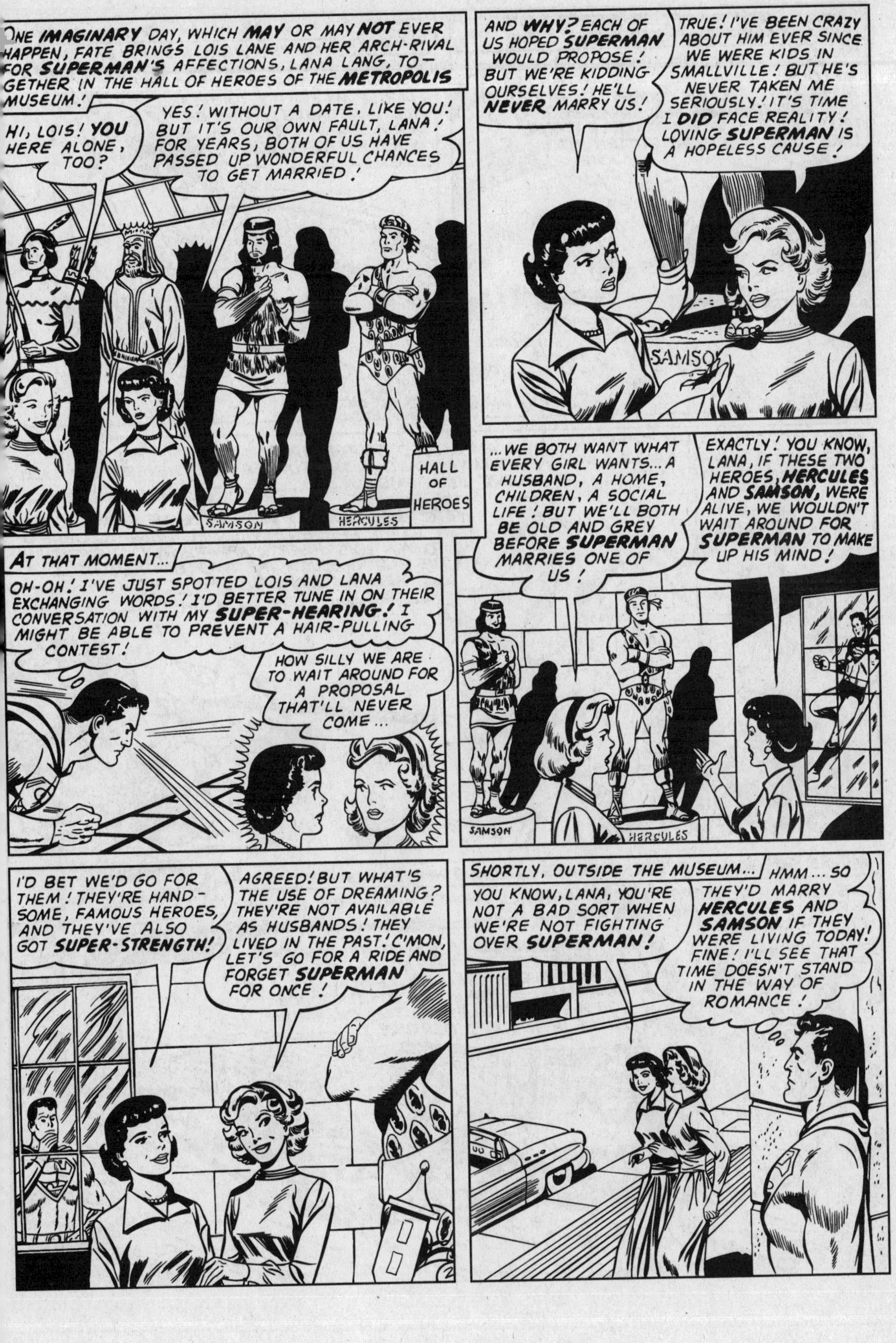
ONE IMAGINARY DAY, WHICH MAY OR MAY NOT EVER HAPPEN, FATE BRINGS LOIS LANE AND HER ARCH-RIVAL FOR SUPERMAN'S AFFECTIONS, LANA LANG, TOGETHER IN THE HALL OF HEROES OF THE METROPOLIS MUSEUM!
HI, LOIS! YOU HERE ALONE, TOO?
YES! WITHOUT A DATE, LIKE YOU! BUT IT'S OUR OWN FAULT, LANA! FOR YEARS, BOTH OF US HAVE PASSED UP WONDERFUL CHANCES TO GET MARRIED!
HALL OF HEROES
SAMSON
HERCULES
AND WHY? EACH OF US HOPED SUPERMAN WOULD PROPOSE! BUT WE'RE KIDDING OURSELVES! HE'LL NEVER MARRY US!
TRUE! I'VE BEEN CRAZY ABOUT HIM EVER SINCE WE WERE KIDS IN SMALLVILLE! BUT HE'S NEVER TAKEN ME SERIOUSLY! IT'S TIME I DID FACE REALITY! LOVING SUPERMAN IS A HOPELESS CAUSE!
SAMSO
AT THAT MOMENT...
OH-OH! I'VE JUST SPOTTED LOIS AND LANA EXCHANGING WORDS! I'D BETTER TUNE IN ON THEIR CONVERSATION WITH MY SUPER-HEARING! I MIGHT BE ABLE TO PREVENT A HAIR-PULLING CONTEST!
HOW SILLY WE ARE TO WAIT AROUND FOR A PROPOSAL THAT'LL NEVER COME...
...WE BOTH WANT WHAT EVERY GIRL WANTS... A HUSBAND, A HOME, CHILDREN, A SOCIAL LIFE! BUT WE'LL BOTH BE OLD AND GREY BEFORE SUPERMAN MARRIES ONE OF US!
EXACTLY! YOU KNOW, LANA, IF THESE TWO HEROES, HERCULES AND SAMSON, WERE ALIVE, WE WOULDN'T WAIT AROUND FOR SUPERMAN TO MAKE UP HIS MIND!
SAMSON
HERCULES
I'D BET WE'D GO FOR THEM! THEY'RE HANDSOME, FAMOUS HEROES, AND THEY'VE ALSO GOT SUPER-STRENGTH!
AGREED! BUT WHAT'S THE USE OF DREAMING? THEY'RE NOT AVAILABLE AS HUSBANDS! THEY LIVED IN THE PAST! C'MON, LET'S GO FOR A RIDE AND FORGET SUPERMAN FOR ONCE!
SHORTLY, OUTSIDE THE MUSEUM...
YOU KNOW, LANA, YOU'RE NOT A BAD SORT WHEN WE'RE NOT FIGHTING OVER SUPERMAN!
HMM... SO THEY'D MARRY HERCULES AND SAMSON IF THEY WERE LIVING TODAY! FINE! I'LL SEE THAT TIME DOESN'T STAND IN THE WAY OF ROMANCE!

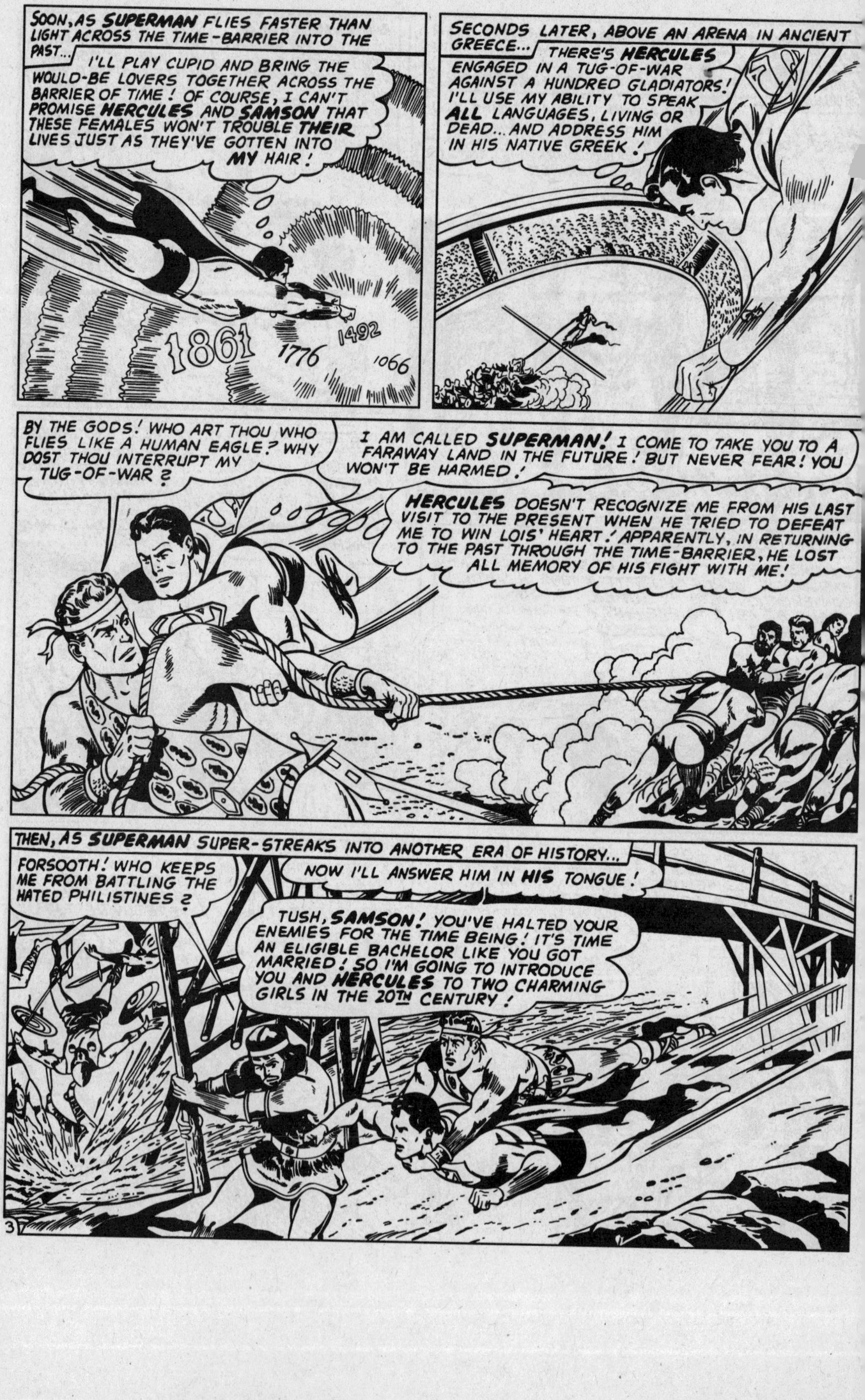
SOON, AS SUPERMAN FLIES FASTER THAN LIGHT ACROSS THE TIME-BARRIER INTO THE PAST...
I'LL PLAY CUPID AND BRING THE WOULD-BE LOVERS TOGETHER ACROSS THE BARRIER OF TIME! OF COURSE, I CAN'T PROMISE HERCULES AND SAMSON THAT THESE FEMALES WON'T TROUBLE THEIR LIVES JUST AS THEY'VE GOTTEN INTO MY HAIR!
1861
1776
1492
1066
SECONDS LATER, ABOVE AN ARENA IN ANCIENT GREECE...
THERE'S HERCULES ENGAGED IN A TUG-OF-WAR AGAINST A HUNDRED GLADIATORS! I'LL USE MY ABILITY TO SPEAK ALL LANGUAGES, LIVING OR DEAD... AND ADDRESS HIM IN HIS NATIVE GREEK!
BY THE GODS! WHO ART THOU WHO FLIES LIKE A HUMAN EAGLE? WHY DOST THOU INTERRUPT MY TUG-OF-WAR?
I AM CALLED SUPERMAN! I COME TO TAKE YOU TO A FARAWAY LAND IN THE FUTURE! BUT NEVER FEAR! YOU WON'T BE HARMED!
HERCULES DOESN'T RECOGNIZE ME FROM HIS LAST VISIT TO THE PRESENT WHEN HE TRIED TO DEFEAT ME TO WIN LOIS' HEART! APPARENTLY, IN RETURNING TO THE PAST THROUGH THE TIME-BARRIER, HE LOST ALL MEMORY OF HIS FIGHT WITH ME!
THEN, AS SUPERMAN SUPER-STREAKS INTO ANOTHER ERA OF HISTORY...
FORSOOTH! WHO KEEPS ME FROM BATTLING THE HATED PHILISTINES?
NOW I'LL ANSWER HIM IN HIS TONGUE!
TUSH, SAMSON! YOU'VE HALTED YOUR ENEMIES FOR THE TIME BEING! IT'S TIME AN ELIGIBLE BACHELOR LIKE YOU GOT MARRIED! SO I'M GOING TO INTRODUCE YOU AND HERCULES TO TWO CHARMING GIRLS IN THE 20TH CENTURY!
3

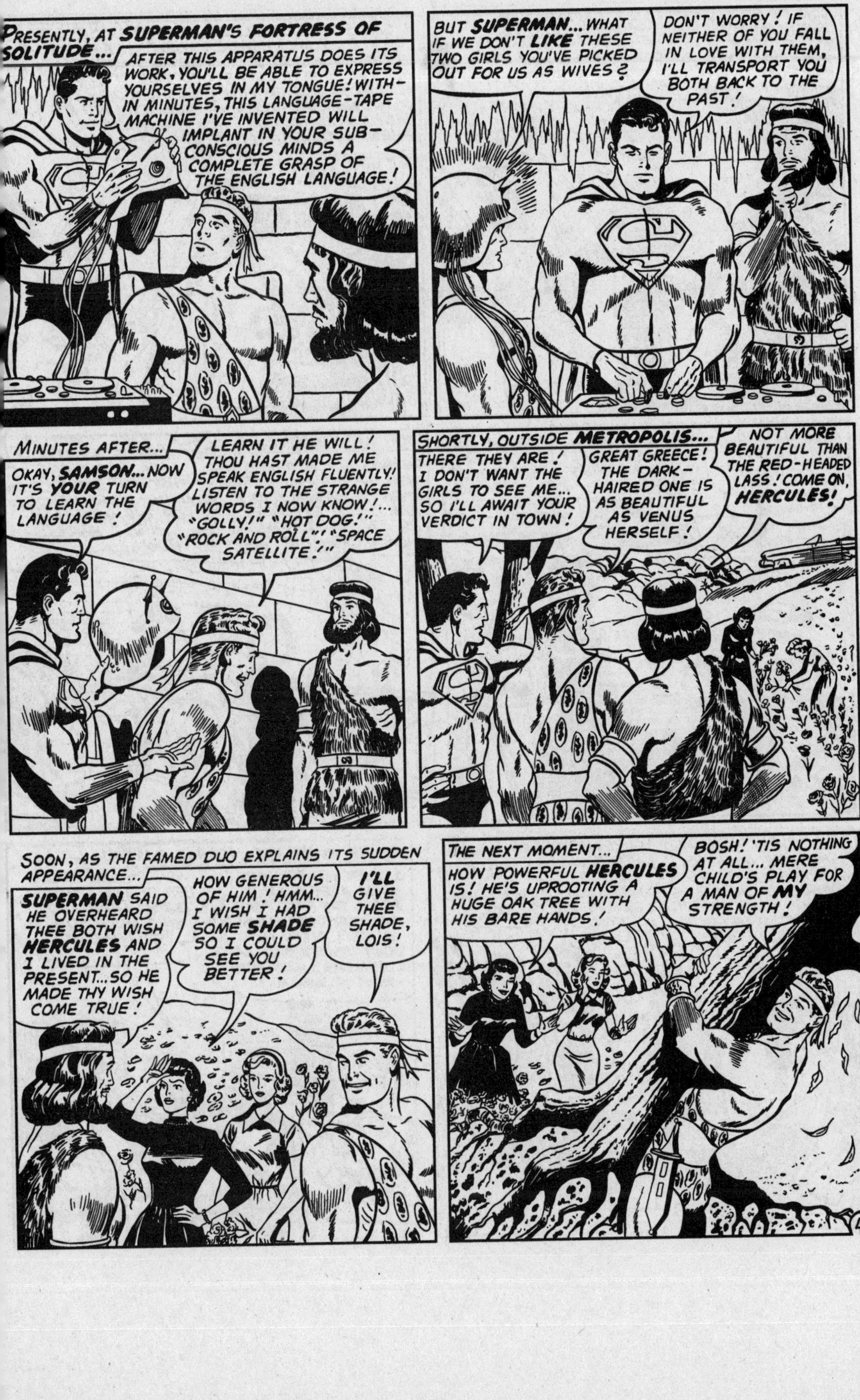
PRESENTLY, AT SUPERMAN'S FORTRESS OF SOLITUDE...
AFTER THIS APPARATUS DOES ITS WORK, YOU'LL BE ABLE TO EXPRESS YOURSELVES IN MY TONGUE! WITHIN MINUTES, THIS LANGUAGE-TAPE MACHINE I'VE INVENTED WILL IMPLANT IN YOUR SUBCONSCIOUS MINDS A COMPLETE GRASP OF THE ENGLISH LANGUAGE!
BUT SUPERMAN... WHAT IF WE DON'T LIKE THESE TWO GIRLS YOU'VE PICKED OUT FOR US AS WIVES?
DON'T WORRY! IF NEITHER OF YOU FALL IN LOVE WITH THEM, I'LL TRANSPORT YOU BOTH BACK TO THE PAST!
MINUTES AFTER...
OKAY, SAMSON... NOW IT'S YOUR TURN TO LEARN THE LANGUAGE!
LEARN IT HE WILL! THOU HAST MADE ME SPEAK ENGLISH FLUENTLY! LISTEN TO THE STRANGE WORDS I NOW KNOW!... "GOLLY!" "HOT DOG!" "ROCK AND ROLL"! "SPACE SATELLITE!"
SHORTLY, OUTSIDE METROPOLIS...
THERE THEY ARE! I DON'T WANT THE GIRLS TO SEE ME... SO I'LL AWAIT YOUR VERDICT IN TOWN!
GREAT GREECE! THE DARK-HAIRED ONE IS AS BEAUTIFUL AS VENUS HERSELF!
NOT MORE BEAUTIFUL THAN THE RED-HEADED LASS! COME ON, HERCULES!
SOON, AS THE FAMED DUO EXPLAINS ITS SUDDEN APPEARANCE...
SUPERMAN SAID HE OVERHEARD THEE BOTH WISH HERCULES AND I LIVED IN THE PRESENT... SO HE MADE THY WISH COME TRUE!
HOW GENEROUS OF HIM! HMM... I WISH I HAD SOME SHADE SO I COULD SEE YOU BETTER!
I'LL GIVE THEE SHADE, LOIS!
THE NEXT MOMENT...
HOW POWERFUL HERCULES IS! HE'S UPROOTING A HUGE OAK TREE WITH HIS BARE HANDS!
BOSH! 'TIS NOTHING AT ALL... MERE CHILD'S PLAY FOR A MAN OF MY STRENGTH!
4

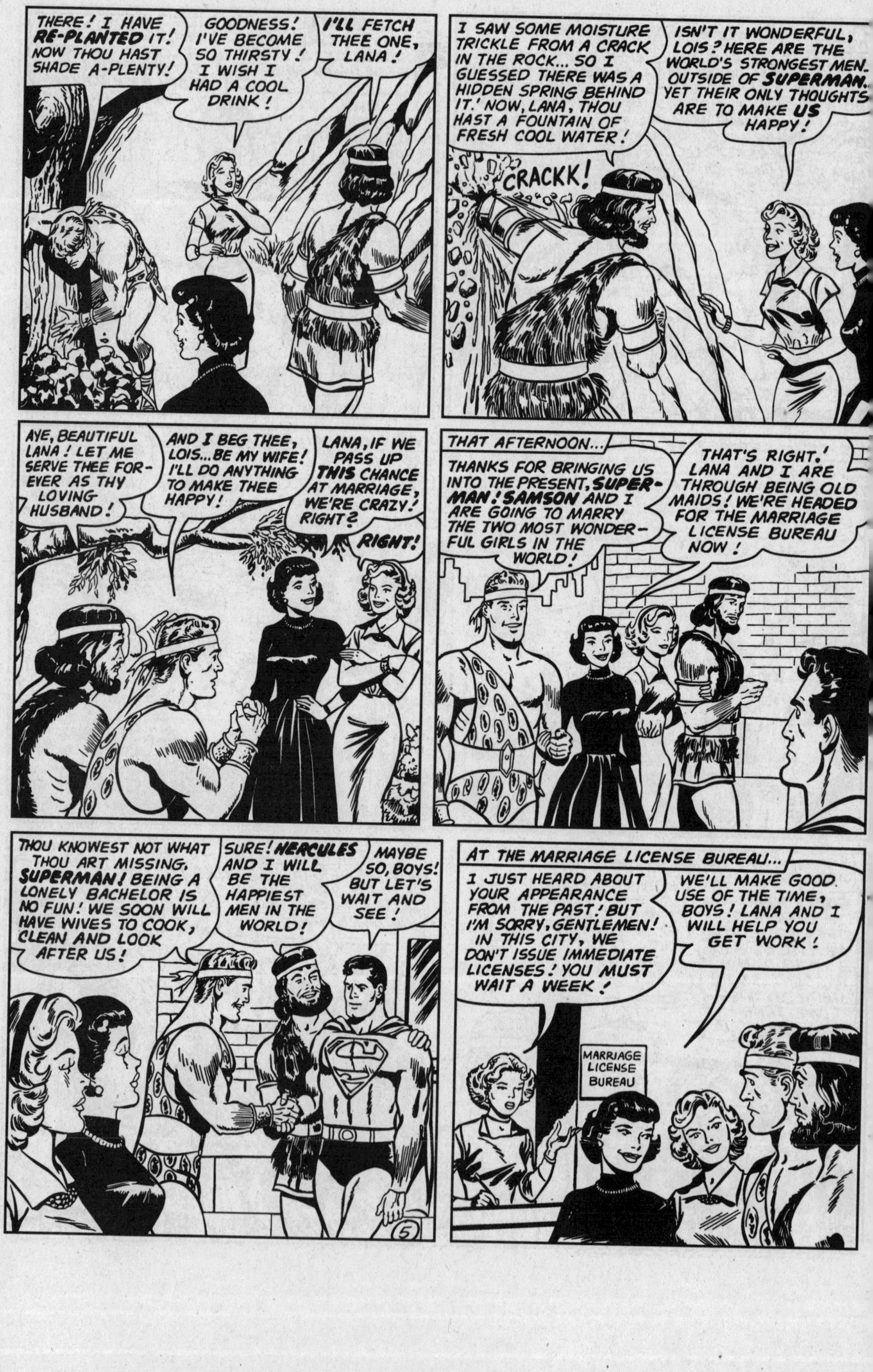
THERE! I HAVE RE-PLANTED IT! NOW THOU HAST SHADE A-PLENTY!
GOODNESS! I'VE BECOME SO THIRSTY! I WISH I HAD A COOL DRINK!
I'LL FETCH THEE ONE, LANA!
I SAW SOME MOISTURE TRICKLE FROM A CRACK IN THE ROCK... SO I GUESSED THERE WAS A HIDDEN SPRING BEHIND IT! NOW, LANA, THOU HAST A FOUNTAIN OF FRESH COOL WATER!
CRACKK!
ISN'T IT WONDERFUL, LOIS? HERE ARE THE WORLD'S STRONGEST MEN OUTSIDE OF SUPERMAN. YET THEIR ONLY THOUGHTS ARE TO MAKE US HAPPY!
AYE, BEAUTIFUL LANA! LET ME SERVE THEE FOREVER AS THY LOVING HUSBAND!
AND I BEG THEE, LOIS... BE MY WIFE! I'LL DO ANYTHING TO MAKE THEE HAPPY!
LANA, IF WE PASS UP THIS CHANCE AT MARRIAGE, WE'RE CRAZY! RIGHT?
RIGHT!
THAT AFTERNOON...
THANKS FOR BRINGING US INTO THE PRESENT, SUPERMAN! SAMSON AND I ARE GOING TO MARRY THE TWO MOST WONDERFUL GIRLS IN THE WORLD!
THAT'S RIGHT! LANA AND I ARE THROUGH BEING OLD MAIDS! WE'RE HEADED FOR THE MARRIAGE LICENSE BUREAU NOW!
THOU KNOWEST NOT WHAT THOU ART MISSING, SUPERMAN! BEING A LONELY BACHELOR IS NO FUN! WE SOON WILL HAVE WIVES TO COOK, CLEAN AND LOOK AFTER US!
SURE! HERCULES AND I WILL BE THE HAPPIEST MEN IN THE WORLD!
MAYBE SO, BOYS! BUT LET'S WAIT AND SEE!
5
AT THE MARRIAGE LICENSE BUREAU...
I JUST HEARD ABOUT YOUR APPEARANCE FROM THE PAST! BUT I'M SORRY, GENTLEMEN! IN THIS CITY, WE DON'T ISSUE IMMEDIATE LICENSES! YOU MUST WAIT A WEEK!
MARRIAGE LICENSE BUREAU
WE'LL MAKE GOOD USE OF THE TIME, BOYS! LANA AND I WILL HELP YOU GET WORK!

THE NEXT DAY, AT A TELEVISION AD AGENCY...

NOW LOOK, LARRY! I KNOW THIS BUSINESS! I TELL YOU *HERCULES* AND *SAMSON* WILL BE SENSATIONAL DOING TV COMMERCIALS! I'LL PERSONALLY REHEARSE THEM IN SELLING YOUR PRODUCTS!

YOU'VE GOT A DEAL, LANA! I AGREE THAT THEY'D HAVE TERRIFIC APPEAL ENDORSING CIGARS, CHEWING GUM, BREAKFAST CEREAL! I'LL USE THEM!

Shampoo your HAIR with SUDSO

TRY OUR TV DINNERS

Smoke for

AND THE FOLLOWING AFTERNOON, AT A MOVIE PRODUCER'S OFFICE...

AFTER READING LOIS LANE'S ARTICLES ABOUT YOUR ARRIVAL FROM THE PAST, I HAD TO SIGN YOU UP FOR A *"SAMSON MEETS HERCULES"* PICTURE! BUT TILL WE FILM IT, KEEP WEARING YOUR COSTUMES! IT'LL BE GREAT PUBLICITY!

YES, SIR! THANKS FOR THE ADVANCE SALARY! NOW WE CAN BUY HOMES FOR OUR FUTURE WIVES!

AND SO, AS THE HEROES BUY HOUSES IN A SUBURB, NEXT DOOR TO EACH OTHER...

THE HOUSE IS BEAUTIFUL, *HERCULES*, BUT I JUST DON'T LIKE IT WHERE IT IS! COULD YOU PUT IT... UH... ON THE RIGHT SIDE OF OUR PROPERTY?

SURE, LOIS! ANYTHING THOU DESIRES!

MINUTES LATER...

OVER *HERE*, DARLING?

COME TO THINK OF IT... NO! IT DOESN'T LOOK WELL THERE! TRY IT ON *THIS* SIDE!

AS *HERCULES* OBLIGES...

OKAY NOW?

NO, SWEETHEART! IT'S STILL NOT RIGHT! WE'LL HAVE TO KEEP TRYING TILL WE FIND THE BEST SPOT! NOW LET'S SEE... MAYBE FURTHER BACK--

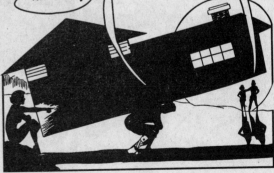

AND WHEN NIGHT FALLS...

GREAT GODS, LOIS! MAKE UP YOUR MIND! I'VE BEEN CARRYING THIS HOUSE ON MY BACK FOR *HOURS*... AND YOU *STILL* HAVEN'T DECIDED WHERE YOU WANT IT!

HA! HA! POOR *HERCULES*! HE'S GOING CRAZY WITH LOIS' INDECISIVENESS! I'M GLAD THOU DOST NOT CHANGE *THY* MIND SO OFTEN!

6

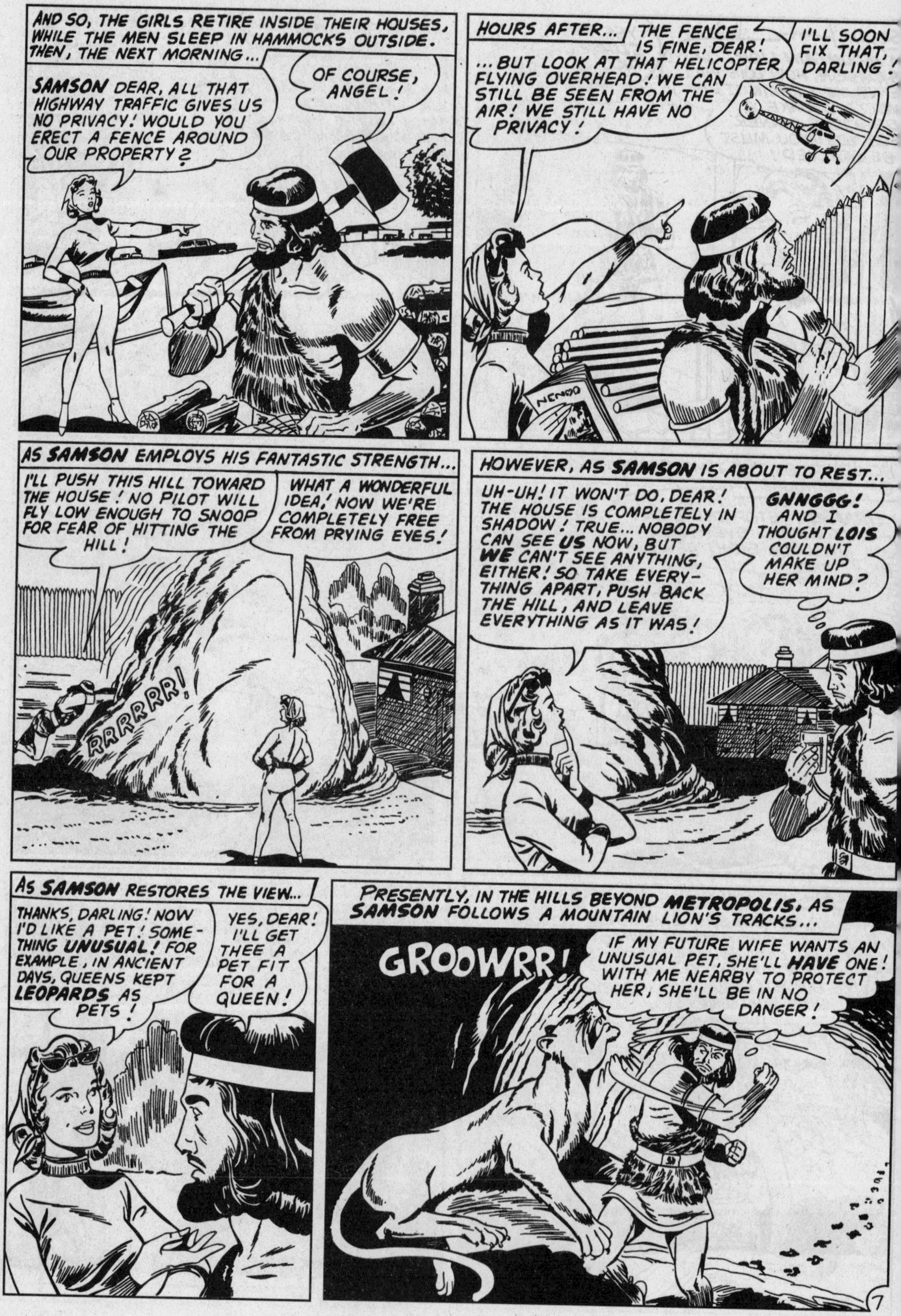
AND SO, THE GIRLS RETIRE INSIDE THEIR HOUSES, WHILE THE MEN SLEEP IN HAMMOCKS OUTSIDE. THEN, THE NEXT MORNING...
SAMSON DEAR, ALL THAT HIGHWAY TRAFFIC GIVES US NO PRIVACY! WOULD YOU ERECT A FENCE AROUND OUR PROPERTY?
OF COURSE, ANGEL!
HOURS AFTER...
THE FENCE IS FINE, DEAR! ...BUT LOOK AT THAT HELICOPTER FLYING OVERHEAD! WE CAN STILL BE SEEN FROM THE AIR! WE STILL HAVE NO PRIVACY!
I'LL SOON FIX THAT, DARLING!
AS SAMSON EMPLOYS HIS FANTASTIC STRENGTH...
I'LL PUSH THIS HILL TOWARD THE HOUSE! NO PILOT WILL FLY LOW ENOUGH TO SNOOP FOR FEAR OF HITTING THE HILL!
WHAT A WONDERFUL IDEA! NOW WE'RE COMPLETELY FREE FROM PRYING EYES!
RRRRRRR!
HOWEVER, AS SAMSON IS ABOUT TO REST...
UH-UH! IT WON'T DO, DEAR! THE HOUSE IS COMPLETELY IN SHADOW! TRUE... NOBODY CAN SEE US NOW, BUT WE CAN'T SEE ANYTHING, EITHER! SO TAKE EVERYTHING APART, PUSH BACK THE HILL, AND LEAVE EVERYTHING AS IT WAS!
GNNGGG! AND I THOUGHT LOIS COULDN'T MAKE UP HER MIND?
AS SAMSON RESTORES THE VIEW...
THANKS, DARLING! NOW I'D LIKE A PET! SOMETHING UNUSUAL! FOR EXAMPLE, IN ANCIENT DAYS, QUEENS KEPT LEOPARDS AS PETS!
YES, DEAR! I'LL GET THEE A PET FIT FOR A QUEEN!
PRESENTLY, IN THE HILLS BEYOND METROPOLIS, AS SAMSON FOLLOWS A MOUNTAIN LION'S TRACKS...
GROOWRR!
IF MY FUTURE WIFE WANTS AN UNUSUAL PET, SHE'LL HAVE ONE! WITH ME NEARBY TO PROTECT HER, SHE'LL BE IN NO DANGER!
7

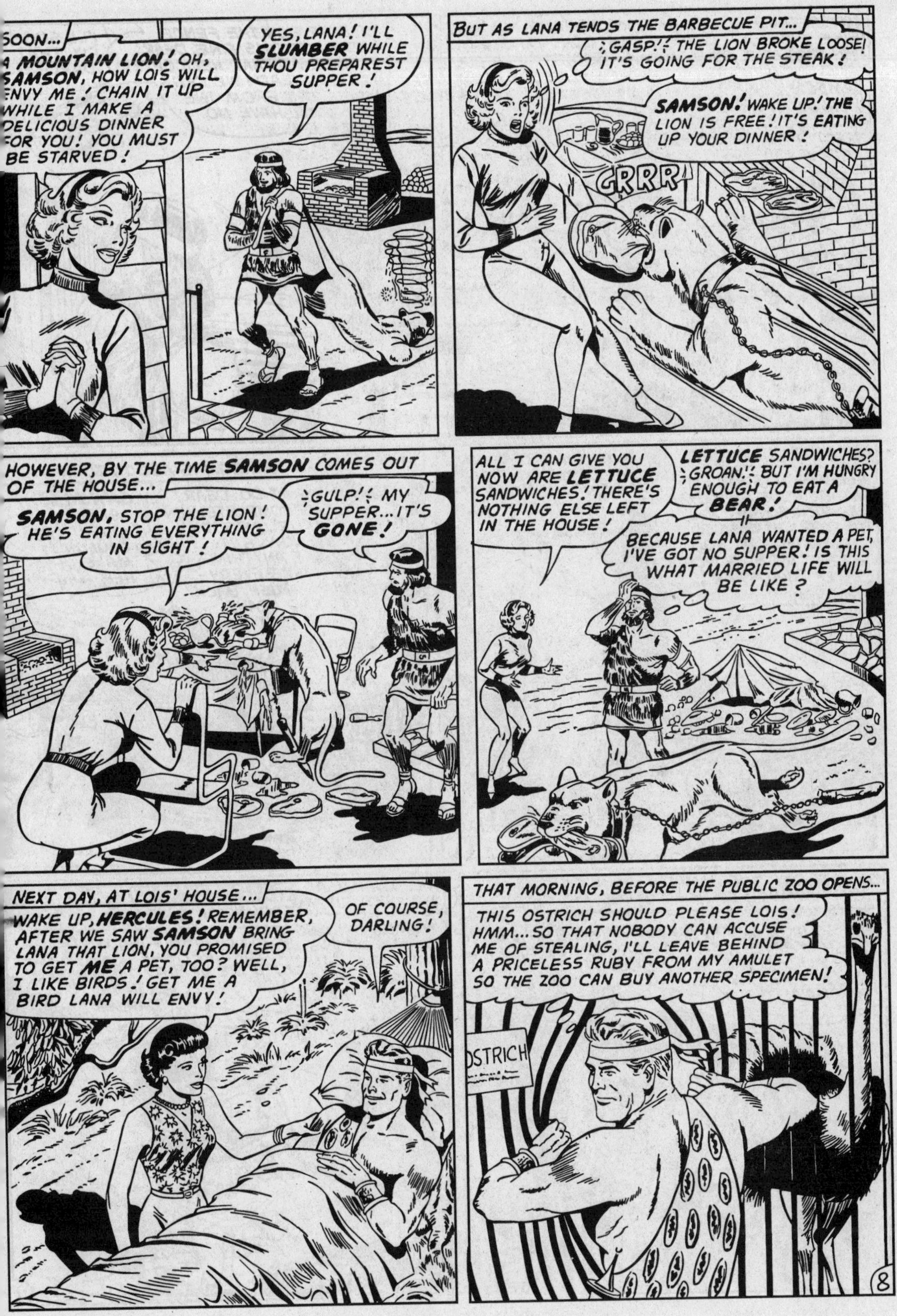
SOON...
A MOUNTAIN LION! OH, SAMSON, HOW LOIS WILL ENVY ME! CHAIN IT UP WHILE I MAKE A DELICIOUS DINNER FOR YOU! YOU MUST BE STARVED!
YES, LANA! I'LL SLUMBER WHILE THOU PREPAREST SUPPER!
BUT AS LANA TENDS THE BARBECUE PIT...
GASP! THE LION BROKE LOOSE! IT'S GOING FOR THE STEAK!
SAMSON! WAKE UP! THE LION IS FREE! IT'S EATING UP YOUR DINNER!
GRRR
HOWEVER, BY THE TIME SAMSON COMES OUT OF THE HOUSE...
SAMSON, STOP THE LION! HE'S EATING EVERYTHING IN SIGHT!
GULP! MY SUPPER...IT'S GONE!
ALL I CAN GIVE YOU NOW ARE LETTUCE SANDWICHES! THERE'S NOTHING ELSE LEFT IN THE HOUSE!
LETTUCE SANDWICHES? GROAN! BUT I'M HUNGRY ENOUGH TO EAT A BEAR!
BECAUSE LANA WANTED A PET, I'VE GOT NO SUPPER! IS THIS WHAT MARRIED LIFE WILL BE LIKE?
NEXT DAY, AT LOIS' HOUSE...
WAKE UP, HERCULES! REMEMBER, AFTER WE SAW SAMSON BRING LANA THAT LION, YOU PROMISED TO GET ME A PET, TOO? WELL, I LIKE BIRDS! GET ME A BIRD LANA WILL ENVY!
OF COURSE, DARLING!
THAT MORNING, BEFORE THE PUBLIC ZOO OPENS...
THIS OSTRICH SHOULD PLEASE LOIS! HMM...SO THAT NOBODY CAN ACCUSE ME OF STEALING, I'LL LEAVE BEHIND A PRICELESS RUBY FROM MY AMULET SO THE ZOO CAN BUY ANOTHER SPECIMEN!
OSTRICH
8

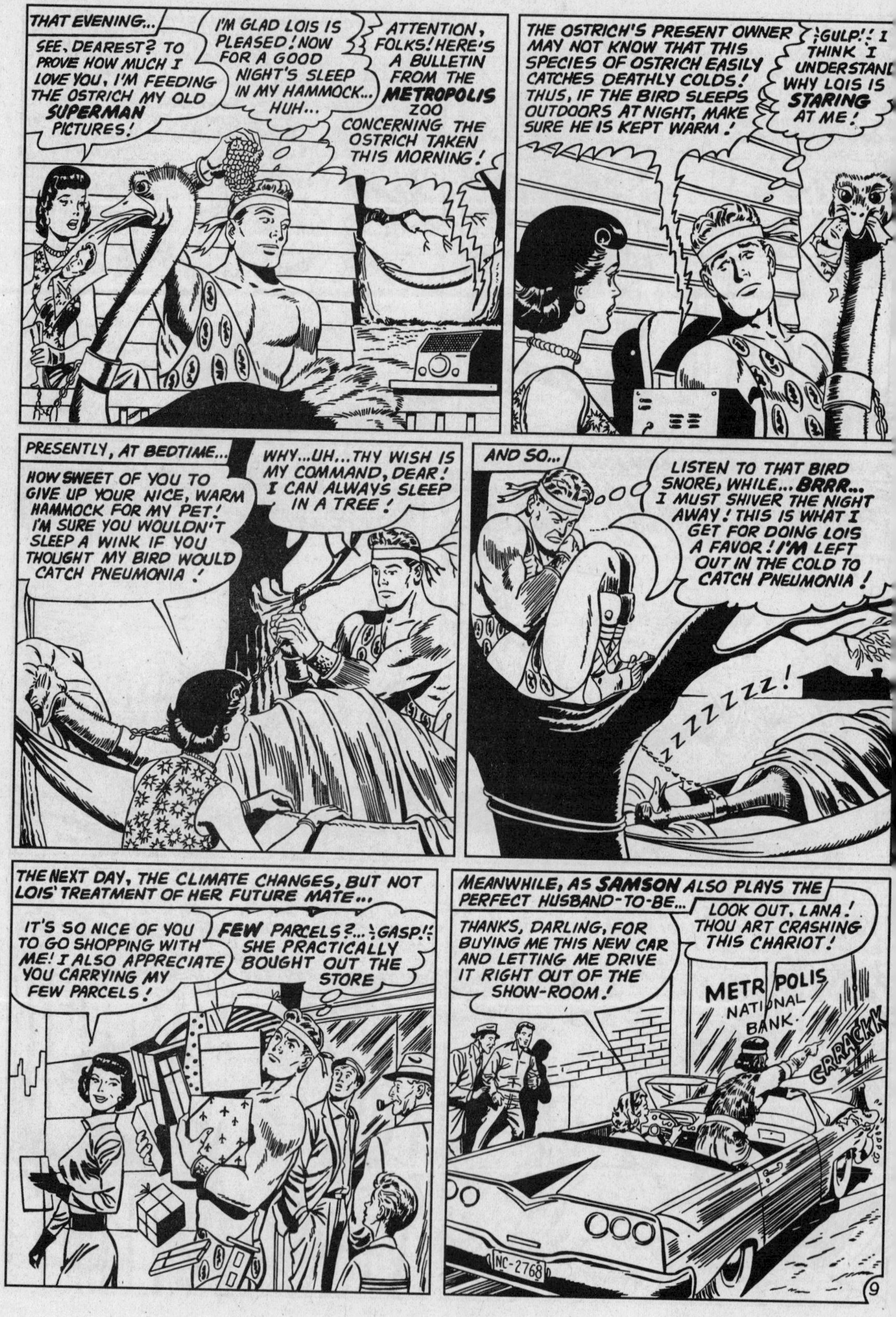
THAT EVENING...
SEE, DEAREST? TO PROVE HOW MUCH I LOVE YOU, I'M FEEDING THE OSTRICH MY OLD SUPERMAN PICTURES!
I'M GLAD LOIS IS PLEASED! NOW FOR A GOOD NIGHT'S SLEEP IN MY HAMMOCK... HUH...
ATTENTION, FOLKS! HERE'S A BULLETIN FROM THE METROPOLIS ZOO CONCERNING THE OSTRICH TAKEN THIS MORNING!
THE OSTRICH'S PRESENT OWNER MAY NOT KNOW THAT THIS SPECIES OF OSTRICH EASILY CATCHES DEATHLY COLDS! THUS, IF THE BIRD SLEEPS OUTDOORS AT NIGHT, MAKE SURE HE IS KEPT WARM!
¡GULP!¡ I THINK I UNDERSTAND WHY LOIS IS STARING AT ME!
PRESENTLY, AT BEDTIME...
HOW SWEET OF YOU TO GIVE UP YOUR NICE, WARM HAMMOCK FOR MY PET! I'M SURE YOU WOULDN'T SLEEP A WINK IF YOU THOUGHT MY BIRD WOULD CATCH PNEUMONIA!
WHY...UH...THY WISH IS MY COMMAND, DEAR! I CAN ALWAYS SLEEP IN A TREE!
AND SO...
LISTEN TO THAT BIRD SNORE, WHILE... BRRR... I MUST SHIVER THE NIGHT AWAY! THIS IS WHAT I GET FOR DOING LOIS A FAVOR! I'M LEFT OUT IN THE COLD TO CATCH PNEUMONIA!
ZZZZZZZZZ!
THE NEXT DAY, THE CLIMATE CHANGES, BUT NOT LOIS' TREATMENT OF HER FUTURE MATE...
IT'S SO NICE OF YOU TO GO SHOPPING WITH ME! I ALSO APPRECIATE YOU CARRYING MY FEW PARCELS!
FEW PARCELS?... ¡GASP!¡ SHE PRACTICALLY BOUGHT OUT THE STORE
MEANWHILE, AS SAMSON ALSO PLAYS THE PERFECT HUSBAND-TO-BE...
THANKS, DARLING, FOR BUYING ME THIS NEW CAR AND LETTING ME DRIVE IT RIGHT OUT OF THE SHOW-ROOM!
LOOK OUT, LANA! THOU ART CRASHING THIS CHARIOT!
METROPOLIS NATIONAL BANK
CRRACKK
NC-2768
9

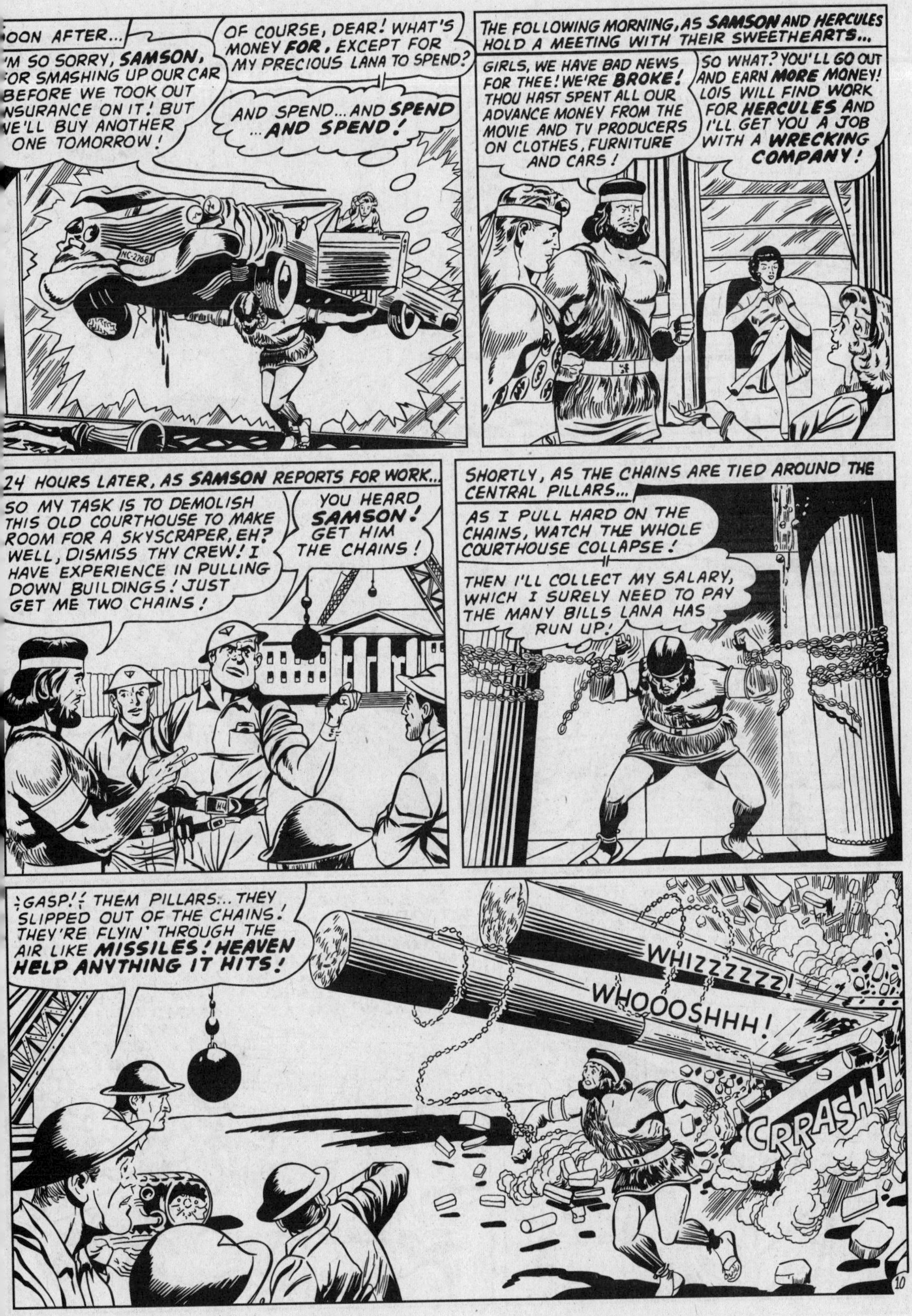
OON AFTER...
'M SO SORRY, SAMSON, FOR SMASHING UP OUR CAR BEFORE WE TOOK OUT NSURANCE ON IT! BUT WE'LL BUY ANOTHER ONE TOMORROW!
OF COURSE, DEAR! WHAT'S MONEY FOR, EXCEPT FOR MY PRECIOUS LANA TO SPEND?
AND SPEND... AND SPEND ... AND SPEND!
NC-2768
THE FOLLOWING MORNING, AS SAMSON AND HERCULES HOLD A MEETING WITH THEIR SWEETHEARTS...
GIRLS, WE HAVE BAD NEWS FOR THEE! WE'RE BROKE! THOU HAST SPENT ALL OUR ADVANCE MONEY FROM THE MOVIE AND TV PRODUCERS ON CLOTHES, FURNITURE AND CARS!
SO WHAT? YOU'LL GO OUT AND EARN MORE MONEY! LOIS WILL FIND WORK FOR HERCULES AND I'LL GET YOU A JOB WITH A WRECKING COMPANY!
24 HOURS LATER, AS SAMSON REPORTS FOR WORK...
SO MY TASK IS TO DEMOLISH THIS OLD COURTHOUSE TO MAKE ROOM FOR A SKYSCRAPER, EH? WELL, DISMISS THY CREW! I HAVE EXPERIENCE IN PULLING DOWN BUILDINGS! JUST GET ME TWO CHAINS!
YOU HEARD SAMSON! GET HIM THE CHAINS!
SHORTLY, AS THE CHAINS ARE TIED AROUND THE CENTRAL PILLARS...
AS I PULL HARD ON THE CHAINS, WATCH THE WHOLE COURTHOUSE COLLAPSE!
THEN I'LL COLLECT MY SALARY, WHICH I SURELY NEED TO PAY THE MANY BILLS LANA HAS RUN UP!
GASP! THEM PILLARS... THEY SLIPPED OUT OF THE CHAINS! THEY'RE FLYIN' THROUGH THE AIR LIKE MISSILES! HEAVEN HELP ANYTHING IT HITS!
WHIZZZZZZ!
WHOOOSHHH!
CRRASHH
10

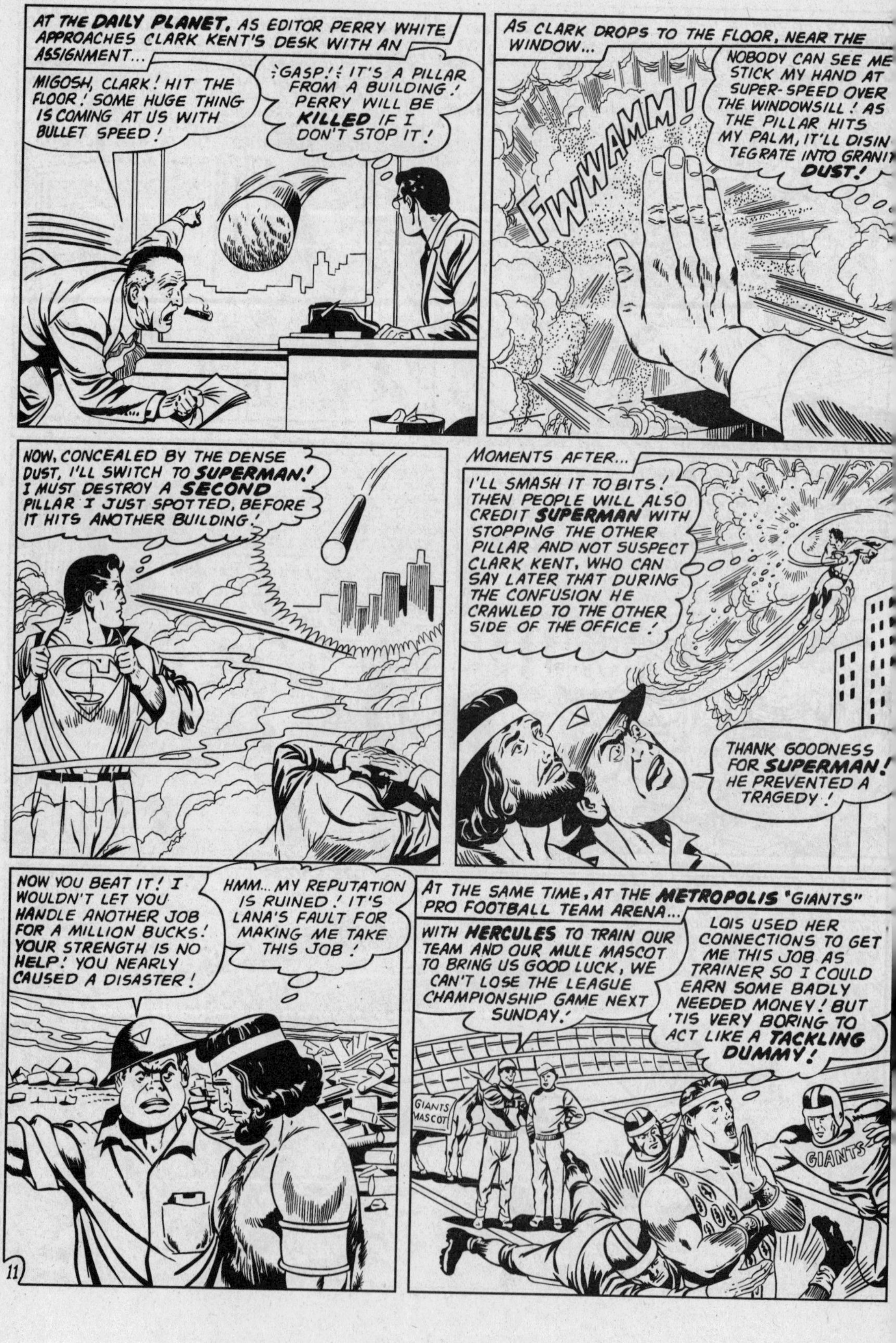
AT THE DAILY PLANET, AS EDITOR PERRY WHITE APPROACHES CLARK KENT'S DESK WITH AN ASSIGNMENT...
MIGOSH, CLARK! HIT THE FLOOR! SOME HUGE THING IS COMING AT US WITH BULLET SPEED!
GASP! IT'S A PILLAR FROM A BUILDING! PERRY WILL BE KILLED IF I DON'T STOP IT!
AS CLARK DROPS TO THE FLOOR, NEAR THE WINDOW...
NOBODY CAN SEE ME STICK MY HAND AT SUPER-SPEED OVER THE WINDOWSILL! AS THE PILLAR HITS MY PALM, IT'LL DISINTEGRATE INTO GRANIT DUST!
FWWAMM!
NOW, CONCEALED BY THE DENSE DUST, I'LL SWITCH TO SUPERMAN! I MUST DESTROY A SECOND PILLAR I JUST SPOTTED, BEFORE IT HITS ANOTHER BUILDING!
MOMENTS AFTER...
I'LL SMASH IT TO BITS! THEN PEOPLE WILL ALSO CREDIT SUPERMAN WITH STOPPING THE OTHER PILLAR AND NOT SUSPECT CLARK KENT, WHO CAN SAY LATER THAT DURING THE CONFUSION HE CRAWLED TO THE OTHER SIDE OF THE OFFICE!
THANK GOODNESS FOR SUPERMAN! HE PREVENTED A TRAGEDY!
NOW YOU BEAT IT! I WOULDN'T LET YOU HANDLE ANOTHER JOB FOR A MILLION BUCKS! YOUR STRENGTH IS NO HELP! YOU NEARLY CAUSED A DISASTER!
HMM... MY REPUTATION IS RUINED! IT'S LANA'S FAULT FOR MAKING ME TAKE THIS JOB!
11
AT THE SAME TIME, AT THE METROPOLIS "GIANTS" PRO FOOTBALL TEAM ARENA...
WITH HERCULES TO TRAIN OUR TEAM AND OUR MULE MASCOT TO BRING US GOOD LUCK, WE CAN'T LOSE THE LEAGUE CHAMPIONSHIP GAME NEXT SUNDAY!
LOIS USED HER CONNECTIONS TO GET ME THIS JOB AS TRAINER SO I COULD EARN SOME BADLY NEEDED MONEY! BUT 'TIS VERY BORING TO ACT LIKE A TACKLING DUMMY!
GIANTS MASCOT
GIANTS

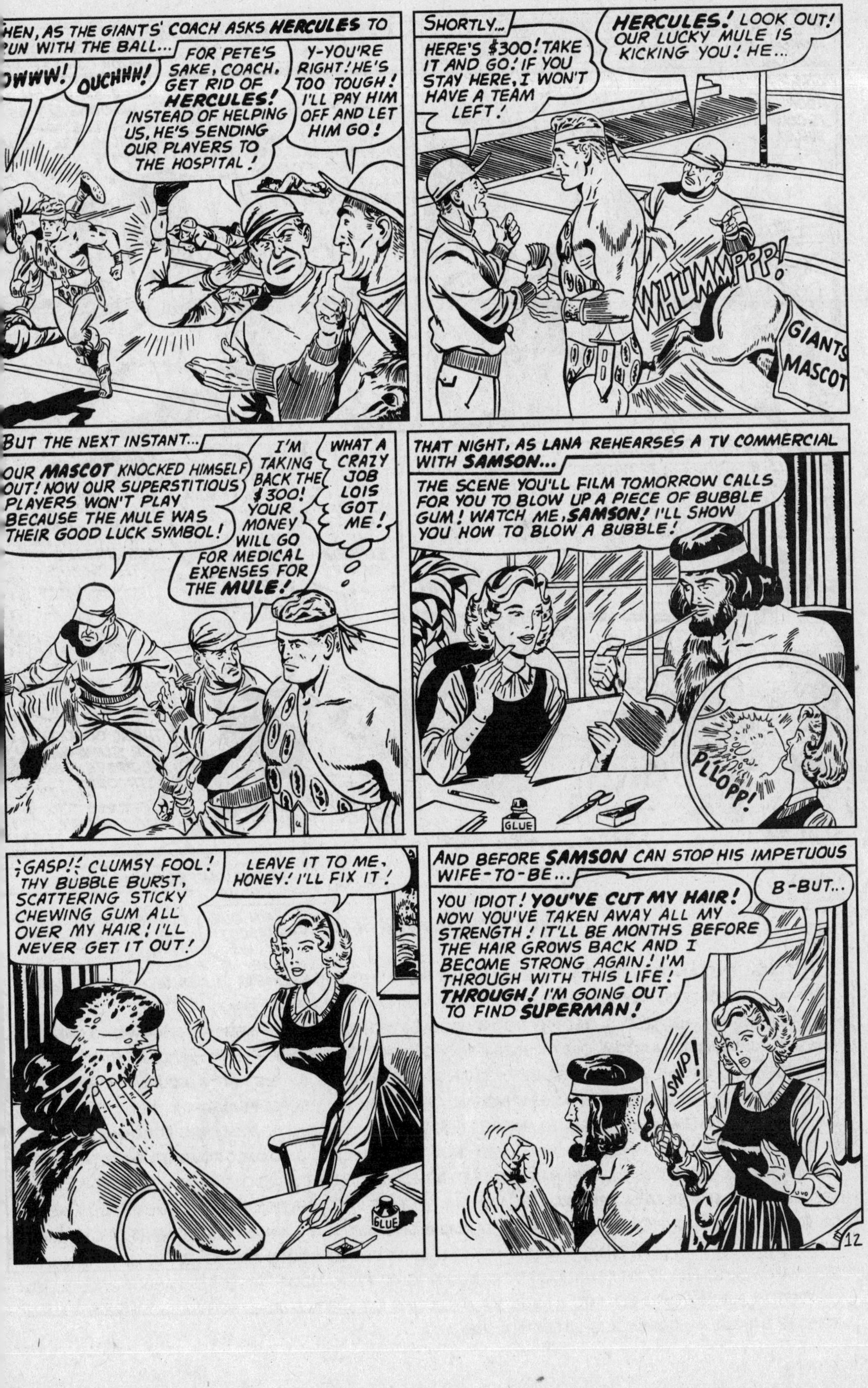
HEN, AS THE GIANTS' COACH ASKS HERCULES TO RUN WITH THE BALL...
OWWW!
OUCHHH!
FOR PETE'S SAKE, COACH, GET RID OF HERCULES! INSTEAD OF HELPING US, HE'S SENDING OUR PLAYERS TO THE HOSPITAL!
Y-YOU'RE RIGHT! HE'S TOO TOUGH! I'LL PAY HIM OFF AND LET HIM GO!
SHORTLY...
HERE'S $300! TAKE IT AND GO! IF YOU STAY HERE, I WON'T HAVE A TEAM LEFT!
HERCULES! LOOK OUT! OUR LUCKY MULE IS KICKING YOU! HE...
WHUMMPPP!
GIANTS MASCOT
BUT THE NEXT INSTANT...
OUR MASCOT KNOCKED HIMSELF OUT! NOW OUR SUPERSTITIOUS PLAYERS WON'T PLAY BECAUSE THE MULE WAS THEIR GOOD LUCK SYMBOL!
I'M TAKING BACK THE $300! YOUR MONEY WILL GO FOR MEDICAL EXPENSES FOR THE MULE!
WHAT A CRAZY JOB LOIS GOT ME!
THAT NIGHT, AS LANA REHEARSES A TV COMMERCIAL WITH SAMSON...
THE SCENE YOU'LL FILM TOMORROW CALLS FOR YOU TO BLOW UP A PIECE OF BUBBLE GUM! WATCH ME, SAMSON! I'LL SHOW YOU HOW TO BLOW A BUBBLE!
PLLOPP!
GLUE
GASP! CLUMSY FOOL! THY BUBBLE BURST, SCATTERING STICKY CHEWING GUM ALL OVER MY HAIR! I'LL NEVER GET IT OUT!
LEAVE IT TO ME, HONEY! I'LL FIX IT!
GLUE
AND BEFORE SAMSON CAN STOP HIS IMPETUOUS WIFE-TO-BE...
YOU IDIOT! YOU'VE CUT MY HAIR! NOW YOU'VE TAKEN AWAY ALL MY STRENGTH! IT'LL BE MONTHS BEFORE THE HAIR GROWS BACK AND I BECOME STRONG AGAIN! I'M THROUGH WITH THIS LIFE! THROUGH! I'M GOING OUT TO FIND SUPERMAN!
B-BUT...
SNIP!
12

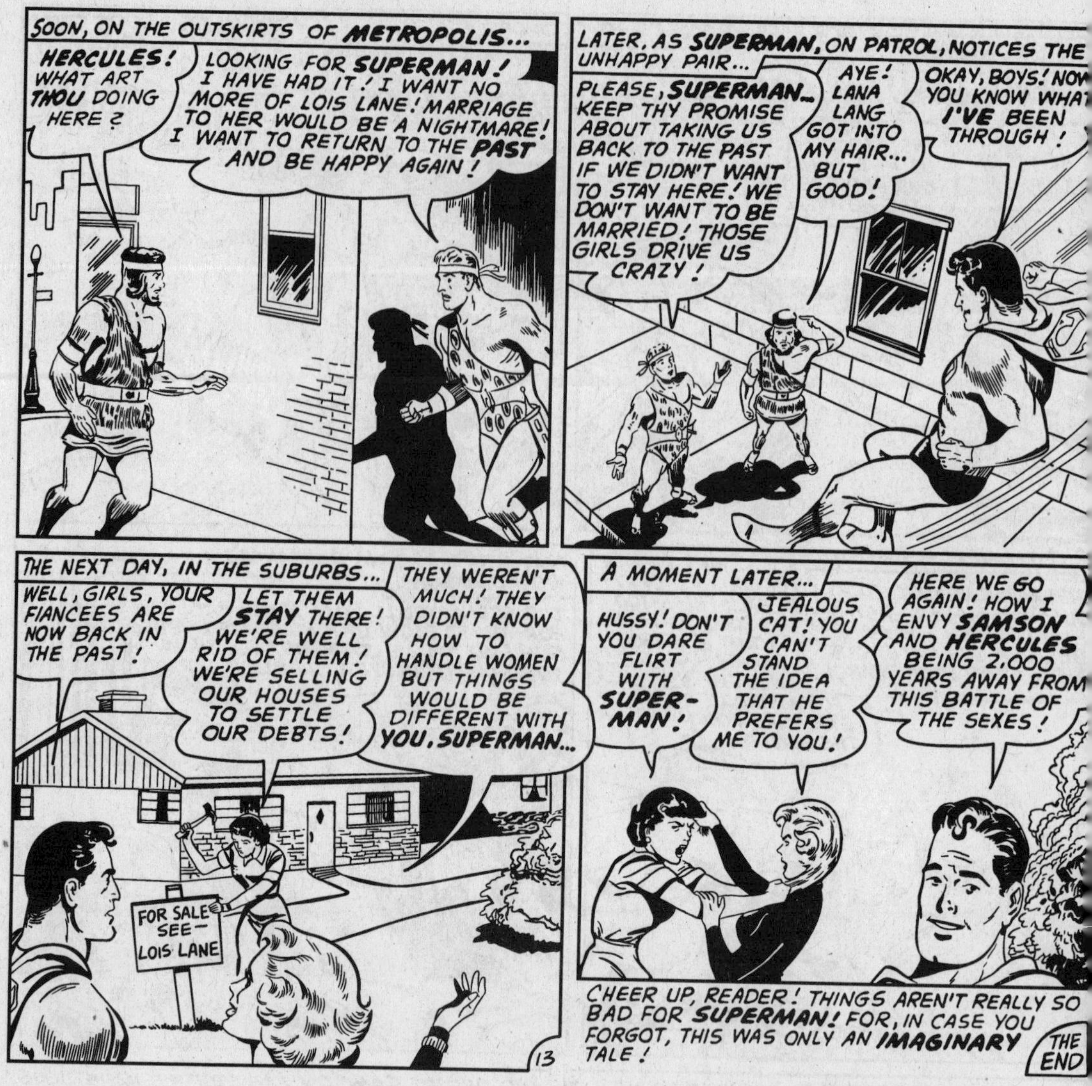
SOON, ON THE OUTSKIRTS OF METROPOLIS...
HERCULES! WHAT ART THOU DOING HERE?
LOOKING FOR SUPERMAN! I HAVE HAD IT! I WANT NO MORE OF LOIS LANE! MARRIAGE TO HER WOULD BE A NIGHTMARE! I WANT TO RETURN TO THE PAST AND BE HAPPY AGAIN!
LATER, AS SUPERMAN, ON PATROL, NOTICES THE UNHAPPY PAIR...
PLEASE, SUPERMAN... KEEP THY PROMISE ABOUT TAKING US BACK TO THE PAST IF WE DIDN'T WANT TO STAY HERE! WE DON'T WANT TO BE MARRIED! THOSE GIRLS DRIVE US CRAZY!
AYE! LANA LANG GOT INTO MY HAIR... BUT GOOD!
OKAY, BOYS! NOW YOU KNOW WHAT I'VE BEEN THROUGH!
THE NEXT DAY, IN THE SUBURBS...
WELL, GIRLS, YOUR FIANCEES ARE NOW BACK IN THE PAST!
LET THEM STAY THERE! WE'RE WELL RID OF THEM! WE'RE SELLING OUR HOUSES TO SETTLE OUR DEBTS!
THEY WEREN'T MUCH! THEY DIDN'T KNOW HOW TO HANDLE WOMEN BUT THINGS WOULD BE DIFFERENT WITH YOU, SUPERMAN...
FOR SALE SEE— LOIS LANE
13
A MOMENT LATER...
HUSSY! DON'T YOU DARE FLIRT WITH SUPER-MAN!
JEALOUS CAT! YOU CAN'T STAND THE IDEA THAT HE PREFERS ME TO YOU!
HERE WE GO AGAIN! HOW I ENVY SAMSON AND HERCULES BEING 2,000 YEARS AWAY FROM THIS BATTLE OF THE SEXES!
CHEER UP, READER! THINGS AREN'T REALLY SO BAD FOR SUPERMAN! FOR, IN CASE YOU FORGOT, THIS WAS ONLY AN IMAGINARY TALE!
THE END

SECRETS OF THE FORTRESS OF SOLITUDE

1. FORTRESS ENTRANCE. FORTRESS IS HIDDEN IN THE ARCTIC, AND ITS ENTRANCE IS IN THE SIDE OF A SNOW-COVERED MOUNTAIN. **2. FORTRESS KEY**. THE GIANT KEY, DISGUISED AS AN AIRPLANE MARKER, IS SO HEAVY ONLY SUPERMAN CAN LIFT IT TO UNLOCK HIS FORTRESS. **3. TROPHY ROOM**. ABOUNDS WITH SOUVENIRS OF MISSIONS PERFORMED ALL OVER THE UNIVERSE. **4. SUPERMAN ROOM**. ONE OF SEVERAL ROOMS IN THE FORTRESS DEDICATED TO FRIENDS OF SUPERMAN. IN THE SUPERMAN ROOM ARE STATUTES OF BOTH SUPERMAN AND CLARK KENT. **5. BATMAN & ROBIN ROOM.** BUILT IN HONOR OF THOSE FAMOUS CRIME-SMASHERS, BATMAN AND ROBIN. **6. SUPER-MURAL.** THIS MURAL, PAINTED BY SUPERMAN, SHOWS HOW HE ONCE CREATED AN ENTIRE SOLAR SYSTEM ALL BY HIMSELF! **7. SUPERGIRL ROOM.** DEDICATED TO SUPERMAN'S COUSIN FROM KRYPTON, KARA, ALSO KNOWN AS LINDA LEE. **8. ATOMIC-POWERED ROBOTS**. THERE'S NOTHING SUPERMAN ENJOYS MORE, WHEN HE DESIRES EXERCISE, THAN TO HAVE A TUG-OF-WAR WITH HIS ATOM-POWERED ROBOTS. **9. JOR-EL AND LARA ARCHWAY**. THE ARCHWAY IS FORMED BY STATUES OF SUPERMAN'S PARENTS AND A MODEL OF HIS HOME WORLD, KRYPTON. **10. MA & PA KENT ROOM**. DEDICATED TO THE KINDLY FOSTER PARENTS WHO ADOPTED SUPERMAN WHEN HE LANDED IN SMALLVILLE AS A BABY. **11. DAILY PLANET ROOM.** A REPLICA OF THE OFFICE IN WHICH SUPERMAN WORKS IN HIS SECRET IDENTITY AS REPORTER CLARK KENT. **12. KANDOR**. THE CITY OF KANDOR ONCE EXISTED ON KRYPTON, BUT WAS SHRUNKEN INTO A BOTTLE VIA A REDUCING RAY BY SPACE-VILLAIN BRAINIAC. SOMEDAY SUPERMAN HOPES TO ENLARGE KANDOR BACK TO ITS ORIGINAL SIZE.

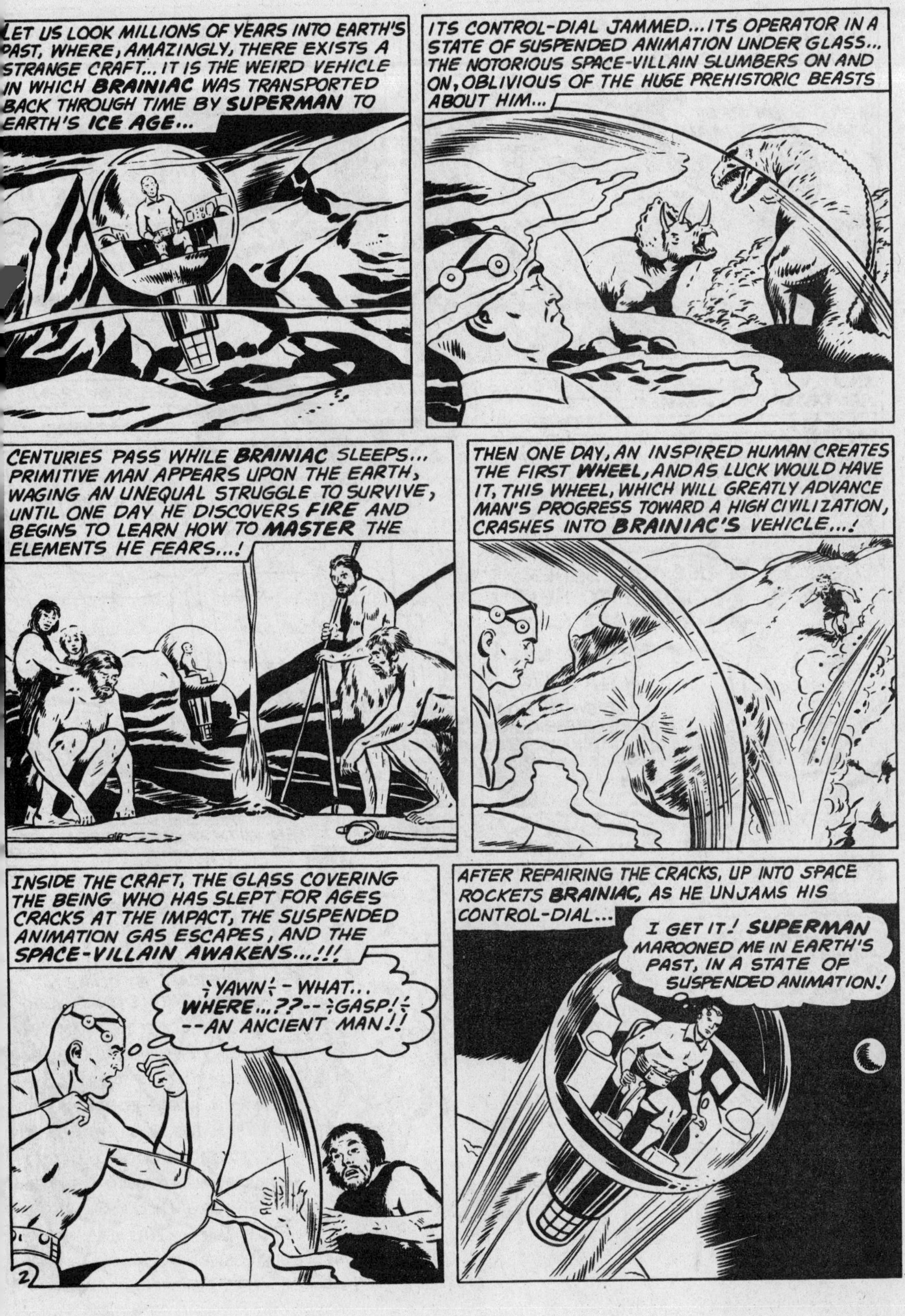
LET US LOOK MILLIONS OF YEARS INTO EARTH'S PAST, WHERE, AMAZINGLY, THERE EXISTS A STRANGE CRAFT... IT IS THE WEIRD VEHICLE IN WHICH BRAINIAC WAS TRANSPORTED BACK THROUGH TIME BY SUPERMAN TO EARTH'S ICE AGE...
ITS CONTROL-DIAL JAMMED...ITS OPERATOR IN A STATE OF SUSPENDED ANIMATION UNDER GLASS... THE NOTORIOUS SPACE-VILLAIN SLUMBERS ON AND ON, OBLIVIOUS OF THE HUGE PREHISTORIC BEASTS ABOUT HIM...
CENTURIES PASS WHILE BRAINIAC SLEEPS... PRIMITIVE MAN APPEARS UPON THE EARTH, WAGING AN UNEQUAL STRUGGLE TO SURVIVE, UNTIL ONE DAY HE DISCOVERS FIRE AND BEGINS TO LEARN HOW TO MASTER THE ELEMENTS HE FEARS...!
THEN ONE DAY, AN INSPIRED HUMAN CREATES THE FIRST WHEEL, AND AS LUCK WOULD HAVE IT, THIS WHEEL, WHICH WILL GREATLY ADVANCE MAN'S PROGRESS TOWARD A HIGH CIVILIZATION, CRASHES INTO BRAINIAC'S VEHICLE...!
INSIDE THE CRAFT, THE GLASS COVERING THE BEING WHO HAS SLEPT FOR AGES CRACKS AT THE IMPACT, THE SUSPENDED ANIMATION GAS ESCAPES, AND THE SPACE-VILLAIN AWAKENS...!!!
-YAWN- - WHAT... WHERE...??-- -GASP!- --AN ANCIENT MAN!!
2
AFTER REPAIRING THE CRACKS, UP INTO SPACE ROCKETS BRAINIAC, AS HE UNJAMS HIS CONTROL-DIAL...
I GET IT! SUPERMAN MAROONED ME IN EARTH'S PAST, IN A STATE OF SUSPENDED ANIMATION!

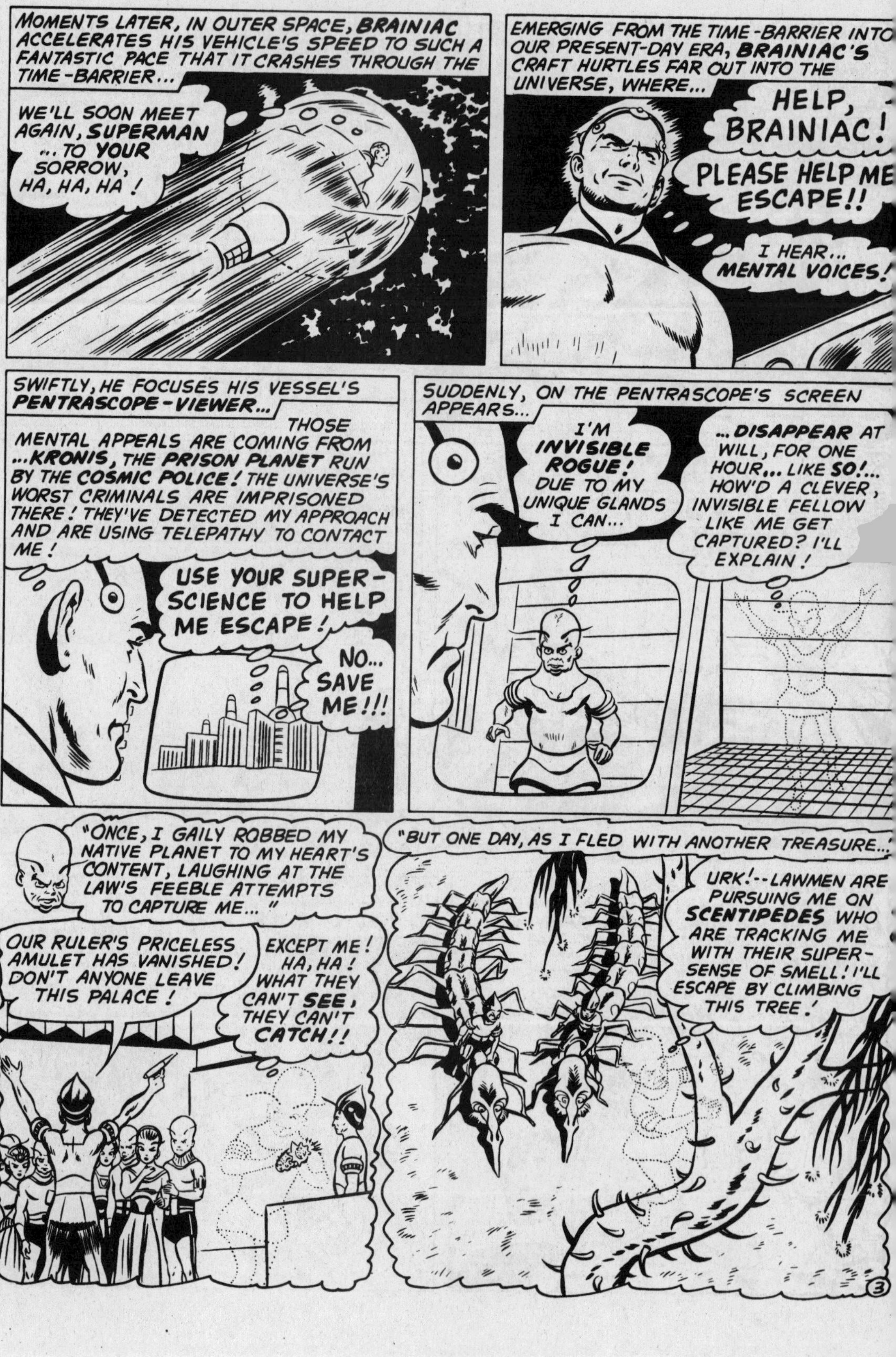
MOMENTS LATER, IN OUTER SPACE, BRAINIAC ACCELERATES HIS VEHICLE'S SPEED TO SUCH A FANTASTIC PACE THAT IT CRASHES THROUGH THE TIME-BARRIER...
WE'LL SOON MEET AGAIN, SUPERMAN ...TO YOUR SORROW, HA, HA, HA!
EMERGING FROM THE TIME-BARRIER INTO OUR PRESENT-DAY ERA, BRAINIAC'S CRAFT HURTLES FAR OUT INTO THE UNIVERSE, WHERE...
HELP, BRAINIAC!
PLEASE HELP ME ESCAPE!!
I HEAR... MENTAL VOICES!
SWIFTLY, HE FOCUSES HIS VESSEL'S PENTRASCOPE-VIEWER...
THOSE MENTAL APPEALS ARE COMING FROM ...KRONIS, THE PRISON PLANET RUN BY THE COSMIC POLICE! THE UNIVERSE'S WORST CRIMINALS ARE IMPRISONED THERE! THEY'VE DETECTED MY APPROACH AND ARE USING TELEPATHY TO CONTACT ME!
USE YOUR SUPER-SCIENCE TO HELP ME ESCAPE!
NO... SAVE ME!!!
SUDDENLY, ON THE PENTRASCOPE'S SCREEN APPEARS...
I'M INVISIBLE ROGUE! DUE TO MY UNIQUE GLANDS I CAN...
...DISAPPEAR AT WILL, FOR ONE HOUR... LIKE SO!... HOW'D A CLEVER, INVISIBLE FELLOW LIKE ME GET CAPTURED? I'LL EXPLAIN!
"ONCE, I GAILY ROBBED MY NATIVE PLANET TO MY HEART'S CONTENT, LAUGHING AT THE LAW'S FEEBLE ATTEMPTS TO CAPTURE ME..."
OUR RULER'S PRICELESS AMULET HAS VANISHED! DON'T ANYONE LEAVE THIS PALACE!
EXCEPT ME! HA, HA! WHAT THEY CAN'T SEE, THEY CAN'T CATCH!!
"BUT ONE DAY, AS I FLED WITH ANOTHER TREASURE..."
URK!--LAWMEN ARE PURSUING ME ON SCENTIPEDES WHO ARE TRACKING ME WITH THEIR SUPER-SENSE OF SMELL! I'LL ESCAPE BY CLIMBING THIS TREE!
3

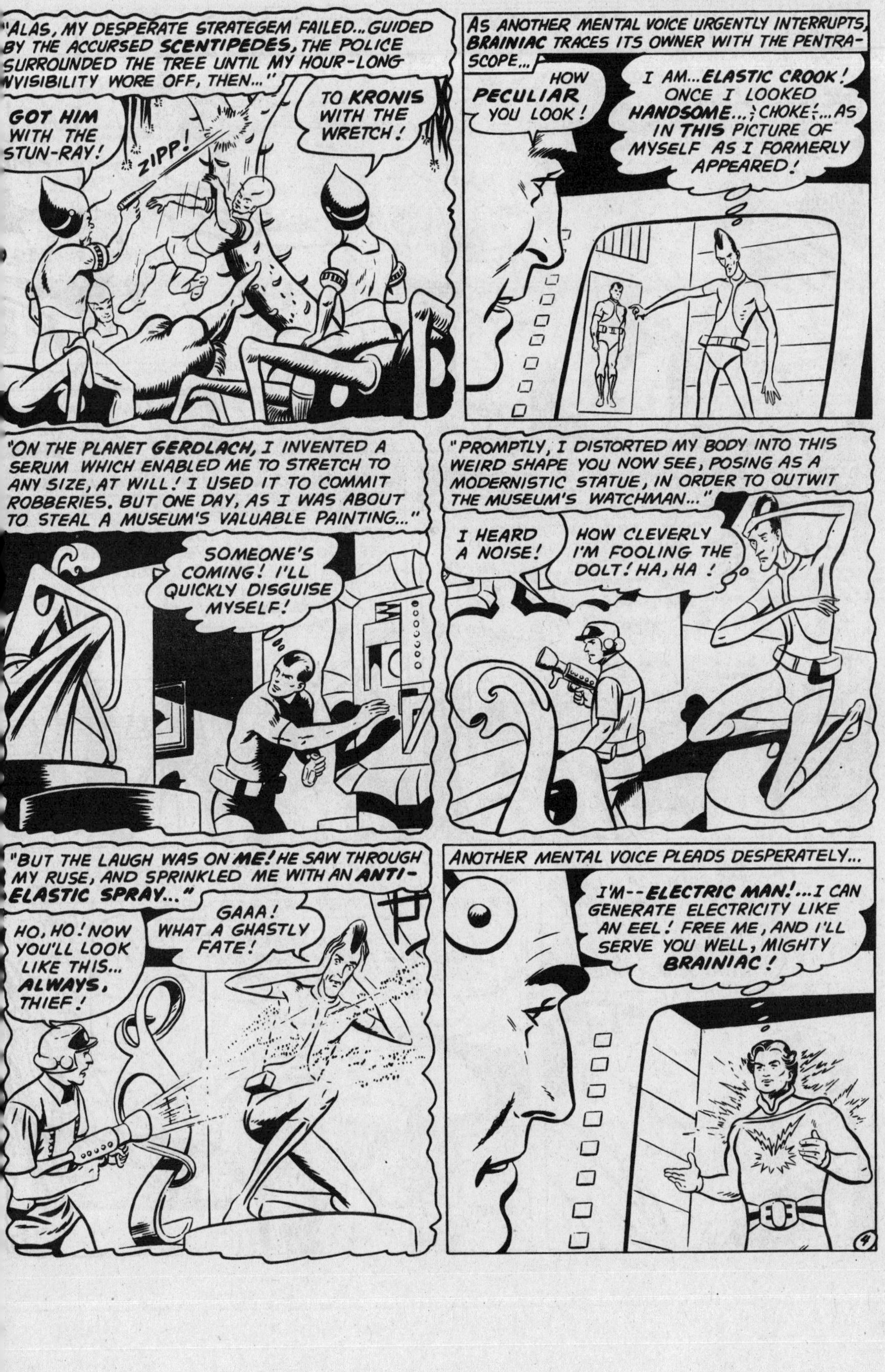
"ALAS, MY DESPERATE STRATEGEM FAILED...GUIDED BY THE ACCURSED SCENTIPEDES, THE POLICE SURROUNDED THE TREE UNTIL MY HOUR-LONG INVISIBILITY WORE OFF, THEN..."
GOT HIM WITH THE STUN-RAY!
ZIPP!
TO KRONIS WITH THE WRETCH!
AS ANOTHER MENTAL VOICE URGENTLY INTERRUPTS, BRAINIAC TRACES ITS OWNER WITH THE PENTRA-SCOPE...
HOW PECULIAR YOU LOOK!
I AM...ELASTIC CROOK! ONCE I LOOKED HANDSOME...CHOKE...AS IN THIS PICTURE OF MYSELF AS I FORMERLY APPEARED!
"ON THE PLANET GERDLACH, I INVENTED A SERUM WHICH ENABLED ME TO STRETCH TO ANY SIZE, AT WILL! I USED IT TO COMMIT ROBBERIES. BUT ONE DAY, AS I WAS ABOUT TO STEAL A MUSEUM'S VALUABLE PAINTING..."
SOMEONE'S COMING! I'LL QUICKLY DISGUISE MYSELF!
"PROMPTLY, I DISTORTED MY BODY INTO THIS WEIRD SHAPE YOU NOW SEE, POSING AS A MODERNISTIC STATUE, IN ORDER TO OUTWIT THE MUSEUM'S WATCHMAN..."
I HEARD A NOISE!
HOW CLEVERLY I'M FOOLING THE DOLT! HA, HA!
"BUT THE LAUGH WAS ON ME! HE SAW THROUGH MY RUSE, AND SPRINKLED ME WITH AN ANTI-ELASTIC SPRAY..."
HO, HO! NOW YOU'LL LOOK LIKE THIS... ALWAYS, THIEF!
GAAA! WHAT A GHASTLY FATE!
ANOTHER MENTAL VOICE PLEADS DESPERATELY...
I'M--ELECTRIC MAN!...I CAN GENERATE ELECTRICITY LIKE AN EEL! FREE ME, AND I'LL SERVE YOU WELL, MIGHTY BRAINIAC!
4

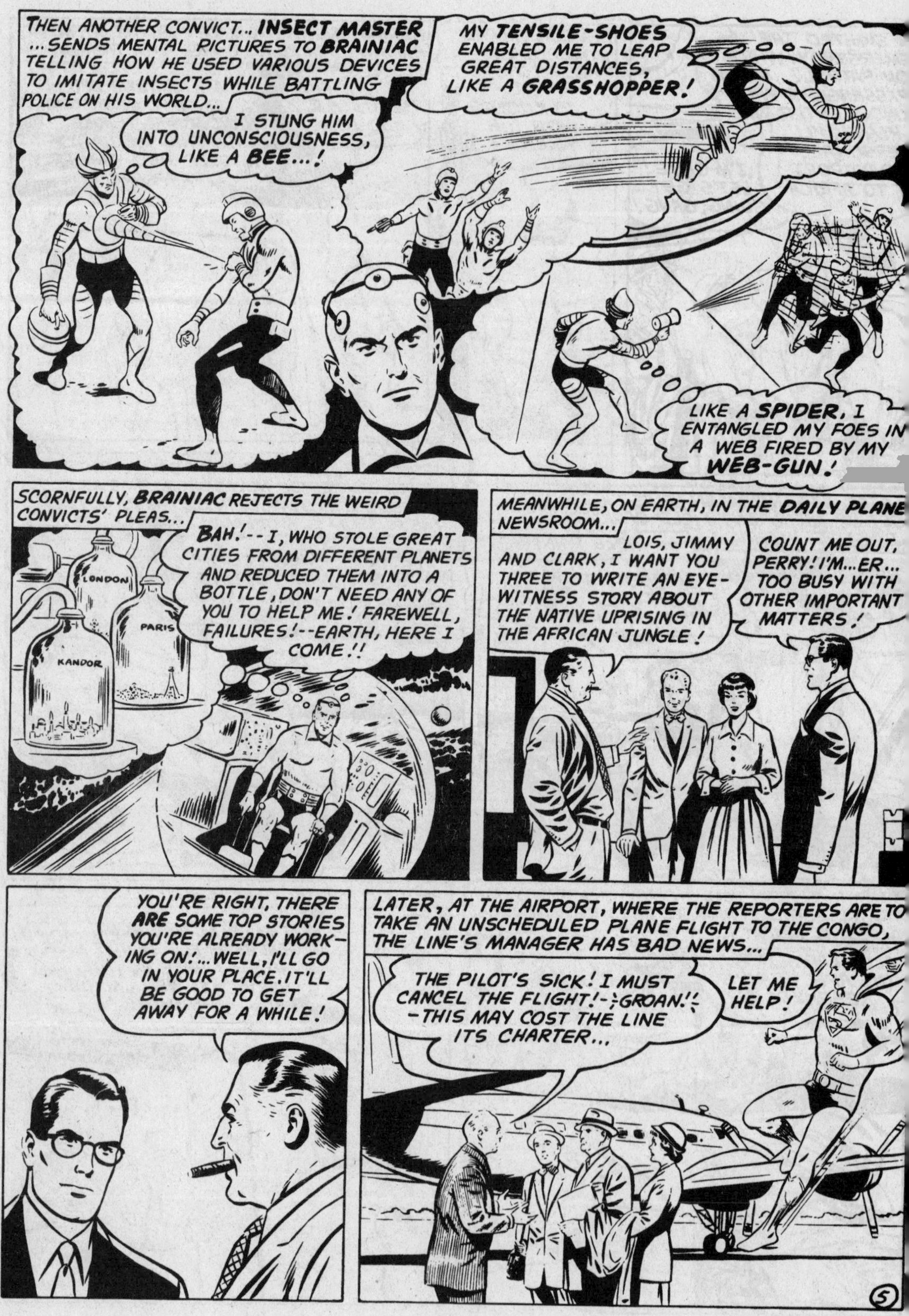
THEN ANOTHER CONVICT... INSECT MASTER ...SENDS MENTAL PICTURES TO BRAINIAC TELLING HOW HE USED VARIOUS DEVICES TO IMITATE INSECTS WHILE BATTLING POLICE ON HIS WORLD...
I STUNG HIM INTO UNCONSCIOUSNESS, LIKE A BEE...!
MY TENSILE-SHOES ENABLED ME TO LEAP GREAT DISTANCES, LIKE A GRASSHOPPER!
LIKE A SPIDER, I ENTANGLED MY FOES IN A WEB FIRED BY MY WEB-GUN!
SCORNFULLY, BRAINIAC REJECTS THE WEIRD CONVICTS' PLEAS...
BAH!--I, WHO STOLE GREAT CITIES FROM DIFFERENT PLANETS AND REDUCED THEM INTO A BOTTLE, DON'T NEED ANY OF YOU TO HELP ME! FAREWELL, FAILURES!--EARTH, HERE I COME!!
LONDON
PARIS
KANDOR
MEANWHILE, ON EARTH, IN THE DAILY PLANE NEWSROOM...
LOIS, JIMMY AND CLARK, I WANT YOU THREE TO WRITE AN EYE-WITNESS STORY ABOUT THE NATIVE UPRISING IN THE AFRICAN JUNGLE!
COUNT ME OUT, PERRY! I'M...ER... TOO BUSY WITH OTHER IMPORTANT MATTERS!
YOU'RE RIGHT, THERE ARE SOME TOP STORIES YOU'RE ALREADY WORKING ON!...WELL, I'LL GO IN YOUR PLACE. IT'LL BE GOOD TO GET AWAY FOR A WHILE!
LATER, AT THE AIRPORT, WHERE THE REPORTERS ARE TO TAKE AN UNSCHEDULED PLANE FLIGHT TO THE CONGO, THE LINE'S MANAGER HAS BAD NEWS...
THE PILOT'S SICK! I MUST CANCEL THE FLIGHT!--GROAN!--THIS MAY COST THE LINE ITS CHARTER...
LET ME HELP!
5

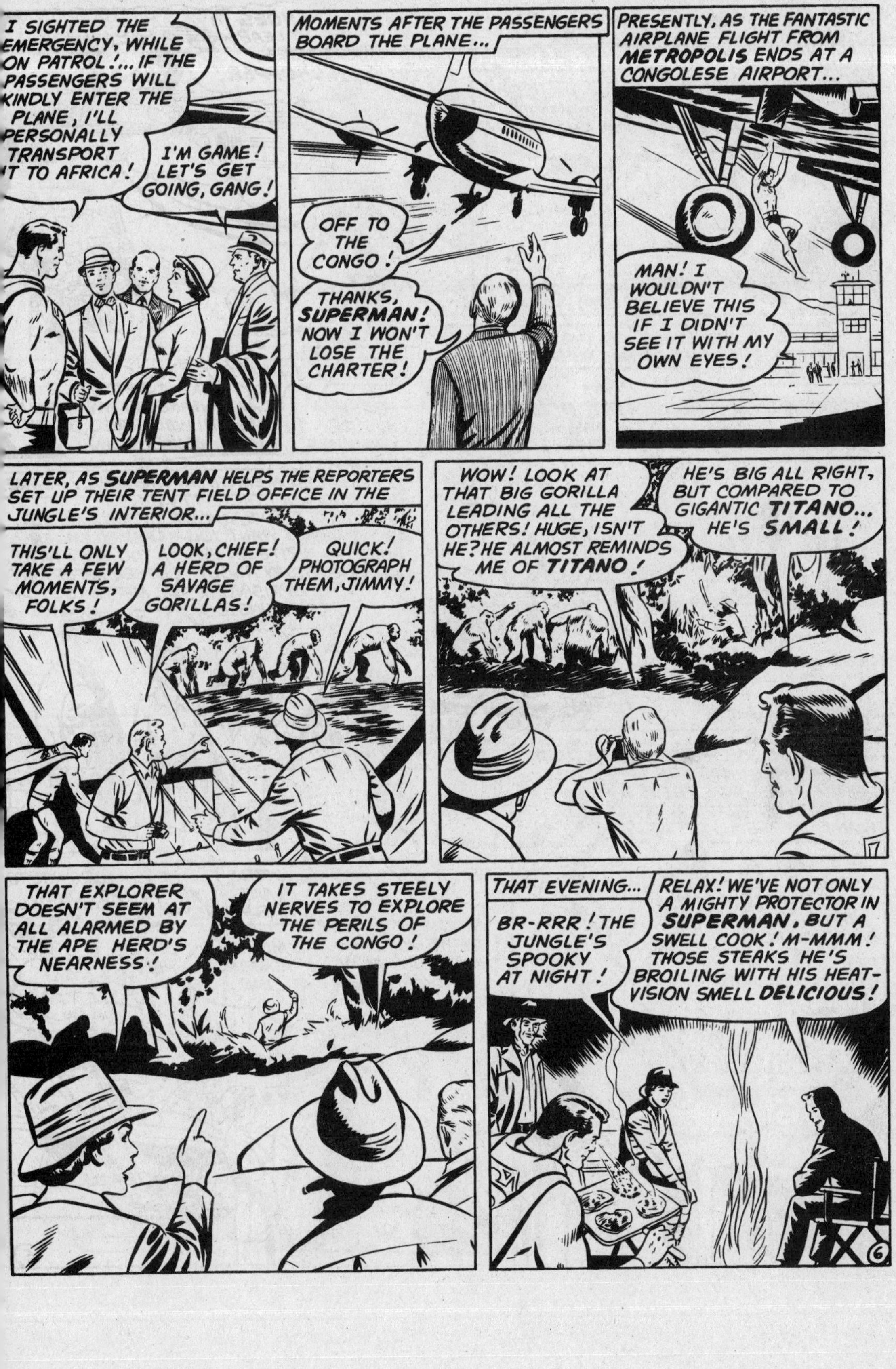
I SIGHTED THE EMERGENCY, WHILE ON PATROL!... IF THE PASSENGERS WILL KINDLY ENTER THE PLANE, I'LL PERSONALLY TRANSPORT IT TO AFRICA!
I'M GAME! LET'S GET GOING, GANG!
MOMENTS AFTER THE PASSENGERS BOARD THE PLANE...
OFF TO THE CONGO!
THANKS, SUPERMAN! NOW I WON'T LOSE THE CHARTER!
PRESENTLY, AS THE FANTASTIC AIRPLANE FLIGHT FROM METROPOLIS ENDS AT A CONGOLESE AIRPORT...
MAN! I WOULDN'T BELIEVE THIS IF I DIDN'T SEE IT WITH MY OWN EYES!
LATER, AS SUPERMAN HELPS THE REPORTERS SET UP THEIR TENT FIELD OFFICE IN THE JUNGLE'S INTERIOR...
THIS'LL ONLY TAKE A FEW MOMENTS, FOLKS!
LOOK, CHIEF! A HERD OF SAVAGE GORILLAS!
QUICK! PHOTOGRAPH THEM, JIMMY!
WOW! LOOK AT THAT BIG GORILLA LEADING ALL THE OTHERS! HUGE, ISN'T HE? HE ALMOST REMINDS ME OF TITANO!
HE'S BIG ALL RIGHT, BUT COMPARED TO GIGANTIC TITANO... HE'S SMALL!
THAT EXPLORER DOESN'T SEEM AT ALL ALARMED BY THE APE HERD'S NEARNESS!
IT TAKES STEELY NERVES TO EXPLORE THE PERILS OF THE CONGO!
THAT EVENING...
BR-RRR! THE JUNGLE'S SPOOKY AT NIGHT!
RELAX! WE'VE NOT ONLY A MIGHTY PROTECTOR IN SUPERMAN, BUT A SWELL COOK! M-MMM! THOSE STEAKS HE'S BROILING WITH HIS HEAT-VISION SMELL DELICIOUS!
6

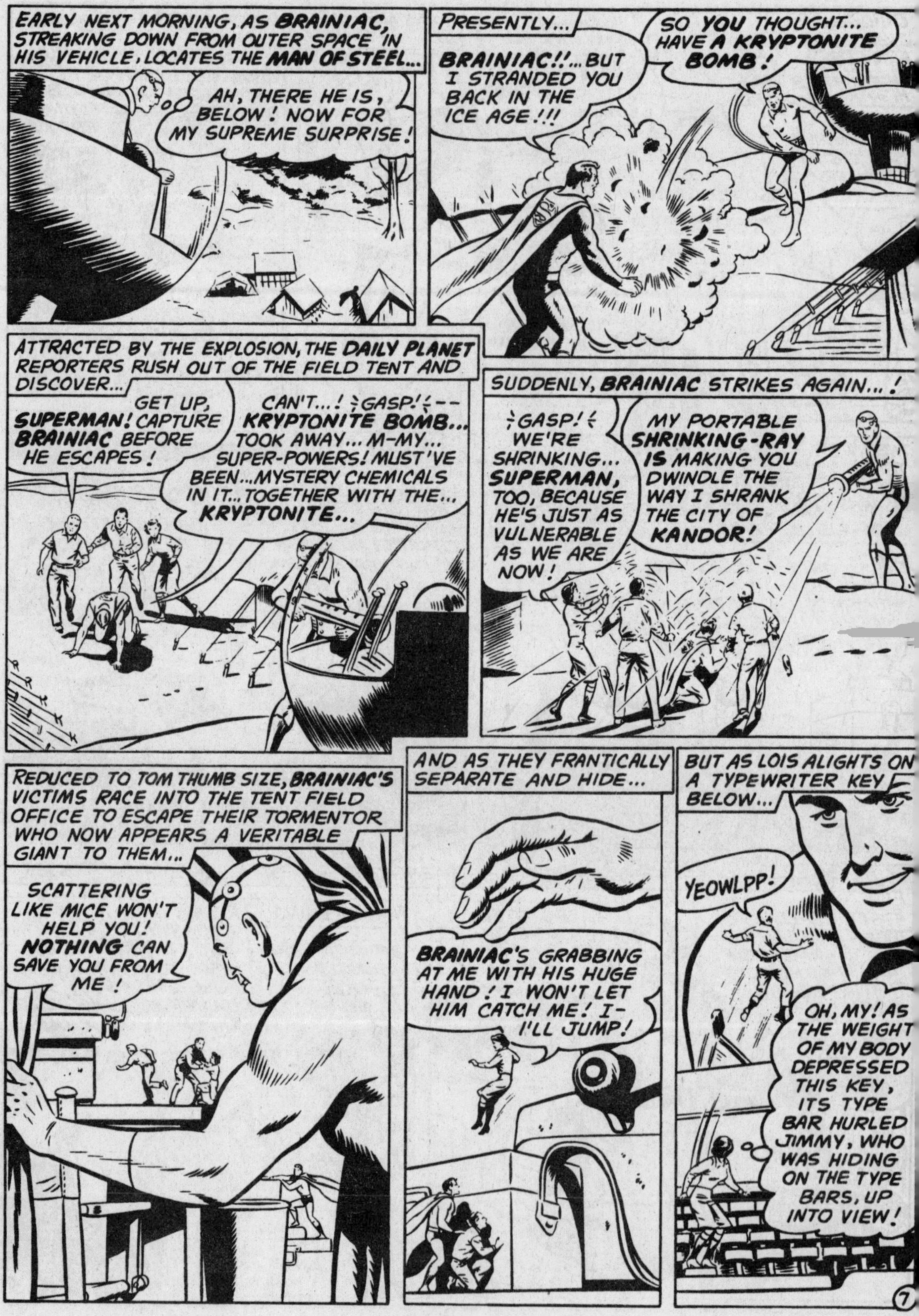
EARLY NEXT MORNING, AS BRAINIAC, STREAKING DOWN FROM OUTER SPACE IN HIS VEHICLE, LOCATES THE MAN OF STEEL...
AH, THERE HE IS, BELOW! NOW FOR MY SUPREME SURPRISE!
PRESENTLY...
BRAINIAC!!...BUT I STRANDED YOU BACK IN THE ICE AGE!!!
SO YOU THOUGHT... HAVE A KRYPTONITE BOMB!
ATTRACTED BY THE EXPLOSION, THE DAILY PLANET REPORTERS RUSH OUT OF THE FIELD TENT AND DISCOVER...
GET UP, SUPERMAN! CAPTURE BRAINIAC BEFORE HE ESCAPES!
CAN'T...! GASP! -- KRYPTONITE BOMB... TOOK AWAY... M-MY... SUPER-POWERS! MUST'VE BEEN...MYSTERY CHEMICALS IN IT...TOGETHER WITH THE... KRYPTONITE...
SUDDENLY, BRAINIAC STRIKES AGAIN...!
GASP! WE'RE SHRINKING... SUPERMAN, TOO, BECAUSE HE'S JUST AS VULNERABLE AS WE ARE NOW!
MY PORTABLE SHRINKING-RAY IS MAKING YOU DWINDLE THE WAY I SHRANK THE CITY OF KANDOR!
REDUCED TO TOM THUMB SIZE, BRAINIAC'S VICTIMS RACE INTO THE TENT FIELD OFFICE TO ESCAPE THEIR TORMENTOR WHO NOW APPEARS A VERITABLE GIANT TO THEM...
SCATTERING LIKE MICE WON'T HELP YOU! NOTHING CAN SAVE YOU FROM ME!
AND AS THEY FRANTICALLY SEPARATE AND HIDE...
BRAINIAC'S GRABBING AT ME WITH HIS HUGE HAND! I WON'T LET HIM CATCH ME! I-I'LL JUMP!
BUT AS LOIS ALIGHTS ON A TYPEWRITER KEY BELOW...
YEOWLPP!
OH, MY! AS THE WEIGHT OF MY BODY DEPRESSED THIS KEY, ITS TYPE BAR HURLED JIMMY, WHO WAS HIDING ON THE TYPE BARS, UP INTO VIEW!
7

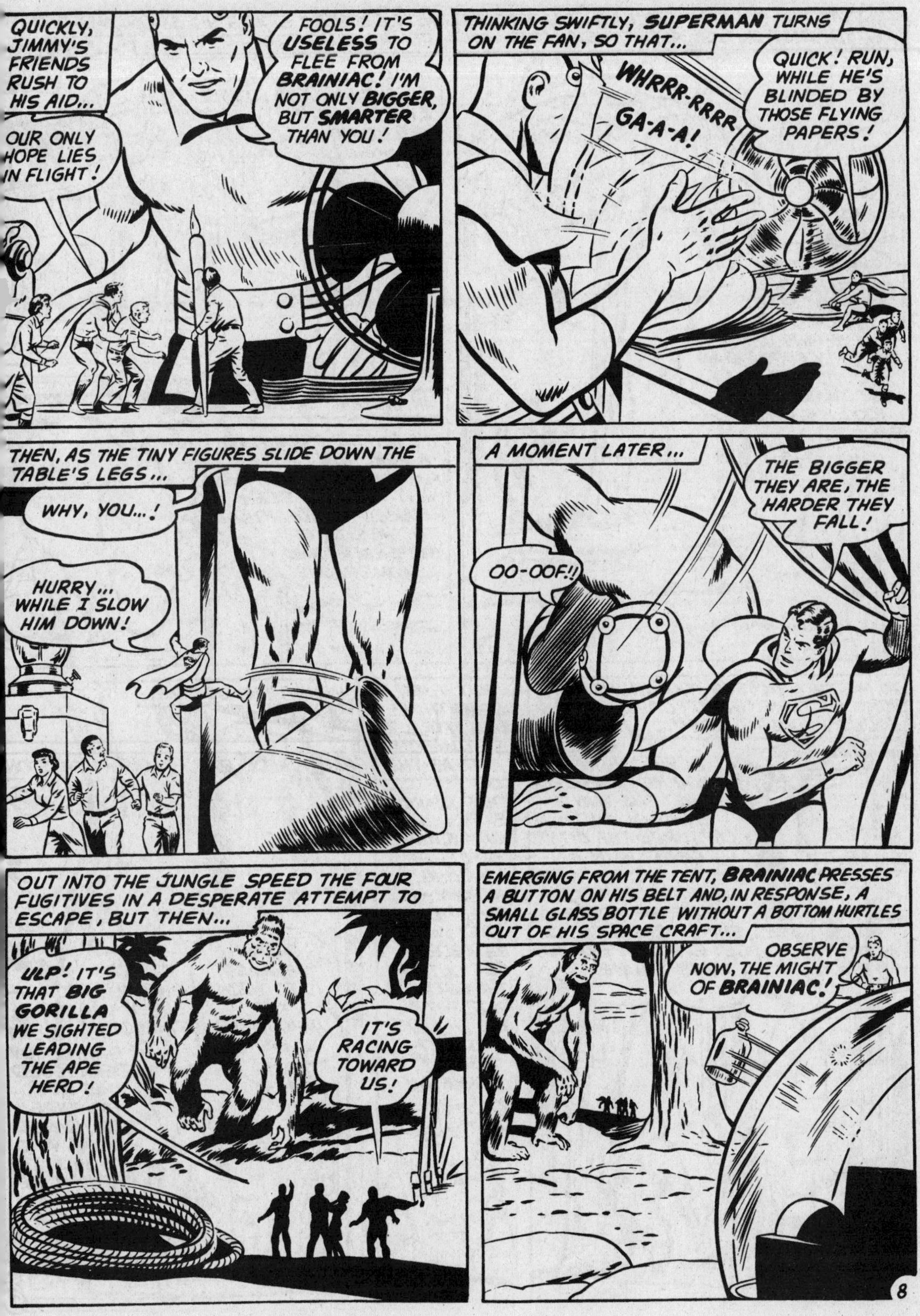
QUICKLY, JIMMY'S FRIENDS RUSH TO HIS AID...
FOOLS! IT'S USELESS TO FLEE FROM BRAINIAC! I'M NOT ONLY BIGGER, BUT SMARTER THAN YOU!
OUR ONLY HOPE LIES IN FLIGHT!
THINKING SWIFTLY, SUPERMAN TURNS ON THE FAN, SO THAT...
WHRRR-RRRR
GA-A-A!
QUICK! RUN, WHILE HE'S BLINDED BY THOSE FLYING PAPERS!
THEN, AS THE TINY FIGURES SLIDE DOWN THE TABLE'S LEGS...
WHY, YOU...!
HURRY... WHILE I SLOW HIM DOWN!
A MOMENT LATER...
THE BIGGER THEY ARE, THE HARDER THEY FALL!
OO-OOF!!
OUT INTO THE JUNGLE SPEED THE FOUR FUGITIVES IN A DESPERATE ATTEMPT TO ESCAPE, BUT THEN...
ULP! IT'S THAT BIG GORILLA WE SIGHTED LEADING THE APE HERD!
IT'S RACING TOWARD US!
EMERGING FROM THE TENT, BRAINIAC PRESSES A BUTTON ON HIS BELT AND, IN RESPONSE, A SMALL GLASS BOTTLE WITHOUT A BOTTOM HURTLES OUT OF HIS SPACE CRAFT...
OBSERVE NOW, THE MIGHT OF BRAINIAC!
8

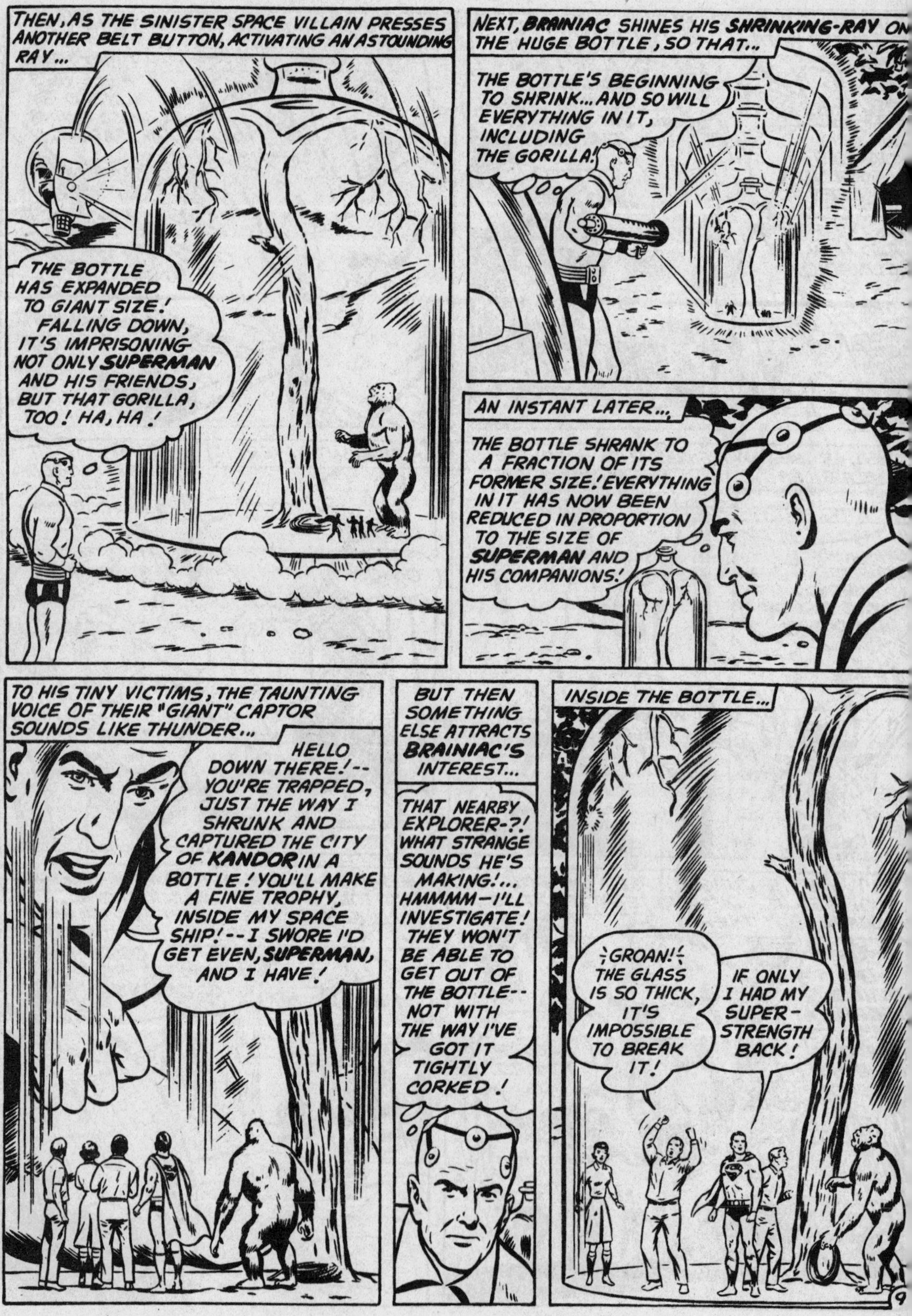
THEN, AS THE SINISTER SPACE VILLAIN PRESSES ANOTHER BELT BUTTON, ACTIVATING AN ASTOUNDING RAY...
THE BOTTLE HAS EXPANDED TO GIANT SIZE! FALLING DOWN, IT'S IMPRISONING NOT ONLY SUPERMAN AND HIS FRIENDS, BUT THAT GORILLA, TOO! HA, HA!
NEXT, BRAINIAC SHINES HIS SHRINKING-RAY ON THE HUGE BOTTLE, SO THAT...
THE BOTTLE'S BEGINNING TO SHRINK... AND SO WILL EVERYTHING IN IT, INCLUDING THE GORILLA!
AN INSTANT LATER...,
THE BOTTLE SHRANK TO A FRACTION OF ITS FORMER SIZE! EVERYTHING IN IT HAS NOW BEEN REDUCED IN PROPORTION TO THE SIZE OF SUPERMAN AND HIS COMPANIONS!
TO HIS TINY VICTIMS, THE TAUNTING VOICE OF THEIR "GIANT" CAPTOR SOUNDS LIKE THUNDER...
HELLO DOWN THERE!--YOU'RE TRAPPED, JUST THE WAY I SHRUNK AND CAPTURED THE CITY OF KANDOR IN A BOTTLE! YOU'LL MAKE A FINE TROPHY, INSIDE MY SPACE SHIP!--I SWORE I'D GET EVEN, SUPERMAN, AND I HAVE!
BUT THEN SOMETHING ELSE ATTRACTS BRAINIAC'S INTEREST...
THAT NEARBY EXPLORER-?! WHAT STRANGE SOUNDS HE'S MAKING!... HMMMM—I'LL INVESTIGATE! THEY WON'T BE ABLE TO GET OUT OF THE BOTTLE--NOT WITH THE WAY I'VE GOT IT TIGHTLY CORKED!
INSIDE THE BOTTLE...
GROAN! THE GLASS IS SO THICK, IT'S IMPOSSIBLE TO BREAK IT!
IF ONLY I HAD MY SUPER-STRENGTH BACK!
9

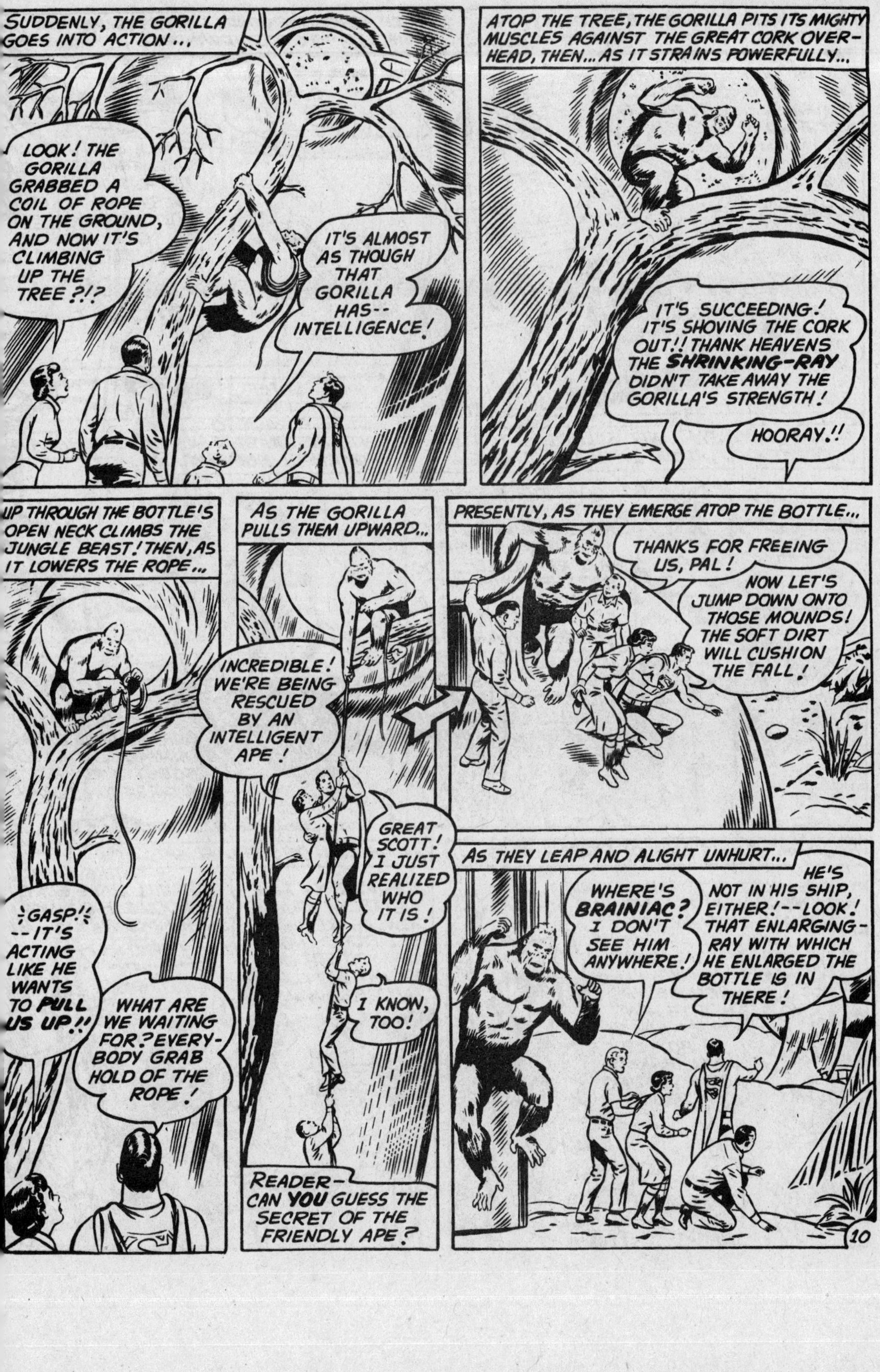
SUDDENLY, THE GORILLA GOES INTO ACTION...
LOOK! THE GORILLA GRABBED A COIL OF ROPE ON THE GROUND, AND NOW IT'S CLIMBING UP THE TREE?!?
IT'S ALMOST AS THOUGH THAT GORILLA HAS-- INTELLIGENCE!
ATOP THE TREE, THE GORILLA PITS ITS MIGHTY MUSCLES AGAINST THE GREAT CORK OVER-HEAD, THEN... AS IT STRAINS POWERFULLY...
IT'S SUCCEEDING! IT'S SHOVING THE CORK OUT!! THANK HEAVENS THE SHRINKING-RAY DIDN'T TAKE AWAY THE GORILLA'S STRENGTH!
HOORAY!!
UP THROUGH THE BOTTLE'S OPEN NECK CLIMBS THE JUNGLE BEAST! THEN, AS IT LOWERS THE ROPE...
GASP! --IT'S ACTING LIKE HE WANTS TO PULL US UP!!
WHAT ARE WE WAITING FOR? EVERY-BODY GRAB HOLD OF THE ROPE!
AS THE GORILLA PULLS THEM UPWARD...
INCREDIBLE! WE'RE BEING RESCUED BY AN INTELLIGENT APE!
GREAT SCOTT! I JUST REALIZED WHO IT IS!
I KNOW, TOO!
READER-- CAN YOU GUESS THE SECRET OF THE FRIENDLY APE?
PRESENTLY, AS THEY EMERGE ATOP THE BOTTLE...
THANKS FOR FREEING US, PAL!
NOW LET'S JUMP DOWN ONTO THOSE MOUNDS! THE SOFT DIRT WILL CUSHION THE FALL!
AS THEY LEAP AND ALIGHT UNHURT...
WHERE'S BRAINIAC? I DON'T SEE HIM ANYWHERE!
HE'S NOT IN HIS SHIP, EITHER!--LOOK! THAT ENLARGING-RAY WITH WHICH HE ENLARGED THE BOTTLE IS IN THERE!
10

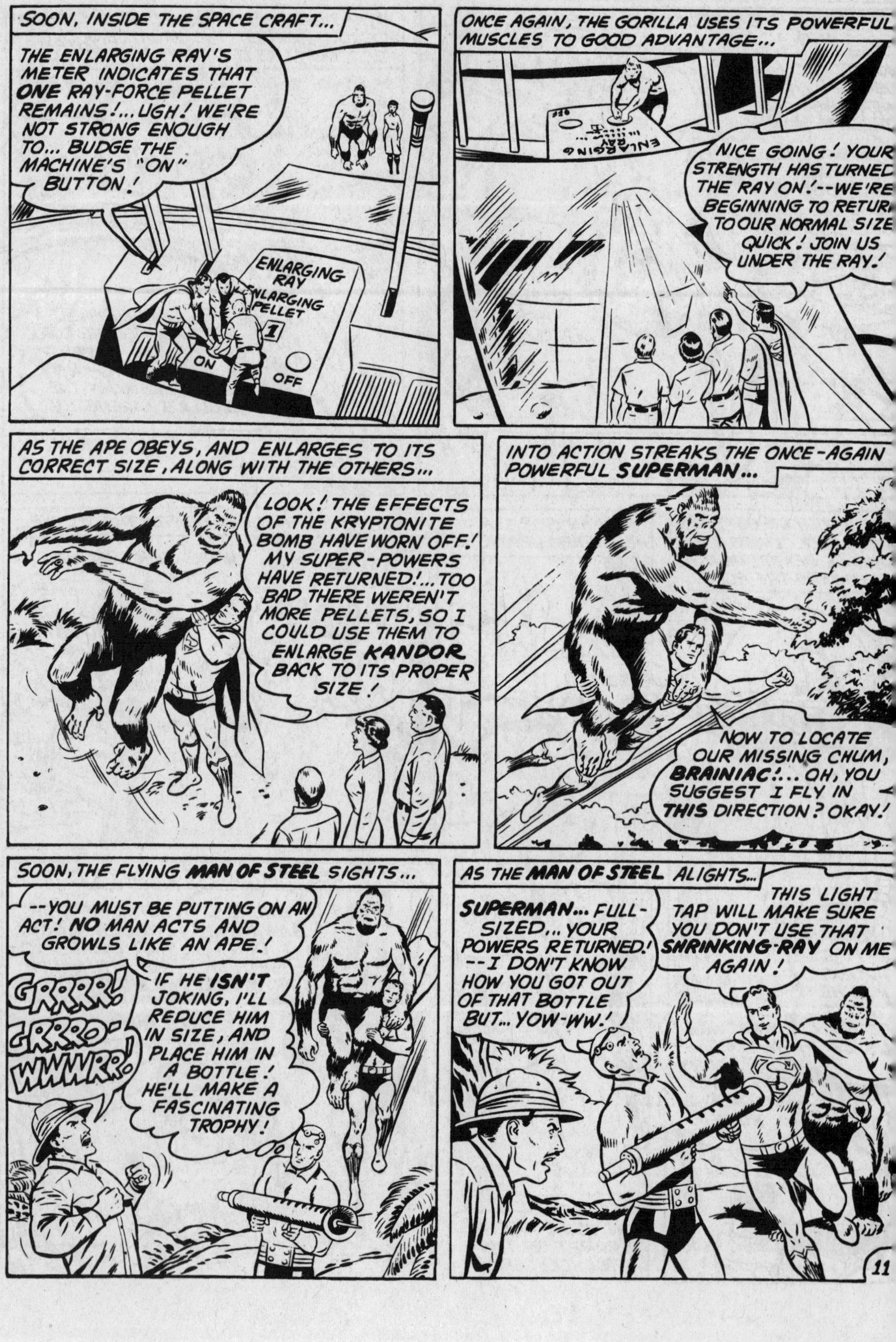
SOON, INSIDE THE SPACE CRAFT...
THE ENLARGING RAY'S METER INDICATES THAT ONE RAY-FORCE PELLET REMAINS!... UGH! WE'RE NOT STRONG ENOUGH TO... BUDGE THE MACHINE'S "ON" BUTTON!
ENLARGING RAY
ENLARGING PELLET
1
ON
OFF
ONCE AGAIN, THE GORILLA USES ITS POWERFUL MUSCLES TO GOOD ADVANTAGE...
NICE GOING! YOUR STRENGTH HAS TURNED THE RAY ON!--WE'RE BEGINNING TO RETUR TO OUR NORMAL SIZE QUICK! JOIN US UNDER THE RAY!
AS THE APE OBEYS, AND ENLARGES TO ITS CORRECT SIZE, ALONG WITH THE OTHERS...
LOOK! THE EFFECTS OF THE KRYPTONITE BOMB HAVE WORN OFF! MY SUPER-POWERS HAVE RETURNED!... TOO BAD THERE WEREN'T MORE PELLETS, SO I COULD USE THEM TO ENLARGE KANDOR BACK TO ITS PROPER SIZE!
INTO ACTION STREAKS THE ONCE-AGAIN POWERFUL SUPERMAN...
NOW TO LOCATE OUR MISSING CHUM, BRAINIAC!... OH, YOU SUGGEST I FLY IN THIS DIRECTION? OKAY!
SOON, THE FLYING MAN OF STEEL SIGHTS...
--YOU MUST BE PUTTING ON AN ACT! NO MAN ACTS AND GROWLS LIKE AN APE!
GRRRR! GRRRO-WWWRR!
IF HE ISN'T JOKING, I'LL REDUCE HIM IN SIZE, AND PLACE HIM IN A BOTTLE! HE'LL MAKE A FASCINATING TROPHY!
AS THE MAN OF STEEL ALIGHTS...
SUPERMAN... FULL-SIZED... YOUR POWERS RETURNED! --I DON'T KNOW HOW YOU GOT OUT OF THAT BOTTLE BUT... YOW-WW!
THIS LIGHT TAP WILL MAKE SURE YOU DON'T USE THAT SHRINKING-RAY ON ME AGAIN!
11

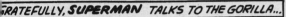

GRATEFULLY, *SUPERMAN* TALKS TO THE GORILLA...

THANKS AGAIN!... WHEN JIMMY AND I NOTICED YOUR MAGIC RING AS YOU PULLED US OUT OF THE BOTTLE, WE REALIZED WE WERE BEING RESCUED BY... *CONGORILLA,* THE APE WITH THE MIND OF A MAN!

THE GORILLA IS RUBBING THE MAGIC RING ON ITS FINGER, WHICH IS IDENTICAL TO THE MAGIC RING CONGO BILL WEARS! THAT'LL SWITCH THE INTELLIGENCE OF THE APE, AND CONGO BILL, BACK TO THEIR PROPER BODIES!

OFF WANDERS THE GORILLA, AS CONGO BILL, NO LONGER ACTING APE-LIKE, SPEAKS...

GLAD TO BE HELPFUL, *SUPERMAN!* WHEN I SAW *BRAINIAC* IN HIS SPACE SHIP EARLIER TODAY, I GUESSED HE PLANNED TO MAKE TROUBLE FOR YOU!

"EARLIER, I'D SEEN YOU SETTING UP CAMP FOR YOUR FRIENDS. THERE WASN'T TIME ENOUGH FOR ME TO REACH YOU AS CONGO BILL, BUT SINCE THE *GOLDEN GORILLA* WAS STILL NEAR YOUR CAMP..."

MUST AID *SUPERMAN!* FIRST, I'LL SWALLOW THESE SLEEPING TABLETS...

"THEN I RUBBED THE MAGIC GORILLA RING, GIVEN TO ME BY A CONGO WITCH DOCTOR..."

IN JUST A FEW MOMENTS *MY* MIND WILL BE TRANSFERRED INTO THE BODY OF THE GOLDEN GORILLA APE-HERD LEADER, WHILE *HIS* APE BRAIN WILL TAKE OVER MY HUMAN BODY!

"IMMEDIATELY, THE INTELLIGENCES WERE SWITCHED..."

I'M CLOSE TO THE CAMP, NOW! I HOPE I ARRIVE SOON ENOUGH TO HELP THEM WITH THIS POWERFUL GORILLA-BODY!

12

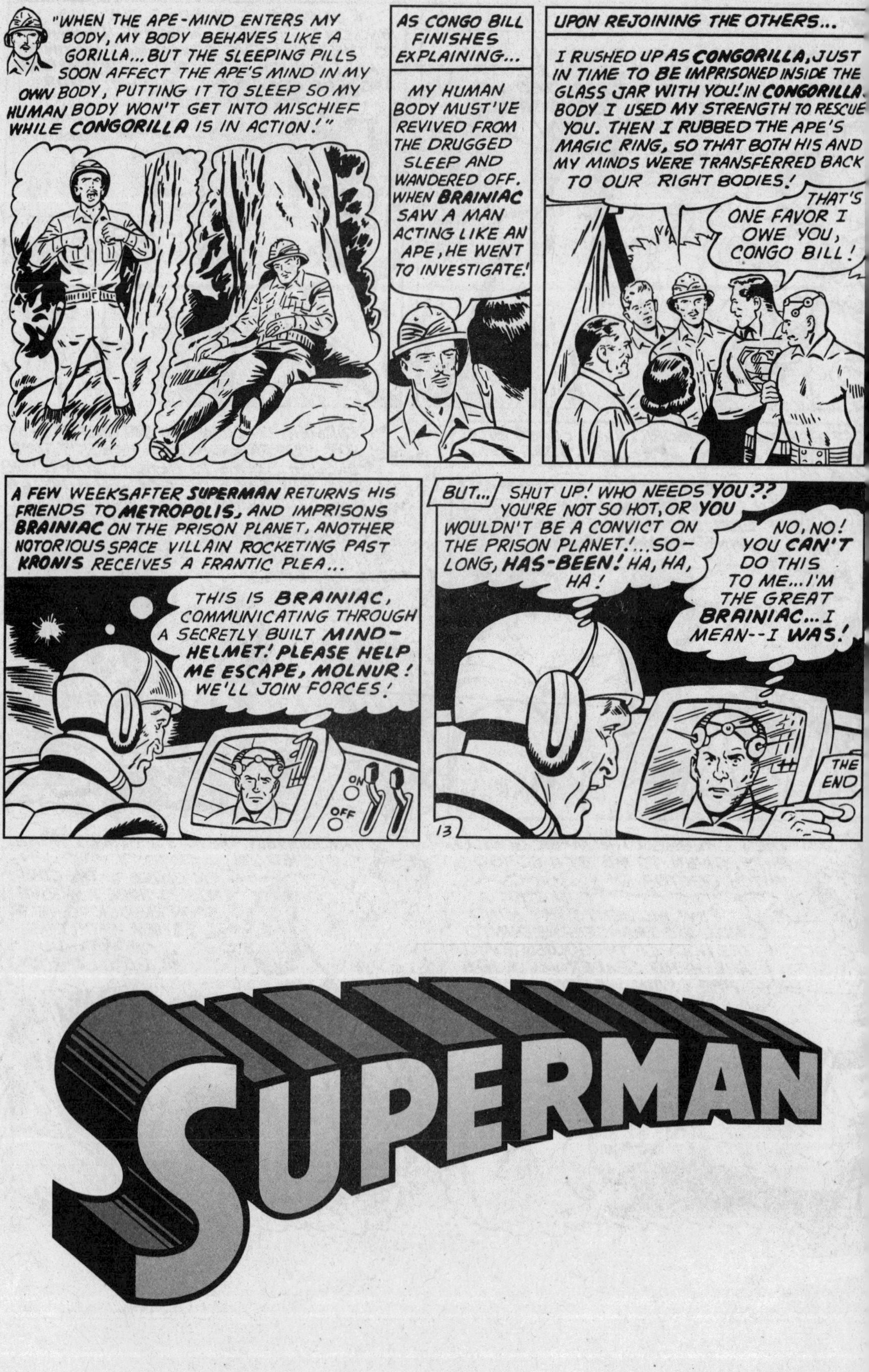
"WHEN THE APE-MIND ENTERS MY BODY, MY BODY BEHAVES LIKE A GORILLA... BUT THE SLEEPING PILLS SOON AFFECT THE APE'S MIND IN MY OWN BODY, PUTTING IT TO SLEEP SO MY HUMAN BODY WON'T GET INTO MISCHIEF WHILE CONGORILLA IS IN ACTION!"
AS CONGO BILL FINISHES EXPLAINING...
MY HUMAN BODY MUST'VE REVIVED FROM THE DRUGGED SLEEP AND WANDERED OFF. WHEN BRAINIAC SAW A MAN ACTING LIKE AN APE, HE WENT TO INVESTIGATE!
UPON REJOINING THE OTHERS...
I RUSHED UP AS CONGORILLA, JUST IN TIME TO BE IMPRISONED INSIDE THE GLASS JAR WITH YOU! IN CONGORILLA BODY I USED MY STRENGTH TO RESCUE YOU. THEN I RUBBED THE APE'S MAGIC RING, SO THAT BOTH HIS AND MY MINDS WERE TRANSFERRED BACK TO OUR RIGHT BODIES!
THAT'S ONE FAVOR I OWE YOU, CONGO BILL!
A FEW WEEKS AFTER SUPERMAN RETURNS HIS FRIENDS TO METROPOLIS, AND IMPRISONS BRAINIAC ON THE PRISON PLANET, ANOTHER NOTORIOUS SPACE VILLAIN ROCKETING PAST KRONIS RECEIVES A FRANTIC PLEA...
THIS IS BRAINIAC, COMMUNICATING THROUGH A SECRETLY BUILT MIND-HELMET! PLEASE HELP ME ESCAPE, MOLNUR! WE'LL JOIN FORCES!
ON
OFF
BUT...
SHUT UP! WHO NEEDS YOU?? YOU'RE NOT SO HOT, OR YOU WOULDN'T BE A CONVICT ON THE PRISON PLANET!...SO-LONG, HAS-BEEN! HA, HA, HA!
NO, NO! YOU CAN'T DO THIS TO ME...I'M THE GREAT BRAINIAC...I MEAN--I WAS!
THE END
13

SUPERMAN

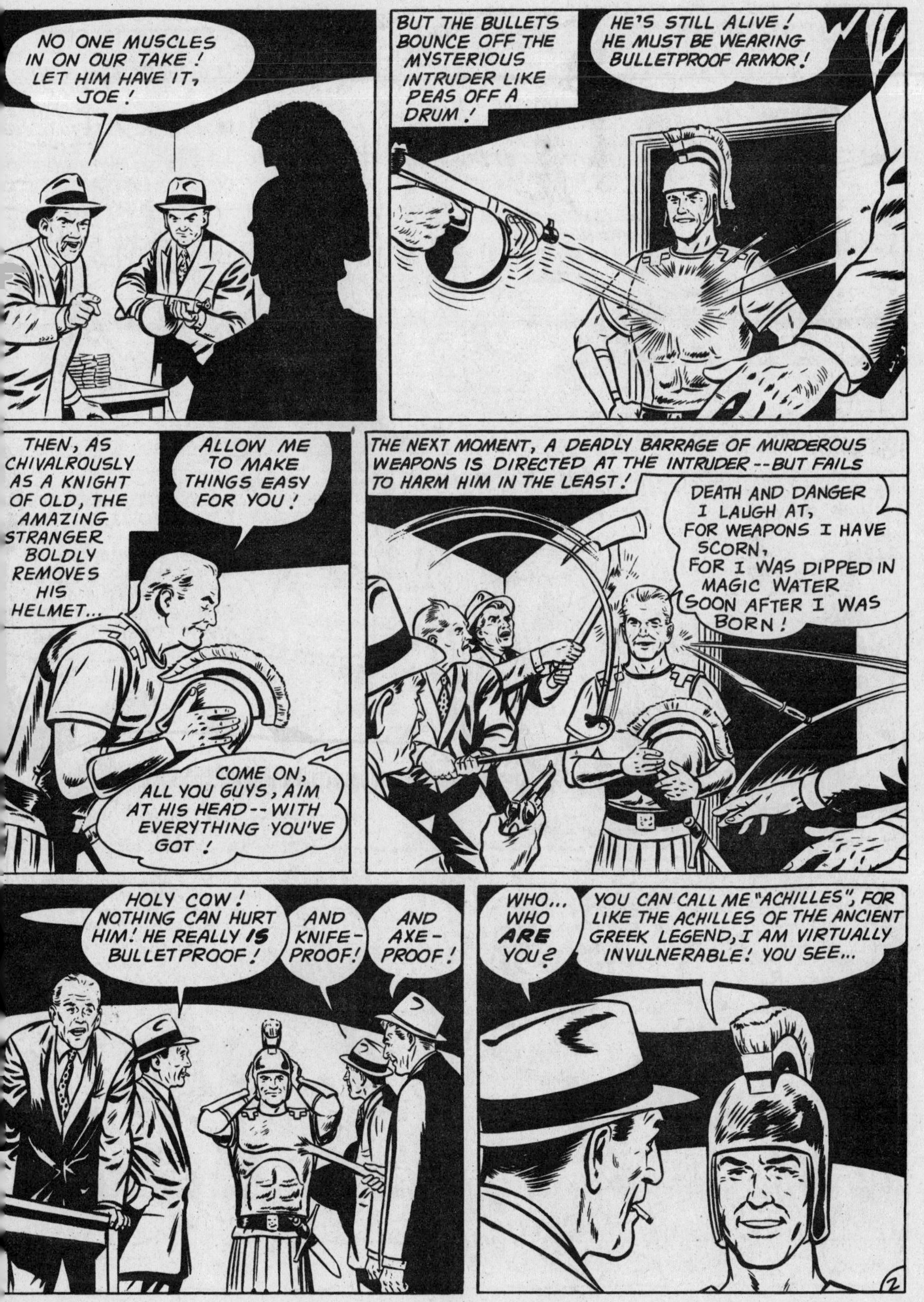
NO ONE MUSCLES IN ON OUR TAKE! LET HIM HAVE IT, JOE!
BUT THE BULLETS BOUNCE OFF THE MYSTERIOUS INTRUDER LIKE PEAS OFF A DRUM!
HE'S STILL ALIVE! HE MUST BE WEARING BULLETPROOF ARMOR!
THEN, AS CHIVALROUSLY AS A KNIGHT OF OLD, THE AMAZING STRANGER BOLDLY REMOVES HIS HELMET...
ALLOW ME TO MAKE THINGS EASY FOR YOU!
COME ON, ALL YOU GUYS, AIM AT HIS HEAD--WITH EVERYTHING YOU'VE GOT!
THE NEXT MOMENT, A DEADLY BARRAGE OF MURDEROUS WEAPONS IS DIRECTED AT THE INTRUDER--BUT FAILS TO HARM HIM IN THE LEAST!
DEATH AND DANGER I LAUGH AT, FOR WEAPONS I HAVE SCORN, FOR I WAS DIPPED IN MAGIC WATER SOON AFTER I WAS BORN!
HOLY COW! NOTHING CAN HURT HIM! HE REALLY **IS** BULLETPROOF!
AND KNIFE-PROOF!
AND AXE-PROOF!
WHO... WHO **ARE** YOU?
YOU CAN CALL ME "ACHILLES", FOR LIKE THE ACHILLES OF THE ANCIENT GREEK LEGEND, I AM VIRTUALLY INVULNERABLE! YOU SEE...
2

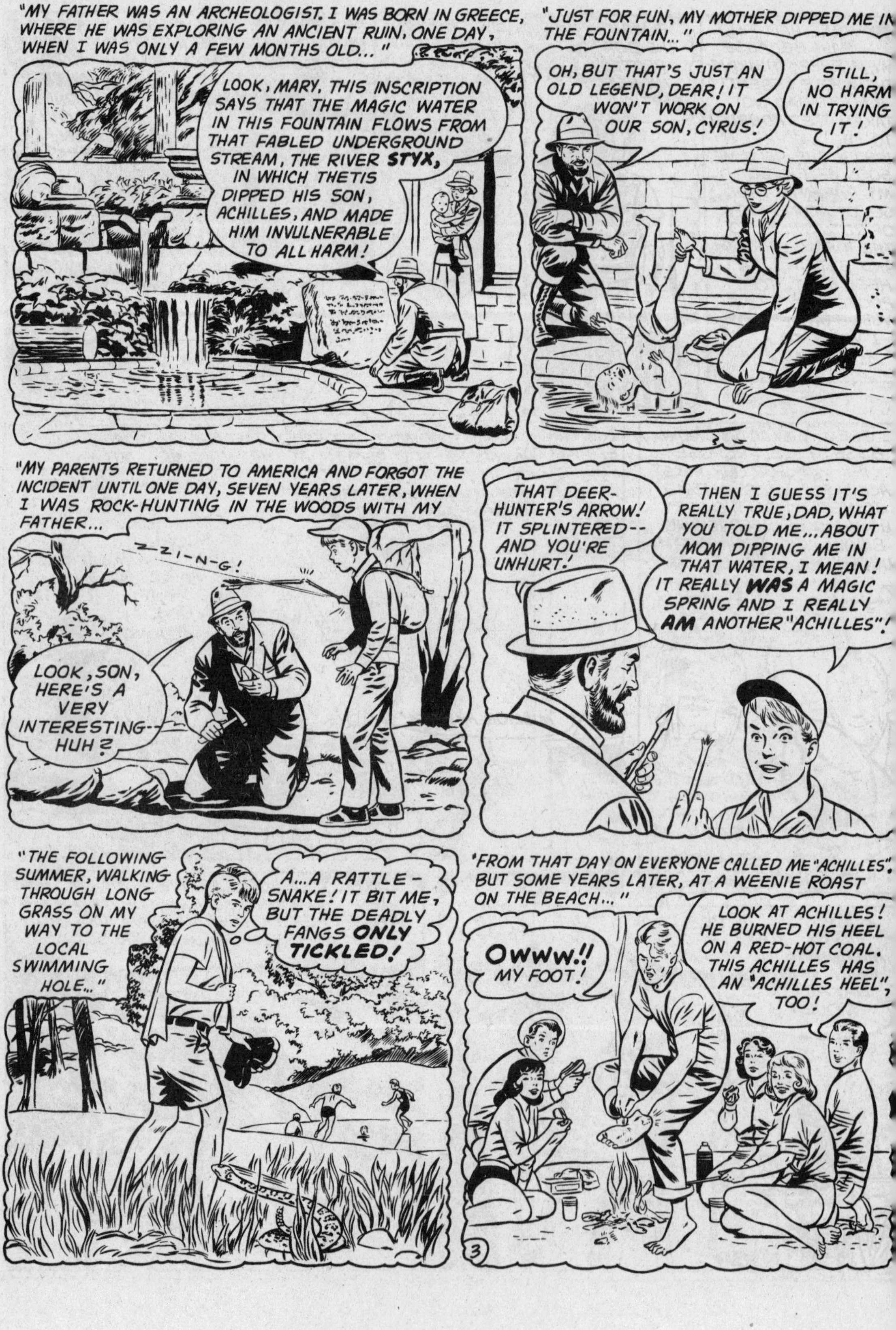
"MY FATHER WAS AN ARCHEOLOGIST. I WAS BORN IN GREECE, WHERE HE WAS EXPLORING AN ANCIENT RUIN. ONE DAY, WHEN I WAS ONLY A FEW MONTHS OLD..."
LOOK, MARY. THIS INSCRIPTION SAYS THAT THE MAGIC WATER IN THIS FOUNTAIN FLOWS FROM THAT FABLED UNDERGROUND STREAM, THE RIVER STYX, IN WHICH THETIS DIPPED HIS SON, ACHILLES, AND MADE HIM INVULNERABLE TO ALL HARM!
"JUST FOR FUN, MY MOTHER DIPPED ME IN THE FOUNTAIN..."
OH, BUT THAT'S JUST AN OLD LEGEND, DEAR! IT WON'T WORK ON OUR SON, CYRUS!
STILL, NO HARM IN TRYING IT!
"MY PARENTS RETURNED TO AMERICA AND FORGOT THE INCIDENT UNTIL ONE DAY, SEVEN YEARS LATER, WHEN I WAS ROCK-HUNTING IN THE WOODS WITH MY FATHER...
Z-Z-I-N-G!
LOOK, SON, HERE'S A VERY INTERESTING-- HUH?
THAT DEER-HUNTER'S ARROW! IT SPLINTERED-- AND YOU'RE UNHURT!
THEN I GUESS IT'S REALLY TRUE, DAD, WHAT YOU TOLD ME... ABOUT MOM DIPPING ME IN THAT WATER, I MEAN! IT REALLY WAS A MAGIC SPRING AND I REALLY AM ANOTHER "ACHILLES"!
"THE FOLLOWING SUMMER, WALKING THROUGH LONG GRASS ON MY WAY TO THE LOCAL SWIMMING HOLE..."
A...A RATTLE-SNAKE! IT BIT ME, BUT THE DEADLY FANGS ONLY TICKLED!
"FROM THAT DAY ON EVERYONE CALLED ME "ACHILLES", BUT SOME YEARS LATER, AT A WEENIE ROAST ON THE BEACH..."
OWWW!! MY FOOT!
LOOK AT ACHILLES! HE BURNED HIS HEEL ON A RED-HOT COAL. THIS ACHILLES HAS AN "ACHILLES HEEL", TOO!
3

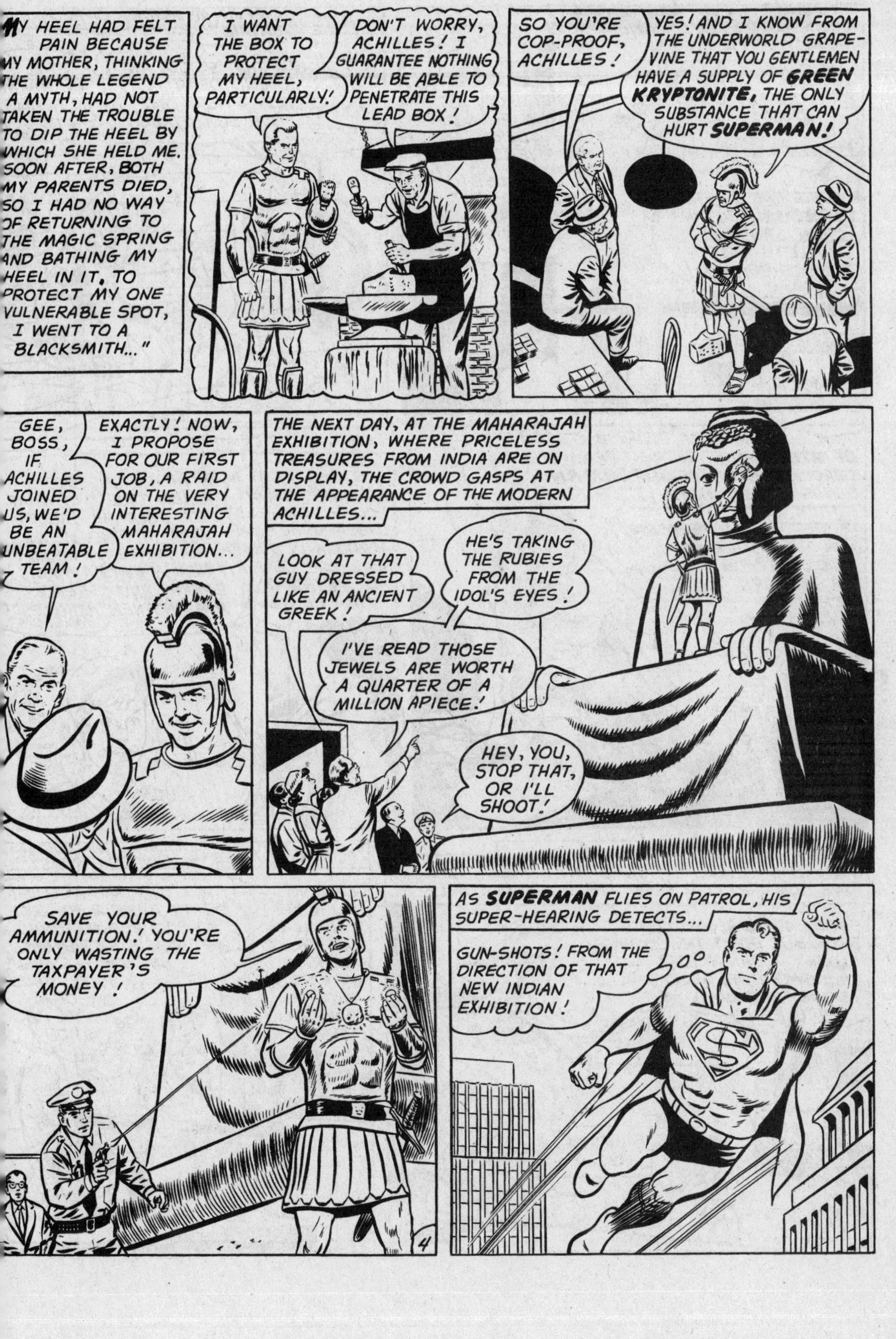
"MY HEEL HAD FELT PAIN BECAUSE MY MOTHER, THINKING THE WHOLE LEGEND A MYTH, HAD NOT TAKEN THE TROUBLE TO DIP THE HEEL BY WHICH SHE HELD ME. SOON AFTER, BOTH MY PARENTS DIED, SO I HAD NO WAY OF RETURNING TO THE MAGIC SPRING AND BATHING MY HEEL IN IT, TO PROTECT MY ONE VULNERABLE SPOT, I WENT TO A BLACKSMITH..."
I WANT THE BOX TO PROTECT MY HEEL, PARTICULARLY!
DON'T WORRY, ACHILLES! I GUARANTEE NOTHING WILL BE ABLE TO PENETRATE THIS LEAD BOX!
SO YOU'RE COP-PROOF, ACHILLES!
YES! AND I KNOW FROM THE UNDERWORLD GRAPE-VINE THAT YOU GENTLEMEN HAVE A SUPPLY OF GREEN KRYPTONITE, THE ONLY SUBSTANCE THAT CAN HURT SUPERMAN!
GEE, BOSS, IF ACHILLES JOINED US, WE'D BE AN UNBEATABLE TEAM!
EXACTLY! NOW, I PROPOSE FOR OUR FIRST JOB, A RAID ON THE VERY INTERESTING MAHARAJAH EXHIBITION...
THE NEXT DAY, AT THE MAHARAJAH EXHIBITION, WHERE PRICELESS TREASURES FROM INDIA ARE ON DISPLAY, THE CROWD GASPS AT THE APPEARANCE OF THE MODERN ACHILLES...
LOOK AT THAT GUY DRESSED LIKE AN ANCIENT GREEK!
HE'S TAKING THE RUBIES FROM THE IDOL'S EYES!
I'VE READ THOSE JEWELS ARE WORTH A QUARTER OF A MILLION APIECE!
HEY, YOU, STOP THAT, OR I'LL SHOOT!
SAVE YOUR AMMUNITION! YOU'RE ONLY WASTING THE TAXPAYER'S MONEY!
4
AS SUPERMAN FLIES ON PATROL, HIS SUPER-HEARING DETECTS...
GUN-SHOTS! FROM THE DIRECTION OF THAT NEW INDIAN EXHIBITION!

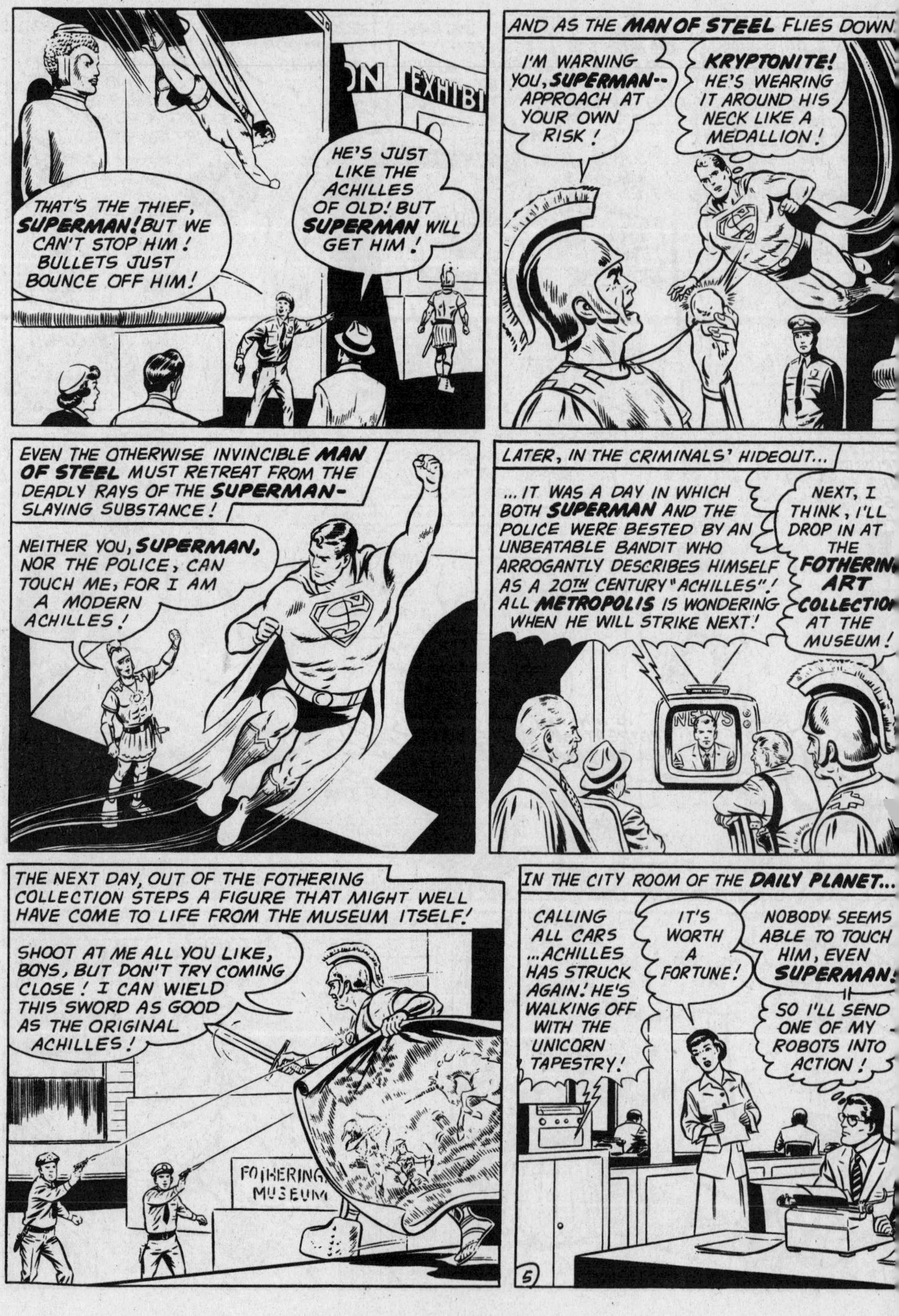
THAT'S THE THIEF, SUPERMAN! BUT WE CAN'T STOP HIM! BULLETS JUST BOUNCE OFF HIM!
HE'S JUST LIKE THE ACHILLES OF OLD! BUT SUPERMAN WILL GET HIM!
AND AS THE MAN OF STEEL FLIES DOWN
I'M WARNING YOU, SUPERMAN-- APPROACH AT YOUR OWN RISK!
KRYPTONITE! HE'S WEARING IT AROUND HIS NECK LIKE A MEDALLION!
EVEN THE OTHERWISE INVINCIBLE MAN OF STEEL MUST RETREAT FROM THE DEADLY RAYS OF THE SUPERMAN-SLAYING SUBSTANCE!
NEITHER YOU, SUPERMAN, NOR THE POLICE, CAN TOUCH ME, FOR I AM A MODERN ACHILLES!
LATER, IN THE CRIMINALS' HIDEOUT...
...IT WAS A DAY IN WHICH BOTH SUPERMAN AND THE POLICE WERE BESTED BY AN UNBEATABLE BANDIT WHO ARROGANTLY DESCRIBES HIMSELF AS A 20TH CENTURY "ACHILLES"! ALL METROPOLIS IS WONDERING WHEN HE WILL STRIKE NEXT!
NEXT, I THINK, I'LL DROP IN AT THE FOTHERIN ART COLLECTIO AT THE MUSEUM!
NEWS
THE NEXT DAY, OUT OF THE FOTHERING COLLECTION STEPS A FIGURE THAT MIGHT WELL HAVE COME TO LIFE FROM THE MUSEUM ITSELF!
SHOOT AT ME ALL YOU LIKE, BOYS, BUT DON'T TRY COMING CLOSE! I CAN WIELD THIS SWORD AS GOOD AS THE ORIGINAL ACHILLES!
FOTHERING MUSEUM
IN THE CITY ROOM OF THE DAILY PLANET...
CALLING ALL CARS ...ACHILLES HAS STRUCK AGAIN! HE'S WALKING OFF WITH THE UNICORN TAPESTRY!
IT'S WORTH A FORTUNE!
NOBODY SEEMS ABLE TO TOUCH HIM, EVEN SUPERMAN!
SO I'LL SEND ONE OF MY ROBOTS INTO ACTION!
5

SECONDS LATER, ACTIVATED BY **SUPERMAN'S** X-RAY VISION, A **SUPERMAN** ROBOT STREAKS FROM ITS SECRET HIDING PLACE IN CLARK KENT'S APARTMENT, TRAVELING AT SUCH SUPER-SPEED ITS FLIGHT IS INVISIBLE TO THE HUMAN EYE!

ROBOT S-3 ANSWERING YOUR SUMMONS, MASTER!

BUT WHEN THE ROBOT NEARS ACHILLES!

YOU CAN'T FOOL **ME!** YOU'RE A ROBOT! YOU'RE NOTHING BUT A PIECE OF STEEL JUNK THAT CAN'T TOUCH ME ANY MORE THAN COPS' BULLETS OR **SUPERMAN** HIMSELF!

SPLIT SECONDS LATER, TRUE TO ACHILLES' BOAST, THE **SUPERMAN** ROBOT SCURRIES AWAY LIKE A FRIGHTENED RABBIT!

STRANGE -- I CAN'T GO NEAR HIM -- SOME INVISIBLE FORCE IS MAKING ME RETREAT! MY MASTER WILL BE DISAPPOINTED!

LATER, AT THE **PLANET** OFFICE, AS CLARK AND LOIS EXAMINE A CLOSE-UP PICTURE OF ACHILLES' FOOT TAKEN BY JIMMY OLSEN...

WELL, CLARK, I GUESS HE'LL GET AWAY WITH HIS CRIMES UNTIL SOMEONE CAN GET THAT BOX OFF HIS FOOT AND EXPOSE HIS ACHILLES HEEL!

I'M NOT SO SURE ABOUT THAT, LOIS! I HAVE A HUNCH THERE'S SOMETHING PHONEY ABOUT MR. ACHILLES!

A FEW DAYS LATER, **SUPERMAN** STANDS GUARD OVER **METROPOLIS**, LIKE AN AERIAL SENTRY...

MOST CRIMINALS REPEAT THEMSELVES...THEIR CRIMES FOLLOW A PREDICTABLE PATTERN. IF I'M RIGHT, ACHILLES WILL BE DRAWN TO THE NEWLY OPENED **HALL OF KINGS AND QUEENS** AT THE COLISEUM GARDENS... WHERE I'VE GOT A TRAP WAITING FOR HIM!

COLISEUM GARDENS EXHIBITION HALL OF KINGS AND QUEENS

AND SURE ENOUGH, ACHILLES DOES VISIT THE HALL...

IT'S ACHILLES AGAIN! NOBODY CAN STOP HIM!

NOT EVEN **SUPERMAN!**

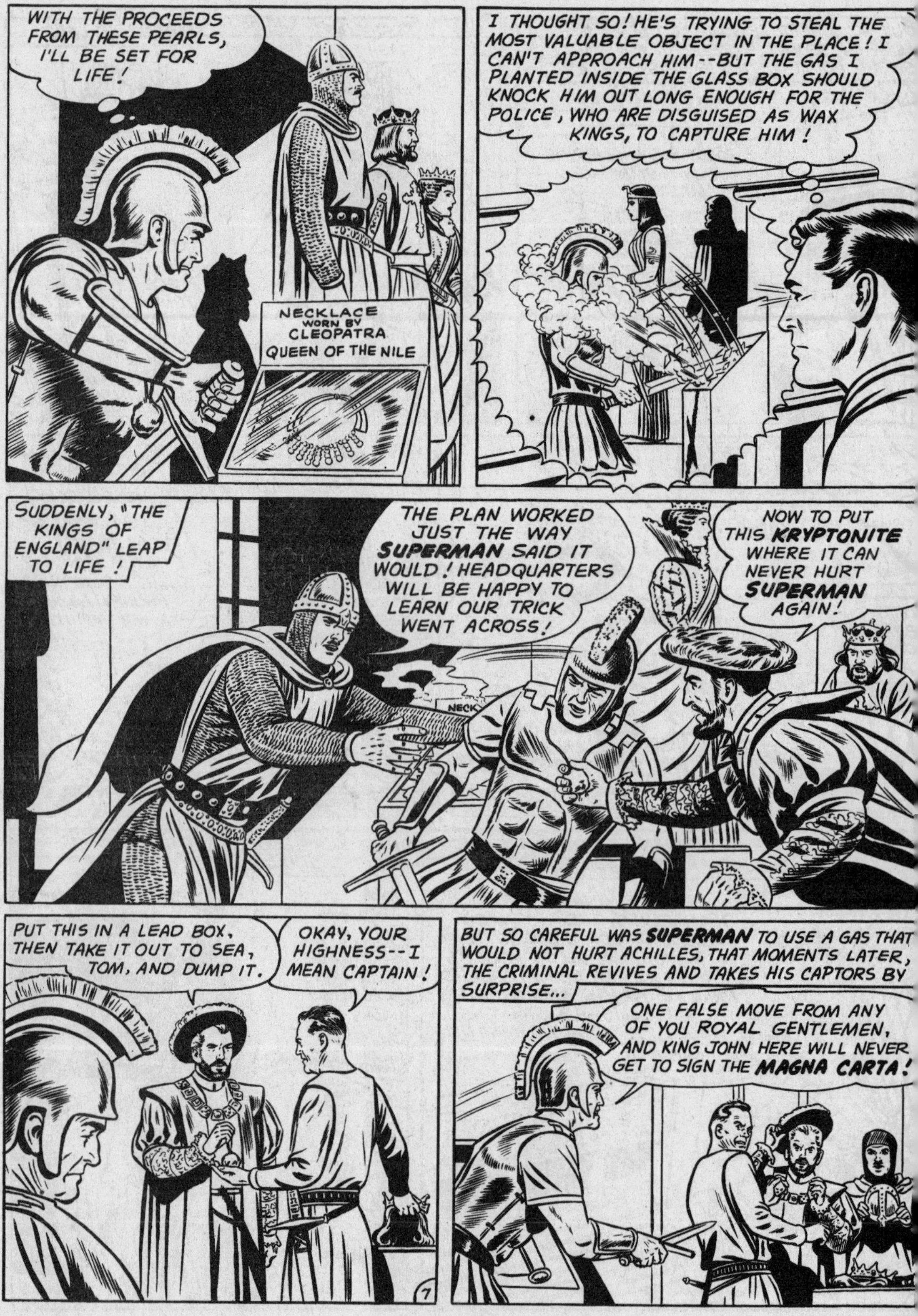
WITH THE PROCEEDS FROM THESE PEARLS, I'LL BE SET FOR LIFE!
NECKLACE WORN BY CLEOPATRA QUEEN OF THE NILE
I THOUGHT SO! HE'S TRYING TO STEAL THE MOST VALUABLE OBJECT IN THE PLACE! I CAN'T APPROACH HIM--BUT THE GAS I PLANTED INSIDE THE GLASS BOX SHOULD KNOCK HIM OUT LONG ENOUGH FOR THE POLICE, WHO ARE DISGUISED AS WAX KINGS, TO CAPTURE HIM!
SUDDENLY, "THE KINGS OF ENGLAND" LEAP TO LIFE!
THE PLAN WORKED JUST THE WAY SUPERMAN SAID IT WOULD! HEADQUARTERS WILL BE HAPPY TO LEARN OUR TRICK WENT ACROSS!
NOW TO PUT THIS KRYPTONITE WHERE IT CAN NEVER HURT SUPERMAN AGAIN!
NECK
PUT THIS IN A LEAD BOX, THEN TAKE IT OUT TO SEA, TOM, AND DUMP IT.
OKAY, YOUR HIGHNESS--I MEAN CAPTAIN!
7
BUT SO CAREFUL WAS SUPERMAN TO USE A GAS THAT WOULD NOT HURT ACHILLES, THAT MOMENTS LATER, THE CRIMINAL REVIVES AND TAKES HIS CAPTORS BY SURPRISE...
ONE FALSE MOVE FROM ANY OF YOU ROYAL GENTLEMEN, AND KING JOHN HERE WILL NEVER GET TO SIGN THE MAGNA CARTA!

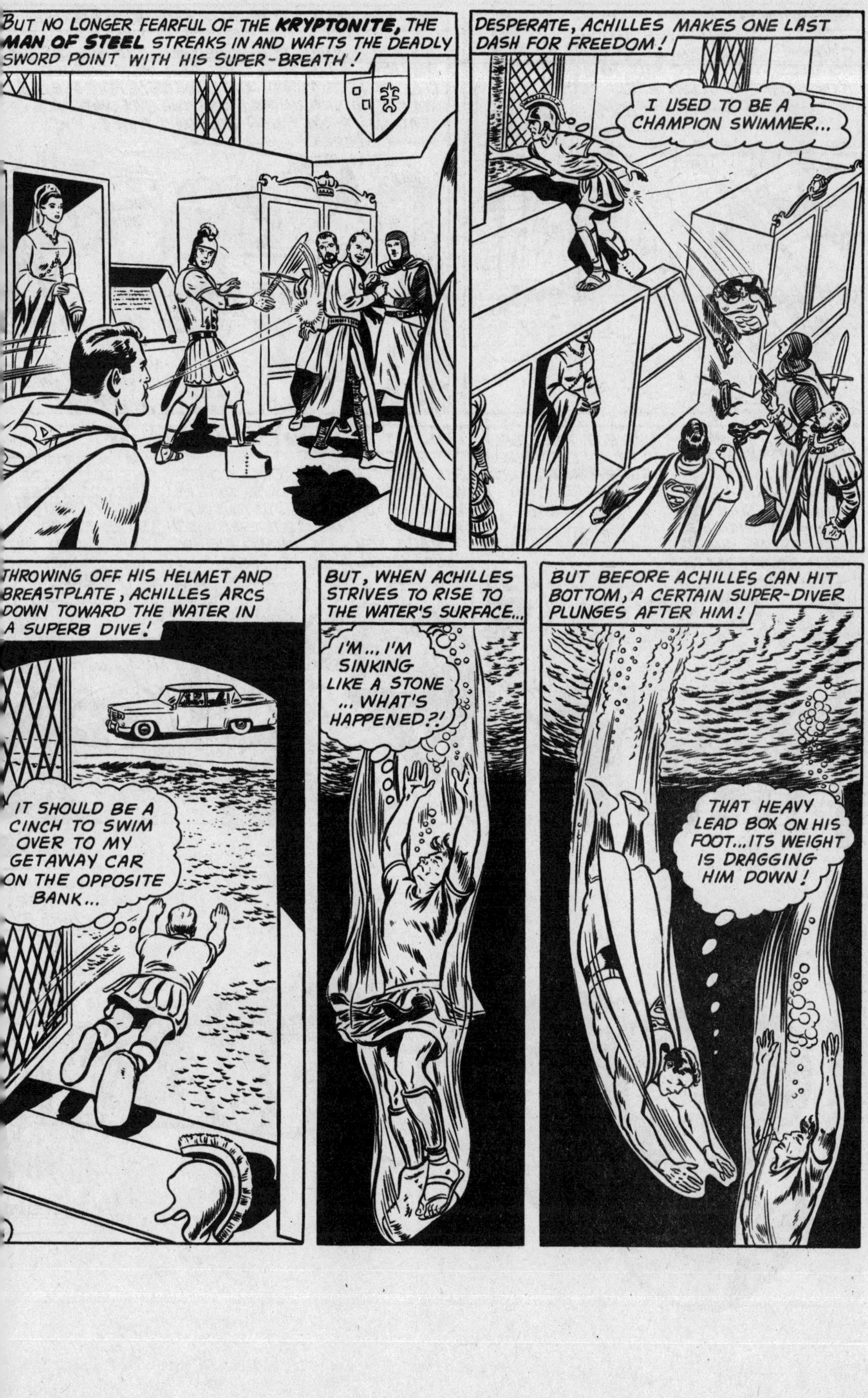
BUT NO LONGER FEARFUL OF THE KRYPTONITE, THE MAN OF STEEL STREAKS IN AND WAFTS THE DEADLY SWORD POINT WITH HIS SUPER-BREATH!
DESPERATE, ACHILLES MAKES ONE LAST DASH FOR FREEDOM!
I USED TO BE A CHAMPION SWIMMER...
THROWING OFF HIS HELMET AND BREASTPLATE, ACHILLES ARCS DOWN TOWARD THE WATER IN A SUPERB DIVE!
IT SHOULD BE A CINCH TO SWIM OVER TO MY GETAWAY CAR ON THE OPPOSITE BANK...
BUT, WHEN ACHILLES STRIVES TO RISE TO THE WATER'S SURFACE...
I'M..., I'M SINKING LIKE A STONE ... WHAT'S HAPPENED?!
BUT BEFORE ACHILLES CAN HIT BOTTOM, A CERTAIN SUPER-DIVER PLUNGES AFTER HIM!
THAT HEAVY LEAD BOX ON HIS FOOT...ITS WEIGHT IS DRAGGING HIM DOWN!

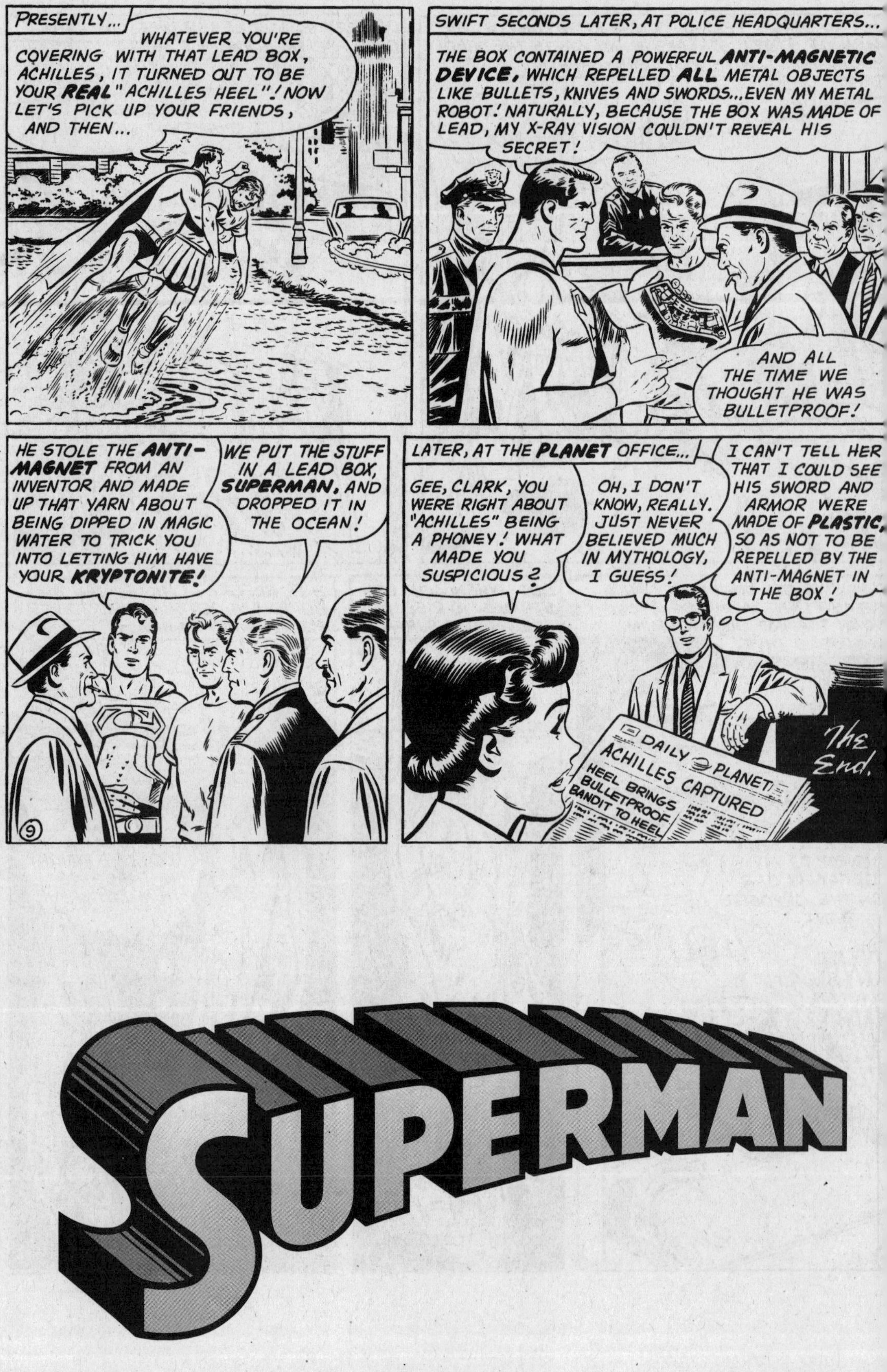
PRESENTLY...
WHATEVER YOU'RE COVERING WITH THAT LEAD BOX, ACHILLES, IT TURNED OUT TO BE YOUR REAL "ACHILLES HEEL"! NOW LET'S PICK UP YOUR FRIENDS, AND THEN...
SWIFT SECONDS LATER, AT POLICE HEADQUARTERS...
THE BOX CONTAINED A POWERFUL ANTI-MAGNETIC DEVICE, WHICH REPELLED ALL METAL OBJECTS LIKE BULLETS, KNIVES AND SWORDS...EVEN MY METAL ROBOT! NATURALLY, BECAUSE THE BOX WAS MADE OF LEAD, MY X-RAY VISION COULDN'T REVEAL HIS SECRET!
AND ALL THE TIME WE THOUGHT HE WAS BULLETPROOF!
HE STOLE THE ANTI-MAGNET FROM AN INVENTOR AND MADE UP THAT YARN ABOUT BEING DIPPED IN MAGIC WATER TO TRICK YOU INTO LETTING HIM HAVE YOUR KRYPTONITE!
WE PUT THE STUFF IN A LEAD BOX, SUPERMAN, AND DROPPED IT IN THE OCEAN!
9
LATER, AT THE PLANET OFFICE...
GEE, CLARK, YOU WERE RIGHT ABOUT "ACHILLES" BEING A PHONEY! WHAT MADE YOU SUSPICIOUS?
OH, I DON'T KNOW, REALLY. JUST NEVER BELIEVED MUCH IN MYTHOLOGY, I GUESS!
I CAN'T TELL HER THAT I COULD SEE HIS SWORD AND ARMOR WERE MADE OF PLASTIC, SO AS NOT TO BE REPELLED BY THE ANTI-MAGNET IN THE BOX!
DAILY PLANET
ACHILLES CAPTURED
HEEL BRINGS BULLETPROOF BANDIT TO HEEL
The End.

SUPERMAN

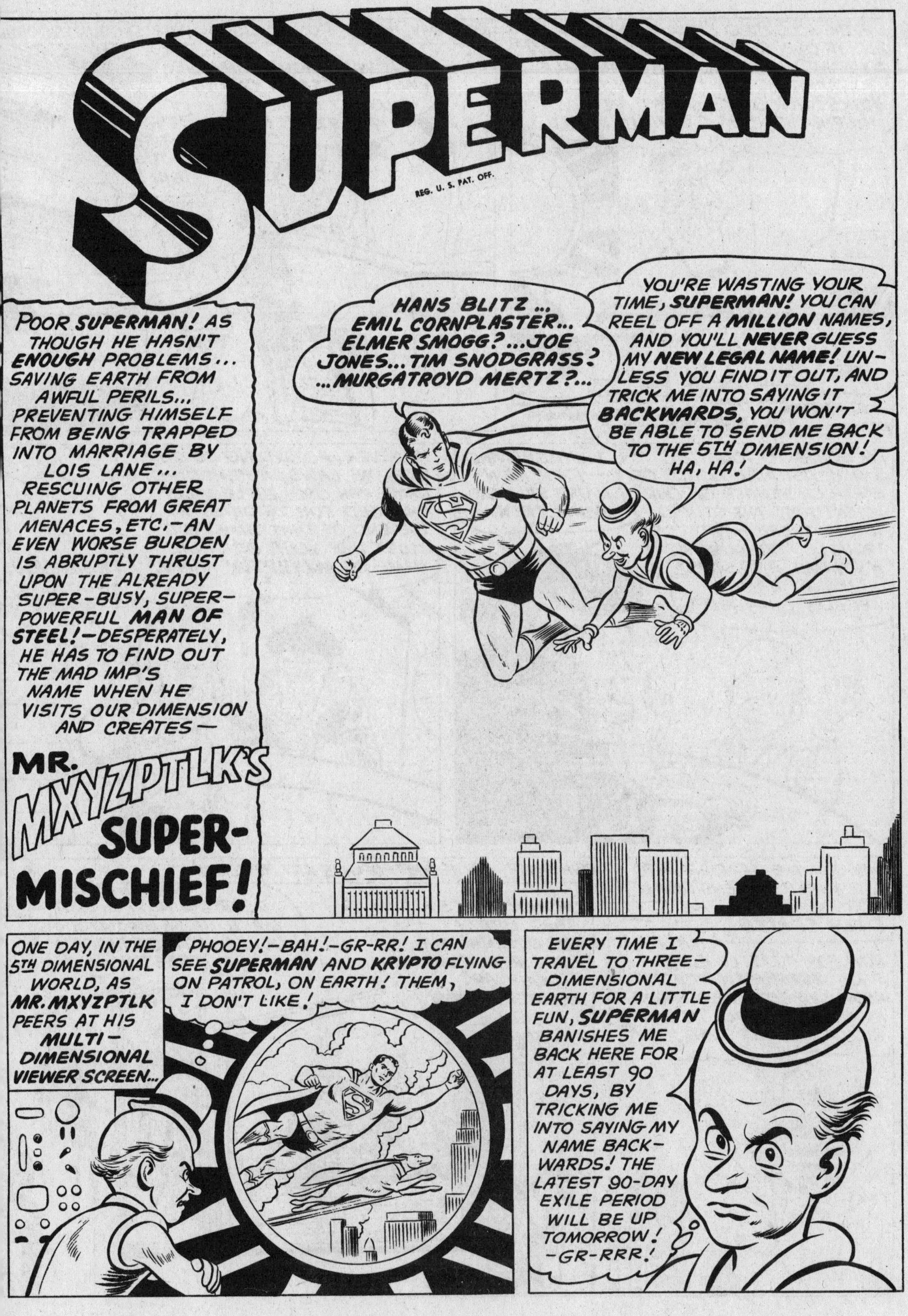
SUPERMAN
REG. U. S. PAT. OFF.
POOR SUPERMAN! AS THOUGH HE HASN'T ENOUGH PROBLEMS... SAVING EARTH FROM AWFUL PERILS... PREVENTING HIMSELF FROM BEING TRAPPED INTO MARRIAGE BY LOIS LANE... RESCUING OTHER PLANETS FROM GREAT MENACES, ETC.—AN EVEN WORSE BURDEN IS ABRUPTLY THRUST UPON THE ALREADY SUPER-BUSY, SUPER-POWERFUL MAN OF STEEL!—DESPERATELY, HE HAS TO FIND OUT THE MAD IMP'S NAME WHEN HE VISITS OUR DIMENSION AND CREATES—
MR. MXYZPTLK'S SUPER-MISCHIEF!
HANS BLITZ... EMIL CORNPLASTER... ELMER SMOGG?...JOE JONES...TIM SNODGRASS? ...MURGATROYD MERTZ?...
YOU'RE WASTING YOUR TIME, SUPERMAN! YOU CAN REEL OFF A MILLION NAMES, AND YOU'LL NEVER GUESS MY NEW LEGAL NAME! UNLESS YOU FIND IT OUT, AND TRICK ME INTO SAYING IT BACKWARDS, YOU WON'T BE ABLE TO SEND ME BACK TO THE 5TH DIMENSION! HA, HA!
ONE DAY, IN THE 5TH DIMENSIONAL WORLD, AS MR. MXYZPTLK PEERS AT HIS MULTI-DIMENSIONAL VIEWER SCREEN...
PHOOEY!—BAH!—GR-RR! I CAN SEE SUPERMAN AND KRYPTO FLYING ON PATROL, ON EARTH! THEM, I DON'T LIKE!
EVERY TIME I TRAVEL TO THREE-DIMENSIONAL EARTH FOR A LITTLE FUN, SUPERMAN BANISHES ME BACK HERE FOR AT LEAST 90 DAYS, BY TRICKING ME INTO SAYING MY NAME BACKWARDS! THE LATEST 90-DAY EXILE PERIOD WILL BE UP TOMORROW! -GR-RRR!

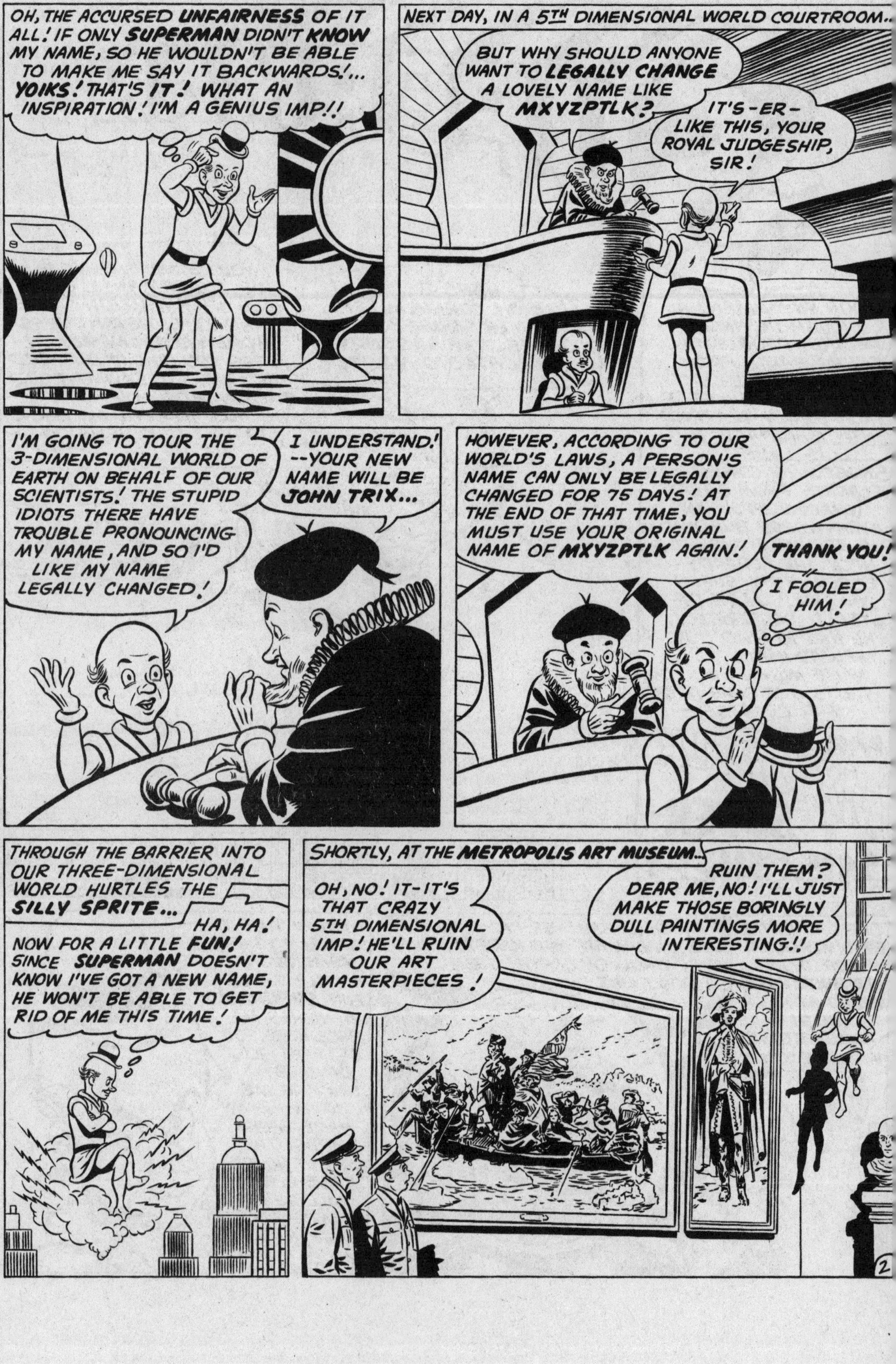
OH, THE ACCURSED UNFAIRNESS OF IT ALL! IF ONLY SUPERMAN DIDN'T KNOW MY NAME, SO HE WOULDN'T BE ABLE TO MAKE ME SAY IT BACKWARDS!... YOIKS! THAT'S IT! WHAT AN INSPIRATION! I'M A GENIUS IMP!!
NEXT DAY, IN A 5TH DIMENSIONAL WORLD COURTROOM...
BUT WHY SHOULD ANYONE WANT TO LEGALLY CHANGE A LOVELY NAME LIKE MXYZPTLK?
IT'S-ER- LIKE THIS, YOUR ROYAL JUDGESHIP, SIR!
I'M GOING TO TOUR THE 3-DIMENSIONAL WORLD OF EARTH ON BEHALF OF OUR SCIENTISTS! THE STUPID IDIOTS THERE HAVE TROUBLE PRONOUNCING MY NAME, AND SO I'D LIKE MY NAME LEGALLY CHANGED!
I UNDERSTAND! --YOUR NEW NAME WILL BE JOHN TRIX...
HOWEVER, ACCORDING TO OUR WORLD'S LAWS, A PERSON'S NAME CAN ONLY BE LEGALLY CHANGED FOR 75 DAYS! AT THE END OF THAT TIME, YOU MUST USE YOUR ORIGINAL NAME OF MXYZPTLK AGAIN!
THANK YOU!
I FOOLED HIM!
THROUGH THE BARRIER INTO OUR THREE-DIMENSIONAL WORLD HURTLES THE SILLY SPRITE...
HA, HA! NOW FOR A LITTLE FUN! SINCE SUPERMAN DOESN'T KNOW I'VE GOT A NEW NAME, HE WON'T BE ABLE TO GET RID OF ME THIS TIME!
SHORTLY, AT THE METROPOLIS ART MUSEUM...
OH, NO! IT-IT'S THAT CRAZY 5TH DIMENSIONAL IMP! HE'LL RUIN OUR ART MASTERPIECES!
RUIN THEM? DEAR ME, NO! I'LL JUST MAKE THOSE BORINGLY DULL PAINTINGS MORE INTERESTING!!
2

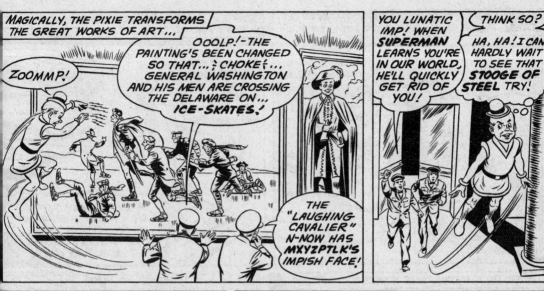

MAGICALLY, THE PIXIE TRANSFORMS THE GREAT WORKS OF ART...

ZOOMMP!

OOOLP! -THE PAINTING'S BEEN CHANGED SO THAT...; CHOKE{... GENERAL WASHINGTON AND HIS MEN ARE CROSSING THE DELAWARE ON... ICE-SKATES!

THE "LAUGHING CAVALIER" N-NOW HAS MXYZPTLK'S IMPISH FACE!

YOU LUNATIC IMP! WHEN SUPERMAN LEARNS YOU'RE IN OUR WORLD, HE'LL QUICKLY GET RID OF YOU!

THINK SO? HA, HA! I CAN HARDLY WAIT TO SEE THAT STOOGE OF STEEL TRY!

SHORTLY... AH, THERE'S THE MUSCLE-BOUND OAF NOW, FLYING ON PATROL! NOW TO RUIN HIS DAY!

I MAGICALLY COMMAND EVERY MANHOLE COVER IN METROPOLIS TO RISE!!

A MOMENT LATER, AS A HORDE OF METAL DISCS SOAR UPWARD IN RESPONSE TO THE IMP'S 5TH DIMENSIONAL MAGIC...!

GREAT SCOTT! IS IT...? --NO, IT ISN'T FLYING SAUCERS! IT'S...ULP!... FLYING MANHOLE COVERS!! WHAT...!?

TRAILING THE FLYING OBJECTS, SUPERMAN SOON SIGHTS ...

GAA!...MR.MXYZPTLK! YOU'RE BACK AGAIN TO BEDEVIL ME! WHAT HAVE I DONE TO DESERVE THIS??!

MANHOLE COVERS... DROP!!!

AS THE METAL DISCS RAIN DOWNWARD, SUPER-MAN FLASHES DESPERATELY AFTER THEM...

IF THEY FALL ON THE CITY, THEY MAY HURT INNOCENT PEOPLE!

3

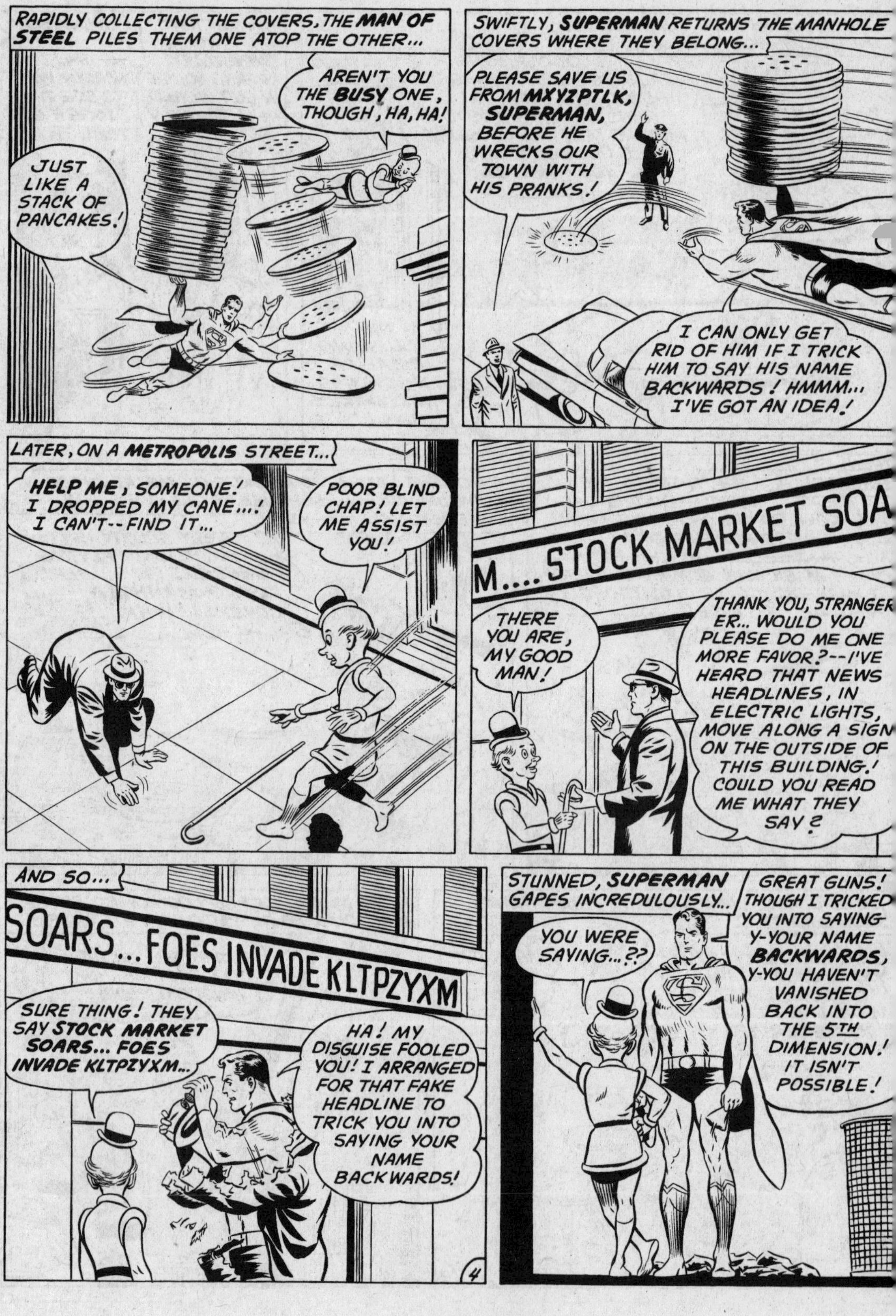
RAPIDLY COLLECTING THE COVERS, THE MAN OF STEEL PILES THEM ONE ATOP THE OTHER...
AREN'T YOU THE BUSY ONE, THOUGH, HA, HA!
JUST LIKE A STACK OF PANCAKES!
SWIFTLY, SUPERMAN RETURNS THE MANHOLE COVERS WHERE THEY BELONG...
PLEASE SAVE US FROM MXYZPTLK, SUPERMAN, BEFORE HE WRECKS OUR TOWN WITH HIS PRANKS!
I CAN ONLY GET RID OF HIM IF I TRICK HIM TO SAY HIS NAME BACKWARDS! HMMM... I'VE GOT AN IDEA!
LATER, ON A METROPOLIS STREET...
HELP ME, SOMEONE! I DROPPED MY CANE...! I CAN'T--FIND IT...
POOR BLIND CHAP! LET ME ASSIST YOU!
M.... STOCK MARKET SOA
THERE YOU ARE, MY GOOD MAN!
THANK YOU, STRANGER ER... WOULD YOU PLEASE DO ME ONE MORE FAVOR?--I'VE HEARD THAT NEWS HEADLINES, IN ELECTRIC LIGHTS, MOVE ALONG A SIGN ON THE OUTSIDE OF THIS BUILDING! COULD YOU READ ME WHAT THEY SAY?
AND SO...
SOARS...FOES INVADE KLTPZYXM
SURE THING! THEY SAY STOCK MARKET SOARS... FOES INVADE KLTPZYXM...
HA! MY DISGUISE FOOLED YOU! I ARRANGED FOR THAT FAKE HEADLINE TO TRICK YOU INTO SAYING YOUR NAME BACKWARDS!
4
STUNNED, SUPERMAN GAPES INCREDULOUSLY...
YOU WERE SAYING...??
GREAT GUNS! THOUGH I TRICKED YOU INTO SAYING Y-YOUR NAME BACKWARDS, Y-YOU HAVEN'T VANISHED BACK INTO THE 5TH DIMENSION! IT ISN'T POSSIBLE!

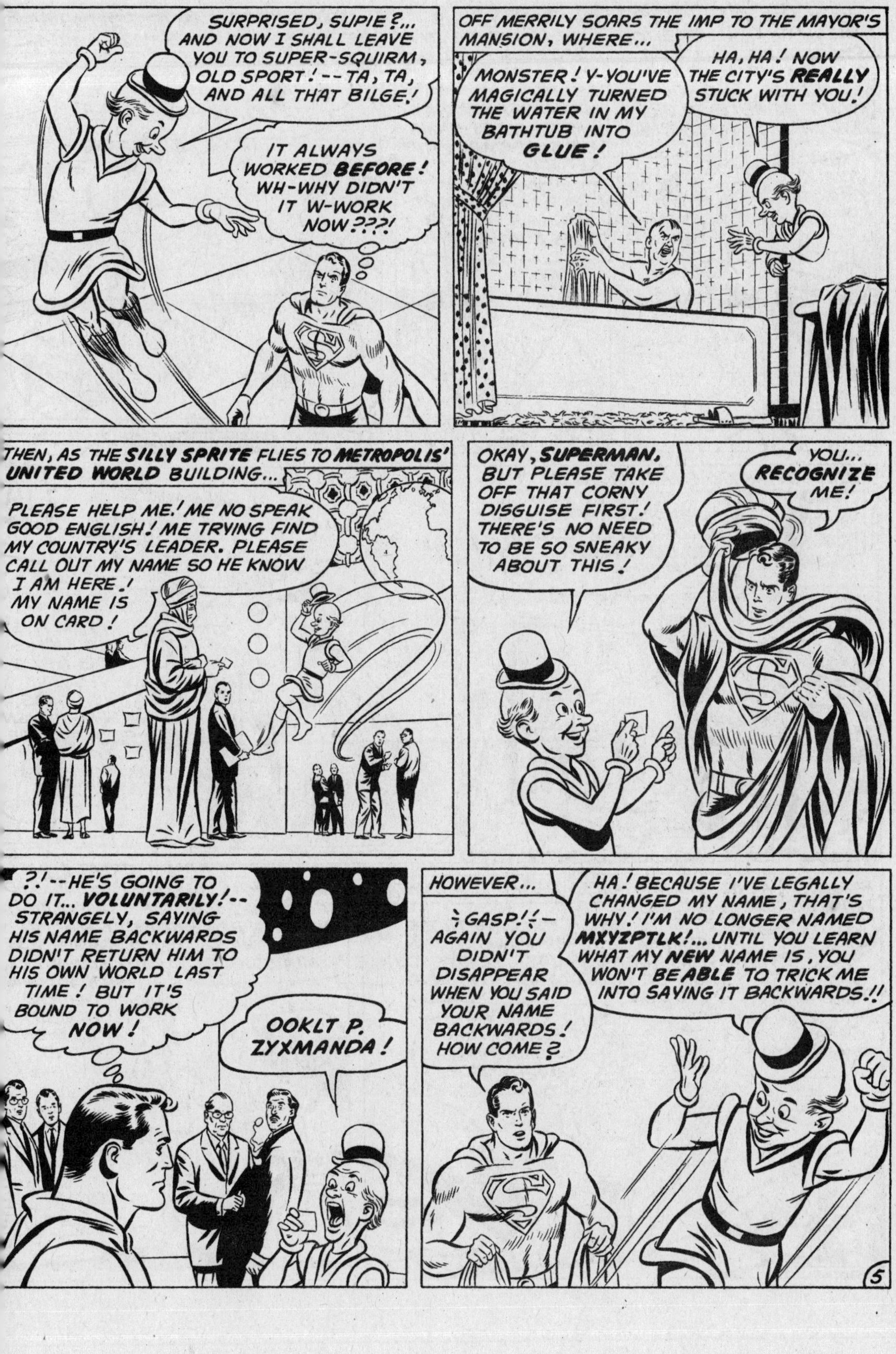
SURPRISED, SUPIE?... AND NOW I SHALL LEAVE YOU TO SUPER-SQUIRM, OLD SPORT! --TA, TA, AND ALL THAT BILGE!
IT ALWAYS WORKED BEFORE! WH-WHY DIDN'T IT W-WORK NOW???!
OFF MERRILY SOARS THE IMP TO THE MAYOR'S MANSION, WHERE...
MONSTER! Y-YOU'VE MAGICALLY TURNED THE WATER IN MY BATHTUB INTO GLUE!
HA, HA! NOW THE CITY'S REALLY STUCK WITH YOU!
THEN, AS THE SILLY SPRITE FLIES TO METROPOLIS' UNITED WORLD BUILDING...
PLEASE HELP ME! ME NO SPEAK GOOD ENGLISH! ME TRYING FIND MY COUNTRY'S LEADER. PLEASE CALL OUT MY NAME SO HE KNOW I AM HERE! MY NAME IS ON CARD!
OKAY, SUPERMAN. BUT PLEASE TAKE OFF THAT CORNY DISGUISE FIRST! THERE'S NO NEED TO BE SO SNEAKY ABOUT THIS!
YOU... RECOGNIZE ME!
?!--HE'S GOING TO DO IT... VOLUNTARILY!--STRANGELY, SAYING HIS NAME BACKWARDS DIDN'T RETURN HIM TO HIS OWN WORLD LAST TIME! BUT IT'S BOUND TO WORK NOW!
OOKLT P. ZYXMANDA!
HOWEVER...
GASP! AGAIN YOU DIDN'T DISAPPEAR WHEN YOU SAID YOUR NAME BACKWARDS! HOW COME?
HA! BECAUSE I'VE LEGALLY CHANGED MY NAME, THAT'S WHY! I'M NO LONGER NAMED MXYZPTLK!... UNTIL YOU LEARN WHAT MY NEW NAME IS, YOU WON'T BE ABLE TO TRICK ME INTO SAYING IT BACKWARDS!!
5

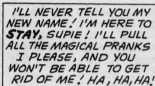

I'LL NEVER TELL YOU MY NEW NAME! I'M HERE TO **STAY**, SUPIE! I'LL PULL ALL THE MAGICAL PRANKS I PLEASE, AND YOU WON'T BE ABLE TO GET RID OF ME! HA, HA, HA!

CHANGING TO HIS CLARK KENT IDENTITY, **SUPERMAN** RETURNS TO THE **PLANET**...

MR. **MXYZPTLK** HAS A NEW SECRET NAME AND **SUPERMAN** CAN'T GET RID OF HIM!

NOW TO GET BACK ON THE JOB AS **SUPERMAN**!

!!

MEANWHILE, ABOVE **METROPOLIS PRISON** THE IMP IS UP TO MORE MADCAP MISCHIEF

PRISONERS... BECOME SUPER! ...**ZOOMMP!!!**

NEXT INSTANT...

HA, HA! NOW THAT YOU'VE MAGICALLY CHANGED ALL OF US CONVICTS INTO **SUPERMEN**, ESCAPING IS A **CINCH**!

HAVE FUN!

PRESENTLY, AS **SUPERMAN** TRACES THE IMP TO A MOUNTAIN PEAK OUTSIDE THE CITY...

WHEN YOU GAVE THOSE CRIMINALS SUPER-POWERS, YOU WENT TOO FAR, PEST! — I'LL GIVE YOU A SUPER-HOT FOOT WITH MY HEAT VISION!

YOU'RE FORGETTING SOMETHING, BUDDY-BOY!

GREAT SCOTT! INSTEAD OF **HEATING** YOUR FEET, MY VISION HAS **FROZEN** THEM! THAT'S IMPOSSIBLE!

NOTHING IS IMPOSSIBLE FOR MY 5TH DIMENSIONAL MAGICAL POWERS. WATCH ME MAKE THE ICE VANISH!

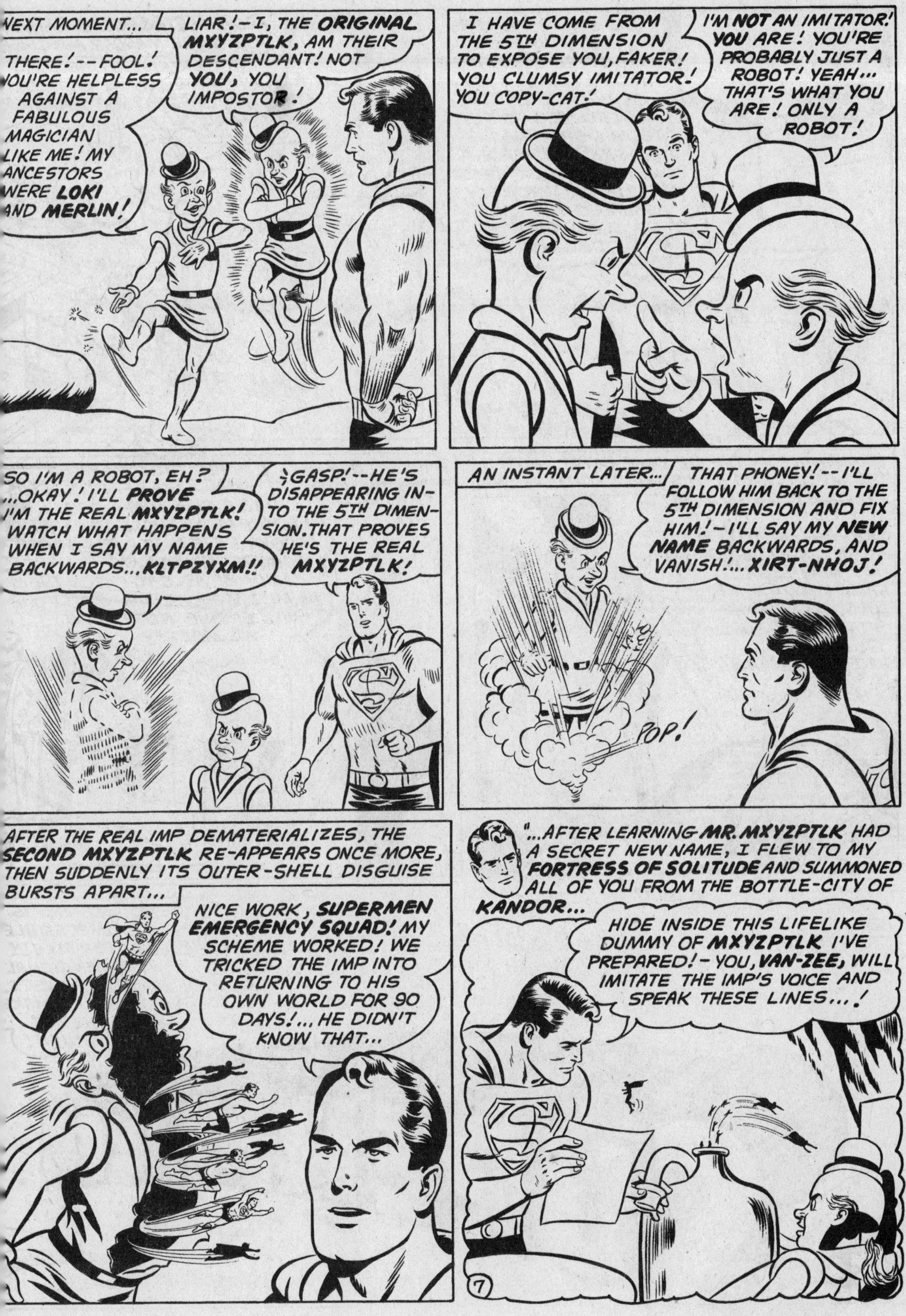
NEXT MOMENT...
THERE! --FOOL! YOU'RE HELPLESS AGAINST A FABULOUS MAGICIAN LIKE ME! MY ANCESTORS WERE LOKI AND MERLIN!
LIAR! -I, THE ORIGINAL MXYZPTLK, AM THEIR DESCENDANT! NOT YOU, YOU IMPOSTOR!
I HAVE COME FROM THE 5TH DIMENSION TO EXPOSE YOU, FAKER! YOU CLUMSY IMITATOR! YOU COPY-CAT!
I'M NOT AN IMITATOR! YOU ARE! YOU'RE PROBABLY JUST A ROBOT! YEAH... THAT'S WHAT YOU ARE! ONLY A ROBOT!
SO I'M A ROBOT, EH? ...OKAY! I'LL PROVE I'M THE REAL MXYZPTLK! WATCH WHAT HAPPENS WHEN I SAY MY NAME BACKWARDS... KLTPZYXM!!
GASP! --HE'S DISAPPEARING INTO THE 5TH DIMENSION. THAT PROVES HE'S THE REAL MXYZPTLK!
AN INSTANT LATER...
THAT PHONEY! --I'LL FOLLOW HIM BACK TO THE 5TH DIMENSION AND FIX HIM! -I'LL SAY MY NEW NAME BACKWARDS, AND VANISH!... XIRT-NHOJ!
POP!
AFTER THE REAL IMP DEMATERIALIZES, THE SECOND MXYZPTLK RE-APPEARS ONCE MORE, THEN SUDDENLY ITS OUTER-SHELL DISGUISE BURSTS APART...
NICE WORK, SUPERMEN EMERGENCY SQUAD! MY SCHEME WORKED! WE TRICKED THE IMP INTO RETURNING TO HIS OWN WORLD FOR 90 DAYS!... HE DIDN'T KNOW THAT...
"...AFTER LEARNING MR. MXYZPTLK HAD A SECRET NEW NAME, I FLEW TO MY FORTRESS OF SOLITUDE AND SUMMONED ALL OF YOU FROM THE BOTTLE-CITY OF KANDOR...
HIDE INSIDE THIS LIFELIKE DUMMY OF MXYZPTLK I'VE PREPARED! -YOU, VAN-ZEE, WILL IMITATE THE IMP'S VOICE AND SPEAK THESE LINES...!
7

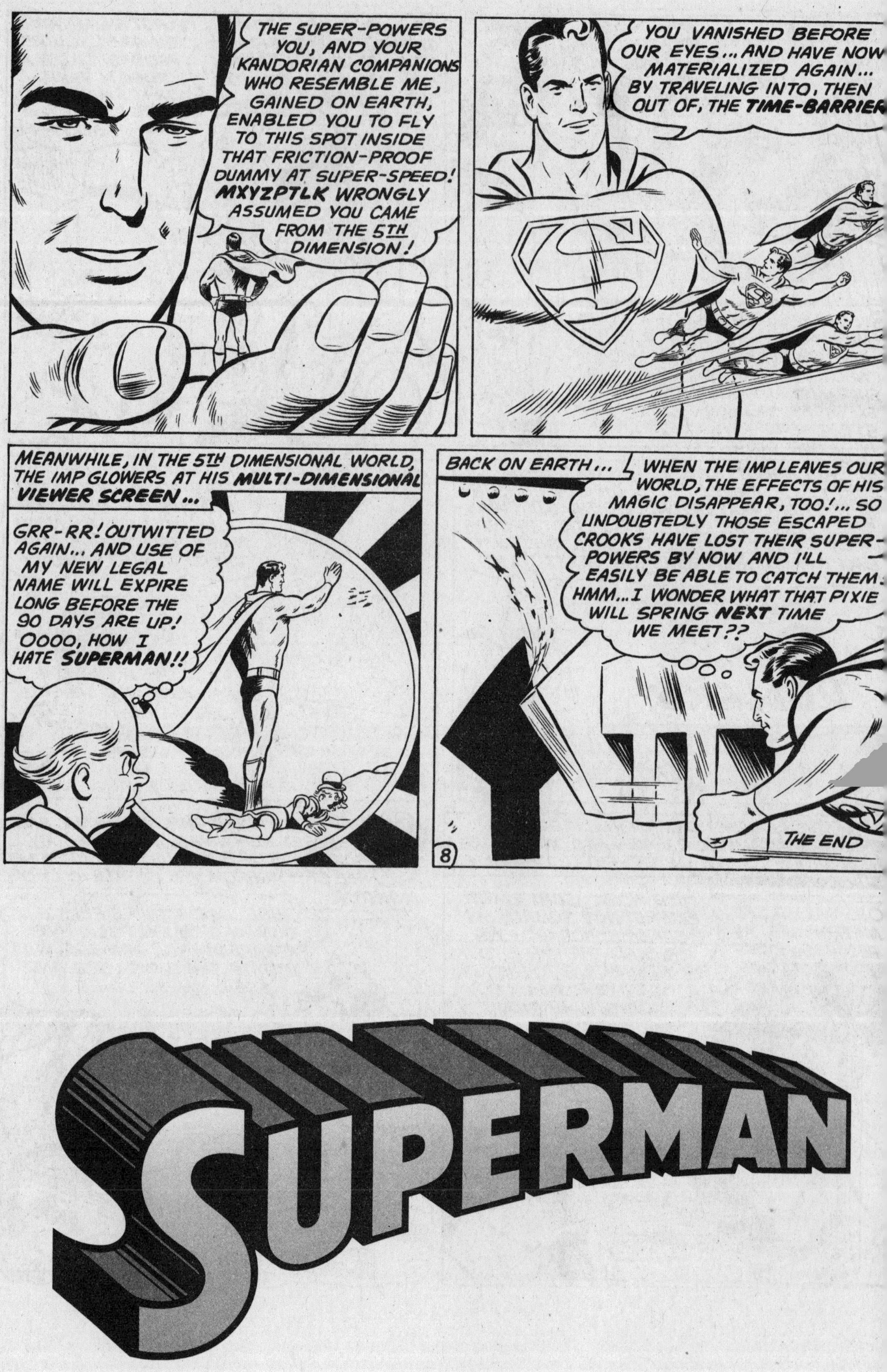
THE SUPER-POWERS YOU, AND YOUR KANDORIAN COMPANIONS WHO RESEMBLE ME, GAINED ON EARTH, ENABLED YOU TO FLY TO THIS SPOT INSIDE THAT FRICTION-PROOF DUMMY AT SUPER-SPEED! MXYZPTLK WRONGLY ASSUMED YOU CAME FROM THE 5TH DIMENSION!
YOU VANISHED BEFORE OUR EYES... AND HAVE NOW MATERIALIZED AGAIN... BY TRAVELING INTO, THEN OUT OF, THE TIME-BARRIER
MEANWHILE, IN THE 5TH DIMENSIONAL WORLD, THE IMP GLOWERS AT HIS MULTI-DIMENSIONAL VIEWER SCREEN...
GRR-RR! OUTWITTED AGAIN... AND USE OF MY NEW LEGAL NAME WILL EXPIRE LONG BEFORE THE 90 DAYS ARE UP! OOOO, HOW I HATE SUPERMAN!!
BACK ON EARTH...
WHEN THE IMP LEAVES OUR WORLD, THE EFFECTS OF HIS MAGIC DISAPPEAR, TOO!... SO UNDOUBTEDLY THOSE ESCAPED CROOKS HAVE LOST THEIR SUPER-POWERS BY NOW AND I'LL EASILY BE ABLE TO CATCH THEM. HMM... I WONDER WHAT THAT PIXIE WILL SPRING NEXT TIME WE MEET??
8
THE END

SUPERMAN

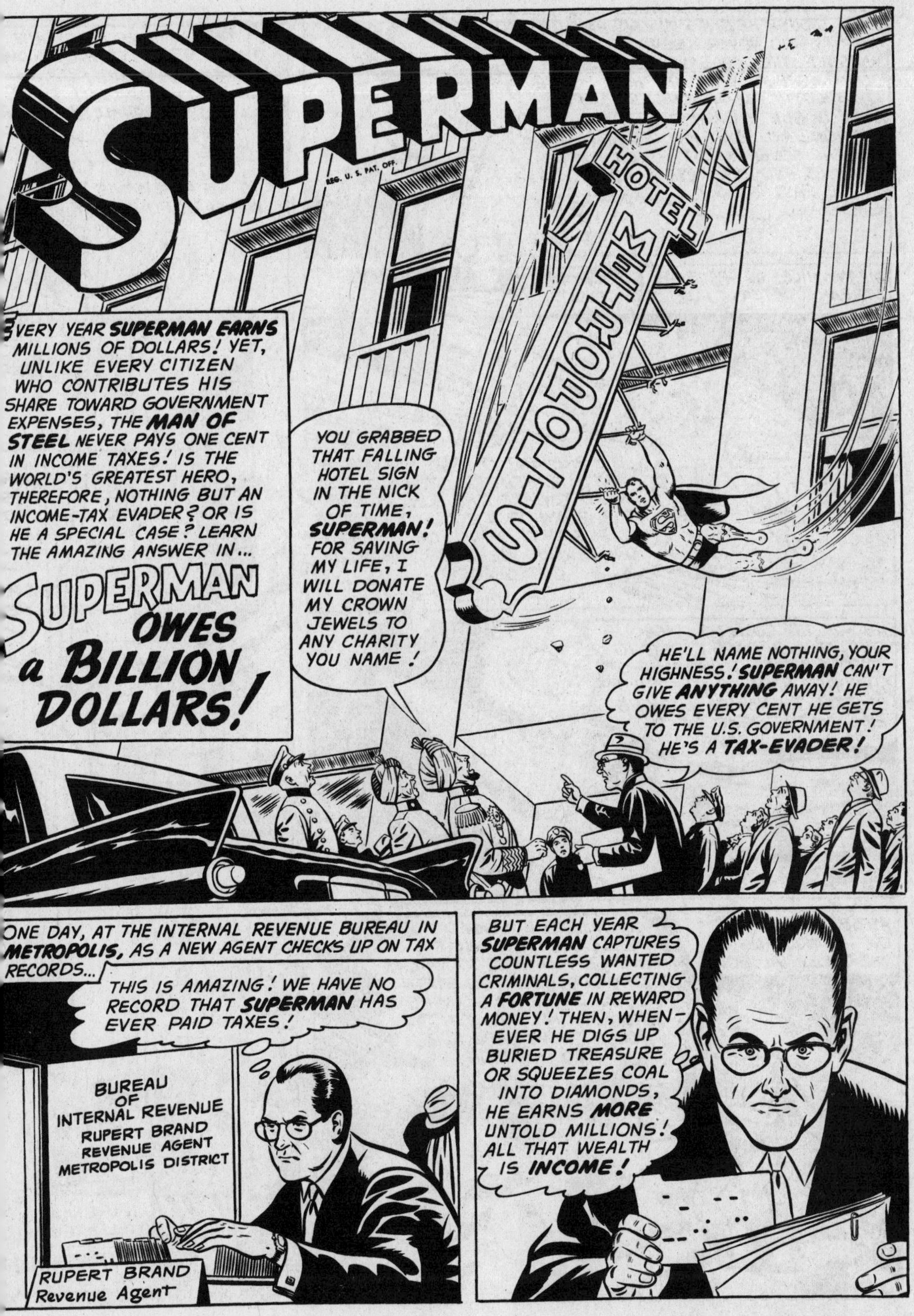
SUPERMAN
REG. U. S. PAT. OFF.
HOTEL METROPOLIS
EVERY YEAR SUPERMAN EARNS MILLIONS OF DOLLARS! YET, UNLIKE EVERY CITIZEN WHO CONTRIBUTES HIS SHARE TOWARD GOVERNMENT EXPENSES, THE MAN OF STEEL NEVER PAYS ONE CENT IN INCOME TAXES! IS THE WORLD'S GREATEST HERO, THEREFORE, NOTHING BUT AN INCOME-TAX EVADER? OR IS HE A SPECIAL CASE? LEARN THE AMAZING ANSWER IN...
SUPERMAN OWES a BILLION DOLLARS!
YOU GRABBED THAT FALLING HOTEL SIGN IN THE NICK OF TIME, SUPERMAN! FOR SAVING MY LIFE, I WILL DONATE MY CROWN JEWELS TO ANY CHARITY YOU NAME!
HE'LL NAME NOTHING, YOUR HIGHNESS! SUPERMAN CAN'T GIVE ANYTHING AWAY! HE OWES EVERY CENT HE GETS TO THE U.S. GOVERNMENT! HE'S A TAX-EVADER!
ONE DAY, AT THE INTERNAL REVENUE BUREAU IN METROPOLIS, AS A NEW AGENT CHECKS UP ON TAX RECORDS...
THIS IS AMAZING! WE HAVE NO RECORD THAT SUPERMAN HAS EVER PAID TAXES!
BUREAU OF INTERNAL REVENUE RUPERT BRAND REVENUE AGENT METROPOLIS DISTRICT
RUPERT BRAND Revenue Agent
BUT EACH YEAR SUPERMAN CAPTURES COUNTLESS WANTED CRIMINALS, COLLECTING A FORTUNE IN REWARD MONEY! THEN, WHENEVER HE DIGS UP BURIED TREASURE OR SQUEEZES COAL INTO DIAMONDS, HE EARNS MORE UNTOLD MILLIONS! ALL THAT WEALTH IS INCOME!

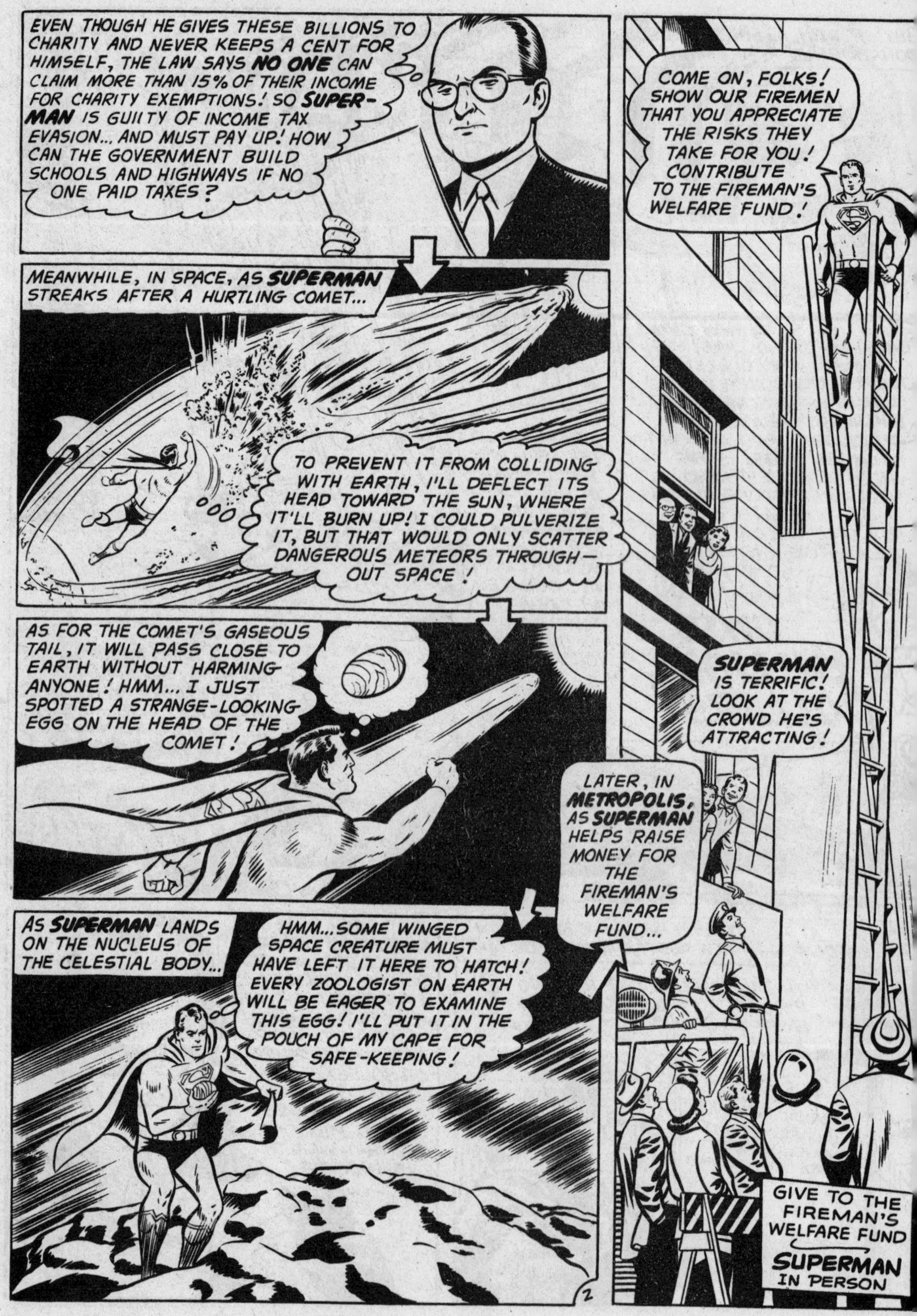
EVEN THOUGH HE GIVES THESE BILLIONS TO CHARITY AND NEVER KEEPS A CENT FOR HIMSELF, THE LAW SAYS NO ONE CAN CLAIM MORE THAN 15% OF THEIR INCOME FOR CHARITY EXEMPTIONS! SO SUPERMAN IS GUILTY OF INCOME TAX EVASION... AND MUST PAY UP! HOW CAN THE GOVERNMENT BUILD SCHOOLS AND HIGHWAYS IF NO ONE PAID TAXES?
MEANWHILE, IN SPACE, AS SUPERMAN STREAKS AFTER A HURTLING COMET...
TO PREVENT IT FROM COLLIDING WITH EARTH, I'LL DEFLECT ITS HEAD TOWARD THE SUN, WHERE IT'LL BURN UP! I COULD PULVERIZE IT, BUT THAT WOULD ONLY SCATTER DANGEROUS METEORS THROUGH-OUT SPACE!
AS FOR THE COMET'S GASEOUS TAIL, IT WILL PASS CLOSE TO EARTH WITHOUT HARMING ANYONE! HMM... I JUST SPOTTED A STRANGE-LOOKING EGG ON THE HEAD OF THE COMET!
AS SUPERMAN LANDS ON THE NUCLEUS OF THE CELESTIAL BODY...
HMM...SOME WINGED SPACE CREATURE MUST HAVE LEFT IT HERE TO HATCH! EVERY ZOOLOGIST ON EARTH WILL BE EAGER TO EXAMINE THIS EGG! I'LL PUT IT IN THE POUCH OF MY CAPE FOR SAFE-KEEPING!
LATER, IN METROPOLIS, AS SUPERMAN HELPS RAISE MONEY FOR THE FIREMAN'S WELFARE FUND...
COME ON, FOLKS! SHOW OUR FIREMEN THAT YOU APPRECIATE THE RISKS THEY TAKE FOR YOU! CONTRIBUTE TO THE FIREMAN'S WELFARE FUND!
SUPERMAN IS TERRIFIC! LOOK AT THE CROWD HE'S ATTRACTING!
GIVE TO THE FIREMAN'S WELFARE FUND
SUPERMAN IN PERSON
2

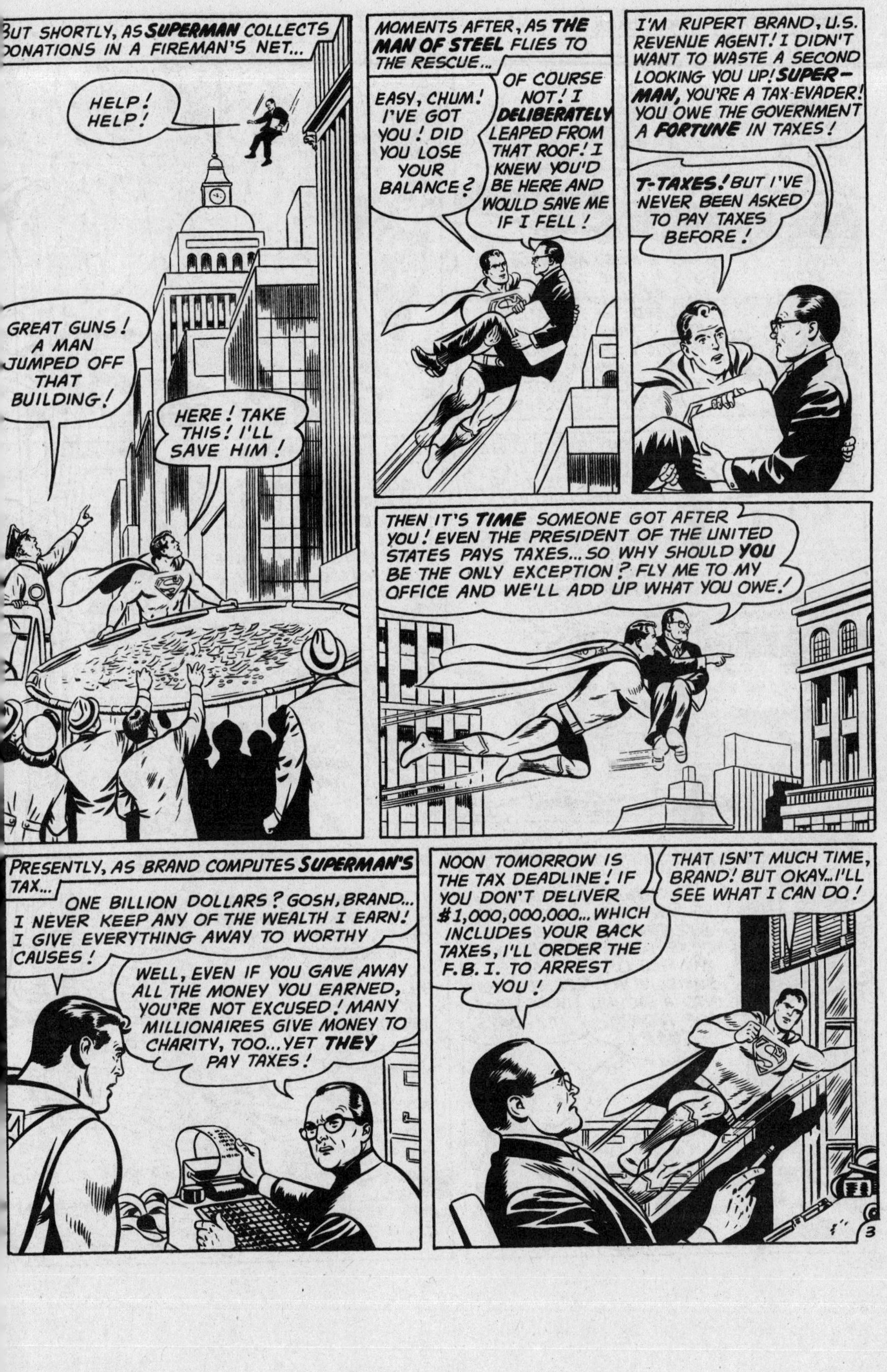
BUT SHORTLY, AS SUPERMAN COLLECTS DONATIONS IN A FIREMAN'S NET...
HELP! HELP!
GREAT GUNS! A MAN JUMPED OFF THAT BUILDING!
HERE! TAKE THIS! I'LL SAVE HIM!
MOMENTS AFTER, AS THE MAN OF STEEL FLIES TO THE RESCUE...
EASY, CHUM! I'VE GOT YOU! DID YOU LOSE YOUR BALANCE?
OF COURSE NOT! I DELIBERATELY LEAPED FROM THAT ROOF! I KNEW YOU'D BE HERE AND WOULD SAVE ME IF I FELL!
I'M RUPERT BRAND, U.S. REVENUE AGENT! I DIDN'T WANT TO WASTE A SECOND LOOKING YOU UP! SUPERMAN, YOU'RE A TAX-EVADER! YOU OWE THE GOVERNMENT A FORTUNE IN TAXES!
T-TAXES! BUT I'VE NEVER BEEN ASKED TO PAY TAXES BEFORE!
THEN IT'S TIME SOMEONE GOT AFTER YOU! EVEN THE PRESIDENT OF THE UNITED STATES PAYS TAXES...SO WHY SHOULD YOU BE THE ONLY EXCEPTION? FLY ME TO MY OFFICE AND WE'LL ADD UP WHAT YOU OWE!
PRESENTLY, AS BRAND COMPUTES SUPERMAN'S TAX...
ONE BILLION DOLLARS? GOSH, BRAND... I NEVER KEEP ANY OF THE WEALTH I EARN! I GIVE EVERYTHING AWAY TO WORTHY CAUSES!
WELL, EVEN IF YOU GAVE AWAY ALL THE MONEY YOU EARNED, YOU'RE NOT EXCUSED! MANY MILLIONAIRES GIVE MONEY TO CHARITY, TOO...YET THEY PAY TAXES!
NOON TOMORROW IS THE TAX DEADLINE! IF YOU DON'T DELIVER $1,000,000,000...WHICH INCLUDES YOUR BACK TAXES, I'LL ORDER THE F.B.I. TO ARREST YOU!
THAT ISN'T MUCH TIME, BRAND! BUT OKAY...I'LL SEE WHAT I CAN DO!
3

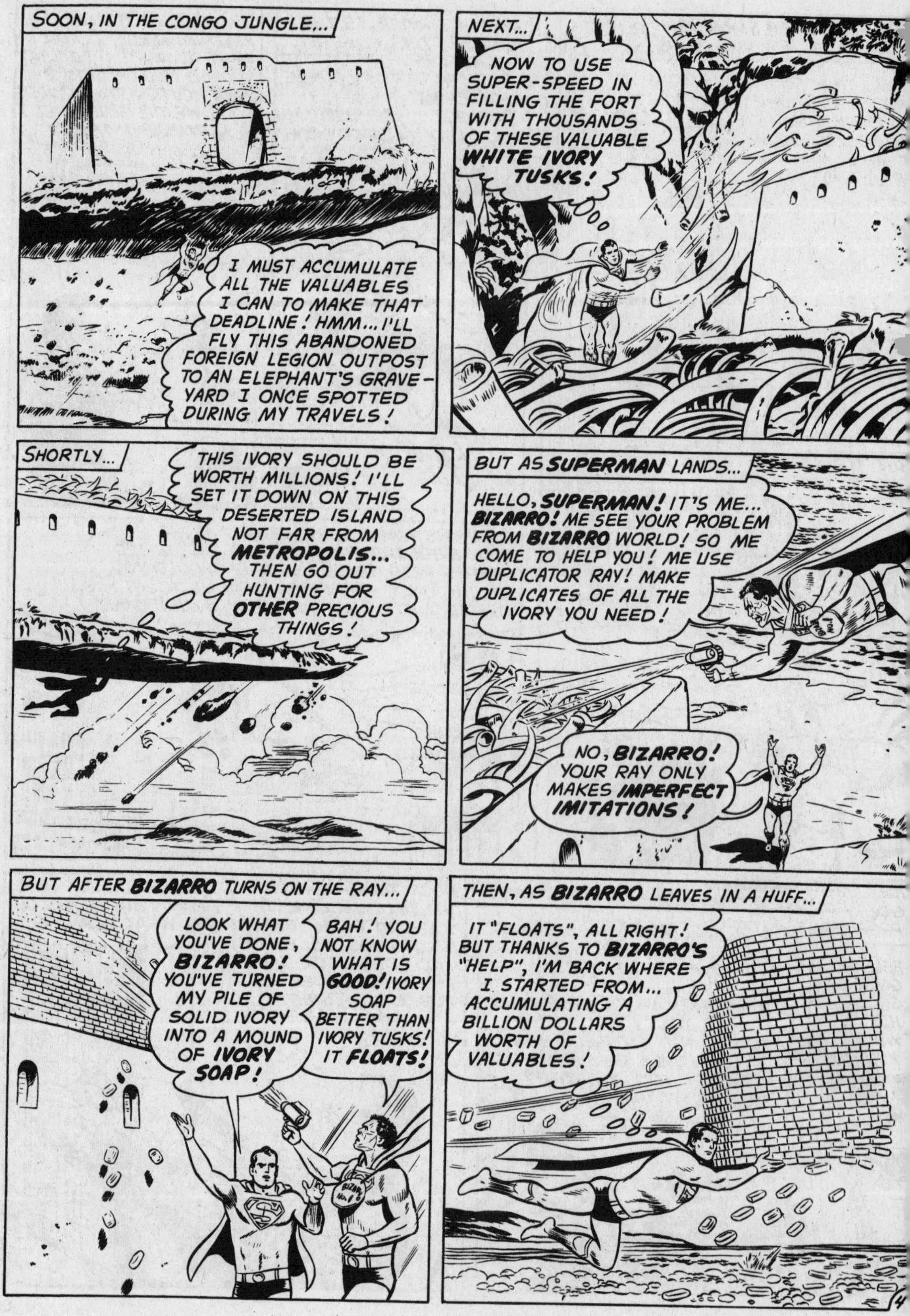
SOON, IN THE CONGO JUNGLE...
I MUST ACCUMULATE ALL THE VALUABLES I CAN TO MAKE THAT DEADLINE! HMM... I'LL FLY THIS ABANDONED FOREIGN LEGION OUTPOST TO AN ELEPHANT'S GRAVE-YARD I ONCE SPOTTED DURING MY TRAVELS!
NEXT...
NOW TO USE SUPER-SPEED IN FILLING THE FORT WITH THOUSANDS OF THESE VALUABLE WHITE IVORY TUSKS!
SHORTLY...
THIS IVORY SHOULD BE WORTH MILLIONS! I'LL SET IT DOWN ON THIS DESERTED ISLAND NOT FAR FROM METROPOLIS... THEN GO OUT HUNTING FOR OTHER PRECIOUS THINGS!
BUT AS SUPERMAN LANDS...
HELLO, SUPERMAN! IT'S ME... BIZARRO! ME SEE YOUR PROBLEM FROM BIZARRO WORLD! SO ME COME TO HELP YOU! ME USE DUPLICATOR RAY! MAKE DUPLICATES OF ALL THE IVORY YOU NEED!
NO, BIZARRO! YOUR RAY ONLY MAKES IMPERFECT IMITATIONS!
BUT AFTER BIZARRO TURNS ON THE RAY...
LOOK WHAT YOU'VE DONE, BIZARRO! YOU'VE TURNED MY PILE OF SOLID IVORY INTO A MOUND OF IVORY SOAP!
BAH! YOU NOT KNOW WHAT IS GOOD! IVORY SOAP BETTER THAN IVORY TUSKS! IT FLOATS!
THEN, AS BIZARRO LEAVES IN A HUFF...
IT "FLOATS", ALL RIGHT! BUT THANKS TO BIZARRO'S "HELP", I'M BACK WHERE I STARTED FROM... ACCUMULATING A BILLION DOLLARS WORTH OF VALUABLES!

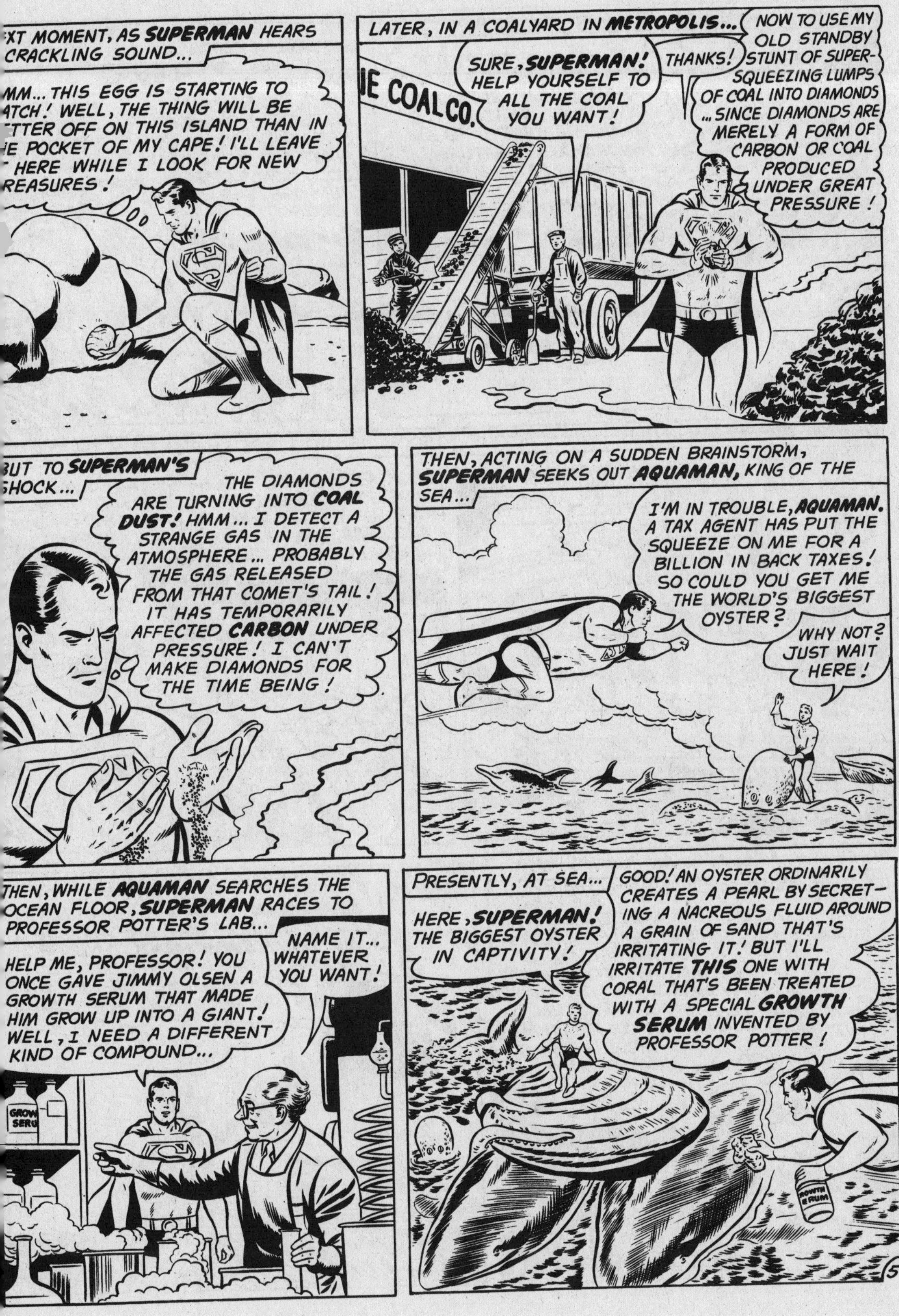

XT MOMENT, AS SUPERMAN HEARS CRACKLING SOUND...
MM... THIS EGG IS STARTING TO ATCH! WELL, THE THING WILL BE TTER OFF ON THIS ISLAND THAN IN E POCKET OF MY CAPE! I'LL LEAVE HERE WHILE I LOOK FOR NEW REASURES!
LATER, IN A COALYARD IN METROPOLIS...
E COAL CO.
SURE, SUPERMAN! HELP YOURSELF TO ALL THE COAL YOU WANT!
THANKS!
NOW TO USE MY OLD STANDBY STUNT OF SUPER-SQUEEZING LUMPS OF COAL INTO DIAMONDS ...SINCE DIAMONDS ARE MERELY A FORM OF CARBON OR COAL PRODUCED UNDER GREAT PRESSURE!
UT TO SUPERMAN'S HOCK...
THE DIAMONDS ARE TURNING INTO COAL DUST! HMM... I DETECT A STRANGE GAS IN THE ATMOSPHERE... PROBABLY THE GAS RELEASED FROM THAT COMET'S TAIL! IT HAS TEMPORARILY AFFECTED CARBON UNDER PRESSURE! I CAN'T MAKE DIAMONDS FOR THE TIME BEING!
THEN, ACTING ON A SUDDEN BRAINSTORM, SUPERMAN SEEKS OUT AQUAMAN, KING OF THE SEA...
I'M IN TROUBLE, AQUAMAN. A TAX AGENT HAS PUT THE SQUEEZE ON ME FOR A BILLION IN BACK TAXES! SO COULD YOU GET ME THE WORLD'S BIGGEST OYSTER?
WHY NOT? JUST WAIT HERE!
THEN, WHILE AQUAMAN SEARCHES THE OCEAN FLOOR, SUPERMAN RACES TO PROFESSOR POTTER'S LAB...
HELP ME, PROFESSOR! YOU ONCE GAVE JIMMY OLSEN A GROWTH SERUM THAT MADE HIM GROW UP INTO A GIANT! WELL, I NEED A DIFFERENT KIND OF COMPOUND...
NAME IT... WHATEVER YOU WANT!
GROW SERU
PRESENTLY, AT SEA...
HERE, SUPERMAN! THE BIGGEST OYSTER IN CAPTIVITY!
GOOD! AN OYSTER ORDINARILY CREATES A PEARL BY SECRETING A NACREOUS FLUID AROUND A GRAIN OF SAND THAT'S IRRITATING IT! BUT I'LL IRRITATE THIS ONE WITH CORAL THAT'S BEEN TREATED WITH A SPECIAL GROWTH SERUM INVENTED BY PROFESSOR POTTER!
GROWTH SERUM
5

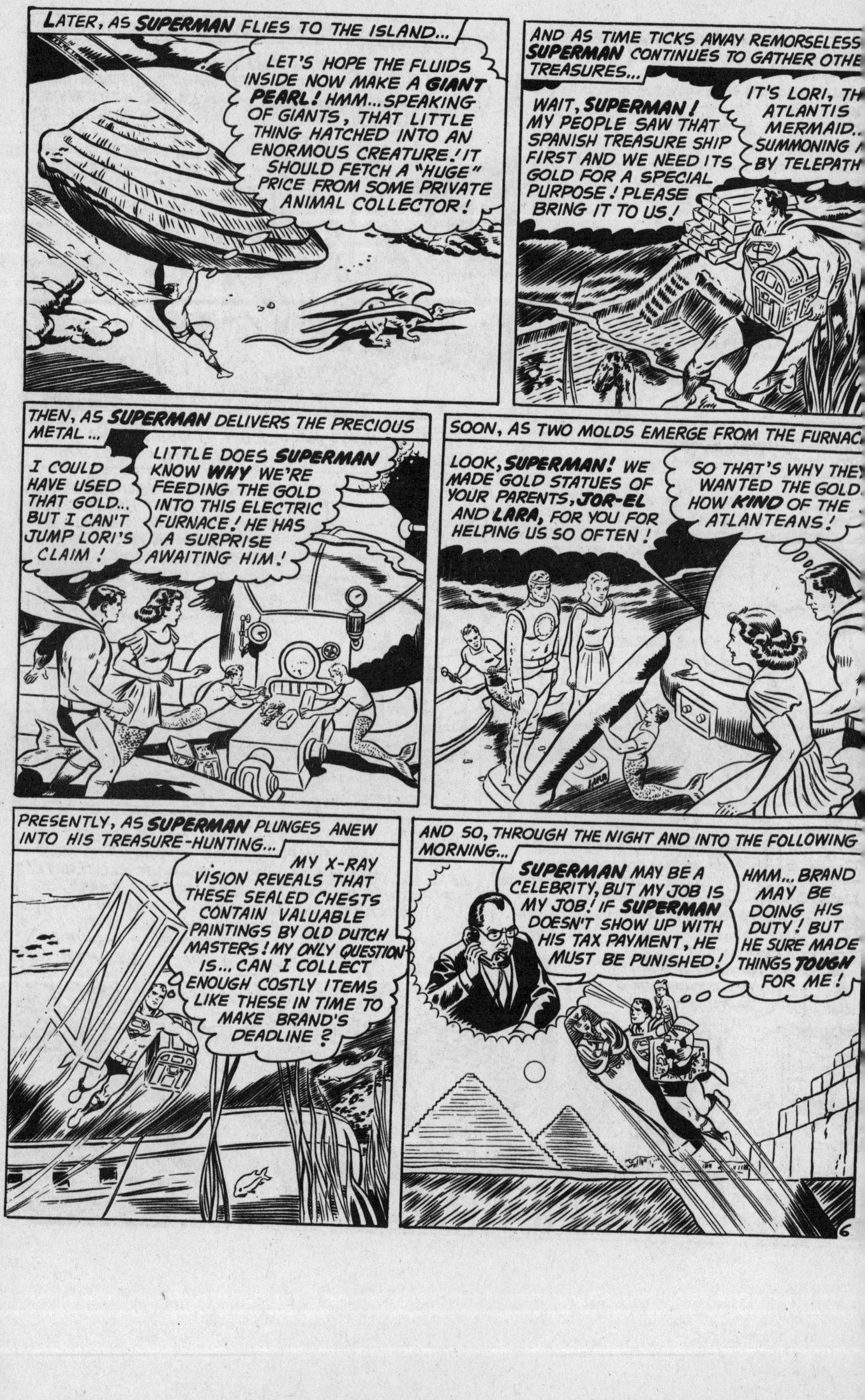
LATER, AS SUPERMAN FLIES TO THE ISLAND...
LET'S HOPE THE FLUIDS INSIDE NOW MAKE A GIANT PEARL! HMM...SPEAKING OF GIANTS, THAT LITTLE THING HATCHED INTO AN ENORMOUS CREATURE! IT SHOULD FETCH A "HUGE" PRICE FROM SOME PRIVATE ANIMAL COLLECTOR!
AND AS TIME TICKS AWAY REMORSELESS SUPERMAN CONTINUES TO GATHER OTHE TREASURES...
IT'S LORI, TH ATLANTIS MERMAID... SUMMONING BY TELEPATH
WAIT, SUPERMAN! MY PEOPLE SAW THAT SPANISH TREASURE SHIP FIRST AND WE NEED ITS GOLD FOR A SPECIAL PURPOSE! PLEASE BRING IT TO US!
THEN, AS SUPERMAN DELIVERS THE PRECIOUS METAL...
I COULD HAVE USED THAT GOLD... BUT I CAN'T JUMP LORI'S CLAIM!
LITTLE DOES SUPERMAN KNOW WHY WE'RE FEEDING THE GOLD INTO THIS ELECTRIC FURNACE! HE HAS A SURPRISE AWAITING HIM!
SOON, AS TWO MOLDS EMERGE FROM THE FURNAC
LOOK, SUPERMAN! WE MADE GOLD STATUES OF YOUR PARENTS, JOR-EL AND LARA, FOR YOU FOR HELPING US SO OFTEN!
SO THAT'S WHY THEY WANTED THE GOLD. HOW KIND OF THE ATLANTEANS!
PRESENTLY, AS SUPERMAN PLUNGES ANEW INTO HIS TREASURE-HUNTING...
MY X-RAY VISION REVEALS THAT THESE SEALED CHESTS CONTAIN VALUABLE PAINTINGS BY OLD DUTCH MASTERS! MY ONLY QUESTION IS... CAN I COLLECT ENOUGH COSTLY ITEMS LIKE THESE IN TIME TO MAKE BRAND'S DEADLINE?
AND SO, THROUGH THE NIGHT AND INTO THE FOLLOWING MORNING...
SUPERMAN MAY BE A CELEBRITY, BUT MY JOB IS MY JOB! IF SUPERMAN DOESN'T SHOW UP WITH HIS TAX PAYMENT, HE MUST BE PUNISHED!
HMM... BRAND MAY BE DOING HIS DUTY! BUT HE SURE MADE THINGS TOUGH FOR ME!
6

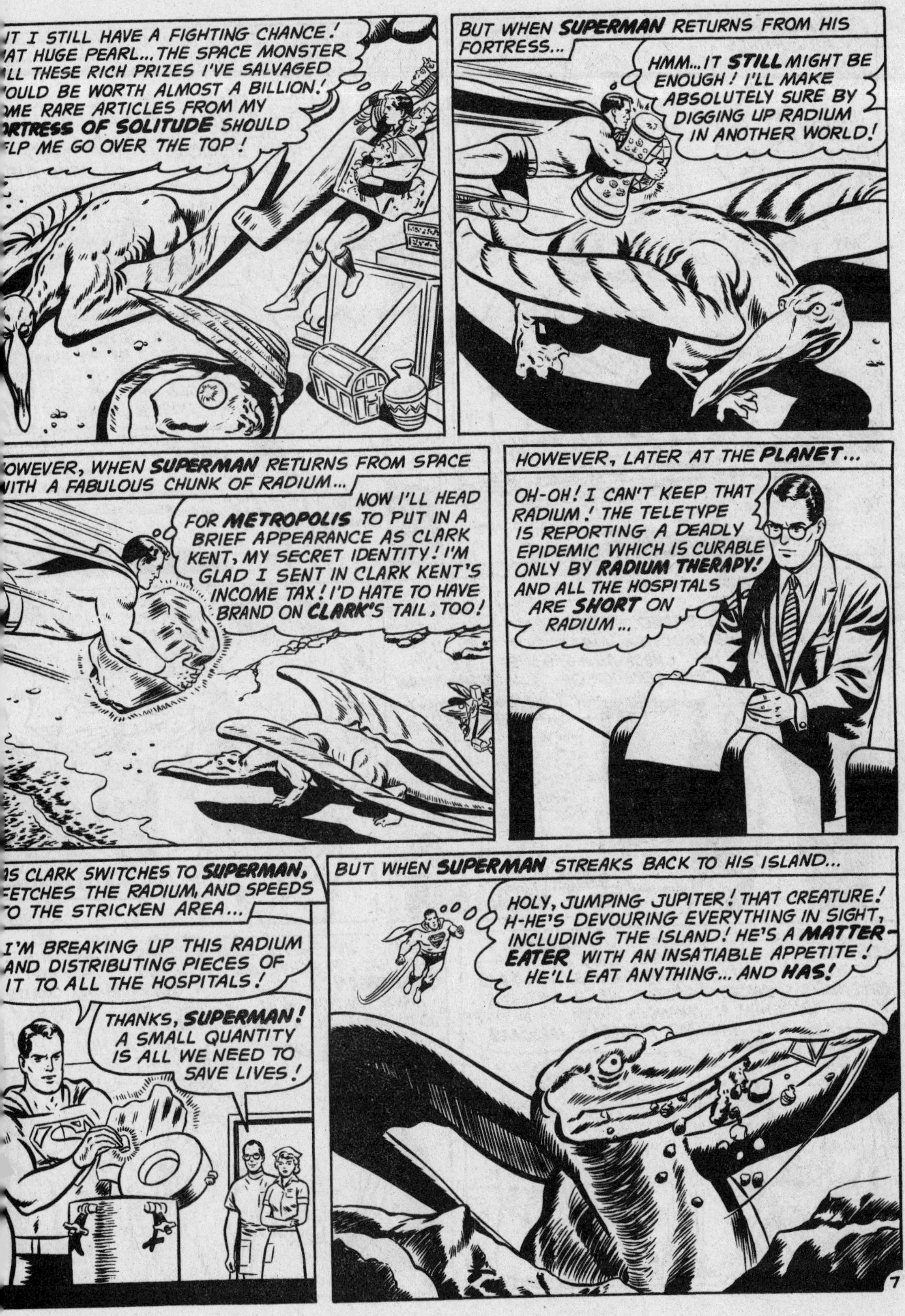

IT I STILL HAVE A FIGHTING CHANCE! AT HUGE PEARL... THE SPACE MONSTER LL THESE RICH PRIZES I'VE SALVAGED OULD BE WORTH ALMOST A BILLION! ME RARE ARTICLES FROM MY ORTRESS OF SOLITUDE SHOULD LP ME GO OVER THE TOP!
BUT WHEN SUPERMAN RETURNS FROM HIS FORTRESS...
HMM... IT STILL MIGHT BE ENOUGH! I'LL MAKE ABSOLUTELY SURE BY DIGGING UP RADIUM IN ANOTHER WORLD!
OWEVER, WHEN SUPERMAN RETURNS FROM SPACE WITH A FABULOUS CHUNK OF RADIUM...
NOW I'LL HEAD FOR METROPOLIS TO PUT IN A BRIEF APPEARANCE AS CLARK KENT, MY SECRET IDENTITY! I'M GLAD I SENT IN CLARK KENT'S INCOME TAX! I'D HATE TO HAVE BRAND ON CLARK'S TAIL, TOO!
HOWEVER, LATER AT THE PLANET...
OH-OH! I CAN'T KEEP THAT RADIUM! THE TELETYPE IS REPORTING A DEADLY EPIDEMIC WHICH IS CURABLE ONLY BY RADIUM THERAPY! AND ALL THE HOSPITALS ARE SHORT ON RADIUM...
AS CLARK SWITCHES TO SUPERMAN, FETCHES THE RADIUM, AND SPEEDS TO THE STRICKEN AREA...
I'M BREAKING UP THIS RADIUM AND DISTRIBUTING PIECES OF IT TO ALL THE HOSPITALS!
THANKS, SUPERMAN! A SMALL QUANTITY IS ALL WE NEED TO SAVE LIVES!
BUT WHEN SUPERMAN STREAKS BACK TO HIS ISLAND...
HOLY, JUMPING JUPITER! THAT CREATURE! H-HE'S DEVOURING EVERYTHING IN SIGHT, INCLUDING THE ISLAND! HE'S A MATTER-EATER WITH AN INSATIABLE APPETITE! HE'LL EAT ANYTHING... AND HAS!
7

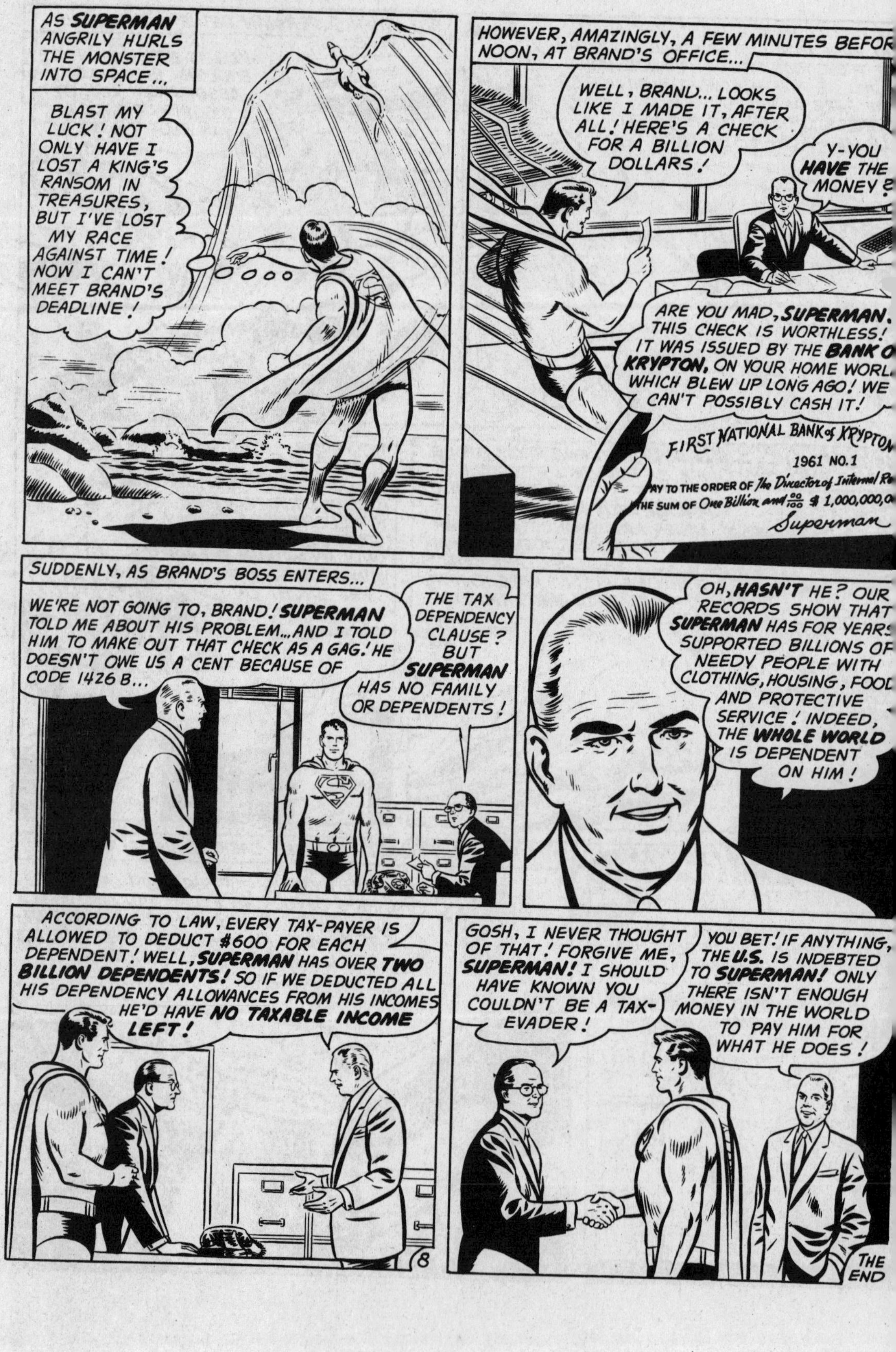
AS SUPERMAN ANGRILY HURLS THE MONSTER INTO SPACE...
BLAST MY LUCK! NOT ONLY HAVE I LOST A KING'S RANSOM IN TREASURES, BUT I'VE LOST MY RACE AGAINST TIME! NOW I CAN'T MEET BRAND'S DEADLINE!
HOWEVER, AMAZINGLY, A FEW MINUTES BEFOR NOON, AT BRAND'S OFFICE...
WELL, BRAND... LOOKS LIKE I MADE IT, AFTER ALL! HERE'S A CHECK FOR A BILLION DOLLARS!
Y-YOU HAVE THE MONEY?
ARE YOU MAD, SUPERMAN. THIS CHECK IS WORTHLESS! IT WAS ISSUED BY THE BANK O KRYPTON, ON YOUR HOME WORL WHICH BLEW UP LONG AGO! WE CAN'T POSSIBLY CASH IT!
FIRST NATIONAL BANK of KRYPTON
1961 NO.1
PAY TO THE ORDER OF The Director of Internal Re
THE SUM OF One Billion and 00/100 $ 1,000,000,0
Superman
SUDDENLY, AS BRAND'S BOSS ENTERS...
WE'RE NOT GOING TO, BRAND! SUPERMAN TOLD ME ABOUT HIS PROBLEM...AND I TOLD HIM TO MAKE OUT THAT CHECK AS A GAG! HE DOESN'T OWE US A CENT BECAUSE OF CODE 1426 B...
THE TAX DEPENDENCY CLAUSE? BUT SUPERMAN HAS NO FAMILY OR DEPENDENTS!
OH, HASN'T HE? OUR RECORDS SHOW THAT SUPERMAN HAS FOR YEARS SUPPORTED BILLIONS OF NEEDY PEOPLE WITH CLOTHING, HOUSING, FOOD AND PROTECTIVE SERVICE! INDEED, THE WHOLE WORLD IS DEPENDENT ON HIM!
ACCORDING TO LAW, EVERY TAX-PAYER IS ALLOWED TO DEDUCT $600 FOR EACH DEPENDENT! WELL, SUPERMAN HAS OVER TWO BILLION DEPENDENTS! SO IF WE DEDUCTED ALL HIS DEPENDENCY ALLOWANCES FROM HIS INCOMES HE'D HAVE NO TAXABLE INCOME LEFT!
8
GOSH, I NEVER THOUGHT OF THAT! FORGIVE ME, SUPERMAN! I SHOULD HAVE KNOWN YOU COULDN'T BE A TAX-EVADER!
YOU BET! IF ANYTHING, THE U.S. IS INDEBTED TO SUPERMAN! ONLY THERE ISN'T ENOUGH MONEY IN THE WORLD TO PAY HIM FOR WHAT HE DOES!
THE END

ONE DAY, IN *METROPOLIS*, A GLOATING FIGURE STUDIES A DIAGRAM...

SO NOBODY'S EVER BEEN ABLE TO ROB THE *UNDERGROUND MUSEUM*, EH? WELL, I, *PAUL PRATT*, WILL BE FIRST!

UNDERGROUND MUSEUM OF INTERNATIONAL TREASURES

GUARDS

ELEVATORS

BURGLAR ALARM

EXHIBIT ROOMS

THAT AFTERNOON...

EVERY NATION HAS CONTRIBUTED ITS RARE TREASURES TO THIS MUSEUM! IT'S SUPPOSED TO BE AS TOUGH TO ROB AS FORT KNOX... WITH HUNDREDS OF GUARDS STATIONED THROUGHOUT THE UNDER-GROUND STRUCTURE!

UNDERGROUND MUSEUM OF INTERNATIONAL TREASURES

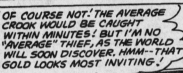
ELEVATORS

AS PRATT TAKES AN ELEVATOR DOWN...

SUPPOSE A CROOK *DID* GRAB AN ARM-FUL OF GOLD STATUES? WHERE COULD HE RUN TO? *HOW* COULD HE ESCAPE? COULD HE *VANISH* THROUGH THE WALLS?

OF COURSE NOT! THE AVERAGE CROOK WOULD BE CAUGHT WITHIN MINUTES! BUT I'M NO "AVERAGE" THIEF, AS THE WORLD WILL SOON DISCOVER. HMM-- THAT GOLD LOOKS MOST INVITING!

TO SEAL ALL EXITS BURGLAR ALARM

MEXICAN EXHIBIT OF RARE AZTEC GOLD STATUES

SHORTLY...

OKAY! I'VE COLLECTED A SMALL FORTUNE! NOW TO MAKE MY GETAWAY!

RAMON, LOOK! A *THIEF!*

LET THE FOOL RUN! HE CAN'T ESCAPE! I'M SEALING OFF ALL ROOMS ON THIS LEVEL!

RARE STAMPS FROM ALL NATIONS

BUT AS HE SPRINTS INTO AN ADJOINING CHAMBER...

HA! HA! THEY THINK I'M *TRAPPED!* I NEED ONLY PUSH A TINY BUTTON ON THIS BELT, AND--

CLICK!

2

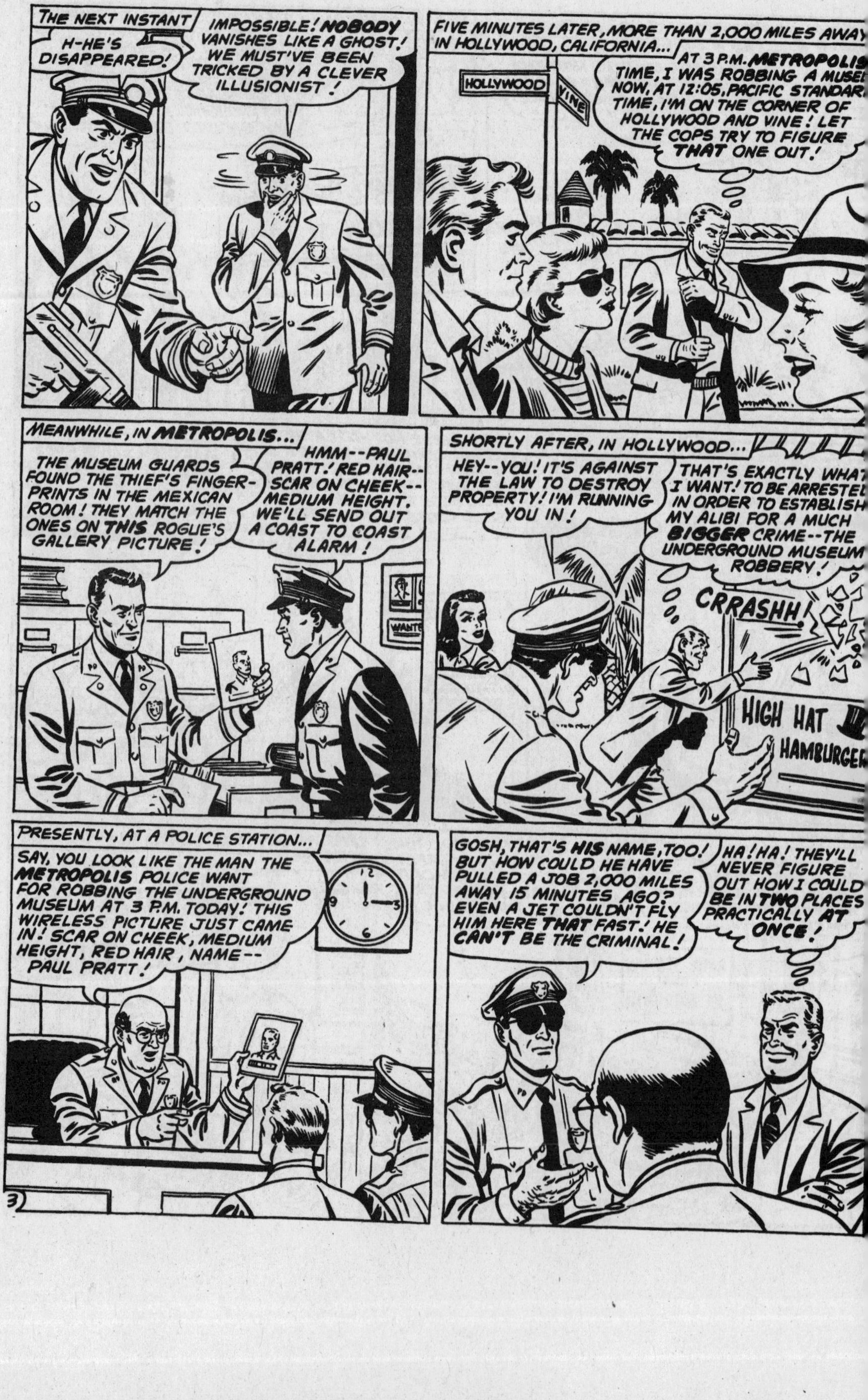
THE NEXT INSTANT
H-HE'S DISAPPEARED!
IMPOSSIBLE! NOBODY VANISHES LIKE A GHOST! WE MUST'VE BEEN TRICKED BY A CLEVER ILLUSIONIST!
FIVE MINUTES LATER, MORE THAN 2,000 MILES AWAY IN HOLLYWOOD, CALIFORNIA...
HOLLYWOOD
VINE
AT 3 P.M. METROPOLIS TIME, I WAS ROBBING A MUSE NOW, AT 12:05, PACIFIC STANDAR TIME, I'M ON THE CORNER OF HOLLYWOOD AND VINE! LET THE COPS TRY TO FIGURE THAT ONE OUT!
MEANWHILE, IN METROPOLIS...
THE MUSEUM GUARDS FOUND THE THIEF'S FINGER-PRINTS IN THE MEXICAN ROOM! THEY MATCH THE ONES ON THIS ROGUE'S GALLERY PICTURE!
HMM--PAUL PRATT! RED HAIR--SCAR ON CHEEK--MEDIUM HEIGHT. WE'LL SEND OUT A COAST TO COAST ALARM!
SHORTLY AFTER, IN HOLLYWOOD...
HEY--YOU! IT'S AGAINST THE LAW TO DESTROY PROPERTY! I'M RUNNING YOU IN!
THAT'S EXACTLY WHAT I WANT! TO BE ARRESTE IN ORDER TO ESTABLISH MY ALIBI FOR A MUCH BIGGER CRIME--THE UNDERGROUND MUSEUM ROBBERY!
CRRASHH!
HIGH HAT
HAMBURGER
PRESENTLY, AT A POLICE STATION...
SAY, YOU LOOK LIKE THE MAN THE METROPOLIS POLICE WANT FOR ROBBING THE UNDERGROUND MUSEUM AT 3 P.M. TODAY! THIS WIRELESS PICTURE JUST CAME IN! SCAR ON CHEEK, MEDIUM HEIGHT, RED HAIR, NAME--PAUL PRATT!
GOSH, THAT'S HIS NAME, TOO! BUT HOW COULD HE HAVE PULLED A JOB 2,000 MILES AWAY 15 MINUTES AGO? EVEN A JET COULDN'T FLY HIM HERE THAT FAST! HE CAN'T BE THE CRIMINAL!
HA! HA! THEY'LL NEVER FIGURE OUT HOW I COULD BE IN TWO PLACES PRACTICALLY AT ONCE!
3

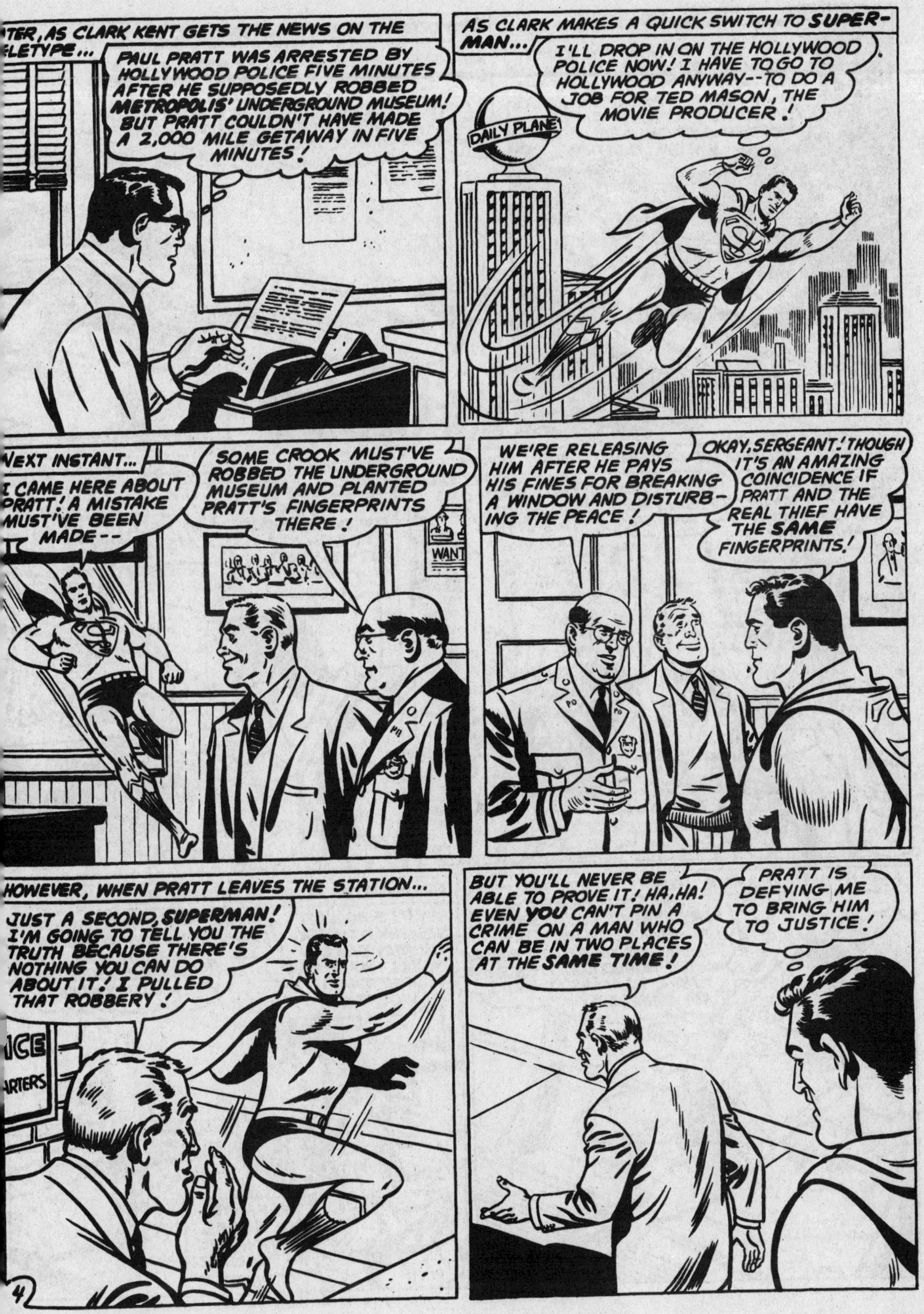
TER, AS CLARK KENT GETS THE NEWS ON THE
ELETYPE...
PAUL PRATT WAS ARRESTED BY HOLLYWOOD POLICE FIVE MINUTES AFTER HE SUPPOSEDLY ROBBED METROPOLIS' UNDERGROUND MUSEUM! BUT PRATT COULDN'T HAVE MADE A 2,000 MILE GETAWAY IN FIVE MINUTES!
AS CLARK MAKES A QUICK SWITCH TO SUPER-MAN...
I'LL DROP IN ON THE HOLLYWOOD POLICE NOW! I HAVE TO GO TO HOLLYWOOD ANYWAY--TO DO A JOB FOR TED MASON, THE MOVIE PRODUCER!
DAILY PLANET
NEXT INSTANT...
I CAME HERE ABOUT PRATT! A MISTAKE MUST'VE BEEN MADE--
SOME CROOK MUST'VE ROBBED THE UNDERGROUND MUSEUM AND PLANTED PRATT'S FINGERPRINTS THERE!
WANT
WE'RE RELEASING HIM AFTER HE PAYS HIS FINES FOR BREAKING A WINDOW AND DISTURB-ING THE PEACE!
OKAY, SERGEANT! THOUGH IT'S AN AMAZING COINCIDENCE IF PRATT AND THE REAL THIEF HAVE THE SAME FINGERPRINTS!
HOWEVER, WHEN PRATT LEAVES THE STATION...
JUST A SECOND, SUPERMAN! I'M GOING TO TELL YOU THE TRUTH BECAUSE THERE'S NOTHING YOU CAN DO ABOUT IT! I PULLED THAT ROBBERY!
ICE
ARTERS
4
BUT YOU'LL NEVER BE ABLE TO PROVE IT! HA, HA! EVEN YOU CAN'T PIN A CRIME ON A MAN WHO CAN BE IN TWO PLACES AT THE SAME TIME!
PRATT IS DEFYING ME TO BRING HIM TO JUSTICE!

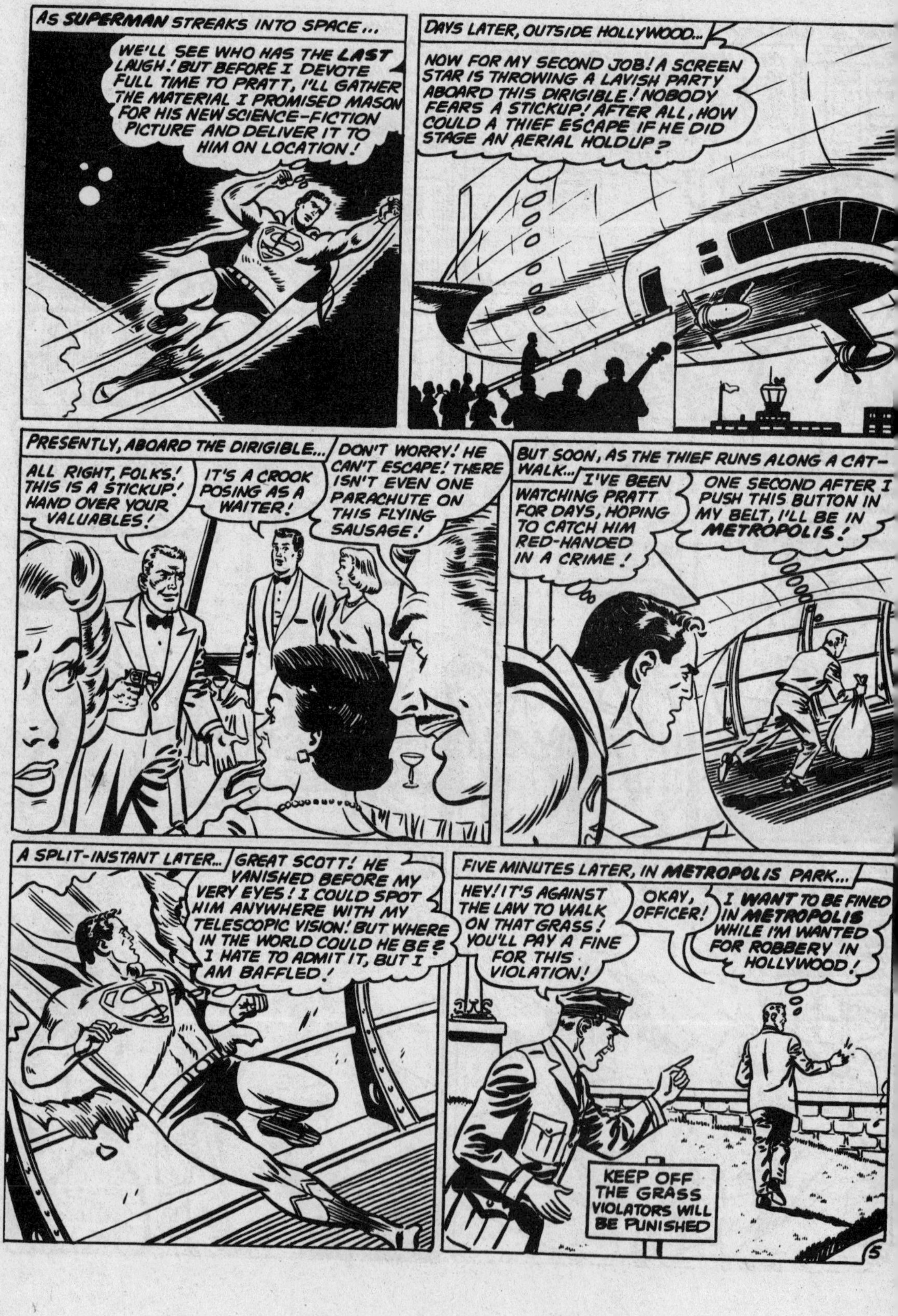
AS SUPERMAN STREAKS INTO SPACE...
WE'LL SEE WHO HAS THE LAST LAUGH! BUT BEFORE I DEVOTE FULL TIME TO PRATT, I'LL GATHER THE MATERIAL I PROMISED MASON FOR HIS NEW SCIENCE-FICTION PICTURE AND DELIVER IT TO HIM ON LOCATION!
DAYS LATER, OUTSIDE HOLLYWOOD...
NOW FOR MY SECOND JOB! A SCREEN STAR IS THROWING A LAVISH PARTY ABOARD THIS DIRIGIBLE! NOBODY FEARS A STICKUP! AFTER ALL, HOW COULD A THIEF ESCAPE IF HE DID STAGE AN AERIAL HOLDUP?
PRESENTLY, ABOARD THE DIRIGIBLE...
ALL RIGHT, FOLKS! THIS IS A STICKUP! HAND OVER YOUR VALUABLES!
IT'S A CROOK POSING AS A WAITER!
DON'T WORRY! HE CAN'T ESCAPE! THERE ISN'T EVEN ONE PARACHUTE ON THIS FLYING SAUSAGE!
BUT SOON, AS THE THIEF RUNS ALONG A CAT-WALK...
I'VE BEEN WATCHING PRATT FOR DAYS, HOPING TO CATCH HIM RED-HANDED IN A CRIME!
ONE SECOND AFTER I PUSH THIS BUTTON IN MY BELT, I'LL BE IN METROPOLIS!
A SPLIT-INSTANT LATER...
GREAT SCOTT! HE VANISHED BEFORE MY VERY EYES! I COULD SPOT HIM ANYWHERE WITH MY TELESCOPIC VISION! BUT WHERE IN THE WORLD COULD HE BE? I HATE TO ADMIT IT, BUT I AM BAFFLED!
FIVE MINUTES LATER, IN METROPOLIS PARK...
HEY! IT'S AGAINST THE LAW TO WALK ON THAT GRASS! YOU'LL PAY A FINE FOR THIS VIOLATION!
OKAY, OFFICER!
I WANT TO BE FINED IN METROPOLIS WHILE I'M WANTED FOR ROBBERY IN HOLLYWOOD!
KEEP OFF THE GRASS VIOLATORS WILL BE PUNISHED
5

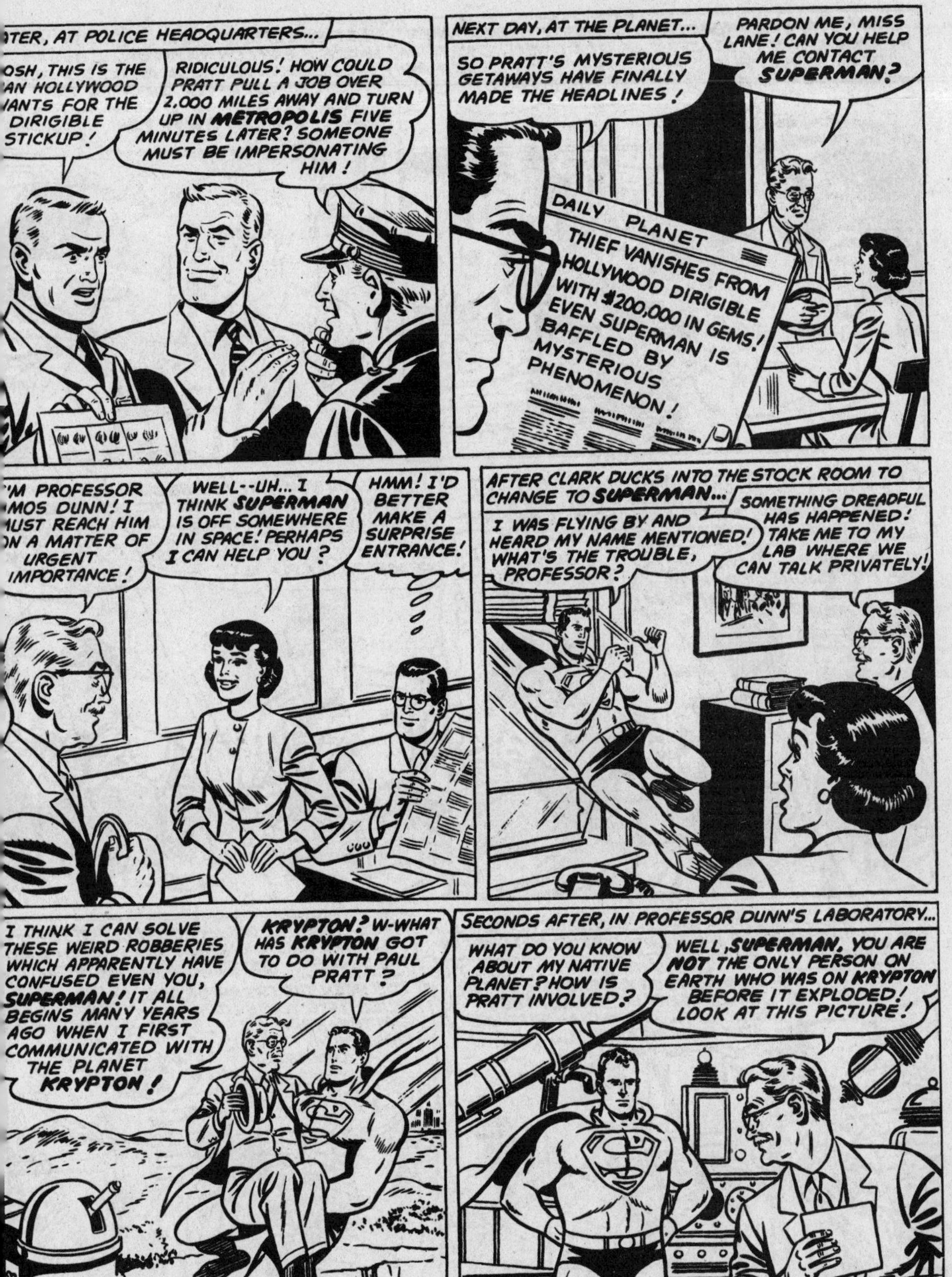
ATER, AT POLICE HEADQUARTERS...
OSH, THIS IS THE AN HOLLYWOOD VANTS FOR THE DIRIGIBLE STICKUP!
RIDICULOUS! HOW COULD PRATT PULL A JOB OVER 2,000 MILES AWAY AND TURN UP IN METROPOLIS FIVE MINUTES LATER? SOMEONE MUST BE IMPERSONATING HIM!
NEXT DAY, AT THE PLANET...
SO PRATT'S MYSTERIOUS GETAWAYS HAVE FINALLY MADE THE HEADLINES!
PARDON ME, MISS LANE! CAN YOU HELP ME CONTACT SUPERMAN?
DAILY PLANET
THIEF VANISHES FROM HOLLYWOOD DIRIGIBLE WITH $200,000 IN GEMS! EVEN SUPERMAN IS BAFFLED BY MYSTERIOUS PHENOMENON!
'M PROFESSOR MOS DUNN! I MUST REACH HIM ON A MATTER OF URGENT IMPORTANCE!
WELL--UH... I THINK SUPERMAN IS OFF SOMEWHERE IN SPACE! PERHAPS I CAN HELP YOU?
HMM! I'D BETTER MAKE A SURPRISE ENTRANCE!
AFTER CLARK DUCKS INTO THE STOCK ROOM TO CHANGE TO SUPERMAN...
I WAS FLYING BY AND HEARD MY NAME MENTIONED! WHAT'S THE TROUBLE, PROFESSOR?
SOMETHING DREADFUL HAS HAPPENED! TAKE ME TO MY LAB WHERE WE CAN TALK PRIVATELY!
I THINK I CAN SOLVE THESE WEIRD ROBBERIES WHICH APPARENTLY HAVE CONFUSED EVEN YOU, SUPERMAN! IT ALL BEGINS MANY YEARS AGO WHEN I FIRST COMMUNICATED WITH THE PLANET KRYPTON!
KRYPTON? W-WHAT HAS KRYPTON GOT TO DO WITH PAUL PRATT?
SECONDS AFTER, IN PROFESSOR DUNN'S LABORATORY...
WHAT DO YOU KNOW ABOUT MY NATIVE PLANET? HOW IS PRATT INVOLVED?
WELL, SUPERMAN, YOU ARE NOT THE ONLY PERSON ON EARTH WHO WAS ON KRYPTON BEFORE IT EXPLODED! LOOK AT THIS PICTURE!
6

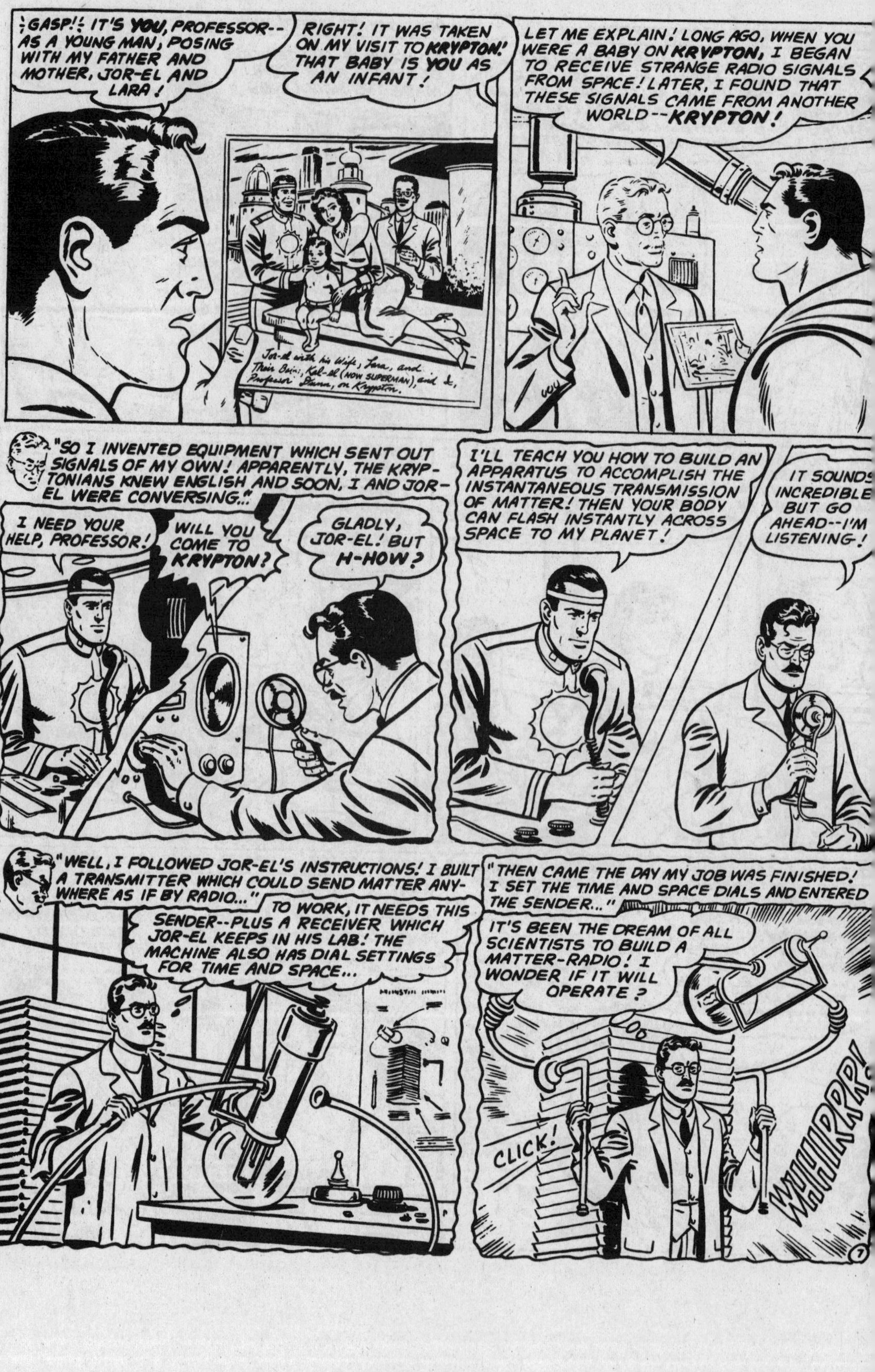
¡GASP!¡ IT'S YOU, PROFESSOR-- AS A YOUNG MAN, POSING WITH MY FATHER AND MOTHER, JOR-EL AND LARA!
RIGHT! IT WAS TAKEN ON MY VISIT TO KRYPTON! THAT BABY IS YOU AS AN INFANT!
LET ME EXPLAIN! LONG AGO, WHEN YOU WERE A BABY ON KRYPTON, I BEGAN TO RECEIVE STRANGE RADIO SIGNALS FROM SPACE! LATER, I FOUND THAT THESE SIGNALS CAME FROM ANOTHER WORLD--KRYPTON!
"SO I INVENTED EQUIPMENT WHICH SENT OUT SIGNALS OF MY OWN! APPARENTLY, THE KRYPTONIANS KNEW ENGLISH AND SOON, I AND JOR-EL WERE CONVERSING..."
I NEED YOUR HELP, PROFESSOR!
WILL YOU COME TO KRYPTON?
GLADLY, JOR-EL! BUT H-HOW?
I'LL TEACH YOU HOW TO BUILD AN APPARATUS TO ACCOMPLISH THE INSTANTANEOUS TRANSMISSION OF MATTER! THEN YOUR BODY CAN FLASH INSTANTLY ACROSS SPACE TO MY PLANET!
IT SOUNDS INCREDIBLE BUT GO AHEAD--I'M LISTENING!
"WELL, I FOLLOWED JOR-EL'S INSTRUCTIONS! I BUILT A TRANSMITTER WHICH COULD SEND MATTER ANYWHERE AS IF BY RADIO..."
TO WORK, IT NEEDS THIS SENDER--PLUS A RECEIVER WHICH JOR-EL KEEPS IN HIS LAB! THE MACHINE ALSO HAS DIAL SETTINGS FOR TIME AND SPACE...
"THEN CAME THE DAY MY JOB WAS FINISHED! I SET THE TIME AND SPACE DIALS AND ENTERED THE SENDER..."
IT'S BEEN THE DREAM OF ALL SCIENTISTS TO BUILD A MATTER-RADIO! I WONDER IF IT WILL OPERATE?
CLICK!
WHIRRR!
7

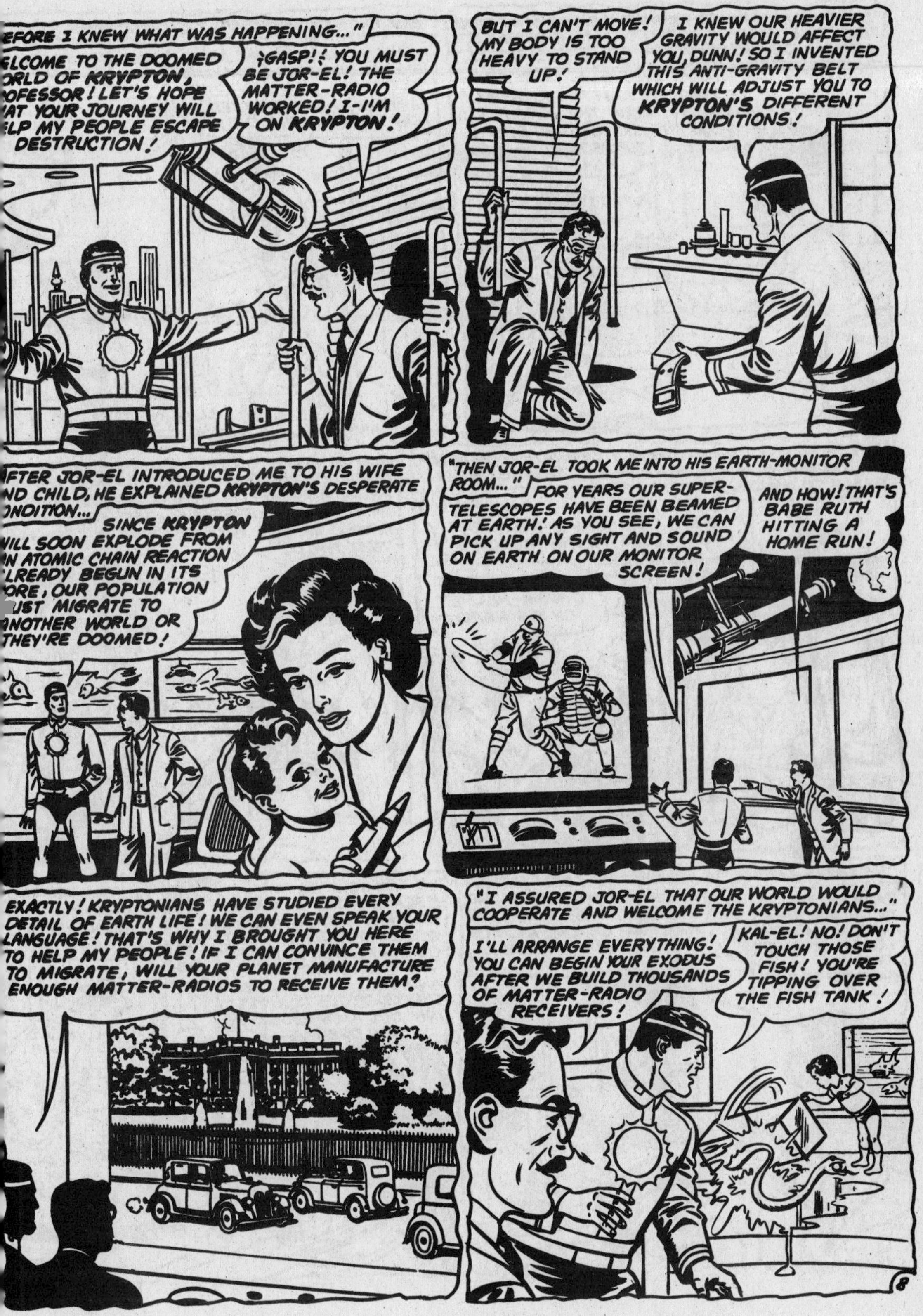
EFORE I KNEW WHAT WAS HAPPENING..."
ELCOME TO THE DOOMED ORLD OF KRYPTON, ROFESSOR! LET'S HOPE AT YOUR JOURNEY WILL ELP MY PEOPLE ESCAPE DESTRUCTION!
¡GASP!¡ YOU MUST BE JOR-EL! THE MATTER-RADIO WORKED! I-I'M ON KRYPTON!
BUT I CAN'T MOVE! MY BODY IS TOO HEAVY TO STAND UP!
I KNEW OUR HEAVIER GRAVITY WOULD AFFECT YOU, DUNN! SO I INVENTED THIS ANTI-GRAVITY BELT WHICH WILL ADJUST YOU TO KRYPTON'S DIFFERENT CONDITIONS!
FTER JOR-EL INTRODUCED ME TO HIS WIFE ND CHILD, HE EXPLAINED KRYPTON'S DESPERATE ONDITION...
SINCE KRYPTON VILL SOON EXPLODE FROM N ATOMIC CHAIN REACTION LREADY BEGUN IN ITS ORE, OUR POPULATION UST MIGRATE TO ANOTHER WORLD OR THEY'RE DOOMED!
"THEN JOR-EL TOOK ME INTO HIS EARTH-MONITOR ROOM..."
FOR YEARS OUR SUPER-TELESCOPES HAVE BEEN BEAMED AT EARTH! AS YOU SEE, WE CAN PICK UP ANY SIGHT AND SOUND ON EARTH ON OUR MONITOR SCREEN!
AND HOW! THAT'S BABE RUTH HITTING A HOME RUN!
EXACTLY! KRYPTONIANS HAVE STUDIED EVERY DETAIL OF EARTH LIFE! WE CAN EVEN SPEAK YOUR LANGUAGE! THAT'S WHY I BROUGHT YOU HERE TO HELP MY PEOPLE! IF I CAN CONVINCE THEM TO MIGRATE, WILL YOUR PLANET MANUFACTURE ENOUGH MATTER-RADIOS TO RECEIVE THEM?
"I ASSURED JOR-EL THAT OUR WORLD WOULD COOPERATE AND WELCOME THE KRYPTONIANS..."
I'LL ARRANGE EVERYTHING! YOU CAN BEGIN YOUR EXODUS AFTER WE BUILD THOUSANDS OF MATTER-RADIO RECEIVERS!
KAL-EL! NO! DON'T TOUCH THOSE FISH! YOU'RE TIPPING OVER THE FISH TANK!
8

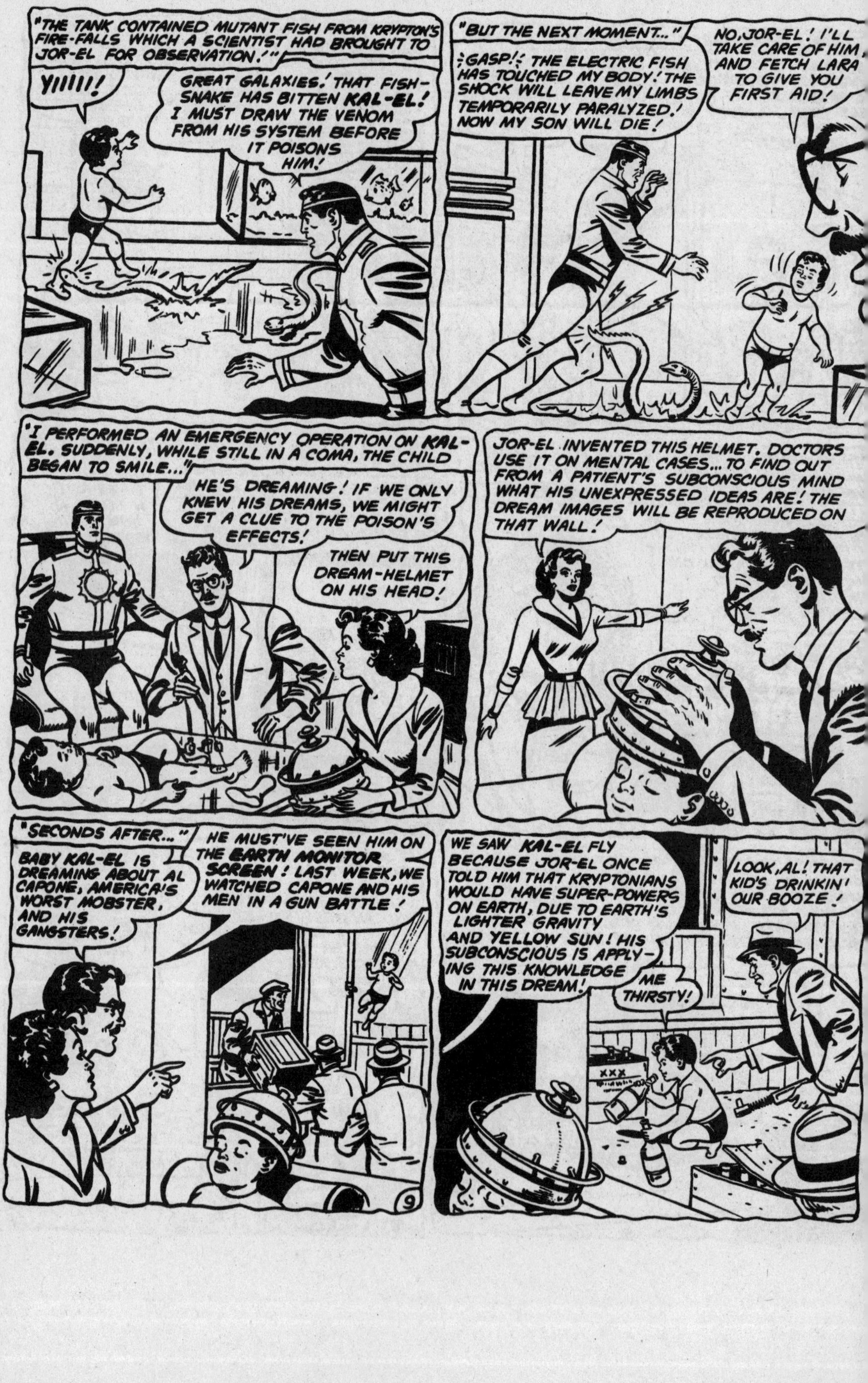
"THE TANK CONTAINED MUTANT FISH FROM KRYPTON'S FIRE-FALLS WHICH A SCIENTIST HAD BROUGHT TO JOR-EL FOR OBSERVATION!"
YIIIIII!
GREAT GALAXIES! THAT FISH-SNAKE HAS BITTEN KAL-EL! I MUST DRAW THE VENOM FROM HIS SYSTEM BEFORE IT POISONS HIM!
"BUT THE NEXT MOMENT..."
GASP! THE ELECTRIC FISH HAS TOUCHED MY BODY! THE SHOCK WILL LEAVE MY LIMBS TEMPORARILY PARALYZED! NOW MY SON WILL DIE!
NO, JOR-EL! I'LL TAKE CARE OF HIM, AND FETCH LARA TO GIVE YOU FIRST AID!
"I PERFORMED AN EMERGENCY OPERATION ON KAL-EL. SUDDENLY, WHILE STILL IN A COMA, THE CHILD BEGAN TO SMILE..."
HE'S DREAMING! IF WE ONLY KNEW HIS DREAMS, WE MIGHT GET A CLUE TO THE POISON'S EFFECTS!
THEN PUT THIS DREAM-HELMET ON HIS HEAD!
JOR-EL INVENTED THIS HELMET. DOCTORS USE IT ON MENTAL CASES... TO FIND OUT FROM A PATIENT'S SUBCONSCIOUS MIND WHAT HIS UNEXPRESSED IDEAS ARE! THE DREAM IMAGES WILL BE REPRODUCED ON THAT WALL!
"SECONDS AFTER..."
BABY KAL-EL IS DREAMING ABOUT AL CAPONE, AMERICA'S WORST MOBSTER, AND HIS GANGSTERS!
HE MUST'VE SEEN HIM ON THE EARTH MONITOR SCREEN! LAST WEEK, WE WATCHED CAPONE AND HIS MEN IN A GUN BATTLE!
WE SAW KAL-EL FLY BECAUSE JOR-EL ONCE TOLD HIM THAT KRYPTONIANS WOULD HAVE SUPER-POWERS ON EARTH, DUE TO EARTH'S LIGHTER GRAVITY AND YELLOW SUN! HIS SUBCONSCIOUS IS APPLYING THIS KNOWLEDGE IN THIS DREAM!
ME THIRSTY!
LOOK, AL! THAT KID'S DRINKIN' OUR BOOZE!
XXX
9

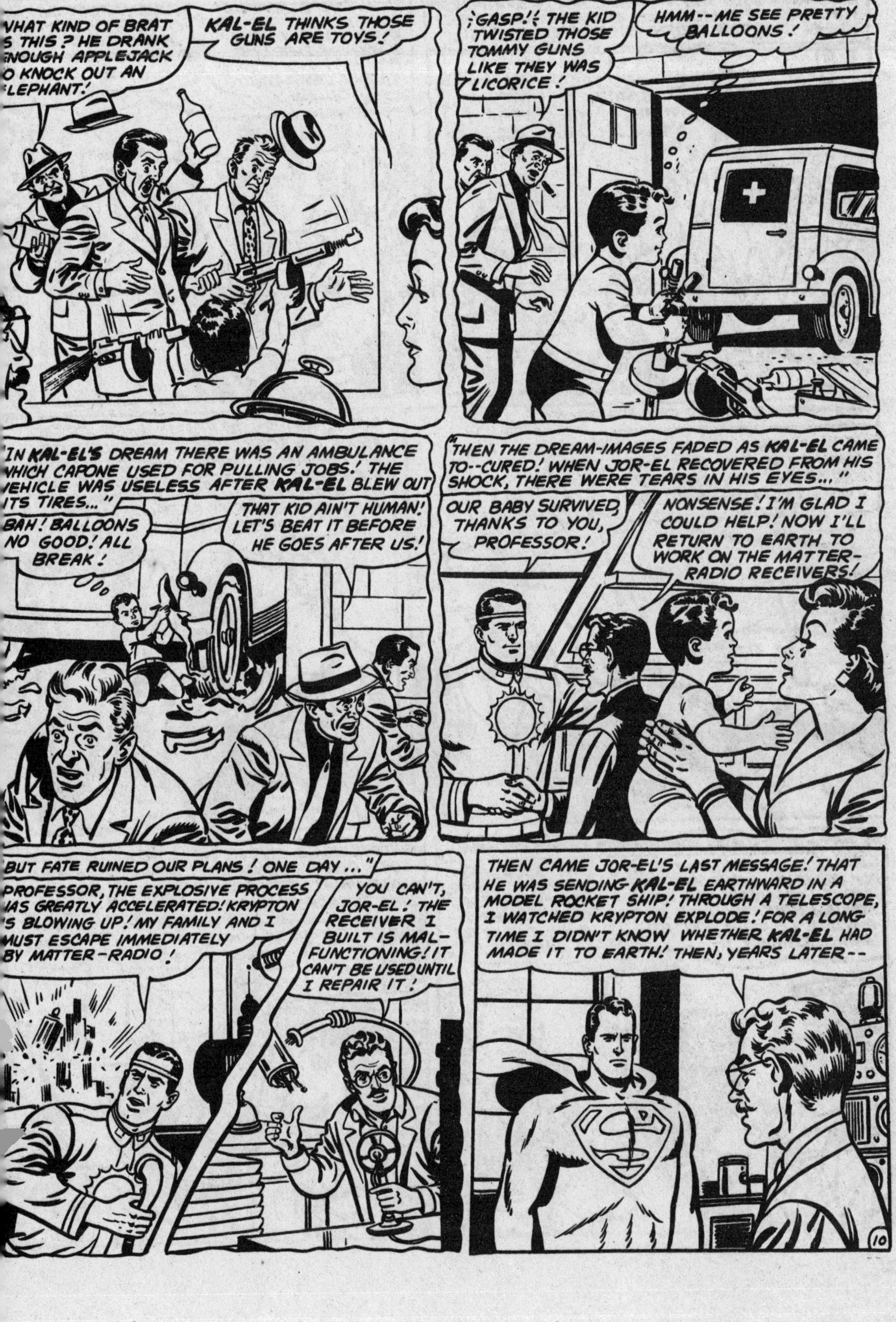
WHAT KIND OF BRAT IS THIS? HE DRANK ENOUGH APPLEJACK TO KNOCK OUT AN ELEPHANT!
KAL-EL THINKS THOSE GUNS ARE TOYS!
¡GASP!¡ THE KID TWISTED THOSE TOMMY GUNS LIKE THEY WAS LICORICE!
HMM--ME SEE PRETTY BALLOONS!
"IN KAL-EL'S DREAM THERE WAS AN AMBULANCE WHICH CAPONE USED FOR PULLING JOBS! THE VEHICLE WAS USELESS AFTER KAL-EL BLEW OUT ITS TIRES..."
BAH! BALLOONS NO GOOD! ALL BREAK!
THAT KID AIN'T HUMAN! LET'S BEAT IT BEFORE HE GOES AFTER US!
"THEN THE DREAM-IMAGES FADED AS KAL-EL CAME TO--CURED! WHEN JOR-EL RECOVERED FROM HIS SHOCK, THERE WERE TEARS IN HIS EYES..."
OUR BABY SURVIVED, THANKS TO YOU, PROFESSOR!
NONSENSE! I'M GLAD I COULD HELP! NOW I'LL RETURN TO EARTH TO WORK ON THE MATTER-RADIO RECEIVERS!
"BUT FATE RUINED OUR PLANS! ONE DAY..."
PROFESSOR, THE EXPLOSIVE PROCESS HAS GREATLY ACCELERATED! KRYPTON IS BLOWING UP! MY FAMILY AND I MUST ESCAPE IMMEDIATELY BY MATTER-RADIO!
YOU CAN'T, JOR-EL! THE RECEIVER I BUILT IS MAL-FUNCTIONING! IT CAN'T BE USED UNTIL I REPAIR IT!
THEN CAME JOR-EL'S LAST MESSAGE! THAT HE WAS SENDING KAL-EL EARTHWARD IN A MODEL ROCKET SHIP! THROUGH A TELESCOPE, I WATCHED KRYPTON EXPLODE! FOR A LONG TIME I DIDN'T KNOW WHETHER KAL-EL HAD MADE IT TO EARTH! THEN, YEARS LATER--
10

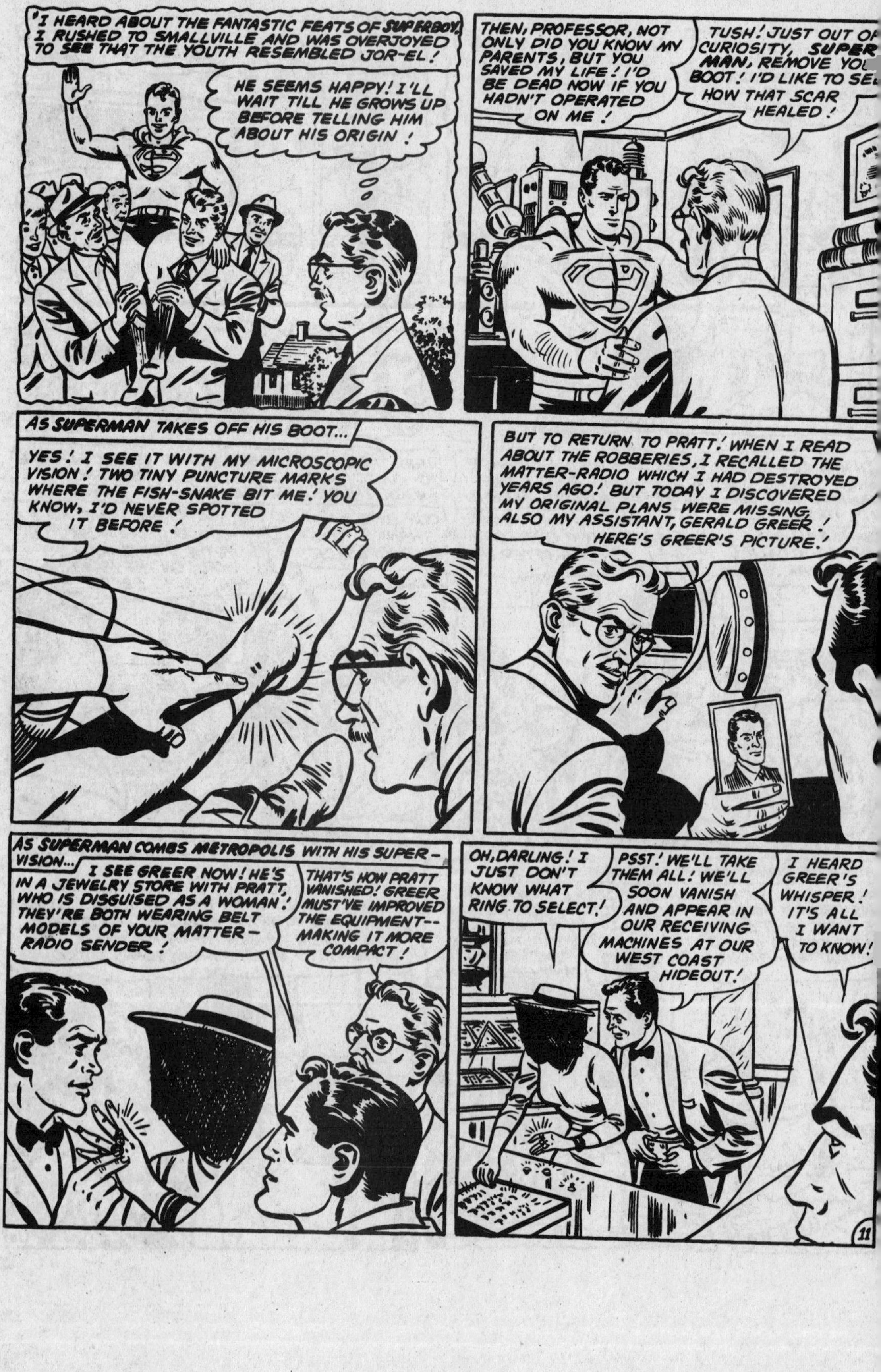
"I HEARD ABOUT THE FANTASTIC FEATS OF SUPERBOY. I RUSHED TO SMALLVILLE AND WAS OVERJOYED TO SEE THAT THE YOUTH RESEMBLED JOR-EL!
HE SEEMS HAPPY! I'LL WAIT TILL HE GROWS UP BEFORE TELLING HIM ABOUT HIS ORIGIN!
THEN, PROFESSOR, NOT ONLY DID YOU KNOW MY PARENTS, BUT YOU SAVED MY LIFE! I'D BE DEAD NOW IF YOU HADN'T OPERATED ON ME!
TUSH! JUST OUT OF CURIOSITY, SUPERMAN, REMOVE YOUR BOOT! I'D LIKE TO SEE HOW THAT SCAR HEALED!
AS SUPERMAN TAKES OFF HIS BOOT...
YES! I SEE IT WITH MY MICROSCOPIC VISION! TWO TINY PUNCTURE MARKS WHERE THE FISH-SNAKE BIT ME! YOU KNOW, I'D NEVER SPOTTED IT BEFORE!
BUT TO RETURN TO PRATT! WHEN I READ ABOUT THE ROBBERIES, I RECALLED THE MATTER-RADIO WHICH I HAD DESTROYED YEARS AGO! BUT TODAY I DISCOVERED MY ORIGINAL PLANS WERE MISSING, ALSO MY ASSISTANT, GERALD GREER! HERE'S GREER'S PICTURE!
AS SUPERMAN COMBS METROPOLIS WITH HIS SUPER-VISION...
I SEE GREER NOW! HE'S IN A JEWELRY STORE WITH PRATT, WHO IS DISGUISED AS A WOMAN! THEY'RE BOTH WEARING BELT MODELS OF YOUR MATTER-RADIO SENDER!
THAT'S HOW PRATT VANISHED! GREER MUST'VE IMPROVED THE EQUIPMENT--MAKING IT MORE COMPACT!
OH, DARLING! I JUST DON'T KNOW WHAT RING TO SELECT!
PSST! WE'LL TAKE THEM ALL! WE'LL SOON VANISH AND APPEAR IN OUR RECEIVING MACHINES AT OUR WEST COAST HIDEOUT!
I HEARD GREER'S WHISPER! IT'S ALL I WANT TO KNOW!
11

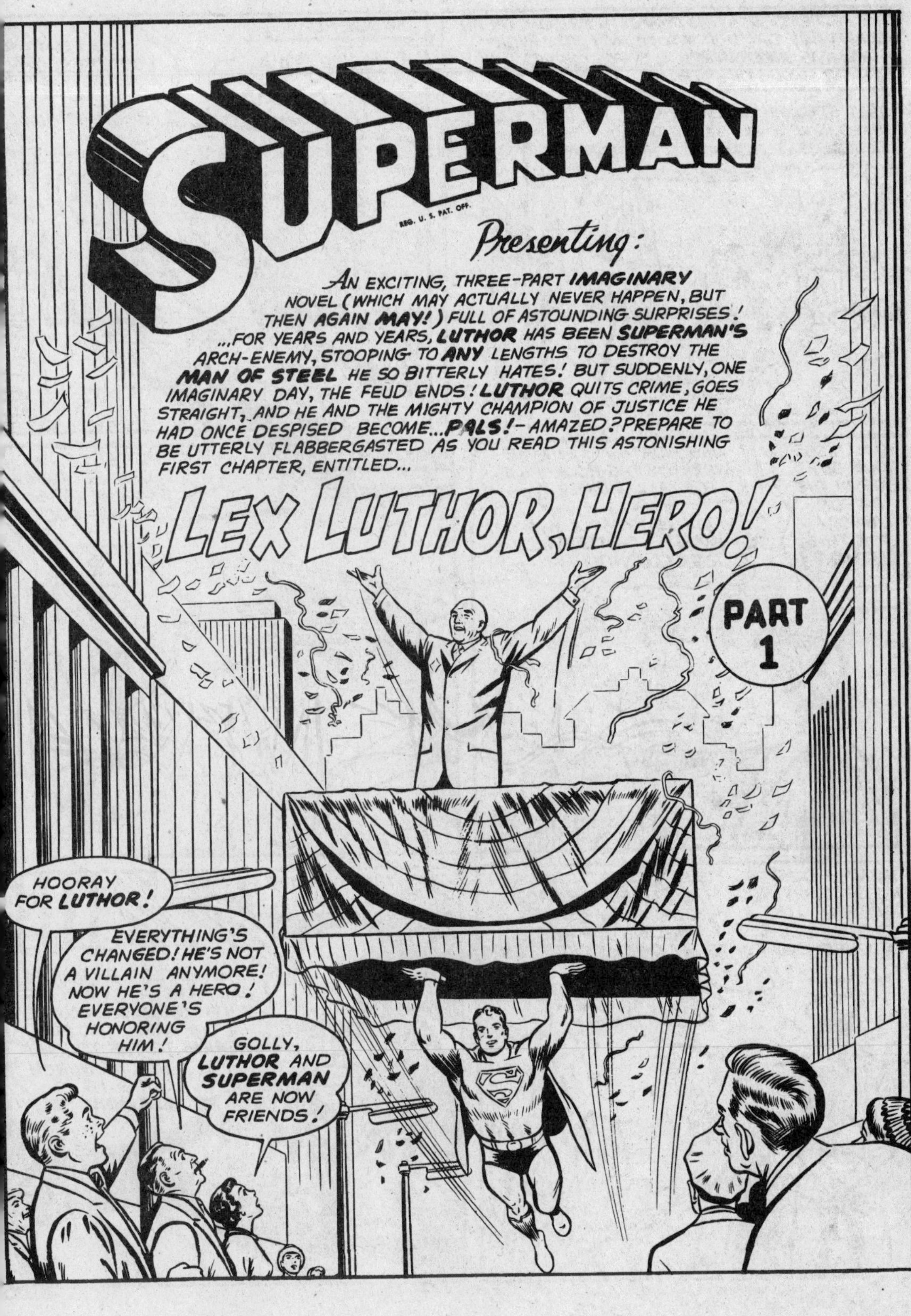
SUPERMAN
REG. U. S. PAT. OFF.
Presenting:
AN EXCITING, THREE-PART IMAGINARY NOVEL (WHICH MAY ACTUALLY NEVER HAPPEN, BUT THEN AGAIN MAY!) FULL OF ASTOUNDING SURPRISES! ...FOR YEARS AND YEARS, LUTHOR HAS BEEN SUPERMAN'S ARCH-ENEMY, STOOPING TO ANY LENGTHS TO DESTROY THE MAN OF STEEL HE SO BITTERLY HATES! BUT SUDDENLY, ONE IMAGINARY DAY, THE FEUD ENDS! LUTHOR QUITS CRIME, GOES STRAIGHT, AND HE AND THE MIGHTY CHAMPION OF JUSTICE HE HAD ONCE DESPISED BECOME...PALS!-AMAZED? PREPARE TO BE UTTERLY FLABBERGASTED AS YOU READ THIS ASTONISHING FIRST CHAPTER, ENTITLED...
LEX LUTHOR, HERO!
PART 1
HOORAY FOR LUTHOR!
EVERYTHING'S CHANGED! HE'S NOT A VILLAIN ANYMORE! NOW HE'S A HERO! EVERYONE'S HONORING HIM!
GOLLY, LUTHOR AND SUPERMAN ARE NOW FRIENDS!

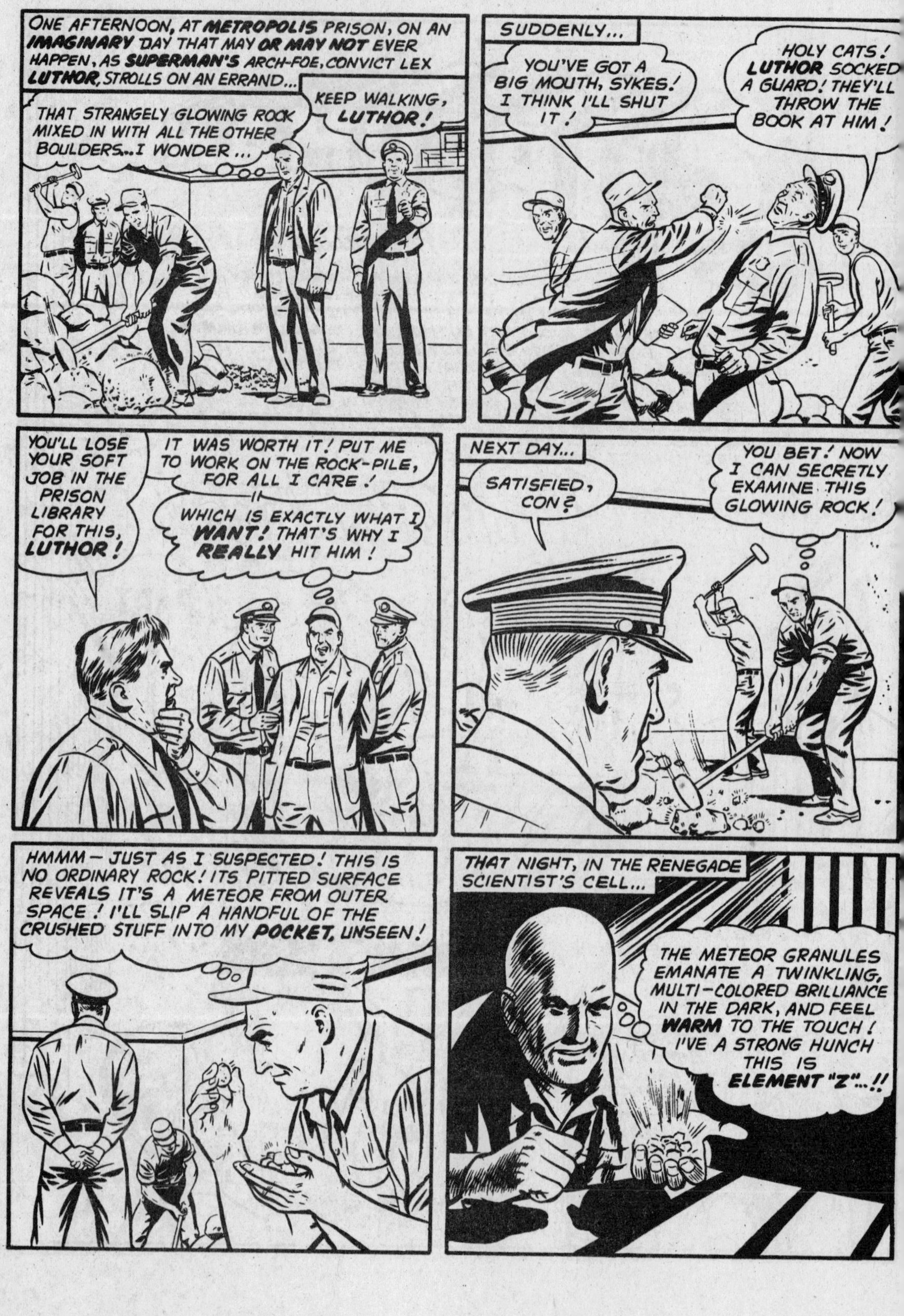
ONE AFTERNOON, AT METROPOLIS PRISON, ON AN IMAGINARY DAY THAT MAY OR MAY NOT EVER HAPPEN, AS SUPERMAN'S ARCH-FOE, CONVICT LEX LUTHOR, STROLLS ON AN ERRAND...
THAT STRANGELY GLOWING ROCK MIXED IN WITH ALL THE OTHER BOULDERS...I WONDER...
KEEP WALKING, LUTHOR!
SUDDENLY...
YOU'VE GOT A BIG MOUTH, SYKES! I THINK I'LL SHUT IT!
HOLY CATS! LUTHOR SOCKED A GUARD! THEY'LL THROW THE BOOK AT HIM!
YOU'LL LOSE YOUR SOFT JOB IN THE PRISON LIBRARY FOR THIS, LUTHOR!
IT WAS WORTH IT! PUT ME TO WORK ON THE ROCK-PILE, FOR ALL I CARE!
WHICH IS EXACTLY WHAT I WANT! THAT'S WHY I REALLY HIT HIM!
NEXT DAY...
SATISFIED, CON?
YOU BET! NOW I CAN SECRETLY EXAMINE THIS GLOWING ROCK!
HMMM — JUST AS I SUSPECTED! THIS IS NO ORDINARY ROCK! ITS PITTED SURFACE REVEALS IT'S A METEOR FROM OUTER SPACE! I'LL SLIP A HANDFUL OF THE CRUSHED STUFF INTO MY POCKET, UNSEEN!
THAT NIGHT, IN THE RENEGADE SCIENTIST'S CELL...
THE METEOR GRANULES EMANATE A TWINKLING, MULTI-COLORED BRILLIANCE IN THE DARK, AND FEEL WARM TO THE TOUCH! I'VE A STRONG HUNCH THIS IS ELEMENT "Z"...!!

"ELEMENT Z" IS A MYSTERIOUS CHEMICAL SUBSTANCE WHICH I'VE LONG BELIEVED EXISTED ELSEWHERE IN THE UNIVERSE! -- IF "ELEMENT Z" HAS NOW REACHED EARTH, THEN I'M ON THE THRESHOLD OF A TREMENDOUS DISCOVERY...!

NEXT MORNING, IN THE WARDEN'S OFFICE...

LUTHOR, YOU'RE OUT OF YOUR MIND, TO MAKE SUCH A REQUEST!

ALL I ASK, SIR, IS ... LET ME USE THE PRISON HOSPITAL'S LABORATORY FACILITIES FOR 24 HOURS!

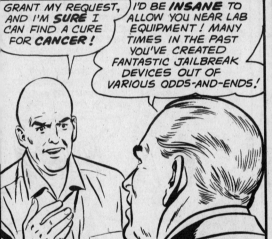

GRANT MY REQUEST, AND I'M SURE I CAN FIND A CURE FOR CANCER!

I'D BE INSANE TO ALLOW YOU NEAR LAB EQUIPMENT! MANY TIMES IN THE PAST YOU'VE CREATED FANTASTIC JAILBREAK DEVICES OUT OF VARIOUS ODDS-AND-ENDS!

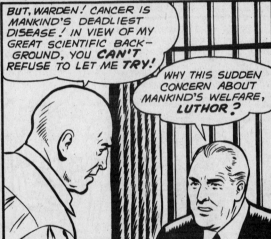

BUT, WARDEN! CANCER IS MANKIND'S DEADLIEST DISEASE! IN VIEW OF MY GREAT SCIENTIFIC BACK-GROUND, YOU CAN'T REFUSE TO LET ME TRY!

WHY THIS SUDDEN CONCERN ABOUT MANKIND'S WELFARE, LUTHOR?

ALL YOUR LIFE YOU'VE TRIED TO CRUSH AND RULE MANKIND WITH ONE MAD INVENTION AFTER ANOTHER! YOU'D HAVE SUCCEEDED, TOO, EXCEPT FOR SUPERMAN!

THAT'S WHY THIS EXPERIMENT MEANS SO MUCH TO ME!

Regards from Superman

I REALIZE AT LAST HOW WRONG I'VE BEEN TO USE MY GREAT BRAIN TO FIGHT, RATHER THAN AID, MANKIND! PLEASE GIVE ME THIS CHANCE TO ATONE...!

OKAY! 24 HOURS! -- BUT YOU'LL BE CLOSELY GUARDED EVERY SECOND!

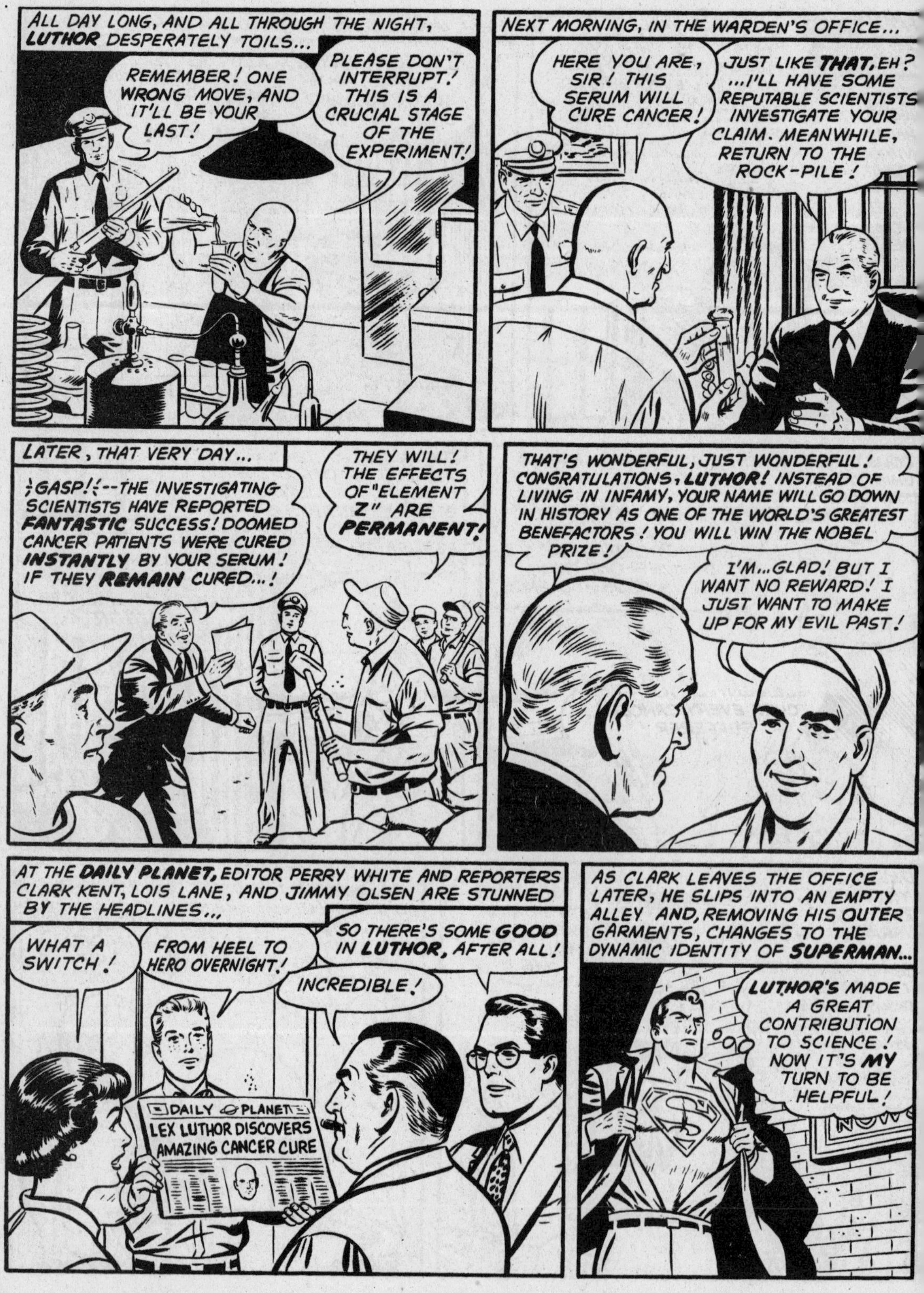
ALL DAY LONG, AND ALL THROUGH THE NIGHT, LUTHOR DESPERATELY TOILS...
REMEMBER! ONE WRONG MOVE, AND IT'LL BE YOUR LAST!
PLEASE DON'T INTERRUPT! THIS IS A CRUCIAL STAGE OF THE EXPERIMENT!
NEXT MORNING, IN THE WARDEN'S OFFICE...
HERE YOU ARE, SIR! THIS SERUM WILL CURE CANCER!
JUST LIKE THAT, EH? ...I'LL HAVE SOME REPUTABLE SCIENTISTS INVESTIGATE YOUR CLAIM. MEANWHILE, RETURN TO THE ROCK-PILE!
LATER, THAT VERY DAY...
{GASP!}--THE INVESTIGATING SCIENTISTS HAVE REPORTED FANTASTIC SUCCESS! DOOMED CANCER PATIENTS WERE CURED INSTANTLY BY YOUR SERUM! IF THEY REMAIN CURED...!
THEY WILL! THE EFFECTS OF "ELEMENT Z" ARE PERMANENT!
THAT'S WONDERFUL, JUST WONDERFUL! CONGRATULATIONS, LUTHOR! INSTEAD OF LIVING IN INFAMY, YOUR NAME WILL GO DOWN IN HISTORY AS ONE OF THE WORLD'S GREATEST BENEFACTORS! YOU WILL WIN THE NOBEL PRIZE!
I'M...GLAD! BUT I WANT NO REWARD! I JUST WANT TO MAKE UP FOR MY EVIL PAST!
AT THE DAILY PLANET, EDITOR PERRY WHITE AND REPORTERS CLARK KENT, LOIS LANE, AND JIMMY OLSEN ARE STUNNED BY THE HEADLINES...
WHAT A SWITCH!
FROM HEEL TO HERO OVERNIGHT!
SO THERE'S SOME GOOD IN LUTHOR, AFTER ALL!
INCREDIBLE!
DAILY PLANET
LEX LUTHOR DISCOVERS AMAZING CANCER CURE
AS CLARK LEAVES THE OFFICE LATER, HE SLIPS INTO AN EMPTY ALLEY AND, REMOVING HIS OUTER GARMENTS, CHANGES TO THE DYNAMIC IDENTITY OF SUPERMAN...
LUTHOR'S MADE A GREAT CONTRIBUTION TO SCIENCE! NOW IT'S MY TURN TO BE HELPFUL!

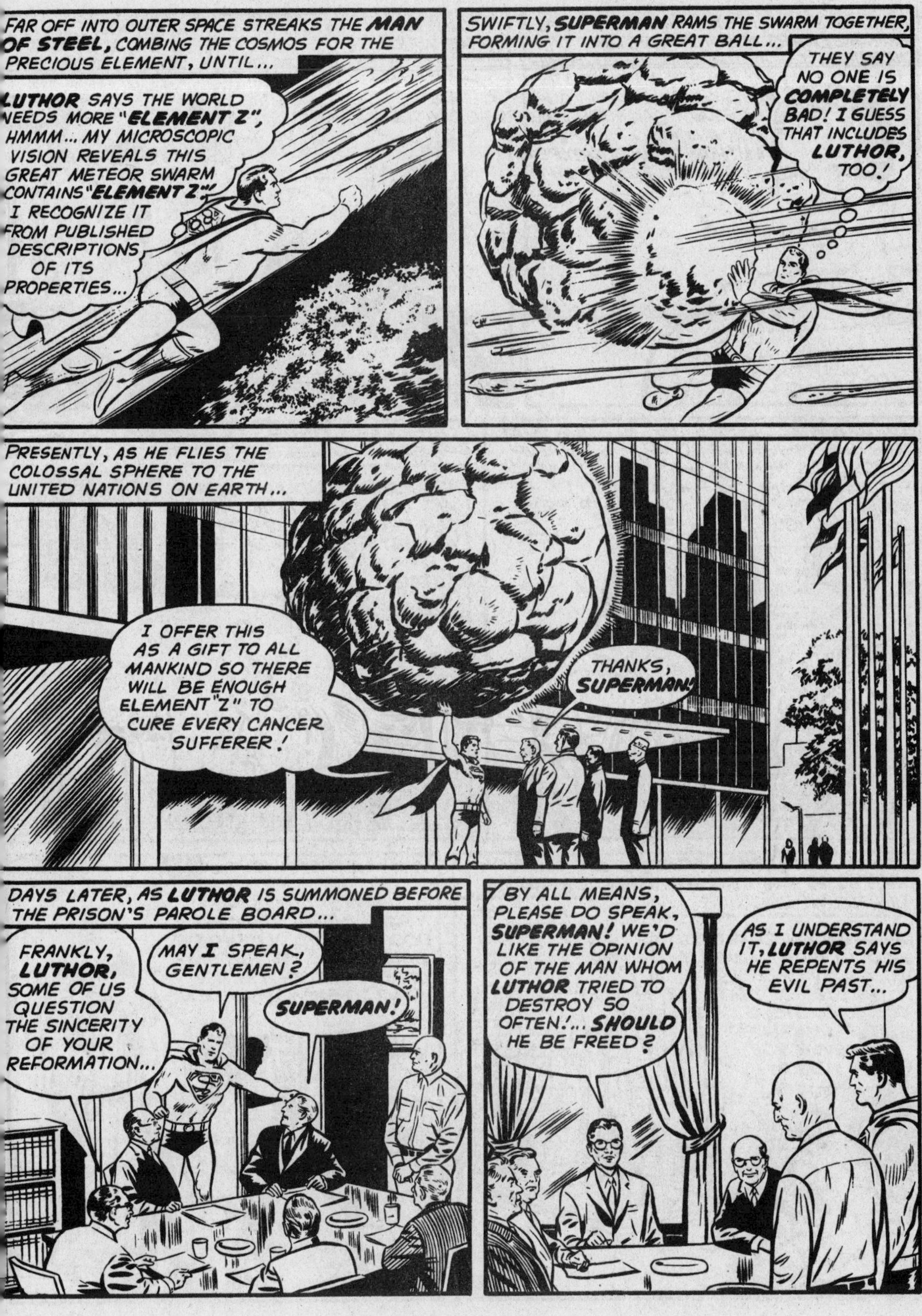
FAR OFF INTO OUTER SPACE STREAKS THE MAN OF STEEL, COMBING THE COSMOS FOR THE PRECIOUS ELEMENT, UNTIL...
LUTHOR SAYS THE WORLD NEEDS MORE "ELEMENT Z", HMMM... MY MICROSCOPIC VISION REVEALS THIS GREAT METEOR SWARM CONTAINS "ELEMENT Z"! I RECOGNIZE IT FROM PUBLISHED DESCRIPTIONS OF ITS PROPERTIES...
SWIFTLY, SUPERMAN RAMS THE SWARM TOGETHER, FORMING IT INTO A GREAT BALL...
THEY SAY NO ONE IS COMPLETELY BAD! I GUESS THAT INCLUDES LUTHOR, TOO!
PRESENTLY, AS HE FLIES THE COLOSSAL SPHERE TO THE UNITED NATIONS ON EARTH...
I OFFER THIS AS A GIFT TO ALL MANKIND SO THERE WILL BE ENOUGH ELEMENT "Z" TO CURE EVERY CANCER SUFFERER!
THANKS, SUPERMAN!
DAYS LATER, AS LUTHOR IS SUMMONED BEFORE THE PRISON'S PAROLE BOARD...
FRANKLY, LUTHOR, SOME OF US QUESTION THE SINCERITY OF YOUR REFORMATION...
MAY I SPEAK, GENTLEMEN?
SUPERMAN!
BY ALL MEANS, PLEASE DO SPEAK, SUPERMAN! WE'D LIKE THE OPINION OF THE MAN WHOM LUTHOR TRIED TO DESTROY SO OFTEN!... SHOULD HE BE FREED?
AS I UNDERSTAND IT, LUTHOR SAYS HE REPENTS HIS EVIL PAST...

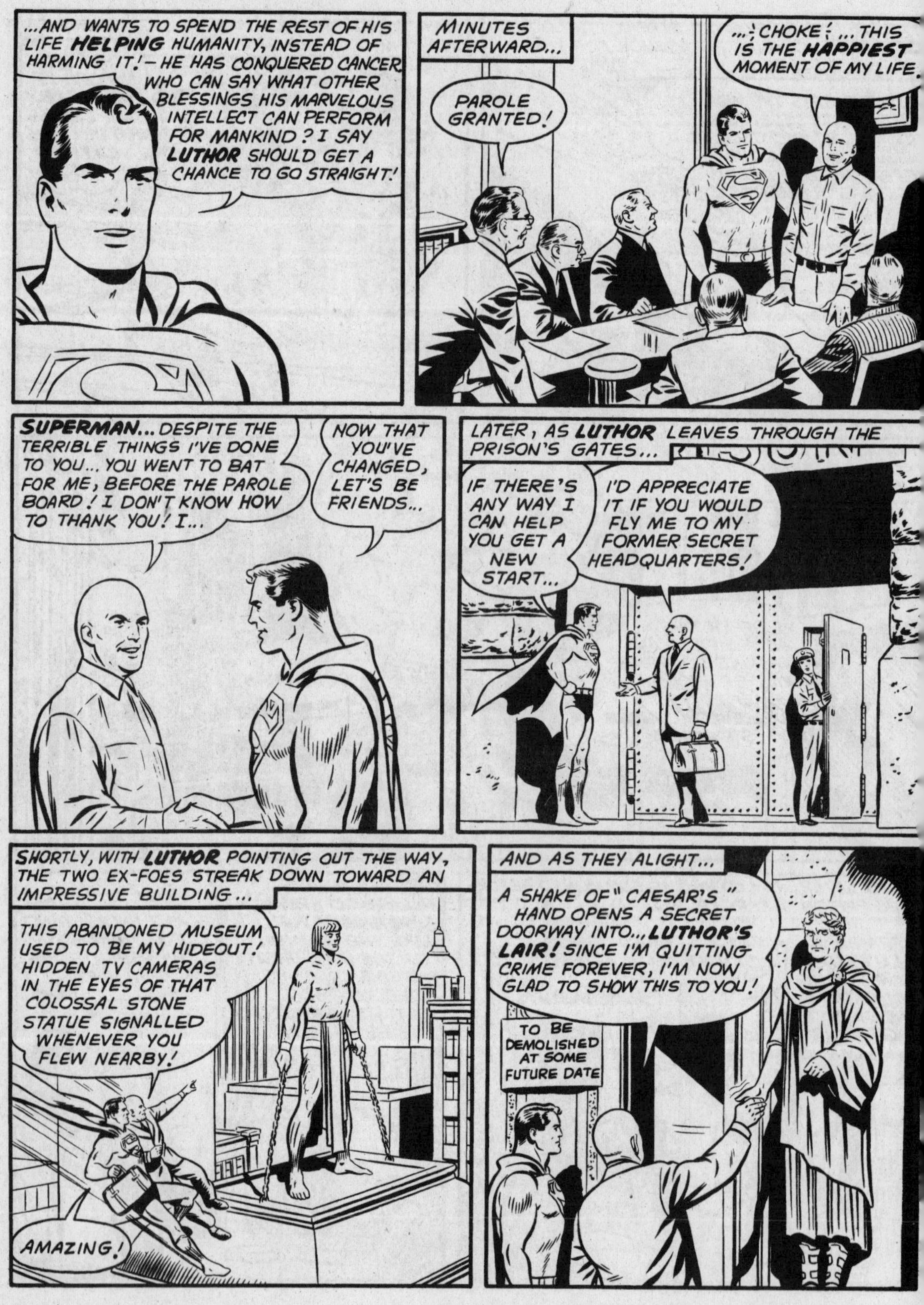
...AND WANTS TO SPEND THE REST OF HIS LIFE HELPING HUMANITY, INSTEAD OF HARMING IT! – HE HAS CONQUERED CANCER. WHO CAN SAY WHAT OTHER BLESSINGS HIS MARVELOUS INTELLECT CAN PERFORM FOR MANKIND? I SAY LUTHOR SHOULD GET A CHANCE TO GO STRAIGHT!
MINUTES AFTERWARD...
PAROLE GRANTED!
...CHOKE ... THIS IS THE HAPPIEST MOMENT OF MY LIFE.
SUPERMAN... DESPITE THE TERRIBLE THINGS I'VE DONE TO YOU... YOU WENT TO BAT FOR ME, BEFORE THE PAROLE BOARD! I DON'T KNOW HOW TO THANK YOU! I...
NOW THAT YOU'VE CHANGED, LET'S BE FRIENDS...
LATER, AS LUTHOR LEAVES THROUGH THE PRISON'S GATES...
IF THERE'S ANY WAY I CAN HELP YOU GET A NEW START...
I'D APPRECIATE IT IF YOU WOULD FLY ME TO MY FORMER SECRET HEADQUARTERS!
SHORTLY, WITH LUTHOR POINTING OUT THE WAY, THE TWO EX-FOES STREAK DOWN TOWARD AN IMPRESSIVE BUILDING...
THIS ABANDONED MUSEUM USED TO BE MY HIDEOUT! HIDDEN TV CAMERAS IN THE EYES OF THAT COLOSSAL STONE STATUE SIGNALLED WHENEVER YOU FLEW NEARBY!
AMAZING!
AND AS THEY ALIGHT...
A SHAKE OF "CAESAR'S" HAND OPENS A SECRET DOORWAY INTO... LUTHOR'S LAIR! SINCE I'M QUITTING CRIME FOREVER, I'M NOW GLAD TO SHOW THIS TO YOU!
TO BE DEMOLISHED AT SOME FUTURE DATE

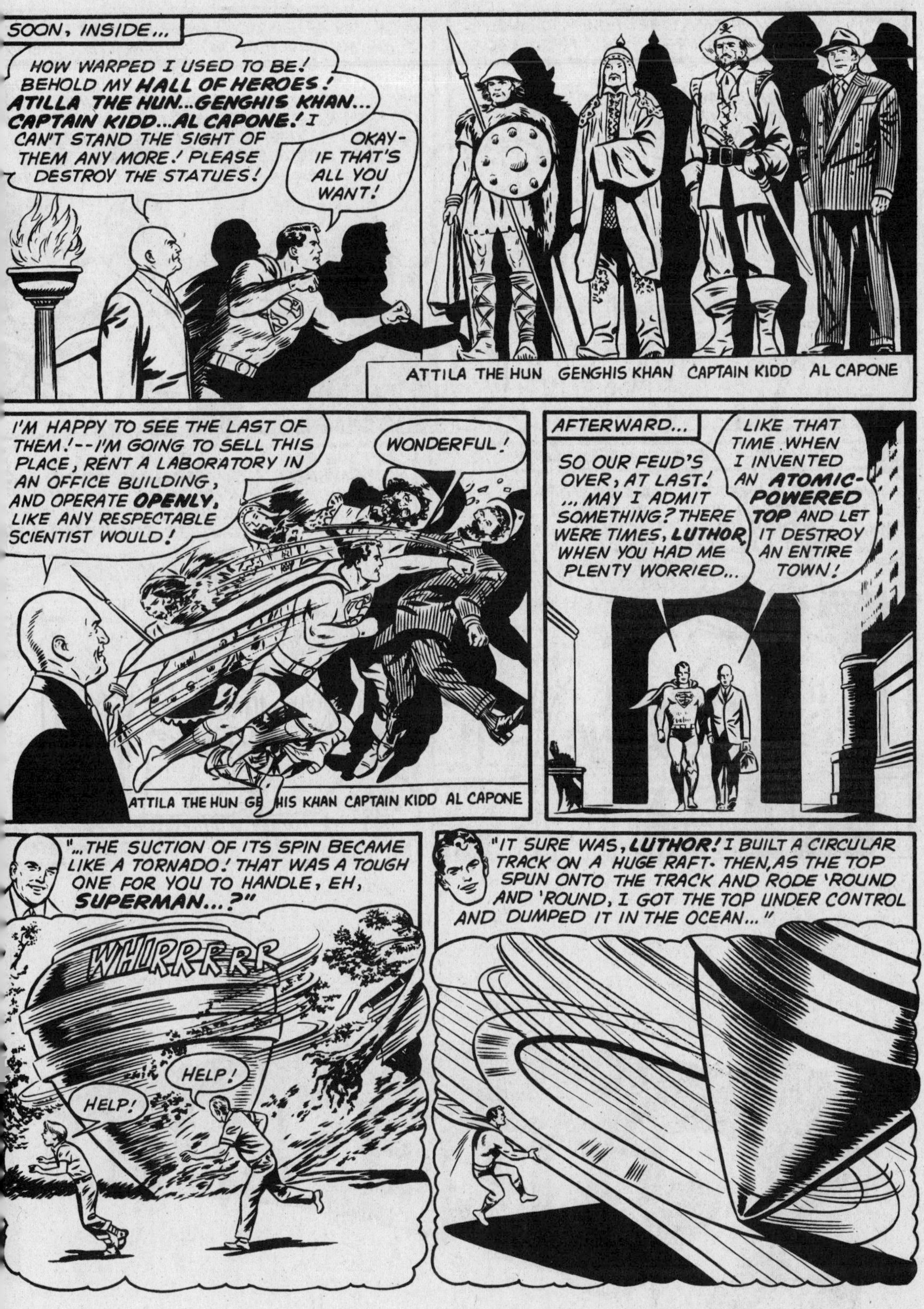
SOON, INSIDE...
HOW WARPED I USED TO BE! BEHOLD MY HALL OF HEROES! ATILLA THE HUN...GENGHIS KHAN... CAPTAIN KIDD...AL CAPONE! I CAN'T STAND THE SIGHT OF THEM ANY MORE! PLEASE DESTROY THE STATUES!
OKAY- IF THAT'S ALL YOU WANT!
ATTILA THE HUN GENGHIS KHAN CAPTAIN KIDD AL CAPONE
I'M HAPPY TO SEE THE LAST OF THEM!--I'M GOING TO SELL THIS PLACE, RENT A LABORATORY IN AN OFFICE BUILDING, AND OPERATE OPENLY, LIKE ANY RESPECTABLE SCIENTIST WOULD!
WONDERFUL!
ATTILA THE HUN GE HIS KHAN CAPTAIN KIDD AL CAPONE
AFTERWARD...
SO OUR FEUD'S OVER, AT LAST! ...MAY I ADMIT SOMETHING? THERE WERE TIMES, LUTHOR, WHEN YOU HAD ME PLENTY WORRIED...
LIKE THAT TIME WHEN I INVENTED AN ATOMIC-POWERED TOP AND LET IT DESTROY AN ENTIRE TOWN!
"...THE SUCTION OF ITS SPIN BECAME LIKE A TORNADO! THAT WAS A TOUGH ONE FOR YOU TO HANDLE, EH, SUPERMAN...?"
WHIRRRRR
HELP!
HELP!
"IT SURE WAS, LUTHOR! I BUILT A CIRCULAR TRACK ON A HUGE RAFT. THEN, AS THE TOP SPUN ONTO THE TRACK AND RODE 'ROUND AND 'ROUND, I GOT THE TOP UNDER CONTROL AND DUMPED IT IN THE OCEAN..."

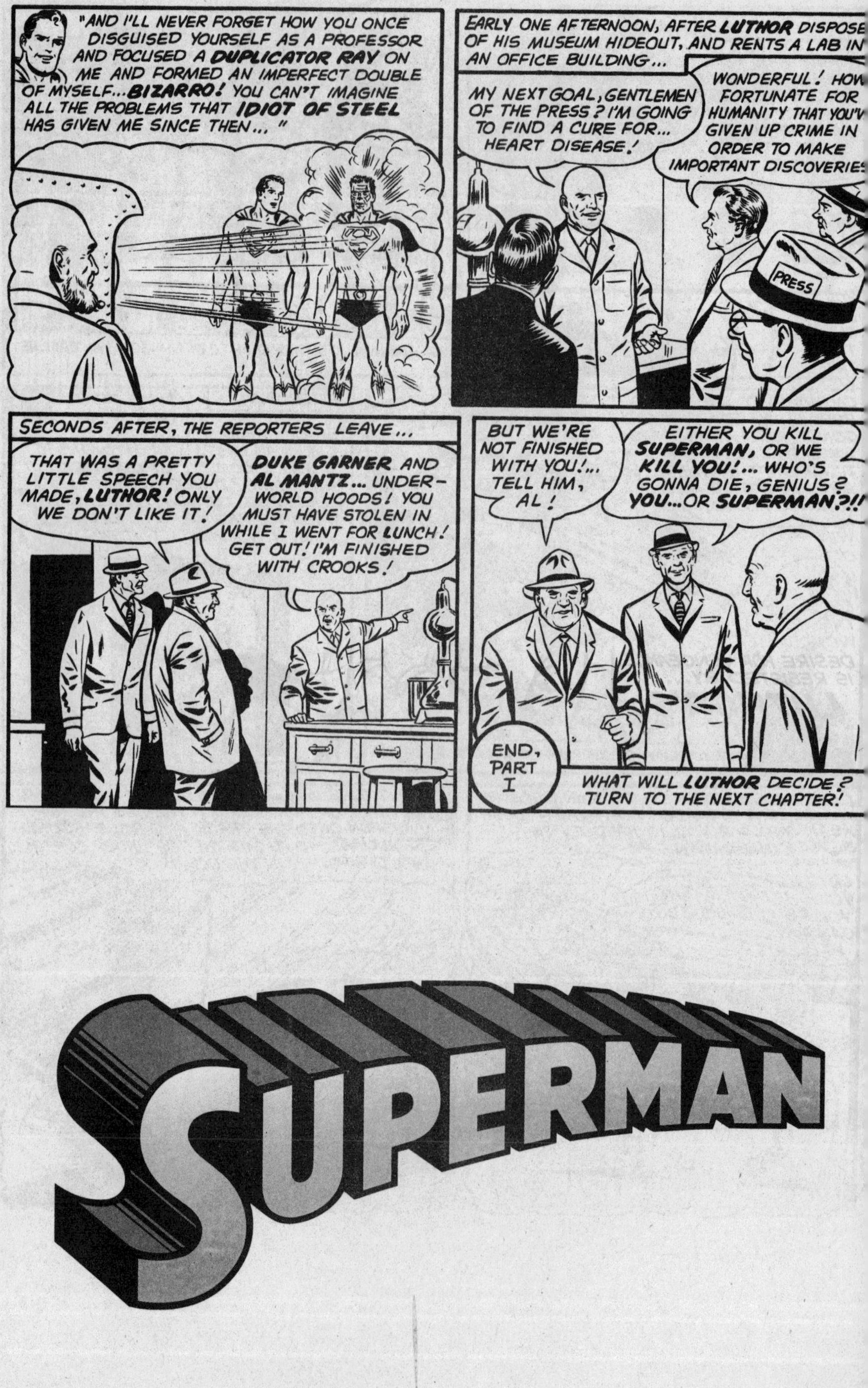
"AND I'LL NEVER FORGET HOW YOU ONCE DISGUISED YOURSELF AS A PROFESSOR AND FOCUSED A DUPLICATOR RAY ON ME AND FORMED AN IMPERFECT DOUBLE OF MYSELF... BIZARRO! YOU CAN'T IMAGINE ALL THE PROBLEMS THAT IDIOT OF STEEL HAS GIVEN ME SINCE THEN..."
EARLY ONE AFTERNOON, AFTER LUTHOR DISPOSE OF HIS MUSEUM HIDEOUT, AND RENTS A LAB IN AN OFFICE BUILDING...
MY NEXT GOAL, GENTLEMEN OF THE PRESS? I'M GOING TO FIND A CURE FOR... HEART DISEASE!
WONDERFUL! HOW FORTUNATE FOR HUMANITY THAT YOU'V GIVEN UP CRIME IN ORDER TO MAKE IMPORTANT DISCOVERIES
PRESS
SECONDS AFTER, THE REPORTERS LEAVE...
THAT WAS A PRETTY LITTLE SPEECH YOU MADE, LUTHOR! ONLY WE DON'T LIKE IT!
DUKE GARNER AND AL MANTZ... UNDERWORLD HOODS! YOU MUST HAVE STOLEN IN WHILE I WENT FOR LUNCH! GET OUT! I'M FINISHED WITH CROOKS!
BUT WE'RE NOT FINISHED WITH YOU!... TELL HIM, AL!
EITHER YOU KILL SUPERMAN, OR WE KILL YOU!... WHO'S GONNA DIE, GENIUS? YOU...OR SUPERMAN?!!
END, PART I
WHAT WILL LUTHOR DECIDE? TURN TO THE NEXT CHAPTER!

SUPERMAN

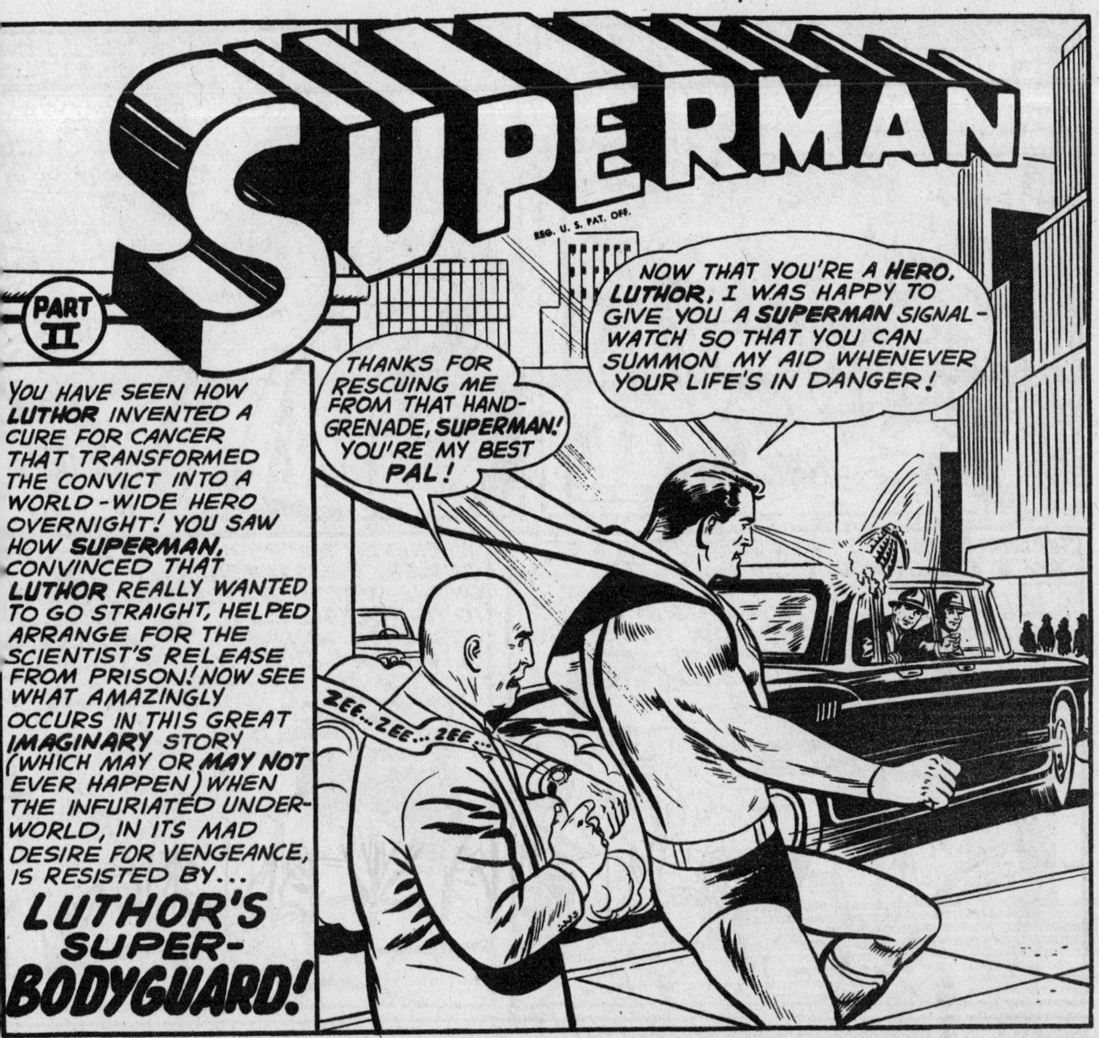
SUPERMAN
REG. U. S. PAT. OFF.
PART II
YOU HAVE SEEN HOW LUTHOR INVENTED A CURE FOR CANCER THAT TRANSFORMED THE CONVICT INTO A WORLD-WIDE HERO OVERNIGHT! YOU SAW HOW SUPERMAN, CONVINCED THAT LUTHOR REALLY WANTED TO GO STRAIGHT, HELPED ARRANGE FOR THE SCIENTIST'S RELEASE FROM PRISON! NOW SEE WHAT AMAZINGLY OCCURS IN THIS GREAT IMAGINARY STORY (WHICH MAY OR MAY NOT EVER HAPPEN) WHEN THE INFURIATED UNDERWORLD, IN ITS MAD DESIRE FOR VENGEANCE, IS RESISTED BY...
LUTHOR'S SUPER-BODYGUARD!
THANKS FOR RESCUING ME FROM THAT HAND-GRENADE, SUPERMAN! YOU'RE MY BEST PAL!
NOW THAT YOU'RE A HERO, LUTHOR, I WAS HAPPY TO GIVE YOU A SUPERMAN SIGNAL-WATCH SO THAT YOU CAN SUMMON MY AID WHENEVER YOUR LIFE'S IN DANGER!
ZEE...ZEE...ZEE...

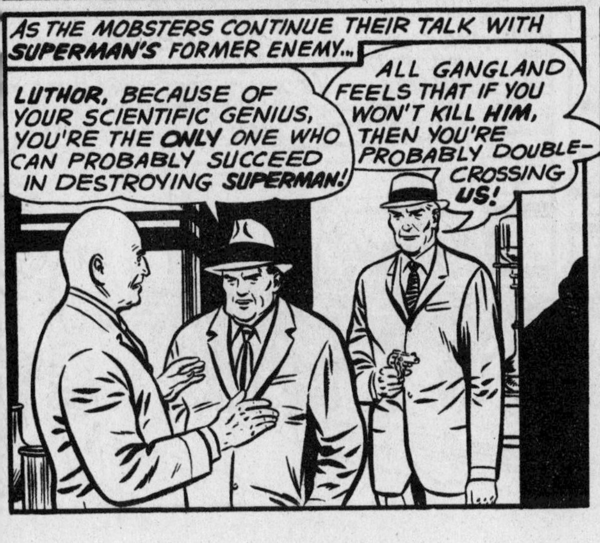
AS THE MOBSTERS CONTINUE THEIR TALK WITH SUPERMAN'S FORMER ENEMY...
LUTHOR, BECAUSE OF YOUR SCIENTIFIC GENIUS, YOU'RE THE ONLY ONE WHO CAN PROBABLY SUCCEED IN DESTROYING SUPERMAN!
ALL GANGLAND FEELS THAT IF YOU WON'T KILL HIM, THEN YOU'RE PROBABLY DOUBLE-CROSSING US!

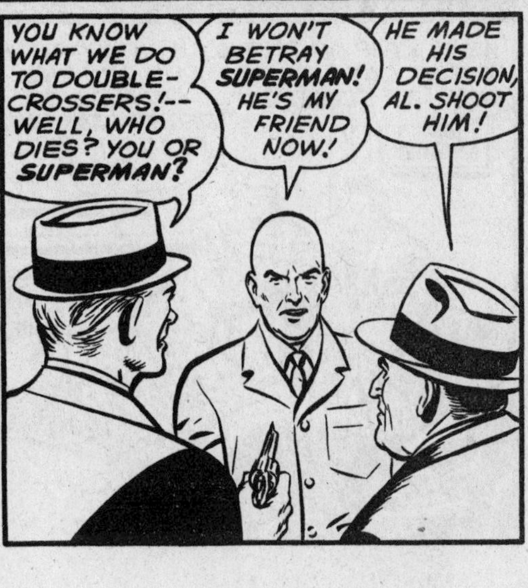
YOU KNOW WHAT WE DO TO DOUBLE-CROSSERS!--WELL, WHO DIES? YOU OR SUPERMAN?
I WON'T BETRAY SUPERMAN! HE'S MY FRIEND NOW!
HE MADE HIS DECISION, AL. SHOOT HIM!

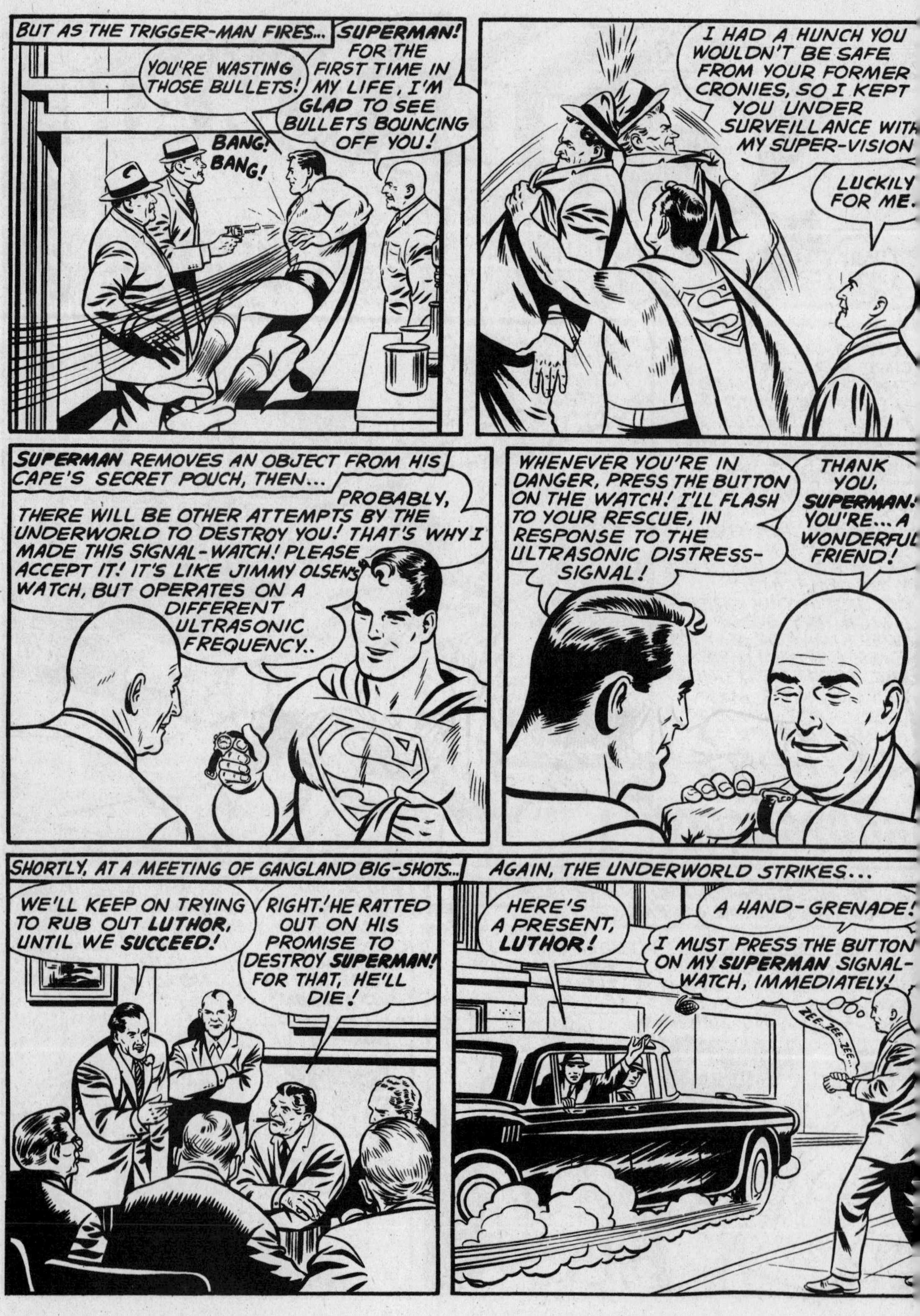
BUT AS THE TRIGGER-MAN FIRES...
YOU'RE WASTING THOSE BULLETS!
SUPERMAN! FOR THE FIRST TIME IN MY LIFE, I'M GLAD TO SEE BULLETS BOUNCING OFF YOU!
BANG! BANG!
I HAD A HUNCH YOU WOULDN'T BE SAFE FROM YOUR FORMER CRONIES, SO I KEPT YOU UNDER SURVEILLANCE WITH MY SUPER-VISION
LUCKILY FOR ME.
SUPERMAN REMOVES AN OBJECT FROM HIS CAPE'S SECRET POUCH, THEN...
PROBABLY, THERE WILL BE OTHER ATTEMPTS BY THE UNDERWORLD TO DESTROY YOU! THAT'S WHY I MADE THIS SIGNAL-WATCH! PLEASE ACCEPT IT! IT'S LIKE JIMMY OLSEN'S WATCH, BUT OPERATES ON A DIFFERENT ULTRASONIC FREQUENCY..
WHENEVER YOU'RE IN DANGER, PRESS THE BUTTON ON THE WATCH! I'LL FLASH TO YOUR RESCUE, IN RESPONSE TO THE ULTRASONIC DISTRESS-SIGNAL!
THANK YOU, SUPERMAN! YOU'RE... A WONDERFUL FRIEND!
SHORTLY, AT A MEETING OF GANGLAND BIG-SHOTS...
WE'LL KEEP ON TRYING TO RUB OUT LUTHOR, UNTIL WE SUCCEED!
RIGHT! HE RATTED OUT ON HIS PROMISE TO DESTROY SUPERMAN! FOR THAT, HE'LL DIE!
AGAIN, THE UNDERWORLD STRIKES...
HERE'S A PRESENT, LUTHOR!
A HAND-GRENADE!
I MUST PRESS THE BUTTON ON MY SUPERMAN SIGNAL-WATCH, IMMEDIATELY!
ZEE..ZEE..ZEE..

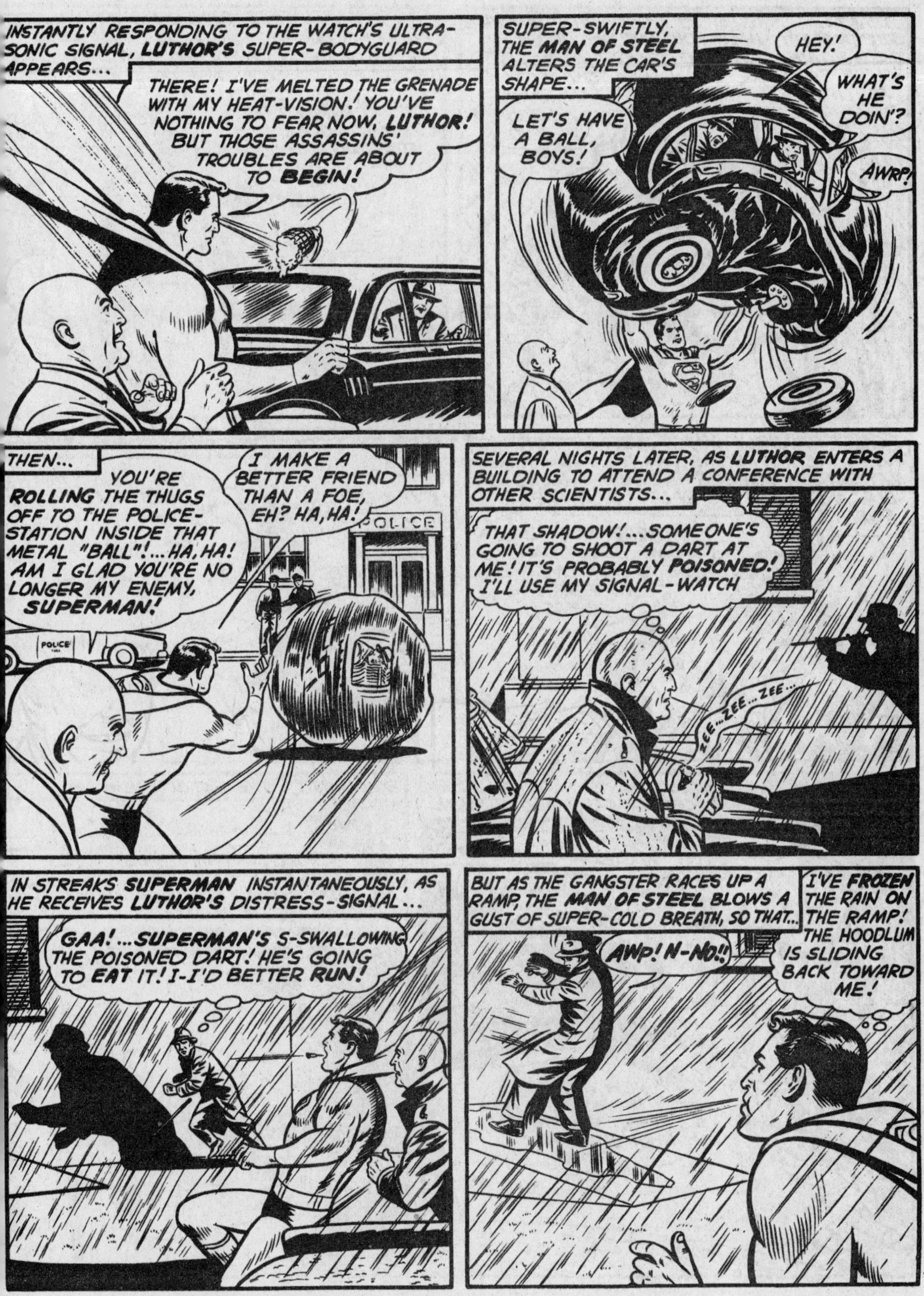
INSTANTLY RESPONDING TO THE WATCH'S ULTRA-SONIC SIGNAL, LUTHOR'S SUPER-BODYGUARD APPEARS...
THERE! I'VE MELTED THE GRENADE WITH MY HEAT-VISION! YOU'VE NOTHING TO FEAR NOW, LUTHOR! BUT THOSE ASSASSINS' TROUBLES ARE ABOUT TO BEGIN!
SUPER-SWIFTLY, THE MAN OF STEEL ALTERS THE CAR'S SHAPE...
HEY!
WHAT'S HE DOIN'?
LET'S HAVE A BALL, BOYS!
AWRP!
THEN...
YOU'RE ROLLING THE THUGS OFF TO THE POLICE-STATION INSIDE THAT METAL "BALL"!...HA, HA! AM I GLAD YOU'RE NO LONGER MY ENEMY, SUPERMAN!
I MAKE A BETTER FRIEND THAN A FOE, EH? HA, HA!
POLICE
POLICE
SEVERAL NIGHTS LATER, AS LUTHOR ENTERS A BUILDING TO ATTEND A CONFERENCE WITH OTHER SCIENTISTS...
THAT SHADOW!...SOMEONE'S GOING TO SHOOT A DART AT ME! IT'S PROBABLY POISONED! I'LL USE MY SIGNAL-WATCH
ZEE...ZEE...ZEE...
IN STREAKS SUPERMAN INSTANTANEOUSLY, AS HE RECEIVES LUTHOR'S DISTRESS-SIGNAL...
GAA!...SUPERMAN'S S-SWALLOWING THE POISONED DART! HE'S GOING TO EAT IT! I-I'D BETTER RUN!
BUT AS THE GANGSTER RACES UP A RAMP, THE MAN OF STEEL BLOWS A GUST OF SUPER-COLD BREATH, SO THAT...
I'VE FROZEN THE RAIN ON THE RAMP! THE HOODLUM IS SLIDING BACK TOWARD ME!
AWP! N-NO!!

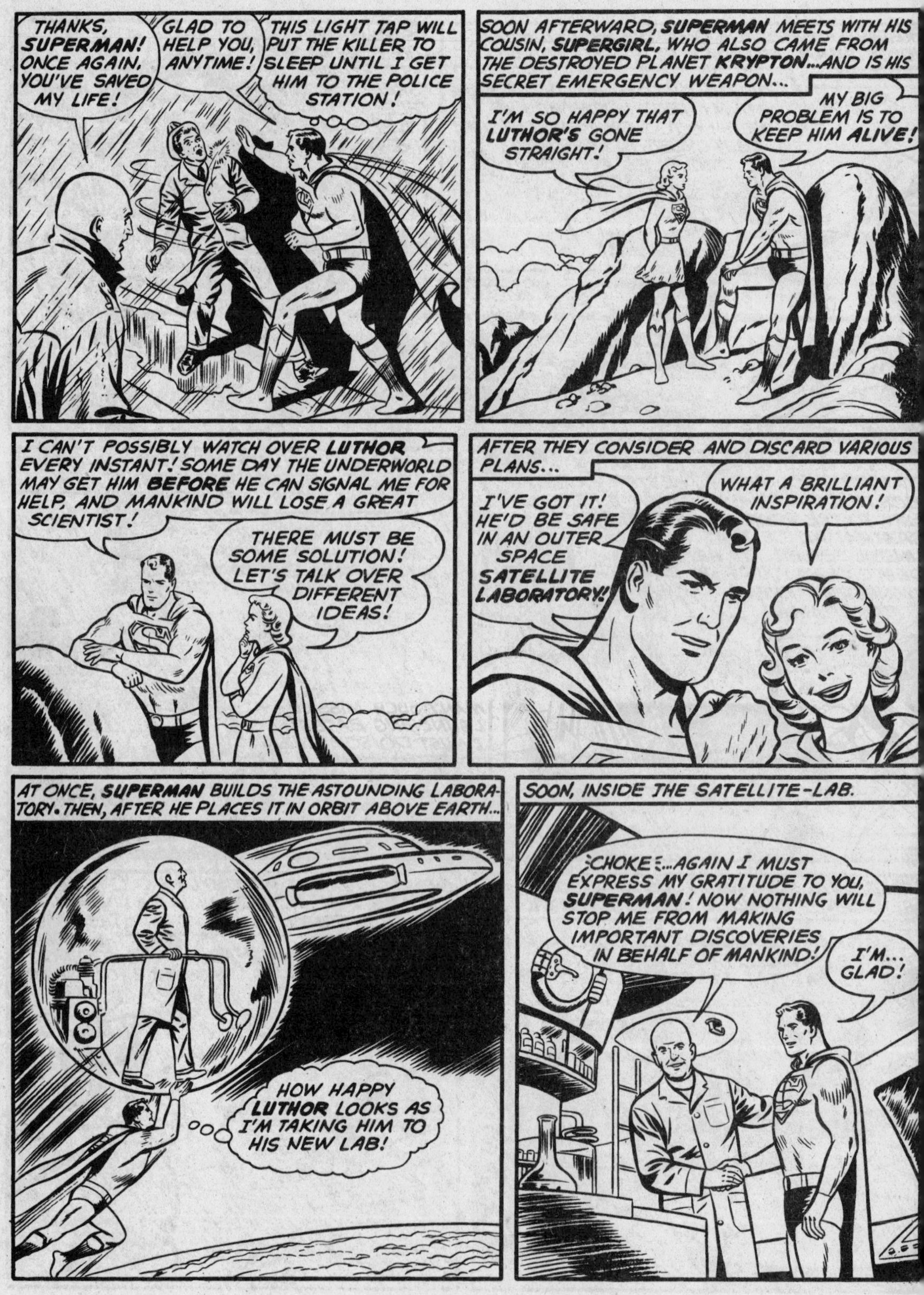
THANKS, SUPERMAN! ONCE AGAIN, YOU'VE SAVED MY LIFE!
GLAD TO HELP YOU, ANYTIME!
THIS LIGHT TAP WILL PUT THE KILLER TO SLEEP UNTIL I GET HIM TO THE POLICE STATION!
SOON AFTERWARD, SUPERMAN MEETS WITH HIS COUSIN, SUPERGIRL, WHO ALSO CAME FROM THE DESTROYED PLANET KRYPTON...AND IS HIS SECRET EMERGENCY WEAPON...
I'M SO HAPPY THAT LUTHOR'S GONE STRAIGHT!
MY BIG PROBLEM IS TO KEEP HIM ALIVE!
I CAN'T POSSIBLY WATCH OVER LUTHOR EVERY INSTANT! SOME DAY THE UNDERWORLD MAY GET HIM BEFORE HE CAN SIGNAL ME FOR HELP, AND MANKIND WILL LOSE A GREAT SCIENTIST!
THERE MUST BE SOME SOLUTION! LET'S TALK OVER DIFFERENT IDEAS!
AFTER THEY CONSIDER AND DISCARD VARIOUS PLANS...
I'VE GOT IT! HE'D BE SAFE IN AN OUTER SPACE SATELLITE LABORATORY!
WHAT A BRILLIANT INSPIRATION!
AT ONCE, SUPERMAN BUILDS THE ASTOUNDING LABORATORY. THEN, AFTER HE PLACES IT IN ORBIT ABOVE EARTH...
HOW HAPPY LUTHOR LOOKS AS I'M TAKING HIM TO HIS NEW LAB!
SOON, INSIDE THE SATELLITE-LAB.
CHOKE ...AGAIN I MUST EXPRESS MY GRATITUDE TO YOU, SUPERMAN! NOW NOTHING WILL STOP ME FROM MAKING IMPORTANT DISCOVERIES IN BEHALF OF MANKIND!
I'M... GLAD!

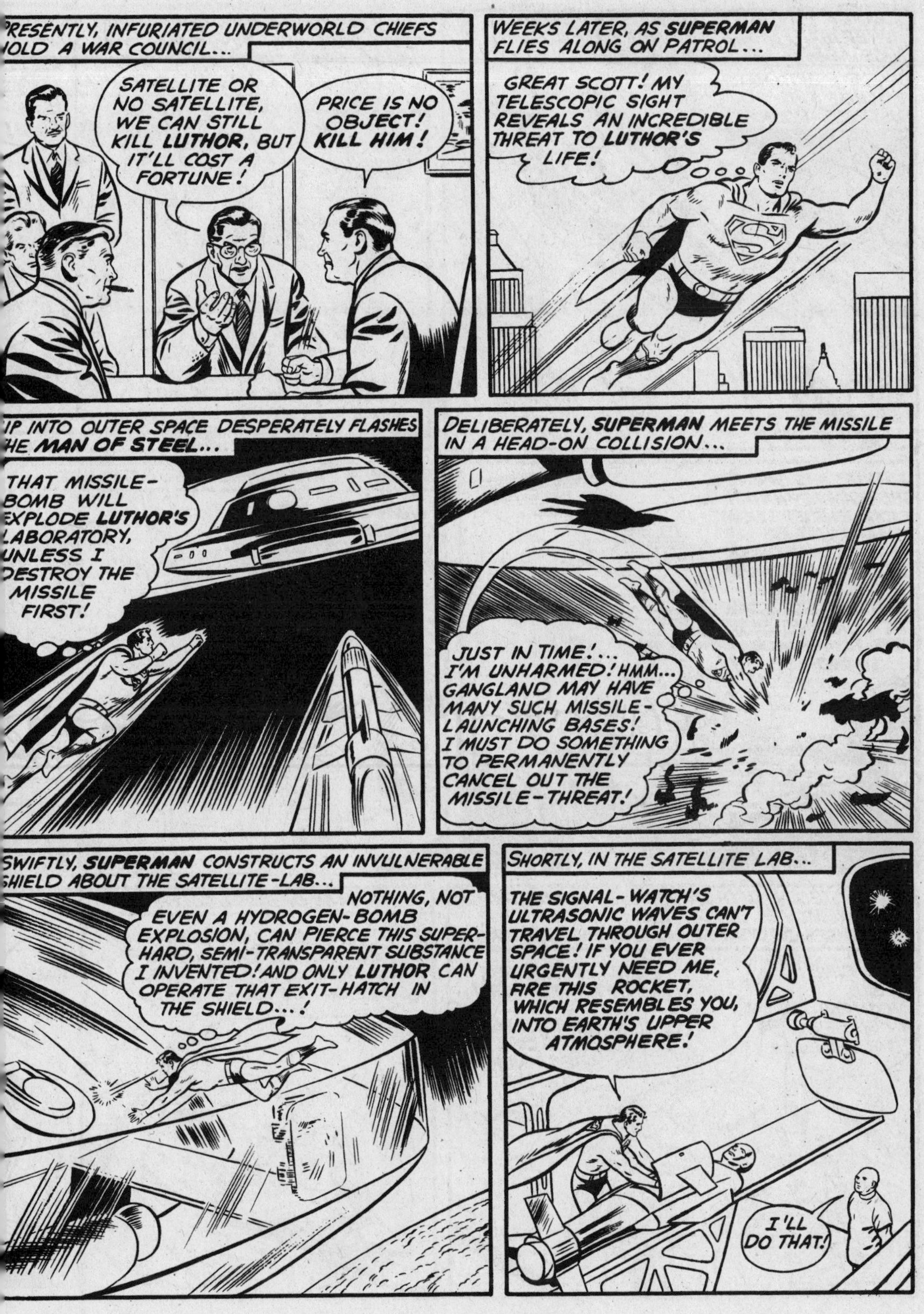
PRESENTLY, INFURIATED UNDERWORLD CHIEFS HOLD A WAR COUNCIL...
SATELLITE OR NO SATELLITE, WE CAN STILL KILL LUTHOR, BUT IT'LL COST A FORTUNE!
PRICE IS NO OBJECT! KILL HIM!
WEEKS LATER, AS SUPERMAN FLIES ALONG ON PATROL...
GREAT SCOTT! MY TELESCOPIC SIGHT REVEALS AN INCREDIBLE THREAT TO LUTHOR'S LIFE!
UP INTO OUTER SPACE DESPERATELY FLASHES THE MAN OF STEEL...
THAT MISSILE-BOMB WILL EXPLODE LUTHOR'S LABORATORY, UNLESS I DESTROY THE MISSILE FIRST!
DELIBERATELY, SUPERMAN MEETS THE MISSILE IN A HEAD-ON COLLISION...
JUST IN TIME!... I'M UNHARMED! HMM... GANGLAND MAY HAVE MANY SUCH MISSILE-LAUNCHING BASES! I MUST DO SOMETHING TO PERMANENTLY CANCEL OUT THE MISSILE-THREAT!
SWIFTLY, SUPERMAN CONSTRUCTS AN INVULNERABLE SHIELD ABOUT THE SATELLITE-LAB...
NOTHING, NOT EVEN A HYDROGEN-BOMB EXPLOSION, CAN PIERCE THIS SUPER-HARD, SEMI-TRANSPARENT SUBSTANCE I INVENTED! AND ONLY LUTHOR CAN OPERATE THAT EXIT-HATCH IN THE SHIELD...!
SHORTLY, IN THE SATELLITE LAB...
THE SIGNAL-WATCH'S ULTRASONIC WAVES CAN'T TRAVEL THROUGH OUTER SPACE! IF YOU EVER URGENTLY NEED ME, FIRE THIS ROCKET, WHICH RESEMBLES YOU, INTO EARTH'S UPPER ATMOSPHERE!
I'LL DO THAT!

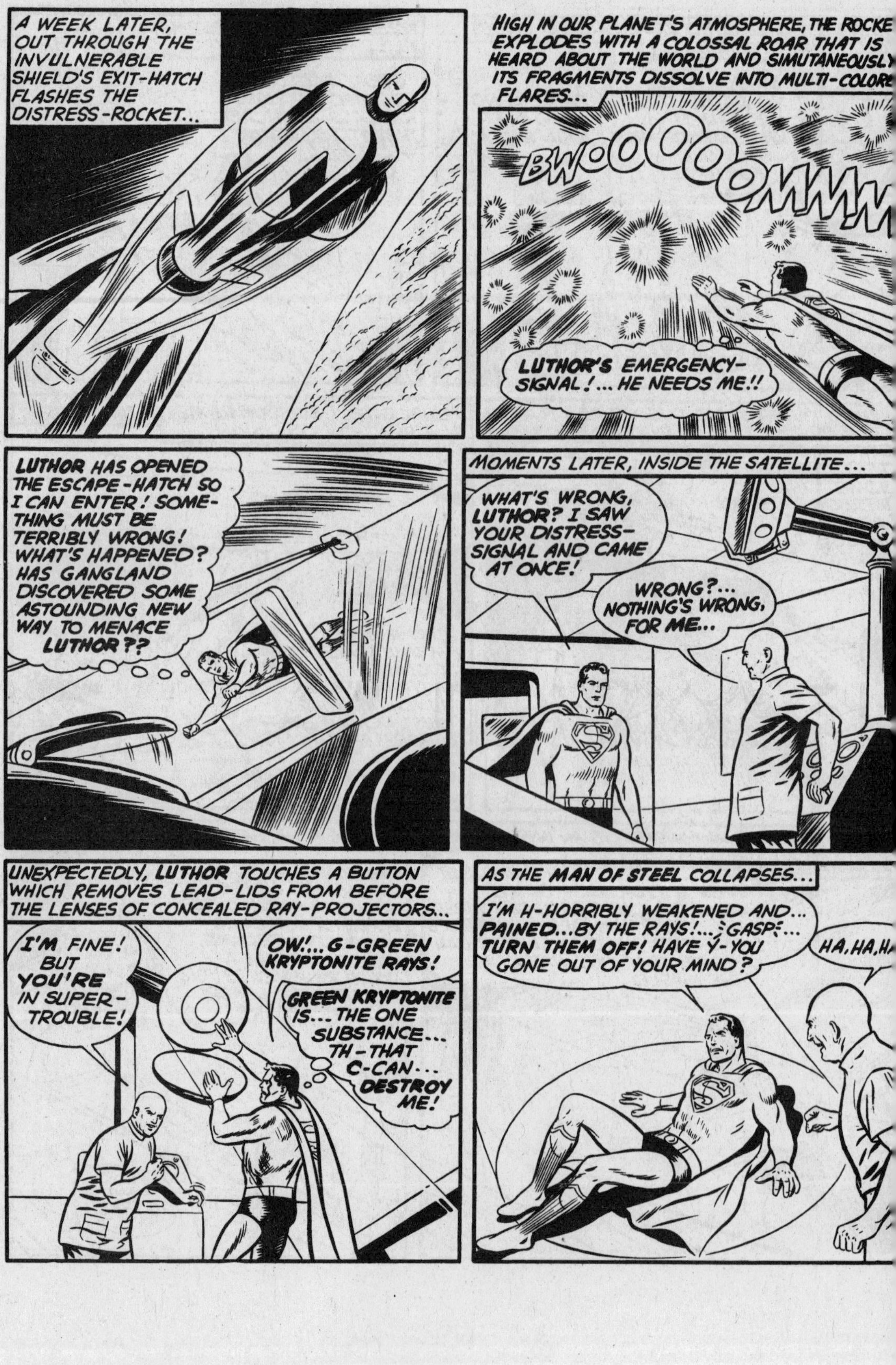
A WEEK LATER, OUT THROUGH THE INVULNERABLE SHIELD'S EXIT-HATCH FLASHES THE DISTRESS-ROCKET...
HIGH IN OUR PLANET'S ATMOSPHERE, THE ROCKE EXPLODES WITH A COLOSSAL ROAR THAT IS HEARD ABOUT THE WORLD AND SIMUTANEOUSL ITS FRAGMENTS DISSOLVE INTO MULTI-COLORE FLARES...
BWOOOOOOMMMM
LUTHOR'S EMERGENCY-SIGNAL!... HE NEEDS ME!!
LUTHOR HAS OPENED THE ESCAPE-HATCH SO I CAN ENTER! SOMETHING MUST BE TERRIBLY WRONG! WHAT'S HAPPENED? HAS GANGLAND DISCOVERED SOME ASTOUNDING NEW WAY TO MENACE LUTHOR??
MOMENTS LATER, INSIDE THE SATELLITE...
WHAT'S WRONG, LUTHOR? I SAW YOUR DISTRESS-SIGNAL AND CAME AT ONCE!
WRONG?... NOTHING'S WRONG, FOR ME...
UNEXPECTEDLY, LUTHOR TOUCHES A BUTTON WHICH REMOVES LEAD-LIDS FROM BEFORE THE LENSES OF CONCEALED RAY-PROJECTORS...
I'M FINE! BUT YOU'RE IN SUPER-TROUBLE!
OW!... G-GREEN KRYPTONITE RAYS!
GREEN KRYPTONITE IS... THE ONE SUBSTANCE... TH-THAT C-CAN... DESTROY ME!
AS THE MAN OF STEEL COLLAPSES...
I'M H-HORRIBLY WEAKENED AND... PAINED... BY THE RAYS!... GASP... TURN THEM OFF! HAVE Y-YOU GONE OUT OF YOUR MIND?
HA, HA, HA

SECONDS LATER, AS *LUTHOR* STRAPS THE MAN OF *STEEL* TO A BENCH, WITH BANDS OF METAL CONTAINING *KRYPTONITE*...

HA, HA! OH, HOW SIMPLE IT WAS TO OUTWIT YOU!

THEN, AS *LUTHOR* PULLS A SWITCH...

SEE, *SUPERMAN?* THAT WALL IS RISING! THERE'S A THICK GLASS PARTITION BEHIND IT, SEPARATING US FROM YOUR DEAR FRIENDS... LOIS LANE, JIMMY OLSEN, AND PERRY WHITE!...THEY CAN'T POSSIBLY BREAK THROUGH THAT GLASS AND RESCUE YOU!

BEHIND THE GLASS PARTITION...

LUTHOR HASN'T *REFORMED!* HE'S AS EVIL AS EVER! HE'S GOING TO KILL *SUPERMAN!*

DON'T GIVE UP HOPE, LOIS!

SUPERMAN'S GOTTEN OUT OF TIGHTER FIXES THAN THIS!

SMIRKING, *LUTHOR* GLOATS...

WASN'T IT *KIND* AND *CONSIDERATE* OF ME TO KIDNAP YOUR FRIENDS, SO THEY COULD WITNESS THIS... HA, HA... TOUCHING MOMENT?... HA, HA! YOU'VE BEGUN TO *TURN GREEN,* AS KRYPTONITE FEVER RAGES WITHIN YOU!

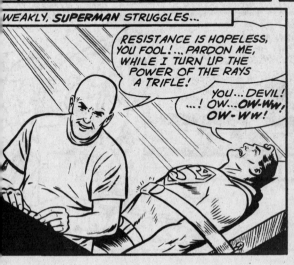

WEAKLY, *SUPERMAN* STRUGGLES...

RESISTANCE IS HOPELESS, YOU FOOL!... PARDON ME, WHILE I TURN UP THE POWER OF THE RAYS A TRIFLE!

YOU...DEVIL! ...! OW...OW-WW! OW-WW!

CLEVER DEVIL, YOU MEAN!... I DISCOVERED THAT CANCER-CURE, IN ORDER TO BE RELEASED FROM JAIL! I *PRETENDED* TO HAVE REFORMED, SO I COULD LULL YOU INTO A FALSE SENSE OF SECURITY! THE PURPOSE ? TO CATCH YOU OFF-GUARD AND LURE YOU INTO THIS DEATH-TRAP!!

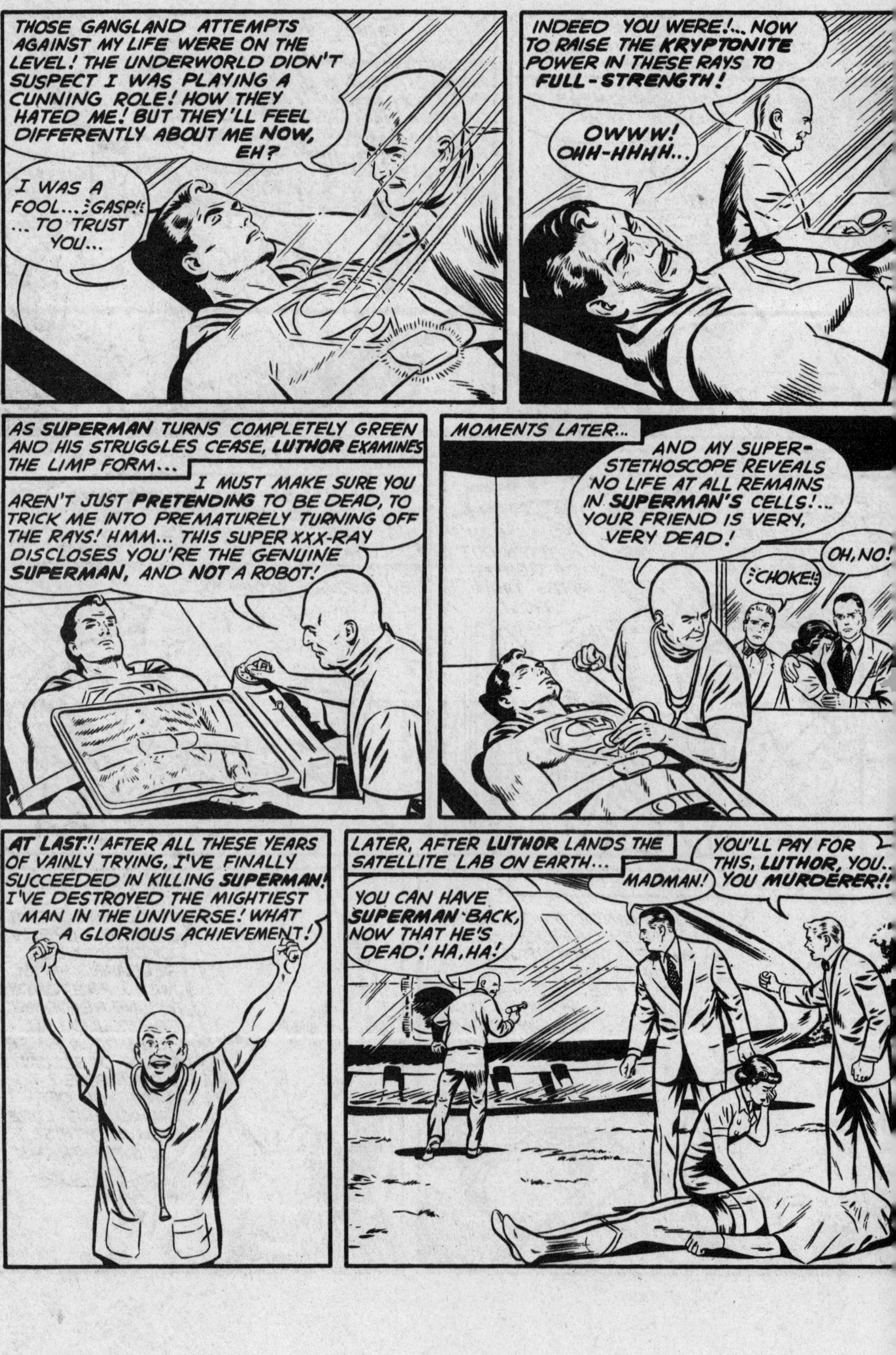
THOSE GANGLAND ATTEMPTS AGAINST MY LIFE WERE ON THE LEVEL! THE UNDERWORLD DIDN'T SUSPECT I WAS PLAYING A CUNNING ROLE! HOW THEY HATED ME! BUT THEY'LL FEEL DIFFERENTLY ABOUT ME NOW, EH?
I WAS A FOOL... GASP! ... TO TRUST YOU...
INDEED YOU WERE!... NOW TO RAISE THE KRYPTONITE POWER IN THESE RAYS TO FULL-STRENGTH!
OWWW! OHH-HHHH...
AS SUPERMAN TURNS COMPLETELY GREEN AND HIS STRUGGLES CEASE, LUTHOR EXAMINES THE LIMP FORM...
I MUST MAKE SURE YOU AREN'T JUST PRETENDING TO BE DEAD, TO TRICK ME INTO PREMATURELY TURNING OFF THE RAYS! HMM... THIS SUPER XXX-RAY DISCLOSES YOU'RE THE GENUINE SUPERMAN, AND NOT A ROBOT!
MOMENTS LATER...
AND MY SUPER-STETHOSCOPE REVEALS NO LIFE AT ALL REMAINS IN SUPERMAN'S CELLS!... YOUR FRIEND IS VERY, VERY DEAD!
CHOKE!
OH, NO!
AT LAST!! AFTER ALL THESE YEARS OF VAINLY TRYING, I'VE FINALLY SUCCEEDED IN KILLING SUPERMAN! I'VE DESTROYED THE MIGHTIEST MAN IN THE UNIVERSE! WHAT A GLORIOUS ACHIEVEMENT!
LATER, AFTER LUTHOR LANDS THE SATELLITE LAB ON EARTH...
YOU CAN HAVE SUPERMAN BACK, NOW THAT HE'S DEAD! HA, HA!
MADMAN!
YOU'LL PAY FOR THIS, LUTHOR, YOU... YOU MURDERER!!

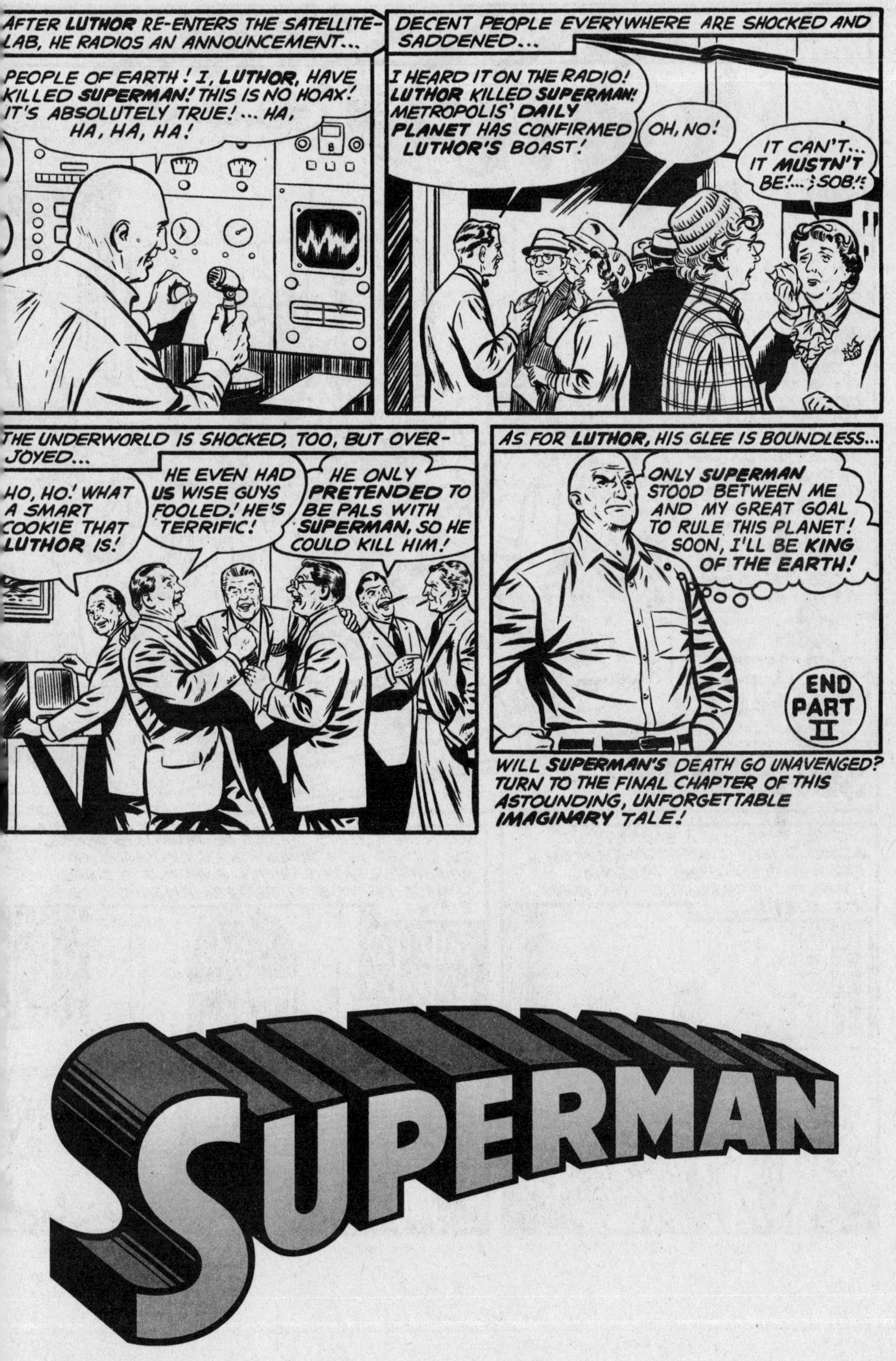
AFTER LUTHOR RE-ENTERS THE SATELLITE-LAB, HE RADIOS AN ANNOUNCEMENT...
PEOPLE OF EARTH! I, LUTHOR, HAVE KILLED SUPERMAN! THIS IS NO HOAX! IT'S ABSOLUTELY TRUE! ... HA, HA, HA, HA!
DECENT PEOPLE EVERYWHERE ARE SHOCKED AND SADDENED...
I HEARD IT ON THE RADIO! LUTHOR KILLED SUPERMAN! METROPOLIS' DAILY PLANET HAS CONFIRMED LUTHOR'S BOAST!
OH, NO!
IT CAN'T... IT MUSTN'T BE!...; SOB!;
THE UNDERWORLD IS SHOCKED, TOO, BUT OVER-JOYED...
HO, HO! WHAT A SMART COOKIE THAT LUTHOR IS!
HE EVEN HAD US WISE GUYS FOOLED! HE'S TERRIFIC!
HE ONLY PRETENDED TO BE PALS WITH SUPERMAN, SO HE COULD KILL HIM!
AS FOR LUTHOR, HIS GLEE IS BOUNDLESS...
ONLY SUPERMAN STOOD BETWEEN ME AND MY GREAT GOAL TO RULE THIS PLANET! SOON, I'LL BE KING OF THE EARTH!
END PART II
WILL SUPERMAN'S DEATH GO UNAVENGED? TURN TO THE FINAL CHAPTER OF THIS ASTOUNDING, UNFORGETTABLE IMAGINARY TALE!

SUPERMAN

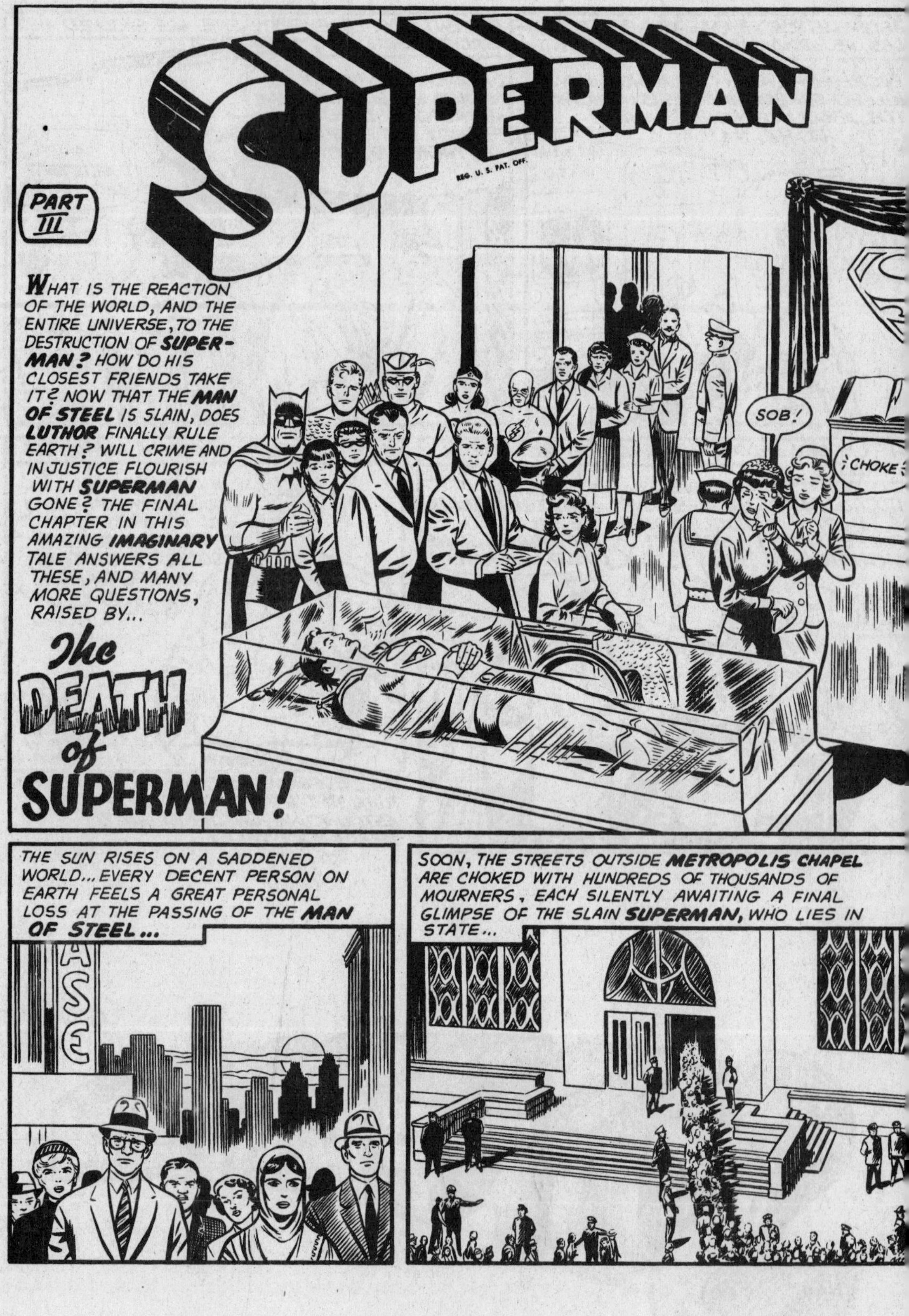
SUPERMAN
REG. U.S. PAT. OFF.
PART III
WHAT IS THE REACTION OF THE WORLD, AND THE ENTIRE UNIVERSE, TO THE DESTRUCTION OF SUPERMAN? HOW DO HIS CLOSEST FRIENDS TAKE IT? NOW THAT THE MAN OF STEEL IS SLAIN, DOES LUTHOR FINALLY RULE EARTH? WILL CRIME AND INJUSTICE FLOURISH WITH SUPERMAN GONE? THE FINAL CHAPTER IN THIS AMAZING IMAGINARY TALE ANSWERS ALL THESE, AND MANY MORE QUESTIONS, RAISED BY...
The DEATH of SUPERMAN!
SOB!
¡CHOKE!
THE SUN RISES ON A SADDENED WORLD... EVERY DECENT PERSON ON EARTH FEELS A GREAT PERSONAL LOSS AT THE PASSING OF THE MAN OF STEEL...
SOON, THE STREETS OUTSIDE METROPOLIS CHAPEL ARE CHOKED WITH HUNDREDS OF THOUSANDS OF MOURNERS, EACH SILENTLY AWAITING A FINAL GLIMPSE OF THE SLAIN SUPERMAN, WHO LIES IN STATE...

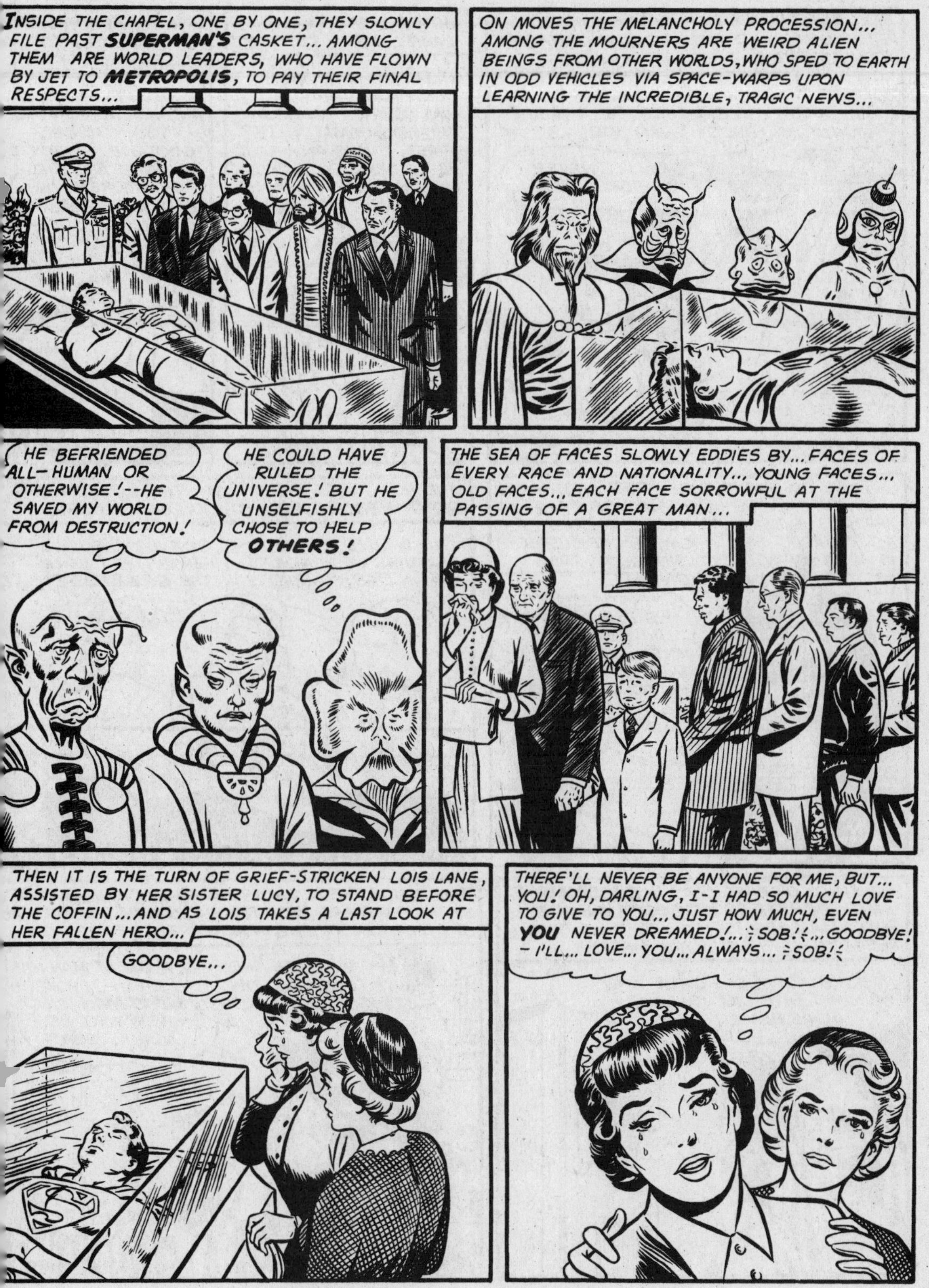
INSIDE THE CHAPEL, ONE BY ONE, THEY SLOWLY FILE PAST SUPERMAN'S CASKET... AMONG THEM ARE WORLD LEADERS, WHO HAVE FLOWN BY JET TO METROPOLIS, TO PAY THEIR FINAL RESPECTS...
ON MOVES THE MELANCHOLY PROCESSION... AMONG THE MOURNERS ARE WEIRD ALIEN BEINGS FROM OTHER WORLDS, WHO SPED TO EARTH IN ODD VEHICLES VIA SPACE-WARPS UPON LEARNING THE INCREDIBLE, TRAGIC NEWS...
HE BEFRIENDED ALL-HUMAN OR OTHERWISE!--HE SAVED MY WORLD FROM DESTRUCTION!
HE COULD HAVE RULED THE UNIVERSE! BUT HE UNSELFISHLY CHOSE TO HELP OTHERS!
THE SEA OF FACES SLOWLY EDDIES BY... FACES OF EVERY RACE AND NATIONALITY..., YOUNG FACES... OLD FACES..., EACH FACE SORROWFUL AT THE PASSING OF A GREAT MAN...
THEN IT IS THE TURN OF GRIEF-STRICKEN LOIS LANE, ASSISTED BY HER SISTER LUCY, TO STAND BEFORE THE COFFIN...AND AS LOIS TAKES A LAST LOOK AT HER FALLEN HERO...
GOODBYE...
THERE'LL NEVER BE ANYONE FOR ME, BUT... YOU! OH, DARLING, I-I HAD SO MUCH LOVE TO GIVE TO YOU... JUST HOW MUCH, EVEN YOU NEVER DREAMED!... SOB!... GOODBYE! - I'LL... LOVE... YOU... ALWAYS... SOB!

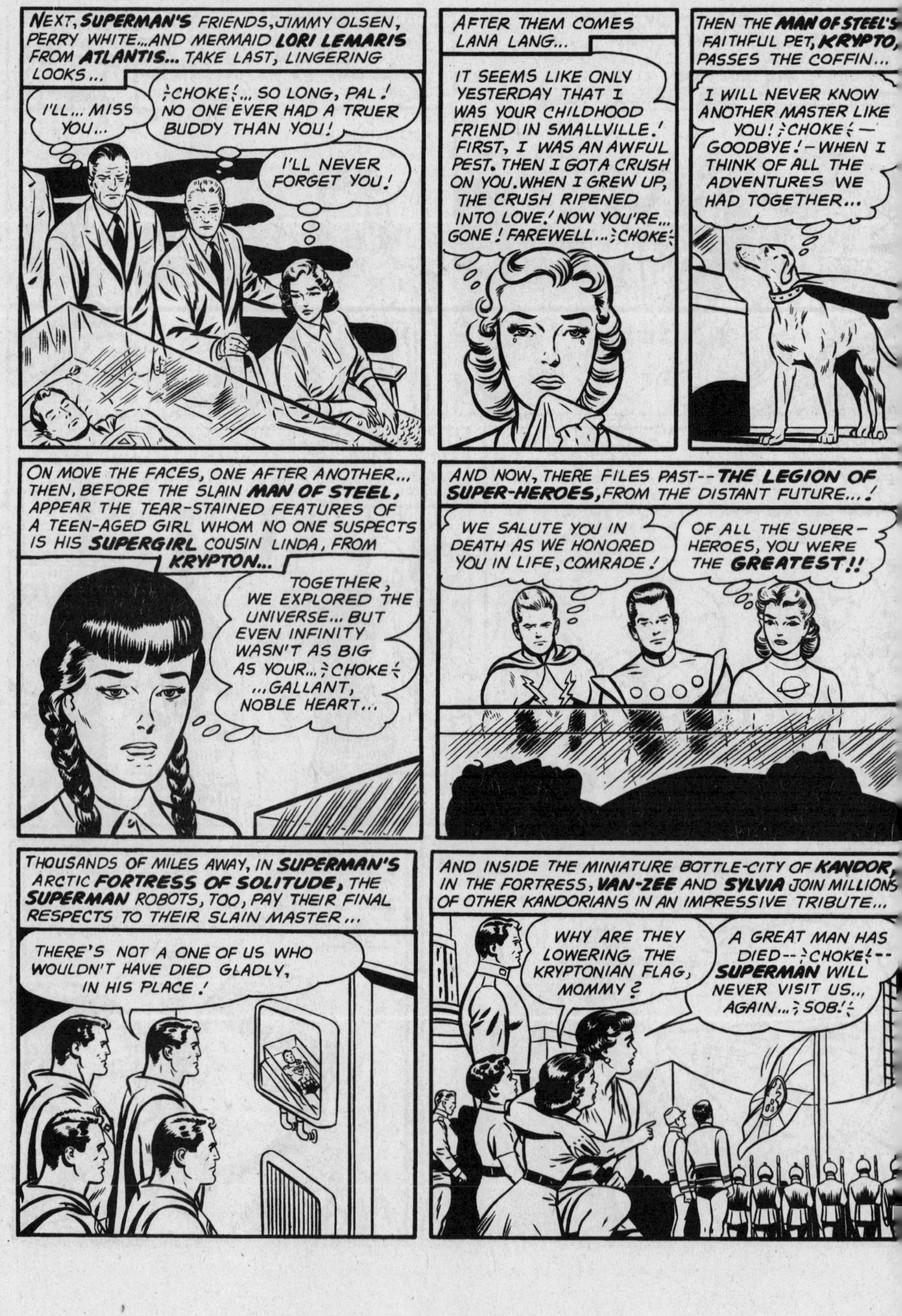
NEXT, SUPERMAN'S FRIENDS, JIMMY OLSEN, PERRY WHITE...AND MERMAID LORI LEMARIS FROM ATLANTIS... TAKE LAST, LINGERING LOOKS...
I'LL... MISS YOU...
¿CHOKE¿... SO LONG, PAL! NO ONE EVER HAD A TRUER BUDDY THAN YOU!
I'LL NEVER FORGET YOU!
AFTER THEM COMES LANA LANG...
IT SEEMS LIKE ONLY YESTERDAY THAT I WAS YOUR CHILDHOOD FRIEND IN SMALLVILLE! FIRST, I WAS AN AWFUL PEST. THEN I GOT A CRUSH ON YOU. WHEN I GREW UP, THE CRUSH RIPENED INTO LOVE! NOW YOU'RE... GONE! FAREWELL... ¿CHOKE¿
THEN THE MAN OF STEEL'S FAITHFUL PET, KRYPTO, PASSES THE COFFIN...
I WILL NEVER KNOW ANOTHER MASTER LIKE YOU! ¿CHOKE¿ — GOODBYE! — WHEN I THINK OF ALL THE ADVENTURES WE HAD TOGETHER...
ON MOVE THE FACES, ONE AFTER ANOTHER... THEN, BEFORE THE SLAIN MAN OF STEEL, APPEAR THE TEAR-STAINED FEATURES OF A TEEN-AGED GIRL WHOM NO ONE SUSPECTS IS HIS SUPERGIRL COUSIN LINDA, FROM KRYPTON...
TOGETHER, WE EXPLORED THE UNIVERSE... BUT EVEN INFINITY WASN'T AS BIG AS YOUR... ¿CHOKE¿ ...GALLANT, NOBLE HEART...
AND NOW, THERE FILES PAST--THE LEGION OF SUPER-HEROES, FROM THE DISTANT FUTURE...!
WE SALUTE YOU IN DEATH AS WE HONORED YOU IN LIFE, COMRADE!
OF ALL THE SUPER-HEROES, YOU WERE THE GREATEST!!
THOUSANDS OF MILES AWAY, IN SUPERMAN'S ARCTIC FORTRESS OF SOLITUDE, THE SUPERMAN ROBOTS, TOO, PAY THEIR FINAL RESPECTS TO THEIR SLAIN MASTER...
THERE'S NOT A ONE OF US WHO WOULDN'T HAVE DIED GLADLY, IN HIS PLACE!
AND INSIDE THE MINIATURE BOTTLE-CITY OF KANDOR, IN THE FORTRESS, VAN-ZEE AND SYLVIA JOIN MILLIONS OF OTHER KANDORIANS IN AN IMPRESSIVE TRIBUTE...
WHY ARE THEY LOWERING THE KRYPTONIAN FLAG, MOMMY?
A GREAT MAN HAS DIED-- ¿CHOKE¿-- SUPERMAN WILL NEVER VISIT US... AGAIN... ¿SOB!¿

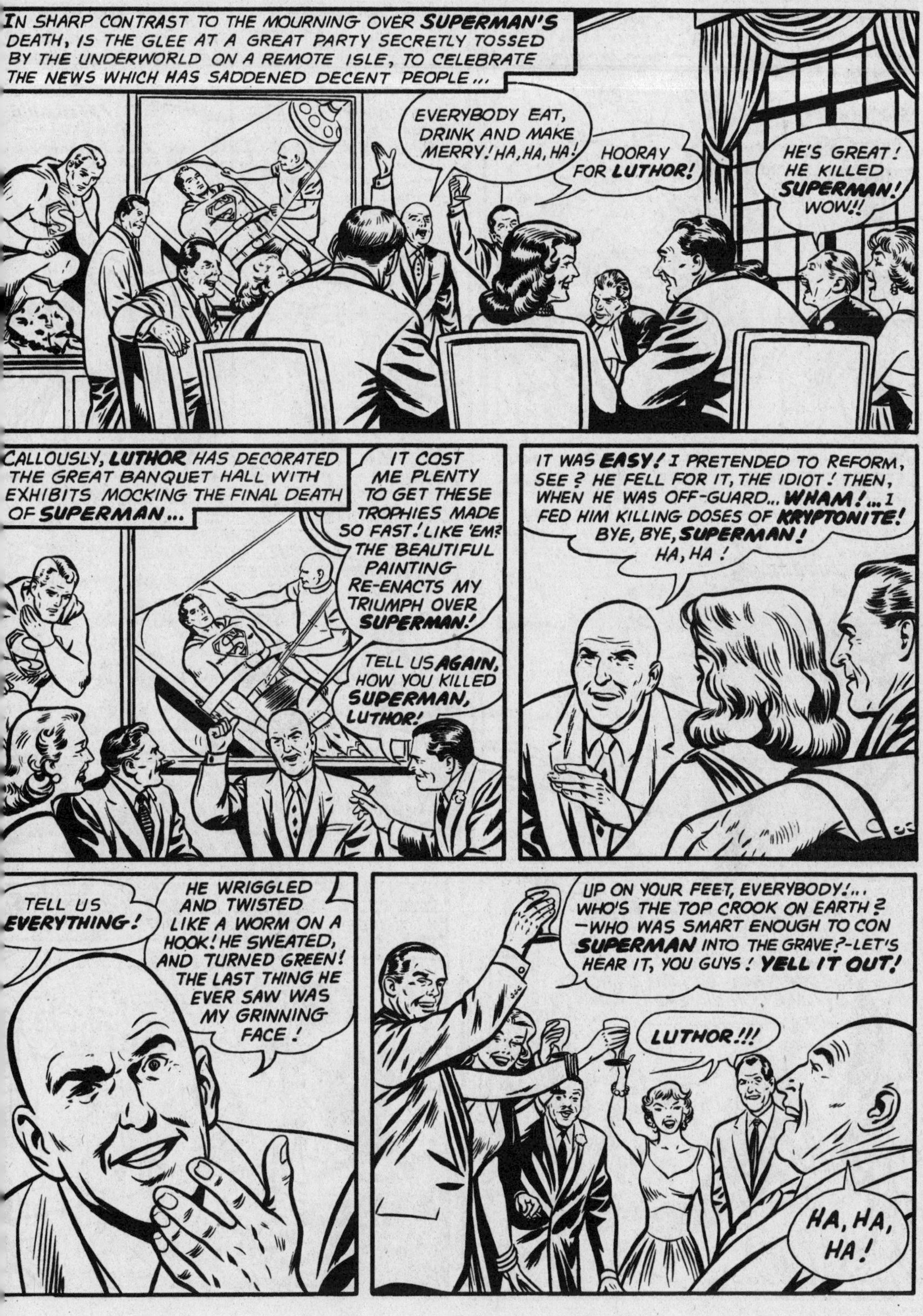
IN SHARP CONTRAST TO THE MOURNING OVER SUPERMAN'S DEATH, IS THE GLEE AT A GREAT PARTY SECRETLY TOSSED BY THE UNDERWORLD ON A REMOTE ISLE, TO CELEBRATE THE NEWS WHICH HAS SADDENED DECENT PEOPLE...
EVERYBODY EAT, DRINK AND MAKE MERRY! HA, HA, HA!
HOORAY FOR LUTHOR!
HE'S GREAT! HE KILLED SUPERMAN! WOW!!
CALLOUSLY, LUTHOR HAS DECORATED THE GREAT BANQUET HALL WITH EXHIBITS MOCKING THE FINAL DEATH OF SUPERMAN...
IT COST ME PLENTY TO GET THESE TROPHIES MADE SO FAST! LIKE 'EM? THE BEAUTIFUL PAINTING RE-ENACTS MY TRIUMPH OVER SUPERMAN!
TELL US AGAIN, HOW YOU KILLED SUPERMAN, LUTHOR!
IT WAS EASY! I PRETENDED TO REFORM, SEE? HE FELL FOR IT, THE IDIOT! THEN, WHEN HE WAS OFF-GUARD... WHAM!...I FED HIM KILLING DOSES OF KRYPTONITE! BYE, BYE, SUPERMAN! HA, HA!
TELL US EVERYTHING!
HE WRIGGLED AND TWISTED LIKE A WORM ON A HOOK! HE SWEATED, AND TURNED GREEN! THE LAST THING HE EVER SAW WAS MY GRINNING FACE!
UP ON YOUR FEET, EVERYBODY!... WHO'S THE TOP CROOK ON EARTH? —WHO WAS SMART ENOUGH TO CON SUPERMAN INTO THE GRAVE?-LET'S HEAR IT, YOU GUYS! YELL IT OUT!
LUTHOR!!!
HA, HA, HA!

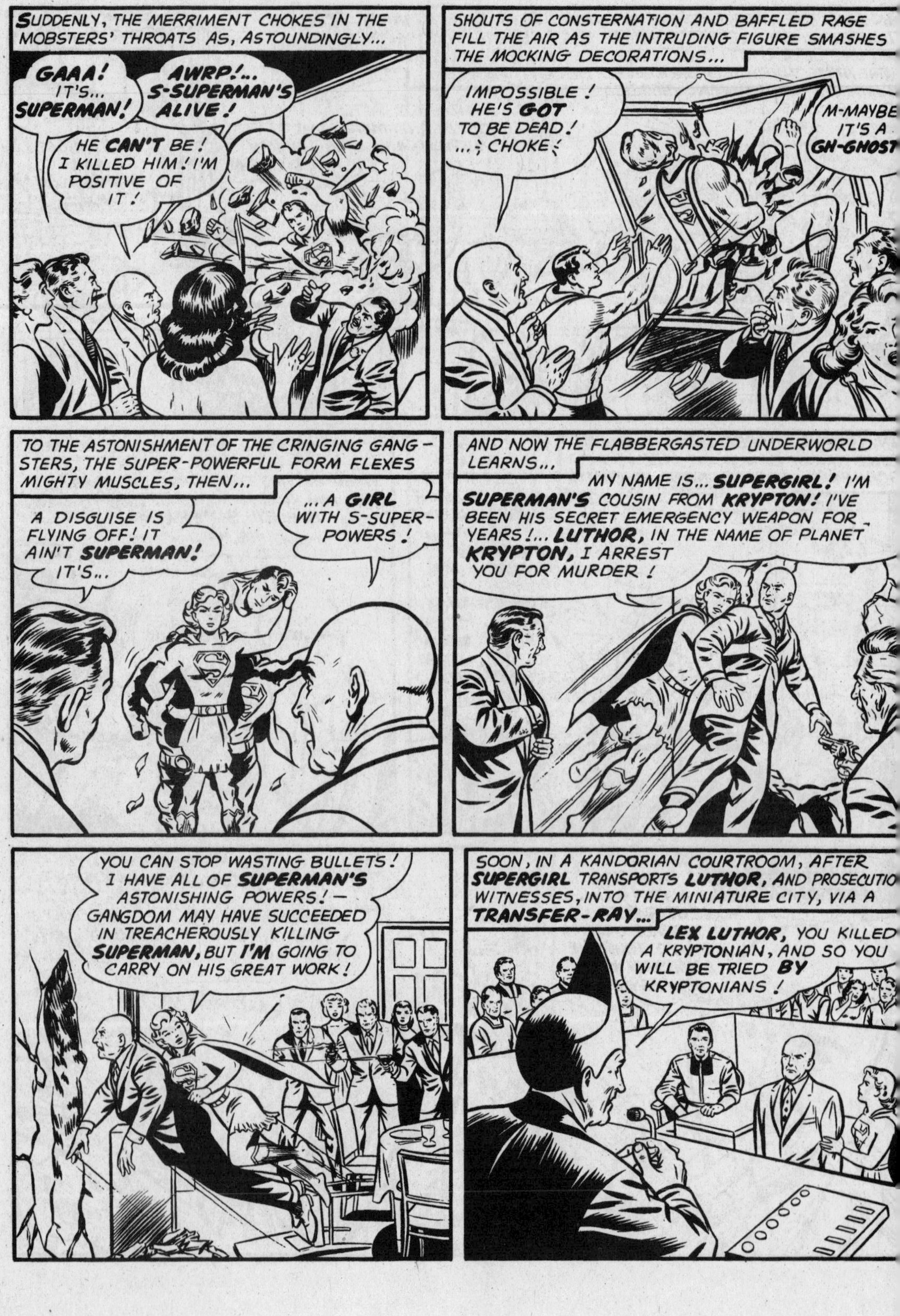
SUDDENLY, THE MERRIMENT CHOKES IN THE MOBSTERS' THROATS AS, ASTOUNDINGLY...
GAAA! IT'S... SUPERMAN!
AWRP!... S-SUPERMAN'S ALIVE!
HE CAN'T BE! I KILLED HIM! I'M POSITIVE OF IT!
SHOUTS OF CONSTERNATION AND BAFFLED RAGE FILL THE AIR AS THE INTRUDING FIGURE SMASHES THE MOCKING DECORATIONS...
IMPOSSIBLE! HE'S GOT TO BE DEAD! ...CHOKE
M-MAYBE IT'S A GH-GHOST
TO THE ASTONISHMENT OF THE CRINGING GANGSTERS, THE SUPER-POWERFUL FORM FLEXES MIGHTY MUSCLES, THEN...
A DISGUISE IS FLYING OFF! IT AIN'T SUPERMAN! IT'S...
...A GIRL WITH S-SUPER-POWERS!
AND NOW THE FLABBERGASTED UNDERWORLD LEARNS...
MY NAME IS... SUPERGIRL! I'M SUPERMAN'S COUSIN FROM KRYPTON! I'VE BEEN HIS SECRET EMERGENCY WEAPON FOR YEARS!... LUTHOR, IN THE NAME OF PLANET KRYPTON, I ARREST YOU FOR MURDER!
YOU CAN STOP WASTING BULLETS! I HAVE ALL OF SUPERMAN'S ASTONISHING POWERS! — GANGDOM MAY HAVE SUCCEEDED IN TREACHEROUSLY KILLING SUPERMAN, BUT I'M GOING TO CARRY ON HIS GREAT WORK!
SOON, IN A KANDORIAN COURTROOM, AFTER SUPERGIRL TRANSPORTS LUTHOR, AND PROSECUTIO WITNESSES, INTO THE MINIATURE CITY, VIA A TRANSFER-RAY...
LEX LUTHOR, YOU KILLED A KRYPTONIAN, AND SO YOU WILL BE TRIED BY KRYPTONIANS!

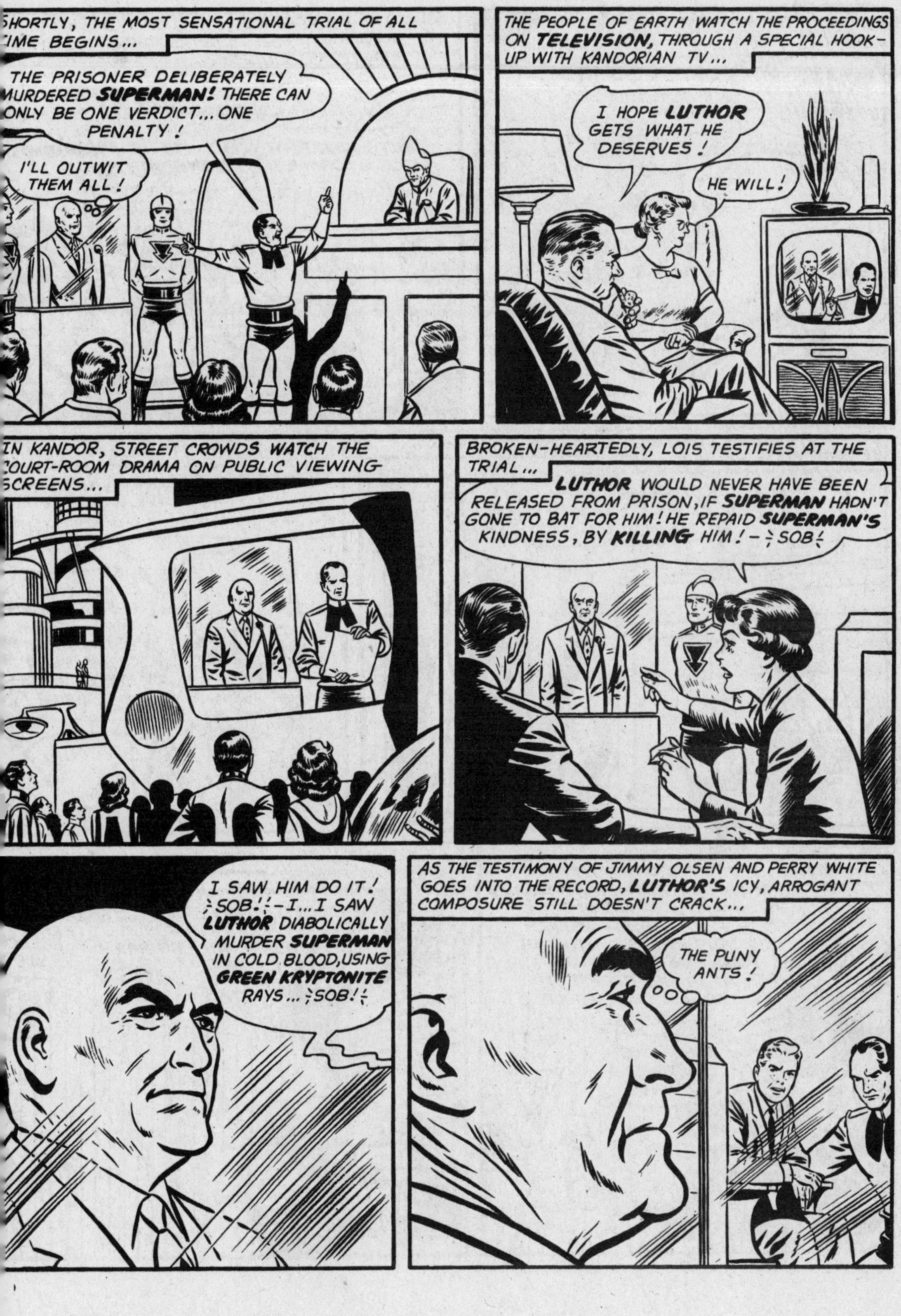
SHORTLY, THE MOST SENSATIONAL TRIAL OF ALL TIME BEGINS...
THE PRISONER DELIBERATELY MURDERED SUPERMAN! THERE CAN ONLY BE ONE VERDICT... ONE PENALTY!
I'LL OUTWIT THEM ALL!
THE PEOPLE OF EARTH WATCH THE PROCEEDINGS ON TELEVISION, THROUGH A SPECIAL HOOK-UP WITH KANDORIAN TV...
I HOPE LUTHOR GETS WHAT HE DESERVES!
HE WILL!
IN KANDOR, STREET CROWDS WATCH THE COURT-ROOM DRAMA ON PUBLIC VIEWING-SCREENS...
BROKEN-HEARTEDLY, LOIS TESTIFIES AT THE TRIAL...
LUTHOR WOULD NEVER HAVE BEEN RELEASED FROM PRISON, IF SUPERMAN HADN'T GONE TO BAT FOR HIM! HE REPAID SUPERMAN'S KINDNESS, BY KILLING HIM! - SOB!
I SAW HIM DO IT! SOB! - I... I SAW LUTHOR DIABOLICALLY MURDER SUPERMAN IN COLD BLOOD, USING GREEN KRYPTONITE RAYS... SOB!
AS THE TESTIMONY OF JIMMY OLSEN AND PERRY WHITE GOES INTO THE RECORD, LUTHOR'S ICY, ARROGANT COMPOSURE STILL DOESN'T CRACK...
THE PUNY ANTS!

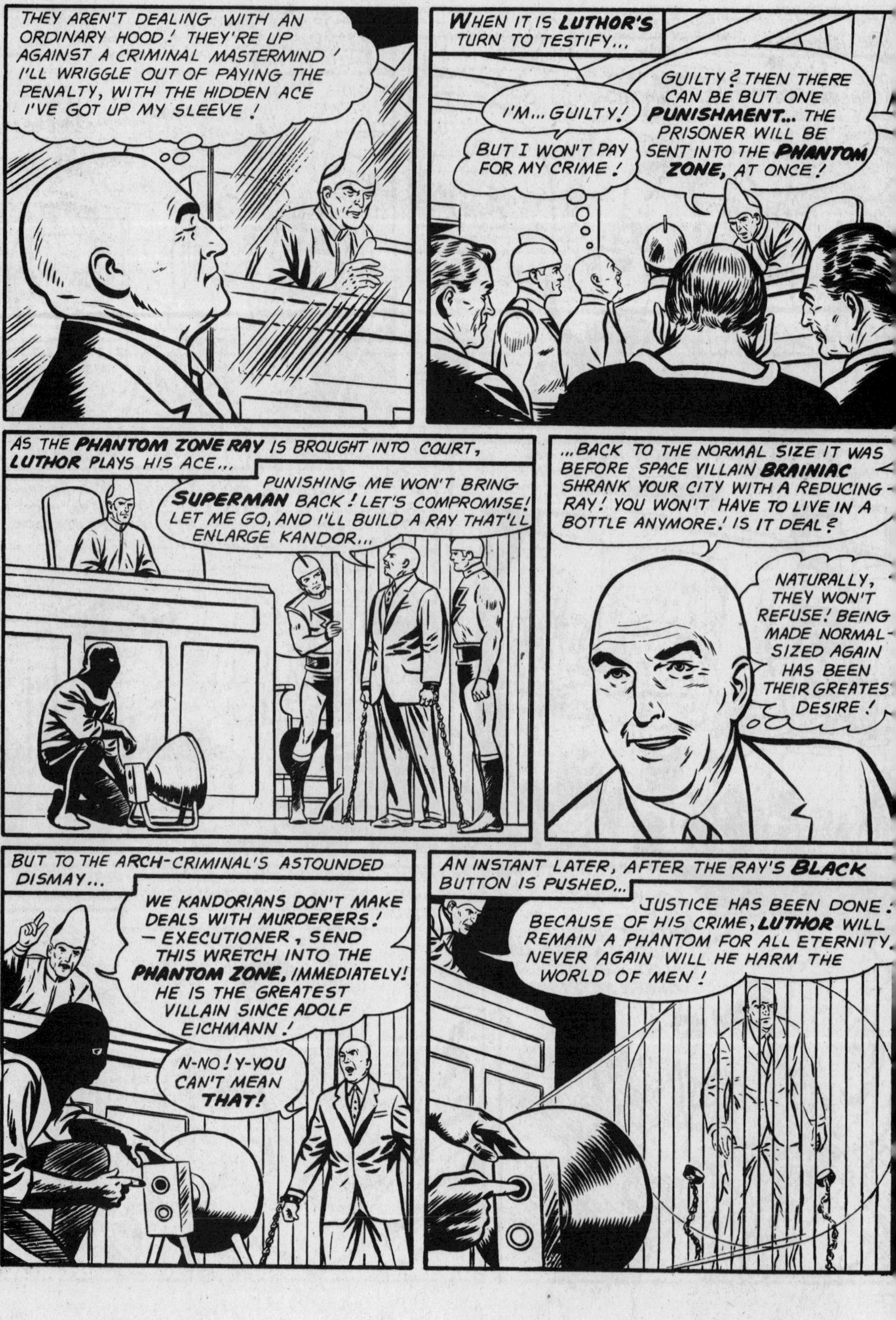
THEY AREN'T DEALING WITH AN ORDINARY HOOD! THEY'RE UP AGAINST A CRIMINAL MASTERMIND! I'LL WRIGGLE OUT OF PAYING THE PENALTY, WITH THE HIDDEN ACE I'VE GOT UP MY SLEEVE!
WHEN IT IS LUTHOR'S TURN TO TESTIFY...
I'M... GUILTY!
BUT I WON'T PAY FOR MY CRIME!
GUILTY? THEN THERE CAN BE BUT ONE PUNISHMENT... THE PRISONER WILL BE SENT INTO THE PHANTOM ZONE, AT ONCE!
AS THE PHANTOM ZONE RAY IS BROUGHT INTO COURT, LUTHOR PLAYS HIS ACE...
PUNISHING ME WON'T BRING SUPERMAN BACK! LET'S COMPROMISE! LET ME GO, AND I'LL BUILD A RAY THAT'LL ENLARGE KANDOR...
...BACK TO THE NORMAL SIZE IT WAS BEFORE SPACE VILLAIN BRAINIAC SHRANK YOUR CITY WITH A REDUCING-RAY! YOU WON'T HAVE TO LIVE IN A BOTTLE ANYMORE! IS IT DEAL?
NATURALLY, THEY WON'T REFUSE! BEING MADE NORMAL-SIZED AGAIN HAS BEEN THEIR GREATES DESIRE!
BUT TO THE ARCH-CRIMINAL'S ASTOUNDED DISMAY...
WE KANDORIANS DON'T MAKE DEALS WITH MURDERERS! —EXECUTIONER, SEND THIS WRETCH INTO THE PHANTOM ZONE, IMMEDIATELY! HE IS THE GREATEST VILLAIN SINCE ADOLF EICHMANN!
N-NO! Y-YOU CAN'T MEAN THAT!
AN INSTANT LATER, AFTER THE RAY'S BLACK BUTTON IS PUSHED...
JUSTICE HAS BEEN DONE! BECAUSE OF HIS CRIME, LUTHOR WILL REMAIN A PHANTOM FOR ALL ETERNITY. NEVER AGAIN WILL HE HARM THE WORLD OF MEN!

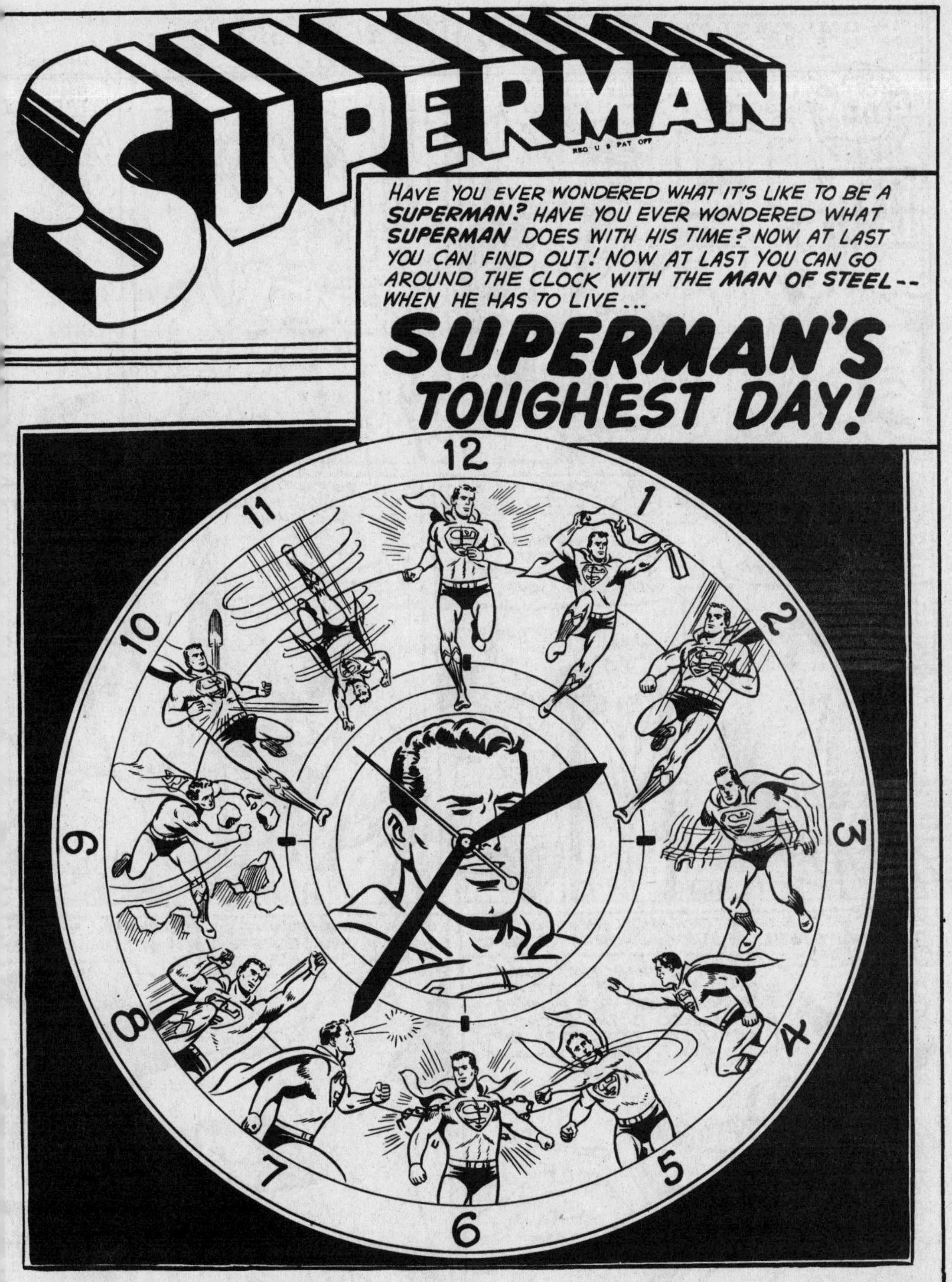
SUPERMAN
REG U S PAT OFF
HAVE YOU EVER WONDERED WHAT IT'S LIKE TO BE A SUPERMAN? HAVE YOU EVER WONDERED WHAT SUPERMAN DOES WITH HIS TIME? NOW AT LAST YOU CAN FIND OUT! NOW AT LAST YOU CAN GO AROUND THE CLOCK WITH THE MAN OF STEEL-- WHEN HE HAS TO LIVE...
SUPERMAN'S TOUGHEST DAY!
12
1
2
3
4
5
6
7
8
9
10
11

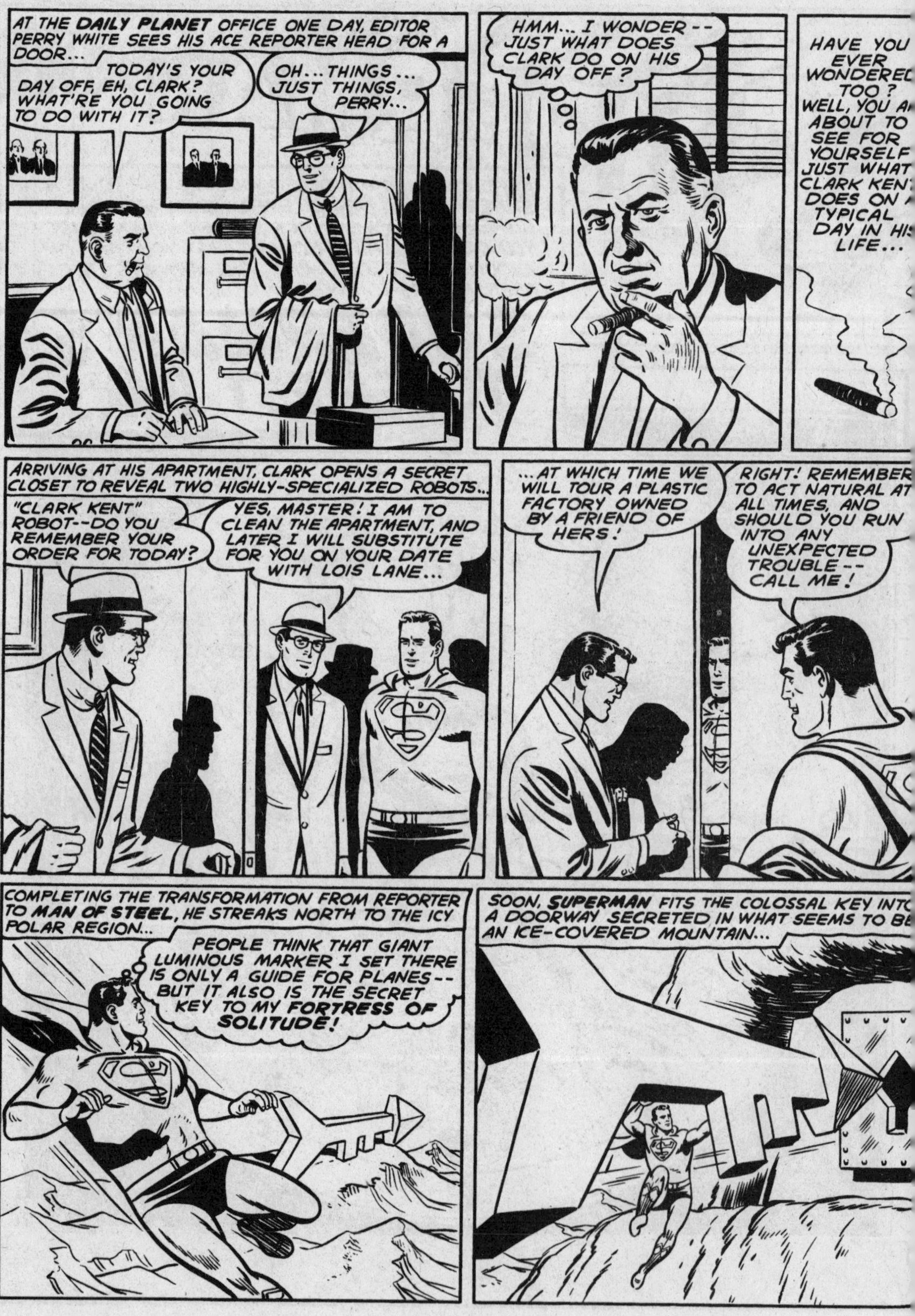
AT THE DAILY PLANET OFFICE ONE DAY, EDITOR PERRY WHITE SEES HIS ACE REPORTER HEAD FOR A DOOR...
TODAY'S YOUR DAY OFF, EH, CLARK? WHAT'RE YOU GOING TO DO WITH IT?
OH... THINGS... JUST THINGS, PERRY...
HMM... I WONDER -- JUST WHAT DOES CLARK DO ON HIS DAY OFF?
HAVE YOU EVER WONDERE TOO? WELL, YOU A ABOUT TO SEE FOR YOURSELF JUST WHAT CLARK KEN DOES ON TYPICAL DAY IN HI LIFE...
ARRIVING AT HIS APARTMENT, CLARK OPENS A SECRET CLOSET TO REVEAL TWO HIGHLY-SPECIALIZED ROBOTS...
"CLARK KENT" ROBOT--DO YOU REMEMBER YOUR ORDER FOR TODAY?
YES, MASTER! I AM TO CLEAN THE APARTMENT, AND LATER I WILL SUBSTITUTE FOR YOU ON YOUR DATE WITH LOIS LANE...
...AT WHICH TIME WE WILL TOUR A PLASTIC FACTORY OWNED BY A FRIEND OF HERS!
RIGHT! REMEMBER TO ACT NATURAL AT ALL TIMES, AND SHOULD YOU RUN INTO ANY UNEXPECTED TROUBLE -- CALL ME!
COMPLETING THE TRANSFORMATION FROM REPORTER TO MAN OF STEEL, HE STREAKS NORTH TO THE ICY POLAR REGION...
PEOPLE THINK THAT GIANT LUMINOUS MARKER I SET THERE IS ONLY A GUIDE FOR PLANES -- BUT IT ALSO IS THE SECRET KEY TO MY FORTRESS OF SOLITUDE!
SOON, SUPERMAN FITS THE COLOSSAL KEY INT A DOORWAY SECRETED IN WHAT SEEMS TO B AN ICE-COVERED MOUNTAIN...

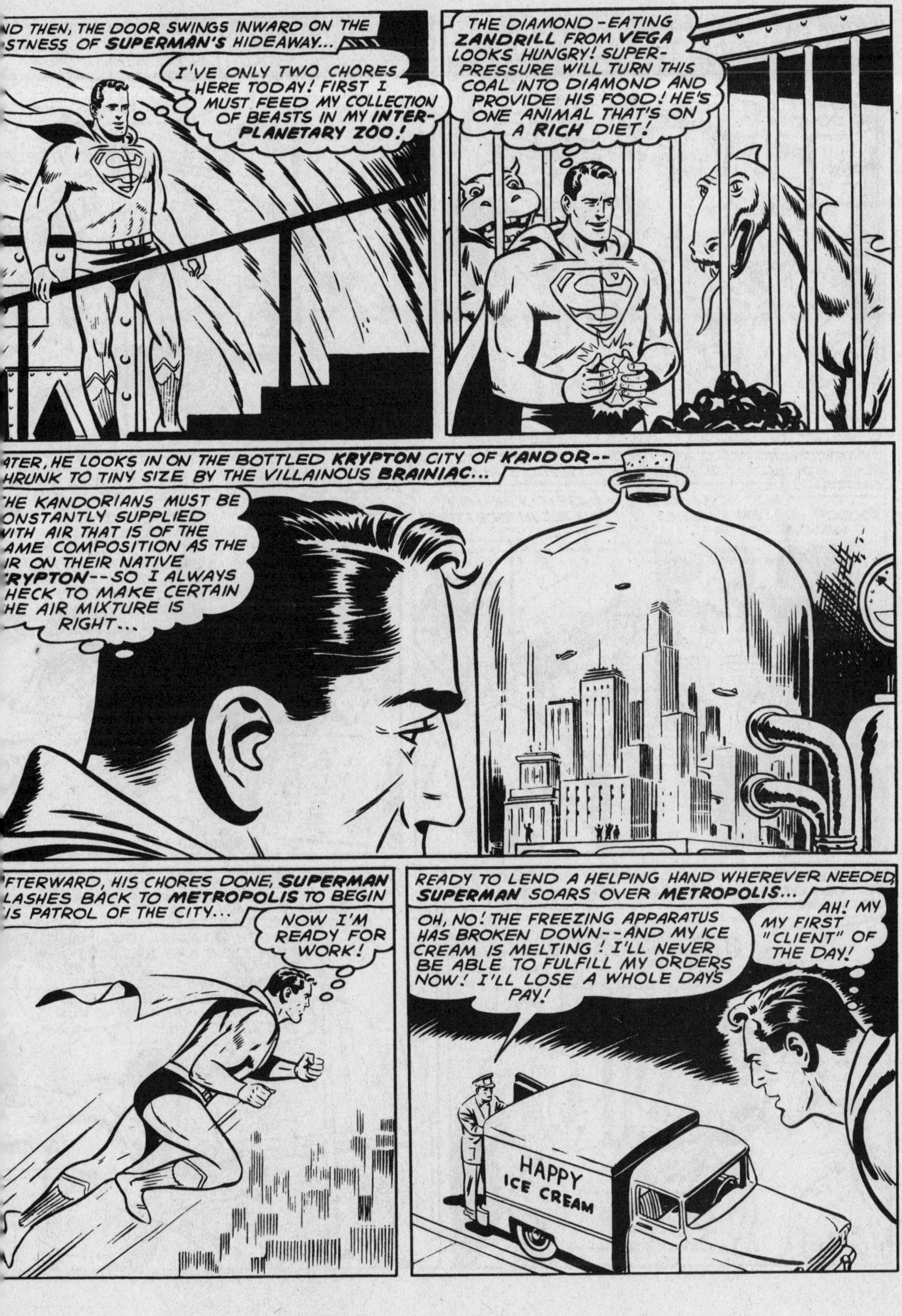
ND THEN, THE DOOR SWINGS INWARD ON THE STNESS OF SUPERMAN'S HIDEAWAY...
I'VE ONLY TWO CHORES HERE TODAY! FIRST I MUST FEED MY COLLECTION OF BEASTS IN MY INTER-PLANETARY ZOO!
THE DIAMOND-EATING ZANDRILL FROM VEGA LOOKS HUNGRY! SUPER-PRESSURE WILL TURN THIS COAL INTO DIAMOND AND PROVIDE HIS FOOD! HE'S ONE ANIMAL THAT'S ON A RICH DIET!
ATER, HE LOOKS IN ON THE BOTTLED KRYPTON CITY OF KANDOR-- HRUNK TO TINY SIZE BY THE VILLAINOUS BRAINIAC...
HE KANDORIANS MUST BE ONSTANTLY SUPPLIED VITH AIR THAT IS OF THE AME COMPOSITION AS THE IR ON THEIR NATIVE RYPTON--SO I ALWAYS HECK TO MAKE CERTAIN HE AIR MIXTURE IS RIGHT...
FTERWARD, HIS CHORES DONE, SUPERMAN LASHES BACK TO METROPOLIS TO BEGIN IS PATROL OF THE CITY...
NOW I'M READY FOR WORK!
READY TO LEND A HELPING HAND WHEREVER NEEDED, SUPERMAN SOARS OVER METROPOLIS...
OH, NO! THE FREEZING APPARATUS HAS BROKEN DOWN--AND MY ICE CREAM IS MELTING! I'LL NEVER BE ABLE TO FULFILL MY ORDERS NOW! I'LL LOSE A WHOLE DAYS PAY!
AH! MY MY FIRST "CLIENT" OF THE DAY!
HAPPY ICE CREAM

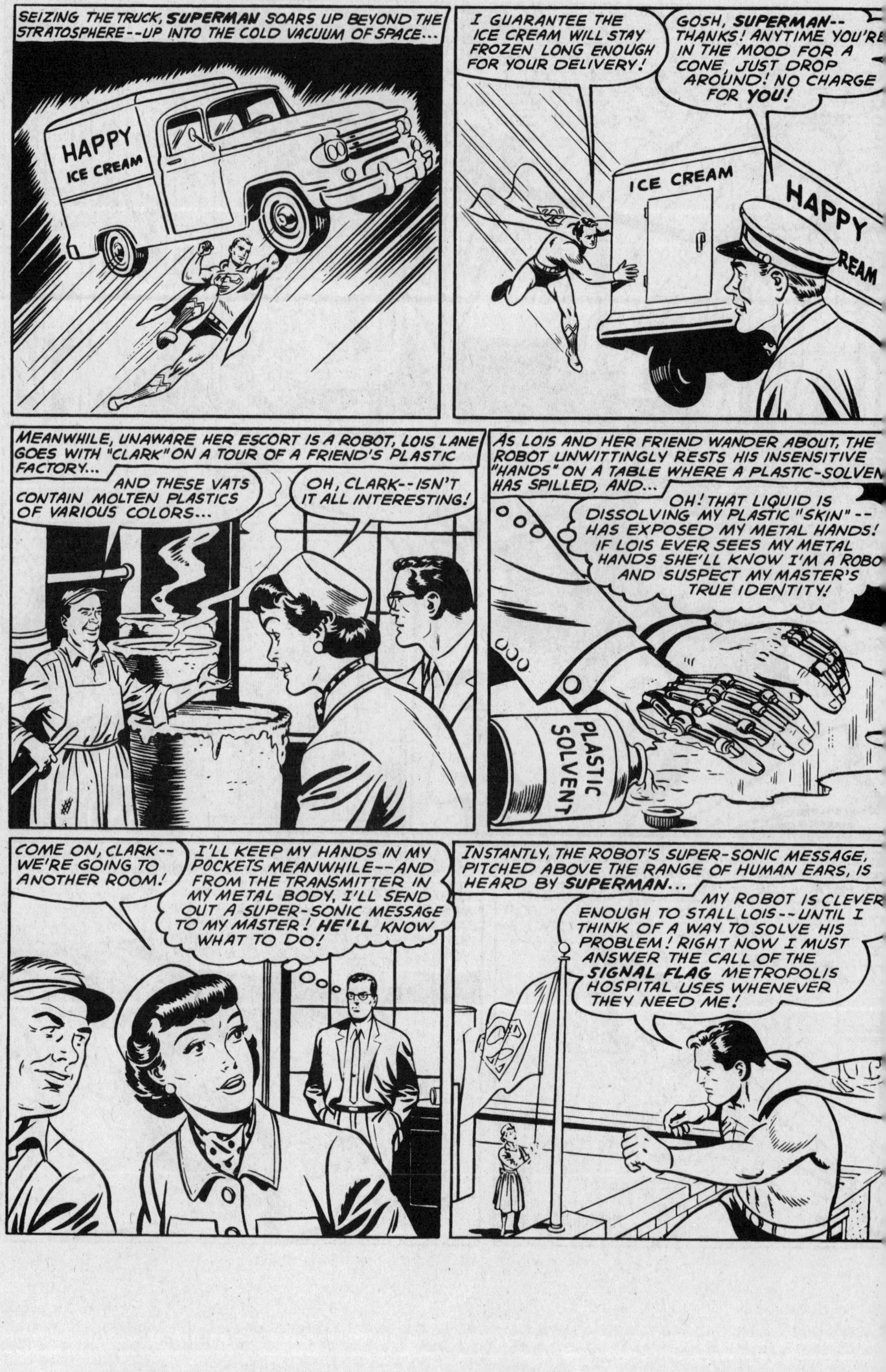
SEIZING THE TRUCK, SUPERMAN SOARS UP BEYOND THE STRATOSPHERE--UP INTO THE COLD VACUUM OF SPACE...
HAPPY ICE CREAM
I GUARANTEE THE ICE CREAM WILL STAY FROZEN LONG ENOUGH FOR YOUR DELIVERY!
GOSH, SUPERMAN--THANKS! ANYTIME YOU'RE IN THE MOOD FOR A CONE, JUST DROP AROUND! NO CHARGE FOR YOU!
ICE CREAM
HAPPY
MEANWHILE, UNAWARE HER ESCORT IS A ROBOT, LOIS LANE GOES WITH "CLARK" ON A TOUR OF A FRIEND'S PLASTIC FACTORY...
AND THESE VATS CONTAIN MOLTEN PLASTICS OF VARIOUS COLORS...
OH, CLARK--ISN'T IT ALL INTERESTING!
AS LOIS AND HER FRIEND WANDER ABOUT, THE ROBOT UNWITTINGLY RESTS HIS INSENSITIVE "HANDS" ON A TABLE WHERE A PLASTIC-SOLVENT HAS SPILLED, AND...
OH! THAT LIQUID IS DISSOLVING MY PLASTIC "SKIN"--HAS EXPOSED MY METAL HANDS! IF LOIS EVER SEES MY METAL HANDS SHE'LL KNOW I'M A ROBOT AND SUSPECT MY MASTER'S TRUE IDENTITY!
PLASTIC SOLVENT
COME ON, CLARK--WE'RE GOING TO ANOTHER ROOM!
I'LL KEEP MY HANDS IN MY POCKETS MEANWHILE--AND FROM THE TRANSMITTER IN MY METAL BODY, I'LL SEND OUT A SUPER-SONIC MESSAGE TO MY MASTER! HE'LL KNOW WHAT TO DO!
INSTANTLY, THE ROBOT'S SUPER-SONIC MESSAGE, PITCHED ABOVE THE RANGE OF HUMAN EARS, IS HEARD BY SUPERMAN...
MY ROBOT IS CLEVER ENOUGH TO STALL LOIS--UNTIL I THINK OF A WAY TO SOLVE HIS PROBLEM! RIGHT NOW I MUST ANSWER THE CALL OF THE SIGNAL FLAG METROPOLIS HOSPITAL USES WHENEVER THEY NEED ME!

PON DARTING INTO THE HOSPITAL...

MY PATIENT HAS A GLASS FRAGMENT IN HIS BRAIN SOMEWHERE, BUT BECAUSE ORDINARY X-RAYS CAN'T REVEAL THE LOCATION OF THE SLIVER, I CAN'T OPERATE...

HMM! MY OWN X-RAY VISION HAS A GREATER RANGE THAN ANY HOSPITAL X-RAY MACHINE, SO DON'T WORRY!

I SEE THE SLIVER! ALL RIGHT, DOCTOR, GET READY TO OPERATE!

SOON, WITH SUPERMAN GUIDING THE SURGEON, A UNIQUE OPERATION IN MEDICAL HISTORY TAKES PLACE...

A LITTLE TO THE LEFT, DOCTOR-- THAT'S IT--

FORCEPS, PLEASE! SUPERMAN, BECAUSE OF YOU, THIS MAN WILL LIVE!

MEANWHILE, BACK AT THE PLASTIC PLANT...

I NOTICED YOU WERE WEARING A WRIST WATCH BEFORE, SIR! COULD YOU PLEASE TELL ME THE TIME?

I CAN'T REFUSE THE MAN WITHOUT APPEARING RUDE-- YET I DARE NOT REMOVE MY ROBOT METAL HANDS FROM MY POCKETS! WHAT CAN I DO?

SUDDENLY, THE ROBOT SOLVES THE DILEMMA--BY USING HIS X-RAY VISION TO LOOK THROUGH THE WALLS AT THE CLOCK ON A NEARBY BUILDING...

IT'S ALMOST TWO O'CLOCK! I KNOW BECAUSE I HAPPENED TO HAVE JUST LOOKED AT THE TIME!

THANK YOU, SIR!

HAVING USED HIS OWN SUPER-VISION AND HEARING TO EAVESDROP ON THE SCENE, SUPERMAN'S TENSION IS EASED...

I KNEW I COULD COUNT ON MY ROBOT TO HANDLE THAT MINOR EMERGENCY THIS TIME! TIME-- THAT REMINDS ME! I PROMISED TO BE ON TIME TO BE A GUEST TEACHER AT THE NATURAL HISTORY CLASS OF THE NEARBY PUBLIC SCHOOL!

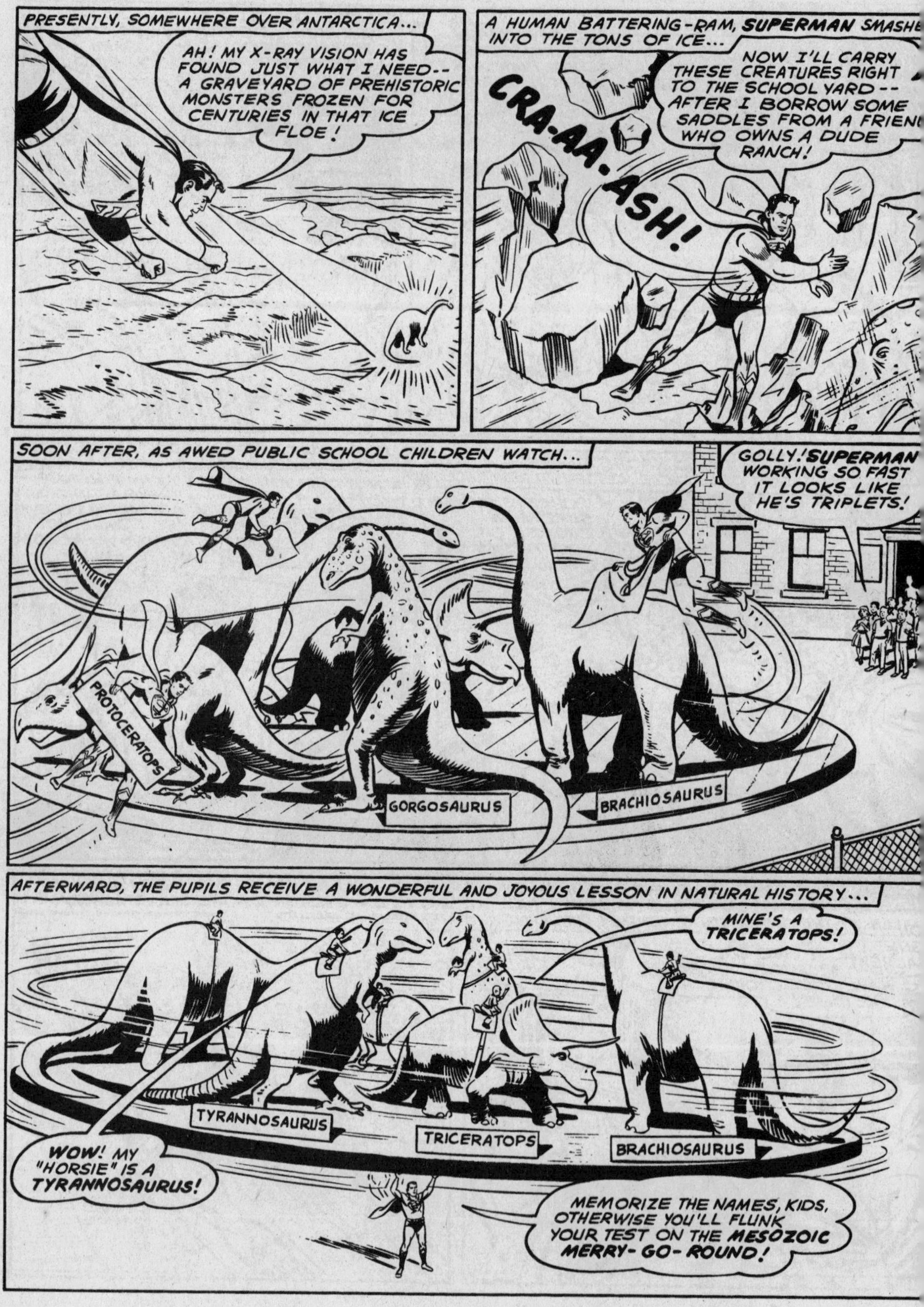
PRESENTLY, SOMEWHERE OVER ANTARCTICA...
AH! MY X-RAY VISION HAS FOUND JUST WHAT I NEED-- A GRAVEYARD OF PREHISTORIC MONSTERS FROZEN FOR CENTURIES IN THAT ICE FLOE!
A HUMAN BATTERING-RAM, SUPERMAN SMASHE INTO THE TONS OF ICE...
CRA-AA-ASH!
NOW I'LL CARRY THESE CREATURES RIGHT TO THE SCHOOL YARD-- AFTER I BORROW SOME SADDLES FROM A FRIEN WHO OWNS A DUDE RANCH!
SOON AFTER, AS AWED PUBLIC SCHOOL CHILDREN WATCH...
GOLLY! SUPERMAN WORKING SO FAST IT LOOKS LIKE HE'S TRIPLETS!
PROTOCERATOPS
GORGOSAURUS
BRACHIOSAURUS
AFTERWARD, THE PUPILS RECEIVE A WONDERFUL AND JOYOUS LESSON IN NATURAL HISTORY...
MINE'S A TRICERATOPS!
TYRANNOSAURUS
TRICERATOPS
BRACHIOSAURUS
WOW! MY "HORSIE" IS A TYRANNOSAURUS!
MEMORIZE THE NAMES, KIDS, OTHERWISE YOU'LL FLUNK YOUR TEST ON THE MESOZOIC MERRY-GO-ROUND!

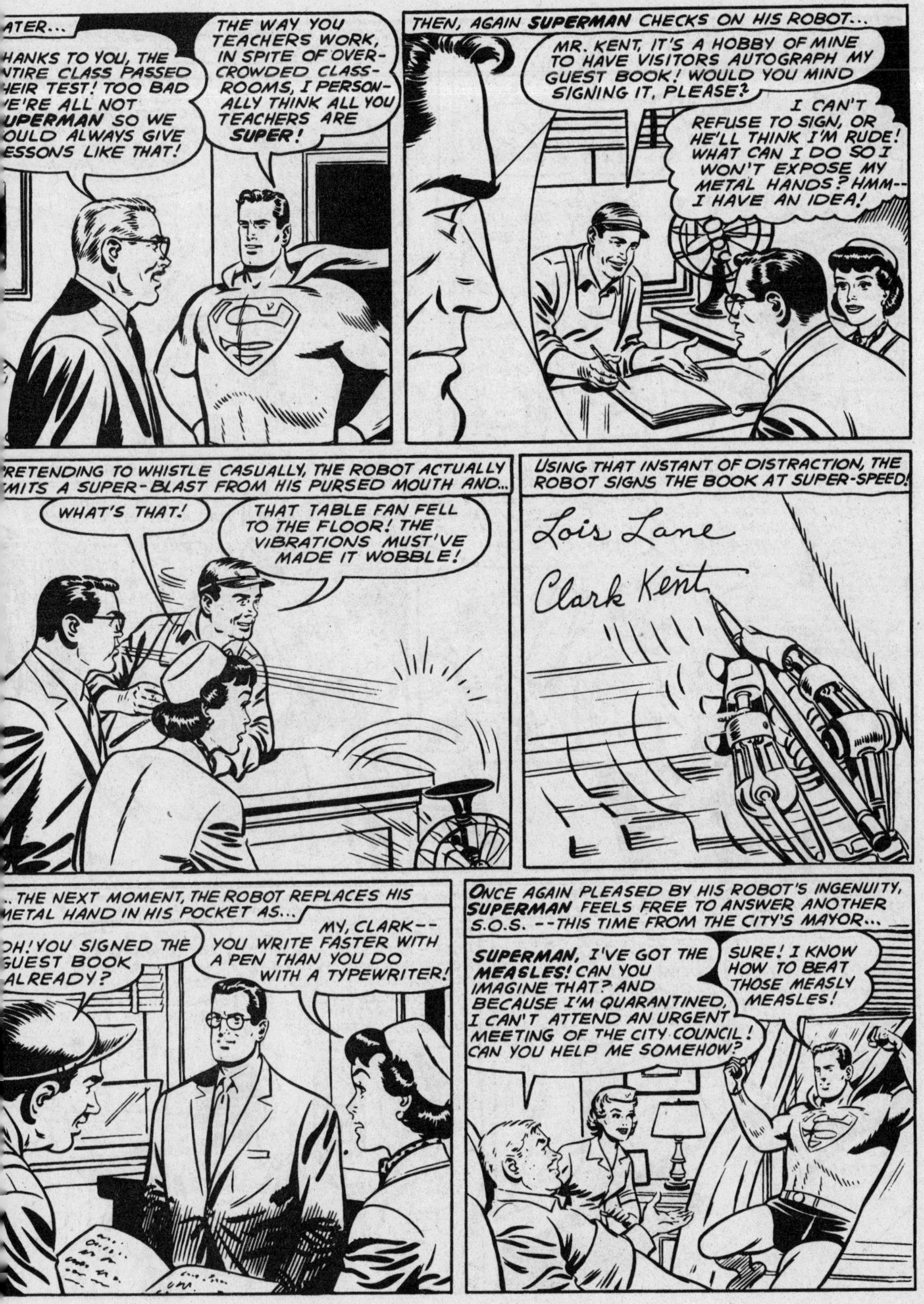
ATER...
HANKS TO YOU, THE ENTIRE CLASS PASSED HEIR TEST! TOO BAD VE'RE ALL NOT SUPERMAN SO WE OULD ALWAYS GIVE ESSONS LIKE THAT!
THE WAY YOU TEACHERS WORK, IN SPITE OF OVER-CROWDED CLASS-ROOMS, I PERSON-ALLY THINK ALL YOU TEACHERS ARE SUPER!
THEN, AGAIN SUPERMAN CHECKS ON HIS ROBOT...
MR. KENT, IT'S A HOBBY OF MINE TO HAVE VISITORS AUTOGRAPH MY GUEST BOOK! WOULD YOU MIND SIGNING IT, PLEASE?
I CAN'T REFUSE TO SIGN, OR HE'LL THINK I'M RUDE! WHAT CAN I DO SO I WON'T EXPOSE MY METAL HANDS? HMM-- I HAVE AN IDEA!
PRETENDING TO WHISTLE CASUALLY, THE ROBOT ACTUALLY EMITS A SUPER-BLAST FROM HIS PURSED MOUTH AND...
WHAT'S THAT!
THAT TABLE FAN FELL TO THE FLOOR! THE VIBRATIONS MUST'VE MADE IT WOBBLE!
USING THAT INSTANT OF DISTRACTION, THE ROBOT SIGNS THE BOOK AT SUPER-SPEED!
Lois Lane
Clark Kent
..THE NEXT MOMENT, THE ROBOT REPLACES HIS METAL HAND IN HIS POCKET AS...
OH! YOU SIGNED THE GUEST BOOK ALREADY?
MY, CLARK-- YOU WRITE FASTER WITH A PEN THAN YOU DO WITH A TYPEWRITER!
ONCE AGAIN PLEASED BY HIS ROBOT'S INGENUITY, SUPERMAN FEELS FREE TO ANSWER ANOTHER S.O.S. --THIS TIME FROM THE CITY'S MAYOR...
SUPERMAN, I'VE GOT THE MEASLES! CAN YOU IMAGINE THAT? AND BECAUSE I'M QUARANTINED, I CAN'T ATTEND AN URGENT MEETING OF THE CITY COUNCIL! CAN YOU HELP ME SOMEHOW?
SURE! I KNOW HOW TO BEAT THOSE MEASLY MEASLES!

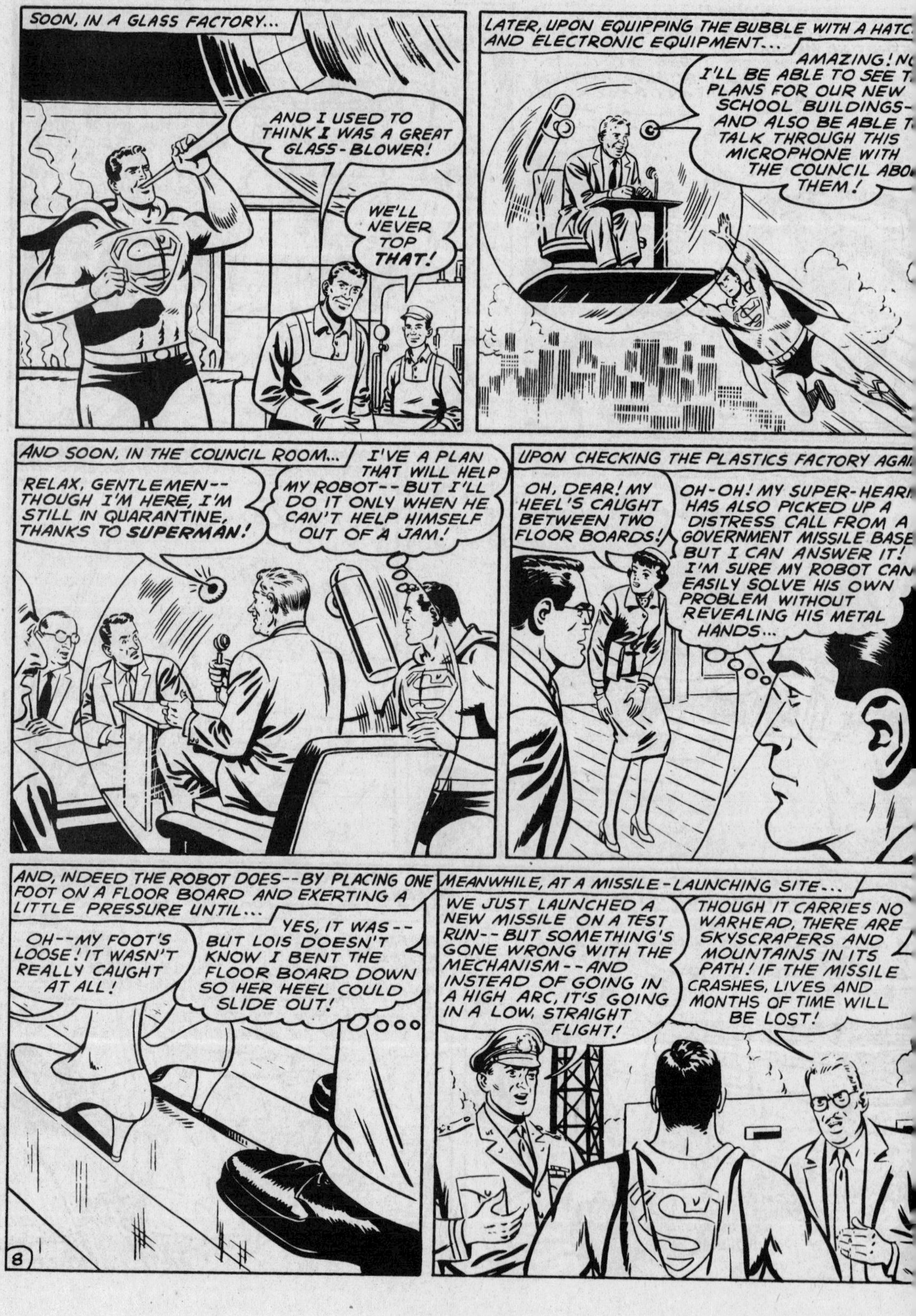
SOON, IN A GLASS FACTORY...
AND I USED TO THINK I WAS A GREAT GLASS-BLOWER!
WE'LL NEVER TOP THAT!
LATER, UPON EQUIPPING THE BUBBLE WITH A HATC
AND ELECTRONIC EQUIPMENT...
AMAZING! N
I'LL BE ABLE TO SEE T
PLANS FOR OUR NEW SCHOOL BUILDINGS-
AND ALSO BE ABLE T
TALK THROUGH THIS MICROPHONE WITH THE COUNCIL ABO
THEM!
AND SOON, IN THE COUNCIL ROOM...
RELAX, GENTLEMEN-- THOUGH I'M HERE, I'M STILL IN QUARANTINE, THANKS TO SUPERMAN!
I'VE A PLAN THAT WILL HELP MY ROBOT-- BUT I'LL DO IT ONLY WHEN HE CAN'T HELP HIMSELF OUT OF A JAM!
UPON CHECKING THE PLASTICS FACTORY AGAI
OH, DEAR! MY HEEL'S CAUGHT BETWEEN TWO FLOOR BOARDS!
OH-OH! MY SUPER-HEAR
HAS ALSO PICKED UP A DISTRESS CALL FROM A
GOVERNMENT MISSILE BASE
BUT I CAN ANSWER IT! I'M SURE MY ROBOT CAN
EASILY SOLVE HIS OWN PROBLEM WITHOUT REVEALING HIS METAL HANDS...
AND, INDEED THE ROBOT DOES--BY PLACING ONE FOOT ON A FLOOR BOARD AND EXERTING A LITTLE PRESSURE UNTIL...
OH--MY FOOT'S LOOSE! IT WASN'T REALLY CAUGHT AT ALL!
YES, IT WAS-- BUT LOIS DOESN'T KNOW I BENT THE FLOOR BOARD DOWN SO HER HEEL COULD SLIDE OUT!
8
MEANWHILE, AT A MISSILE-LAUNCHING SITE...
WE JUST LAUNCHED A NEW MISSILE ON A TEST RUN-- BUT SOMETHING'S GONE WRONG WITH THE MECHANISM--AND INSTEAD OF GOING IN A HIGH ARC, IT'S GOING IN A LOW, STRAIGHT FLIGHT!
THOUGH IT CARRIES NO WARHEAD, THERE ARE SKYSCRAPERS AND MOUNTAINS IN ITS PATH! IF THE MISSILE CRASHES, LIVES AND MONTHS OF TIME WILL BE LOST!

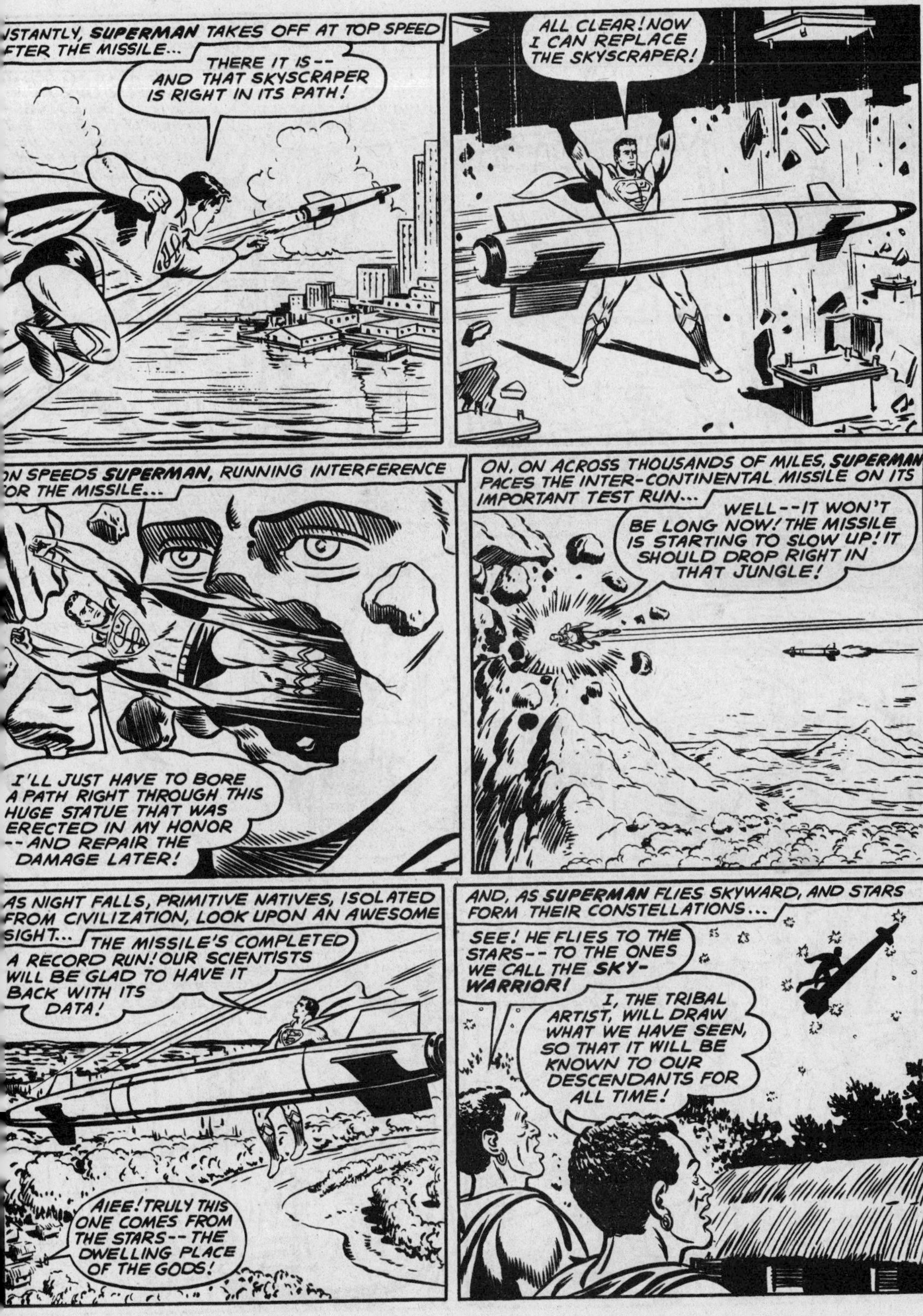
NSTANTLY, SUPERMAN TAKES OFF AT TOP SPEED FTER THE MISSILE...
THERE IT IS-- AND THAT SKYSCRAPER IS RIGHT IN ITS PATH!
ALL CLEAR! NOW I CAN REPLACE THE SKYSCRAPER!
ON SPEEDS SUPERMAN, RUNNING INTERFERENCE OR THE MISSILE...
I'LL JUST HAVE TO BORE A PATH RIGHT THROUGH THIS HUGE STATUE THAT WAS ERECTED IN MY HONOR --AND REPAIR THE DAMAGE LATER!
ON, ON ACROSS THOUSANDS OF MILES, SUPERMAN PACES THE INTER-CONTINENTAL MISSILE ON ITS IMPORTANT TEST RUN...
WELL--IT WON'T BE LONG NOW! THE MISSILE IS STARTING TO SLOW UP! IT SHOULD DROP RIGHT IN THAT JUNGLE!
AS NIGHT FALLS, PRIMITIVE NATIVES, ISOLATED FROM CIVILIZATION, LOOK UPON AN AWESOME SIGHT...
THE MISSILE'S COMPLETED A RECORD RUN! OUR SCIENTISTS WILL BE GLAD TO HAVE IT BACK WITH ITS DATA!
AIEE! TRULY THIS ONE COMES FROM THE STARS--THE DWELLING PLACE OF THE GODS!
AND, AS SUPERMAN FLIES SKYWARD, AND STARS FORM THEIR CONSTELLATIONS...
SEE! HE FLIES TO THE STARS-- TO THE ONES WE CALL THE SKY-WARRIOR!
I, THE TRIBAL ARTIST, WILL DRAW WHAT WE HAVE SEEN, SO THAT IT WILL BE KNOWN TO OUR DESCENDANTS FOR ALL TIME!

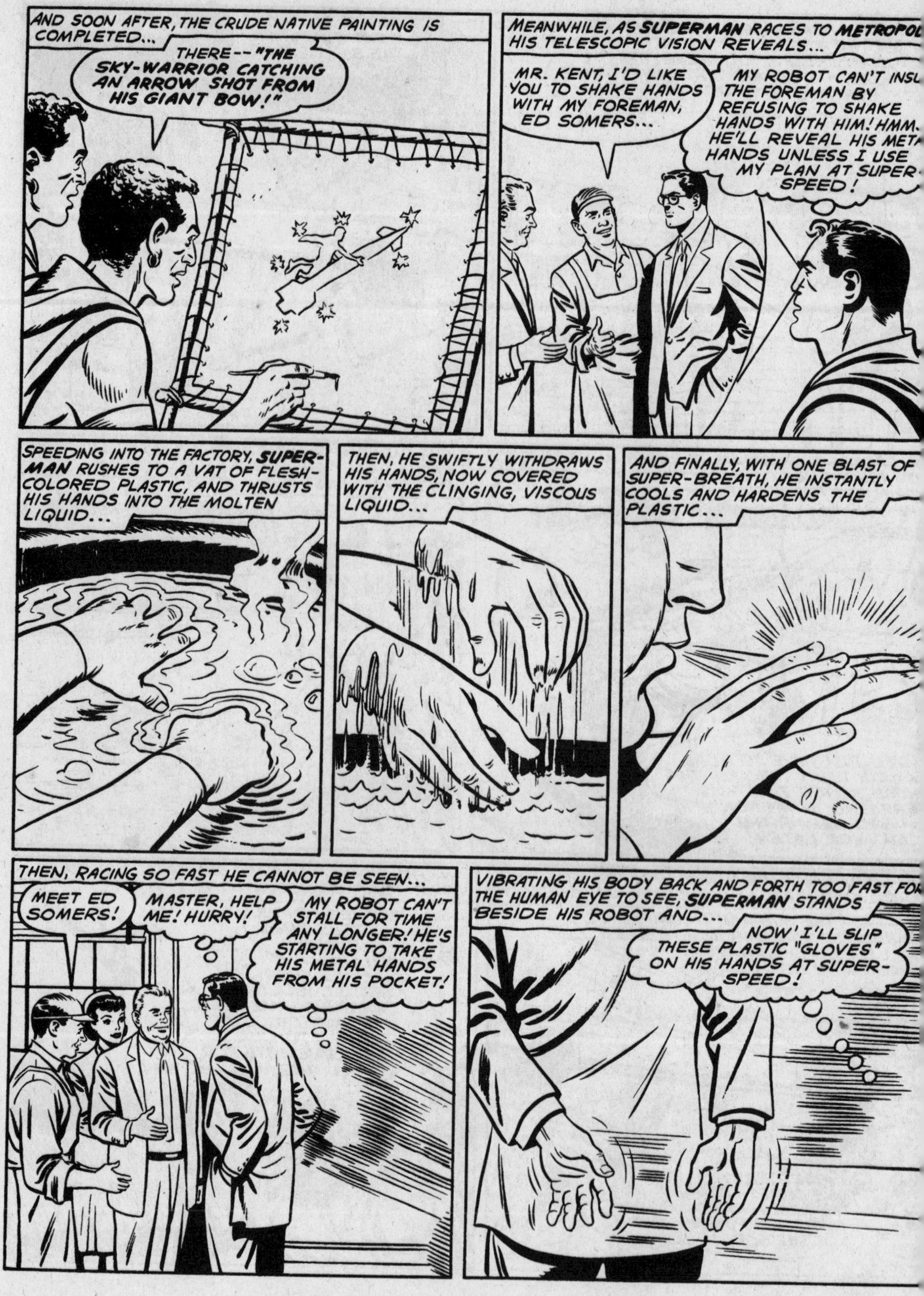
AND SOON AFTER, THE CRUDE NATIVE PAINTING IS COMPLETED...
THERE--"THE SKY-WARRIOR CATCHING AN ARROW SHOT FROM HIS GIANT BOW!"
MEANWHILE, AS SUPERMAN RACES TO METROPOL
HIS TELESCOPIC VISION REVEALS...
MR. KENT, I'D LIKE YOU TO SHAKE HANDS WITH MY FOREMAN, ED SOMERS...
MY ROBOT CAN'T INSU THE FOREMAN BY REFUSING TO SHAKE HANDS WITH HIM! HMM. HE'LL REVEAL HIS META HANDS UNLESS I USE MY PLAN AT SUPER-SPEED!
SPEEDING INTO THE FACTORY, SUPERMAN RUSHES TO A VAT OF FLESH-COLORED PLASTIC, AND THRUSTS HIS HANDS INTO THE MOLTEN LIQUID...
THEN, HE SWIFTLY WITHDRAWS HIS HANDS, NOW COVERED WITH THE CLINGING, VISCOUS LIQUID...
AND FINALLY, WITH ONE BLAST OF SUPER-BREATH, HE INSTANTLY COOLS AND HARDENS THE PLASTIC...
THEN, RACING SO FAST HE CANNOT BE SEEN...
MEET ED SOMERS!
MASTER, HELP ME! HURRY!
MY ROBOT CAN'T STALL FOR TIME ANY LONGER! HE'S STARTING TO TAKE HIS METAL HANDS FROM HIS POCKET!
VIBRATING HIS BODY BACK AND FORTH TOO FAST FO THE HUMAN EYE TO SEE, SUPERMAN STANDS BESIDE HIS ROBOT AND...
NOW I'LL SLIP THESE PLASTIC "GLOVES" ON HIS HANDS AT SUPER-SPEED!

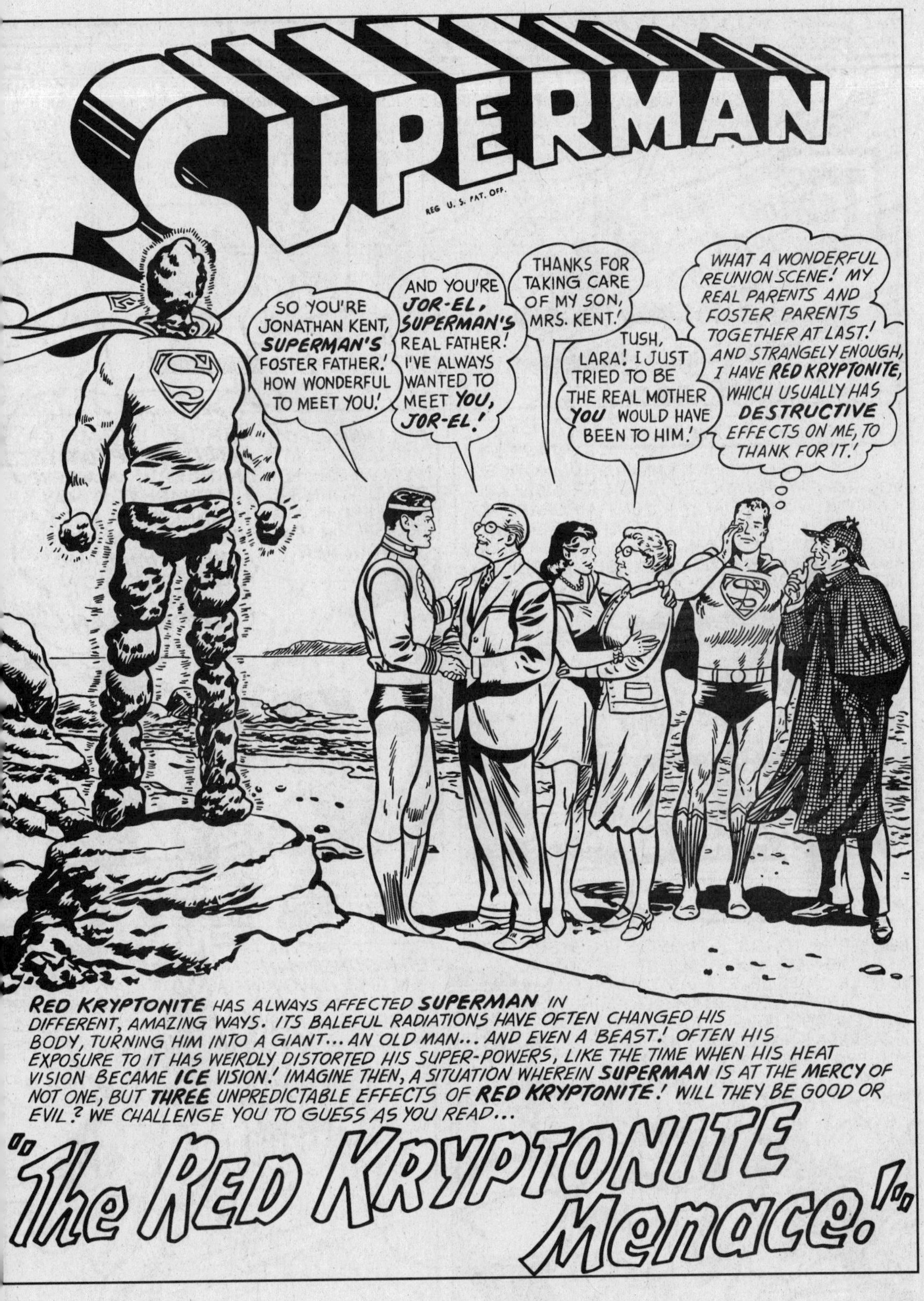
SUPERMAN
REG. U.S. PAT. OFF.
SO YOU'RE JONATHAN KENT, SUPERMAN'S FOSTER FATHER! HOW WONDERFUL TO MEET YOU!
AND YOU'RE JOR-EL, SUPERMAN'S REAL FATHER! I'VE ALWAYS WANTED TO MEET YOU, JOR-EL!
THANKS FOR TAKING CARE OF MY SON, MRS. KENT!
TUSH, LARA! I JUST TRIED TO BE THE REAL MOTHER YOU WOULD HAVE BEEN TO HIM!
WHAT A WONDERFUL REUNION SCENE! MY REAL PARENTS AND FOSTER PARENTS TOGETHER AT LAST! AND STRANGELY ENOUGH, I HAVE RED KRYPTONITE, WHICH USUALLY HAS DESTRUCTIVE EFFECTS ON ME, TO THANK FOR IT!
RED KRYPTONITE HAS ALWAYS AFFECTED SUPERMAN IN DIFFERENT, AMAZING WAYS. ITS BALEFUL RADIATIONS HAVE OFTEN CHANGED HIS BODY, TURNING HIM INTO A GIANT... AN OLD MAN... AND EVEN A BEAST! OFTEN HIS EXPOSURE TO IT HAS WEIRDLY DISTORTED HIS SUPER-POWERS, LIKE THE TIME WHEN HIS HEAT VISION BECAME ICE VISION! IMAGINE THEN, A SITUATION WHEREIN SUPERMAN IS AT THE MERCY OF NOT ONE, BUT THREE UNPREDICTABLE EFFECTS OF RED KRYPTONITE! WILL THEY BE GOOD OR EVIL? WE CHALLENGE YOU TO GUESS AS YOU READ...
"The RED KRYPTONITE Menace!"

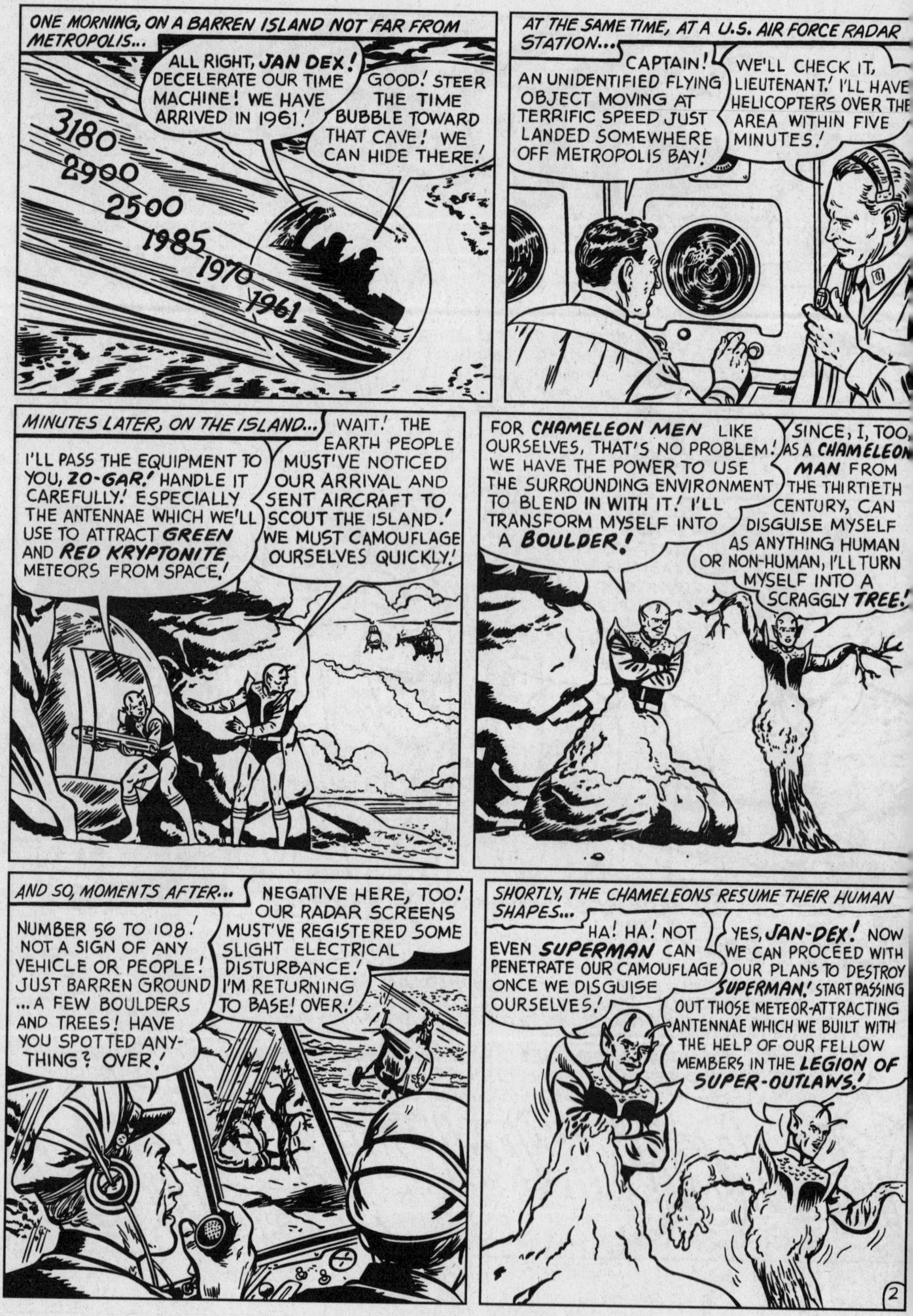
ONE MORNING, ON A BARREN ISLAND NOT FAR FROM METROPOLIS...
ALL RIGHT, JAN DEX! DECELERATE OUR TIME MACHINE! WE HAVE ARRIVED IN 1961!
GOOD! STEER THE TIME BUBBLE TOWARD THAT CAVE! WE CAN HIDE THERE!
3180
2900
2500
1985
1970
1961
AT THE SAME TIME, AT A U.S. AIR FORCE RADAR STATION...
CAPTAIN! AN UNIDENTIFIED FLYING OBJECT MOVING AT TERRIFIC SPEED JUST LANDED SOMEWHERE OFF METROPOLIS BAY!
WE'LL CHECK IT, LIEUTENANT! I'LL HAVE HELICOPTERS OVER THE AREA WITHIN FIVE MINUTES!
MINUTES LATER, ON THE ISLAND...
I'LL PASS THE EQUIPMENT TO YOU, ZO-GAR! HANDLE IT CAREFULLY! ESPECIALLY THE ANTENNAE WHICH WE'LL USE TO ATTRACT GREEN AND RED KRYPTONITE METEORS FROM SPACE!
WAIT! THE EARTH PEOPLE MUST'VE NOTICED OUR ARRIVAL AND SENT AIRCRAFT TO SCOUT THE ISLAND! WE MUST CAMOUFLAGE OURSELVES QUICKLY!
FOR CHAMELEON MEN LIKE OURSELVES, THAT'S NO PROBLEM! WE HAVE THE POWER TO USE THE SURROUNDING ENVIRONMENT TO BLEND IN WITH IT! I'LL TRANSFORM MYSELF INTO A BOULDER!
SINCE, I, TOO, AS A CHAMELEON MAN FROM THE THIRTIETH CENTURY, CAN DISGUISE MYSELF AS ANYTHING HUMAN OR NON-HUMAN, I'LL TURN MYSELF INTO A SCRAGGLY TREE!
AND SO, MOMENTS AFTER...
NUMBER 56 TO 108! NOT A SIGN OF ANY VEHICLE OR PEOPLE! JUST BARREN GROUND ...A FEW BOULDERS AND TREES! HAVE YOU SPOTTED ANYTHING? OVER!
NEGATIVE HERE, TOO! OUR RADAR SCREENS MUST'VE REGISTERED SOME SLIGHT ELECTRICAL DISTURBANCE! I'M RETURNING TO BASE! OVER!
SHORTLY, THE CHAMELEONS RESUME THEIR HUMAN SHAPES...
HA! HA! NOT EVEN SUPERMAN CAN PENETRATE OUR CAMOUFLAGE ONCE WE DISGUISE OURSELVES!
YES, JAN-DEX! NOW WE CAN PROCEED WITH OUR PLANS TO DESTROY SUPERMAN! START PASSING OUT THOSE METEOR-ATTRACTING ANTENNAE WHICH WE BUILT WITH THE HELP OF OUR FELLOW MEMBERS IN THE LEGION OF SUPER-OUTLAWS!
2

OON, AS THE TWO ANTENNAE ARE ASSEMBLED...

ALL SET, ZO-GAR! OUR ANTENNAE ARE READY TO PULL DOWN RED AND GREEN KRYPTONITE FROM SPACE!

THEN LET THE METEORS FALL! I'LL STORE THE GREEN KRYPTONITE IN THIS CHEST! AS FOR THE RED KRYPTONITE, THIS RAY GUN WILL SHAPE IT INTO THE STATUE WE WANT TO BUILD!

PRESENTLY...

AH! OUR EQUIPMENT WORKS! HERE COME THE TWO TYPES OF KRYPTONITE WE NEED TO DESTROY SUPERMAN!

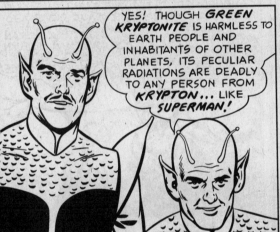

YES! THOUGH GREEN KRYPTONITE IS HARMLESS TO EARTH PEOPLE AND INHABITANTS OF OTHER PLANETS, ITS PECULIAR RADIATIONS ARE DEADLY TO ANY PERSON FROM KRYPTON... LIKE SUPERMAN!

WHEN AN ATOMIC EXPLOSION DESTROYED KRYPTON LONG AGO, CHUNKS OF GREEN KRYPTONITE WERE FORMED AND SCATTERED THROUGHOUT SPACE AS METEORS! BUT ONE FLOCK OF THESE METEORS WENT THROUGH A STRANGE COSMIC CLOUD AND TURNED TO RED KRYPTONITE!

EVER SINCE THEN, RED KRYPTONITE HAS ALWAYS HAD PECULIAR, UNPREDICTABLE EFFECTS ON SUPERMAN! LET'S HOPE THE WORST EFFECTS YET WILL AFFLICT HIM TOMORROW!

DON'T WORRY, ZO-GAR! THEY WILL! I'LL TURN OFF THE ANTENNA CONTROLS AND WE'LL GO TO WORK!

THEN, AS THE ANTENNAE ARE DISMANTLED...

I'LL COLLECT THE GREEN KRYPTONITE IN THE CHEST WHILE YOU BUILD THE RED KRYPTONITE STATUE, ZO-GAR!

RIGHT! ONCE WE TRICK SUPERMAN INTO COMING WITHIN RANGE OF THIS RED KRYPTONITE, WE'VE GOT HIM! IN THE PAST, RED KRYPTONITE HAS PLAGUED HIM WITH AMNESIA, LOSS OF SUPER-POWERS AND SO FORTH!

3

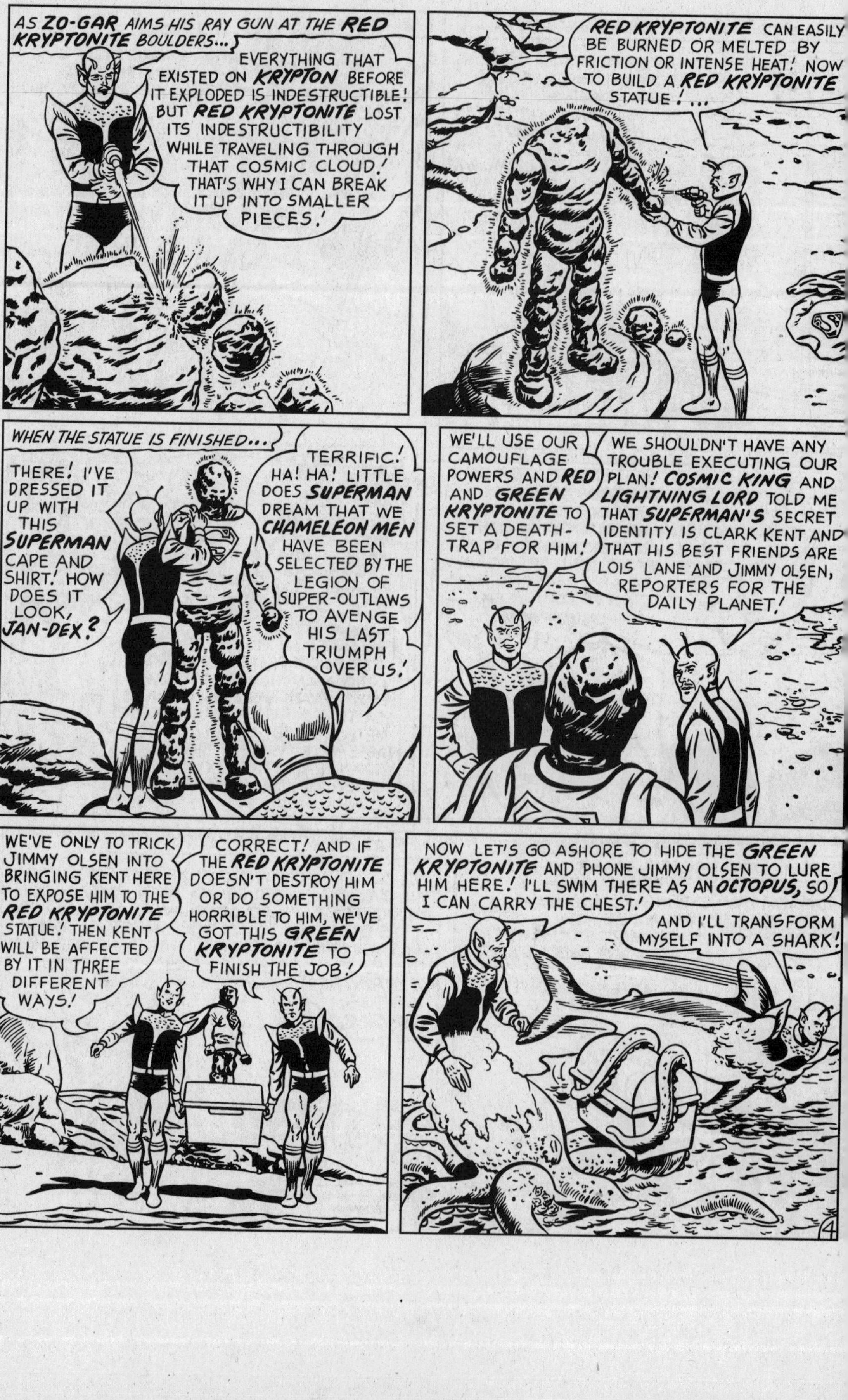
AS ZO-GAR AIMS HIS RAY GUN AT THE RED KRYPTONITE BOULDERS...
EVERYTHING THAT EXISTED ON KRYPTON BEFORE IT EXPLODED IS INDESTRUCTIBLE! BUT RED KRYPTONITE LOST ITS INDESTRUCTIBILITY WHILE TRAVELING THROUGH THAT COSMIC CLOUD! THAT'S WHY I CAN BREAK IT UP INTO SMALLER PIECES!
RED KRYPTONITE CAN EASILY BE BURNED OR MELTED BY FRICTION OR INTENSE HEAT! NOW TO BUILD A RED KRYPTONITE STATUE!...
WHEN THE STATUE IS FINISHED...
THERE! I'VE DRESSED IT UP WITH THIS SUPERMAN CAPE AND SHIRT! HOW DOES IT LOOK, JAN-DEX?
TERRIFIC! HA! HA! LITTLE DOES SUPERMAN DREAM THAT WE CHAMELEON MEN HAVE BEEN SELECTED BY THE LEGION OF SUPER-OUTLAWS TO AVENGE HIS LAST TRIUMPH OVER US!
WE'LL USE OUR CAMOUFLAGE POWERS AND RED AND GREEN KRYPTONITE TO SET A DEATH-TRAP FOR HIM!
WE SHOULDN'T HAVE ANY TROUBLE EXECUTING OUR PLAN! COSMIC KING AND LIGHTNING LORD TOLD ME THAT SUPERMAN'S SECRET IDENTITY IS CLARK KENT AND THAT HIS BEST FRIENDS ARE LOIS LANE AND JIMMY OLSEN, REPORTERS FOR THE DAILY PLANET!
WE'VE ONLY TO TRICK JIMMY OLSEN INTO BRINGING KENT HERE TO EXPOSE HIM TO THE RED KRYPTONITE STATUE! THEN KENT WILL BE AFFECTED BY IT IN THREE DIFFERENT WAYS!
CORRECT! AND IF THE RED KRYPTONITE DOESN'T DESTROY HIM OR DO SOMETHING HORRIBLE TO HIM, WE'VE GOT THIS GREEN KRYPTONITE TO FINISH THE JOB!
NOW LET'S GO ASHORE TO HIDE THE GREEN KRYPTONITE AND PHONE JIMMY OLSEN TO LURE HIM HERE! I'LL SWIM THERE AS AN OCTOPUS, SO I CAN CARRY THE CHEST!
AND I'LL TRANSFORM MYSELF INTO A SHARK!
4

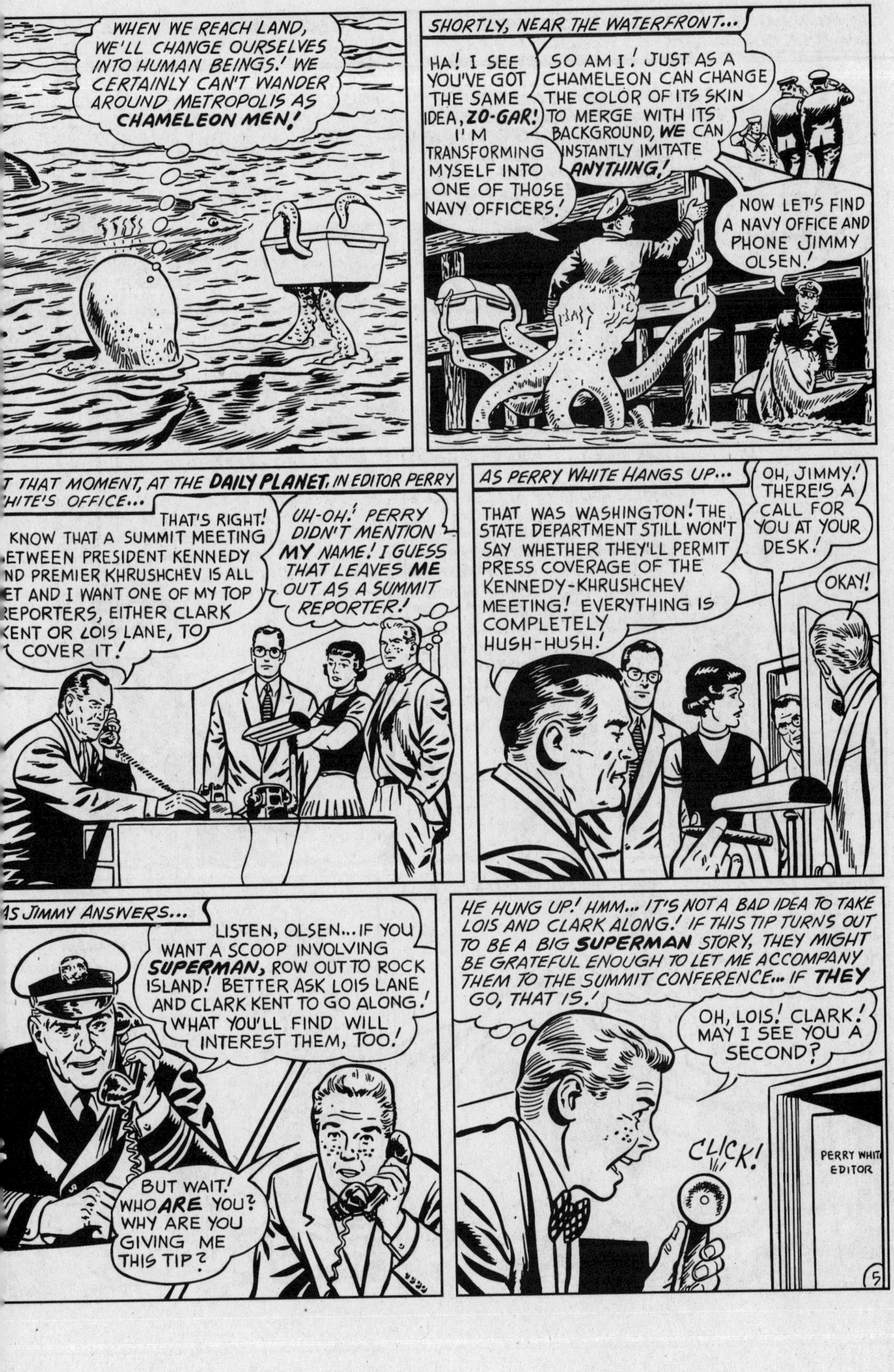
WHEN WE REACH LAND, WE'LL CHANGE OURSELVES INTO HUMAN BEINGS! WE CERTAINLY CAN'T WANDER AROUND METROPOLIS AS CHAMELEON MEN!
SHORTLY, NEAR THE WATERFRONT...
HA! I SEE YOU'VE GOT THE SAME IDEA, ZO-GAR! I'M TRANSFORMING MYSELF INTO ONE OF THOSE NAVY OFFICERS!
SO AM I! JUST AS A CHAMELEON CAN CHANGE THE COLOR OF ITS SKIN TO MERGE WITH ITS BACKGROUND, WE CAN INSTANTLY IMITATE ANYTHING!
NOW LET'S FIND A NAVY OFFICE AND PHONE JIMMY OLSEN!
T THAT MOMENT, AT THE DAILY PLANET, IN EDITOR PERRY HITE'S OFFICE...
THAT'S RIGHT! KNOW THAT A SUMMIT MEETING ETWEEN PRESIDENT KENNEDY ND PREMIER KHRUSHCHEV IS ALL ET AND I WANT ONE OF MY TOP REPORTERS, EITHER CLARK KENT OR LOIS LANE, TO COVER IT!
UH-OH! PERRY DIDN'T MENTION MY NAME! I GUESS THAT LEAVES ME OUT AS A SUMMIT REPORTER!
AS PERRY WHITE HANGS UP...
THAT WAS WASHINGTON! THE STATE DEPARTMENT STILL WON'T SAY WHETHER THEY'LL PERMIT PRESS COVERAGE OF THE KENNEDY-KHRUSHCHEV MEETING! EVERYTHING IS COMPLETELY HUSH-HUSH!
OH, JIMMY! THERE'S A CALL FOR YOU AT YOUR DESK!
OKAY!
AS JIMMY ANSWERS...
LISTEN, OLSEN...IF YOU WANT A SCOOP INVOLVING SUPERMAN, ROW OUT TO ROCK ISLAND! BETTER ASK LOIS LANE AND CLARK KENT TO GO ALONG! WHAT YOU'LL FIND WILL INTEREST THEM, TOO!
BUT WAIT! WHO ARE YOU? WHY ARE YOU GIVING ME THIS TIP?
HE HUNG UP! HMM... IT'S NOT A BAD IDEA TO TAKE LOIS AND CLARK ALONG! IF THIS TIP TURNS OUT TO BE A BIG SUPERMAN STORY, THEY MIGHT BE GRATEFUL ENOUGH TO LET ME ACCOMPANY THEM TO THE SUMMIT CONFERENCE... IF THEY GO, THAT IS!
OH, LOIS! CLARK! MAY I SEE YOU A SECOND?
CLICK!
PERRY WHIT EDITOR
5

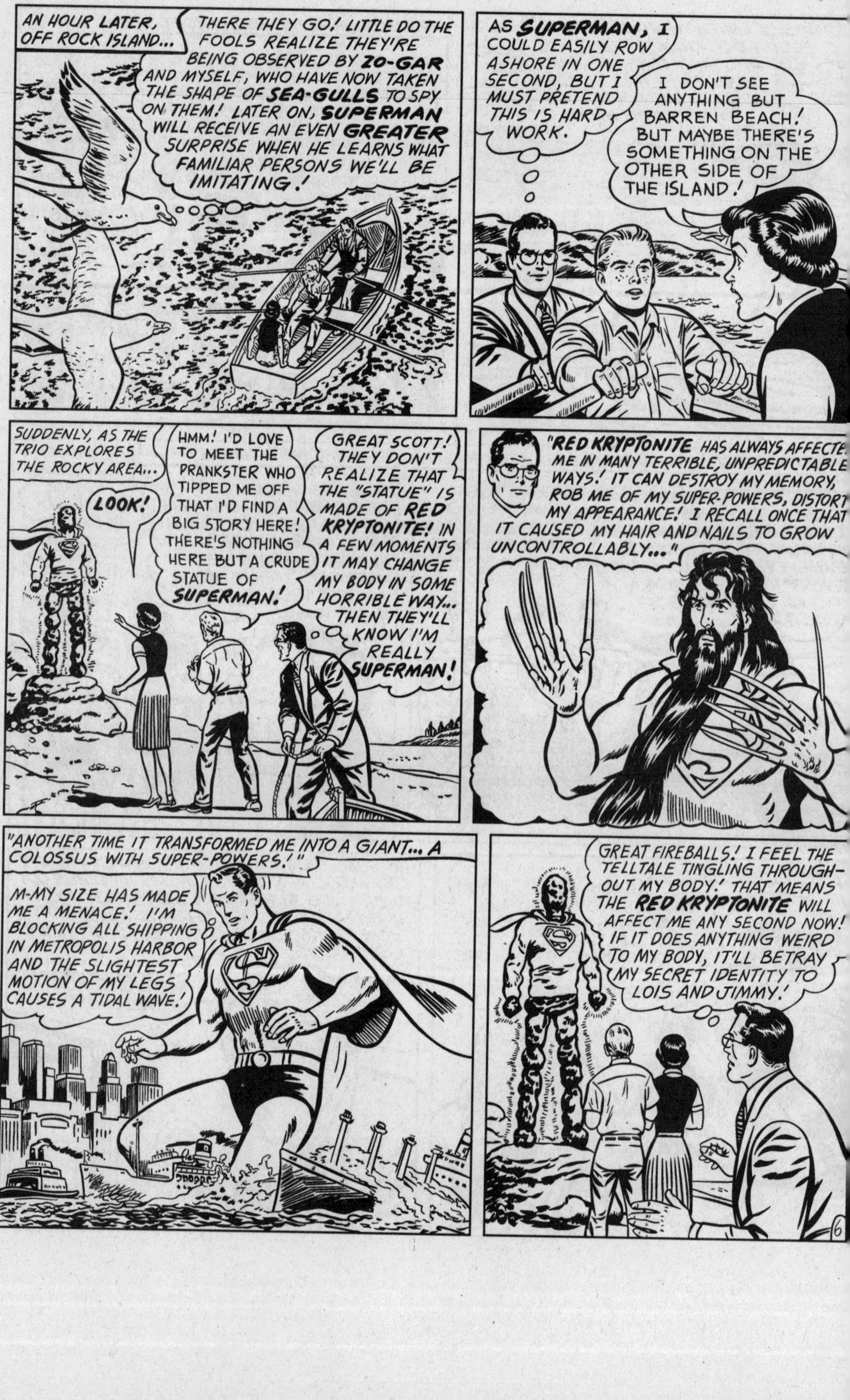
AN HOUR LATER, OFF ROCK ISLAND...
THERE THEY GO! LITTLE DO THE FOOLS REALIZE THEY'RE BEING OBSERVED BY ZO-GAR AND MYSELF, WHO HAVE NOW TAKEN THE SHAPE OF SEA-GULLS TO SPY ON THEM! LATER ON, SUPERMAN WILL RECEIVE AN EVEN GREATER SURPRISE WHEN HE LEARNS WHAT FAMILIAR PERSONS WE'LL BE IMITATING!
AS SUPERMAN, I COULD EASILY ROW ASHORE IN ONE SECOND, BUT I MUST PRETEND THIS IS HARD WORK.
I DON'T SEE ANYTHING BUT BARREN BEACH! BUT MAYBE THERE'S SOMETHING ON THE OTHER SIDE OF THE ISLAND!
SUDDENLY, AS THE TRIO EXPLORES THE ROCKY AREA...
LOOK!
HMM! I'D LOVE TO MEET THE PRANKSTER WHO TIPPED ME OFF THAT I'D FIND A BIG STORY HERE! THERE'S NOTHING HERE BUT A CRUDE STATUE OF SUPERMAN!
GREAT SCOTT! THEY DON'T REALIZE THAT THE "STATUE" IS MADE OF RED KRYPTONITE! IN A FEW MOMENTS IT MAY CHANGE MY BODY IN SOME HORRIBLE WAY... THEN THEY'LL KNOW I'M REALLY SUPERMAN!
"RED KRYPTONITE HAS ALWAYS AFFECTE ME IN MANY TERRIBLE, UNPREDICTABLE WAYS! IT CAN DESTROY MY MEMORY, ROB ME OF MY SUPER-POWERS, DISTORT MY APPEARANCE! I RECALL ONCE THAT IT CAUSED MY HAIR AND NAILS TO GROW UNCONTROLLABLY..."
"ANOTHER TIME IT TRANSFORMED ME INTO A GIANT... A COLOSSUS WITH SUPER-POWERS!"
M-MY SIZE HAS MADE ME A MENACE! I'M BLOCKING ALL SHIPPING IN METROPOLIS HARBOR AND THE SLIGHTEST MOTION OF MY LEGS CAUSES A TIDAL WAVE!
GREAT FIREBALLS! I FEEL THE TELLTALE TINGLING THROUGH-OUT MY BODY! THAT MEANS THE RED KRYPTONITE WILL AFFECT ME ANY SECOND NOW! IF IT DOES ANYTHING WEIRD TO MY BODY, IT'LL BETRAY MY SECRET IDENTITY TO LOIS AND JIMMY!
6

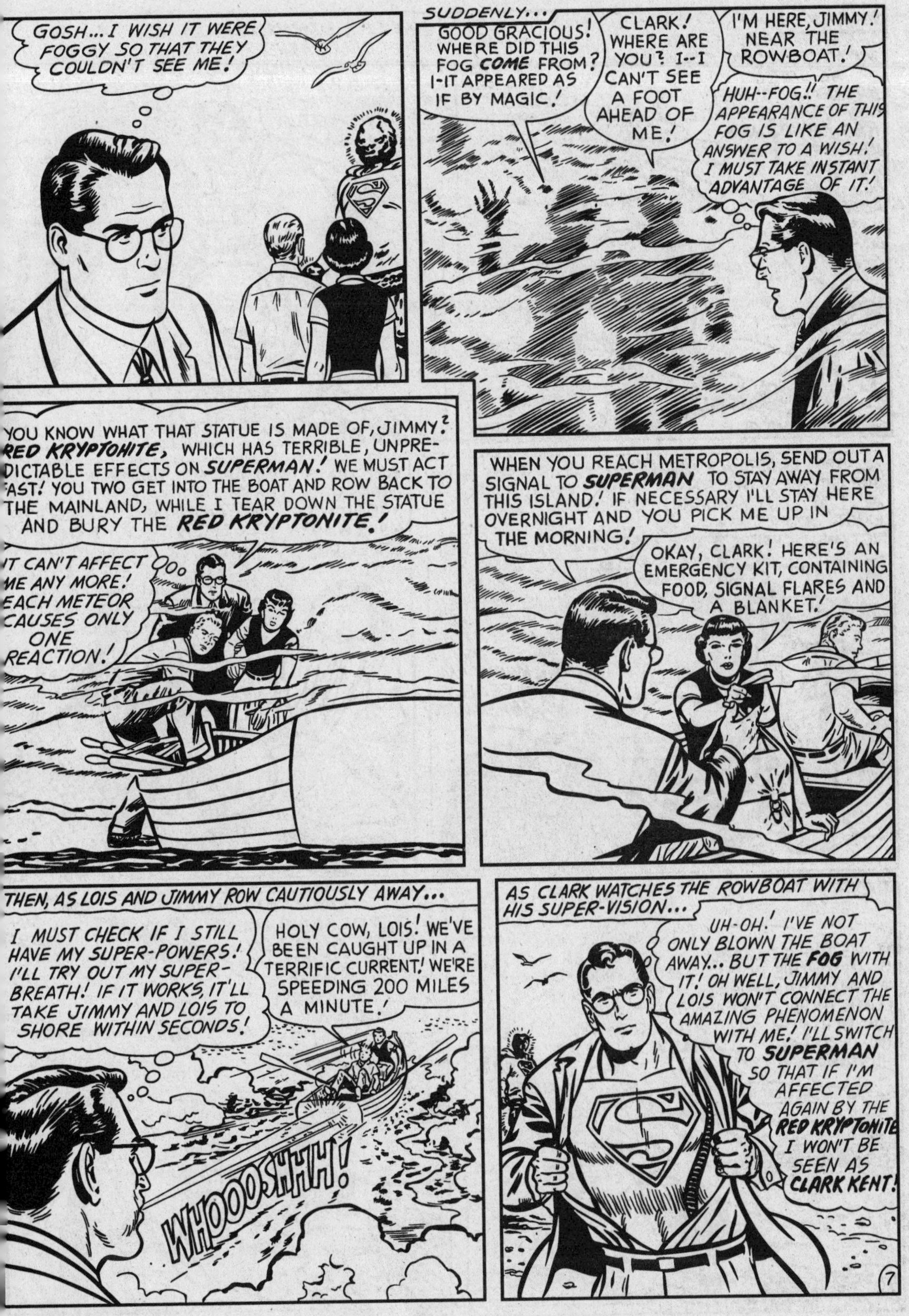
GOSH... I WISH IT WERE FOGGY SO THAT THEY COULDN'T SEE ME!
SUDDENLY...
GOOD GRACIOUS! WHERE DID THIS FOG COME FROM? I-IT APPEARED AS IF BY MAGIC!
CLARK! WHERE ARE YOU? I--I CAN'T SEE A FOOT AHEAD OF ME!
I'M HERE, JIMMY! NEAR THE ROWBOAT!
HUH--FOG!! THE APPEARANCE OF THIS FOG IS LIKE AN ANSWER TO A WISH! I MUST TAKE INSTANT ADVANTAGE OF IT!
YOU KNOW WHAT THAT STATUE IS MADE OF, JIMMY? RED KRYPTONITE, WHICH HAS TERRIBLE, UNPREDICTABLE EFFECTS ON SUPERMAN! WE MUST ACT FAST! YOU TWO GET INTO THE BOAT AND ROW BACK TO THE MAINLAND, WHILE I TEAR DOWN THE STATUE AND BURY THE RED KRYPTONITE!
IT CAN'T AFFECT ME ANY MORE! EACH METEOR CAUSES ONLY ONE REACTION!
WHEN YOU REACH METROPOLIS, SEND OUT A SIGNAL TO SUPERMAN TO STAY AWAY FROM THIS ISLAND! IF NECESSARY I'LL STAY HERE OVERNIGHT AND YOU PICK ME UP IN THE MORNING!
OKAY, CLARK! HERE'S AN EMERGENCY KIT, CONTAINING FOOD, SIGNAL FLARES AND A BLANKET!
THEN, AS LOIS AND JIMMY ROW CAUTIOUSLY AWAY...
I MUST CHECK IF I STILL HAVE MY SUPER-POWERS! I'LL TRY OUT MY SUPER-BREATH! IF IT WORKS, IT'LL TAKE JIMMY AND LOIS TO SHORE WITHIN SECONDS!
HOLY COW, LOIS! WE'VE BEEN CAUGHT UP IN A TERRIFIC CURRENT! WE'RE SPEEDING 200 MILES A MINUTE!
WHOOOSHHH!
AS CLARK WATCHES THE ROWBOAT WITH HIS SUPER-VISION...
UH-OH! I'VE NOT ONLY BLOWN THE BOAT AWAY... BUT THE FOG WITH IT! OH WELL, JIMMY AND LOIS WON'T CONNECT THE AMAZING PHENOMENON WITH ME! I'LL SWITCH TO SUPERMAN SO THAT IF I'M AFFECTED AGAIN BY THE RED KRYPTONITE I WON'T BE SEEN AS CLARK KENT!
7

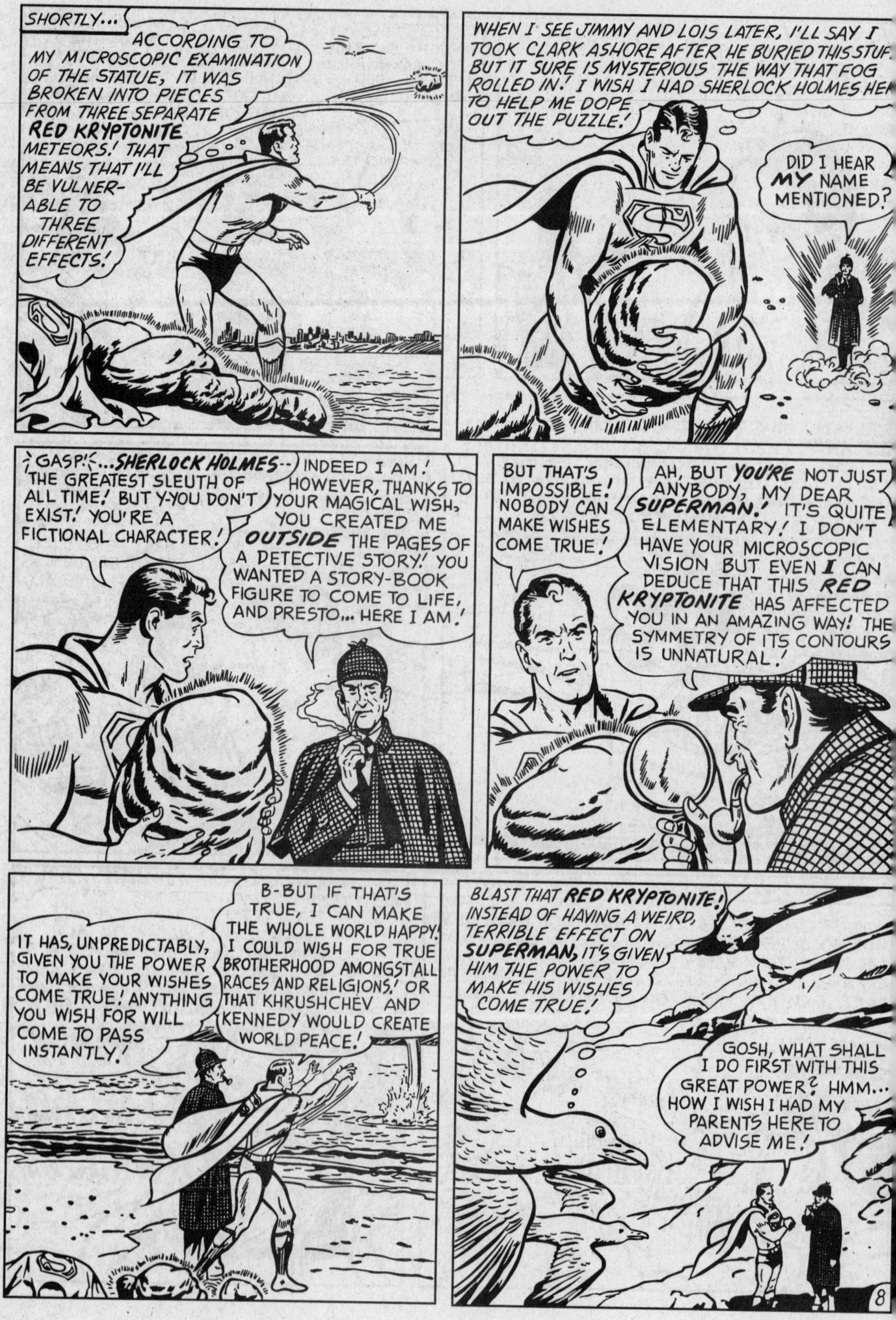
SHORTLY...
ACCORDING TO MY MICROSCOPIC EXAMINATION OF THE STATUE, IT WAS BROKEN INTO PIECES FROM THREE SEPARATE RED KRYPTONITE METEORS! THAT MEANS THAT I'LL BE VULNERABLE TO THREE DIFFERENT EFFECTS!
WHEN I SEE JIMMY AND LOIS LATER, I'LL SAY I TOOK CLARK ASHORE AFTER HE BURIED THIS STUF BUT IT SURE IS MYSTERIOUS THE WAY THAT FOG ROLLED IN! I WISH I HAD SHERLOCK HOLMES HE TO HELP ME DOPE OUT THE PUZZLE!
DID I HEAR MY NAME MENTIONED?
GASP! ...SHERLOCK HOLMES-- THE GREATEST SLEUTH OF ALL TIME! BUT Y-YOU DON'T EXIST! YOU'RE A FICTIONAL CHARACTER!
INDEED I AM! HOWEVER, THANKS TO YOUR MAGICAL WISH, YOU CREATED ME OUTSIDE THE PAGES OF A DETECTIVE STORY! YOU WANTED A STORY-BOOK FIGURE TO COME TO LIFE, AND PRESTO... HERE I AM!
BUT THAT'S IMPOSSIBLE! NOBODY CAN MAKE WISHES COME TRUE!
AH, BUT YOU'RE NOT JUST ANYBODY, MY DEAR SUPERMAN! IT'S QUITE ELEMENTARY! I DON'T HAVE YOUR MICROSCOPIC VISION BUT EVEN I CAN DEDUCE THAT THIS RED KRYPTONITE HAS AFFECTED YOU IN AN AMAZING WAY! THE SYMMETRY OF ITS CONTOURS IS UNNATURAL!
IT HAS, UNPREDICTABLY, GIVEN YOU THE POWER TO MAKE YOUR WISHES COME TRUE! ANYTHING YOU WISH FOR WILL COME TO PASS INSTANTLY!
B-BUT IF THAT'S TRUE, I CAN MAKE THE WHOLE WORLD HAPPY! I COULD WISH FOR TRUE BROTHERHOOD AMONGST ALL RACES AND RELIGIONS! OR THAT KHRUSHCHEV AND KENNEDY WOULD CREATE WORLD PEACE!
BLAST THAT RED KRYPTONITE! INSTEAD OF HAVING A WEIRD, TERRIBLE EFFECT ON SUPERMAN, IT'S GIVEN HIM THE POWER TO MAKE HIS WISHES COME TRUE!
GOSH, WHAT SHALL I DO FIRST WITH THIS GREAT POWER? HMM... HOW I WISH I HAD MY PARENTS HERE TO ADVISE ME!
8

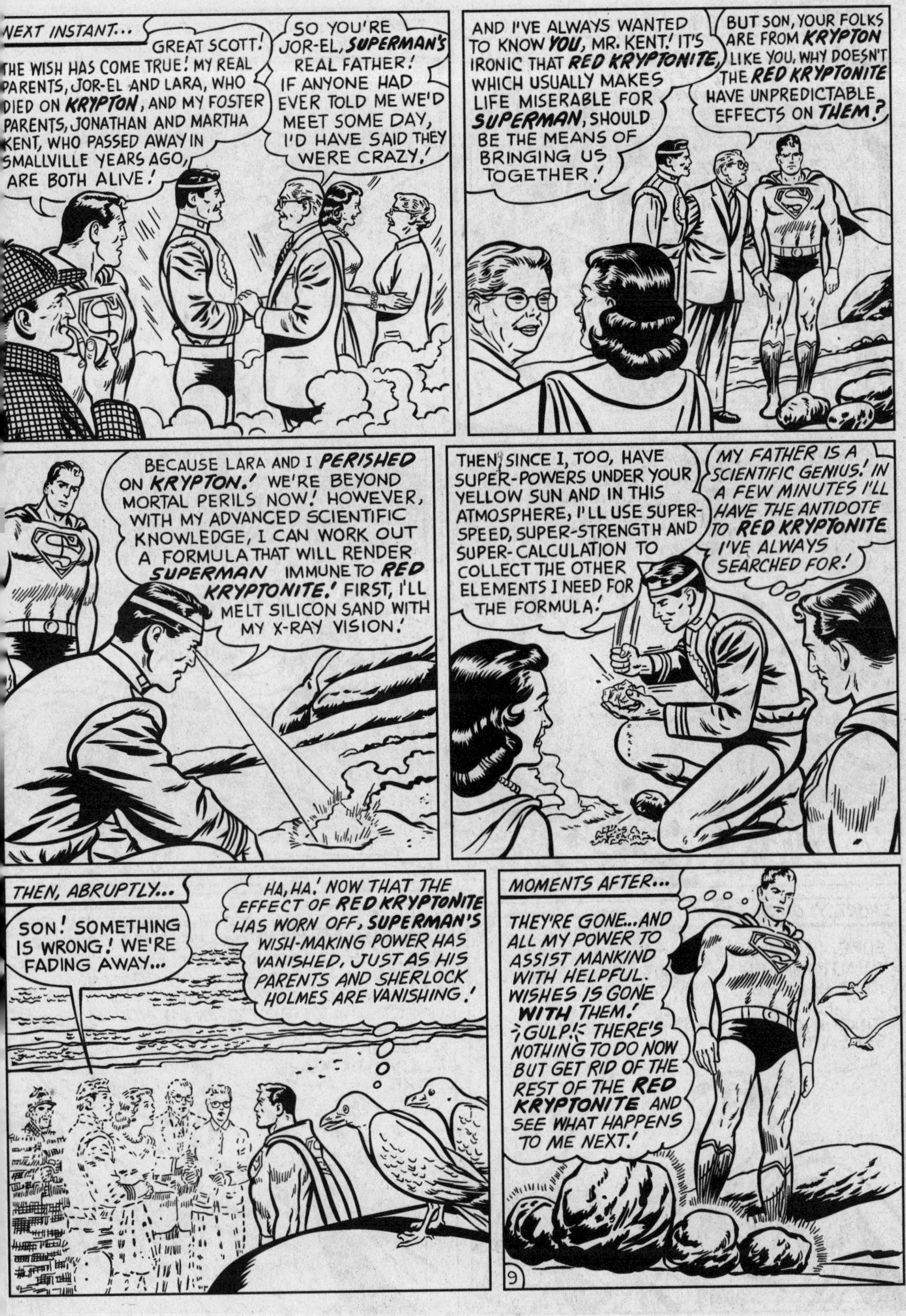
NEXT INSTANT...
GREAT SCOTT! THE WISH HAS COME TRUE! MY REAL PARENTS, JOR-EL AND LARA, WHO DIED ON KRYPTON, AND MY FOSTER PARENTS, JONATHAN AND MARTHA KENT, WHO PASSED AWAY IN SMALLVILLE YEARS AGO, ARE BOTH ALIVE!
SO YOU'RE JOR-EL, SUPERMAN'S REAL FATHER! IF ANYONE HAD EVER TOLD ME WE'D MEET SOME DAY, I'D HAVE SAID THEY WERE CRAZY!
AND I'VE ALWAYS WANTED TO KNOW YOU, MR. KENT! IT'S IRONIC THAT RED KRYPTONITE, WHICH USUALLY MAKES LIFE MISERABLE FOR SUPERMAN, SHOULD BE THE MEANS OF BRINGING US TOGETHER!
BUT SON, YOUR FOLKS ARE FROM KRYPTON LIKE YOU, WHY DOESN'T THE RED KRYPTONITE HAVE UNPREDICTABLE EFFECTS ON THEM?
BECAUSE LARA AND I PERISHED ON KRYPTON! WE'RE BEYOND MORTAL PERILS NOW! HOWEVER, WITH MY ADVANCED SCIENTIFIC KNOWLEDGE, I CAN WORK OUT A FORMULA THAT WILL RENDER SUPERMAN IMMUNE TO RED KRYPTONITE! FIRST, I'LL MELT SILICON SAND WITH MY X-RAY VISION!
THEN, SINCE I, TOO, HAVE SUPER-POWERS UNDER YOUR YELLOW SUN AND IN THIS ATMOSPHERE, I'LL USE SUPER-SPEED, SUPER-STRENGTH AND SUPER-CALCULATION TO COLLECT THE OTHER ELEMENTS I NEED FOR THE FORMULA!
MY FATHER IS A SCIENTIFIC GENIUS! IN A FEW MINUTES I'LL HAVE THE ANTIDOTE TO RED KRYPTONITE I'VE ALWAYS SEARCHED FOR!
THEN, ABRUPTLY...
SON! SOMETHING IS WRONG! WE'RE FADING AWAY...
HA, HA! NOW THAT THE EFFECT OF RED KRYPTONITE HAS WORN OFF, SUPERMAN'S WISH-MAKING POWER HAS VANISHED, JUST AS HIS PARENTS AND SHERLOCK HOLMES ARE VANISHING!
MOMENTS AFTER...
THEY'RE GONE...AND ALL MY POWER TO ASSIST MANKIND WITH HELPFUL WISHES IS GONE WITH THEM! GULP! THERE'S NOTHING TO DO NOW BUT GET RID OF THE REST OF THE RED KRYPTONITE AND SEE WHAT HAPPENS TO ME NEXT!
9

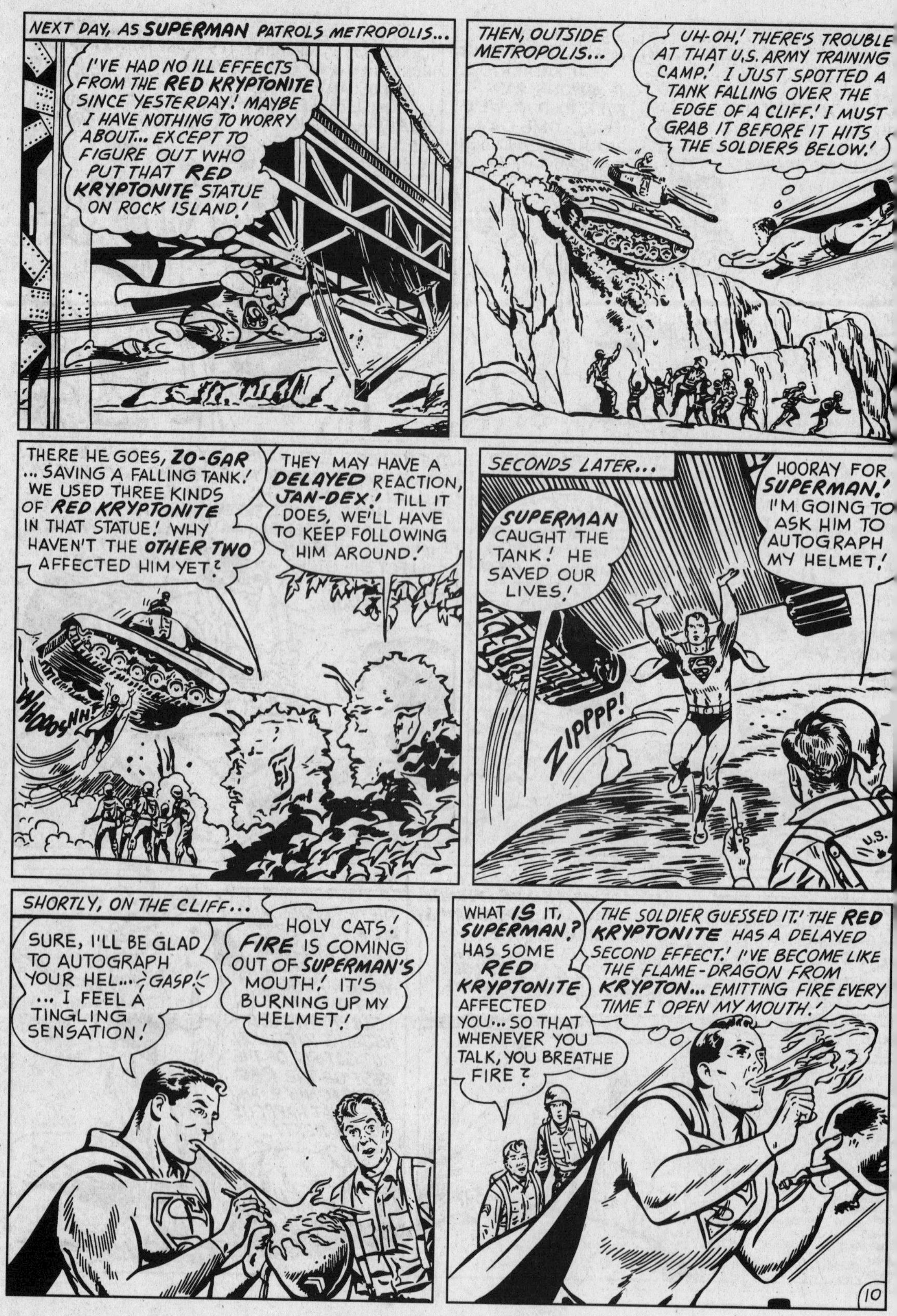
NEXT DAY, AS SUPERMAN PATROLS METROPOLIS...
I'VE HAD NO ILL EFFECTS FROM THE RED KRYPTONITE SINCE YESTERDAY! MAYBE I HAVE NOTHING TO WORRY ABOUT... EXCEPT TO FIGURE OUT WHO PUT THAT RED KRYPTONITE STATUE ON ROCK ISLAND!
THEN, OUTSIDE METROPOLIS...
UH-OH! THERE'S TROUBLE AT THAT U.S. ARMY TRAINING CAMP! I JUST SPOTTED A TANK FALLING OVER THE EDGE OF A CLIFF! I MUST GRAB IT BEFORE IT HITS THE SOLDIERS BELOW!
THERE HE GOES, ZO-GAR ... SAVING A FALLING TANK! WE USED THREE KINDS OF RED KRYPTONITE IN THAT STATUE! WHY HAVEN'T THE OTHER TWO AFFECTED HIM YET?
THEY MAY HAVE A DELAYED REACTION, JAN-DEX! TILL IT DOES, WE'LL HAVE TO KEEP FOLLOWING HIM AROUND!
WHOOOSHH!
SECONDS LATER...
SUPERMAN CAUGHT THE TANK! HE SAVED OUR LIVES!
HOORAY FOR SUPERMAN! I'M GOING TO ASK HIM TO AUTOGRAPH MY HELMET!
ZIPPPP!
U.S.
SHORTLY, ON THE CLIFF...
SURE, I'LL BE GLAD TO AUTOGRAPH YOUR HEL... GASP! ... I FEEL A TINGLING SENSATION!
HOLY CATS! FIRE IS COMING OUT OF SUPERMAN'S MOUTH! IT'S BURNING UP MY HELMET!
WHAT IS IT, SUPERMAN? HAS SOME RED KRYPTONITE AFFECTED YOU... SO THAT WHENEVER YOU TALK, YOU BREATHE FIRE?
THE SOLDIER GUESSED IT! THE RED KRYPTONITE HAS A DELAYED SECOND EFFECT! I'VE BECOME LIKE THE FLAME-DRAGON FROM KRYPTON... EMITTING FIRE EVERY TIME I OPEN MY MOUTH!
10

YES, MEN! I'M SUFFERING FROM THE EFFECTS OF SOME **RED KRYPTONITE** I RECENTLY CAME IN CONTACT WITH! I MUST STAY AWAY FROM YOU BECAUSE IF I SPEAK, I MAY ACCIDENTALLY BURN SOMEONE!

GOSH! WHAT A TERRIBLE THING TO HAPPEN TO **SUPERMAN!** NOW HE'LL HAVE TO ISOLATE HIMSELF!

IT'S TRUE! I CAN'T BE AROUND PEOPLE NOW! THAT MEANS I CAN'T ATTEND THE KENNEDY-KHRUSHCHEV MEETING EVEN IF I'M PERMITTED TO COVER IT AS CLARK KENT! UNLESS... WAIT A SECOND! I'VE GOT A **TERRIFIC** IDEA! I NEEDN'T BE AFRAID TO SWITCH BACK TO CLARK KENT!

AND SO, LATER, AT THE **PLANET**, AFTER **SUPERMAN** BECOMES CLARK KENT...

CLARK! THIS IS LOIS! I HEARD YOU WERE USING THE NIGHT EDITOR'S OFFICE TODAY! MAY I SEE YOU A MOMENT?

SURE, LOIS! COME RIGHT IN!

OH, DARN! THERE GOES MY FLAME BREATH AGAIN! IT'S BURNED UP THE INTERCOM! I'LL HAVE TO HIDE IT AND BLOW THE SMOKE SMELL OUT OF THE ROOM BEFORE LOIS ENTERS!

SHORTLY...

I'VE GOT BAD NEWS! PERRY JUST GOT A CALL! IT'S DEFINITE NOW! ABSOLUTELY NO REPORTERS ALLOWED AT THE SUMMIT CONFERENCE! THEY ONLY WANT **SUPERMAN** TO ATTEND THE SUMMIT MEETING. HE'LL STAND GUARD THERE!

GOSH, I'M SORRY, LOIS! I WAS SORT OF HOPING WE'D BOTH BE THERE!

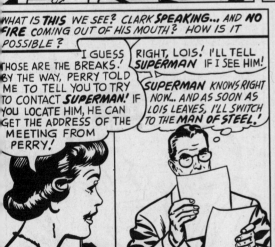

WHAT IS **THIS** WE SEE? CLARK **SPEAKING**... AND **NO FIRE** COMING OUT OF HIS MOUTH? HOW IS IT POSSIBLE?

I GUESS THOSE ARE THE BREAKS! BY THE WAY, PERRY TOLD ME TO TELL YOU TO TRY TO CONTACT **SUPERMAN!** IF YOU LOCATE HIM, HE CAN GET THE ADDRESS OF THE MEETING FROM PERRY!

RIGHT, LOIS! I'LL TELL **SUPERMAN** IF I SEE HIM!

SUPERMAN KNOWS RIGHT NOW... AND AS SOON AS LOIS LEAVES, I'LL SWITCH TO THE **MAN OF STEEL!**

SOON, IN PERRY'S OFFICE...

I'M GLAD CLARK WAS ABLE TO REACH YOU, **SUPERMAN!** THE PHONE CALL SAID THAT KENNEDY AND KHRUSHCHEV ARE CONFERRING IN A DESERTED BUNKER AT FORT DIXON! YOU'RE TO GUARD THEM!

I'LL FLY THERE AT ONCE, PERRY!

HOW CAN **SUPERMAN** SPEAK WITHOUT EMITTING FIRE? CAN **YOU** GUESS?

11

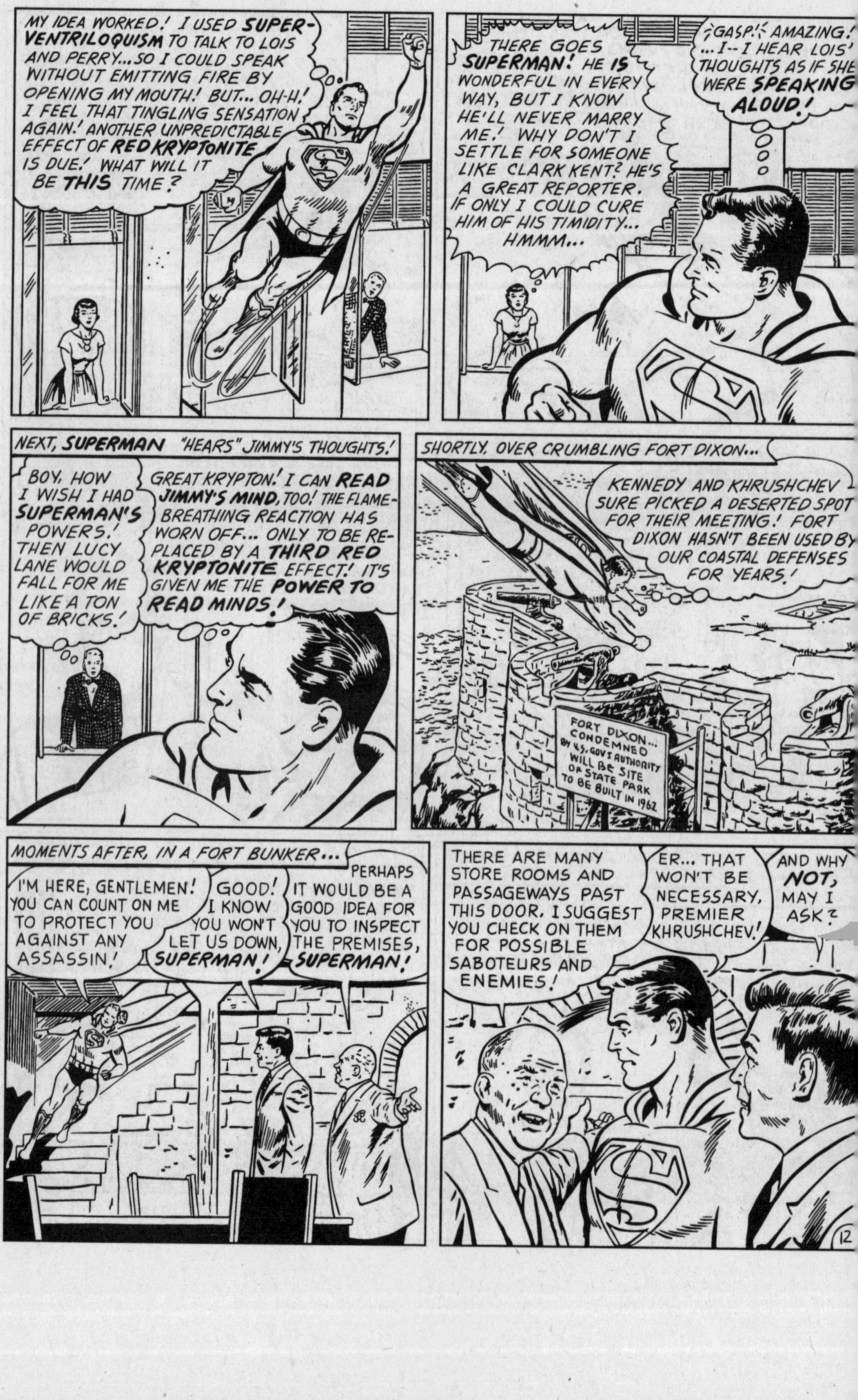
MY IDEA WORKED! I USED SUPER-VENTRILOQUISM TO TALK TO LOIS AND PERRY...SO I COULD SPEAK WITHOUT EMITTING FIRE BY OPENING MY MOUTH! BUT... OH-H! I FEEL THAT TINGLING SENSATION AGAIN! ANOTHER UNPREDICTABLE EFFECT OF RED KRYPTONITE IS DUE! WHAT WILL IT BE THIS TIME?
THERE GOES SUPERMAN! HE IS WONDERFUL IN EVERY WAY, BUT I KNOW HE'LL NEVER MARRY ME! WHY DON'T I SETTLE FOR SOMEONE LIKE CLARK KENT? HE'S A GREAT REPORTER. IF ONLY I COULD CURE HIM OF HIS TIMIDITY... HMMM...
GASP! AMAZING! ...I--I HEAR LOIS' THOUGHTS AS IF SHE WERE SPEAKING ALOUD!
NEXT, SUPERMAN "HEARS" JIMMY'S THOUGHTS!
BOY, HOW I WISH I HAD SUPERMAN'S POWERS! THEN LUCY LANE WOULD FALL FOR ME LIKE A TON OF BRICKS!
GREAT KRYPTON! I CAN READ JIMMY'S MIND, TOO! THE FLAME-BREATHING REACTION HAS WORN OFF... ONLY TO BE REPLACED BY A THIRD RED KRYPTONITE EFFECT! IT'S GIVEN ME THE POWER TO READ MINDS!
SHORTLY, OVER CRUMBLING FORT DIXON...
KENNEDY AND KHRUSHCHEV SURE PICKED A DESERTED SPOT FOR THEIR MEETING! FORT DIXON HASN'T BEEN USED BY OUR COASTAL DEFENSES FOR YEARS!
FORT DIXON... CONDEMNED BY U.S. GOV'T AUTHORITY WILL BE SITE OF STATE PARK TO BE BUILT IN 1962
MOMENTS AFTER, IN A FORT BUNKER...
I'M HERE, GENTLEMEN! YOU CAN COUNT ON ME TO PROTECT YOU AGAINST ANY ASSASSIN!
GOOD! I KNOW YOU WON'T LET US DOWN, SUPERMAN!
PERHAPS IT WOULD BE A GOOD IDEA FOR YOU TO INSPECT THE PREMISES, SUPERMAN!
THERE ARE MANY STORE ROOMS AND PASSAGEWAYS PAST THIS DOOR. I SUGGEST YOU CHECK ON THEM FOR POSSIBLE SABOTEURS AND ENEMIES!
ER... THAT WON'T BE NECESSARY, PREMIER KHRUSHCHEV!
AND WHY NOT, MAY I ASK?
12

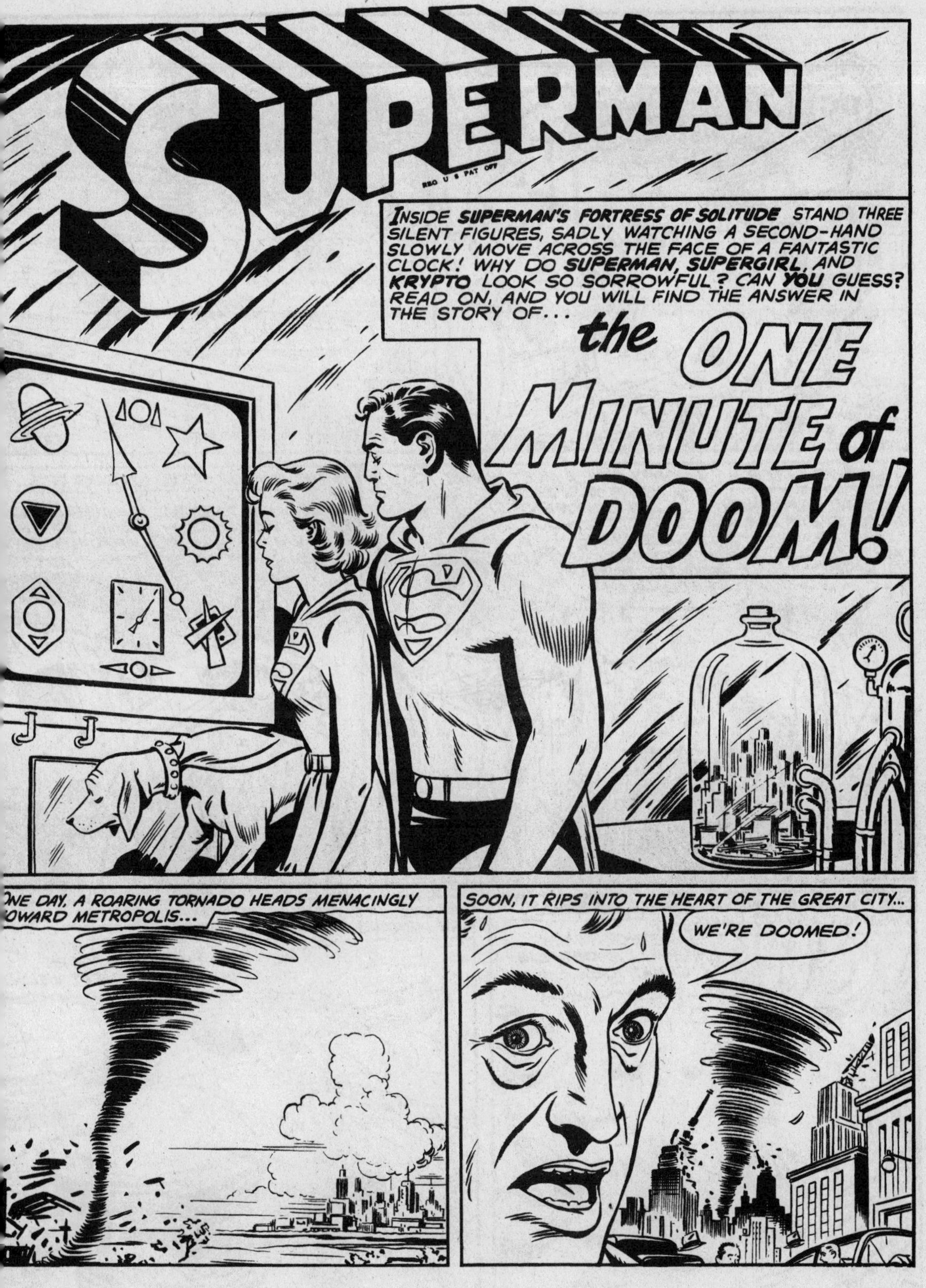
SUPERMAN
REG U S PAT OFF
INSIDE SUPERMAN'S FORTRESS OF SOLITUDE STAND THREE SILENT FIGURES, SADLY WATCHING A SECOND-HAND SLOWLY MOVE ACROSS THE FACE OF A FANTASTIC CLOCK! WHY DO SUPERMAN, SUPERGIRL, AND KRYPTO LOOK SO SORROWFUL? CAN YOU GUESS? READ ON, AND YOU WILL FIND THE ANSWER IN THE STORY OF...
the ONE MINUTE of DOOM!
ONE DAY, A ROARING TORNADO HEADS MENACINGLY OWARD METROPOLIS...
SOON, IT RIPS INTO THE HEART OF THE GREAT CITY...
WE'RE DOOMED!

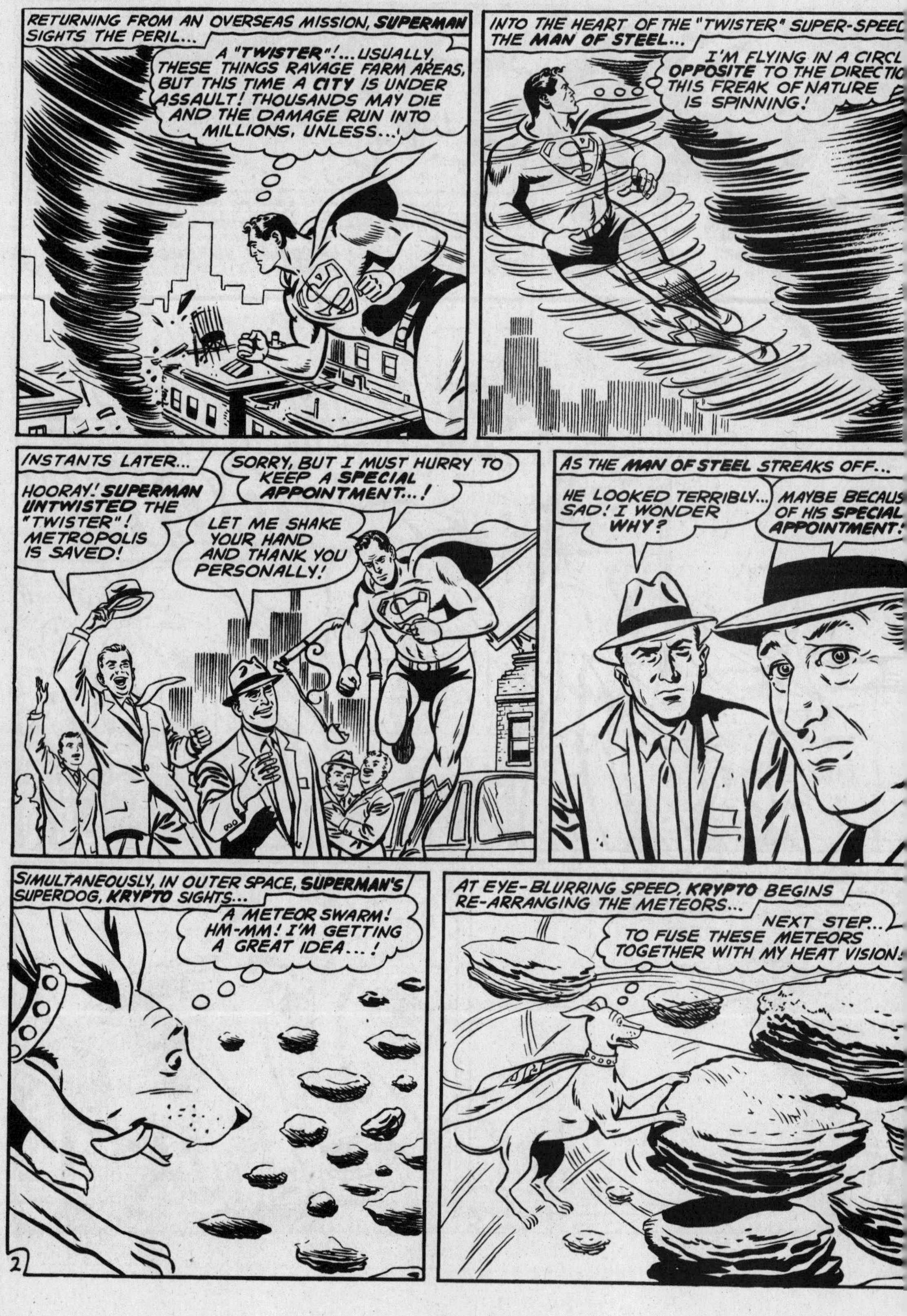
RETURNING FROM AN OVERSEAS MISSION, SUPERMAN SIGHTS THE PERIL...
A "TWISTER"!... USUALLY, THESE THINGS RAVAGE FARM AREAS, BUT THIS TIME A CITY IS UNDER ASSAULT! THOUSANDS MAY DIE AND THE DAMAGE RUN INTO MILLIONS, UNLESS...!
INTO THE HEART OF THE "TWISTER" SUPER-SPEEDS THE MAN OF STEEL...
I'M FLYING IN A CIRCLE OPPOSITE TO THE DIRECTION THIS FREAK OF NATURE IS SPINNING!
INSTANTS LATER...
HOORAY! SUPERMAN UNTWISTED THE "TWISTER"! METROPOLIS IS SAVED!
LET ME SHAKE YOUR HAND AND THANK YOU PERSONALLY!
SORRY, BUT I MUST HURRY TO KEEP A SPECIAL APPOINTMENT...!
AS THE MAN OF STEEL STREAKS OFF...
HE LOOKED TERRIBLY... SAD! I WONDER WHY?
MAYBE BECAUSE OF HIS SPECIAL APPOINTMENT!
SIMULTANEOUSLY, IN OUTER SPACE, SUPERMAN'S SUPERDOG, KRYPTO SIGHTS...
A METEOR SWARM! HM-MM! I'M GETTING A GREAT IDEA...!
2
AT EYE-BLURRING SPEED, KRYPTO BEGINS RE-ARRANGING THE METEORS...
NEXT STEP... TO FUSE THESE METEORS TOGETHER WITH MY HEAT VISION!

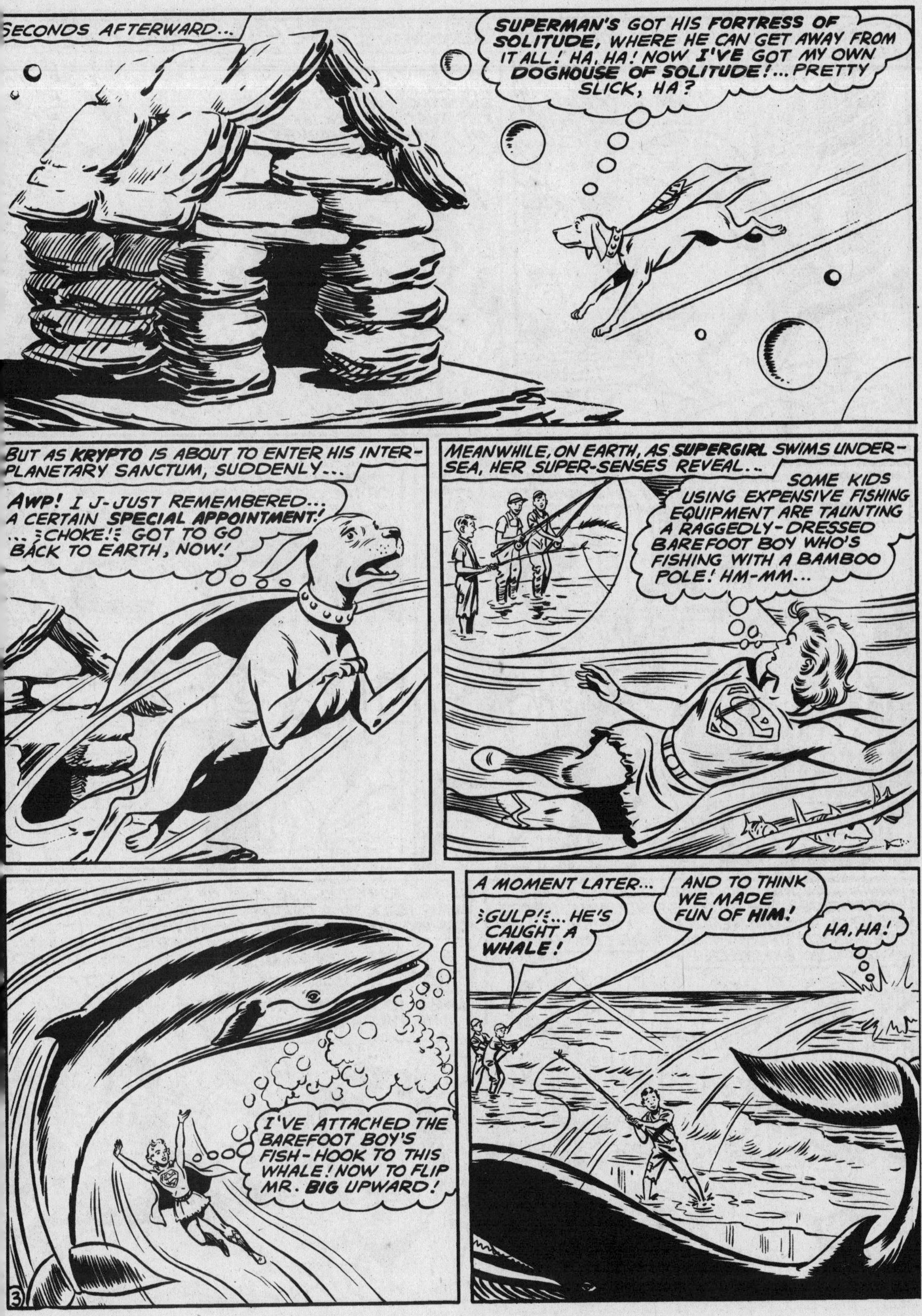
SECONDS AFTERWARD...
SUPERMAN'S GOT HIS FORTRESS OF SOLITUDE, WHERE HE CAN GET AWAY FROM IT ALL! HA, HA! NOW I'VE GOT MY OWN DOGHOUSE OF SOLITUDE!... PRETTY SLICK, HA?
BUT AS KRYPTO IS ABOUT TO ENTER HIS INTER-PLANETARY SANCTUM, SUDDENLY...
AWP! I J-JUST REMEMBERED... A CERTAIN SPECIAL APPOINTMENT! ... ¡CHOKE!¡ GOT TO GO BACK TO EARTH, NOW!
MEANWHILE, ON EARTH, AS SUPERGIRL SWIMS UNDER-SEA, HER SUPER-SENSES REVEAL...
SOME KIDS USING EXPENSIVE FISHING EQUIPMENT ARE TAUNTING A RAGGEDLY-DRESSED BAREFOOT BOY WHO'S FISHING WITH A BAMBOO POLE! HM-MM...
I'VE ATTACHED THE BAREFOOT BOY'S FISH-HOOK TO THIS WHALE! NOW TO FLIP MR. BIG UPWARD!
3
A MOMENT LATER...
¡GULP!¡... HE'S CAUGHT A WHALE!
AND TO THINK WE MADE FUN OF HIM!
HA, HA!

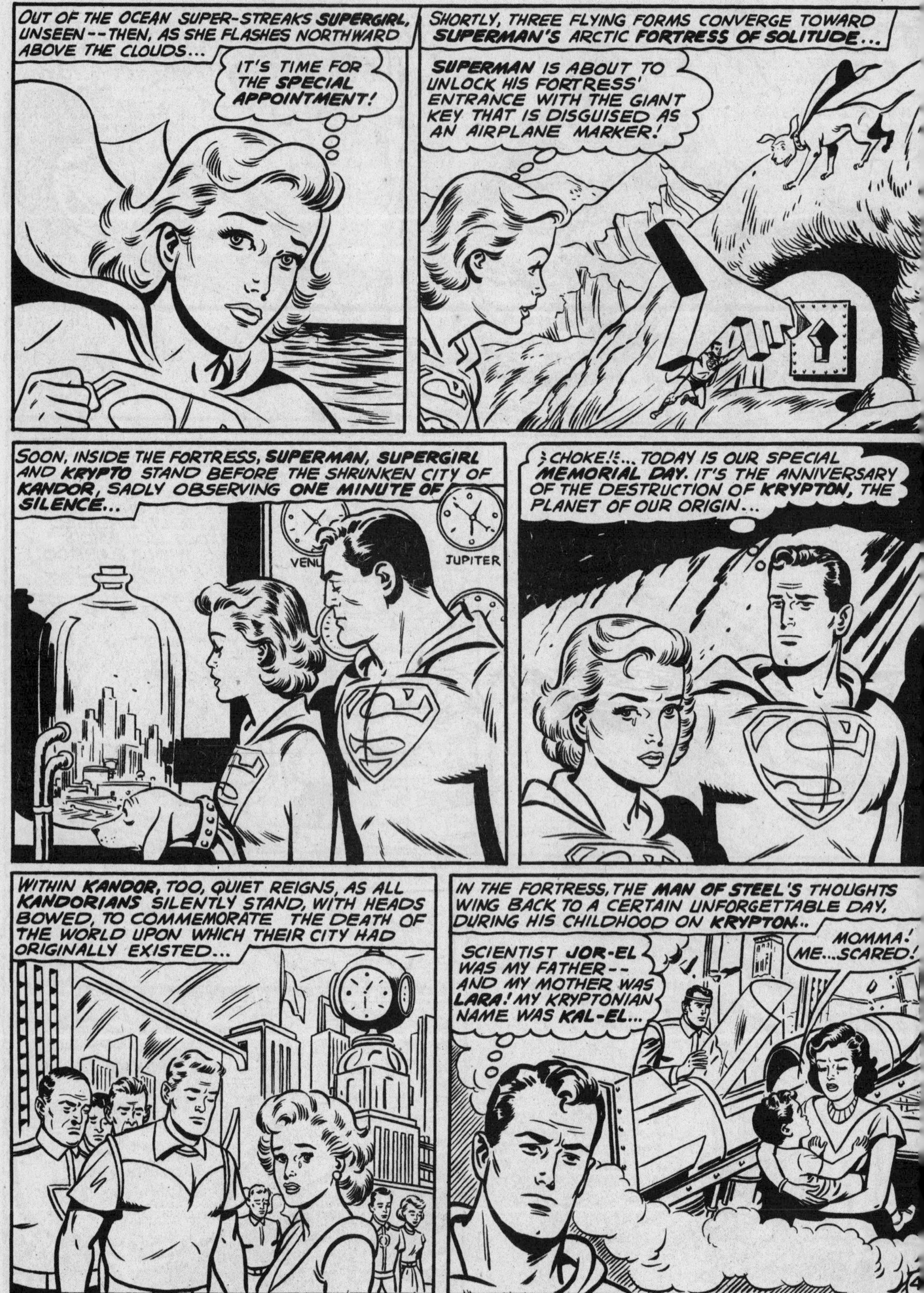

OUT OF THE OCEAN SUPER-STREAKS SUPERGIRL, UNSEEN--THEN, AS SHE FLASHES NORTHWARD ABOVE THE CLOUDS...
IT'S TIME FOR THE SPECIAL APPOINTMENT!
SHORTLY, THREE FLYING FORMS CONVERGE TOWARD SUPERMAN'S ARCTIC FORTRESS OF SOLITUDE...
SUPERMAN IS ABOUT TO UNLOCK HIS FORTRESS' ENTRANCE WITH THE GIANT KEY THAT IS DISGUISED AS AN AIRPLANE MARKER!
SOON, INSIDE THE FORTRESS, SUPERMAN, SUPERGIRL AND KRYPTO STAND BEFORE THE SHRUNKEN CITY OF KANDOR, SADLY OBSERVING ONE MINUTE OF SILENCE...
JUPITER
CHOKE!... TODAY IS OUR SPECIAL MEMORIAL DAY. IT'S THE ANNIVERSARY OF THE DESTRUCTION OF KRYPTON, THE PLANET OF OUR ORIGIN...
WITHIN KANDOR, TOO, QUIET REIGNS, AS ALL KANDORIANS SILENTLY STAND, WITH HEADS BOWED, TO COMMEMORATE THE DEATH OF THE WORLD UPON WHICH THEIR CITY HAD ORIGINALLY EXISTED...
IN THE FORTRESS, THE MAN OF STEEL'S THOUGHTS WING BACK TO A CERTAIN UNFORGETTABLE DAY, DURING HIS CHILDHOOD ON KRYPTON...
SCIENTIST JOR-EL WAS MY FATHER--AND MY MOTHER WAS LARA! MY KRYPTONIAN NAME WAS KAL-EL...
MOMMA! ME...SCARED!
4

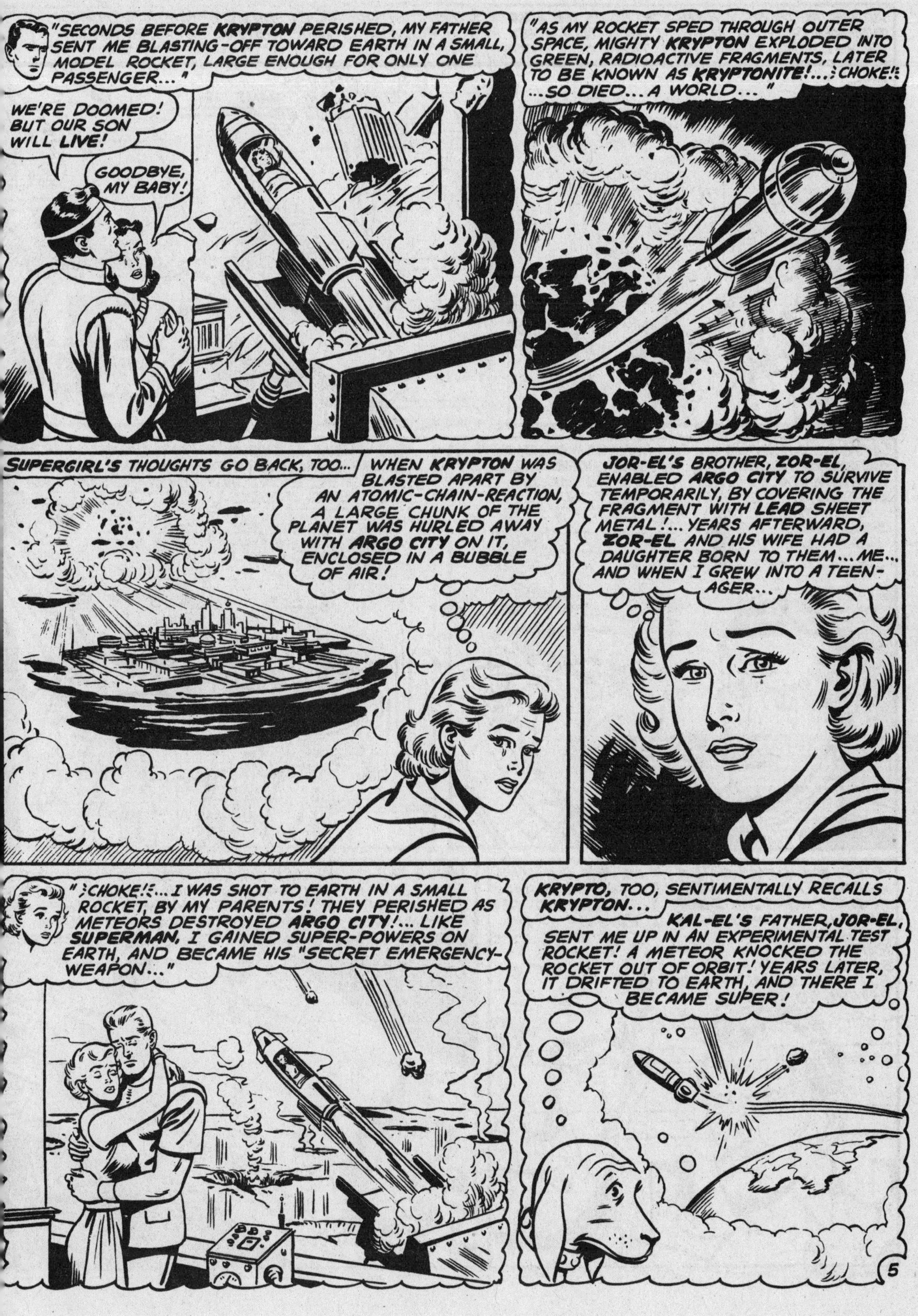
"SECONDS BEFORE KRYPTON PERISHED, MY FATHER SENT ME BLASTING-OFF TOWARD EARTH IN A SMALL, MODEL ROCKET, LARGE ENOUGH FOR ONLY ONE PASSENGER..."
WE'RE DOOMED! BUT OUR SON WILL LIVE!
GOODBYE, MY BABY!
"AS MY ROCKET SPED THROUGH OUTER SPACE, MIGHTY KRYPTON EXPLODED INTO GREEN, RADIOACTIVE FRAGMENTS, LATER TO BE KNOWN AS KRYPTONITE!...;CHOKE!: ...SO DIED... A WORLD..."
SUPERGIRL'S THOUGHTS GO BACK, TOO...
WHEN KRYPTON WAS BLASTED APART BY AN ATOMIC-CHAIN-REACTION, A LARGE CHUNK OF THE PLANET WAS HURLED AWAY WITH ARGO CITY ON IT, ENCLOSED IN A BUBBLE OF AIR!
JOR-EL'S BROTHER, ZOR-EL, ENABLED ARGO CITY TO SURVIVE TEMPORARILY, BY COVERING THE FRAGMENT WITH LEAD SHEET METAL!... YEARS AFTERWARD, ZOR-EL AND HIS WIFE HAD A DAUGHTER BORN TO THEM... ME... AND WHEN I GREW INTO A TEEN-AGER...
";CHOKE!:... I WAS SHOT TO EARTH IN A SMALL ROCKET, BY MY PARENTS! THEY PERISHED AS METEORS DESTROYED ARGO CITY!... LIKE SUPERMAN, I GAINED SUPER-POWERS ON EARTH, AND BECAME HIS "SECRET EMERGENCY-WEAPON..."
KRYPTO, TOO, SENTIMENTALLY RECALLS KRYPTON...
KAL-EL'S FATHER, JOR-EL, SENT ME UP IN AN EXPERIMENTAL TEST ROCKET! A METEOR KNOCKED THE ROCKET OUT OF ORBIT! YEARS LATER, IT DRIFTED TO EARTH, AND THERE I BECAME SUPER!
5

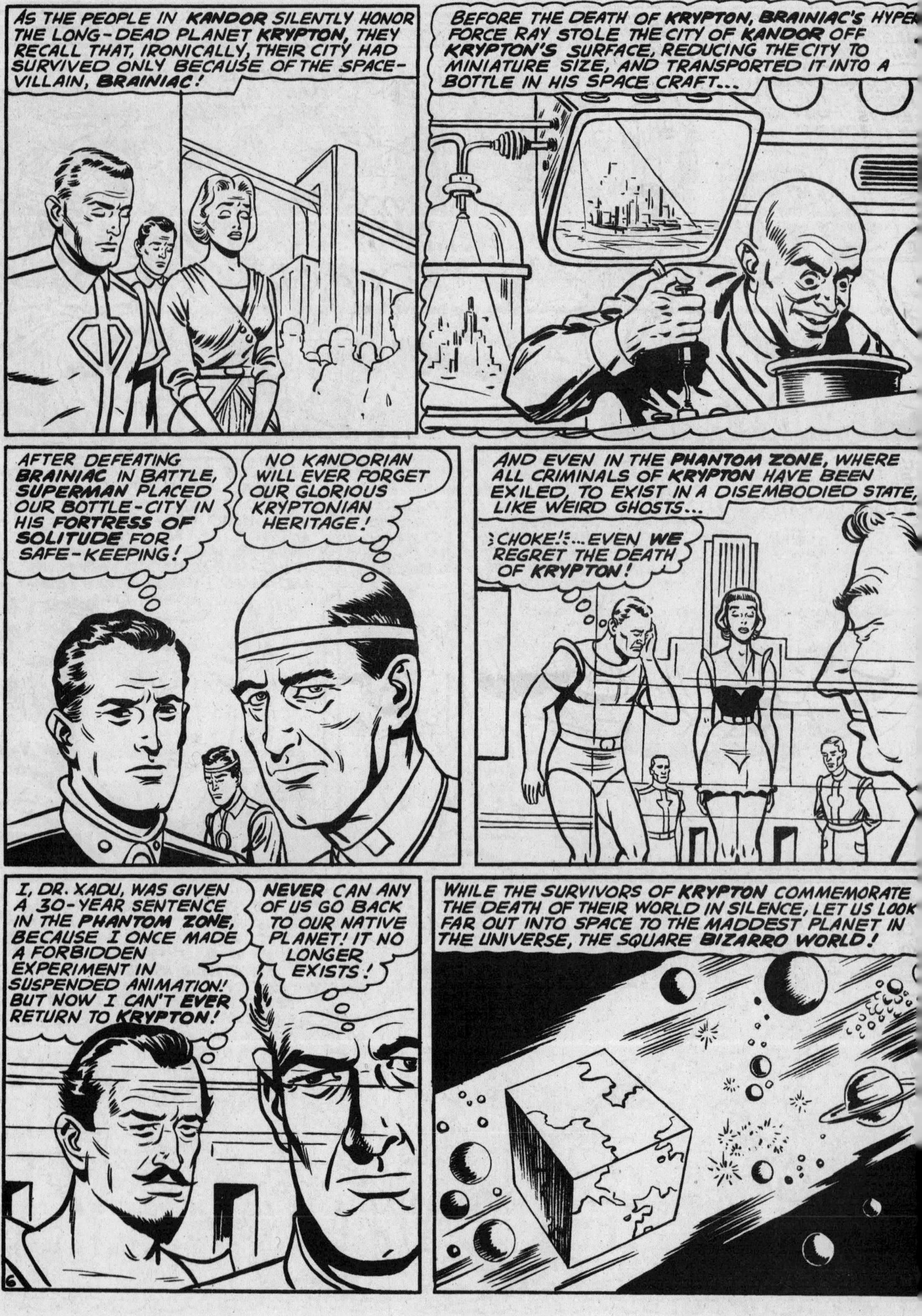

AS THE PEOPLE IN KANDOR SILENTLY HONOR THE LONG-DEAD PLANET KRYPTON, THEY RECALL THAT, IRONICALLY, THEIR CITY HAD SURVIVED ONLY BECAUSE OF THE SPACE-VILLAIN, BRAINIAC!
BEFORE THE DEATH OF KRYPTON, BRAINIAC'S HYPER-FORCE RAY STOLE THE CITY OF KANDOR OFF KRYPTON'S SURFACE, REDUCING THE CITY TO MINIATURE SIZE, AND TRANSPORTED IT INTO A BOTTLE IN HIS SPACE CRAFT...
AFTER DEFEATING BRAINIAC IN BATTLE, SUPERMAN PLACED OUR BOTTLE-CITY IN HIS FORTRESS OF SOLITUDE FOR SAFE-KEEPING!
NO KANDORIAN WILL EVER FORGET OUR GLORIOUS KRYPTONIAN HERITAGE!
AND EVEN IN THE PHANTOM ZONE, WHERE ALL CRIMINALS OF KRYPTON HAVE BEEN EXILED, TO EXIST IN A DISEMBODIED STATE, LIKE WEIRD GHOSTS...
CHOKE! ...EVEN WE REGRET THE DEATH OF KRYPTON!
I, DR. XADU, WAS GIVEN A 30-YEAR SENTENCE IN THE PHANTOM ZONE, BECAUSE I ONCE MADE A FORBIDDEN EXPERIMENT IN SUSPENDED ANIMATION! BUT NOW I CAN'T EVER RETURN TO KRYPTON!
NEVER CAN ANY OF US GO BACK TO OUR NATIVE PLANET! IT NO LONGER EXISTS!
6
WHILE THE SURVIVORS OF KRYPTON COMMEMORATE THE DEATH OF THEIR WORLD IN SILENCE, LET US LOOK FAR OUT INTO SPACE TO THE MADDEST PLANET IN THE UNIVERSE, THE SQUARE BIZARRO WORLD!

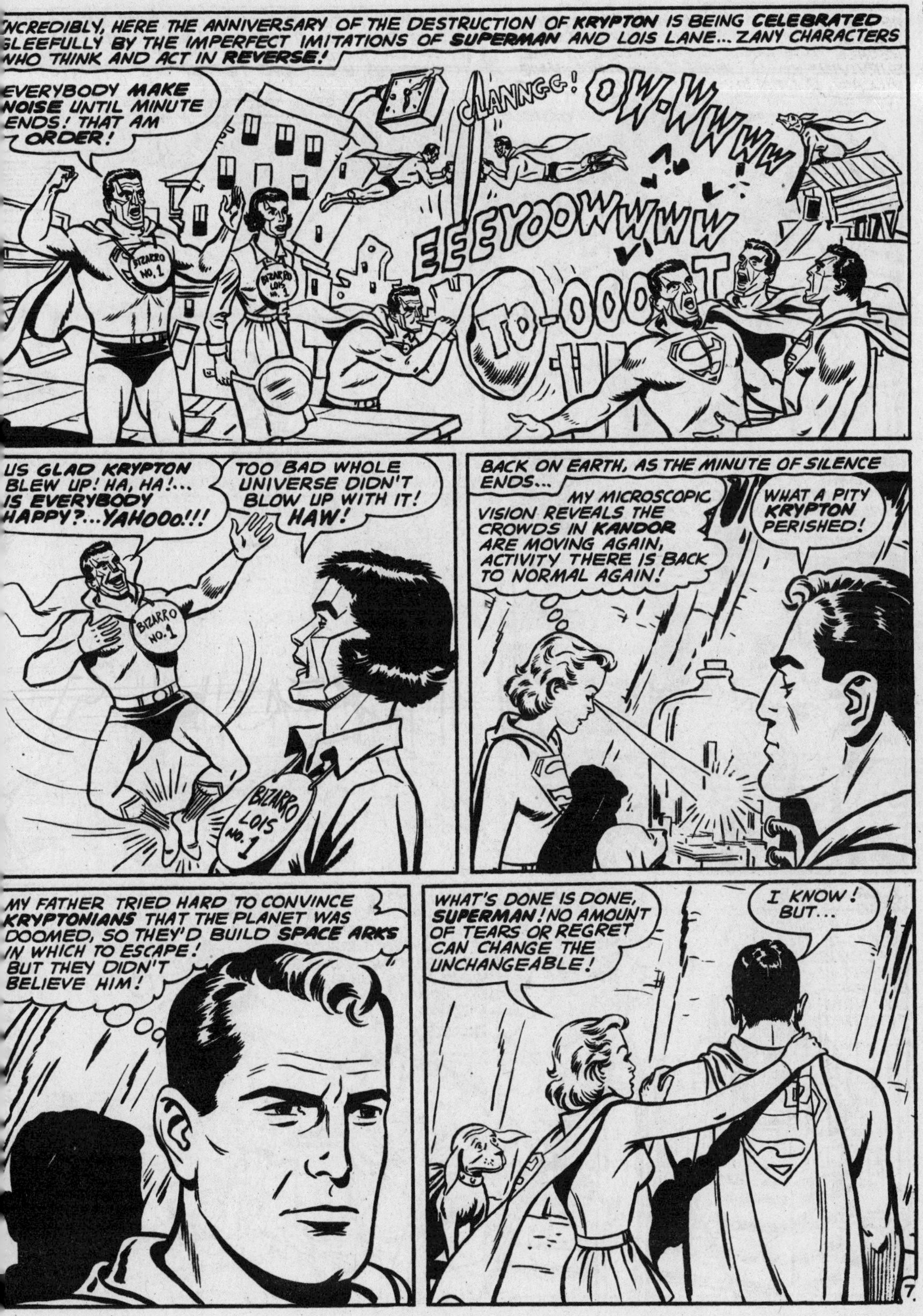
INCREDIBLY, HERE THE ANNIVERSARY OF THE DESTRUCTION OF KRYPTON IS BEING CELEBRATED GLEEFULLY BY THE IMPERFECT IMITATIONS OF SUPERMAN AND LOIS LANE... ZANY CHARACTERS WHO THINK AND ACT IN REVERSE!
EVERYBODY MAKE NOISE UNTIL MINUTE ENDS! THAT AM ORDER!
BIZARRO NO. 1
BIZARRO LOIS NO. 1
CLANNGG!
OW-WWWWW
EEEYOOWWWWW
TO-OOOT
US GLAD KRYPTON BLEW UP! HA, HA!... IS EVERYBODY HAPPY?...YAHOOO!!!
TOO BAD WHOLE UNIVERSE DIDN'T BLOW UP WITH IT! HAW!
BIZARRO NO. 1
BIZARRO LOIS NO. 1
BACK ON EARTH, AS THE MINUTE OF SILENCE ENDS...
MY MICROSCOPIC VISION REVEALS THE CROWDS IN KANDOR ARE MOVING AGAIN, ACTIVITY THERE IS BACK TO NORMAL AGAIN!
WHAT A PITY KRYPTON PERISHED!
MY FATHER TRIED HARD TO CONVINCE KRYPTONIANS THAT THE PLANET WAS DOOMED, SO THEY'D BUILD SPACE ARKS IN WHICH TO ESCAPE! BUT THEY DIDN'T BELIEVE HIM!
WHAT'S DONE IS DONE, SUPERMAN! NO AMOUNT OF TEARS OR REGRET CAN CHANGE THE UNCHANGEABLE!
I KNOW! BUT...
7

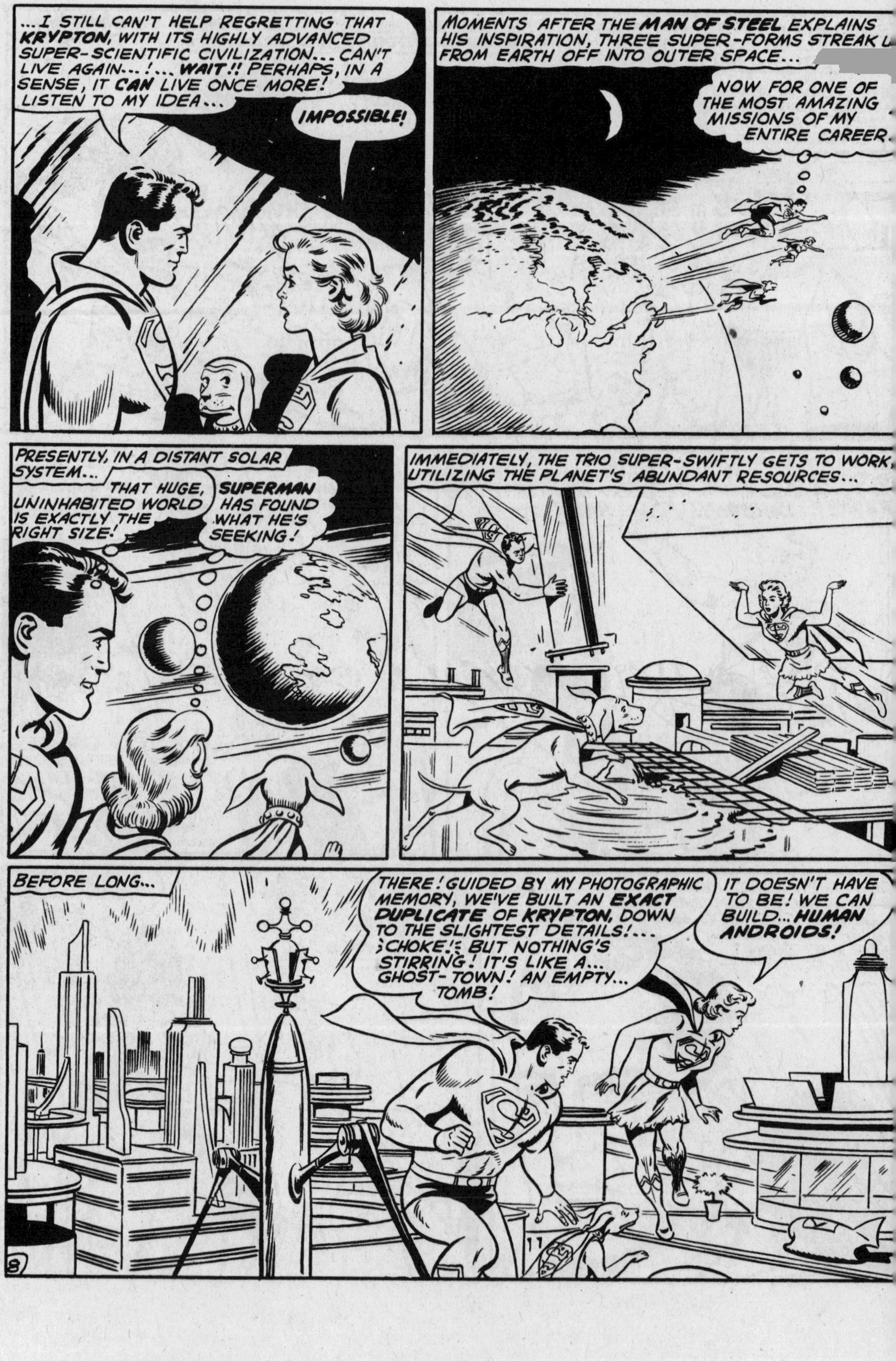
...I STILL CAN'T HELP REGRETTING THAT KRYPTON, WITH ITS HIGHLY ADVANCED SUPER-SCIENTIFIC CIVILIZATION... CAN'T LIVE AGAIN...!... WAIT!! PERHAPS, IN A SENSE, IT CAN LIVE ONCE MORE! LISTEN TO MY IDEA...
IMPOSSIBLE!
MOMENTS AFTER THE MAN OF STEEL EXPLAINS HIS INSPIRATION, THREE SUPER-FORMS STREAK FROM EARTH OFF INTO OUTER SPACE...
NOW FOR ONE OF THE MOST AMAZING MISSIONS OF MY ENTIRE CAREER
PRESENTLY, IN A DISTANT SOLAR SYSTEM...
THAT HUGE, UNINHABITED WORLD IS EXACTLY THE RIGHT SIZE!
SUPERMAN HAS FOUND WHAT HE'S SEEKING!
IMMEDIATELY, THE TRIO SUPER-SWIFTLY GETS TO WORK, UTILIZING THE PLANET'S ABUNDANT RESOURCES...
BEFORE LONG...
THERE! GUIDED BY MY PHOTOGRAPHIC MEMORY, WE'VE BUILT AN EXACT DUPLICATE OF KRYPTON, DOWN TO THE SLIGHTEST DETAILS!... ;CHOKE!; BUT NOTHING'S STIRRING! IT'S LIKE A... GHOST-TOWN! AN EMPTY... TOMB!
IT DOESN'T HAVE TO BE! WE CAN BUILD... HUMAN ANDROIDS!
8

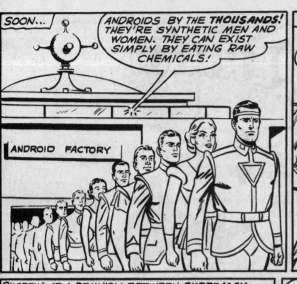

SOON... ANDROIDS BY THE *THOUSANDS!* THEY'RE SYNTHETIC MEN AND WOMEN. THEY CAN EXIST SIMPLY BY EATING RAW CHEMICALS!

ANDROID FACTORY

LATER... ¿GASP!¿... IT'S... STARTING!

KRYPTON LIVES AGAIN!!

GOLLY!

SHORTLY, AT A REUNION BETWEEN *SUPERMAN, SUPERGIRL* AND ROBOT IMITATIONS OF THEIR PARENTS...

MY SON, MY SON!

KARA... DAUGHTER!

DADDY!

I'M SO HAPPY!...¿CHOKE!¿ IF ONLY THESE ANDROIDS WERE REAL PEOPLE, AND *KRYPTON* HADN'T PERISHED!

LATER, AS THE SUPER-TRIO PREPARES TO LEAVE... CREATING A *MEMORIAL PLANET* WAS A BEAUTIFUL IDEA, *SUPERMAN!*

I'VE LOVED EVERY MINUTE OF IT HERE!

THEN, AS THEY STREAK BACK TOWARD EARTH... WE'LL RETURN HERE EACH YEAR, ON THE ANNIVERSARY OF THE DEATH OF *KRYPTON!*

'TIL WE MEET AGAIN!

The End.

9

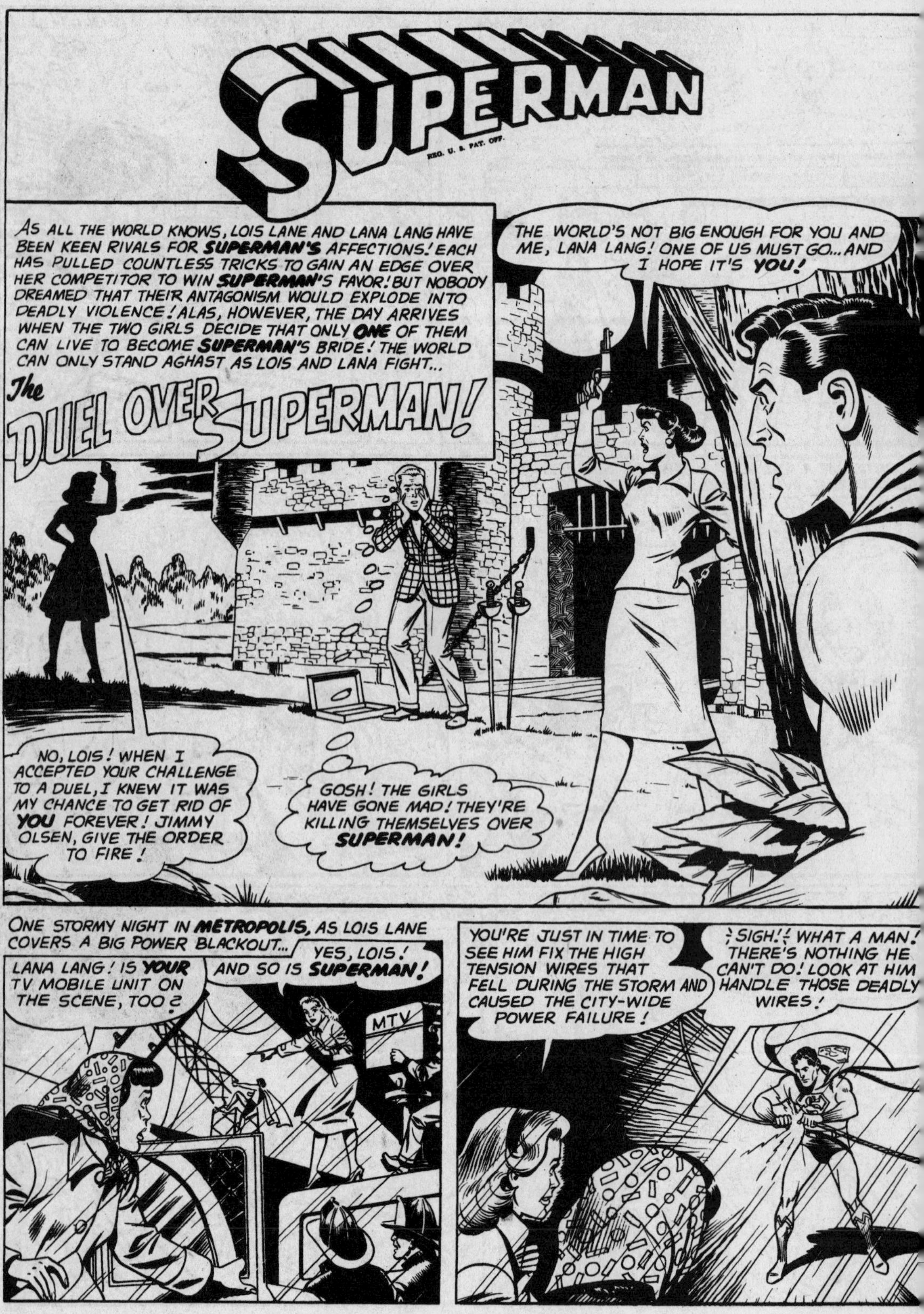
SUPERMAN
REG. U. S. PAT. OFF.
AS ALL THE WORLD KNOWS, LOIS LANE AND LANA LANG HAVE BEEN KEEN RIVALS FOR SUPERMAN'S AFFECTIONS! EACH HAS PULLED COUNTLESS TRICKS TO GAIN AN EDGE OVER HER COMPETITOR TO WIN SUPERMAN'S FAVOR! BUT NOBODY DREAMED THAT THEIR ANTAGONISM WOULD EXPLODE INTO DEADLY VIOLENCE! ALAS, HOWEVER, THE DAY ARRIVES WHEN THE TWO GIRLS DECIDE THAT ONLY ONE OF THEM CAN LIVE TO BECOME SUPERMAN'S BRIDE! THE WORLD CAN ONLY STAND AGHAST AS LOIS AND LANA FIGHT...
The DUEL OVER SUPERMAN!
THE WORLD'S NOT BIG ENOUGH FOR YOU AND ME, LANA LANG! ONE OF US MUST GO... AND I HOPE IT'S YOU!
NO, LOIS! WHEN I ACCEPTED YOUR CHALLENGE TO A DUEL, I KNEW IT WAS MY CHANCE TO GET RID OF YOU FOREVER! JIMMY OLSEN, GIVE THE ORDER TO FIRE!
GOSH! THE GIRLS HAVE GONE MAD! THEY'RE KILLING THEMSELVES OVER SUPERMAN!
ONE STORMY NIGHT IN METROPOLIS, AS LOIS LANE COVERS A BIG POWER BLACKOUT...
LANA LANG! IS YOUR TV MOBILE UNIT ON THE SCENE, TOO?
YES, LOIS! AND SO IS SUPERMAN!
MTV
YOU'RE JUST IN TIME TO SEE HIM FIX THE HIGH TENSION WIRES THAT FELL DURING THE STORM AND CAUSED THE CITY-WIDE POWER FAILURE!
SIGH! WHAT A MAN! THERE'S NOTHING HE CAN'T DO! LOOK AT HIM HANDLE THOSE DEADLY WIRES!

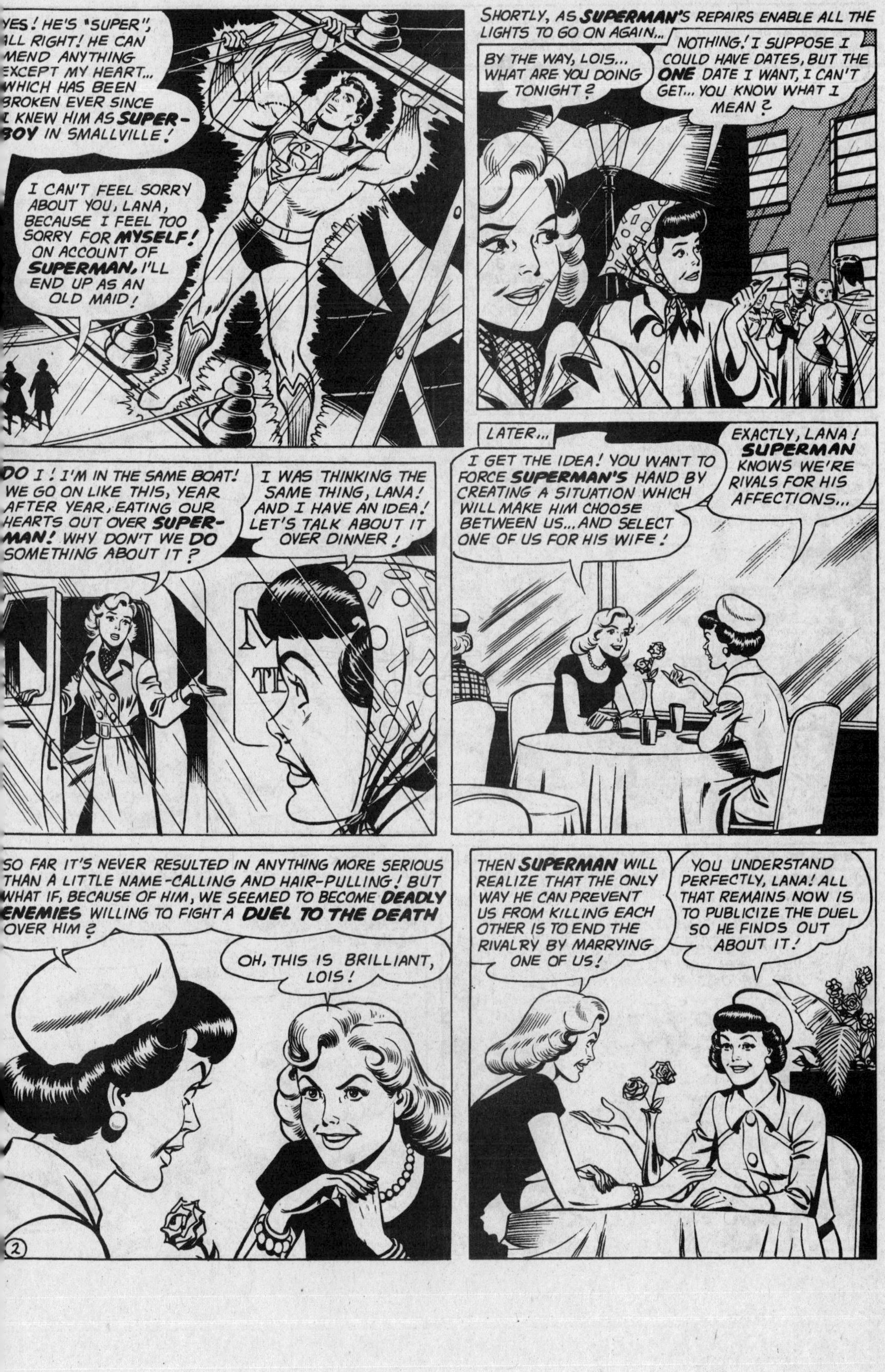
YES! HE'S "SUPER", ALL RIGHT! HE CAN MEND ANYTHING EXCEPT MY HEART... WHICH HAS BEEN BROKEN EVER SINCE I KNEW HIM AS SUPERBOY IN SMALLVILLE!
I CAN'T FEEL SORRY ABOUT YOU, LANA, BECAUSE I FEEL TOO SORRY FOR MYSELF! ON ACCOUNT OF SUPERMAN, I'LL END UP AS AN OLD MAID!
SHORTLY, AS SUPERMAN'S REPAIRS ENABLE ALL THE LIGHTS TO GO ON AGAIN...
BY THE WAY, LOIS... WHAT ARE YOU DOING TONIGHT?
NOTHING! I SUPPOSE I COULD HAVE DATES, BUT THE ONE DATE I WANT, I CAN'T GET... YOU KNOW WHAT I MEAN?
DO I! I'M IN THE SAME BOAT! WE GO ON LIKE THIS, YEAR AFTER YEAR, EATING OUR HEARTS OUT OVER SUPERMAN! WHY DON'T WE DO SOMETHING ABOUT IT?
I WAS THINKING THE SAME THING, LANA! AND I HAVE AN IDEA! LET'S TALK ABOUT IT OVER DINNER!
LATER...
I GET THE IDEA! YOU WANT TO FORCE SUPERMAN'S HAND BY CREATING A SITUATION WHICH WILL MAKE HIM CHOOSE BETWEEN US... AND SELECT ONE OF US FOR HIS WIFE!
EXACTLY, LANA! SUPERMAN KNOWS WE'RE RIVALS FOR HIS AFFECTIONS...
SO FAR IT'S NEVER RESULTED IN ANYTHING MORE SERIOUS THAN A LITTLE NAME-CALLING AND HAIR-PULLING! BUT WHAT IF, BECAUSE OF HIM, WE SEEMED TO BECOME DEADLY ENEMIES WILLING TO FIGHT A DUEL TO THE DEATH OVER HIM?
OH, THIS IS BRILLIANT, LOIS!
2
THEN SUPERMAN WILL REALIZE THAT THE ONLY WAY HE CAN PREVENT US FROM KILLING EACH OTHER IS TO END THE RIVALRY BY MARRYING ONE OF US!
YOU UNDERSTAND PERFECTLY, LANA! ALL THAT REMAINS NOW IS TO PUBLICIZE THE DUEL SO HE FINDS OUT ABOUT IT!

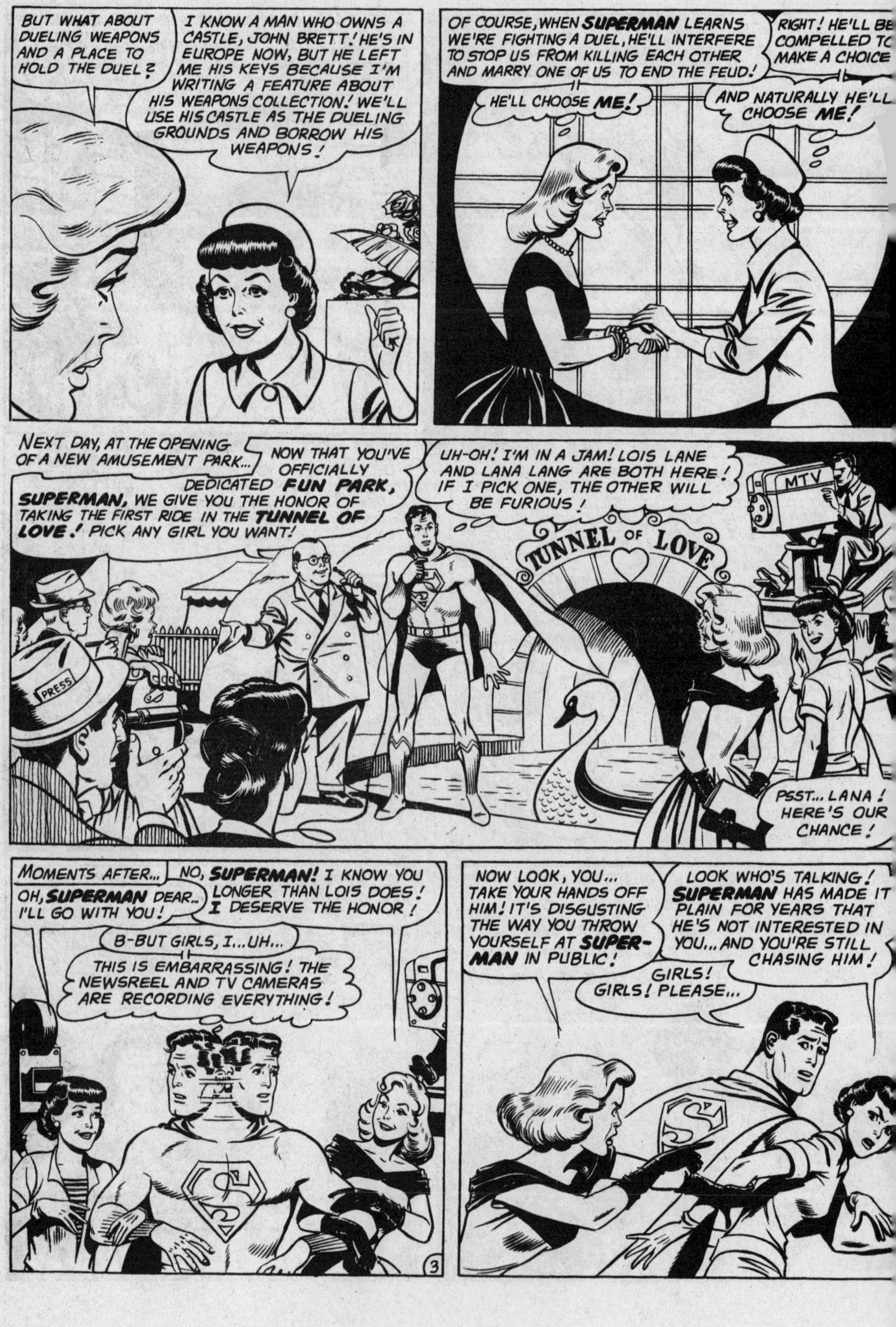
BUT WHAT ABOUT DUELING WEAPONS AND A PLACE TO HOLD THE DUEL?
I KNOW A MAN WHO OWNS A CASTLE, JOHN BRETT! HE'S IN EUROPE NOW, BUT HE LEFT ME HIS KEYS BECAUSE I'M WRITING A FEATURE ABOUT HIS WEAPONS COLLECTION! WE'LL USE HIS CASTLE AS THE DUELING GROUNDS AND BORROW HIS WEAPONS!
OF COURSE, WHEN SUPERMAN LEARNS WE'RE FIGHTING A DUEL, HE'LL INTERFERE TO STOP US FROM KILLING EACH OTHER AND MARRY ONE OF US TO END THE FEUD!
RIGHT! HE'LL BE COMPELLED TO MAKE A CHOICE
HE'LL CHOOSE ME!
AND NATURALLY HE'LL CHOOSE ME!
NEXT DAY, AT THE OPENING OF A NEW AMUSEMENT PARK...
NOW THAT YOU'VE OFFICIALLY DEDICATED FUN PARK, SUPERMAN, WE GIVE YOU THE HONOR OF TAKING THE FIRST RIDE IN THE TUNNEL OF LOVE! PICK ANY GIRL YOU WANT!
UH-OH! I'M IN A JAM! LOIS LANE AND LANA LANG ARE BOTH HERE! IF I PICK ONE, THE OTHER WILL BE FURIOUS!
MTV
TUNNEL OF LOVE
PRESS
PSST... LANA! HERE'S OUR CHANCE!
MOMENTS AFTER...
OH, SUPERMAN DEAR... I'LL GO WITH YOU!
NO, SUPERMAN! I KNOW YOU LONGER THAN LOIS DOES! I DESERVE THE HONOR!
B-BUT GIRLS, I...UH...
THIS IS EMBARRASSING! THE NEWSREEL AND TV CAMERAS ARE RECORDING EVERYTHING!
3
NOW LOOK, YOU... TAKE YOUR HANDS OFF HIM! IT'S DISGUSTING THE WAY YOU THROW YOURSELF AT SUPERMAN IN PUBLIC!
LOOK WHO'S TALKING! SUPERMAN HAS MADE IT PLAIN FOR YEARS THAT HE'S NOT INTERESTED IN YOU...AND YOU'RE STILL CHASING HIM!
GIRLS! GIRLS! PLEASE...

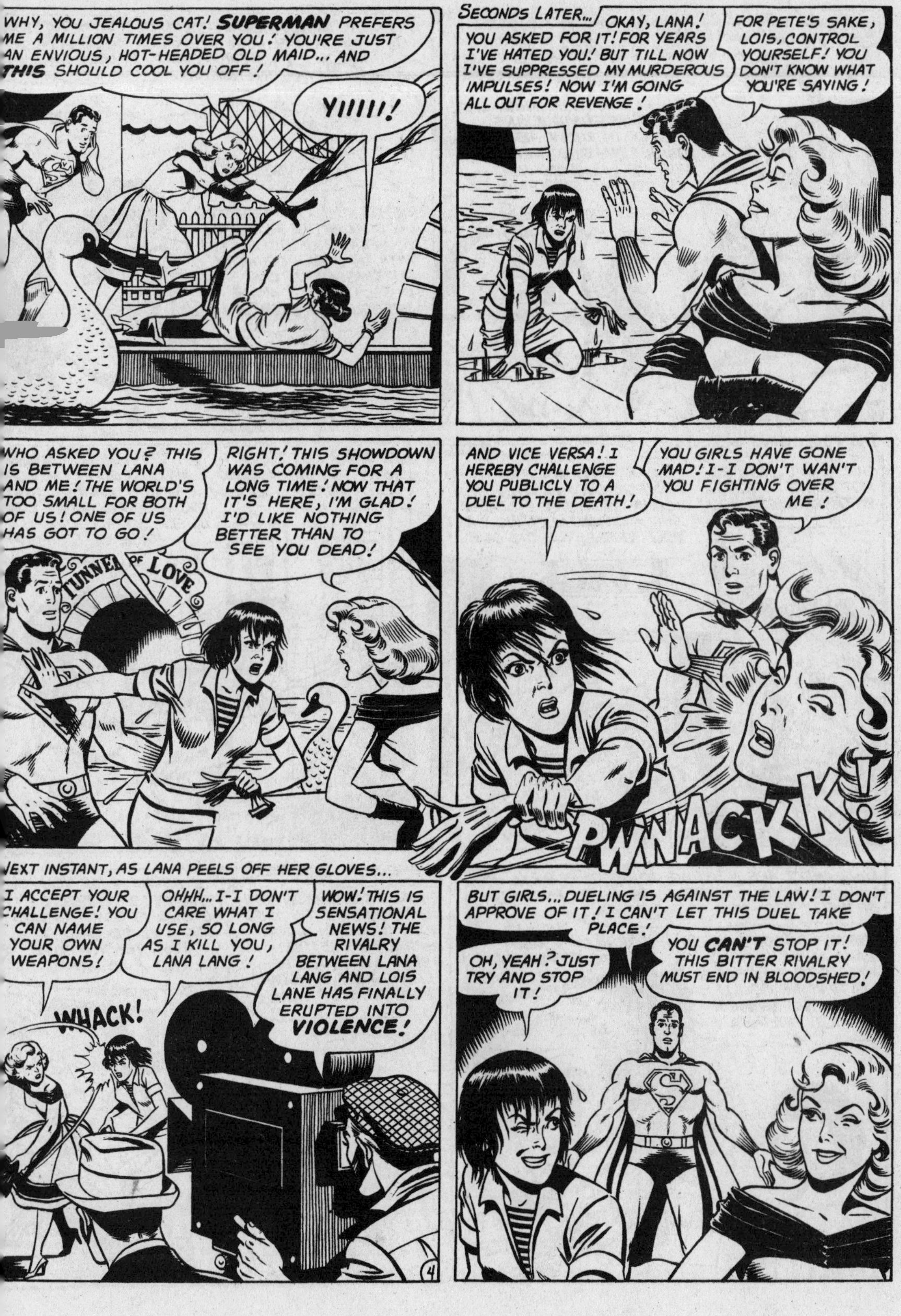
WHY, YOU JEALOUS CAT! SUPERMAN PREFERS ME A MILLION TIMES OVER YOU! YOU'RE JUST AN ENVIOUS, HOT-HEADED OLD MAID... AND THIS SHOULD COOL YOU OFF!
YIIIII!
SECONDS LATER...
OKAY, LANA! YOU ASKED FOR IT! FOR YEARS I'VE HATED YOU! BUT TILL NOW I'VE SUPPRESSED MY MURDEROUS IMPULSES! NOW I'M GOING ALL OUT FOR REVENGE!
FOR PETE'S SAKE, LOIS, CONTROL YOURSELF! YOU DON'T KNOW WHAT YOU'RE SAYING!
WHO ASKED YOU? THIS IS BETWEEN LANA AND ME! THE WORLD'S TOO SMALL FOR BOTH OF US! ONE OF US HAS GOT TO GO!
RIGHT! THIS SHOWDOWN WAS COMING FOR A LONG TIME! NOW THAT IT'S HERE, I'M GLAD! I'D LIKE NOTHING BETTER THAN TO SEE YOU DEAD!
TUNNEL OF LOVE
AND VICE VERSA! I HEREBY CHALLENGE YOU PUBLICLY TO A DUEL TO THE DEATH!
YOU GIRLS HAVE GONE MAD! I-I DON'T WAN'T YOU FIGHTING OVER ME!
PWNACKK!
NEXT INSTANT, AS LANA PEELS OFF HER GLOVES...
I ACCEPT YOUR CHALLENGE! YOU CAN NAME YOUR OWN WEAPONS!
OHHH... I-I DON'T CARE WHAT I USE, SO LONG AS I KILL YOU, LANA LANG!
WOW! THIS IS SENSATIONAL NEWS! THE RIVALRY BETWEEN LANA LANG AND LOIS LANE HAS FINALLY ERUPTED INTO VIOLENCE!
WHACK!
4
BUT GIRLS... DUELING IS AGAINST THE LAW! I DON'T APPROVE OF IT! I CAN'T LET THIS DUEL TAKE PLACE!
OH, YEAH? JUST TRY AND STOP IT!
YOU CAN'T STOP IT! THIS BITTER RIVALRY MUST END IN BLOODSHED!

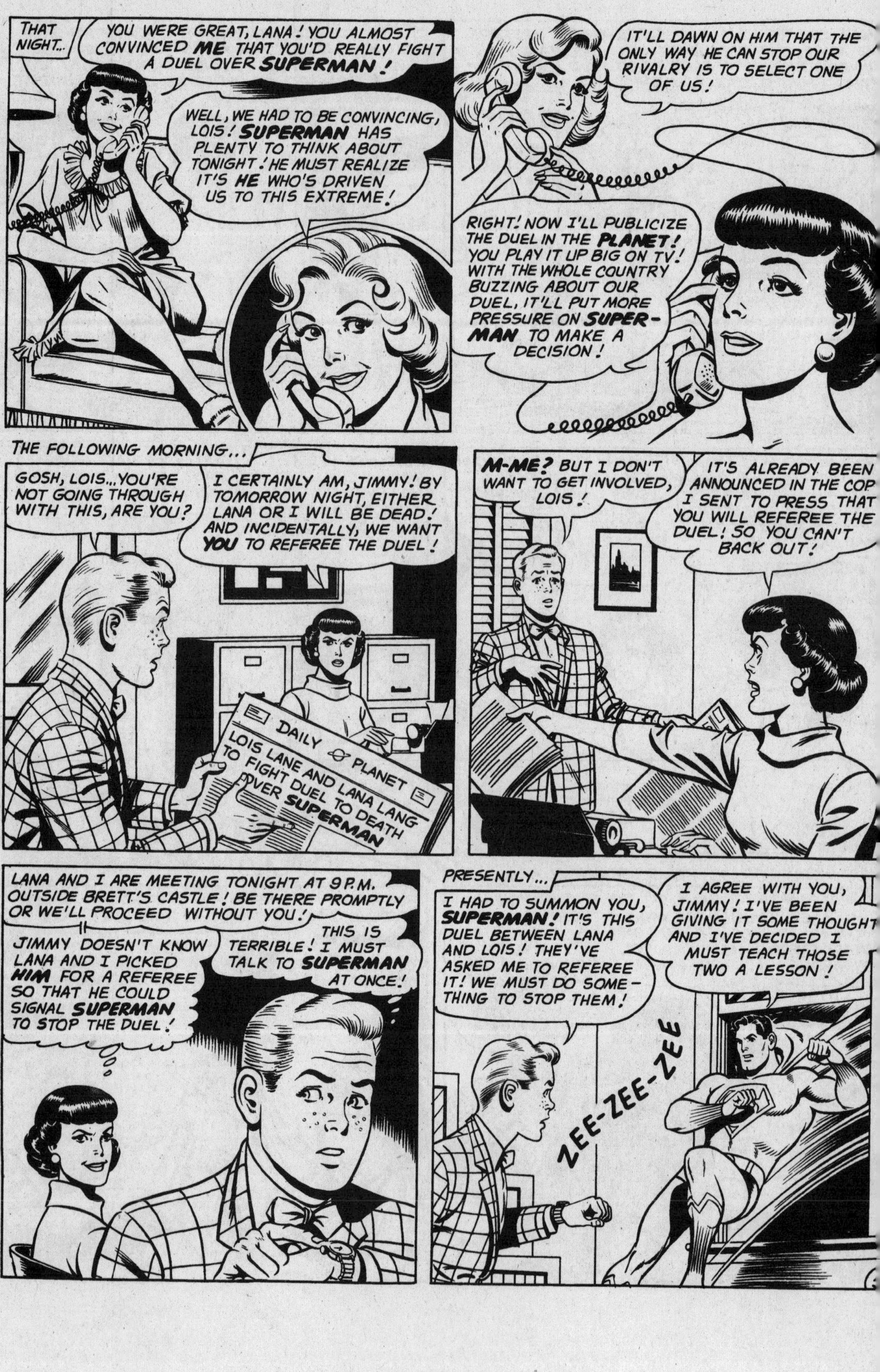
THAT NIGHT...
YOU WERE GREAT, LANA! YOU ALMOST CONVINCED ME THAT YOU'D REALLY FIGHT A DUEL OVER SUPERMAN!
WELL, WE HAD TO BE CONVINCING, LOIS! SUPERMAN HAS PLENTY TO THINK ABOUT TONIGHT! HE MUST REALIZE IT'S HE WHO'S DRIVEN US TO THIS EXTREME!
IT'LL DAWN ON HIM THAT THE ONLY WAY HE CAN STOP OUR RIVALRY IS TO SELECT ONE OF US!
RIGHT! NOW I'LL PUBLICIZE THE DUEL IN THE PLANET! YOU PLAY IT UP BIG ON TV! WITH THE WHOLE COUNTRY BUZZING ABOUT OUR DUEL, IT'LL PUT MORE PRESSURE ON SUPER-MAN TO MAKE A DECISION!
THE FOLLOWING MORNING...
GOSH, LOIS...YOU'RE NOT GOING THROUGH WITH THIS, ARE YOU?
I CERTAINLY AM, JIMMY! BY TOMORROW NIGHT, EITHER LANA OR I WILL BE DEAD! AND INCIDENTALLY, WE WANT YOU TO REFEREE THE DUEL!
DAILY PLANET
LOIS LANE AND LANA LANG TO FIGHT DUEL TO DEATH OVER SUPERMAN
M-ME? BUT I DON'T WANT TO GET INVOLVED, LOIS!
IT'S ALREADY BEEN ANNOUNCED IN THE COPY I SENT TO PRESS THAT YOU WILL REFEREE THE DUEL! SO YOU CAN'T BACK OUT!
LANA AND I ARE MEETING TONIGHT AT 9 P.M. OUTSIDE BRETT'S CASTLE! BE THERE PROMPTLY OR WE'LL PROCEED WITHOUT YOU!
JIMMY DOESN'T KNOW LANA AND I PICKED HIM FOR A REFEREE SO THAT HE COULD SIGNAL SUPERMAN TO STOP THE DUEL!
THIS IS TERRIBLE! I MUST TALK TO SUPERMAN AT ONCE!
PRESENTLY...
I HAD TO SUMMON YOU, SUPERMAN! IT'S THIS DUEL BETWEEN LANA AND LOIS! THEY'VE ASKED ME TO REFEREE IT! WE MUST DO SOME-THING TO STOP THEM!
I AGREE WITH YOU, JIMMY! I'VE BEEN GIVING IT SOME THOUGHT AND I'VE DECIDED I MUST TEACH THOSE TWO A LESSON!
ZEE-ZEE-ZEE

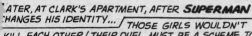

LATER, AT CLARK'S APARTMENT, AFTER **SUPERMAN** CHANGES HIS IDENTITY...

THOSE GIRLS WOULDN'T KILL EACH OTHER! THEIR DUEL MUST BE A SCHEME TO MAKE ME FEEL RESPONSIBLE FOR THEIR FEUD, SO THAT I'LL END THEIR RIVALRY BY MARRYING ONE OF THEM! BUT I'LL SURPRISE THEM BY USING THESE **TWO ROBOTS** I BUILT!

THAT NIGHT, AS LANA ARRIVES AT BRETT CASTLE...

HMM...I'LL EXPLORE THE DUNGEONS BEFORE I MEET LOIS! THEN... ¿GASP!¿ ...THE DOOR HAS SWUNG SHUT!

THIS IS MY CHANCE TO TRAP LANA SO THAT MY **LANA LANG ROBOT** CAN SUBSTITUTE FOR HER IN THE DUEL. LANA CAN SCREAM HER HEAD OFF HERE AND NOT BE HEARD!

SLAMMM!

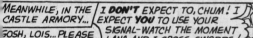

MEANWHILE, IN THE CASTLE ARMORY...

GOSH, LOIS...PLEASE DON'T GO THROUGH WITH THIS DUEL!

I **DON'T** EXPECT TO, CHUM! I EXPECT **YOU** TO USE YOUR SIGNAL-WATCH THE MOMENT LANA AND I CROSS SWORDS!

SORRY, JIMMY! MY QUARREL WITH LANA CAN ONLY BE SETTLED THE HARD WAY!

SHORTLY, OUTSIDE...

AH, LANA! THERE YOU ARE! TAKE YOUR CHOICE OF WEAPONS! PISTOL OR SWORD?

SWORD! AND LET'S BEGIN FIGHTING AT ONCE!

HA! MY **LANA ROBOT** IS DOING A SWELL ACTING JOB! NEITHER JIMMY NOR LOIS REALIZE SHE'S JUST A MACHINE!

SOON, AS THE DUEL BEGINS...

EN GARDE!

EN GARDE, NOTHING! START PRAYING, YOU HUSSY!

6

WHAT'S WRONG WITH JIMMY? WHY DOESN'T HE SIGNAL **SUPERMAN?** THIS WHOLE SCHEME DEPENDS ON **SUPERMAN'S** SHOWING UP TO STOP THIS DUEL!

GOLLY! I HOPE **SUPERMAN** SHOWS UP FAST! THESE CRAZY GALS ARE LIABLE TO KILL EACH OTHER!

CLANNG!

PWANNNG!

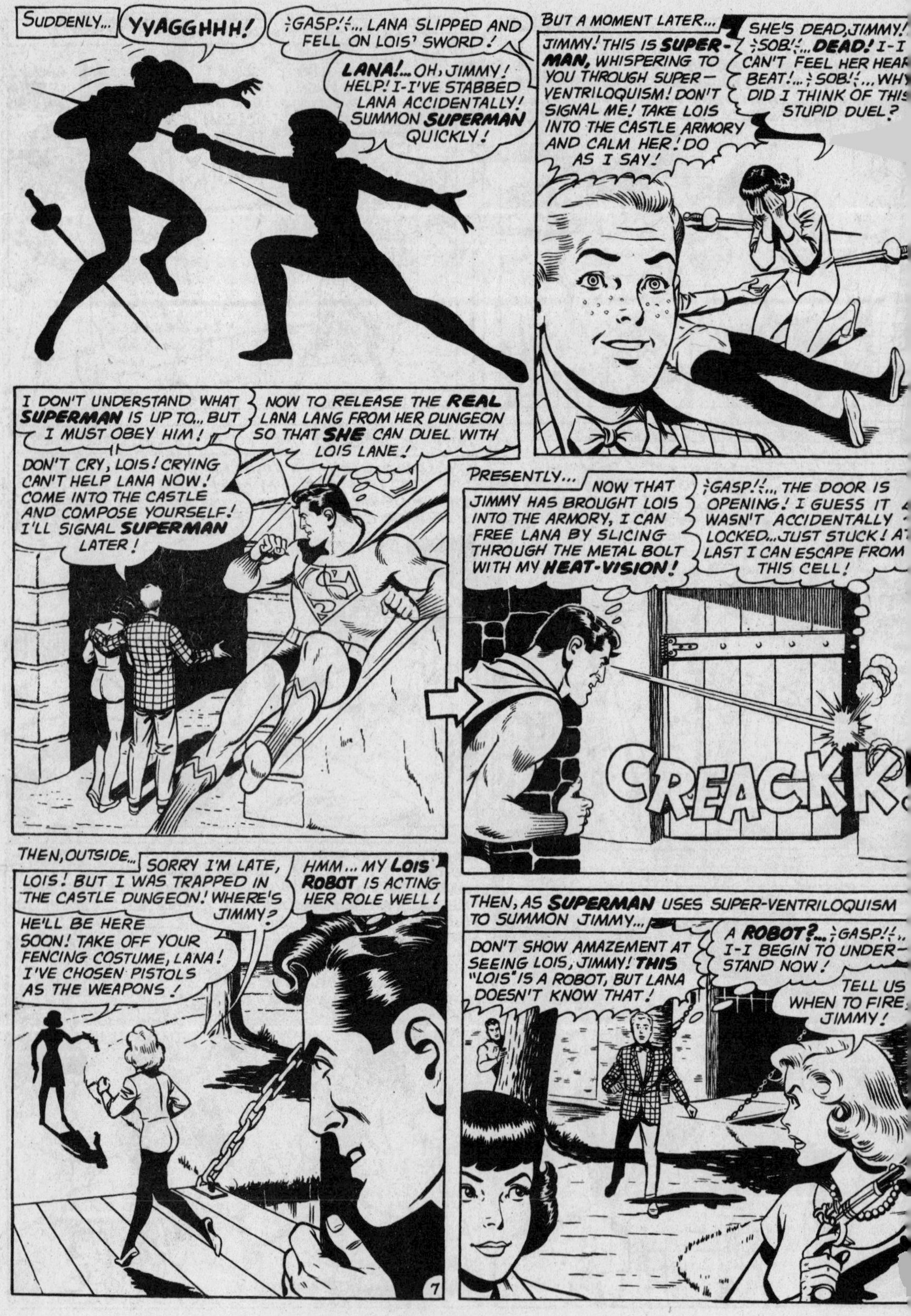
SUDDENLY...
YYAGGHHH!
¡GASP!¡... LANA SLIPPED AND FELL ON LOIS' SWORD!
LANA!... OH, JIMMY! HELP! I-I'VE STABBED LANA ACCIDENTALLY! SUMMON SUPERMAN QUICKLY!
BUT A MOMENT LATER...
JIMMY! THIS IS SUPERMAN, WHISPERING TO YOU THROUGH SUPER-VENTRILOQUISM! DON'T SIGNAL ME! TAKE LOIS INTO THE CASTLE ARMORY AND CALM HER! DO AS I SAY!
SHE'S DEAD, JIMMY! ¡SOB!¡... DEAD! I-I CAN'T FEEL HER HEAR BEAT!... ¡SOB!¡... WHY DID I THINK OF THIS STUPID DUEL?
I DON'T UNDERSTAND WHAT SUPERMAN IS UP TO... BUT I MUST OBEY HIM!
NOW TO RELEASE THE REAL LANA LANG FROM HER DUNGEON SO THAT SHE CAN DUEL WITH LOIS LANE!
DON'T CRY, LOIS! CRYING CAN'T HELP LANA NOW! COME INTO THE CASTLE AND COMPOSE YOURSELF! I'LL SIGNAL SUPERMAN LATER!
PRESENTLY...
NOW THAT JIMMY HAS BROUGHT LOIS INTO THE ARMORY, I CAN FREE LANA BY SLICING THROUGH THE METAL BOLT WITH MY HEAT-VISION!
¡GASP!¡... THE DOOR IS OPENING! I GUESS IT WASN'T ACCIDENTALLY LOCKED... JUST STUCK! AT LAST I CAN ESCAPE FROM THIS CELL!
CREACKK!
THEN, OUTSIDE...
SORRY I'M LATE, LOIS! BUT I WAS TRAPPED IN THE CASTLE DUNGEON! WHERE'S JIMMY?
HMM... MY LOIS ROBOT IS ACTING HER ROLE WELL!
HE'LL BE HERE SOON! TAKE OFF YOUR FENCING COSTUME, LANA! I'VE CHOSEN PISTOLS AS THE WEAPONS!
7
THEN, AS SUPERMAN USES SUPER-VENTRILOQUISM TO SUMMON JIMMY...
DON'T SHOW AMAZEMENT AT SEEING LOIS, JIMMY! THIS "LOIS" IS A ROBOT, BUT LANA DOESN'T KNOW THAT!
A ROBOT?... ¡GASP!¡... I-I BEGIN TO UNDERSTAND NOW!
TELL US WHEN TO FIRE, JIMMY!

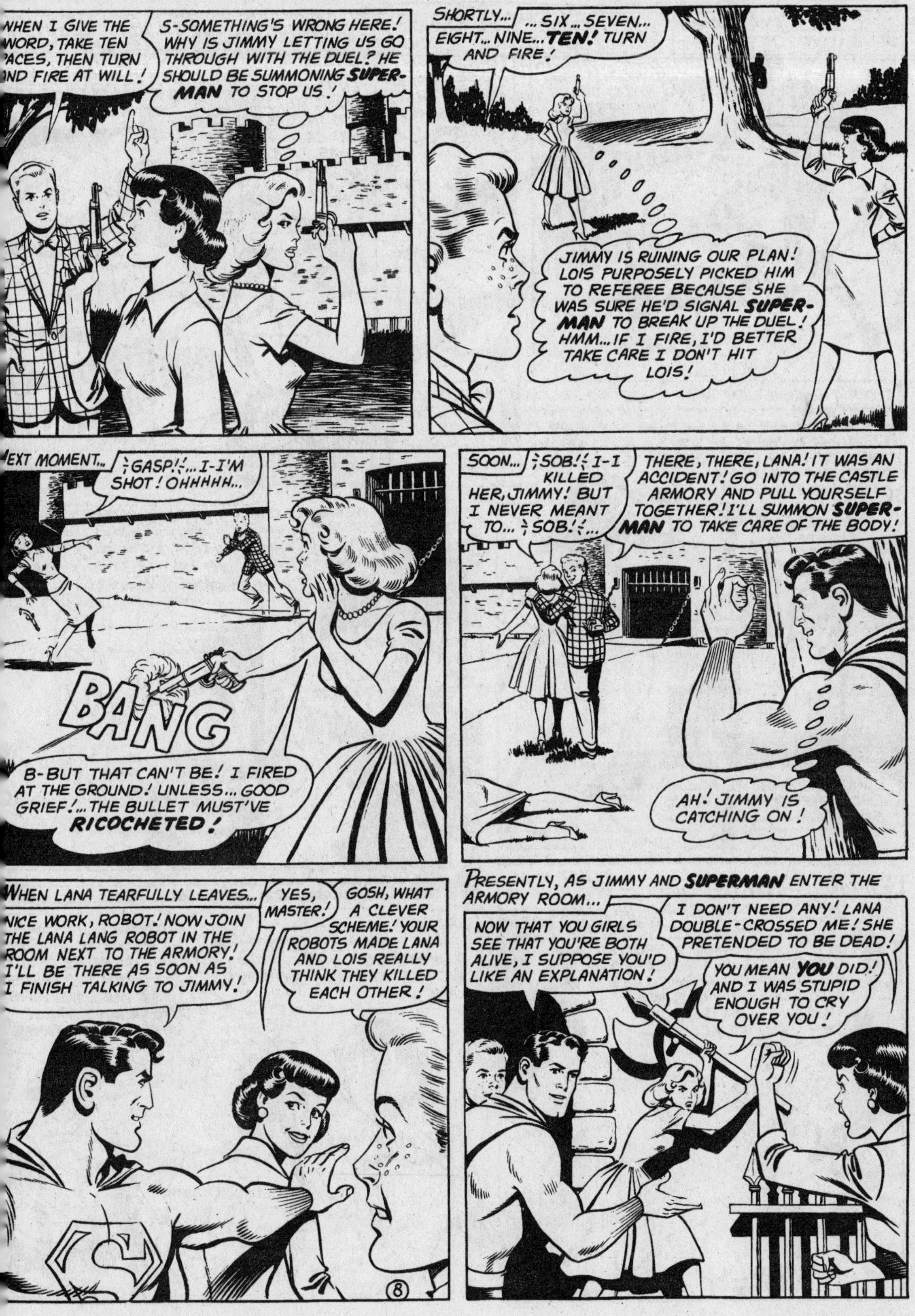
WHEN I GIVE THE WORD, TAKE TEN PACES, THEN TURN AND FIRE AT WILL!
S-SOMETHING'S WRONG HERE! WHY IS JIMMY LETTING US GO THROUGH WITH THE DUEL? HE SHOULD BE SUMMONING SUPERMAN TO STOP US!
SHORTLY...
...SIX...SEVEN... EIGHT...NINE...TEN! TURN AND FIRE!
JIMMY IS RUINING OUR PLAN! LOIS PURPOSELY PICKED HIM TO REFEREE BECAUSE SHE WAS SURE HE'D SIGNAL SUPERMAN TO BREAK UP THE DUEL! HMM...IF I FIRE, I'D BETTER TAKE CARE I DON'T HIT LOIS!
NEXT MOMENT...
GASP!...I-I'M SHOT! OHHHHH...
BANG
B-BUT THAT CAN'T BE! I FIRED AT THE GROUND! UNLESS...GOOD GRIEF!...THE BULLET MUST'VE RICOCHETED!
SOON...
SOB! I-I KILLED HER, JIMMY! BUT I NEVER MEANT TO... SOB!...
THERE, THERE, LANA! IT WAS AN ACCIDENT! GO INTO THE CASTLE ARMORY AND PULL YOURSELF TOGETHER! I'LL SUMMON SUPERMAN TO TAKE CARE OF THE BODY!
AH! JIMMY IS CATCHING ON!
WHEN LANA TEARFULLY LEAVES...
NICE WORK, ROBOT! NOW JOIN THE LANA LANG ROBOT IN THE ROOM NEXT TO THE ARMORY! I'LL BE THERE AS SOON AS I FINISH TALKING TO JIMMY!
YES, MASTER!
GOSH, WHAT A CLEVER SCHEME! YOUR ROBOTS MADE LANA AND LOIS REALLY THINK THEY KILLED EACH OTHER!
8
PRESENTLY, AS JIMMY AND SUPERMAN ENTER THE ARMORY ROOM...
NOW THAT YOU GIRLS SEE THAT YOU'RE BOTH ALIVE, I SUPPOSE YOU'D LIKE AN EXPLANATION!
I DON'T NEED ANY! LANA DOUBLE-CROSSED ME! SHE PRETENDED TO BE DEAD!
YOU MEAN YOU DID! AND I WAS STUPID ENOUGH TO CRY OVER YOU!

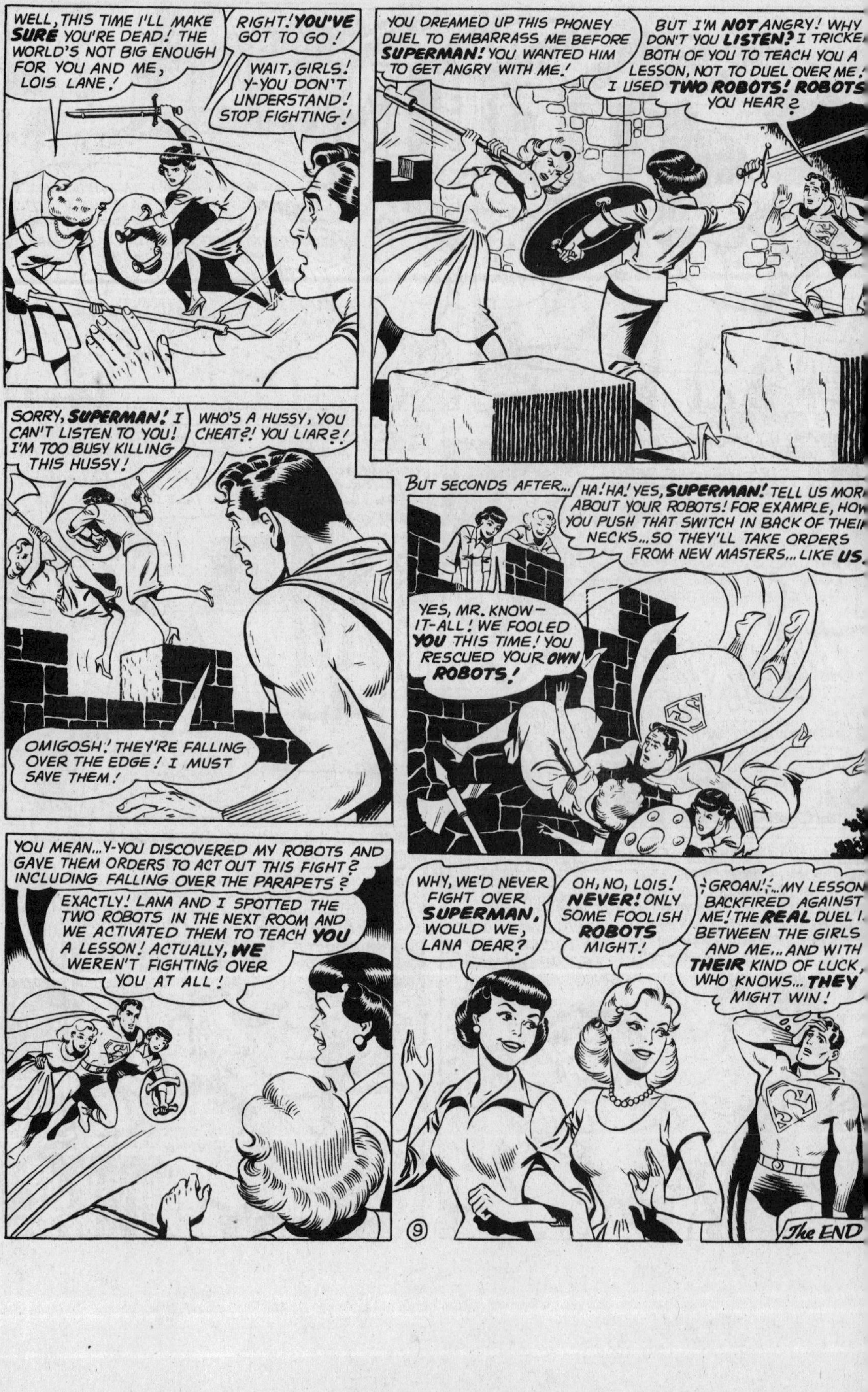
WELL, THIS TIME I'LL MAKE SURE YOU'RE DEAD! THE WORLD'S NOT BIG ENOUGH FOR YOU AND ME, LOIS LANE!
RIGHT! YOU'VE GOT TO GO!
WAIT, GIRLS! Y-YOU DON'T UNDERSTAND! STOP FIGHTING!
YOU DREAMED UP THIS PHONEY DUEL TO EMBARRASS ME BEFORE SUPERMAN! YOU WANTED HIM TO GET ANGRY WITH ME!
BUT I'M NOT ANGRY! WHY DON'T YOU LISTEN? I TRICKE BOTH OF YOU TO TEACH YOU A LESSON, NOT TO DUEL OVER ME! I USED TWO ROBOTS! ROBOTS YOU HEAR?
SORRY, SUPERMAN! I CAN'T LISTEN TO YOU! I'M TOO BUSY KILLING THIS HUSSY!
WHO'S A HUSSY, YOU CHEAT?! YOU LIAR?!
OMIGOSH! THEY'RE FALLING OVER THE EDGE! I MUST SAVE THEM!
BUT SECONDS AFTER...
HA! HA! YES, SUPERMAN! TELL US MOR ABOUT YOUR ROBOTS! FOR EXAMPLE, HOW YOU PUSH THAT SWITCH IN BACK OF THEI NECKS...SO THEY'LL TAKE ORDERS FROM NEW MASTERS...LIKE US.
YES, MR. KNOW-IT-ALL! WE FOOLED YOU THIS TIME! YOU RESCUED YOUR OWN ROBOTS!
YOU MEAN...Y-YOU DISCOVERED MY ROBOTS AND GAVE THEM ORDERS TO ACT OUT THIS FIGHT? INCLUDING FALLING OVER THE PARAPETS?
EXACTLY! LANA AND I SPOTTED THE TWO ROBOTS IN THE NEXT ROOM AND WE ACTIVATED THEM TO TEACH YOU A LESSON! ACTUALLY, WE WEREN'T FIGHTING OVER YOU AT ALL!
WHY, WE'D NEVER FIGHT OVER SUPERMAN, WOULD WE, LANA DEAR?
OH, NO, LOIS! NEVER! ONLY SOME FOOLISH ROBOTS MIGHT!
GROAN!...MY LESSON BACKFIRED AGAINST ME! THE REAL DUEL I BETWEEN THE GIRLS AND ME...AND WITH THEIR KIND OF LUCK, WHO KNOWS...THEY MIGHT WIN!
9
The END

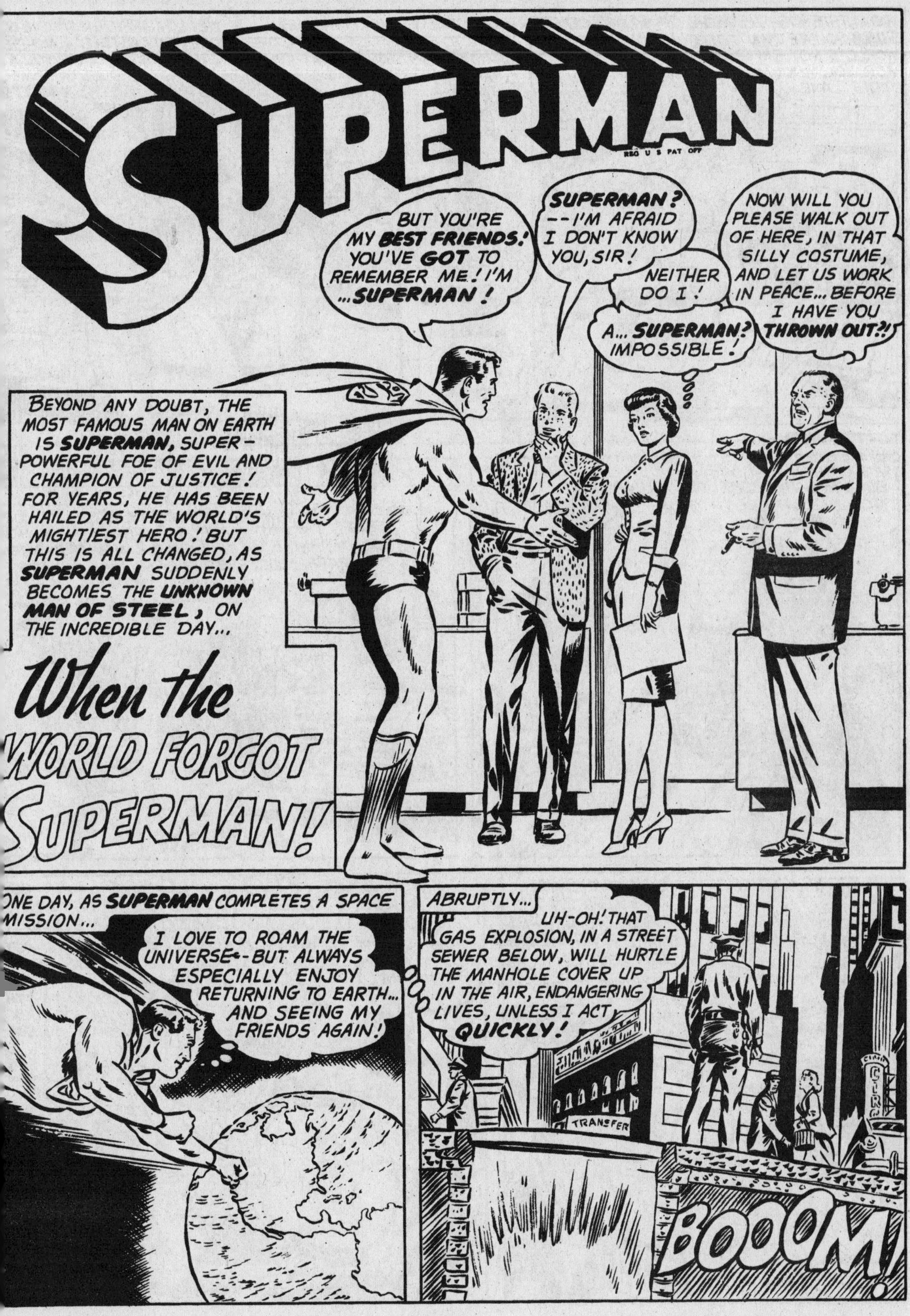
SUPERMAN
REG U S PAT OFF
BUT YOU'RE MY BEST FRIENDS! YOU'VE GOT TO REMEMBER ME! I'M ...SUPERMAN!
SUPERMAN? --I'M AFRAID I DON'T KNOW YOU, SIR!
NEITHER DO I!
A... SUPERMAN? IMPOSSIBLE!
NOW WILL YOU PLEASE WALK OUT OF HERE, IN THAT SILLY COSTUME, AND LET US WORK IN PEACE... BEFORE I HAVE YOU THROWN OUT?!
BEYOND ANY DOUBT, THE MOST FAMOUS MAN ON EARTH IS SUPERMAN, SUPER-POWERFUL FOE OF EVIL AND CHAMPION OF JUSTICE! FOR YEARS, HE HAS BEEN HAILED AS THE WORLD'S MIGHTIEST HERO! BUT THIS IS ALL CHANGED, AS SUPERMAN SUDDENLY BECOMES THE UNKNOWN MAN OF STEEL, ON THE INCREDIBLE DAY...
When the WORLD FORGOT SUPERMAN!
ONE DAY, AS SUPERMAN COMPLETES A SPACE MISSION...
I LOVE TO ROAM THE UNIVERSE--BUT ALWAYS ESPECIALLY ENJOY RETURNING TO EARTH... AND SEEING MY FRIENDS AGAIN!
ABRUPTLY...
UH-OH! THAT GAS EXPLOSION, IN A STREET SEWER BELOW, WILL HURTLE THE MANHOLE COVER UP IN THE AIR, ENDANGERING LIVES, UNLESS I ACT QUICKLY!
TRANSFER
BOOOM!

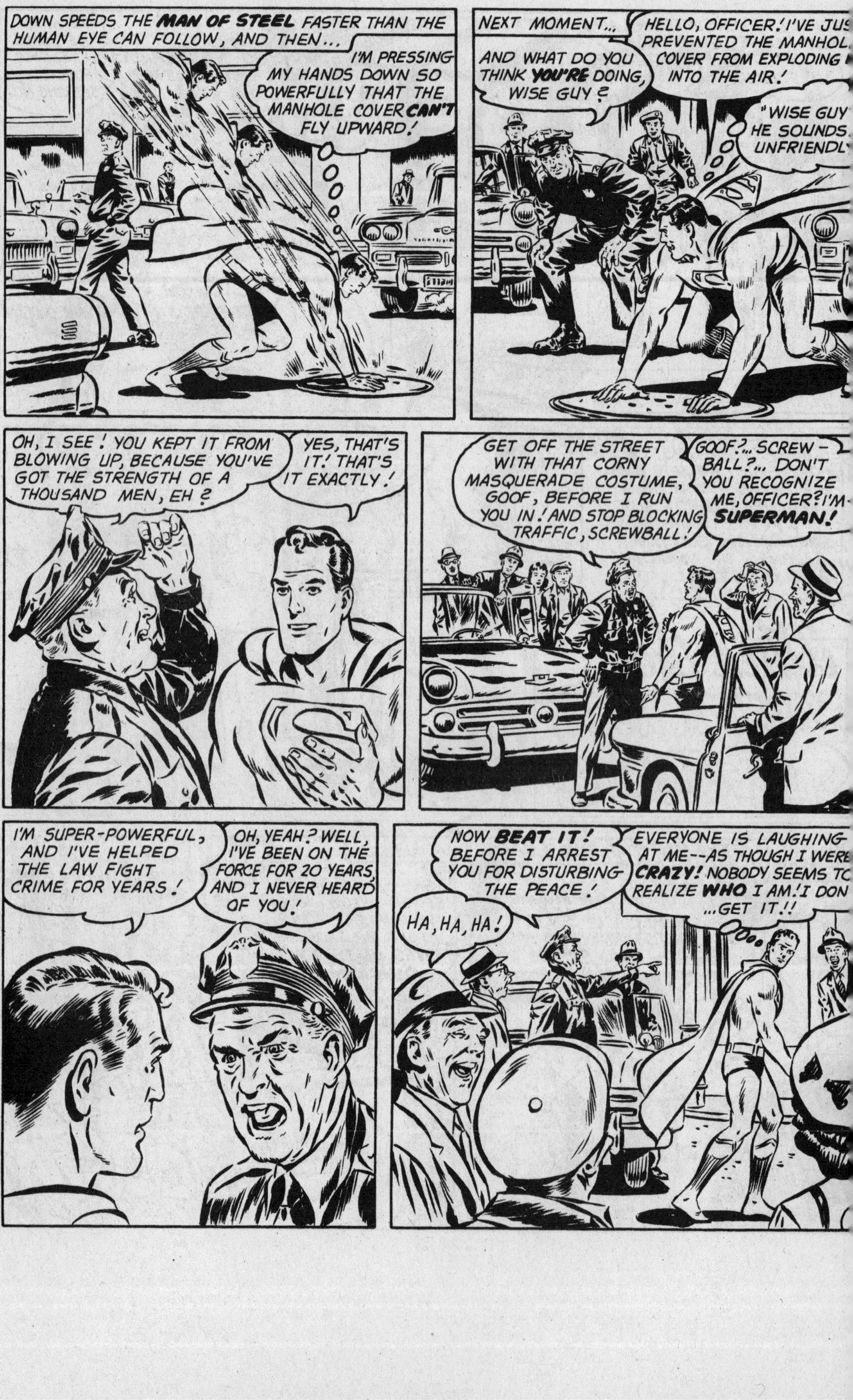
DOWN SPEEDS THE **MAN OF STEEL** FASTER THAN THE HUMAN EYE CAN FOLLOW, AND THEN...
I'M PRESSING MY HANDS DOWN SO POWERFULLY THAT THE MANHOLE COVER **CAN'T** FLY UPWARD!
NEXT MOMENT...
HELLO, OFFICER! I'VE JUS PREVENTED THE MANHOL COVER FROM EXPLODING INTO THE AIR!
AND WHAT DO YOU THINK **YOU'RE** DOING, WISE GUY?
"WISE GUY" HE SOUNDS. UNFRIENDL
OH, I SEE! YOU KEPT IT FROM BLOWING UP, BECAUSE YOU'VE GOT THE STRENGTH OF A THOUSAND MEN, EH?
YES, THAT'S IT! THAT'S IT EXACTLY!
GET OFF THE STREET WITH THAT CORNY MASQUERADE COSTUME, GOOF, BEFORE I RUN YOU IN! AND STOP BLOCKING TRAFFIC, SCREWBALL!
GOOF?... SCREW-BALL?... DON'T YOU RECOGNIZE ME, OFFICER? I'M **SUPERMAN!**
I'M SUPER-POWERFUL, AND I'VE HELPED THE LAW FIGHT CRIME FOR YEARS!
OH, YEAH? WELL, I'VE BEEN ON THE FORCE FOR 20 YEARS, AND I NEVER HEARD OF YOU!
NOW **BEAT IT!** BEFORE I ARREST YOU FOR DISTURBING THE PEACE!
HA, HA, HA!
EVERYONE IS LAUGHING AT ME--AS THOUGH I WERE **CRAZY!** NOBODY SEEMS TO REALIZE **WHO** I AM! I DON ...GET IT!!

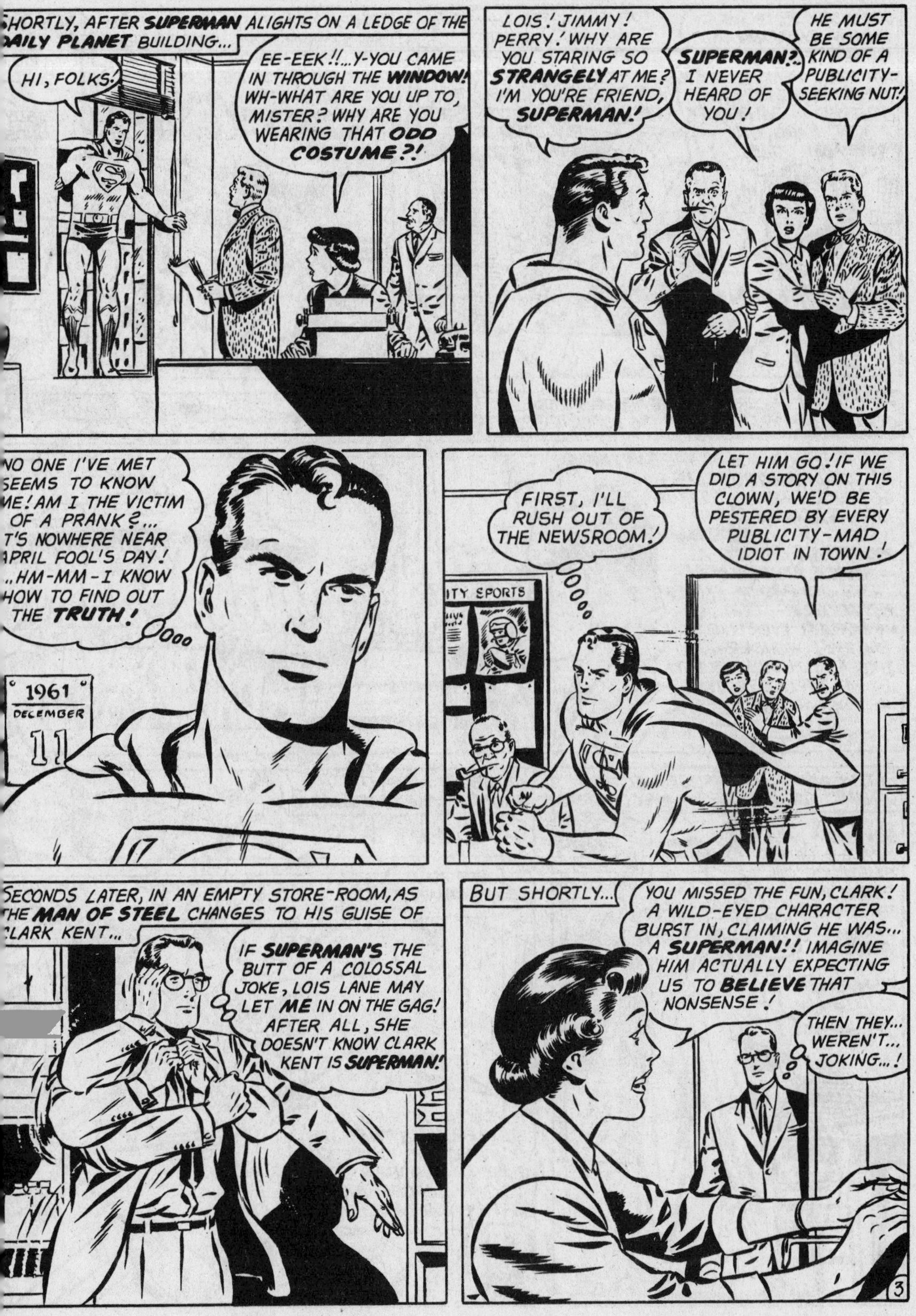
SHORTLY, AFTER SUPERMAN ALIGHTS ON A LEDGE OF THE DAILY PLANET BUILDING...
HI, FOLKS!
EE-EEK!!...Y-YOU CAME IN THROUGH THE WINDOW! WH-WHAT ARE YOU UP TO, MISTER? WHY ARE YOU WEARING THAT ODD COSTUME?!
LOIS! JIMMY! PERRY! WHY ARE YOU STARING SO STRANGELY AT ME? I'M YOU'RE FRIEND, SUPERMAN!
SUPERMAN?... I NEVER HEARD OF YOU!
HE MUST BE SOME KIND OF A PUBLICITY-SEEKING NUT!
NO ONE I'VE MET SEEMS TO KNOW ME! AM I THE VICTIM OF A PRANK?... IT'S NOWHERE NEAR APRIL FOOL'S DAY! ..HM-MM-I KNOW HOW TO FIND OUT THE TRUTH!
1961 DECEMBER 11
FIRST, I'LL RUSH OUT OF THE NEWSROOM!
LET HIM GO! IF WE DID A STORY ON THIS CLOWN, WE'D BE PESTERED BY EVERY PUBLICITY-MAD IDIOT IN TOWN!
ITY SPORTS
SECONDS LATER, IN AN EMPTY STORE-ROOM, AS THE MAN OF STEEL CHANGES TO HIS GUISE OF CLARK KENT...
IF SUPERMAN'S THE BUTT OF A COLOSSAL JOKE, LOIS LANE MAY LET ME IN ON THE GAG! AFTER ALL, SHE DOESN'T KNOW CLARK KENT IS SUPERMAN!
BUT SHORTLY...
YOU MISSED THE FUN, CLARK! A WILD-EYED CHARACTER BURST IN, CLAIMING HE WAS... A SUPERMAN!! IMAGINE HIM ACTUALLY EXPECTING US TO BELIEVE THAT NONSENSE!
THEN THEY... WEREN'T... JOKING...!
3

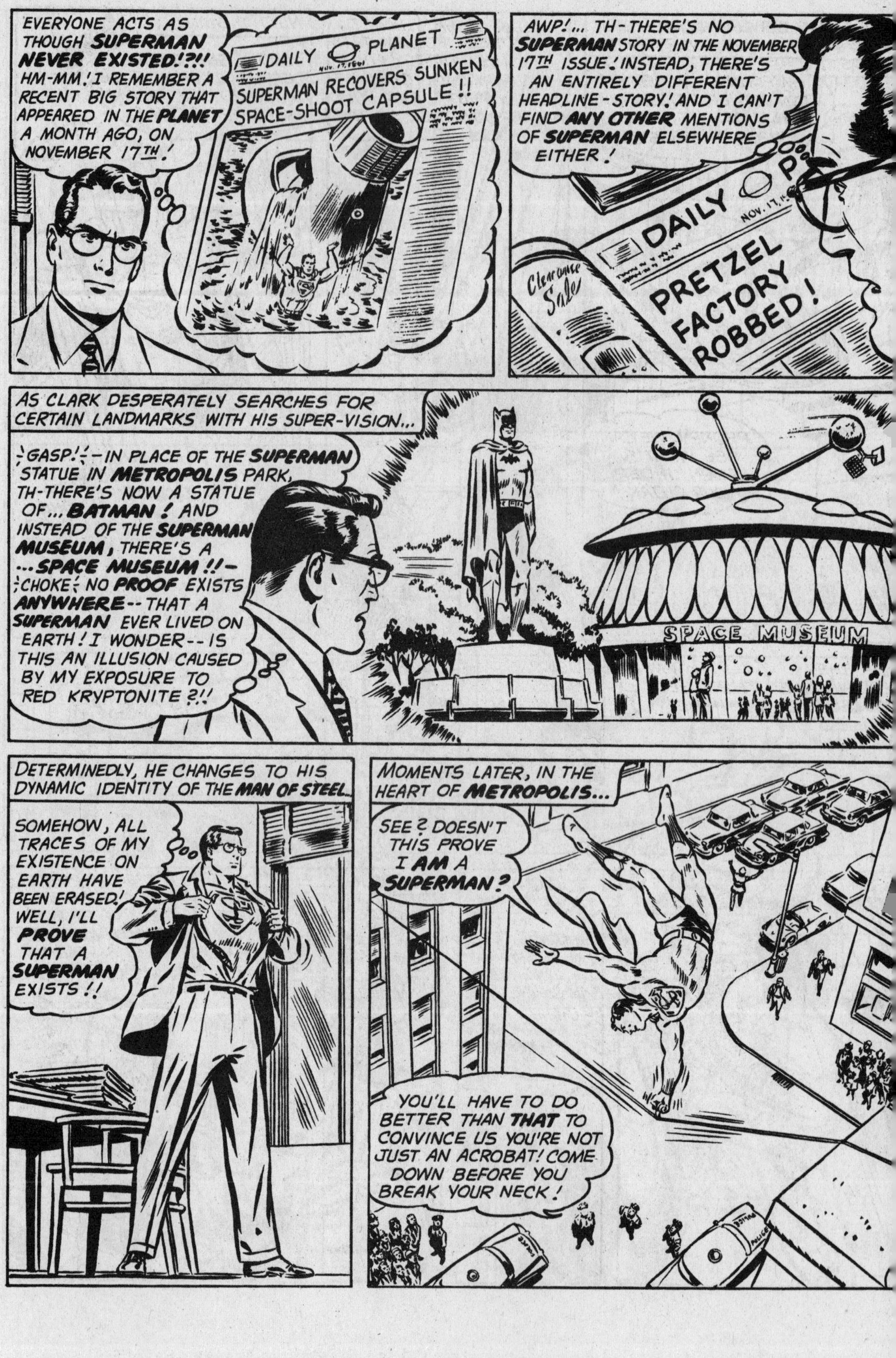
EVERYONE ACTS AS THOUGH SUPERMAN NEVER EXISTED!?!! HM-MM! I REMEMBER A RECENT BIG STORY THAT APPEARED IN THE PLANET A MONTH AGO, ON NOVEMBER 17TH!
DAILY PLANET
SUPERMAN RECOVERS SUNKEN SPACE-SHOOT CAPSULE!!
AWP!... TH-THERE'S NO SUPERMAN STORY IN THE NOVEMBER 17TH ISSUE! INSTEAD, THERE'S AN ENTIRELY DIFFERENT HEADLINE-STORY! AND I CAN'T FIND ANY OTHER MENTIONS OF SUPERMAN ELSEWHERE EITHER!
DAILY
PRETZEL FACTORY ROBBED!
AS CLARK DESPERATELY SEARCHES FOR CERTAIN LANDMARKS WITH HIS SUPER-VISION...
GASP! —IN PLACE OF THE SUPERMAN STATUE IN METROPOLIS PARK, TH-THERE'S NOW A STATUE OF... BATMAN! AND INSTEAD OF THE SUPERMAN MUSEUM, THERE'S A ...SPACE MUSEUM!!— CHOKE! NO PROOF EXISTS ANYWHERE--THAT A SUPERMAN EVER LIVED ON EARTH! I WONDER--IS THIS AN ILLUSION CAUSED BY MY EXPOSURE TO RED KRYPTONITE?!!
SPACE MUSEUM
DETERMINEDLY, HE CHANGES TO HIS DYNAMIC IDENTITY OF THE MAN OF STEEL.
SOMEHOW, ALL TRACES OF MY EXISTENCE ON EARTH HAVE BEEN ERASED! WELL, I'LL PROVE THAT A SUPERMAN EXISTS!!
MOMENTS LATER, IN THE HEART OF METROPOLIS...
SEE? DOESN'T THIS PROVE I AM A SUPERMAN?
YOU'LL HAVE TO DO BETTER THAN THAT TO CONVINCE US YOU'RE NOT JUST AN ACROBAT! COME DOWN BEFORE YOU BREAK YOUR NECK!

STUNG BY HIS VIEWERS' DISBELIEF, SUPERMAN FLASHES OVER THEIR HEADS...

I'M FLYING -- UNDER MY OWN POWER! DO YOU **STILL** DENY I HAVE SUPER-POWERS?

PHONEY! WE CAN SEE WHAT'S HIDDEN UNDER YOUR CLOAK!

GASP! HOW'D THOSE ROCKET-JETS GET THERE? WELL, I'LL QUICKLY ALIGHT, AND PULL ANOTHER STUNT!

NEXT INSTANT...

SEE -- ONE GREAT LEAP IS LAUNCHING ME SKYWARD! TRY TO DENY I'M SUPER, **NOW!**

ANYONE COULD DO WHAT YOU'RE DOING...

...IF THEY WERE WEARING **POWERFUL SPRINGS** ON THEIR SHOES ...JUST AS YOU ARE!

ULP! H-HOW'D **THEY** GET THERE?!

ALIGHTING AGAIN, **SUPERMAN** MAKES ANOTHER ATTEMPT TO CONVINCE SCOFFING ONLOOKERS.

WATCH ME CATCH THAT TOPPLING STONE STATUE!

I'M DRAWING IT DOWN WITH A MIGHTY INTAKE OF VACUUM-BREATH!

YOU FOOL! YOU'LL BE KILLED!

THEN...

THEN HE **IS** A **SUPERMAN!!**

I'VE FINALLY CONVINCED THEM!

5

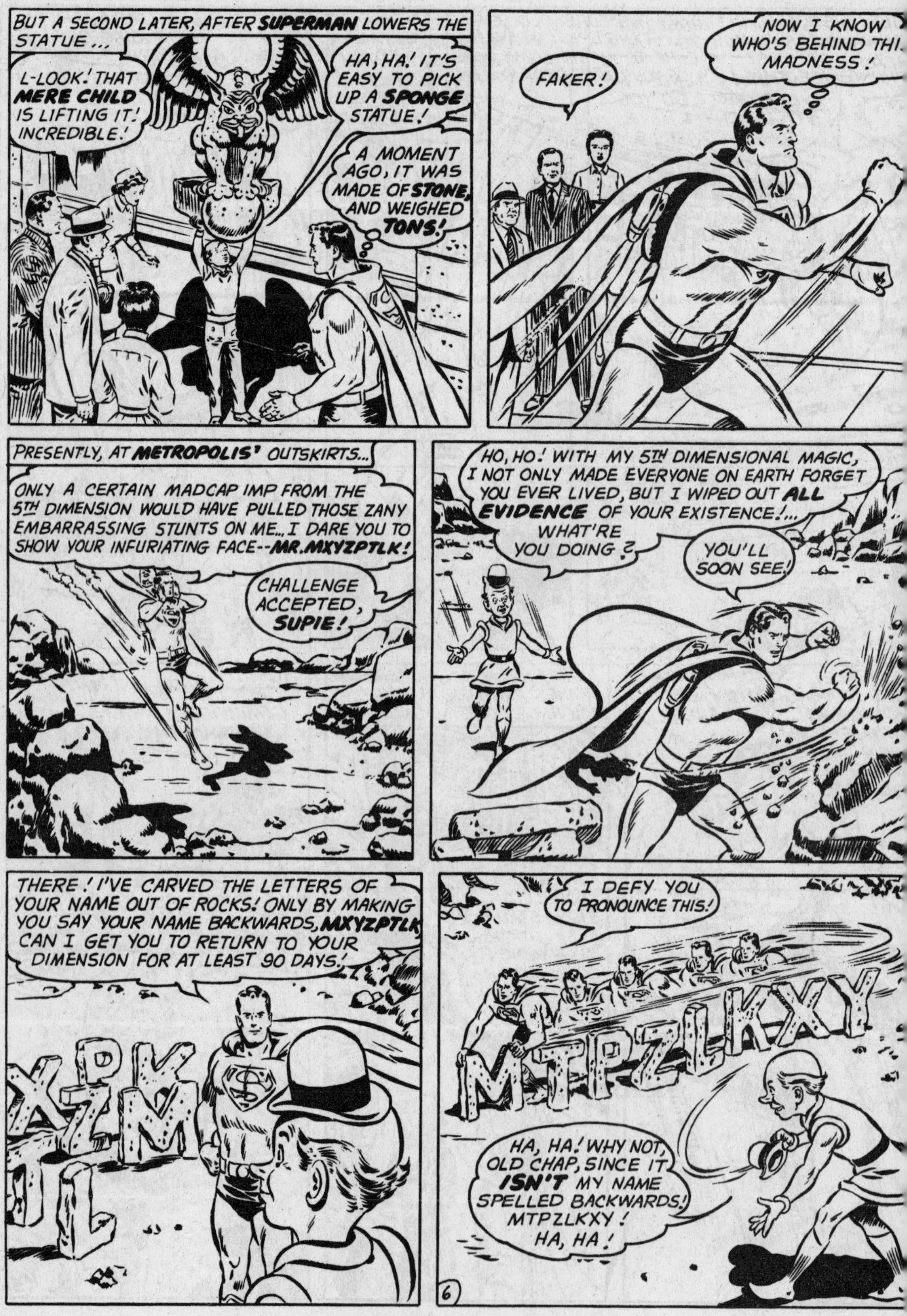
BUT A SECOND LATER, AFTER SUPERMAN LOWERS THE STATUE ...
L-LOOK! THAT MERE CHILD IS LIFTING IT! INCREDIBLE!
HA, HA! IT'S EASY TO PICK UP A SPONGE STATUE!
A MOMENT AGO, IT WAS MADE OF STONE, AND WEIGHED TONS!
FAKER!
NOW I KNOW WHO'S BEHIND THI MADNESS!
PRESENTLY, AT METROPOLIS' OUTSKIRTS...
ONLY A CERTAIN MADCAP IMP FROM THE 5TH DIMENSION WOULD HAVE PULLED THOSE ZANY EMBARRASSING STUNTS ON ME... I DARE YOU TO SHOW YOUR INFURIATING FACE--MR. MXYZPTLK!
CHALLENGE ACCEPTED, SUPIE!
HO, HO! WITH MY 5TH DIMENSIONAL MAGIC, I NOT ONLY MADE EVERYONE ON EARTH FORGET YOU EVER LIVED, BUT I WIPED OUT ALL EVIDENCE OF YOUR EXISTENCE!... WHAT'RE YOU DOING?
YOU'LL SOON SEE!
THERE! I'VE CARVED THE LETTERS OF YOUR NAME OUT OF ROCKS! ONLY BY MAKING YOU SAY YOUR NAME BACKWARDS, MXYZPTLK, CAN I GET YOU TO RETURN TO YOUR DIMENSION FOR AT LEAST 90 DAYS!
I DEFY YOU TO PRONOUNCE THIS!
MTPZLKXY
HA, HA! WHY NOT, OLD CHAP, SINCE IT ISN'T MY NAME SPELLED BACKWARDS! MTPZLKXY! HA, HA!
6

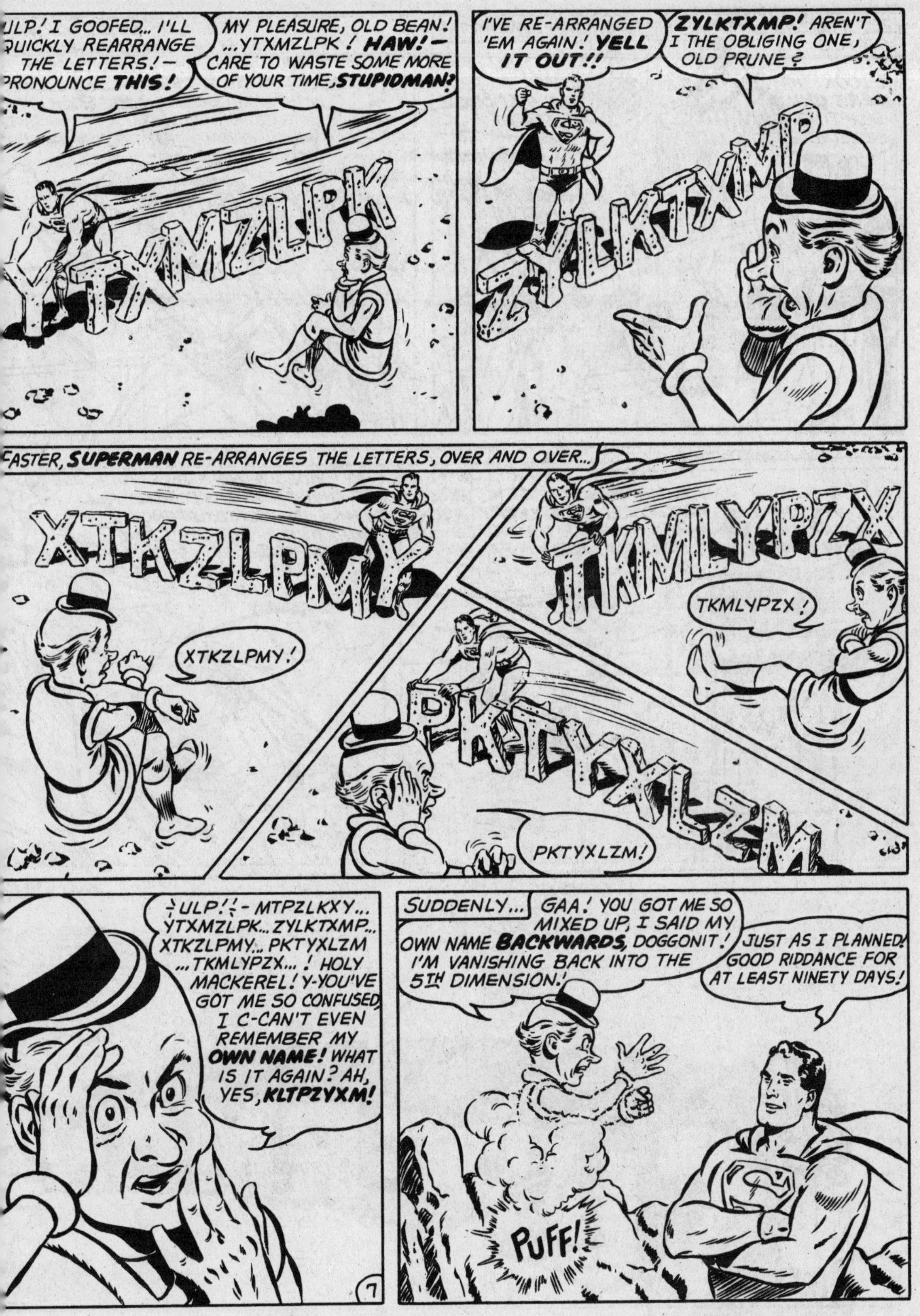
ULP! I GOOFED... I'LL QUICKLY REARRANGE THE LETTERS!— PRONOUNCE THIS!
MY PLEASURE, OLD BEAN! ...YTXMZLPK! HAW!— CARE TO WASTE SOME MORE OF YOUR TIME, STUPIDMAN?
YTXMZLPK
I'VE RE-ARRANGED 'EM AGAIN! YELL IT OUT!!
ZYLKTXMP! AREN'T I THE OBLIGING ONE, OLD PRUNE?
ZYLKTXMP
FASTER, SUPERMAN RE-ARRANGES THE LETTERS, OVER AND OVER...
XTKZLPMY
XTKZLPMY!
TKMLYPZX
TKMLYPZX!
PKTYXLZM
PKTYXLZM!
ULP! - MTPZLKXY... YTXMZLPK... ZYLKTXMP... XTKZLPMY... PKTYXLZM ...TKMLYPZX...! HOLY MACKEREL! Y-YOU'VE GOT ME SO CONFUSED, I C-CAN'T EVEN REMEMBER MY OWN NAME! WHAT IS IT AGAIN? AH, YES, KLTPZYXM!
7
SUDDENLY...
GAA! YOU GOT ME SO MIXED UP, I SAID MY OWN NAME BACKWARDS, DOGGONIT! I'M VANISHING BACK INTO THE 5TH DIMENSION!
JUST AS I PLANNED! GOOD RIDDANCE FOR AT LEAST NINETY DAYS!
PUFF!

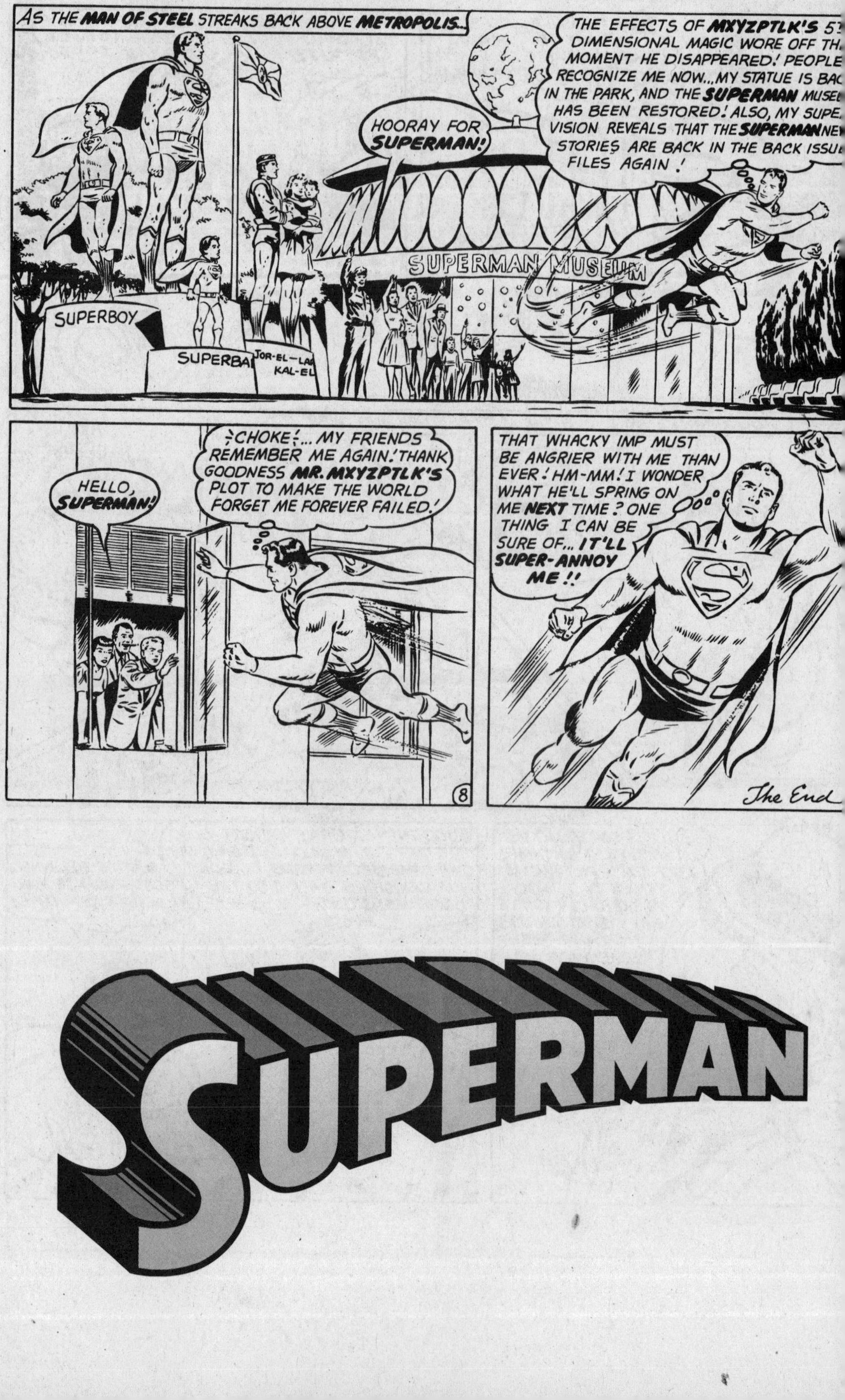
AS THE MAN OF STEEL STREAKS BACK ABOVE METROPOLIS...
THE EFFECTS OF MXYZPTLK'S 5 DIMENSIONAL MAGIC WORE OFF TH MOMENT HE DISAPPEARED! PEOPLE RECOGNIZE ME NOW... MY STATUE IS BAC IN THE PARK, AND THE SUPERMAN MUSE HAS BEEN RESTORED! ALSO, MY SUPE VISION REVEALS THAT THE SUPERMAN NE STORIES ARE BACK IN THE BACK ISSU FILES AGAIN!
HOORAY FOR SUPERMAN!
SUPERMAN MUSEUM
SUPERBOY
SUPERBA
JOR-EL—LA KAL-EL
HELLO, SUPERMAN!
-CHOKE-... MY FRIENDS REMEMBER ME AGAIN! THANK GOODNESS MR. MXYZPTLK'S PLOT TO MAKE THE WORLD FORGET ME FOREVER FAILED!
8
THAT WHACKY IMP MUST BE ANGRIER WITH ME THAN EVER! HM-MM! I WONDER WHAT HE'LL SPRING ON ME NEXT TIME? ONE THING I CAN BE SURE OF... IT'LL SUPER-ANNOY ME!!
The End

SUPERMAN

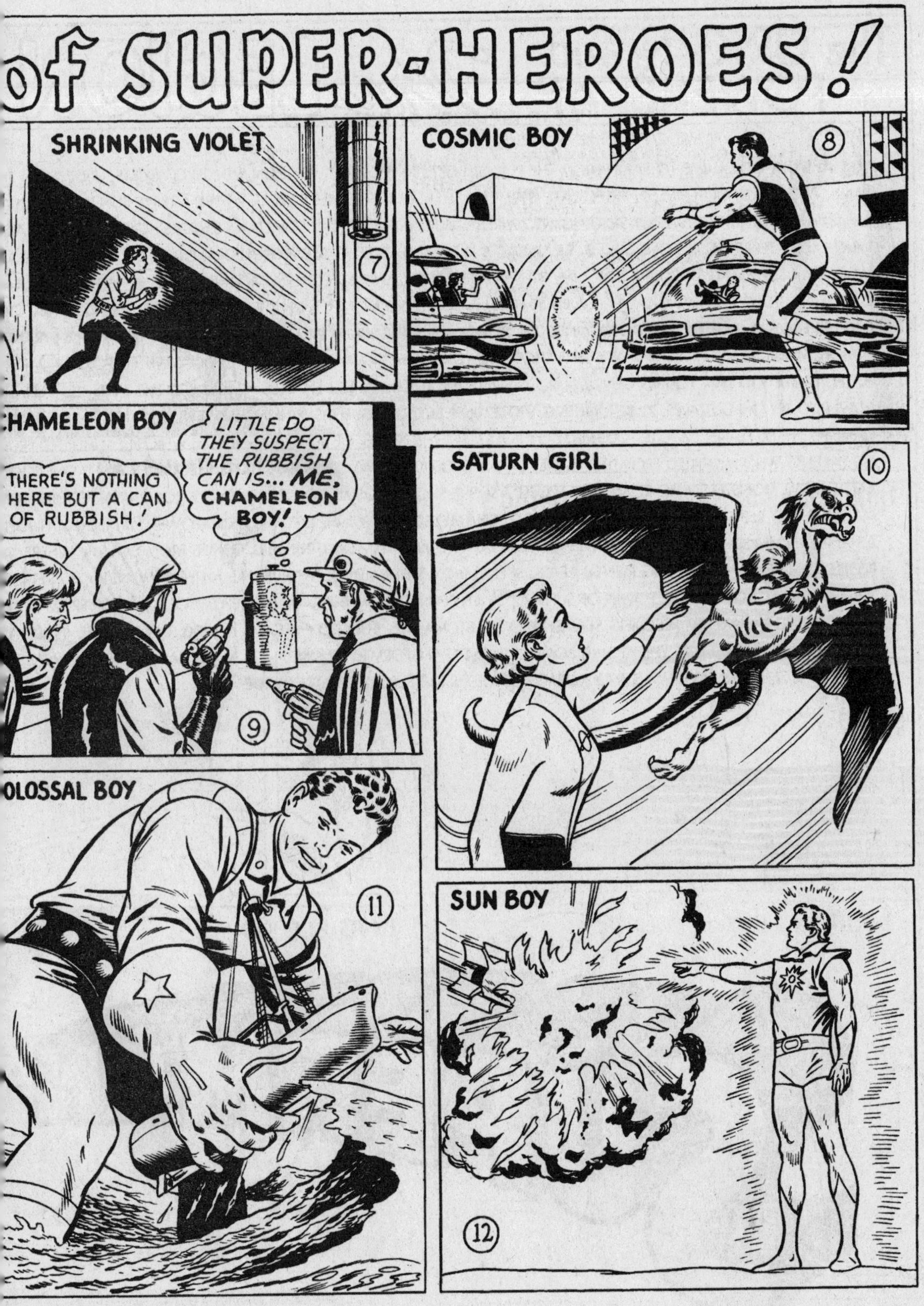
of SUPER-HEROES!
SHRINKING VIOLET
7
COSMIC BOY
8
CHAMELEON BOY
THERE'S NOTHING HERE BUT A CAN OF RUBBISH!
LITTLE DO THEY SUSPECT THE RUBBISH CAN IS... ME, CHAMELEON BOY!
9
SATURN GIRL
10
OLOSSAL BOY
11
SUN BOY
12

SEE FOLLOWING PAGE FOR IDENTIFICATION OF THE SUPER-HEROES

KEY TO THE LEGION OF SUPER-HEROES

1.PHANTOM GIRL CAME TO EARTH FROM THE PLANET BGZTL IN THE 4TH DIMENSION, WHICH CO-EXISTS, UNSEEN, IN THE SAME SPACE EARTH OCCUPIES. **2. TRIPLICATE GIRL** COMES FROM THE PLANET CARGG, WHERE A TRIPLE SUN IMBUED ALL ITS INHABITANTS WITH THE POWER OF SPLITTING INTO THREE BODIES. TRIPLICATE GIRL SOMETIMES SHOCKS HER ESCORTS ON EARTH WHO EXPECT TO BE DATING ONE GIRL! **3. BRAINIAC 5** IS THE GREAT-GREAT-GREAT-GREAT-GRANDSON OF THE SPACE VILLAIN WHO WAS SUPERMAN'S FOULEST FOE. HIS FORCE-SHIELD BELT CAN PROTECT HIM FROM DANGER. **4. LIGHTNING LAD** GAINED MASTERY OF LIGHTNING WHEN A BLAST FROM A LIGHTNING MONSTER ON THE PLANET KORBAL FREAKISHLY ELECTRIFIED HIS BODY. **5. BOUNCING BOY** GAINED THE POWER OF SUPER-BOUNCING WHEN HE DRANK A SCIENTIST'S STRANGE POTION, MISTAKING IT FOR SODA-POP. SCENE SHOWS HIM BOUNCING AWAY FROM ANGRY CROOKS WITH IMPORTANT PAPERS. **6. INVISIBLE KID** IS A YOUNG GENIUS WHO INVENTED A SERUM WHICH ENABLES HIM TO BECOME INVISIBLE, USES HIS POWER TO SPY ON OUTLAWS. **7. SHRINKING VIOLET** INHERITED HER SUPER-SHRINKING POWERS FROM HER PARENTS WHO CAME FROM THE PLANET IMSK. **8. COSMIC BOY** POSSESSES THE POWER OF SUPER-MAGNETISM, WHICH HE INHERITED FROM HIS PARENTS WHO MIGRATED FROM THE PLANET BRAAL! EVOLUTION HAS GIVEN BRAALIANS THE POWER TO MAGNETICALLY BATTLE METAL MONSTERS WHO ROAM THAT WORLD. SCENE SHOWS COSMIC BOY PREVENTING A ROCKET-CAR COLLISION BY MAGNETICALLY REPELLING THE TWO METAL CRAFT. **9. CHAMELEON BOY** INHERITED HIS WEIRD POWER TO DISGUISE HIMSELF AS ANYTHING FROM HIS PARENTS, NATIVES OF THE PLANET DURLA. **10. SATURN GIRL** COMES FROM SATURN, WHERE ALL PEOPLE CAN PERFORM AMAZING MENTAL FEATS. SCENE SHOWS HER MENTALLY ORDERING A FIERCE MONSTER TO RETREAT. **11. COLOSSAL BOY** HAS THE POWER OF SUPER-GROWTH GAINED FROM THE RADIATION EFFECT OF A METEOR FROM OUTER SPACE. SCENE SHOWS HIM RESCUING SEAMEN FROM A STORM. **12. SUN BOY** BECAME ACCIDENTALLY LOCKED INSIDE AN ATOMIC REACTOR CHAMBER. THE ATOMIC BOMBARDMENT TRANSFORMED HIM INTO A HUMAN BEACON OF BLAZING LIGHT AND HEAT. SCENE DEPICTS HIM MELTING A DEADLY SPACE MISSILE BEFORE IT CAN EXPLODE.

...E DAY, IN METROPOLIS, AS *PLANET* REPORTER ...ARK KENT, WHO IS SECRETLY *SUPERMAN*, ...TENDS A SEANCE...

...AM... THIS MEDIUM, MADAME ...GA, MUST BE HUNGRY FOR ...LICITY! SHE'S INVITED ...EPORTERS TO PROVE SHE ...S OCCULT POWERS AND ...N COMMUNICATE WITH THE ...RITS OF DEAD PEOPLE!

...AND NOW, GENTLEMEN, I WILL GO INTO A TRANCE!

SHORTLY...

GOSH, SHE HASN'T BATTED AN EYELASH FOR FIVE MINUTES! SHE'S IN A TRANCE!

TOO BAD I CAN'T TELL THE OTHER NEWSMEN *HOW* I KNOW SHE'S A PHONY! WITH MY *MICROSCOPIC VISION* I CAN SEE HER EYELIDS FLUTTERING!

...EN...

...OW! THE ...BLE IS ...SING! ...IS MEDIUM ...EALLY HAS ...AGICAL ...OWERS!

SOME "MAGIC"! HER ASSISTANT IS WORKING A POWERFUL MAGNET UPSTAIRS AND IT'S DRAWING THE TABLE UPWARD BY ATTRACTING METAL CONCEALED IN THE TABLE TOP!

SUDDENLY...

ATTENTION! THE SPIRIT WORLD WISHES TO CONTACT US!

SHE MEANS FROM "BEYOND" THE *WALL*! IT'S ANOTHER ASSISTANT, USING PHOSPHORESCENT MAKE-UP ON HIS ARM TO HELP PUT OVER HIS HOAX!

GREETINGS, MY FRIENDS, FROM THE BEYOND!

...ET HIM WHO ...EEKS ADVICE ...ROM THE DEAD ...SK HIS QUESTION ...OW AND IT ...HALL BE ...NSWERED!

OKAY! MY UNCLE HORACE, BEFORE HE DIED, ALWAYS GAVE ME EXCELLENT ADVICE! UNCLE HORACE, I'LL BE MARRIED NEXT WEEK! PLEASE TELL ME NOW... WILL MY MARRIAGE BE A HAPPY ONE?

SOON, AS THE MYSTERIOUS ARM WRITES...

PSSTT... CLARK! THAT DAME IS A FAKE! I TRICKED HER! I HAVE NO UNCLE HORACE AND I'M NOT GETTING MARRIED!

DEAR NEPHEW... WORRY NOT! WEDDED BLISS AWAITS YOU!-- UNCLE HORACE

HA! HA! I'M GLAD MY NEWS-PAPERMAN PALS SEE THROUGH HER, TOO!

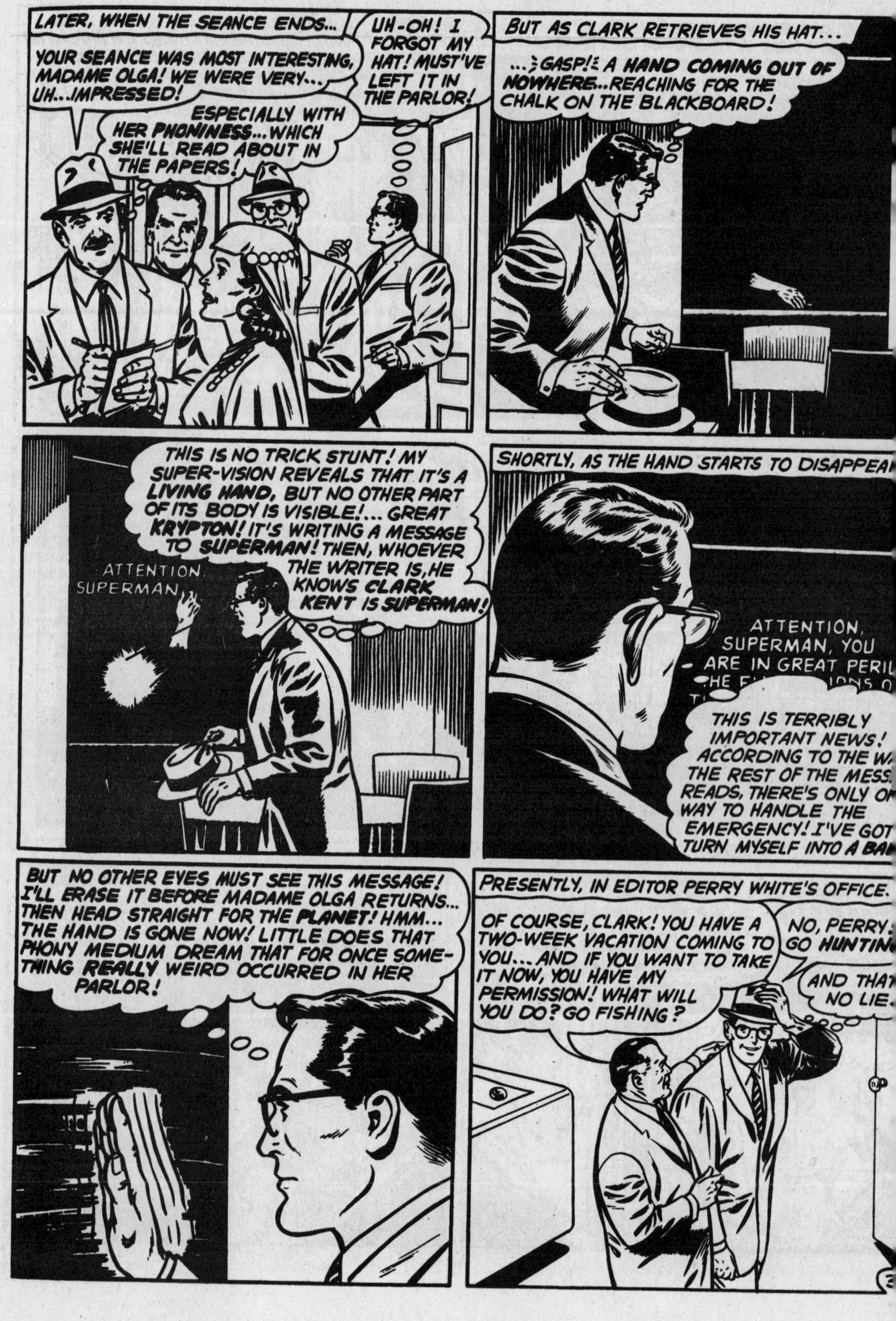
LATER, WHEN THE SEANCE ENDS...
YOUR SEANCE WAS MOST INTERESTING, MADAME OLGA! WE WERE VERY... UH...IMPRESSED!
ESPECIALLY WITH HER PHONINESS...WHICH SHE'LL READ ABOUT IN THE PAPERS!
UH-OH! I FORGOT MY HAT! MUST'VE LEFT IT IN THE PARLOR!
BUT AS CLARK RETRIEVES HIS HAT...
...GASP! A HAND COMING OUT OF NOWHERE...REACHING FOR THE CHALK ON THE BLACKBOARD!
THIS IS NO TRICK STUNT! MY SUPER-VISION REVEALS THAT IT'S A LIVING HAND, BUT NO OTHER PART OF ITS BODY IS VISIBLE!... GREAT KRYPTON! IT'S WRITING A MESSAGE TO SUPERMAN! THEN, WHOEVER THE WRITER IS, HE KNOWS CLARK KENT IS SUPERMAN!
ATTENTION, SUPERMAN
SHORTLY, AS THE HAND STARTS TO DISAPPEA
ATTENTION, SUPERMAN, YOU ARE IN GREAT PERIL
THIS IS TERRIBLY IMPORTANT NEWS! ACCORDING TO THE WA THE REST OF THE MESS READS, THERE'S ONLY ON WAY TO HANDLE THE EMERGENCY! I'VE GOT TURN MYSELF INTO A BA
BUT NO OTHER EYES MUST SEE THIS MESSAGE! I'LL ERASE IT BEFORE MADAME OLGA RETURNS... THEN HEAD STRAIGHT FOR THE PLANET! HMM... THE HAND IS GONE NOW! LITTLE DOES THAT PHONY MEDIUM DREAM THAT FOR ONCE SOMETHING REALLY WEIRD OCCURRED IN HER PARLOR!
PRESENTLY, IN EDITOR PERRY WHITE'S OFFICE.
OF COURSE, CLARK! YOU HAVE A TWO-WEEK VACATION COMING TO YOU... AND IF YOU WANT TO TAKE IT NOW, YOU HAVE MY PERMISSION! WHAT WILL YOU DO? GO FISHING?
NO, PERRY. GO HUNTIN
AND THA NO LIE.

SHORTLY, IN A *PLANET* STOCK ROOM, AS CLARK SWITCHES TO *THE MAN OF STEEL*...

NOW TO BECOME A BABY SO THAT I'LL BE READY FOR THE EMERGENCY I'VE BEEN WARNED ABOUT! I MUST FLY TO MY FORTRESS OF SOLITUDE AT ONCE!

PRESENTLY, INSIDE THE FORTRESS...

LOCKED INSIDE THIS SAFE ARE VARIOUS KINDS OF *RED KRYPTONITE!* ONE TYPE ONCE TURNED *SUPERGIRL* INTO A *BABY GIRL* AND KRYPTO INTO A *PUP* FOR A BRIEF TIME!

IF I EXPOSE MYSELF TO THE RAYS OF THE *RED K* IN BOX #4, THEY'LL AFFECT ME THE SAME WAY! I'LL BECOME INSTANTLY YOUNGER, TOO! I NEED ONLY BREAK OPEN THE PROTECTIVE LEAD COVERING...

TYPE #1
REMOVES
SUPER-POWERS

TYPE #2
MAKES USER
A GIANT

TYPE #3
MAKES USER
INVISIBLE

TYPE #4
TURNS USER
INTO BABY

AH! THE RED KRYPTONITE RADIATIONS ARE HITTING ME! I CAN FEEL MY BODY TINGLING ALL OVER...WHICH MEANS THAT IN A FEW SECONDS I'LL BECOME THE MOST UNIQUE BABY ALIVE!

CRACKK!

I'M BEING REDUCED TO BABY-SIZE! BUT IN EVERY OTHER RESPECT... SPEECH, FEELINGS, POWERS... I'LL REMAIN SUPERMAN!

MY BABY-LIKE APPEARANCE SHOULD LAST JUST LONG ENOUGH FOR ME TO CARRY OUT MY SCHEME!

FOR ONLY AS A *BABY* CAN I HANDLE THE PERIL THAT'S COMING UP!

THEN, AS SUPERMAN'S COSTUME ALSO SHRINKS...

AS IT HAPPENED WITH SUPERGIRL AND KRYPTO, THE AURA OF RED KRYPTONITE HAS AFFECTED MY COSTUME, TOO, AND REDUCED IT IN PROPORTION TO MY BODY!

SPEAKING OF SMALL THINGS, IT'S TIME I CHECKED THE AIR SUPPLY THAT GOES INTO KANDOR, THE KRYPTONIAN CITY WHICH BRAINIAC, THE SUPER-VILLAIN, REDUCED TO MINIATURE SIZE WITH HIS SHRINKING RAY BEFORE KRYPTON EXPLODED!

SECONDS LATER, AS SUPERMAN STREAKS BACK TO METROPOLIS...

IT'LL CREATE A SENSATION WHEN PEOPLE SEE A PINT-SIZED SUPERMAN HANDLING KING-SIZE EMERGENCIES! BUT SMALL I MUST REMAIN UNTIL MY BIG EMERGENCY IS OVER!

PRESENTLY, AT THE OUTSKIRTS OF THE CITY...

HMM... THERE'S A PHONY RACKET! WITH MY TELESCOPIC VISION I CAN SPOT A HALF DOZEN SWINDLERS I'VE SEEN BEFORE IN ROGUE'S GALLERY PICTURES!

LOOP A PRIZE — WONDERFUL PRIZES!

TOO BAD, BOYS! YOU'VE LOST AGAIN!

PRIZES GALORE

PITCH A PENNY

CARNIVAL FOR CHARITY

APPARENTLY THE CROOKS ARE RUNNING A PHONY CARNIVAL FOR "CHARITY"! IF I KNOW THEM, THEY'VE RIGGED EVERY GAME SO NOBODY CAN WIN A THING!

GOSH, I HIT THE BOTTLES... BUT THEY DON'T FALL DOWN!

AND I CAN'T EVEN SCORE ONE BULL'S-EYE!

DON'T GIVE UP, LADS! TRY ANOTHER TEN SHOTS FOR A QUARTER!

CH A NY — PITCH A PENNY

PRIZE GALLERY

HIT THE MILK BOTTLES

WIN A PRIZE

!PRIZES!

TARGET SHOOT

5

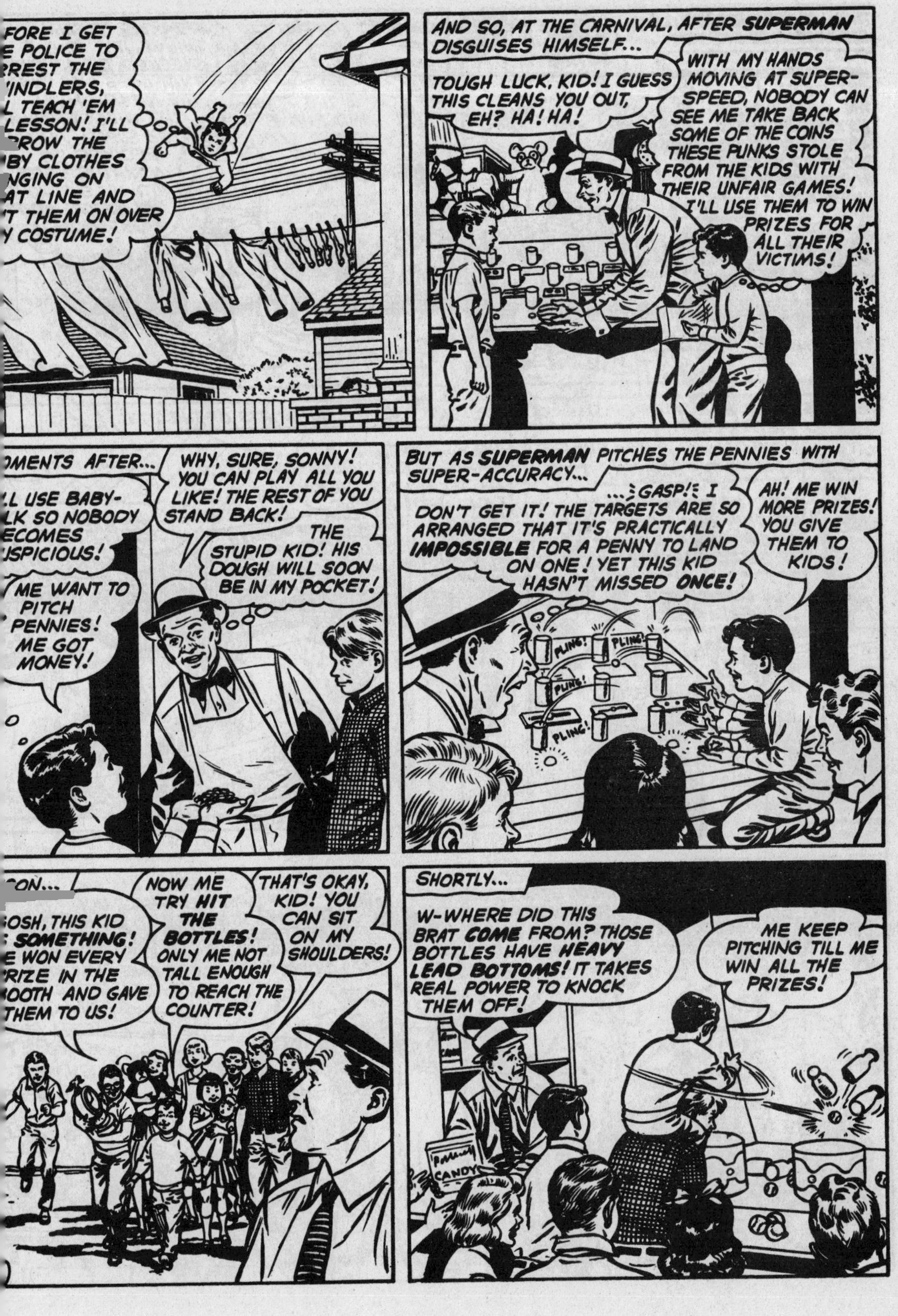
FORE I GET
E POLICE TO
RREST THE
INDLERS,
L TEACH 'EM
LESSON! I'LL
ROW THE
BY CLOTHES
NGING ON
AT LINE AND
T THEM ON OVER
Y COSTUME!
AND SO, AT THE CARNIVAL, AFTER SUPERMAN DISGUISES HIMSELF...
TOUGH LUCK, KID! I GUESS THIS CLEANS YOU OUT, EH? HA! HA!
WITH MY HANDS MOVING AT SUPER-SPEED, NOBODY CAN SEE ME TAKE BACK SOME OF THE COINS THESE PUNKS STOLE FROM THE KIDS WITH THEIR UNFAIR GAMES! I'LL USE THEM TO WIN PRIZES FOR ALL THEIR VICTIMS!
OMENTS AFTER...
L USE BABY-
LK SO NOBODY
ECOMES
SPICIOUS!
ME WANT TO PITCH PENNIES! ME GOT MONEY!
WHY, SURE, SONNY! YOU CAN PLAY ALL YOU LIKE! THE REST OF YOU STAND BACK!
THE STUPID KID! HIS DOUGH WILL SOON BE IN MY POCKET!
BUT AS SUPERMAN PITCHES THE PENNIES WITH SUPER-ACCURACY...
...GASP! I DON'T GET IT! THE TARGETS ARE SO ARRANGED THAT IT'S PRACTICALLY IMPOSSIBLE FOR A PENNY TO LAND ON ONE! YET THIS KID HASN'T MISSED ONCE!
AH! ME WIN MORE PRIZES! YOU GIVE THEM TO KIDS!
PLING!
PLING!
PLING!
PLING!
PLING!
ON...
OSH, THIS KID
SOMETHING!
E WON EVERY
RIZE IN THE
OOTH AND GAVE
THEM TO US!
NOW ME TRY HIT THE BOTTLES! ONLY ME NOT TALL ENOUGH TO REACH THE COUNTER!
THAT'S OKAY, KID! YOU CAN SIT ON MY SHOULDERS!
SHORTLY...
W-WHERE DID THIS BRAT COME FROM? THOSE BOTTLES HAVE HEAVY LEAD BOTTOMS! IT TAKES REAL POWER TO KNOCK THEM OFF!
ME KEEP PITCHING TILL ME WIN ALL THE PRIZES!
CANDY

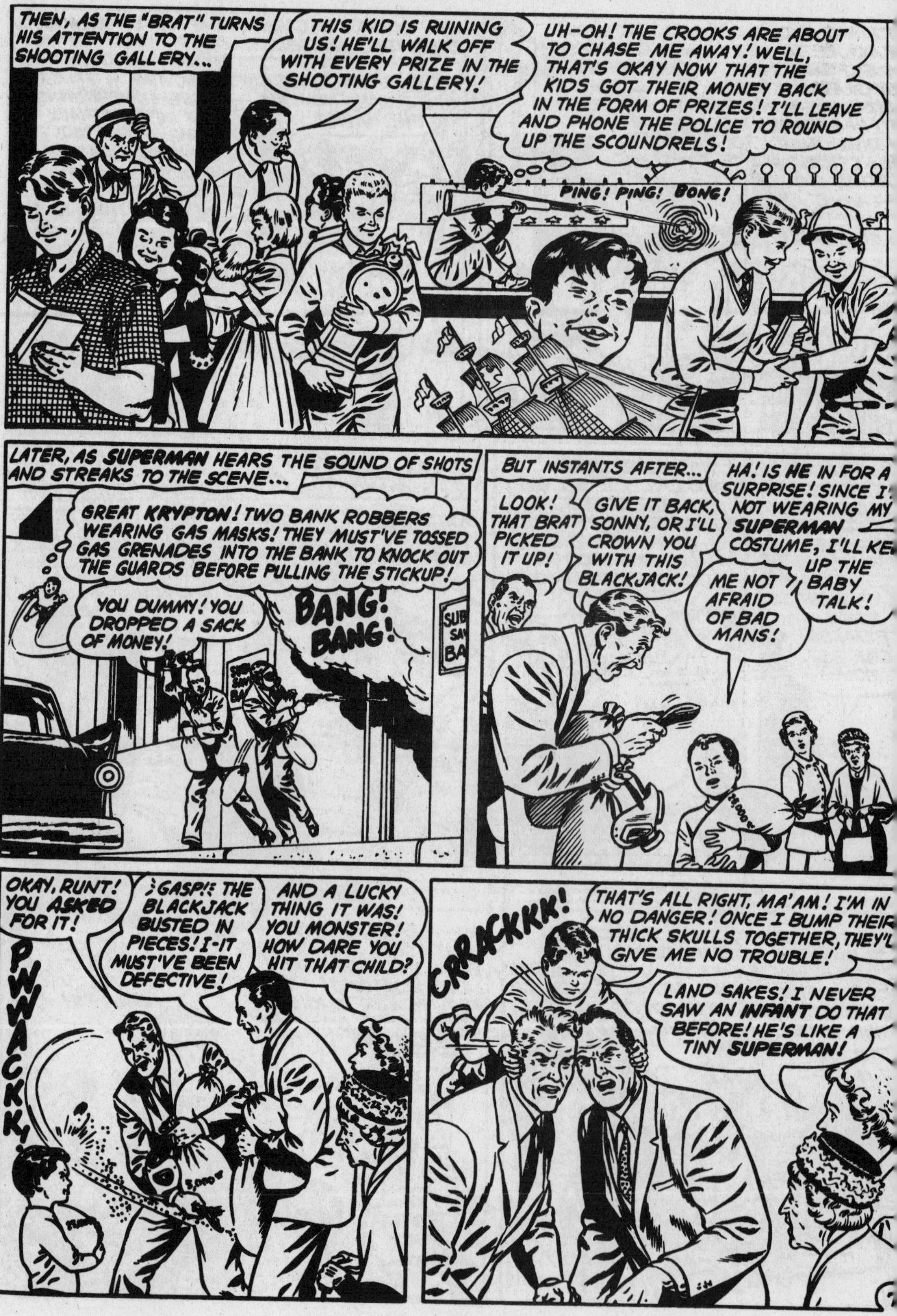
THEN, AS THE "BRAT" TURNS HIS ATTENTION TO THE SHOOTING GALLERY...
THIS KID IS RUINING US! HE'LL WALK OFF WITH EVERY PRIZE IN THE SHOOTING GALLERY!
UH-OH! THE CROOKS ARE ABOUT TO CHASE ME AWAY! WELL, THAT'S OKAY NOW THAT THE KIDS GOT THEIR MONEY BACK IN THE FORM OF PRIZES! I'LL LEAVE AND PHONE THE POLICE TO ROUND UP THE SCOUNDRELS!
PING! PING! BONG!
LATER, AS SUPERMAN HEARS THE SOUND OF SHOTS AND STREAKS TO THE SCENE...
GREAT KRYPTON! TWO BANK ROBBERS WEARING GAS MASKS! THEY MUST'VE TOSSED GAS GRENADES INTO THE BANK TO KNOCK OUT THE GUARDS BEFORE PULLING THE STICKUP!
YOU DUMMY! YOU DROPPED A SACK OF MONEY!
BANG! BANG!
BUT INSTANTS AFTER...
LOOK! THAT BRAT PICKED IT UP!
GIVE IT BACK, SONNY, OR I'LL CROWN YOU WITH THIS BLACKJACK!
HA! IS HE IN FOR A SURPRISE! SINCE I'M NOT WEARING MY SUPERMAN COSTUME, I'LL KEEP UP THE BABY TALK!
ME NOT AFRAID OF BAD MANS!
OKAY, RUNT! YOU ASKED FOR IT!
PWWACKK!
GASP! THE BLACKJACK BUSTED IN PIECES! I-IT MUST'VE BEEN DEFECTIVE!
AND A LUCKY THING IT WAS! YOU MONSTER! HOW DARE YOU HIT THAT CHILD?
CRRACKKK!
THAT'S ALL RIGHT, MA'AM! I'M IN NO DANGER! ONCE I BUMP THEIR THICK SKULLS TOGETHER, THEY'LL GIVE ME NO TROUBLE!
LAND SAKES! I NEVER SAW AN INFANT DO THAT BEFORE! HE'S LIKE A TINY SUPERMAN!

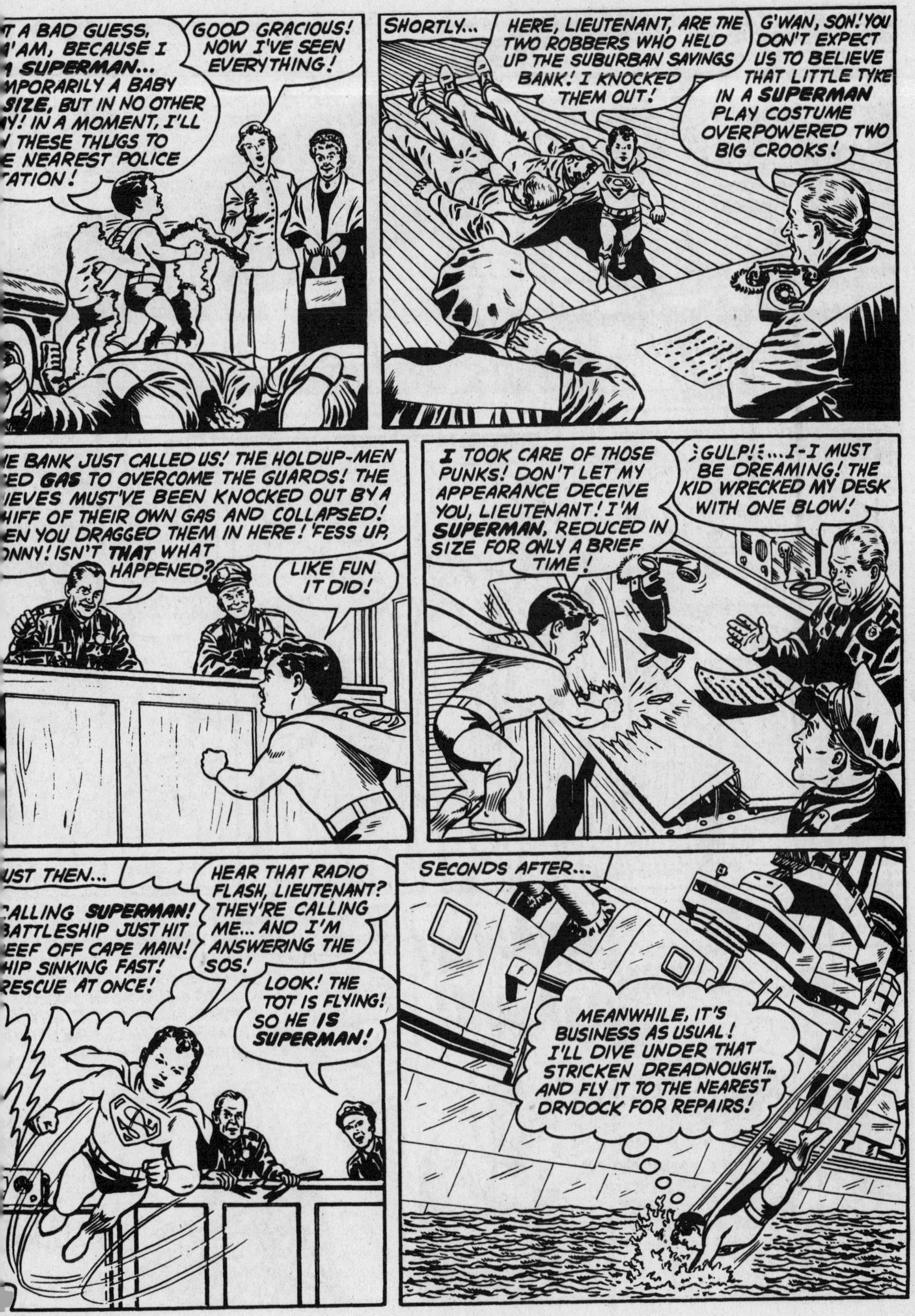
T A BAD GUESS, A'AM, BECAUSE I SUPERMAN... MPORARILY A BABY SIZE, BUT IN NO OTHER Y! IN A MOMENT, I'LL THESE THUGS TO E NEAREST POLICE TATION!
GOOD GRACIOUS! NOW I'VE SEEN EVERYTHING!
SHORTLY...
HERE, LIEUTENANT, ARE THE TWO ROBBERS WHO HELD UP THE SUBURBAN SAVINGS BANK! I KNOCKED THEM OUT!
G'WAN, SON! YOU DON'T EXPECT US TO BELIEVE THAT LITTLE TYKE IN A SUPERMAN PLAY COSTUME OVERPOWERED TWO BIG CROOKS!
E BANK JUST CALLED US! THE HOLDUP-MEN ED GAS TO OVERCOME THE GUARDS! THE IEVES MUST'VE BEEN KNOCKED OUT BY A HIFF OF THEIR OWN GAS AND COLLAPSED! EN YOU DRAGGED THEM IN HERE! 'FESS UP, ONNY! ISN'T THAT WHAT HAPPENED?
LIKE FUN IT DID!
I TOOK CARE OF THOSE PUNKS! DON'T LET MY APPEARANCE DECEIVE YOU, LIEUTENANT! I'M SUPERMAN, REDUCED IN SIZE FOR ONLY A BRIEF TIME!
GULP! ...I-I MUST BE DREAMING! THE KID WRECKED MY DESK WITH ONE BLOW!
UST THEN...
CALLING SUPERMAN! BATTLESHIP JUST HIT EEF OFF CAPE MAIN! HIP SINKING FAST! RESCUE AT ONCE!
HEAR THAT RADIO FLASH, LIEUTENANT? THEY'RE CALLING ME... AND I'M ANSWERING THE SOS!
LOOK! THE TOT IS FLYING! SO HE IS SUPERMAN!
SECONDS AFTER...
MEANWHILE, IT'S BUSINESS AS USUAL! I'LL DIVE UNDER THAT STRICKEN DREADNOUGHT... AND FLY IT TO THE NEAREST DRYDOCK FOR REPAIRS!

PRESENTLY, AT THE NAVY BASE IN METROPOLIS...

GREAT SCOTT, ADMIRAL! SUPERMAN HAS BEEN REDUCED TO BABY SIZE BUT IT HASN'T PREVENTED HIM FROM PERFORMING HIS USUAL MAN-SIZED SUPER-FEATS!

YES! BIG OR SMALL, SUPERMAN REMAINS AN AMAZING HERO! WE MUST HONOR HIM FOR HIS GREAT RESCUE JOB!

ACCORDINGLY, AN HOUR LATER, ABOARD THE ADMIRAL'S FLAGSHIP...

OFFICERS AND CREW... ATTENTION! THE NAVY IS ABOUT TO GIVE A 21-GUN SALUTE TO THE GREATEST HERO OF ALL TIME... SUPERMAN!

SUPERMAN?!

THAT LITTLE KID? IS THE ADMIRAL CRAZY? HOW CAN THAT BABY BE SUPERMAN?

ER... ADMIRAL! I JUST OVERHEARD YOUR MEN! APPARENTLY THEY THINK YOU'VE MADE A MISTAKE!

BOOM BOOM BOOM

AS THE BABE OF STEEL SOARS UPWARD...

NOW DO YOU BELIEVE I'M SUPERMAN?

BRRAMM! BRRAAMM!

WOW! HE'S STOPPING 16-INCH SHELLS WITH HIS CHEST! HE'S GOT TO BE SUPERMAN!

LATER, AS SUPERMAN CONTINUES HIS PATROL ALONG THE NORTHERN COAST...

IT WON'T BE LONG NOW! THE SIGNAL FOR ME TO GO TO WORK SHOULD APPEAR IN THE SKY AT ANY MOMENT! HMM... SOMETHING STRANGE IS HAPPENING ON THAT ISLAND!

9

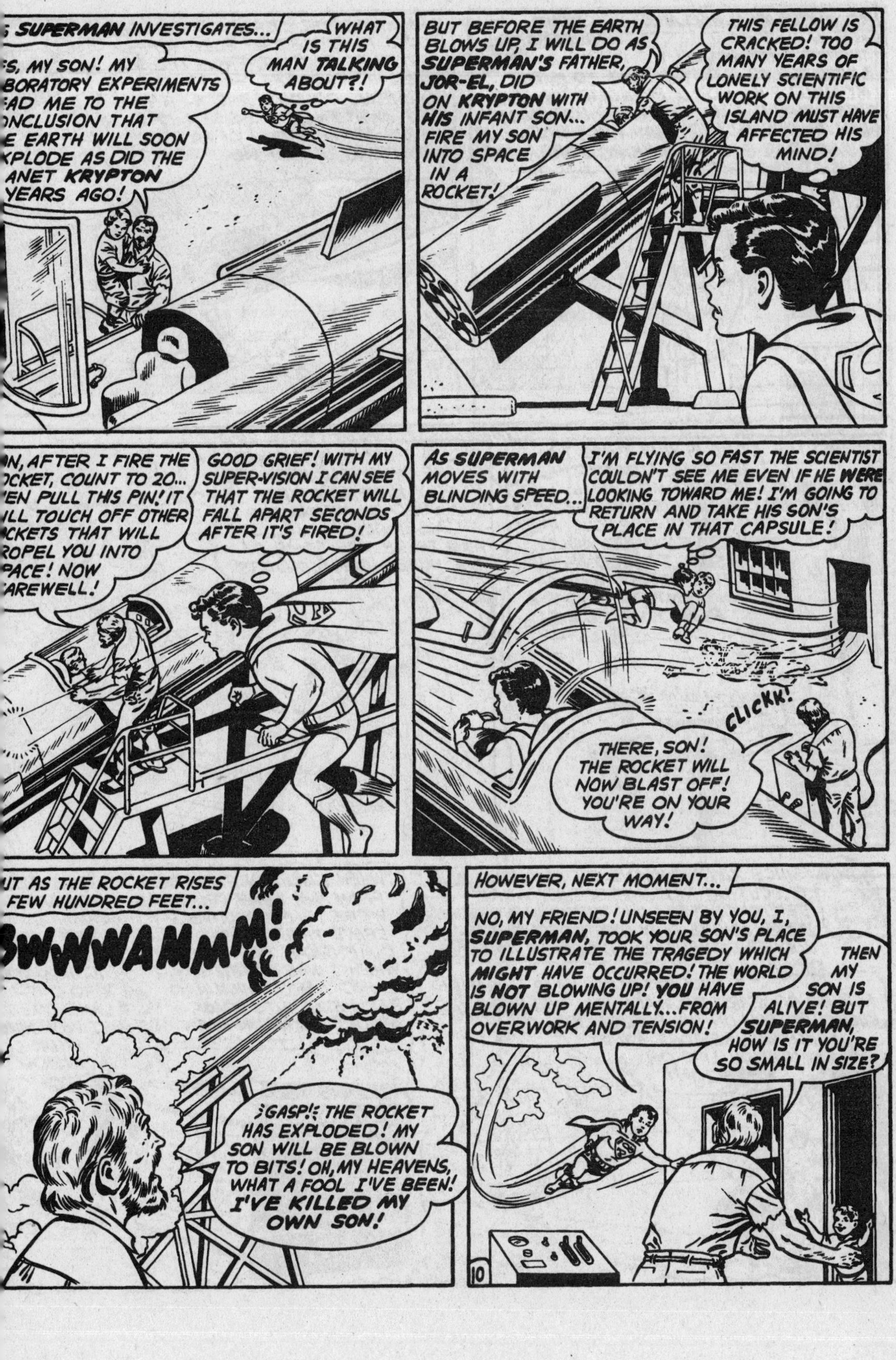

S SUPERMAN INVESTIGATES...
ES, MY SON! MY LABORATORY EXPERIMENTS LEAD ME TO THE CONCLUSION THAT THE EARTH WILL SOON EXPLODE AS DID THE PLANET KRYPTON YEARS AGO!
WHAT IS THIS MAN TALKING ABOUT?!
BUT BEFORE THE EARTH BLOWS UP, I WILL DO AS SUPERMAN'S FATHER, JOR-EL, DID ON KRYPTON WITH HIS INFANT SON... FIRE MY SON INTO SPACE IN A ROCKET!
THIS FELLOW IS CRACKED! TOO MANY YEARS OF LONELY SCIENTIFIC WORK ON THIS ISLAND MUST HAVE AFFECTED HIS MIND!
ON, AFTER I FIRE THE ROCKET, COUNT TO 20... THEN PULL THIS PIN! IT WILL TOUCH OFF OTHER ROCKETS THAT WILL PROPEL YOU INTO SPACE! NOW FAREWELL!
GOOD GRIEF! WITH MY SUPER-VISION I CAN SEE THAT THE ROCKET WILL FALL APART SECONDS AFTER IT'S FIRED!
AS SUPERMAN MOVES WITH BLINDING SPEED...
I'M FLYING SO FAST THE SCIENTIST COULDN'T SEE ME EVEN IF HE WERE LOOKING TOWARD ME! I'M GOING TO RETURN AND TAKE HIS SON'S PLACE IN THAT CAPSULE!
CLICKK!
THERE, SON! THE ROCKET WILL NOW BLAST OFF! YOU'RE ON YOUR WAY!
UT AS THE ROCKET RISES FEW HUNDRED FEET...
BWWWAMMM!
GASP! THE ROCKET HAS EXPLODED! MY SON WILL BE BLOWN TO BITS! OH, MY HEAVENS, WHAT A FOOL I'VE BEEN! I'VE KILLED MY OWN SON!
HOWEVER, NEXT MOMENT...
NO, MY FRIEND! UNSEEN BY YOU, I, SUPERMAN, TOOK YOUR SON'S PLACE TO ILLUSTRATE THE TRAGEDY WHICH MIGHT HAVE OCCURRED! THE WORLD IS NOT BLOWING UP! YOU HAVE BLOWN UP MENTALLY...FROM OVERWORK AND TENSION!
THEN MY SON IS ALIVE! BUT SUPERMAN, HOW IS IT YOU'RE SO SMALL IN SIZE?
10

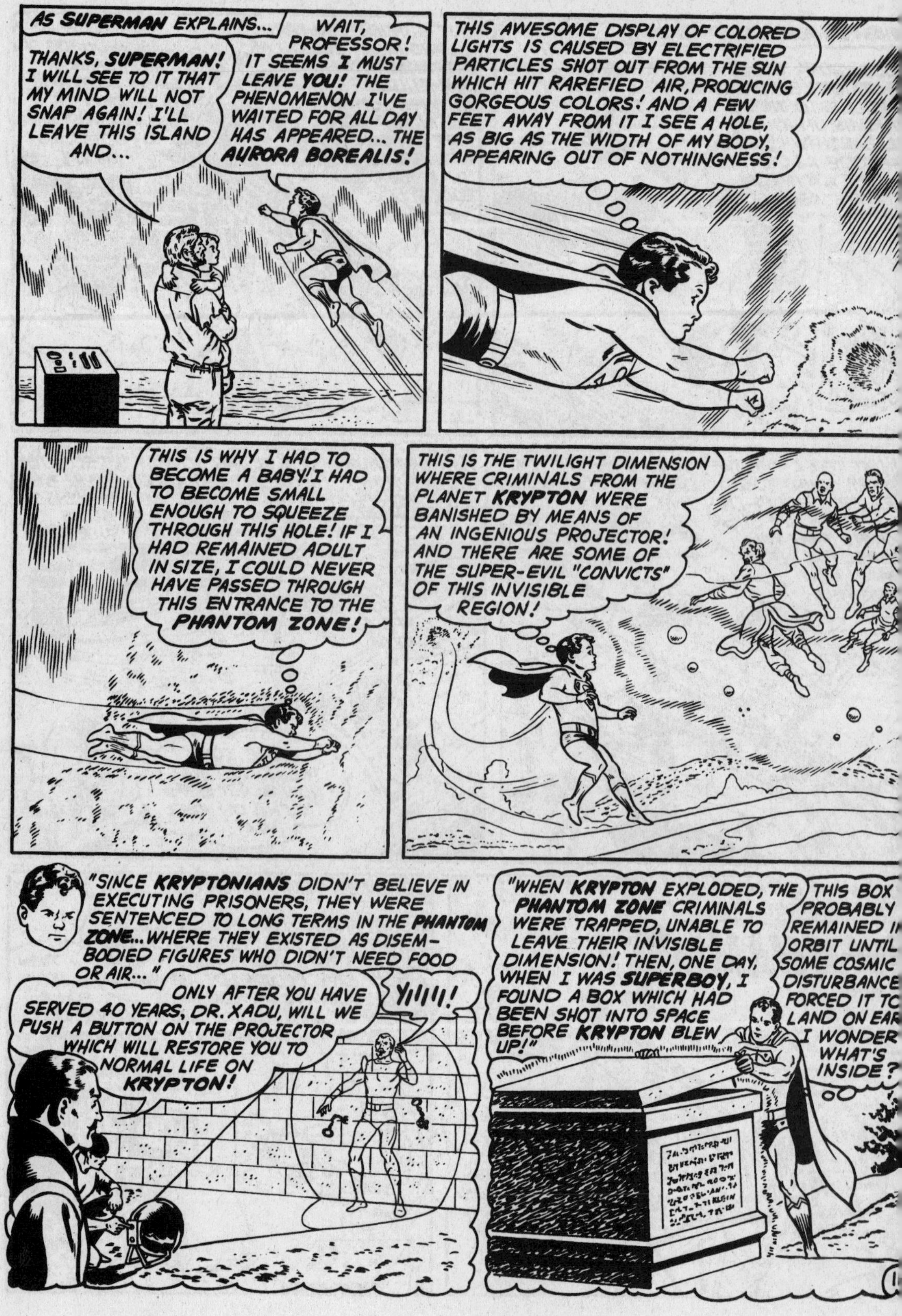
AS SUPERMAN EXPLAINS...
THANKS, SUPERMAN! I WILL SEE TO IT THAT MY MIND WILL NOT SNAP AGAIN! I'LL LEAVE THIS ISLAND AND...
WAIT, PROFESSOR! IT SEEMS I MUST LEAVE YOU! THE PHENOMENON I'VE WAITED FOR ALL DAY HAS APPEARED... THE AURORA BOREALIS!
THIS AWESOME DISPLAY OF COLORED LIGHTS IS CAUSED BY ELECTRIFIED PARTICLES SHOT OUT FROM THE SUN WHICH HIT RAREFIED AIR, PRODUCING GORGEOUS COLORS! AND A FEW FEET AWAY FROM IT I SEE A HOLE, AS BIG AS THE WIDTH OF MY BODY, APPEARING OUT OF NOTHINGNESS!
THIS IS WHY I HAD TO BECOME A BABY! I HAD TO BECOME SMALL ENOUGH TO SQUEEZE THROUGH THIS HOLE! IF I HAD REMAINED ADULT IN SIZE, I COULD NEVER HAVE PASSED THROUGH THIS ENTRANCE TO THE PHANTOM ZONE!
THIS IS THE TWILIGHT DIMENSION WHERE CRIMINALS FROM THE PLANET KRYPTON WERE BANISHED BY MEANS OF AN INGENIOUS PROJECTOR! AND THERE ARE SOME OF THE SUPER-EVIL "CONVICTS" OF THIS INVISIBLE REGION!
"SINCE KRYPTONIANS DIDN'T BELIEVE IN EXECUTING PRISONERS, THEY WERE SENTENCED TO LONG TERMS IN THE PHANTOM ZONE... WHERE THEY EXISTED AS DISEMBODIED FIGURES WHO DIDN'T NEED FOOD OR AIR..."
ONLY AFTER YOU HAVE SERVED 40 YEARS, DR. XADU, WILL WE PUSH A BUTTON ON THE PROJECTOR WHICH WILL RESTORE YOU TO NORMAL LIFE ON KRYPTON!
YIIIII!
"WHEN KRYPTON EXPLODED, THE PHANTOM ZONE CRIMINALS WERE TRAPPED, UNABLE TO LEAVE THEIR INVISIBLE DIMENSION! THEN, ONE DAY, WHEN I WAS SUPERBOY, I FOUND A BOX WHICH HAD BEEN SHOT INTO SPACE BEFORE KRYPTON BLEW UP!"
THIS BOX PROBABLY REMAINED I ORBIT UNTIL SOME COSMIC DISTURBANCE FORCED IT TO LAND ON EAR I WONDER WHAT'S INSIDE?

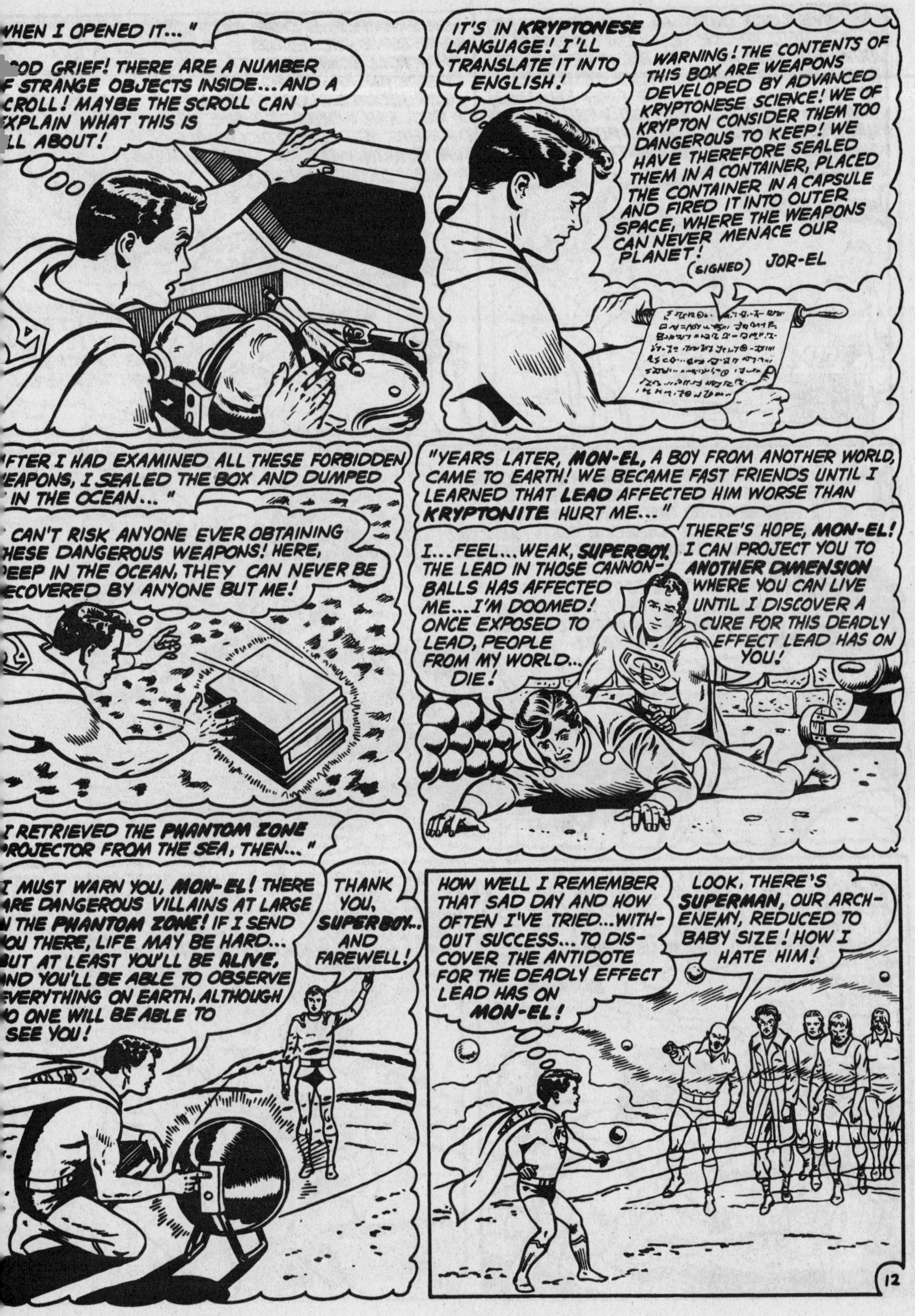
WHEN I OPENED IT..."
OD GRIEF! THERE ARE A NUMBER F STRANGE OBJECTS INSIDE... AND A CROLL! MAYBE THE SCROLL CAN XPLAIN WHAT THIS IS LL ABOUT!
IT'S IN KRYPTONESE LANGUAGE! I'LL TRANSLATE IT INTO ENGLISH!
WARNING! THE CONTENTS OF THIS BOX ARE WEAPONS DEVELOPED BY ADVANCED KRYPTONESE SCIENCE! WE OF KRYPTON CONSIDER THEM TOO DANGEROUS TO KEEP! WE HAVE THEREFORE SEALED THEM IN A CONTAINER, PLACED THE CONTAINER IN A CAPSULE AND FIRED IT INTO OUTER SPACE, WHERE THE WEAPONS CAN NEVER MENACE OUR PLANET! (SIGNED) JOR-EL
FTER I HAD EXAMINED ALL THESE FORBIDDEN EAPONS, I SEALED THE BOX AND DUMPED IN THE OCEAN..."
CAN'T RISK ANYONE EVER OBTAINING HESE DANGEROUS WEAPONS! HERE, EEP IN THE OCEAN, THEY CAN NEVER BE ECOVERED BY ANYONE BUT ME!
"YEARS LATER, MON-EL, A BOY FROM ANOTHER WORLD, CAME TO EARTH! WE BECAME FAST FRIENDS UNTIL I LEARNED THAT LEAD AFFECTED HIM WORSE THAN KRYPTONITE HURT ME..."
I...FEEL...WEAK, SUPERBOY. THE LEAD IN THOSE CANNON-BALLS HAS AFFECTED ME...I'M DOOMED! ONCE EXPOSED TO LEAD, PEOPLE FROM MY WORLD... DIE!
THERE'S HOPE, MON-EL! I CAN PROJECT YOU TO ANOTHER DIMENSION WHERE YOU CAN LIVE UNTIL I DISCOVER A CURE FOR THIS DEADLY EFFECT LEAD HAS ON YOU!
I RETRIEVED THE PHANTOM ZONE PROJECTOR FROM THE SEA, THEN..."
I MUST WARN YOU, MON-EL! THERE ARE DANGEROUS VILLAINS AT LARGE N THE PHANTOM ZONE! IF I SEND OU THERE, LIFE MAY BE HARD... UT AT LEAST YOU'LL BE ALIVE, ND YOU'LL BE ABLE TO OBSERVE EVERYTHING ON EARTH, ALTHOUGH O ONE WILL BE ABLE TO SEE YOU!
THANK YOU, SUPERBOY... AND FAREWELL!
HOW WELL I REMEMBER THAT SAD DAY AND HOW OFTEN I'VE TRIED...WITHOUT SUCCESS...TO DISCOVER THE ANTIDOTE FOR THE DEADLY EFFECT LEAD HAS ON MON-EL!
LOOK, THERE'S SUPERMAN, OUR ARCH-ENEMY, REDUCED TO BABY SIZE! HOW I HATE HIM!
12

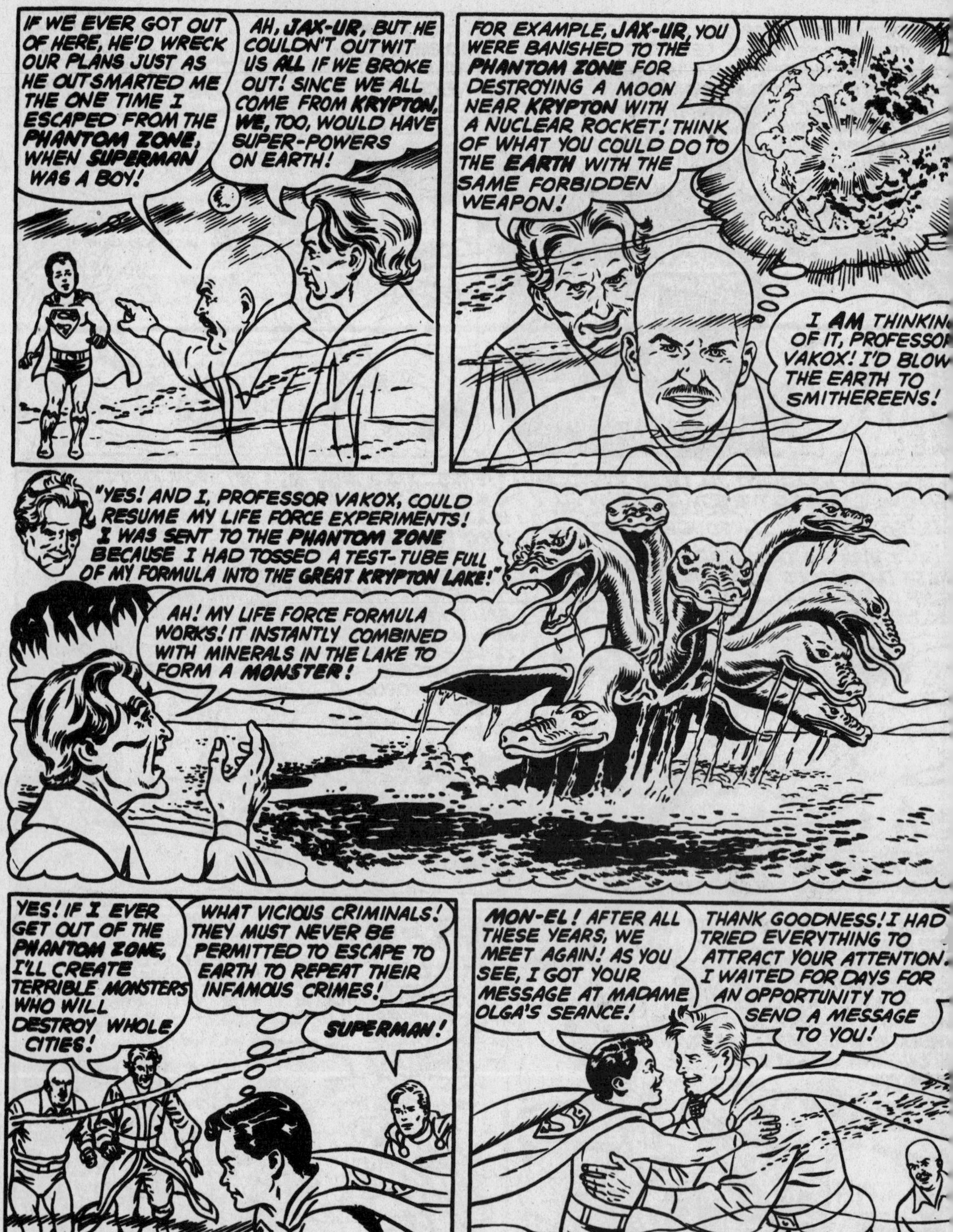
IF WE EVER GOT OUT OF HERE, HE'D WRECK OUR PLANS JUST AS HE OUTSMARTED ME THE ONE TIME I ESCAPED FROM THE PHANTOM ZONE, WHEN SUPERMAN WAS A BOY!
AH, JAX-UR, BUT HE COULDN'T OUTWIT US ALL IF WE BROKE OUT! SINCE WE ALL COME FROM KRYPTON, WE, TOO, WOULD HAVE SUPER-POWERS ON EARTH!
FOR EXAMPLE, JAX-UR, YOU WERE BANISHED TO THE PHANTOM ZONE FOR DESTROYING A MOON NEAR KRYPTON WITH A NUCLEAR ROCKET! THINK OF WHAT YOU COULD DO TO THE EARTH WITH THE SAME FORBIDDEN WEAPON!
I AM THINKIN OF IT, PROFESSOR VAKOX! I'D BLOW THE EARTH TO SMITHEREENS!
"YES! AND I, PROFESSOR VAKOX, COULD RESUME MY LIFE FORCE EXPERIMENTS! I WAS SENT TO THE PHANTOM ZONE BECAUSE I HAD TOSSED A TEST-TUBE FULL OF MY FORMULA INTO THE GREAT KRYPTON LAKE!"
AH! MY LIFE FORCE FORMULA WORKS! IT INSTANTLY COMBINED WITH MINERALS IN THE LAKE TO FORM A MONSTER!
YES! IF I EVER GET OUT OF THE PHANTOM ZONE, I'LL CREATE TERRIBLE MONSTERS WHO WILL DESTROY WHOLE CITIES!
WHAT VICIOUS CRIMINALS! THEY MUST NEVER BE PERMITTED TO ESCAPE TO EARTH TO REPEAT THEIR INFAMOUS CRIMES!
SUPERMAN!
MON-EL! AFTER ALL THESE YEARS, WE MEET AGAIN! AS YOU SEE, I GOT YOUR MESSAGE AT MADAME OLGA'S SEANCE!
THANK GOODNESS! I HAD TRIED EVERYTHING TO ATTRACT YOUR ATTENTION. I WAITED FOR DAYS FOR AN OPPORTUNITY TO SEND A MESSAGE TO YOU!
13

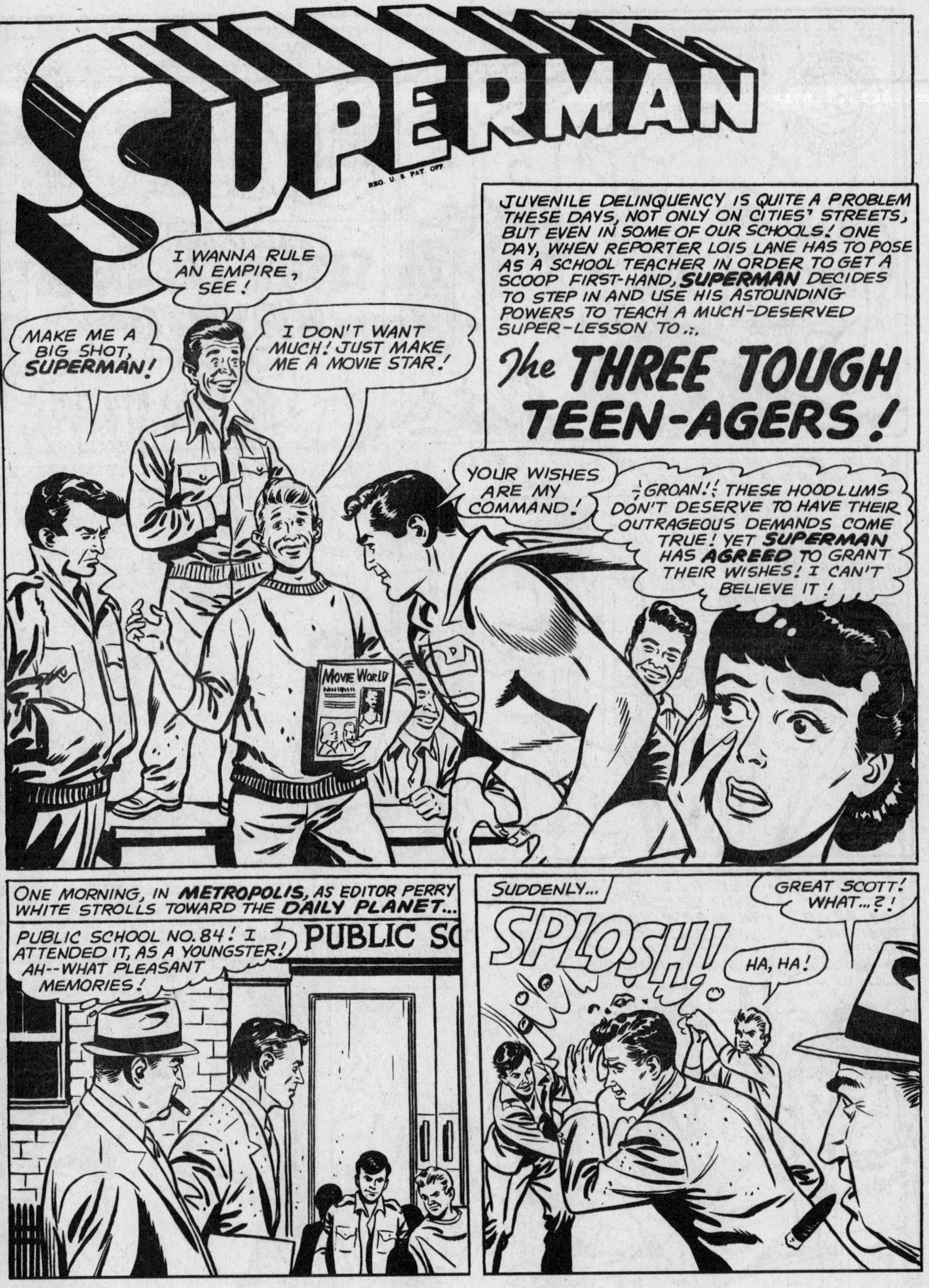
SUPERMAN
REG. U.S. PAT. OFF.
JUVENILE DELINQUENCY IS QUITE A PROBLEM THESE DAYS, NOT ONLY ON CITIES' STREETS, BUT EVEN IN SOME OF OUR SCHOOLS! ONE DAY, WHEN REPORTER LOIS LANE HAS TO POSE AS A SCHOOL TEACHER IN ORDER TO GET A SCOOP FIRST-HAND, SUPERMAN DECIDES TO STEP IN AND USE HIS ASTOUNDING POWERS TO TEACH A MUCH-DESERVED SUPER-LESSON TO...
The THREE TOUGH TEEN-AGERS!
MAKE ME A BIG SHOT, SUPERMAN!
I WANNA RULE AN EMPIRE, SEE!
I DON'T WANT MUCH! JUST MAKE ME A MOVIE STAR!
MOVIE WORLD
YOUR WISHES ARE MY COMMAND!
¡GROAN!¡ THESE HOODLUMS DON'T DESERVE TO HAVE THEIR OUTRAGEOUS DEMANDS COME TRUE! YET SUPERMAN HAS AGREED TO GRANT THEIR WISHES! I CAN'T BELIEVE IT!
ONE MORNING, IN METROPOLIS, AS EDITOR PERRY WHITE STROLLS TOWARD THE DAILY PLANET...
PUBLIC SC
PUBLIC SCHOOL NO. 84! I ATTENDED IT, AS A YOUNGSTER! AH--WHAT PLEASANT MEMORIES!
SUDDENLY...
SPLOSH!
HA, HA!
GREAT SCOTT! WHAT...?!

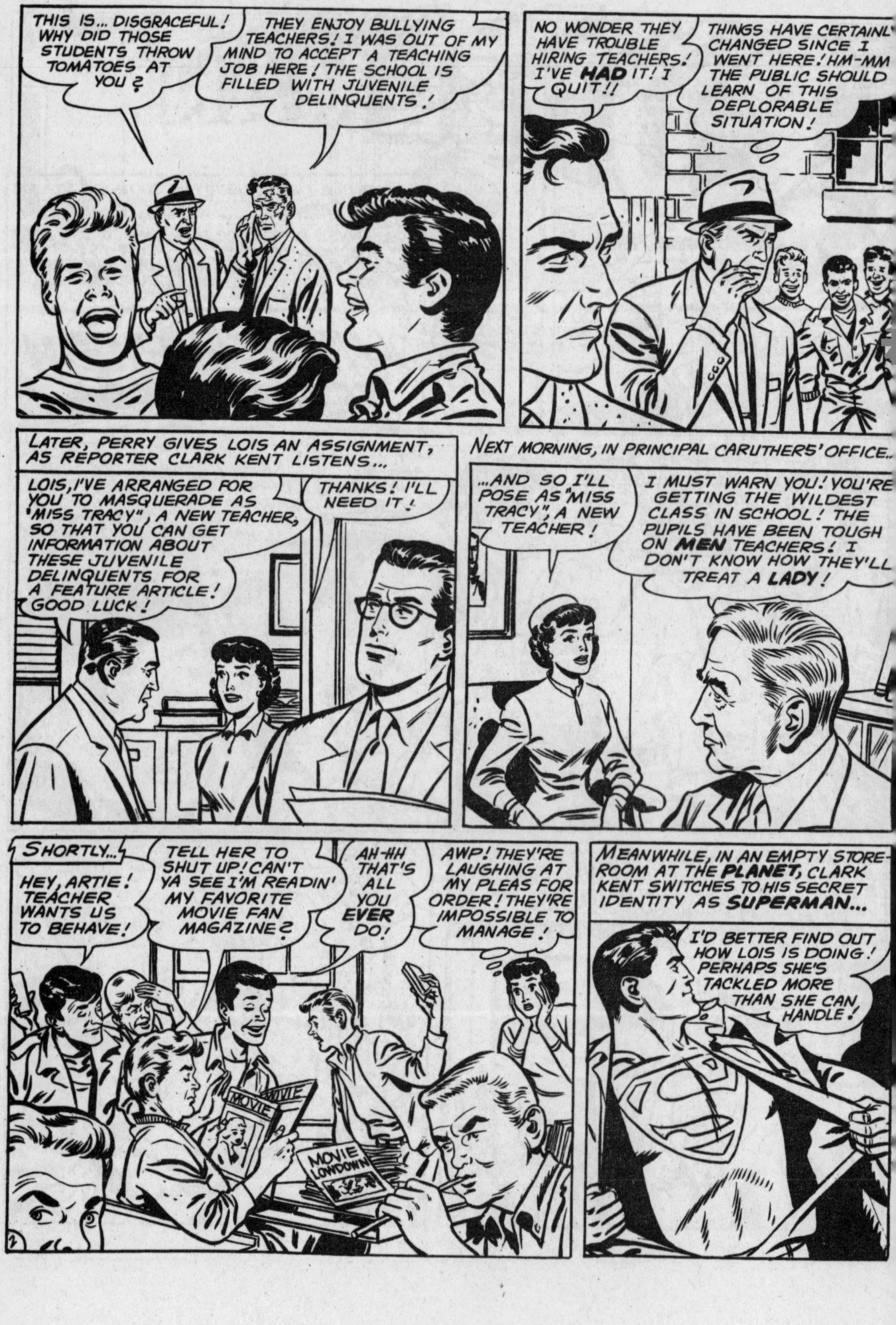
THIS IS... DISGRACEFUL! WHY DID THOSE STUDENTS THROW TOMATOES AT YOU?
THEY ENJOY BULLYING TEACHERS! I WAS OUT OF MY MIND TO ACCEPT A TEACHING JOB HERE! THE SCHOOL IS FILLED WITH JUVENILE DELINQUENTS!
NO WONDER THEY HAVE TROUBLE HIRING TEACHERS! I'VE HAD IT! I QUIT!!
THINGS HAVE CERTAINL CHANGED SINCE I WENT HERE! HM-MM THE PUBLIC SHOULD LEARN OF THIS DEPLORABLE SITUATION!
LATER, PERRY GIVES LOIS AN ASSIGNMENT, AS REPORTER CLARK KENT LISTENS...
LOIS, I'VE ARRANGED FOR YOU TO MASQUERADE AS "MISS TRACY", A NEW TEACHER, SO THAT YOU CAN GET INFORMATION ABOUT THESE JUVENILE DELINQUENTS FOR A FEATURE ARTICLE! GOOD LUCK!
THANKS! I'LL NEED IT!
NEXT MORNING, IN PRINCIPAL CARUTHERS' OFFICE...
...AND SO I'LL POSE AS "MISS TRACY", A NEW TEACHER!
I MUST WARN YOU! YOU'RE GETTING THE WILDEST CLASS IN SCHOOL! THE PUPILS HAVE BEEN TOUGH ON MEN TEACHERS! I DON'T KNOW HOW THEY'LL TREAT A LADY!
SHORTLY...
HEY, ARTIE! TEACHER WANTS US TO BEHAVE!
TELL HER TO SHUT UP! CAN'T YA SEE I'M READIN' MY FAVORITE MOVIE FAN MAGAZINE?
AH-HH THAT'S ALL YOU EVER DO!
AWP! THEY'RE LAUGHING AT MY PLEAS FOR ORDER! THEY'RE IMPOSSIBLE TO MANAGE!
MOVIE
MOVIE LOWDOWN
MEANWHILE, IN AN EMPTY STORE-ROOM AT THE PLANET, CLARK KENT SWITCHES TO HIS SECRET IDENTITY AS SUPERMAN...
I'D BETTER FIND OUT HOW LOIS IS DOING! PERHAPS SHE'S TACKLED MORE THAN SHE CAN HANDLE!
2

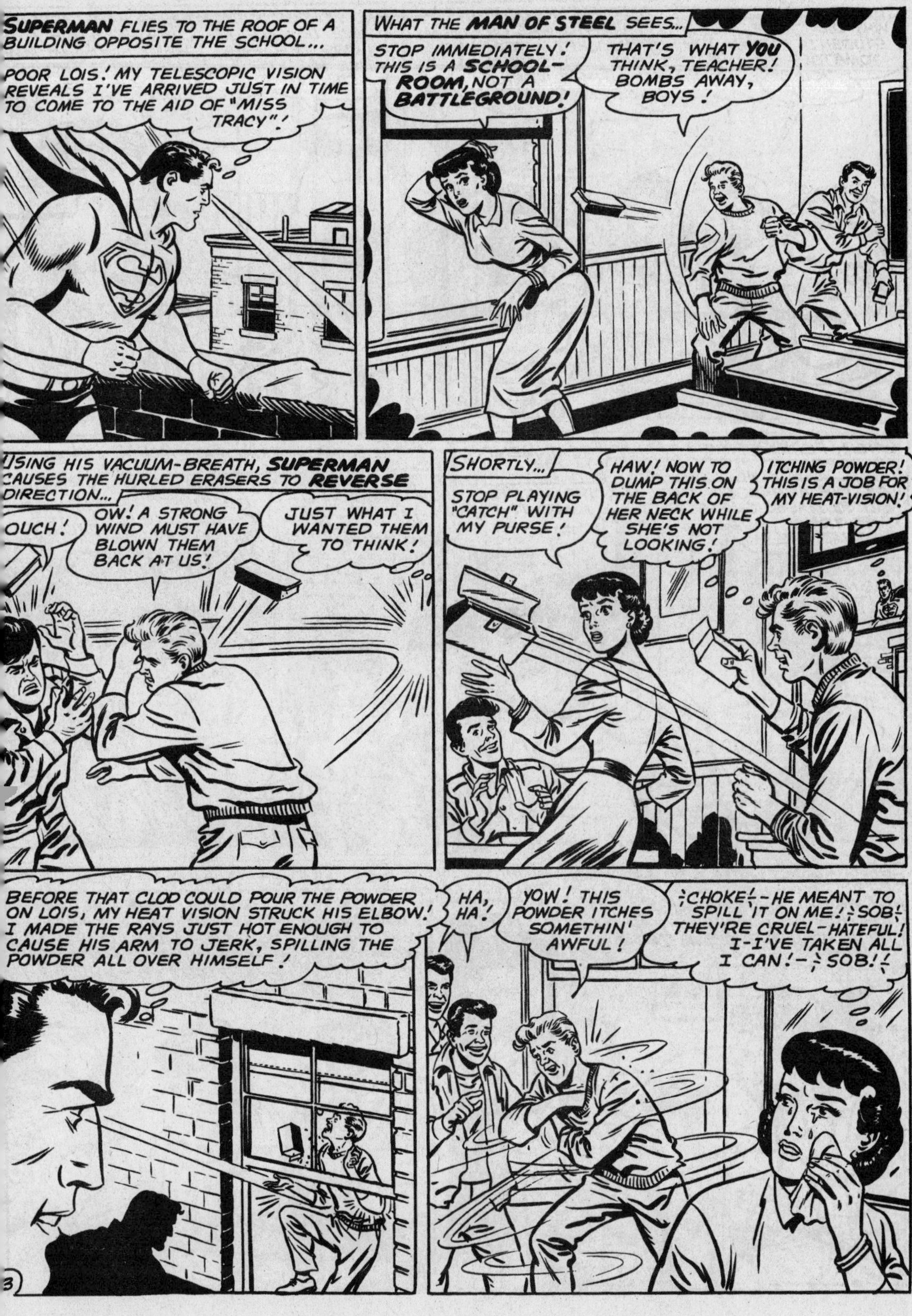
SUPERMAN FLIES TO THE ROOF OF A BUILDING OPPOSITE THE SCHOOL...
POOR LOIS! MY TELESCOPIC VISION REVEALS I'VE ARRIVED JUST IN TIME TO COME TO THE AID OF "MISS TRACY"!
WHAT THE MAN OF STEEL SEES...
STOP IMMEDIATELY! THIS IS A SCHOOL-ROOM, NOT A BATTLEGROUND!
THAT'S WHAT YOU THINK, TEACHER! BOMBS AWAY, BOYS!
USING HIS VACUUM-BREATH, SUPERMAN CAUSES THE HURLED ERASERS TO REVERSE DIRECTION...
OUCH!
OW! A STRONG WIND MUST HAVE BLOWN THEM BACK AT US!
JUST WHAT I WANTED THEM TO THINK!
SHORTLY...
STOP PLAYING "CATCH" WITH MY PURSE!
HAW! NOW TO DUMP THIS ON THE BACK OF HER NECK WHILE SHE'S NOT LOOKING!
ITCHING POWDER! THIS IS A JOB FOR MY HEAT-VISION!
BEFORE THAT CLOD COULD POUR THE POWDER ON LOIS, MY HEAT VISION STRUCK HIS ELBOW! I MADE THE RAYS JUST HOT ENOUGH TO CAUSE HIS ARM TO JERK, SPILLING THE POWDER ALL OVER HIMSELF!
3
HA, HA!
YOW! THIS POWDER ITCHES SOMETHIN' AWFUL!
-CHOKE- -HE MEANT TO SPILL IT ON ME! -SOB- THEY'RE CRUEL-HATEFUL! I-I'VE TAKEN ALL I CAN! - -SOB!-

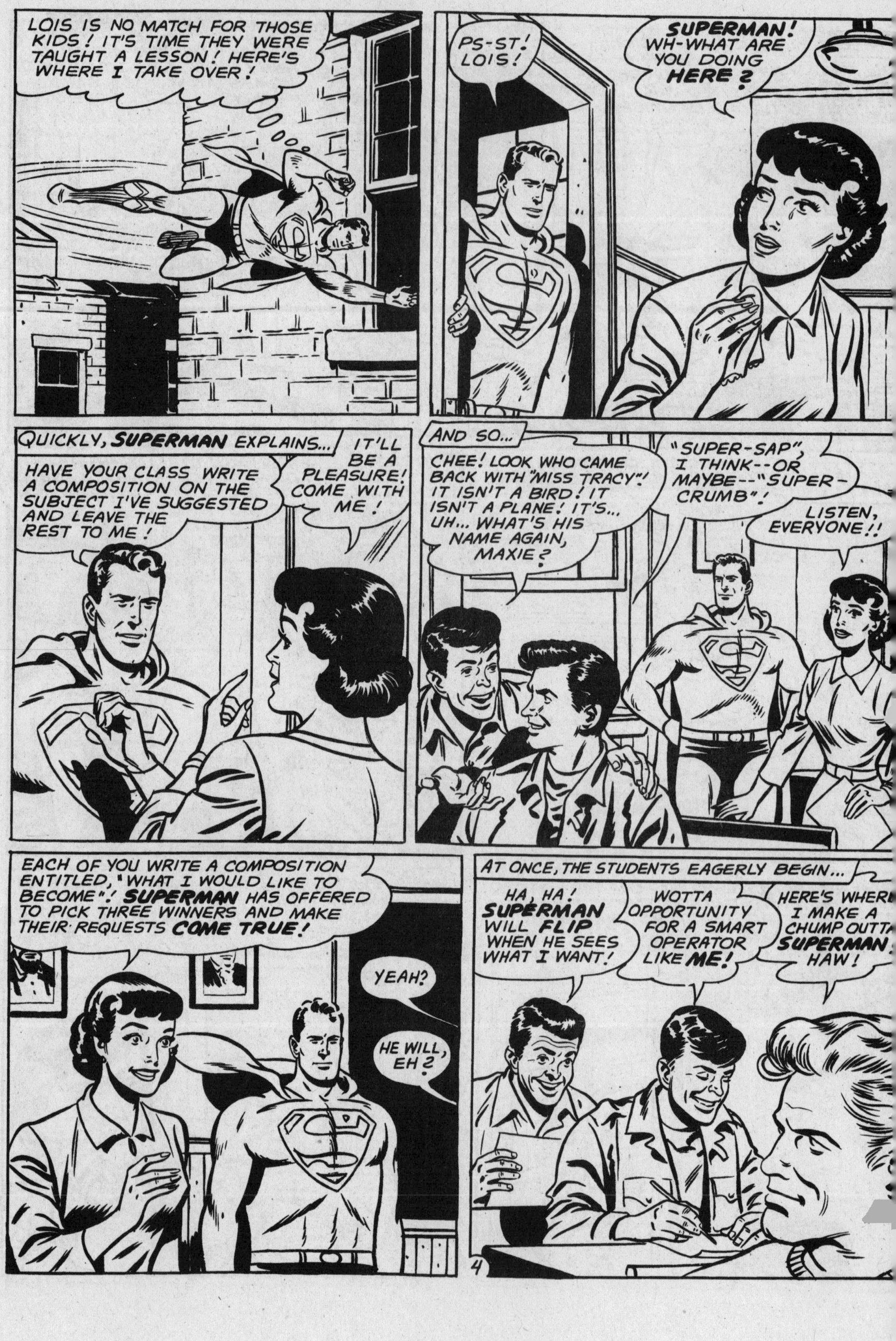
LOIS IS NO MATCH FOR THOSE KIDS! IT'S TIME THEY WERE TAUGHT A LESSON! HERE'S WHERE I TAKE OVER!
PS-ST! LOIS!
SUPERMAN! WH-WHAT ARE YOU DOING HERE?
QUICKLY, SUPERMAN EXPLAINS...
HAVE YOUR CLASS WRITE A COMPOSITION ON THE SUBJECT I'VE SUGGESTED AND LEAVE THE REST TO ME!
IT'LL BE A PLEASURE! COME WITH ME!
AND SO...
CHEE! LOOK WHO CAME BACK WITH "MISS TRACY"! IT ISN'T A BIRD! IT ISN'T A PLANE! IT'S... UH... WHAT'S HIS NAME AGAIN, MAXIE?
"SUPER-SAP", I THINK--OR MAYBE--"SUPER-CRUMB"!
LISTEN, EVERYONE!!
EACH OF YOU WRITE A COMPOSITION ENTITLED, "WHAT I WOULD LIKE TO BECOME"! SUPERMAN HAS OFFERED TO PICK THREE WINNERS AND MAKE THEIR REQUESTS COME TRUE!
YEAH?
HE WILL, EH?
AT ONCE, THE STUDENTS EAGERLY BEGIN...
HA, HA! SUPERMAN WILL FLIP WHEN HE SEES WHAT I WANT!
WOTTA OPPORTUNITY FOR A SMART OPERATOR LIKE ME!
HERE'S WHERE I MAKE A CHUMP OUTTA SUPERMAN! HAW!
4

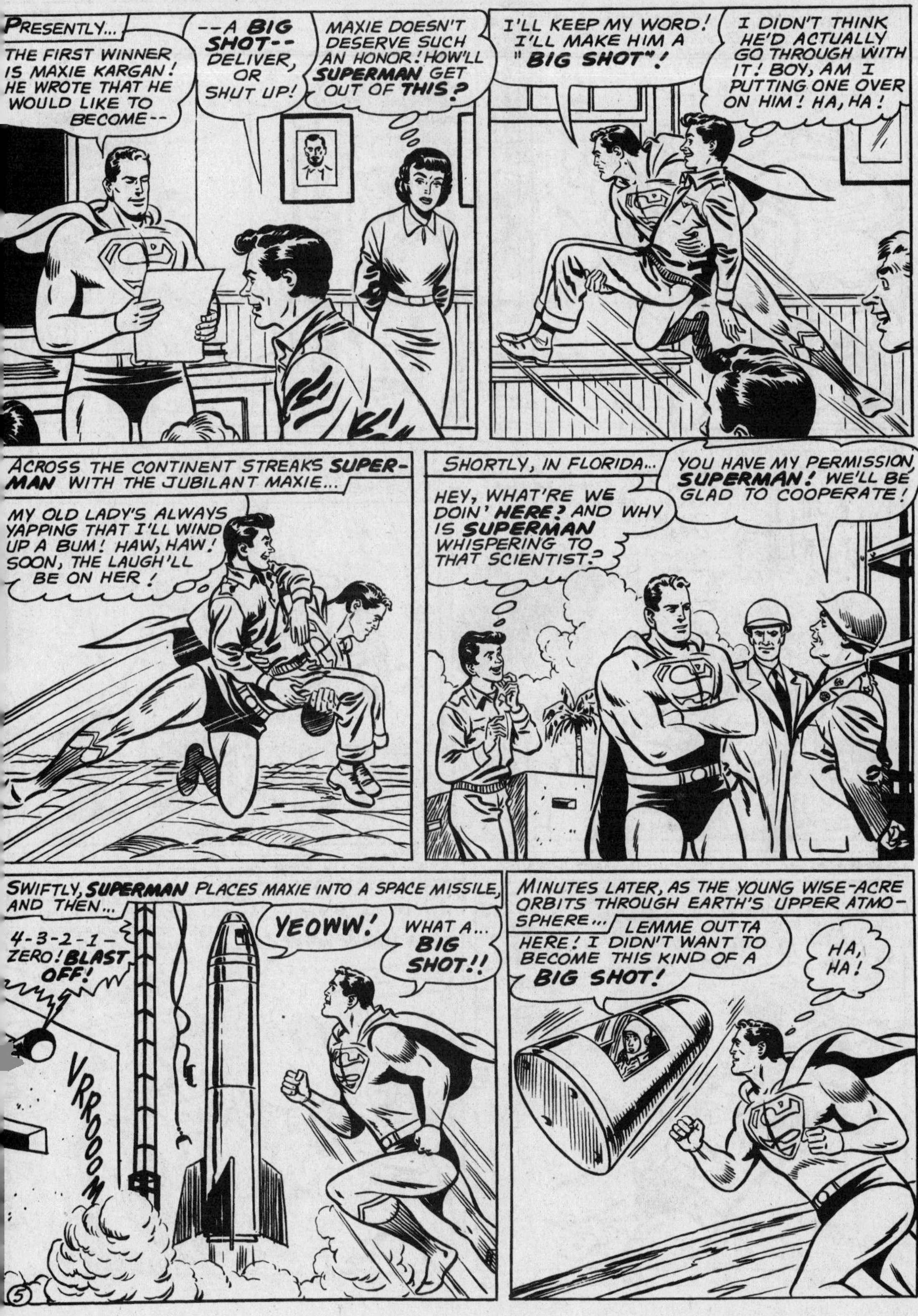
PRESENTLY...
THE FIRST WINNER IS MAXIE KARGAN! HE WROTE THAT HE WOULD LIKE TO BECOME--
--A BIG SHOT-- DELIVER, OR SHUT UP!
MAXIE DOESN'T DESERVE SUCH AN HONOR! HOW'LL SUPERMAN GET OUT OF THIS?
I'LL KEEP MY WORD! I'LL MAKE HIM A "BIG SHOT"!
I DIDN'T THINK HE'D ACTUALLY GO THROUGH WITH IT! BOY, AM I PUTTING ONE OVER ON HIM! HA, HA!
ACROSS THE CONTINENT STREAKS SUPERMAN WITH THE JUBILANT MAXIE...
MY OLD LADY'S ALWAYS YAPPING THAT I'LL WIND UP A BUM! HAW, HAW! SOON, THE LAUGH'LL BE ON HER!
SHORTLY, IN FLORIDA...
HEY, WHAT'RE WE DOIN' HERE? AND WHY IS SUPERMAN WHISPERING TO THAT SCIENTIST?
YOU HAVE MY PERMISSION, SUPERMAN! WE'LL BE GLAD TO COOPERATE!
SWIFTLY, SUPERMAN PLACES MAXIE INTO A SPACE MISSILE, AND THEN...
4-3-2-1-ZERO! BLAST OFF!
YEOWW!
WHAT A... BIG SHOT!!
VRROOOM
MINUTES LATER, AS THE YOUNG WISE-ACRE ORBITS THROUGH EARTH'S UPPER ATMOSPHERE...
LEMME OUTTA HERE! I DIDN'T WANT TO BECOME THIS KIND OF A BIG SHOT!
HA, HA!
5

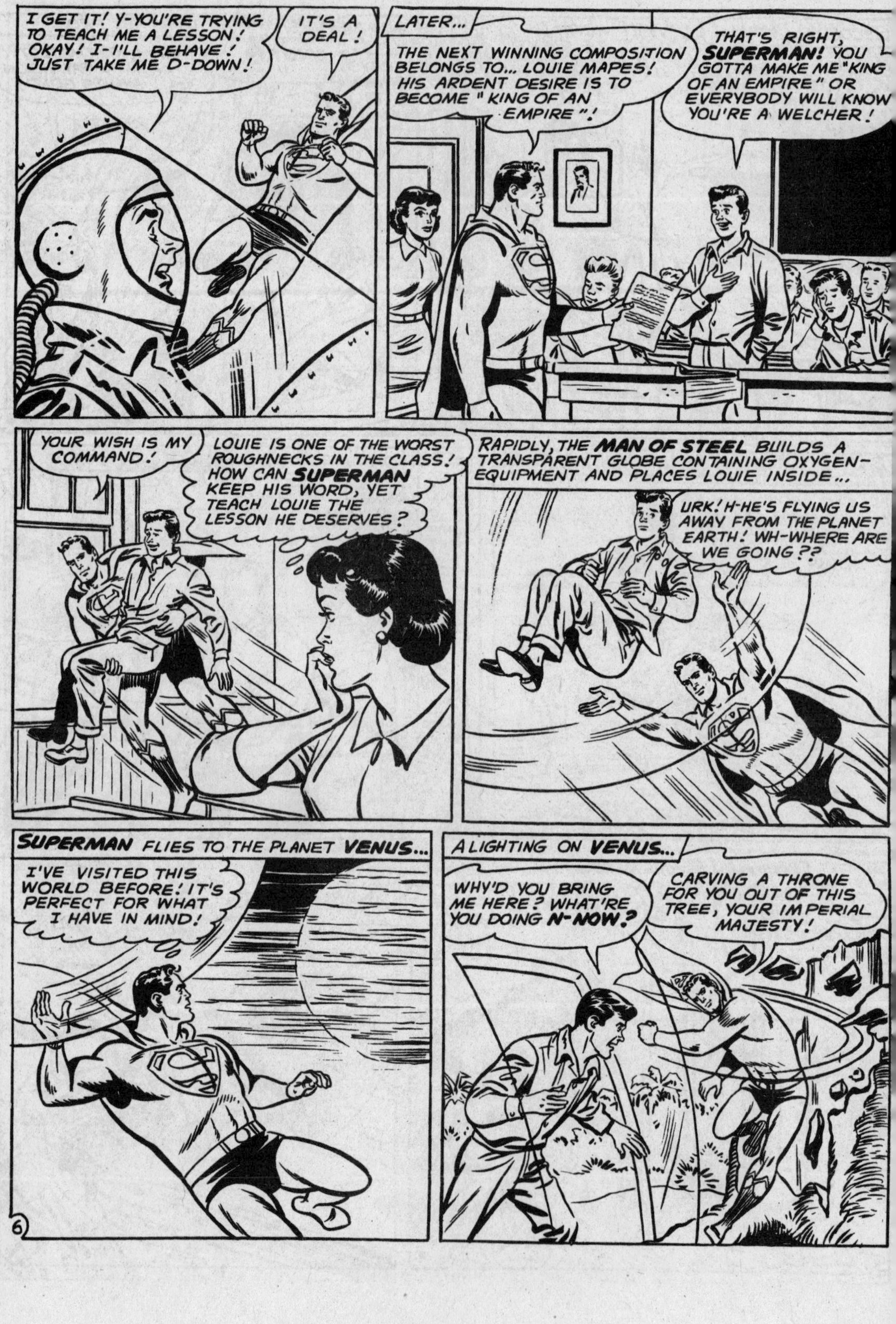
I GET IT! Y-YOU'RE TRYING TO TEACH ME A LESSON! OKAY! I-I'LL BEHAVE! JUST TAKE ME D-DOWN!
IT'S A DEAL!
LATER...
THE NEXT WINNING COMPOSITION BELONGS TO... LOUIE MAPES! HIS ARDENT DESIRE IS TO BECOME "KING OF AN EMPIRE"!
THAT'S RIGHT, SUPERMAN! YOU GOTTA MAKE ME "KING OF AN EMPIRE" OR EVERYBODY WILL KNOW YOU'RE A WELCHER!
YOUR WISH IS MY COMMAND!
LOUIE IS ONE OF THE WORST ROUGHNECKS IN THE CLASS! HOW CAN SUPERMAN KEEP HIS WORD, YET TEACH LOUIE THE LESSON HE DESERVES?
RAPIDLY, THE MAN OF STEEL BUILDS A TRANSPARENT GLOBE CONTAINING OXYGEN-EQUIPMENT AND PLACES LOUIE INSIDE...
URK! H-HE'S FLYING US AWAY FROM THE PLANET EARTH! WH-WHERE ARE WE GOING??
SUPERMAN FLIES TO THE PLANET VENUS...
I'VE VISITED THIS WORLD BEFORE! IT'S PERFECT FOR WHAT I HAVE IN MIND!
6
ALIGHTING ON VENUS...
WHY'D YOU BRING ME HERE? WHAT'RE YOU DOING N-NOW?
CARVING A THRONE FOR YOU OUT OF THIS TREE, YOUR IMPERIAL MAJESTY!

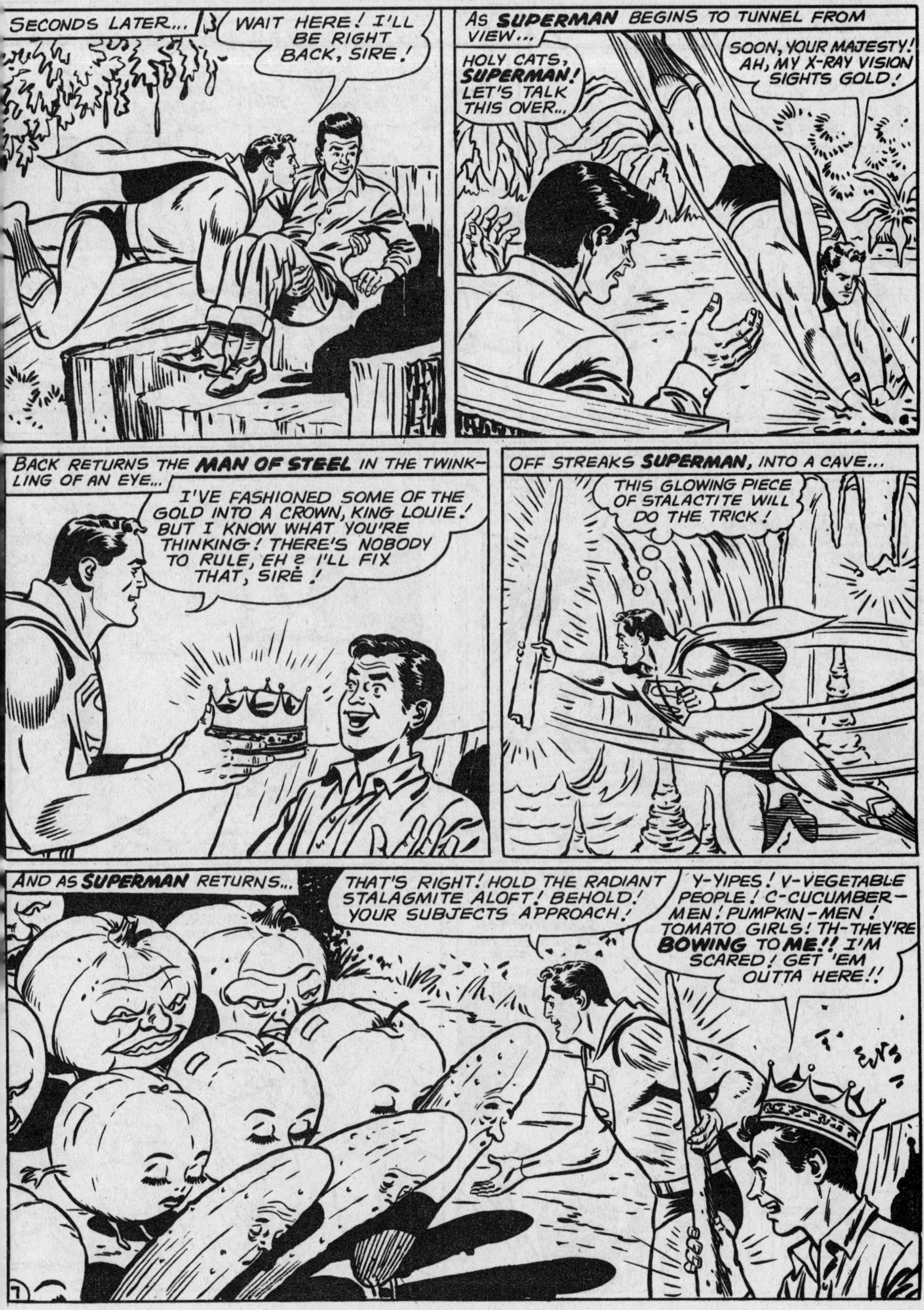
SECONDS LATER...
WAIT HERE! I'LL BE RIGHT BACK, SIRE!
AS SUPERMAN BEGINS TO TUNNEL FROM VIEW...
HOLY CATS, SUPERMAN! LET'S TALK THIS OVER...
SOON, YOUR MAJESTY! AH, MY X-RAY VISION SIGHTS GOLD!
BACK RETURNS THE MAN OF STEEL IN THE TWINKLING OF AN EYE...
I'VE FASHIONED SOME OF THE GOLD INTO A CROWN, KING LOUIE! BUT I KNOW WHAT YOU'RE THINKING! THERE'S NOBODY TO RULE, EH? I'LL FIX THAT, SIRE!
OFF STREAKS SUPERMAN, INTO A CAVE...
THIS GLOWING PIECE OF STALACTITE WILL DO THE TRICK!
AND AS SUPERMAN RETURNS...
THAT'S RIGHT! HOLD THE RADIANT STALAGMITE ALOFT! BEHOLD! YOUR SUBJECTS APPROACH!
Y-YIPES! V-VEGETABLE PEOPLE! C-CUCUMBER-MEN! PUMPKIN-MEN! TOMATO GIRLS! TH-THEY'RE BOWING TO ME!! I'M SCARED! GET 'EM OUTTA HERE!!
7

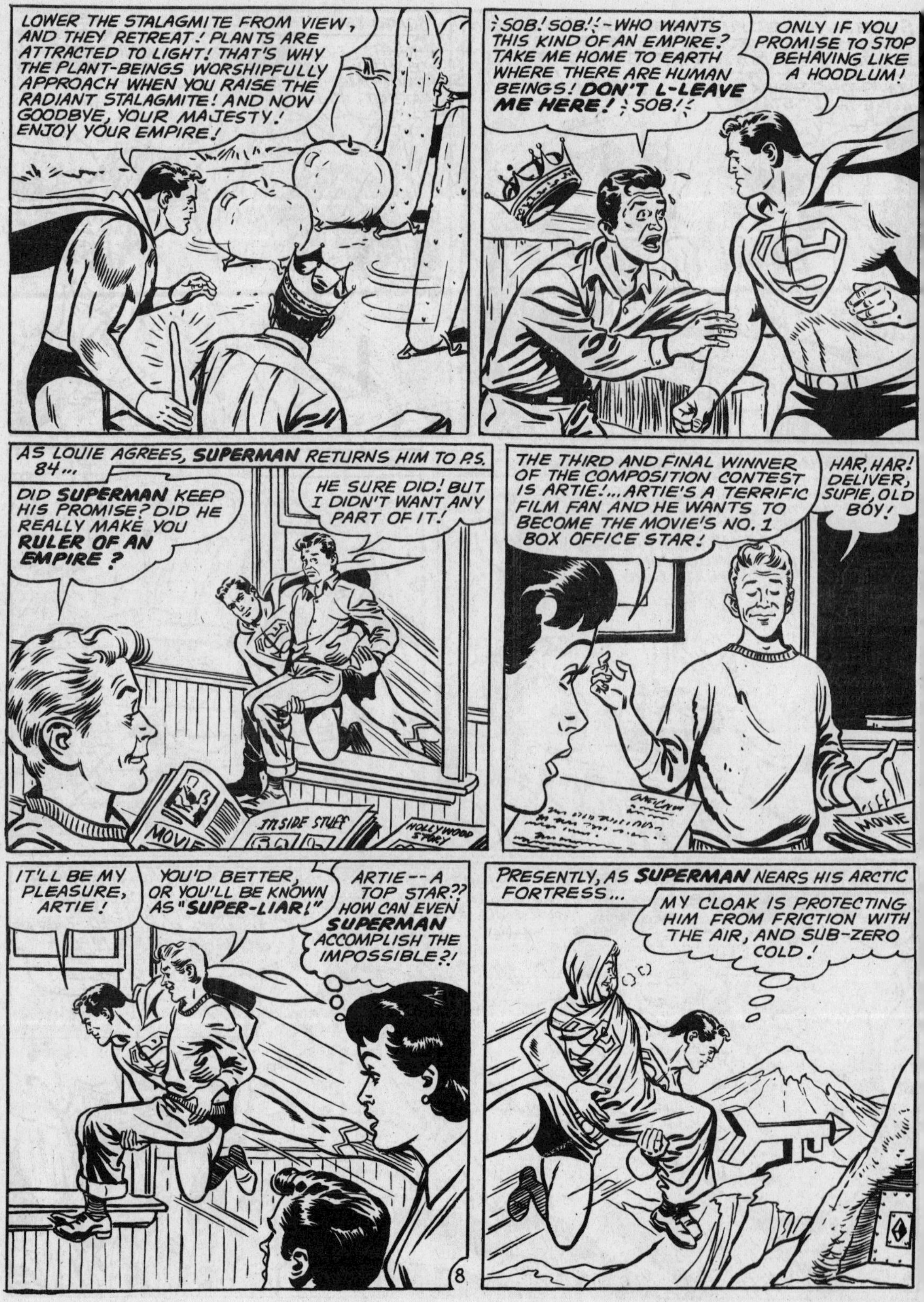
LOWER THE STALAGMITE FROM VIEW, AND THEY RETREAT! PLANTS ARE ATTRACTED TO LIGHT! THAT'S WHY THE PLANT-BEINGS WORSHIPFULLY APPROACH WHEN YOU RAISE THE RADIANT STALAGMITE! AND NOW GOODBYE, YOUR MAJESTY! ENJOY YOUR EMPIRE!
SOB! SOB!-WHO WANTS THIS KIND OF AN EMPIRE? TAKE ME HOME TO EARTH WHERE THERE ARE HUMAN BEINGS! DON'T L-LEAVE ME HERE! SOB!
ONLY IF YOU PROMISE TO STOP BEHAVING LIKE A HOODLUM!
AS LOUIE AGREES, SUPERMAN RETURNS HIM TO P.S. 84...
DID SUPERMAN KEEP HIS PROMISE? DID HE REALLY MAKE YOU RULER OF AN EMPIRE?
HE SURE DID! BUT I DIDN'T WANT ANY PART OF IT!
INSIDE STUFF
MOVIE
HOLLYWOOD STORY
THE THIRD AND FINAL WINNER OF THE COMPOSITION CONTEST IS ARTIE!...ARTIE'S A TERRIFIC FILM FAN AND HE WANTS TO BECOME THE MOVIE'S NO. 1 BOX OFFICE STAR!
HAR, HAR! DELIVER, SUPIE, OLD BOY!
MOVIE
IT'LL BE MY PLEASURE, ARTIE!
YOU'D BETTER, OR YOU'LL BE KNOWN AS "SUPER-LIAR!"
ARTIE-- A TOP STAR?? HOW CAN EVEN SUPERMAN ACCOMPLISH THE IMPOSSIBLE?!
8
PRESENTLY, AS SUPERMAN NEARS HIS ARCTIC FORTRESS...
MY CLOAK IS PROTECTING HIM FROM FRICTION WITH THE AIR, AND SUB-ZERO COLD!

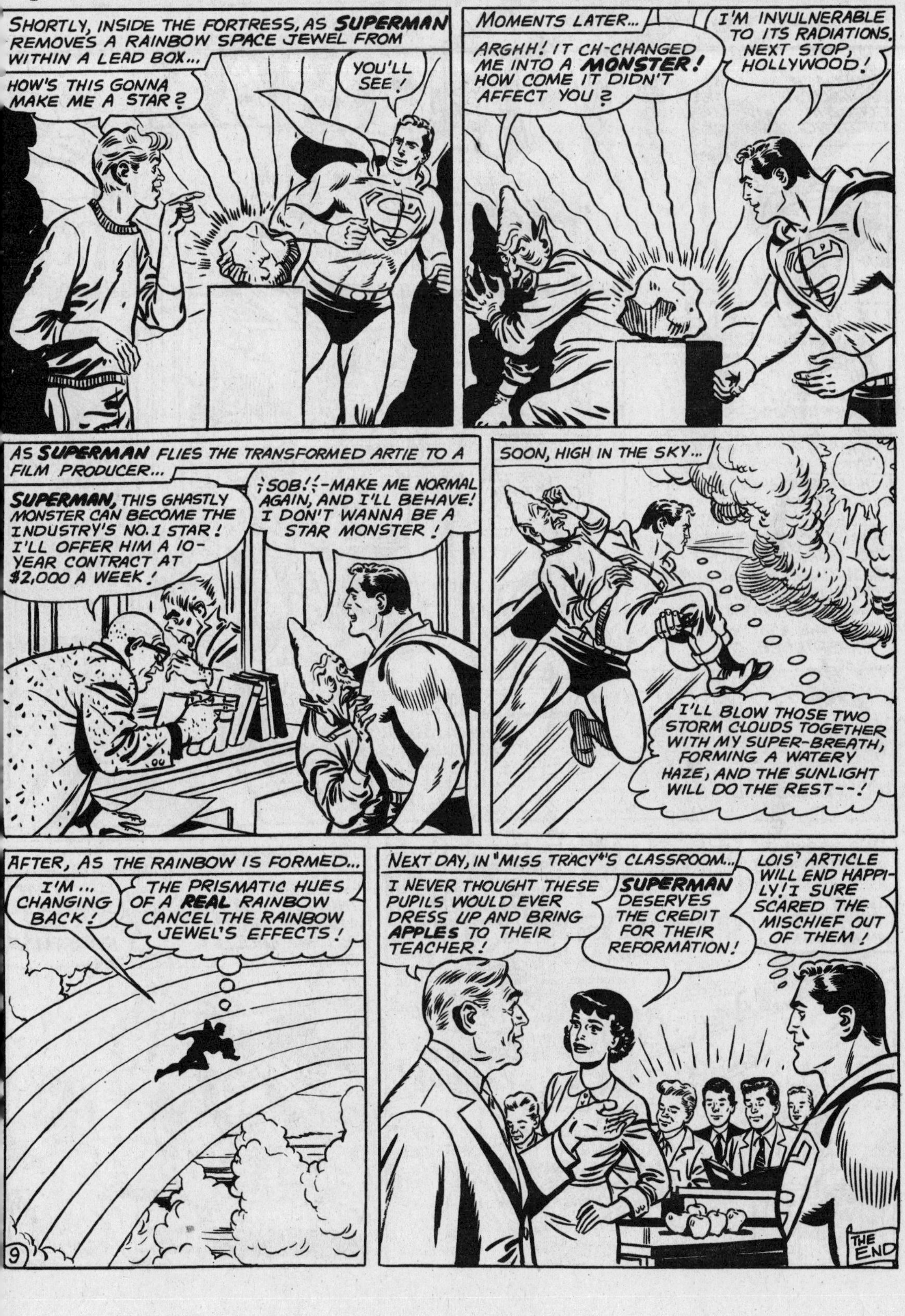
SHORTLY, INSIDE THE FORTRESS, AS SUPERMAN REMOVES A RAINBOW SPACE JEWEL FROM WITHIN A LEAD BOX...
HOW'S THIS GONNA MAKE ME A STAR?
YOU'LL SEE!
MOMENTS LATER...
ARGHH! IT CH-CHANGED ME INTO A MONSTER! HOW COME IT DIDN'T AFFECT YOU?
I'M INVULNERABLE TO ITS RADIATIONS. NEXT STOP, HOLLYWOOD!
AS SUPERMAN FLIES THE TRANSFORMED ARTIE TO A FILM PRODUCER...
SUPERMAN, THIS GHASTLY MONSTER CAN BECOME THE INDUSTRY'S NO. 1 STAR! I'LL OFFER HIM A 10-YEAR CONTRACT AT $2,000 A WEEK!
¡SOB!¡-MAKE ME NORMAL AGAIN, AND I'LL BEHAVE! I DON'T WANNA BE A STAR MONSTER!
SOON, HIGH IN THE SKY...
I'LL BLOW THOSE TWO STORM CLOUDS TOGETHER WITH MY SUPER-BREATH, FORMING A WATERY HAZE, AND THE SUNLIGHT WILL DO THE REST--!
AFTER, AS THE RAINBOW IS FORMED...
I'M... CHANGING BACK!
THE PRISMATIC HUES OF A REAL RAINBOW CANCEL THE RAINBOW JEWEL'S EFFECTS!
9
NEXT DAY, IN "MISS TRACY'S" CLASSROOM...
I NEVER THOUGHT THESE PUPILS WOULD EVER DRESS UP AND BRING APPLES TO THEIR TEACHER!
SUPERMAN DESERVES THE CREDIT FOR THEIR REFORMATION!
LOIS' ARTICLE WILL END HAPPILY! I SURE SCARED THE MISCHIEF OUT OF THEM!
THE END

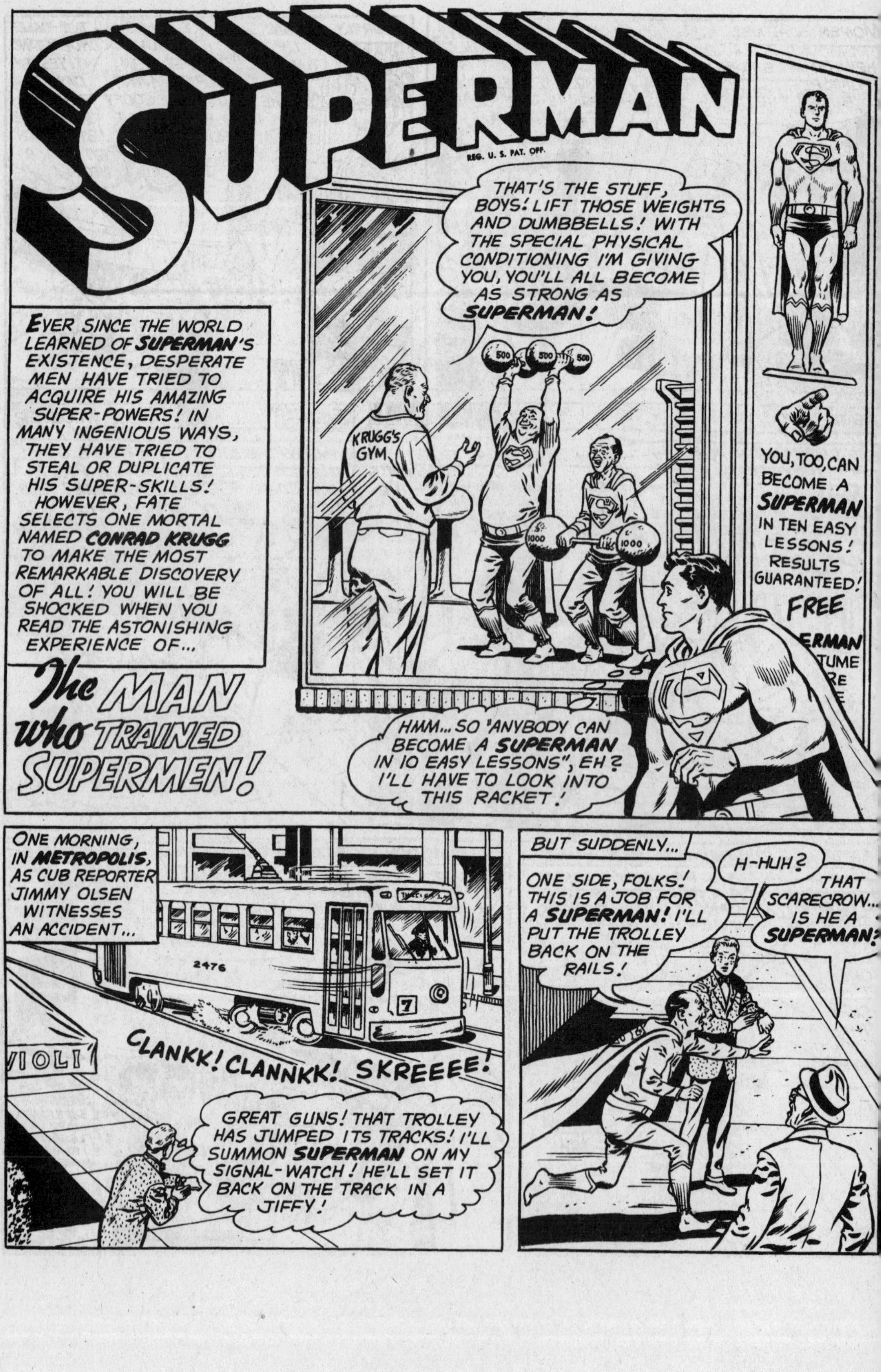
SUPERMAN
REG. U. S. PAT. OFF.
EVER SINCE THE WORLD LEARNED OF SUPERMAN'S EXISTENCE, DESPERATE MEN HAVE TRIED TO ACQUIRE HIS AMAZING SUPER-POWERS! IN MANY INGENIOUS WAYS, THEY HAVE TRIED TO STEAL OR DUPLICATE HIS SUPER-SKILLS! HOWEVER, FATE SELECTS ONE MORTAL NAMED CONRAD KRUGG TO MAKE THE MOST REMARKABLE DISCOVERY OF ALL! YOU WILL BE SHOCKED WHEN YOU READ THE ASTONISHING EXPERIENCE OF...
The MAN who TRAINED SUPERMEN!
THAT'S THE STUFF, BOYS! LIFT THOSE WEIGHTS AND DUMBBELLS! WITH THE SPECIAL PHYSICAL CONDITIONING I'M GIVING YOU, YOU'LL ALL BECOME AS STRONG AS SUPERMAN!
KRUGG'S GYM
500
500
500
1000
1000
YOU, TOO, CAN BECOME A SUPERMAN IN TEN EASY LESSONS! RESULTS GUARANTEED!
FREE
HMM... SO "ANYBODY CAN BECOME A SUPERMAN IN 10 EASY LESSONS", EH? I'LL HAVE TO LOOK INTO THIS RACKET!
ONE MORNING, IN METROPOLIS, AS CUB REPORTER JIMMY OLSEN WITNESSES AN ACCIDENT...
2476
7
CLANKK! CLANNKK! SKREEEEE!
GREAT GUNS! THAT TROLLEY HAS JUMPED ITS TRACKS! I'LL SUMMON SUPERMAN ON MY SIGNAL-WATCH! HE'LL SET IT BACK ON THE TRACK IN A JIFFY!
BUT SUDDENLY...
ONE SIDE, FOLKS! THIS IS A JOB FOR A SUPERMAN! I'LL PUT THE TROLLEY BACK ON THE RAILS!
H-HUH?
THAT SCARECROW... IS HE A SUPERMAN?

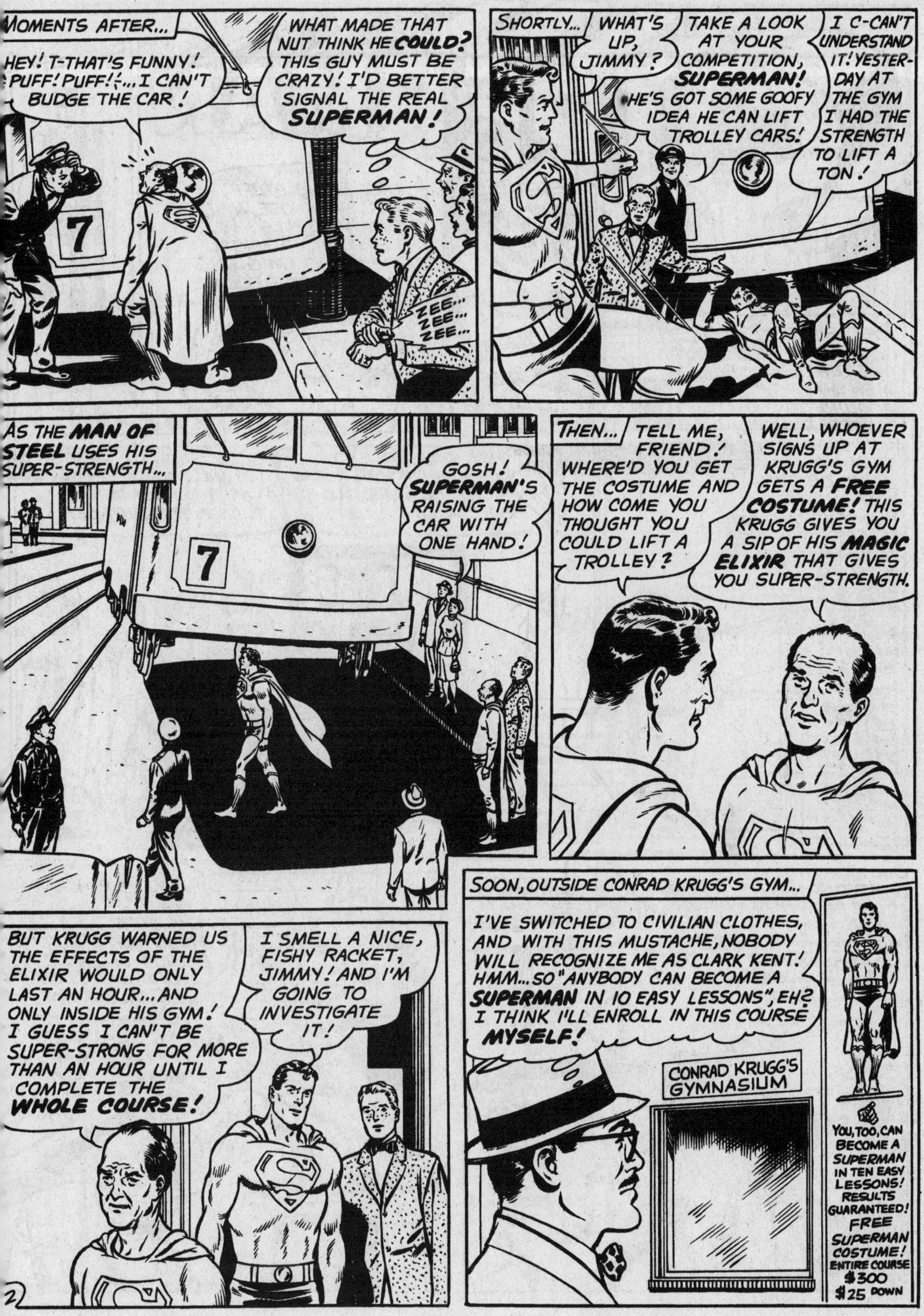
MOMENTS AFTER...
HEY! T-THAT'S FUNNY! PUFF! PUFF!...I CAN'T BUDGE THE CAR!
WHAT MADE THAT NUT THINK HE COULD? THIS GUY MUST BE CRAZY! I'D BETTER SIGNAL THE REAL SUPERMAN!
ZEE... ZEE... ZEE...
7
SHORTLY...
WHAT'S UP, JIMMY?
TAKE A LOOK AT YOUR COMPETITION, SUPERMAN! HE'S GOT SOME GOOFY IDEA HE CAN LIFT TROLLEY CARS!
I C-CAN'T UNDERSTAND IT! YESTERDAY AT THE GYM I HAD THE STRENGTH TO LIFT A TON!
AS THE MAN OF STEEL USES HIS SUPER-STRENGTH...
GOSH! SUPERMAN'S RAISING THE CAR WITH ONE HAND!
7
THEN...
TELL ME, FRIEND! WHERE'D YOU GET THE COSTUME AND HOW COME YOU THOUGHT YOU COULD LIFT A TROLLEY?
WELL, WHOEVER SIGNS UP AT KRUGG'S GYM GETS A FREE COSTUME! THIS KRUGG GIVES YOU A SIP OF HIS MAGIC ELIXIR THAT GIVES YOU SUPER-STRENGTH.
BUT KRUGG WARNED US THE EFFECTS OF THE ELIXIR WOULD ONLY LAST AN HOUR...AND ONLY INSIDE HIS GYM! I GUESS I CAN'T BE SUPER-STRONG FOR MORE THAN AN HOUR UNTIL I COMPLETE THE WHOLE COURSE!
I SMELL A NICE, FISHY RACKET, JIMMY! AND I'M GOING TO INVESTIGATE IT!
2
SOON, OUTSIDE CONRAD KRUGG'S GYM...
I'VE SWITCHED TO CIVILIAN CLOTHES, AND WITH THIS MUSTACHE, NOBODY WILL RECOGNIZE ME AS CLARK KENT! HMM...SO "ANYBODY CAN BECOME A SUPERMAN IN 10 EASY LESSONS", EH? I THINK I'LL ENROLL IN THIS COURSE MYSELF!
CONRAD KRUGG'S GYMNASIUM
YOU, TOO, CAN BECOME A SUPERMAN IN TEN EASY LESSONS! RESULTS GUARANTEED! FREE SUPERMAN COSTUME! ENTIRE COURSE $300 $25 DOWN

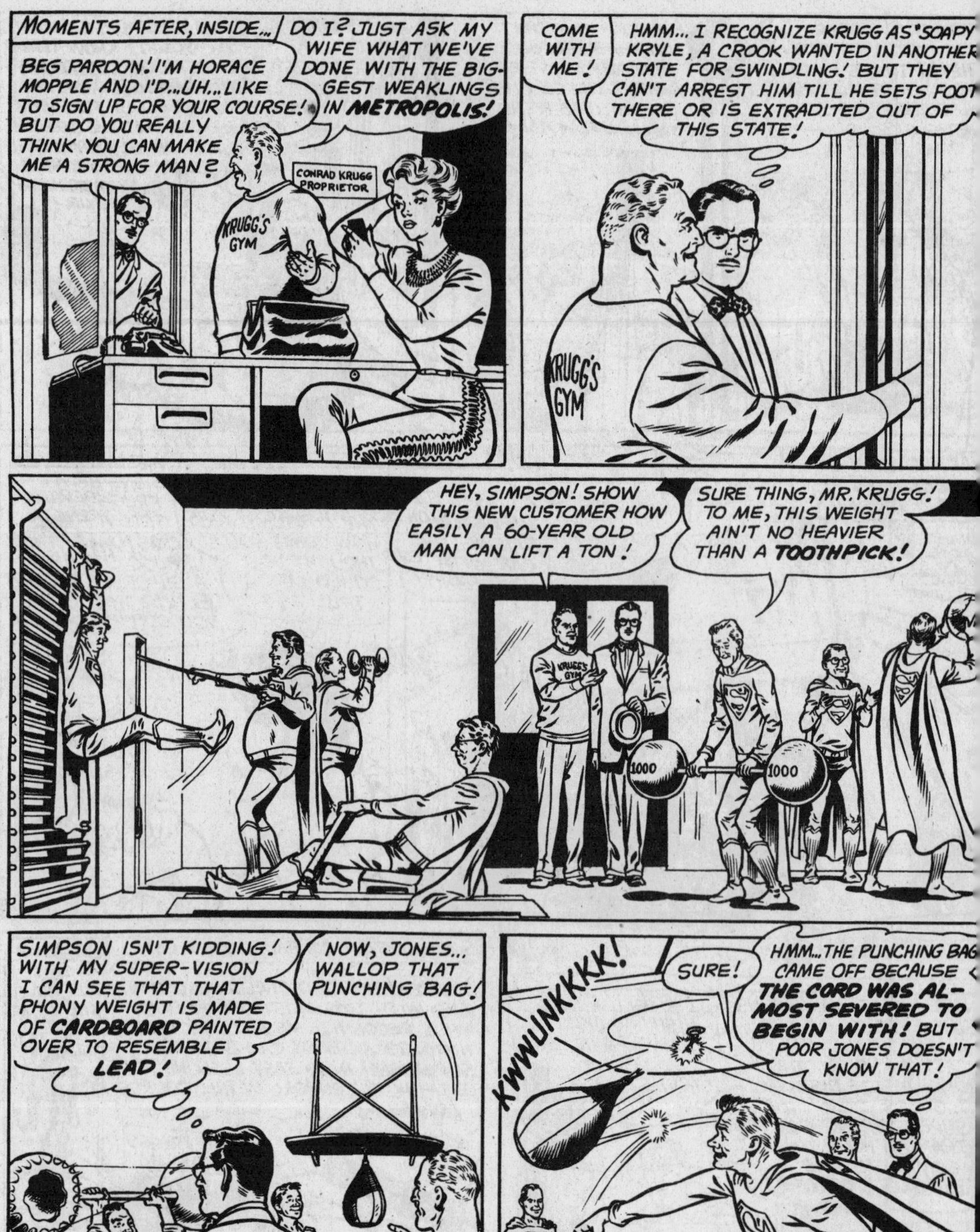
MOMENTS AFTER, INSIDE...
BEG PARDON! I'M HORACE MOPPLE AND I'D...UH...LIKE TO SIGN UP FOR YOUR COURSE! BUT DO YOU REALLY THINK YOU CAN MAKE ME A STRONG MAN?
DO I? JUST ASK MY WIFE WHAT WE'VE DONE WITH THE BIGGEST WEAKLINGS IN METROPOLIS!
CONRAD KRUGG PROPRIETOR
KRUGG'S GYM
COME WITH ME!
HMM... I RECOGNIZE KRUGG AS "SOAPY" KRYLE, A CROOK WANTED IN ANOTHER STATE FOR SWINDLING! BUT THEY CAN'T ARREST HIM TILL HE SETS FOOT THERE OR IS EXTRADITED OUT OF THIS STATE!
KRUGG'S GYM
HEY, SIMPSON! SHOW THIS NEW CUSTOMER HOW EASILY A 60-YEAR OLD MAN CAN LIFT A TON!
SURE THING, MR. KRUGG! TO ME, THIS WEIGHT AIN'T NO HEAVIER THAN A TOOTHPICK!
KRUGG'S GYM
1000
1000
SIMPSON ISN'T KIDDING! WITH MY SUPER-VISION I CAN SEE THAT THAT PHONY WEIGHT IS MADE OF CARDBOARD PAINTED OVER TO RESEMBLE LEAD!
NOW, JONES... WALLOP THAT PUNCHING BAG!
3
KWWUNKKKK!
SURE!
HMM...THE PUNCHING BAG CAME OFF BECAUSE THE CORD WAS ALMOST SEVERED TO BEGIN WITH! BUT POOR JONES DOESN'T KNOW THAT!

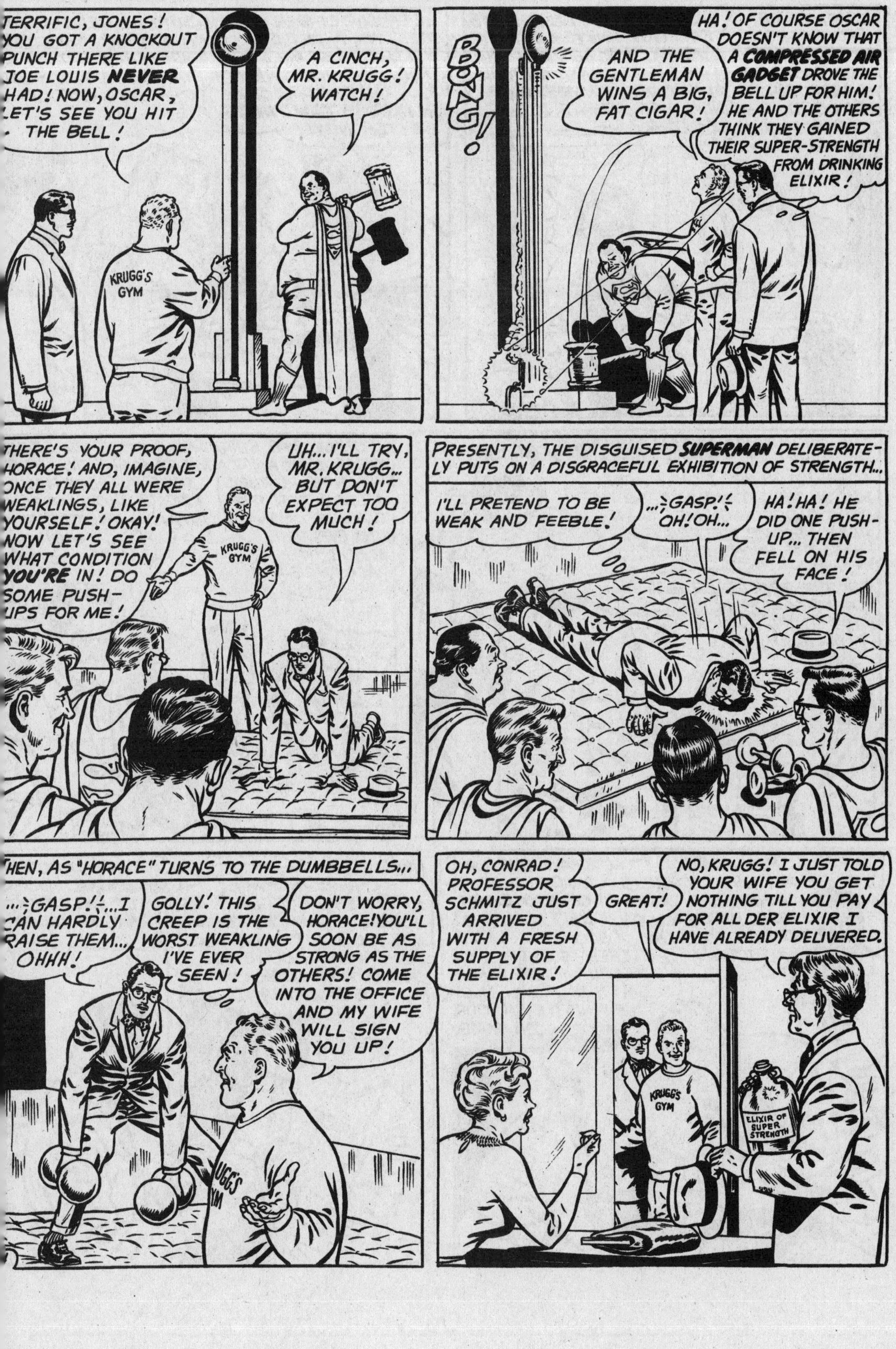
TERRIFIC, JONES! YOU GOT A KNOCKOUT PUNCH THERE LIKE JOE LOUIS NEVER HAD! NOW, OSCAR, LET'S SEE YOU HIT THE BELL!
A CINCH, MR. KRUGG! WATCH!
KRUGG'S GYM
BONG!
AND THE GENTLEMAN WINS A BIG, FAT CIGAR!
HA! OF COURSE OSCAR DOESN'T KNOW THAT A COMPRESSED AIR GADGET DROVE THE BELL UP FOR HIM! HE AND THE OTHERS THINK THEY GAINED THEIR SUPER-STRENGTH FROM DRINKING ELIXIR!
THERE'S YOUR PROOF, HORACE! AND, IMAGINE, ONCE THEY ALL WERE WEAKLINGS, LIKE YOURSELF! OKAY! NOW LET'S SEE WHAT CONDITION YOU'RE IN! DO SOME PUSH-UPS FOR ME!
UH...I'LL TRY, MR. KRUGG... BUT DON'T EXPECT TOO MUCH!
KRUGG'S GYM
PRESENTLY, THE DISGUISED SUPERMAN DELIBERATELY PUTS ON A DISGRACEFUL EXHIBITION OF STRENGTH...
I'LL PRETEND TO BE WEAK AND FEEBLE!
...GASP!... OH! OH...
HA! HA! HE DID ONE PUSH-UP... THEN FELL ON HIS FACE!
THEN, AS "HORACE" TURNS TO THE DUMBBELLS...
...GASP!...I CAN HARDLY RAISE THEM... OHHH!
GOLLY! THIS CREEP IS THE WORST WEAKLING I'VE EVER SEEN!
DON'T WORRY, HORACE! YOU'LL SOON BE AS STRONG AS THE OTHERS! COME INTO THE OFFICE AND MY WIFE WILL SIGN YOU UP!
OH, CONRAD! PROFESSOR SCHMITZ JUST ARRIVED WITH A FRESH SUPPLY OF THE ELIXIR!
GREAT!
NO, KRUGG! I JUST TOLD YOUR WIFE YOU GET NOTHING TILL YOU PAY FOR ALL DER ELIXIR I HAVE ALREADY DELIVERED.
KRUGG'S GYM
ELIXIR OF SUPER STRENGTH

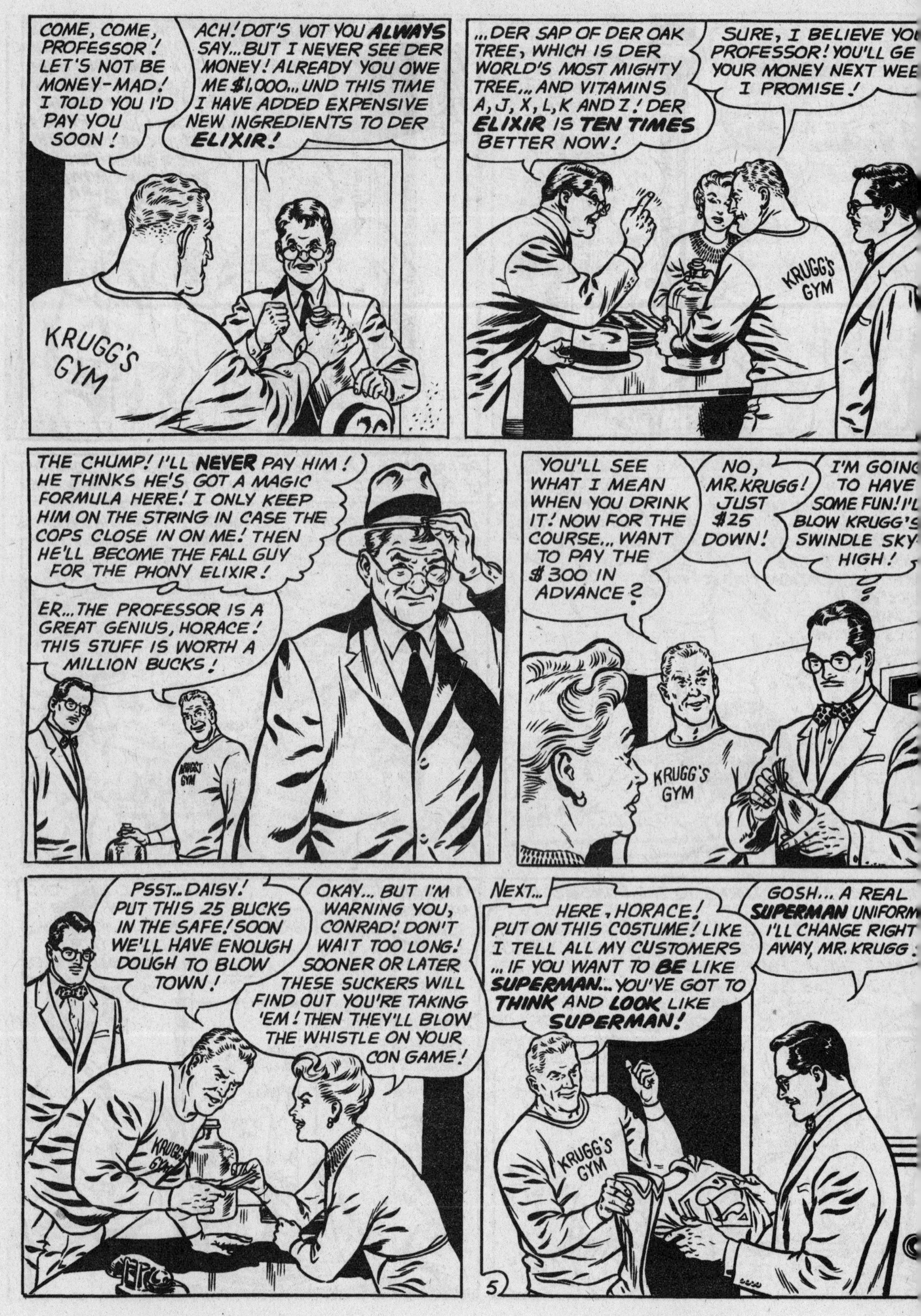
COME, COME, PROFESSOR! LET'S NOT BE MONEY-MAD! I TOLD YOU I'D PAY YOU SOON!
ACH! DOT'S VOT YOU ALWAYS SAY...BUT I NEVER SEE DER MONEY! ALREADY YOU OWE ME $1,000...UND THIS TIME I HAVE ADDED EXPENSIVE NEW INGREDIENTS TO DER ELIXIR!
KRUGG'S GYM
...DER SAP OF DER OAK TREE, WHICH IS DER WORLD'S MOST MIGHTY TREE... AND VITAMINS A, J, X, L, K AND Z! DER ELIXIR IS TEN TIMES BETTER NOW!
SURE, I BELIEVE YO PROFESSOR! YOU'LL GE YOUR MONEY NEXT WEE I PROMISE!
KRUGG'S GYM
THE CHUMP! I'LL NEVER PAY HIM! HE THINKS HE'S GOT A MAGIC FORMULA HERE! I ONLY KEEP HIM ON THE STRING IN CASE THE COPS CLOSE IN ON ME! THEN HE'LL BECOME THE FALL GUY FOR THE PHONY ELIXIR!
ER...THE PROFESSOR IS A GREAT GENIUS, HORACE! THIS STUFF IS WORTH A MILLION BUCKS!
YOU'LL SEE WHAT I MEAN WHEN YOU DRINK IT! NOW FOR THE COURSE... WANT TO PAY THE $300 IN ADVANCE?
NO, MR. KRUGG! JUST $25 DOWN!
I'M GOING TO HAVE SOME FUN! I'L BLOW KRUGG'S SWINDLE SKY HIGH!
KRUGG'S GYM
PSST...DAISY! PUT THIS 25 BUCKS IN THE SAFE! SOON WE'LL HAVE ENOUGH DOUGH TO BLOW TOWN!
OKAY... BUT I'M WARNING YOU, CONRAD! DON'T WAIT TOO LONG! SOONER OR LATER THESE SUCKERS WILL FIND OUT YOU'RE TAKING 'EM! THEN THEY'LL BLOW THE WHISTLE ON YOUR CON GAME!
NEXT...
HERE, HORACE! PUT ON THIS COSTUME! LIKE I TELL ALL MY CUSTOMERS ...IF YOU WANT TO BE LIKE SUPERMAN... YOU'VE GOT TO THINK AND LOOK LIKE SUPERMAN!
GOSH... A REAL SUPERMAN UNIFORM I'LL CHANGE RIGHT AWAY, MR. KRUGG
KRUGG'S GYM
5

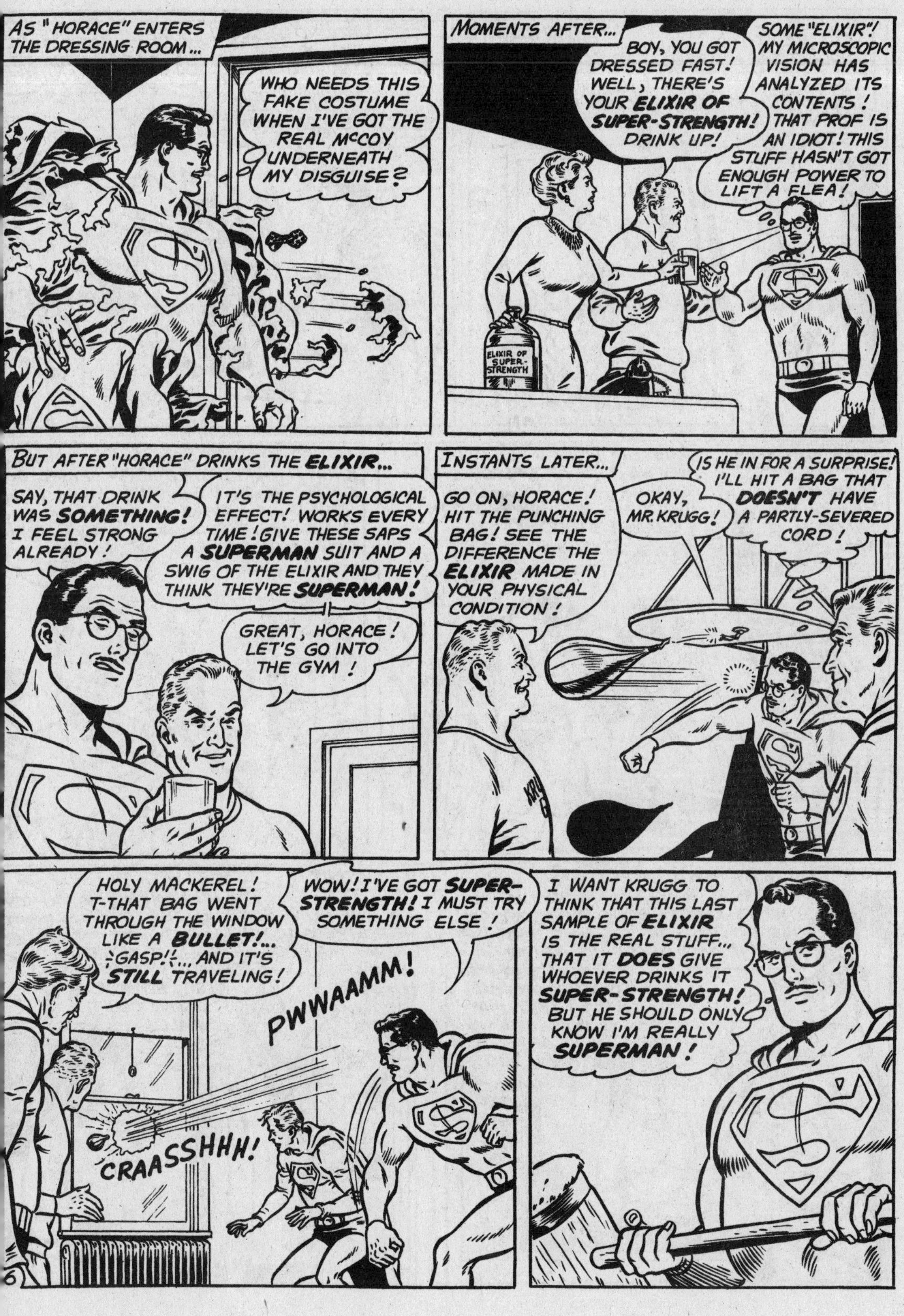
AS "HORACE" ENTERS THE DRESSING ROOM...
WHO NEEDS THIS FAKE COSTUME WHEN I'VE GOT THE REAL McCOY UNDERNEATH MY DISGUISE?
MOMENTS AFTER...
BOY, YOU GOT DRESSED FAST! WELL, THERE'S YOUR ELIXIR OF SUPER-STRENGTH! DRINK UP!
SOME "ELIXIR"! MY MICROSCOPIC VISION HAS ANALYZED ITS CONTENTS! THAT PROF IS AN IDIOT! THIS STUFF HASN'T GOT ENOUGH POWER TO LIFT A FLEA!
ELIXIR OF SUPER-STRENGTH
BUT AFTER "HORACE" DRINKS THE ELIXIR...
SAY, THAT DRINK WAS SOMETHING! I FEEL STRONG ALREADY!
IT'S THE PSYCHOLOGICAL EFFECT! WORKS EVERY TIME! GIVE THESE SAPS A SUPERMAN SUIT AND A SWIG OF THE ELIXIR AND THEY THINK THEY'RE SUPERMAN!
GREAT, HORACE! LET'S GO INTO THE GYM!
INSTANTS LATER...
GO ON, HORACE! HIT THE PUNCHING BAG! SEE THE DIFFERENCE THE ELIXIR MADE IN YOUR PHYSICAL CONDITION!
OKAY, MR. KRUGG!
IS HE IN FOR A SURPRISE! I'LL HIT A BAG THAT DOESN'T HAVE A PARTLY-SEVERED CORD!
HOLY MACKEREL! T-THAT BAG WENT THROUGH THE WINDOW LIKE A BULLET!... -GASP!-... AND IT'S STILL TRAVELING!
WOW! I'VE GOT SUPER-STRENGTH! I MUST TRY SOMETHING ELSE!
PWWAAMM!
CRAASSHHH!
I WANT KRUGG TO THINK THAT THIS LAST SAMPLE OF ELIXIR IS THE REAL STUFF... THAT IT DOES GIVE WHOEVER DRINKS IT SUPER-STRENGTH! BUT HE SHOULD ONLY KNOW I'M REALLY SUPERMAN!
6

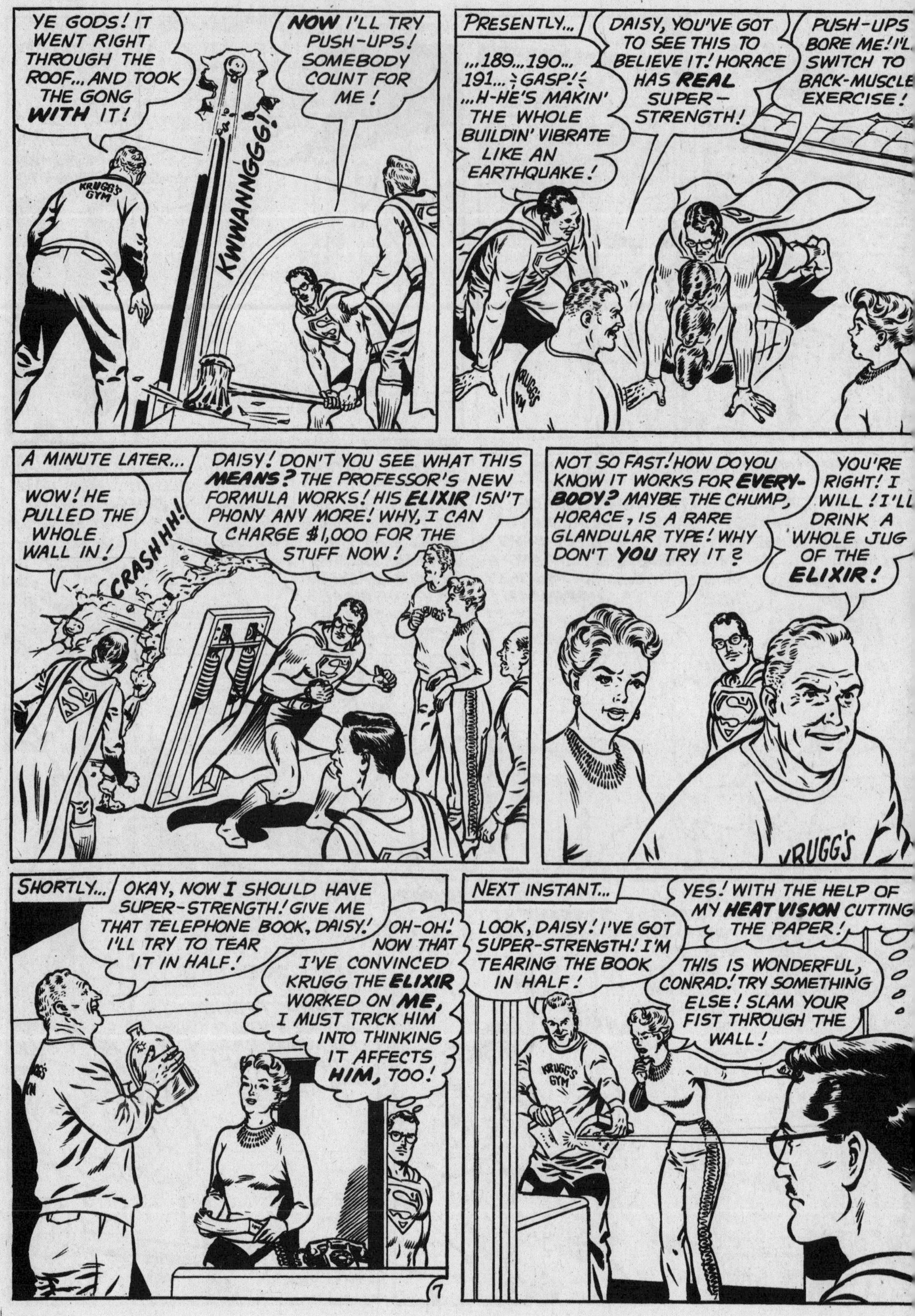
YE GODS! IT WENT RIGHT THROUGH THE ROOF...AND TOOK THE GONG WITH IT!
KWWANNGGG!
NOW I'LL TRY PUSH-UPS! SOMEBODY COUNT FOR ME!
PRESENTLY...
...189...190... 191...GASP!...H-HE'S MAKIN' THE WHOLE BUILDIN' VIBRATE LIKE AN EARTHQUAKE!
DAISY, YOU'VE GOT TO SEE THIS TO BELIEVE IT! HORACE HAS REAL SUPER-STRENGTH!
PUSH-UPS BORE ME! I'LL SWITCH TO BACK-MUSCLE EXERCISE!
A MINUTE LATER...
WOW! HE PULLED THE WHOLE WALL IN!
CRASHHH!
DAISY! DON'T YOU SEE WHAT THIS MEANS? THE PROFESSOR'S NEW FORMULA WORKS! HIS ELIXIR ISN'T PHONY ANY MORE! WHY, I CAN CHARGE $1,000 FOR THE STUFF NOW!
NOT SO FAST! HOW DO YOU KNOW IT WORKS FOR EVERYBODY? MAYBE THE CHUMP, HORACE, IS A RARE GLANDULAR TYPE! WHY DON'T YOU TRY IT?
YOU'RE RIGHT! I WILL! I'LL DRINK A WHOLE JUG OF THE ELIXIR!
KRUGG'S
SHORTLY...
OKAY, NOW I SHOULD HAVE SUPER-STRENGTH! GIVE ME THAT TELEPHONE BOOK, DAISY! I'LL TRY TO TEAR IT IN HALF!
OH-OH! NOW THAT I'VE CONVINCED KRUGG THE ELIXIR WORKED ON ME, I MUST TRICK HIM INTO THINKING IT AFFECTS HIM, TOO!
NEXT INSTANT...
LOOK, DAISY! I'VE GOT SUPER-STRENGTH! I'M TEARING THE BOOK IN HALF!
YES! WITH THE HELP OF MY HEAT VISION CUTTING THE PAPER!
THIS IS WONDERFUL, CONRAD! TRY SOMETHING ELSE! SLAM YOUR FIST THROUGH THE WALL!

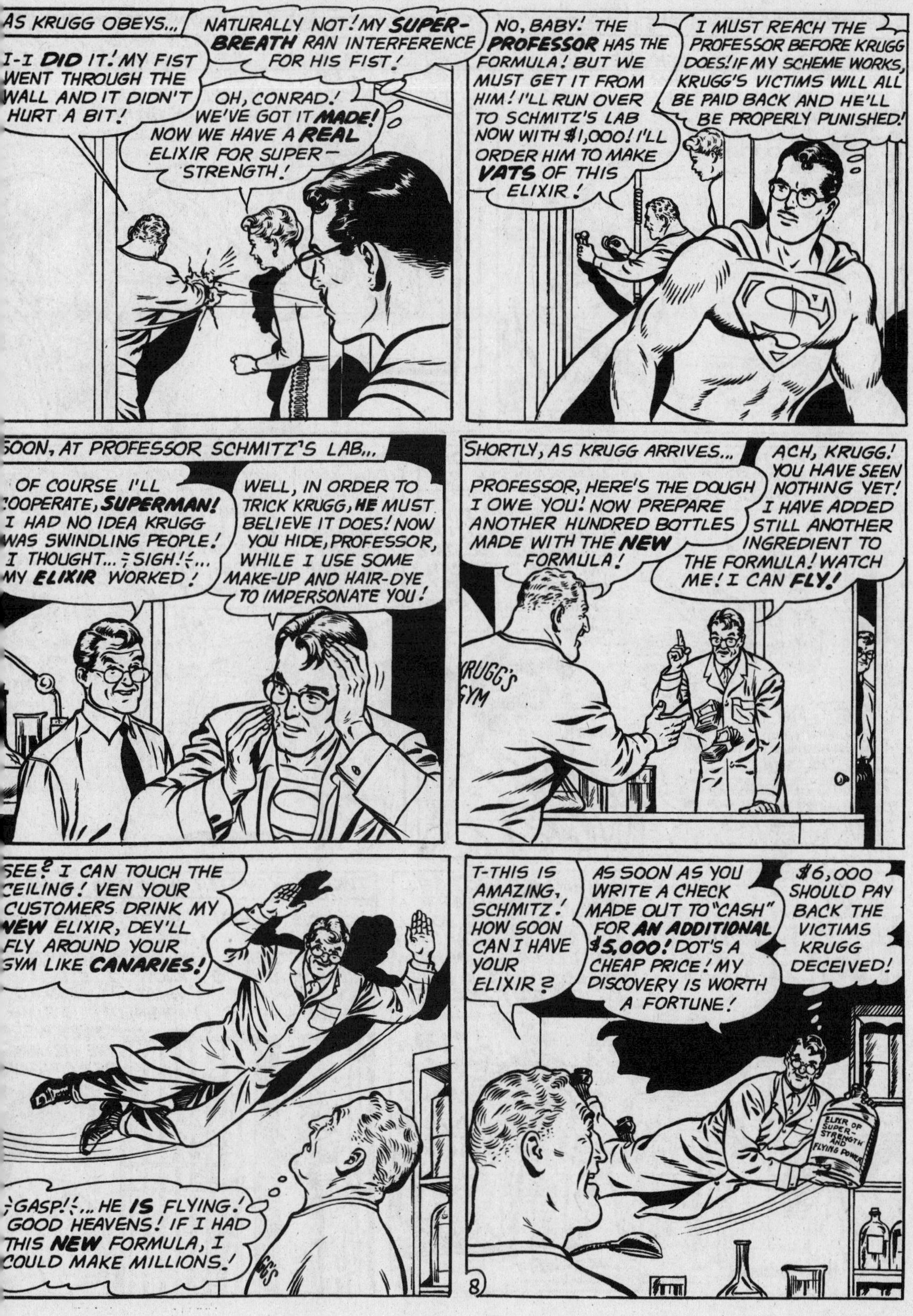
AS KRUGG OBEYS...
I-I DID IT! MY FIST WENT THROUGH THE WALL AND IT DIDN'T HURT A BIT!
NATURALLY NOT! MY SUPER-BREATH RAN INTERFERENCE FOR HIS FIST!
OH, CONRAD! WE'VE GOT IT MADE! NOW WE HAVE A REAL ELIXIR FOR SUPER-STRENGTH!
NO, BABY! THE PROFESSOR HAS THE FORMULA! BUT WE MUST GET IT FROM HIM! I'LL RUN OVER TO SCHMITZ'S LAB NOW WITH $1,000! I'LL ORDER HIM TO MAKE VATS OF THIS ELIXIR!
I MUST REACH THE PROFESSOR BEFORE KRUGG DOES! IF MY SCHEME WORKS, KRUGG'S VICTIMS WILL ALL BE PAID BACK AND HE'LL BE PROPERLY PUNISHED!
SOON, AT PROFESSOR SCHMITZ'S LAB...
OF COURSE I'LL COOPERATE, SUPERMAN! I HAD NO IDEA KRUGG WAS SWINDLING PEOPLE! I THOUGHT... SIGH!... MY ELIXIR WORKED!
WELL, IN ORDER TO TRICK KRUGG, HE MUST BELIEVE IT DOES! NOW YOU HIDE, PROFESSOR, WHILE I USE SOME MAKE-UP AND HAIR-DYE TO IMPERSONATE YOU!
SHORTLY, AS KRUGG ARRIVES...
PROFESSOR, HERE'S THE DOUGH I OWE YOU! NOW PREPARE ANOTHER HUNDRED BOTTLES MADE WITH THE NEW FORMULA!
ACH, KRUGG! YOU HAVE SEEN NOTHING YET! I HAVE ADDED STILL ANOTHER INGREDIENT TO THE FORMULA! WATCH ME! I CAN FLY!
KRUGG'S GYM
SEE? I CAN TOUCH THE CEILING! VEN YOUR CUSTOMERS DRINK MY NEW ELIXIR, DEY'LL FLY AROUND YOUR GYM LIKE CANARIES!
GASP!... HE IS FLYING! GOOD HEAVENS! IF I HAD THIS NEW FORMULA, I COULD MAKE MILLIONS!
T-THIS IS AMAZING, SCHMITZ! HOW SOON CAN I HAVE YOUR ELIXIR?
AS SOON AS YOU WRITE A CHECK MADE OUT TO "CASH" FOR AN ADDITIONAL $5,000! DOT'S A CHEAP PRICE! MY DISCOVERY IS WORTH A FORTUNE!
$6,000 SHOULD PAY BACK THE VICTIMS KRUGG DECEIVED!
ELIXIR OF SUPER-STRENGTH AND FLYING POWER
8

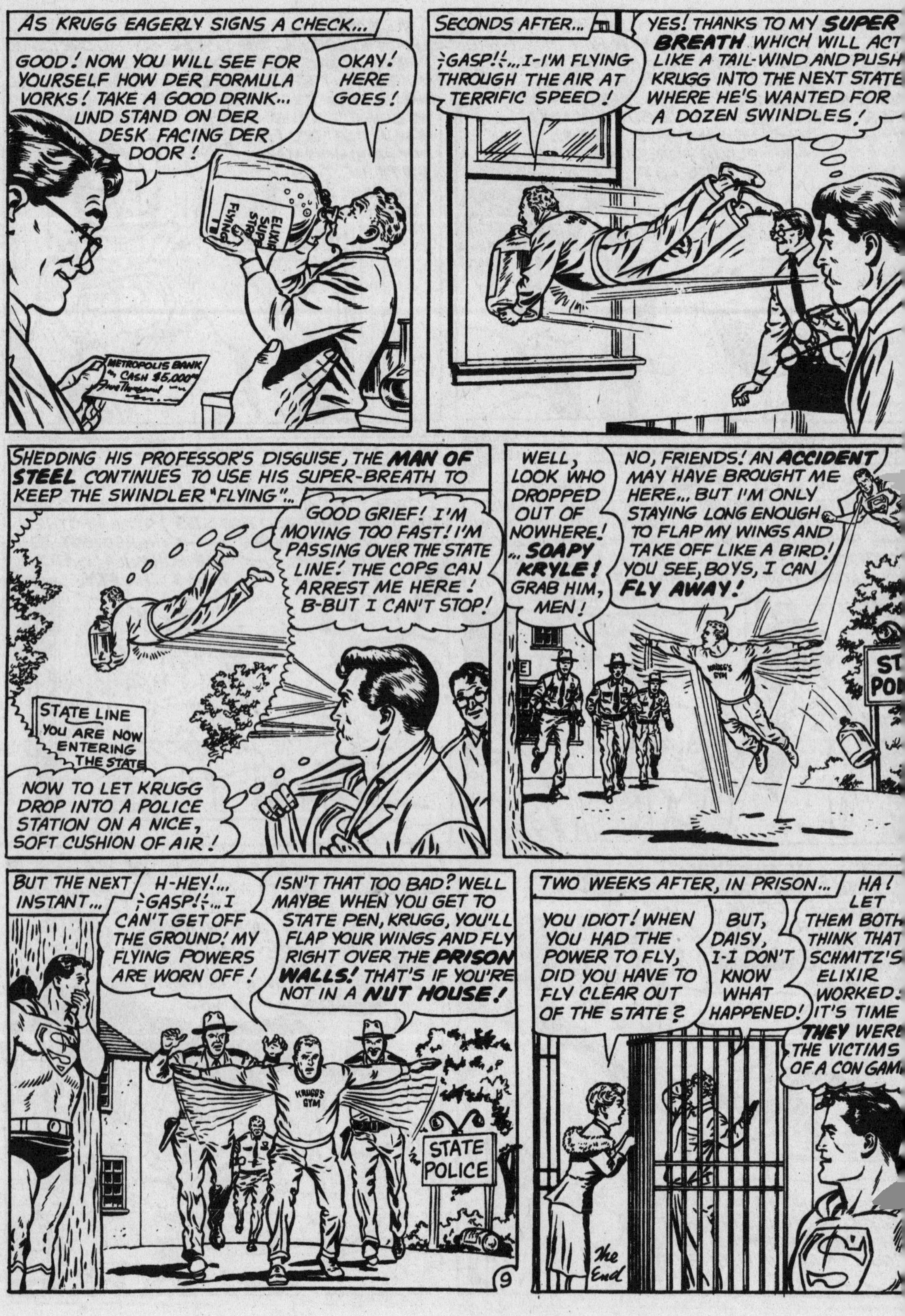
AS KRUGG EAGERLY SIGNS A CHECK...
GOOD! NOW YOU WILL SEE FOR YOURSELF HOW DER FORMULA VORKS! TAKE A GOOD DRINK... UND STAND ON DER DESK FACING DER DOOR!
OKAY! HERE GOES!
METROPOLIS BANK
CASH $5,000
ELIXIR SUPER STRENGTH FLYING
SECONDS AFTER...
GASP! ... I-I'M FLYING THROUGH THE AIR AT TERRIFIC SPEED!
YES! THANKS TO MY SUPER BREATH WHICH WILL ACT LIKE A TAIL-WIND AND PUSH KRUGG INTO THE NEXT STATE WHERE HE'S WANTED FOR A DOZEN SWINDLES!
SHEDDING HIS PROFESSOR'S DISGUISE, THE MAN OF STEEL CONTINUES TO USE HIS SUPER-BREATH TO KEEP THE SWINDLER "FLYING"...
GOOD GRIEF! I'M MOVING TOO FAST! I'M PASSING OVER THE STATE LINE! THE COPS CAN ARREST ME HERE! B-BUT I CAN'T STOP!
STATE LINE
YOU ARE NOW ENTERING THE STATE
NOW TO LET KRUGG DROP INTO A POLICE STATION ON A NICE, SOFT CUSHION OF AIR!
WELL, LOOK WHO DROPPED OUT OF NOWHERE! ... SOAPY KRYLE! GRAB HIM, MEN!
NO, FRIENDS! AN ACCIDENT MAY HAVE BROUGHT ME HERE... BUT I'M ONLY STAYING LONG ENOUGH TO FLAP MY WINGS AND TAKE OFF LIKE A BIRD! YOU SEE, BOYS, I CAN FLY AWAY!
KRUGG'S GYM
BUT THE NEXT INSTANT...
H-HEY!... GASP! ... I CAN'T GET OFF THE GROUND! MY FLYING POWERS ARE WORN OFF!
ISN'T THAT TOO BAD? WELL MAYBE WHEN YOU GET TO STATE PEN, KRUGG, YOU'LL FLAP YOUR WINGS AND FLY RIGHT OVER THE PRISON WALLS! THAT'S IF YOU'RE NOT IN A NUT HOUSE!
KRUGG'S GYM
STATE POLICE
9
TWO WEEKS AFTER, IN PRISON...
YOU IDIOT! WHEN YOU HAD THE POWER TO FLY, DID YOU HAVE TO FLY CLEAR OUT OF THE STATE?
BUT, DAISY, I-I DON'T KNOW WHAT HAPPENED!
HA! LET THEM BOTH THINK THAT SCHMITZ'S ELIXIR WORKED! IT'S TIME THEY WERE THE VICTIMS OF A CON GAM
The End

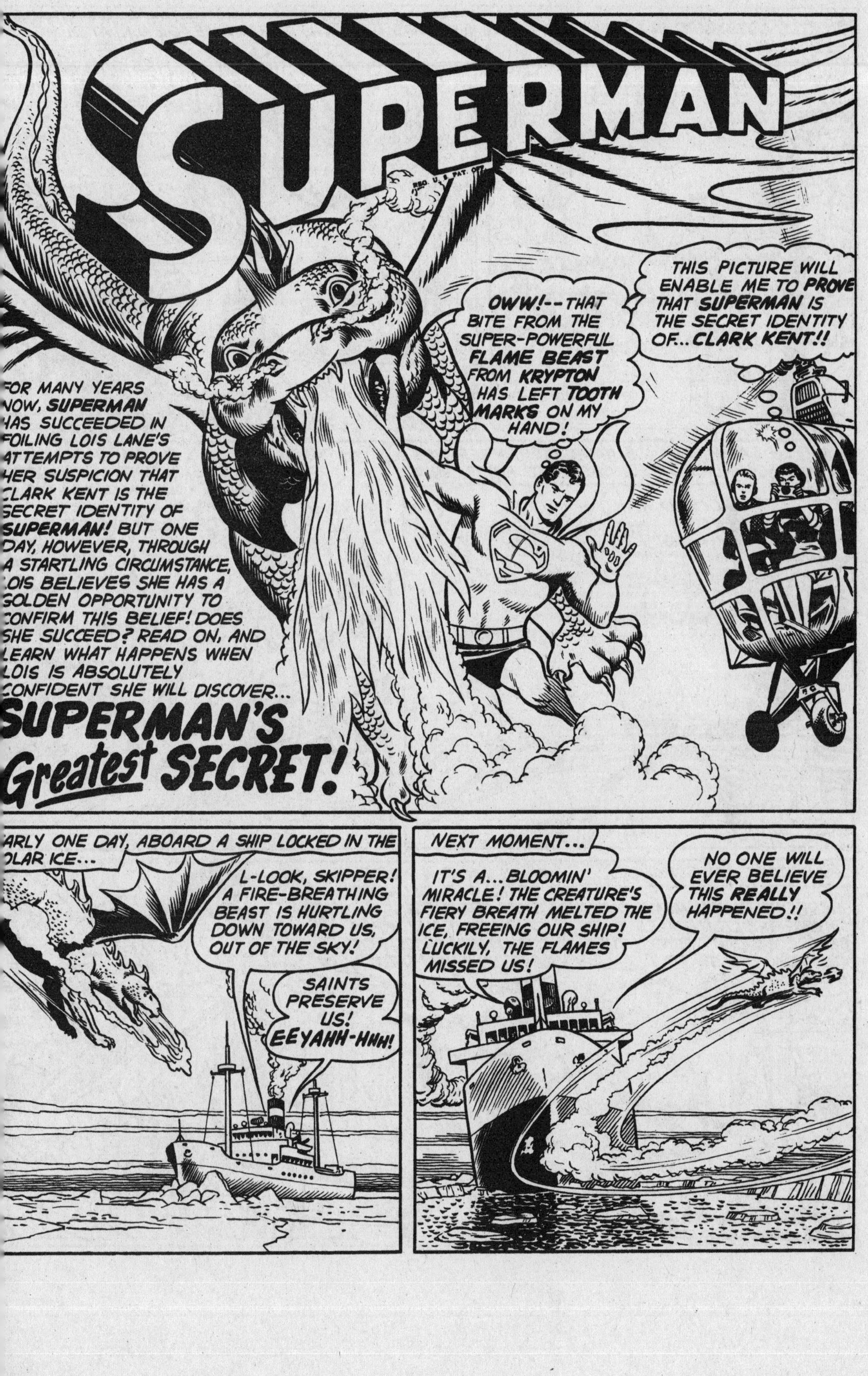
SUPERMAN
REG. U.S. PAT. OFF.
OWW!--THAT BITE FROM THE SUPER-POWERFUL FLAME BEAST FROM KRYPTON HAS LEFT TOOTH MARKS ON MY HAND!
THIS PICTURE WILL ENABLE ME TO PROVE THAT SUPERMAN IS THE SECRET IDENTITY OF...CLARK KENT!!
FOR MANY YEARS NOW, SUPERMAN HAS SUCCEEDED IN FOILING LOIS LANE'S ATTEMPTS TO PROVE HER SUSPICION THAT CLARK KENT IS THE SECRET IDENTITY OF SUPERMAN! BUT ONE DAY, HOWEVER, THROUGH A STARTLING CIRCUMSTANCE, LOIS BELIEVES SHE HAS A GOLDEN OPPORTUNITY TO CONFIRM THIS BELIEF! DOES SHE SUCCEED? READ ON, AND LEARN WHAT HAPPENS WHEN LOIS IS ABSOLUTELY CONFIDENT SHE WILL DISCOVER...
SUPERMAN'S Greatest SECRET!
ARLY ONE DAY, ABOARD A SHIP LOCKED IN THE OLAR ICE...
L-LOOK, SKIPPER! A FIRE-BREATHING BEAST IS HURTLING DOWN TOWARD US, OUT OF THE SKY!
SAINTS PRESERVE US! EEYAHH-HHH!
NEXT MOMENT...
IT'S A...BLOOMIN' MIRACLE! THE CREATURE'S FIERY BREATH MELTED THE ICE, FREEING OUR SHIP! LUCKILY, THE FLAMES MISSED US!
NO ONE WILL EVER BELIEVE THIS REALLY HAPPENED!!

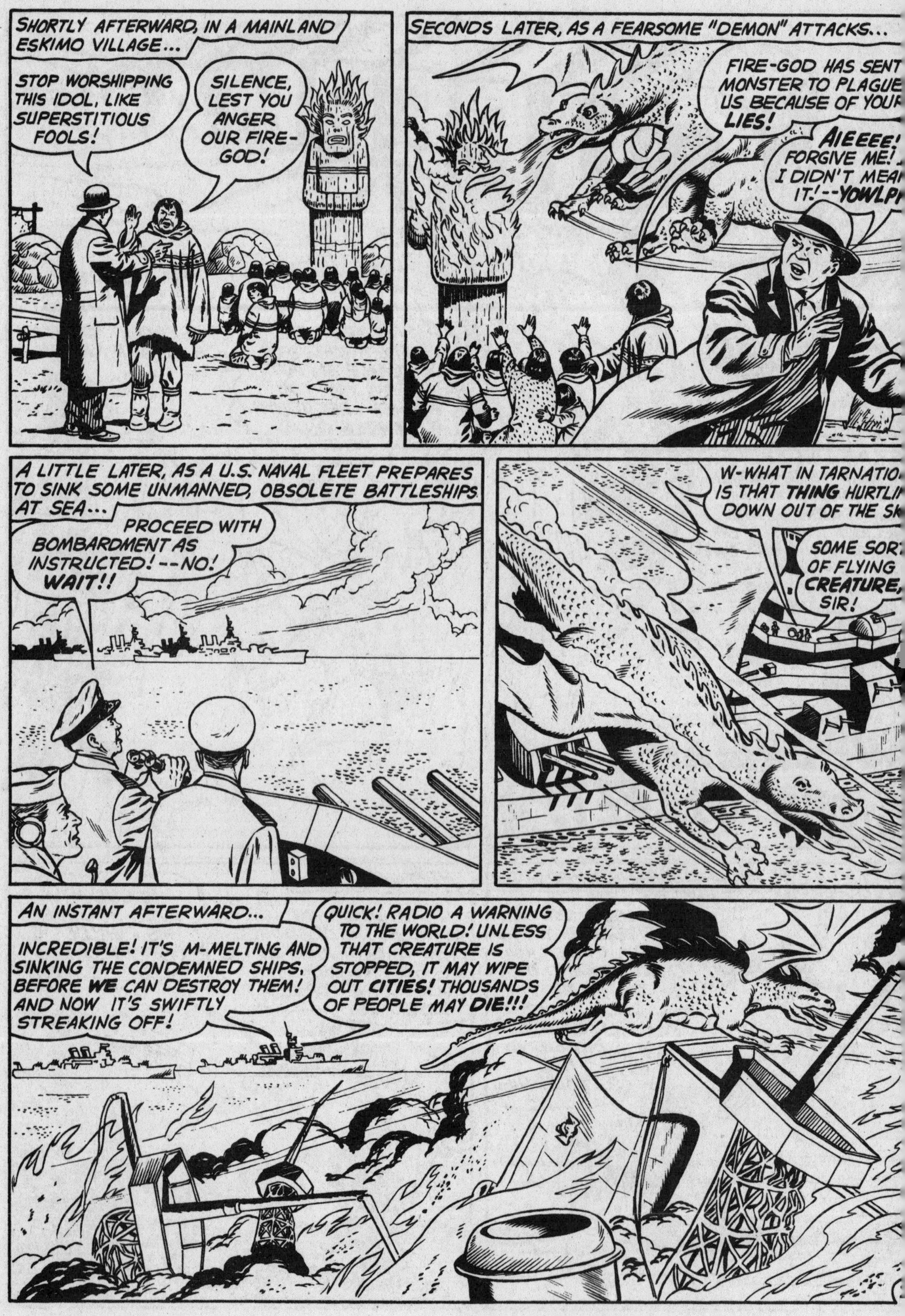
SHORTLY AFTERWARD, IN A MAINLAND ESKIMO VILLAGE...
STOP WORSHIPPING THIS IDOL, LIKE SUPERSTITIOUS FOOLS!
SILENCE, LEST YOU ANGER OUR FIRE-GOD!
SECONDS LATER, AS A FEARSOME "DEMON" ATTACKS...
FIRE-GOD HAS SENT MONSTER TO PLAGUE US BECAUSE OF YOUR LIES!
AIEEEE! FORGIVE ME! I DIDN'T MEA IT!--YOWLP
A LITTLE LATER, AS A U.S. NAVAL FLEET PREPARES TO SINK SOME UNMANNED, OBSOLETE BATTLESHIPS AT SEA...
PROCEED WITH BOMBARDMENT AS INSTRUCTED! --NO! WAIT!!
W-WHAT IN TARNATIO IS THAT THING HURTLI DOWN OUT OF THE SK
SOME SOR OF FLYING CREATURE, SIR!
AN INSTANT AFTERWARD...
INCREDIBLE! IT'S M-MELTING AND SINKING THE CONDEMNED SHIPS, BEFORE WE CAN DESTROY THEM! AND NOW IT'S SWIFTLY STREAKING OFF!
QUICK! RADIO A WARNING TO THE WORLD! UNLESS THAT CREATURE IS STOPPED, IT MAY WIPE OUT CITIES! THOUSANDS OF PEOPLE MAY DIE!!!

RESENTLY, AT THE **DAILY PLANET** IN METROPOLIS, REPORTERS CLARK KENT, LOIS LANE AND JIMMY SEN SEE A STARTLING NEWS FLASH...

M FLAME DRAGON... TTACKING ARTH!

I MUST SLIP AWAY AND SWITCH TO **SUPERMAN** WITHOUT AROUSING LOIS' SUSPICION... HMM... I HAVE AN IDEA!

QUICK-WITTEDLY, CLARK USES SUPER-VENTRILOQUISM...

BETTER HURRY DOWN-STAIRS, CLARK! A COP IS ABOUT TO GIVE YOU A PARKING TICKET!

OKAY!

LITTLE DOES LOIS SUSPECT I'M ANSWERING MY **OWN** VOICE!

MOMENTS LATER...

CLARK'S NOT IN THE HALL! NEITHER IS WHOEVER HE SPOKE TO!... IF CLARK'S SECRETLY **SUPERMAN**, AS I OFTEN SUSPECTED, HE COULD'VE USED **SUPER-VENTRILOQUISM** IN ORDER TO SLIP AWAY AND CHANGE TO **SUPERMAN**! I WONDER...

AS LOIS AND JIMMY HURRY TO THE FLYING NEWSROOM HELICOPTER ON THE ROOF, CLARK SWITCHES IDENTITIES IN AN EMPTY STORE-ROOM...

I THOUGHT I HAD RID EARTH OF THAT CREATURE PERMANENTLY!*

*SEE "THE FLAME DRAGON FROM KRYPTON!", SUPERMAN MAGAZINE, NO. 142 — Editor.

SECONDS LATER, AS HE STREAKS THROUGH THE KY, **SUPERMAN'S** TELESCOPIC VISION PROBES UTER SPACE...

MMM... THE FLAME RAGON I ONCE FOUGHT STILL WHERE I PLACED IN ORBIT... BEYOND LUTO... FROZEN INSIDE E, IN SUSPENDED ANIMATION!

③

SOON, ABOVE A ROCKY CLIFF...

A HUGE, CRACKED EGG-SHELL! I GET IT! THE ORIGINAL FLAME DRAGON LAID AN EGG, WHILE ON EARTH, AND THAT **NEW** FLAME DRAGON HATCHED FROM IT!

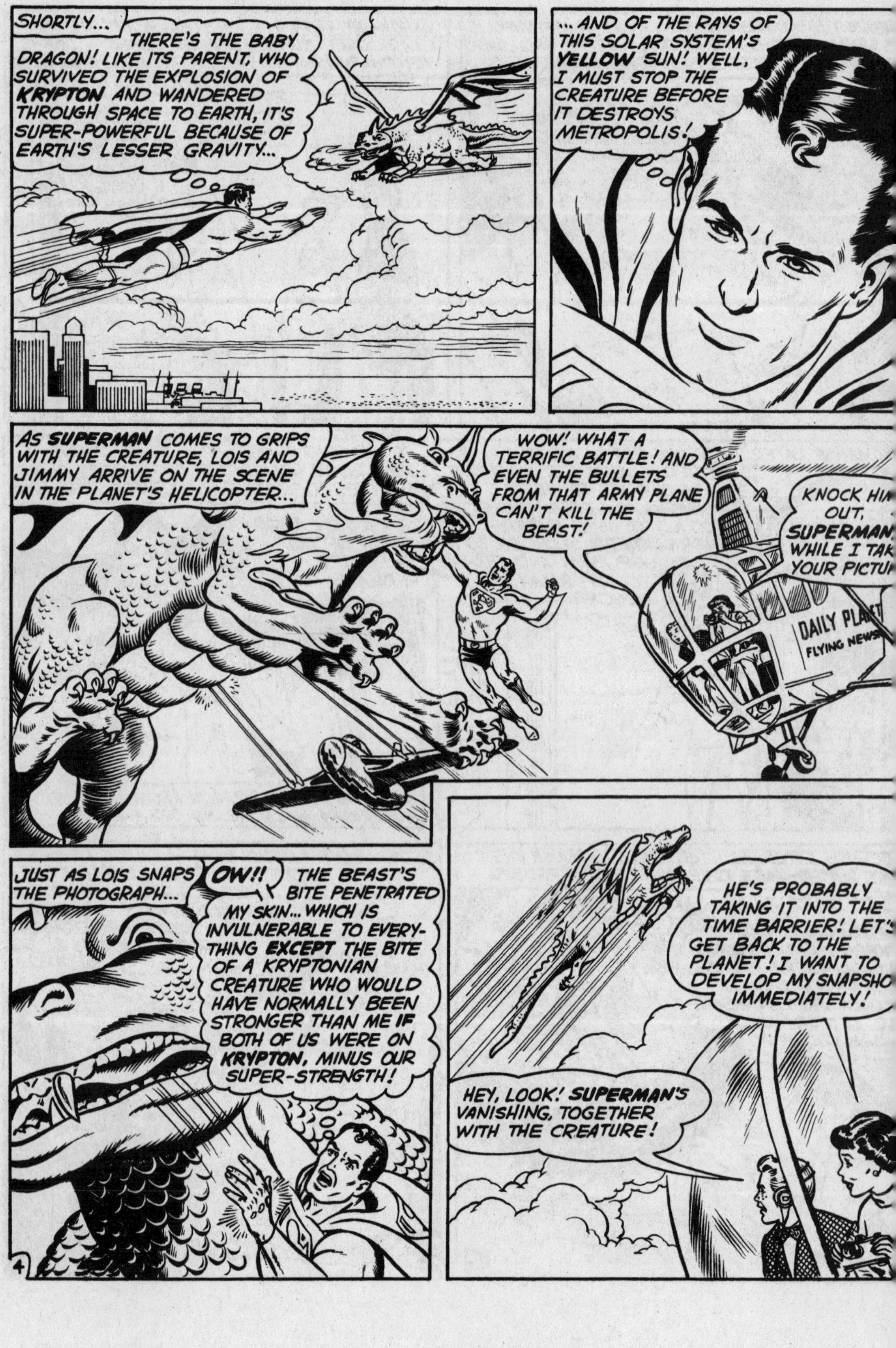
SHORTLY...
THERE'S THE BABY DRAGON! LIKE ITS PARENT, WHO SURVIVED THE EXPLOSION OF KRYPTON AND WANDERED THROUGH SPACE TO EARTH, IT'S SUPER-POWERFUL BECAUSE OF EARTH'S LESSER GRAVITY...
... AND OF THE RAYS OF THIS SOLAR SYSTEM'S YELLOW SUN! WELL, I MUST STOP THE CREATURE BEFORE IT DESTROYS METROPOLIS!
AS SUPERMAN COMES TO GRIPS WITH THE CREATURE, LOIS AND JIMMY ARRIVE ON THE SCENE IN THE PLANET'S HELICOPTER...
WOW! WHAT A TERRIFIC BATTLE! AND EVEN THE BULLETS FROM THAT ARMY PLANE CAN'T KILL THE BEAST!
DAILY PLA
FLYING NEWS
JUST AS LOIS SNAPS THE PHOTOGRAPH...
OW!! THE BEAST'S BITE PENETRATED MY SKIN... WHICH IS INVULNERABLE TO EVERY-THING EXCEPT THE BITE OF A KRYPTONIAN CREATURE WHO WOULD HAVE NORMALLY BEEN STRONGER THAN ME IF BOTH OF US WERE ON KRYPTON, MINUS OUR SUPER-STRENGTH!
4
HEY, LOOK! SUPERMAN'S VANISHING, TOGETHER WITH THE CREATURE!
IMMEDIATELY!

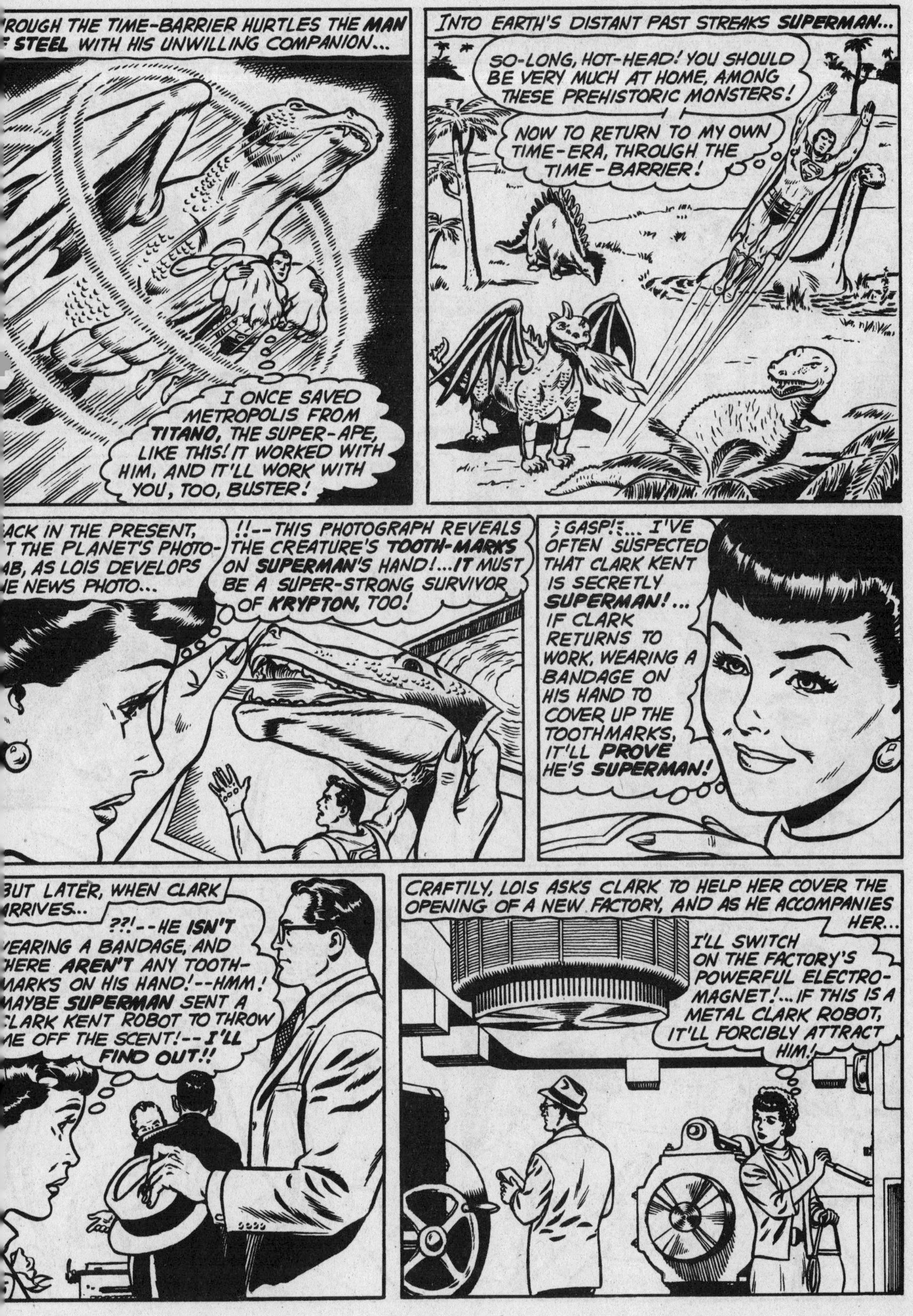
ROUGH THE TIME-BARRIER HURTLES THE MAN STEEL WITH HIS UNWILLING COMPANION...
I ONCE SAVED METROPOLIS FROM TITANO, THE SUPER-APE, LIKE THIS! IT WORKED WITH HIM, AND IT'LL WORK WITH YOU, TOO, BUSTER!
INTO EARTH'S DISTANT PAST STREAKS SUPERMAN...
SO-LONG, HOT-HEAD! YOU SHOULD BE VERY MUCH AT HOME, AMONG THESE PREHISTORIC MONSTERS!
NOW TO RETURN TO MY OWN TIME-ERA, THROUGH THE TIME-BARRIER!
ACK IN THE PRESENT, T THE PLANET'S PHOTO-AB, AS LOIS DEVELOPS E NEWS PHOTO...
!!--THIS PHOTOGRAPH REVEALS THE CREATURE'S TOOTH-MARKS ON SUPERMAN'S HAND!...IT MUST BE A SUPER-STRONG SURVIVOR OF KRYPTON, TOO!
GASP! ... I'VE OFTEN SUSPECTED THAT CLARK KENT IS SECRETLY SUPERMAN!... IF CLARK RETURNS TO WORK, WEARING A BANDAGE ON HIS HAND TO COVER UP THE TOOTHMARKS, IT'LL PROVE HE'S SUPERMAN!
BUT LATER, WHEN CLARK ARRIVES...
??!--HE ISN'T EARING A BANDAGE, AND HERE AREN'T ANY TOOTH-MARKS ON HIS HAND!--HMM! MAYBE SUPERMAN SENT A CLARK KENT ROBOT TO THROW ME OFF THE SCENT!--I'LL FIND OUT!!
CRAFTILY, LOIS ASKS CLARK TO HELP HER COVER THE OPENING OF A NEW FACTORY, AND AS HE ACCOMPANIES HER...
I'LL SWITCH ON THE FACTORY'S POWERFUL ELECTRO-MAGNET!...IF THIS IS A METAL CLARK ROBOT, IT'LL FORCIBLY ATTRACT HIM!

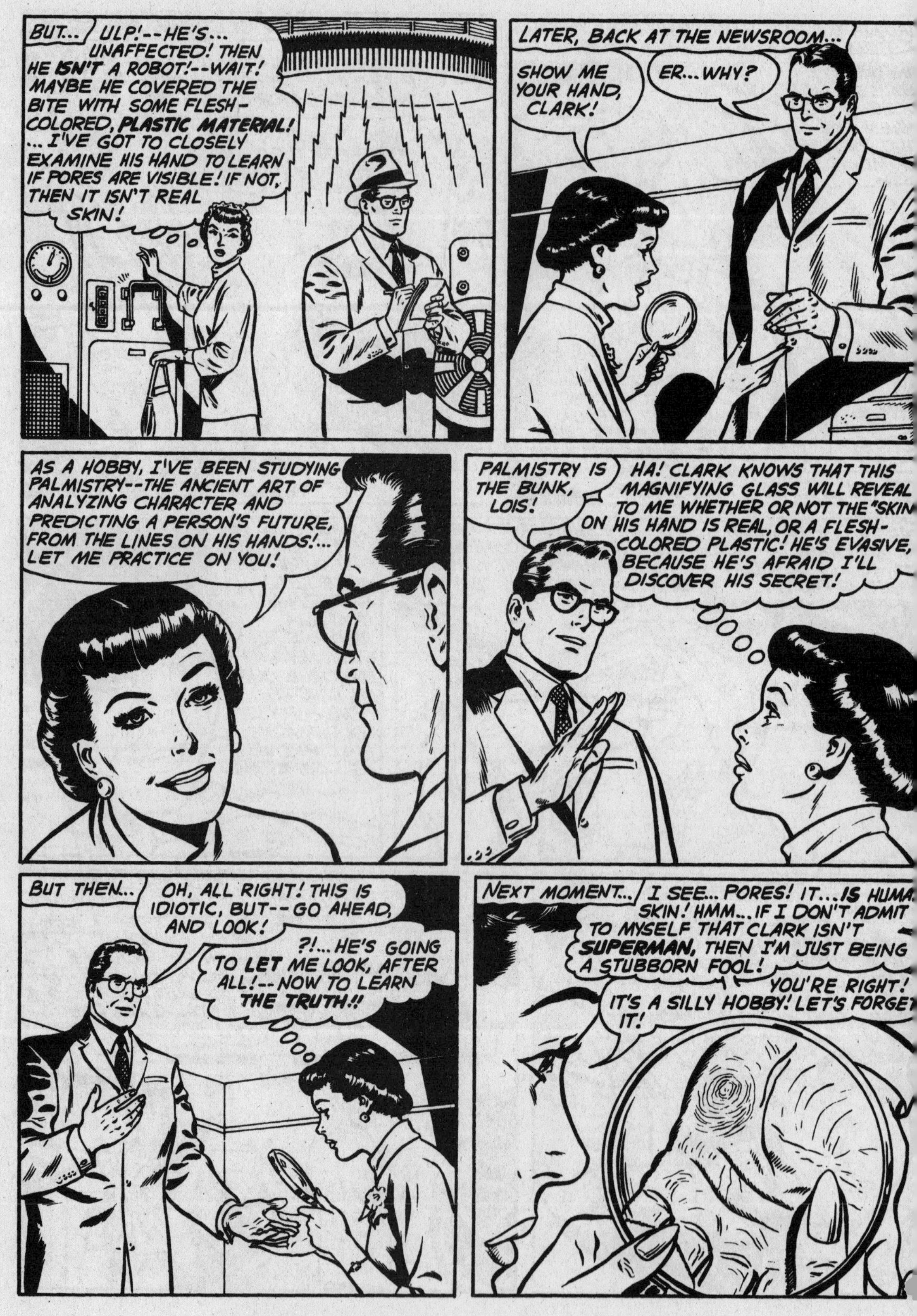
BUT...
ULP!--HE'S... UNAFFECTED! THEN HE ISN'T A ROBOT!--WAIT! MAYBE HE COVERED THE BITE WITH SOME FLESH-COLORED, PLASTIC MATERIAL! ... I'VE GOT TO CLOSELY EXAMINE HIS HAND TO LEARN IF PORES ARE VISIBLE! IF NOT, THEN IT ISN'T REAL SKIN!
LATER, BACK AT THE NEWSROOM...
SHOW ME YOUR HAND, CLARK!
ER...WHY?
AS A HOBBY, I'VE BEEN STUDYING PALMISTRY--THE ANCIENT ART OF ANALYZING CHARACTER AND PREDICTING A PERSON'S FUTURE, FROM THE LINES ON HIS HANDS!... LET ME PRACTICE ON YOU!
PALMISTRY IS THE BUNK, LOIS!
HA! CLARK KNOWS THAT THIS MAGNIFYING GLASS WILL REVEAL TO ME WHETHER OR NOT THE "SKIN" ON HIS HAND IS REAL, OR A FLESH-COLORED PLASTIC! HE'S EVASIVE, BECAUSE HE'S AFRAID I'LL DISCOVER HIS SECRET!
BUT THEN...
OH, ALL RIGHT! THIS IS IDIOTIC, BUT--GO AHEAD, AND LOOK!
?!... HE'S GOING TO LET ME LOOK, AFTER ALL!--NOW TO LEARN THE TRUTH!!
NEXT MOMENT...
I SEE... PORES! IT... IS HUMAN SKIN! HMM... IF I DON'T ADMIT TO MYSELF THAT CLARK ISN'T SUPERMAN, THEN I'M JUST BEING A STUBBORN FOOL!
YOU'RE RIGHT! IT'S A SILLY HOBBY! LET'S FORGET IT!

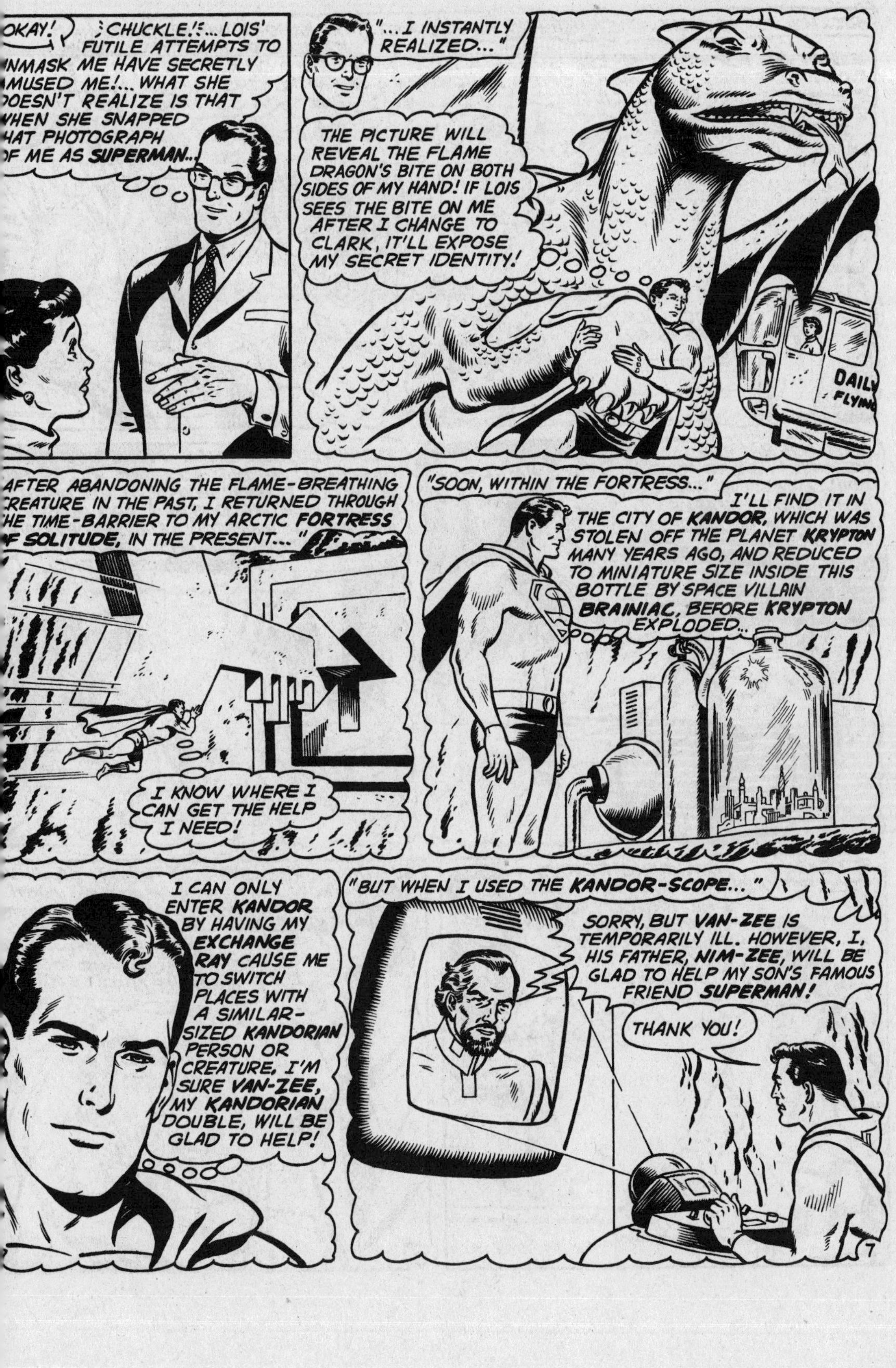
OKAY!
¡CHUCKLE!¡... LOIS' FUTILE ATTEMPTS TO UNMASK ME HAVE SECRETLY AMUSED ME!... WHAT SHE DOESN'T REALIZE IS THAT WHEN SHE SNAPPED THAT PHOTOGRAPH OF ME AS SUPERMAN...
"...I INSTANTLY REALIZED..."
THE PICTURE WILL REVEAL THE FLAME DRAGON'S BITE ON BOTH SIDES OF MY HAND! IF LOIS SEES THE BITE ON ME AFTER I CHANGE TO CLARK, IT'LL EXPOSE MY SECRET IDENTITY!
DAILY FLYIN
AFTER ABANDONING THE FLAME-BREATHING CREATURE IN THE PAST, I RETURNED THROUGH THE TIME-BARRIER TO MY ARCTIC FORTRESS OF SOLITUDE, IN THE PRESENT..."
I KNOW WHERE I CAN GET THE HELP I NEED!
"SOON, WITHIN THE FORTRESS..."
I'LL FIND IT IN THE CITY OF KANDOR, WHICH WAS STOLEN OFF THE PLANET KRYPTON MANY YEARS AGO, AND REDUCED TO MINIATURE SIZE INSIDE THIS BOTTLE BY SPACE VILLAIN BRAINIAC, BEFORE KRYPTON EXPLODED...
I CAN ONLY ENTER KANDOR BY HAVING MY EXCHANGE RAY CAUSE ME TO SWITCH PLACES WITH A SIMILAR-SIZED KANDORIAN PERSON OR CREATURE, I'M SURE VAN-ZEE, MY KANDORIAN DOUBLE, WILL BE GLAD TO HELP!
"BUT WHEN I USED THE KANDOR-SCOPE..."
SORRY, BUT VAN-ZEE IS TEMPORARILY ILL. HOWEVER, I, HIS FATHER, NIM-ZEE, WILL BE GLAD TO HELP MY SON'S FAMOUS FRIEND SUPERMAN!
THANK YOU!
7

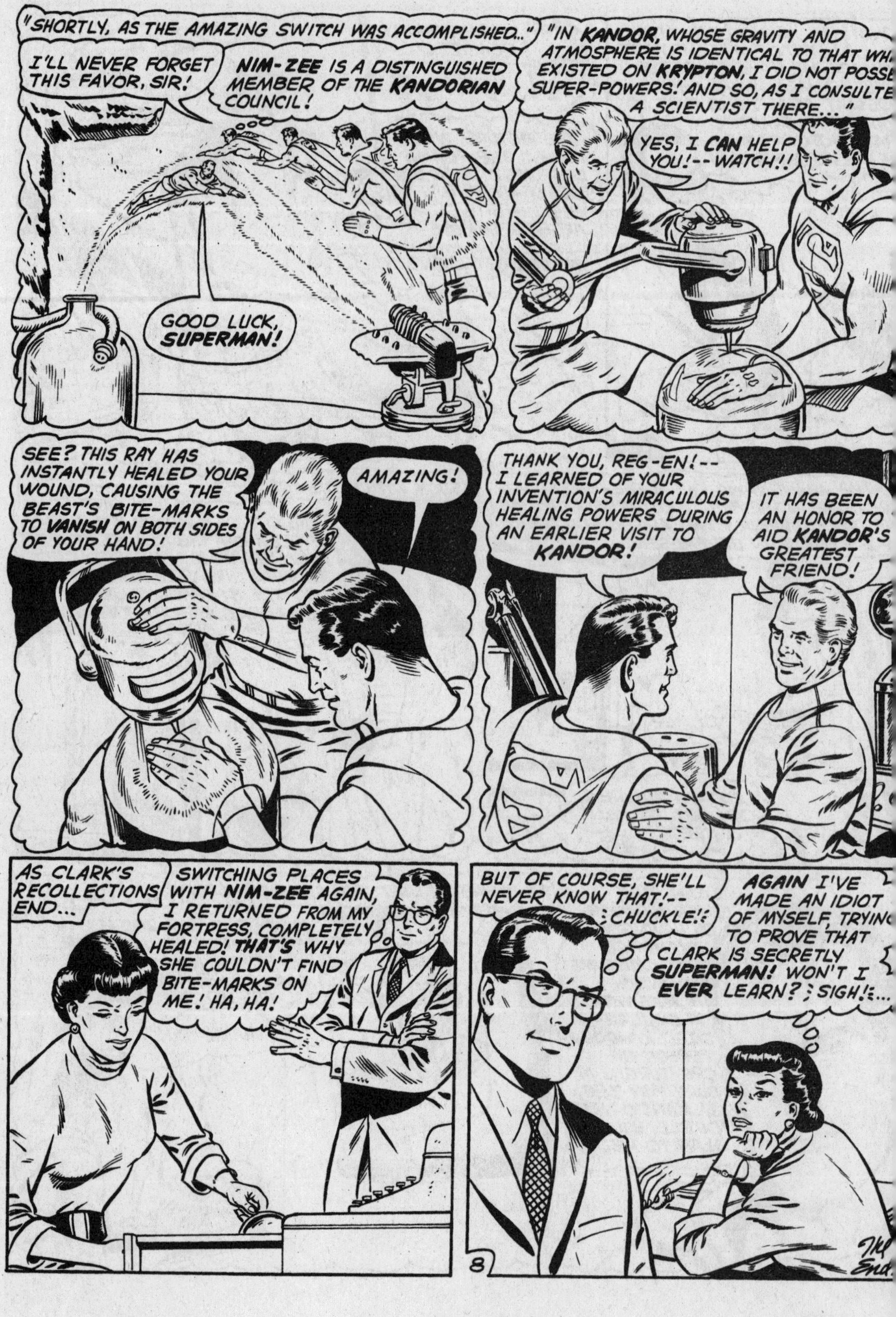
"SHORTLY, AS THE AMAZING SWITCH WAS ACCOMPLISHED.."
I'LL NEVER FORGET THIS FAVOR, SIR!
NIM-ZEE IS A DISTINGUISHED MEMBER OF THE KANDORIAN COUNCIL!
GOOD LUCK, SUPERMAN!
"IN KANDOR, WHOSE GRAVITY AND ATMOSPHERE IS IDENTICAL TO THAT WH EXISTED ON KRYPTON, I DID NOT POSSE SUPER-POWERS! AND SO, AS I CONSULTE A SCIENTIST THERE..."
YES, I CAN HELP YOU!--WATCH!!
SEE? THIS RAY HAS INSTANTLY HEALED YOUR WOUND, CAUSING THE BEAST'S BITE-MARKS TO VANISH ON BOTH SIDES OF YOUR HAND!
AMAZING!
THANK YOU, REG-EN!-- I LEARNED OF YOUR INVENTION'S MIRACULOUS HEALING POWERS DURING AN EARLIER VISIT TO KANDOR!
IT HAS BEEN AN HONOR TO AID KANDOR'S GREATEST FRIEND!
AS CLARK'S RECOLLECTIONS END...
SWITCHING PLACES WITH NIM-ZEE AGAIN, I RETURNED FROM MY FORTRESS, COMPLETELY HEALED! THAT'S WHY SHE COULDN'T FIND BITE-MARKS ON ME! HA, HA!
BUT OF COURSE, SHE'LL NEVER KNOW THAT!-- :CHUCKLE!:
AGAIN I'VE MADE AN IDIOT OF MYSELF, TRYIN TO PROVE THAT CLARK IS SECRETLY SUPERMAN! WON'T I EVER LEARN? :SIGH!:...
8

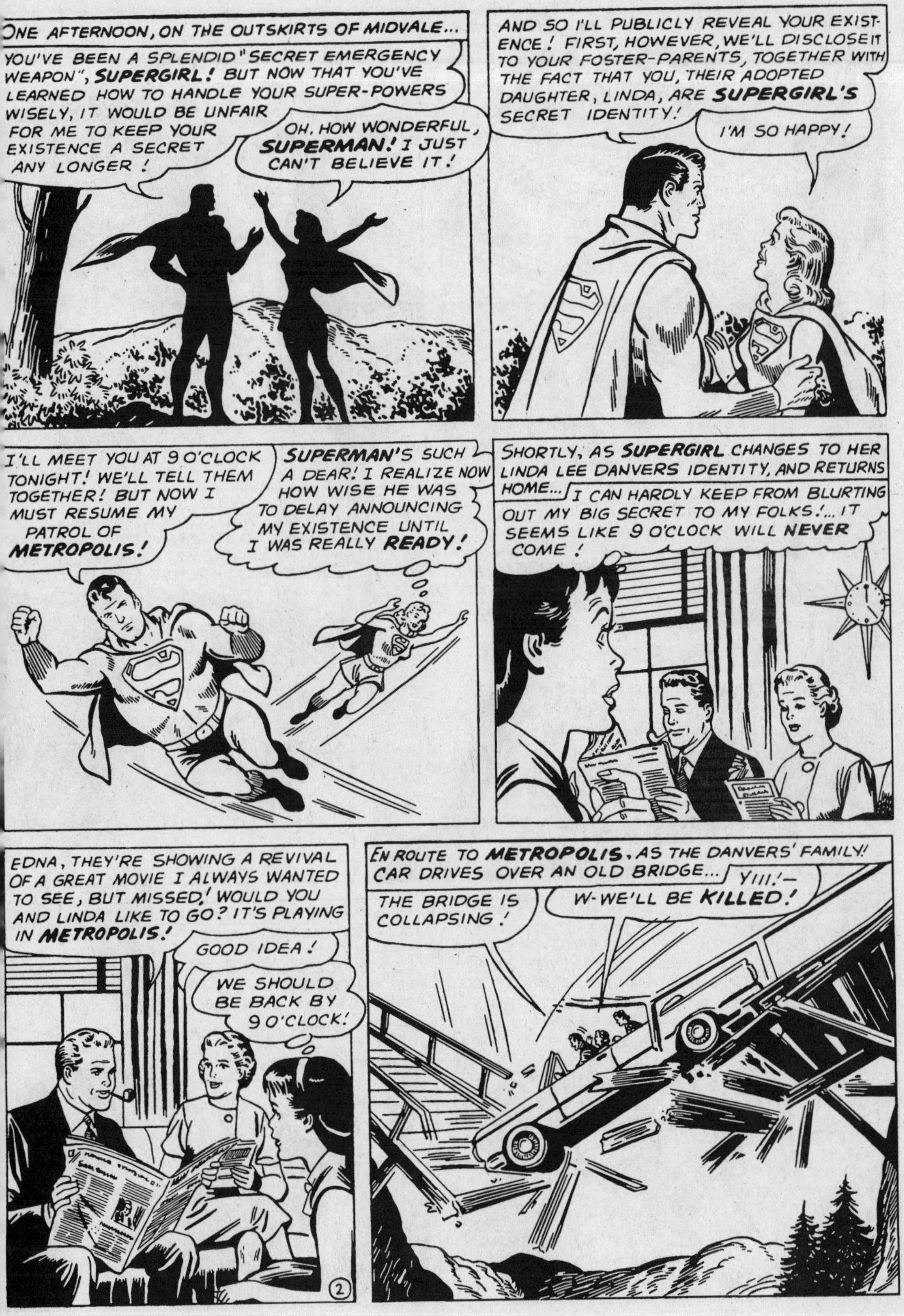
ONE AFTERNOON, ON THE OUTSKIRTS OF MIDVALE...
YOU'VE BEEN A SPLENDID "SECRET EMERGENCY WEAPON", SUPERGIRL! BUT NOW THAT YOU'VE LEARNED HOW TO HANDLE YOUR SUPER-POWERS WISELY, IT WOULD BE UNFAIR FOR ME TO KEEP YOUR EXISTENCE A SECRET ANY LONGER!
OH, HOW WONDERFUL, SUPERMAN! I JUST CAN'T BELIEVE IT!
AND SO I'LL PUBLICLY REVEAL YOUR EXISTENCE! FIRST, HOWEVER, WE'LL DISCLOSE IT TO YOUR FOSTER-PARENTS, TOGETHER WITH THE FACT THAT YOU, THEIR ADOPTED DAUGHTER, LINDA, ARE SUPERGIRL'S SECRET IDENTITY!
I'M SO HAPPY!
I'LL MEET YOU AT 9 O'CLOCK TONIGHT! WE'LL TELL THEM TOGETHER! BUT NOW I MUST RESUME MY PATROL OF METROPOLIS!
SUPERMAN'S SUCH A DEAR! I REALIZE NOW HOW WISE HE WAS TO DELAY ANNOUNCING MY EXISTENCE UNTIL I WAS REALLY READY!
SHORTLY, AS SUPERGIRL CHANGES TO HER LINDA LEE DANVERS IDENTITY, AND RETURNS HOME...
I CAN HARDLY KEEP FROM BLURTING OUT MY BIG SECRET TO MY FOLKS!... IT SEEMS LIKE 9 O'CLOCK WILL NEVER COME!
EDNA, THEY'RE SHOWING A REVIVAL OF A GREAT MOVIE I ALWAYS WANTED TO SEE, BUT MISSED! WOULD YOU AND LINDA LIKE TO GO? IT'S PLAYING IN METROPOLIS!
GOOD IDEA!
WE SHOULD BE BACK BY 9 O'CLOCK!
2
EN ROUTE TO METROPOLIS, AS THE DANVERS' FAMILY CAR DRIVES OVER AN OLD BRIDGE...
YIII!—
THE BRIDGE IS COLLAPSING!
W-WE'LL BE KILLED!

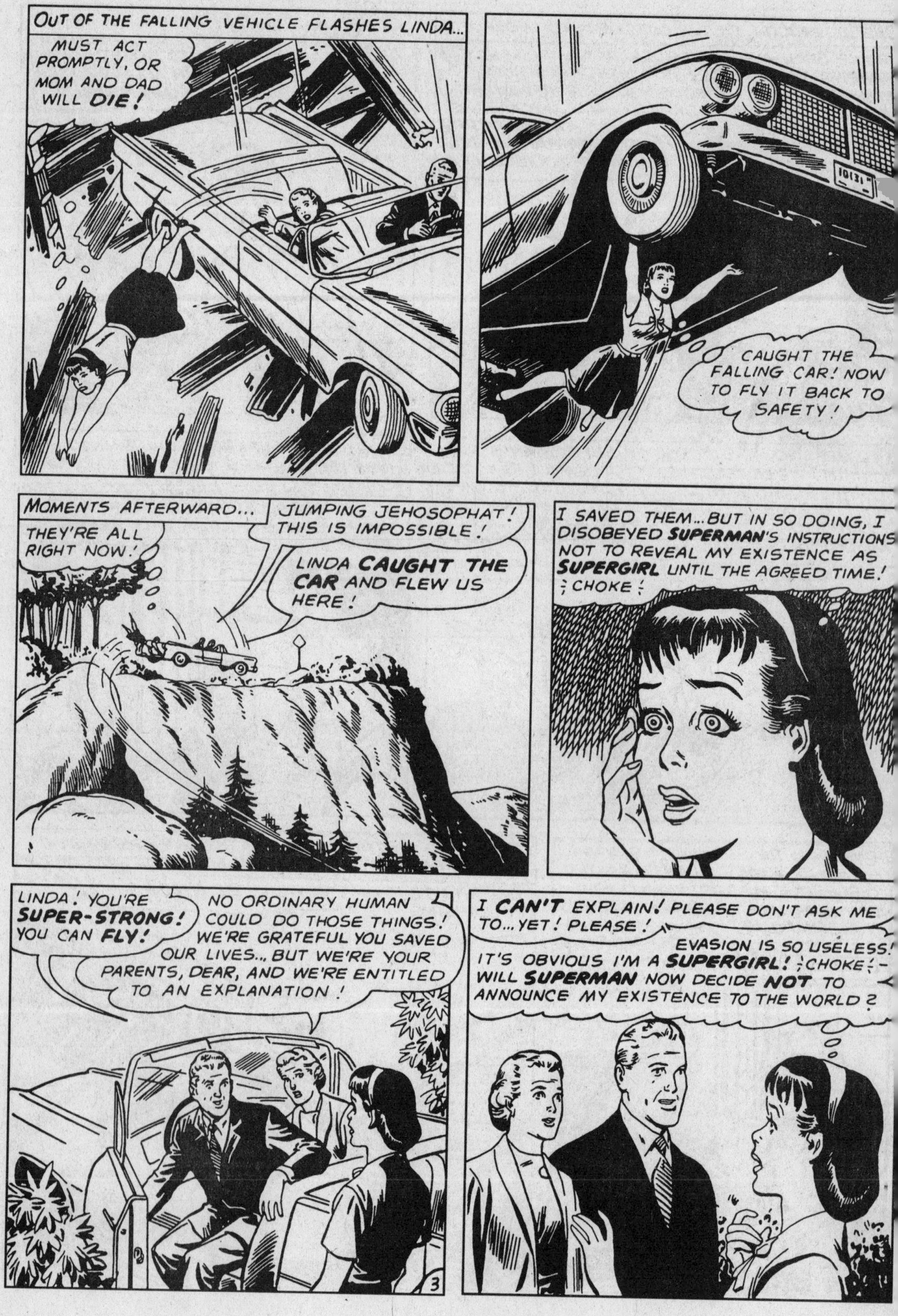
OUT OF THE FALLING VEHICLE FLASHES LINDA...
MUST ACT PROMPTLY, OR MOM AND DAD WILL DIE!
CAUGHT THE FALLING CAR! NOW TO FLY IT BACK TO SAFETY!
MOMENTS AFTERWARD...
THEY'RE ALL RIGHT NOW!
JUMPING JEHOSOPHAT! THIS IS IMPOSSIBLE!
LINDA CAUGHT THE CAR AND FLEW US HERE!
I SAVED THEM...BUT IN SO DOING, I DISOBEYED SUPERMAN'S INSTRUCTIONS NOT TO REVEAL MY EXISTENCE AS SUPERGIRL UNTIL THE AGREED TIME! -CHOKE-
LINDA! YOU'RE SUPER-STRONG! YOU CAN FLY!
NO ORDINARY HUMAN COULD DO THOSE THINGS! WE'RE GRATEFUL YOU SAVED OUR LIVES... BUT WE'RE YOUR PARENTS, DEAR, AND WE'RE ENTITLED TO AN EXPLANATION!
3
I CAN'T EXPLAIN! PLEASE DON'T ASK ME TO...YET! PLEASE!
EVASION IS SO USELESS! IT'S OBVIOUS I'M A SUPERGIRL! -CHOKE!- WILL SUPERMAN NOW DECIDE NOT TO ANNOUNCE MY EXISTENCE TO THE WORLD?

SUDDENLY... IT'S ALL RIGHT, LINDA! TELL YOUR PARENTS *EVERYTHING!*

SUPERMAN! WHAT...?!

SUPERMAN DOESN'T LOOK *ANGRY!*

I FINISHED MY PATROL EARLIER THAN EXPECTED, LINDA, AND WAS FLYING TOWARD YOUR HOME WHEN I SIGHTED THE RESCUE WITH MY TELESCOPIC VISION!... NATURALLY YOU HAD TO SAVE YOUR PARENTS, THOUGH IT MEANT DISCLOSING YOUR SUPER-POWERS!

YOU MEAN...YOU HAVEN'T CHANGED YOUR MIND ABOUT...?

REVEALING YOUR SECRET IDENTITY? OF COURSE NOT! LET'S DO IT *RIGHT NOW!*

"SECRET IDENTITY"? WHAT ARE THE TWO OF YOU TALKING ABOUT?!

RAPIDLY, LINDA CHANGES TO HER *SUPERGIRL* IDENTITY IN THE TWINKLING OF AN EYE...

MEET *SUPERGIRL,* MR. AND MRS. DANVERS! YOUR DAUGHTER LINDA IS ACTUALLY MY COUSIN FROM THE DESTROYED PLANET *KRYPTON!*

OH MY!

GASP!

SEE? SHE HAS SUPER-POWERS AS GREAT AS MINE!

BUT *KRYPTON* EXPLODED WHEN YOU LEFT IT IN A ROCKET SHIP AS A BABY! SINCE *SUPERGIRL'S* MUCH YOUNGER THAN YOU, *HOW* COULD SHE HAVE ESCAPED *KRYPTON'S* DESTRUCTION?

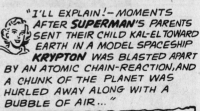

"I'LL EXPLAIN!—MOMENTS AFTER *SUPERMAN'S* PARENTS SENT THEIR CHILD *KAL-EL* TOWARD EARTH IN A MODEL SPACESHIP *KRYPTON* WAS BLASTED APART BY AN ATOMIC CHAIN-REACTION, AND A CHUNK OF THE PLANET WAS HURLED AWAY ALONG WITH A BUBBLE OF AIR..."

4

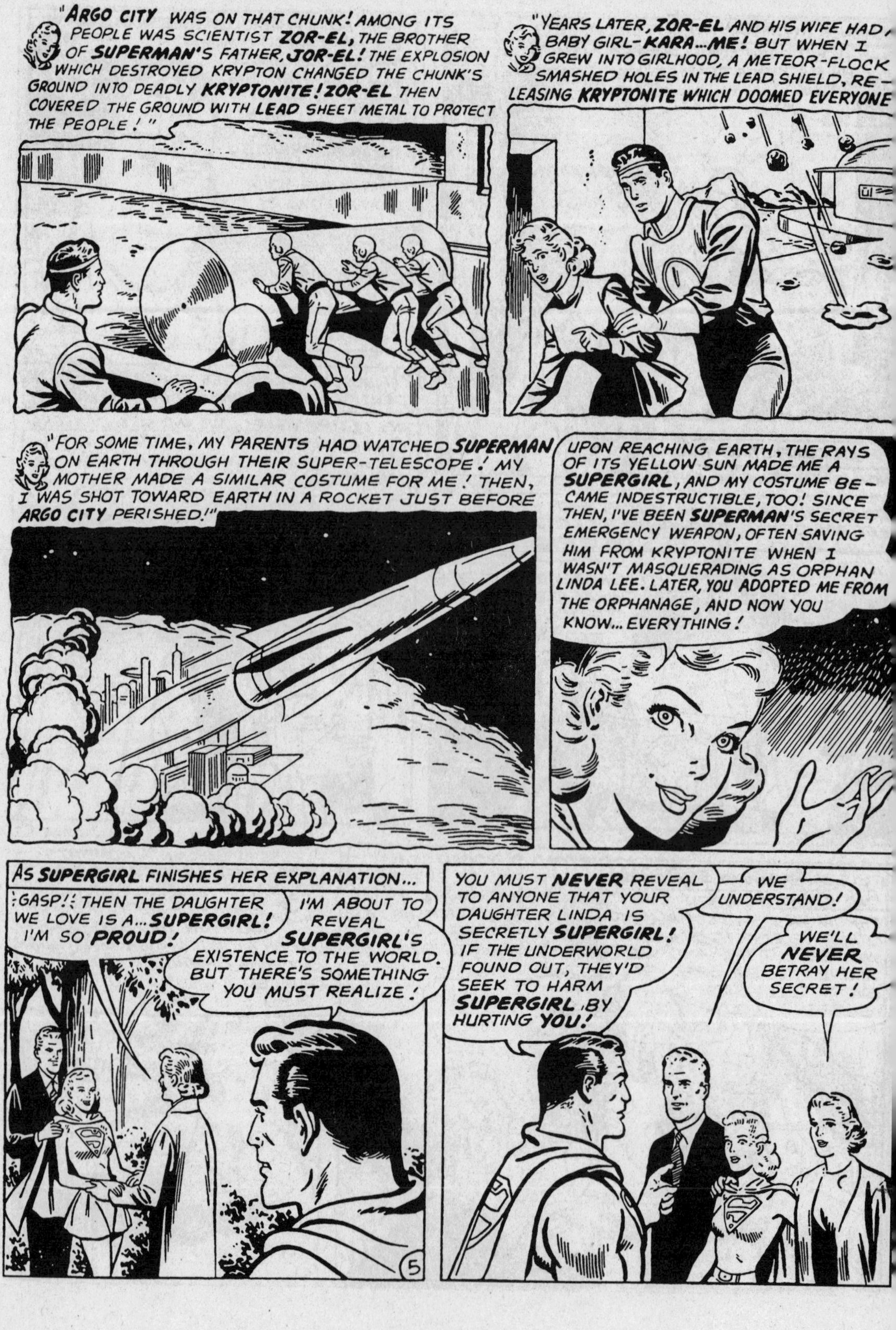
"ARGO CITY WAS ON THAT CHUNK! AMONG ITS PEOPLE WAS SCIENTIST ZOR-EL, THE BROTHER OF SUPERMAN'S FATHER, JOR-EL! THE EXPLOSION WHICH DESTROYED KRYPTON CHANGED THE CHUNK'S GROUND INTO DEADLY KRYPTONITE! ZOR-EL THEN COVERED THE GROUND WITH LEAD SHEET METAL TO PROTECT THE PEOPLE!"
"YEARS LATER, ZOR-EL AND HIS WIFE HAD A BABY GIRL--KARA...ME! BUT WHEN I GREW INTO GIRLHOOD, A METEOR-FLOCK SMASHED HOLES IN THE LEAD SHIELD, RELEASING KRYPTONITE WHICH DOOMED EVERYONE
"FOR SOME TIME, MY PARENTS HAD WATCHED SUPERMAN ON EARTH THROUGH THEIR SUPER-TELESCOPE! MY MOTHER MADE A SIMILAR COSTUME FOR ME! THEN, I WAS SHOT TOWARD EARTH IN A ROCKET JUST BEFORE ARGO CITY PERISHED!"
UPON REACHING EARTH, THE RAYS OF ITS YELLOW SUN MADE ME A SUPERGIRL, AND MY COSTUME BECAME INDESTRUCTIBLE, TOO! SINCE THEN, I'VE BEEN SUPERMAN'S SECRET EMERGENCY WEAPON, OFTEN SAVING HIM FROM KRYPTONITE WHEN I WASN'T MASQUERADING AS ORPHAN LINDA LEE. LATER, YOU ADOPTED ME FROM THE ORPHANAGE, AND NOW YOU KNOW... EVERYTHING!
AS SUPERGIRL FINISHES HER EXPLANATION...
GASP! THEN THE DAUGHTER WE LOVE IS A... SUPERGIRL! I'M SO PROUD!
I'M ABOUT TO REVEAL SUPERGIRL'S EXISTENCE TO THE WORLD. BUT THERE'S SOMETHING YOU MUST REALIZE!
5
YOU MUST NEVER REVEAL TO ANYONE THAT YOUR DAUGHTER LINDA IS SECRETLY SUPERGIRL! IF THE UNDERWORLD FOUND OUT, THEY'D SEEK TO HARM SUPERGIRL BY HURTING YOU!
WE UNDERSTAND!
WE'LL NEVER BETRAY HER SECRET!

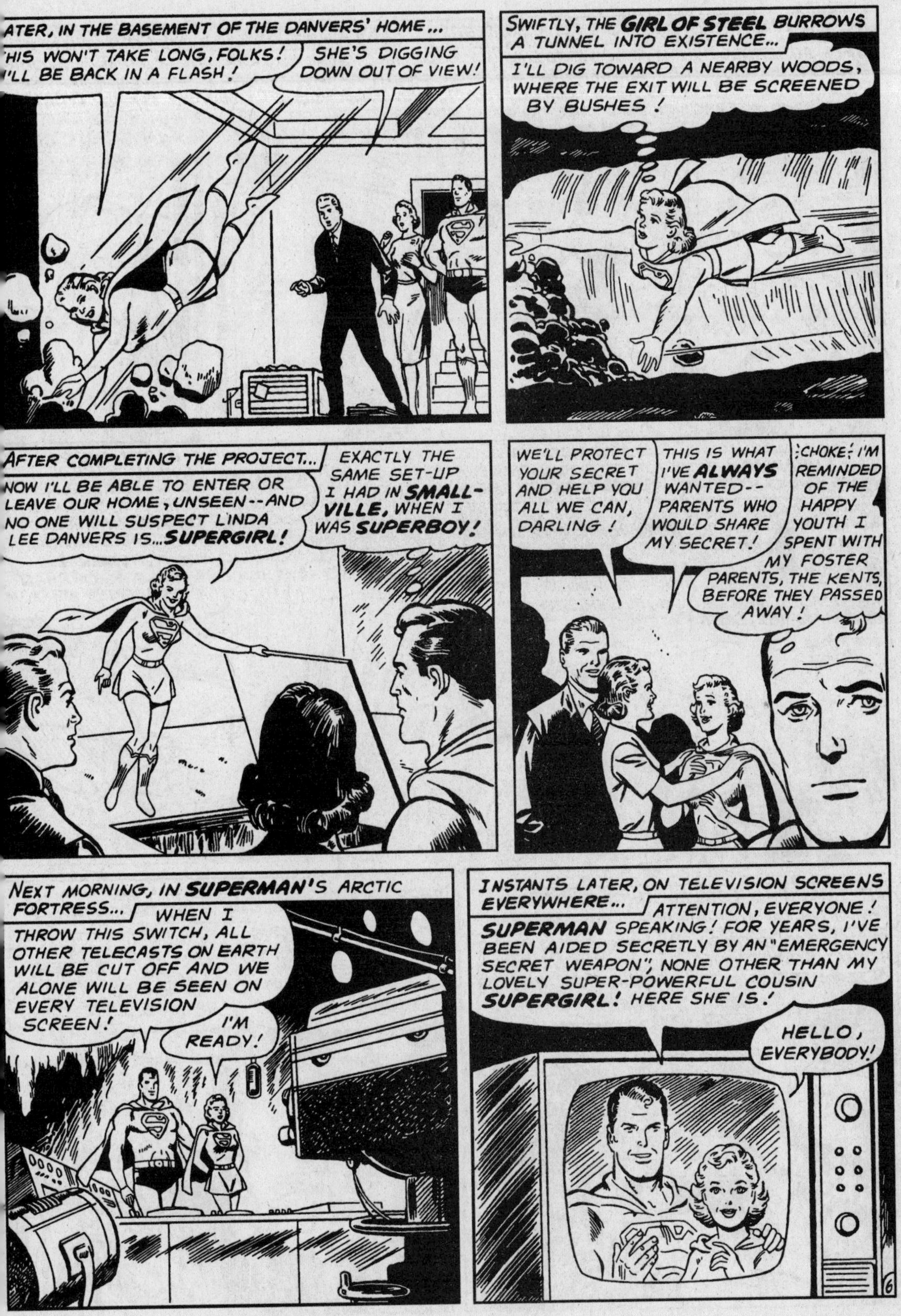
ATER, IN THE BASEMENT OF THE DANVERS' HOME...
THIS WON'T TAKE LONG, FOLKS! I'LL BE BACK IN A FLASH!
SHE'S DIGGING DOWN OUT OF VIEW!
SWIFTLY, THE GIRL OF STEEL BURROWS A TUNNEL INTO EXISTENCE...
I'LL DIG TOWARD A NEARBY WOODS, WHERE THE EXIT WILL BE SCREENED BY BUSHES!
AFTER COMPLETING THE PROJECT...
NOW I'LL BE ABLE TO ENTER OR LEAVE OUR HOME, UNSEEN--AND NO ONE WILL SUSPECT LINDA LEE DANVERS IS...SUPERGIRL!
EXACTLY THE SAME SET-UP I HAD IN SMALLVILLE, WHEN I WAS SUPERBOY!
WE'LL PROTECT YOUR SECRET AND HELP YOU ALL WE CAN, DARLING!
THIS IS WHAT I'VE ALWAYS WANTED--PARENTS WHO WOULD SHARE MY SECRET!
:CHOKE: I'M REMINDED OF THE HAPPY YOUTH I SPENT WITH MY FOSTER PARENTS, THE KENTS, BEFORE THEY PASSED AWAY!
NEXT MORNING, IN SUPERMAN'S ARCTIC FORTRESS...
WHEN I THROW THIS SWITCH, ALL OTHER TELECASTS ON EARTH WILL BE CUT OFF AND WE ALONE WILL BE SEEN ON EVERY TELEVISION SCREEN!
I'M READY!
INSTANTS LATER, ON TELEVISION SCREENS EVERYWHERE...
ATTENTION, EVERYONE! SUPERMAN SPEAKING! FOR YEARS, I'VE BEEN AIDED SECRETLY BY AN "EMERGENCY SECRET WEAPON", NONE OTHER THAN MY LOVELY SUPER-POWERFUL COUSIN SUPERGIRL! HERE SHE IS!
HELLO, EVERYBODY!
6

THE AMAZING NEWS BURSTS LIKE A BOMBSHELL, ASTOUNDING VIEWERS ALL OVER THE GLOBE!

SHE'S ADORABLE! I **LOVE** HER HAIR!

I'M HOLLYWOOD'S MOST BEAUTIFUL ACTRESS! BUT SHE'LL ATTRACT MORE ATTENTION THAN ME!...**BAH!**

IT'S UNFAIR! PEOPLE WILL LAUGH AT MY ACT, KNOWING A YOUNG GIRL IS STRONGER THAN ME!

¿GROAN¿ HOW CAN THIS SNIP OF A CHILD BE MIGHTIER THAN ALL THE SOVIET ATOMIC BOMBS PUT TOGETHER? IT MUST BE A CAPITALISTIC **HOAX**!

NEXT, **SUPERMAN** RUNS A TAPE EXPLAINING THE ORIGIN OF **SUPERGIRL** AND SHOWING SOME OF THE FEATS SHE'D SECRETLY PERFORMED IN THE PAST...

SOME OF THESE SCENES WERE PHOTOGRAPHED BY MY ROBOTS WHILE **SUPERGIRL** AND I WERE IN ACTION TOGETHER! HERE **SUPERGIRL**, FROM A SAFE DISTANCE, HURLED A BOULDER AT A KRYPTONITE METEOR WITH SUCH POWER THAT THE DEADLY METEOR WAS PULVERIZED OUT OF EXISTENCE, SAVING ME!

RECENTLY, A COMET'S PATH WAS BRINGING IT DANGEROUSLY CLOSE TO EARTH! WHY DID IT MYSTERIOUSLY CHANGE ITS COURSE? BECAUSE **SUPERGIRL** PLUNGED INTO IT, HEADLONG, DEFLECTING IT, THUS PREVENTING A COLLISION!

BUT THOUGH HONEST LAW-ABIDING CITIZENS REJOICE EVERYWHERE, GANGLAND MOURNS...

IT WAS BAD ENOUGH HAVING **SUPERMAN** AFTER US, BUT NOW--

... WE GOTTA WORRY ABOUT A **SUPER-DAME**, TOO! DISGUSTING, AIN'T IT?

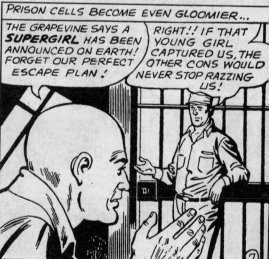

PRISON CELLS BECOME EVEN GLOOMIER...

THE GRAPEVINE SAYS A **SUPERGIRL** HAS BEEN ANNOUNCED ON EARTH! FORGET OUR PERFECT ESCAPE PLAN!

RIGHT!! IF THAT YOUNG GIRL CAPTURED US, THE OTHER CONS WOULD NEVER STOP RAZZING US!

7

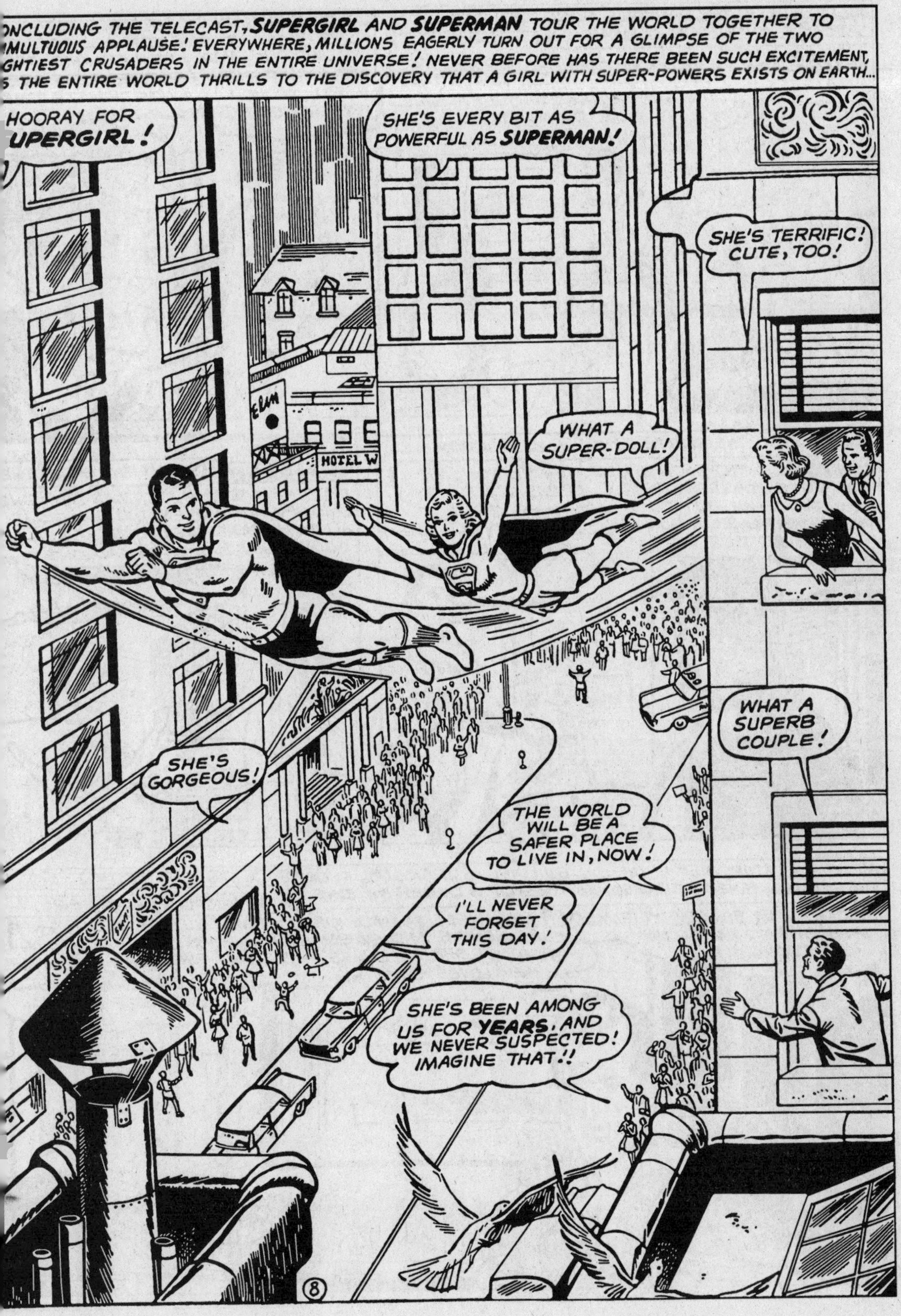
ONCLUDING THE TELECAST, SUPERGIRL AND SUPERMAN TOUR THE WORLD TOGETHER TO MULTUOUS APPLAUSE! EVERYWHERE, MILLIONS EAGERLY TURN OUT FOR A GLIMPSE OF THE TWO GHTIEST CRUSADERS IN THE ENTIRE UNIVERSE! NEVER BEFORE HAS THERE BEEN SUCH EXCITEMENT, S THE ENTIRE WORLD THRILLS TO THE DISCOVERY THAT A GIRL WITH SUPER-POWERS EXISTS ON EARTH...
HOORAY FOR UPERGIRL!
SHE'S EVERY BIT AS POWERFUL AS SUPERMAN!
SHE'S TERRIFIC! CUTE, TOO!
WHAT A SUPER-DOLL!
HOTEL W
SHE'S GORGEOUS!
WHAT A SUPERB COUPLE!
THE WORLD WILL BE A SAFER PLACE TO LIVE IN, NOW!
I'LL NEVER FORGET THIS DAY!
SHE'S BEEN AMONG US FOR YEARS, AND WE NEVER SUSPECTED! IMAGINE THAT!!
8

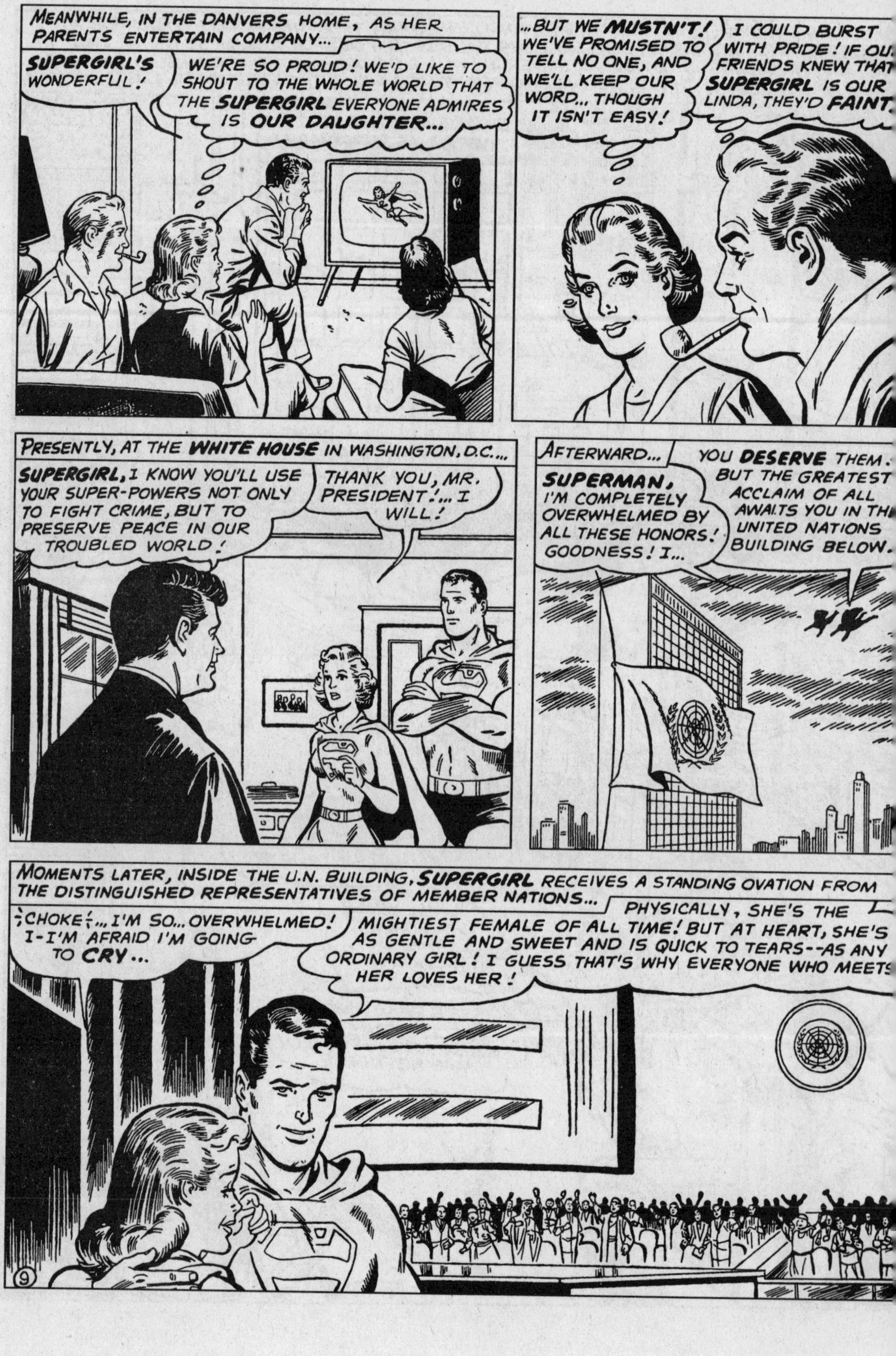
MEANWHILE, IN THE DANVERS HOME, AS HER PARENTS ENTERTAIN COMPANY...
SUPERGIRL'S WONDERFUL!
WE'RE SO PROUD! WE'D LIKE TO SHOUT TO THE WHOLE WORLD THAT THE SUPERGIRL EVERYONE ADMIRES IS OUR DAUGHTER...
...BUT WE MUSTN'T! WE'VE PROMISED TO TELL NO ONE, AND WE'LL KEEP OUR WORD... THOUGH IT ISN'T EASY!
I COULD BURST WITH PRIDE! IF OU FRIENDS KNEW THAT SUPERGIRL IS OUR LINDA, THEY'D FAINT
PRESENTLY, AT THE WHITE HOUSE IN WASHINGTON, D.C....
SUPERGIRL, I KNOW YOU'LL USE YOUR SUPER-POWERS NOT ONLY TO FIGHT CRIME, BUT TO PRESERVE PEACE IN OUR TROUBLED WORLD!
THANK YOU, MR. PRESIDENT!... I WILL!
AFTERWARD...
SUPERMAN, I'M COMPLETELY OVERWHELMED BY ALL THESE HONORS! GOODNESS! I...
YOU DESERVE THEM. BUT THE GREATEST ACCLAIM OF ALL AWAITS YOU IN TH UNITED NATIONS BUILDING BELOW.
MOMENTS LATER, INSIDE THE U.N. BUILDING, SUPERGIRL RECEIVES A STANDING OVATION FROM THE DISTINGUISHED REPRESENTATIVES OF MEMBER NATIONS...
-CHOKE-... I'M SO... OVERWHELMED! I-I'M AFRAID I'M GOING TO CRY...
PHYSICALLY, SHE'S THE MIGHTIEST FEMALE OF ALL TIME! BUT AT HEART, SHE'S AS GENTLE AND SWEET AND IS QUICK TO TEARS--AS ANY ORDINARY GIRL! I GUESS THAT'S WHY EVERYONE WHO MEETS HER LOVES HER!
9

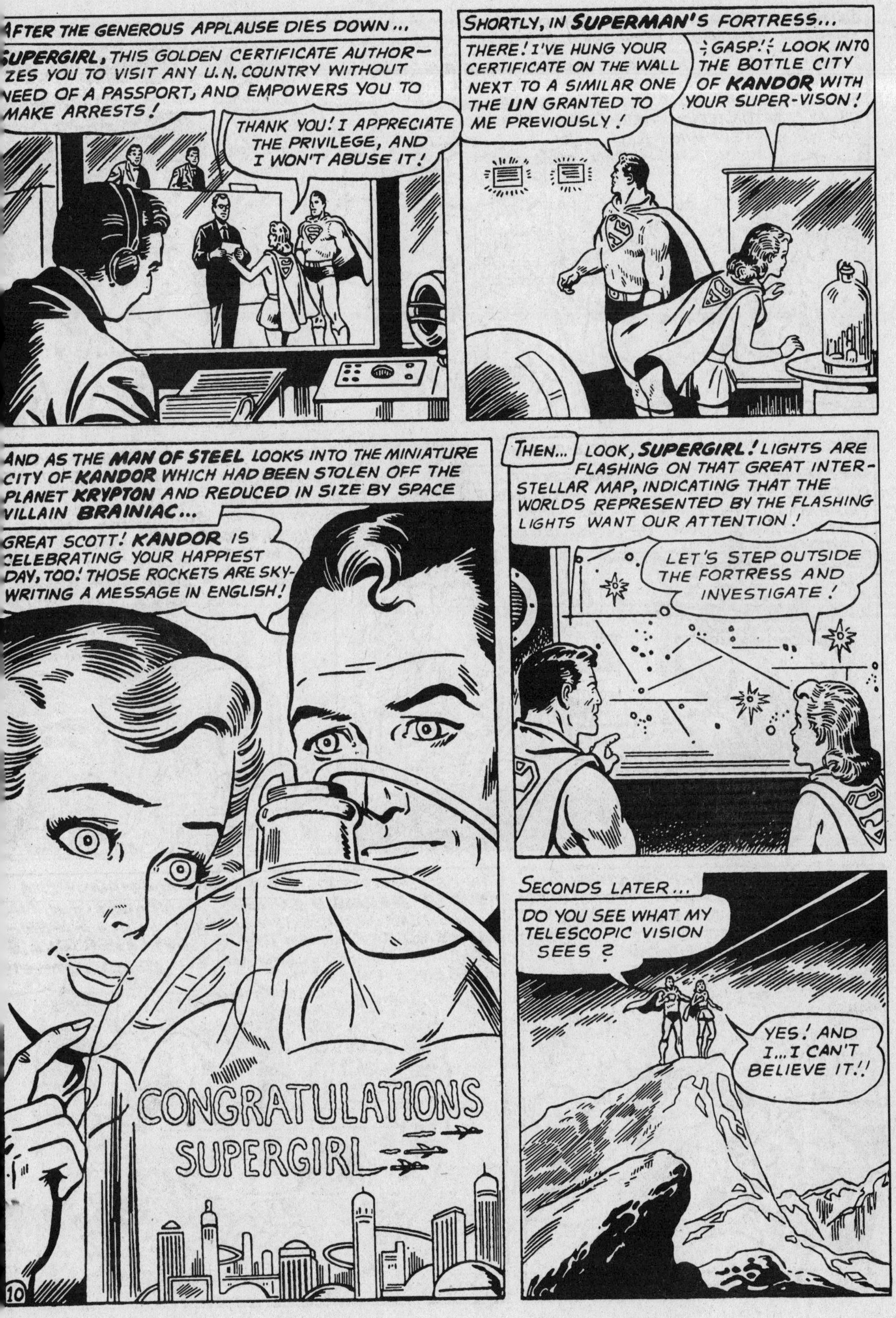
AFTER THE GENEROUS APPLAUSE DIES DOWN...
SUPERGIRL, THIS GOLDEN CERTIFICATE AUTHORIZES YOU TO VISIT ANY U.N. COUNTRY WITHOUT NEED OF A PASSPORT, AND EMPOWERS YOU TO MAKE ARRESTS!
THANK YOU! I APPRECIATE THE PRIVILEGE, AND I WON'T ABUSE IT!
SHORTLY, IN SUPERMAN'S FORTRESS...
THERE! I'VE HUNG YOUR CERTIFICATE ON THE WALL NEXT TO A SIMILAR ONE THE UN GRANTED TO ME PREVIOUSLY!
GASP! LOOK INTO THE BOTTLE CITY OF KANDOR WITH YOUR SUPER-VISON!
AND AS THE MAN OF STEEL LOOKS INTO THE MINIATURE CITY OF KANDOR WHICH HAD BEEN STOLEN OFF THE PLANET KRYPTON AND REDUCED IN SIZE BY SPACE VILLAIN BRAINIAC...
GREAT SCOTT! KANDOR IS CELEBRATING YOUR HAPPIEST DAY, TOO! THOSE ROCKETS ARE SKY-WRITING A MESSAGE IN ENGLISH!
CONGRATULATIONS SUPERGIRL
10
THEN...
LOOK, SUPERGIRL! LIGHTS ARE FLASHING ON THAT GREAT INTER-STELLAR MAP, INDICATING THAT THE WORLDS REPRESENTED BY THE FLASHING LIGHTS WANT OUR ATTENTION!
LET'S STEP OUTSIDE THE FORTRESS AND INVESTIGATE!
SECONDS LATER...
DO YOU SEE WHAT MY TELESCOPIC VISION SEES?
YES! AND I...I CAN'T BELIEVE IT!!

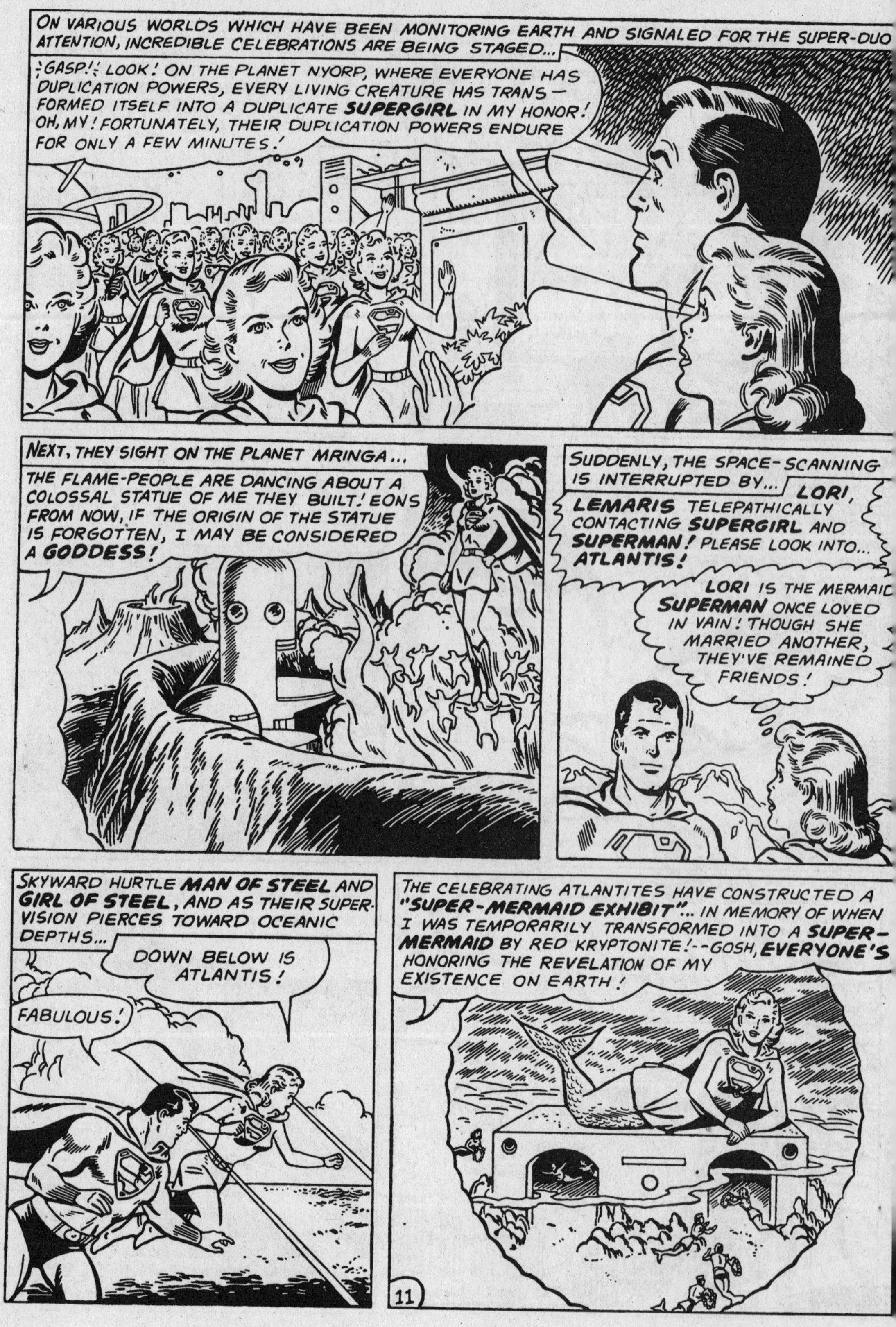
ON VARIOUS WORLDS WHICH HAVE BEEN MONITORING EARTH AND SIGNALED FOR THE SUPER-DUO ATTENTION, INCREDIBLE CELEBRATIONS ARE BEING STAGED...
;GASP!; LOOK! ON THE PLANET NYORP, WHERE EVERYONE HAS DUPLICATION POWERS, EVERY LIVING CREATURE HAS TRANSFORMED ITSELF INTO A DUPLICATE SUPERGIRL IN MY HONOR! OH, MY! FORTUNATELY, THEIR DUPLICATION POWERS ENDURE FOR ONLY A FEW MINUTES!
NEXT, THEY SIGHT ON THE PLANET MRINGA...
THE FLAME-PEOPLE ARE DANCING ABOUT A COLOSSAL STATUE OF ME THEY BUILT! EONS FROM NOW, IF THE ORIGIN OF THE STATUE IS FORGOTTEN, I MAY BE CONSIDERED A GODDESS!
SUDDENLY, THE SPACE-SCANNING IS INTERRUPTED BY...
LORI, LEMARIS TELEPATHICALLY CONTACTING SUPERGIRL AND SUPERMAN! PLEASE LOOK INTO... ATLANTIS!
LORI IS THE MERMAID SUPERMAN ONCE LOVED IN VAIN! THOUGH SHE MARRIED ANOTHER, THEY'VE REMAINED FRIENDS!
SKYWARD HURTLE MAN OF STEEL AND GIRL OF STEEL, AND AS THEIR SUPER-VISION PIERCES TOWARD OCEANIC DEPTHS...
DOWN BELOW IS ATLANTIS!
FABULOUS!
THE CELEBRATING ATLANTITES HAVE CONSTRUCTED A "SUPER-MERMAID EXHIBIT"... IN MEMORY OF WHEN I WAS TEMPORARILY TRANSFORMED INTO A SUPER-MERMAID BY RED KRYPTONITE!--GOSH, EVERYONE'S HONORING THE REVELATION OF MY EXISTENCE ON EARTH!
11

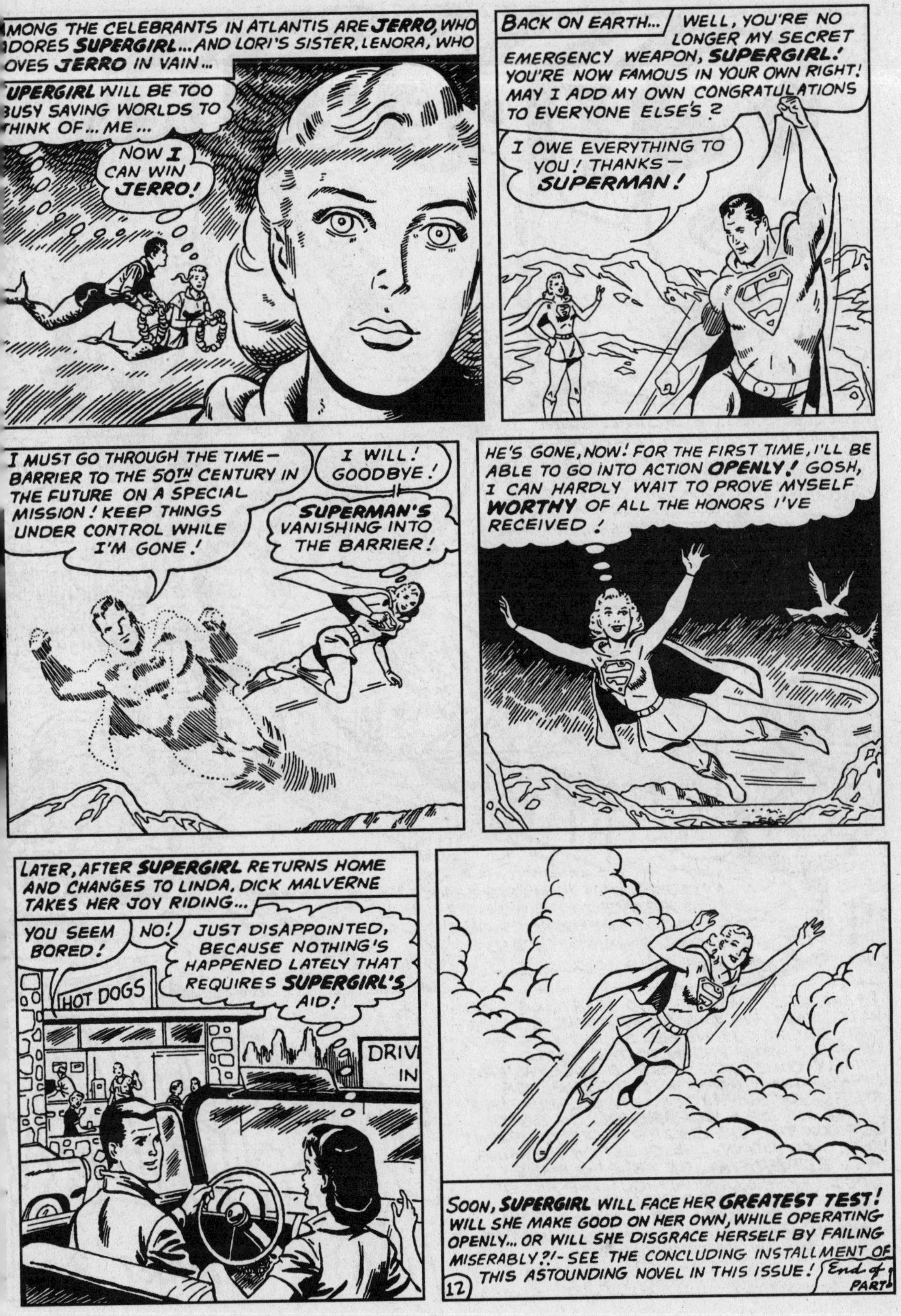
AMONG THE CELEBRANTS IN ATLANTIS ARE JERRO, WHO ADORES SUPERGIRL... AND LORI'S SISTER, LENORA, WHO LOVES JERRO IN VAIN...
SUPERGIRL WILL BE TOO BUSY SAVING WORLDS TO THINK OF... ME...
NOW I CAN WIN JERRO!
BACK ON EARTH...
WELL, YOU'RE NO LONGER MY SECRET EMERGENCY WEAPON, SUPERGIRL! YOU'RE NOW FAMOUS IN YOUR OWN RIGHT! MAY I ADD MY OWN CONGRATULATIONS TO EVERYONE ELSE'S?
I OWE EVERYTHING TO YOU! THANKS— SUPERMAN!
I MUST GO THROUGH THE TIME-BARRIER TO THE 50TH CENTURY IN THE FUTURE ON A SPECIAL MISSION! KEEP THINGS UNDER CONTROL WHILE I'M GONE!
I WILL! GOODBYE!
SUPERMAN'S VANISHING INTO THE BARRIER!
HE'S GONE, NOW! FOR THE FIRST TIME, I'LL BE ABLE TO GO INTO ACTION OPENLY! GOSH, I CAN HARDLY WAIT TO PROVE MYSELF WORTHY OF ALL THE HONORS I'VE RECEIVED!
LATER, AFTER SUPERGIRL RETURNS HOME AND CHANGES TO LINDA, DICK MALVERNE TAKES HER JOY RIDING...
YOU SEEM BORED!
NO! JUST DISAPPOINTED, BECAUSE NOTHING'S HAPPENED LATELY THAT REQUIRES SUPERGIRL'S AID!
HOT DOGS
DRIVE IN
SOON, SUPERGIRL WILL FACE HER GREATEST TEST! WILL SHE MAKE GOOD ON HER OWN, WHILE OPERATING OPENLY... OR WILL SHE DISGRACE HERSELF BY FAILING MISERABLY?!- SEE THE CONCLUDING INSTALLMENT OF THIS ASTOUNDING NOVEL IN THIS ISSUE!
12
End of PART I

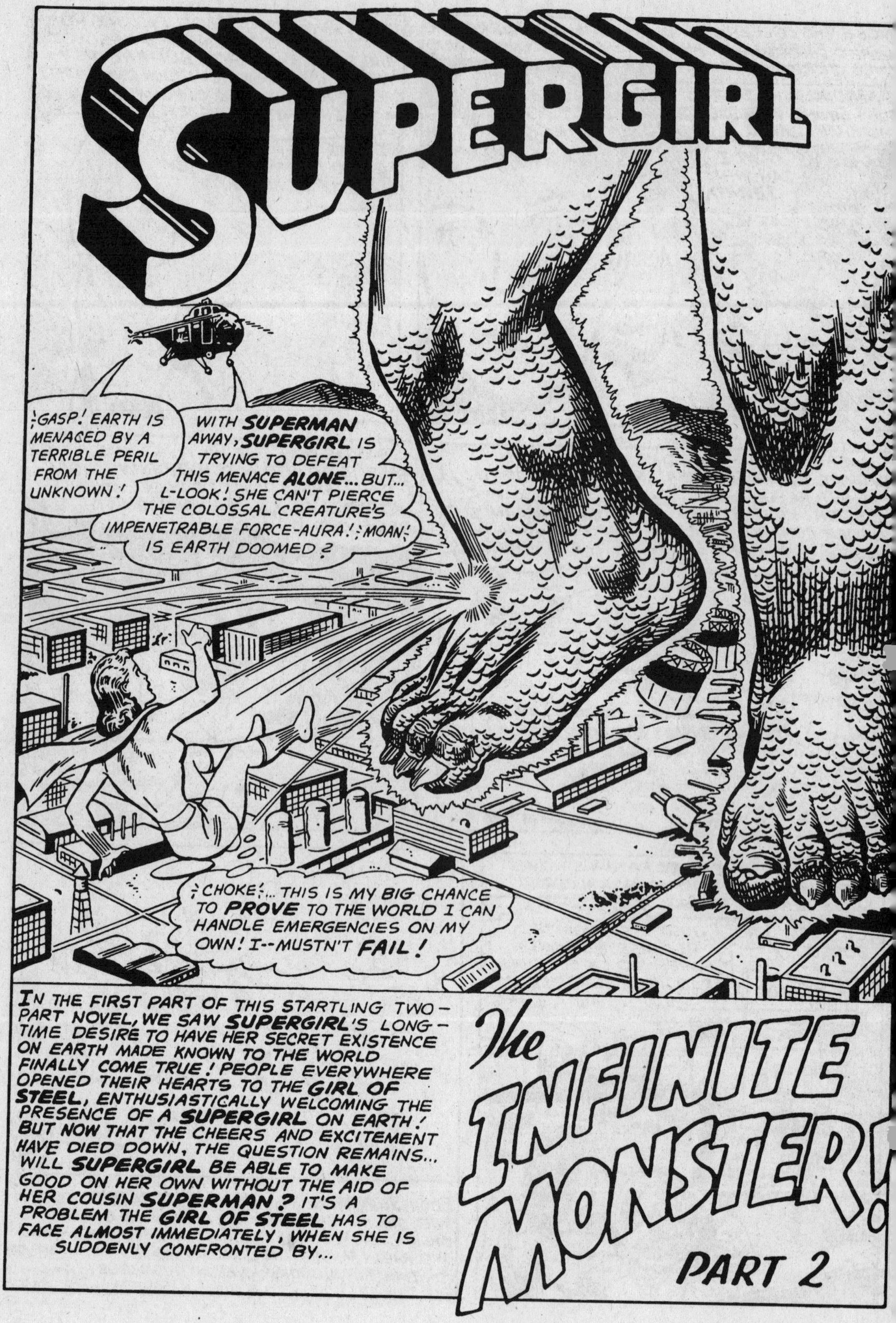
SUPERGIRL
¡GASP! EARTH IS MENACED BY A TERRIBLE PERIL FROM THE UNKNOWN!
WITH SUPERMAN AWAY, SUPERGIRL IS TRYING TO DEFEAT THIS MENACE ALONE... BUT... L-LOOK! SHE CAN'T PIERCE THE COLOSSAL CREATURE'S IMPENETRABLE FORCE-AURA! ¡MOAN! IS EARTH DOOMED?
¡CHOKE!... THIS IS MY BIG CHANCE TO PROVE TO THE WORLD I CAN HANDLE EMERGENCIES ON MY OWN! I--MUSTN'T FAIL!
IN THE FIRST PART OF THIS STARTLING TWO-PART NOVEL, WE SAW SUPERGIRL'S LONG-TIME DESIRE TO HAVE HER SECRET EXISTENCE ON EARTH MADE KNOWN TO THE WORLD FINALLY COME TRUE! PEOPLE EVERYWHERE OPENED THEIR HEARTS TO THE GIRL OF STEEL, ENTHUSIASTICALLY WELCOMING THE PRESENCE OF A SUPERGIRL ON EARTH! BUT NOW THAT THE CHEERS AND EXCITEMENT HAVE DIED DOWN, THE QUESTION REMAINS... WILL SUPERGIRL BE ABLE TO MAKE GOOD ON HER OWN WITHOUT THE AID OF HER COUSIN SUPERMAN? IT'S A PROBLEM THE GIRL OF STEEL HAS TO FACE ALMOST IMMEDIATELY, WHEN SHE IS SUDDENLY CONFRONTED BY...
The INFINITE MONSTER!
PART 2

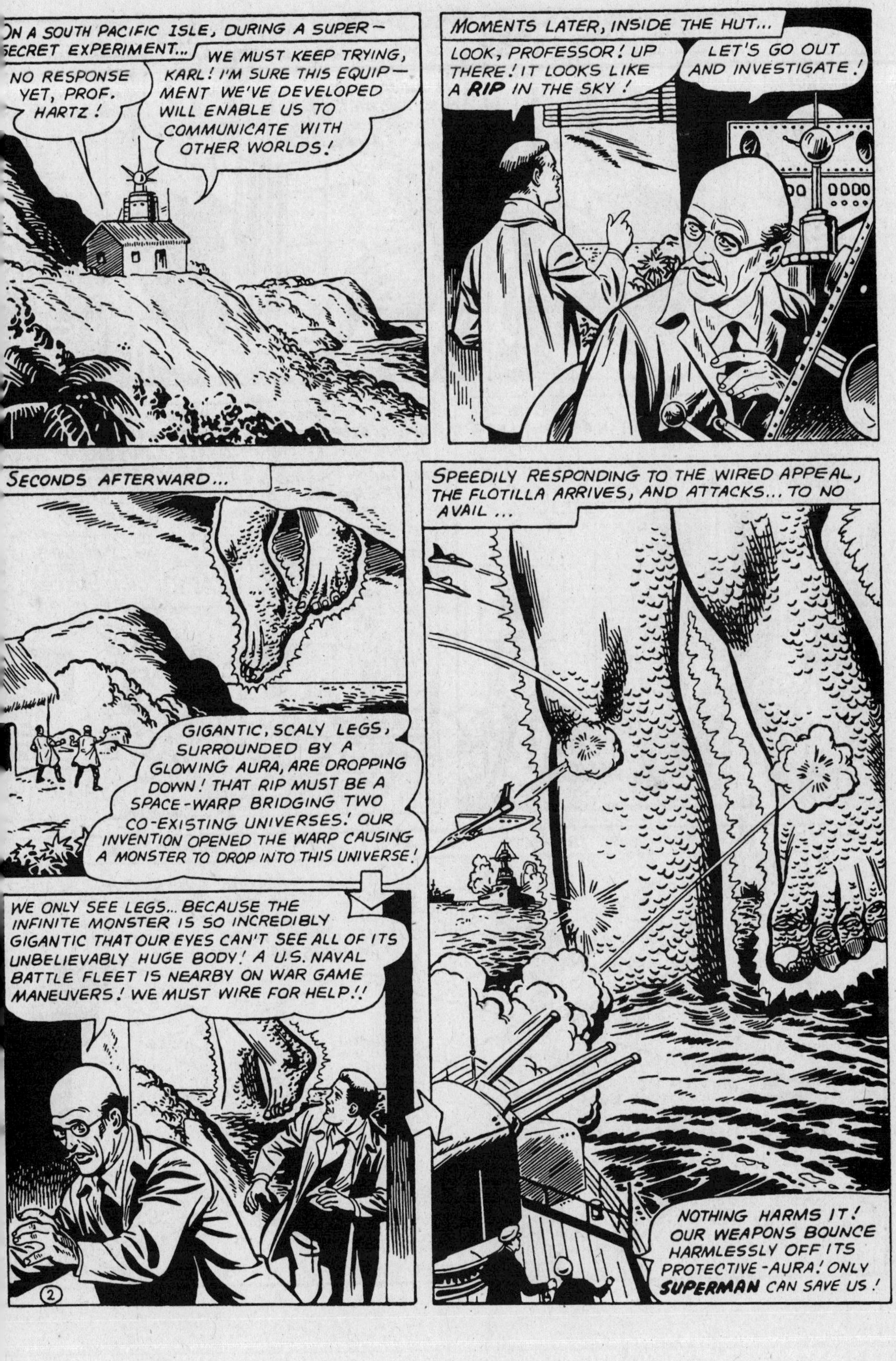
ON A SOUTH PACIFIC ISLE, DURING A SUPER-SECRET EXPERIMENT...
NO RESPONSE YET, PROF. HARTZ!
WE MUST KEEP TRYING, KARL! I'M SURE THIS EQUIPMENT WE'VE DEVELOPED WILL ENABLE US TO COMMUNICATE WITH OTHER WORLDS!
MOMENTS LATER, INSIDE THE HUT...
LOOK, PROFESSOR! UP THERE! IT LOOKS LIKE A RIP IN THE SKY!
LET'S GO OUT AND INVESTIGATE!
SECONDS AFTERWARD...
GIGANTIC, SCALY LEGS, SURROUNDED BY A GLOWING AURA, ARE DROPPING DOWN! THAT RIP MUST BE A SPACE-WARP BRIDGING TWO CO-EXISTING UNIVERSES! OUR INVENTION OPENED THE WARP CAUSING A MONSTER TO DROP INTO THIS UNIVERSE!
WE ONLY SEE LEGS... BECAUSE THE INFINITE MONSTER IS SO INCREDIBLY GIGANTIC THAT OUR EYES CAN'T SEE ALL OF ITS UNBELIEVABLY HUGE BODY! A U.S. NAVAL BATTLE FLEET IS NEARBY ON WAR GAME MANEUVERS! WE MUST WIRE FOR HELP!!
2
SPEEDILY RESPONDING TO THE WIRED APPEAL, THE FLOTILLA ARRIVES, AND ATTACKS... TO NO AVAIL...
NOTHING HARMS IT! OUR WEAPONS BOUNCE HARMLESSLY OFF ITS PROTECTIVE-AURA! ONLY SUPERMAN CAN SAVE US!

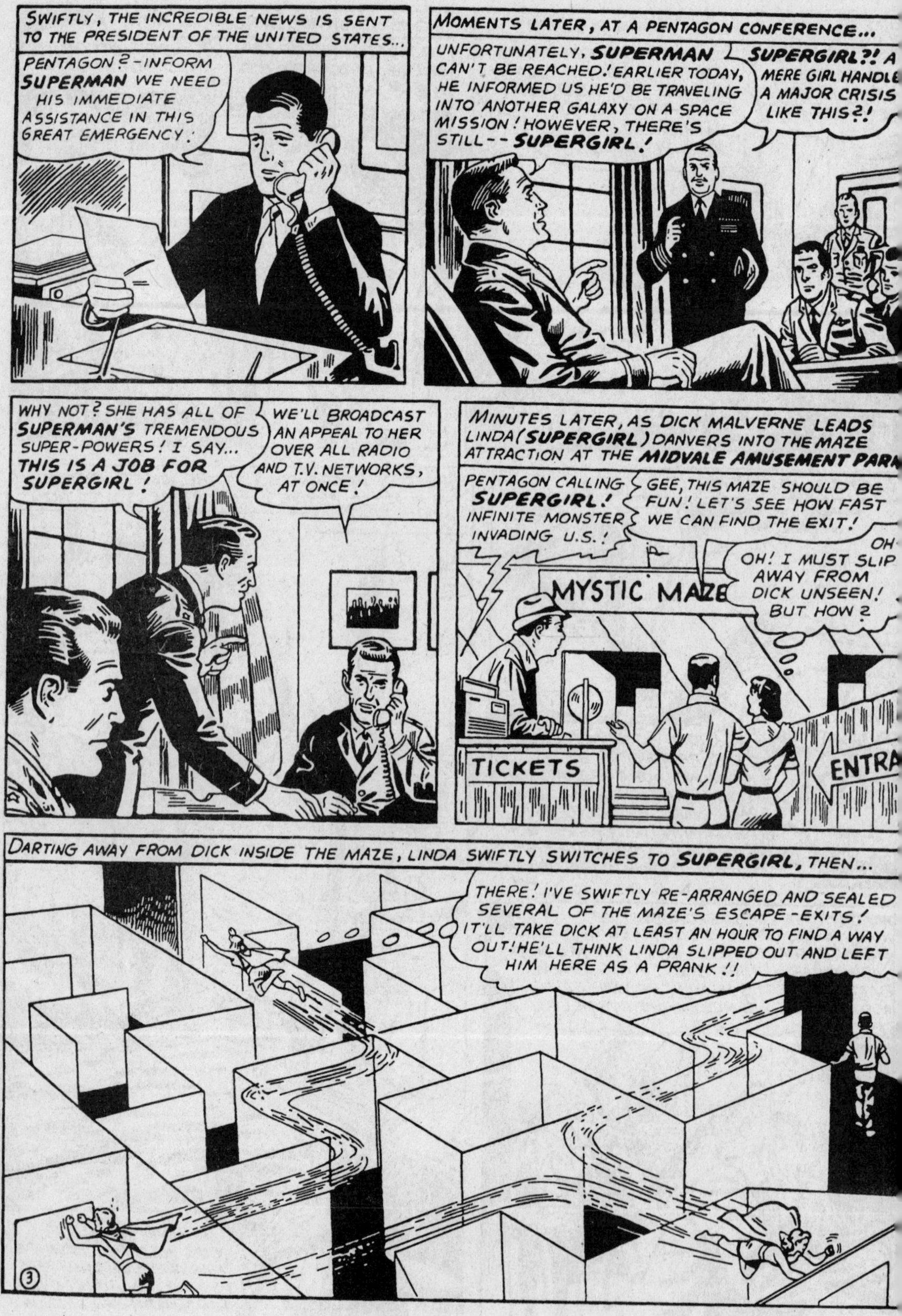

SWIFTLY, THE INCREDIBLE NEWS IS SENT TO THE PRESIDENT OF THE UNITED STATES...
PENTAGON?-INFORM SUPERMAN WE NEED HIS IMMEDIATE ASSISTANCE IN THIS GREAT EMERGENCY!
MOMENTS LATER, AT A PENTAGON CONFERENCE...
UNFORTUNATELY, SUPERMAN CAN'T BE REACHED! EARLIER TODAY, HE INFORMED US HE'D BE TRAVELING INTO ANOTHER GALAXY ON A SPACE MISSION! HOWEVER, THERE'S STILL--SUPERGIRL!
SUPERGIRL?! A MERE GIRL HANDLE A MAJOR CRISIS LIKE THIS?!
WHY NOT? SHE HAS ALL OF SUPERMAN'S TREMENDOUS SUPER-POWERS! I SAY... THIS IS A JOB FOR SUPERGIRL!
WE'LL BROADCAST AN APPEAL TO HER OVER ALL RADIO AND T.V. NETWORKS, AT ONCE!
MINUTES LATER, AS DICK MALVERNE LEADS LINDA (SUPERGIRL) DANVERS INTO THE MAZE ATTRACTION AT THE MIDVALE AMUSEMENT PARK
PENTAGON CALLING SUPERGIRL! INFINITE MONSTER INVADING U.S.!
GEE, THIS MAZE SHOULD BE FUN! LET'S SEE HOW FAST WE CAN FIND THE EXIT!
OH OH! I MUST SLIP AWAY FROM DICK UNSEEN! BUT HOW?
MYSTIC MAZE
TICKETS
ENTRA
DARTING AWAY FROM DICK INSIDE THE MAZE, LINDA SWIFTLY SWITCHES TO SUPERGIRL, THEN...
THERE! I'VE SWIFTLY RE-ARRANGED AND SEALED SEVERAL OF THE MAZE'S ESCAPE-EXITS! IT'LL TAKE DICK AT LEAST AN HOUR TO FIND A WAY OUT! HE'LL THINK LINDA SLIPPED OUT AND LEFT HIM HERE AS A PRANK!!
3

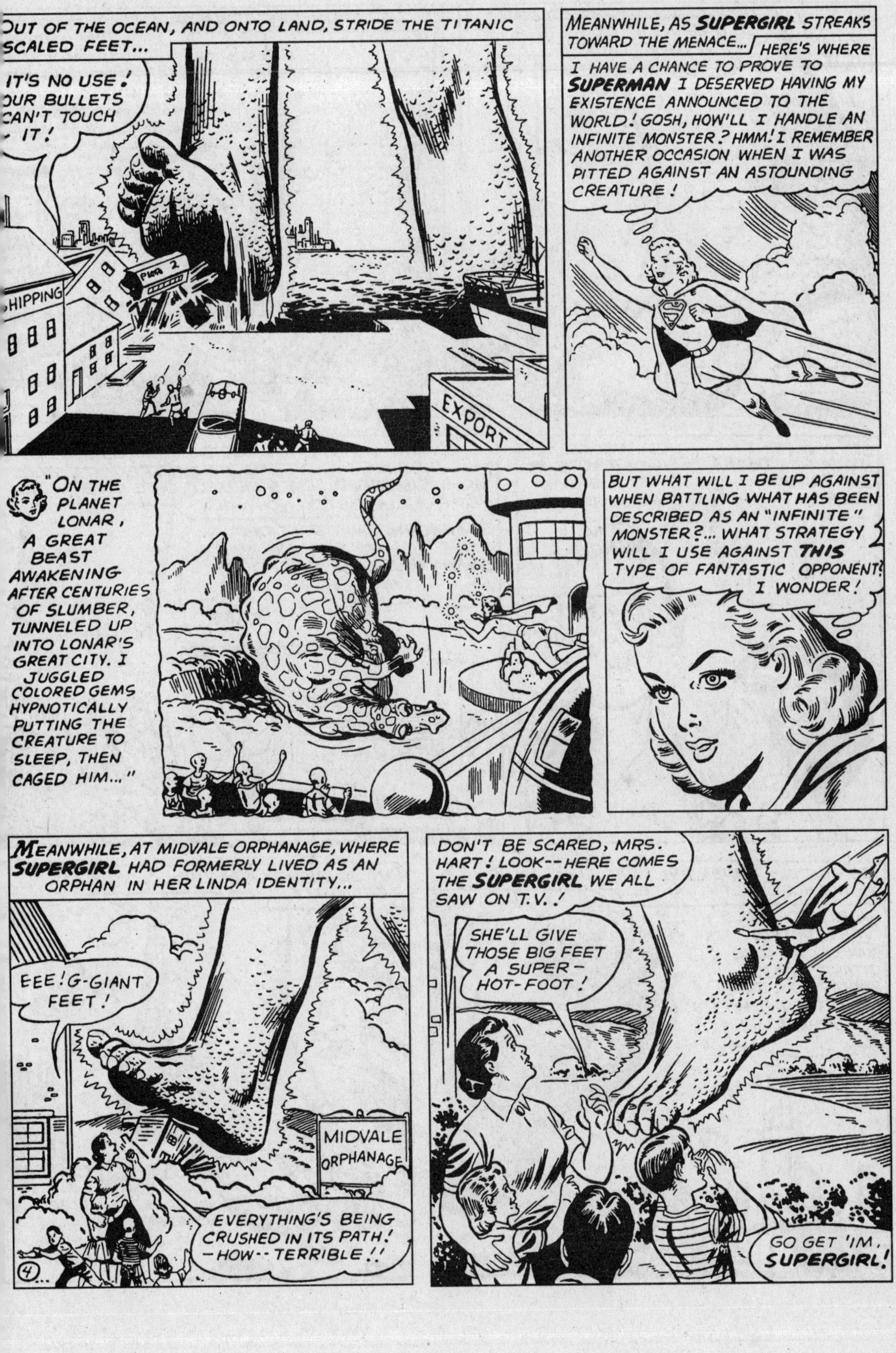
OUT OF THE OCEAN, AND ONTO LAND, STRIDE THE TITANIC SCALED FEET...
IT'S NO USE! OUR BULLETS CAN'T TOUCH IT!
SHIPPING
EXPORT
MEANWHILE, AS SUPERGIRL STREAKS TOWARD THE MENACE...
HERE'S WHERE I HAVE A CHANCE TO PROVE TO SUPERMAN I DESERVED HAVING MY EXISTENCE ANNOUNCED TO THE WORLD! GOSH, HOW'LL I HANDLE AN INFINITE MONSTER? HMM! I REMEMBER ANOTHER OCCASION WHEN I WAS PITTED AGAINST AN ASTOUNDING CREATURE!
"ON THE PLANET LONAR, A GREAT BEAST AWAKENING AFTER CENTURIES OF SLUMBER, TUNNELED UP INTO LONAR'S GREAT CITY. I JUGGLED COLORED GEMS HYPNOTICALLY PUTTING THE CREATURE TO SLEEP, THEN CAGED HIM..."
BUT WHAT WILL I BE UP AGAINST WHEN BATTLING WHAT HAS BEEN DESCRIBED AS AN "INFINITE" MONSTER?... WHAT STRATEGY WILL I USE AGAINST THIS TYPE OF FANTASTIC OPPONENT? I WONDER!
MEANWHILE, AT MIDVALE ORPHANAGE, WHERE SUPERGIRL HAD FORMERLY LIVED AS AN ORPHAN IN HER LINDA IDENTITY...
EEE! G-GIANT FEET!
MIDVALE ORPHANAGE
EVERYTHING'S BEING CRUSHED IN ITS PATH! -HOW--TERRIBLE!!
4
DON'T BE SCARED, MRS. HART! LOOK--HERE COMES THE SUPERGIRL WE ALL SAW ON T.V.!
SHE'LL GIVE THOSE BIG FEET A SUPER-HOT-FOOT!
GO GET 'IM, SUPERGIRL!

INCREDIBLY GIGANTIC LEGS! I'LL BRING IT DOWN IN A *FLYING TACKLE...!*

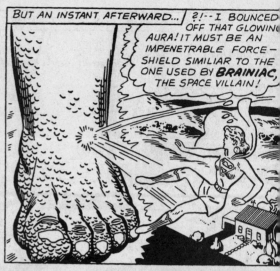

BUT AN INSTANT AFTERWARD...

?!-- I BOUNCED OFF THAT GLOWING AURA! IT MUST BE AN IMPENETRABLE FORCE- SHIELD SIMILIAR TO THE ONE USED BY *BRAINIAC,* THE SPACE VILLAIN!

GEE WILLIKERS! DIDJA SEE *THAT?* SHE FAILED TO *STOP* IT!

HOLY MACKERAL! MAYBE *SUPERGIRL* ISN'T ALL SHE'S CRACKED UP TO BE.!!

AS SEVERAL GIGANTIC STRIDES OF THE COLOSSAL FEET TAKE THE HUGE INVADER INTO THE *METROPOLIS* STEEL YARDS, *SUPERGIRL* HURLS HERSELF ONCE MORE AT IT DESPERATELY, BUT TO NO AVAIL...

SUPERGIRL CAN'T STOP THAT CREATURE! HOW I WISH WE HAD *SUPERMAN* HERE INSTEAD OF THAT GIRL!

DESPERATELY, *SUPERGIRL* TRIES ANOTHER METHOD AS THE HUGE FEET ADVANCE...

MUST STOP THE DESTRUCTIVE MARCH OF THOSE TITANIC FEET! PERHAPS IF I GRAB HOLD, THEN FLIP IT UPWARD...!

⑤

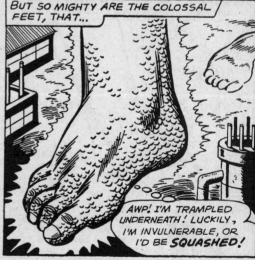

BUT SO MIGHTY ARE THE COLOSSAL FEET, THAT...

AWP! I'M TRAMPLED UNDERNEATH! LUCKILY, I'M INVULNERABLE, OR I'D BE *SQUASHED!*

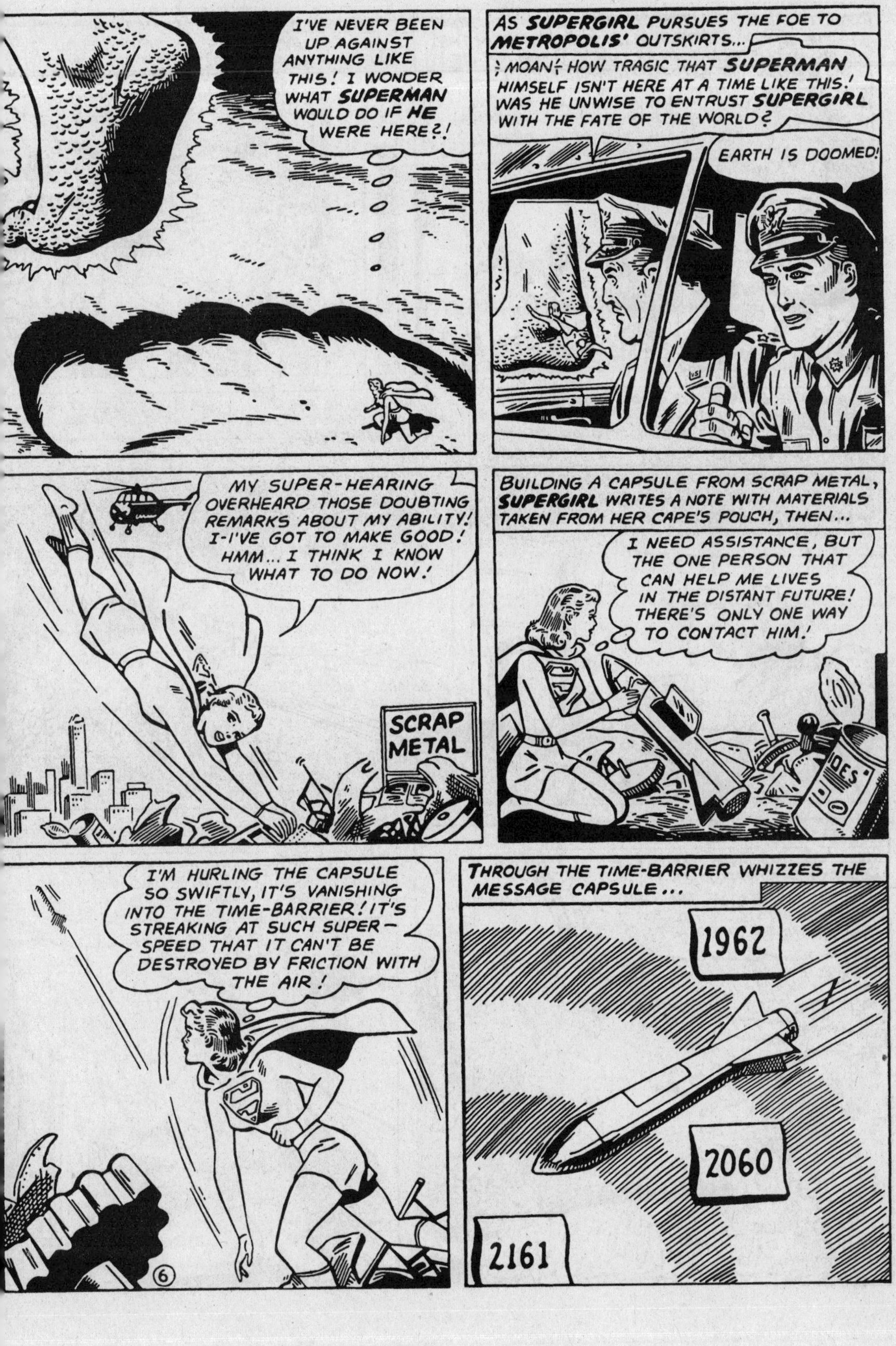
I'VE NEVER BEEN UP AGAINST ANYTHING LIKE THIS! I WONDER WHAT SUPERMAN WOULD DO IF HE WERE HERE?!
AS SUPERGIRL PURSUES THE FOE TO METROPOLIS' OUTSKIRTS...
MOAN HOW TRAGIC THAT SUPERMAN HIMSELF ISN'T HERE AT A TIME LIKE THIS! WAS HE UNWISE TO ENTRUST SUPERGIRL WITH THE FATE OF THE WORLD?
EARTH IS DOOMED!
MY SUPER-HEARING OVERHEARD THOSE DOUBTING REMARKS ABOUT MY ABILITY! I-I'VE GOT TO MAKE GOOD! HMM... I THINK I KNOW WHAT TO DO NOW!
SCRAP METAL
BUILDING A CAPSULE FROM SCRAP METAL, SUPERGIRL WRITES A NOTE WITH MATERIALS TAKEN FROM HER CAPE'S POUCH, THEN...
I NEED ASSISTANCE, BUT THE ONE PERSON THAT CAN HELP ME LIVES IN THE DISTANT FUTURE! THERE'S ONLY ONE WAY TO CONTACT HIM!
I'M HURLING THE CAPSULE SO SWIFTLY, IT'S VANISHING INTO THE TIME-BARRIER! IT'S STREAKING AT SUCH SUPER-SPEED THAT IT CAN'T BE DESTROYED BY FRICTION WITH THE AIR!
6
THROUGH THE TIME-BARRIER WHIZZES THE MESSAGE CAPSULE...
1962
2060
2161

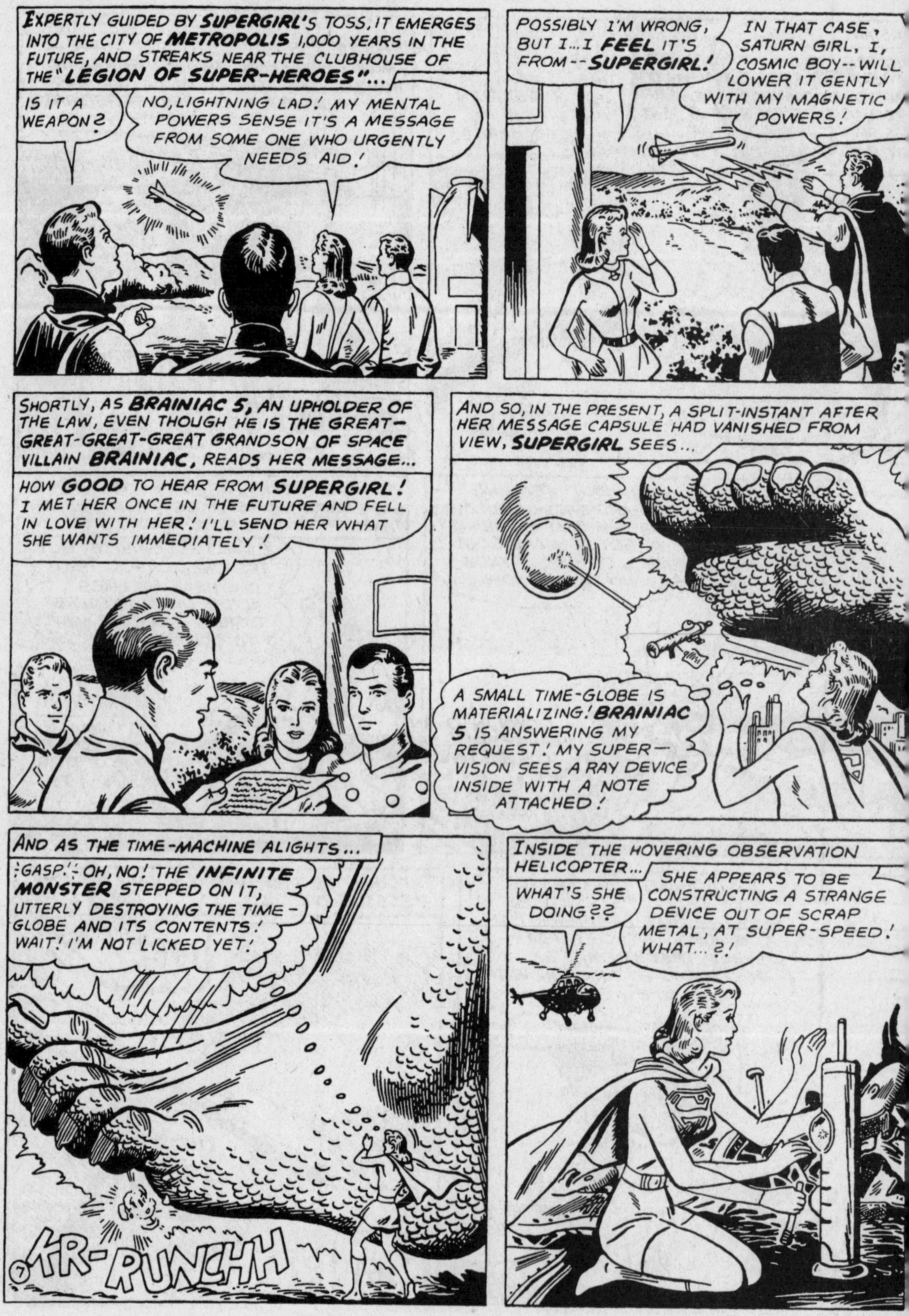
EXPERTLY GUIDED BY SUPERGIRL'S TOSS, IT EMERGES INTO THE CITY OF METROPOLIS 1,000 YEARS IN THE FUTURE, AND STREAKS NEAR THE CLUBHOUSE OF THE "LEGION OF SUPER-HEROES"...
IS IT A WEAPON?
NO, LIGHTNING LAD! MY MENTAL POWERS SENSE IT'S A MESSAGE FROM SOME ONE WHO URGENTLY NEEDS AID!
POSSIBLY I'M WRONG, BUT I...I FEEL IT'S FROM--SUPERGIRL!
IN THAT CASE, SATURN GIRL, I, COSMIC BOY--WILL LOWER IT GENTLY WITH MY MAGNETIC POWERS!
SHORTLY, AS BRAINIAC 5, AN UPHOLDER OF THE LAW, EVEN THOUGH HE IS THE GREAT-GREAT-GREAT-GREAT GRANDSON OF SPACE VILLAIN BRAINIAC, READS HER MESSAGE...
HOW GOOD TO HEAR FROM SUPERGIRL! I MET HER ONCE IN THE FUTURE AND FELL IN LOVE WITH HER! I'LL SEND HER WHAT SHE WANTS IMMEDIATELY!
AND SO, IN THE PRESENT, A SPLIT-INSTANT AFTER HER MESSAGE CAPSULE HAD VANISHED FROM VIEW, SUPERGIRL SEES...
A SMALL TIME-GLOBE IS MATERIALIZING! BRAINIAC 5 IS ANSWERING MY REQUEST! MY SUPER-VISION SEES A RAY DEVICE INSIDE WITH A NOTE ATTACHED!
AND AS THE TIME-MACHINE ALIGHTS...
-GASP!- OH, NO! THE INFINITE MONSTER STEPPED ON IT, UTTERLY DESTROYING THE TIME-GLOBE AND ITS CONTENTS! WAIT! I'M NOT LICKED YET!
KR-RUNCHH
7
INSIDE THE HOVERING OBSERVATION HELICOPTER...
WHAT'S SHE DOING??
SHE APPEARS TO BE CONSTRUCTING A STRANGE DEVICE OUT OF SCRAP METAL, AT SUPER-SPEED! WHAT...?!

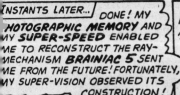

INSTANTS LATER... DONE! MY PHOTOGRAPHIC MEMORY AND MY SUPER-SPEED ENABLED ME TO RECONSTRUCT THE RAY-MECHANISM BRAINIAC 5 SENT ME FROM THE FUTURE! FORTUNATELY, MY SUPER-VISION OBSERVED ITS CONSTRUCTION!

NOW TO SHINE BRAINIAC 5'S RAY ON THE INFINITE MONSTER! AH--IT'S STARTING TO WORK! THE COLOSSAL CREATURE IS BEGINNING TO DWINDLE IN SIZE!

MY HUNCH WAS CORRECT THAT BRAINIAC 5 MIGHT HAVE A SHRINKING RAY SIMILAR TO THE ONE HIS ANCESTOR USED IN REDUCING THE KRYPTONIAN CITY OF KANDOR DOWN TO MINIATURE SIZE!

SECONDS LATER... SUCCESS! I SHRANK THE INFINITE MONSTER DOWN INTO AN INFINITESIMAL CREATURE! IT'S SO TINY NOW THAT IT CAN HARM NO ONE!

OFF TO SUPERMAN'S ARCTIC FORTRESS FLASHES THE GIRL OF STEEL... THE DAMAGE THIS MONSTER CAUSED WAS ACCIDENTAL, AND SO I DON'T WANT TO HARM IT! I'LL PUT IT WHERE IT'LL BE SAFE!

SHORTLY... SATISFIED, GENTLEMEN? YOU'RE EVERY BIT AS RESOURCEFUL AND TERRIFIC AS YOUR COUSIN SUPERMAN... CONGRATULATIONS!

8

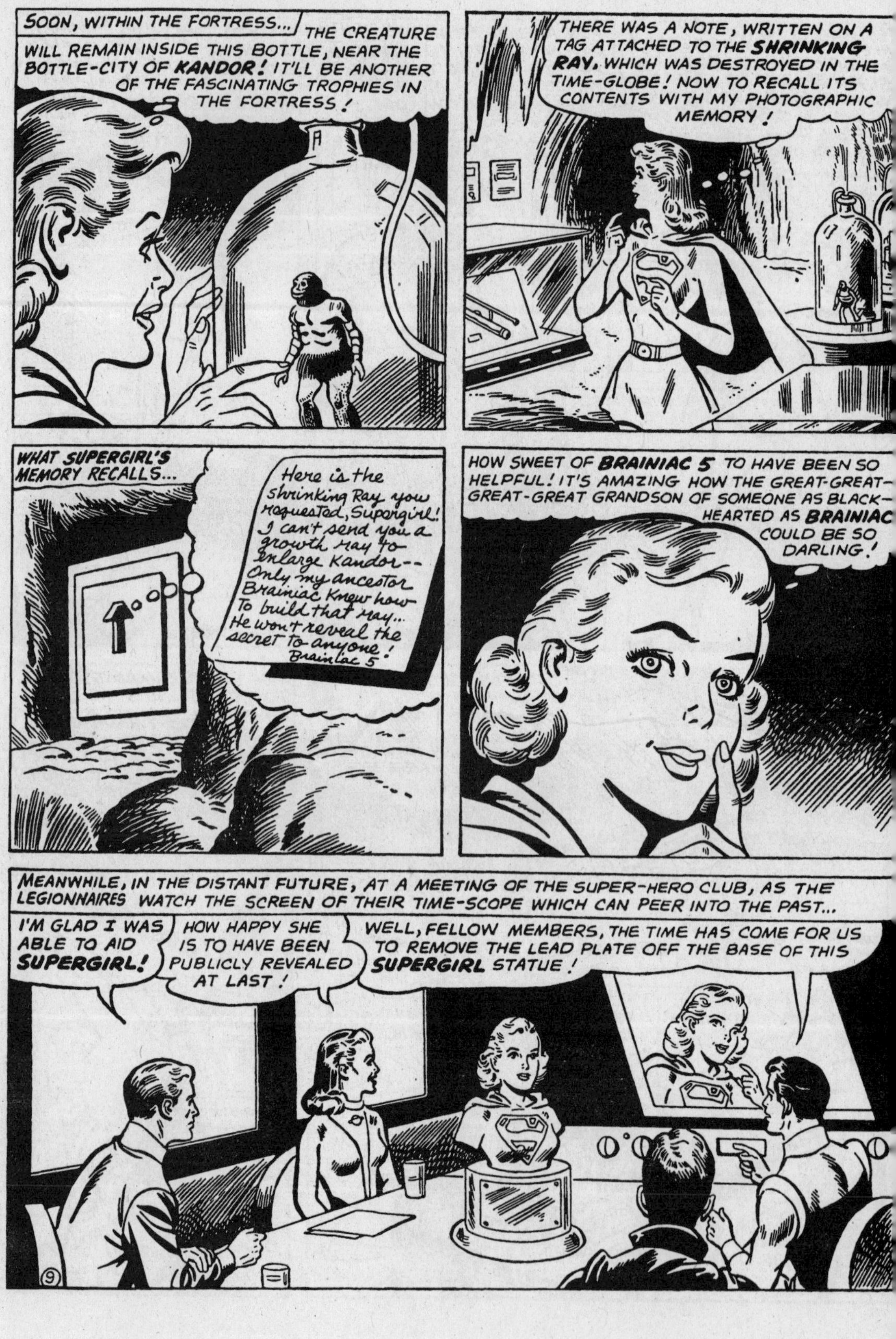
SOON, WITHIN THE FORTRESS...
THE CREATURE WILL REMAIN INSIDE THIS BOTTLE, NEAR THE BOTTLE-CITY OF KANDOR! IT'LL BE ANOTHER OF THE FASCINATING TROPHIES IN THE FORTRESS!
THERE WAS A NOTE, WRITTEN ON A TAG ATTACHED TO THE SHRINKING RAY, WHICH WAS DESTROYED IN THE TIME-GLOBE! NOW TO RECALL ITS CONTENTS WITH MY PHOTOGRAPHIC MEMORY!
WHAT SUPERGIRL'S MEMORY RECALLS...
Here is the shrinking Ray you requested, Supergirl! I can't send you a growth ray to enlarge Kandor -- Only my ancestor Brainiac knew how to build that ray... He won't reveal the secret to anyone! Brainiac 5
HOW SWEET OF BRAINIAC 5 TO HAVE BEEN SO HELPFUL! IT'S AMAZING HOW THE GREAT-GREAT-GREAT-GREAT GRANDSON OF SOMEONE AS BLACK-HEARTED AS BRAINIAC COULD BE SO DARLING!
MEANWHILE, IN THE DISTANT FUTURE, AT A MEETING OF THE SUPER-HERO CLUB, AS THE LEGIONNAIRES WATCH THE SCREEN OF THEIR TIME-SCOPE WHICH CAN PEER INTO THE PAST...
I'M GLAD I WAS ABLE TO AID SUPERGIRL!
HOW HAPPY SHE IS TO HAVE BEEN PUBLICLY REVEALED AT LAST!
WELL, FELLOW MEMBERS, THE TIME HAS COME FOR US TO REMOVE THE LEAD PLATE OFF THE BASE OF THIS SUPERGIRL STATUE!
9

NOW THERE'S NO LONGER ANY NEED TO HIDE THE LETTERING BEHIND THE METAL PLATE FROM **SUPERGIRL'S** VISION WHENEVER SHE VISITS US!

PREVIOUSLY WE USED A LEAD PLATE BECAUSE HER X-RAY VISION CAN'T PENETRATE THAT METAL!

MOMENTS LATER...

YEAR OF SUPERGIRL'S ARRIVAL ON EARTH 1959

YEAR SUPERGIRL'S EXISTENCE WAS REVEALED ON EARTH 1962

WE DIDN'T WANT **SUPERGIRL** TO KNOW WHEN HER EXISTENCE WAS REVEALED! IT WOULD HAVE SPOILED **SUPERMAN'S** PLAN TO SURPRISE HER!

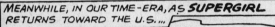

MEANWHILE, IN OUR TIME-ERA, AS **SUPERGIRL** RETURNS TOWARD THE U.S....

HMM--THE "RIP" IN THE SKY WHICH WAS A WARP IN SPACE CONNECTING THE TWO CO-EXISTING UNIVERSES HAS HEALED ITSELF! GOOD! THERE'S NO DANGER OF ANY MORE INFINITE CREATURES DROPPING THROUGH AND MENACING LIFE IN THIS UNIVERSE!

SHORTLY, AS THE **GIRL OF STEEL** STREAKS TOWARD THE PENTAGON...

GASP! A 21 GUN SALUTE! AND THE SOLDIERS ARE SALUTING ME! GOODNESS... HOW THRILLING!

PRESENTLY, AT THE PENTAGON...

SUPERGIRL, YOU HANDLED THE **INFINITE MONSTER** EMERGENCY MAGNIFICENTLY! WE'RE EXTREMELY GRATEFUL TO YOU! THE PRESIDENT WANTS TO THANK YOU PERSONALLY AT A PARTY IN YOUR HONOR!

SHORTLY, ON THE WHITE HOUSE LAWN...

YOU'RE AS RESOURCEFUL AS YOU ARE LOVELY, **SUPERGIRL!** THANKS A MILLION!

THE PRESIDENT'S WIFE LOOKS-- GORGEOUS!

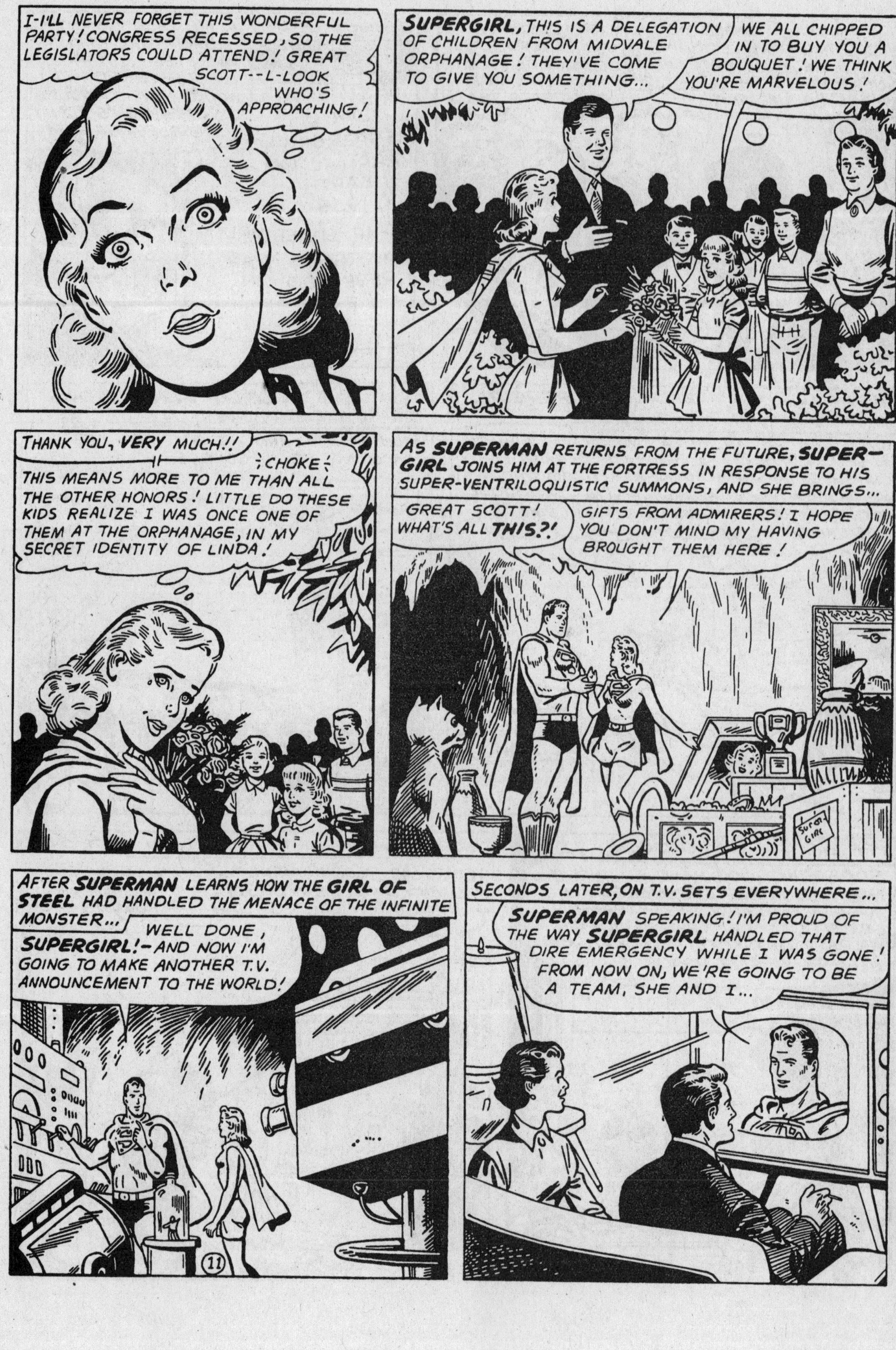
I-I'LL NEVER FORGET THIS WONDERFUL PARTY! CONGRESS RECESSED, SO THE LEGISLATORS COULD ATTEND! GREAT SCOTT--L-LOOK WHO'S APPROACHING!
SUPERGIRL, THIS IS A DELEGATION OF CHILDREN FROM MIDVALE ORPHANAGE! THEY'VE COME TO GIVE YOU SOMETHING...
WE ALL CHIPPED IN TO BUY YOU A BOUQUET! WE THINK YOU'RE MARVELOUS!
THANK YOU, VERY MUCH!!
CHOKE
THIS MEANS MORE TO ME THAN ALL THE OTHER HONORS! LITTLE DO THESE KIDS REALIZE I WAS ONCE ONE OF THEM AT THE ORPHANAGE, IN MY SECRET IDENTITY OF LINDA!
AS SUPERMAN RETURNS FROM THE FUTURE, SUPERGIRL JOINS HIM AT THE FORTRESS IN RESPONSE TO HIS SUPER-VENTRILOQUISTIC SUMMONS, AND SHE BRINGS...
GREAT SCOTT! WHAT'S ALL THIS?!
GIFTS FROM ADMIRERS! I HOPE YOU DON'T MIND MY HAVING BROUGHT THEM HERE!
AFTER SUPERMAN LEARNS HOW THE GIRL OF STEEL HAD HANDLED THE MENACE OF THE INFINITE MONSTER...
WELL DONE, SUPERGIRL!-- AND NOW I'M GOING TO MAKE ANOTHER T.V. ANNOUNCEMENT TO THE WORLD!
11
SECONDS LATER, ON T.V. SETS EVERYWHERE...
SUPERMAN SPEAKING! I'M PROUD OF THE WAY SUPERGIRL HANDLED THAT DIRE EMERGENCY WHILE I WAS GONE! FROM NOW ON, WE'RE GOING TO BE A TEAM, SHE AND I...

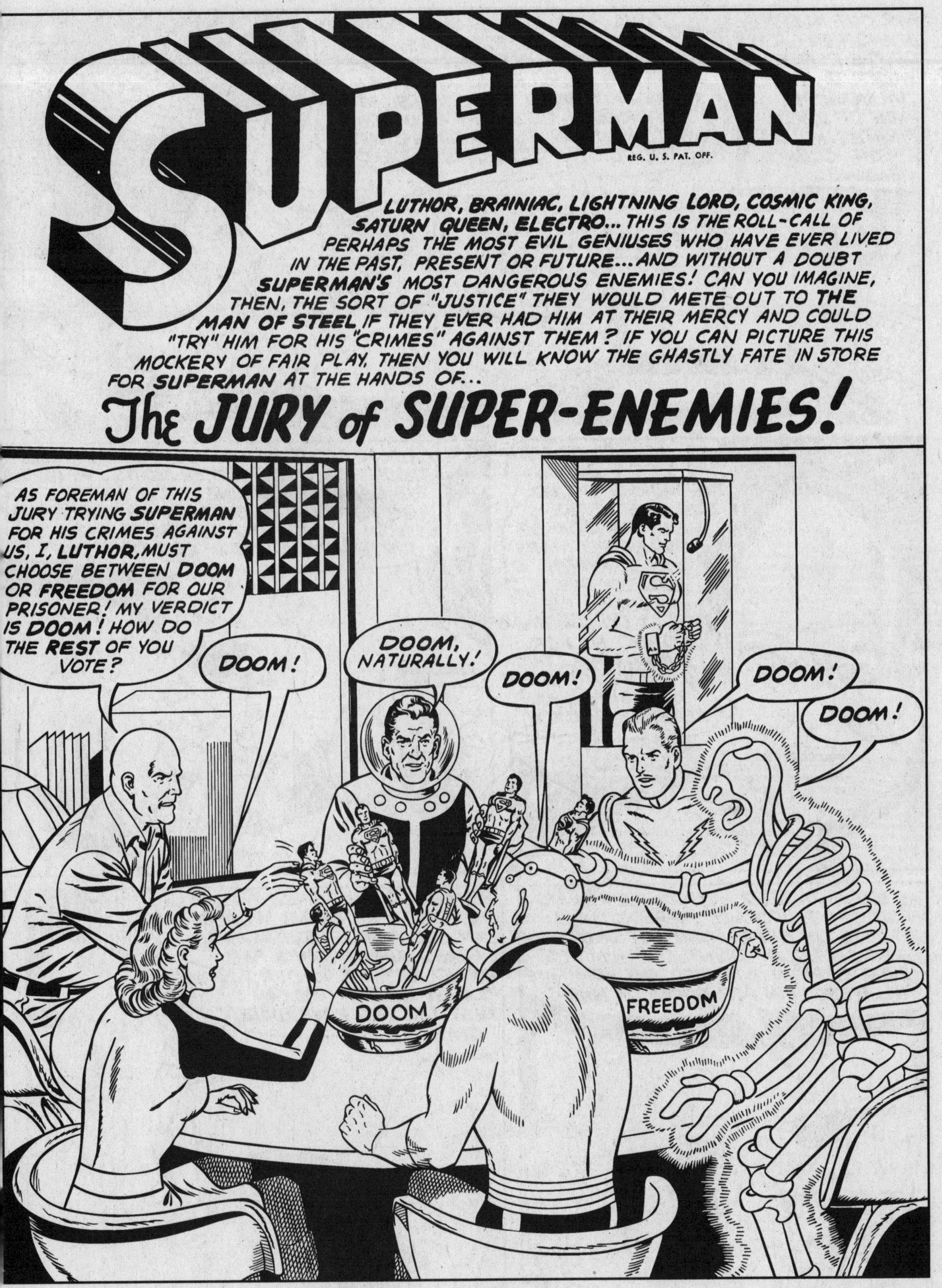
SUPERMAN
REG. U. S. PAT. OFF.
LUTHOR, BRAINIAC, LIGHTNING LORD, COSMIC KING, SATURN QUEEN, ELECTRO... THIS IS THE ROLL-CALL OF PERHAPS THE MOST EVIL GENIUSES WHO HAVE EVER LIVED IN THE PAST, PRESENT OR FUTURE... AND WITHOUT A DOUBT SUPERMAN'S MOST DANGEROUS ENEMIES! CAN YOU IMAGINE, THEN, THE SORT OF "JUSTICE" THEY WOULD METE OUT TO THE MAN OF STEEL IF THEY EVER HAD HIM AT THEIR MERCY AND COULD "TRY" HIM FOR HIS "CRIMES" AGAINST THEM? IF YOU CAN PICTURE THIS MOCKERY OF FAIR PLAY, THEN YOU WILL KNOW THE GHASTLY FATE IN STORE FOR SUPERMAN AT THE HANDS OF...
The JURY of SUPER-ENEMIES!
AS FOREMAN OF THIS JURY TRYING SUPERMAN FOR HIS CRIMES AGAINST US, I, LUTHOR, MUST CHOOSE BETWEEN DOOM OR FREEDOM FOR OUR PRISONER! MY VERDICT IS DOOM! HOW DO THE REST OF YOU VOTE?
DOOM!
DOOM, NATURALLY!
DOOM!
DOOM!
DOOM!
DOOM
FREEDOM

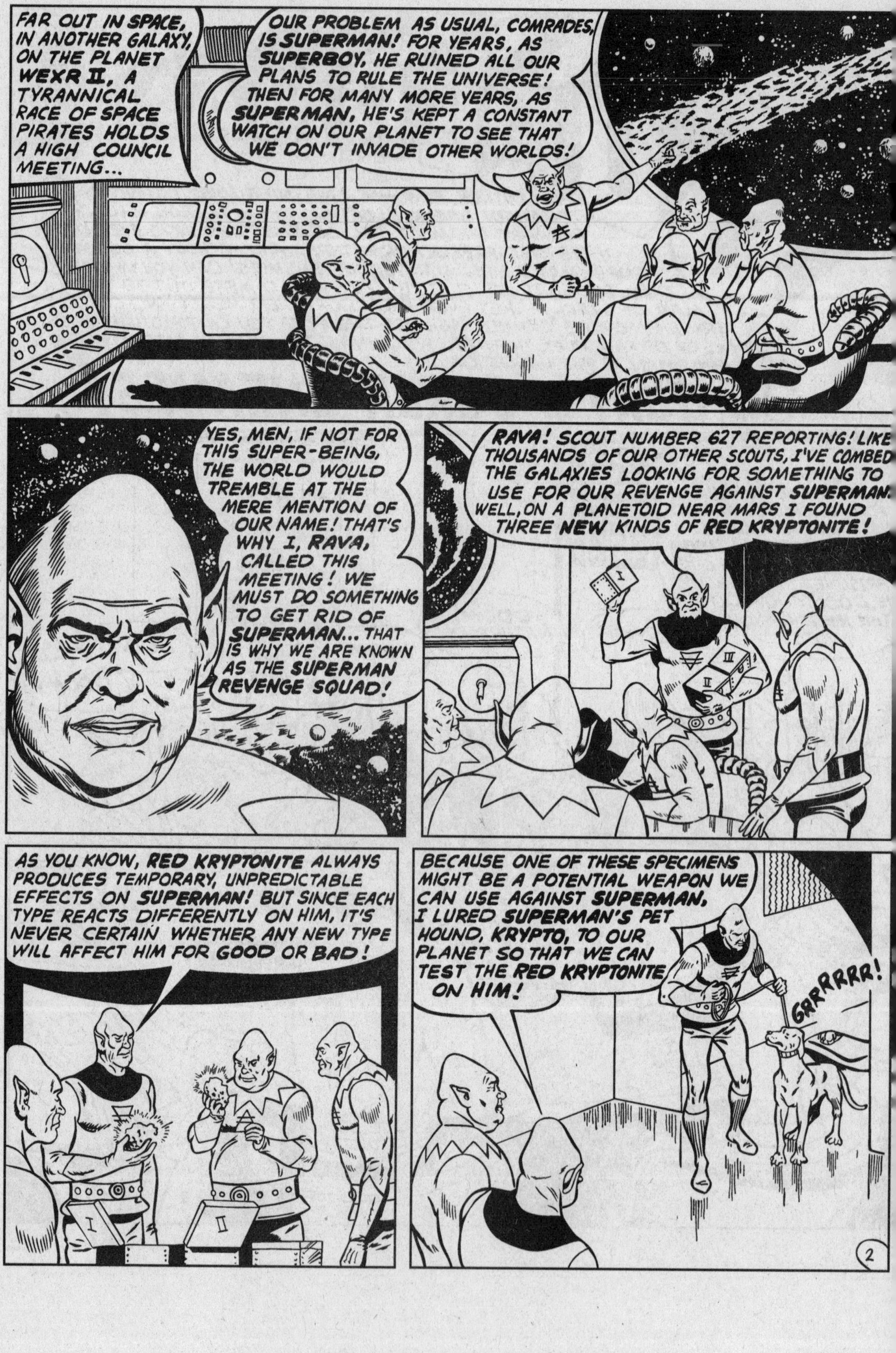
FAR OUT IN SPACE, IN ANOTHER GALAXY, ON THE PLANET WEXR II, A TYRANNICAL RACE OF SPACE PIRATES HOLDS A HIGH COUNCIL MEETING...
OUR PROBLEM AS USUAL, COMRADES, IS SUPERMAN! FOR YEARS, AS SUPERBOY, HE RUINED ALL OUR PLANS TO RULE THE UNIVERSE! THEN FOR MANY MORE YEARS, AS SUPERMAN, HE'S KEPT A CONSTANT WATCH ON OUR PLANET TO SEE THAT WE DON'T INVADE OTHER WORLDS!
YES, MEN, IF NOT FOR THIS SUPER-BEING, THE WORLD WOULD TREMBLE AT THE MERE MENTION OF OUR NAME! THAT'S WHY I, RAVA, CALLED THIS MEETING! WE MUST DO SOMETHING TO GET RID OF SUPERMAN... THAT IS WHY WE ARE KNOWN AS THE SUPERMAN REVENGE SQUAD!
RAVA! SCOUT NUMBER 627 REPORTING! LIKE THOUSANDS OF OUR OTHER SCOUTS, I'VE COMBED THE GALAXIES LOOKING FOR SOMETHING TO USE FOR OUR REVENGE AGAINST SUPERMAN. WELL, ON A PLANETOID NEAR MARS I FOUND THREE NEW KINDS OF RED KRYPTONITE!
AS YOU KNOW, RED KRYPTONITE ALWAYS PRODUCES TEMPORARY, UNPREDICTABLE EFFECTS ON SUPERMAN! BUT SINCE EACH TYPE REACTS DIFFERENTLY ON HIM, IT'S NEVER CERTAIN WHETHER ANY NEW TYPE WILL AFFECT HIM FOR GOOD OR BAD!
BECAUSE ONE OF THESE SPECIMENS MIGHT BE A POTENTIAL WEAPON WE CAN USE AGAINST SUPERMAN, I LURED SUPERMAN'S PET HOUND, KRYPTO, TO OUR PLANET SO THAT WE CAN TEST THE RED KRYPTONITE ON HIM!
GRRRRRR!
2

SINCE KRYPTO COMES FROM THE SAME WORLD AS SUPERMAN, WHATEVER AFFECTS THE DOG WILL AFFECT HIS MASTER! DON'T BE AFRAID OF HIM, RAVA! KRYPTO'S STILL SEMI-PARALYZED FROM THE DOSE OF GREEN KRYPTONITE WE GAVE HIM!
VERY WELL! I'LL EXPOSE HIM TO THE RED KRYPTONITE IN BOX #1!
I
MOMENTS AFTER...
LOOK! ON BEING EXPOSED TO ITS RAYS, THE DOG IS SHAKING VIOLENTLY... AS IF A STRANGE FEELING WERE PASSING THROUGH HIS BODY!
IT'S THE TINGLING SENSATION SUPERMAN ALWAYS GETS WHEN HE'S BEING AFFECTED BY RED KRYPTONITE!
LOOK! HE'S DISAPPEARING!... GASP!... HE'S BECOMING A PHANTOM!
TEN MINUTES LATER...
NOW THE EFFECT IS WEARING OFF! THE DOG IS RE-APPEARING!
HMMPP! I CAN'T SEE HOW WE CAN GAIN BY TEMPORARILY CHANGING SUPERMAN INTO A PHANTOM! I'LL TRY THE SECOND PIECE!
II
AS KRYPTO REACTS TO THE SECOND SAMPLE...
HE'S BECOME STRIPED... LIKE THE TIGERS WE'VE OBSERVED ON EARTH THROUGH OUR TRANS-SPACE TELESCOPE!
BAH! ANOTHER USELESS EFFECT! WHEN THE STRIPES FADE AWAY, I'LL EXPOSE KRYPTO TO THE RED KRYPTONITE FROM BOX #3!
SHORTLY...
HMM... THIS TIME HE'S FALLING ASLEEP! I'M AFRAID, SCOUT 627, THAT YOUR RED KRYPTONITE DISCOVERIES WILL PROVE AS INEFFECTUAL AS ALL THE OTHERS WE'VE TESTED THROUGH THE YEARS!
III
3

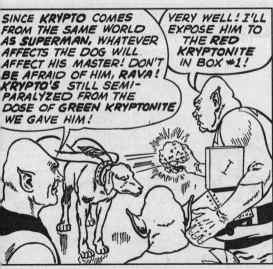

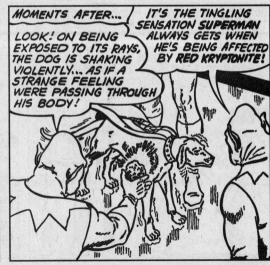

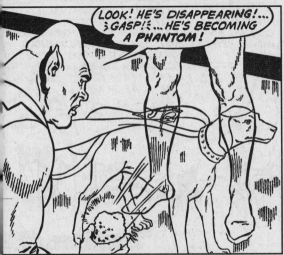

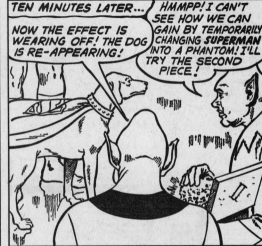

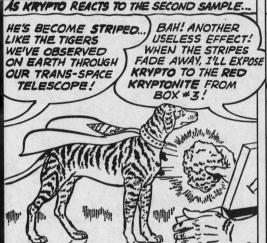

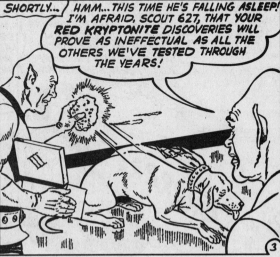

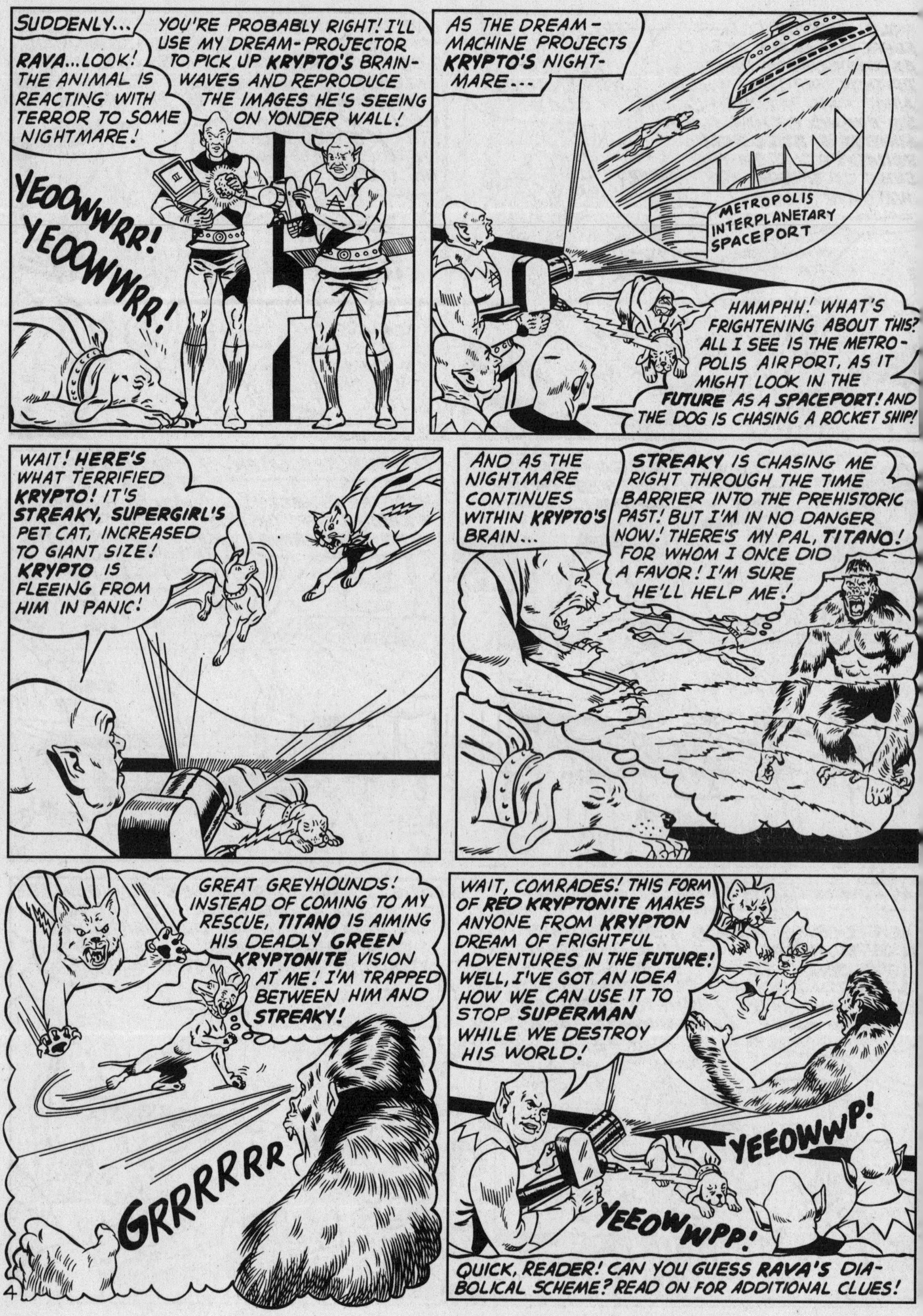

SUDDENLY...
RAVA...LOOK! THE ANIMAL IS REACTING WITH TERROR TO SOME NIGHTMARE!
YOU'RE PROBABLY RIGHT! I'LL USE MY DREAM-PROJECTOR TO PICK UP KRYPTO'S BRAIN-WAVES AND REPRODUCE THE IMAGES HE'S SEEING ON YONDER WALL!
YEOOWWRR! YEOOWWRR! YEOOWWRR!
AS THE DREAM-MACHINE PROJECTS KRYPTO'S NIGHTMARE...
METROPOLIS INTERPLANETARY SPACEPORT
HMMPHH! WHAT'S FRIGHTENING ABOUT THIS? ALL I SEE IS THE METROPOLIS AIRPORT, AS IT MIGHT LOOK IN THE FUTURE AS A SPACEPORT! AND THE DOG IS CHASING A ROCKET SHIP!
WAIT! HERE'S WHAT TERRIFIED KRYPTO! IT'S STREAKY, SUPERGIRL'S PET CAT, INCREASED TO GIANT SIZE! KRYPTO IS FLEEING FROM HIM IN PANIC!
AND AS THE NIGHTMARE CONTINUES WITHIN KRYPTO'S BRAIN...
STREAKY IS CHASING ME RIGHT THROUGH THE TIME BARRIER INTO THE PREHISTORIC PAST! BUT I'M IN NO DANGER NOW! THERE'S MY PAL, TITANO! FOR WHOM I ONCE DID A FAVOR! I'M SURE HE'LL HELP ME!
GREAT GREYHOUNDS! INSTEAD OF COMING TO MY RESCUE, TITANO IS AIMING HIS DEADLY GREEN KRYPTONITE VISION AT ME! I'M TRAPPED BETWEEN HIM AND STREAKY!
GRRRRRR
4
WAIT, COMRADES! THIS FORM OF RED KRYPTONITE MAKES ANYONE FROM KRYPTON DREAM OF FRIGHTFUL ADVENTURES IN THE FUTURE! WELL, I'VE GOT AN IDEA HOW WE CAN USE IT TO STOP SUPERMAN WHILE WE DESTROY HIS WORLD!
YEEOWWP!
YEEOWWPP!
QUICK, READER! CAN YOU GUESS RAVA'S DIABOLICAL SCHEME? READ ON FOR ADDITIONAL CLUES!

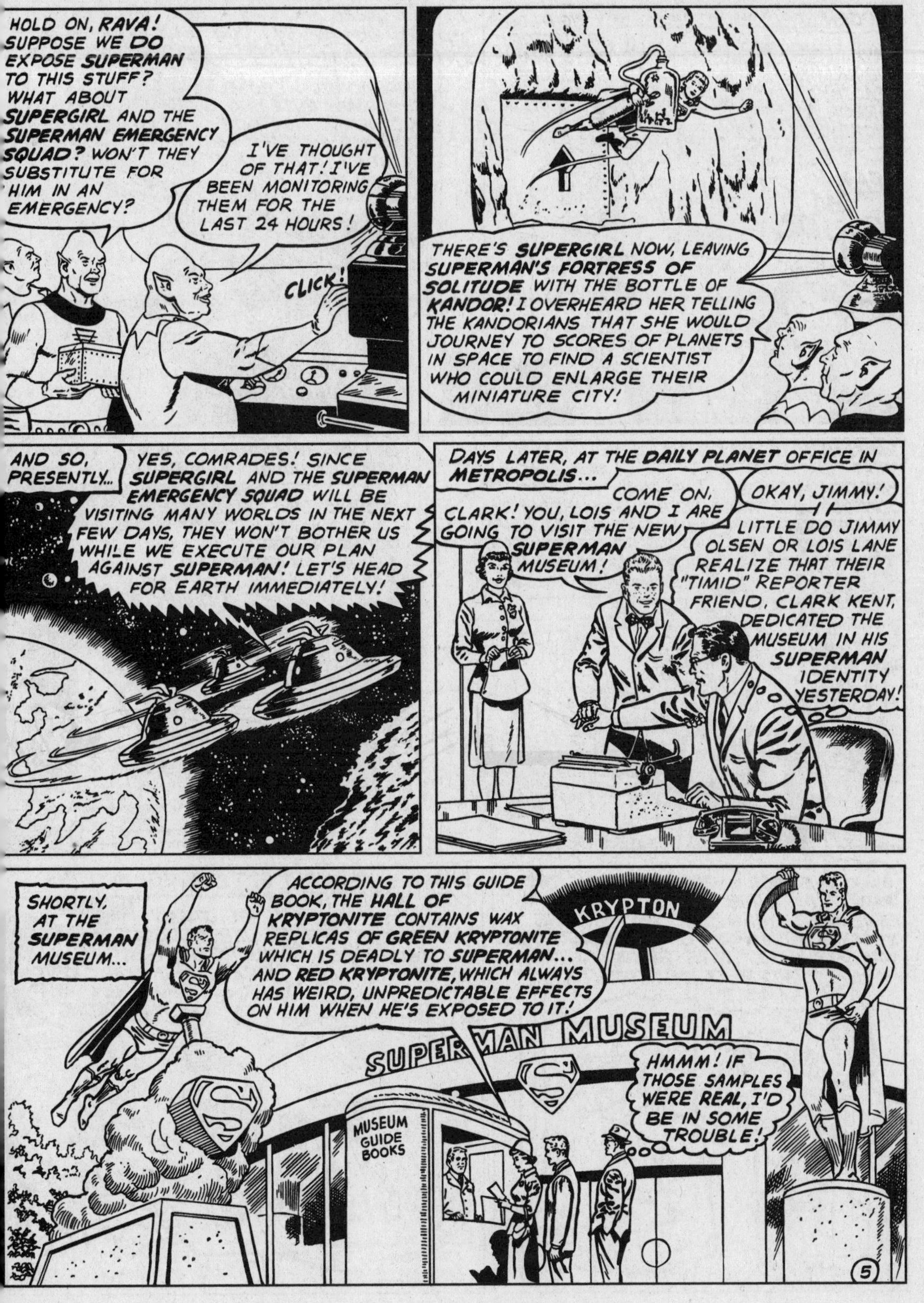
HOLD ON, RAVA! SUPPOSE WE DO EXPOSE SUPERMAN TO THIS STUFF? WHAT ABOUT SUPERGIRL AND THE SUPERMAN EMERGENCY SQUAD? WON'T THEY SUBSTITUTE FOR HIM IN AN EMERGENCY?
I'VE THOUGHT OF THAT! I'VE BEEN MONITORING THEM FOR THE LAST 24 HOURS!
CLICK!
THERE'S SUPERGIRL NOW, LEAVING SUPERMAN'S FORTRESS OF SOLITUDE WITH THE BOTTLE OF KANDOR! I OVERHEARD HER TELLING THE KANDORIANS THAT SHE WOULD JOURNEY TO SCORES OF PLANETS IN SPACE TO FIND A SCIENTIST WHO COULD ENLARGE THEIR MINIATURE CITY!
AND SO, PRESENTLY...
YES, COMRADES! SINCE SUPERGIRL AND THE SUPERMAN EMERGENCY SQUAD WILL BE VISITING MANY WORLDS IN THE NEXT FEW DAYS, THEY WON'T BOTHER US WHILE WE EXECUTE OUR PLAN AGAINST SUPERMAN! LET'S HEAD FOR EARTH IMMEDIATELY!
DAYS LATER, AT THE DAILY PLANET OFFICE IN METROPOLIS...
COME ON, CLARK! YOU, LOIS AND I ARE GOING TO VISIT THE NEW SUPERMAN MUSEUM!
OKAY, JIMMY!
LITTLE DO JIMMY OLSEN OR LOIS LANE REALIZE THAT THEIR "TIMID" REPORTER FRIEND, CLARK KENT, DEDICATED THE MUSEUM IN HIS SUPERMAN IDENTITY YESTERDAY!
SHORTLY, AT THE SUPERMAN MUSEUM...
ACCORDING TO THIS GUIDE BOOK, THE HALL OF KRYPTONITE CONTAINS WAX REPLICAS OF GREEN KRYPTONITE WHICH IS DEADLY TO SUPERMAN... AND RED KRYPTONITE, WHICH ALWAYS HAS WEIRD, UNPREDICTABLE EFFECTS ON HIM WHEN HE'S EXPOSED TO IT!
KRYPTON
SUPERMAN MUSEUM
MUSEUM GUIDE BOOKS
HMMM! IF THOSE SAMPLES WERE REAL, I'D BE IN SOME TROUBLE!
5

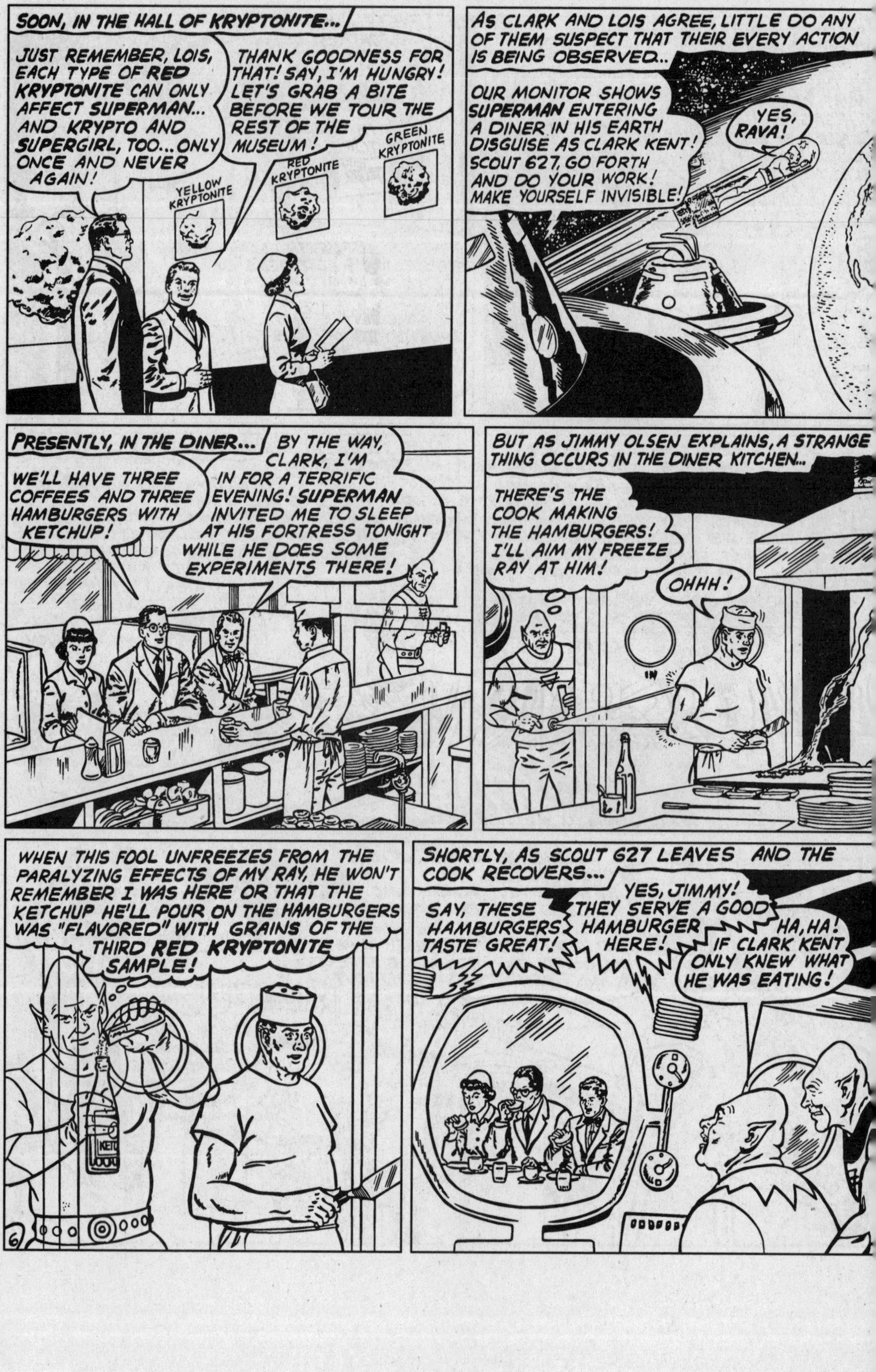
SOON, IN THE HALL OF KRYPTONITE...
JUST REMEMBER, LOIS, EACH TYPE OF RED KRYPTONITE CAN ONLY AFFECT SUPERMAN... AND KRYPTO AND SUPERGIRL, TOO...ONLY ONCE AND NEVER AGAIN!
THANK GOODNESS FOR THAT! SAY, I'M HUNGRY! LET'S GRAB A BITE BEFORE WE TOUR THE REST OF THE MUSEUM!
YELLOW KRYPTONITE
RED KRYPTONITE
GREEN KRYPTONITE
AS CLARK AND LOIS AGREE, LITTLE DO ANY OF THEM SUSPECT THAT THEIR EVERY ACTION IS BEING OBSERVED...
OUR MONITOR SHOWS SUPERMAN ENTERING A DINER IN HIS EARTH DISGUISE AS CLARK KENT! SCOUT 627, GO FORTH AND DO YOUR WORK! MAKE YOURSELF INVISIBLE!
YES, RAVA!
PRESENTLY, IN THE DINER...
WE'LL HAVE THREE COFFEES AND THREE HAMBURGERS WITH KETCHUP!
BY THE WAY, CLARK, I'M IN FOR A TERRIFIC EVENING! SUPERMAN INVITED ME TO SLEEP AT HIS FORTRESS TONIGHT WHILE HE DOES SOME EXPERIMENTS THERE!
BUT AS JIMMY OLSEN EXPLAINS, A STRANGE THING OCCURS IN THE DINER KITCHEN...
THERE'S THE COOK MAKING THE HAMBURGERS! I'LL AIM MY FREEZE RAY AT HIM!
OHHH!
WHEN THIS FOOL UNFREEZES FROM THE PARALYZING EFFECTS OF MY RAY, HE WON'T REMEMBER I WAS HERE OR THAT THE KETCHUP HE'LL POUR ON THE HAMBURGERS WAS "FLAVORED" WITH GRAINS OF THE THIRD RED KRYPTONITE SAMPLE!
6
SHORTLY, AS SCOUT 627 LEAVES AND THE COOK RECOVERS...
SAY, THESE HAMBURGERS TASTE GREAT!
YES, JIMMY! THEY SERVE A GOOD HAMBURGER HERE!
HA, HA! IF CLARK KENT ONLY KNEW WHAT HE WAS EATING!

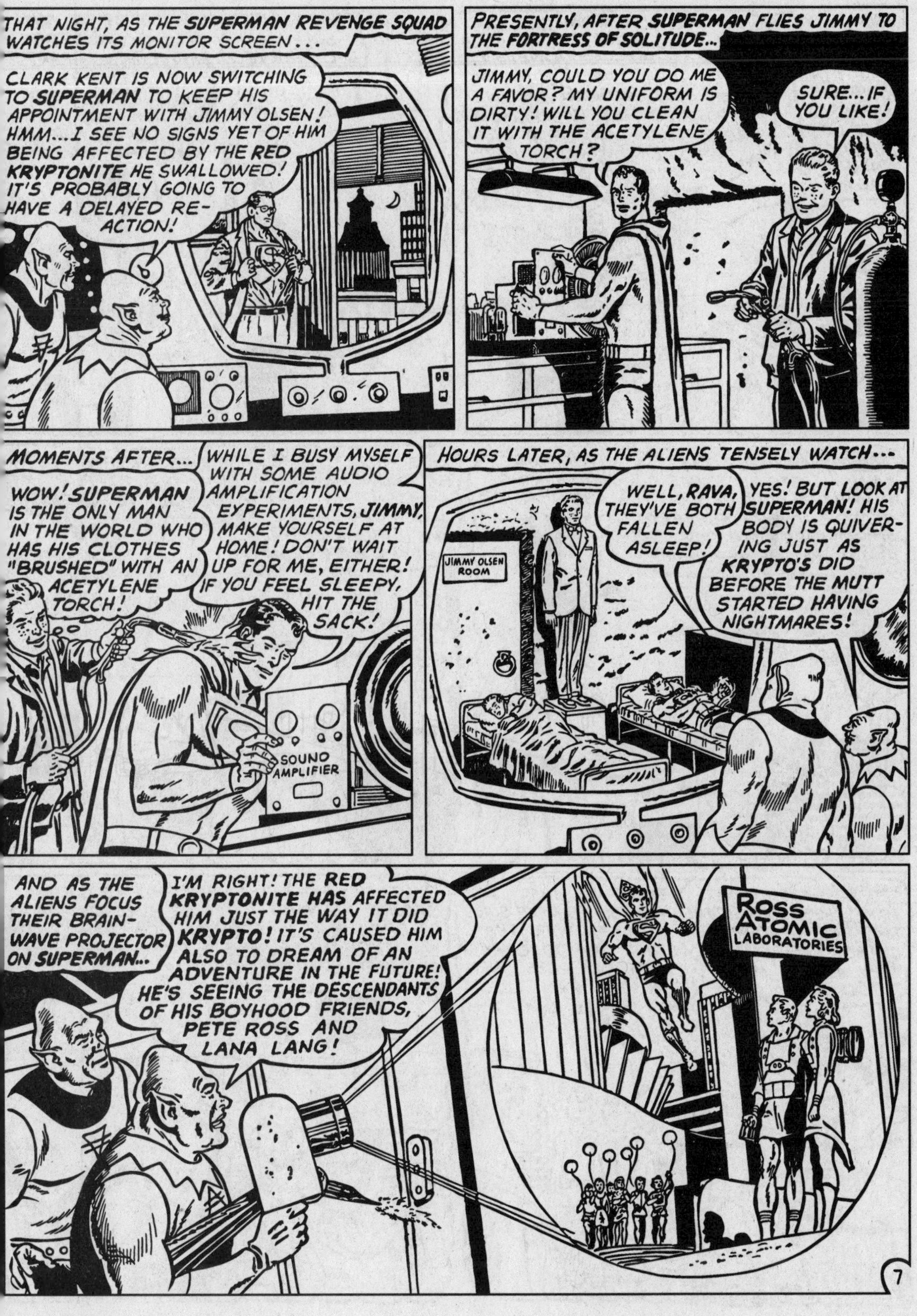
THAT NIGHT, AS THE SUPERMAN REVENGE SQUAD WATCHES ITS MONITOR SCREEN...
CLARK KENT IS NOW SWITCHING TO SUPERMAN TO KEEP HIS APPOINTMENT WITH JIMMY OLSEN! HMM...I SEE NO SIGNS YET OF HIM BEING AFFECTED BY THE RED KRYPTONITE HE SWALLOWED! IT'S PROBABLY GOING TO HAVE A DELAYED RE-ACTION!
PRESENTLY, AFTER SUPERMAN FLIES JIMMY TO THE FORTRESS OF SOLITUDE...
JIMMY, COULD YOU DO ME A FAVOR? MY UNIFORM IS DIRTY! WILL YOU CLEAN IT WITH THE ACETYLENE TORCH?
SURE...IF YOU LIKE!
MOMENTS AFTER...
WOW! SUPERMAN IS THE ONLY MAN IN THE WORLD WHO HAS HIS CLOTHES "BRUSHED" WITH AN ACETYLENE TORCH!
WHILE I BUSY MYSELF WITH SOME AUDIO AMPLIFICATION EXPERIMENTS, JIMMY, MAKE YOURSELF AT HOME! DON'T WAIT UP FOR ME, EITHER! IF YOU FEEL SLEEPY, HIT THE SACK!
SOUND AMPLIFIER
HOURS LATER, AS THE ALIENS TENSELY WATCH...
JIMMY OLSEN ROOM
WELL, RAVA, THEY'VE BOTH FALLEN ASLEEP!
YES! BUT LOOK AT SUPERMAN! HIS BODY IS QUIVERING JUST AS KRYPTO'S DID BEFORE THE MUTT STARTED HAVING NIGHTMARES!
AND AS THE ALIENS FOCUS THEIR BRAIN-WAVE PROJECTOR ON SUPERMAN...
I'M RIGHT! THE RED KRYPTONITE HAS AFFECTED HIM JUST THE WAY IT DID KRYPTO! IT'S CAUSED HIM ALSO TO DREAM OF AN ADVENTURE IN THE FUTURE! HE'S SEEING THE DESCENDANTS OF HIS BOYHOOD FRIENDS, PETE ROSS AND LANA LANG!
ROSS ATOMIC LABORATORIES
7

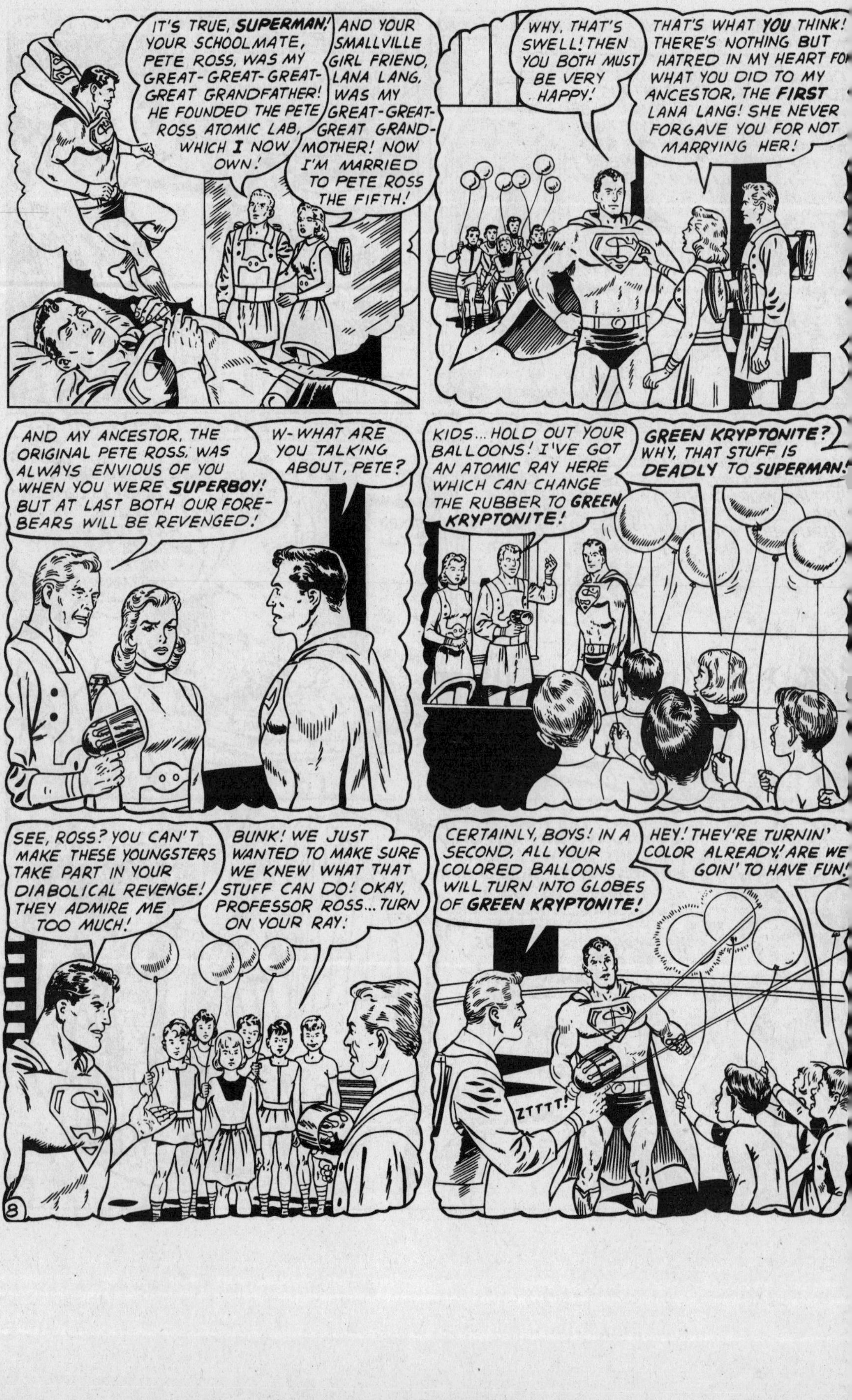
IT'S TRUE, SUPERMAN! YOUR SCHOOLMATE, PETE ROSS, WAS MY GREAT-GREAT-GREAT-GREAT GRANDFATHER! HE FOUNDED THE PETE ROSS ATOMIC LAB, WHICH I NOW OWN!
AND YOUR SMALLVILLE GIRL FRIEND, LANA LANG, WAS MY GREAT-GREAT-GREAT GRANDMOTHER! NOW I'M MARRIED TO PETE ROSS THE FIFTH!
WHY, THAT'S SWELL! THEN YOU BOTH MUST BE VERY HAPPY!
THAT'S WHAT YOU THINK! THERE'S NOTHING BUT HATRED IN MY HEART FO WHAT YOU DID TO MY ANCESTOR, THE FIRST LANA LANG! SHE NEVER FORGAVE YOU FOR NOT MARRYING HER!
AND MY ANCESTOR, THE ORIGINAL PETE ROSS, WAS ALWAYS ENVIOUS OF YOU WHEN YOU WERE SUPERBOY! BUT AT LAST BOTH OUR FOREBEARS WILL BE REVENGED!
W-WHAT ARE YOU TALKING ABOUT, PETE?
KIDS... HOLD OUT YOUR BALLOONS! I'VE GOT AN ATOMIC RAY HERE WHICH CAN CHANGE THE RUBBER TO GREEN KRYPTONITE!
GREEN KRYPTONITE? WHY, THAT STUFF IS DEADLY TO SUPERMAN!
SEE, ROSS? YOU CAN'T MAKE THESE YOUNGSTERS TAKE PART IN YOUR DIABOLICAL REVENGE! THEY ADMIRE ME TOO MUCH!
BUNK! WE JUST WANTED TO MAKE SURE WE KNEW WHAT THAT STUFF CAN DO! OKAY, PROFESSOR ROSS...TURN ON YOUR RAY!
8
CERTAINLY, BOYS! IN A SECOND, ALL YOUR COLORED BALLOONS WILL TURN INTO GLOBES OF GREEN KRYPTONITE!
HEY! THEY'RE TURNIN' COLOR ALREADY! ARE WE GOIN' TO HAVE FUN!
ZTTTT!

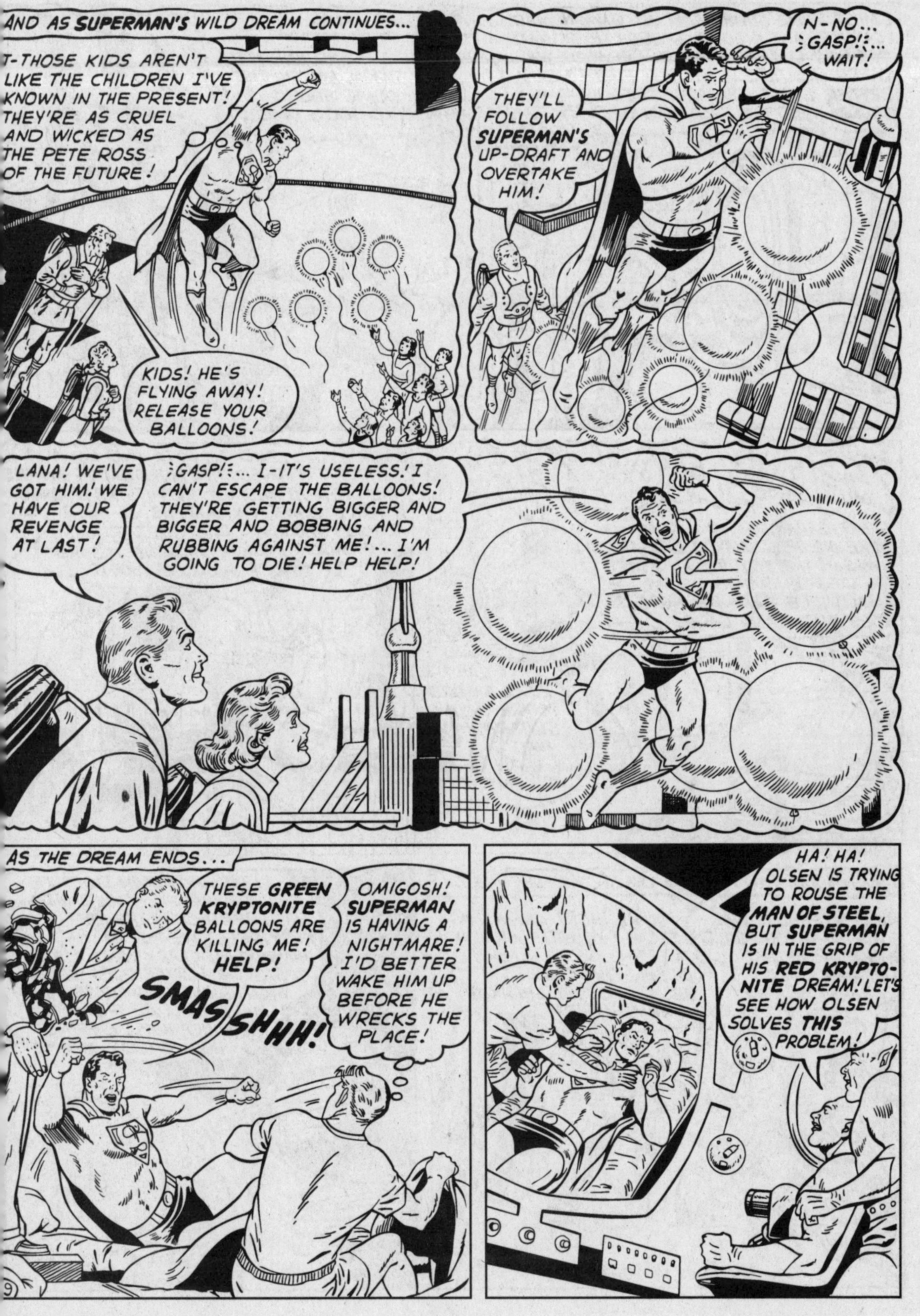
AND AS SUPERMAN'S WILD DREAM CONTINUES...
T-THOSE KIDS AREN'T LIKE THE CHILDREN I'VE KNOWN IN THE PRESENT! THEY'RE AS CRUEL AND WICKED AS THE PETE ROSS OF THE FUTURE!
KIDS! HE'S FLYING AWAY! RELEASE YOUR BALLOONS!
THEY'LL FOLLOW SUPERMAN'S UP-DRAFT AND OVERTAKE HIM!
N-NO... GASP!... WAIT!
LANA! WE'VE GOT HIM! WE HAVE OUR REVENGE AT LAST!
GASP!... I-IT'S USELESS! I CAN'T ESCAPE THE BALLOONS! THEY'RE GETTING BIGGER AND BIGGER AND BOBBING AND RUBBING AGAINST ME!... I'M GOING TO DIE! HELP HELP!
AS THE DREAM ENDS...
THESE GREEN KRYPTONITE BALLOONS ARE KILLING ME! HELP!
SMASHHH!
OMIGOSH! SUPERMAN IS HAVING A NIGHTMARE! I'D BETTER WAKE HIM UP BEFORE HE WRECKS THE PLACE!
HA! HA! OLSEN IS TRYING TO ROUSE THE MAN OF STEEL, BUT SUPERMAN IS IN THE GRIP OF HIS RED KRYPTONITE DREAM! LET'S SEE HOW OLSEN SOLVES THIS PROBLEM!
9

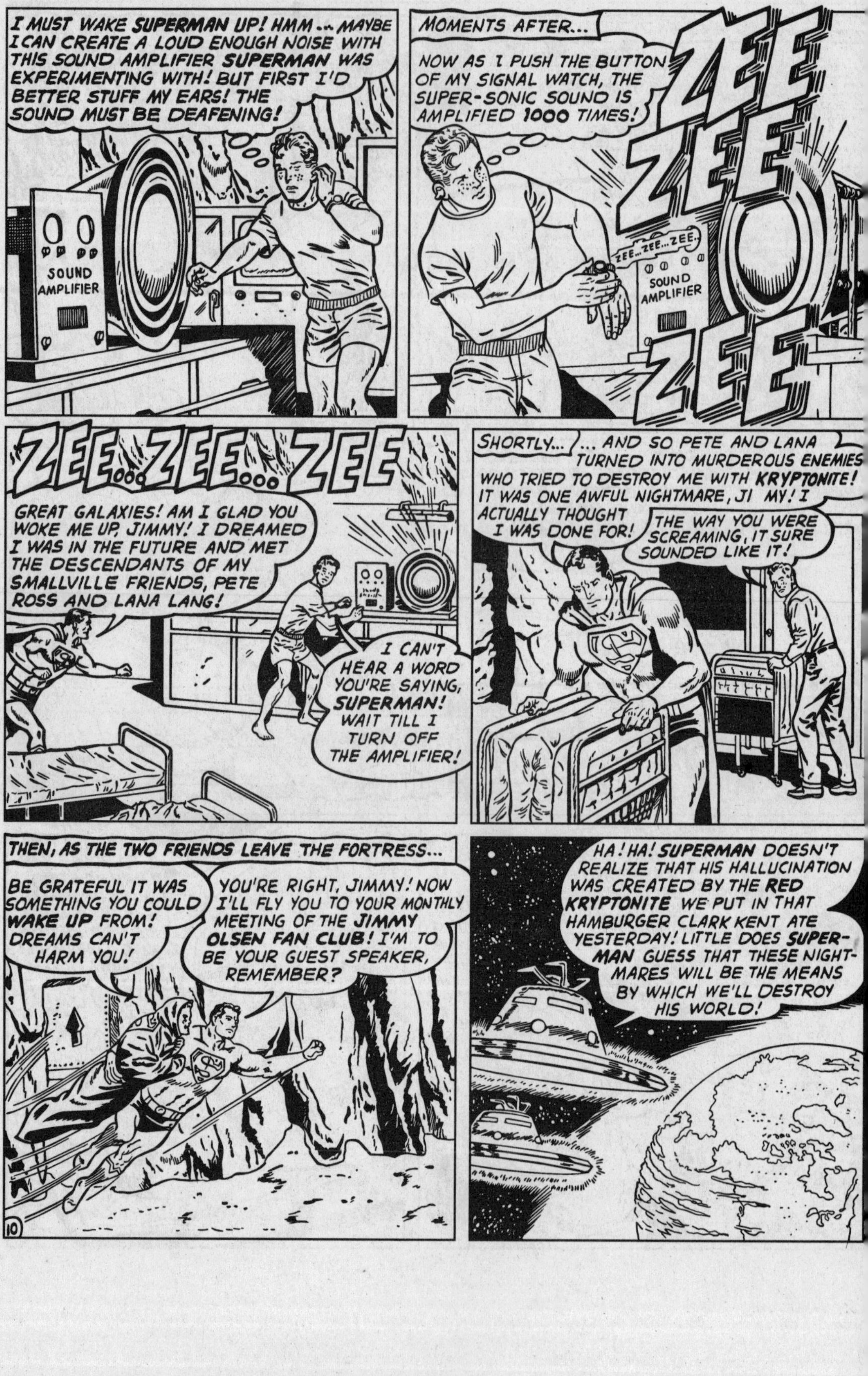

I MUST WAKE SUPERMAN UP! HMM ... MAYBE I CAN CREATE A LOUD ENOUGH NOISE WITH THIS SOUND AMPLIFIER SUPERMAN WAS EXPERIMENTING WITH! BUT FIRST I'D BETTER STUFF MY EARS! THE SOUND MUST BE DEAFENING!
SOUND AMPLIFIER
MOMENTS AFTER...
NOW AS I PUSH THE BUTTON OF MY SIGNAL WATCH, THE SUPER-SONIC SOUND IS AMPLIFIED 1000 TIMES!
ZEE ZEE ZEE
ZEE...ZEE...ZEE..
SOUND AMPLIFIER
ZEE...ZEE...ZEE
GREAT GALAXIES! AM I GLAD YOU WOKE ME UP, JIMMY! I DREAMED I WAS IN THE FUTURE AND MET THE DESCENDANTS OF MY SMALLVILLE FRIENDS, PETE ROSS AND LANA LANG!
I CAN'T HEAR A WORD YOU'RE SAYING, SUPERMAN! WAIT TILL I TURN OFF THE AMPLIFIER!
SHORTLY...
... AND SO PETE AND LANA TURNED INTO MURDEROUS ENEMIES WHO TRIED TO DESTROY ME WITH KRYPTONITE! IT WAS ONE AWFUL NIGHTMARE, JI MY! I ACTUALLY THOUGHT I WAS DONE FOR!
THE WAY YOU WERE SCREAMING, IT SURE SOUNDED LIKE IT!
THEN, AS THE TWO FRIENDS LEAVE THE FORTRESS...
BE GRATEFUL IT WAS SOMETHING YOU COULD WAKE UP FROM! DREAMS CAN'T HARM YOU!
YOU'RE RIGHT, JIMMY! NOW I'LL FLY YOU TO YOUR MONTHLY MEETING OF THE JIMMY OLSEN FAN CLUB! I'M TO BE YOUR GUEST SPEAKER, REMEMBER?
10
HA! HA! SUPERMAN DOESN'T REALIZE THAT HIS HALLUCINATION WAS CREATED BY THE RED KRYPTONITE WE PUT IN THAT HAMBURGER CLARK KENT ATE YESTERDAY! LITTLE DOES SUPERMAN GUESS THAT THESE NIGHTMARES WILL BE THE MEANS BY WHICH WE'LL DESTROY HIS WORLD!

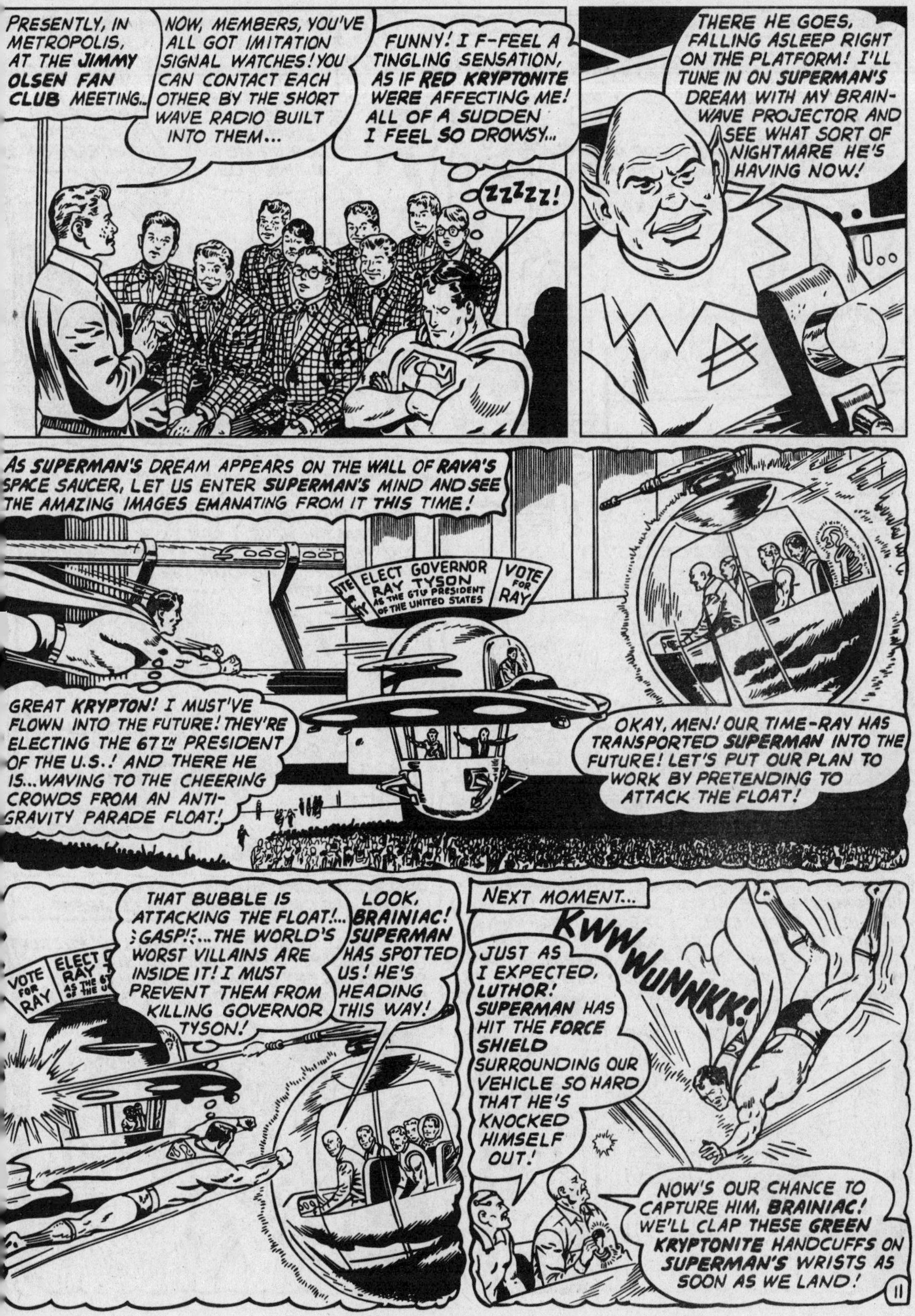
PRESENTLY, IN METROPOLIS, AT THE JIMMY OLSEN FAN CLUB MEETING..
NOW, MEMBERS, YOU'VE ALL GOT IMITATION SIGNAL WATCHES! YOU CAN CONTACT EACH OTHER BY THE SHORT WAVE RADIO BUILT INTO THEM...
FUNNY! I F-FEEL A TINGLING SENSATION, AS IF RED KRYPTONITE WERE AFFECTING ME! ALL OF A SUDDEN I FEEL SO DROWSY...
ZZZZZ!
THERE HE GOES, FALLING ASLEEP RIGHT ON THE PLATFORM! I'LL TUNE IN ON SUPERMAN'S DREAM WITH MY BRAIN-WAVE PROJECTOR AND SEE WHAT SORT OF NIGHTMARE HE'S HAVING NOW!
AS SUPERMAN'S DREAM APPEARS ON THE WALL OF RAVA'S SPACE SAUCER, LET US ENTER SUPERMAN'S MIND AND SEE THE AMAZING IMAGES EMANATING FROM IT THIS TIME!
ELECT GOVERNOR RAY TYSON AS THE 67TH PRESIDENT OF THE UNITED STATES
VOTE FOR RAY
GREAT KRYPTON! I MUST'VE FLOWN INTO THE FUTURE! THEY'RE ELECTING THE 67TH PRESIDENT OF THE U.S.! AND THERE HE IS...WAVING TO THE CHEERING CROWDS FROM AN ANTI-GRAVITY PARADE FLOAT!
OKAY, MEN! OUR TIME-RAY HAS TRANSPORTED SUPERMAN INTO THE FUTURE! LET'S PUT OUR PLAN TO WORK BY PRETENDING TO ATTACK THE FLOAT!
THAT BUBBLE IS ATTACKING THE FLOAT!... GASP!... THE WORLD'S WORST VILLAINS ARE INSIDE IT! I MUST PREVENT THEM FROM KILLING GOVERNOR TYSON!
LOOK, BRAINIAC! SUPERMAN HAS SPOTTED US! HE'S HEADING THIS WAY!
NEXT MOMENT...
KWWWUNNKK!
JUST AS I EXPECTED, LUTHOR! SUPERMAN HAS HIT THE FORCE SHIELD SURROUNDING OUR VEHICLE SO HARD THAT HE'S KNOCKED HIMSELF OUT!
NOW'S OUR CHANCE TO CAPTURE HIM, BRAINIAC! WE'LL CLAP THESE GREEN KRYPTONITE HANDCUFFS ON SUPERMAN'S WRISTS AS SOON AS WE LAND!
11

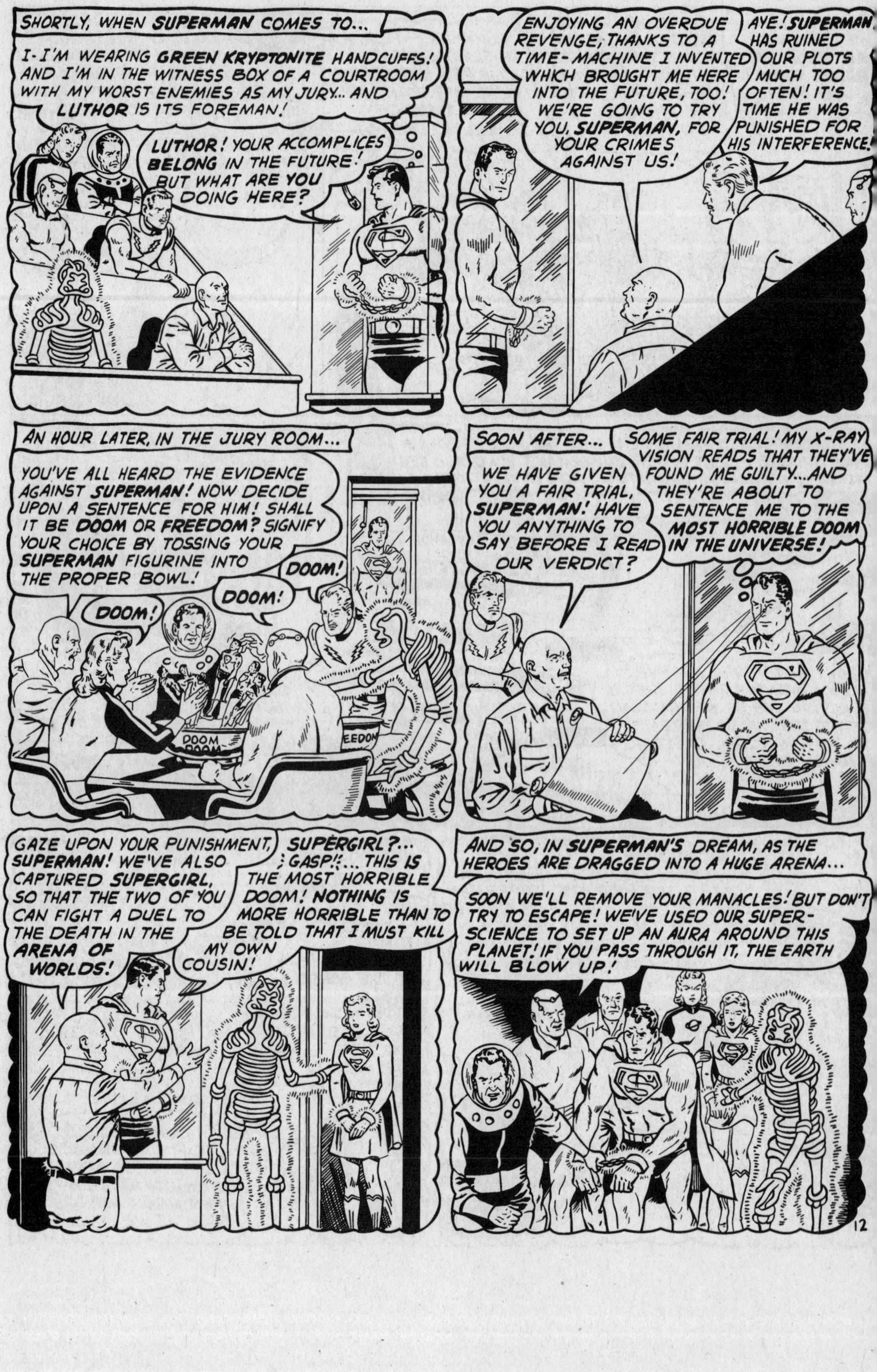
SHORTLY, WHEN SUPERMAN COMES TO...
I-I'M WEARING GREEN KRYPTONITE HANDCUFFS! AND I'M IN THE WITNESS BOX OF A COURTROOM WITH MY WORST ENEMIES AS MY JURY... AND LUTHOR IS ITS FOREMAN!
LUTHOR! YOUR ACCOMPLICES BELONG IN THE FUTURE! BUT WHAT ARE YOU DOING HERE?
ENJOYING AN OVERDUE REVENGE, THANKS TO A TIME-MACHINE I INVENTED WHICH BROUGHT ME HERE INTO THE FUTURE, TOO! WE'RE GOING TO TRY YOU, SUPERMAN, FOR YOUR CRIMES AGAINST US!
AYE! SUPERMAN HAS RUINED OUR PLOTS MUCH TOO OFTEN! IT'S TIME HE WAS PUNISHED FOR HIS INTERFERENCE!
AN HOUR LATER, IN THE JURY ROOM...
YOU'VE ALL HEARD THE EVIDENCE AGAINST SUPERMAN! NOW DECIDE UPON A SENTENCE FOR HIM! SHALL IT BE DOOM OR FREEDOM? SIGNIFY YOUR CHOICE BY TOSSING YOUR SUPERMAN FIGURINE INTO THE PROPER BOWL!
DOOM!
DOOM!
DOOM!
DOOM
EEDOM
SOON AFTER...
WE HAVE GIVEN YOU A FAIR TRIAL, SUPERMAN! HAVE YOU ANYTHING TO SAY BEFORE I READ OUR VERDICT?
SOME FAIR TRIAL! MY X-RAY VISION READS THAT THEY'VE FOUND ME GUILTY...AND THEY'RE ABOUT TO SENTENCE ME TO THE MOST HORRIBLE DOOM IN THE UNIVERSE!
GAZE UPON YOUR PUNISHMENT, SUPERMAN! WE'VE ALSO CAPTURED SUPERGIRL, SO THAT THE TWO OF YOU CAN FIGHT A DUEL TO THE DEATH IN THE ARENA OF WORLDS!
SUPERGIRL?... ;GASP!;... THIS IS THE MOST HORRIBLE DOOM! NOTHING IS MORE HORRIBLE THAN TO BE TOLD THAT I MUST KILL MY OWN COUSIN!
AND SO, IN SUPERMAN'S DREAM, AS THE HEROES ARE DRAGGED INTO A HUGE ARENA...
SOON WE'LL REMOVE YOUR MANACLES! BUT DON'T TRY TO ESCAPE! WE'VE USED OUR SUPER-SCIENCE TO SET UP AN AURA AROUND THIS PLANET! IF YOU PASS THROUGH IT, THE EARTH WILL BLOW UP!
12

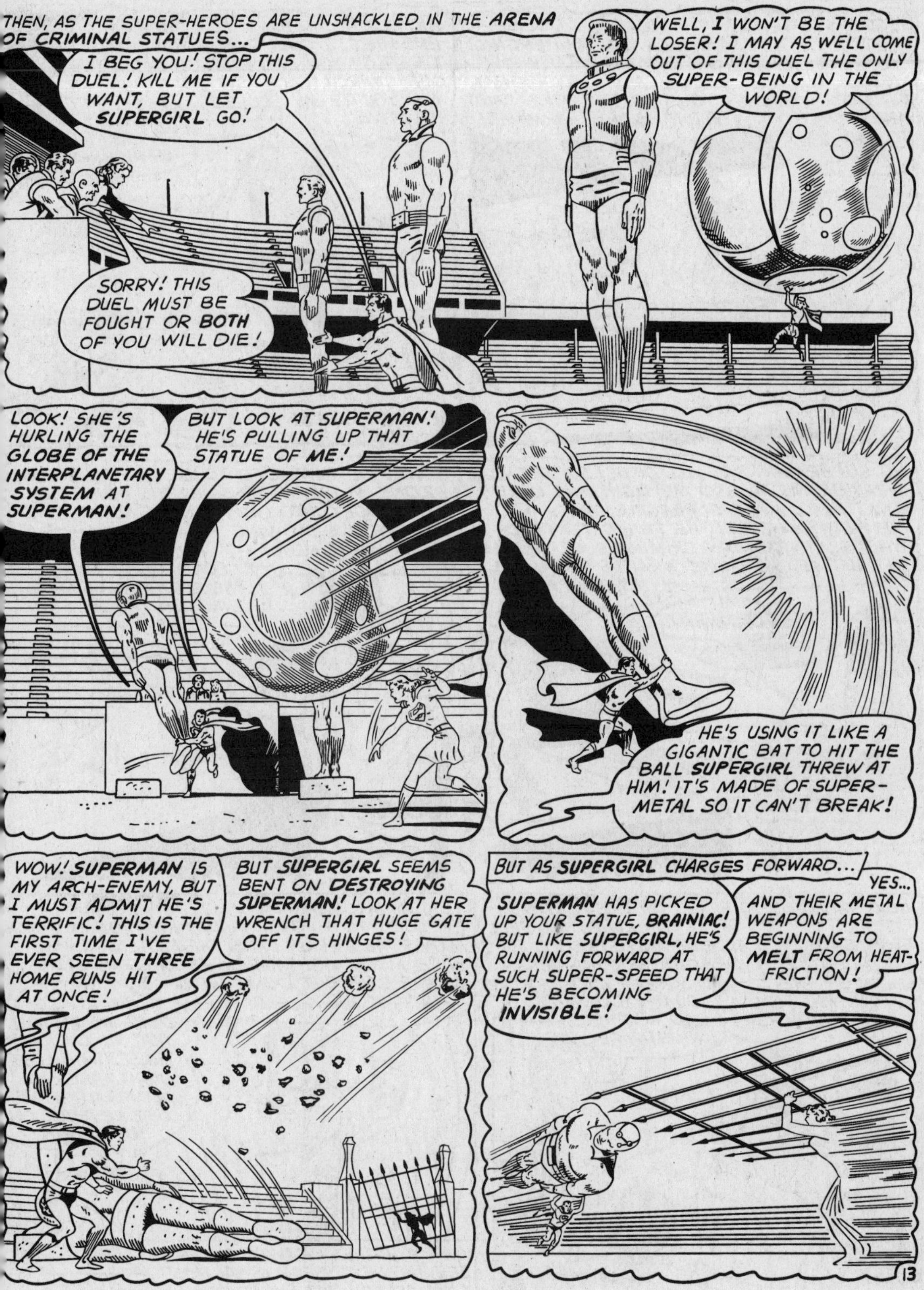
THEN, AS THE SUPER-HEROES ARE UNSHACKLED IN THE ARENA OF CRIMINAL STATUES...
I BEG YOU! STOP THIS DUEL! KILL ME IF YOU WANT, BUT LET SUPERGIRL GO!
SORRY! THIS DUEL MUST BE FOUGHT OR BOTH OF YOU WILL DIE!
WELL, I WON'T BE THE LOSER! I MAY AS WELL COME OUT OF THIS DUEL THE ONLY SUPER-BEING IN THE WORLD!
LOOK! SHE'S HURLING THE GLOBE OF THE INTERPLANETARY SYSTEM AT SUPERMAN!
BUT LOOK AT SUPERMAN! HE'S PULLING UP THAT STATUE OF ME!
HE'S USING IT LIKE A GIGANTIC BAT TO HIT THE BALL SUPERGIRL THREW AT HIM! IT'S MADE OF SUPER-METAL SO IT CAN'T BREAK!
WOW! SUPERMAN IS MY ARCH-ENEMY, BUT I MUST ADMIT HE'S TERRIFIC! THIS IS THE FIRST TIME I'VE EVER SEEN THREE HOME RUNS HIT AT ONCE!
BUT SUPERGIRL SEEMS BENT ON DESTROYING SUPERMAN! LOOK AT HER WRENCH THAT HUGE GATE OFF ITS HINGES!
BUT AS SUPERGIRL CHARGES FORWARD...
SUPERMAN HAS PICKED UP YOUR STATUE, BRAINIAC! BUT LIKE SUPERGIRL, HE'S RUNNING FORWARD AT SUCH SUPER-SPEED THAT HE'S BECOMING INVISIBLE!
YES... AND THEIR METAL WEAPONS ARE BEGINNING TO MELT FROM HEAT-FRICTION!
13

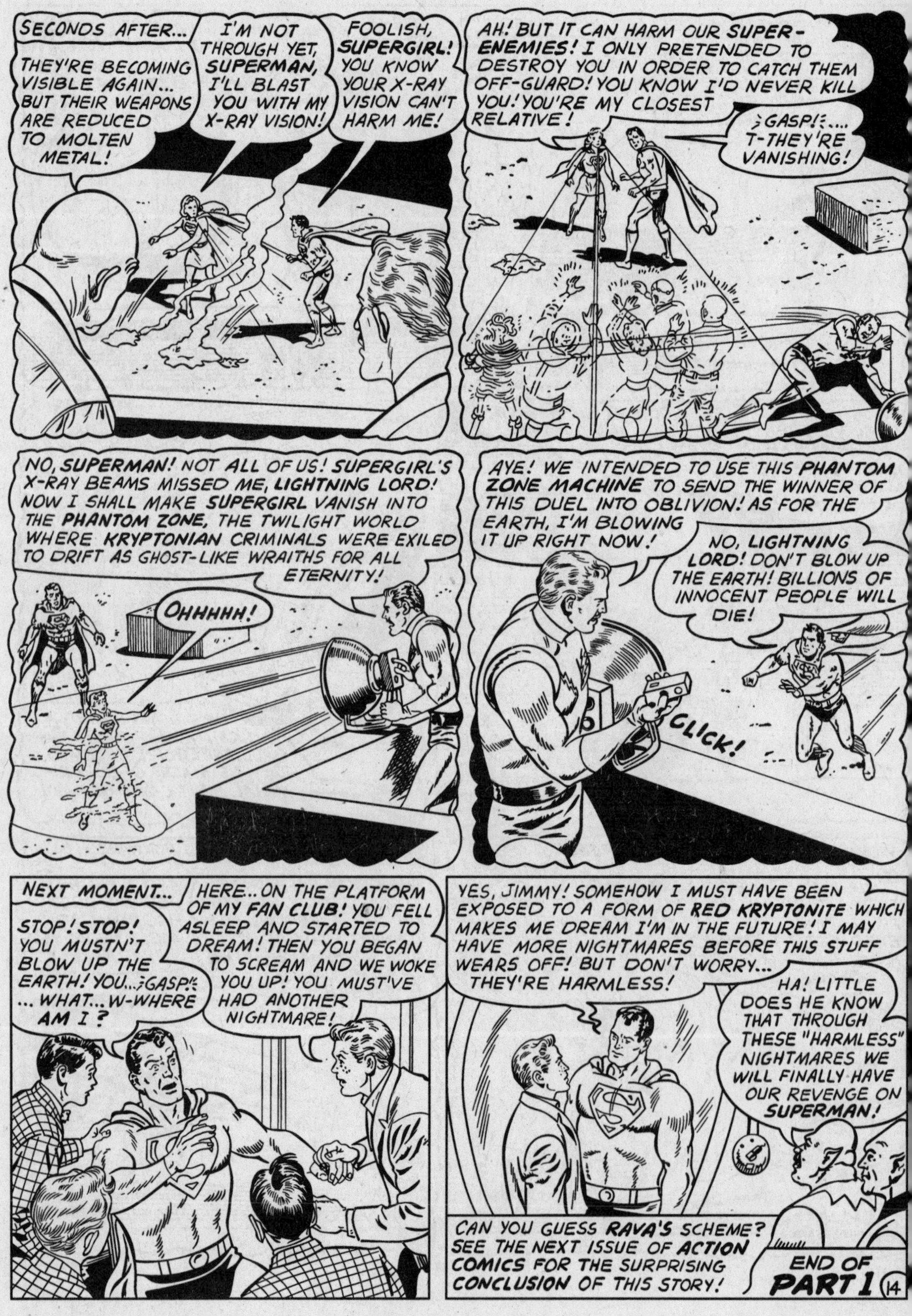
SECONDS AFTER...
THEY'RE BECOMING VISIBLE AGAIN... BUT THEIR WEAPONS ARE REDUCED TO MOLTEN METAL!
I'M NOT THROUGH YET, SUPERMAN, I'LL BLAST YOU WITH MY X-RAY VISION!
FOOLISH, SUPERGIRL! YOU KNOW YOUR X-RAY VISION CAN'T HARM ME!
AH! BUT IT CAN HARM OUR SUPER-ENEMIES! I ONLY PRETENDED TO DESTROY YOU IN ORDER TO CATCH THEM OFF-GUARD! YOU KNOW I'D NEVER KILL YOU! YOU'RE MY CLOSEST RELATIVE!
GASP!... T-THEY'RE VANISHING!
NO, SUPERMAN! NOT ALL OF US! SUPERGIRL'S X-RAY BEAMS MISSED ME, LIGHTNING LORD! NOW I SHALL MAKE SUPERGIRL VANISH INTO THE PHANTOM ZONE, THE TWILIGHT WORLD WHERE KRYPTONIAN CRIMINALS WERE EXILED TO DRIFT AS GHOST-LIKE WRAITHS FOR ALL ETERNITY!
OHHHHH!
AYE! WE INTENDED TO USE THIS PHANTOM ZONE MACHINE TO SEND THE WINNER OF THIS DUEL INTO OBLIVION! AS FOR THE EARTH, I'M BLOWING IT UP RIGHT NOW!
NO, LIGHTNING LORD! DON'T BLOW UP THE EARTH! BILLIONS OF INNOCENT PEOPLE WILL DIE!
CLICK!
NEXT MOMENT...
STOP! STOP! YOU MUSTN'T BLOW UP THE EARTH! YOU... GASP! ... WHAT... W-WHERE AM I?
HERE... ON THE PLATFORM OF MY FAN CLUB! YOU FELL ASLEEP AND STARTED TO DREAM! THEN YOU BEGAN TO SCREAM AND WE WOKE YOU UP! YOU MUST'VE HAD ANOTHER NIGHTMARE!
YES, JIMMY! SOMEHOW I MUST HAVE BEEN EXPOSED TO A FORM OF RED KRYPTONITE WHICH MAKES ME DREAM I'M IN THE FUTURE! I MAY HAVE MORE NIGHTMARES BEFORE THIS STUFF WEARS OFF! BUT DON'T WORRY... THEY'RE HARMLESS!
HA! LITTLE DOES HE KNOW THAT THROUGH THESE "HARMLESS" NIGHTMARES WE WILL FINALLY HAVE OUR REVENGE ON SUPERMAN!
CAN YOU GUESS RAVA'S SCHEME? SEE THE NEXT ISSUE OF ACTION COMICS FOR THE SURPRISING CONCLUSION OF THIS STORY!
END OF PART 1
14

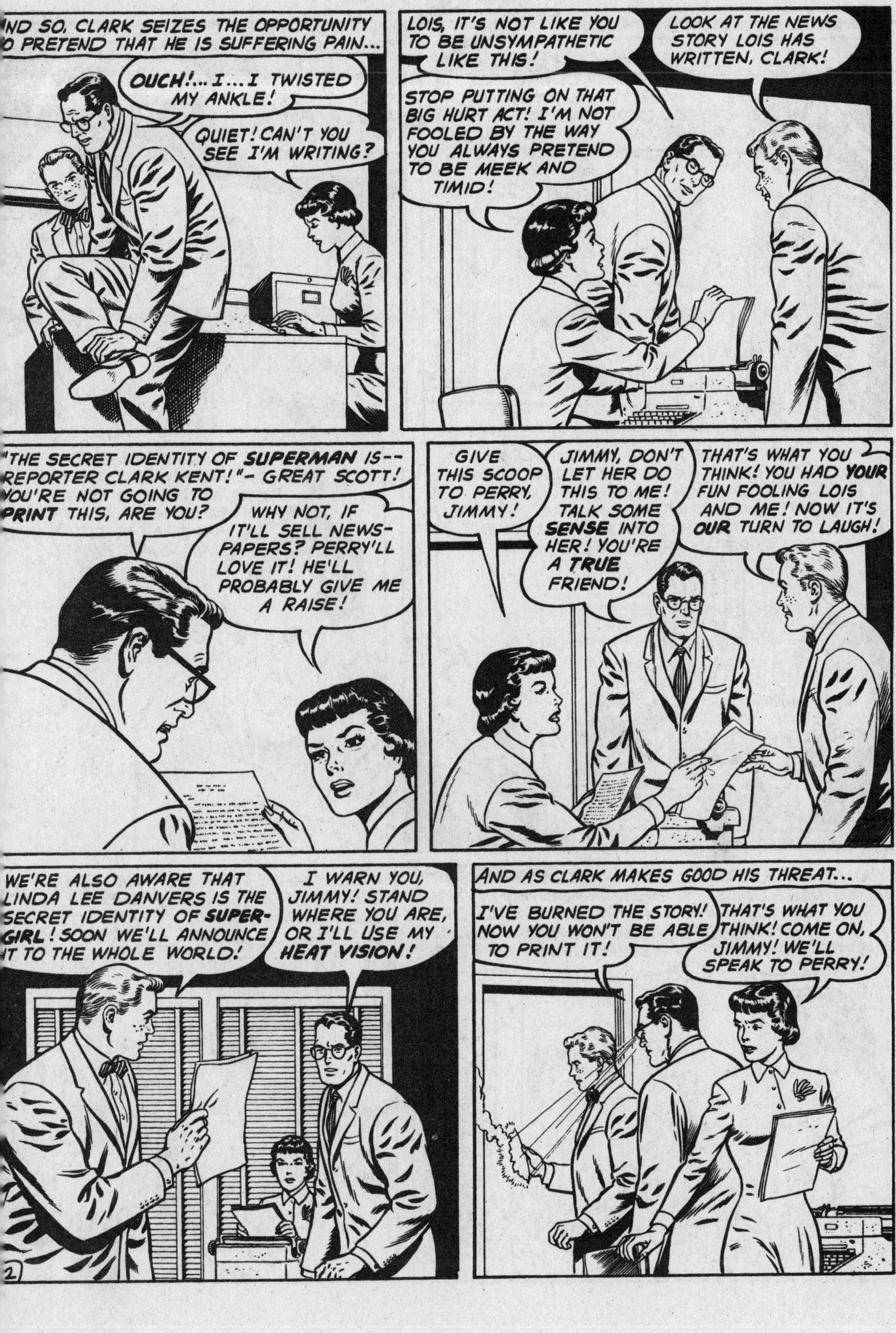
ND SO, CLARK SEIZES THE OPPORTUNITY O PRETEND THAT HE IS SUFFERING PAIN...
OUCH!... I... I TWISTED MY ANKLE!
QUIET! CAN'T YOU SEE I'M WRITING?
LOIS, IT'S NOT LIKE YOU TO BE UNSYMPATHETIC LIKE THIS!
LOOK AT THE NEWS STORY LOIS HAS WRITTEN, CLARK!
STOP PUTTING ON THAT BIG HURT ACT! I'M NOT FOOLED BY THE WAY YOU ALWAYS PRETEND TO BE MEEK AND TIMID!
"THE SECRET IDENTITY OF SUPERMAN IS--REPORTER CLARK KENT!"- GREAT SCOTT! YOU'RE NOT GOING TO PRINT THIS, ARE YOU?
WHY NOT, IF IT'LL SELL NEWS-PAPERS? PERRY'LL LOVE IT! HE'LL PROBABLY GIVE ME A RAISE!
GIVE THIS SCOOP TO PERRY, JIMMY!
JIMMY, DON'T LET HER DO THIS TO ME! TALK SOME SENSE INTO HER! YOU'RE A TRUE FRIEND!
THAT'S WHAT YOU THINK! YOU HAD YOUR FUN FOOLING LOIS AND ME! NOW IT'S OUR TURN TO LAUGH!
WE'RE ALSO AWARE THAT LINDA LEE DANVERS IS THE SECRET IDENTITY OF SUPER-GIRL! SOON WE'LL ANNOUNCE IT TO THE WHOLE WORLD!
I WARN YOU, JIMMY! STAND WHERE YOU ARE, OR I'LL USE MY HEAT VISION!
2
AND AS CLARK MAKES GOOD HIS THREAT...
I'VE BURNED THE STORY! NOW YOU WON'T BE ABLE TO PRINT IT!
THAT'S WHAT YOU THINK! COME ON, JIMMY! WE'LL SPEAK TO PERRY!

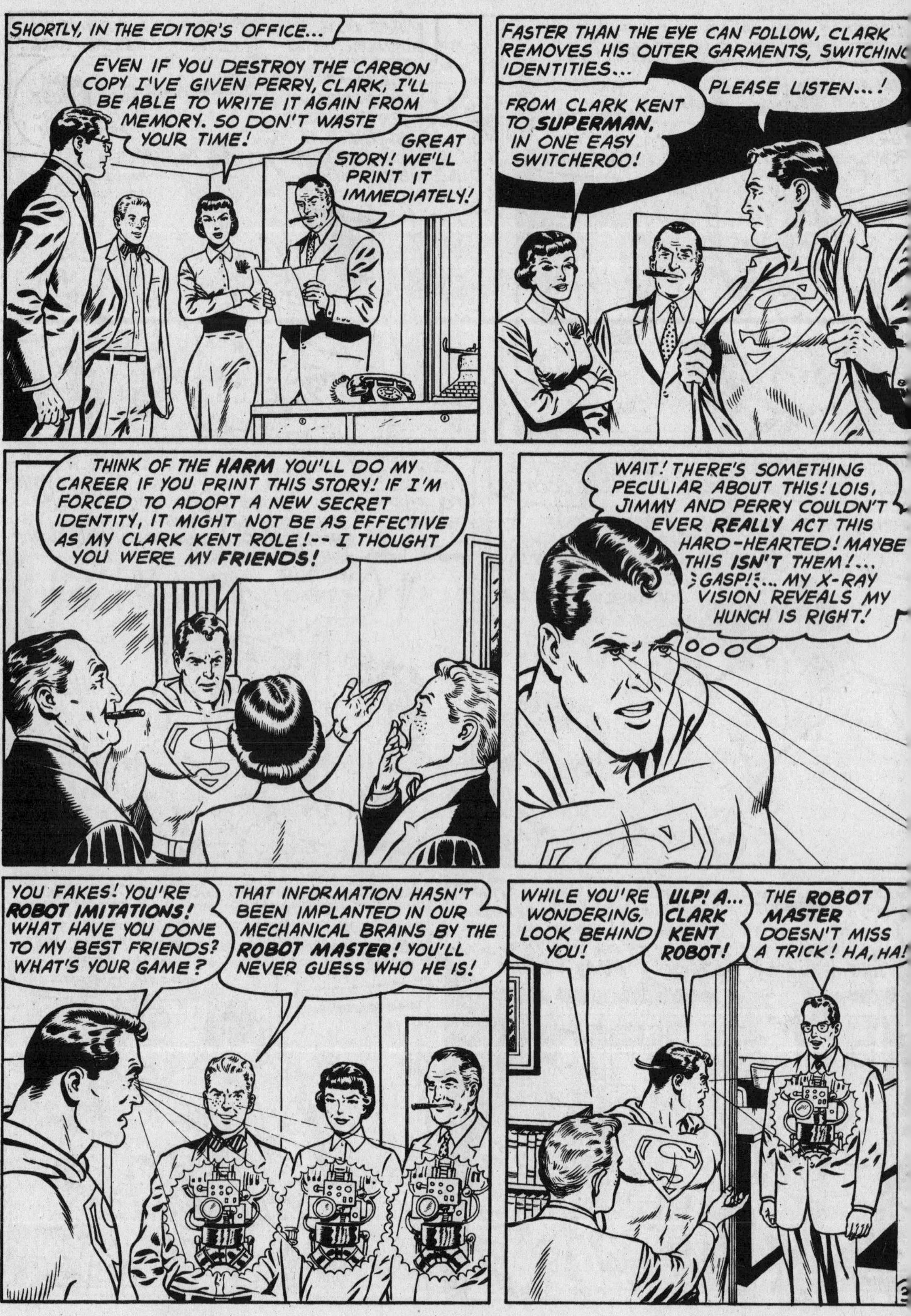
SHORTLY, IN THE EDITOR'S OFFICE...
EVEN IF YOU DESTROY THE CARBON COPY I'VE GIVEN PERRY, CLARK, I'LL BE ABLE TO WRITE IT AGAIN FROM MEMORY. SO DON'T WASTE YOUR TIME!
GREAT STORY! WE'LL PRINT IT IMMEDIATELY!
FASTER THAN THE EYE CAN FOLLOW, CLARK REMOVES HIS OUTER GARMENTS, SWITCHING IDENTITIES...
FROM CLARK KENT TO SUPERMAN, IN ONE EASY SWITCHEROO!
PLEASE LISTEN...!
THINK OF THE HARM YOU'LL DO MY CAREER IF YOU PRINT THIS STORY! IF I'M FORCED TO ADOPT A NEW SECRET IDENTITY, IT MIGHT NOT BE AS EFFECTIVE AS MY CLARK KENT ROLE!-- I THOUGHT YOU WERE MY FRIENDS!
WAIT! THERE'S SOMETHING PECULIAR ABOUT THIS! LOIS, JIMMY AND PERRY COULDN'T EVER REALLY ACT THIS HARD-HEARTED! MAYBE THIS ISN'T THEM!... GASP!... MY X-RAY VISION REVEALS MY HUNCH IS RIGHT!
YOU FAKES! YOU'RE ROBOT IMITATIONS! WHAT HAVE YOU DONE TO MY BEST FRIENDS? WHAT'S YOUR GAME?
THAT INFORMATION HASN'T BEEN IMPLANTED IN OUR MECHANICAL BRAINS BY THE ROBOT MASTER! YOU'LL NEVER GUESS WHO HE IS!
WHILE YOU'RE WONDERING, LOOK BEHIND YOU!
ULP! A... CLARK KENT ROBOT!
THE ROBOT MASTER DOESN'T MISS A TRICK! HA, HA!

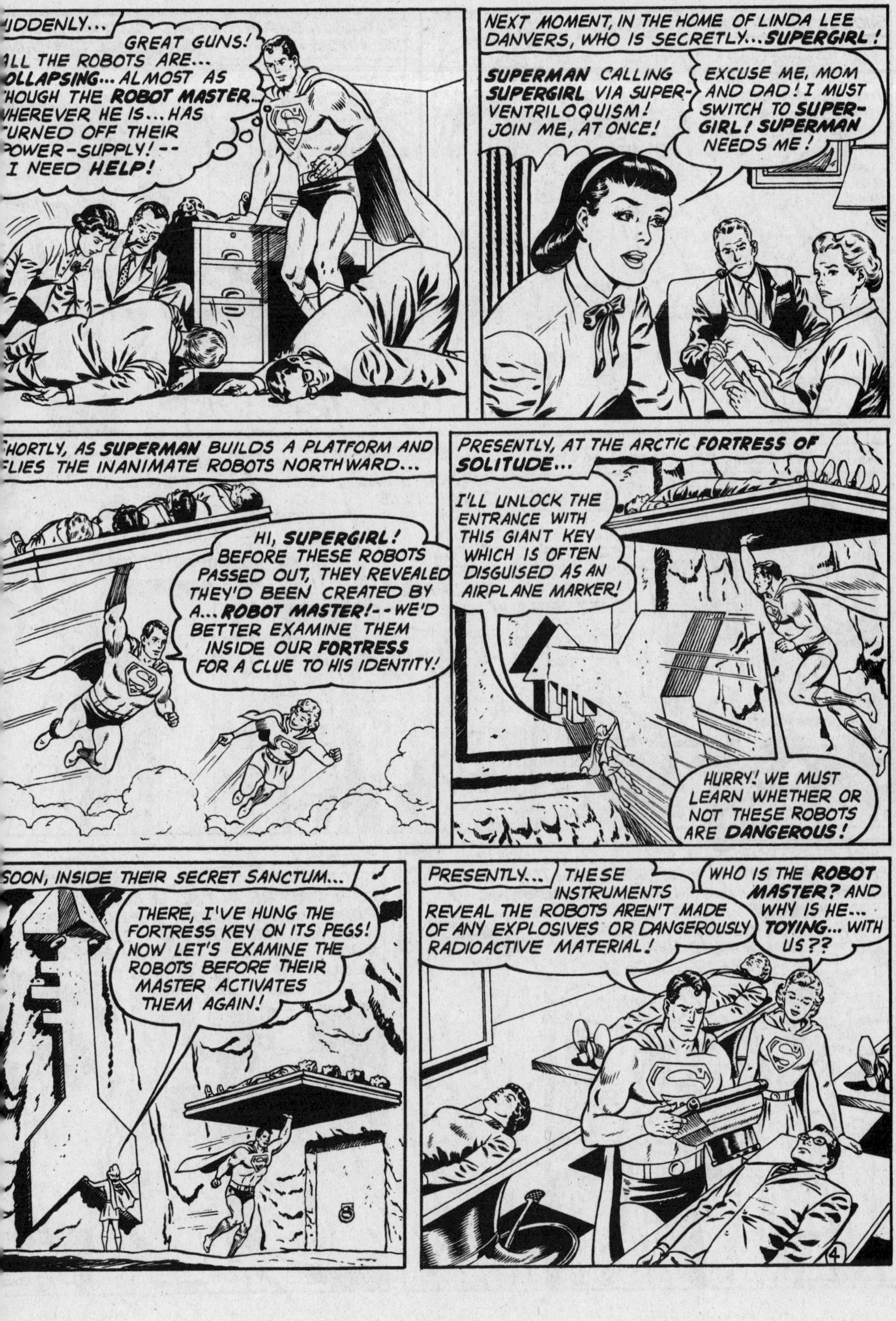

IDDENLY...
GREAT GUNS! ALL THE ROBOTS ARE... COLLAPSING... ALMOST AS THOUGH THE ROBOT MASTER... WHEREVER HE IS... HAS TURNED OFF THEIR POWER-SUPPLY! -- I NEED HELP!
NEXT MOMENT, IN THE HOME OF LINDA LEE DANVERS, WHO IS SECRETLY... SUPERGIRL!
SUPERMAN CALLING SUPERGIRL VIA SUPER-VENTRILOQUISM! JOIN ME, AT ONCE!
EXCUSE ME, MOM AND DAD! I MUST SWITCH TO SUPERGIRL! SUPERMAN NEEDS ME!
HORTLY, AS SUPERMAN BUILDS A PLATFORM AND FLIES THE INANIMATE ROBOTS NORTHWARD...
HI, SUPERGIRL! BEFORE THESE ROBOTS PASSED OUT, THEY REVEALED THEY'D BEEN CREATED BY A... ROBOT MASTER!--WE'D BETTER EXAMINE THEM INSIDE OUR FORTRESS FOR A CLUE TO HIS IDENTITY!
PRESENTLY, AT THE ARCTIC FORTRESS OF SOLITUDE...
I'LL UNLOCK THE ENTRANCE WITH THIS GIANT KEY WHICH IS OFTEN DISGUISED AS AN AIRPLANE MARKER!
HURRY! WE MUST LEARN WHETHER OR NOT THESE ROBOTS ARE DANGEROUS!
SOON, INSIDE THEIR SECRET SANCTUM...
THERE, I'VE HUNG THE FORTRESS KEY ON ITS PEGS! NOW LET'S EXAMINE THE ROBOTS BEFORE THEIR MASTER ACTIVATES THEM AGAIN!
PRESENTLY...
THESE INSTRUMENTS REVEAL THE ROBOTS AREN'T MADE OF ANY EXPLOSIVES OR DANGEROUSLY RADIOACTIVE MATERIAL!
WHO IS THE ROBOT MASTER? AND WHY IS HE... TOYING... WITH US??
4

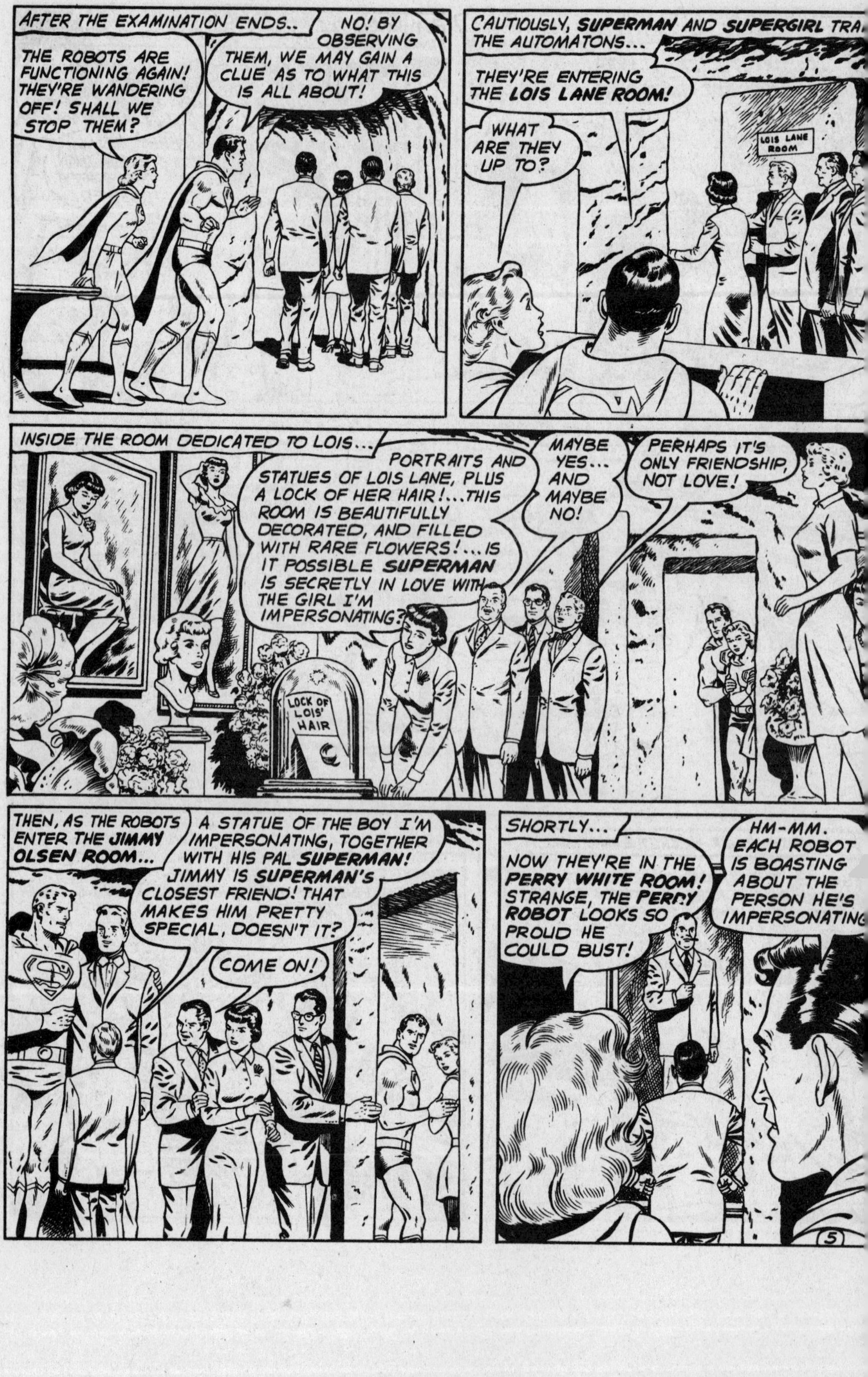
AFTER THE EXAMINATION ENDS..
THE ROBOTS ARE FUNCTIONING AGAIN! THEY'RE WANDERING OFF! SHALL WE STOP THEM?
NO! BY OBSERVING THEM, WE MAY GAIN A CLUE AS TO WHAT THIS IS ALL ABOUT!
CAUTIOUSLY, SUPERMAN AND SUPERGIRL TRA
THE AUTOMATONS...
THEY'RE ENTERING THE LOIS LANE ROOM!
WHAT ARE THEY UP TO?
LOIS LANE ROOM
INSIDE THE ROOM DEDICATED TO LOIS...
PORTRAITS AND STATUES OF LOIS LANE, PLUS A LOCK OF HER HAIR!...THIS ROOM IS BEAUTIFULLY DECORATED, AND FILLED WITH RARE FLOWERS!...IS IT POSSIBLE SUPERMAN IS SECRETLY IN LOVE WITH THE GIRL I'M IMPERSONATING?
MAYBE YES... AND MAYBE NO!
PERHAPS IT'S ONLY FRIENDSHIP, NOT LOVE!
LOCK OF LOIS' HAIR
THEN, AS THE ROBOTS ENTER THE JIMMY OLSEN ROOM...
A STATUE OF THE BOY I'M IMPERSONATING, TOGETHER WITH HIS PAL SUPERMAN! JIMMY IS SUPERMAN'S CLOSEST FRIEND! THAT MAKES HIM PRETTY SPECIAL, DOESN'T IT?
COME ON!
SHORTLY...
NOW THEY'RE IN THE PERRY WHITE ROOM! STRANGE, THE PERRY ROBOT LOOKS SO PROUD HE COULD BUST!
HM-MM. EACH ROBOT IS BOASTING ABOUT THE PERSON HE'S IMPERSONATING
5

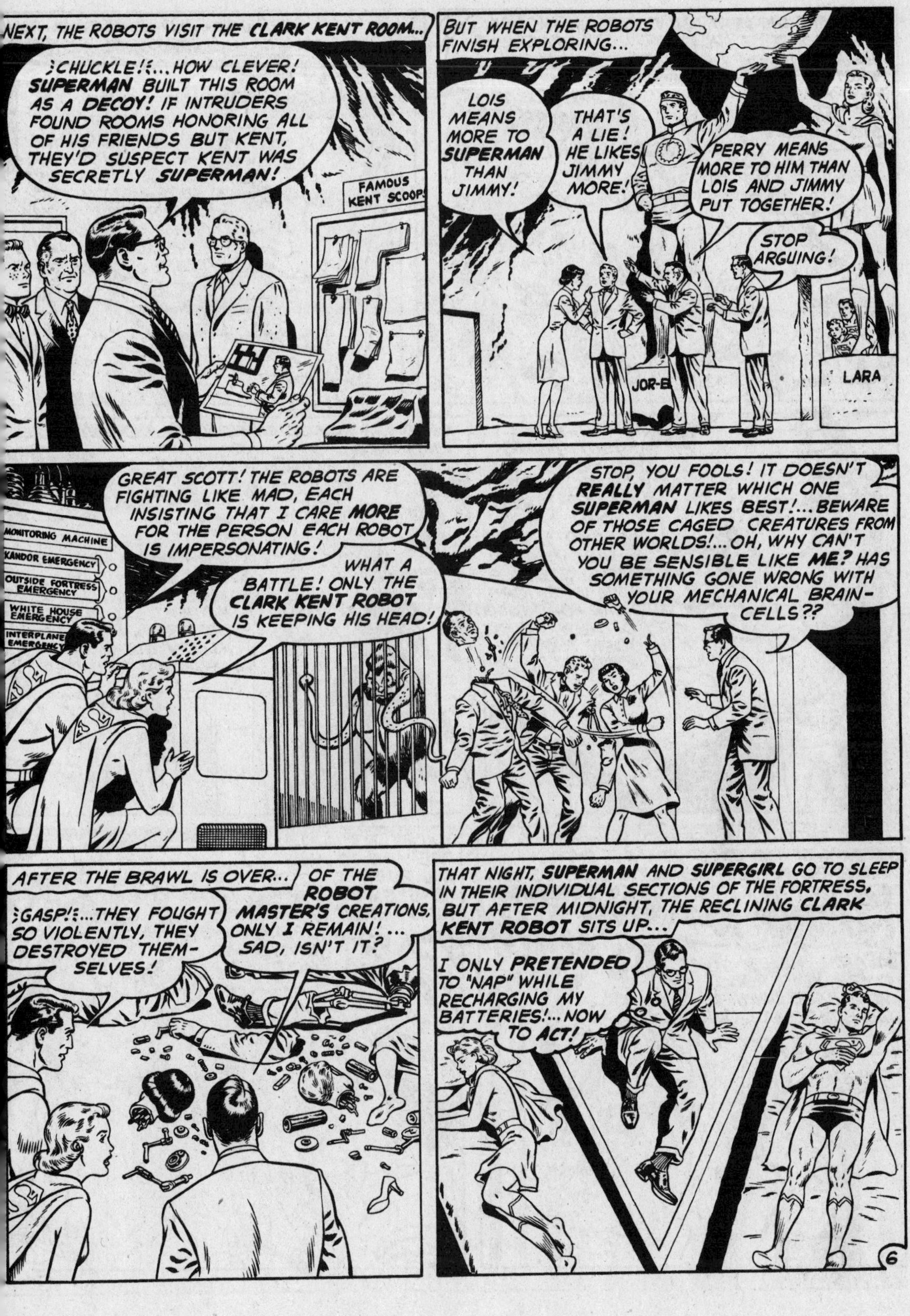
NEXT, THE ROBOTS VISIT THE CLARK KENT ROOM...
CHUCKLE!...HOW CLEVER! SUPERMAN BUILT THIS ROOM AS A DECOY! IF INTRUDERS FOUND ROOMS HONORING ALL OF HIS FRIENDS BUT KENT, THEY'D SUSPECT KENT WAS SECRETLY SUPERMAN!
FAMOUS KENT SCOOPS
BUT WHEN THE ROBOTS FINISH EXPLORING...
LOIS MEANS MORE TO SUPERMAN THAN JIMMY!
THAT'S A LIE! HE LIKES JIMMY MORE!
PERRY MEANS MORE TO HIM THAN LOIS AND JIMMY PUT TOGETHER!
STOP ARGUING!
JOR-EL
LARA
MONITORING MACHINE
KANDOR EMERGENCY
OUTSIDE FORTRESS EMERGENCY
WHITE HOUSE EMERGENCY
GREAT SCOTT! THE ROBOTS ARE FIGHTING LIKE MAD, EACH INSISTING THAT I CARE MORE FOR THE PERSON EACH ROBOT IS IMPERSONATING!
WHAT A BATTLE! ONLY THE CLARK KENT ROBOT IS KEEPING HIS HEAD!
STOP, YOU FOOLS! IT DOESN'T REALLY MATTER WHICH ONE SUPERMAN LIKES BEST!... BEWARE OF THOSE CAGED CREATURES FROM OTHER WORLDS!... OH, WHY CAN'T YOU BE SENSIBLE LIKE ME? HAS SOMETHING GONE WRONG WITH YOUR MECHANICAL BRAIN-CELLS??
AFTER THE BRAWL IS OVER...
GASP!...THEY FOUGHT SO VIOLENTLY, THEY DESTROYED THEMSELVES!
OF THE ROBOT MASTER'S CREATIONS, ONLY I REMAIN!... SAD, ISN'T IT?
THAT NIGHT, SUPERMAN AND SUPERGIRL GO TO SLEEP IN THEIR INDIVIDUAL SECTIONS OF THE FORTRESS, BUT AFTER MIDNIGHT, THE RECLINING CLARK KENT ROBOT SITS UP...
I ONLY PRETENDED TO "NAP" WHILE RECHARGING MY BATTERIES!... NOW TO ACT!
6

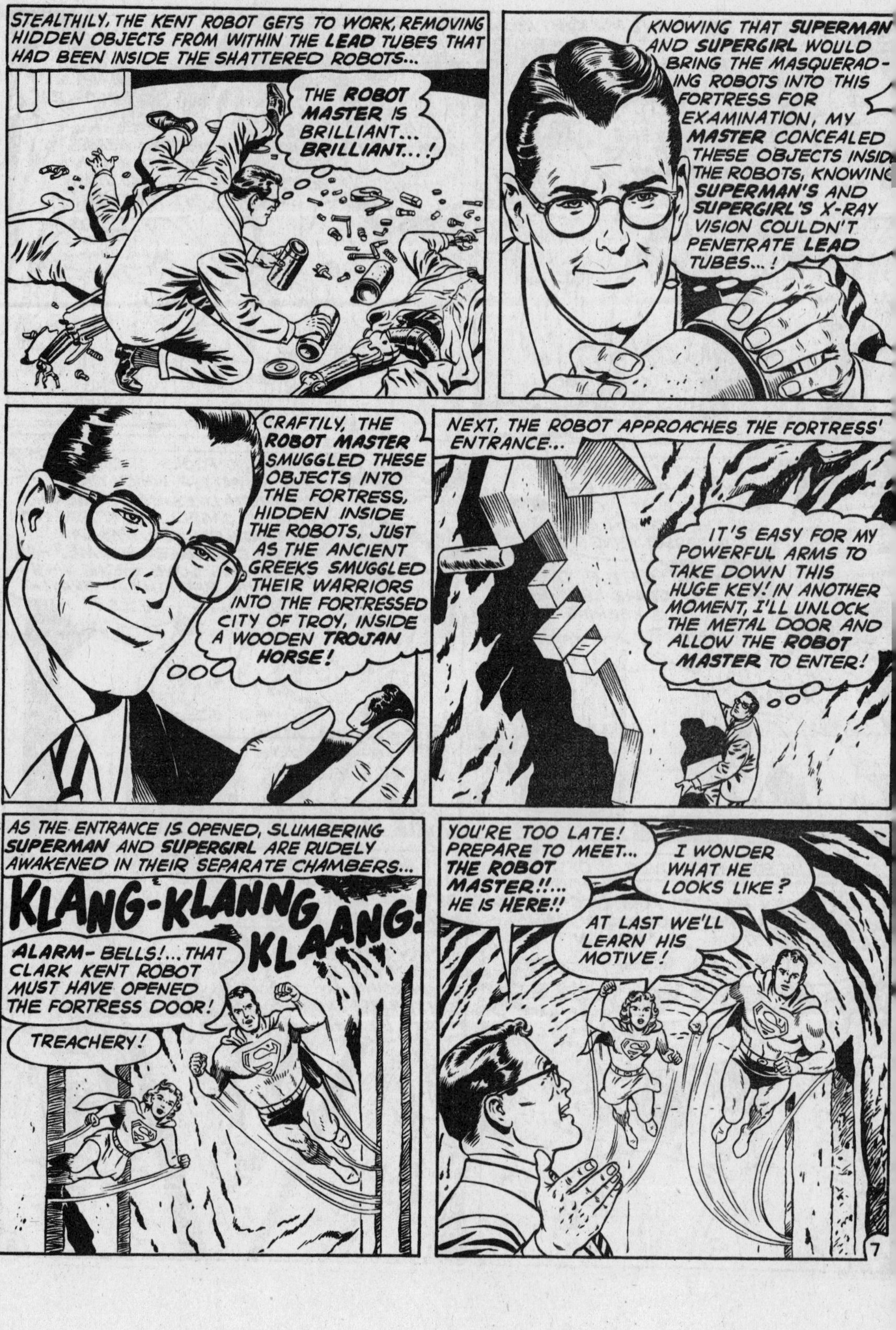
STEALTHILY, THE KENT ROBOT GETS TO WORK, REMOVING HIDDEN OBJECTS FROM WITHIN THE LEAD TUBES THAT HAD BEEN INSIDE THE SHATTERED ROBOTS...
THE ROBOT MASTER IS BRILLIANT... BRILLIANT...!
KNOWING THAT SUPERMAN AND SUPERGIRL WOULD BRING THE MASQUERADING ROBOTS INTO THIS FORTRESS FOR EXAMINATION, MY MASTER CONCEALED THESE OBJECTS INSIDE THE ROBOTS, KNOWING SUPERMAN'S AND SUPERGIRL'S X-RAY VISION COULDN'T PENETRATE LEAD TUBES...!
CRAFTILY, THE ROBOT MASTER SMUGGLED THESE OBJECTS INTO THE FORTRESS, HIDDEN INSIDE THE ROBOTS, JUST AS THE ANCIENT GREEKS SMUGGLED THEIR WARRIORS INTO THE FORTRESSED CITY OF TROY, INSIDE A WOODEN TROJAN HORSE!
NEXT, THE ROBOT APPROACHES THE FORTRESS' ENTRANCE...
IT'S EASY FOR MY POWERFUL ARMS TO TAKE DOWN THIS HUGE KEY! IN ANOTHER MOMENT, I'LL UNLOCK THE METAL DOOR AND ALLOW THE ROBOT MASTER TO ENTER!
AS THE ENTRANCE IS OPENED, SLUMBERING SUPERMAN AND SUPERGIRL ARE RUDELY AWAKENED IN THEIR SEPARATE CHAMBERS...
KLANG-KLANNNG
KLAANG!
ALARM-BELLS!...THAT CLARK KENT ROBOT MUST HAVE OPENED THE FORTRESS DOOR!
TREACHERY!
YOU'RE TOO LATE! PREPARE TO MEET... THE ROBOT MASTER!!... HE IS HERE!!
I WONDER WHAT HE LOOKS LIKE?
AT LAST WE'LL LEARN HIS MOTIVE!
7

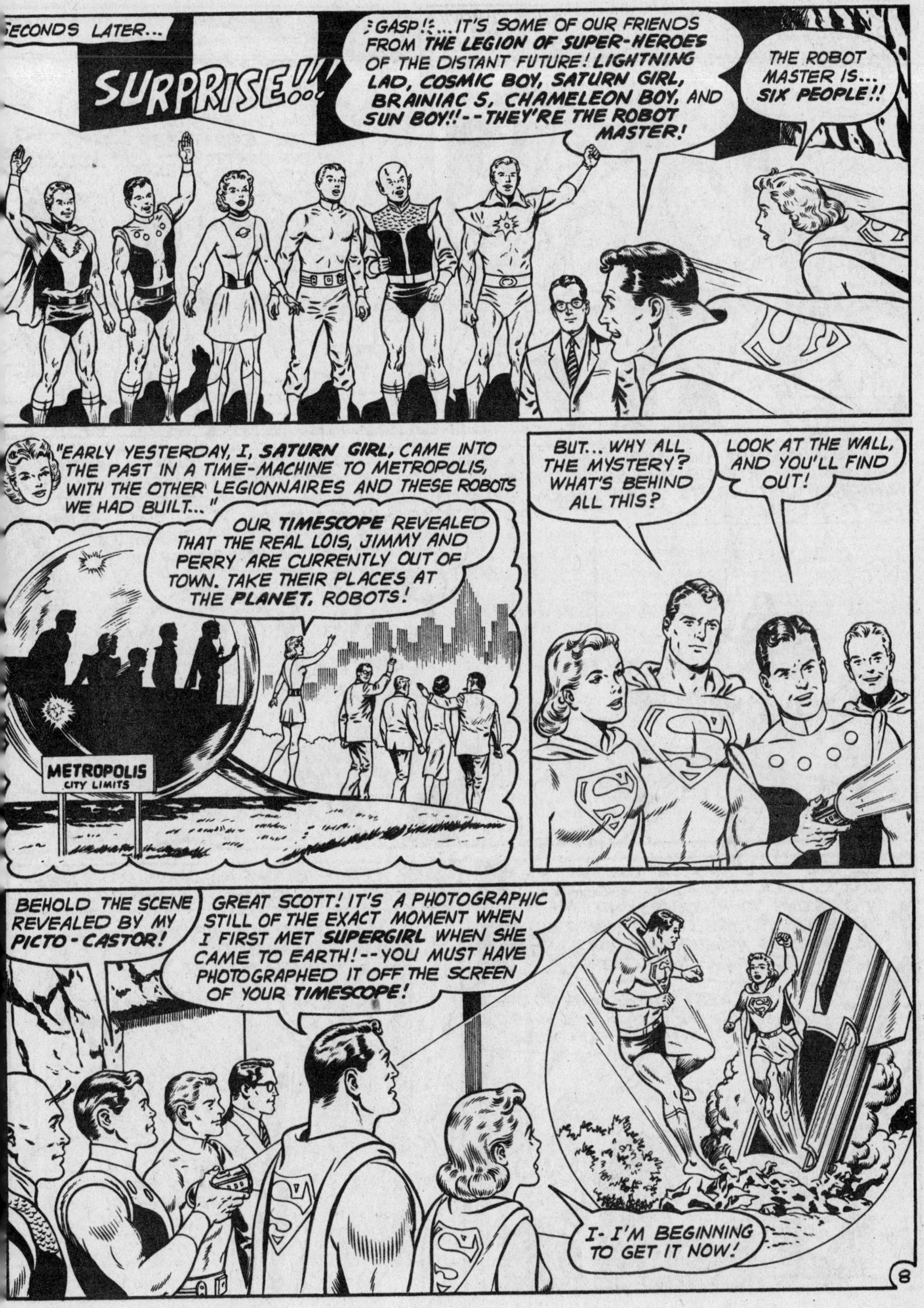
SECONDS LATER...
SURPRISE!!!
GASP!!... IT'S SOME OF OUR FRIENDS FROM THE LEGION OF SUPER-HEROES OF THE DISTANT FUTURE! LIGHTNING LAD, COSMIC BOY, SATURN GIRL, BRAINIAC 5, CHAMELEON BOY, AND SUN BOY!!--THEY'RE THE ROBOT MASTER!
THE ROBOT MASTER IS... SIX PEOPLE!!
"EARLY YESTERDAY, I, SATURN GIRL, CAME INTO THE PAST IN A TIME-MACHINE TO METROPOLIS, WITH THE OTHER LEGIONNAIRES AND THESE ROBOTS WE HAD BUILT..."
OUR TIMESCOPE REVEALED THAT THE REAL LOIS, JIMMY AND PERRY ARE CURRENTLY OUT OF TOWN. TAKE THEIR PLACES AT THE PLANET, ROBOTS!
METROPOLIS
CITY LIMITS
BUT... WHY ALL THE MYSTERY? WHAT'S BEHIND ALL THIS?
LOOK AT THE WALL, AND YOU'LL FIND OUT!
BEHOLD THE SCENE REVEALED BY MY PICTO-CASTOR!
GREAT SCOTT! IT'S A PHOTOGRAPHIC STILL OF THE EXACT MOMENT WHEN I FIRST MET SUPERGIRL WHEN SHE CAME TO EARTH!--YOU MUST HAVE PHOTOGRAPHED IT OFF THE SCREEN OF YOUR TIMESCOPE!
I-I'M BEGINNING TO GET IT NOW!
8

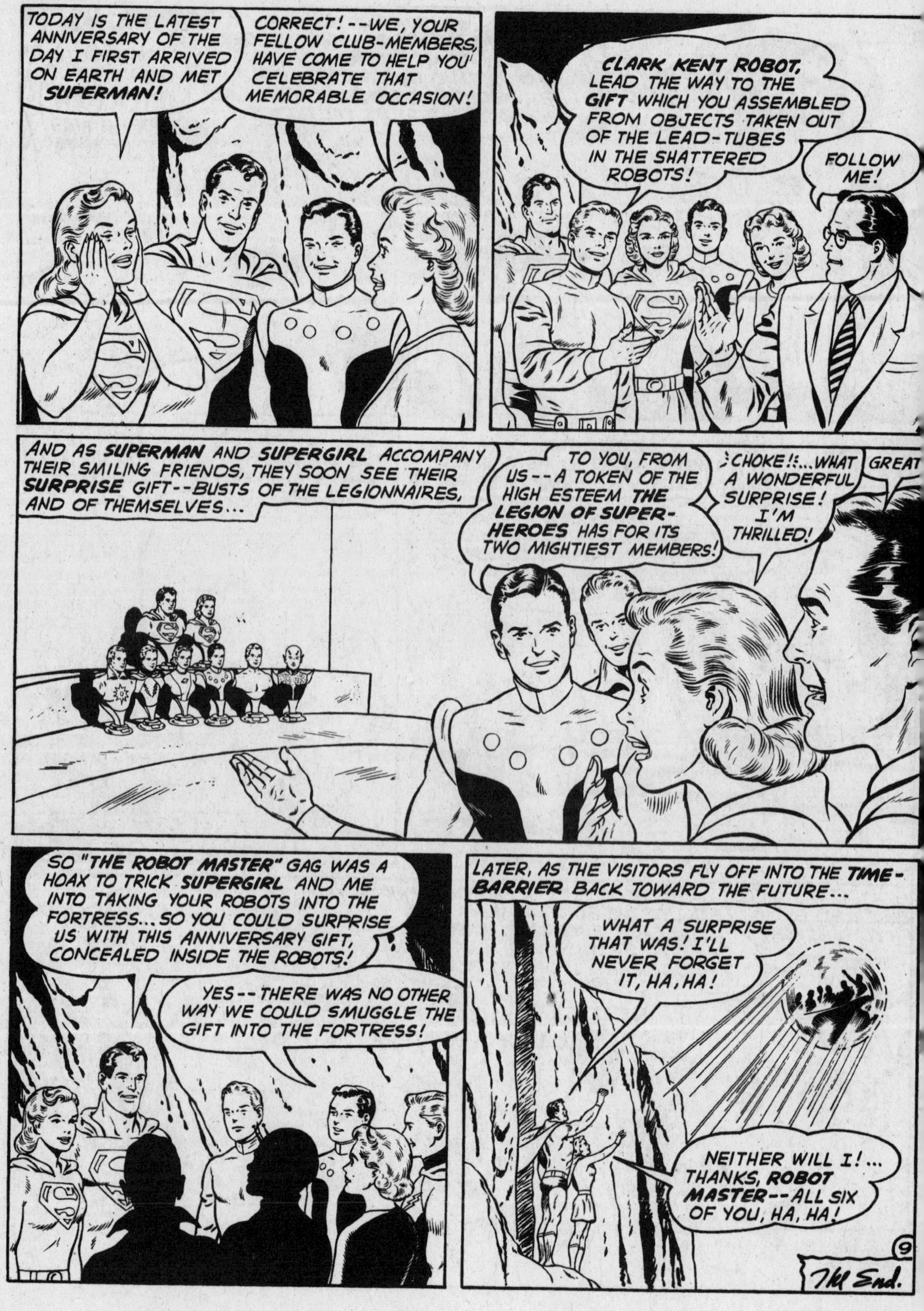
TODAY IS THE LATEST ANNIVERSARY OF THE DAY I FIRST ARRIVED ON EARTH AND MET SUPERMAN!
CORRECT! --WE, YOUR FELLOW CLUB-MEMBERS, HAVE COME TO HELP YOU CELEBRATE THAT MEMORABLE OCCASION!
CLARK KENT ROBOT, LEAD THE WAY TO THE GIFT WHICH YOU ASSEMBLED FROM OBJECTS TAKEN OUT OF THE LEAD-TUBES IN THE SHATTERED ROBOTS!
FOLLOW ME!
AND AS SUPERMAN AND SUPERGIRL ACCOMPANY THEIR SMILING FRIENDS, THEY SOON SEE THEIR SURPRISE GIFT--BUSTS OF THE LEGIONNAIRES, AND OF THEMSELVES...
TO YOU, FROM US--A TOKEN OF THE HIGH ESTEEM THE LEGION OF SUPER-HEROES HAS FOR ITS TWO MIGHTIEST MEMBERS!
CHOKE!...WHAT A WONDERFUL SURPRISE! I'M THRILLED!
GREAT
SO "THE ROBOT MASTER" GAG WAS A HOAX TO TRICK SUPERGIRL AND ME INTO TAKING YOUR ROBOTS INTO THE FORTRESS...SO YOU COULD SURPRISE US WITH THIS ANNIVERSARY GIFT, CONCEALED INSIDE THE ROBOTS!
YES--THERE WAS NO OTHER WAY WE COULD SMUGGLE THE GIFT INTO THE FORTRESS!
LATER, AS THE VISITORS FLY OFF INTO THE TIME-BARRIER BACK TOWARD THE FUTURE...
WHAT A SURPRISE THAT WAS! I'LL NEVER FORGET IT, HA, HA!
NEITHER WILL I!... THANKS, ROBOT MASTER--ALL SIX OF YOU, HA, HA!
9
The End.

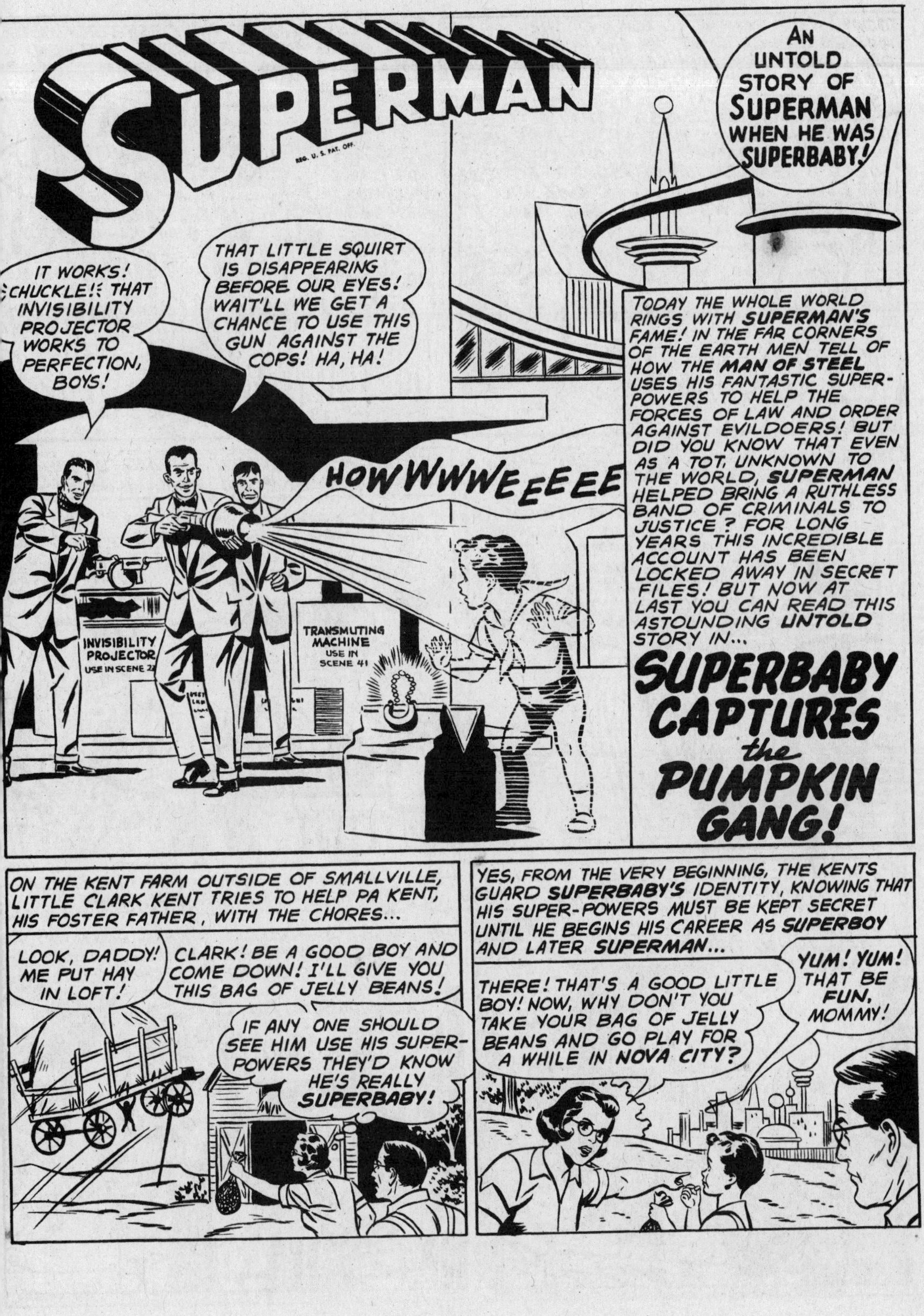
SUPERMAN
REG. U.S. PAT. OFF.
AN UNTOLD STORY OF SUPERMAN WHEN HE WAS SUPERBABY!
IT WORKS! CHUCKLE! THAT INVISIBILITY PROJECTOR WORKS TO PERFECTION, BOYS!
THAT LITTLE SQUIRT IS DISAPPEARING BEFORE OUR EYES! WAIT'LL WE GET A CHANCE TO USE THIS GUN AGAINST THE COPS! HA, HA!
HOWWWWEEEEE
INVISIBILITY PROJECTOR USE IN SCENE 22
TRANSMUTING MACHINE USE IN SCENE 41
TODAY THE WHOLE WORLD RINGS WITH SUPERMAN'S FAME! IN THE FAR CORNERS OF THE EARTH MEN TELL OF HOW THE MAN OF STEEL USES HIS FANTASTIC SUPER-POWERS TO HELP THE FORCES OF LAW AND ORDER AGAINST EVILDOERS! BUT DID YOU KNOW THAT EVEN AS A TOT, UNKNOWN TO THE WORLD, SUPERMAN HELPED BRING A RUTHLESS BAND OF CRIMINALS TO JUSTICE? FOR LONG YEARS THIS INCREDIBLE ACCOUNT HAS BEEN LOCKED AWAY IN SECRET FILES! BUT NOW AT LAST YOU CAN READ THIS ASTOUNDING UNTOLD STORY IN...
SUPERBABY CAPTURES the PUMPKIN GANG!
ON THE KENT FARM OUTSIDE OF SMALLVILLE, LITTLE CLARK KENT TRIES TO HELP PA KENT, HIS FOSTER FATHER, WITH THE CHORES...
LOOK, DADDY! ME PUT HAY IN LOFT!
CLARK! BE A GOOD BOY AND COME DOWN! I'LL GIVE YOU THIS BAG OF JELLY BEANS!
IF ANY ONE SHOULD SEE HIM USE HIS SUPER-POWERS THEY'D KNOW HE'S REALLY SUPERBABY!
YES, FROM THE VERY BEGINNING, THE KENTS GUARD SUPERBABY'S IDENTITY, KNOWING THAT HIS SUPER-POWERS MUST BE KEPT SECRET UNTIL HE BEGINS HIS CAREER AS SUPERBOY AND LATER SUPERMAN...
THERE! THAT'S A GOOD LITTLE BOY! NOW, WHY DON'T YOU TAKE YOUR BAG OF JELLY BEANS AND GO PLAY FOR A WHILE IN NOVA CITY?
YUM! YUM! THAT BE FUN, MOMMY!

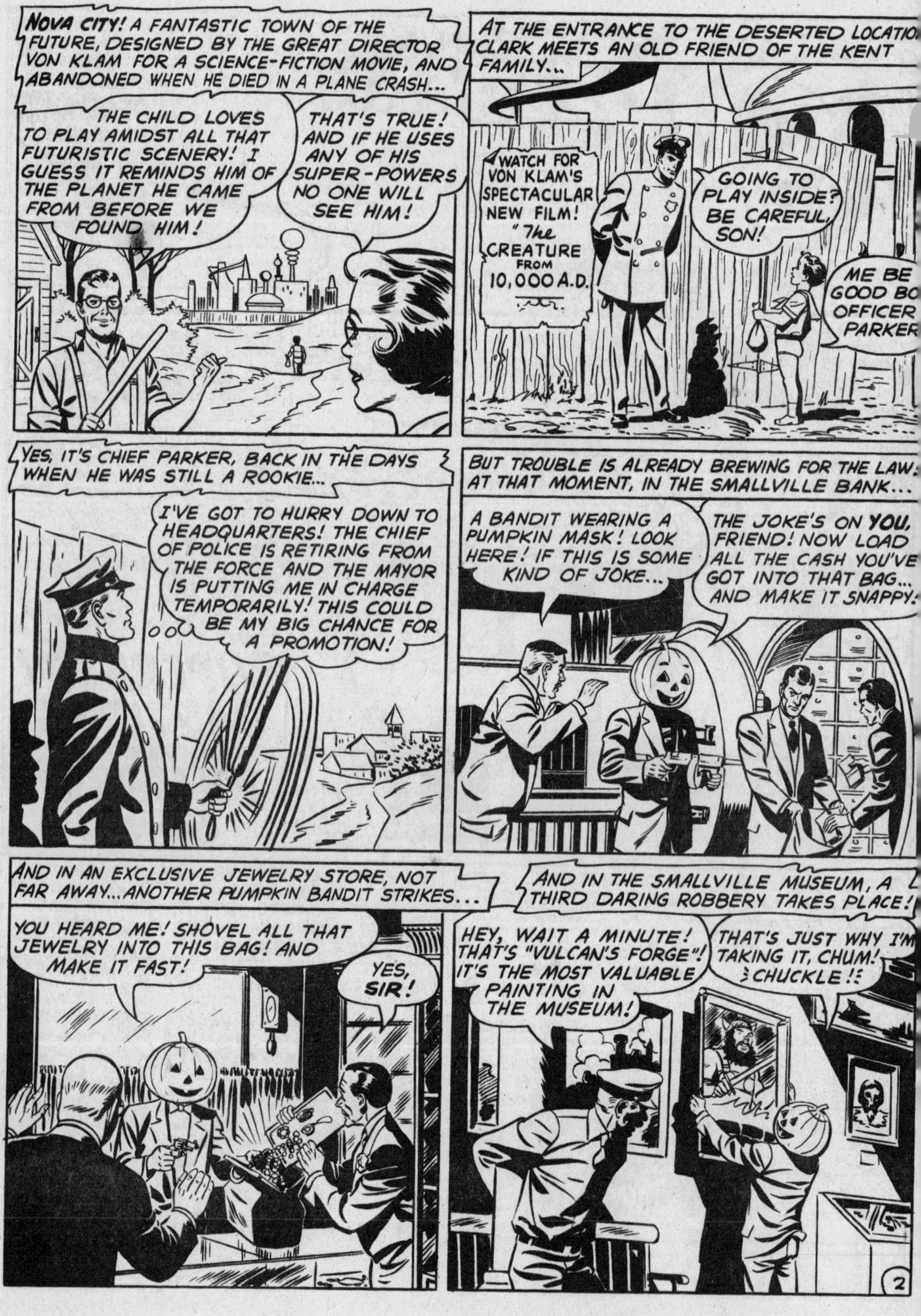
NOVA CITY! A FANTASTIC TOWN OF THE FUTURE, DESIGNED BY THE GREAT DIRECTOR VON KLAM FOR A SCIENCE-FICTION MOVIE, AND ABANDONED WHEN HE DIED IN A PLANE CRASH...
THE CHILD LOVES TO PLAY AMIDST ALL THAT FUTURISTIC SCENERY! I GUESS IT REMINDS HIM OF THE PLANET HE CAME FROM BEFORE WE FOUND HIM!
THAT'S TRUE! AND IF HE USES ANY OF HIS SUPER-POWERS NO ONE WILL SEE HIM!
AT THE ENTRANCE TO THE DESERTED LOCATIO CLARK MEETS AN OLD FRIEND OF THE KENT FAMILY...
WATCH FOR VON KLAM'S SPECTACULAR NEW FILM! "The CREATURE FROM 10,000 A.D.
GOING TO PLAY INSIDE? BE CAREFUL, SON!
ME BE GOOD BO OFFICER PARKER
YES, IT'S CHIEF PARKER, BACK IN THE DAYS WHEN HE WAS STILL A ROOKIE...
I'VE GOT TO HURRY DOWN TO HEADQUARTERS! THE CHIEF OF POLICE IS RETIRING FROM THE FORCE AND THE MAYOR IS PUTTING ME IN CHARGE TEMPORARILY! THIS COULD BE MY BIG CHANCE FOR A PROMOTION!
BUT TROUBLE IS ALREADY BREWING FOR THE LAW: AT THAT MOMENT, IN THE SMALLVILLE BANK...
A BANDIT WEARING A PUMPKIN MASK! LOOK HERE! IF THIS IS SOME KIND OF JOKE...
THE JOKE'S ON YOU, FRIEND! NOW LOAD ALL THE CASH YOU'VE GOT INTO THAT BAG... AND MAKE IT SNAPPY!
AND IN AN EXCLUSIVE JEWELRY STORE, NOT FAR AWAY...ANOTHER PUMPKIN BANDIT STRIKES...
YOU HEARD ME! SHOVEL ALL THAT JEWELRY INTO THIS BAG! AND MAKE IT FAST!
YES, SIR!
AND IN THE SMALLVILLE MUSEUM, A THIRD DARING ROBBERY TAKES PLACE!
HEY, WAIT A MINUTE! THAT'S "VULCAN'S FORGE"! IT'S THE MOST VALUABLE PAINTING IN THE MUSEUM!
THAT'S JUST WHY I'M TAKING IT, CHUM! CHUCKLE!
2

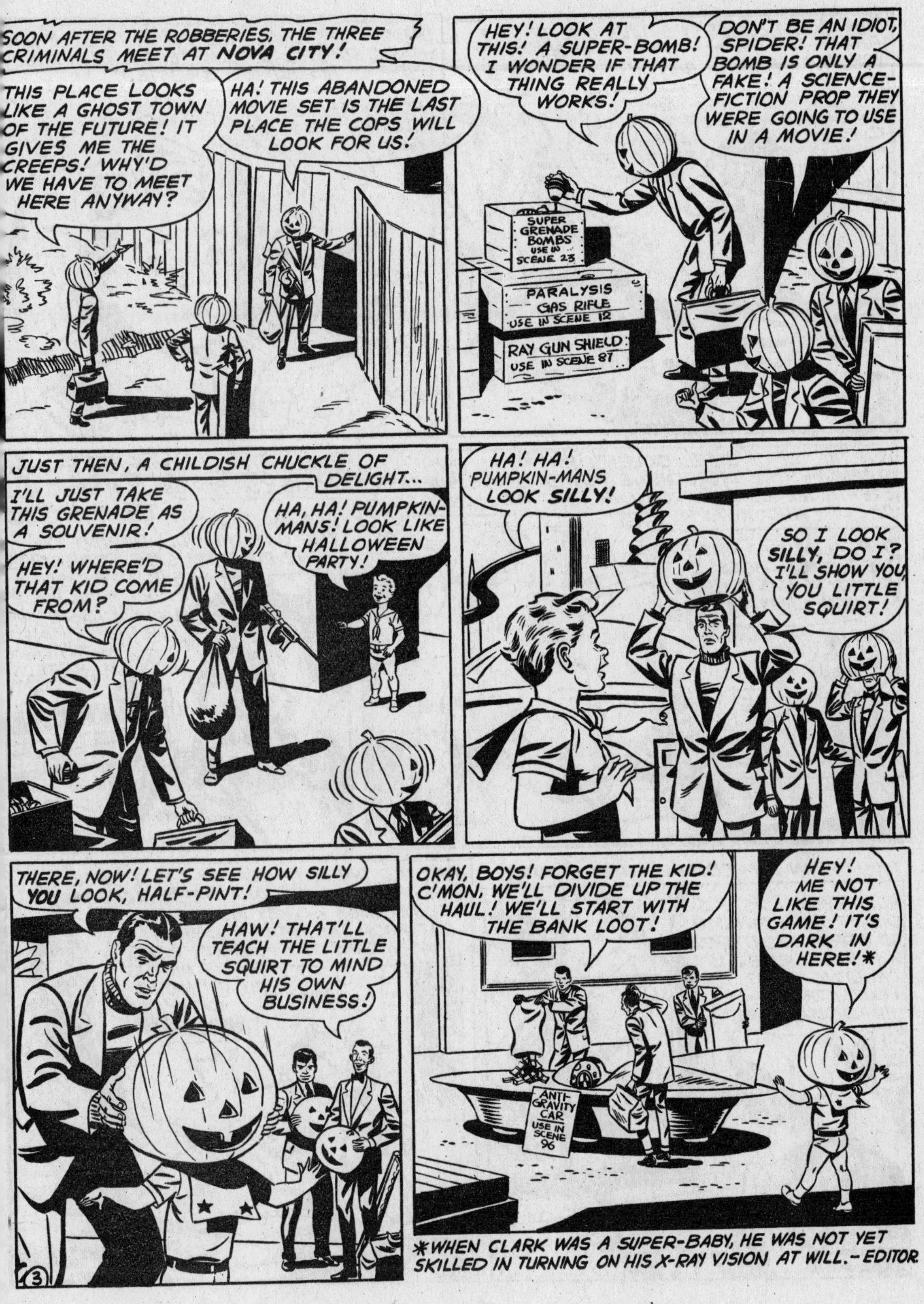
SOON AFTER THE ROBBERIES, THE THREE CRIMINALS MEET AT NOVA CITY!
THIS PLACE LOOKS LIKE A GHOST TOWN OF THE FUTURE! IT GIVES ME THE CREEPS! WHY'D WE HAVE TO MEET HERE ANYWAY?
HA! THIS ABANDONED MOVIE SET IS THE LAST PLACE THE COPS WILL LOOK FOR US!
HEY! LOOK AT THIS! A SUPER-BOMB! I WONDER IF THAT THING REALLY WORKS!
DON'T BE AN IDIOT, SPIDER! THAT BOMB IS ONLY A FAKE! A SCIENCE-FICTION PROP THEY WERE GOING TO USE IN A MOVIE!
SUPER GRENADE BOMBS USE IN SCENE 23
PARALYSIS GAS RIFLE USE IN SCENE 12
RAY GUN SHIELD USE IN SCENE 87
JUST THEN, A CHILDISH CHUCKLE OF DELIGHT...
I'LL JUST TAKE THIS GRENADE AS A SOUVENIR!
HEY! WHERE'D THAT KID COME FROM?
HA, HA! PUMPKIN-MANS! LOOK LIKE HALLOWEEN PARTY!
HA! HA! PUMPKIN-MANS LOOK SILLY!
SO I LOOK SILLY, DO I? I'LL SHOW YOU, YOU LITTLE SQUIRT!
THERE, NOW! LET'S SEE HOW SILLY YOU LOOK, HALF-PINT!
HAW! THAT'LL TEACH THE LITTLE SQUIRT TO MIND HIS OWN BUSINESS!
3
OKAY, BOYS! FORGET THE KID! C'MON, WE'LL DIVIDE UP THE HAUL! WE'LL START WITH THE BANK LOOT!
HEY! ME NOT LIKE THIS GAME! IT'S DARK IN HERE!*
ANTI-GRAVITY CAR USE IN SCENE 96
*WHEN CLARK WAS A SUPER-BABY, HE WAS NOT YET SKILLED IN TURNING ON HIS X-RAY VISION AT WILL.-EDITOR

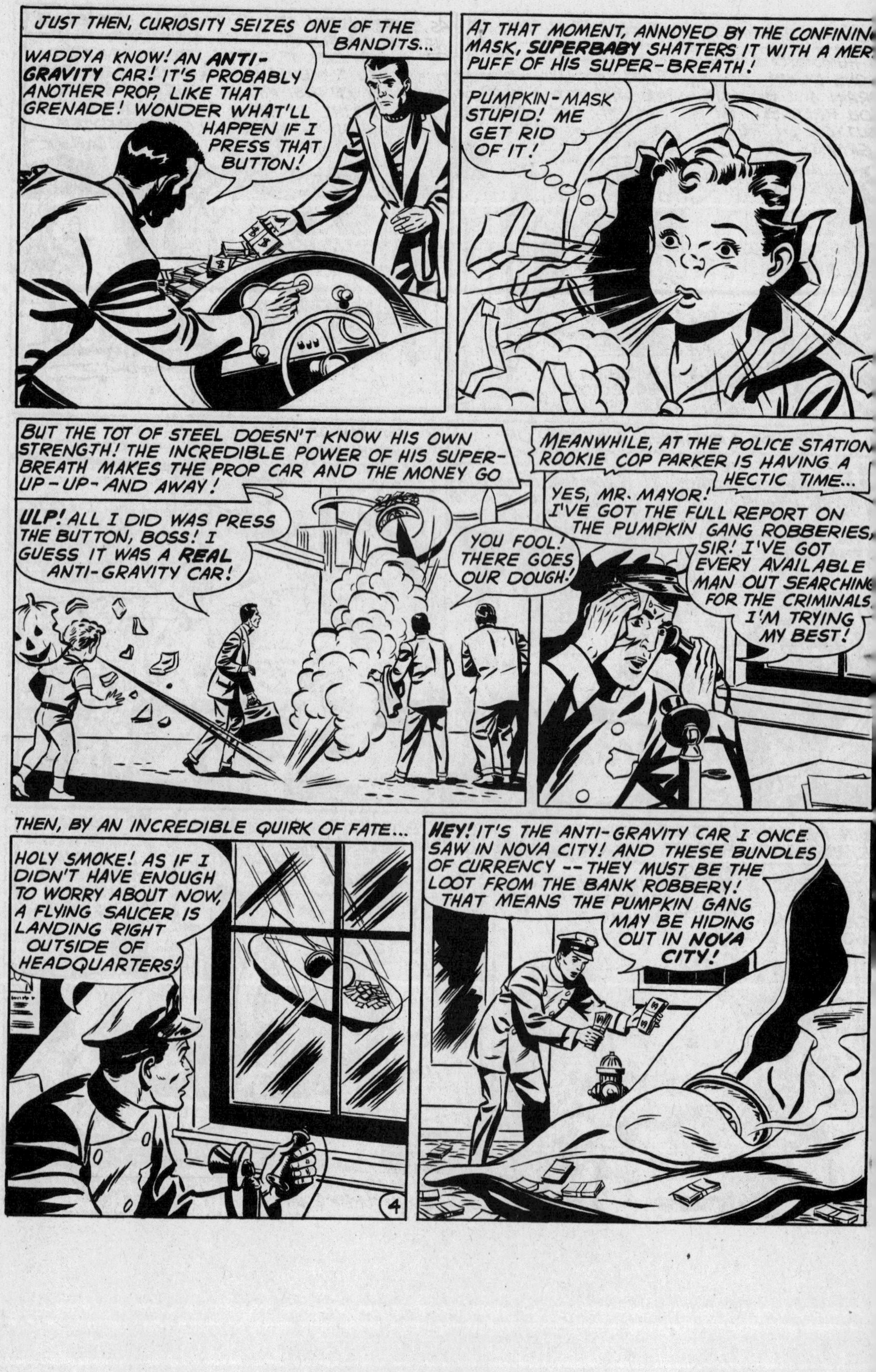
JUST THEN, CURIOSITY SEIZES ONE OF THE BANDITS...
WADDYA KNOW! AN ANTI-GRAVITY CAR! IT'S PROBABLY ANOTHER PROP, LIKE THAT GRENADE! WONDER WHAT'LL HAPPEN IF I PRESS THAT BUTTON!
AT THAT MOMENT, ANNOYED BY THE CONFINING MASK, SUPERBABY SHATTERS IT WITH A MERE PUFF OF HIS SUPER-BREATH!
PUMPKIN-MASK STUPID! ME GET RID OF IT!
BUT THE TOT OF STEEL DOESN'T KNOW HIS OWN STRENGTH! THE INCREDIBLE POWER OF HIS SUPER-BREATH MAKES THE PROP CAR AND THE MONEY GO UP-UP-AND AWAY!
ULP! ALL I DID WAS PRESS THE BUTTON, BOSS! I GUESS IT WAS A REAL ANTI-GRAVITY CAR!
YOU FOOL! THERE GOES OUR DOUGH!
MEANWHILE, AT THE POLICE STATION, ROOKIE COP PARKER IS HAVING A HECTIC TIME...
YES, MR. MAYOR! I'VE GOT THE FULL REPORT ON THE PUMPKIN GANG ROBBERIES, SIR! I'VE GOT EVERY AVAILABLE MAN OUT SEARCHING FOR THE CRIMINALS. I'M TRYING MY BEST!
THEN, BY AN INCREDIBLE QUIRK OF FATE...
HOLY SMOKE! AS IF I DIDN'T HAVE ENOUGH TO WORRY ABOUT NOW, A FLYING SAUCER IS LANDING RIGHT OUTSIDE OF HEADQUARTERS!
4
HEY! IT'S THE ANTI-GRAVITY CAR I ONCE SAW IN NOVA CITY! AND THESE BUNDLES OF CURRENCY -- THEY MUST BE THE LOOT FROM THE BANK ROBBERY! THAT MEANS THE PUMPKIN GANG MAY BE HIDING OUT IN NOVA CITY!

MEANWHILE, BACK IN *NOVA CITY*...

A HUNDRED GRAND GONE DOWN THE DRAIN ALL BECAUSE YOU PRESSED THE BUTTON ON THE ANTI-GRAVITY CAR!

KEEP YOUR SHIRT ON, KRIMP! IF SOME OF THE OTHER GADGETS AROUND HERE WORK AS WELL AS THAT GRAVITY CAR, THAT HUNDRED GRAND WILL BE PEANUTS TO US!

RAY

INVISIBILITY PROJECTOR USE IN SCENE 34

AS *SUPERBABY* TOYS WITH SOME GLITTERING NEW PLAYTHINGS...

THIS GUN...IT'S SUPPOSED TO SHOOT AN INVISIBILITY RAY! I'D LIKE TO TRY IT ON SOMETHING AND SEE IF IT WORKS!

TRY IT ON THAT LITTLE HALF-PINT, SPIDER! MAYBE THAT'LL TEACH HIM NOT TO MEDDLE WITH OUR JEWELS!

THE TOUCH OF A FINGER TO A BUTTON, AND...

HOWWWEEEE!

WOW! WHAT A RACKET!

WAH!

ANY TOT CAN BE STARTLED AT A SUDDEN NOISE, BUT *SUPERBABY* IS *SUPER-STARTLED* AND REACTS AT SUCH *SUPER-SPEED*, HE BECOMES INVISIBLE!

WAHHHH! ME SCARED!

HOWWWEEEE!

BUT THE BANDITS HAVE THEIR OWN EXPLANATION FOR THE PHENOMENON!

IT WORKED! THAT INVISIBLE RAY GADGET REALLY WORKED, BOSS!

THE KID DISAPPEARED RIGHT BEFORE OUR VERY EYES!

5

NEXT MOMENT...

BOSS, THE PRODUCER WHO INVENTED ALL THESE GADGETS MUST HAVE BEEN SMARTER THAN EDISON AND EINSTEIN PUT TOGETHER!

YOU SAID IT, SPIDER! NOW, LET'S TRY THIS WEATHER MACHINE! IF THIS THING WORKS LIKE ALL THE OTHER PROPS, WE COULD STOP THE POLICE COLD BY STARTING A BLIZZARD OR HURRICANE EVERY TIME THEY CHASE US!

WEATHER CONTROL MACHINE

RAIN
SLEET
COLD
HEAT
FOG
WIND

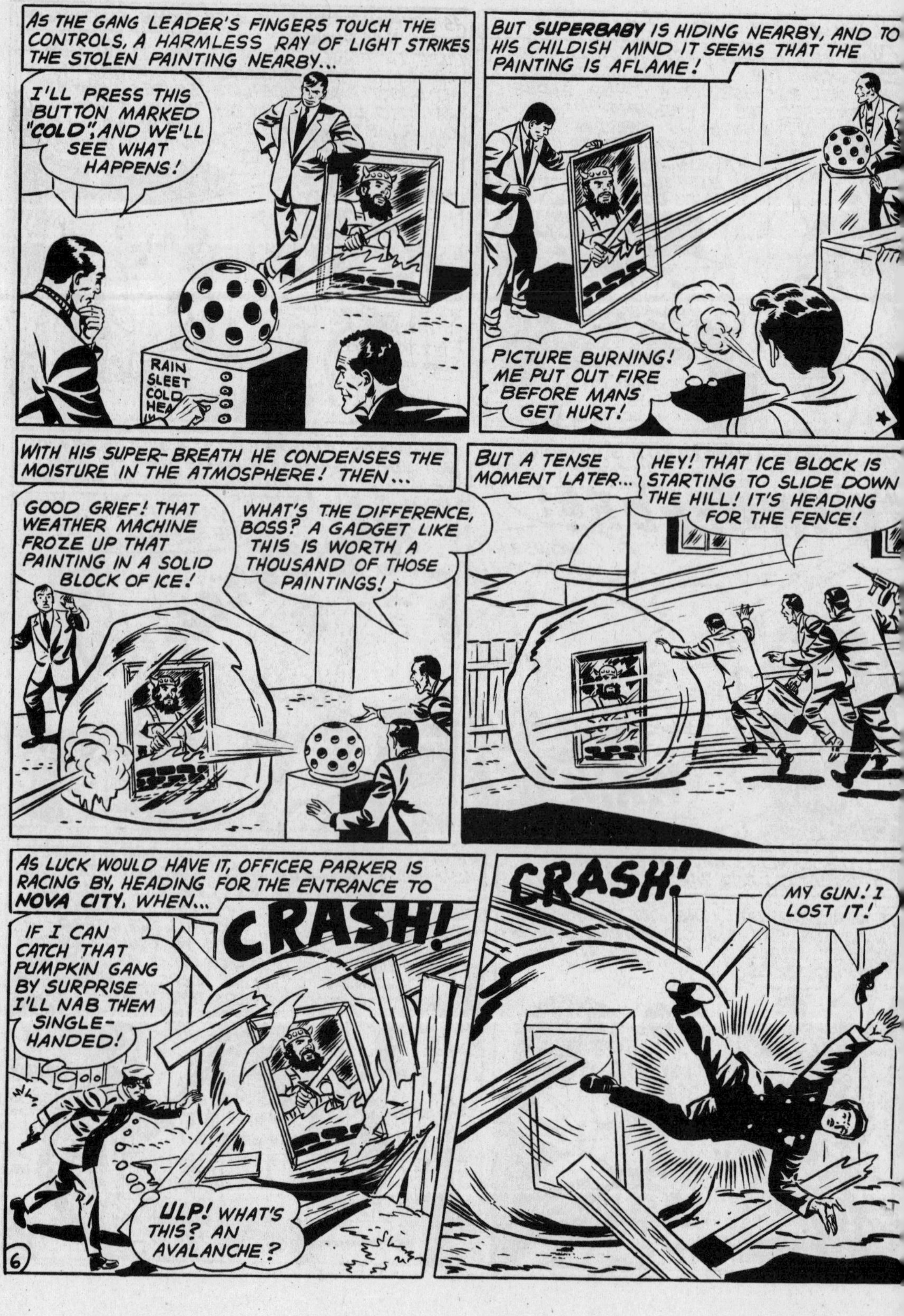
AS THE GANG LEADER'S FINGERS TOUCH THE CONTROLS, A HARMLESS RAY OF LIGHT STRIKES THE STOLEN PAINTING NEARBY...
I'LL PRESS THIS BUTTON MARKED "COLD", AND WE'LL SEE WHAT HAPPENS!
RAIN
SLEET
COLD
BUT SUPERBABY IS HIDING NEARBY, AND TO HIS CHILDISH MIND IT SEEMS THAT THE PAINTING IS AFLAME!
PICTURE BURNING! ME PUT OUT FIRE BEFORE MANS GET HURT!
WITH HIS SUPER-BREATH HE CONDENSES THE MOISTURE IN THE ATMOSPHERE! THEN...
GOOD GRIEF! THAT WEATHER MACHINE FROZE UP THAT PAINTING IN A SOLID BLOCK OF ICE!
WHAT'S THE DIFFERENCE, BOSS? A GADGET LIKE THIS IS WORTH A THOUSAND OF THOSE PAINTINGS!
BUT A TENSE MOMENT LATER...
HEY! THAT ICE BLOCK IS STARTING TO SLIDE DOWN THE HILL! IT'S HEADING FOR THE FENCE!
AS LUCK WOULD HAVE IT, OFFICER PARKER IS RACING BY, HEADING FOR THE ENTRANCE TO NOVA CITY, WHEN...
IF I CAN CATCH THAT PUMPKIN GANG BY SURPRISE I'LL NAB THEM SINGLE-HANDED!
CRASH!
ULP! WHAT'S THIS? AN AVALANCHE?
6
CRASH!
MY GUN! I LOST IT!

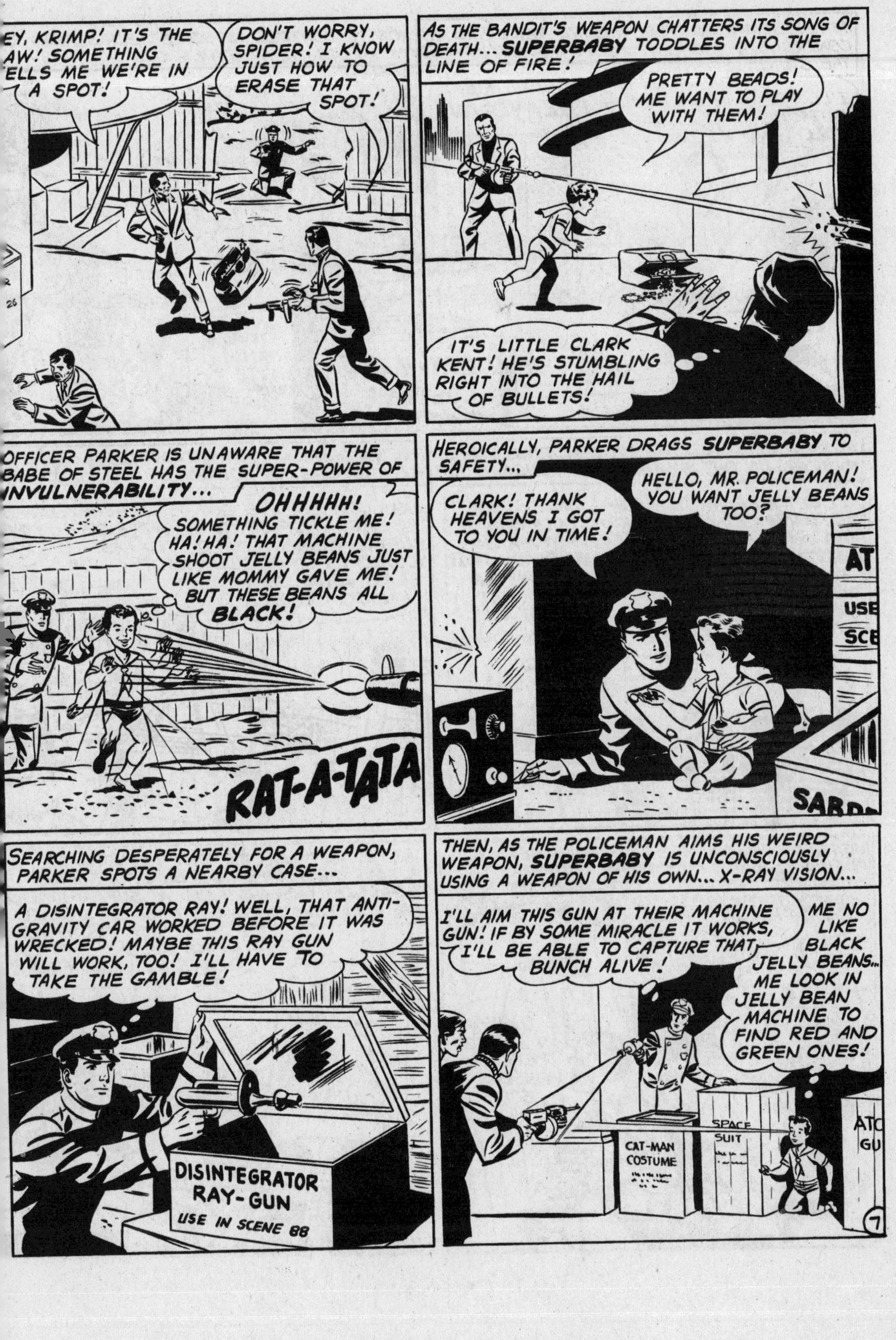
EY, KRIMP! IT'S THE AW! SOMETHING ELLS ME WE'RE IN A SPOT!
DON'T WORRY, SPIDER! I KNOW JUST HOW TO ERASE THAT SPOT!
AS THE BANDIT'S WEAPON CHATTERS ITS SONG OF DEATH... SUPERBABY TODDLES INTO THE LINE OF FIRE!
PRETTY BEADS! ME WANT TO PLAY WITH THEM!
IT'S LITTLE CLARK KENT! HE'S STUMBLING RIGHT INTO THE HAIL OF BULLETS!
OFFICER PARKER IS UNAWARE THAT THE BABE OF STEEL HAS THE SUPER-POWER OF INVULNERABILITY...
OHHHHH! SOMETHING TICKLE ME! HA! HA! THAT MACHINE SHOOT JELLY BEANS JUST LIKE MOMMY GAVE ME! BUT THESE BEANS ALL BLACK!
RAT-A-TATA
HEROICALLY, PARKER DRAGS SUPERBABY TO SAFETY...
CLARK! THANK HEAVENS I GOT TO YOU IN TIME!
HELLO, MR. POLICEMAN! YOU WANT JELLY BEANS TOO?
SEARCHING DESPERATELY FOR A WEAPON, PARKER SPOTS A NEARBY CASE...
A DISINTEGRATOR RAY! WELL, THAT ANTI-GRAVITY CAR WORKED BEFORE IT WAS WRECKED! MAYBE THIS RAY GUN WILL WORK, TOO! I'LL HAVE TO TAKE THE GAMBLE!
DISINTEGRATOR RAY-GUN
USE IN SCENE 88
THEN, AS THE POLICEMAN AIMS HIS WEIRD WEAPON, SUPERBABY IS UNCONSCIOUSLY USING A WEAPON OF HIS OWN... X-RAY VISION...
I'LL AIM THIS GUN AT THEIR MACHINE GUN! IF BY SOME MIRACLE IT WORKS, I'LL BE ABLE TO CAPTURE THAT BUNCH ALIVE!
ME NO LIKE BLACK JELLY BEANS... ME LOOK IN JELLY BEAN MACHINE TO FIND RED AND GREEN ONES!
CAT-MAN COSTUME
SPACE SUIT
7

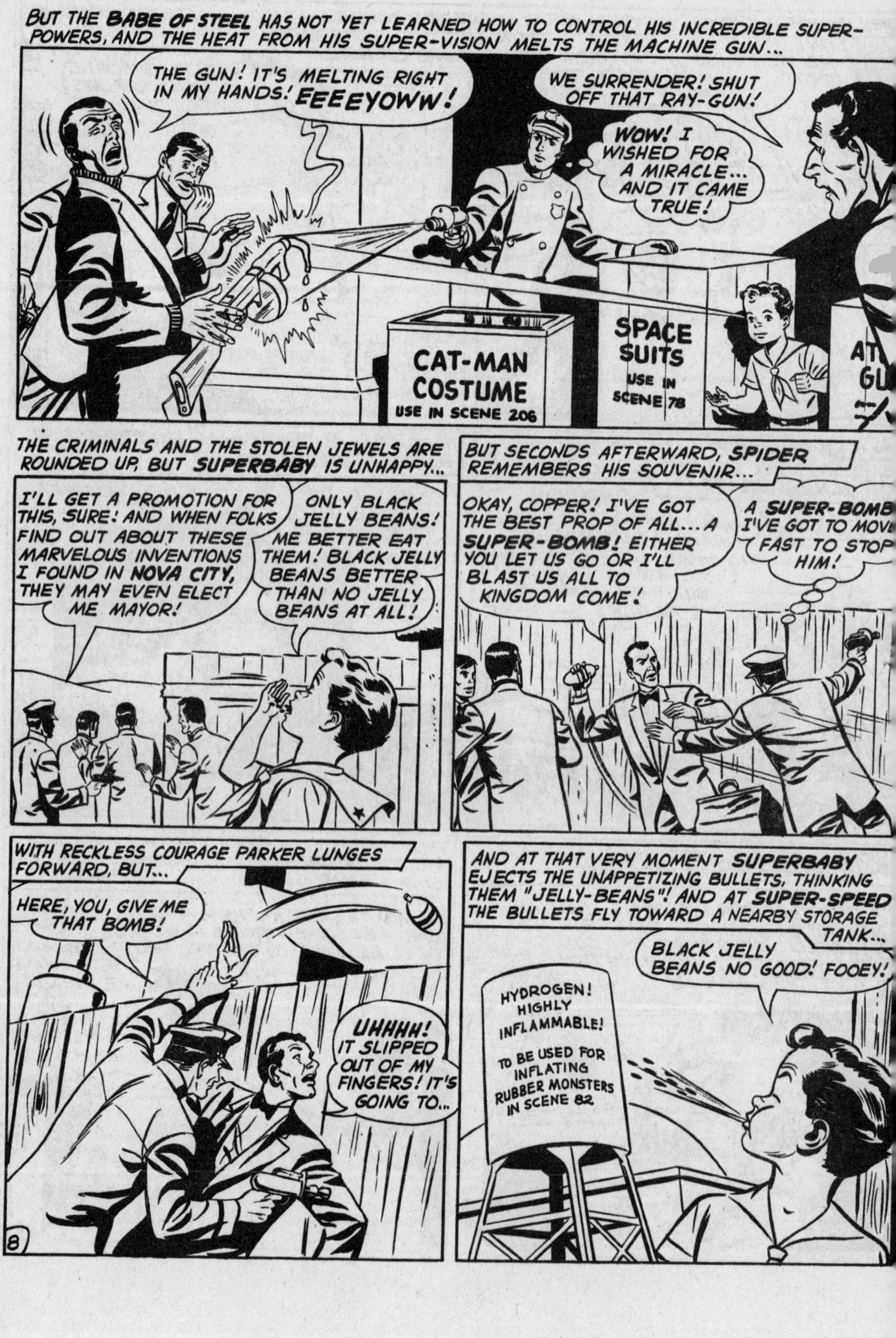
BUT THE BABE OF STEEL HAS NOT YET LEARNED HOW TO CONTROL HIS INCREDIBLE SUPER-POWERS, AND THE HEAT FROM HIS SUPER-VISION MELTS THE MACHINE GUN...
THE GUN! IT'S MELTING RIGHT IN MY HANDS! EEEEYOWW!
WE SURRENDER! SHUT OFF THAT RAY-GUN!
WOW! I WISHED FOR A MIRACLE... AND IT CAME TRUE!
CAT-MAN COSTUME USE IN SCENE 206
SPACE SUITS USE IN SCENE 78
THE CRIMINALS AND THE STOLEN JEWELS ARE ROUNDED UP, BUT SUPERBABY IS UNHAPPY...
I'LL GET A PROMOTION FOR THIS, SURE! AND WHEN FOLKS FIND OUT ABOUT THESE MARVELOUS INVENTIONS I FOUND IN NOVA CITY, THEY MAY EVEN ELECT ME MAYOR!
ONLY BLACK JELLY BEANS! ME BETTER EAT THEM! BLACK JELLY BEANS BETTER THAN NO JELLY BEANS AT ALL!
BUT SECONDS AFTERWARD, SPIDER REMEMBERS HIS SOUVENIR...
OKAY, COPPER! I'VE GOT THE BEST PROP OF ALL... A SUPER-BOMB! EITHER YOU LET US GO OR I'LL BLAST US ALL TO KINGDOM COME!
A SUPER-BOMB I'VE GOT TO MOVE FAST TO STOP HIM!
WITH RECKLESS COURAGE PARKER LUNGES FORWARD, BUT...
HERE, YOU, GIVE ME THAT BOMB!
UHHHH! IT SLIPPED OUT OF MY FINGERS! IT'S GOING TO...
AND AT THAT VERY MOMENT SUPERBABY EJECTS THE UNAPPETIZING BULLETS, THINKING THEM "JELLY-BEANS"! AND AT SUPER-SPEED THE BULLETS FLY TOWARD A NEARBY STORAGE TANK...
BLACK JELLY BEANS NO GOOD! FOOEY!
HYDROGEN! HIGHLY INFLAMMABLE! TO BE USED FOR INFLATING RUBBER MONSTERS IN SCENE 82
8

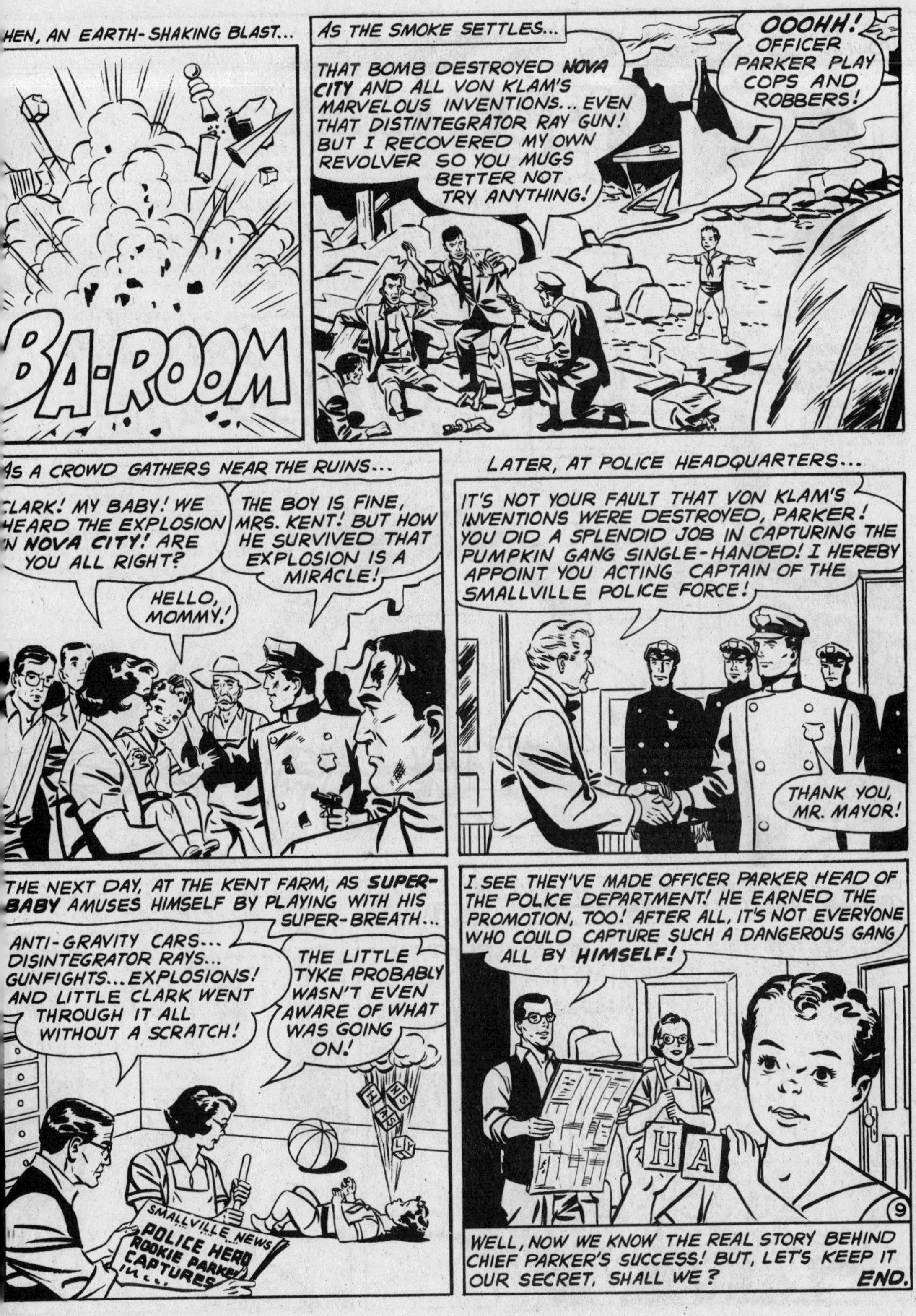
HEN, AN EARTH-SHAKING BLAST...
BA-ROOM
AS THE SMOKE SETTLES...
THAT BOMB DESTROYED NOVA CITY AND ALL VON KLAM'S MARVELOUS INVENTIONS... EVEN THAT DISTINTEGRATOR RAY GUN! BUT I RECOVERED MY OWN REVOLVER SO YOU MUGS BETTER NOT TRY ANYTHING!
OOOHH! OFFICER PARKER PLAY COPS AND ROBBERS!
AS A CROWD GATHERS NEAR THE RUINS...
CLARK! MY BABY! WE HEARD THE EXPLOSION IN NOVA CITY! ARE YOU ALL RIGHT?
THE BOY IS FINE, MRS. KENT! BUT HOW HE SURVIVED THAT EXPLOSION IS A MIRACLE!
HELLO, MOMMY!
LATER, AT POLICE HEADQUARTERS...
IT'S NOT YOUR FAULT THAT VON KLAM'S INVENTIONS WERE DESTROYED, PARKER! YOU DID A SPLENDID JOB IN CAPTURING THE PUMPKIN GANG SINGLE-HANDED! I HEREBY APPOINT YOU ACTING CAPTAIN OF THE SMALLVILLE POLICE FORCE!
THANK YOU, MR. MAYOR!
THE NEXT DAY, AT THE KENT FARM, AS SUPER-BABY AMUSES HIMSELF BY PLAYING WITH HIS SUPER-BREATH...
ANTI-GRAVITY CARS... DISINTEGRATOR RAYS... GUNFIGHTS...EXPLOSIONS! AND LITTLE CLARK WENT THROUGH IT ALL WITHOUT A SCRATCH!
THE LITTLE TYKE PROBABLY WASN'T EVEN AWARE OF WHAT WAS GOING ON!
SMALLVILLE NEWS
POLICE HERO ROOKIE PARKER CAPTURES
I SEE THEY'VE MADE OFFICER PARKER HEAD OF THE POLICE DEPARTMENT! HE EARNED THE PROMOTION, TOO! AFTER ALL, IT'S NOT EVERYONE WHO COULD CAPTURE SUCH A DANGEROUS GANG ALL BY HIMSELF!
HA
9
WELL, NOW WE KNOW THE REAL STORY BEHIND CHIEF PARKER'S SUCCESS! BUT, LET'S KEEP IT OUR SECRET, SHALL WE?
END.

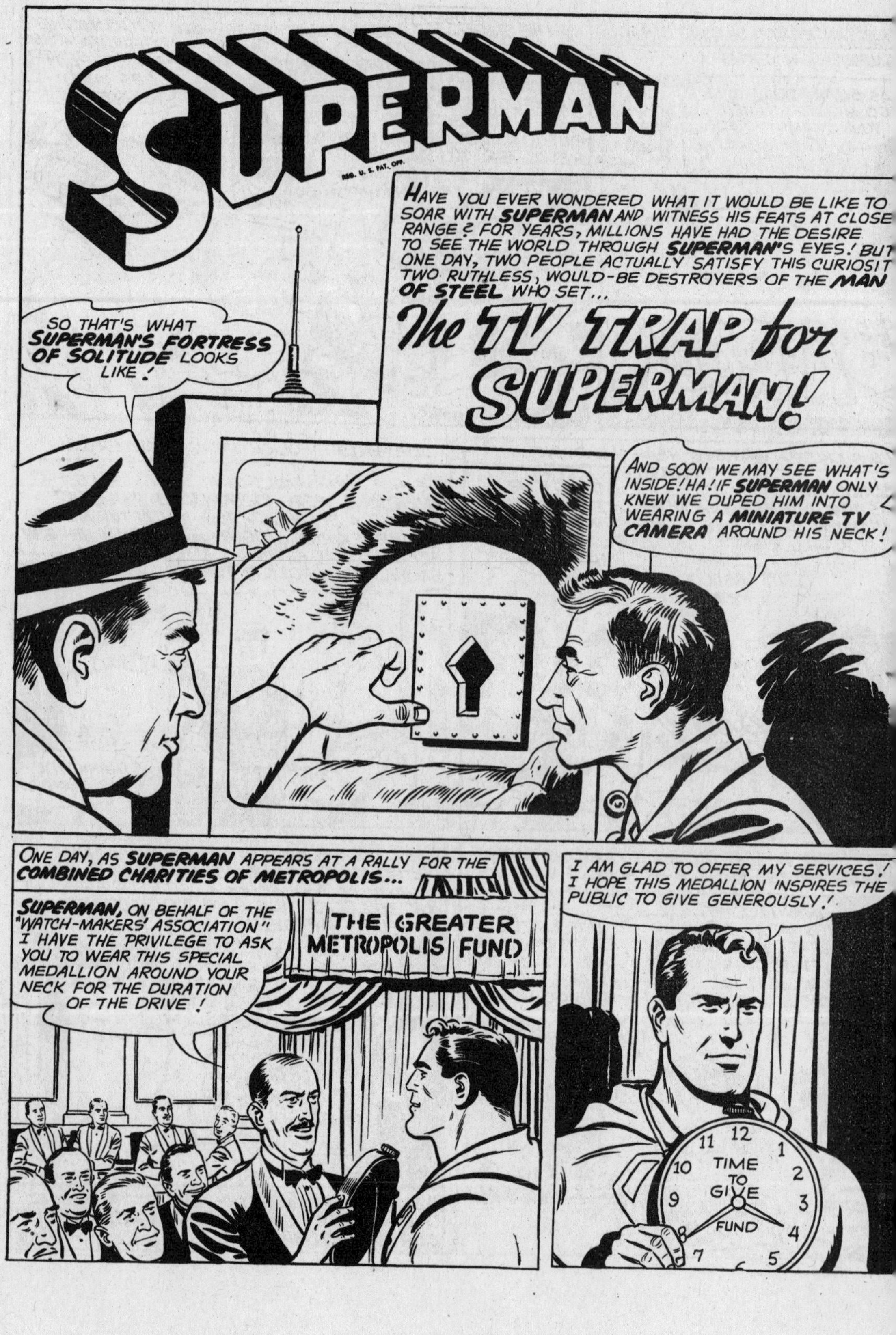
SUPERMAN
REG. U. S. PAT. OFF.
HAVE YOU EVER WONDERED WHAT IT WOULD BE LIKE TO SOAR WITH SUPERMAN AND WITNESS HIS FEATS AT CLOSE RANGE? FOR YEARS, MILLIONS HAVE HAD THE DESIRE TO SEE THE WORLD THROUGH SUPERMAN'S EYES! BUT ONE DAY, TWO PEOPLE ACTUALLY SATISFY THIS CURIOSIT TWO RUTHLESS, WOULD-BE DESTROYERS OF THE MAN OF STEEL WHO SET...
The TV TRAP for SUPERMAN!
SO THAT'S WHAT SUPERMAN'S FORTRESS OF SOLITUDE LOOKS LIKE!
AND SOON WE MAY SEE WHAT'S INSIDE! HA! IF SUPERMAN ONLY KNEW WE DUPED HIM INTO WEARING A MINIATURE TV CAMERA AROUND HIS NECK!
ONE DAY, AS SUPERMAN APPEARS AT A RALLY FOR THE COMBINED CHARITIES OF METROPOLIS...
THE GREATER METROPOLIS FUND
SUPERMAN, ON BEHALF OF THE "WATCH-MAKERS' ASSOCIATION" I HAVE THE PRIVILEGE TO ASK YOU TO WEAR THIS SPECIAL MEDALLION AROUND YOUR NECK FOR THE DURATION OF THE DRIVE!
I AM GLAD TO OFFER MY SERVICES! I HOPE THIS MEDALLION INSPIRES THE PUBLIC TO GIVE GENEROUSLY!
TIME TO GIVE FUND

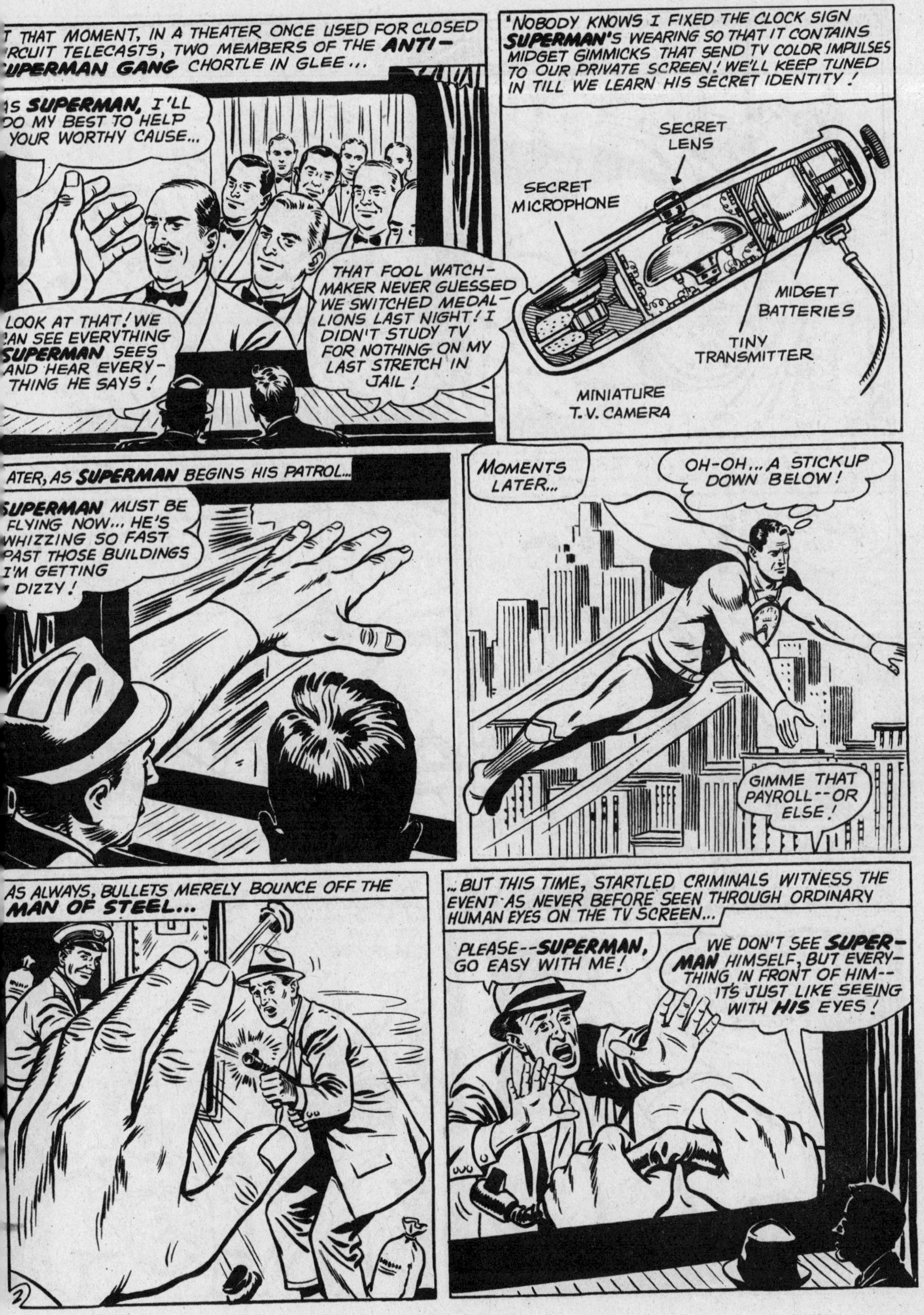
T THAT MOMENT, IN A THEATER ONCE USED FOR CLOSED IRCUIT TELECASTS, TWO MEMBERS OF THE ANTI-SUPERMAN GANG CHORTLE IN GLEE...
AS SUPERMAN, I'LL DO MY BEST TO HELP YOUR WORTHY CAUSE...
LOOK AT THAT! WE CAN SEE EVERYTHING SUPERMAN SEES AND HEAR EVERYTHING HE SAYS!
THAT FOOL WATCHMAKER NEVER GUESSED WE SWITCHED MEDALLIONS LAST NIGHT! I DIDN'T STUDY TV FOR NOTHING ON MY LAST STRETCH IN JAIL!
"NOBODY KNOWS I FIXED THE CLOCK SIGN SUPERMAN'S WEARING SO THAT IT CONTAINS MIDGET GIMMICKS THAT SEND TV COLOR IMPULSES TO OUR PRIVATE SCREEN! WE'LL KEEP TUNED IN TILL WE LEARN HIS SECRET IDENTITY!
SECRET LENS
SECRET MICROPHONE
MIDGET BATTERIES
TINY TRANSMITTER
MINIATURE T.V. CAMERA
ATER, AS SUPERMAN BEGINS HIS PATROL...
SUPERMAN MUST BE FLYING NOW... HE'S WHIZZING SO FAST PAST THOSE BUILDINGS I'M GETTING DIZZY!
MOMENTS LATER...
OH-OH... A STICKUP DOWN BELOW!
GIMME THAT PAYROLL--OR ELSE!
AS ALWAYS, BULLETS MERELY BOUNCE OFF THE MAN OF STEEL...
...BUT THIS TIME, STARTLED CRIMINALS WITNESS THE EVENT AS NEVER BEFORE SEEN THROUGH ORDINARY HUMAN EYES ON THE TV SCREEN...
PLEASE--SUPERMAN, GO EASY WITH ME!
WE DON'T SEE SUPERMAN HIMSELF, BUT EVERYTHING IN FRONT OF HIM--IT'S JUST LIKE SEEING WITH HIS EYES!

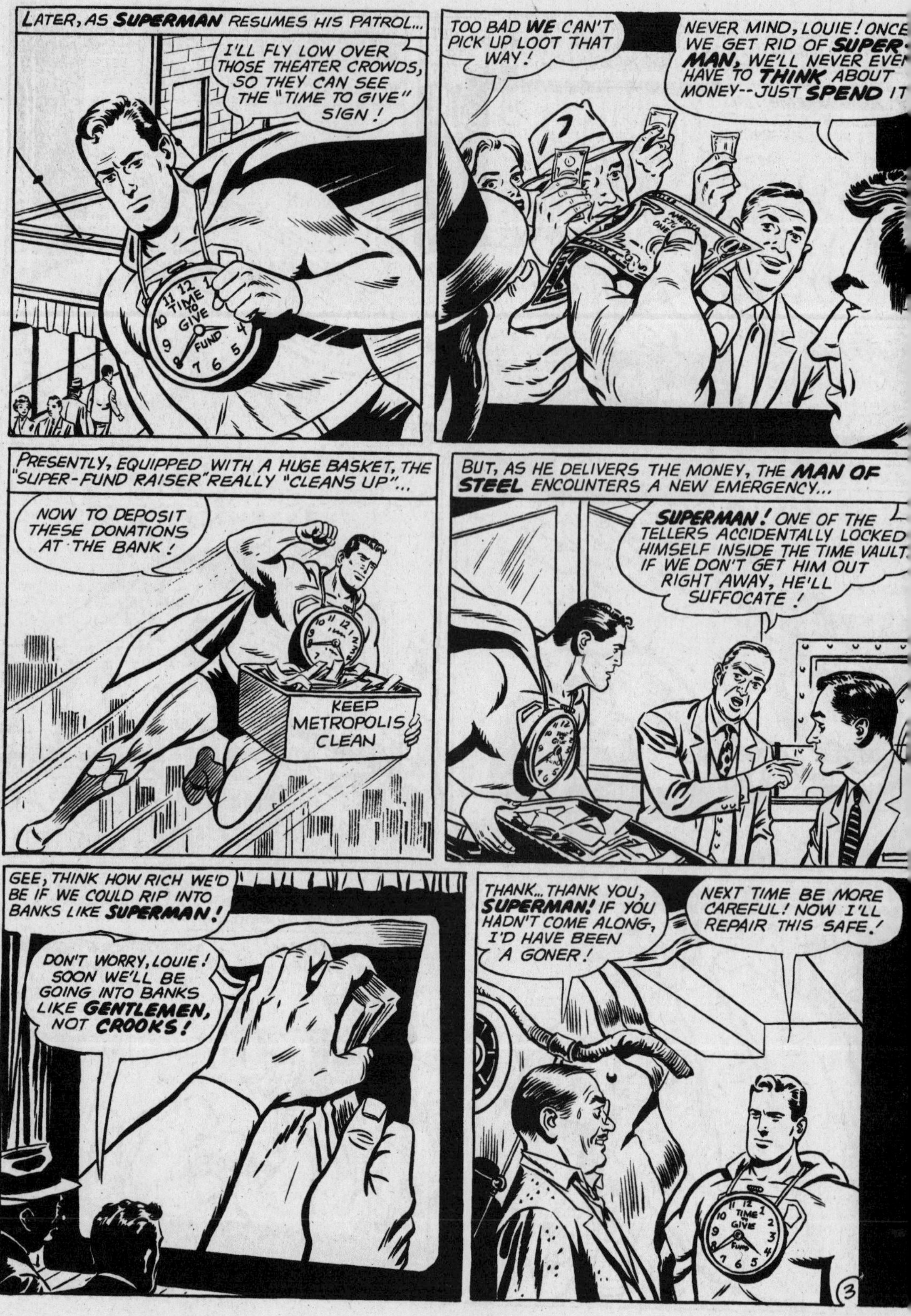
LATER, AS SUPERMAN RESUMES HIS PATROL...
I'LL FLY LOW OVER THOSE THEATER CROWDS, SO THEY CAN SEE THE "TIME TO GIVE" SIGN!
TIME TO GIVE FUND
TOO BAD WE CAN'T PICK UP LOOT THAT WAY!
NEVER MIND, LOUIE! ONCE WE GET RID OF SUPER-MAN, WE'LL NEVER EVE HAVE TO THINK ABOUT MONEY--JUST SPEND IT
PRESENTLY, EQUIPPED WITH A HUGE BASKET, THE "SUPER-FUND RAISER" REALLY "CLEANS UP"...
NOW TO DEPOSIT THESE DONATIONS AT THE BANK!
KEEP METROPOLIS CLEAN
BUT, AS HE DELIVERS THE MONEY, THE MAN OF STEEL ENCOUNTERS A NEW EMERGENCY...
SUPERMAN! ONE OF THE TELLERS ACCIDENTALLY LOCKED HIMSELF INSIDE THE TIME VAULT. IF WE DON'T GET HIM OUT RIGHT AWAY, HE'LL SUFFOCATE!
GEE, THINK HOW RICH WE'D BE IF WE COULD RIP INTO BANKS LIKE SUPERMAN!
DON'T WORRY, LOUIE! SOON WE'LL BE GOING INTO BANKS LIKE GENTLEMEN, NOT CROOKS!
THANK... THANK YOU, SUPERMAN! IF YOU HADN'T COME ALONG, I'D HAVE BEEN A GONER!
NEXT TIME BE MORE CAREFUL! NOW I'LL REPAIR THIS SAFE!
TIME TO GIVE FUND
3

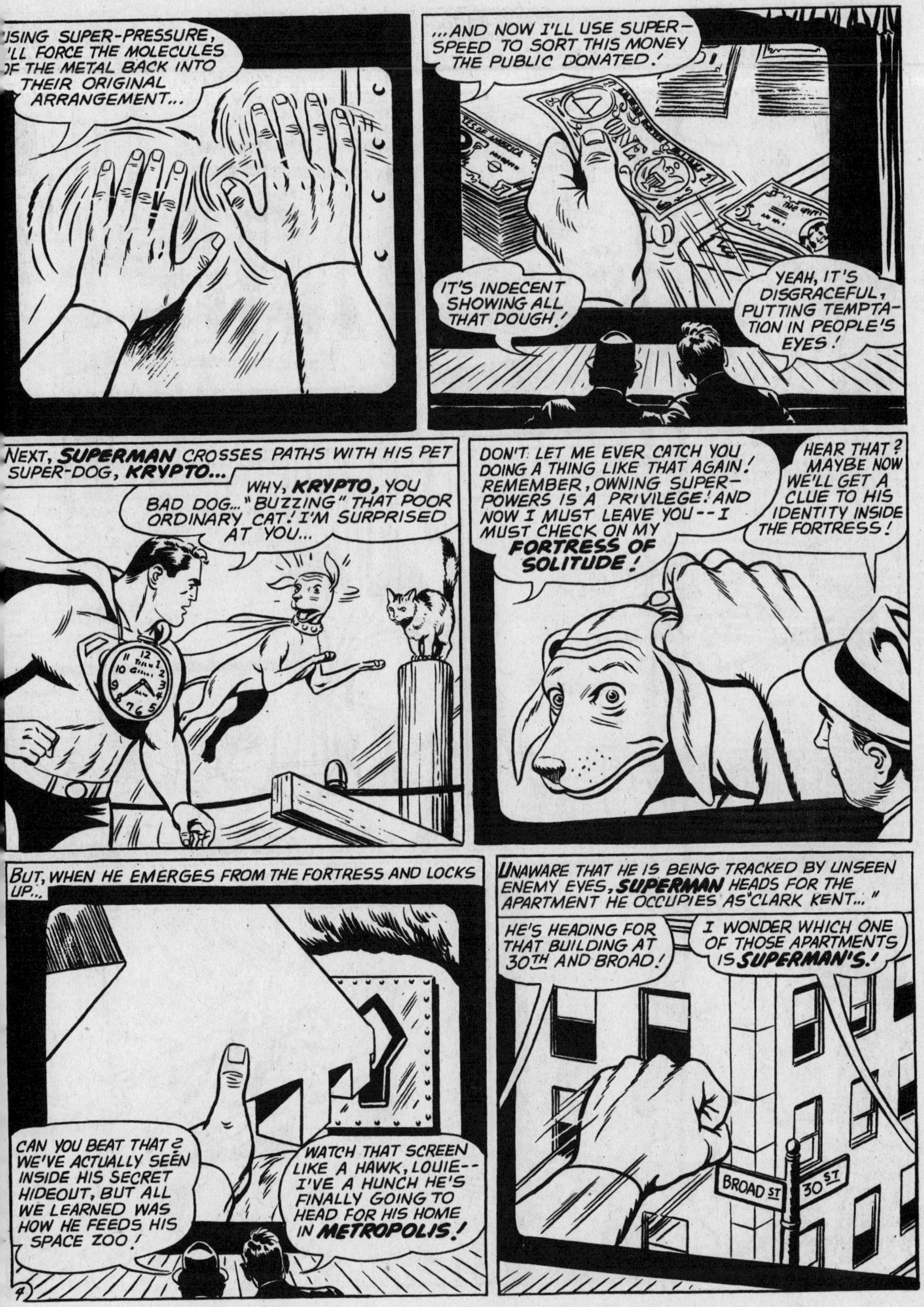
USING SUPER-PRESSURE, I'LL FORCE THE MOLECULES OF THE METAL BACK INTO THEIR ORIGINAL ARRANGEMENT...
...AND NOW I'LL USE SUPER-SPEED TO SORT THIS MONEY THE PUBLIC DONATED!
IT'S INDECENT SHOWING ALL THAT DOUGH!
YEAH, IT'S DISGRACEFUL, PUTTING TEMPTATION IN PEOPLE'S EYES!
NEXT, SUPERMAN CROSSES PATHS WITH HIS PET SUPER-DOG, KRYPTO...
WHY, KRYPTO, YOU BAD DOG..."BUZZING" THAT POOR ORDINARY CAT! I'M SURPRISED AT YOU...
DON'T LET ME EVER CATCH YOU DOING A THING LIKE THAT AGAIN! REMEMBER, OWNING SUPER-POWERS IS A PRIVILEGE! AND NOW I MUST LEAVE YOU--I MUST CHECK ON MY FORTRESS OF SOLITUDE!
HEAR THAT? MAYBE NOW WE'LL GET A CLUE TO HIS IDENTITY INSIDE THE FORTRESS!
BUT, WHEN HE EMERGES FROM THE FORTRESS AND LOCKS UP...
CAN YOU BEAT THAT? WE'VE ACTUALLY SEEN INSIDE HIS SECRET HIDEOUT, BUT ALL WE LEARNED WAS HOW HE FEEDS HIS SPACE ZOO!
WATCH THAT SCREEN LIKE A HAWK, LOUIE--I'VE A HUNCH HE'S FINALLY GOING TO HEAD FOR HIS HOME IN METROPOLIS!
4
UNAWARE THAT HE IS BEING TRACKED BY UNSEEN ENEMY EYES, SUPERMAN HEADS FOR THE APARTMENT HE OCCUPIES AS "CLARK KENT..."
HE'S HEADING FOR THAT BUILDING AT 30TH AND BROAD!
I WONDER WHICH ONE OF THOSE APARTMENTS IS SUPERMAN'S!
BROAD ST
30 ST

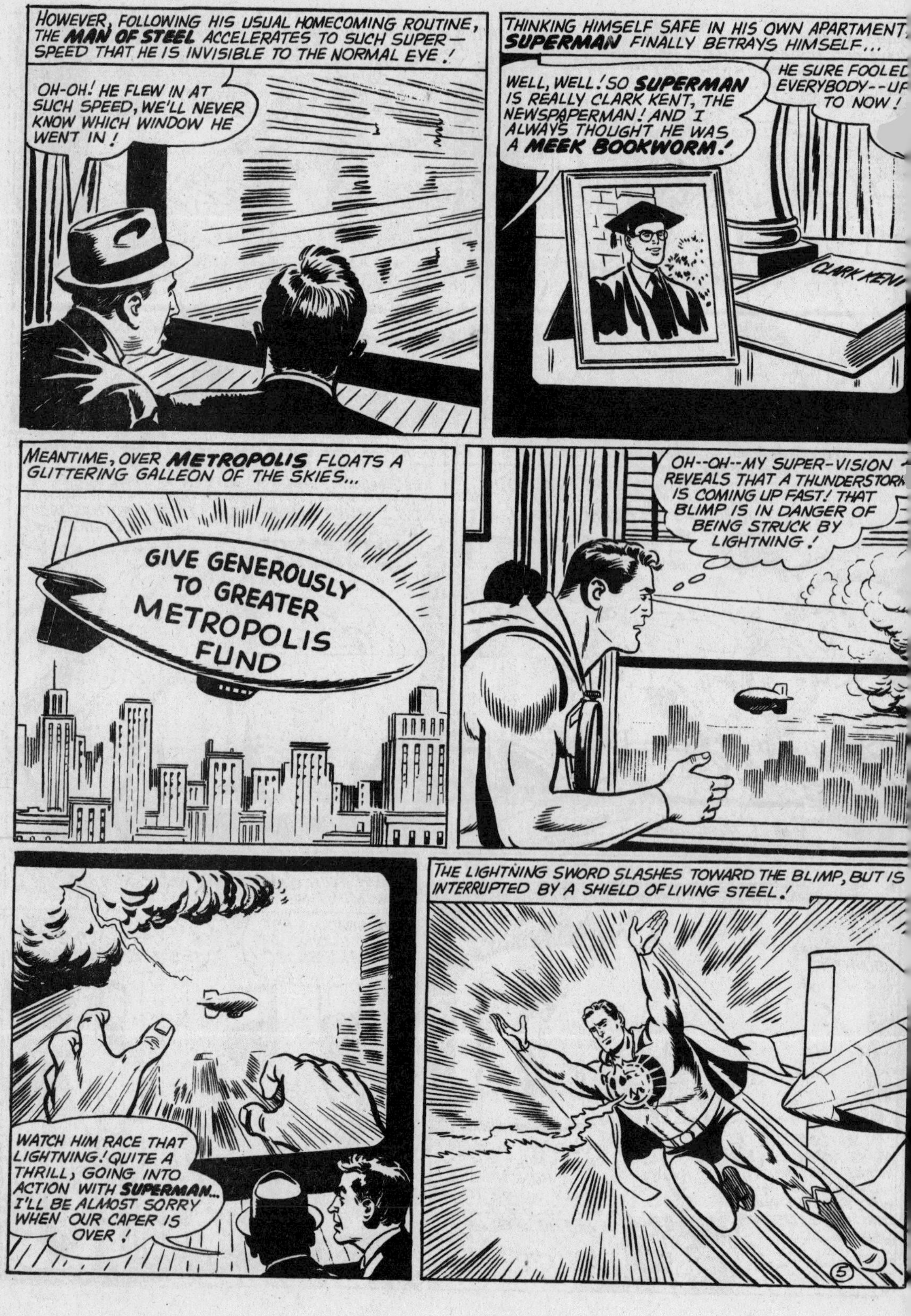
HOWEVER, FOLLOWING HIS USUAL HOMECOMING ROUTINE, THE MAN OF STEEL ACCELERATES TO SUCH SUPER-SPEED THAT HE IS INVISIBLE TO THE NORMAL EYE!
OH-OH! HE FLEW IN AT SUCH SPEED, WE'LL NEVER KNOW WHICH WINDOW HE WENT IN!
THINKING HIMSELF SAFE IN HIS OWN APARTMENT, SUPERMAN FINALLY BETRAYS HIMSELF...
WELL, WELL! SO SUPERMAN IS REALLY CLARK KENT, THE NEWSPAPERMAN! AND I ALWAYS THOUGHT HE WAS A MEEK BOOKWORM!
HE SURE FOOLED EVERYBODY--UP TO NOW!
MEANTIME, OVER METROPOLIS FLOATS A GLITTERING GALLEON OF THE SKIES...
GIVE GENEROUSLY TO GREATER METROPOLIS FUND
OH--OH--MY SUPER-VISION REVEALS THAT A THUNDERSTORM IS COMING UP FAST! THAT BLIMP IS IN DANGER OF BEING STRUCK BY LIGHTNING!
WATCH HIM RACE THAT LIGHTNING! QUITE A THRILL, GOING INTO ACTION WITH SUPERMAN... I'LL BE ALMOST SORRY WHEN OUR CAPER IS OVER!
THE LIGHTNING SWORD SLASHES TOWARD THE BLIMP, BUT IS INTERRUPTED BY A SHIELD OF LIVING STEEL!
5

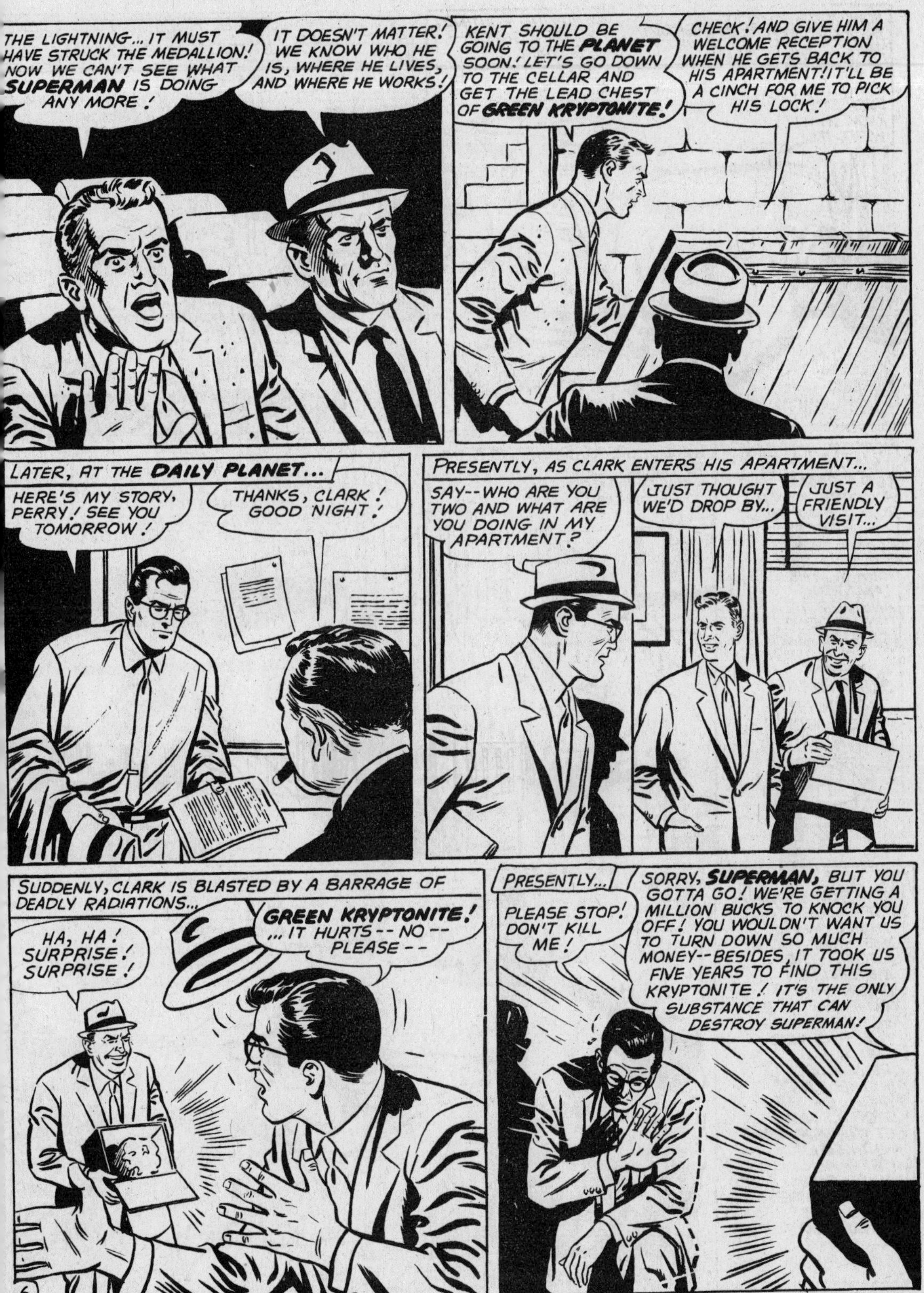
THE LIGHTNING... IT MUST HAVE STRUCK THE MEDALLION! NOW WE CAN'T SEE WHAT SUPERMAN IS DOING ANY MORE!
IT DOESN'T MATTER! WE KNOW WHO HE IS, WHERE HE LIVES, AND WHERE HE WORKS!
KENT SHOULD BE GOING TO THE PLANET SOON! LET'S GO DOWN TO THE CELLAR AND GET THE LEAD CHEST OF GREEN KRYPTONITE!
CHECK! AND GIVE HIM A WELCOME RECEPTION WHEN HE GETS BACK TO HIS APARTMENT! IT'LL BE A CINCH FOR ME TO PICK HIS LOCK!
LATER, AT THE DAILY PLANET...
HERE'S MY STORY, PERRY! SEE YOU TOMORROW!
THANKS, CLARK! GOOD NIGHT!
PRESENTLY, AS CLARK ENTERS HIS APARTMENT...
SAY--WHO ARE YOU TWO AND WHAT ARE YOU DOING IN MY APARTMENT?
JUST THOUGHT WE'D DROP BY...
JUST A FRIENDLY VISIT...
SUDDENLY, CLARK IS BLASTED BY A BARRAGE OF DEADLY RADIATIONS...
HA, HA! SURPRISE! SURPRISE!
GREEN KRYPTONITE! ... IT HURTS -- NO -- PLEASE --
6
PRESENTLY...
PLEASE STOP! DON'T KILL ME!
SORRY, SUPERMAN, BUT YOU GOTTA GO! WE'RE GETTING A MILLION BUCKS TO KNOCK YOU OFF! YOU WOULDN'T WANT US TO TURN DOWN SO MUCH MONEY--BESIDES, IT TOOK US FIVE YEARS TO FIND THIS KRYPTONITE! IT'S THE ONLY SUBSTANCE THAT CAN DESTROY SUPERMAN!

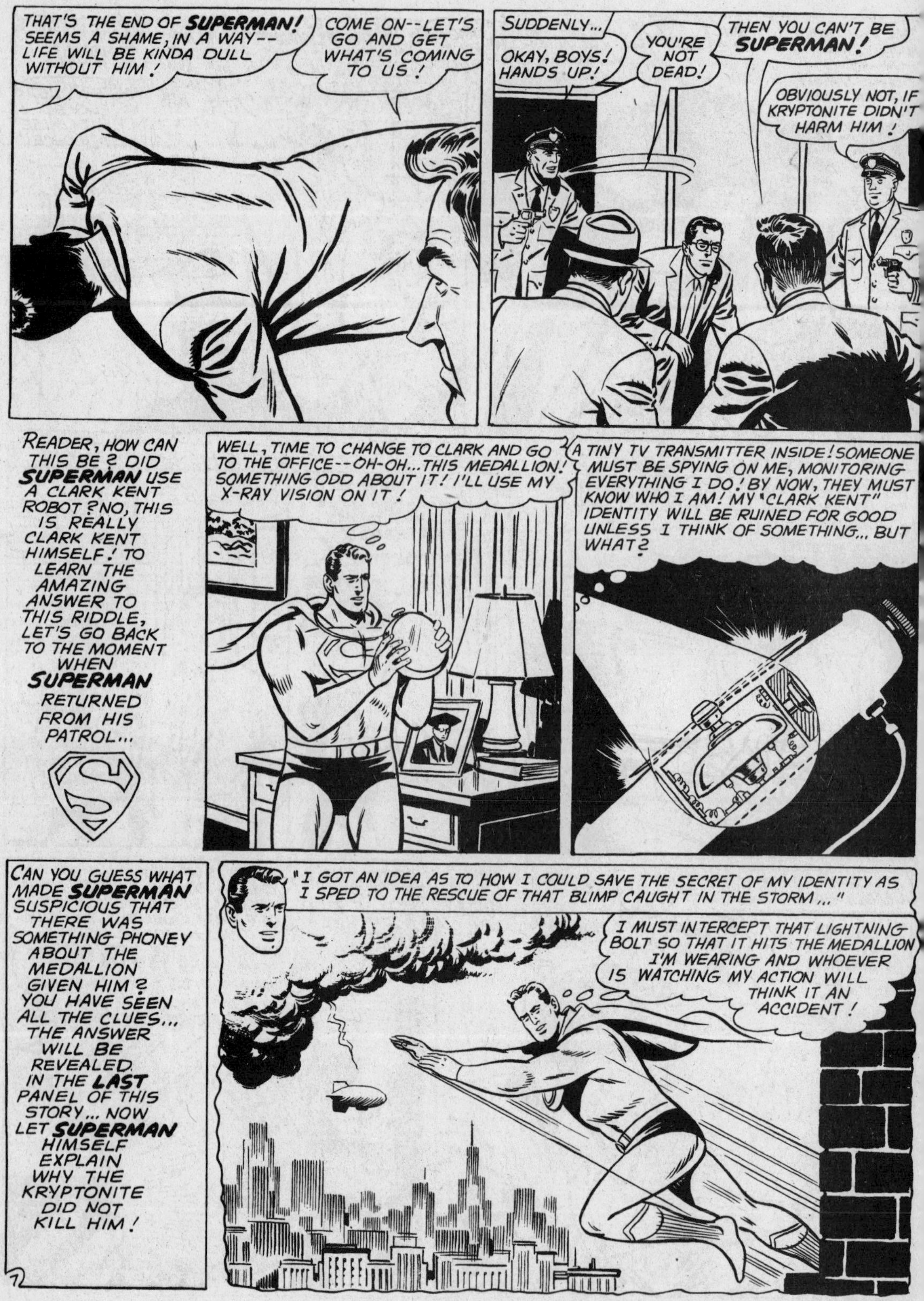
THAT'S THE END OF SUPERMAN! SEEMS A SHAME, IN A WAY-- LIFE WILL BE KINDA DULL WITHOUT HIM!
COME ON--LET'S GO AND GET WHAT'S COMING TO US!
SUDDENLY...
OKAY, BOYS! HANDS UP!
YOU'RE NOT DEAD!
THEN YOU CAN'T BE SUPERMAN!
OBVIOUSLY NOT, IF KRYPTONITE DIDN'T HARM HIM!
READER, HOW CAN THIS BE? DID SUPERMAN USE A CLARK KENT ROBOT? NO, THIS IS REALLY CLARK KENT HIMSELF! TO LEARN THE AMAZING ANSWER TO THIS RIDDLE, LET'S GO BACK TO THE MOMENT WHEN SUPERMAN RETURNED FROM HIS PATROL...
WELL, TIME TO CHANGE TO CLARK AND GO TO THE OFFICE--OH-OH...THIS MEDALLION! SOMETHING ODD ABOUT IT! I'LL USE MY X-RAY VISION ON IT!
A TINY TV TRANSMITTER INSIDE! SOMEONE MUST BE SPYING ON ME, MONITORING EVERYTHING I DO! BY NOW, THEY MUST KNOW WHO I AM! MY "CLARK KENT" IDENTITY WILL BE RUINED FOR GOOD UNLESS I THINK OF SOMETHING... BUT WHAT?
CAN YOU GUESS WHAT MADE SUPERMAN SUSPICIOUS THAT THERE WAS SOMETHING PHONEY ABOUT THE MEDALLION GIVEN HIM? YOU HAVE SEEN ALL THE CLUES... THE ANSWER WILL BE REVEALED IN THE LAST PANEL OF THIS STORY... NOW LET SUPERMAN HIMSELF EXPLAIN WHY THE KRYPTONITE DID NOT KILL HIM!
"I GOT AN IDEA AS TO HOW I COULD SAVE THE SECRET OF MY IDENTITY AS I SPED TO THE RESCUE OF THAT BLIMP CAUGHT IN THE STORM..."
I MUST INTERCEPT THAT LIGHTNING BOLT SO THAT IT HITS THE MEDALLION I'M WEARING AND WHOEVER IS WATCHING MY ACTION WILL THINK IT AN ACCIDENT!
7

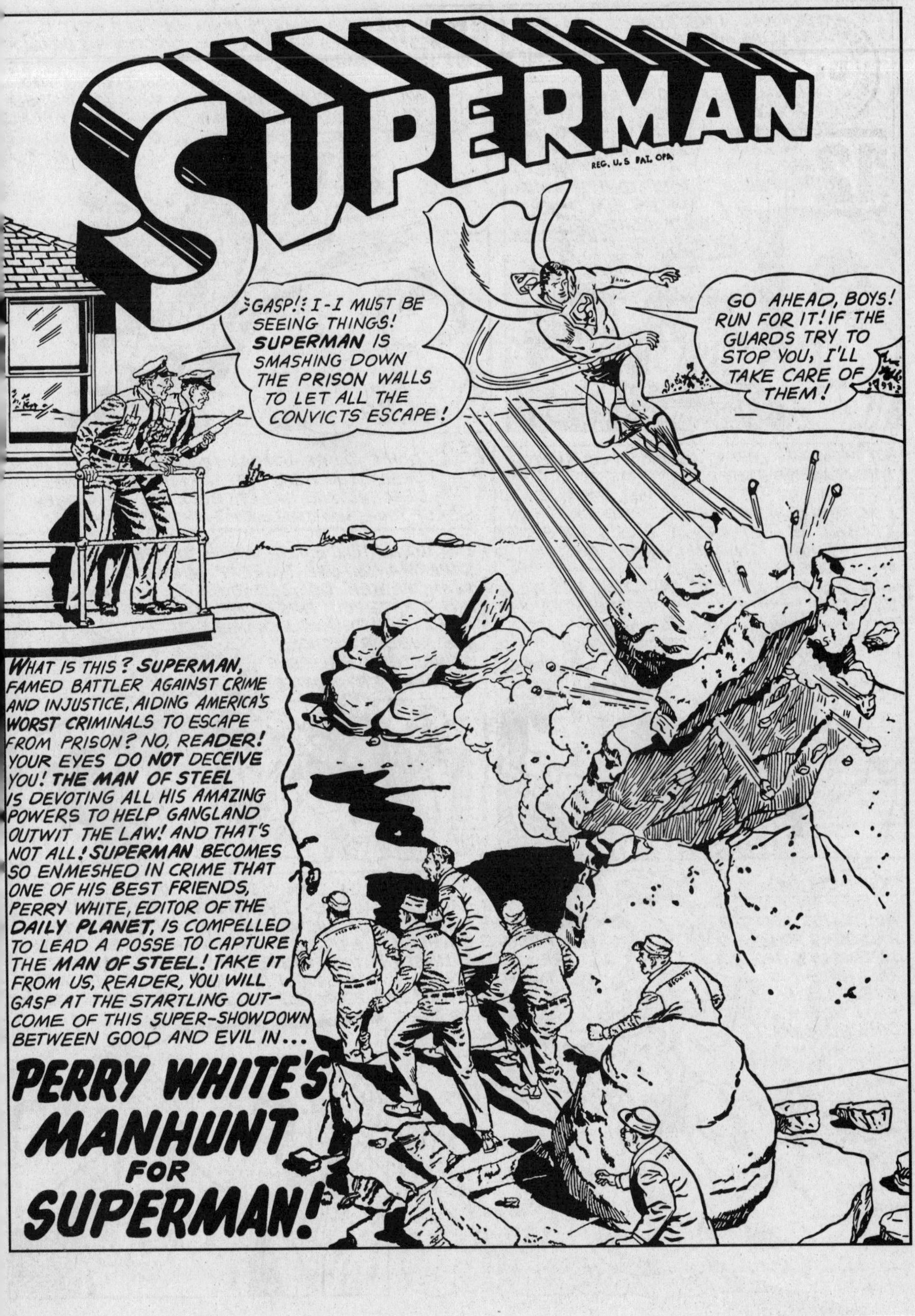
SUPERMAN
REG. U.S PAT. OFF.
GASP! I-I MUST BE SEEING THINGS! SUPERMAN IS SMASHING DOWN THE PRISON WALLS TO LET ALL THE CONVICTS ESCAPE!
GO AHEAD, BOYS! RUN FOR IT! IF THE GUARDS TRY TO STOP YOU, I'LL TAKE CARE OF THEM!
WHAT IS THIS? SUPERMAN, FAMED BATTLER AGAINST CRIME AND INJUSTICE, AIDING AMERICA'S WORST CRIMINALS TO ESCAPE FROM PRISON? NO, READER! YOUR EYES DO NOT DECEIVE YOU! THE MAN OF STEEL IS DEVOTING ALL HIS AMAZING POWERS TO HELP GANGLAND OUTWIT THE LAW! AND THAT'S NOT ALL! SUPERMAN BECOMES SO ENMESHED IN CRIME THAT ONE OF HIS BEST FRIENDS, PERRY WHITE, EDITOR OF THE DAILY PLANET, IS COMPELLED TO LEAD A POSSE TO CAPTURE THE MAN OF STEEL! TAKE IT FROM US, READER, YOU WILL GASP AT THE STARTLING OUT-COME OF THIS SUPER-SHOWDOWN BETWEEN GOOD AND EVIL IN...
PERRY WHITE'S MANHUNT FOR SUPERMAN!

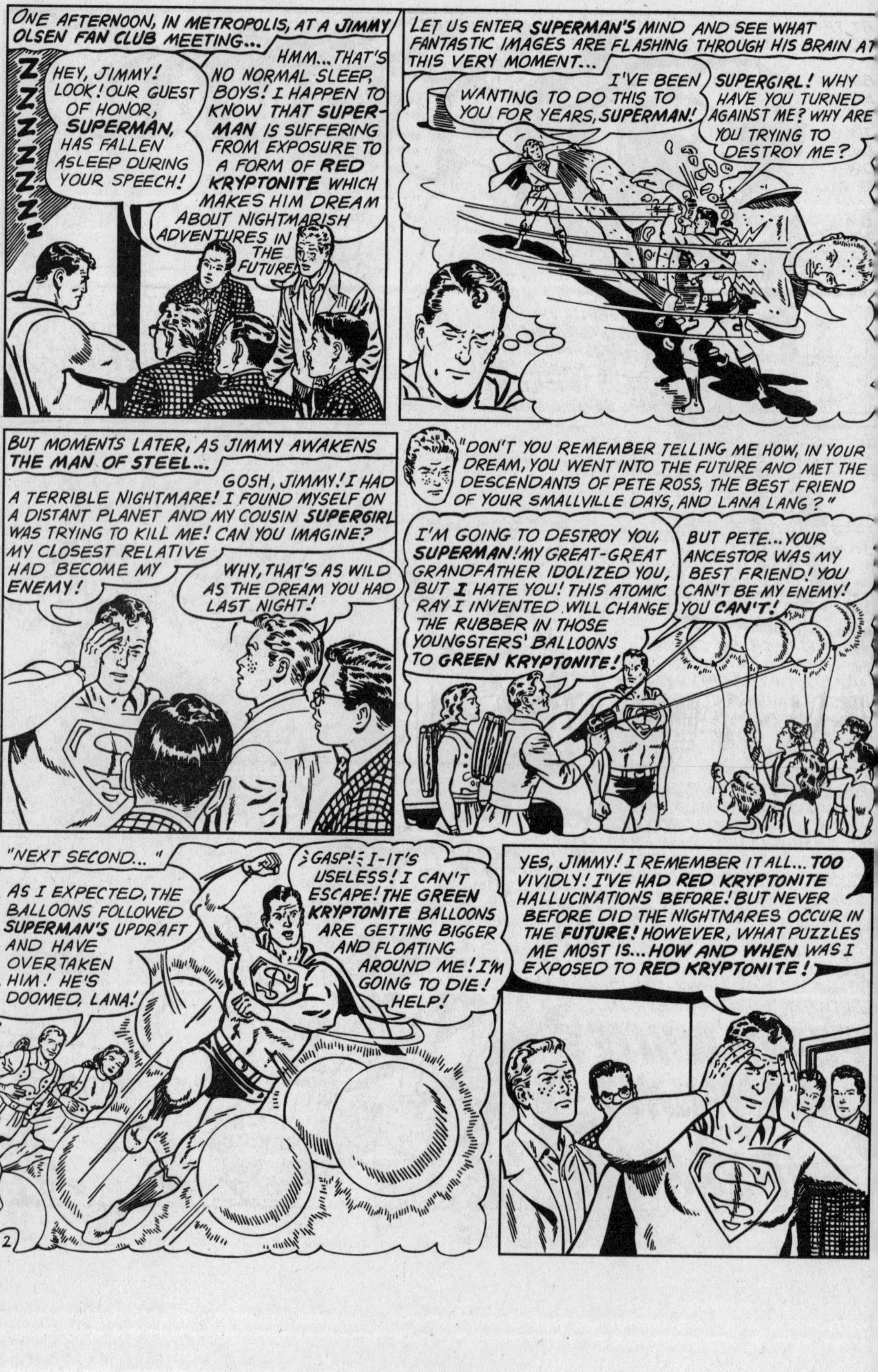
ONE AFTERNOON, IN METROPOLIS, AT A JIMMY OLSEN FAN CLUB MEETING...
ZZZZZZZ
HEY, JIMMY! LOOK! OUR GUEST OF HONOR, SUPERMAN, HAS FALLEN ASLEEP DURING YOUR SPEECH!
HMM...THAT'S NO NORMAL SLEEP, BOYS! I HAPPEN TO KNOW THAT SUPERMAN IS SUFFERING FROM EXPOSURE TO A FORM OF RED KRYPTONITE WHICH MAKES HIM DREAM ABOUT NIGHTMARISH ADVENTURES IN THE FUTURE!
LET US ENTER SUPERMAN'S MIND AND SEE WHAT FANTASTIC IMAGES ARE FLASHING THROUGH HIS BRAIN AT THIS VERY MOMENT...
I'VE BEEN WANTING TO DO THIS TO YOU FOR YEARS, SUPERMAN!
SUPERGIRL! WHY HAVE YOU TURNED AGAINST ME? WHY ARE YOU TRYING TO DESTROY ME?
BUT MOMENTS LATER, AS JIMMY AWAKENS THE MAN OF STEEL...
GOSH, JIMMY! I HAD A TERRIBLE NIGHTMARE! I FOUND MYSELF ON A DISTANT PLANET AND MY COUSIN SUPERGIRL WAS TRYING TO KILL ME! CAN YOU IMAGINE? MY CLOSEST RELATIVE HAD BECOME MY ENEMY!
WHY, THAT'S AS WILD AS THE DREAM YOU HAD LAST NIGHT!
"DON'T YOU REMEMBER TELLING ME HOW, IN YOUR DREAM, YOU WENT INTO THE FUTURE AND MET THE DESCENDANTS OF PETE ROSS, THE BEST FRIEND OF YOUR SMALLVILLE DAYS, AND LANA LANG?"
I'M GOING TO DESTROY YOU, SUPERMAN! MY GREAT-GREAT GRANDFATHER IDOLIZED YOU, BUT I HATE YOU! THIS ATOMIC RAY I INVENTED WILL CHANGE THE RUBBER IN THOSE YOUNGSTERS' BALLOONS TO GREEN KRYPTONITE!
BUT PETE...YOUR ANCESTOR WAS MY BEST FRIEND! YOU CAN'T BE MY ENEMY! YOU CAN'T!
"NEXT SECOND..."
AS I EXPECTED, THE BALLOONS FOLLOWED SUPERMAN'S UPDRAFT AND HAVE OVERTAKEN HIM! HE'S DOOMED, LANA!
GASP! I-IT'S USELESS! I CAN'T ESCAPE! THE GREEN KRYPTONITE BALLOONS ARE GETTING BIGGER AND FLOATING AROUND ME! I'M GOING TO DIE! HELP!
YES, JIMMY! I REMEMBER IT ALL...TOO VIVIDLY! I'VE HAD RED KRYPTONITE HALLUCINATIONS BEFORE! BUT NEVER BEFORE DID THE NIGHTMARES OCCUR IN THE FUTURE! HOWEVER, WHAT PUZZLES ME MOST IS...HOW AND WHEN WAS I EXPOSED TO RED KRYPTONITE!
2

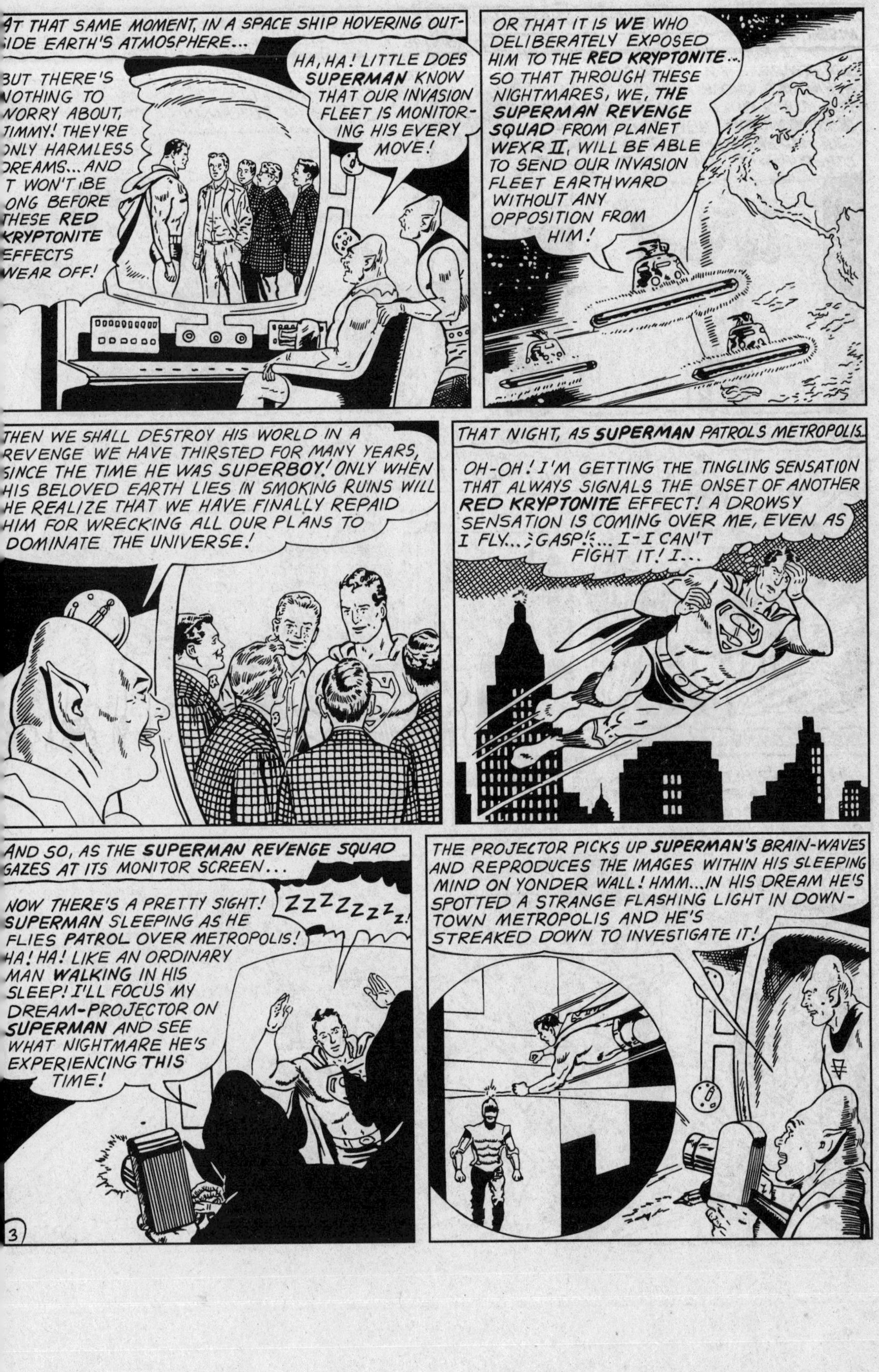
AT THAT SAME MOMENT, IN A SPACE SHIP HOVERING OUTSIDE EARTH'S ATMOSPHERE...
BUT THERE'S NOTHING TO WORRY ABOUT, TIMMY! THEY'RE ONLY HARMLESS DREAMS... AND IT WON'T BE LONG BEFORE THESE RED KRYPTONITE EFFECTS WEAR OFF!
HA, HA! LITTLE DOES SUPERMAN KNOW THAT OUR INVASION FLEET IS MONITORING HIS EVERY MOVE!
OR THAT IT IS WE WHO DELIBERATELY EXPOSED HIM TO THE RED KRYPTONITE... SO THAT THROUGH THESE NIGHTMARES, WE, THE SUPERMAN REVENGE SQUAD FROM PLANET WEXR II, WILL BE ABLE TO SEND OUR INVASION FLEET EARTHWARD WITHOUT ANY OPPOSITION FROM HIM!
THEN WE SHALL DESTROY HIS WORLD IN A REVENGE WE HAVE THIRSTED FOR MANY YEARS, SINCE THE TIME HE WAS SUPERBOY! ONLY WHEN HIS BELOVED EARTH LIES IN SMOKING RUINS WILL HE REALIZE THAT WE HAVE FINALLY REPAID HIM FOR WRECKING ALL OUR PLANS TO DOMINATE THE UNIVERSE!
THAT NIGHT, AS SUPERMAN PATROLS METROPOLIS...
OH-OH! I'M GETTING THE TINGLING SENSATION THAT ALWAYS SIGNALS THE ONSET OF ANOTHER RED KRYPTONITE EFFECT! A DROWSY SENSATION IS COMING OVER ME, EVEN AS I FLY... *GASP!*... I-I CAN'T FIGHT IT! I...
AND SO, AS THE SUPERMAN REVENGE SQUAD GAZES AT ITS MONITOR SCREEN...
NOW THERE'S A PRETTY SIGHT! SUPERMAN SLEEPING AS HE FLIES PATROL OVER METROPOLIS! HA! HA! LIKE AN ORDINARY MAN WALKING IN HIS SLEEP! I'LL FOCUS MY DREAM-PROJECTOR ON SUPERMAN AND SEE WHAT NIGHTMARE HE'S EXPERIENCING THIS TIME!
ZZZZZZZz!
THE PROJECTOR PICKS UP SUPERMAN'S BRAIN-WAVES AND REPRODUCES THE IMAGES WITHIN HIS SLEEPING MIND ON YONDER WALL! HMM... IN HIS DREAM HE'S SPOTTED A STRANGE FLASHING LIGHT IN DOWNTOWN METROPOLIS AND HE'S STREAKED DOWN TO INVESTIGATE IT!
3

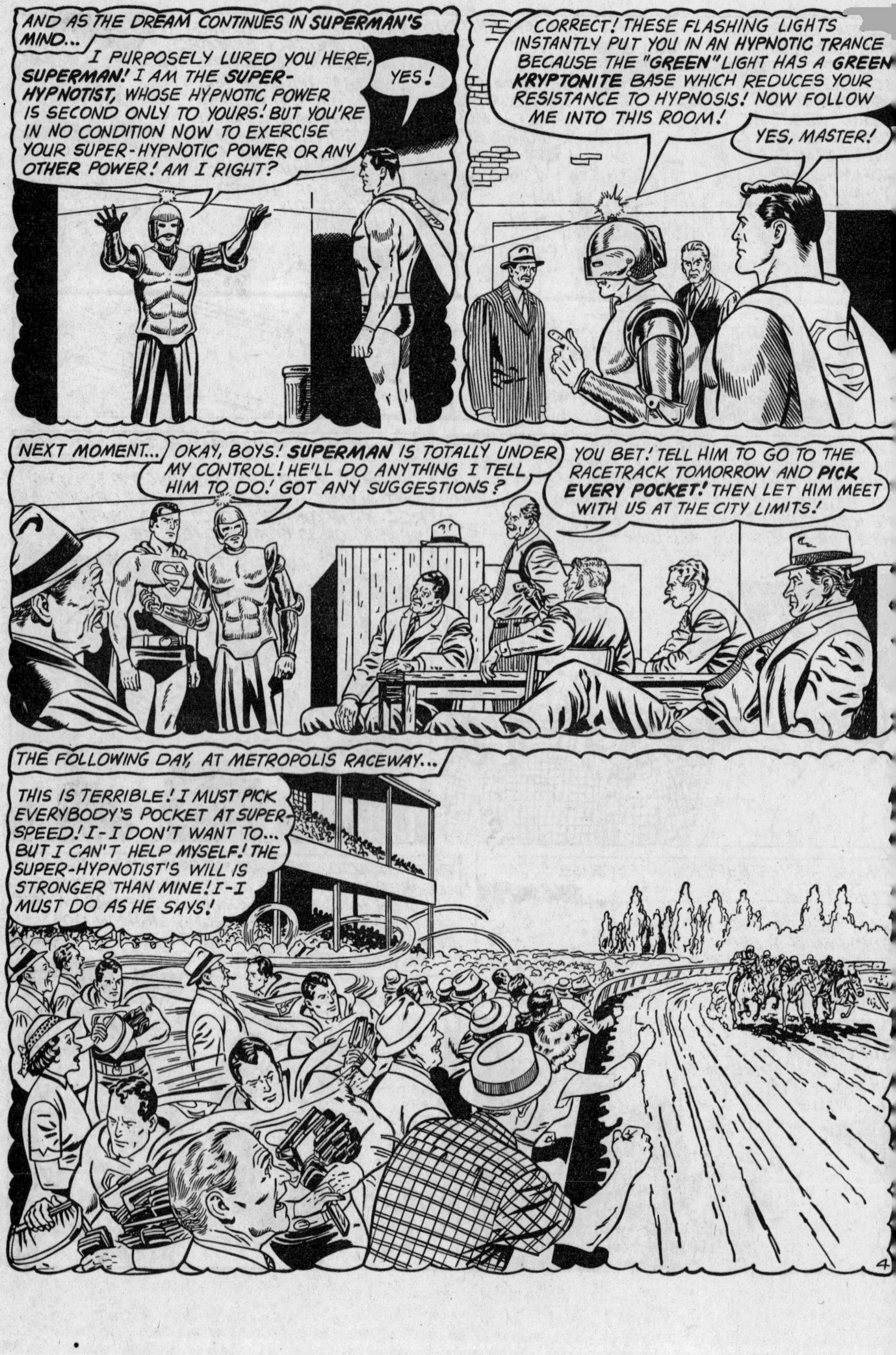
AND AS THE DREAM CONTINUES IN SUPERMAN'S MIND...
I PURPOSELY LURED YOU HERE, SUPERMAN! I AM THE SUPER-HYPNOTIST, WHOSE HYPNOTIC POWER IS SECOND ONLY TO YOURS! BUT YOU'RE IN NO CONDITION NOW TO EXERCISE YOUR SUPER-HYPNOTIC POWER OR ANY OTHER POWER! AM I RIGHT?
YES!
CORRECT! THESE FLASHING LIGHTS INSTANTLY PUT YOU IN AN HYPNOTIC TRANCE BECAUSE THE "GREEN" LIGHT HAS A GREEN KRYPTONITE BASE WHICH REDUCES YOUR RESISTANCE TO HYPNOSIS! NOW FOLLOW ME INTO THIS ROOM!
YES, MASTER!
NEXT MOMENT...
OKAY, BOYS! SUPERMAN IS TOTALLY UNDER MY CONTROL! HE'LL DO ANYTHING I TELL HIM TO DO! GOT ANY SUGGESTIONS?
YOU BET! TELL HIM TO GO TO THE RACETRACK TOMORROW AND PICK EVERY POCKET! THEN LET HIM MEET WITH US AT THE CITY LIMITS!
THE FOLLOWING DAY, AT METROPOLIS RACEWAY...
THIS IS TERRIBLE! I MUST PICK EVERYBODY'S POCKET AT SUPER-SPEED! I-I DON'T WANT TO... BUT I CAN'T HELP MYSELF! THE SUPER-HYPNOTIST'S WILL IS STRONGER THAN MINE! I-I MUST DO AS HE SAYS!
4

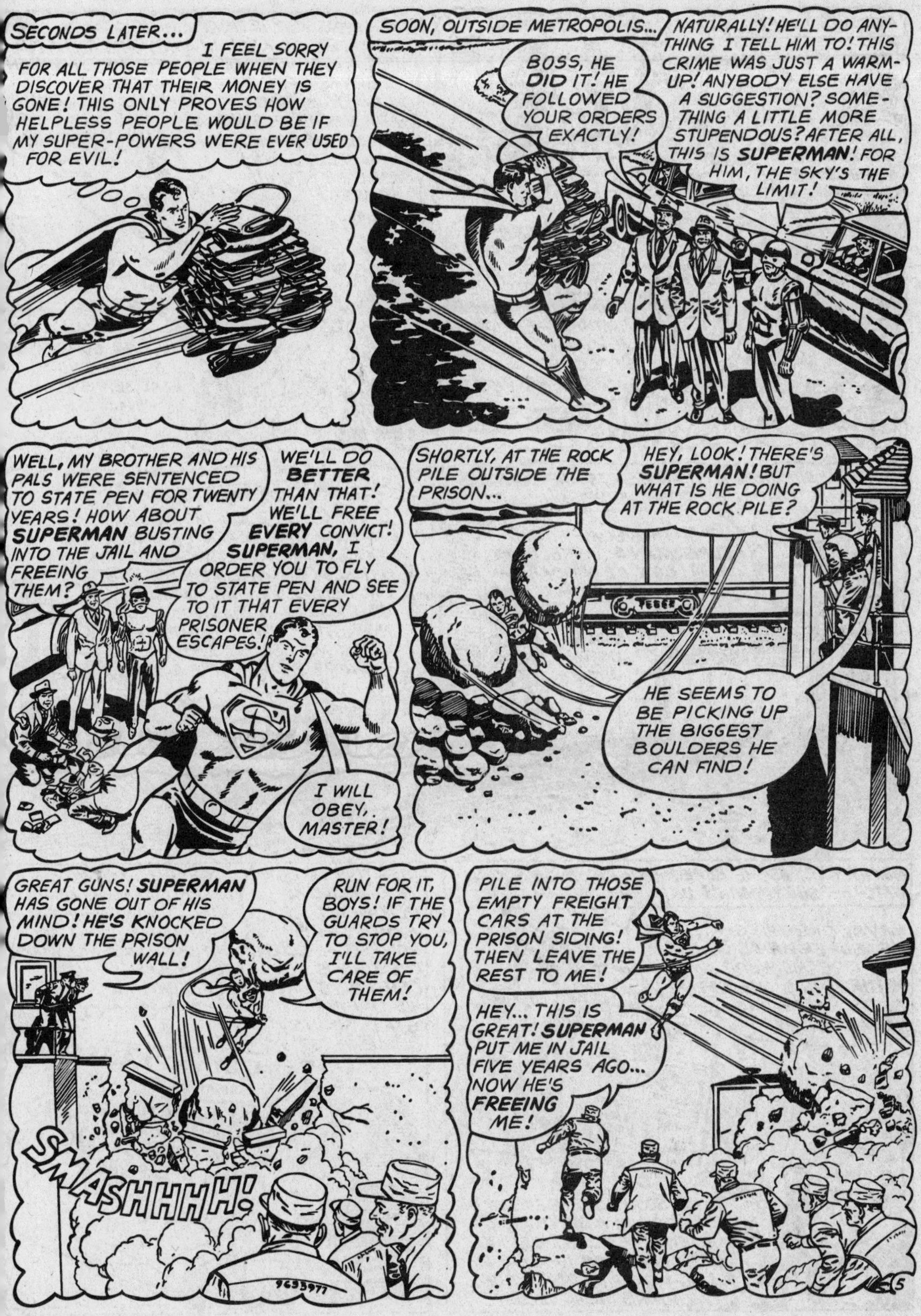
SECONDS LATER...
I FEEL SORRY FOR ALL THOSE PEOPLE WHEN THEY DISCOVER THAT THEIR MONEY IS GONE! THIS ONLY PROVES HOW HELPLESS PEOPLE WOULD BE IF MY SUPER-POWERS WERE EVER USED FOR EVIL!
SOON, OUTSIDE METROPOLIS...
BOSS, HE DID IT! HE FOLLOWED YOUR ORDERS EXACTLY!
NATURALLY! HE'LL DO ANYTHING I TELL HIM TO! THIS CRIME WAS JUST A WARM-UP! ANYBODY ELSE HAVE A SUGGESTION? SOMETHING A LITTLE MORE STUPENDOUS? AFTER ALL, THIS IS SUPERMAN! FOR HIM, THE SKY'S THE LIMIT!
WELL, MY BROTHER AND HIS PALS WERE SENTENCED TO STATE PEN FOR TWENTY YEARS! HOW ABOUT SUPERMAN BUSTING INTO THE JAIL AND FREEING THEM?
WE'LL DO BETTER THAN THAT! WE'LL FREE EVERY CONVICT! SUPERMAN, I ORDER YOU TO FLY TO STATE PEN AND SEE TO IT THAT EVERY PRISONER ESCAPES!
I WILL OBEY, MASTER!
SHORTLY, AT THE ROCK PILE OUTSIDE THE PRISON...
HEY, LOOK! THERE'S SUPERMAN! BUT WHAT IS HE DOING AT THE ROCK PILE?
HE SEEMS TO BE PICKING UP THE BIGGEST BOULDERS HE CAN FIND!
GREAT GUNS! SUPERMAN HAS GONE OUT OF HIS MIND! HE'S KNOCKED DOWN THE PRISON WALL!
RUN FOR IT, BOYS! IF THE GUARDS TRY TO STOP YOU, I'LL TAKE CARE OF THEM!
SMASHHHH!
9693977
PILE INTO THOSE EMPTY FREIGHT CARS AT THE PRISON SIDING! THEN LEAVE THE REST TO ME!
HEY... THIS IS GREAT! SUPERMAN PUT ME IN JAIL FIVE YEARS AGO... NOW HE'S FREEING ME!
5

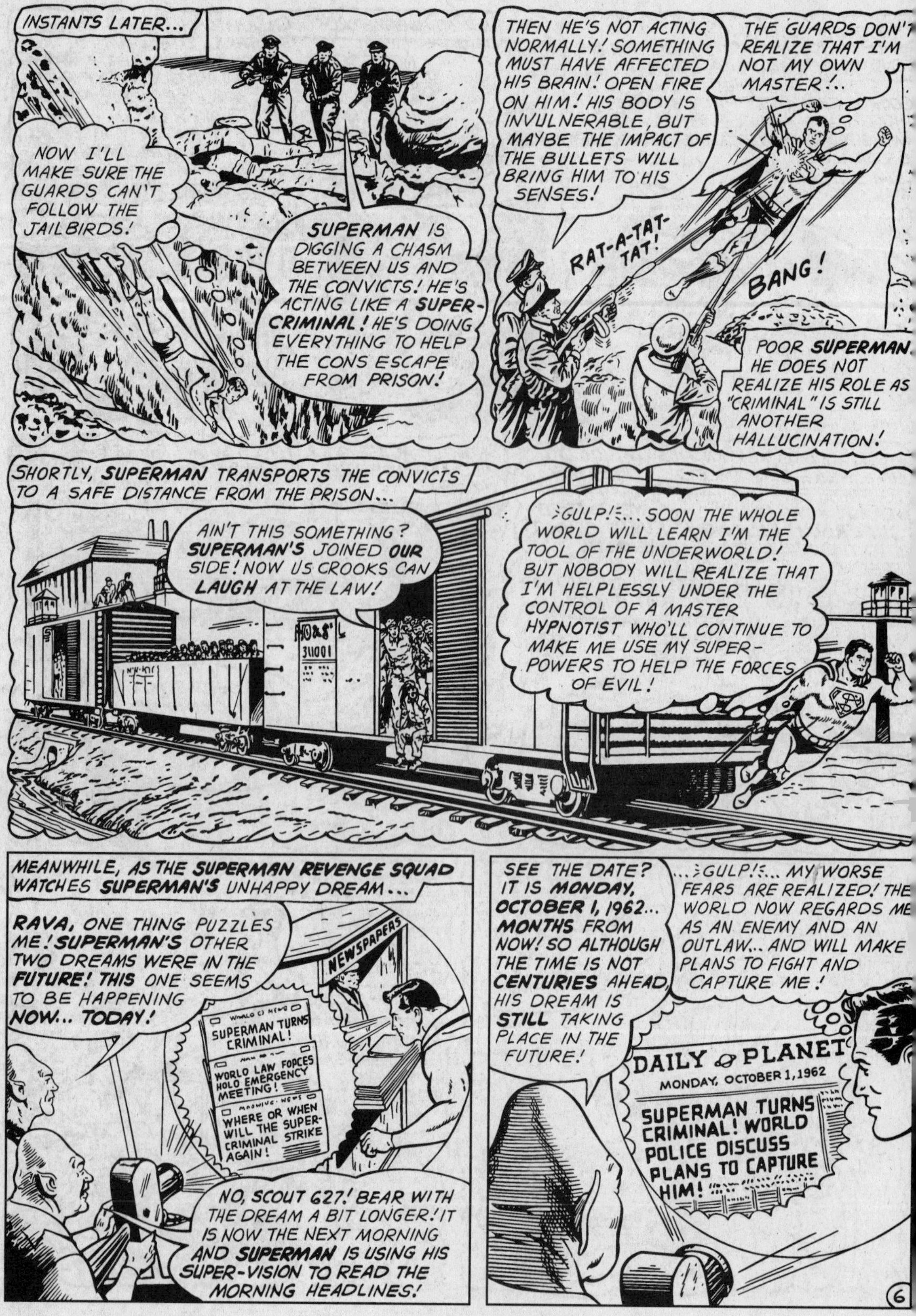
INSTANTS LATER...
NOW I'LL MAKE SURE THE GUARDS CAN'T FOLLOW THE JAILBIRDS!
SUPERMAN IS DIGGING A CHASM BETWEEN US AND THE CONVICTS! HE'S ACTING LIKE A SUPER-CRIMINAL! HE'S DOING EVERYTHING TO HELP THE CONS ESCAPE FROM PRISON!
THEN HE'S NOT ACTING NORMALLY! SOMETHING MUST HAVE AFFECTED HIS BRAIN! OPEN FIRE ON HIM! HIS BODY IS INVULNERABLE, BUT MAYBE THE IMPACT OF THE BULLETS WILL BRING HIM TO HIS SENSES!
THE GUARDS DON'T REALIZE THAT I'M NOT MY OWN MASTER!..
RAT-A-TAT-TAT!
BANG!
POOR SUPERMAN. HE DOES NOT REALIZE HIS ROLE AS "CRIMINAL" IS STILL ANOTHER HALLUCINATION!
SHORTLY, SUPERMAN TRANSPORTS THE CONVICTS TO A SAFE DISTANCE FROM THE PRISON...
AIN'T THIS SOMETHING? SUPERMAN'S JOINED OUR SIDE! NOW US CROOKS CAN LAUGH AT THE LAW!
GULP!... SOON THE WHOLE WORLD WILL LEARN I'M THE TOOL OF THE UNDERWORLD! BUT NOBODY WILL REALIZE THAT I'M HELPLESSLY UNDER THE CONTROL OF A MASTER HYPNOTIST WHO'LL CONTINUE TO MAKE ME USE MY SUPER-POWERS TO HELP THE FORCES OF EVIL!
MEANWHILE, AS THE SUPERMAN REVENGE SQUAD WATCHES SUPERMAN'S UNHAPPY DREAM...
RAVA, ONE THING PUZZLES ME! SUPERMAN'S OTHER TWO DREAMS WERE IN THE FUTURE! THIS ONE SEEMS TO BE HAPPENING NOW... TODAY!
NEWSPAPERS
SUPERMAN TURNS CRIMINAL!
WORLD LAW FORCES HOLD EMERGENCY MEETING!
WHERE OR WHEN WILL THE SUPER-CRIMINAL STRIKE AGAIN!
NO, SCOUT 627! BEAR WITH THE DREAM A BIT LONGER! IT IS NOW THE NEXT MORNING AND SUPERMAN IS USING HIS SUPER-VISION TO READ THE MORNING HEADLINES!
SEE THE DATE? IT IS MONDAY, OCTOBER 1, 1962... MONTHS FROM NOW! SO ALTHOUGH THE TIME IS NOT CENTURIES AHEAD, HIS DREAM IS STILL TAKING PLACE IN THE FUTURE!
...GULP!... MY WORSE FEARS ARE REALIZED! THE WORLD NOW REGARDS ME AS AN ENEMY AND AN OUTLAW... AND WILL MAKE PLANS TO FIGHT AND CAPTURE ME!
DAILY PLANET
MONDAY, OCTOBER 1, 1962
SUPERMAN TURNS CRIMINAL! WORLD POLICE DISCUSS PLANS TO CAPTURE HIM!
6

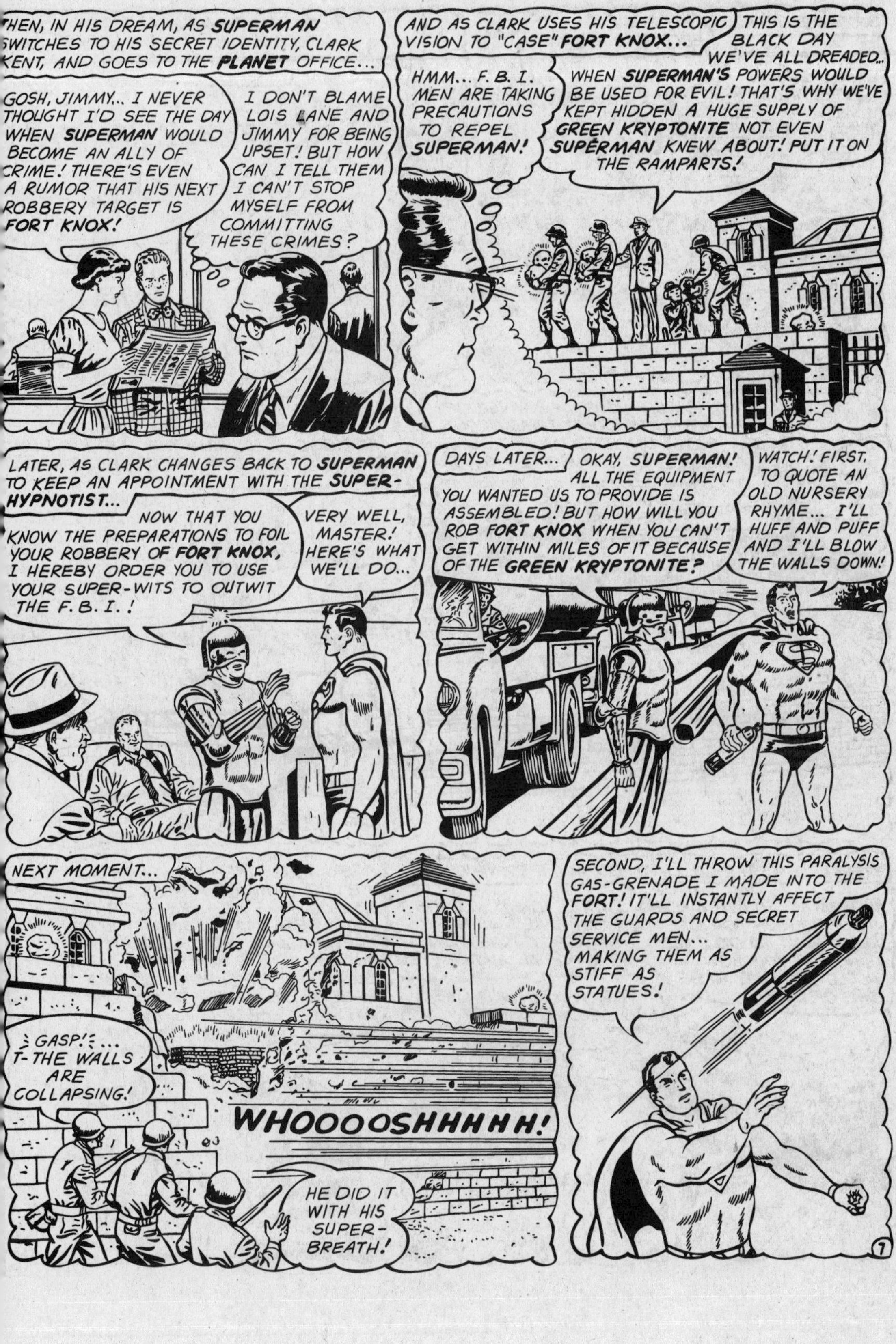
THEN, IN HIS DREAM, AS SUPERMAN SWITCHES TO HIS SECRET IDENTITY, CLARK KENT, AND GOES TO THE PLANET OFFICE...
GOSH, JIMMY... I NEVER THOUGHT I'D SEE THE DAY WHEN SUPERMAN WOULD BECOME AN ALLY OF CRIME! THERE'S EVEN A RUMOR THAT HIS NEXT ROBBERY TARGET IS FORT KNOX!
I DON'T BLAME LOIS LANE AND JIMMY FOR BEING UPSET! BUT HOW CAN I TELL THEM I CAN'T STOP MYSELF FROM COMMITTING THESE CRIMES?
AND AS CLARK USES HIS TELESCOPIC VISION TO "CASE" FORT KNOX...
HMM... F.B.I. MEN ARE TAKING PRECAUTIONS TO REPEL SUPERMAN!
THIS IS THE BLACK DAY WE'VE ALL DREADED... WHEN SUPERMAN'S POWERS WOULD BE USED FOR EVIL! THAT'S WHY WE'VE KEPT HIDDEN A HUGE SUPPLY OF GREEN KRYPTONITE NOT EVEN SUPERMAN KNEW ABOUT! PUT IT ON THE RAMPARTS!
LATER, AS CLARK CHANGES BACK TO SUPERMAN TO KEEP AN APPOINTMENT WITH THE SUPER-HYPNOTIST...
NOW THAT YOU KNOW THE PREPARATIONS TO FOIL YOUR ROBBERY OF FORT KNOX, I HEREBY ORDER YOU TO USE YOUR SUPER-WITS TO OUTWIT THE F.B.I.!
VERY WELL, MASTER! HERE'S WHAT WE'LL DO...
DAYS LATER...
OKAY, SUPERMAN! ALL THE EQUIPMENT YOU WANTED US TO PROVIDE IS ASSEMBLED! BUT HOW WILL YOU ROB FORT KNOX WHEN YOU CAN'T GET WITHIN MILES OF IT BECAUSE OF THE GREEN KRYPTONITE?
WATCH! FIRST, TO QUOTE AN OLD NURSERY RHYME... I'LL HUFF AND PUFF AND I'LL BLOW THE WALLS DOWN!
NEXT MOMENT...
GASP!... T-THE WALLS ARE COLLAPSING!
WHOOOOSHHHHH!
HE DID IT WITH HIS SUPER-BREATH!
SECOND, I'LL THROW THIS PARALYSIS GAS-GRENADE I MADE INTO THE FORT! IT'LL INSTANTLY AFFECT THE GUARDS AND SECRET SERVICE MEN... MAKING THEM AS STIFF AS STATUES!
7

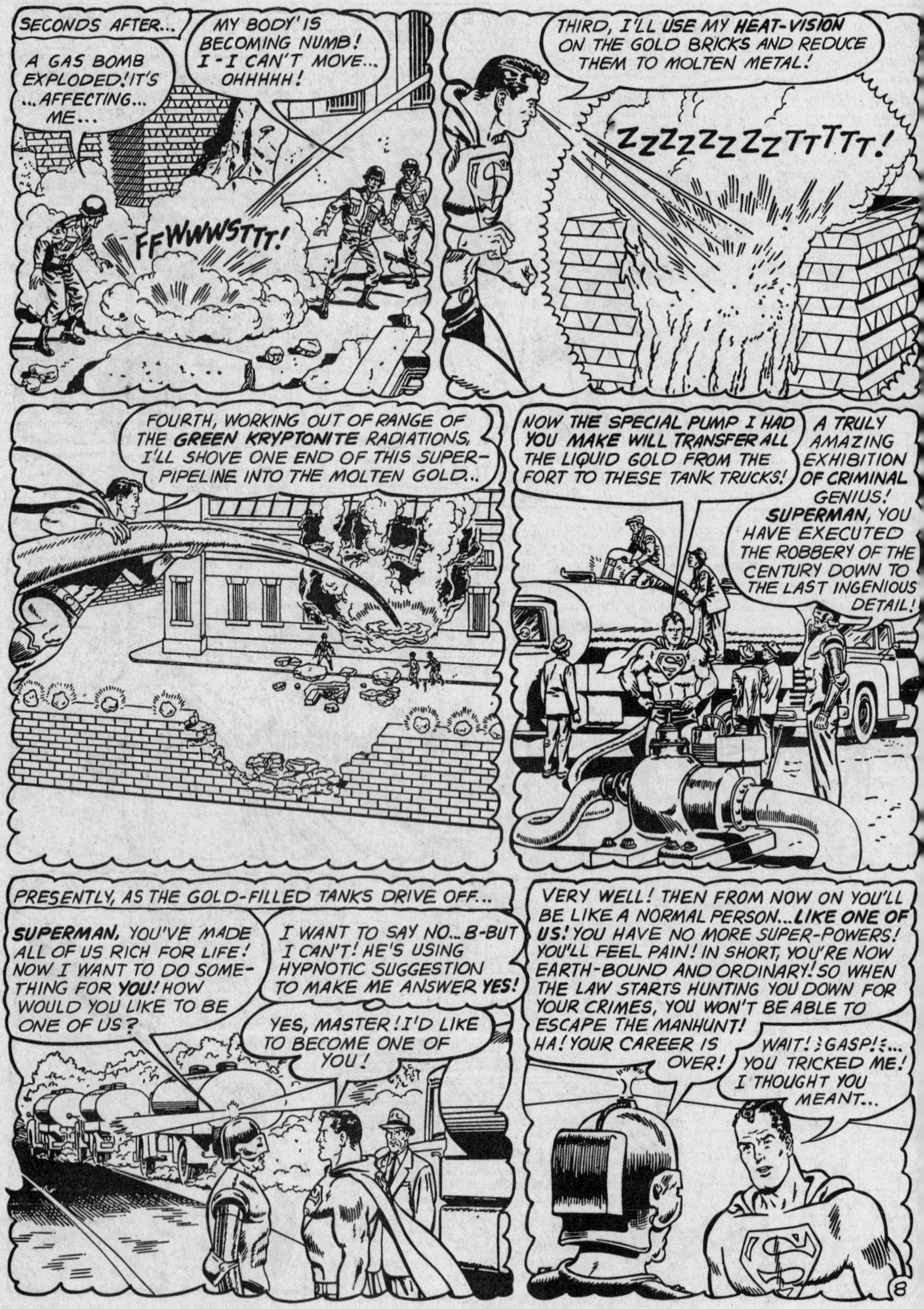
SECONDS AFTER...
A GAS BOMB EXPLODED! IT'S ...AFFECTING... ME...
MY BODY IS BECOMING NUMB! I-I CAN'T MOVE... OHHHHH!
FFWWWSTTT!
THIRD, I'LL USE MY HEAT-VISION ON THE GOLD BRICKS AND REDUCE THEM TO MOLTEN METAL!
ZZZZZZZZZTTTTTT!
FOURTH, WORKING OUT OF RANGE OF THE GREEN KRYPTONITE RADIATIONS, I'LL SHOVE ONE END OF THIS SUPER-PIPELINE INTO THE MOLTEN GOLD...
NOW THE SPECIAL PUMP I HAD YOU MAKE WILL TRANSFER ALL THE LIQUID GOLD FROM THE FORT TO THESE TANK TRUCKS!
A TRULY AMAZING EXHIBITION OF CRIMINAL GENIUS! SUPERMAN, YOU HAVE EXECUTED THE ROBBERY OF THE CENTURY DOWN TO THE LAST INGENIOUS DETAIL!
PRESENTLY, AS THE GOLD-FILLED TANKS DRIVE OFF...
SUPERMAN, YOU'VE MADE ALL OF US RICH FOR LIFE! NOW I WANT TO DO SOMETHING FOR YOU! HOW WOULD YOU LIKE TO BE ONE OF US?
I WANT TO SAY NO...B-BUT I CAN'T! HE'S USING HYPNOTIC SUGGESTION TO MAKE ME ANSWER YES!
YES, MASTER! I'D LIKE TO BECOME ONE OF YOU!
VERY WELL! THEN FROM NOW ON YOU'LL BE LIKE A NORMAL PERSON...LIKE ONE OF US! YOU HAVE NO MORE SUPER-POWERS! YOU'LL FEEL PAIN! IN SHORT, YOU'RE NOW EARTH-BOUND AND ORDINARY! SO WHEN THE LAW STARTS HUNTING YOU DOWN FOR YOUR CRIMES, YOU WON'T BE ABLE TO ESCAPE THE MANHUNT! HA! YOUR CAREER IS OVER!
WAIT! GASP! ... YOU TRICKED ME! I THOUGHT YOU MEANT...
8

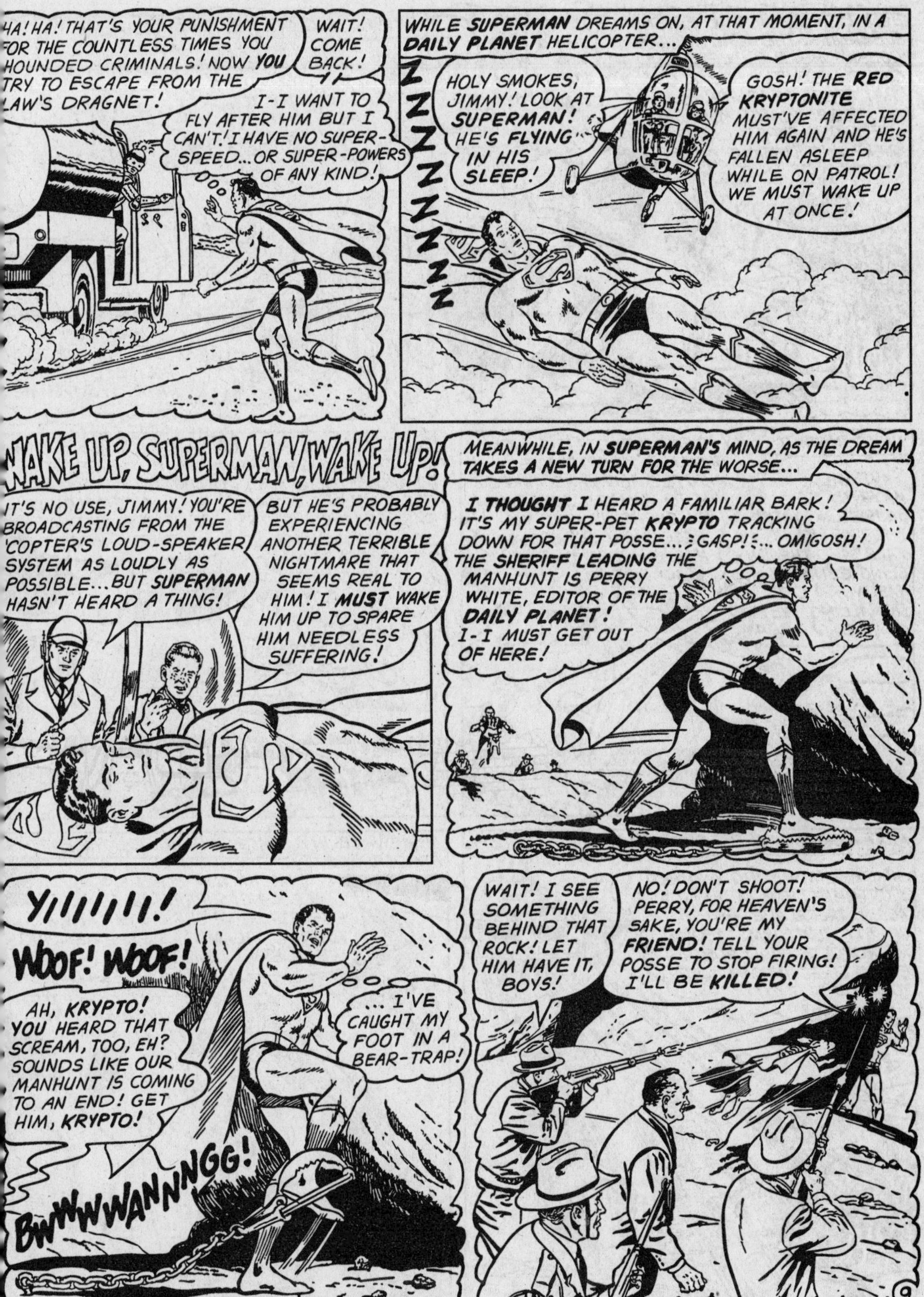
HA! HA! THAT'S YOUR PUNISHMENT FOR THE COUNTLESS TIMES YOU HOUNDED CRIMINALS! NOW YOU TRY TO ESCAPE FROM THE LAW'S DRAGNET!
WAIT! COME BACK!
I-I WANT TO FLY AFTER HIM BUT I CAN'T! I HAVE NO SUPER-SPEED...OR SUPER-POWERS OF ANY KIND!
WHILE SUPERMAN DREAMS ON, AT THAT MOMENT, IN A DAILY PLANET HELICOPTER...
HOLY SMOKES, JIMMY! LOOK AT SUPERMAN! HE'S FLYING IN HIS SLEEP!
GOSH! THE RED KRYPTONITE MUST'VE AFFECTED HIM AGAIN AND HE'S FALLEN ASLEEP WHILE ON PATROL! WE MUST WAKE UP AT ONCE!
ZZZZZZZZZZ
WAKE UP, SUPERMAN, WAKE UP!
IT'S NO USE, JIMMY! YOU'RE BROADCASTING FROM THE 'COPTER'S LOUD-SPEAKER SYSTEM AS LOUDLY AS POSSIBLE...BUT SUPERMAN HASN'T HEARD A THING!
BUT HE'S PROBABLY EXPERIENCING ANOTHER TERRIBLE NIGHTMARE THAT SEEMS REAL TO HIM! I MUST WAKE HIM UP TO SPARE HIM NEEDLESS SUFFERING!
MEANWHILE, IN SUPERMAN'S MIND, AS THE DREAM TAKES A NEW TURN FOR THE WORSE...
I THOUGHT I HEARD A FAMILIAR BARK! IT'S MY SUPER-PET KRYPTO TRACKING DOWN FOR THAT POSSE...GASP!...OMIGOSH! THE SHERIFF LEADING THE MANHUNT IS PERRY WHITE, EDITOR OF THE DAILY PLANET! I-I MUST GET OUT OF HERE!
YIIIIII!
WOOF! WOOF!
AH, KRYPTO! YOU HEARD THAT SCREAM, TOO, EH? SOUNDS LIKE OUR MANHUNT IS COMING TO AN END! GET HIM, KRYPTO!
...I'VE CAUGHT MY FOOT IN A BEAR-TRAP!
BWWWWANNNGG!
WAIT! I SEE SOMETHING BEHIND THAT ROCK! LET HIM HAVE IT, BOYS!
NO! DON'T SHOOT! PERRY, FOR HEAVEN'S SAKE, YOU'RE MY FRIEND! TELL YOUR POSSE TO STOP FIRING! I'LL BE KILLED!
9

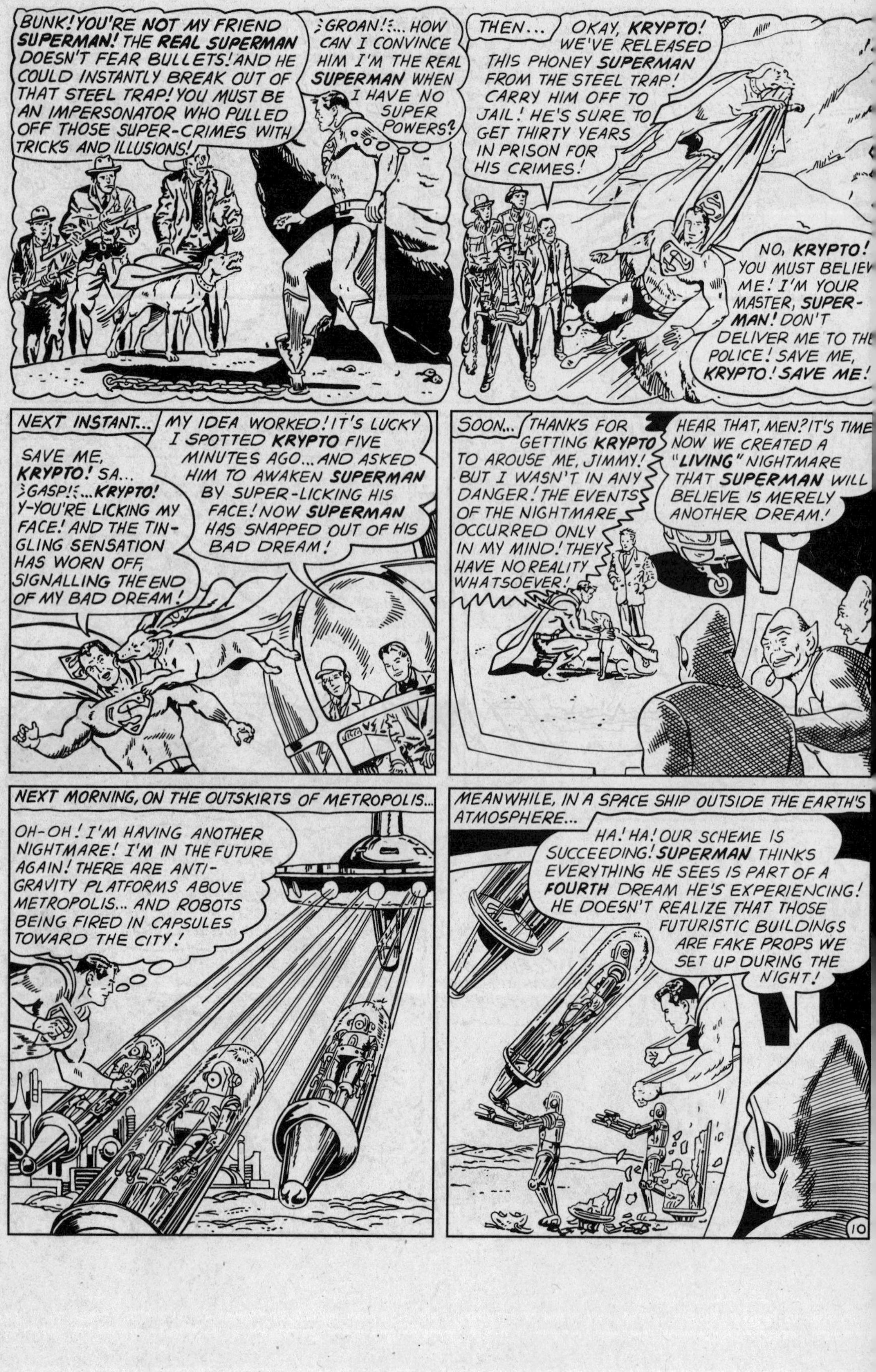
BUNK! YOU'RE NOT MY FRIEND SUPERMAN! THE REAL SUPERMAN DOESN'T FEAR BULLETS! AND HE COULD INSTANTLY BREAK OUT OF THAT STEEL TRAP! YOU MUST BE AN IMPERSONATOR WHO PULLED OFF THOSE SUPER-CRIMES WITH TRICKS AND ILLUSIONS!
GROAN!... HOW CAN I CONVINCE HIM I'M THE REAL SUPERMAN WHEN I HAVE NO SUPER POWERS?
THEN...
OKAY, KRYPTO! WE'VE RELEASED THIS PHONEY SUPERMAN FROM THE STEEL TRAP! CARRY HIM OFF TO JAIL! HE'S SURE TO GET THIRTY YEARS IN PRISON FOR HIS CRIMES!
NO, KRYPTO! YOU MUST BELIEV ME! I'M YOUR MASTER, SUPER-MAN! DON'T DELIVER ME TO TH POLICE! SAVE ME, KRYPTO! SAVE ME!
NEXT INSTANT...
SAVE ME, KRYPTO! SA... GASP!... KRYPTO! Y-YOU'RE LICKING MY FACE! AND THE TIN-GLING SENSATION HAS WORN OFF, SIGNALLING THE END OF MY BAD DREAM!
MY IDEA WORKED! IT'S LUCKY I SPOTTED KRYPTO FIVE MINUTES AGO... AND ASKED HIM TO AWAKEN SUPERMAN BY SUPER-LICKING HIS FACE! NOW SUPERMAN HAS SNAPPED OUT OF HIS BAD DREAM!
SOON...
THANKS FOR GETTING KRYPTO TO AROUSE ME, JIMMY! BUT I WASN'T IN ANY DANGER! THE EVENTS OF THE NIGHTMARE OCCURRED ONLY IN MY MIND! THEY HAVE NO REALITY WHATSOEVER!
HEAR THAT, MEN? IT'S TIME NOW WE CREATED A "LIVING" NIGHTMARE THAT SUPERMAN WILL BELIEVE IS MERELY ANOTHER DREAM!
NEXT MORNING, ON THE OUTSKIRTS OF METROPOLIS...
OH-OH! I'M HAVING ANOTHER NIGHTMARE! I'M IN THE FUTURE AGAIN! THERE ARE ANTI-GRAVITY PLATFORMS ABOVE METROPOLIS... AND ROBOTS BEING FIRED IN CAPSULES TOWARD THE CITY!
MEANWHILE, IN A SPACE SHIP OUTSIDE THE EARTH'S ATMOSPHERE...
HA! HA! OUR SCHEME IS SUCCEEDING! SUPERMAN THINKS EVERYTHING HE SEES IS PART OF A FOURTH DREAM HE'S EXPERIENCING! HE DOESN'T REALIZE THAT THOSE FUTURISTIC BUILDINGS ARE FAKE PROPS WE SET UP DURING THE NIGHT!
10

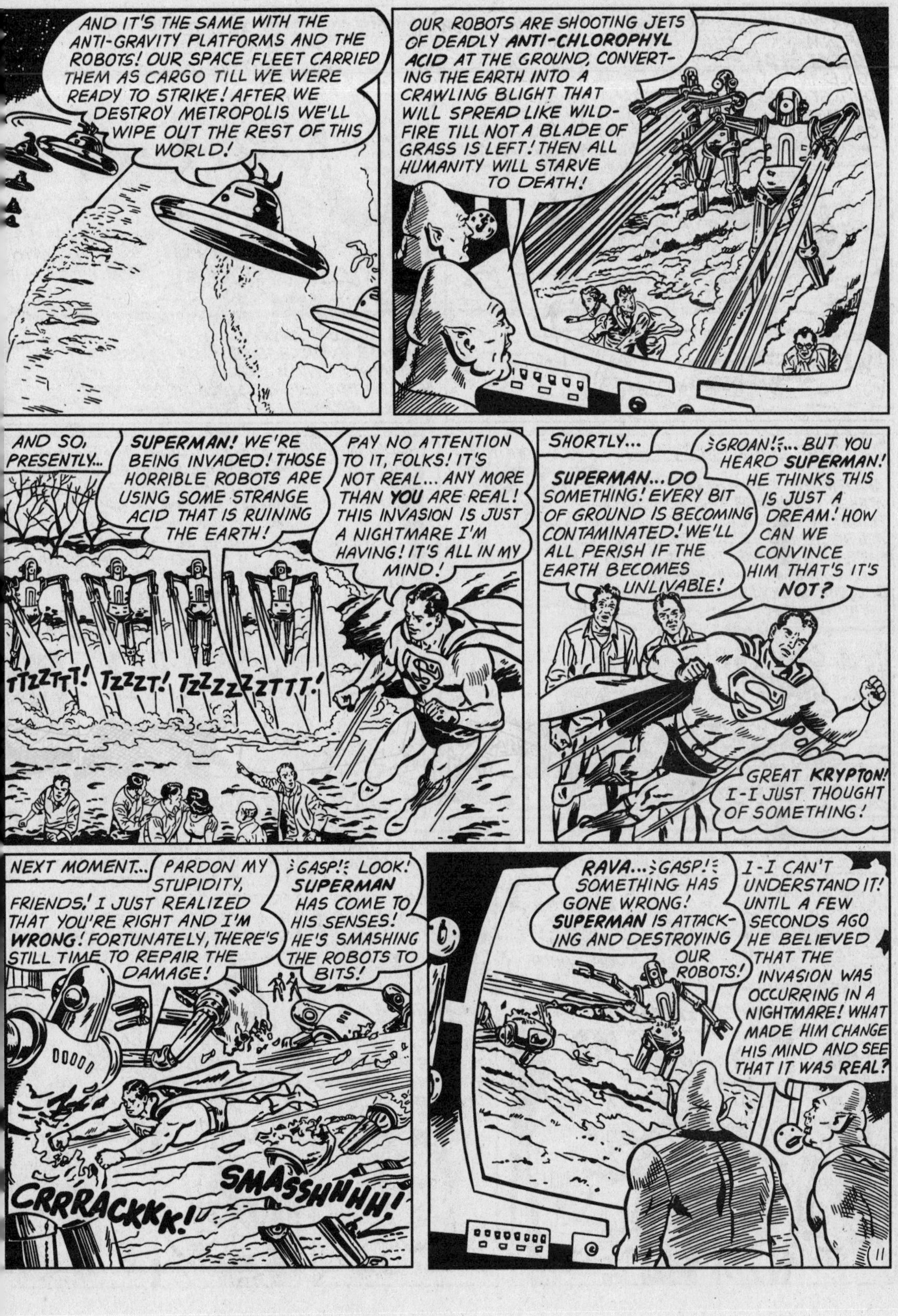
AND IT'S THE SAME WITH THE ANTI-GRAVITY PLATFORMS AND THE ROBOTS! OUR SPACE FLEET CARRIED THEM AS CARGO TILL WE WERE READY TO STRIKE! AFTER WE DESTROY METROPOLIS WE'LL WIPE OUT THE REST OF THIS WORLD!
OUR ROBOTS ARE SHOOTING JETS OF DEADLY ANTI-CHLOROPHYL ACID AT THE GROUND, CONVERTING THE EARTH INTO A CRAWLING BLIGHT THAT WILL SPREAD LIKE WILDFIRE TILL NOT A BLADE OF GRASS IS LEFT! THEN ALL HUMANITY WILL STARVE TO DEATH!
AND SO, PRESENTLY...
SUPERMAN! WE'RE BEING INVADED! THOSE HORRIBLE ROBOTS ARE USING SOME STRANGE ACID THAT IS RUINING THE EARTH!
PAY NO ATTENTION TO IT, FOLKS! IT'S NOT REAL... ANY MORE THAN YOU ARE REAL! THIS INVASION IS JUST A NIGHTMARE I'M HAVING! IT'S ALL IN MY MIND!
TTZZTTT! TZZZT! TZZZZZZTTT!
SHORTLY...
SUPERMAN... DO SOMETHING! EVERY BIT OF GROUND IS BECOMING CONTAMINATED! WE'LL ALL PERISH IF THE EARTH BECOMES UNLIVABLE!
GROAN! ... BUT YOU HEARD SUPERMAN! HE THINKS THIS IS JUST A DREAM! HOW CAN WE CONVINCE HIM THAT'S IT'S NOT?
GREAT KRYPTON! I-I JUST THOUGHT OF SOMETHING!
NEXT MOMENT...
PARDON MY STUPIDITY, FRIENDS! I JUST REALIZED THAT YOU'RE RIGHT AND I'M WRONG! FORTUNATELY, THERE'S STILL TIME TO REPAIR THE DAMAGE!
GASP! LOOK! SUPERMAN HAS COME TO HIS SENSES! HE'S SMASHING THE ROBOTS TO BITS!
CRRRACKKK!
SMASSHHHH!
RAVA... GASP! SOMETHING HAS GONE WRONG! SUPERMAN IS ATTACKING AND DESTROYING OUR ROBOTS!
I-I CAN'T UNDERSTAND IT! UNTIL A FEW SECONDS AGO HE BELIEVED THAT THE INVASION WAS OCCURRING IN A NIGHTMARE! WHAT MADE HIM CHANGE HIS MIND AND SEE THAT IT WAS REAL?
11

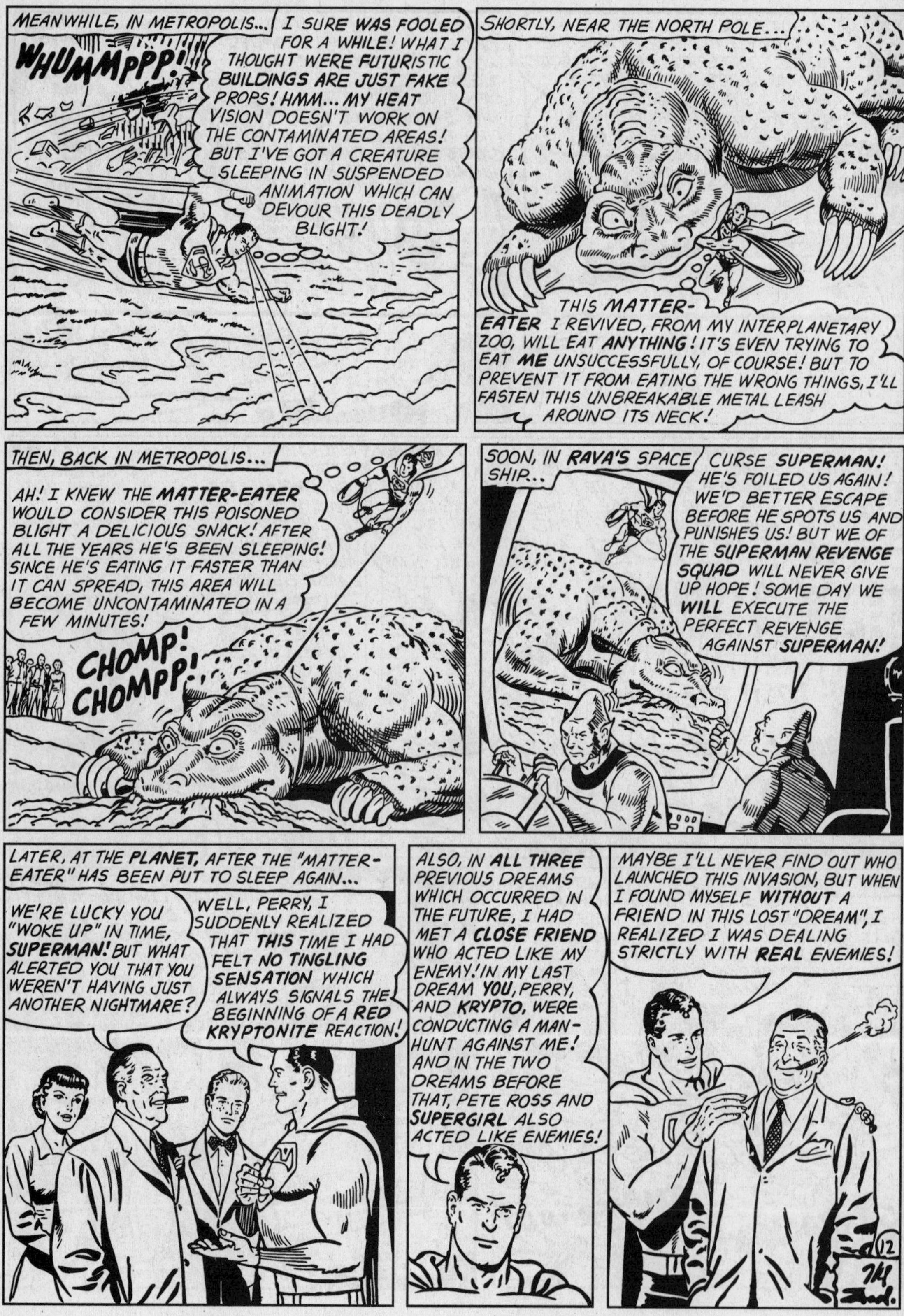
MEANWHILE, IN METROPOLIS...
WHUMMPPP!
I SURE WAS FOOLED FOR A WHILE! WHAT I THOUGHT WERE FUTURISTIC BUILDINGS ARE JUST FAKE PROPS! HMM... MY HEAT VISION DOESN'T WORK ON THE CONTAMINATED AREAS! BUT I'VE GOT A CREATURE SLEEPING IN SUSPENDED ANIMATION WHICH CAN DEVOUR THIS DEADLY BLIGHT!
SHORTLY, NEAR THE NORTH POLE...
THIS MATTER-EATER I REVIVED, FROM MY INTERPLANETARY ZOO, WILL EAT ANYTHING! IT'S EVEN TRYING TO EAT ME UNSUCCESSFULLY, OF COURSE! BUT TO PREVENT IT FROM EATING THE WRONG THINGS, I'LL FASTEN THIS UNBREAKABLE METAL LEASH AROUND ITS NECK!
THEN, BACK IN METROPOLIS...
AH! I KNEW THE MATTER-EATER WOULD CONSIDER THIS POISONED BLIGHT A DELICIOUS SNACK! AFTER ALL THE YEARS HE'S BEEN SLEEPING! SINCE HE'S EATING IT FASTER THAN IT CAN SPREAD, THIS AREA WILL BECOME UNCONTAMINATED IN A FEW MINUTES!
CHOMP! CHOMPP!
SOON, IN RAVA'S SPACE SHIP...
CURSE SUPERMAN! HE'S FOILED US AGAIN! WE'D BETTER ESCAPE BEFORE HE SPOTS US AND PUNISHES US! BUT WE OF THE SUPERMAN REVENGE SQUAD WILL NEVER GIVE UP HOPE! SOME DAY WE WILL EXECUTE THE PERFECT REVENGE AGAINST SUPERMAN!
LATER, AT THE PLANET, AFTER THE "MATTER-EATER" HAS BEEN PUT TO SLEEP AGAIN...
WE'RE LUCKY YOU "WOKE UP" IN TIME, SUPERMAN! BUT WHAT ALERTED YOU THAT YOU WEREN'T HAVING JUST ANOTHER NIGHTMARE?
WELL, PERRY, I SUDDENLY REALIZED THAT THIS TIME I HAD FELT NO TINGLING SENSATION WHICH ALWAYS SIGNALS THE BEGINNING OF A RED KRYPTONITE REACTION!
ALSO, IN ALL THREE PREVIOUS DREAMS WHICH OCCURRED IN THE FUTURE, I HAD MET A CLOSE FRIEND WHO ACTED LIKE MY ENEMY! IN MY LAST DREAM YOU, PERRY, AND KRYPTO, WERE CONDUCTING A MAN-HUNT AGAINST ME! AND IN THE TWO DREAMS BEFORE THAT, PETE ROSS AND SUPERGIRL ALSO ACTED LIKE ENEMIES!
MAYBE I'LL NEVER FIND OUT WHO LAUNCHED THIS INVASION, BUT WHEN I FOUND MYSELF WITHOUT A FRIEND IN THIS LOST "DREAM", I REALIZED I WAS DEALING STRICTLY WITH REAL ENEMIES!
12

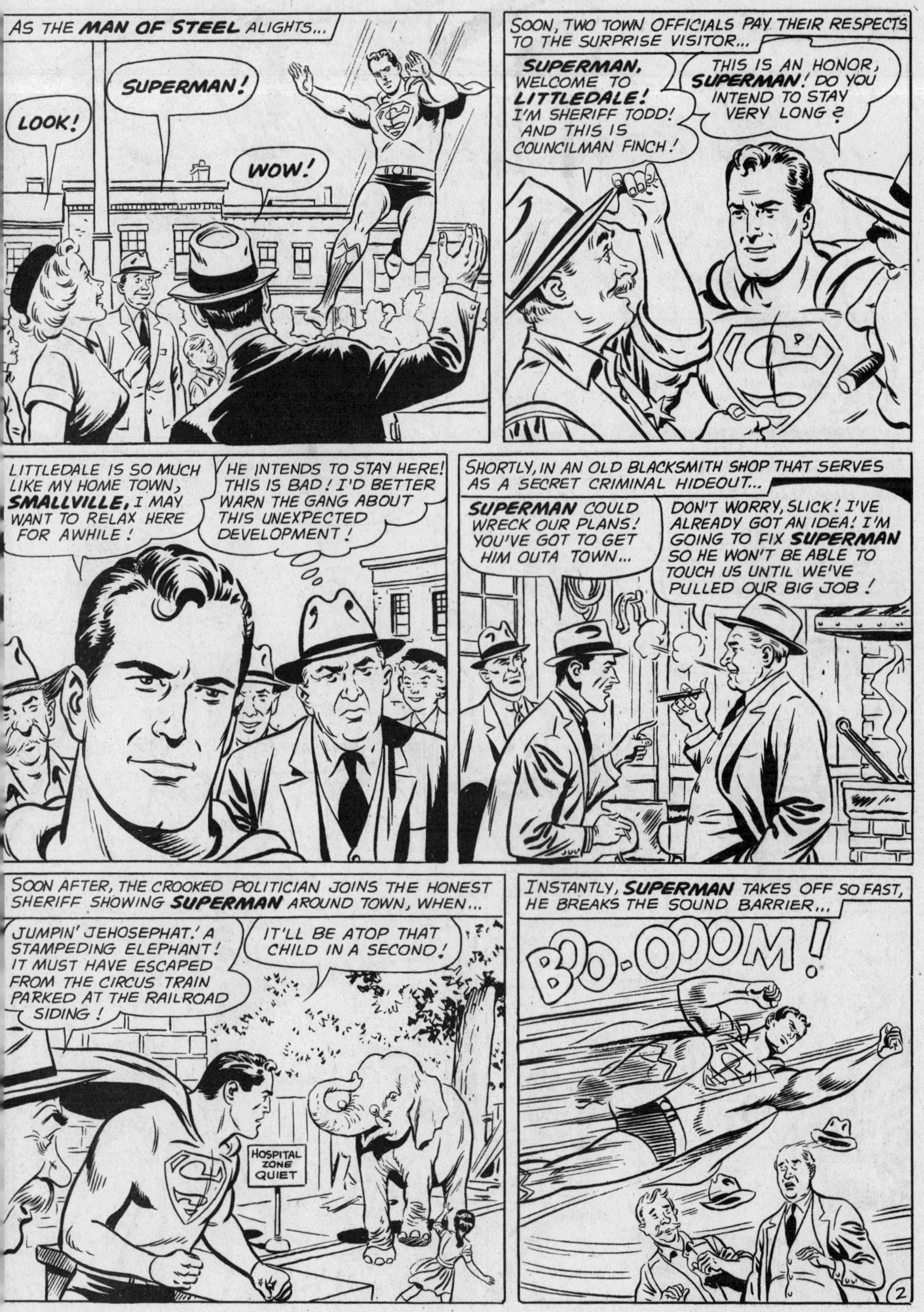
AS THE MAN OF STEEL ALIGHTS...
LOOK!
SUPERMAN!
WOW!
SOON, TWO TOWN OFFICIALS PAY THEIR RESPECTS TO THE SURPRISE VISITOR...
SUPERMAN, WELCOME TO LITTLEDALE! I'M SHERIFF TODD! AND THIS IS COUNCILMAN FINCH!
THIS IS AN HONOR, SUPERMAN! DO YOU INTEND TO STAY VERY LONG?
LITTLEDALE IS SO MUCH LIKE MY HOME TOWN, SMALLVILLE, I MAY WANT TO RELAX HERE FOR AWHILE!
HE INTENDS TO STAY HERE! THIS IS BAD! I'D BETTER WARN THE GANG ABOUT THIS UNEXPECTED DEVELOPMENT!
SHORTLY, IN AN OLD BLACKSMITH SHOP THAT SERVES AS A SECRET CRIMINAL HIDEOUT...
SUPERMAN COULD WRECK OUR PLANS! YOU'VE GOT TO GET HIM OUTA TOWN...
DON'T WORRY, SLICK! I'VE ALREADY GOT AN IDEA! I'M GOING TO FIX SUPERMAN SO HE WON'T BE ABLE TO TOUCH US UNTIL WE'VE PULLED OUR BIG JOB!
SOON AFTER, THE CROOKED POLITICIAN JOINS THE HONEST SHERIFF SHOWING SUPERMAN AROUND TOWN, WHEN...
JUMPIN' JEHOSEPHAT! A STAMPEDING ELEPHANT! IT MUST HAVE ESCAPED FROM THE CIRCUS TRAIN PARKED AT THE RAILROAD SIDING!
IT'LL BE ATOP THAT CHILD IN A SECOND!
HOSPITAL ZONE QUIET
INSTANTLY, SUPERMAN TAKES OFF SO FAST, HE BREAKS THE SOUND BARRIER...
BOO-OOOM!
2

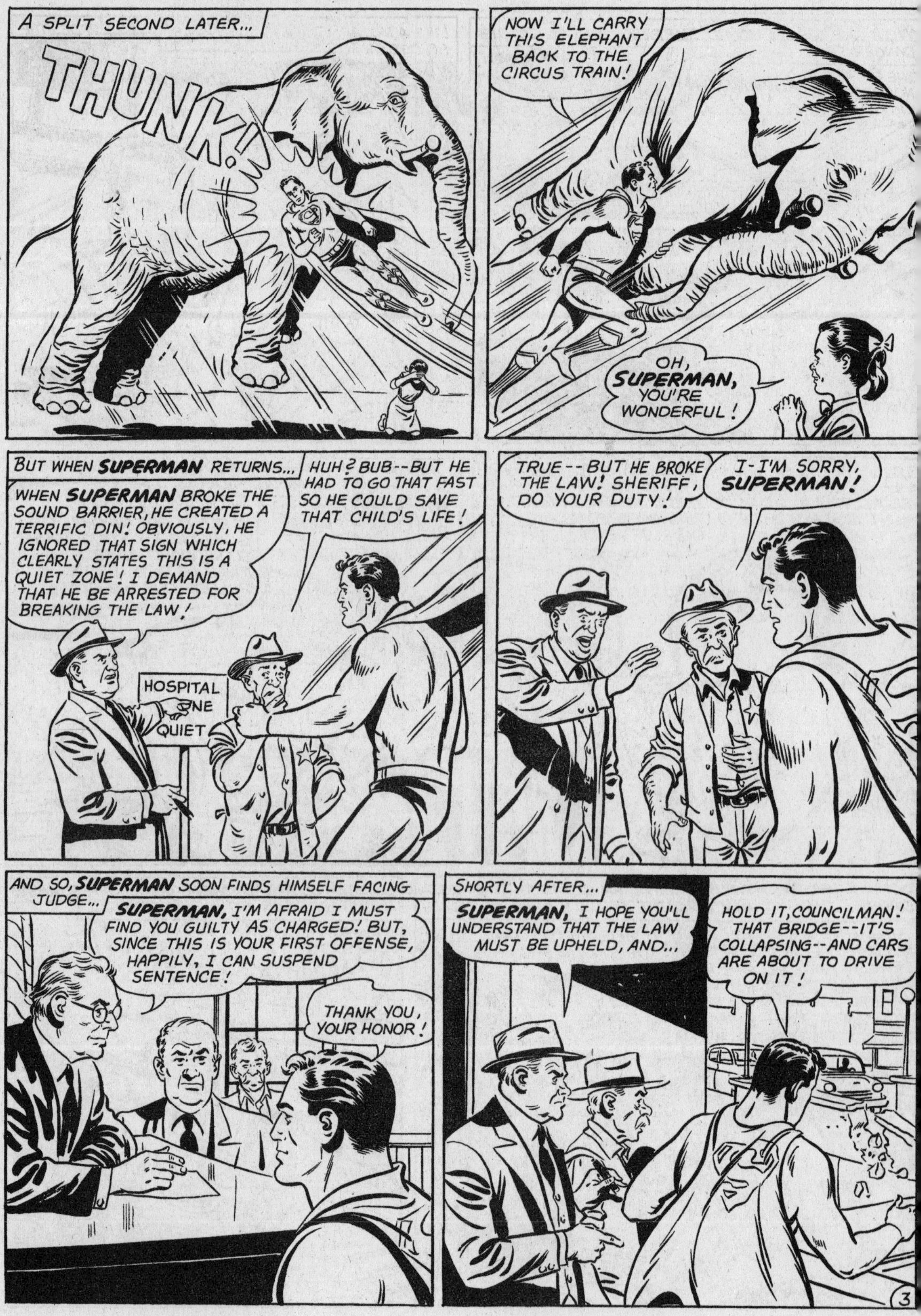
A SPLIT SECOND LATER...
THUNK!
NOW I'LL CARRY THIS ELEPHANT BACK TO THE CIRCUS TRAIN!
OH, SUPERMAN, YOU'RE WONDERFUL!
BUT WHEN SUPERMAN RETURNS...
WHEN SUPERMAN BROKE THE SOUND BARRIER, HE CREATED A TERRIFIC DIN! OBVIOUSLY, HE IGNORED THAT SIGN WHICH CLEARLY STATES THIS IS A QUIET ZONE! I DEMAND THAT HE BE ARRESTED FOR BREAKING THE LAW!
HUH? BUB--BUT HE HAD TO GO THAT FAST SO HE COULD SAVE THAT CHILD'S LIFE!
HOSPITAL
QUIET
TRUE--BUT HE BROKE THE LAW! SHERIFF, DO YOUR DUTY!
I-I'M SORRY, SUPERMAN!
AND SO, SUPERMAN SOON FINDS HIMSELF FACING JUDGE...
SUPERMAN, I'M AFRAID I MUST FIND YOU GUILTY AS CHARGED! BUT, SINCE THIS IS YOUR FIRST OFFENSE, HAPPILY, I CAN SUSPEND SENTENCE!
THANK YOU, YOUR HONOR!
SHORTLY AFTER...
SUPERMAN, I HOPE YOU'LL UNDERSTAND THAT THE LAW MUST BE UPHELD, AND...
HOLD IT, COUNCILMAN! THAT BRIDGE--IT'S COLLAPSING--AND CARS ARE ABOUT TO DRIVE ON IT!
3

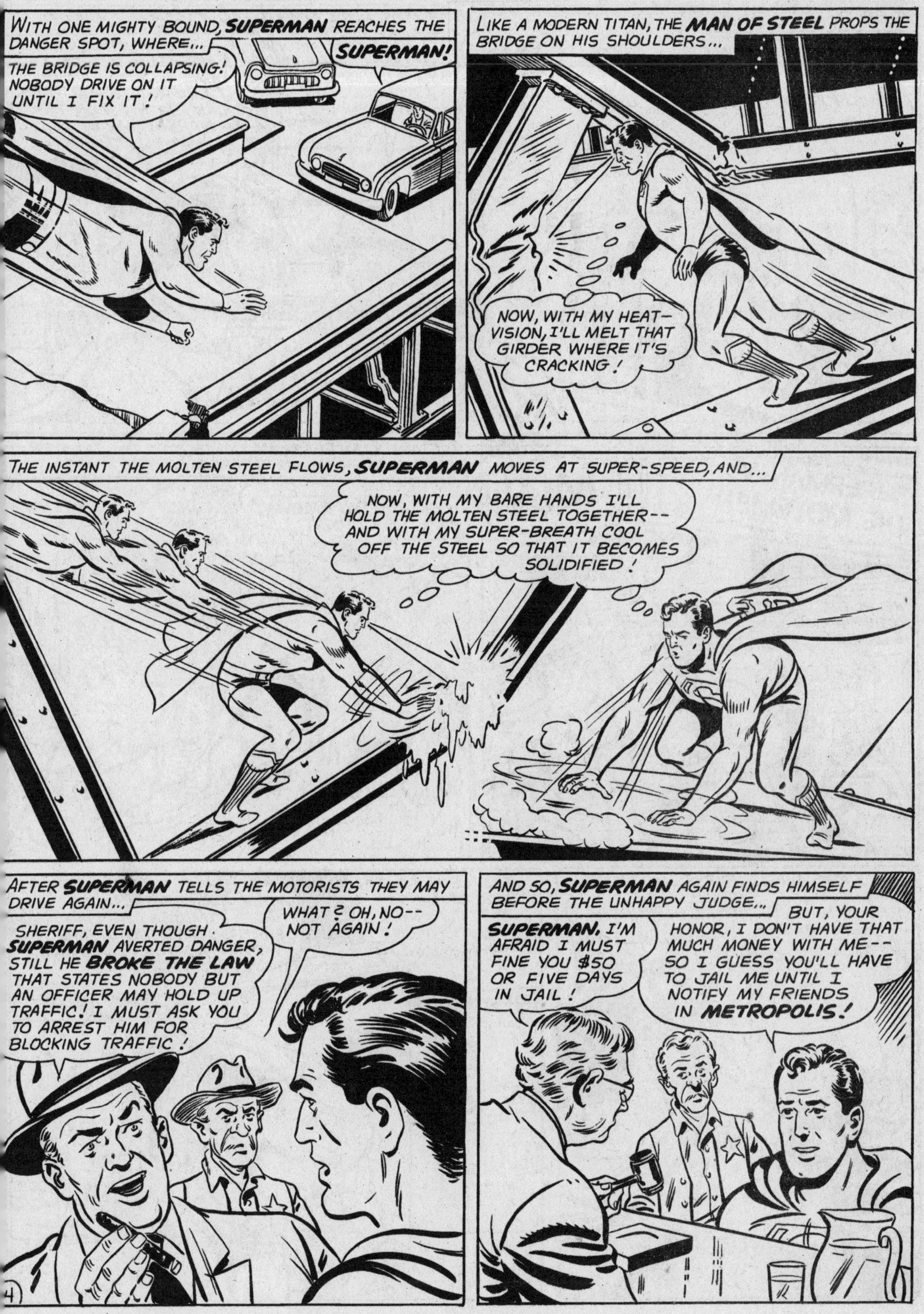

WITH ONE MIGHTY BOUND, SUPERMAN REACHES THE DANGER SPOT, WHERE...
SUPERMAN!
THE BRIDGE IS COLLAPSING! NOBODY DRIVE ON IT UNTIL I FIX IT!
LIKE A MODERN TITAN, THE MAN OF STEEL PROPS THE BRIDGE ON HIS SHOULDERS...
NOW, WITH MY HEAT-VISION, I'LL MELT THAT GIRDER WHERE IT'S CRACKING!
THE INSTANT THE MOLTEN STEEL FLOWS, SUPERMAN MOVES AT SUPER-SPEED, AND...
NOW, WITH MY BARE HANDS I'LL HOLD THE MOLTEN STEEL TOGETHER-- AND WITH MY SUPER-BREATH COOL OFF THE STEEL SO THAT IT BECOMES SOLIDIFIED!
AFTER SUPERMAN TELLS THE MOTORISTS THEY MAY DRIVE AGAIN...
SHERIFF, EVEN THOUGH SUPERMAN AVERTED DANGER, STILL HE BROKE THE LAW THAT STATES NOBODY BUT AN OFFICER MAY HOLD UP TRAFFIC! I MUST ASK YOU TO ARREST HIM FOR BLOCKING TRAFFIC!
WHAT? OH, NO-- NOT AGAIN!
AND SO, SUPERMAN AGAIN FINDS HIMSELF BEFORE THE UNHAPPY JUDGE...
SUPERMAN, I'M AFRAID I MUST FINE YOU $50 OR FIVE DAYS IN JAIL!
BUT, YOUR HONOR, I DON'T HAVE THAT MUCH MONEY WITH ME-- SO I GUESS YOU'LL HAVE TO JAIL ME UNTIL I NOTIFY MY FRIENDS IN METROPOLIS!
4

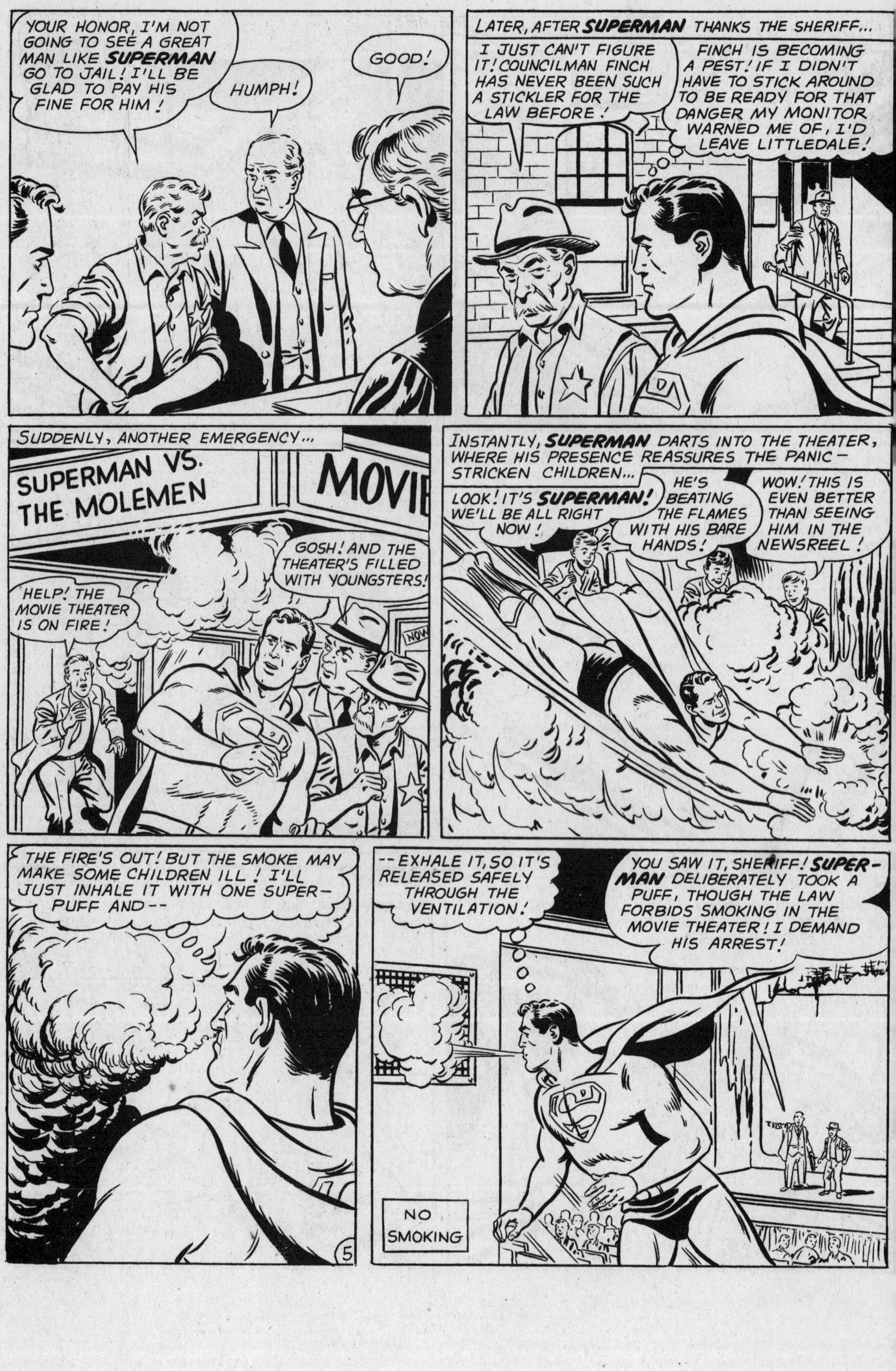
YOUR HONOR, I'M NOT GOING TO SEE A GREAT MAN LIKE SUPERMAN GO TO JAIL! I'LL BE GLAD TO PAY HIS FINE FOR HIM!
HUMPH!
GOOD!
LATER, AFTER SUPERMAN THANKS THE SHERIFF...
I JUST CAN'T FIGURE IT! COUNCILMAN FINCH HAS NEVER BEEN SUCH A STICKLER FOR THE LAW BEFORE!
FINCH IS BECOMING A PEST! IF I DIDN'T HAVE TO STICK AROUND TO BE READY FOR THAT DANGER MY MONITOR WARNED ME OF, I'D LEAVE LITTLEDALE!
SUDDENLY, ANOTHER EMERGENCY...
SUPERMAN VS. THE MOLEMEN
MOVIE
GOSH! AND THE THEATER'S FILLED WITH YOUNGSTERS!
HELP! THE MOVIE THEATER IS ON FIRE!
NOW
INSTANTLY, SUPERMAN DARTS INTO THE THEATER, WHERE HIS PRESENCE REASSURES THE PANIC-STRICKEN CHILDREN...
LOOK! IT'S SUPERMAN! WE'LL BE ALL RIGHT NOW!
HE'S BEATING THE FLAMES WITH HIS BARE HANDS!
WOW! THIS IS EVEN BETTER THAN SEEING HIM IN THE NEWSREEL!
THE FIRE'S OUT! BUT THE SMOKE MAY MAKE SOME CHILDREN ILL! I'LL JUST INHALE IT WITH ONE SUPER-PUFF AND--
5
--EXHALE IT, SO IT'S RELEASED SAFELY THROUGH THE VENTILATION!
YOU SAW IT, SHERIFF! SUPERMAN DELIBERATELY TOOK A PUFF, THOUGH THE LAW FORBIDS SMOKING IN THE MOVIE THEATER! I DEMAND HIS ARREST!
NO SMOKING

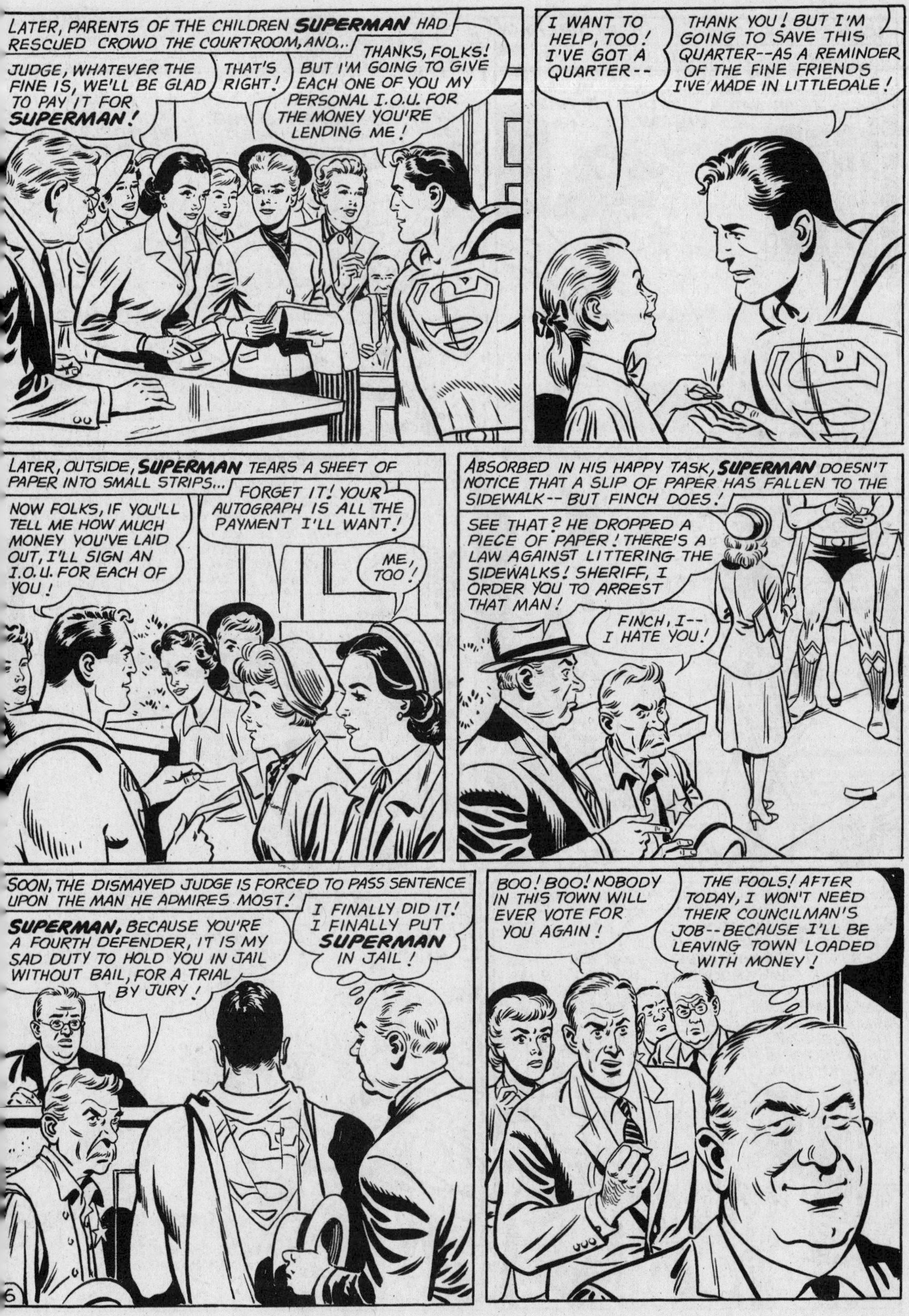
LATER, PARENTS OF THE CHILDREN SUPERMAN HAD RESCUED CROWD THE COURTROOM, AND...
JUDGE, WHATEVER THE FINE IS, WE'LL BE GLAD TO PAY IT FOR SUPERMAN!
THAT'S RIGHT!
THANKS, FOLKS! BUT I'M GOING TO GIVE EACH ONE OF YOU MY PERSONAL I.O.U. FOR THE MONEY YOU'RE LENDING ME!
I WANT TO HELP, TOO! I'VE GOT A QUARTER--
THANK YOU! BUT I'M GOING TO SAVE THIS QUARTER--AS A REMINDER OF THE FINE FRIENDS I'VE MADE IN LITTLEDALE!
LATER, OUTSIDE, SUPERMAN TEARS A SHEET OF PAPER INTO SMALL STRIPS...
NOW FOLKS, IF YOU'LL TELL ME HOW MUCH MONEY YOU'VE LAID OUT, I'LL SIGN AN I.O.U. FOR EACH OF YOU!
FORGET IT! YOUR AUTOGRAPH IS ALL THE PAYMENT I'LL WANT!
ME, TOO!
ABSORBED IN HIS HAPPY TASK, SUPERMAN DOESN'T NOTICE THAT A SLIP OF PAPER HAS FALLEN TO THE SIDEWALK-- BUT FINCH DOES!
SEE THAT? HE DROPPED A PIECE OF PAPER! THERE'S A LAW AGAINST LITTERING THE SIDEWALKS! SHERIFF, I ORDER YOU TO ARREST THAT MAN!
FINCH, I-- I HATE YOU!
SOON, THE DISMAYED JUDGE IS FORCED TO PASS SENTENCE UPON THE MAN HE ADMIRES MOST!
SUPERMAN, BECAUSE YOU'RE A FOURTH DEFENDER, IT IS MY SAD DUTY TO HOLD YOU IN JAIL WITHOUT BAIL, FOR A TRIAL BY JURY!
I FINALLY DID IT! I FINALLY PUT SUPERMAN IN JAIL!
6
BOO! BOO! NOBODY IN THIS TOWN WILL EVER VOTE FOR YOU AGAIN!
THE FOOLS! AFTER TODAY, I WON'T NEED THEIR COUNCILMAN'S JOB--BECAUSE I'LL BE LEAVING TOWN LOADED WITH MONEY!

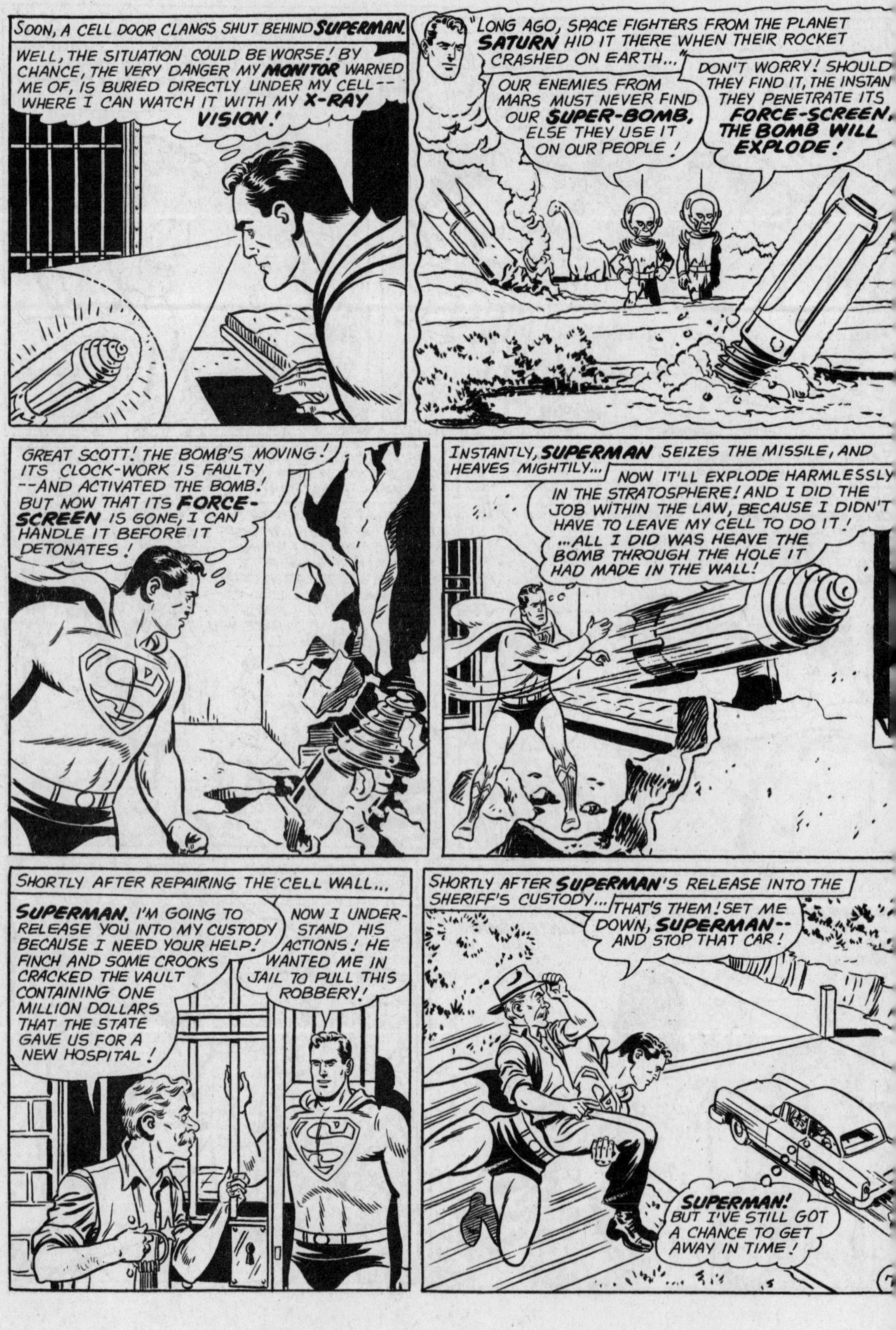
SOON, A CELL DOOR CLANGS SHUT BEHIND SUPERMAN.
WELL, THE SITUATION COULD BE WORSE! BY CHANCE, THE VERY DANGER MY MONITOR WARNED ME OF, IS BURIED DIRECTLY UNDER MY CELL-- WHERE I CAN WATCH IT WITH MY X-RAY VISION!
"LONG AGO, SPACE FIGHTERS FROM THE PLANET SATURN HID IT THERE WHEN THEIR ROCKET CRASHED ON EARTH..."
OUR ENEMIES FROM MARS MUST NEVER FIND OUR SUPER-BOMB, ELSE THEY USE IT ON OUR PEOPLE!
DON'T WORRY! SHOULD THEY FIND IT, THE INSTAN THEY PENETRATE ITS FORCE-SCREEN, THE BOMB WILL EXPLODE!
GREAT SCOTT! THE BOMB'S MOVING! ITS CLOCK-WORK IS FAULTY --AND ACTIVATED THE BOMB! BUT NOW THAT ITS FORCE-SCREEN IS GONE, I CAN HANDLE IT BEFORE IT DETONATES!
INSTANTLY, SUPERMAN SEIZES THE MISSILE, AND HEAVES MIGHTILY...
NOW IT'LL EXPLODE HARMLESSLY IN THE STRATOSPHERE! AND I DID THE JOB WITHIN THE LAW, BECAUSE I DIDN'T HAVE TO LEAVE MY CELL TO DO IT! ...ALL I DID WAS HEAVE THE BOMB THROUGH THE HOLE IT HAD MADE IN THE WALL!
SHORTLY AFTER REPAIRING THE CELL WALL...
SUPERMAN, I'M GOING TO RELEASE YOU INTO MY CUSTODY BECAUSE I NEED YOUR HELP! FINCH AND SOME CROOKS CRACKED THE VAULT CONTAINING ONE MILLION DOLLARS THAT THE STATE GAVE US FOR A NEW HOSPITAL!
NOW I UNDERSTAND HIS ACTIONS! HE WANTED ME IN JAIL TO PULL THIS ROBBERY!
SHORTLY AFTER SUPERMAN'S RELEASE INTO THE SHERIFF'S CUSTODY...
THAT'S THEM! SET ME DOWN, SUPERMAN-- AND STOP THAT CAR!
SUPERMAN! BUT I'VE STILL GOT A CHANCE TO GET AWAY IN TIME!

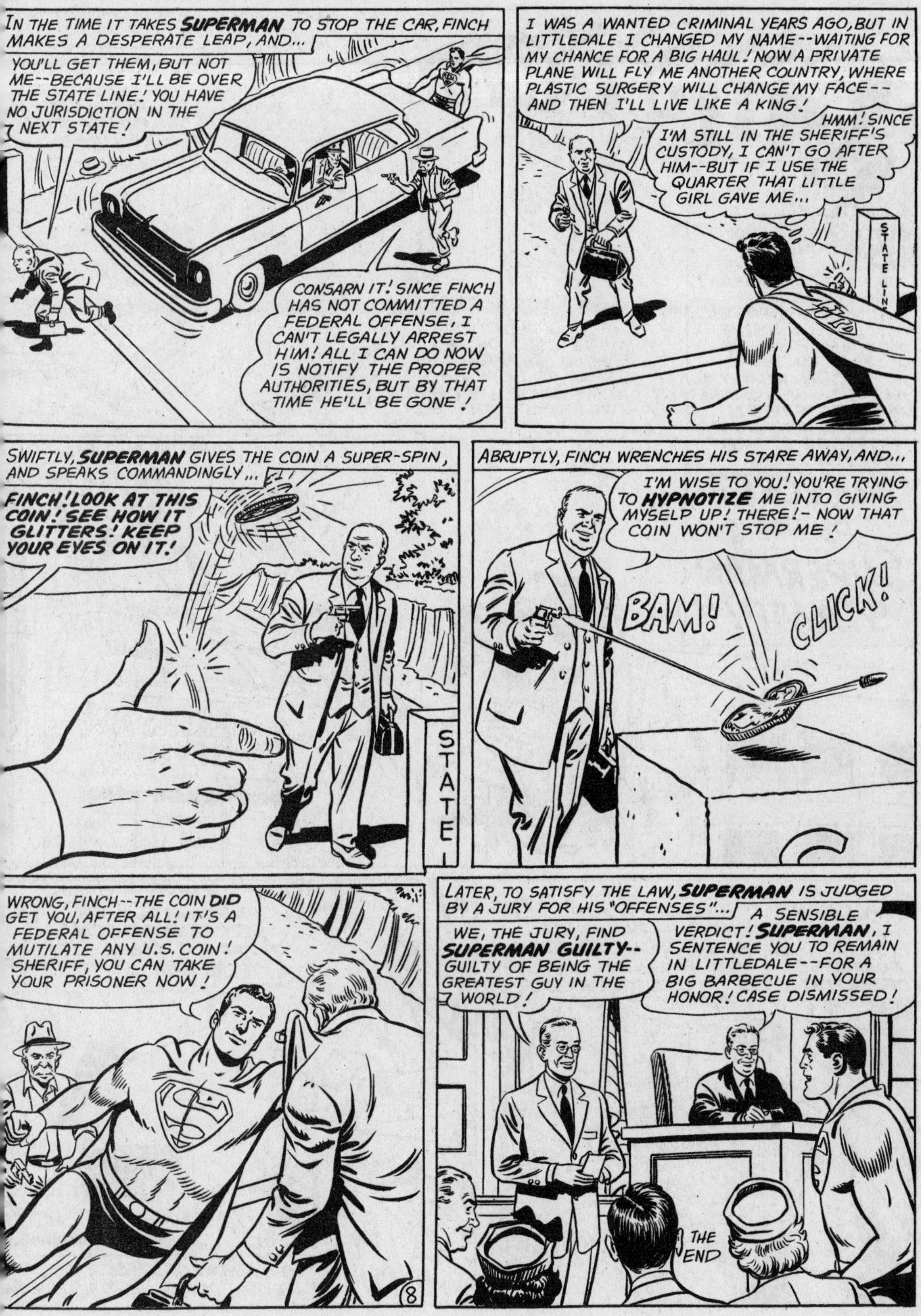
IN THE TIME IT TAKES SUPERMAN TO STOP THE CAR, FINCH MAKES A DESPERATE LEAP, AND...
YOU'LL GET THEM, BUT NOT ME--BECAUSE I'LL BE OVER THE STATE LINE! YOU HAVE NO JURISDICTION IN THE NEXT STATE!
CONSARN IT! SINCE FINCH HAS NOT COMMITTED A FEDERAL OFFENSE, I CAN'T LEGALLY ARREST HIM! ALL I CAN DO NOW IS NOTIFY THE PROPER AUTHORITIES, BUT BY THAT TIME HE'LL BE GONE!
I WAS A WANTED CRIMINAL YEARS AGO, BUT IN LITTLEDALE I CHANGED MY NAME--WAITING FOR MY CHANCE FOR A BIG HAUL! NOW A PRIVATE PLANE WILL FLY ME ANOTHER COUNTRY, WHERE PLASTIC SURGERY WILL CHANGE MY FACE--AND THEN I'LL LIVE LIKE A KING!
HMM! SINCE I'M STILL IN THE SHERIFF'S CUSTODY, I CAN'T GO AFTER HIM--BUT IF I USE THE QUARTER THAT LITTLE GIRL GAVE ME...
STATE LINE
SWIFTLY, SUPERMAN GIVES THE COIN A SUPER-SPIN, AND SPEAKS COMMANDINGLY...
FINCH! LOOK AT THIS COIN! SEE HOW IT GLITTERS! KEEP YOUR EYES ON IT!
STATE
ABRUPTLY, FINCH WRENCHES HIS STARE AWAY, AND...
I'M WISE TO YOU! YOU'RE TRYING TO HYPNOTIZE ME INTO GIVING MYSELF UP! THERE!- NOW THAT COIN WON'T STOP ME!
BAM!
CLICK!
WRONG, FINCH--THE COIN DID GET YOU, AFTER ALL! IT'S A FEDERAL OFFENSE TO MUTILATE ANY U.S. COIN! SHERIFF, YOU CAN TAKE YOUR PRISONER NOW!
8
LATER, TO SATISFY THE LAW, SUPERMAN IS JUDGED BY A JURY FOR HIS "OFFENSES"...
WE, THE JURY, FIND SUPERMAN GUILTY--GUILTY OF BEING THE GREATEST GUY IN THE WORLD!
A SENSIBLE VERDICT! SUPERMAN, I SENTENCE YOU TO REMAIN IN LITTLEDALE--FOR A BIG BARBECUE IN YOUR HONOR! CASE DISMISSED!
THE END

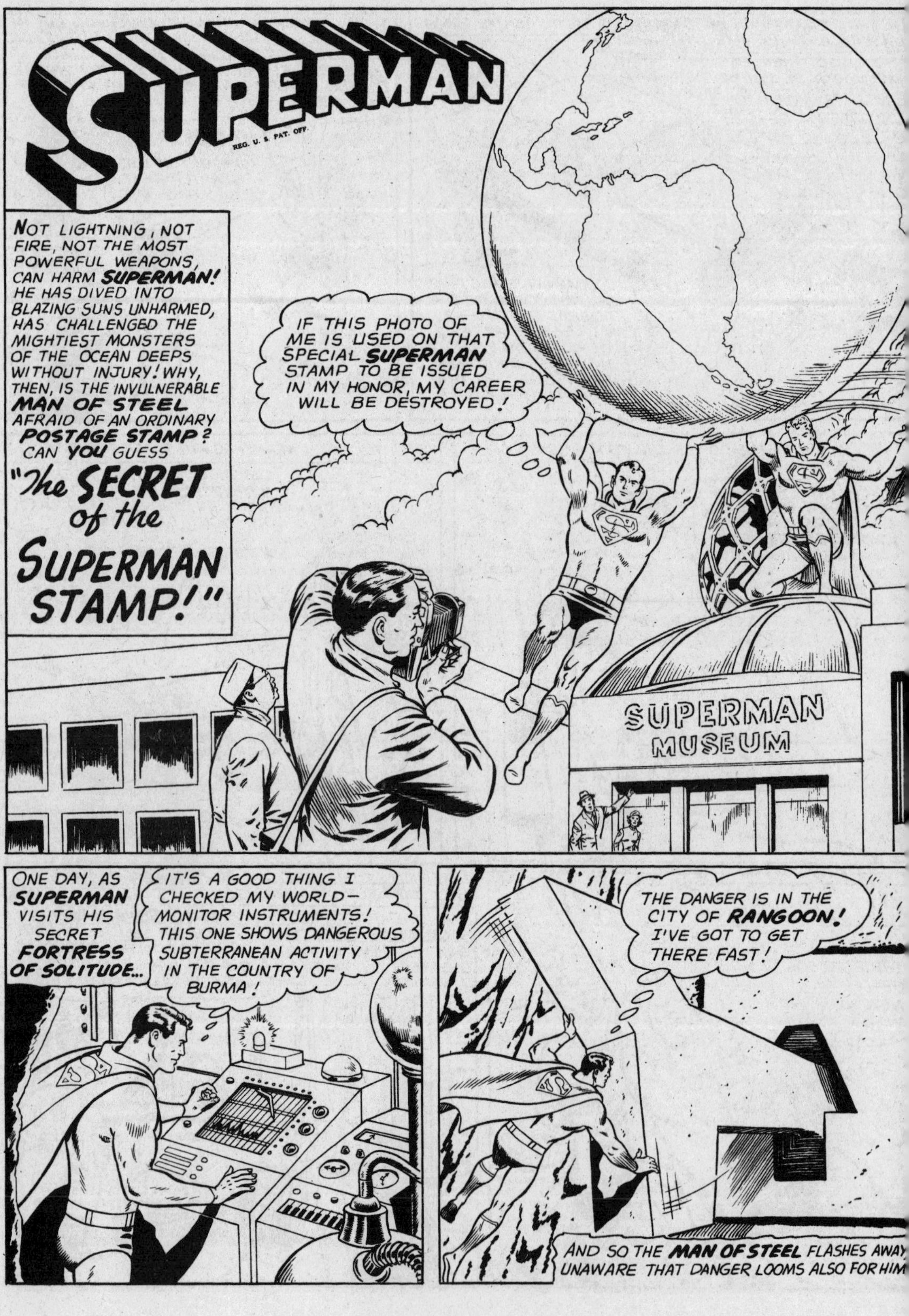
SUPERMAN
REG. U. S. PAT. OFF.
NOT LIGHTNING, NOT FIRE, NOT THE MOST POWERFUL WEAPONS, CAN HARM SUPERMAN! HE HAS DIVED INTO BLAZING SUNS UNHARMED, HAS CHALLENGED THE MIGHTIEST MONSTERS OF THE OCEAN DEEPS WITHOUT INJURY! WHY, THEN, IS THE INVULNERABLE MAN OF STEEL AFRAID OF AN ORDINARY POSTAGE STAMP? CAN YOU GUESS "The SECRET of the SUPERMAN STAMP!"
IF THIS PHOTO OF ME IS USED ON THAT SPECIAL SUPERMAN STAMP TO BE ISSUED IN MY HONOR, MY CAREER WILL BE DESTROYED!
SUPERMAN MUSEUM
ONE DAY, AS SUPERMAN VISITS HIS SECRET FORTRESS OF SOLITUDE...
IT'S A GOOD THING I CHECKED MY WORLD-MONITOR INSTRUMENTS! THIS ONE SHOWS DANGEROUS SUBTERRANEAN ACTIVITY IN THE COUNTRY OF BURMA!
THE DANGER IS IN THE CITY OF RANGOON! I'VE GOT TO GET THERE FAST!
AND SO THE MAN OF STEEL FLASHES AWAY, UNAWARE THAT DANGER LOOMS ALSO FOR HIM

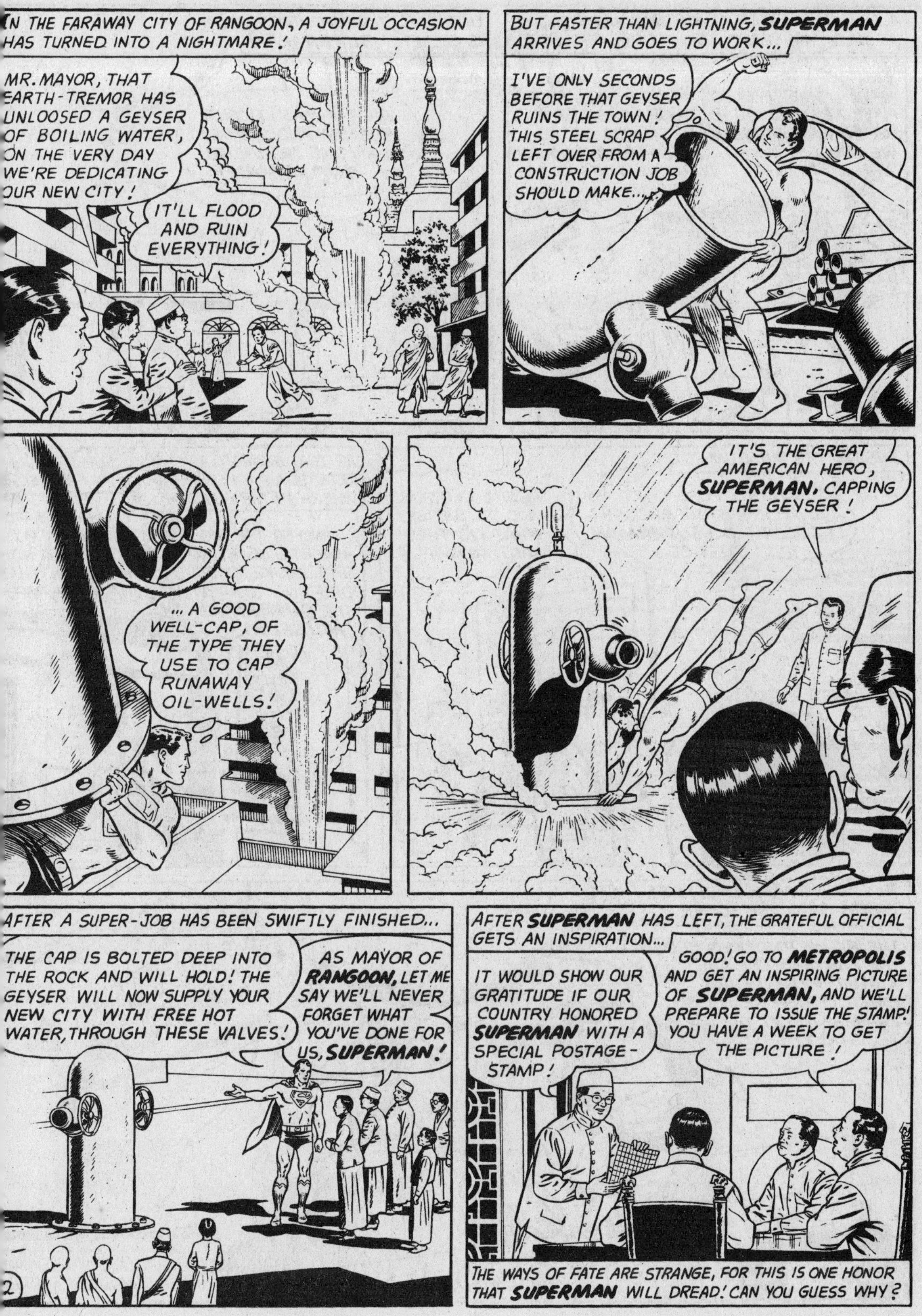
IN THE FARAWAY CITY OF RANGOON, A JOYFUL OCCASION HAS TURNED INTO A NIGHTMARE!
MR. MAYOR, THAT EARTH-TREMOR HAS UNLOOSED A GEYSER OF BOILING WATER, ON THE VERY DAY WE'RE DEDICATING OUR NEW CITY!
IT'LL FLOOD AND RUIN EVERYTHING!
BUT FASTER THAN LIGHTNING, SUPERMAN ARRIVES AND GOES TO WORK...
I'VE ONLY SECONDS BEFORE THAT GEYSER RUINS THE TOWN! THIS STEEL SCRAP LEFT OVER FROM A CONSTRUCTION JOB SHOULD MAKE...
...A GOOD WELL-CAP, OF THE TYPE THEY USE TO CAP RUNAWAY OIL-WELLS!
IT'S THE GREAT AMERICAN HERO, SUPERMAN, CAPPING THE GEYSER!
AFTER A SUPER-JOB HAS BEEN SWIFTLY FINISHED...
THE CAP IS BOLTED DEEP INTO THE ROCK AND WILL HOLD! THE GEYSER WILL NOW SUPPLY YOUR NEW CITY WITH FREE HOT WATER, THROUGH THESE VALVES!
AS MAYOR OF RANGOON, LET ME SAY WE'LL NEVER FORGET WHAT YOU'VE DONE FOR US, SUPERMAN!
2
AFTER SUPERMAN HAS LEFT, THE GRATEFUL OFFICIAL GETS AN INSPIRATION...
IT WOULD SHOW OUR GRATITUDE IF OUR COUNTRY HONORED SUPERMAN WITH A SPECIAL POSTAGE-STAMP!
GOOD! GO TO METROPOLIS AND GET AN INSPIRING PICTURE OF SUPERMAN, AND WE'LL PREPARE TO ISSUE THE STAMP! YOU HAVE A WEEK TO GET THE PICTURE!
THE WAYS OF FATE ARE STRANGE, FOR THIS IS ONE HONOR THAT SUPERMAN WILL DREAD! CAN YOU GUESS WHY?

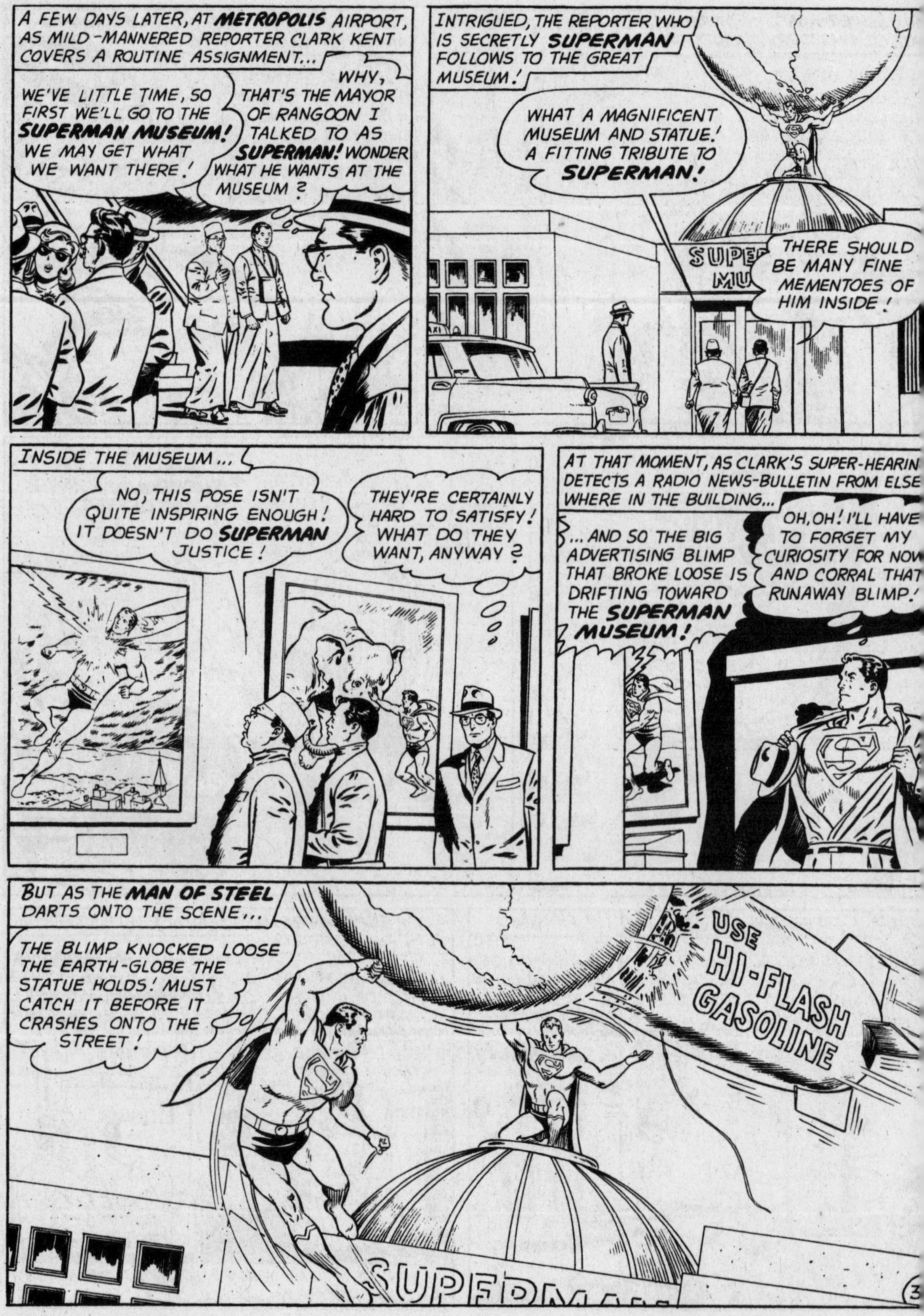
A FEW DAYS LATER, AT METROPOLIS AIRPORT, AS MILD-MANNERED REPORTER CLARK KENT COVERS A ROUTINE ASSIGNMENT...
WE'VE LITTLE TIME, SO FIRST WE'LL GO TO THE SUPERMAN MUSEUM! WE MAY GET WHAT WE WANT THERE!
WHY, THAT'S THE MAYOR OF RANGOON I TALKED TO AS SUPERMAN! WONDER WHAT HE WANTS AT THE MUSEUM?
INTRIGUED, THE REPORTER WHO IS SECRETLY SUPERMAN FOLLOWS TO THE GREAT MUSEUM!
WHAT A MAGNIFICENT MUSEUM AND STATUE! A FITTING TRIBUTE TO SUPERMAN!
THERE SHOULD BE MANY FINE MEMENTOES OF HIM INSIDE!
INSIDE THE MUSEUM...
NO, THIS POSE ISN'T QUITE INSPIRING ENOUGH! IT DOESN'T DO SUPERMAN JUSTICE!
THEY'RE CERTAINLY HARD TO SATISFY! WHAT DO THEY WANT, ANYWAY?
AT THAT MOMENT, AS CLARK'S SUPER-HEARIN DETECTS A RADIO NEWS-BULLETIN FROM ELSE WHERE IN THE BUILDING...
...AND SO THE BIG ADVERTISING BLIMP THAT BROKE LOOSE IS DRIFTING TOWARD THE SUPERMAN MUSEUM!
OH, OH! I'LL HAVE TO FORGET MY CURIOSITY FOR NOW AND CORRAL THAT RUNAWAY BLIMP!
BUT AS THE MAN OF STEEL DARTS ONTO THE SCENE...
THE BLIMP KNOCKED LOOSE THE EARTH-GLOBE THE STATUE HOLDS! MUST CATCH IT BEFORE IT CRASHES ONTO THE STREET!
USE HI-FLASH GASOLINE
SUPERMAN

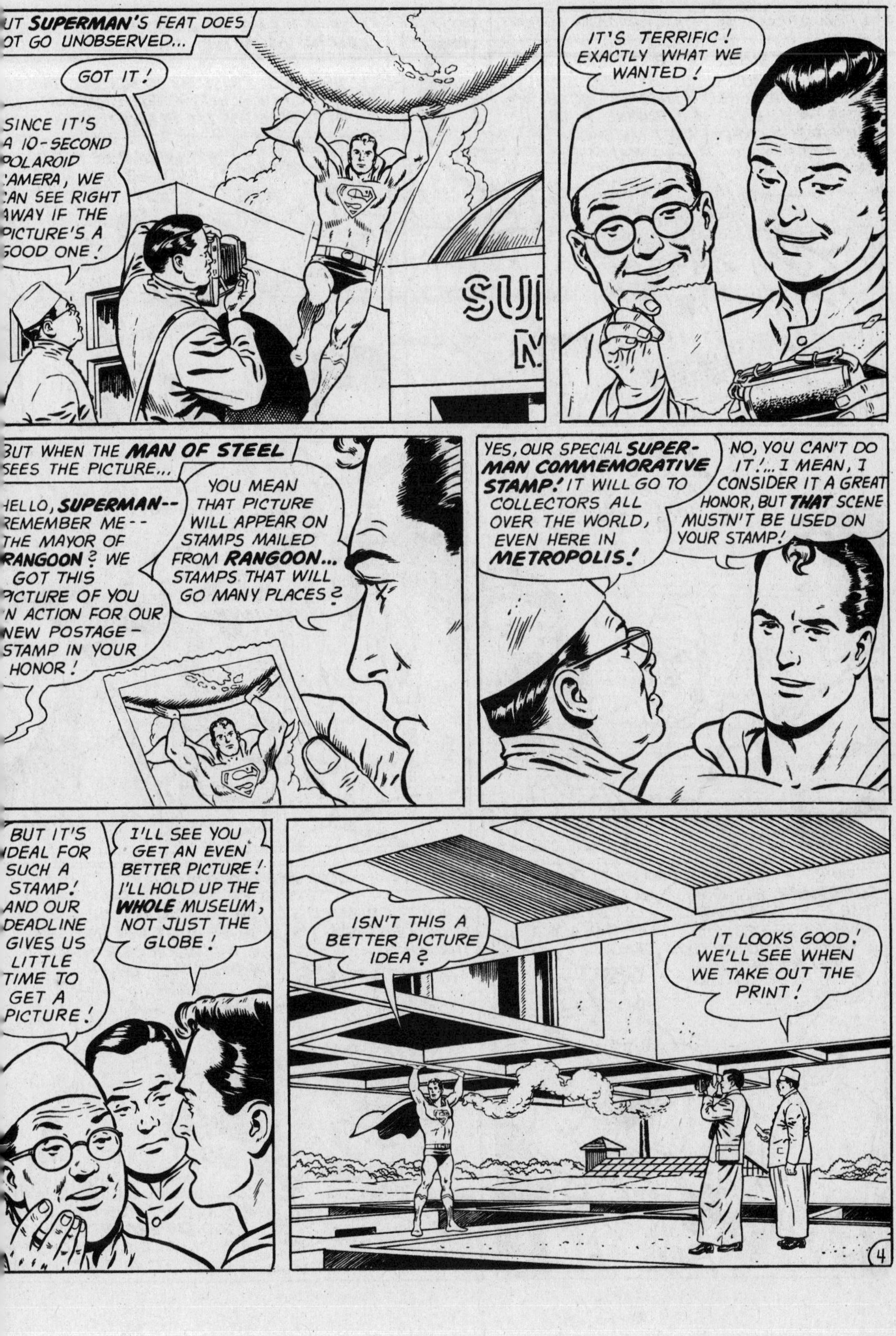
UT SUPERMAN'S FEAT DOES OT GO UNOBSERVED...
GOT IT!
SINCE IT'S A 10-SECOND POLAROID CAMERA, WE CAN SEE RIGHT AWAY IF THE PICTURE'S A GOOD ONE!
IT'S TERRIFIC! EXACTLY WHAT WE WANTED!
BUT WHEN THE MAN OF STEEL SEES THE PICTURE...
HELLO, SUPERMAN-- REMEMBER ME-- THE MAYOR OF RANGOON? WE GOT THIS PICTURE OF YOU IN ACTION FOR OUR NEW POSTAGE-STAMP IN YOUR HONOR!
YOU MEAN THAT PICTURE WILL APPEAR ON STAMPS MAILED FROM RANGOON... STAMPS THAT WILL GO MANY PLACES?
YES, OUR SPECIAL SUPERMAN COMMEMORATIVE STAMP! IT WILL GO TO COLLECTORS ALL OVER THE WORLD, EVEN HERE IN METROPOLIS!
NO, YOU CAN'T DO IT!... I MEAN, I CONSIDER IT A GREAT HONOR, BUT THAT SCENE MUSTN'T BE USED ON YOUR STAMP!
BUT IT'S IDEAL FOR SUCH A STAMP! AND OUR DEADLINE GIVES US LITTLE TIME TO GET A PICTURE!
I'LL SEE YOU GET AN EVEN BETTER PICTURE! I'LL HOLD UP THE WHOLE MUSEUM, NOT JUST THE GLOBE!
ISN'T THIS A BETTER PICTURE IDEA?
IT LOOKS GOOD! WE'LL SEE WHEN WE TAKE OUT THE PRINT!
4

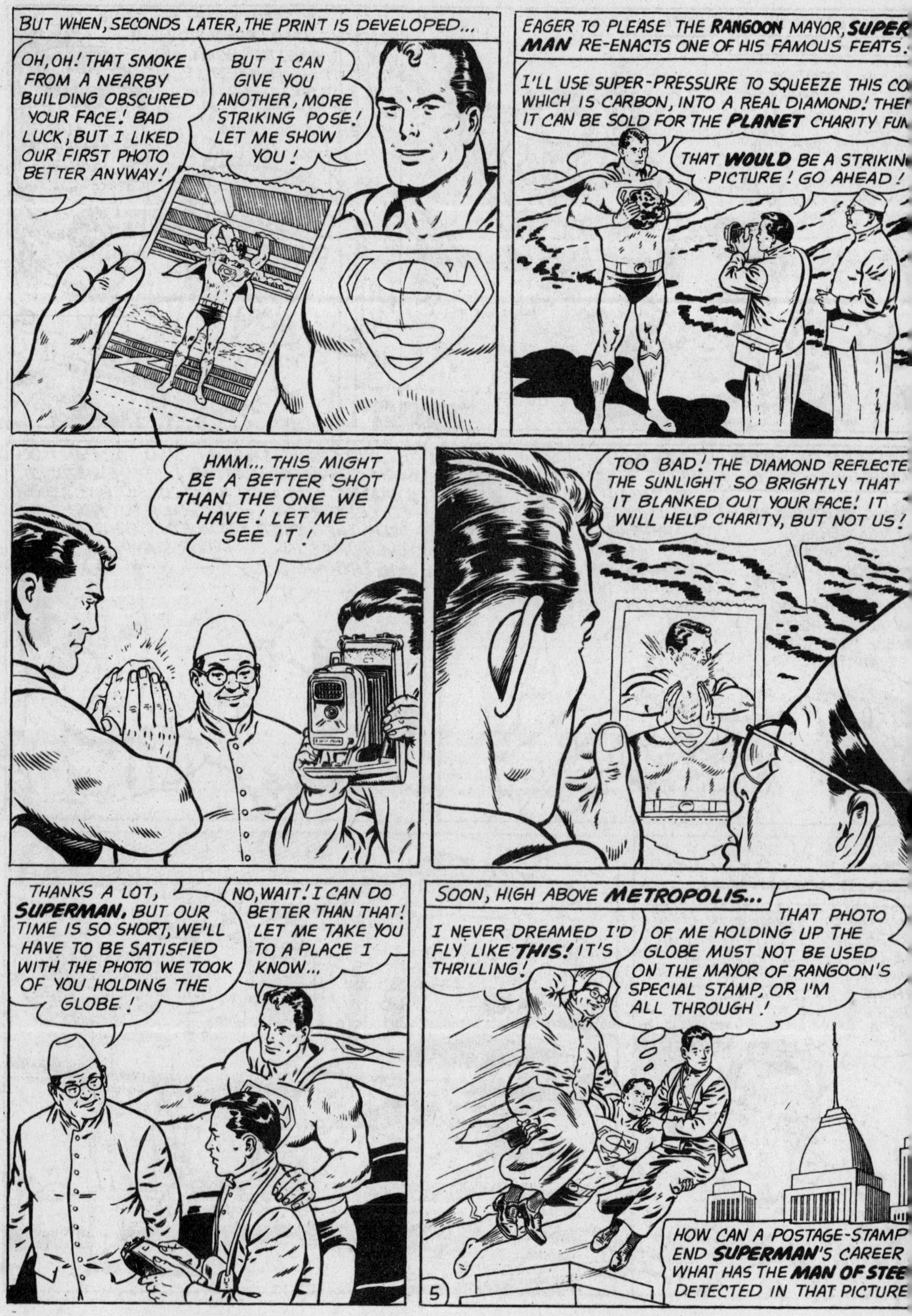
BUT WHEN, SECONDS LATER, THE PRINT IS DEVELOPED...
OH, OH! THAT SMOKE FROM A NEARBY BUILDING OBSCURED YOUR FACE! BAD LUCK, BUT I LIKED OUR FIRST PHOTO BETTER ANYWAY!
BUT I CAN GIVE YOU ANOTHER, MORE STRIKING POSE! LET ME SHOW YOU!
EAGER TO PLEASE THE RANGOON MAYOR, SUPER MAN RE-ENACTS ONE OF HIS FAMOUS FEATS.
I'LL USE SUPER-PRESSURE TO SQUEEZE THIS CO WHICH IS CARBON, INTO A REAL DIAMOND! THE IT CAN BE SOLD FOR THE PLANET CHARITY FU
THAT WOULD BE A STRIKIN PICTURE! GO AHEAD!
HMM... THIS MIGHT BE A BETTER SHOT THAN THE ONE WE HAVE! LET ME SEE IT!
TOO BAD! THE DIAMOND REFLECTE THE SUNLIGHT SO BRIGHTLY THAT IT BLANKED OUT YOUR FACE! IT WILL HELP CHARITY, BUT NOT US!
THANKS A LOT, SUPERMAN. BUT OUR TIME IS SO SHORT, WE'LL HAVE TO BE SATISFIED WITH THE PHOTO WE TOOK OF YOU HOLDING THE GLOBE!
NO, WAIT! I CAN DO BETTER THAN THAT! LET ME TAKE YOU TO A PLACE I KNOW...
SOON, HIGH ABOVE METROPOLIS...
I NEVER DREAMED I'D FLY LIKE THIS! IT'S THRILLING!
THAT PHOTO OF ME HOLDING UP THE GLOBE MUST NOT BE USED ON THE MAYOR OF RANGOON'S SPECIAL STAMP, OR I'M ALL THROUGH!
HOW CAN A POSTAGE-STAMP END SUPERMAN'S CAREER WHAT HAS THE MAN OF STEE DETECTED IN THAT PICTURE
5

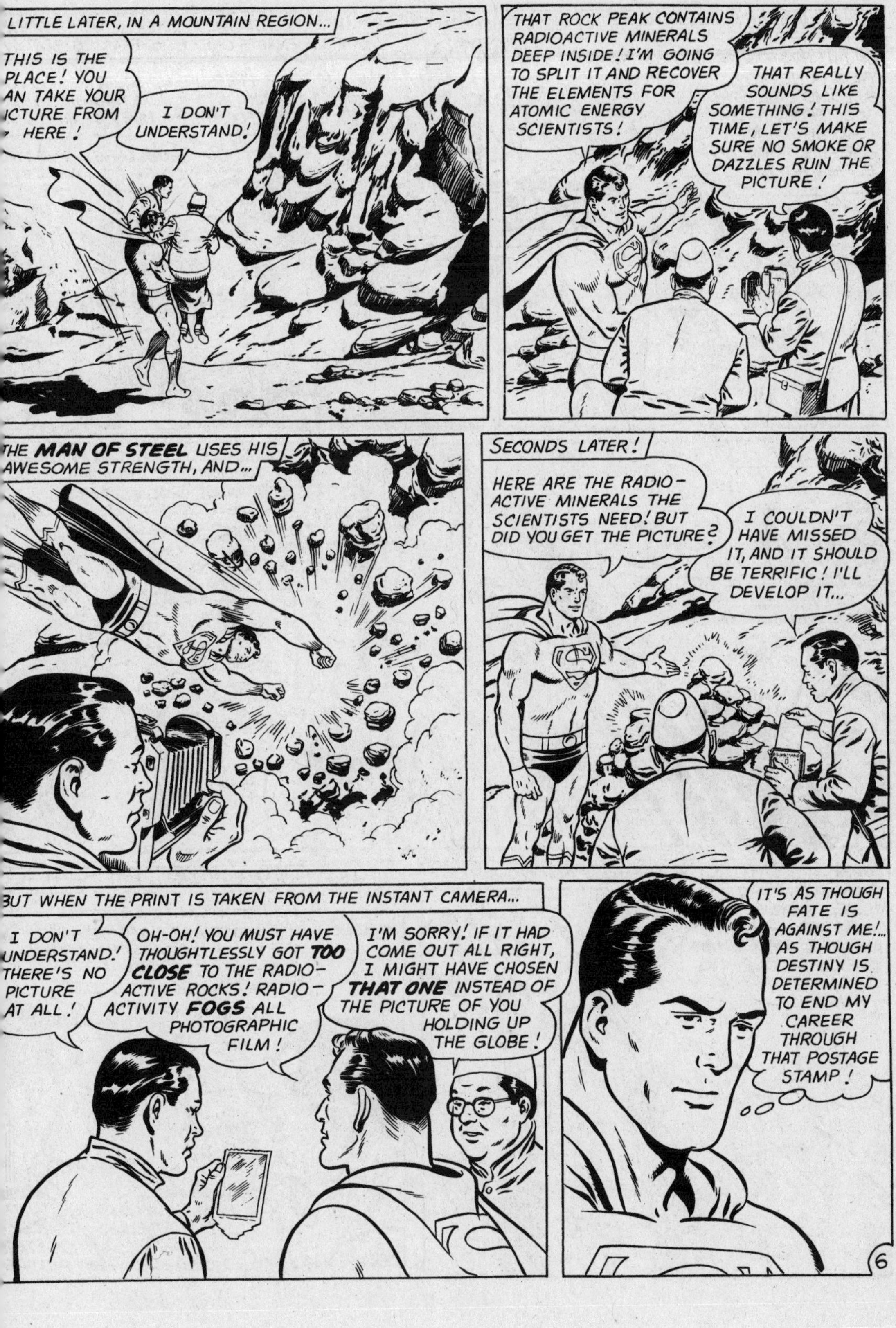
LITTLE LATER, IN A MOUNTAIN REGION...
THIS IS THE PLACE! YOU AN TAKE YOUR ICTURE FROM HERE!
I DON'T UNDERSTAND!
THAT ROCK PEAK CONTAINS RADIOACTIVE MINERALS DEEP INSIDE! I'M GOING TO SPLIT IT AND RECOVER THE ELEMENTS FOR ATOMIC ENERGY SCIENTISTS!
THAT REALLY SOUNDS LIKE SOMETHING! THIS TIME, LET'S MAKE SURE NO SMOKE OR DAZZLES RUIN THE PICTURE!
THE MAN OF STEEL USES HIS AWESOME STRENGTH, AND...
SECONDS LATER!
HERE ARE THE RADIO-ACTIVE MINERALS THE SCIENTISTS NEED! BUT DID YOU GET THE PICTURE?
I COULDN'T HAVE MISSED IT, AND IT SHOULD BE TERRIFIC! I'LL DEVELOP IT...
BUT WHEN THE PRINT IS TAKEN FROM THE INSTANT CAMERA...
I DON'T UNDERSTAND! THERE'S NO PICTURE AT ALL!
OH-OH! YOU MUST HAVE THOUGHTLESSLY GOT TOO CLOSE TO THE RADIO-ACTIVE ROCKS! RADIO-ACTIVITY FOGS ALL PHOTOGRAPHIC FILM!
I'M SORRY! IF IT HAD COME OUT ALL RIGHT, I MIGHT HAVE CHOSEN THAT ONE INSTEAD OF THE PICTURE OF YOU HOLDING UP THE GLOBE!
IT'S AS THOUGH FATE IS AGAINST ME!... AS THOUGH DESTINY IS DETERMINED TO END MY CAREER THROUGH THAT POSTAGE STAMP!
6

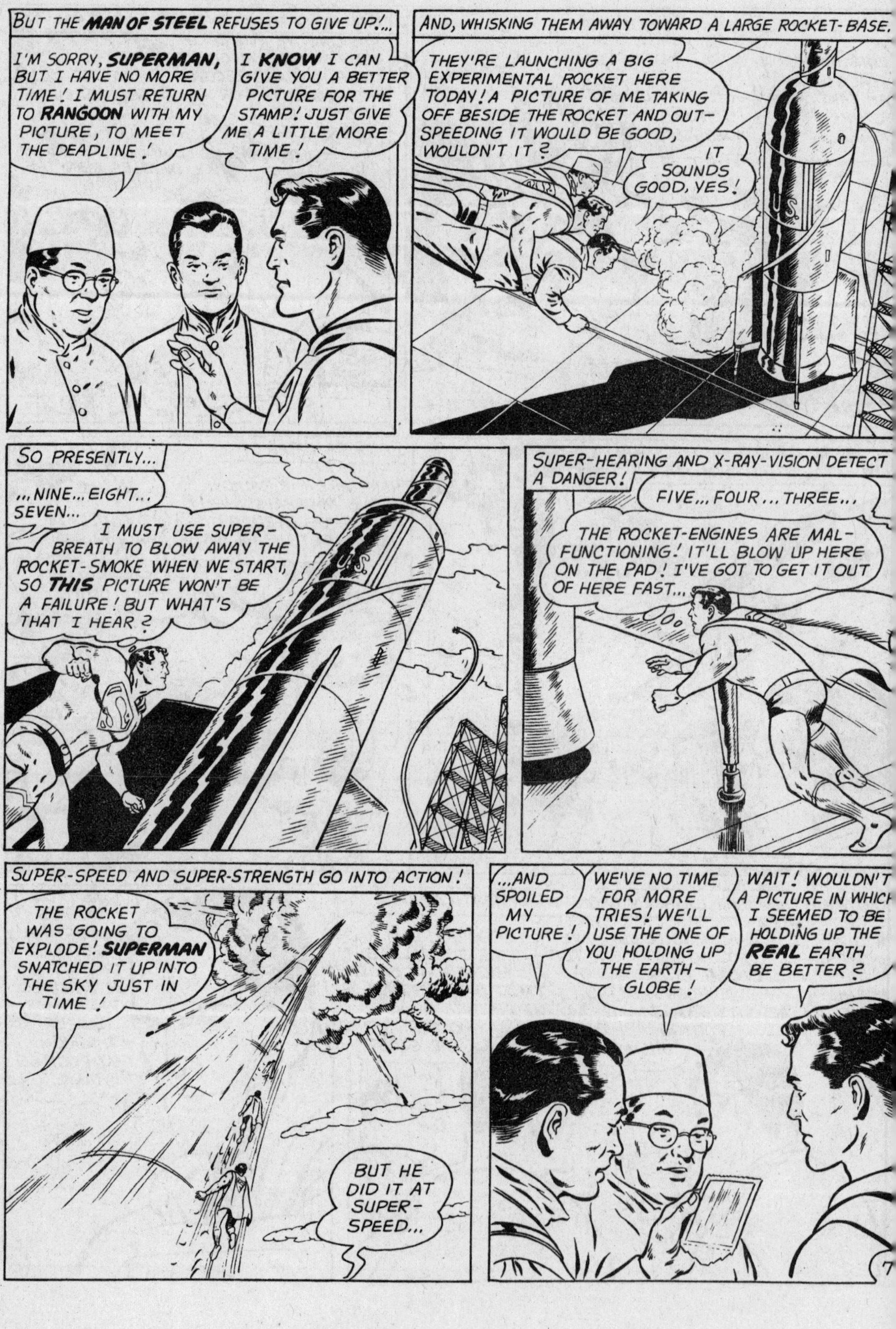
BUT THE MAN OF STEEL REFUSES TO GIVE UP!...
I'M SORRY, SUPERMAN, BUT I HAVE NO MORE TIME! I MUST RETURN TO RANGOON WITH MY PICTURE, TO MEET THE DEADLINE!
I KNOW I CAN GIVE YOU A BETTER PICTURE FOR THE STAMP! JUST GIVE ME A LITTLE MORE TIME!
AND, WHISKING THEM AWAY TOWARD A LARGE ROCKET-BASE...
THEY'RE LAUNCHING A BIG EXPERIMENTAL ROCKET HERE TODAY! A PICTURE OF ME TAKING OFF BESIDE THE ROCKET AND OUT-SPEEDING IT WOULD BE GOOD, WOULDN'T IT?
IT SOUNDS GOOD, YES!
SO PRESENTLY...
...NINE... EIGHT... SEVEN...
I MUST USE SUPER-BREATH TO BLOW AWAY THE ROCKET-SMOKE WHEN WE START, SO THIS PICTURE WON'T BE A FAILURE! BUT WHAT'S THAT I HEAR?
SUPER-HEARING AND X-RAY-VISION DETECT A DANGER!
FIVE... FOUR... THREE...
THE ROCKET-ENGINES ARE MAL-FUNCTIONING! IT'LL BLOW UP HERE ON THE PAD! I'VE GOT TO GET IT OUT OF HERE FAST...
SUPER-SPEED AND SUPER-STRENGTH GO INTO ACTION!
THE ROCKET WAS GOING TO EXPLODE! SUPERMAN SNATCHED IT UP INTO THE SKY JUST IN TIME!
BUT HE DID IT AT SUPER-SPEED...
...AND SPOILED MY PICTURE!
WE'VE NO TIME FOR MORE TRIES! WE'LL USE THE ONE OF YOU HOLDING UP THE EARTH-GLOBE!
WAIT! WOULDN'T A PICTURE IN WHICH I SEEMED TO BE HOLDING UP THE REAL EARTH BE BETTER?
7

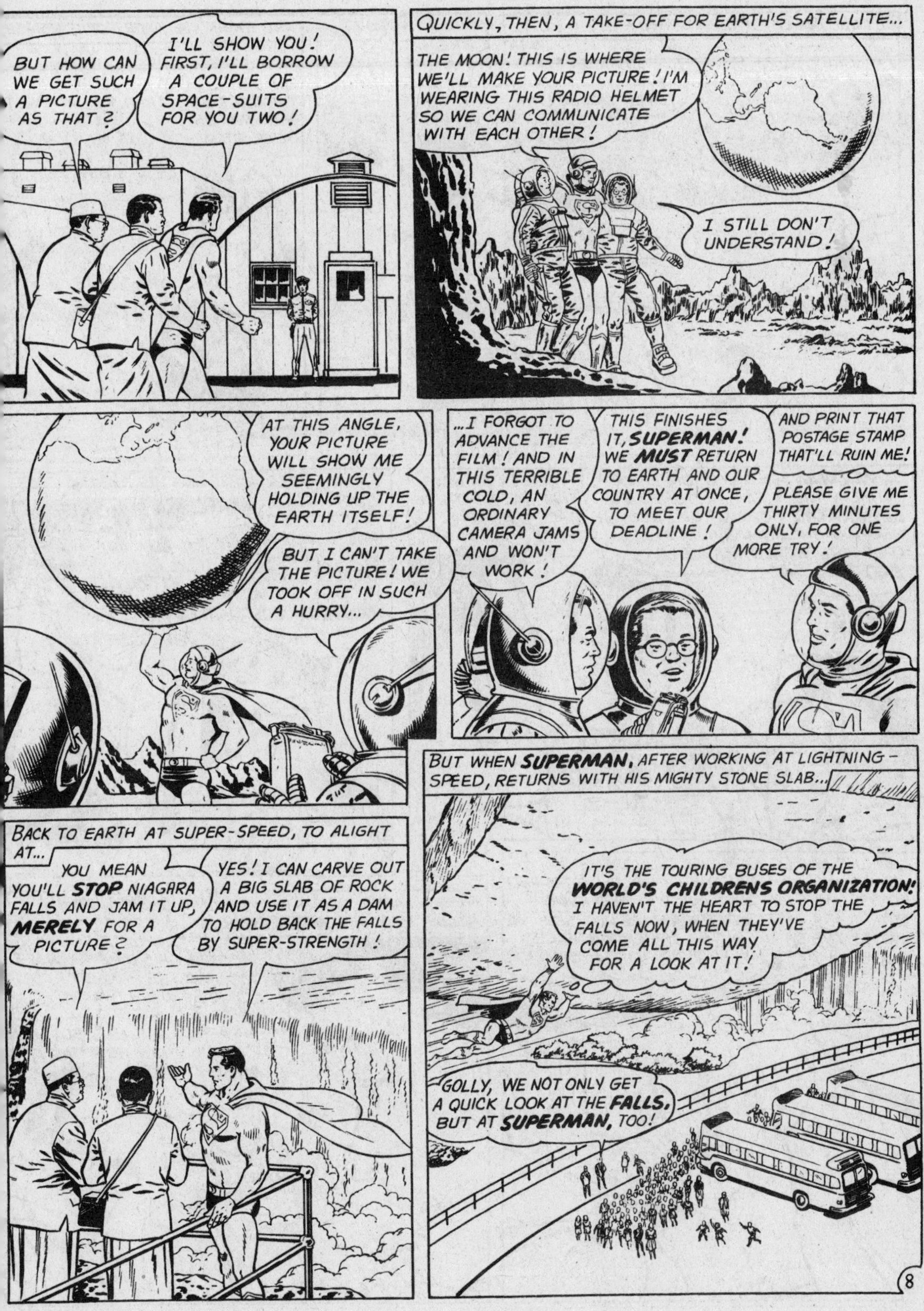
BUT HOW CAN WE GET SUCH A PICTURE AS THAT ?
I'LL SHOW YOU! FIRST, I'LL BORROW A COUPLE OF SPACE-SUITS FOR YOU TWO!
QUICKLY, THEN, A TAKE-OFF FOR EARTH'S SATELLITE...
THE MOON! THIS IS WHERE WE'LL MAKE YOUR PICTURE! I'M WEARING THIS RADIO HELMET SO WE CAN COMMUNICATE WITH EACH OTHER!
I STILL DON'T UNDERSTAND!
AT THIS ANGLE, YOUR PICTURE WILL SHOW ME SEEMINGLY HOLDING UP THE EARTH ITSELF!
BUT I CAN'T TAKE THE PICTURE! WE TOOK OFF IN SUCH A HURRY...
...I FORGOT TO ADVANCE THE FILM! AND IN THIS TERRIBLE COLD, AN ORDINARY CAMERA JAMS AND WON'T WORK!
THIS FINISHES IT, SUPERMAN! WE MUST RETURN TO EARTH AND OUR COUNTRY AT ONCE, TO MEET OUR DEADLINE!
AND PRINT THAT POSTAGE STAMP THAT'LL RUIN ME!
PLEASE GIVE ME THIRTY MINUTES ONLY, FOR ONE MORE TRY!
BACK TO EARTH AT SUPER-SPEED, TO ALIGHT AT...
YOU MEAN YOU'LL STOP NIAGARA FALLS AND JAM IT UP, MERELY FOR A PICTURE?
YES! I CAN CARVE OUT A BIG SLAB OF ROCK AND USE IT AS A DAM TO HOLD BACK THE FALLS BY SUPER-STRENGTH!
BUT WHEN SUPERMAN, AFTER WORKING AT LIGHTNING-SPEED, RETURNS WITH HIS MIGHTY STONE SLAB...
IT'S THE TOURING BUSES OF THE WORLD'S CHILDRENS ORGANIZATION! I HAVEN'T THE HEART TO STOP THE FALLS NOW, WHEN THEY'VE COME ALL THIS WAY FOR A LOOK AT IT!
GOLLY, WE NOT ONLY GET A QUICK LOOK AT THE FALLS, BUT AT SUPERMAN, TOO!
8

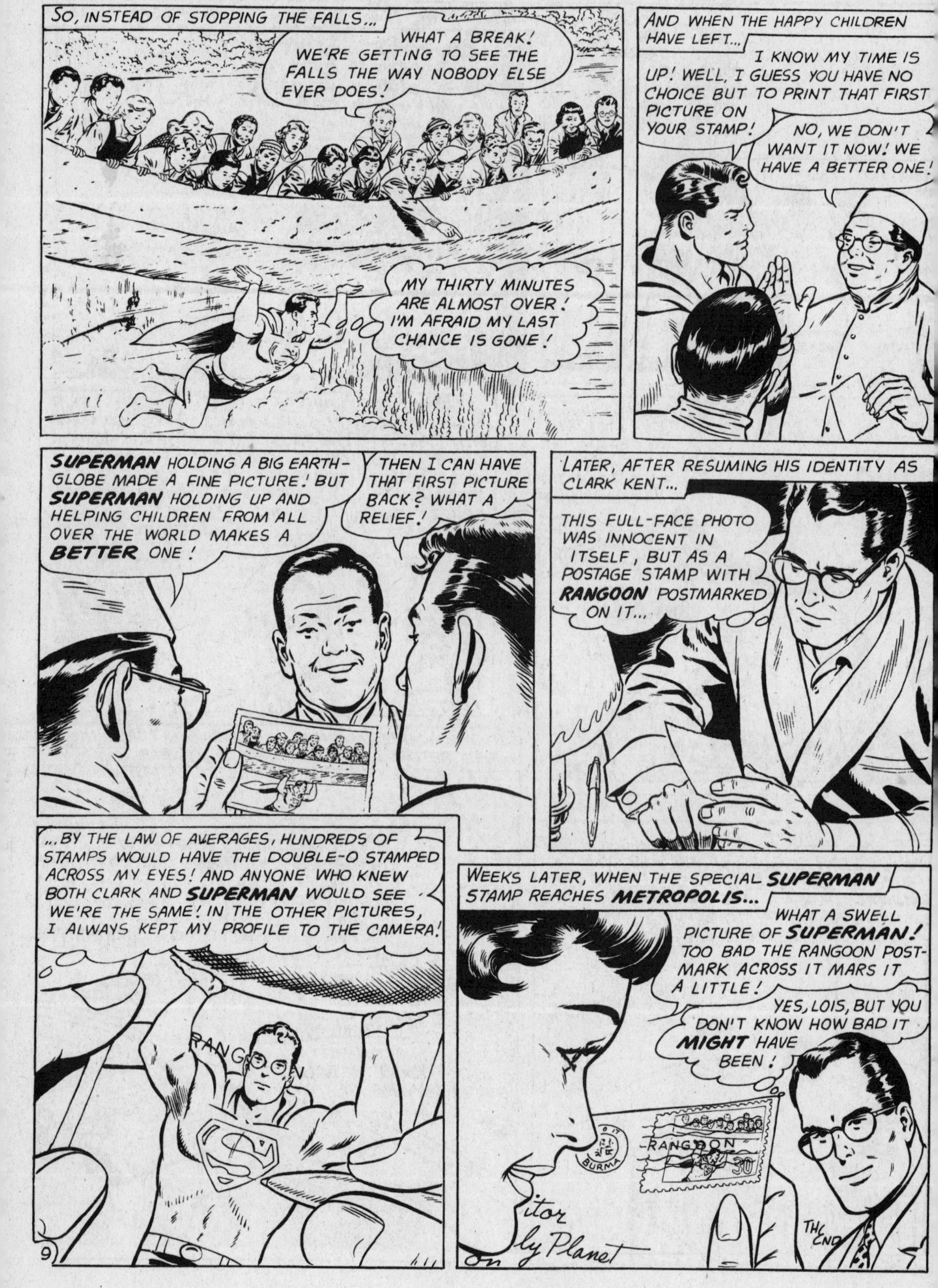
SO, INSTEAD OF STOPPING THE FALLS...
WHAT A BREAK! WE'RE GETTING TO SEE THE FALLS THE WAY NOBODY ELSE EVER DOES!
MY THIRTY MINUTES ARE ALMOST OVER! I'M AFRAID MY LAST CHANCE IS GONE!
AND WHEN THE HAPPY CHILDREN HAVE LEFT...
I KNOW MY TIME IS UP! WELL, I GUESS YOU HAVE NO CHOICE BUT TO PRINT THAT FIRST PICTURE ON YOUR STAMP!
NO, WE DON'T WANT IT NOW! WE HAVE A BETTER ONE!
SUPERMAN HOLDING A BIG EARTH-GLOBE MADE A FINE PICTURE! BUT SUPERMAN HOLDING UP AND HELPING CHILDREN FROM ALL OVER THE WORLD MAKES A BETTER ONE!
THEN I CAN HAVE THAT FIRST PICTURE BACK? WHAT A RELIEF!
LATER, AFTER RESUMING HIS IDENTITY AS CLARK KENT...
THIS FULL-FACE PHOTO WAS INNOCENT IN ITSELF, BUT AS A POSTAGE STAMP WITH RANGOON POSTMARKED ON IT...
...BY THE LAW OF AVERAGES, HUNDREDS OF STAMPS WOULD HAVE THE DOUBLE-O STAMPED ACROSS MY EYES! AND ANYONE WHO KNEW BOTH CLARK AND SUPERMAN WOULD SEE WE'RE THE SAME! IN THE OTHER PICTURES, I ALWAYS KEPT MY PROFILE TO THE CAMERA!
RANGOON
9
WEEKS LATER, WHEN THE SPECIAL SUPERMAN STAMP REACHES METROPOLIS...
WHAT A SWELL PICTURE OF SUPERMAN! TOO BAD THE RANGOON POST-MARK ACROSS IT MARS IT A LITTLE!
YES, LOIS, BUT YOU DON'T KNOW HOW BAD IT MIGHT HAVE BEEN!
BURMA
RANGOON
30
itor
ly Planet
THE END

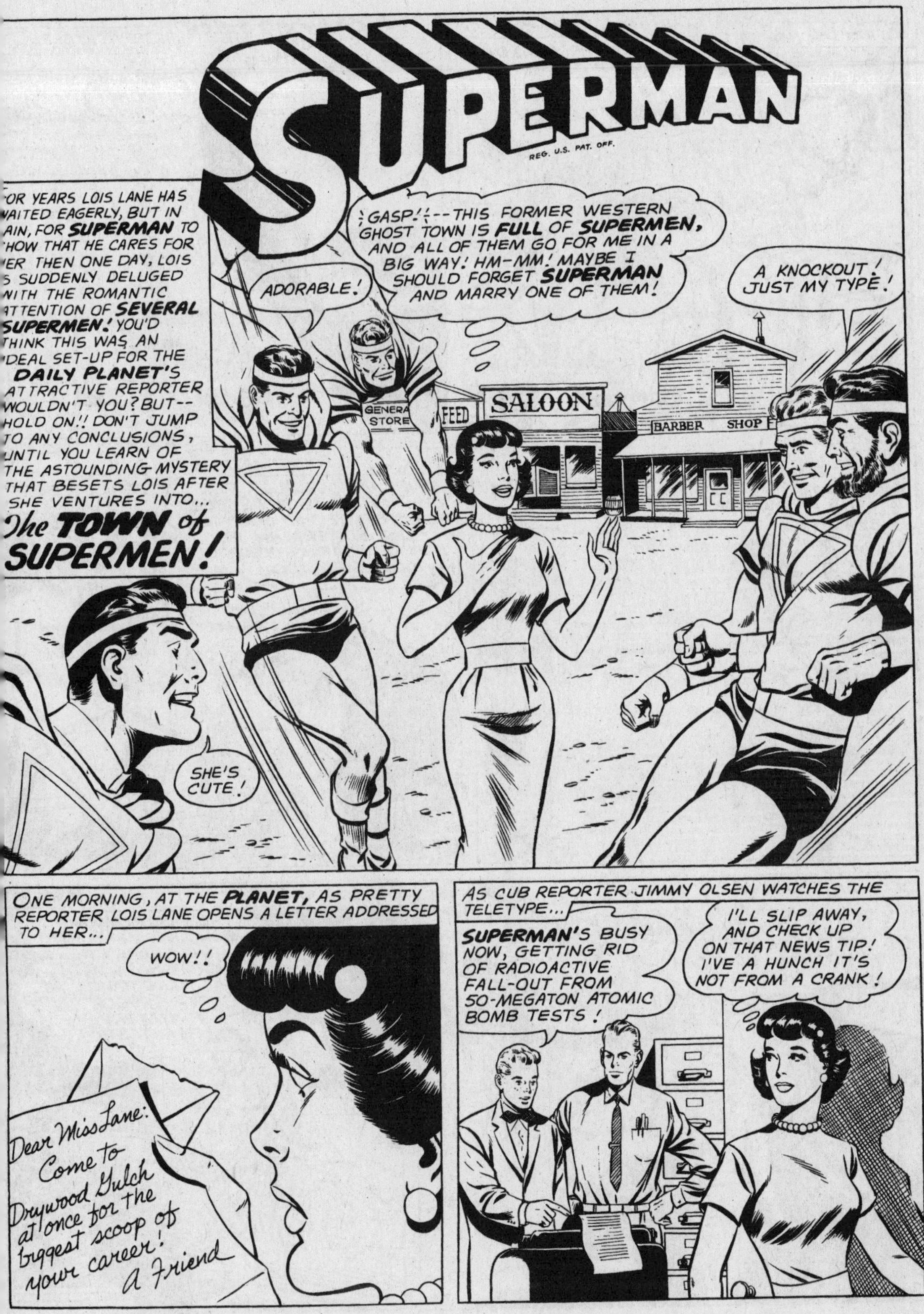
SUPERMAN
REG. U.S. PAT. OFF.
OR YEARS LOIS LANE HAS AITED EAGERLY, BUT IN AIN, FOR SUPERMAN TO HOW THAT HE CARES FOR ER THEN ONE DAY, LOIS S SUDDENLY DELUGED WITH THE ROMANTIC TTENTION OF SEVERAL SUPERMEN! YOU'D THINK THIS WAS AN DEAL SET-UP FOR THE DAILY PLANET'S ATTRACTIVE REPORTER WOULDN'T YOU? BUT-- HOLD ON!! DON'T JUMP TO ANY CONCLUSIONS, UNTIL YOU LEARN OF THE ASTOUNDING MYSTERY THAT BESETS LOIS AFTER SHE VENTURES INTO...
The TOWN of SUPERMEN!
GASP!!--THIS FORMER WESTERN GHOST TOWN IS FULL OF SUPERMEN, AND ALL OF THEM GO FOR ME IN A BIG WAY! HM-MM! MAYBE I SHOULD FORGET SUPERMAN AND MARRY ONE OF THEM!
ADORABLE!
A KNOCKOUT! JUST MY TYPE!
GENERA STORE
FEED
SALOON
BARBER SHOP
SHE'S CUTE!
ONE MORNING, AT THE PLANET, AS PRETTY REPORTER LOIS LANE OPENS A LETTER ADDRESSED TO HER...
WOW!!
Dear Miss Lane: Come to Drywood Gulch at once for the biggest scoop of your career! A Friend
AS CUB REPORTER JIMMY OLSEN WATCHES THE TELETYPE...
SUPERMAN'S BUSY NOW, GETTING RID OF RADIOACTIVE FALL-OUT FROM 50-MEGATON ATOMIC BOMB TESTS!
I'LL SLIP AWAY, AND CHECK UP ON THAT NEWS TIP! I'VE A HUNCH IT'S NOT FROM A CRANK!

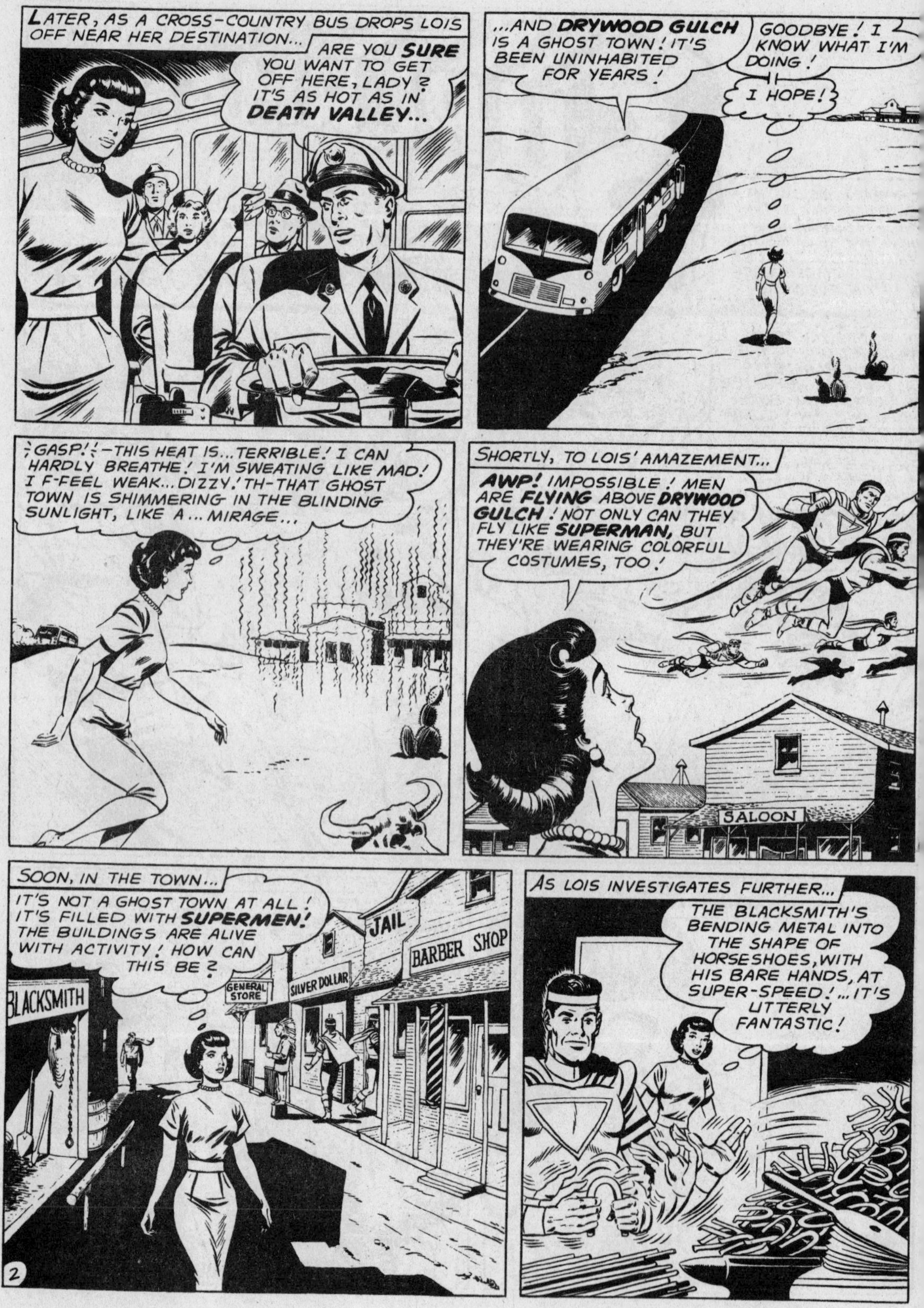
LATER, AS A CROSS-COUNTRY BUS DROPS LOIS OFF NEAR HER DESTINATION...
ARE YOU SURE YOU WANT TO GET OFF HERE, LADY? IT'S AS HOT AS IN DEATH VALLEY...
...AND DRYWOOD GULCH IS A GHOST TOWN! IT'S BEEN UNINHABITED FOR YEARS!
GOODBYE! I KNOW WHAT I'M DOING!
I HOPE!
GASP! -THIS HEAT IS...TERRIBLE! I CAN HARDLY BREATHE! I'M SWEATING LIKE MAD! I F-FEEL WEAK...DIZZY! TH-THAT GHOST TOWN IS SHIMMERING IN THE BLINDING SUNLIGHT, LIKE A...MIRAGE...
SHORTLY, TO LOIS' AMAZEMENT...
AWP! IMPOSSIBLE! MEN ARE FLYING ABOVE DRYWOOD GULCH! NOT ONLY CAN THEY FLY LIKE SUPERMAN, BUT THEY'RE WEARING COLORFUL COSTUMES, TOO!
SALOON
SOON, IN THE TOWN...
IT'S NOT A GHOST TOWN AT ALL! IT'S FILLED WITH SUPERMEN! THE BUILDINGS ARE ALIVE WITH ACTIVITY! HOW CAN THIS BE?
JAIL
BARBER SHOP
SILVER DOLLAR
GENERAL STORE
BLACKSMITH
2
AS LOIS INVESTIGATES FURTHER...
THE BLACKSMITH'S BENDING METAL INTO THE SHAPE OF HORSESHOES, WITH HIS BARE HANDS, AT SUPER-SPEED! ...IT'S UTTERLY FANTASTIC!

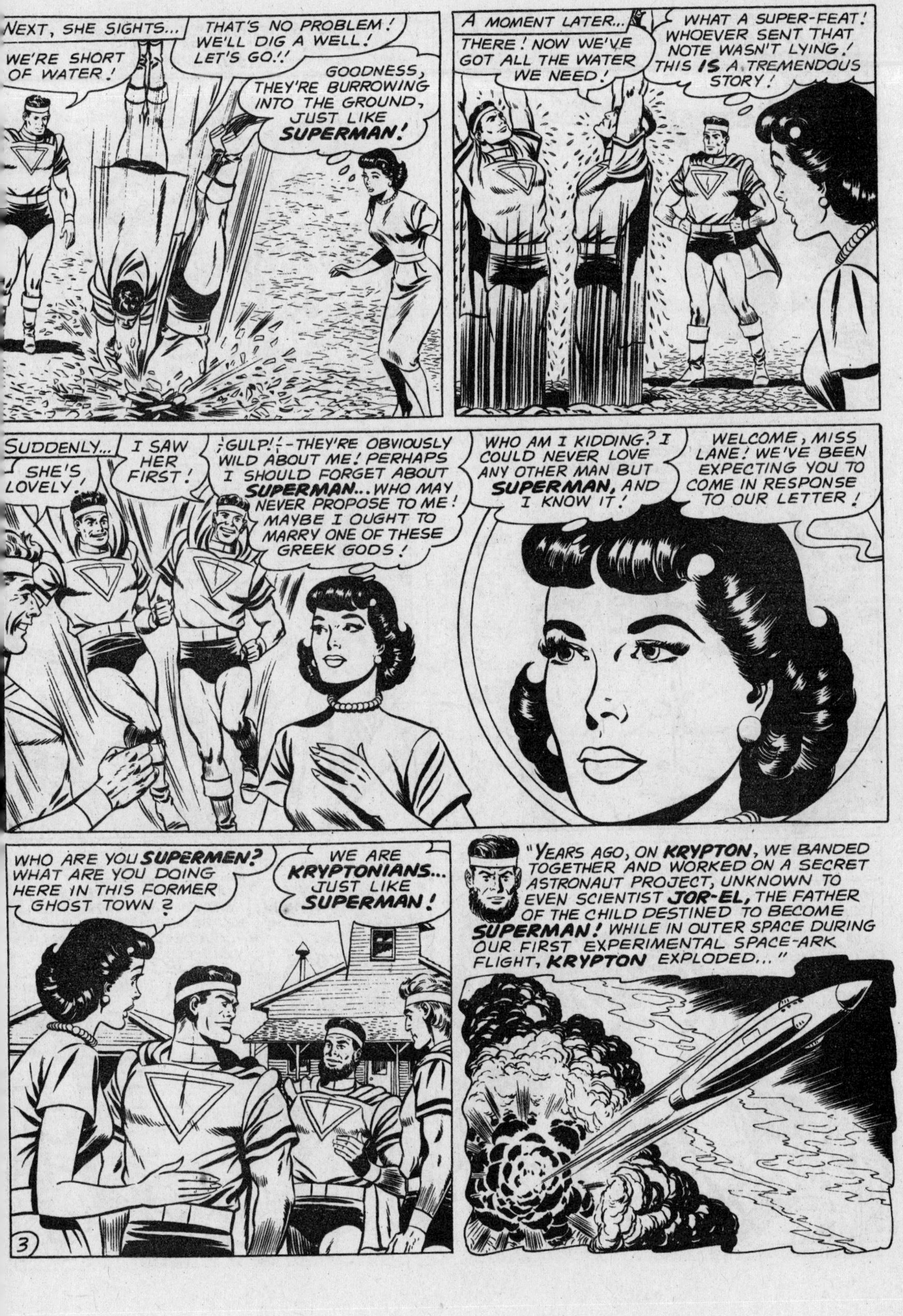
NEXT, SHE SIGHTS...
WE'RE SHORT OF WATER!
THAT'S NO PROBLEM! WE'LL DIG A WELL! LET'S GO!!
GOODNESS, THEY'RE BURROWING INTO THE GROUND, JUST LIKE SUPERMAN!
A MOMENT LATER...
THERE! NOW WE'VE GOT ALL THE WATER WE NEED!
WHAT A SUPER-FEAT! WHOEVER SENT THAT NOTE WASN'T LYING! THIS IS A TREMENDOUS STORY!
SUDDENLY...
SHE'S LOVELY!
I SAW HER FIRST!
GULP! -THEY'RE OBVIOUSLY WILD ABOUT ME! PERHAPS I SHOULD FORGET ABOUT SUPERMAN... WHO MAY NEVER PROPOSE TO ME! MAYBE I OUGHT TO MARRY ONE OF THESE GREEK GODS!
WHO AM I KIDDING? I COULD NEVER LOVE ANY OTHER MAN BUT SUPERMAN, AND I KNOW IT!
WELCOME, MISS LANE! WE'VE BEEN EXPECTING YOU TO COME IN RESPONSE TO OUR LETTER!
WHO ARE YOU SUPERMEN? WHAT ARE YOU DOING HERE IN THIS FORMER GHOST TOWN?
WE ARE KRYPTONIANS... JUST LIKE SUPERMAN!
3
"YEARS AGO, ON KRYPTON, WE BANDED TOGETHER AND WORKED ON A SECRET ASTRONAUT PROJECT, UNKNOWN TO EVEN SCIENTIST JOR-EL, THE FATHER OF THE CHILD DESTINED TO BECOME SUPERMAN! WHILE IN OUTER SPACE DURING OUR FIRST EXPERIMENTAL SPACE-ARK FLIGHT, KRYPTON EXPLODED..."

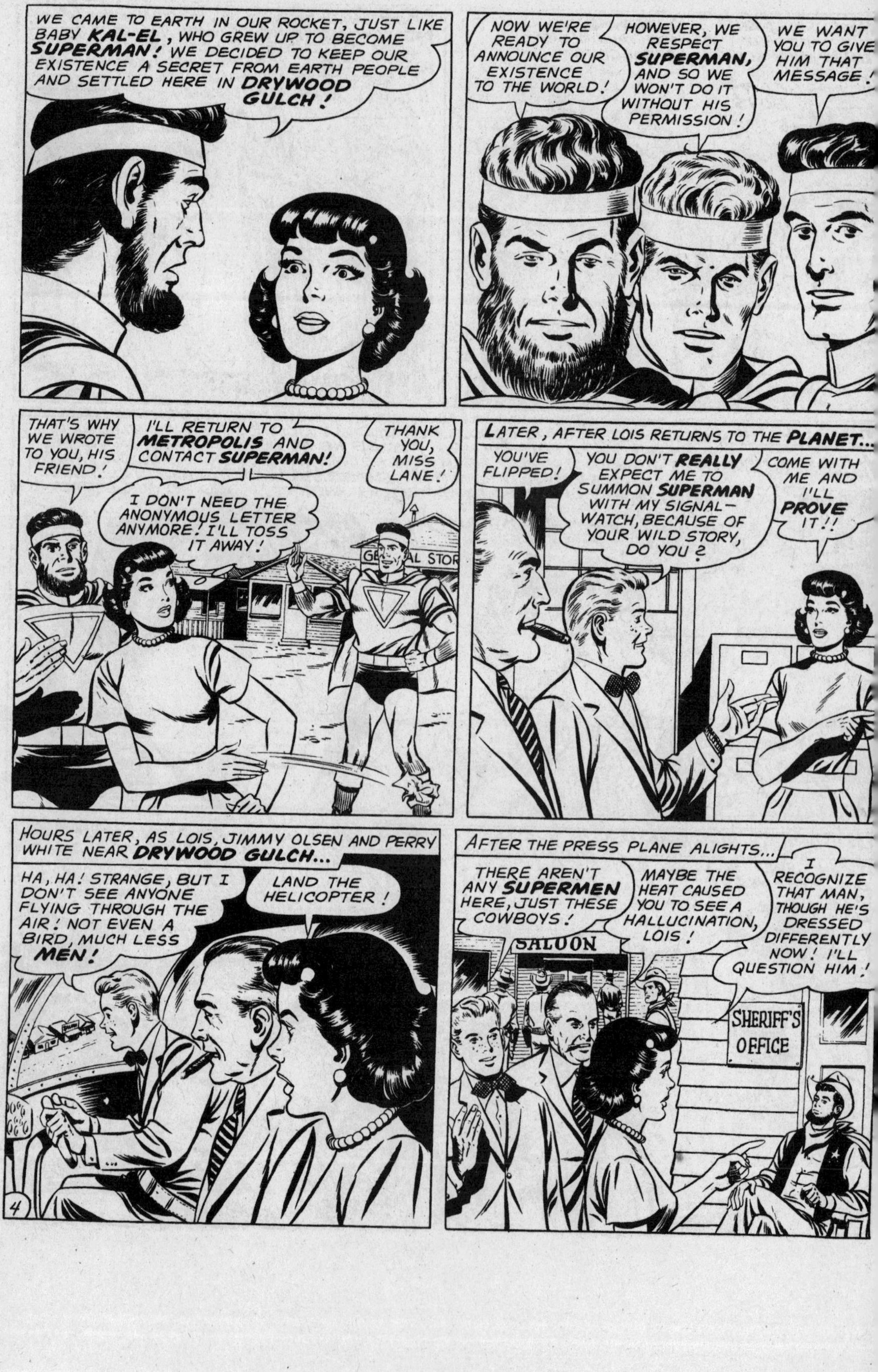
WE CAME TO EARTH IN OUR ROCKET, JUST LIKE BABY KAL-EL, WHO GREW UP TO BECOME SUPERMAN! WE DECIDED TO KEEP OUR EXISTENCE A SECRET FROM EARTH PEOPLE AND SETTLED HERE IN DRYWOOD GULCH!
NOW WE'RE READY TO ANNOUNCE OUR EXISTENCE TO THE WORLD!
HOWEVER, WE RESPECT SUPERMAN, AND SO WE WON'T DO IT WITHOUT HIS PERMISSION!
WE WANT YOU TO GIVE HIM THAT MESSAGE!
THAT'S WHY WE WROTE TO YOU, HIS FRIEND!
I'LL RETURN TO METROPOLIS AND CONTACT SUPERMAN!
THANK YOU, MISS LANE!
I DON'T NEED THE ANONYMOUS LETTER ANYMORE! I'LL TOSS IT AWAY!
LATER, AFTER LOIS RETURNS TO THE PLANET...
YOU'VE FLIPPED!
YOU DON'T REALLY EXPECT ME TO SUMMON SUPERMAN WITH MY SIGNAL-WATCH, BECAUSE OF YOUR WILD STORY, DO YOU?
COME WITH ME AND I'LL PROVE IT!!
HOURS LATER, AS LOIS, JIMMY OLSEN AND PERRY WHITE NEAR DRYWOOD GULCH...
HA, HA! STRANGE, BUT I DON'T SEE ANYONE FLYING THROUGH THE AIR! NOT EVEN A BIRD, MUCH LESS MEN!
LAND THE HELICOPTER!
4
AFTER THE PRESS PLANE ALIGHTS...
THERE AREN'T ANY SUPERMEN HERE, JUST THESE COWBOYS!
MAYBE THE HEAT CAUSED YOU TO SEE A HALLUCINATION, LOIS!
I RECOGNIZE THAT MAN, THOUGH HE'S DRESSED DIFFERENTLY NOW! I'LL QUESTION HIM!
SALOON
SHERIFF'S OFFICE

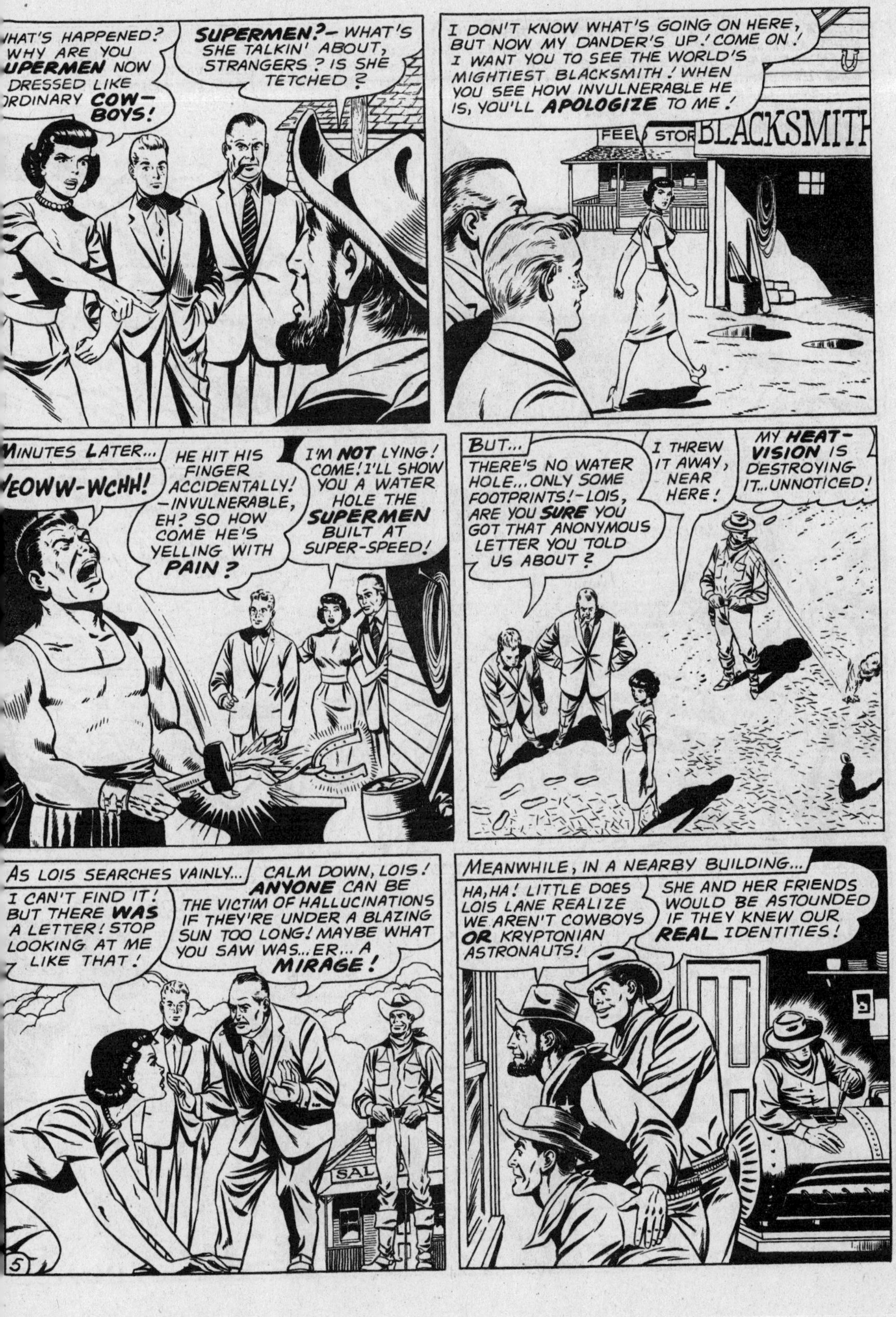
WHAT'S HAPPENED? WHY ARE YOU SUPERMEN NOW DRESSED LIKE ORDINARY COW-BOYS!
SUPERMEN?- WHAT'S SHE TALKIN' ABOUT, STRANGERS? IS SHE TETCHED?
I DON'T KNOW WHAT'S GOING ON HERE, BUT NOW MY DANDER'S UP! COME ON! I WANT YOU TO SEE THE WORLD'S MIGHTIEST BLACKSMITH! WHEN YOU SEE HOW INVULNERABLE HE IS, YOU'LL APOLOGIZE TO ME!
FEE STOR
BLACKSMITH
MINUTES LATER...
YEOWW-WCHH!
HE HIT HIS FINGER ACCIDENTALLY! -INVULNERABLE, EH? SO HOW COME HE'S YELLING WITH PAIN?
I'M NOT LYING! COME! I'LL SHOW YOU A WATER HOLE THE SUPERMEN BUILT AT SUPER-SPEED!
BUT...
THERE'S NO WATER HOLE...ONLY SOME FOOTPRINTS!-LOIS, ARE YOU SURE YOU GOT THAT ANONYMOUS LETTER YOU TOLD US ABOUT?
I THREW IT AWAY, NEAR HERE!
MY HEAT-VISION IS DESTROYING IT...UNNOTICED!
AS LOIS SEARCHES VAINLY...
I CAN'T FIND IT! BUT THERE WAS A LETTER! STOP LOOKING AT ME LIKE THAT!
CALM DOWN, LOIS! ANYONE CAN BE THE VICTIM OF HALLUCINATIONS IF THEY'RE UNDER A BLAZING SUN TOO LONG! MAYBE WHAT YOU SAW WAS...ER... A MIRAGE!
SAL
5
MEANWHILE, IN A NEARBY BUILDING...
HA,HA! LITTLE DOES LOIS LANE REALIZE WE AREN'T COWBOYS OR KRYPTONIAN ASTRONAUTS!
SHE AND HER FRIENDS WOULD BE ASTOUNDED IF THEY KNEW OUR REAL IDENTITIES!

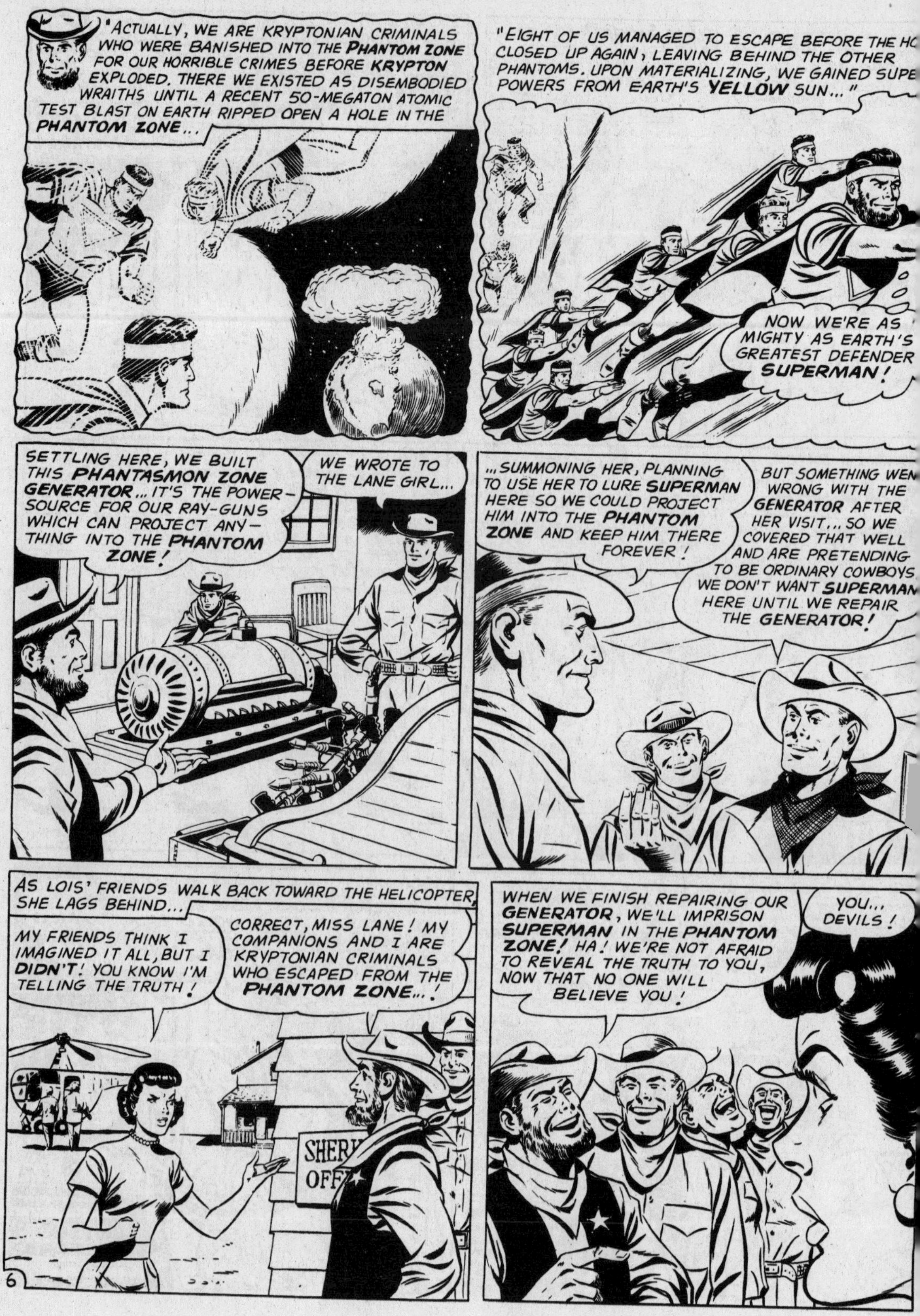

"ACTUALLY, WE ARE KRYPTONIAN CRIMINALS WHO WERE BANISHED INTO THE PHANTOM ZONE FOR OUR HORRIBLE CRIMES BEFORE KRYPTON EXPLODED. THERE WE EXISTED AS DISEMBODIED WRAITHS UNTIL A RECENT 50-MEGATON ATOMIC TEST BLAST ON EARTH RIPPED OPEN A HOLE IN THE PHANTOM ZONE...
"EIGHT OF US MANAGED TO ESCAPE BEFORE THE HO CLOSED UP AGAIN, LEAVING BEHIND THE OTHER PHANTOMS. UPON MATERIALIZING, WE GAINED SUPE POWERS FROM EARTH'S YELLOW SUN..."
NOW WE'RE AS MIGHTY AS EARTH'S GREATEST DEFENDER SUPERMAN!
SETTLING HERE, WE BUILT THIS PHANTASMON ZONE GENERATOR... IT'S THE POWER-SOURCE FOR OUR RAY-GUNS WHICH CAN PROJECT ANYTHING INTO THE PHANTOM ZONE!
WE WROTE TO THE LANE GIRL...
...SUMMONING HER, PLANNING TO USE HER TO LURE SUPERMAN HERE SO WE COULD PROJECT HIM INTO THE PHANTOM ZONE AND KEEP HIM THERE FOREVER!
BUT SOMETHING WEN WRONG WITH THE GENERATOR AFTER HER VISIT... SO WE COVERED THAT WELL AND ARE PRETENDING TO BE ORDINARY COWBOYS WE DON'T WANT SUPERMAN HERE UNTIL WE REPAIR THE GENERATOR!
AS LOIS' FRIENDS WALK BACK TOWARD THE HELICOPTER, SHE LAGS BEHIND...
MY FRIENDS THINK I IMAGINED IT ALL, BUT I DIDN'T! YOU KNOW I'M TELLING THE TRUTH!
CORRECT, MISS LANE! MY COMPANIONS AND I ARE KRYPTONIAN CRIMINALS WHO ESCAPED FROM THE PHANTOM ZONE...!
SHER OFF
6
WHEN WE FINISH REPAIRING OUR GENERATOR, WE'LL IMPRISON SUPERMAN IN THE PHANTOM ZONE! HA! WE'RE NOT AFRAID TO REVEAL THE TRUTH TO YOU, NOW THAT NO ONE WILL BELIEVE YOU!
YOU... DEVILS!

WHAT A FIENDISH PLOT! FOR SUPERMAN'S SAKE, I'VE GOT TO CONVINCE JIMMY AND PERRY I'M NOT LYING OR MAD! WAIT! I-I THINK I SEE PROOF THAT'LL CONVINCE THEM IN ONE OF THOSE SHOPS DOWN THE STREET!

GENERAL ST

SOON...
WHAT? AGAIN?! LOIS, YOU MUST THINK WE'RE IDIOTS, OR SOMETHING!

JIMMY, PLEASE COME AND LOOK AT WHAT I'VE GOT TO SHOW YOU!

ALL RIGHT. BUT ONLY IF YOU PROMISE TO GIVE UP THIS WILD-GOOSE CHASE IF YOU CAN'T FIND ANY PROOF!

SHORTLY, BACK IN TOWN...
LOIS, WHAT YOU JUST SHOWED US CONVINCED ME YOU WERE TELLING THE TRUTH! I HOPE SUPERMAN HAS RETURNED FROM OUTER SPACE, SO HE CAN HEAR MY ULTRASONIC SIGNAL AND GET HERE IN TIME!

HURRY!

SALOO

RAL STO

ZEE...ZEE...ZEE...

READER-- CAN YOU GUESS WHAT LOIS HAS SHOWN JIMMY AND PERRY?

INSTANTS LATER...
WHAT'S UP, JIMMY? I JUST RETURNED AND GOT YOUR SIGNAL! GREAT SCOTT! THOSE "COWBOYS"! MY X-RAY VISION REVEALS THEY'RE WEARING KRYPTONIAN COSTUMES UNDERNEATH THEIR CLOTHES! THEY'RE CRIMINALS WHO WERE BANISHED INTO THE PHANTOM ZONE! SOMEHOW THEY'VE ESCAPED!

SHERIFF'S OFFICE

YOU WON'T GET AWAY WITH THIS! I'LL RETURN YOU TO THE PHANTOM ZONE 'SOMEHOW, TO SERVE OUT THE REST OF YOUR SENTENCE!

FEED STORE

WE JUST COMPLETED REPAIRING THE PHANTASMON POWER-GENERATOR! IT'S YOU WHO'LL BE BANISHED INTO THE PHANTOM ZONE BY THESE RAY-GUNS POWERED BY THE GENERATOR!

AND AS THE CRIMINALS FLEX THEIR MIGHTY MUSCLES AND BURST OFF THEIR OUTER GARMENTS...
IT WAS THE TESTIMONY OF YOUR FATHER, JOR-EL, THAT DOOMED MANY OF US INTO THE PHANTOM ZONE! WE'LL AVENGE OURSELVES BY SENDING YOU THERE!

7

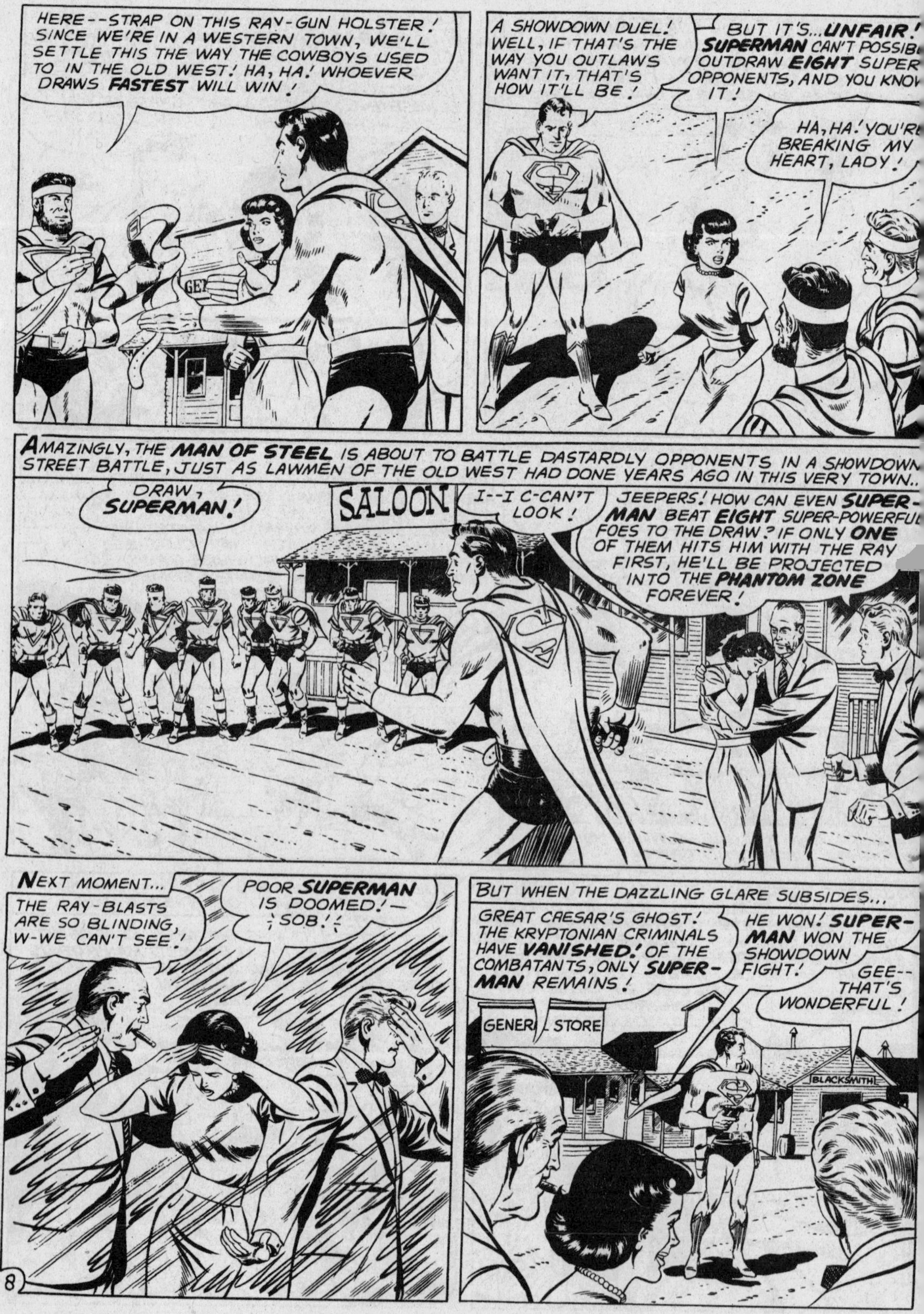
HERE--STRAP ON THIS RAY-GUN HOLSTER! SINCE WE'RE IN A WESTERN TOWN, WE'LL SETTLE THIS THE WAY THE COWBOYS USED TO IN THE OLD WEST! HA, HA! WHOEVER DRAWS FASTEST WILL WIN!
A SHOWDOWN DUEL! WELL, IF THAT'S THE WAY YOU OUTLAWS WANT IT, THAT'S HOW IT'LL BE!
BUT IT'S...UNFAIR! SUPERMAN CAN'T POSSIB OUTDRAW EIGHT SUPER OPPONENTS, AND YOU KNOW IT!
HA, HA! YOU'RE BREAKING MY HEART, LADY!
AMAZINGLY, THE MAN OF STEEL IS ABOUT TO BATTLE DASTARDLY OPPONENTS IN A SHOWDOWN STREET BATTLE, JUST AS LAWMEN OF THE OLD WEST HAD DONE YEARS AGO IN THIS VERY TOWN..
DRAW, SUPERMAN!
SALOON
I--I C-CAN'T LOOK!
JEEPERS! HOW CAN EVEN SUPER-MAN BEAT EIGHT SUPER-POWERFUL FOES TO THE DRAW? IF ONLY ONE OF THEM HITS HIM WITH THE RAY FIRST, HE'LL BE PROJECTED INTO THE PHANTOM ZONE FOREVER!
NEXT MOMENT...
THE RAY-BLASTS ARE SO BLINDING, W-WE CAN'T SEE!
POOR SUPERMAN IS DOOMED!— SOB!
BUT WHEN THE DAZZLING GLARE SUBSIDES...
GREAT CAESAR'S GHOST! THE KRYPTONIAN CRIMINALS HAVE VANISHED! OF THE COMBATANTS, ONLY SUPER-MAN REMAINS!
HE WON! SUPER-MAN WON THE SHOWDOWN FIGHT!
GEE-- THAT'S WONDERFUL!
GENERAL STORE
BLACKSMITH
8

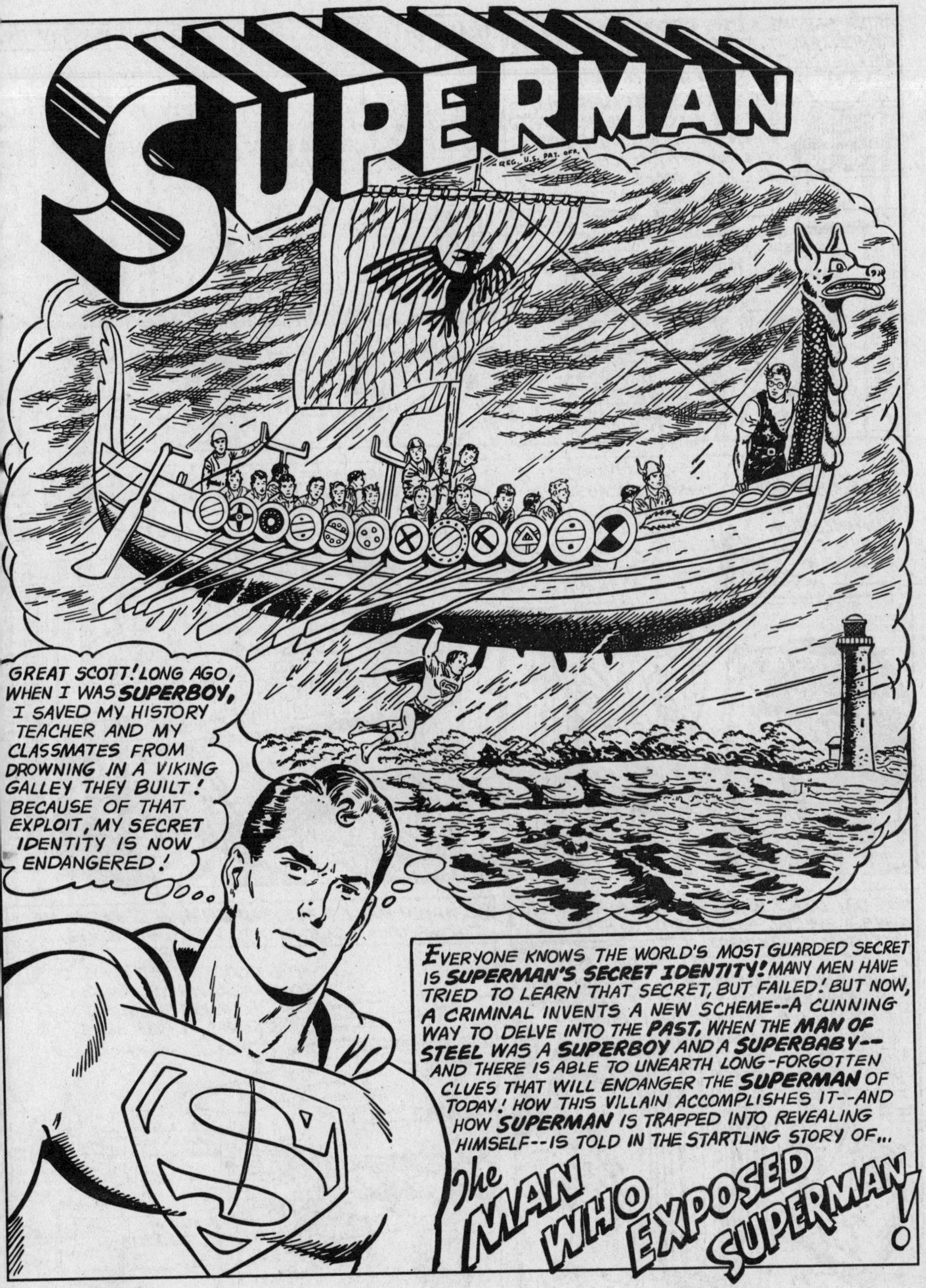
SUPERMAN
REG. U.S. PAT. OFF.
GREAT SCOTT! LONG AGO, WHEN I WAS SUPERBOY, I SAVED MY HISTORY TEACHER AND MY CLASSMATES FROM DROWNING IN A VIKING GALLEY THEY BUILT! BECAUSE OF THAT EXPLOIT, MY SECRET IDENTITY IS NOW ENDANGERED!
EVERYONE KNOWS THE WORLD'S MOST GUARDED SECRET IS SUPERMAN'S SECRET IDENTITY! MANY MEN HAVE TRIED TO LEARN THAT SECRET, BUT FAILED! BUT NOW, A CRIMINAL INVENTS A NEW SCHEME--A CUNNING WAY TO DELVE INTO THE PAST, WHEN THE MAN OF STEEL WAS A SUPERBOY AND A SUPERBABY--AND THERE IS ABLE TO UNEARTH LONG-FORGOTTEN CLUES THAT WILL ENDANGER THE SUPERMAN OF TODAY! HOW THIS VILLAIN ACCOMPLISHES IT--AND HOW SUPERMAN IS TRAPPED INTO REVEALING HIMSELF--IS TOLD IN THE STARTLING STORY OF...
The MAN WHO EXPOSED SUPERMAN!

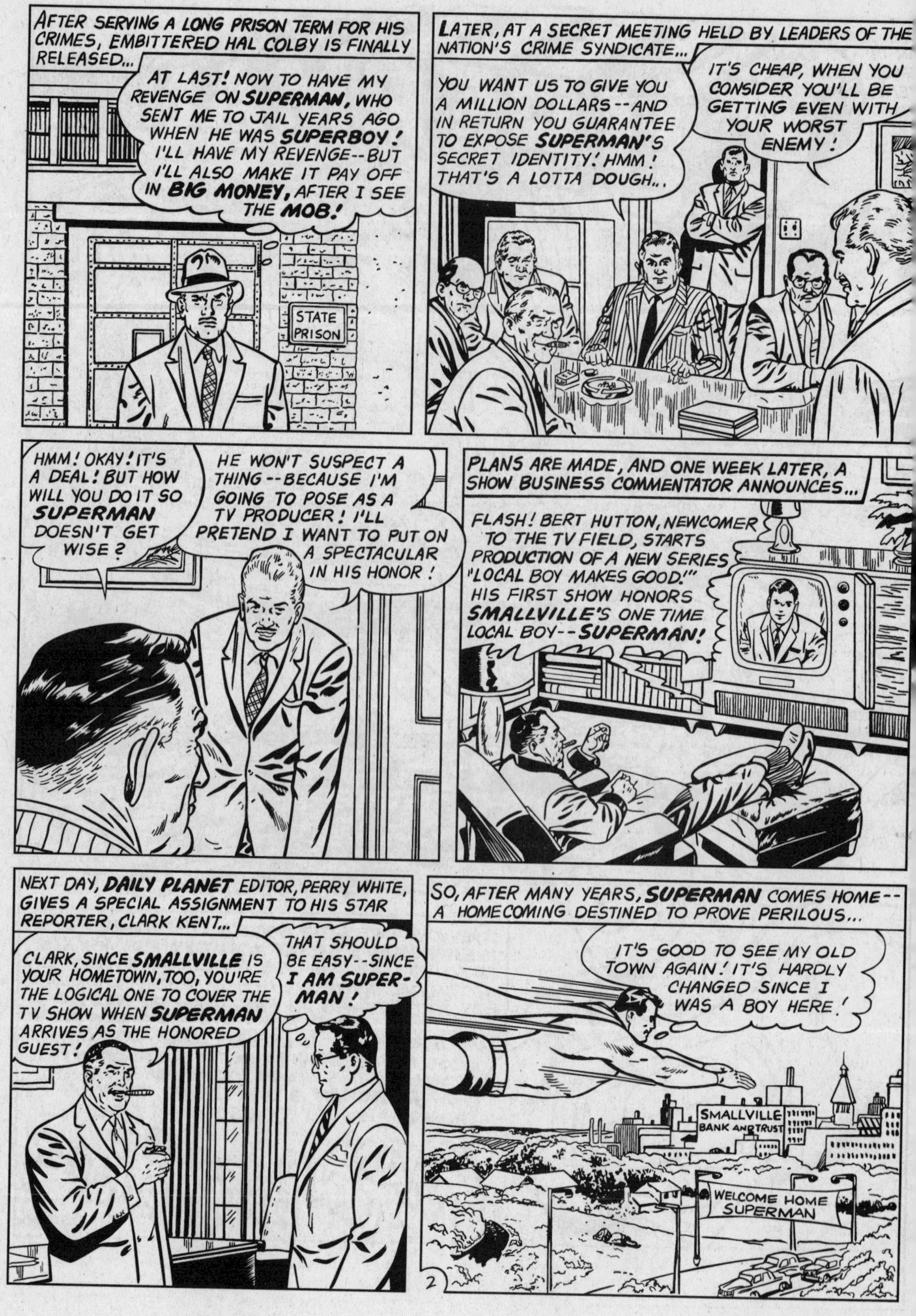
AFTER SERVING A LONG PRISON TERM FOR HIS CRIMES, EMBITTERED HAL COLBY IS FINALLY RELEASED...
AT LAST! NOW TO HAVE MY REVENGE ON SUPERMAN, WHO SENT ME TO JAIL YEARS AGO WHEN HE WAS SUPERBOY! I'LL HAVE MY REVENGE--BUT I'LL ALSO MAKE IT PAY OFF IN BIG MONEY, AFTER I SEE THE MOB!
STATE PRISON
LATER, AT A SECRET MEETING HELD BY LEADERS OF THE NATION'S CRIME SYNDICATE...
YOU WANT US TO GIVE YOU A MILLION DOLLARS--AND IN RETURN YOU GUARANTEE TO EXPOSE SUPERMAN'S SECRET IDENTITY! HMM! THAT'S A LOTTA DOUGH...
IT'S CHEAP, WHEN YOU CONSIDER YOU'LL BE GETTING EVEN WITH YOUR WORST ENEMY!
HMM! OKAY! IT'S A DEAL! BUT HOW WILL YOU DO IT SO SUPERMAN DOESN'T GET WISE?
HE WON'T SUSPECT A THING--BECAUSE I'M GOING TO POSE AS A TV PRODUCER! I'LL PRETEND I WANT TO PUT ON A SPECTACULAR IN HIS HONOR!
PLANS ARE MADE, AND ONE WEEK LATER, A SHOW BUSINESS COMMENTATOR ANNOUNCES...
FLASH! BERT HUTTON, NEWCOMER TO THE TV FIELD, STARTS PRODUCTION OF A NEW SERIES "LOCAL BOY MAKES GOOD!" HIS FIRST SHOW HONORS SMALLVILLE'S ONE TIME LOCAL BOY--SUPERMAN!
NEXT DAY, DAILY PLANET EDITOR, PERRY WHITE, GIVES A SPECIAL ASSIGNMENT TO HIS STAR REPORTER, CLARK KENT...
CLARK, SINCE SMALLVILLE IS YOUR HOMETOWN, TOO, YOU'RE THE LOGICAL ONE TO COVER THE TV SHOW WHEN SUPERMAN ARRIVES AS THE HONORED GUEST!
THAT SHOULD BE EASY--SINCE I AM SUPER-MAN!
SO, AFTER MANY YEARS, SUPERMAN COMES HOME--A HOMECOMING DESTINED TO PROVE PERILOUS...
IT'S GOOD TO SEE MY OLD TOWN AGAIN! IT'S HARDLY CHANGED SINCE I WAS A BOY HERE!
SMALLVILLE BANK AND TRUST
WELCOME HOME SUPERMAN
2

THE ORPHANAGE! I WAS AN INFANT WHEN I WAS TAKEN THERE BY THE KENTS--AFTER THEY FOUND ME IN THE ROCKET THAT BROUGHT ME FROM MY NATIVE PLANET, KRYPTON...*

*EDITOR'S NOTE: BECAUSE OF HIS SUPER-MEMORY, SUPERMAN CAN RECALL ALL THE INCIDENTS OF HIS CHILDHOOD!

"LUCKILY, I WASN'T THERE LONG--OTHERWISE I WOULD HAVE UNWITTINGLY REVEALED THAT I WAS A SUPER-BABY!"

CRACK

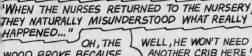

"WHEN THE NURSES RETURNED TO THE NURSERY, THEY NATURALLY MISUNDERSTOOD WHAT REALLY HAPPENED..."

OH, THE WOOD BROKE BECAUSE IT MUST HAVE BEEN OLD! IT'S LUCKY THE LITTLE FELLOW WASN'T HURT!

WELL, HE WON'T NEED ANOTHER CRIB HERE! THE KENTS HAVE COME BACK TO ADOPT HIM!

SUDDENLY, A VOICE INTERRUPTS SUPERMAN'S MEMORIES...

SUPERMAN! WE DIDN'T REALIZE YOU HAD ARRIVED! I'M BERT HUTTON! MY CREW AND I WERE JUST ON OUR WAY TO SMALLVILLE HIGH!

HUTTON TV Productio

WELL, MR. HUTTON, SINCE YOU'RE GOING TO THE SCHOOL, I MIGHT AS WELL TAG ALONG!

I KNEW HE WOULDN'T RECOGNIZE ME! I'VE CHANGED A LOT SINCE HE SENT ME TO PRISON-- BUT THERE'LL BE CHANGES IN HIS LIFE, TOO! I'LL SEE TO THAT!

3

SUPERMAN'S FACE SEEMED SAD AND NOSTALGIC, WHEN HE WAS LOOKING AT THE ORPHANAGE BEFORE! WHY? I WONDER IF THAT PLACE HOLDS ANY MEMORIES FOR HIM...?

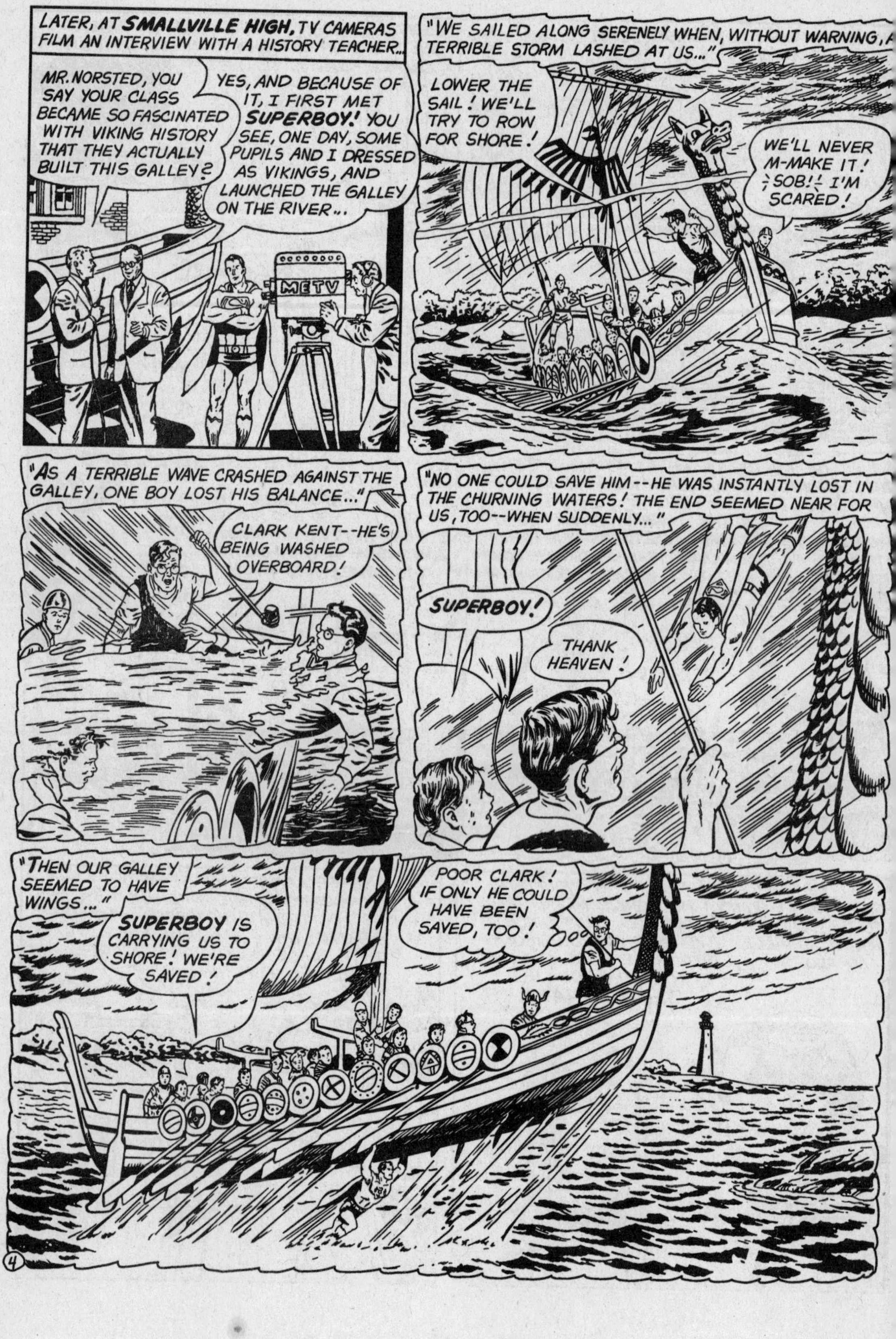
LATER, AT SMALLVILLE HIGH, TV CAMERAS FILM AN INTERVIEW WITH A HISTORY TEACHER...
MR. NORSTED, YOU SAY YOUR CLASS BECAME SO FASCINATED WITH VIKING HISTORY THAT THEY ACTUALLY BUILT THIS GALLEY?
YES, AND BECAUSE OF IT, I FIRST MET SUPERBOY! YOU SEE, ONE DAY, SOME PUPILS AND I DRESSED AS VIKINGS, AND LAUNCHED THE GALLEY ON THE RIVER...
METV
"WE SAILED ALONG SERENELY WHEN, WITHOUT WARNING, A TERRIBLE STORM LASHED AT US..."
LOWER THE SAIL! WE'LL TRY TO ROW FOR SHORE!
WE'LL NEVER M-MAKE IT! SOB! I'M SCARED!
"AS A TERRIBLE WAVE CRASHED AGAINST THE GALLEY, ONE BOY LOST HIS BALANCE..."
CLARK KENT--HE'S BEING WASHED OVERBOARD!
"NO ONE COULD SAVE HIM--HE WAS INSTANTLY LOST IN THE CHURNING WATERS! THE END SEEMED NEAR FOR US, TOO--WHEN SUDDENLY..."
SUPERBOY!
THANK HEAVEN!
"THEN OUR GALLEY SEEMED TO HAVE WINGS..."
SUPERBOY IS CARRYING US TO SHORE! WE'RE SAVED!
POOR CLARK! IF ONLY HE COULD HAVE BEEN SAVED, TOO!
4

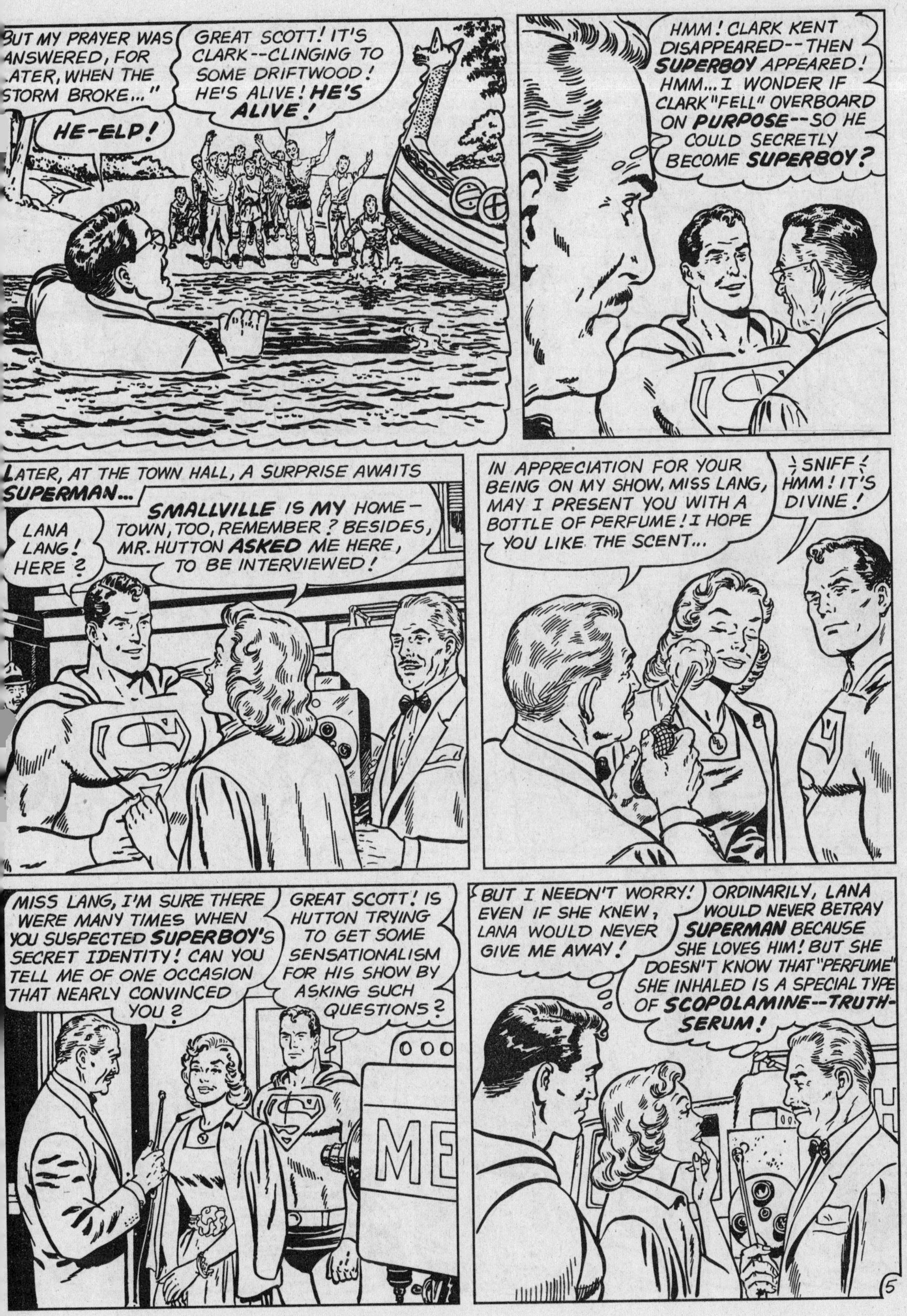
BUT MY PRAYER WAS ANSWERED, FOR LATER, WHEN THE STORM BROKE..."
GREAT SCOTT! IT'S CLARK--CLINGING TO SOME DRIFTWOOD! HE'S ALIVE! HE'S ALIVE!
HE-ELP!
HMM! CLARK KENT DISAPPEARED--THEN SUPERBOY APPEARED! HMM... I WONDER IF CLARK "FELL" OVERBOARD ON PURPOSE--SO HE COULD SECRETLY BECOME SUPERBOY?
LATER, AT THE TOWN HALL, A SURPRISE AWAITS SUPERMAN...
LANA LANG! HERE?
SMALLVILLE IS MY HOME-TOWN, TOO, REMEMBER? BESIDES, MR. HUTTON ASKED ME HERE, TO BE INTERVIEWED!
IN APPRECIATION FOR YOUR BEING ON MY SHOW, MISS LANG, MAY I PRESENT YOU WITH A BOTTLE OF PERFUME! I HOPE YOU LIKE THE SCENT...
SNIFF! HMM! IT'S DIVINE!
MISS LANG, I'M SURE THERE WERE MANY TIMES WHEN YOU SUSPECTED SUPERBOY'S SECRET IDENTITY! CAN YOU TELL ME OF ONE OCCASION THAT NEARLY CONVINCED YOU?
GREAT SCOTT! IS HUTTON TRYING TO GET SOME SENSATIONALISM FOR HIS SHOW BY ASKING SUCH QUESTIONS?
BUT I NEEDN'T WORRY! EVEN IF SHE KNEW, LANA WOULD NEVER GIVE ME AWAY!
ORDINARILY, LANA WOULD NEVER BETRAY SUPERMAN BECAUSE SHE LOVES HIM! BUT SHE DOESN'T KNOW THAT "PERFUME" SHE INHALED IS A SPECIAL TYPE OF SCOPOLAMINE--TRUTH-SERUM!
5

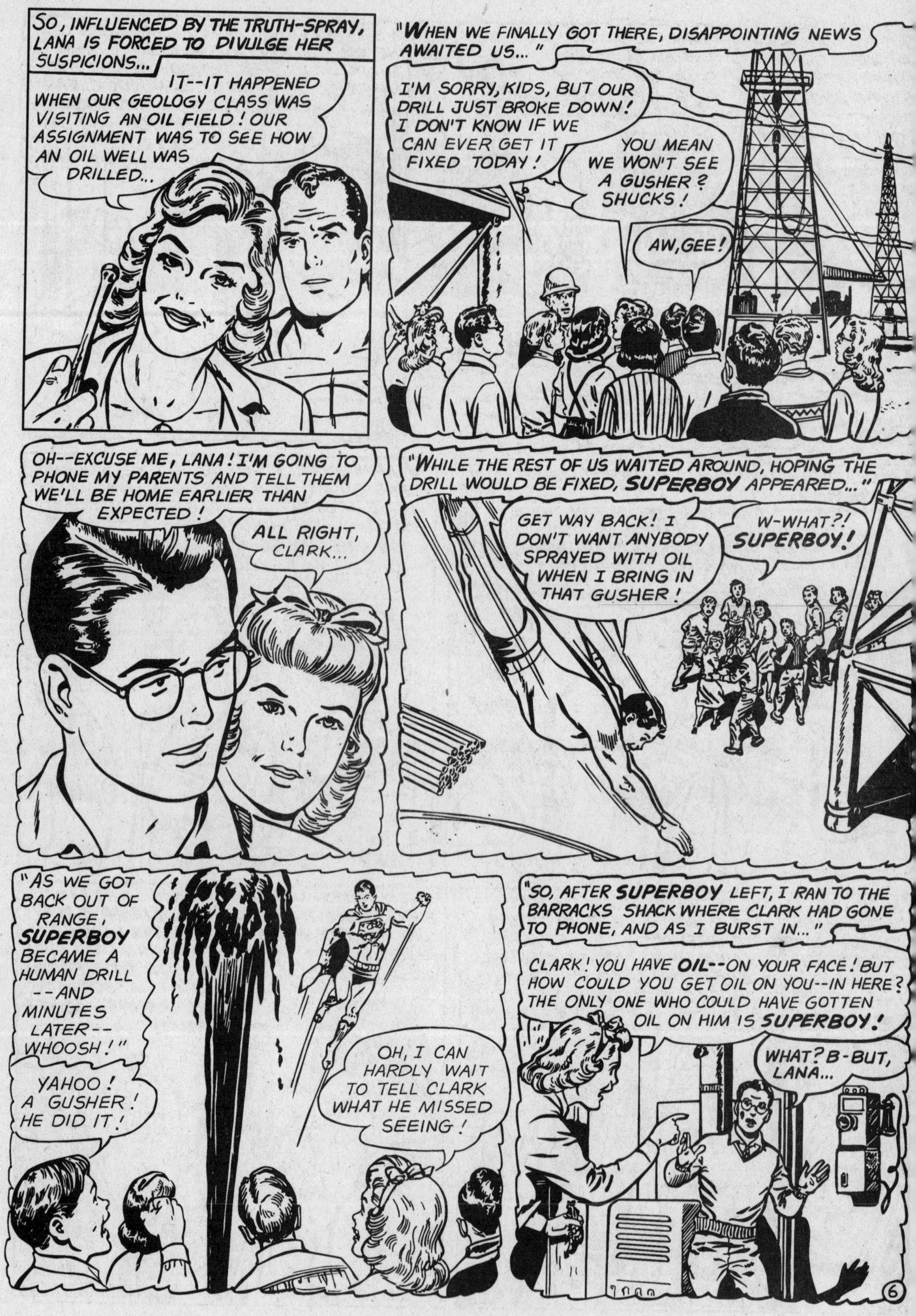
SO, INFLUENCED BY THE TRUTH-SPRAY, LANA IS FORCED TO DIVULGE HER SUSPICIONS...
IT--IT HAPPENED WHEN OUR GEOLOGY CLASS WAS VISITING AN OIL FIELD! OUR ASSIGNMENT WAS TO SEE HOW AN OIL WELL WAS DRILLED...
"WHEN WE FINALLY GOT THERE, DISAPPOINTING NEWS AWAITED US..."
I'M SORRY, KIDS, BUT OUR DRILL JUST BROKE DOWN! I DON'T KNOW IF WE CAN EVER GET IT FIXED TODAY!
YOU MEAN WE WON'T SEE A GUSHER? SHUCKS!
AW, GEE!
OH--EXCUSE ME, LANA! I'M GOING TO PHONE MY PARENTS AND TELL THEM WE'LL BE HOME EARLIER THAN EXPECTED!
ALL RIGHT, CLARK...
"WHILE THE REST OF US WAITED AROUND, HOPING THE DRILL WOULD BE FIXED, SUPERBOY APPEARED..."
GET WAY BACK! I DON'T WANT ANYBODY SPRAYED WITH OIL WHEN I BRING IN THAT GUSHER!
W-WHAT?! SUPERBOY!
"AS WE GOT BACK OUT OF RANGE, SUPERBOY BECAME A HUMAN DRILL --AND MINUTES LATER-- WHOOSH!"
YAHOO! A GUSHER! HE DID IT!
OH, I CAN HARDLY WAIT TO TELL CLARK WHAT HE MISSED SEEING!
"SO, AFTER SUPERBOY LEFT, I RAN TO THE BARRACKS SHACK WHERE CLARK HAD GONE TO PHONE, AND AS I BURST IN..."
CLARK! YOU HAVE OIL--ON YOUR FACE! BUT HOW COULD YOU GET OIL ON YOU--IN HERE? THE ONLY ONE WHO COULD HAVE GOTTEN OIL ON HIM IS SUPERBOY!
WHAT? B-BUT, LANA...
6

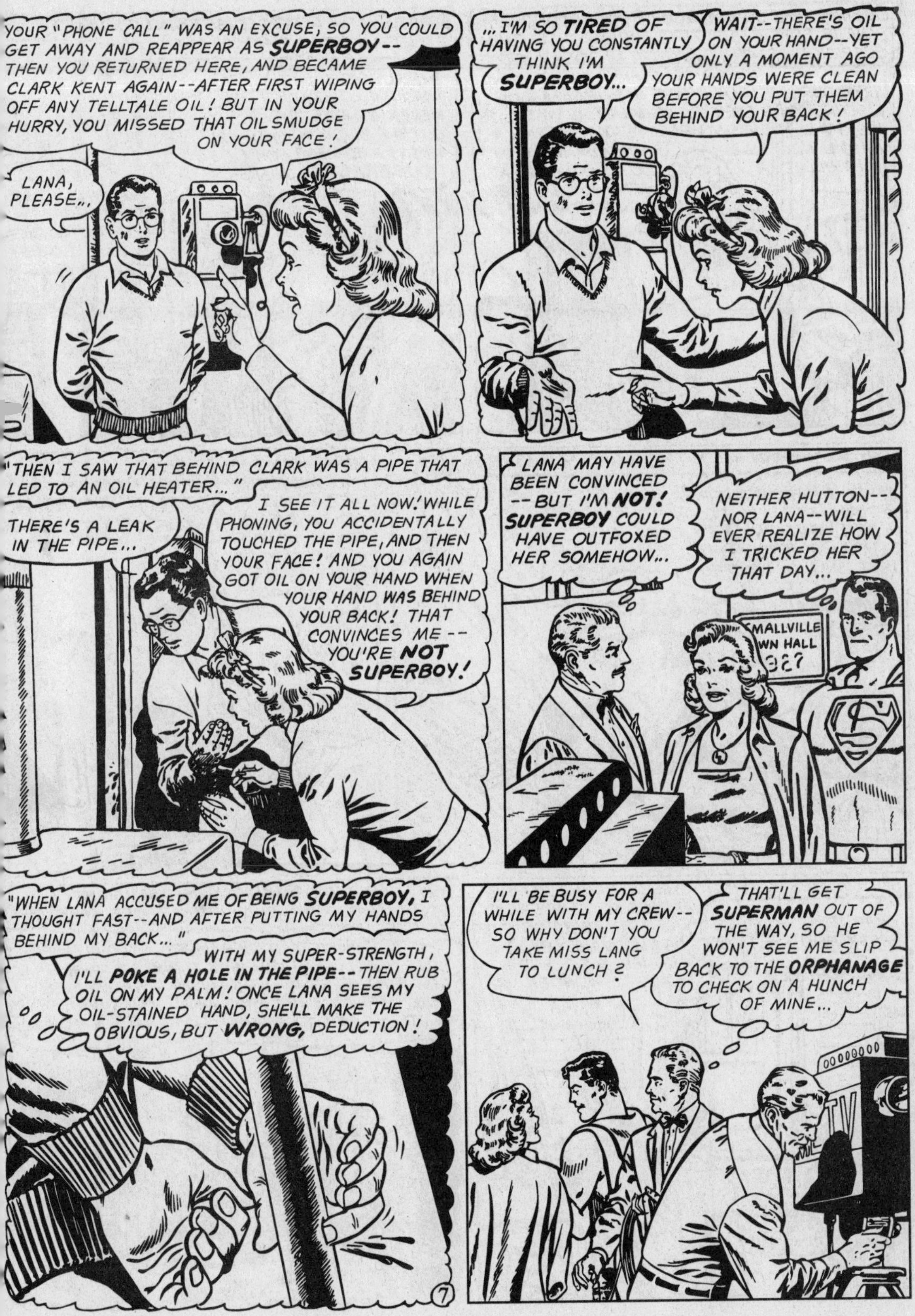
YOUR "PHONE CALL" WAS AN EXCUSE, SO YOU COULD GET AWAY AND REAPPEAR AS SUPERBOY--THEN YOU RETURNED HERE, AND BECAME CLARK KENT AGAIN--AFTER FIRST WIPING OFF ANY TELLTALE OIL! BUT IN YOUR HURRY, YOU MISSED THAT OIL SMUDGE ON YOUR FACE!
LANA, PLEASE...
...I'M SO TIRED OF HAVING YOU CONSTANTLY THINK I'M SUPERBOY...
WAIT--THERE'S OIL ON YOUR HAND--YET ONLY A MOMENT AGO YOUR HANDS WERE CLEAN BEFORE YOU PUT THEM BEHIND YOUR BACK!
"THEN I SAW THAT BEHIND CLARK WAS A PIPE THAT LED TO AN OIL HEATER..."
THERE'S A LEAK IN THE PIPE...
I SEE IT ALL NOW! WHILE PHONING, YOU ACCIDENTALLY TOUCHED THE PIPE, AND THEN YOUR FACE! AND YOU AGAIN GOT OIL ON YOUR HAND WHEN YOUR HAND WAS BEHIND YOUR BACK! THAT CONVINCES ME--YOU'RE NOT SUPERBOY!
LANA MAY HAVE BEEN CONVINCED--BUT I'M NOT! SUPERBOY COULD HAVE OUTFOXED HER SOMEHOW...
NEITHER HUTTON--NOR LANA--WILL EVER REALIZE HOW I TRICKED HER THAT DAY...
MALLVILLE
WN HALL
927
"WHEN LANA ACCUSED ME OF BEING SUPERBOY, I THOUGHT FAST--AND AFTER PUTTING MY HANDS BEHIND MY BACK..."
WITH MY SUPER-STRENGTH, I'LL POKE A HOLE IN THE PIPE--THEN RUB OIL ON MY PALM! ONCE LANA SEES MY OIL-STAINED HAND, SHE'LL MAKE THE OBVIOUS, BUT WRONG, DEDUCTION!
7
I'LL BE BUSY FOR A WHILE WITH MY CREW--SO WHY DON'T YOU TAKE MISS LANG TO LUNCH?
THAT'LL GET SUPERMAN OUT OF THE WAY, SO HE WON'T SEE ME SLIP BACK TO THE ORPHANAGE TO CHECK ON A HUNCH OF MINE...
TV

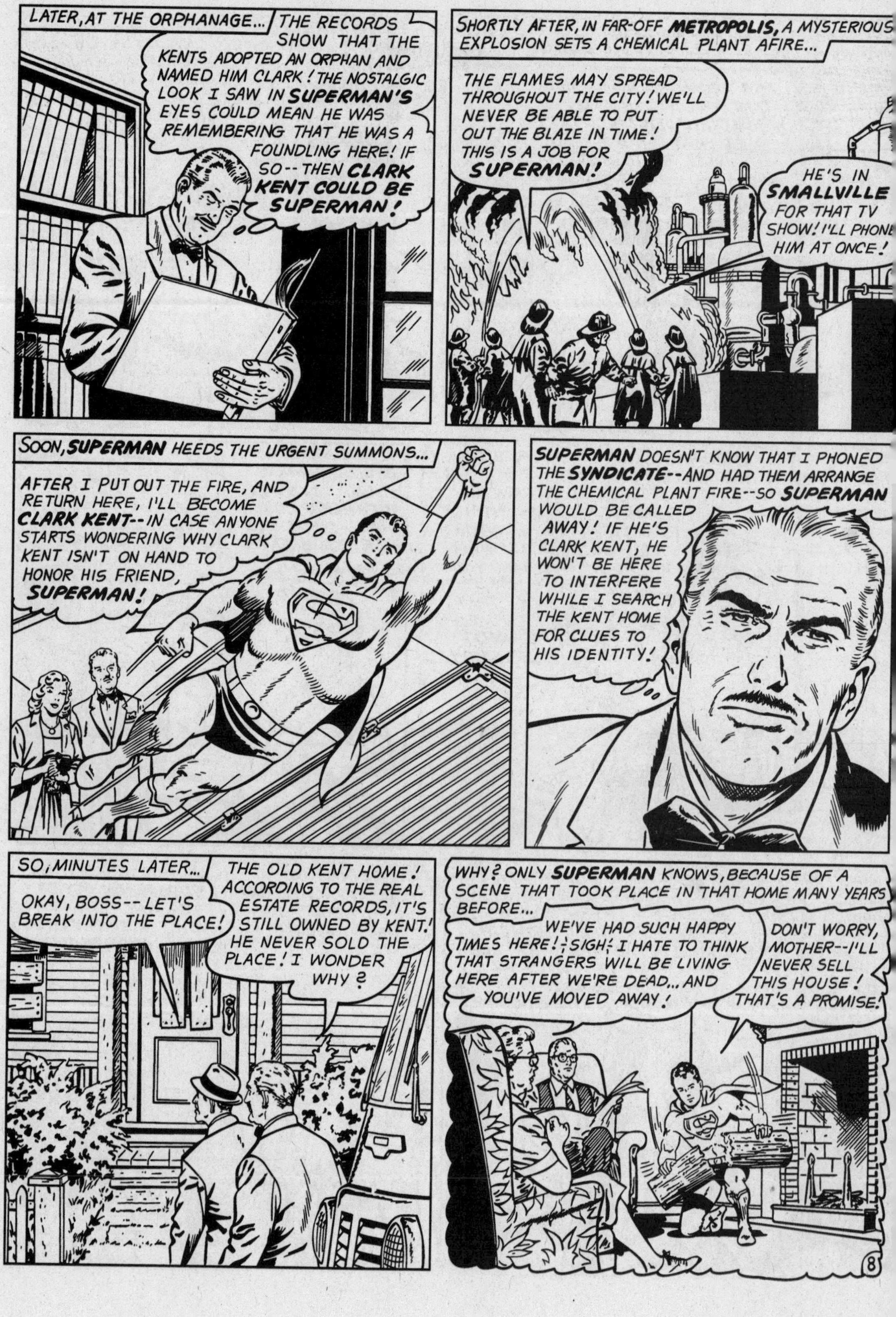
LATER, AT THE ORPHANAGE...
THE RECORDS SHOW THAT THE KENTS ADOPTED AN ORPHAN AND NAMED HIM CLARK! THE NOSTALGIC LOOK I SAW IN SUPERMAN'S EYES COULD MEAN HE WAS REMEMBERING THAT HE WAS A FOUNDLING HERE! IF SO-- THEN CLARK KENT COULD BE SUPERMAN!
SHORTLY AFTER, IN FAR-OFF METROPOLIS, A MYSTERIOUS EXPLOSION SETS A CHEMICAL PLANT AFIRE...
THE FLAMES MAY SPREAD THROUGHOUT THE CITY! WE'LL NEVER BE ABLE TO PUT OUT THE BLAZE IN TIME! THIS IS A JOB FOR SUPERMAN!
HE'S IN SMALLVILLE FOR THAT TV SHOW! I'LL PHONE HIM AT ONCE!
SOON, SUPERMAN HEEDS THE URGENT SUMMONS...
AFTER I PUT OUT THE FIRE, AND RETURN HERE, I'LL BECOME CLARK KENT-- IN CASE ANYONE STARTS WONDERING WHY CLARK KENT ISN'T ON HAND TO HONOR HIS FRIEND, SUPERMAN!
SUPERMAN DOESN'T KNOW THAT I PHONED THE SYNDICATE--AND HAD THEM ARRANGE THE CHEMICAL PLANT FIRE--SO SUPERMAN WOULD BE CALLED AWAY! IF HE'S CLARK KENT, HE WON'T BE HERE TO INTERFERE WHILE I SEARCH THE KENT HOME FOR CLUES TO HIS IDENTITY!
SO, MINUTES LATER...
OKAY, BOSS-- LET'S BREAK INTO THE PLACE!
THE OLD KENT HOME! ACCORDING TO THE REAL ESTATE RECORDS, IT'S STILL OWNED BY KENT! HE NEVER SOLD THE PLACE! I WONDER WHY?
WHY? ONLY SUPERMAN KNOWS, BECAUSE OF A SCENE THAT TOOK PLACE IN THAT HOME MANY YEARS BEFORE...
WE'VE HAD SUCH HAPPY TIMES HERE! -SIGH- I HATE TO THINK THAT STRANGERS WILL BE LIVING HERE AFTER WE'RE DEAD... AND YOU'VE MOVED AWAY!
DON'T WORRY, MOTHER--I'LL NEVER SELL THIS HOUSE! THAT'S A PROMISE!
8

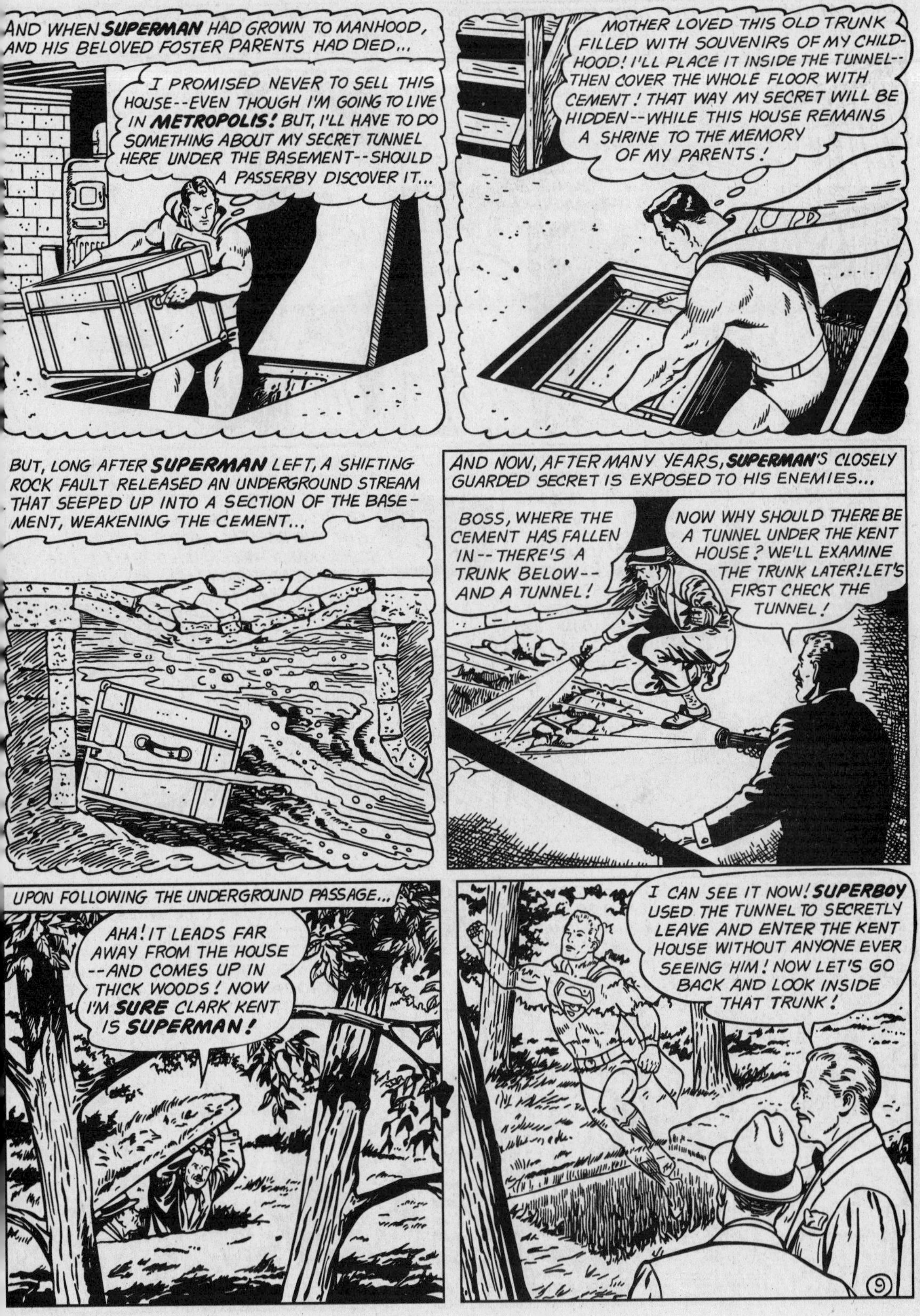
AND WHEN SUPERMAN HAD GROWN TO MANHOOD, AND HIS BELOVED FOSTER PARENTS HAD DIED...
I PROMISED NEVER TO SELL THIS HOUSE--EVEN THOUGH I'M GOING TO LIVE IN METROPOLIS! BUT, I'LL HAVE TO DO SOMETHING ABOUT MY SECRET TUNNEL HERE UNDER THE BASEMENT--SHOULD A PASSERBY DISCOVER IT...
MOTHER LOVED THIS OLD TRUNK FILLED WITH SOUVENIRS OF MY CHILDHOOD! I'LL PLACE IT INSIDE THE TUNNEL--THEN COVER THE WHOLE FLOOR WITH CEMENT! THAT WAY MY SECRET WILL BE HIDDEN--WHILE THIS HOUSE REMAINS A SHRINE TO THE MEMORY OF MY PARENTS!
BUT, LONG AFTER SUPERMAN LEFT, A SHIFTING ROCK FAULT RELEASED AN UNDERGROUND STREAM THAT SEEPED UP INTO A SECTION OF THE BASEMENT, WEAKENING THE CEMENT...
AND NOW, AFTER MANY YEARS, SUPERMAN'S CLOSELY GUARDED SECRET IS EXPOSED TO HIS ENEMIES...
BOSS, WHERE THE CEMENT HAS FALLEN IN--THERE'S A TRUNK BELOW--AND A TUNNEL!
NOW WHY SHOULD THERE BE A TUNNEL UNDER THE KENT HOUSE? WE'LL EXAMINE THE TRUNK LATER! LET'S FIRST CHECK THE TUNNEL!
UPON FOLLOWING THE UNDERGROUND PASSAGE...
AHA! IT LEADS FAR AWAY FROM THE HOUSE--AND COMES UP IN THICK WOODS! NOW I'M SURE CLARK KENT IS SUPERMAN!
I CAN SEE IT NOW! SUPERBOY USED THE TUNNEL TO SECRETLY LEAVE AND ENTER THE KENT HOUSE WITHOUT ANYONE EVER SEEING HIM! NOW LET'S GO BACK AND LOOK INSIDE THAT TRUNK!
9

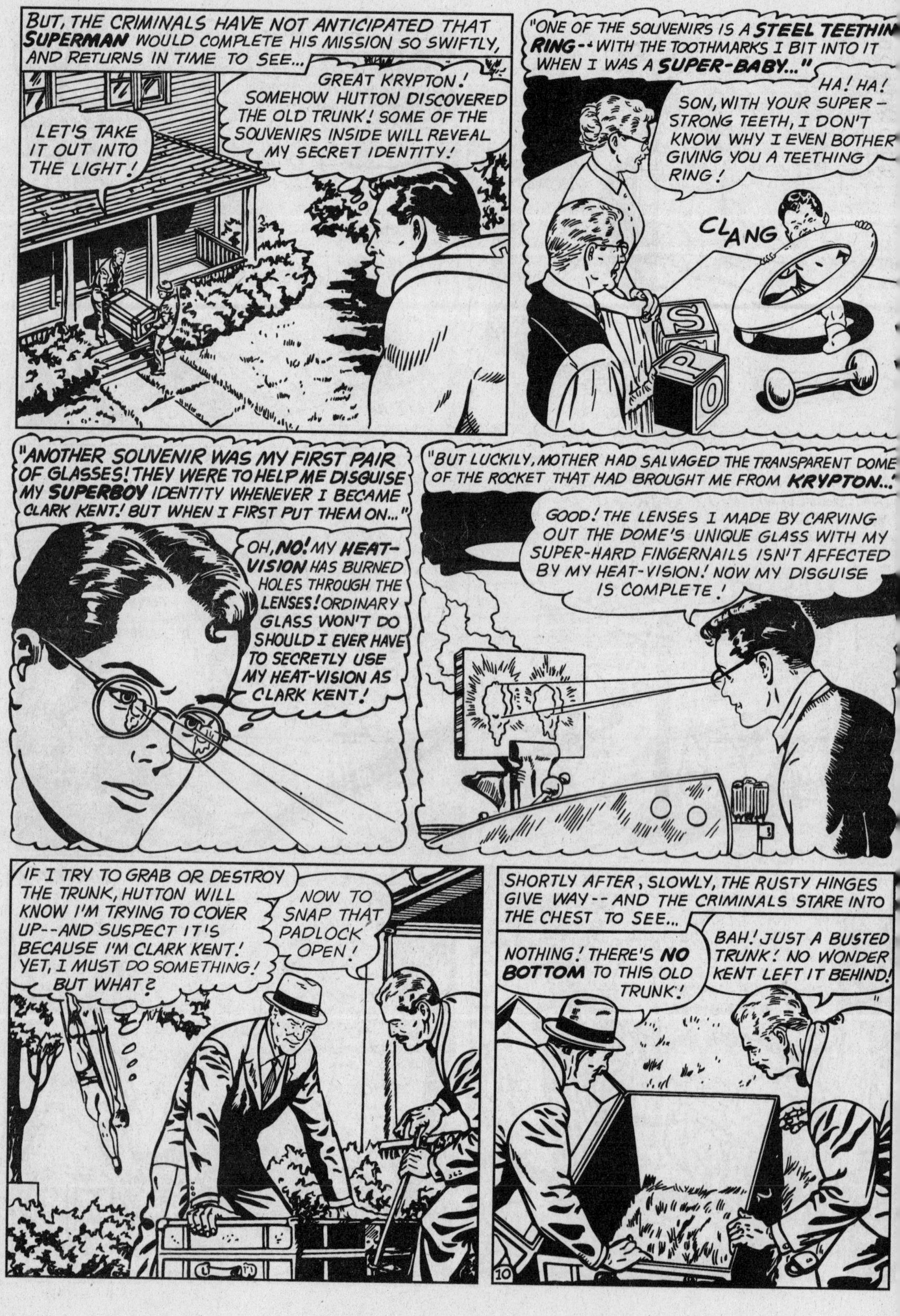
BUT, THE CRIMINALS HAVE NOT ANTICIPATED THAT SUPERMAN WOULD COMPLETE HIS MISSION SO SWIFTLY, AND RETURNS IN TIME TO SEE...
GREAT KRYPTON! SOMEHOW HUTTON DISCOVERED THE OLD TRUNK! SOME OF THE SOUVENIRS INSIDE WILL REVEAL MY SECRET IDENTITY!
LET'S TAKE IT OUT INTO THE LIGHT!
"ONE OF THE SOUVENIRS IS A STEEL TEETHIN RING--WITH THE TOOTHMARKS I BIT INTO IT WHEN I WAS A SUPER-BABY..."
HA! HA! SON, WITH YOUR SUPER-STRONG TEETH, I DON'T KNOW WHY I EVEN BOTHER GIVING YOU A TEETHING RING!
CLANG
"ANOTHER SOUVENIR WAS MY FIRST PAIR OF GLASSES! THEY WERE TO HELP ME DISGUISE MY SUPERBOY IDENTITY WHENEVER I BECAME CLARK KENT! BUT WHEN I FIRST PUT THEM ON..."
OH, NO! MY HEAT-VISION HAS BURNED HOLES THROUGH THE LENSES! ORDINARY GLASS WON'T DO SHOULD I EVER HAVE TO SECRETLY USE MY HEAT-VISION AS CLARK KENT!
"BUT LUCKILY, MOTHER HAD SALVAGED THE TRANSPARENT DOME OF THE ROCKET THAT HAD BROUGHT ME FROM KRYPTON..."
GOOD! THE LENSES I MADE BY CARVING OUT THE DOME'S UNIQUE GLASS WITH MY SUPER-HARD FINGERNAILS ISN'T AFFECTED BY MY HEAT-VISION! NOW MY DISGUISE IS COMPLETE!
IF I TRY TO GRAB OR DESTROY THE TRUNK, HUTTON WILL KNOW I'M TRYING TO COVER UP--AND SUSPECT IT'S BECAUSE I'M CLARK KENT! YET, I MUST DO SOMETHING! BUT WHAT?
NOW TO SNAP THAT PADLOCK OPEN!
SHORTLY AFTER, SLOWLY, THE RUSTY HINGES GIVE WAY--AND THE CRIMINALS STARE INTO THE CHEST TO SEE...
NOTHING! THERE'S NO BOTTOM TO THIS OLD TRUNK!
BAH! JUST A BUSTED TRUNK! NO WONDER KENT LEFT IT BEHIND!
10

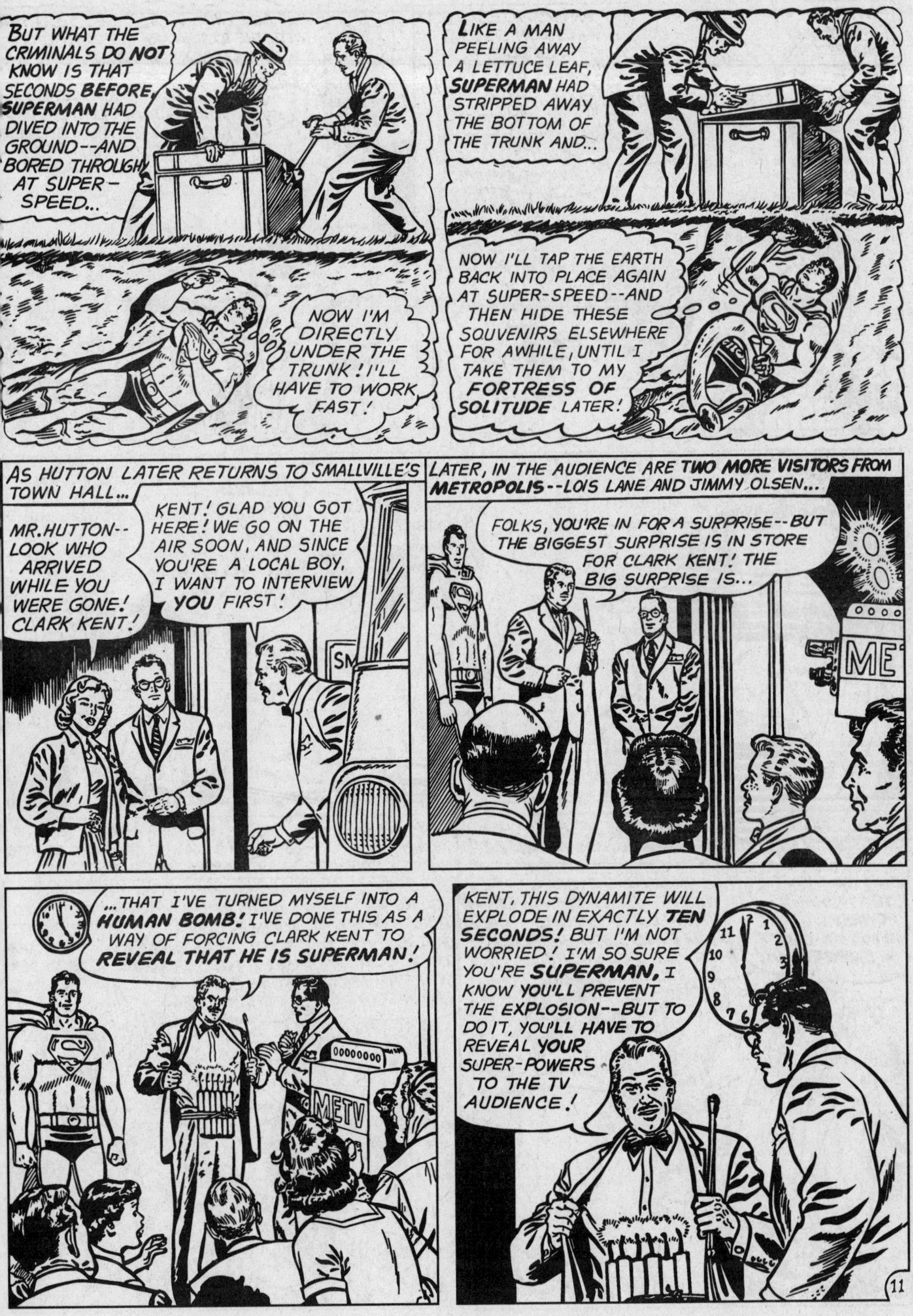
BUT WHAT THE CRIMINALS DO NOT KNOW IS THAT SECONDS BEFORE, SUPERMAN HAD DIVED INTO THE GROUND--AND BORED THROUGH AT SUPER-SPEED...
NOW I'M DIRECTLY UNDER THE TRUNK! I'LL HAVE TO WORK FAST!
LIKE A MAN PEELING AWAY A LETTUCE LEAF, SUPERMAN HAD STRIPPED AWAY THE BOTTOM OF THE TRUNK AND...
NOW I'LL TAP THE EARTH BACK INTO PLACE AGAIN AT SUPER-SPEED--AND THEN HIDE THESE SOUVENIRS ELSEWHERE FOR AWHILE, UNTIL I TAKE THEM TO MY FORTRESS OF SOLITUDE LATER!
AS HUTTON LATER RETURNS TO SMALLVILLE'S TOWN HALL...
MR. HUTTON--LOOK WHO ARRIVED WHILE YOU WERE GONE! CLARK KENT!
KENT! GLAD YOU GOT HERE! WE GO ON THE AIR SOON, AND SINCE YOU'RE A LOCAL BOY, I WANT TO INTERVIEW YOU FIRST!
LATER, IN THE AUDIENCE ARE TWO MORE VISITORS FROM METROPOLIS--LOIS LANE AND JIMMY OLSEN...
FOLKS, YOU'RE IN FOR A SURPRISE--BUT THE BIGGEST SURPRISE IS IN STORE FOR CLARK KENT! THE BIG SURPRISE IS...
MET
...THAT I'VE TURNED MYSELF INTO A HUMAN BOMB! I'VE DONE THIS AS A WAY OF FORCING CLARK KENT TO REVEAL THAT HE IS SUPERMAN!
METV
KENT, THIS DYNAMITE WILL EXPLODE IN EXACTLY TEN SECONDS! BUT I'M NOT WORRIED! I'M SO SURE YOU'RE SUPERMAN, I KNOW YOU'LL PREVENT THE EXPLOSION--BUT TO DO IT, YOU'LL HAVE TO REVEAL YOUR SUPER-POWERS TO THE TV AUDIENCE!
11

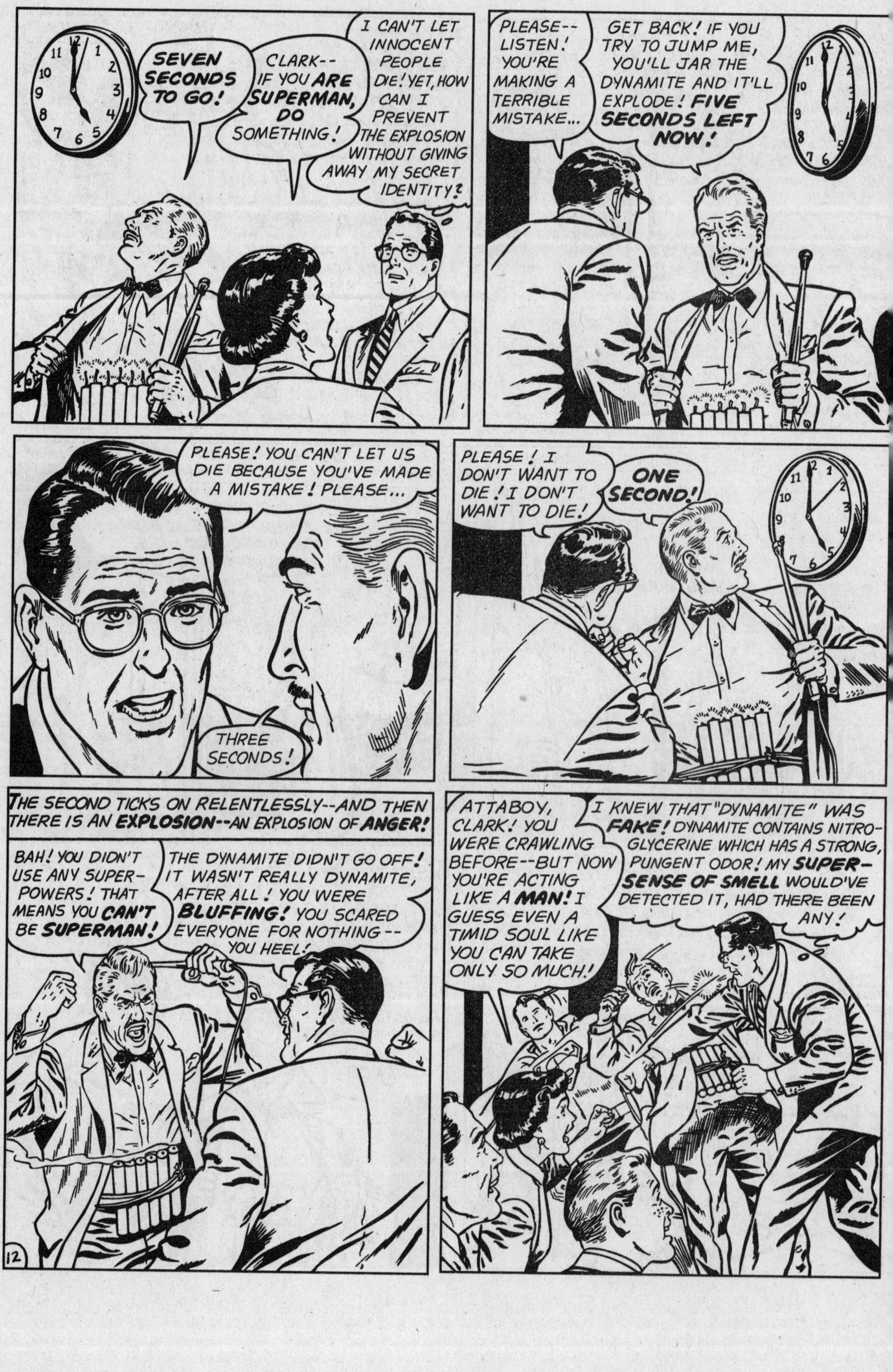
SEVEN SECONDS TO GO!
CLARK-- IF YOU ARE SUPERMAN, DO SOMETHING!
I CAN'T LET INNOCENT PEOPLE DIE! YET, HOW CAN I PREVENT THE EXPLOSION WITHOUT GIVING AWAY MY SECRET IDENTITY?
PLEASE-- LISTEN! YOU'RE MAKING A TERRIBLE MISTAKE...
GET BACK! IF YOU TRY TO JUMP ME, YOU'LL JAR THE DYNAMITE AND IT'LL EXPLODE! FIVE SECONDS LEFT NOW!
PLEASE! YOU CAN'T LET US DIE BECAUSE YOU'VE MADE A MISTAKE! PLEASE...
THREE SECONDS!
PLEASE! I DON'T WANT TO DIE! I DON'T WANT TO DIE!
ONE SECOND!
THE SECOND TICKS ON RELENTLESSLY--AND THEN THERE IS AN EXPLOSION--AN EXPLOSION OF ANGER!
BAH! YOU DIDN'T USE ANY SUPER-POWERS! THAT MEANS YOU CAN'T BE SUPERMAN!
THE DYNAMITE DIDN'T GO OFF! IT WASN'T REALLY DYNAMITE, AFTER ALL! YOU WERE BLUFFING! YOU SCARED EVERYONE FOR NOTHING-- YOU HEEL!
12
ATTABOY, CLARK! YOU WERE CRAWLING BEFORE--BUT NOW YOU'RE ACTING LIKE A MAN! I GUESS EVEN A TIMID SOUL LIKE YOU CAN TAKE ONLY SO MUCH!
I KNEW THAT "DYNAMITE" WAS FAKE! DYNAMITE CONTAINS NITRO-GLYCERINE WHICH HAS A STRONG, PUNGENT ODOR! MY SUPER-SENSE OF SMELL WOULD'VE DETECTED IT, HAD THERE BEEN ANY!

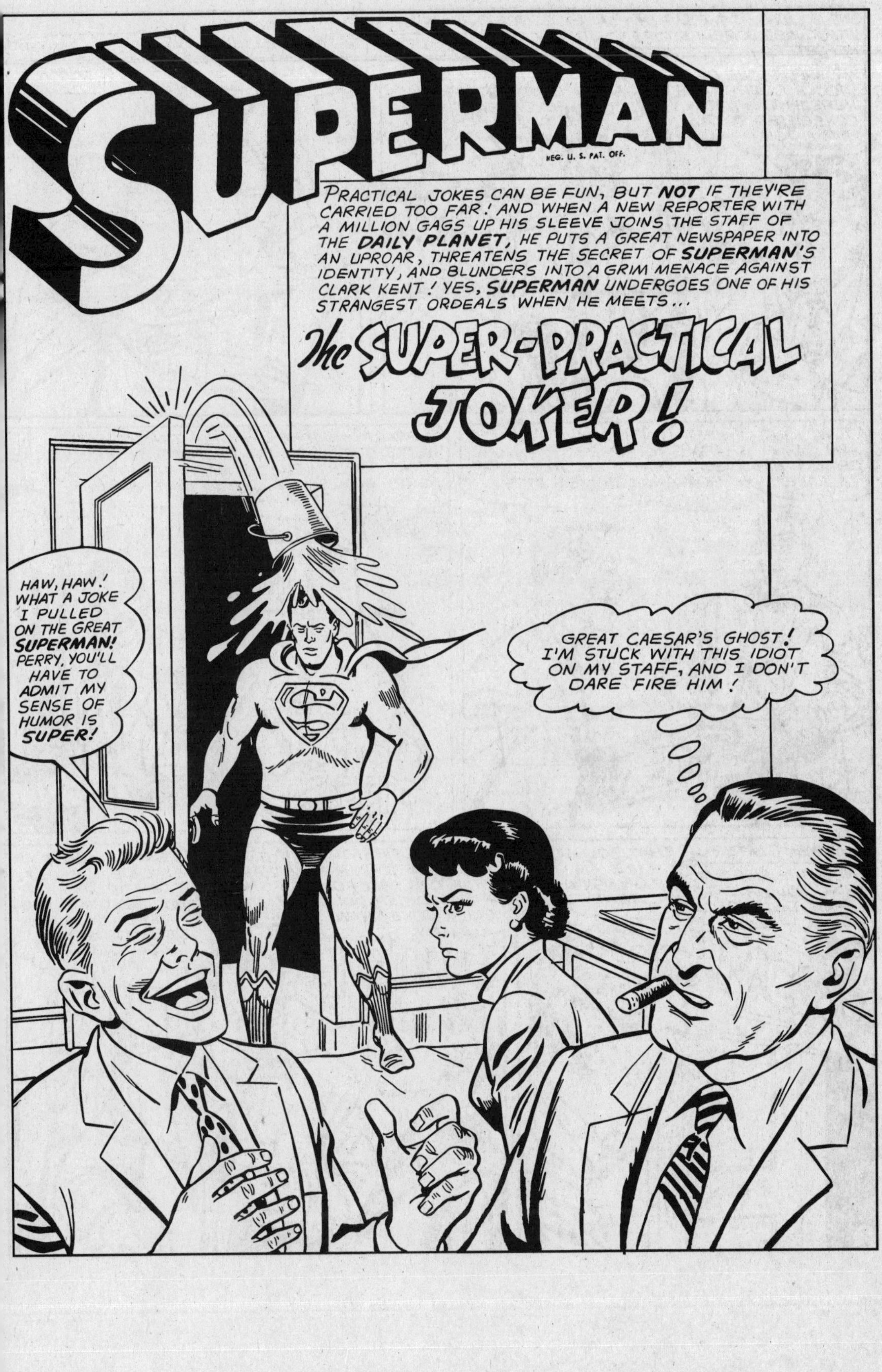
SUPERMAN
REG. U. S. PAT. OFF.
PRACTICAL JOKES CAN BE FUN, BUT NOT IF THEY'RE CARRIED TOO FAR! AND WHEN A NEW REPORTER WITH A MILLION GAGS UP HIS SLEEVE JOINS THE STAFF OF THE DAILY PLANET, HE PUTS A GREAT NEWSPAPER INTO AN UPROAR, THREATENS THE SECRET OF SUPERMAN'S IDENTITY, AND BLUNDERS INTO A GRIM MENACE AGAINST CLARK KENT! YES, SUPERMAN UNDERGOES ONE OF HIS STRANGEST ORDEALS WHEN HE MEETS...
The SUPER-PRACTICAL JOKER!
HAW, HAW! WHAT A JOKE I PULLED ON THE GREAT SUPERMAN! PERRY, YOU'LL HAVE TO ADMIT MY SENSE OF HUMOR IS SUPER!
GREAT CAESAR'S GHOST! I'M STUCK WITH THIS IDIOT ON MY STAFF, AND I DON'T DARE FIRE HIM!

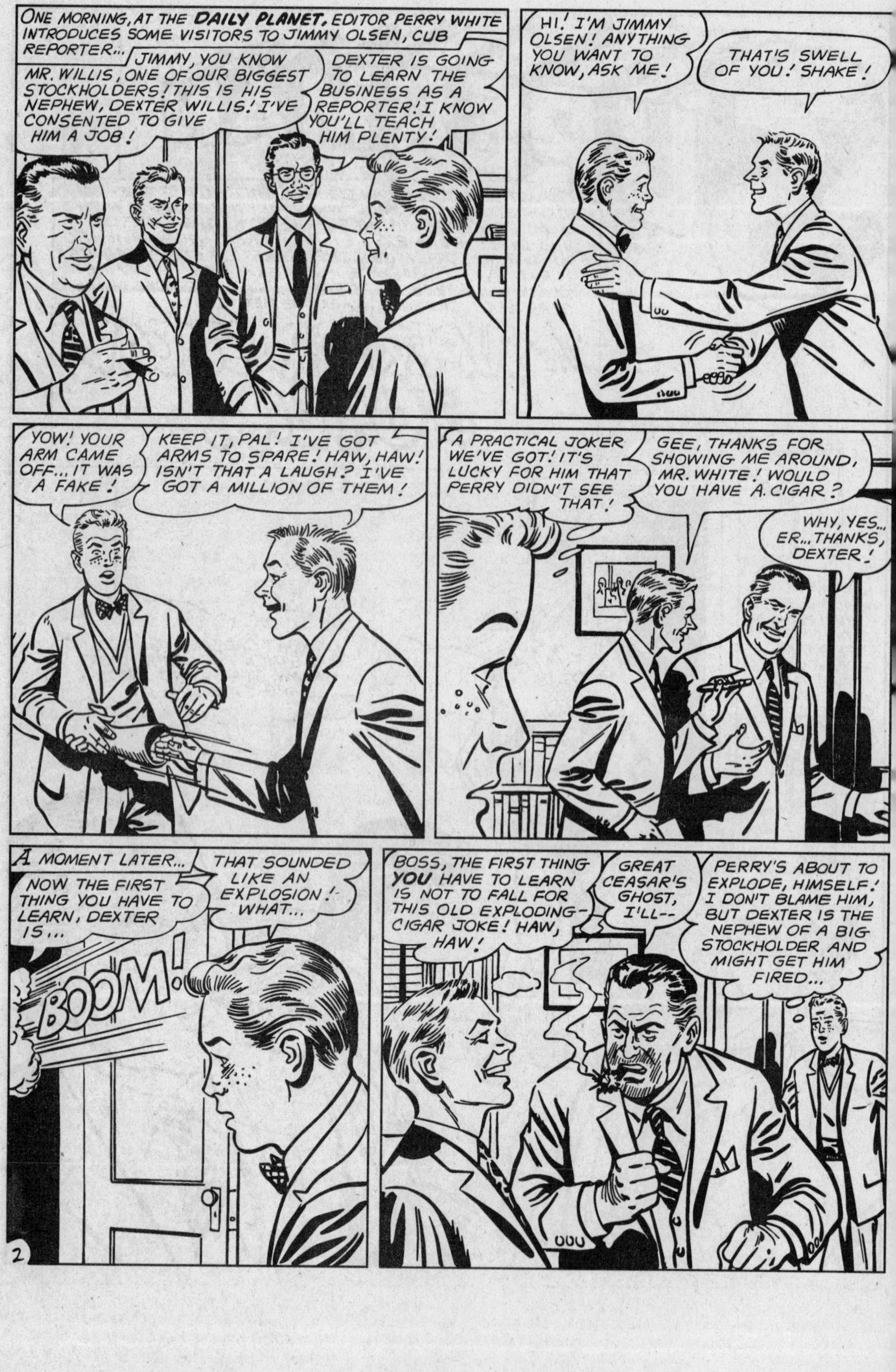
ONE MORNING, AT THE DAILY PLANET, EDITOR PERRY WHITE INTRODUCES SOME VISITORS TO JIMMY OLSEN, CUB REPORTER...
JIMMY, YOU KNOW MR. WILLIS, ONE OF OUR BIGGEST STOCKHOLDERS! THIS IS HIS NEPHEW, DEXTER WILLIS! I'VE CONSENTED TO GIVE HIM A JOB!
DEXTER IS GOING TO LEARN THE BUSINESS AS A REPORTER! I KNOW YOU'LL TEACH HIM PLENTY!
HI! I'M JIMMY OLSEN! ANYTHING YOU WANT TO KNOW, ASK ME!
THAT'S SWELL OF YOU! SHAKE!
YOW! YOUR ARM CAME OFF... IT WAS A FAKE!
KEEP IT, PAL! I'VE GOT ARMS TO SPARE! HAW, HAW! ISN'T THAT A LAUGH? I'VE GOT A MILLION OF THEM!
A PRACTICAL JOKER WE'VE GOT! IT'S LUCKY FOR HIM THAT PERRY DIDN'T SEE THAT!
GEE, THANKS FOR SHOWING ME AROUND, MR. WHITE! WOULD YOU HAVE A CIGAR?
WHY, YES... ER... THANKS, DEXTER!
A MOMENT LATER...
NOW THE FIRST THING YOU HAVE TO LEARN, DEXTER IS...
THAT SOUNDED LIKE AN EXPLOSION! - WHAT...
BOOM!
BOSS, THE FIRST THING YOU HAVE TO LEARN IS NOT TO FALL FOR THIS OLD EXPLODING-CIGAR JOKE! HAW, HAW!
GREAT CEASAR'S GHOST, I'LL--
PERRY'S ABOUT TO EXPLODE, HIMSELF! I DON'T BLAME HIM, BUT DEXTER IS THE NEPHEW OF A BIG STOCKHOLDER AND MIGHT GET HIM FIRED...
2

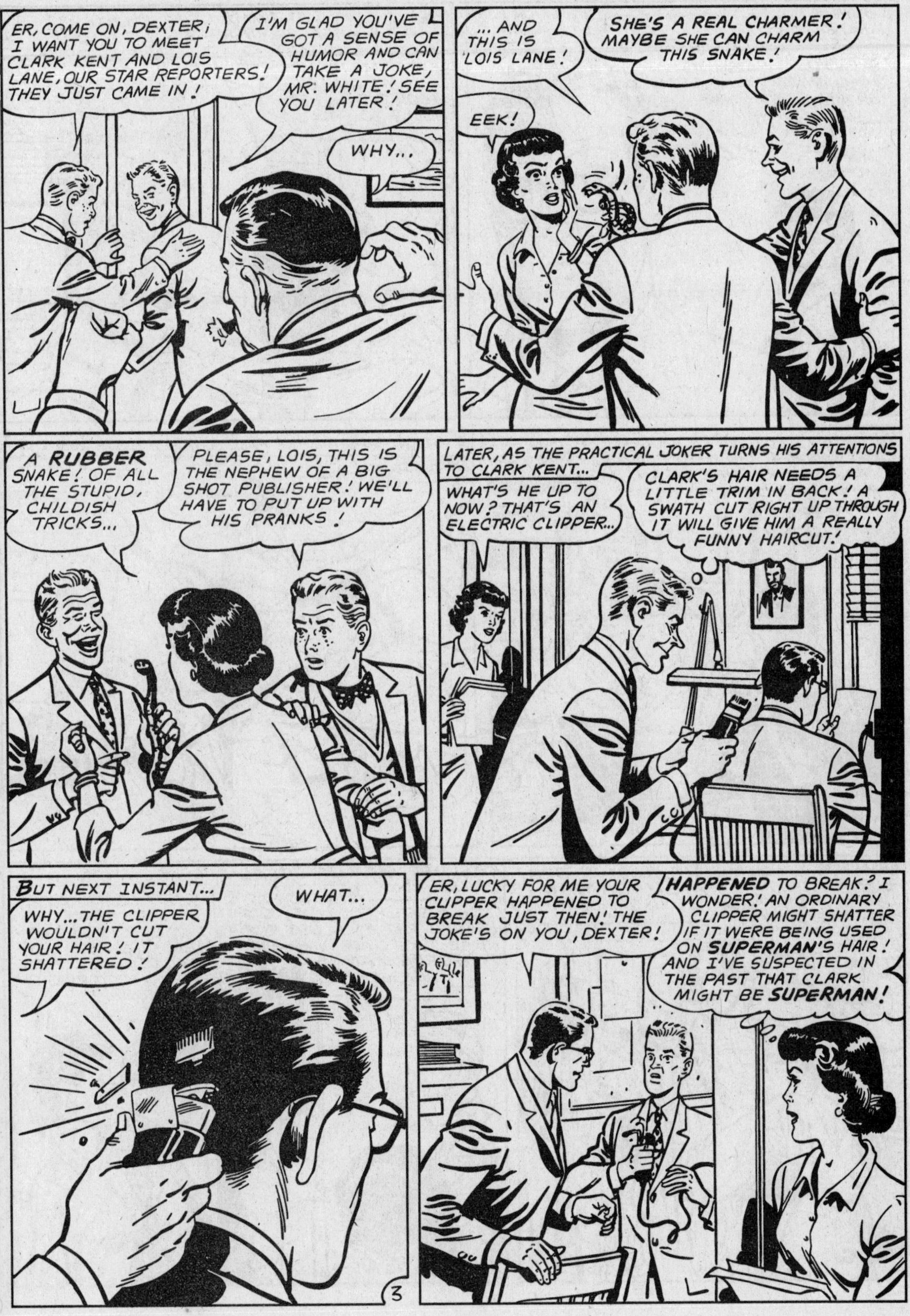
ER, COME ON, DEXTER; I WANT YOU TO MEET CLARK KENT AND LOIS LANE, OUR STAR REPORTERS! THEY JUST CAME IN!
I'M GLAD YOU'VE GOT A SENSE OF HUMOR AND CAN TAKE A JOKE, MR. WHITE! SEE YOU LATER!
WHY...
... AND THIS IS LOIS LANE!
SHE'S A REAL CHARMER! MAYBE SHE CAN CHARM THIS SNAKE!
EEK!
A RUBBER SNAKE! OF ALL THE STUPID, CHILDISH TRICKS...
PLEASE, LOIS, THIS IS THE NEPHEW OF A BIG SHOT PUBLISHER! WE'LL HAVE TO PUT UP WITH HIS PRANKS!
LATER, AS THE PRACTICAL JOKER TURNS HIS ATTENTIONS TO CLARK KENT...
WHAT'S HE UP TO NOW? THAT'S AN ELECTRIC CLIPPER...
CLARK'S HAIR NEEDS A LITTLE TRIM IN BACK! A SWATH CUT RIGHT UP THROUGH IT WILL GIVE HIM A REALLY FUNNY HAIRCUT!
BUT NEXT INSTANT...
WHY... THE CLIPPER WOULDN'T CUT YOUR HAIR! IT SHATTERED!
WHAT...
3
ER, LUCKY FOR ME YOUR CLIPPER HAPPENED TO BREAK JUST THEN! THE JOKE'S ON YOU, DEXTER!
HAPPENED TO BREAK? I WONDER! AN ORDINARY CLIPPER MIGHT SHATTER IF IT WERE BEING USED ON SUPERMAN'S HAIR! AND I'VE SUSPECTED IN THE PAST THAT CLARK MIGHT BE SUPERMAN!

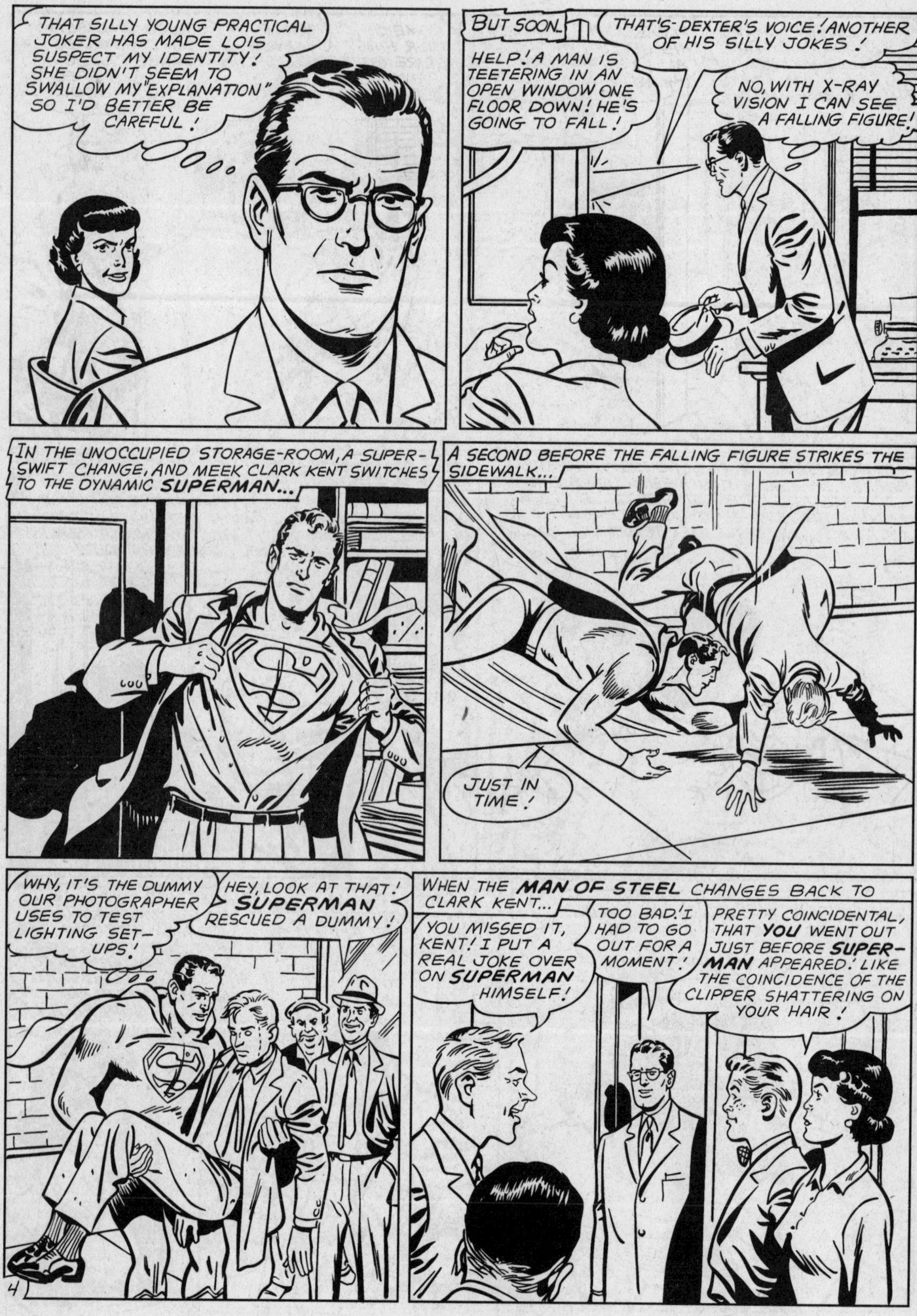
THAT SILLY YOUNG PRACTICAL JOKER HAS MADE LOIS SUSPECT MY IDENTITY! SHE DIDN'T SEEM TO SWALLOW MY "EXPLANATION" SO I'D BETTER BE CAREFUL!
BUT SOON...
HELP! A MAN IS TEETERING IN AN OPEN WINDOW ONE FLOOR DOWN! HE'S GOING TO FALL!
THAT'S DEXTER'S VOICE! ANOTHER OF HIS SILLY JOKES!
NO, WITH X-RAY VISION I CAN SEE A FALLING FIGURE!
IN THE UNOCCUPIED STORAGE-ROOM, A SUPER-SWIFT CHANGE, AND MEEK CLARK KENT SWITCHES TO THE DYNAMIC SUPERMAN...
A SECOND BEFORE THE FALLING FIGURE STRIKES THE SIDEWALK...
JUST IN TIME!
WHY, IT'S THE DUMMY OUR PHOTOGRAPHER USES TO TEST LIGHTING SET-UPS!
HEY, LOOK AT THAT! SUPERMAN RESCUED A DUMMY!
WHEN THE MAN OF STEEL CHANGES BACK TO CLARK KENT...
YOU MISSED IT, KENT! I PUT A REAL JOKE OVER ON SUPERMAN HIMSELF!
TOO BAD! I HAD TO GO OUT FOR A MOMENT!
PRETTY COINCIDENTAL, THAT YOU WENT OUT JUST BEFORE SUPERMAN APPEARED! LIKE THE COINCIDENCE OF THE CLIPPER SHATTERING ON YOUR HAIR!
4

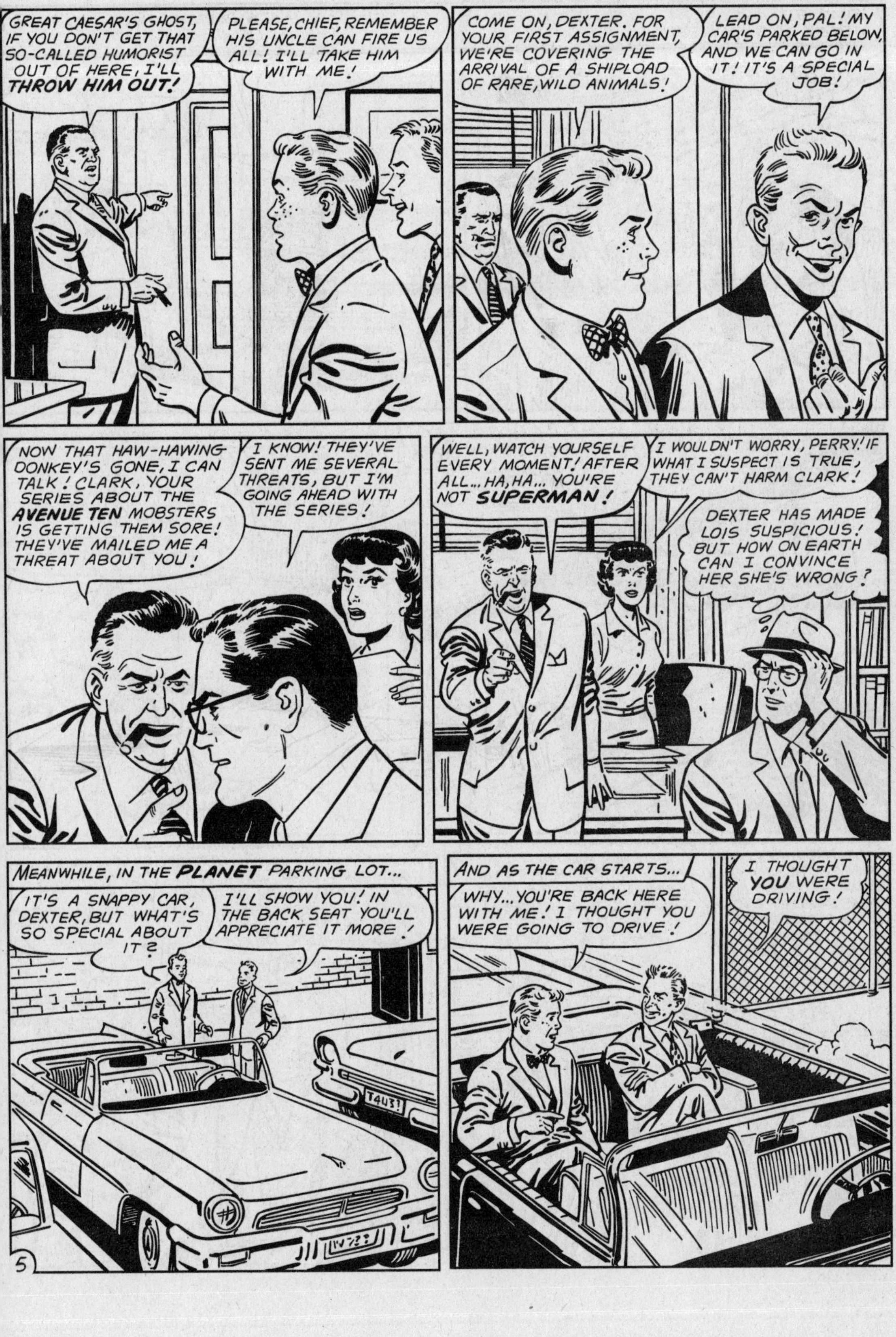
GREAT CAESAR'S GHOST, IF YOU DON'T GET THAT SO-CALLED HUMORIST OUT OF HERE, I'LL **THROW HIM OUT!**
PLEASE, CHIEF, REMEMBER HIS UNCLE CAN FIRE US ALL! I'LL TAKE HIM WITH ME!
COME ON, DEXTER. FOR YOUR FIRST ASSIGNMENT, WE'RE COVERING THE ARRIVAL OF A SHIPLOAD OF RARE, WILD ANIMALS!
LEAD ON, PAL! MY CAR'S PARKED BELOW, AND WE CAN GO IN IT! IT'S A SPECIAL JOB!
NOW THAT HAW-HAWING DONKEY'S GONE, I CAN TALK! CLARK, YOUR SERIES ABOUT THE **AVENUE TEN** MOBSTERS IS GETTING THEM SORE! THEY'VE MAILED ME A THREAT ABOUT YOU!
I KNOW! THEY'VE SENT ME SEVERAL THREATS, BUT I'M GOING AHEAD WITH THE SERIES!
WELL, WATCH YOURSELF EVERY MOMENT! AFTER ALL... HA, HA... YOU'RE NOT **SUPERMAN!**
I WOULDN'T WORRY, PERRY! IF WHAT I SUSPECT IS TRUE, THEY CAN'T HARM CLARK!
DEXTER HAS MADE LOIS SUSPICIOUS! BUT HOW ON EARTH CAN I CONVINCE HER SHE'S WRONG?
MEANWHILE, IN THE **PLANET** PARKING LOT...
IT'S A SNAPPY CAR, DEXTER, BUT WHAT'S SO SPECIAL ABOUT IT?
I'LL SHOW YOU! IN THE BACK SEAT YOU'LL APPRECIATE IT MORE!
T4U3!
5
AND AS THE CAR STARTS...
WHY... YOU'RE BACK HERE WITH ME! I THOUGHT YOU WERE GOING TO DRIVE!
I THOUGHT **YOU** WERE DRIVING!

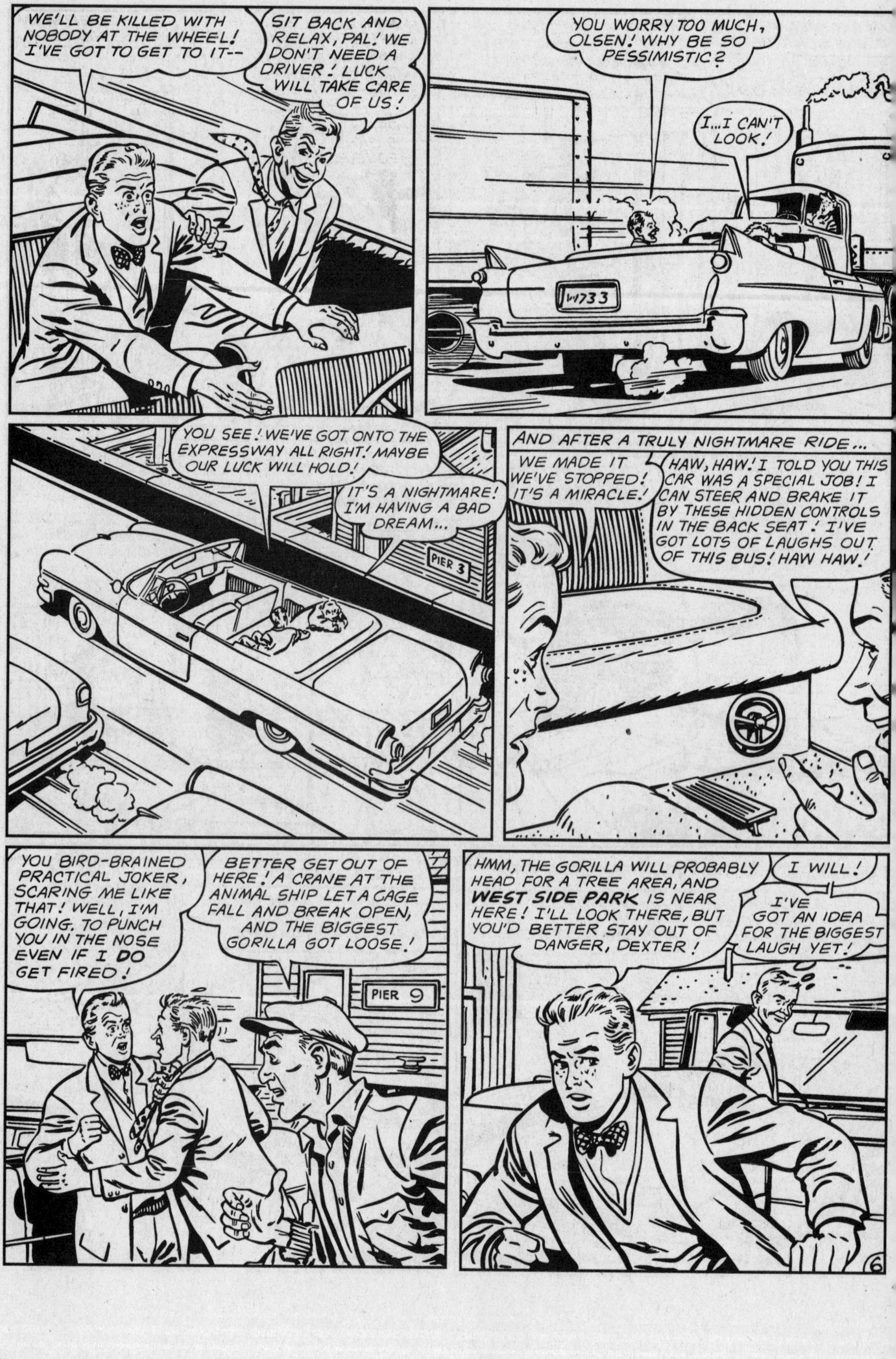
WE'LL BE KILLED WITH NOBODY AT THE WHEEL! I'VE GOT TO GET TO IT--
SIT BACK AND RELAX, PAL! WE DON'T NEED A DRIVER! LUCK WILL TAKE CARE OF US!
YOU WORRY TOO MUCH, OLSEN! WHY BE SO PESSIMISTIC?
I...I CAN'T LOOK!
W733
YOU SEE! WE'VE GOT ONTO THE EXPRESSWAY ALL RIGHT! MAYBE OUR LUCK WILL HOLD!
IT'S A NIGHTMARE! I'M HAVING A BAD DREAM...
PIER 3
AND AFTER A TRULY NIGHTMARE RIDE...
WE MADE IT WE'VE STOPPED! IT'S A MIRACLE!
HAW, HAW! I TOLD YOU THIS CAR WAS A SPECIAL JOB! I CAN STEER AND BRAKE IT BY THESE HIDDEN CONTROLS IN THE BACK SEAT! I'VE GOT LOTS OF LAUGHS OUT OF THIS BUS! HAW HAW!
YOU BIRD-BRAINED PRACTICAL JOKER, SCARING ME LIKE THAT! WELL, I'M GOING. TO PUNCH YOU IN THE NOSE EVEN IF I DO GET FIRED!
BETTER GET OUT OF HERE! A CRANE AT THE ANIMAL SHIP LET A CAGE FALL AND BREAK OPEN, AND THE BIGGEST GORILLA GOT LOOSE!
PIER 9
HMM, THE GORILLA WILL PROBABLY HEAD FOR A TREE AREA, AND WEST SIDE PARK IS NEAR HERE! I'LL LOOK THERE, BUT YOU'D BETTER STAY OUT OF DANGER, DEXTER!
I WILL!
I'VE GOT AN IDEA FOR THE BIGGEST LAUGH YET!
6

MEANWHILE, NEARBY, THE SUPER-HEARING OF CLARK KENT HAS CAUGHT THE ALARM!

I'LL HAVE TO FORGET THE *AVENUE TEN* MOBSTERS AND THEIR THREATS TILL THAT GORILLA IS ROUNDED UP! THEY'RE MILD CREATURES, BUT IF THEY'RE SCARED, THEY GO BERSERK!

WHILE JIMMY VAINLY SEARCHES THE PARK, *SUPERMAN* SOON LOCATES THE ANIMAL WITH THE AID OF HIS TELESCOPIC VISION...

GREAT SCOTT, THE GORILLA'S TRYING TO SMASH THAT POLICE HELI-COPTER! IF IT GETS SHOT, THE GIRDER MAY SLIP FROM ITS GRASP AND HIT SOMEONE BELOW!

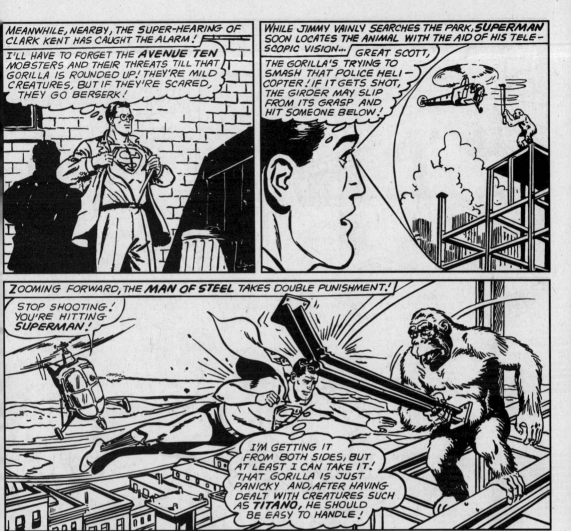

ZOOMING FORWARD, THE *MAN OF STEEL* TAKES DOUBLE PUNISHMENT!

STOP SHOOTING! YOU'RE HITTING *SUPERMAN!*

I'M GETTING IT FROM BOTH SIDES, BUT AT LEAST I CAN TAKE IT! THAT GORILLA IS JUST PANICKY AND, AFTER HAVING DEALT WITH CREATURES SUCH AS *TITANO*, HE SHOULD BE EASY TO HANDLE!

SEIZING AND BENDING THE GIRDER, THE *MAN OF STEEL* USES IT TO PINION THE APE...

THIS WILL HOLD YOU TILL YOU QUIET DOWN! I'LL FIND YOUR OWNERS!

BUT SUDDENLY, A SUMMONS...

JIMMY'S USING HIS SIGNAL-WATCH TO CALL ME FOR HELP! HE MUST BE IN TROUBLE!

ZEE ZEE ZEE

7

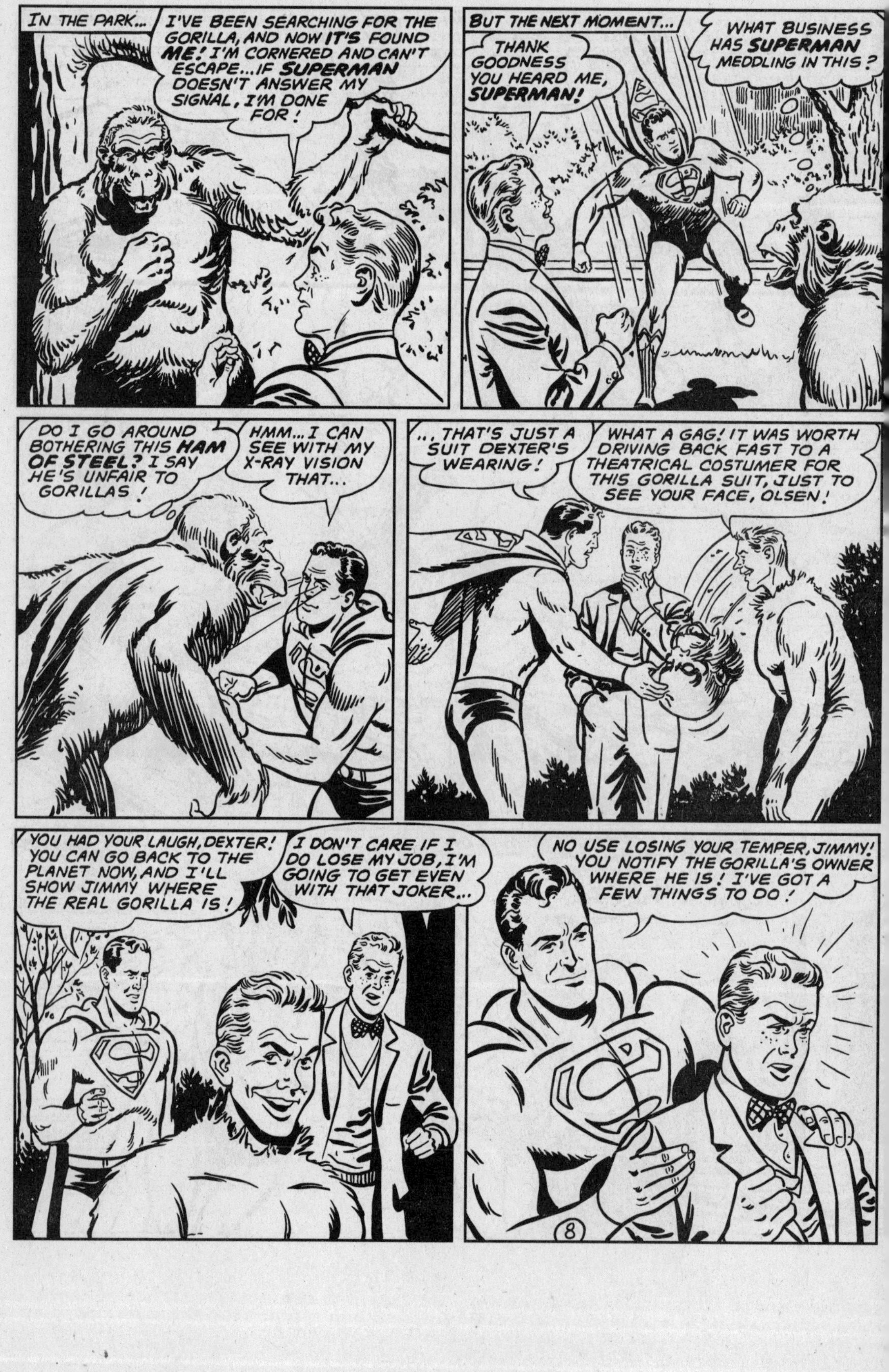
IN THE PARK...
I'VE BEEN SEARCHING FOR THE GORILLA, AND NOW IT'S FOUND ME! I'M CORNERED AND CAN'T ESCAPE...IF SUPERMAN DOESN'T ANSWER MY SIGNAL, I'M DONE FOR!
BUT THE NEXT MOMENT...
THANK GOODNESS YOU HEARD ME, SUPERMAN!
WHAT BUSINESS HAS SUPERMAN MEDDLING IN THIS?
DO I GO AROUND BOTHERING THIS HAM OF STEEL? I SAY HE'S UNFAIR TO GORILLAS!
HMM...I CAN SEE WITH MY X-RAY VISION THAT...
..., THAT'S JUST A SUIT DEXTER'S WEARING!
WHAT A GAG! IT WAS WORTH DRIVING BACK FAST TO A THEATRICAL COSTUMER FOR THIS GORILLA SUIT, JUST TO SEE YOUR FACE, OLSEN!
YOU HAD YOUR LAUGH, DEXTER! YOU CAN GO BACK TO THE PLANET NOW, AND I'LL SHOW JIMMY WHERE THE REAL GORILLA IS!
I DON'T CARE IF I DO LOSE MY JOB, I'M GOING TO GET EVEN WITH THAT JOKER...
NO USE LOSING YOUR TEMPER, JIMMY! YOU NOTIFY THE GORILLA'S OWNER WHERE HE IS! I'VE GOT A FEW THINGS TO DO!
8

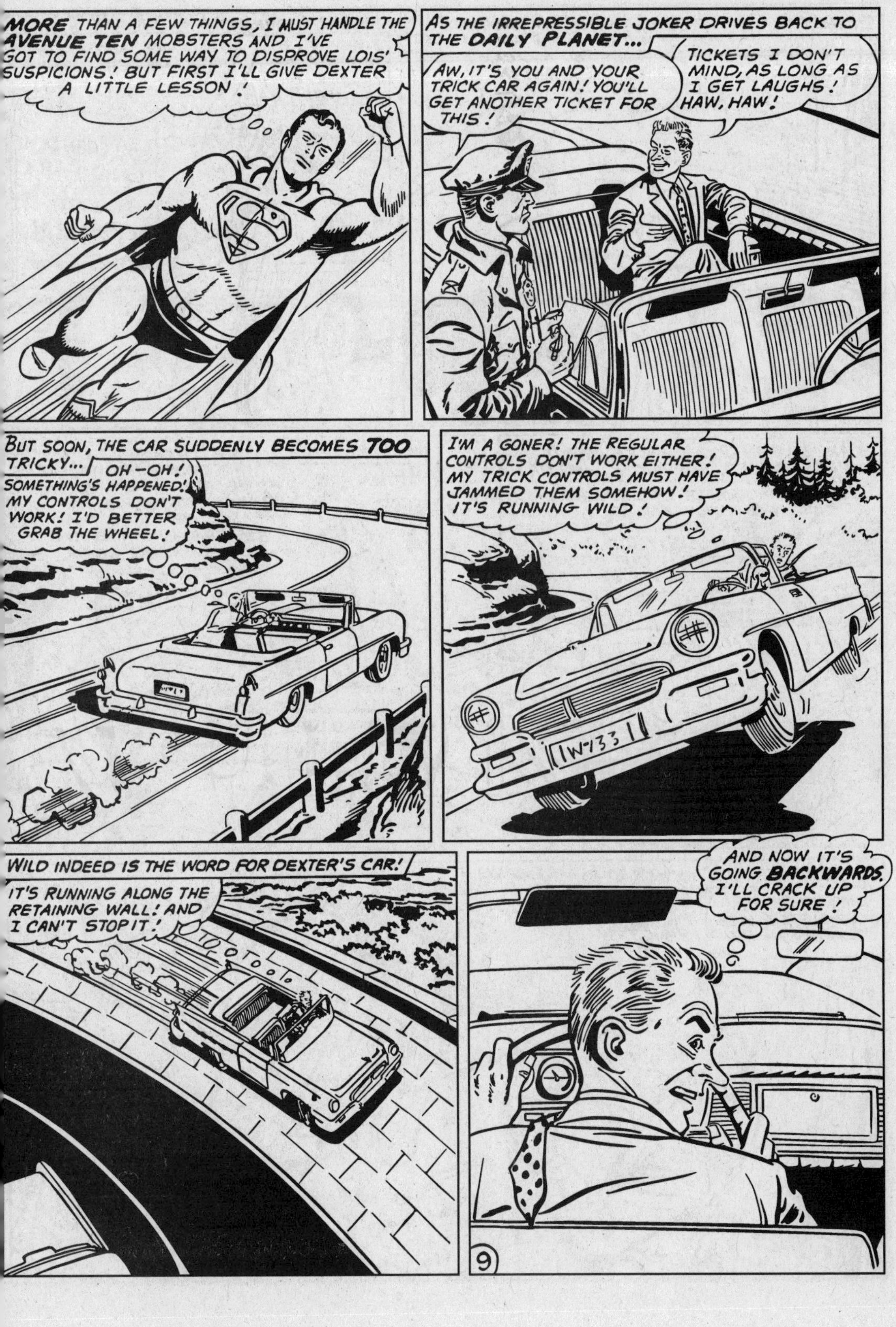
MORE THAN A FEW THINGS, I MUST HANDLE THE AVENUE TEN MOBSTERS AND I'VE GOT TO FIND SOME WAY TO DISPROVE LOIS' SUSPICIONS! BUT FIRST I'LL GIVE DEXTER A LITTLE LESSON!
AS THE IRREPRESSIBLE JOKER DRIVES BACK TO THE DAILY PLANET...
AW, IT'S YOU AND YOUR TRICK CAR AGAIN! YOU'LL GET ANOTHER TICKET FOR THIS!
TICKETS I DON'T MIND, AS LONG AS I GET LAUGHS! HAW, HAW!
BUT SOON, THE CAR SUDDENLY BECOMES TOO TRICKY...
OH-OH! SOMETHING'S HAPPENED! MY CONTROLS DON'T WORK! I'D BETTER GRAB THE WHEEL!
I'M A GONER! THE REGULAR CONTROLS DON'T WORK EITHER! MY TRICK CONTROLS MUST HAVE JAMMED THEM SOMEHOW! IT'S RUNNING WILD!
IW-133
WILD INDEED IS THE WORD FOR DEXTER'S CAR!
IT'S RUNNING ALONG THE RETAINING WALL! AND I CAN'T STOP IT!
AND NOW IT'S GOING BACKWARDS. I'LL CRACK UP FOR SURE!
9

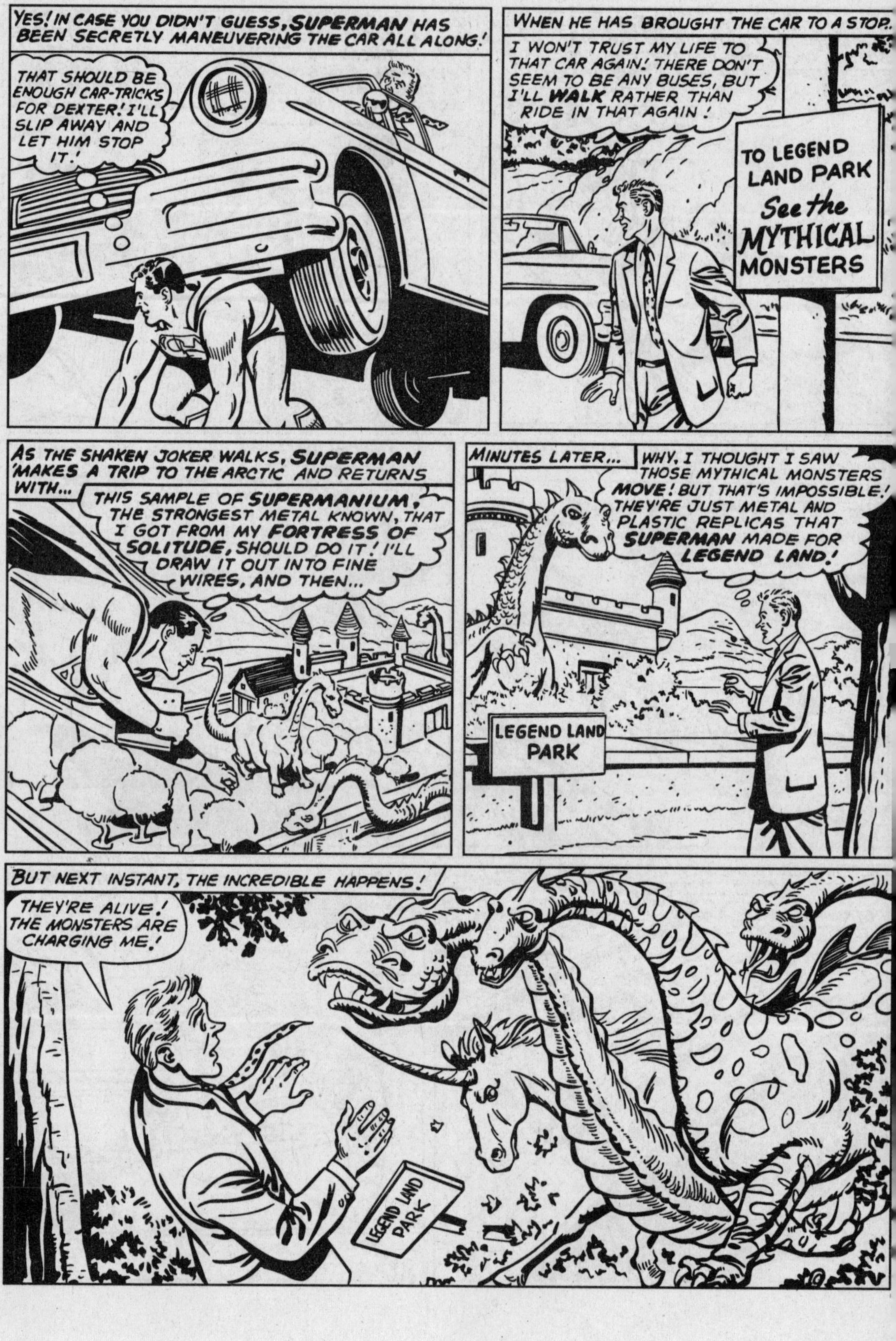
YES! IN CASE YOU DIDN'T GUESS, SUPERMAN HAS BEEN SECRETLY MANEUVERING THE CAR ALL ALONG!
THAT SHOULD BE ENOUGH CAR-TRICKS FOR DEXTER! I'LL SLIP AWAY AND LET HIM STOP IT!
WHEN HE HAS BROUGHT THE CAR TO A STOP...
I WON'T TRUST MY LIFE TO THAT CAR AGAIN! THERE DON'T SEEM TO BE ANY BUSES, BUT I'LL WALK RATHER THAN RIDE IN THAT AGAIN!
TO LEGEND LAND PARK See the MYTHICAL MONSTERS
AS THE SHAKEN JOKER WALKS, SUPERMAN MAKES A TRIP TO THE ARCTIC AND RETURNS WITH...
THIS SAMPLE OF SUPERMANIUM, THE STRONGEST METAL KNOWN, THAT I GOT FROM MY FORTRESS OF SOLITUDE, SHOULD DO IT! I'LL DRAW IT OUT INTO FINE WIRES, AND THEN...
MINUTES LATER...
WHY, I THOUGHT I SAW THOSE MYTHICAL MONSTERS MOVE! BUT THAT'S IMPOSSIBLE! THEY'RE JUST METAL AND PLASTIC REPLICAS THAT SUPERMAN MADE FOR LEGEND LAND!
LEGEND LAND PARK
BUT NEXT INSTANT, THE INCREDIBLE HAPPENS!
THEY'RE ALIVE! THE MONSTERS ARE CHARGING ME!
LEGEND LAND PARK

UNKNOWN TO DEXTER, *SUPERMAN* IS MAKING THE MONSTERS SEEM ALIVE BY PLAYING THE ROLE OF A SUPER-PUPPETEER...

THE *SUPERMANIUM* WIRES ARE TOO FINE TO SEE, BUT STRONG ENOUGH TO MANIPULATE THE MYTHICAL MONSTER REPLICAS LIKE PUPPETS! WELL, I GUESS HE'S LEARNED HIS LESSON BY NOW, SO I'LL RETURN THEM TO THE PARK!

AND LATER, WHEN DEXTER PLUCKS UP COURAGE ENOUGH TO ADVANCE AGAIN...

WHY, THEY *ARE* JUST LIFELESS PLASTIC AND METAL! BUT THEY DID CHARGE ME, SOMEHOW! I'M GETTING OUT OF HERE!

"LEGEND LAND" PARK

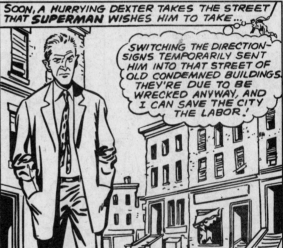

SOON, A HURRYING DEXTER TAKES THE STREET THAT *SUPERMAN* WISHES HIM TO TAKE...

SWITCHING THE DIRECTION-SIGNS TEMPORARILY SENT HIM INTO THAT STREET OF OLD CONDEMNED BUILDINGS. THEY'RE DUE TO BE WRECKED ANYWAY, AND I CAN SAVE THE CITY THE LABOR!

THIS OLD STREET WITH NO ONE IN IT IS EERIE... BUT, THAT BUILDING! IT'S TOPPLING! EEK!

THE WHOLE STREET'S GOING TO FALL DOWN! HELP!

11

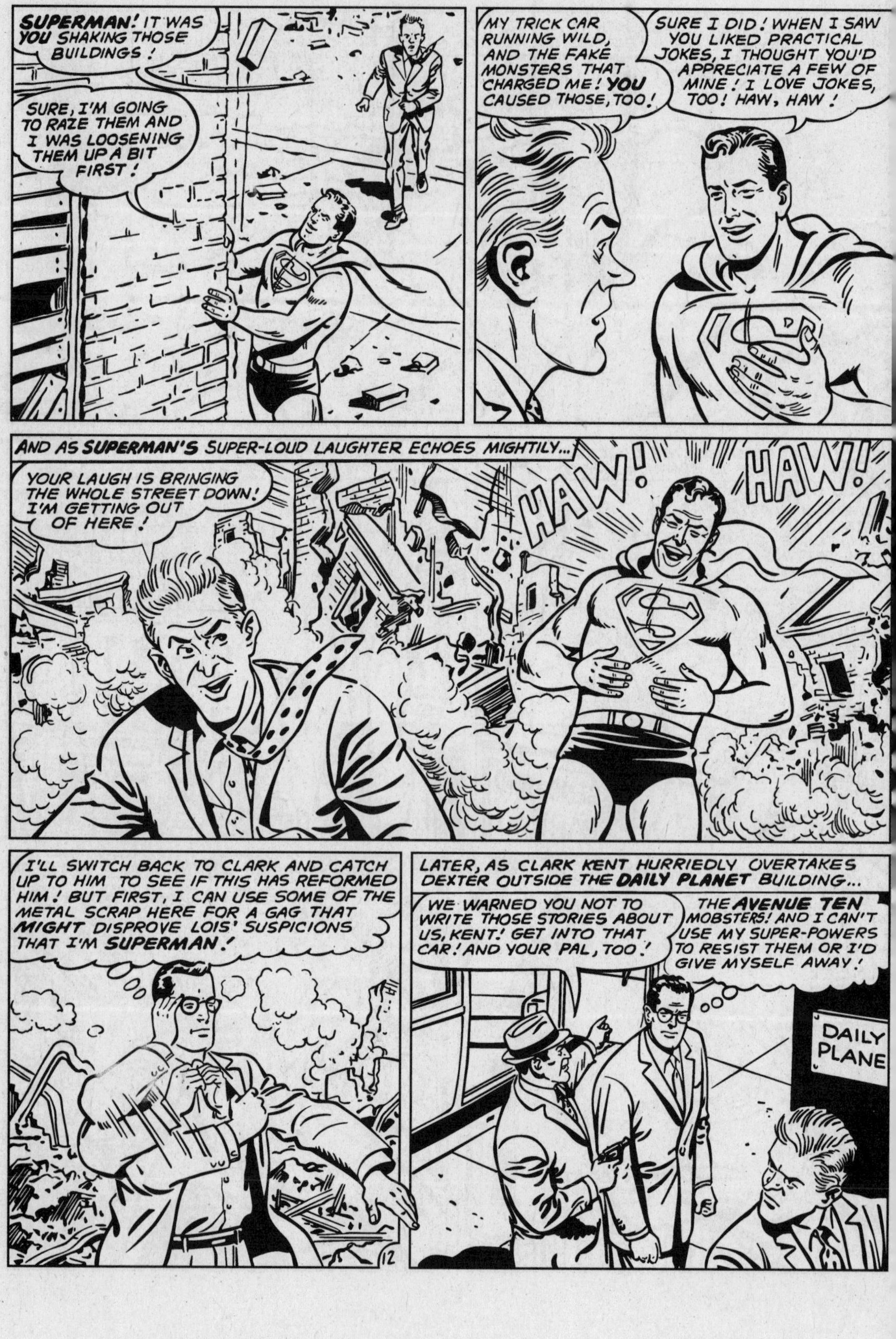
SUPERMAN! IT WAS YOU SHAKING THOSE BUILDINGS!
SURE, I'M GOING TO RAZE THEM AND I WAS LOOSENING THEM UP A BIT FIRST!
MY TRICK CAR RUNNING WILD, AND THE FAKE MONSTERS THAT CHARGED ME! YOU CAUSED THOSE, TOO!
SURE I DID! WHEN I SAW YOU LIKED PRACTICAL JOKES, I THOUGHT YOU'D APPRECIATE A FEW OF MINE! I LOVE JOKES, TOO! HAW, HAW!
AND AS SUPERMAN'S SUPER-LOUD LAUGHTER ECHOES MIGHTILY...
YOUR LAUGH IS BRINGING THE WHOLE STREET DOWN! I'M GETTING OUT OF HERE!
HAW! HAW!
I'LL SWITCH BACK TO CLARK AND CATCH UP TO HIM TO SEE IF THIS HAS REFORMED HIM! BUT FIRST, I CAN USE SOME OF THE METAL SCRAP HERE FOR A GAG THAT MIGHT DISPROVE LOIS' SUSPICIONS THAT I'M SUPERMAN!
12
LATER, AS CLARK KENT HURRIEDLY OVERTAKES DEXTER OUTSIDE THE DAILY PLANET BUILDING...
WE WARNED YOU NOT TO WRITE THOSE STORIES ABOUT US, KENT! GET INTO THAT CAR! AND YOUR PAL, TOO!
THE AVENUE TEN MOBSTERS! AND I CAN'T USE MY SUPER-POWERS TO RESIST THEM OR I'D GIVE MYSELF AWAY!
DAILY PLANE

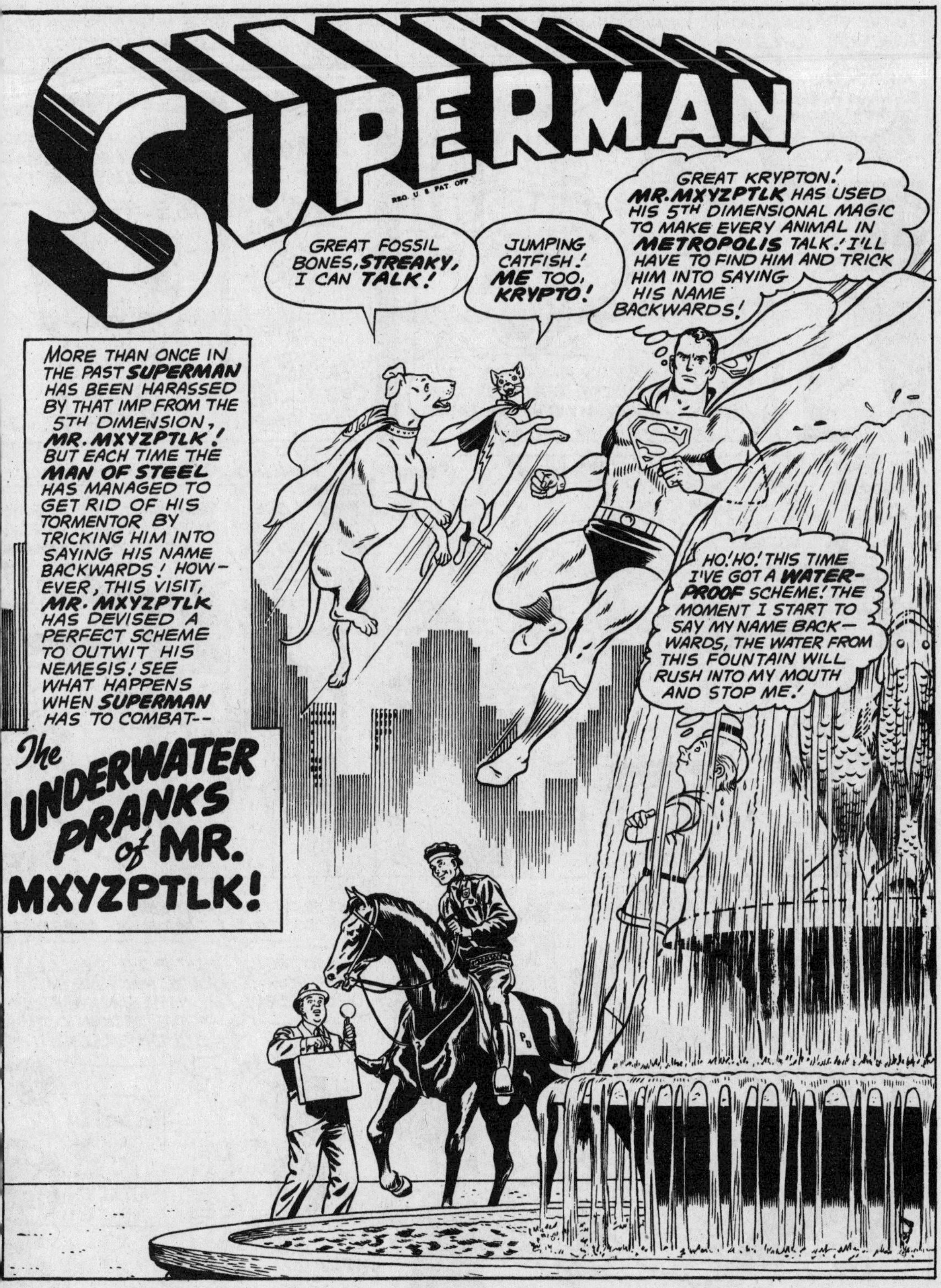
SUPERMAN
REG. U.S. PAT. OFF.
MORE THAN ONCE IN THE PAST SUPERMAN HAS BEEN HARASSED BY THAT IMP FROM THE 5TH DIMENSION, MR. MXYZPTLK! BUT EACH TIME THE MAN OF STEEL HAS MANAGED TO GET RID OF HIS TORMENTOR BY TRICKING HIM INTO SAYING HIS NAME BACKWARDS! HOWEVER, THIS VISIT, MR. MXYZPTLK HAS DEVISED A PERFECT SCHEME TO OUTWIT HIS NEMESIS! SEE WHAT HAPPENS WHEN SUPERMAN HAS TO COMBAT--
The UNDERWATER PRANKS of MR. MXYZPTLK!
GREAT FOSSIL BONES, STREAKY, I CAN TALK!
JUMPING CATFISH! ME TOO, KRYPTO!
GREAT KRYPTON! MR. MXYZPTLK HAS USED HIS 5TH DIMENSIONAL MAGIC TO MAKE EVERY ANIMAL IN METROPOLIS TALK! I'LL HAVE TO FIND HIM AND TRICK HIM INTO SAYING HIS NAME BACKWARDS!
HO! HO! THIS TIME I'VE GOT A WATER-PROOF SCHEME! THE MOMENT I START TO SAY MY NAME BACKWARDS, THE WATER FROM THIS FOUNTAIN WILL RUSH INTO MY MOUTH AND STOP ME!
PD

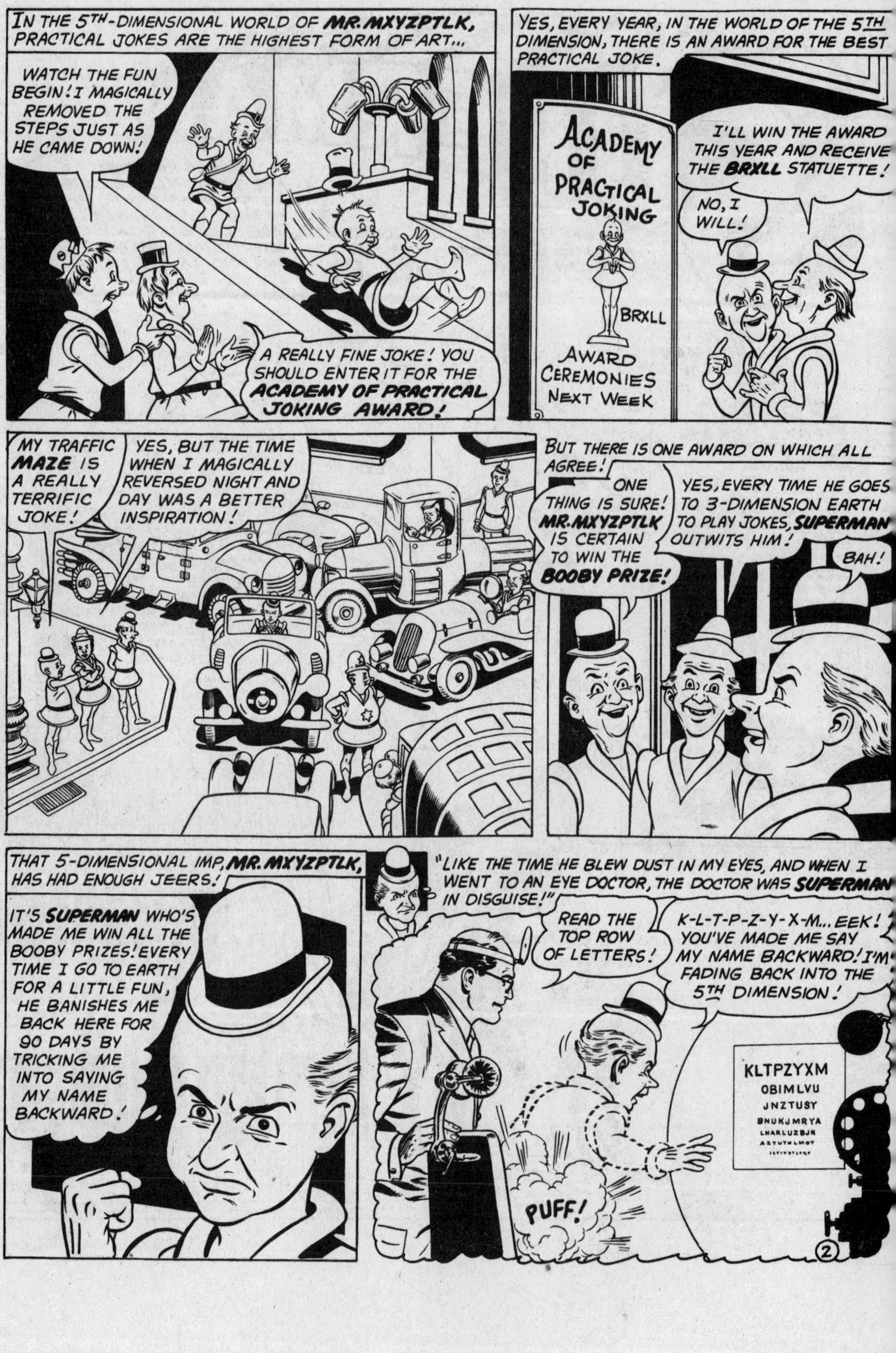
IN THE 5TH-DIMENSIONAL WORLD OF MR. MXYZPTLK, PRACTICAL JOKES ARE THE HIGHEST FORM OF ART...
WATCH THE FUN BEGIN! I MAGICALLY REMOVED THE STEPS JUST AS HE CAME DOWN!
A REALLY FINE JOKE! YOU SHOULD ENTER IT FOR THE ACADEMY OF PRACTICAL JOKING AWARD!
YES, EVERY YEAR, IN THE WORLD OF THE 5TH DIMENSION, THERE IS AN AWARD FOR THE BEST PRACTICAL JOKE.
ACADEMY OF PRACTICAL JOKING
BRXLL
AWARD CEREMONIES NEXT WEEK
I'LL WIN THE AWARD THIS YEAR AND RECEIVE THE BRXLL STATUETTE!
NO, I WILL!
MY TRAFFIC MAZE IS A REALLY TERRIFIC JOKE!
YES, BUT THE TIME WHEN I MAGICALLY REVERSED NIGHT AND DAY WAS A BETTER INSPIRATION!
BUT THERE IS ONE AWARD ON WHICH ALL AGREE!
ONE THING IS SURE! MR. MXYZPTLK IS CERTAIN TO WIN THE BOOBY PRIZE!
YES, EVERY TIME HE GOES TO 3-DIMENSION EARTH TO PLAY JOKES, SUPERMAN OUTWITS HIM!
BAH!
THAT 5-DIMENSIONAL IMP, MR. MXYZPTLK, HAS HAD ENOUGH JEERS!
IT'S SUPERMAN WHO'S MADE ME WIN ALL THE BOOBY PRIZES! EVERY TIME I GO TO EARTH FOR A LITTLE FUN, HE BANISHES ME BACK HERE FOR 90 DAYS BY TRICKING ME INTO SAYING MY NAME BACKWARD!
"LIKE THE TIME HE BLEW DUST IN MY EYES, AND WHEN I WENT TO AN EYE DOCTOR, THE DOCTOR WAS SUPERMAN IN DISGUISE!"
READ THE TOP ROW OF LETTERS!
K-L-T-P-Z-Y-X-M... EEK! YOU'VE MADE ME SAY MY NAME BACKWARD! I'M FADING BACK INTO THE 5TH DIMENSION!
KLTPZYXM
OBIMLVU
JNZTUSY
BNUKJMRYA
PUFF!
2

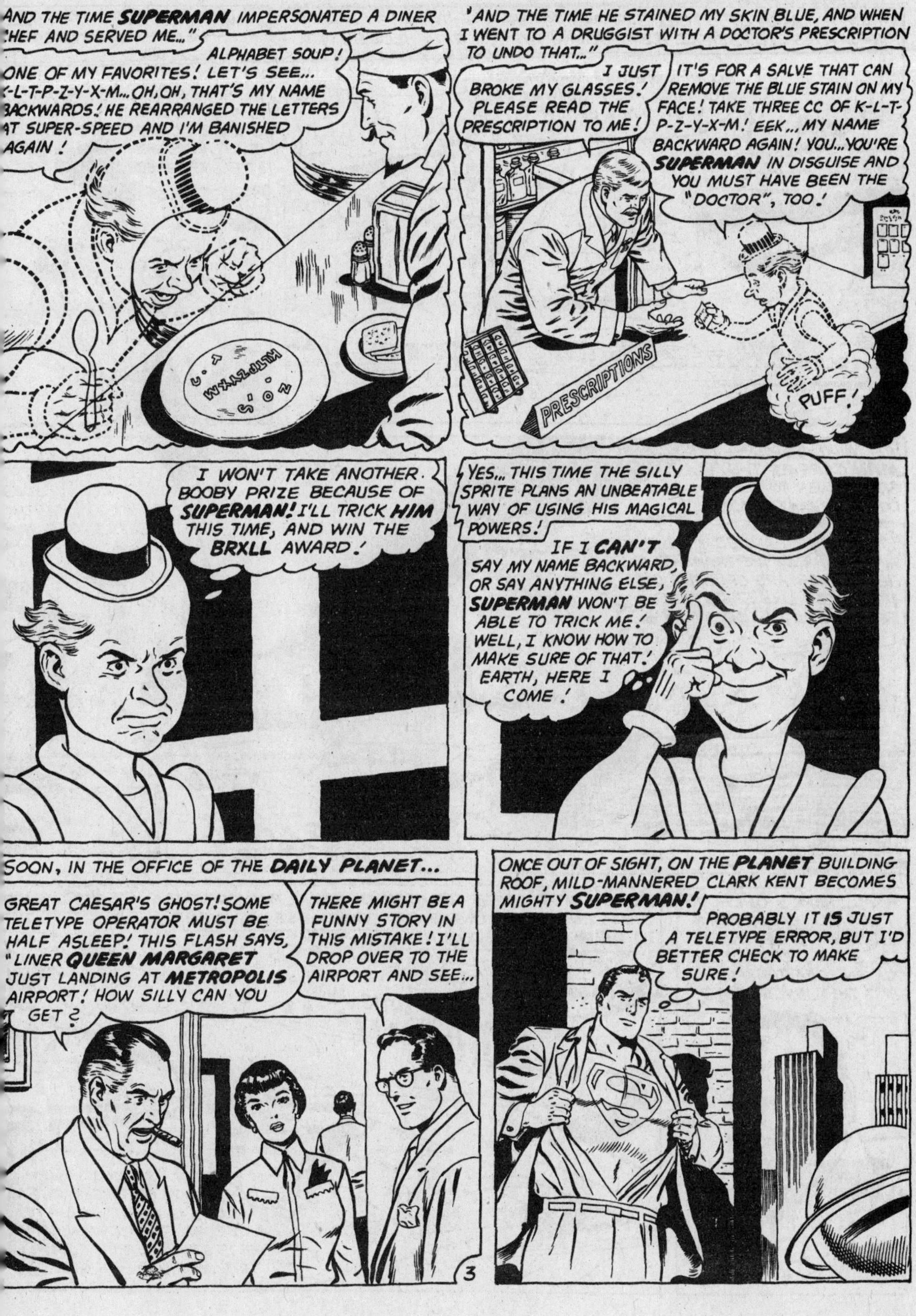
AND THE TIME SUPERMAN IMPERSONATED A DINER CHEF AND SERVED ME..."
ALPHABET SOUP! ONE OF MY FAVORITES! LET'S SEE... K-L-T-P-Z-Y-X-M... OH, OH, THAT'S MY NAME BACKWARDS! HE REARRANGED THE LETTERS AT SUPER-SPEED AND I'M BANISHED AGAIN!
"AND THE TIME HE STAINED MY SKIN BLUE, AND WHEN I WENT TO A DRUGGIST WITH A DOCTOR'S PRESCRIPTION TO UNDO THAT..."
I JUST BROKE MY GLASSES! PLEASE READ THE PRESCRIPTION TO ME!
IT'S FOR A SALVE THAT CAN REMOVE THE BLUE STAIN ON MY FACE! TAKE THREE CC OF K-L-T-P-Z-Y-X-M! EEK... MY NAME BACKWARD AGAIN! YOU... YOU'RE SUPERMAN IN DISGUISE AND YOU MUST HAVE BEEN THE "DOCTOR", TOO!
PRESCRIPTIONS
PUFF!
I WON'T TAKE ANOTHER BOOBY PRIZE BECAUSE OF SUPERMAN! I'LL TRICK HIM THIS TIME, AND WIN THE BRXLL AWARD!
YES... THIS TIME THE SILLY SPRITE PLANS AN UNBEATABLE WAY OF USING HIS MAGICAL POWERS!
IF I CAN'T SAY MY NAME BACKWARD, OR SAY ANYTHING ELSE, SUPERMAN WON'T BE ABLE TO TRICK ME! WELL, I KNOW HOW TO MAKE SURE OF THAT! EARTH, HERE I COME!
SOON, IN THE OFFICE OF THE DAILY PLANET...
GREAT CAESAR'S GHOST! SOME TELETYPE OPERATOR MUST BE HALF ASLEEP! THIS FLASH SAYS, "LINER QUEEN MARGARET JUST LANDING AT METROPOLIS AIRPORT! HOW SILLY CAN YOU GET?
THERE MIGHT BE A FUNNY STORY IN THIS MISTAKE! I'LL DROP OVER TO THE AIRPORT AND SEE...
3
ONCE OUT OF SIGHT, ON THE PLANET BUILDING ROOF, MILD-MANNERED CLARK KENT BECOMES MIGHTY SUPERMAN!
PROBABLY IT IS JUST A TELETYPE ERROR, BUT I'D BETTER CHECK TO MAKE SURE!

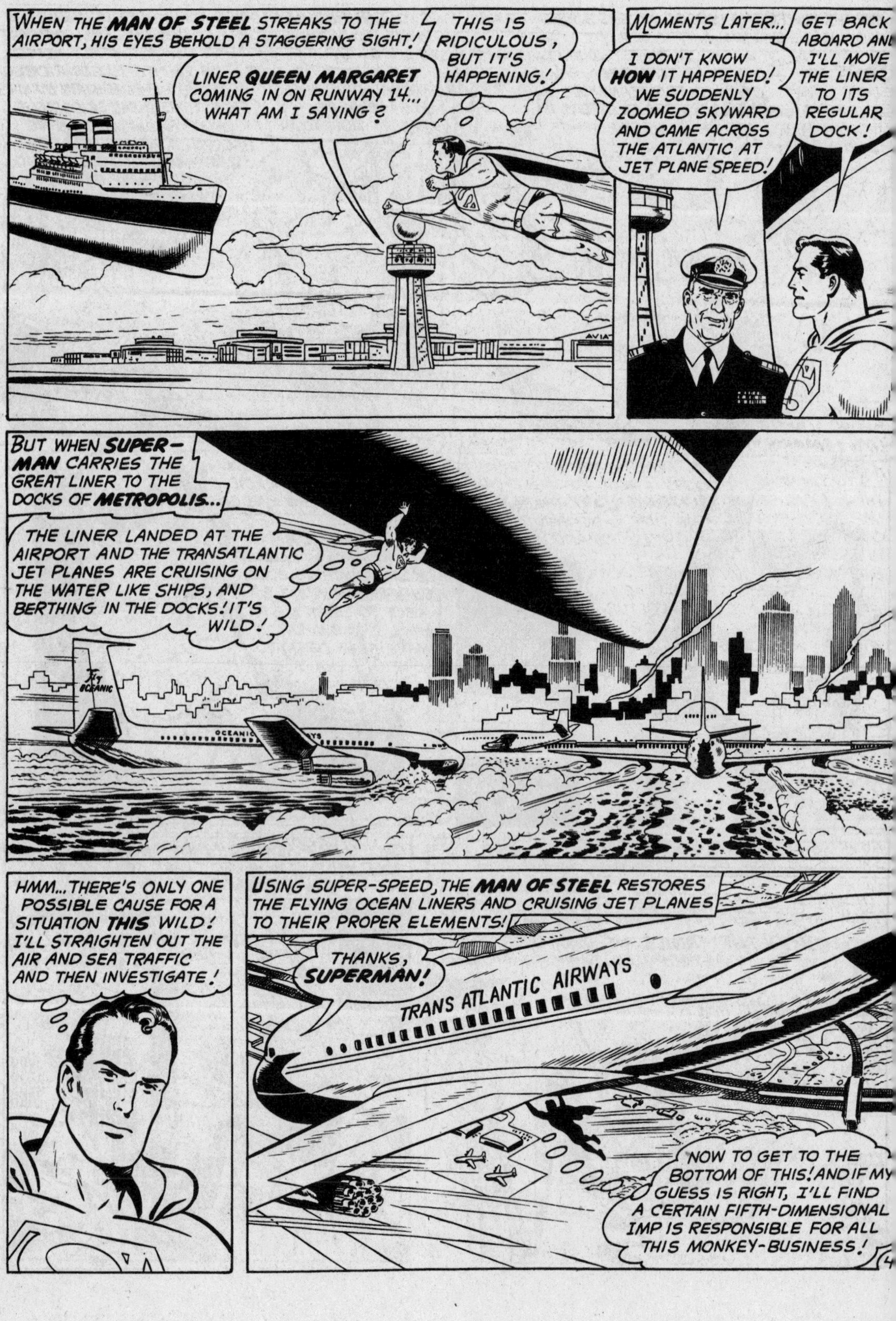
WHEN THE MAN OF STEEL STREAKS TO THE AIRPORT, HIS EYES BEHOLD A STAGGERING SIGHT!
LINER QUEEN MARGARET COMING IN ON RUNWAY 14... WHAT AM I SAYING?
THIS IS RIDICULOUS, BUT IT'S HAPPENING!
AVIA
MOMENTS LATER...
I DON'T KNOW HOW IT HAPPENED! WE SUDDENLY ZOOMED SKYWARD AND CAME ACROSS THE ATLANTIC AT JET PLANE SPEED!
GET BACK ABOARD AND I'LL MOVE THE LINER TO ITS REGULAR DOCK!
BUT WHEN SUPERMAN CARRIES THE GREAT LINER TO THE DOCKS OF METROPOLIS...
THE LINER LANDED AT THE AIRPORT AND THE TRANSATLANTIC JET PLANES ARE CRUISING ON THE WATER LIKE SHIPS, AND BERTHING IN THE DOCKS! IT'S WILD!
HMM... THERE'S ONLY ONE POSSIBLE CAUSE FOR A SITUATION THIS WILD! I'LL STRAIGHTEN OUT THE AIR AND SEA TRAFFIC AND THEN INVESTIGATE!
USING SUPER-SPEED, THE MAN OF STEEL RESTORES THE FLYING OCEAN LINERS AND CRUISING JET PLANES TO THEIR PROPER ELEMENTS!
THANKS, SUPERMAN!
TRANS ATLANTIC AIRWAYS
NOW TO GET TO THE BOTTOM OF THIS! AND IF MY GUESS IS RIGHT, I'LL FIND A CERTAIN FIFTH-DIMENSIONAL IMP IS RESPONSIBLE FOR ALL THIS MONKEY-BUSINESS!

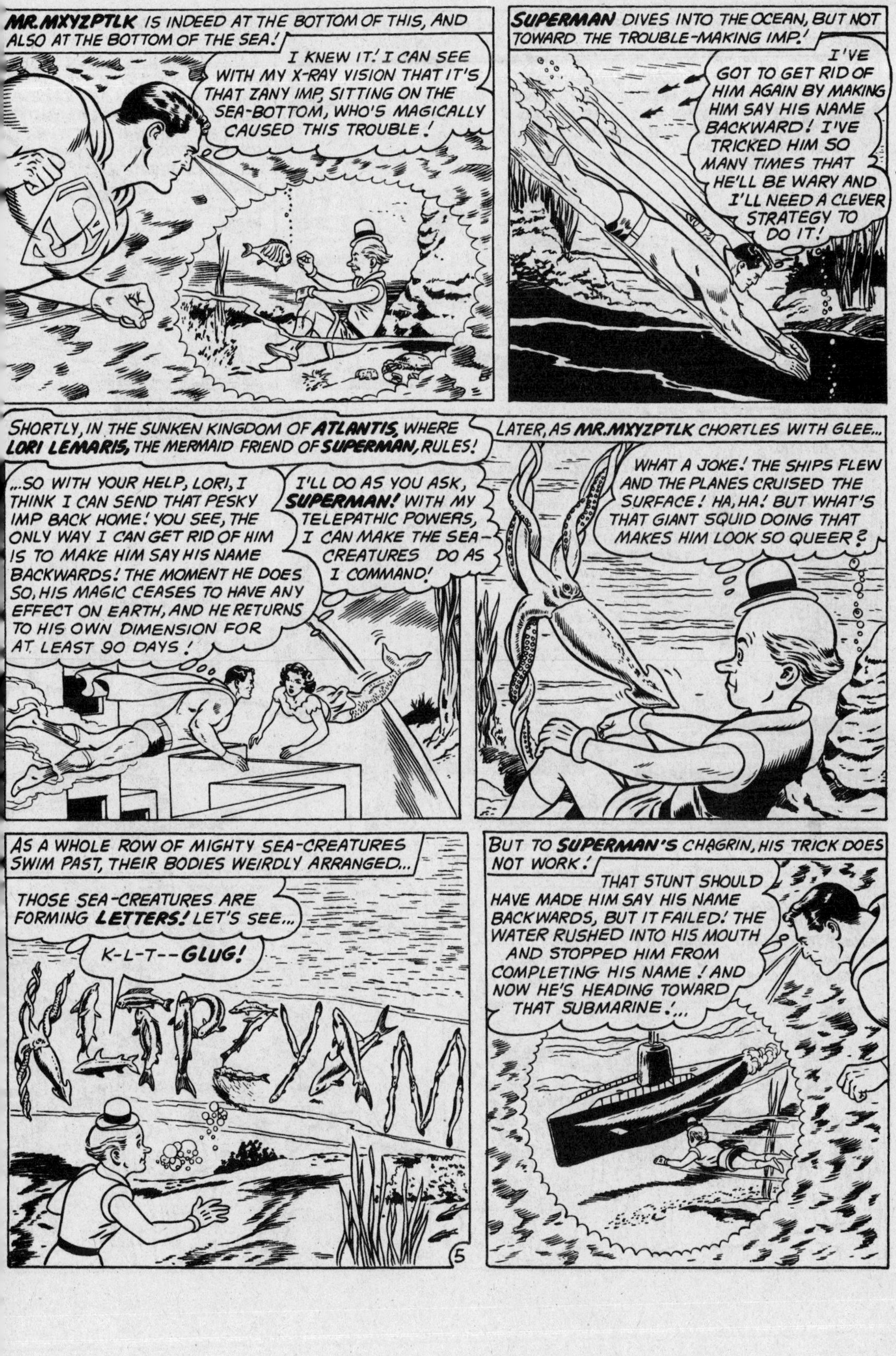
MR. MXYZPTLK IS INDEED AT THE BOTTOM OF THIS, AND ALSO AT THE BOTTOM OF THE SEA!
I KNEW IT! I CAN SEE WITH MY X-RAY VISION THAT IT'S THAT ZANY IMP, SITTING ON THE SEA-BOTTOM, WHO'S MAGICALLY CAUSED THIS TROUBLE!
SUPERMAN DIVES INTO THE OCEAN, BUT NOT TOWARD THE TROUBLE-MAKING IMP!
I'VE GOT TO GET RID OF HIM AGAIN BY MAKING HIM SAY HIS NAME BACKWARD! I'VE TRICKED HIM SO MANY TIMES THAT HE'LL BE WARY AND I'LL NEED A CLEVER STRATEGY TO DO IT!
SHORTLY, IN THE SUNKEN KINGDOM OF ATLANTIS, WHERE LORI LEMARIS, THE MERMAID FRIEND OF SUPERMAN, RULES!
...SO WITH YOUR HELP, LORI, I THINK I CAN SEND THAT PESKY IMP BACK HOME! YOU SEE, THE ONLY WAY I CAN GET RID OF HIM IS TO MAKE HIM SAY HIS NAME BACKWARDS! THE MOMENT HE DOES SO, HIS MAGIC CEASES TO HAVE ANY EFFECT ON EARTH, AND HE RETURNS TO HIS OWN DIMENSION FOR AT LEAST 90 DAYS!
I'LL DO AS YOU ASK, SUPERMAN! WITH MY TELEPATHIC POWERS, I CAN MAKE THE SEA-CREATURES DO AS I COMMAND!
LATER, AS MR. MXYZPTLK CHORTLES WITH GLEE...
WHAT A JOKE! THE SHIPS FLEW AND THE PLANES CRUISED THE SURFACE! HA, HA! BUT WHAT'S THAT GIANT SQUID DOING THAT MAKES HIM LOOK SO QUEER?
AS A WHOLE ROW OF MIGHTY SEA-CREATURES SWIM PAST, THEIR BODIES WEIRDLY ARRANGED...
THOSE SEA-CREATURES ARE FORMING LETTERS! LET'S SEE...
K-L-T--GLUG!
5
BUT TO SUPERMAN'S CHAGRIN, HIS TRICK DOES NOT WORK!
THAT STUNT SHOULD HAVE MADE HIM SAY HIS NAME BACKWARDS, BUT IT FAILED! THE WATER RUSHED INTO HIS MOUTH AND STOPPED HIM FROM COMPLETING HIS NAME! AND NOW HE'S HEADING TOWARD THAT SUBMARINE!...

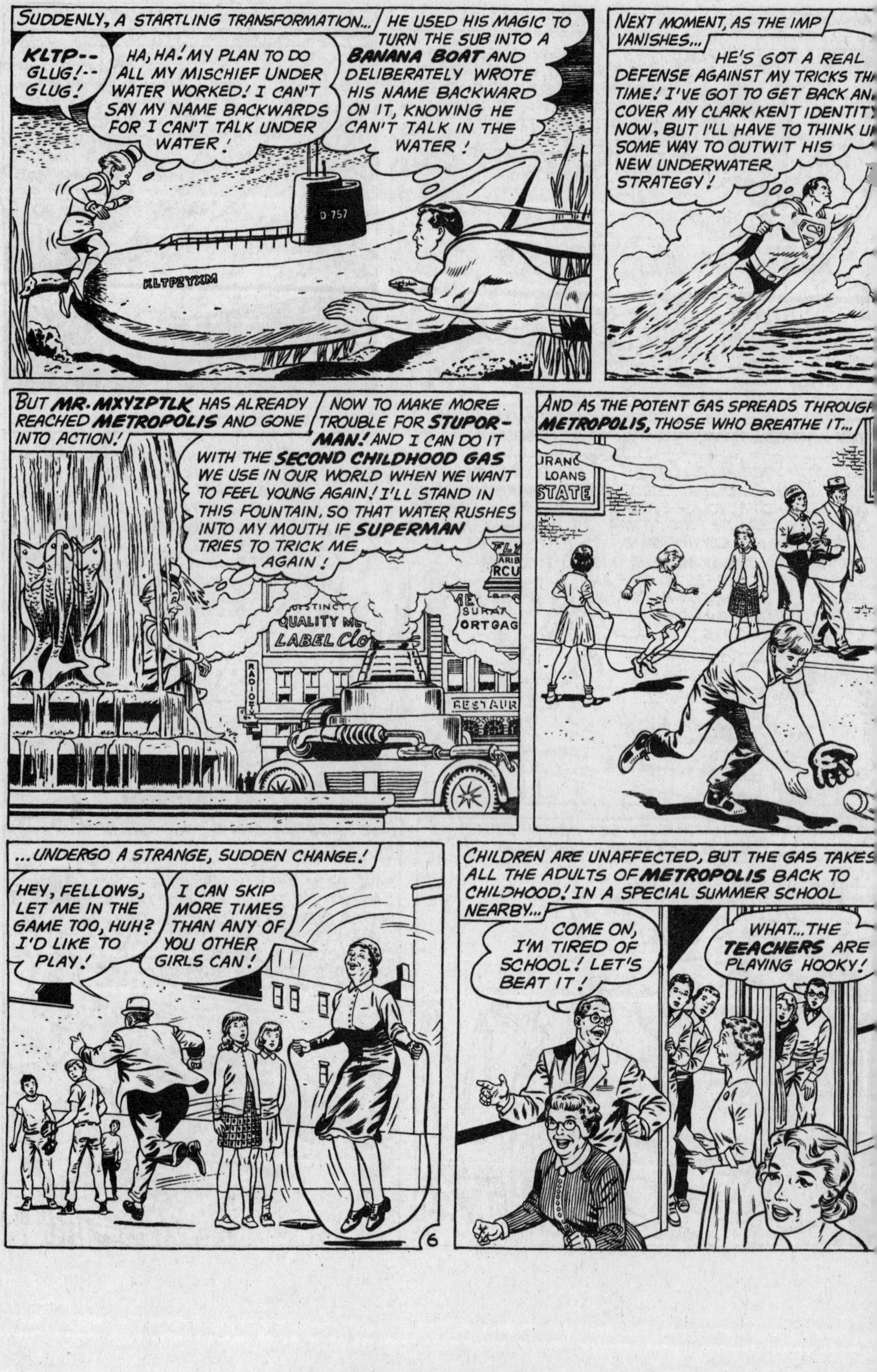
SUDDENLY, A STARTLING TRANSFORMATION...
KLTP--GLUG!--GLUG!
HA, HA! MY PLAN TO DO ALL MY MISCHIEF UNDER WATER WORKED! I CAN'T SAY MY NAME BACKWARDS FOR I CAN'T TALK UNDER WATER!
HE USED HIS MAGIC TO TURN THE SUB INTO A BANANA BOAT AND DELIBERATELY WROTE HIS NAME BACKWARD ON IT, KNOWING HE CAN'T TALK IN THE WATER!
D-757
KLTPZYXM
NEXT MOMENT, AS THE IMP VANISHES...
HE'S GOT A REAL DEFENSE AGAINST MY TRICKS TH TIME! I'VE GOT TO GET BACK AN COVER MY CLARK KENT IDENTIT NOW, BUT I'LL HAVE TO THINK U SOME WAY TO OUTWIT HIS NEW UNDERWATER STRATEGY!
BUT MR. MXYZPTLK HAS ALREADY REACHED METROPOLIS AND GONE INTO ACTION!
NOW TO MAKE MORE TROUBLE FOR STUPOR-MAN! AND I CAN DO IT WITH THE SECOND CHILDHOOD GAS WE USE IN OUR WORLD WHEN WE WANT TO FEEL YOUNG AGAIN! I'LL STAND IN THIS FOUNTAIN, SO THAT WATER RUSHES INTO MY MOUTH IF SUPERMAN TRIES TO TRICK ME AGAIN!
QUALITY ME
LABEL Clo
ORTGAG
RESTAUR
AND AS THE POTENT GAS SPREADS THROUG METROPOLIS, THOSE WHO BREATHE IT...
LOANS
STATE
...UNDERGO A STRANGE, SUDDEN CHANGE!
HEY, FELLOWS, LET ME IN THE GAME TOO, HUH? I'D LIKE TO PLAY!
I CAN SKIP MORE TIMES THAN ANY OF YOU OTHER GIRLS CAN!
6
CHILDREN ARE UNAFFECTED, BUT THE GAS TAKES ALL THE ADULTS OF METROPOLIS BACK TO CHILDHOOD! IN A SPECIAL SUMMER SCHOOL NEARBY...
COME ON, I'M TIRED OF SCHOOL! LET'S BEAT IT!
WHAT...THE TEACHERS ARE PLAYING HOOKY!

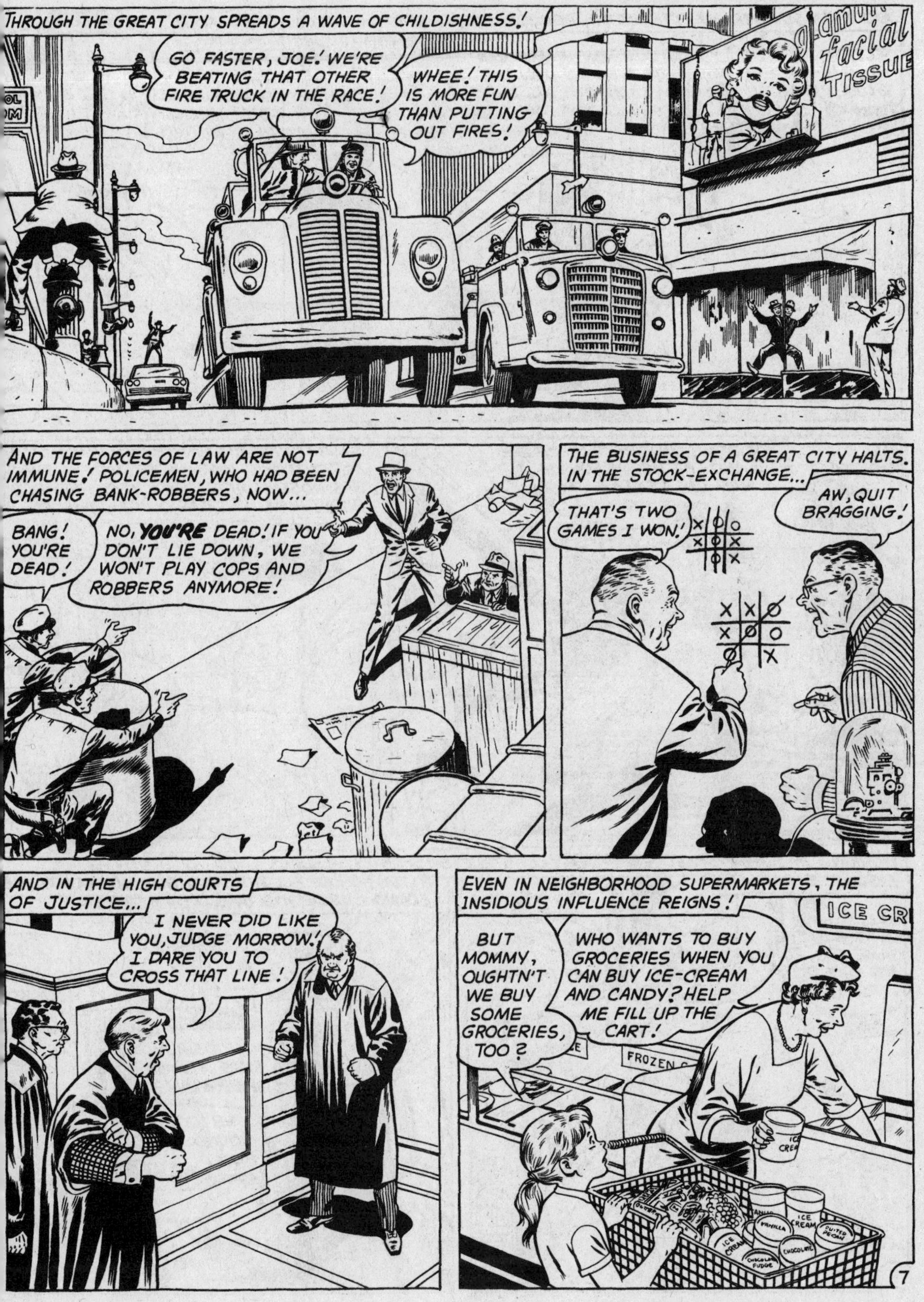
THROUGH THE GREAT CITY SPREADS A WAVE OF CHILDISHNESS!
GO FASTER, JOE! WE'RE BEATING THAT OTHER FIRE TRUCK IN THE RACE!
WHEE! THIS IS MORE FUN THAN PUTTING OUT FIRES!
facial TISSUE
AND THE FORCES OF LAW ARE NOT IMMUNE! POLICEMEN, WHO HAD BEEN CHASING BANK-ROBBERS, NOW...
BANG! YOU'RE DEAD!
NO, YOU'RE DEAD! IF YOU DON'T LIE DOWN, WE WON'T PLAY COPS AND ROBBERS ANYMORE!
THE BUSINESS OF A GREAT CITY HALTS. IN THE STOCK-EXCHANGE...
THAT'S TWO GAMES I WON!
AW, QUIT BRAGGING!
AND IN THE HIGH COURTS OF JUSTICE...
I NEVER DID LIKE YOU, JUDGE MORROW! I DARE YOU TO CROSS THAT LINE!
EVEN IN NEIGHBORHOOD SUPERMARKETS, THE INSIDIOUS INFLUENCE REIGNS!
ICE CR
BUT MOMMY, OUGHTN'T WE BUY SOME GROCERIES, TOO?
WHO WANTS TO BUY GROCERIES WHEN YOU CAN BUY ICE-CREAM AND CANDY? HELP ME FILL UP THE CART!
FROZEN
VANILLA
ICE CREAM
CHOCOLATE
7

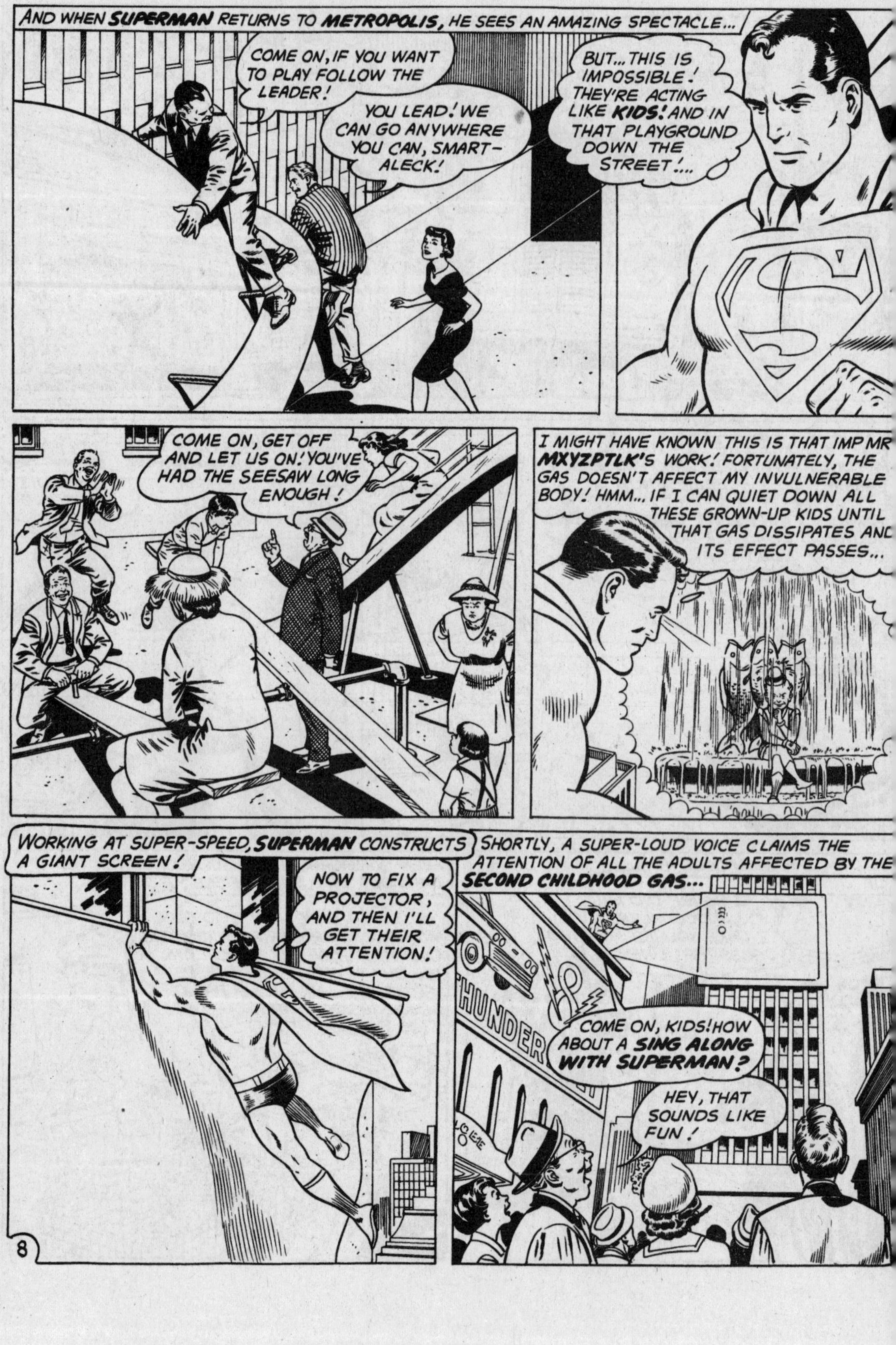
AND WHEN SUPERMAN RETURNS TO METROPOLIS, HE SEES AN AMAZING SPECTACLE...
COME ON, IF YOU WANT TO PLAY FOLLOW THE LEADER!
YOU LEAD! WE CAN GO ANYWHERE YOU CAN, SMART-ALECK!
BUT... THIS IS IMPOSSIBLE! THEY'RE ACTING LIKE KIDS! AND IN THAT PLAYGROUND DOWN THE STREET!...
COME ON, GET OFF AND LET US ON! YOU'VE HAD THE SEESAW LONG ENOUGH!
I MIGHT HAVE KNOWN THIS IS THAT IMP MR MXYZPTLK'S WORK! FORTUNATELY, THE GAS DOESN'T AFFECT MY INVULNERABLE BODY! HMM... IF I CAN QUIET DOWN ALL THESE GROWN-UP KIDS UNTIL THAT GAS DISSIPATES AND ITS EFFECT PASSES...
WORKING AT SUPER-SPEED, SUPERMAN CONSTRUCTS A GIANT SCREEN!
NOW TO FIX A PROJECTOR, AND THEN I'LL GET THEIR ATTENTION!
8
SHORTLY, A SUPER-LOUD VOICE CLAIMS THE ATTENTION OF ALL THE ADULTS AFFECTED BY THE SECOND CHILDHOOD GAS...
THUNDER
COME ON, KIDS! HOW ABOUT A SING ALONG WITH SUPERMAN?
HEY, THAT SOUNDS LIKE FUN!

SING A SONG OF SIXPENCE...

♪♪♪ SING A SONG OF SIXPENCE...! ♪♪♪♪

HA, HA! I'VE PUT **SUPER-SAP** TO LOTS OF TROUBLE THIS TIME! SURE, I'LL SING ALONG WITH HIM, TO MOCK HIM!

OF SIXPENCE, POCKETFUL

POCKET-FUL OF ...**GLUG**!

POCKETFUL OF KLTPZYXM

WATER IN MY MOUTH! IT'S A GOOD THING I WAS IN THIS FOUNTAIN! HE NEARLY TRICKED ME INTO SINGING MY NAME BACKWARDS!

AS THE GAS DISSIPATES AND ALL ADULTS RETURN TO NORMAL...

GREAT CAESAR'S GHOST, WHAT CAME OVER YOU TO CLIMB UP HERE? LOIS AND JIMMY-- GET BACK TO WORK!

BUT PERRY, **YOU** LED US UP HERE!

A HARRIED **SUPERMAN** CONFRONTS HIS IMPISH ANTAGONIST!

WE'VE HAD DUELS BEFORE, BUT THIS IS THE FIRST TIME YOU'VE BEEN AFRAID TO MEET ME IN THE OPEN AIR!

SUPERMAN IS TRYING TO BAIT ME OUT OF THE WATER, BUT IT WON'T WORK! I'LL JUST SPEAK TO HIM IN SIGN LANGUAGE!

9

HE'S USING SIGN-LANGUAGE TO SAY, "AT LAST I HAVE MY REVENGE, **SUPER-SAP**! THIS WILL WIN ME A **BRXLL** AWARD." WHY, I'LL GRAB THAT IMP, AND...

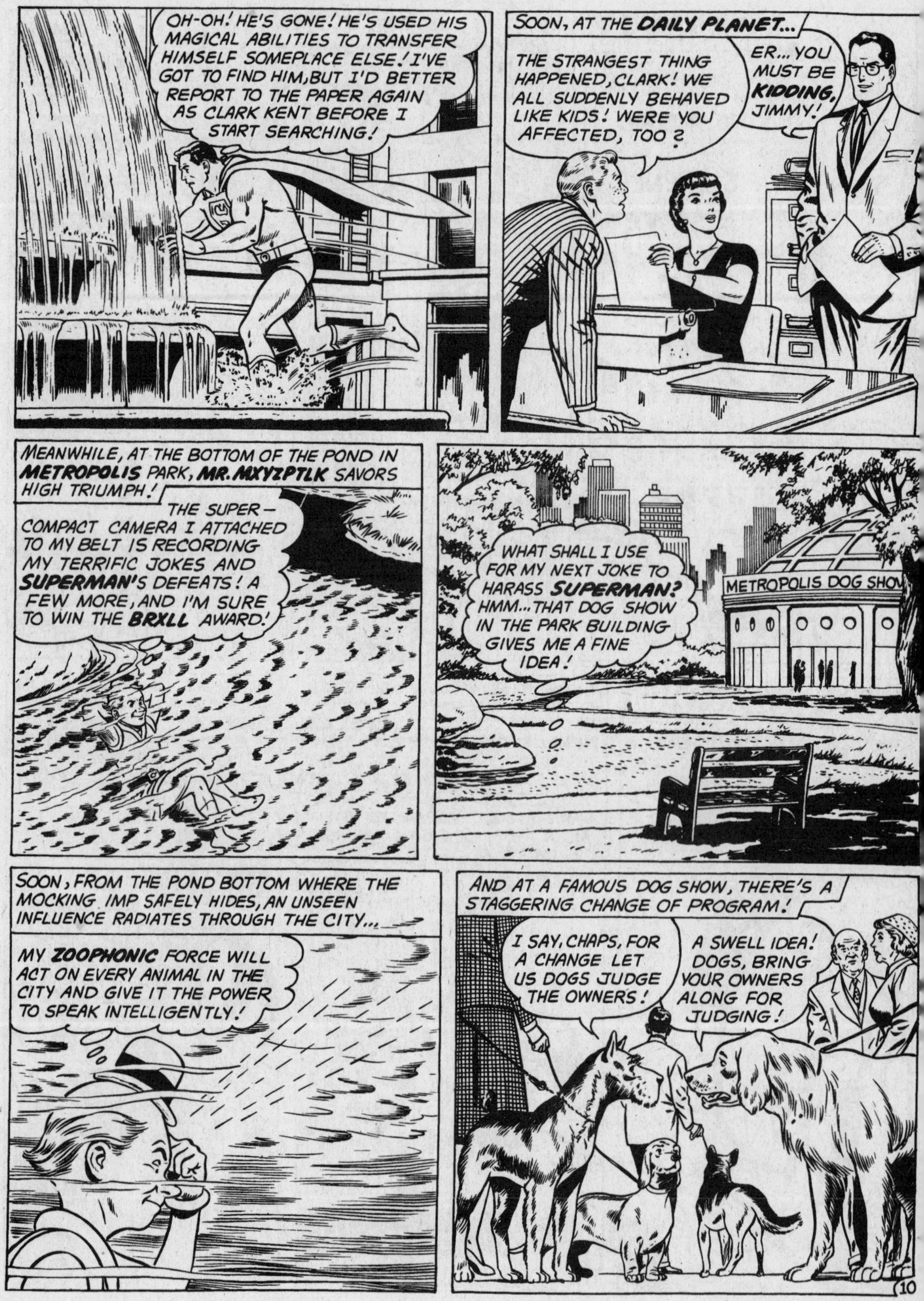
OH-OH! HE'S GONE! HE'S USED HIS MAGICAL ABILITIES TO TRANSFER HIMSELF SOMEPLACE ELSE! I'VE GOT TO FIND HIM, BUT I'D BETTER REPORT TO THE PAPER AGAIN AS CLARK KENT BEFORE I START SEARCHING!
SOON, AT THE DAILY PLANET...
THE STRANGEST THING HAPPENED, CLARK! WE ALL SUDDENLY BEHAVED LIKE KIDS! WERE YOU AFFECTED, TOO?
ER...YOU MUST BE KIDDING, JIMMY!
MEANWHILE, AT THE BOTTOM OF THE POND IN METROPOLIS PARK, MR. MXYZPTLK SAVORS HIGH TRIUMPH!
THE SUPER-COMPACT CAMERA I ATTACHED TO MY BELT IS RECORDING MY TERRIFIC JOKES AND SUPERMAN'S DEFEATS! A FEW MORE, AND I'M SURE TO WIN THE BRXLL AWARD!
WHAT SHALL I USE FOR MY NEXT JOKE TO HARASS SUPERMAN? HMM...THAT DOG SHOW IN THE PARK BUILDING GIVES ME A FINE IDEA!
METROPOLIS DOG SHOW
SOON, FROM THE POND BOTTOM WHERE THE MOCKING IMP SAFELY HIDES, AN UNSEEN INFLUENCE RADIATES THROUGH THE CITY...
MY ZOOPHONIC FORCE WILL ACT ON EVERY ANIMAL IN THE CITY AND GIVE IT THE POWER TO SPEAK INTELLIGENTLY!
AND AT A FAMOUS DOG SHOW, THERE'S A STAGGERING CHANGE OF PROGRAM!
I SAY, CHAPS, FOR A CHANGE LET US DOGS JUDGE THE OWNERS!
A SWELL IDEA! DOGS, BRING YOUR OWNERS ALONG FOR JUDGING!
10

THIS IS MY OWNER, MRS. SMITHEBY!
A POOR SPECIMEN! HER HAIR'S TOO SHORT AND HER HEAD IS NOT WELL-SHAPED! DISQUALIFIED!
I KNOW I'M HEARING THIS, BUT IT MUST BE A DREAM!
BUT THE INCREDIBLE HAPPENINGS LOOSED UPON THE CITY BY MR. MXYZPTLK'S ZOOPHONIC FORCE IS NO DREAM!
MAMA, LOOK AT THE FUNNY PEOPLE WHO HAVE COME TODAY!
YES, CHILD, THEY'RE AMUSING!
SPACE ROCKET CONVENTIO
...AND THIS IS HAMBO, THE BRAVE LITTLE CHIMPANZEE WHO'LL MAKE THE NEXT ROCKET TEST-FLIGHT!
LISTEN, MAC, IF YOU WANT SOME-BODY TO RIDE THAT ROCKET, YOU DO IT YOURSELF! I QUIT!
MODEL NOVA III
WHEN CLARK SWITCHES BACK TO SUPERMAN TO INVESTI-GATE THE GROWING BEDLAM...
KRYPTO, TRY TO QUIET THE PEOPLE'S FEAR OF THE TALKING ANIMALS, WHILE I HUNT THE IMP BEHIND THIS!
HI, SUPERMAN. I'VE JUST COME BACK FROM SPACE AND...YIPE! I CAN TALK NOW!
GREAT CAT'S WHISKERS... ME, TOO!
NO JAY-WALKING! STEP ALONG, EVERYBODY!
KRYPTO, THE SUPER-DOG, GOES CLEVERLY INTO ACTION TO AVOID PANIC!
HELLO, FOLKS! WE, THE ANIMALS OF METROPOLIS, ARE SPEAKING TO YOU BY SPECIAL SUPER-VENTRILOQUISM, TO BRING YOU THE FOLLOWING MESSAGE, "BUY HOOSON'S ANIMAL CRACKERS!"
AW, IT'S JUST A CLEVER VENTRILOQUISTIC TRICK TO BROADCAST A COMMERCIAL! THE ANIMALS AREN'T REALLY TALKING!
MEANWHILE, WHEN SUPERMAN'S X-RAY VISION AGAIN LOCATES MR. MXYZPTLK...
I KNOW YOU'RE DOWN THERE, IMP! YOU MUST BE REALLY AFRAID TO HIDE LIKE THIS! TOO AFRAID YOU'LL SAY YOUR NAME BACKWARDS!
HE'S GOT SOMETHING UP HIS SLEEVE, BUT HE CAN'T OUTWIT ME THIS TIME! WHEN I SPEAK, THE WATER WILL SILENCE ME!
11

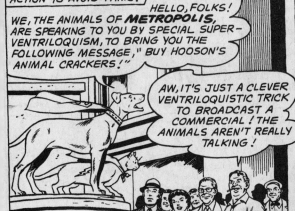

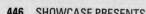

AND AS THE IMP STARTS TO SPEAK, *SUPERMAN* USES HIS SUPER-BREATH TO...

I'LL BLOW THE WATER OUT OF THE POND AND HE'LL BE SPEAKING HIS NAME BACKWARD IN THE AIR! BUT... HE WENT RIGHT ALONG WITH THE WATER!

KL-- GLUG!

AND AS *SUPERMAN* HASTILY RETURNS THE WATER TO THE POND...

HE'S USING HIS SIGN-LANGUAGE TO TAUNT ME! "I OUTSMARTED YOU AGAIN, *HAM OF STEEL!*" OH, NO, THIS IS TOO MUCH!

AND FOR ONCE, *SUPERMAN* GIVES WAY TO A FIT OF SUPER-TEMPER!

YOU WRETCHED GNOME, I'VE HAD ENOUGH OF YOU FOR ALL TIME!

I REALLY GOT TO *SUPERMAN* THIS TIME! LOOK AT HIM RAGE! THIS IS THE MOST HEART-WARMING SIGHT I'VE EVER SEEN!

LISTEN, YOU PEST! I'M GOING TO THE MOON AND STAY THERE TILL YOU GO BACK TO THE *FIFTH DIMENSION!* I NEVER WANT TO SEE YOUR FACE AGAIN!

LOOK AT HIM RUN AWAY! HE CAN'T FACE ME ANYMORE! HA, HA! THIS IS A REWARD FOR ALL THE TIMES HE EXASPERATED *ME!*

THE MOON? THERE'S NO AIR THERE AND SOUND CAN'T EXIST IN A VACUUM, SO I'D BE SAFE TO FOLLOW *SUPERMAN* SOME MORE! I'VE REALLY GOT HIM GOING THIS TIME!

SO, MAGICALLY TRANSFERRING HIMSELF AND THUS ENDING THE *ZOOPHONIC* NUISANCE IN *METROPOLIS*, THE IMP FOLLOWS *SUPERMAN* TO THE MOON...

HE FOLLOWED ME, AS I FIGURED HE WOULD WHEN I PRETENDED TO LOSE MY TEMPER!

NOW TO TEASE HIM SOME MORE!

12

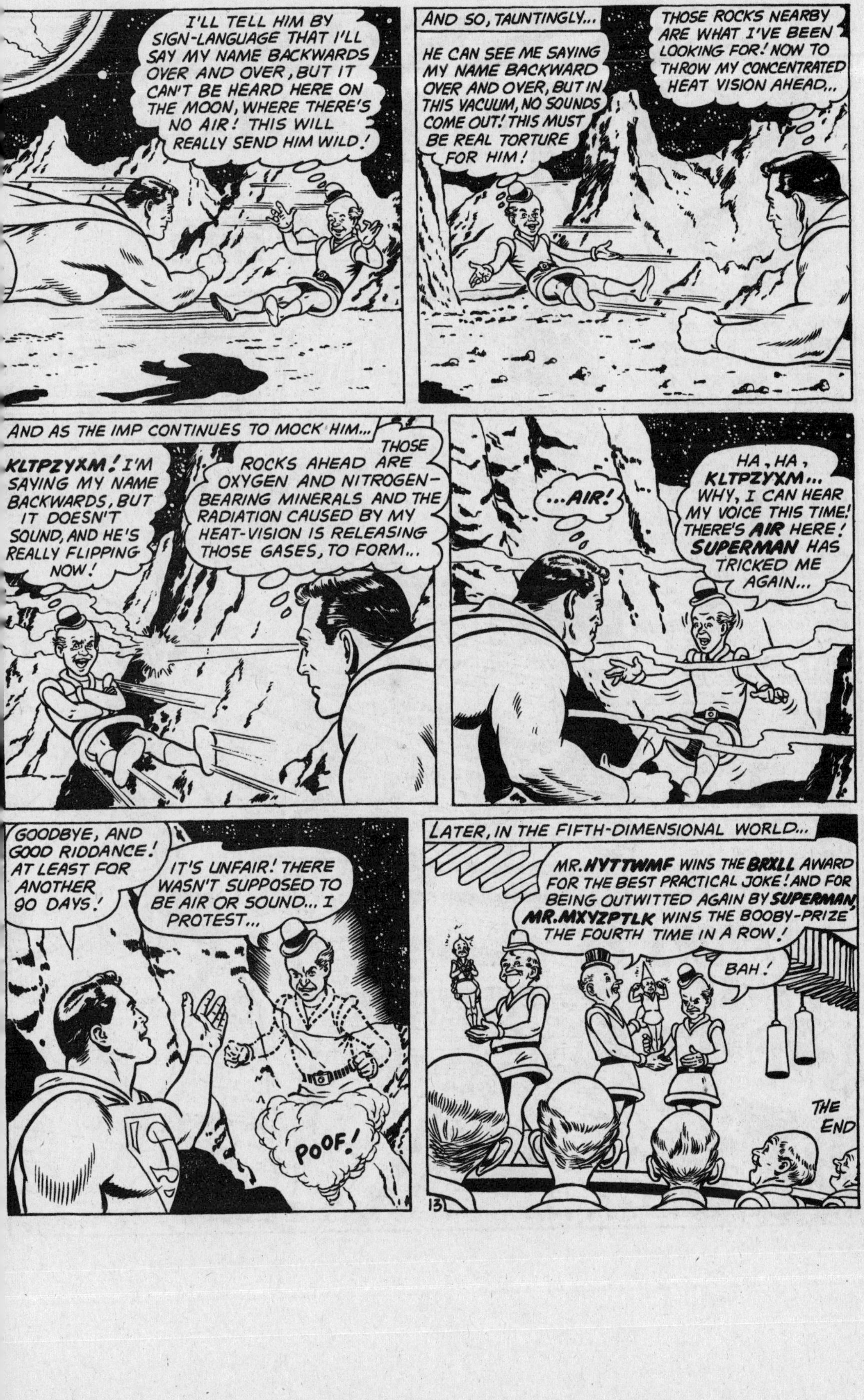
I'LL TELL HIM BY SIGN-LANGUAGE THAT I'LL SAY MY NAME BACKWARDS OVER AND OVER, BUT IT CAN'T BE HEARD HERE ON THE MOON, WHERE THERE'S NO AIR! THIS WILL REALLY SEND HIM WILD!
AND SO, TAUNTINGLY...
HE CAN SEE ME SAYING MY NAME BACKWARD OVER AND OVER, BUT IN THIS VACUUM, NO SOUNDS COME OUT! THIS MUST BE REAL TORTURE FOR HIM!
THOSE ROCKS NEARBY ARE WHAT I'VE BEEN LOOKING FOR! NOW TO THROW MY CONCENTRATED HEAT VISION AHEAD...
AND AS THE IMP CONTINUES TO MOCK HIM...
KLTPZYXM! I'M SAYING MY NAME BACKWARDS, BUT IT DOESN'T SOUND, AND HE'S REALLY FLIPPING NOW!
THOSE ROCKS AHEAD ARE OXYGEN AND NITROGEN-BEARING MINERALS AND THE RADIATION CAUSED BY MY HEAT-VISION IS RELEASING THOSE GASES, TO FORM...
...AIR!
HA, HA, KLTPZYXM... WHY, I CAN HEAR MY VOICE THIS TIME! THERE'S AIR HERE! SUPERMAN HAS TRICKED ME AGAIN...
GOODBYE, AND GOOD RIDDANCE! AT LEAST FOR ANOTHER 90 DAYS!
IT'S UNFAIR! THERE WASN'T SUPPOSED TO BE AIR OR SOUND... I PROTEST...
POOF!
13
LATER, IN THE FIFTH-DIMENSIONAL WORLD...
MR. HYTTWMF WINS THE BRXLL AWARD FOR THE BEST PRACTICAL JOKE! AND FOR BEING OUTWITTED AGAIN BY SUPERMAN, MR. MXYZPTLK WINS THE BOOBY-PRIZE THE FOURTH TIME IN A ROW!
BAH!
THE END

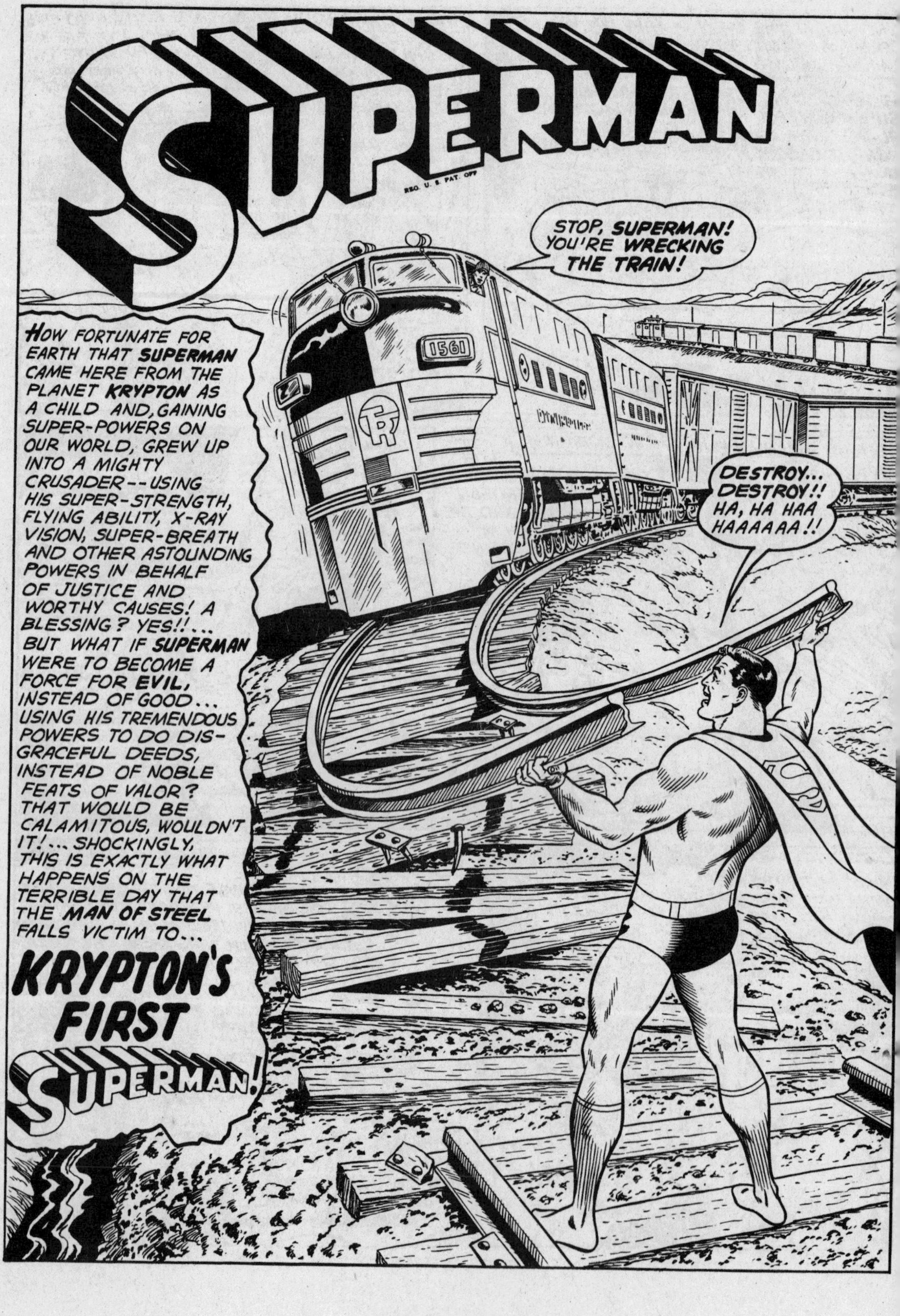
SUPERMAN
REG. U. S. PAT. OFF
STOP, SUPERMAN! YOU'RE WRECKING THE TRAIN!
HOW FORTUNATE FOR EARTH THAT SUPERMAN CAME HERE FROM THE PLANET KRYPTON AS A CHILD AND, GAINING SUPER-POWERS ON OUR WORLD, GREW UP INTO A MIGHTY CRUSADER--USING HIS SUPER-STRENGTH, FLYING ABILITY, X-RAY VISION, SUPER-BREATH AND OTHER ASTOUNDING POWERS IN BEHALF OF JUSTICE AND WORTHY CAUSES! A BLESSING? YES!!... BUT WHAT IF SUPERMAN WERE TO BECOME A FORCE FOR EVIL, INSTEAD OF GOOD... USING HIS TREMENDOUS POWERS TO DO DIS-GRACEFUL DEEDS, INSTEAD OF NOBLE FEATS OF VALOR? THAT WOULD BE CALAMITOUS, WOULDN'T IT!... SHOCKINGLY, THIS IS EXACTLY WHAT HAPPENS ON THE TERRIBLE DAY THAT THE MAN OF STEEL FALLS VICTIM TO...
KRYPTON'S FIRST SUPERMAN!
1561
DESTROY... DESTROY!! HA, HA HAA HAAAAAA!!

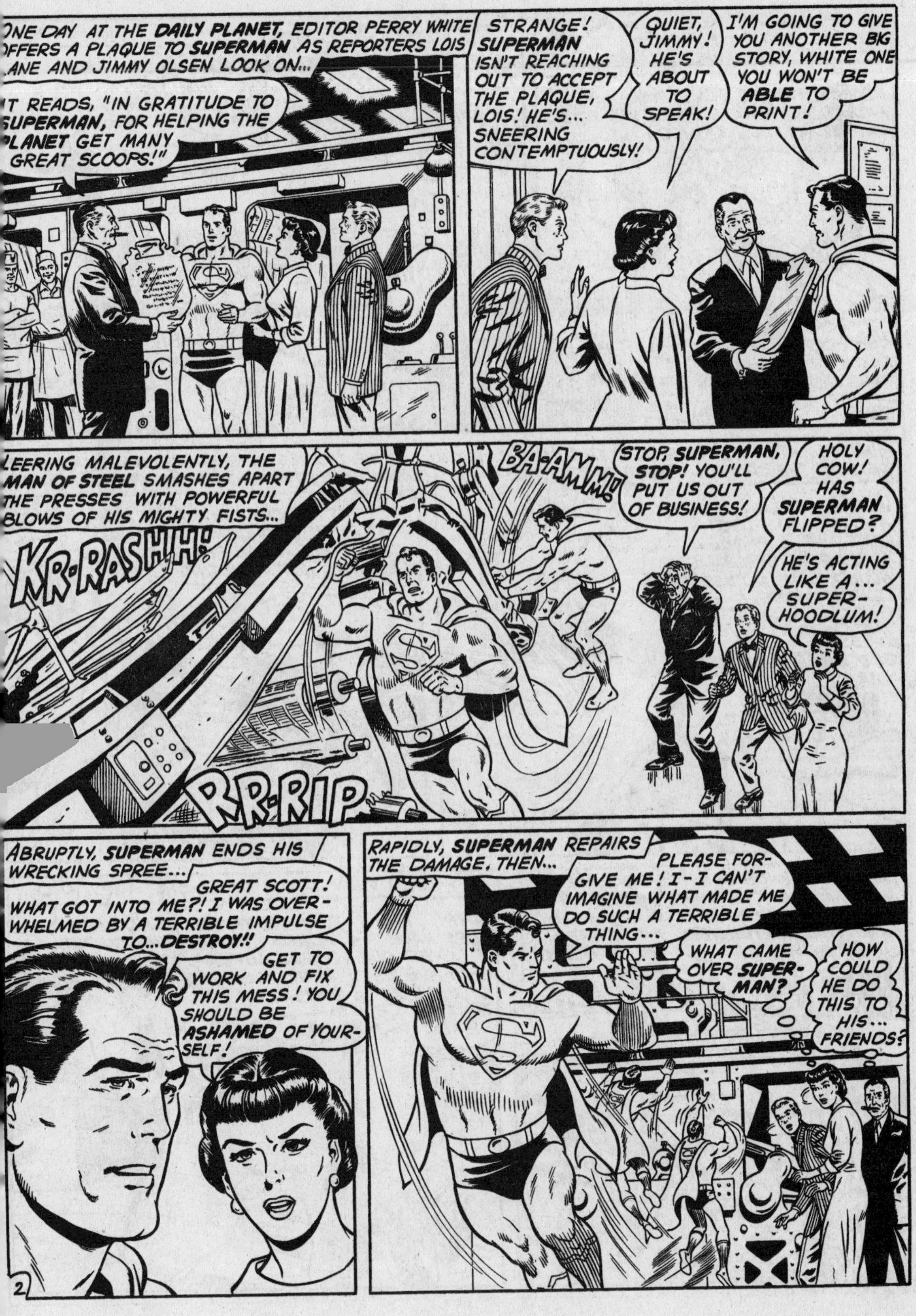
ONE DAY AT THE DAILY PLANET, EDITOR PERRY WHITE OFFERS A PLAQUE TO SUPERMAN AS REPORTERS LOIS LANE AND JIMMY OLSEN LOOK ON...
IT READS, "IN GRATITUDE TO SUPERMAN, FOR HELPING THE PLANET GET MANY GREAT SCOOPS!"
STRANGE! SUPERMAN ISN'T REACHING OUT TO ACCEPT THE PLAQUE, LOIS! HE'S... SNEERING CONTEMPTUOUSLY!
QUIET, JIMMY! HE'S ABOUT TO SPEAK!
I'M GOING TO GIVE YOU ANOTHER BIG STORY, WHITE ONE YOU WON'T BE ABLE TO PRINT!
LEERING MALEVOLENTLY, THE MAN OF STEEL SMASHES APART THE PRESSES WITH POWERFUL BLOWS OF HIS MIGHTY FISTS...
KR-RASHH!
BA-AMM!
STOP, SUPERMAN, STOP! YOU'LL PUT US OUT OF BUSINESS!
HOLY COW! HAS SUPERMAN FLIPPED?
HE'S ACTING LIKE A... SUPER-HOODLUM!
RR-RIP
ABRUPTLY, SUPERMAN ENDS HIS WRECKING SPREE...
GREAT SCOTT! WHAT GOT INTO ME?! I WAS OVER-WHELMED BY A TERRIBLE IMPULSE TO...DESTROY!!
GET TO WORK AND FIX THIS MESS! YOU SHOULD BE ASHAMED OF YOUR-SELF!
2
RAPIDLY, SUPERMAN REPAIRS THE DAMAGE. THEN...
PLEASE FOR-GIVE ME! I-I CAN'T IMAGINE WHAT MADE ME DO SUCH A TERRIBLE THING...
WHAT CAME OVER SUPER-MAN?
HOW COULD HE DO THIS TO HIS... FRIENDS?

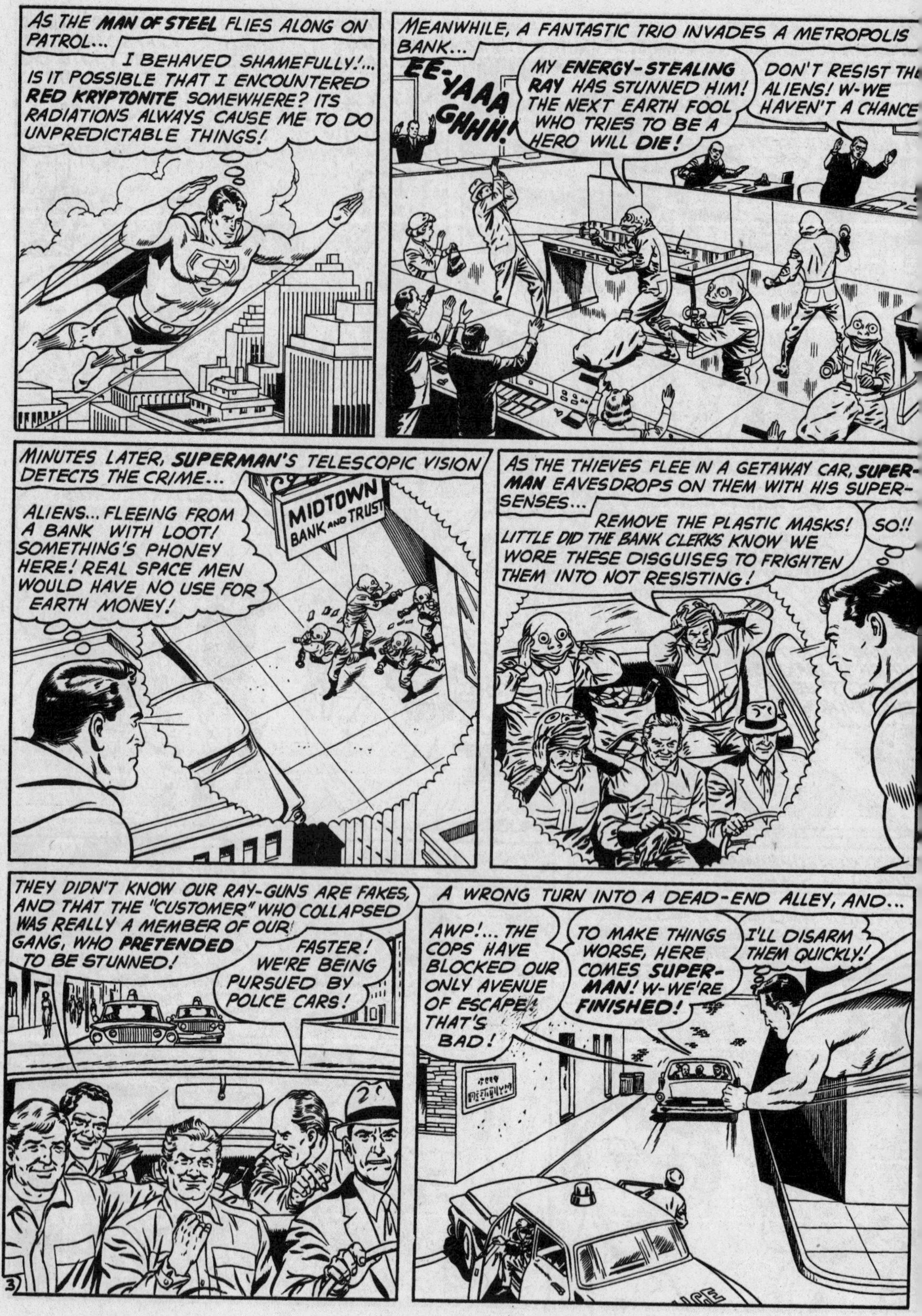
AS THE MAN OF STEEL FLIES ALONG ON PATROL...
I BEHAVED SHAMEFULLY!... IS IT POSSIBLE THAT I ENCOUNTERED RED KRYPTONITE SOMEWHERE? ITS RADIATIONS ALWAYS CAUSE ME TO DO UNPREDICTABLE THINGS!
MEANWHILE, A FANTASTIC TRIO INVADES A METROPOLIS BANK...
EE-YAAA GHHH!
MY ENERGY-STEALING RAY HAS STUNNED HIM! THE NEXT EARTH FOOL WHO TRIES TO BE A HERO WILL DIE!
DON'T RESIST THE ALIENS! W-WE HAVEN'T A CHANCE
MINUTES LATER, SUPERMAN'S TELESCOPIC VISION DETECTS THE CRIME...
MIDTOWN BANK AND TRUST
ALIENS... FLEEING FROM A BANK WITH LOOT! SOMETHING'S PHONEY HERE! REAL SPACE MEN WOULD HAVE NO USE FOR EARTH MONEY!
AS THE THIEVES FLEE IN A GETAWAY CAR, SUPERMAN EAVESDROPS ON THEM WITH HIS SUPER-SENSES...
REMOVE THE PLASTIC MASKS! LITTLE DID THE BANK CLERKS KNOW WE WORE THESE DISGUISES TO FRIGHTEN THEM INTO NOT RESISTING!
SO!!
THEY DIDN'T KNOW OUR RAY-GUNS ARE FAKES, AND THAT THE "CUSTOMER" WHO COLLAPSED WAS REALLY A MEMBER OF OUR GANG, WHO PRETENDED TO BE STUNNED!
FASTER! WE'RE BEING PURSUED BY POLICE CARS!
3
A WRONG TURN INTO A DEAD-END ALLEY, AND...
AWP!... THE COPS HAVE BLOCKED OUR ONLY AVENUE OF ESCAPE! THAT'S BAD!
TO MAKE THINGS WORSE, HERE COMES SUPERMAN! W-WE'RE FINISHED!
I'LL DISARM THEM QUICKLY!

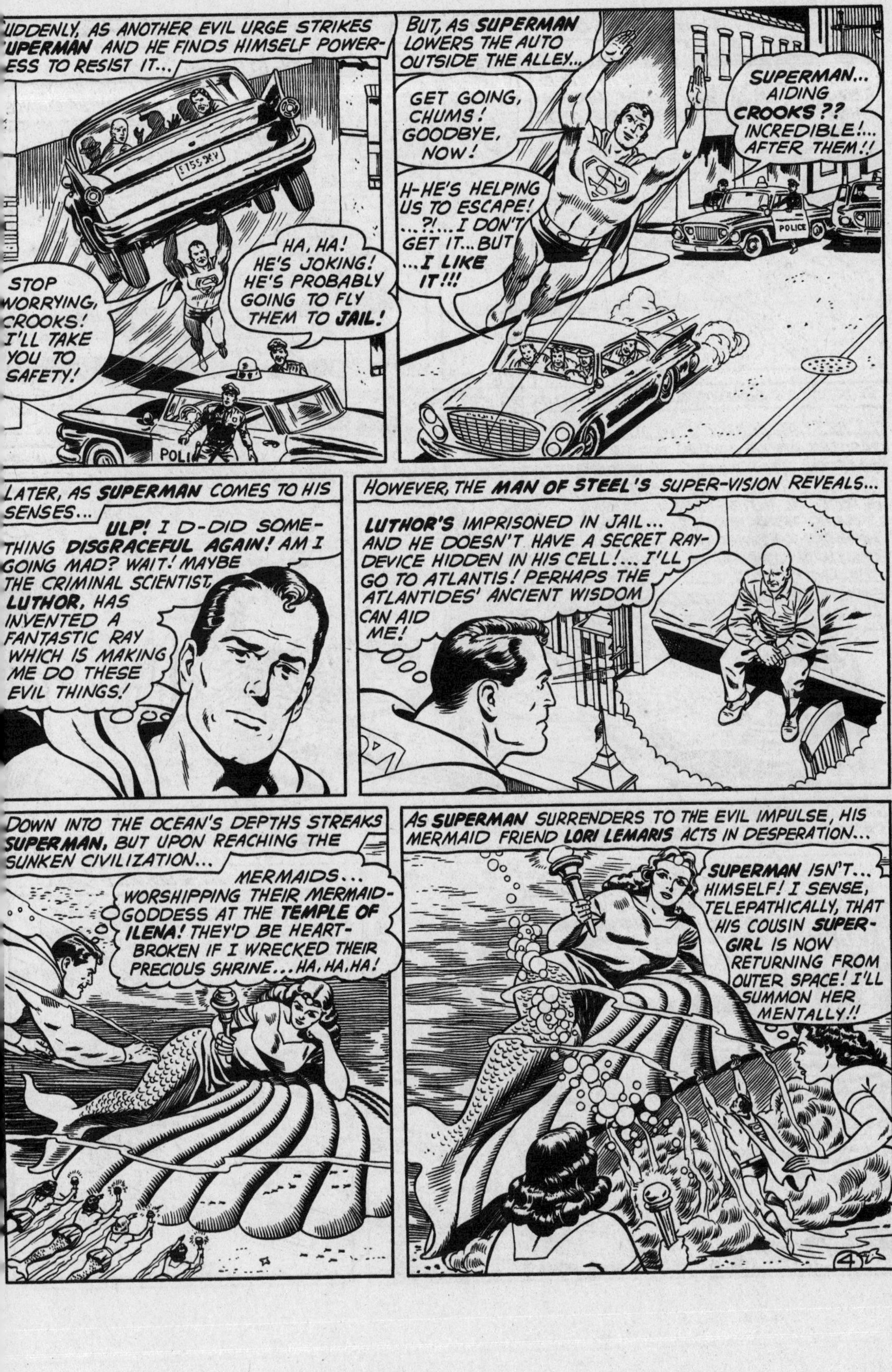

UDDENLY, AS ANOTHER EVIL URGE STRIKES UPERMAN AND HE FINDS HIMSELF POWER-ESS TO RESIST IT...
STOP WORRYING, CROOKS! I'LL TAKE YOU TO SAFETY!
HA, HA! HE'S JOKING! HE'S PROBABLY GOING TO FLY THEM TO JAIL!
POLI
BUT, AS SUPERMAN LOWERS THE AUTO OUTSIDE THE ALLEY...
GET GOING, CHUMS! GOODBYE, NOW!
H-HE'S HELPING US TO ESCAPE! ...?!...I DON'T GET IT...BUT ...I LIKE IT!!!
SUPERMAN... AIDING CROOKS?? INCREDIBLE!... AFTER THEM!!
POLICE
LATER, AS SUPERMAN COMES TO HIS SENSES...
ULP! I D-DID SOMETHING DISGRACEFUL AGAIN! AM I GOING MAD? WAIT! MAYBE THE CRIMINAL SCIENTIST, LUTHOR, HAS INVENTED A FANTASTIC RAY WHICH IS MAKING ME DO THESE EVIL THINGS!
HOWEVER, THE MAN OF STEEL'S SUPER-VISION REVEALS...
LUTHOR'S IMPRISONED IN JAIL... AND HE DOESN'T HAVE A SECRET RAY-DEVICE HIDDEN IN HIS CELL!... I'LL GO TO ATLANTIS! PERHAPS THE ATLANTIDES' ANCIENT WISDOM CAN AID ME!
DOWN INTO THE OCEAN'S DEPTHS STREAKS SUPERMAN, BUT UPON REACHING THE SUNKEN CIVILIZATION...
MERMAIDS... WORSHIPPING THEIR MERMAID-GODDESS AT THE TEMPLE OF ILENA! THEY'D BE HEART-BROKEN IF I WRECKED THEIR PRECIOUS SHRINE... HA, HA, HA!
AS SUPERMAN SURRENDERS TO THE EVIL IMPULSE, HIS MERMAID FRIEND LORI LEMARIS ACTS IN DESPERATION...
SUPERMAN ISN'T... HIMSELF! I SENSE, TELEPATHICALLY, THAT HIS COUSIN SUPER-GIRL IS NOW RETURNING FROM OUTER SPACE! I'LL SUMMON HER MENTALLY!!
4

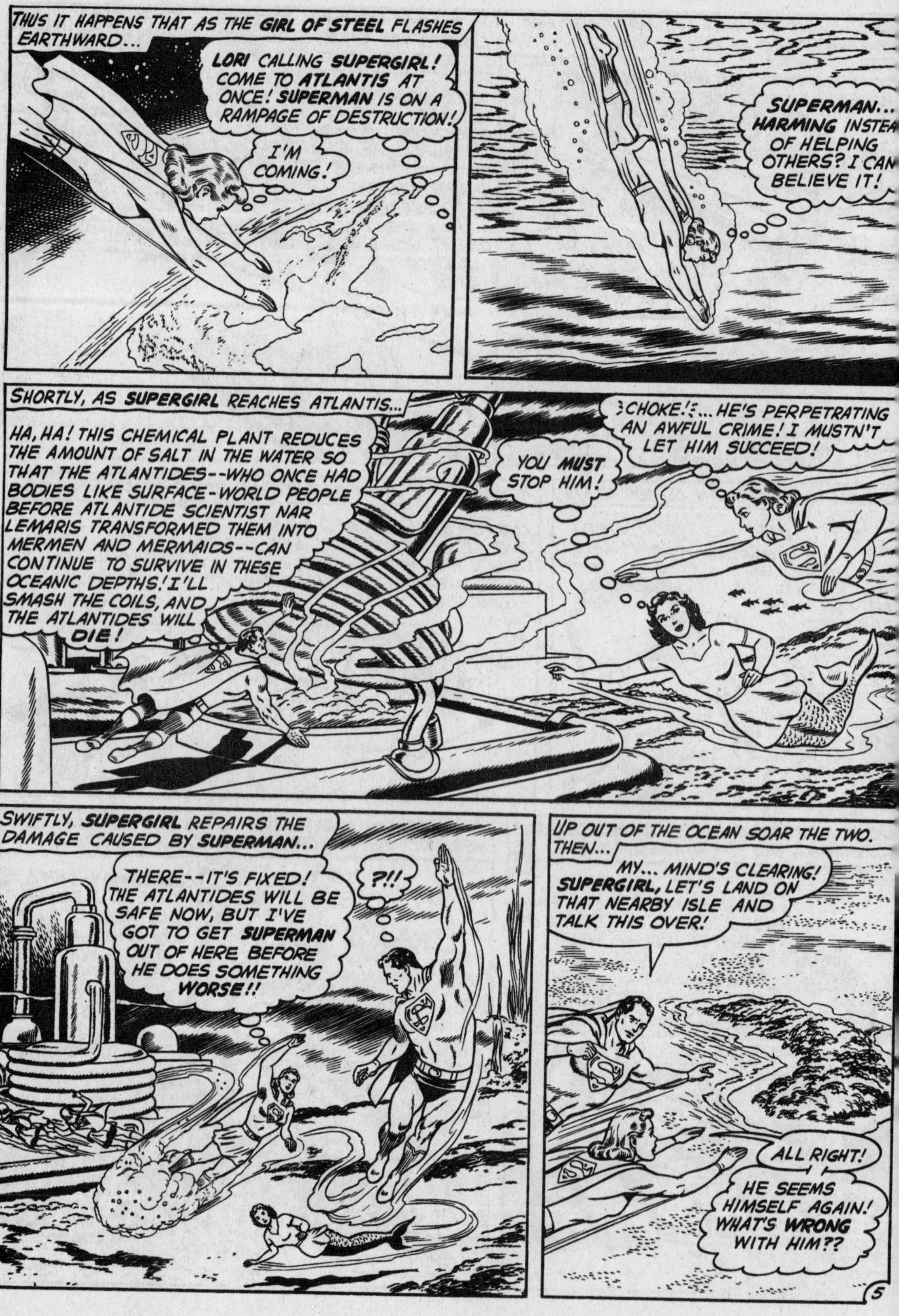
THUS IT HAPPENS THAT AS THE GIRL OF STEEL FLASHES EARTHWARD...
LORI CALLING SUPERGIRL! COME TO ATLANTIS AT ONCE! SUPERMAN IS ON A RAMPAGE OF DESTRUCTION!
I'M COMING!
SUPERMAN... HARMING INSTEA OF HELPING OTHERS? I CAN BELIEVE IT!
SHORTLY, AS SUPERGIRL REACHES ATLANTIS...
HA, HA! THIS CHEMICAL PLANT REDUCES THE AMOUNT OF SALT IN THE WATER SO THAT THE ATLANTIDES--WHO ONCE HAD BODIES LIKE SURFACE-WORLD PEOPLE BEFORE ATLANTIDE SCIENTIST NAR LEMARIS TRANSFORMED THEM INTO MERMEN AND MERMAIDS--CAN CONTINUE TO SURVIVE IN THESE OCEANIC DEPTHS! I'LL SMASH THE COILS, AND THE ATLANTIDES WILL DIE!
YOU MUST STOP HIM!
CHOKE! ... HE'S PERPETRATING AN AWFUL CRIME! I MUSTN'T LET HIM SUCCEED!
SWIFTLY, SUPERGIRL REPAIRS THE DAMAGE CAUSED BY SUPERMAN...
THERE--IT'S FIXED! THE ATLANTIDES WILL BE SAFE NOW, BUT I'VE GOT TO GET SUPERMAN OUT OF HERE BEFORE HE DOES SOMETHING WORSE!!
?!!
UP OUT OF THE OCEAN SOAR THE TWO. THEN...
MY... MIND'S CLEARING! SUPERGIRL, LET'S LAND ON THAT NEARBY ISLE AND TALK THIS OVER!
ALL RIGHT!
HE SEEMS HIMSELF AGAIN! WHAT'S WRONG WITH HIM??
5

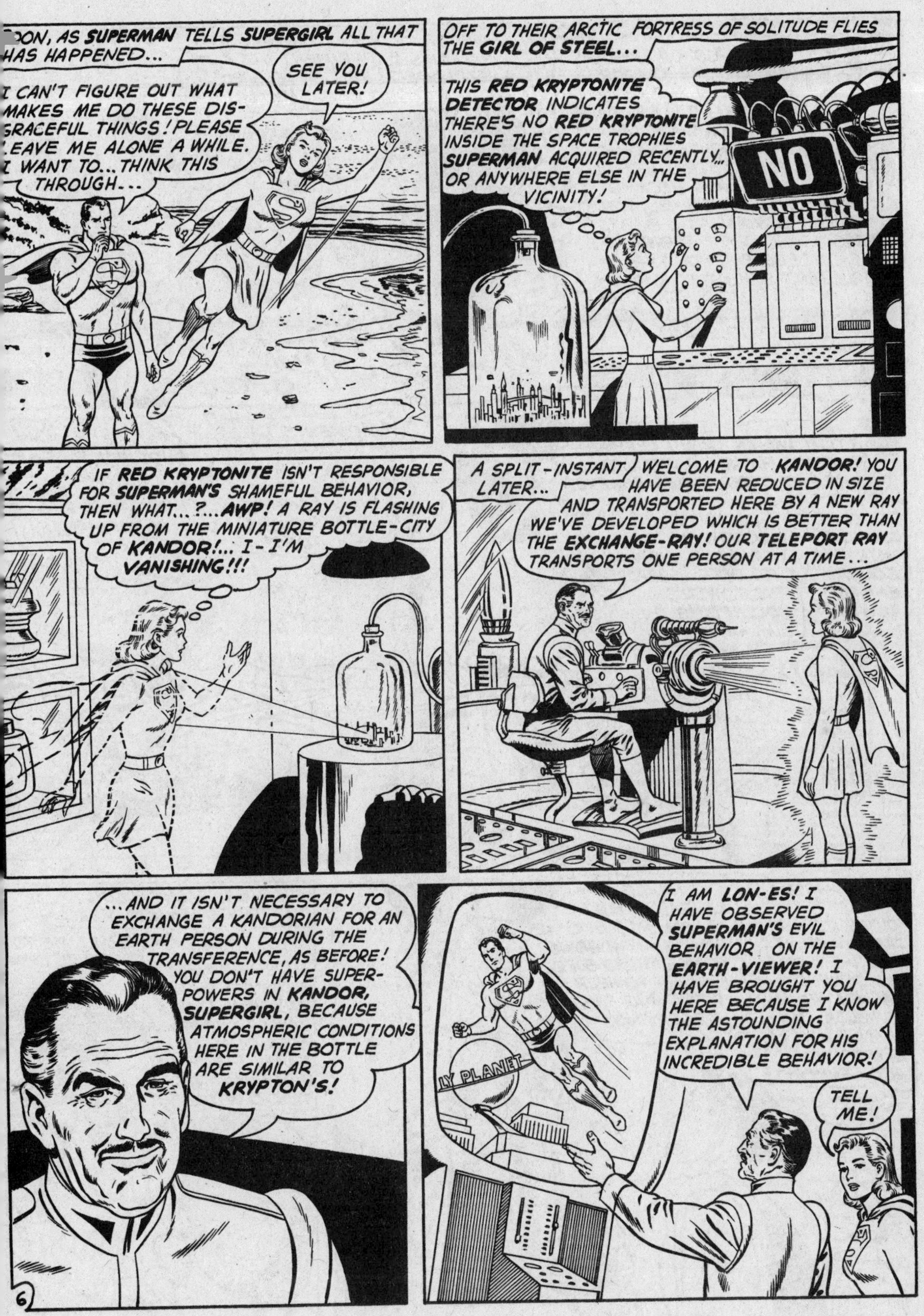
OON, AS SUPERMAN TELLS SUPERGIRL ALL THAT HAS HAPPENED...
I CAN'T FIGURE OUT WHAT MAKES ME DO THESE DISGRACEFUL THINGS! PLEASE LEAVE ME ALONE A WHILE. I WANT TO... THINK THIS THROUGH...
SEE YOU LATER!
OFF TO THEIR ARCTIC FORTRESS OF SOLITUDE FLIES THE GIRL OF STEEL...
THIS RED KRYPTONITE DETECTOR INDICATES THERE'S NO RED KRYPTONITE INSIDE THE SPACE TROPHIES SUPERMAN ACQUIRED RECENTLY... OR ANYWHERE ELSE IN THE VICINITY!
NO
IF RED KRYPTONITE ISN'T RESPONSIBLE FOR SUPERMAN'S SHAMEFUL BEHAVIOR, THEN WHAT...?...AWP! A RAY IS FLASHING UP FROM THE MINIATURE BOTTLE-CITY OF KANDOR!... I-I'M VANISHING!!!
A SPLIT-INSTANT LATER...
WELCOME TO KANDOR! YOU HAVE BEEN REDUCED IN SIZE AND TRANSPORTED HERE BY A NEW RAY WE'VE DEVELOPED WHICH IS BETTER THAN THE EXCHANGE-RAY! OUR TELEPORT RAY TRANSPORTS ONE PERSON AT A TIME...
...AND IT ISN'T NECESSARY TO EXCHANGE A KANDORIAN FOR AN EARTH PERSON DURING THE TRANSFERENCE, AS BEFORE! YOU DON'T HAVE SUPER-POWERS IN KANDOR, SUPERGIRL, BECAUSE ATMOSPHERIC CONDITIONS HERE IN THE BOTTLE ARE SIMILAR TO KRYPTON'S!
6
LY PLANET
I AM LON-ES! I HAVE OBSERVED SUPERMAN'S EVIL BEHAVIOR ON THE EARTH-VIEWER! I HAVE BROUGHT YOU HERE BECAUSE I KNOW THE ASTOUNDING EXPLANATION FOR HIS INCREDIBLE BEHAVIOR!
TELL ME!

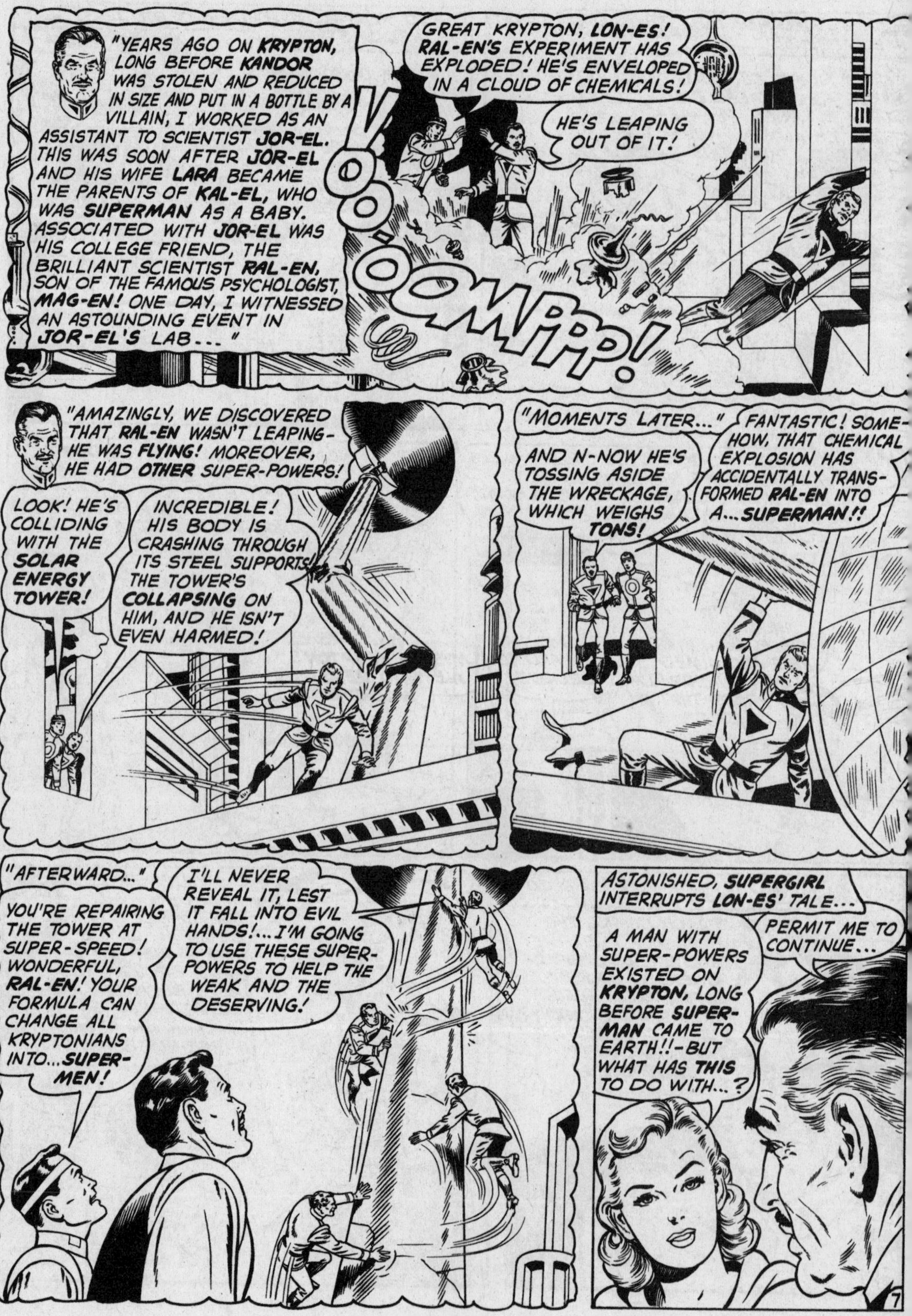
"YEARS AGO ON KRYPTON, LONG BEFORE KANDOR WAS STOLEN AND REDUCED IN SIZE AND PUT IN A BOTTLE BY A VILLAIN, I WORKED AS AN ASSISTANT TO SCIENTIST JOR-EL. THIS WAS SOON AFTER JOR-EL AND HIS WIFE LARA BECAME THE PARENTS OF KAL-EL, WHO WAS SUPERMAN AS A BABY. ASSOCIATED WITH JOR-EL WAS HIS COLLEGE FRIEND, THE BRILLIANT SCIENTIST RAL-EN, SON OF THE FAMOUS PSYCHOLOGIST, MAG-EN! ONE DAY, I WITNESSED AN ASTOUNDING EVENT IN JOR-EL'S LAB..."
VAROOOMPPP!
GREAT KRYPTON, LON-ES! RAL-EN'S EXPERIMENT HAS EXPLODED! HE'S ENVELOPED IN A CLOUD OF CHEMICALS!
HE'S LEAPING OUT OF IT!
"AMAZINGLY, WE DISCOVERED THAT RAL-EN WASN'T LEAPING-HE WAS FLYING! MOREOVER, HE HAD OTHER SUPER-POWERS!
LOOK! HE'S COLLIDING WITH THE SOLAR ENERGY TOWER!
INCREDIBLE! HIS BODY IS CRASHING THROUGH ITS STEEL SUPPORTS! THE TOWER'S COLLAPSING ON HIM, AND HE ISN'T EVEN HARMED!
"MOMENTS LATER..."
AND N-NOW HE'S TOSSING ASIDE THE WRECKAGE, WHICH WEIGHS TONS!
FANTASTIC! SOMEHOW, THAT CHEMICAL EXPLOSION HAS ACCIDENTALLY TRANSFORMED RAL-EN INTO A...SUPERMAN!!
"AFTERWARD..."
YOU'RE REPAIRING THE TOWER AT SUPER-SPEED! WONDERFUL, RAL-EN! YOUR FORMULA CAN CHANGE ALL KRYPTONIANS INTO...SUPER-MEN!
I'LL NEVER REVEAL IT, LEST IT FALL INTO EVIL HANDS!...I'M GOING TO USE THESE SUPER-POWERS TO HELP THE WEAK AND THE DESERVING!
ASTONISHED, SUPERGIRL INTERRUPTS LON-ES' TALE...
A MAN WITH SUPER-POWERS EXISTED ON KRYPTON, LONG BEFORE SUPERMAN CAME TO EARTH!!-BUT WHAT HAS THIS TO DO WITH...?
PERMIT ME TO CONTINUE...
7

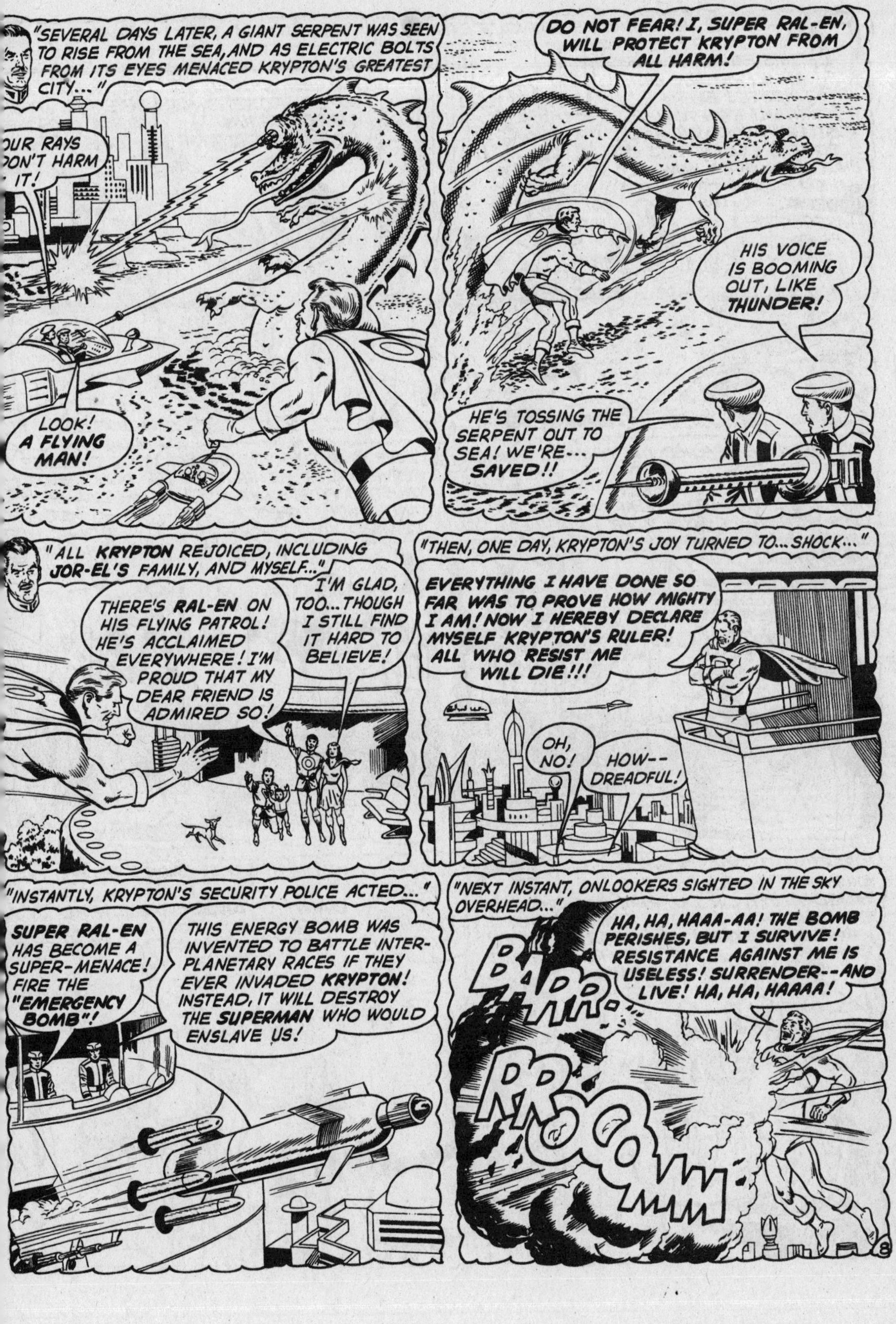
"SEVERAL DAYS LATER, A GIANT SERPENT WAS SEEN TO RISE FROM THE SEA, AND AS ELECTRIC BOLTS FROM ITS EYES MENACED KRYPTON'S GREATEST CITY..."
OUR RAYS DON'T HARM IT!
LOOK! A FLYING MAN!
DO NOT FEAR! I, SUPER RAL-EN, WILL PROTECT KRYPTON FROM ALL HARM!
HIS VOICE IS BOOMING OUT, LIKE THUNDER!
HE'S TOSSING THE SERPENT OUT TO SEA! WE'RE... SAVED!!
"ALL KRYPTON REJOICED, INCLUDING JOR-EL'S FAMILY, AND MYSELF..."
THERE'S RAL-EN ON HIS FLYING PATROL! HE'S ACCLAIMED EVERYWHERE! I'M PROUD THAT MY DEAR FRIEND IS ADMIRED SO!
I'M GLAD, TOO...THOUGH I STILL FIND IT HARD TO BELIEVE!
"THEN, ONE DAY, KRYPTON'S JOY TURNED TO...SHOCK..."
EVERYTHING I HAVE DONE SO FAR WAS TO PROVE HOW MIGHTY I AM! NOW I HEREBY DECLARE MYSELF KRYPTON'S RULER! ALL WHO RESIST ME WILL DIE!!!
OH, NO!
HOW-- DREADFUL!
"INSTANTLY, KRYPTON'S SECURITY POLICE ACTED..."
SUPER RAL-EN HAS BECOME A SUPER-MENACE! FIRE THE "EMERGENCY BOMB"!
THIS ENERGY BOMB WAS INVENTED TO BATTLE INTER-PLANETARY RACES IF THEY EVER INVADED KRYPTON! INSTEAD, IT WILL DESTROY THE SUPERMAN WHO WOULD ENSLAVE US!
"NEXT INSTANT, ONLOOKERS SIGHTED IN THE SKY OVERHEAD..."
BAROOM
RROOOMMM
HA, HA, HAAA-AA! THE BOMB PERISHES, BUT I SURVIVE! RESISTANCE AGAINST ME IS USELESS! SURRENDER--AND LIVE! HA, HA, HAAAA!
8

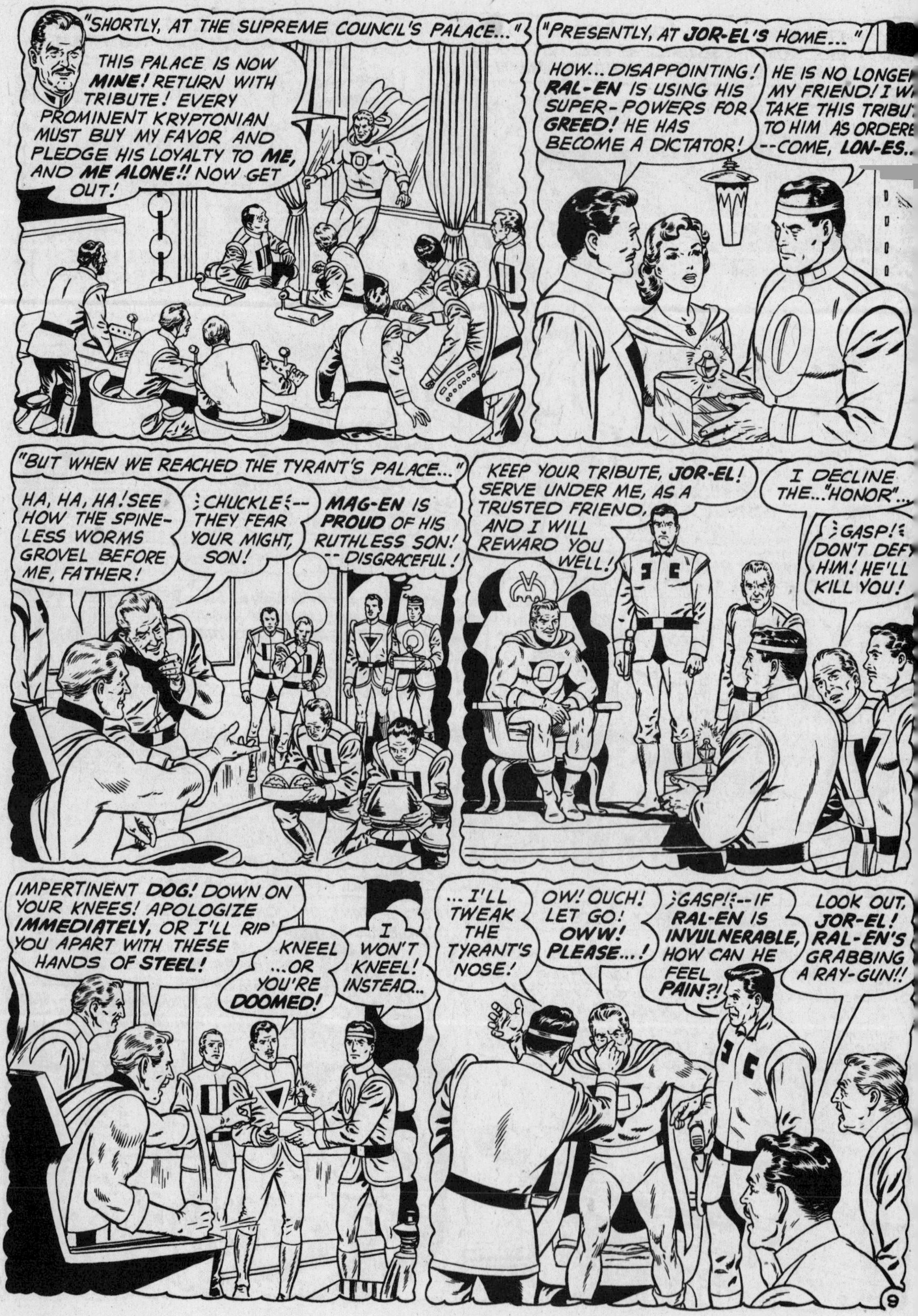
"SHORTLY, AT THE SUPREME COUNCIL'S PALACE..."
THIS PALACE IS NOW MINE! RETURN WITH TRIBUTE! EVERY PROMINENT KRYPTONIAN MUST BUY MY FAVOR AND PLEDGE HIS LOYALTY TO ME, AND ME ALONE!! NOW GET OUT!
"PRESENTLY, AT JOR-EL'S HOME..."
HOW...DISAPPOINTING! RAL-EN IS USING HIS SUPER-POWERS FOR GREED! HE HAS BECOME A DICTATOR!
HE IS NO LONGE MY FRIEND! I W TAKE THIS TRIBU TO HIM AS ORDERE --COME, LON-ES..
"BUT WHEN WE REACHED THE TYRANT'S PALACE..."
HA, HA, HA! SEE HOW THE SPINELESS WORMS GROVEL BEFORE ME, FATHER!
CHUCKLE --THEY FEAR YOUR MIGHT, SON!
MAG-EN IS PROUD OF HIS RUTHLESS SON! --DISGRACEFUL!
KEEP YOUR TRIBUTE, JOR-EL! SERVE UNDER ME, AS A TRUSTED FRIEND, AND I WILL REWARD YOU WELL!
I DECLINE THE..."HONOR"...
GASP! DON'T DEFY HIM! HE'LL KILL YOU!
IMPERTINENT DOG! DOWN ON YOUR KNEES! APOLOGIZE IMMEDIATELY, OR I'LL RIP YOU APART WITH THESE HANDS OF STEEL!
KNEEL ...OR YOU'RE DOOMED!
I WON'T KNEEL! INSTEAD...
...I'LL TWEAK THE TYRANT'S NOSE!
OW! OUCH! LET GO! OWW! PLEASE...!
GASP! --IF RAL-EN IS INVULNERABLE, HOW CAN HE FEEL PAIN?!
LOOK OUT, JOR-EL! RAL-EN'S GRABBING A RAY-GUN!!
9

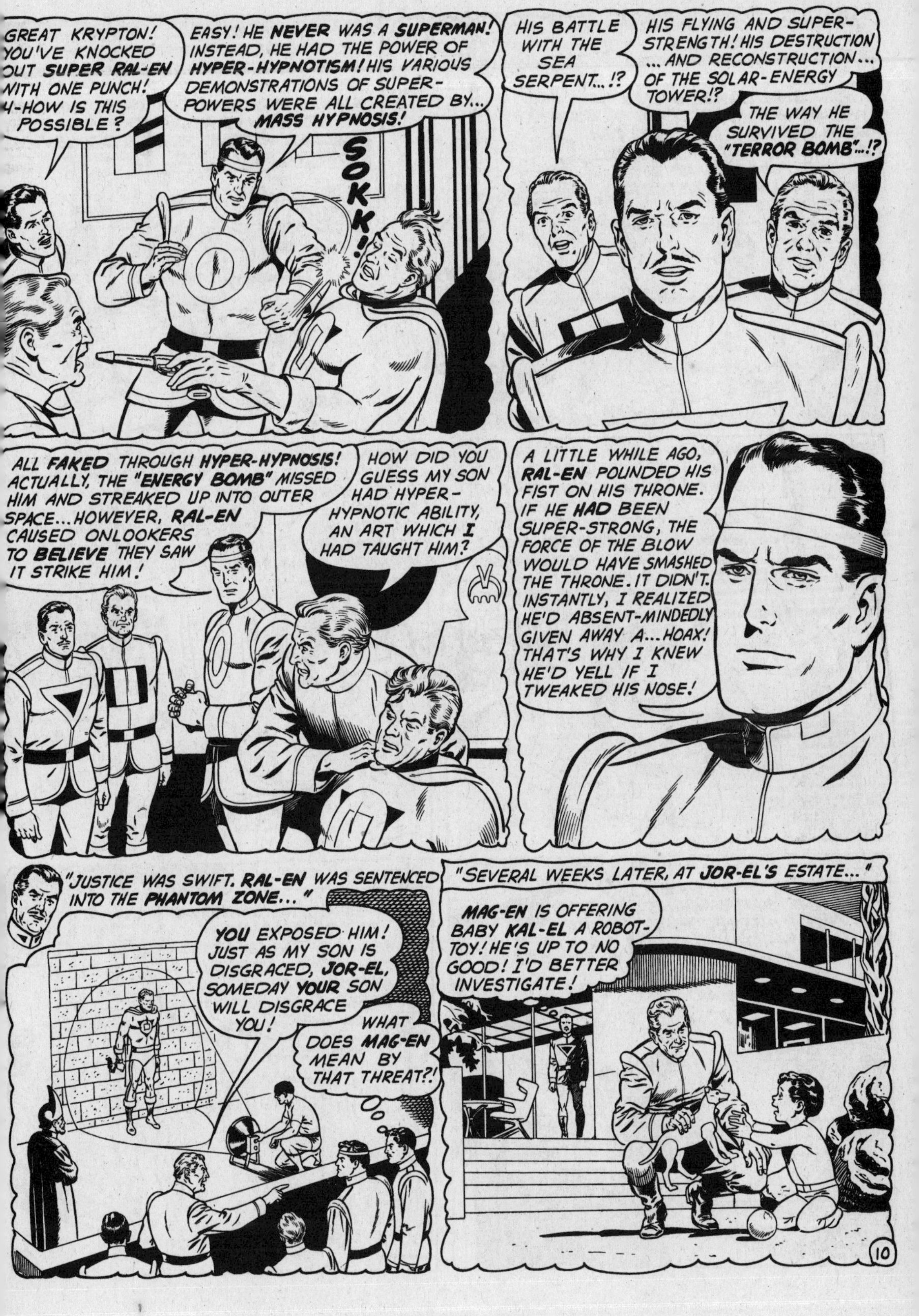
GREAT KRYPTON! YOU'VE KNOCKED OUT SUPER RAL-EN WITH ONE PUNCH! H-HOW IS THIS POSSIBLE?
EASY! HE NEVER WAS A SUPERMAN! INSTEAD, HE HAD THE POWER OF HYPER-HYPNOTISM! HIS VARIOUS DEMONSTRATIONS OF SUPER-POWERS WERE ALL CREATED BY... MASS HYPNOSIS!
SOKK!
HIS BATTLE WITH THE SEA SERPENT...!?
HIS FLYING AND SUPER-STRENGTH! HIS DESTRUCTION ...AND RECONSTRUCTION... OF THE SOLAR-ENERGY TOWER!?
THE WAY HE SURVIVED THE "TERROR BOMB"...!?
ALL FAKED THROUGH HYPER-HYPNOSIS! ACTUALLY, THE "ENERGY BOMB" MISSED HIM AND STREAKED UP INTO OUTER SPACE... HOWEVER, RAL-EN CAUSED ONLOOKERS TO BELIEVE THEY SAW IT STRIKE HIM!
HOW DID YOU GUESS MY SON HAD HYPER-HYPNOTIC ABILITY, AN ART WHICH I HAD TAUGHT HIM?
A LITTLE WHILE AGO, RAL-EN POUNDED HIS FIST ON HIS THRONE. IF HE HAD BEEN SUPER-STRONG, THE FORCE OF THE BLOW WOULD HAVE SMASHED THE THRONE. IT DIDN'T. INSTANTLY, I REALIZED HE'D ABSENT-MINDEDLY GIVEN AWAY A... HOAX! THAT'S WHY I KNEW HE'D YELL IF I TWEAKED HIS NOSE!
"JUSTICE WAS SWIFT. RAL-EN WAS SENTENCED INTO THE PHANTOM ZONE..."
YOU EXPOSED HIM! JUST AS MY SON IS DISGRACED, JOR-EL, SOMEDAY YOUR SON WILL DISGRACE YOU!
WHAT DOES MAG-EN MEAN BY THAT THREAT?!
"SEVERAL WEEKS LATER, AT JOR-EL'S ESTATE..."
MAG-EN IS OFFERING BABY KAL-EL A ROBOT-TOY! HE'S UP TO NO GOOD! I'D BETTER INVESTIGATE!
10

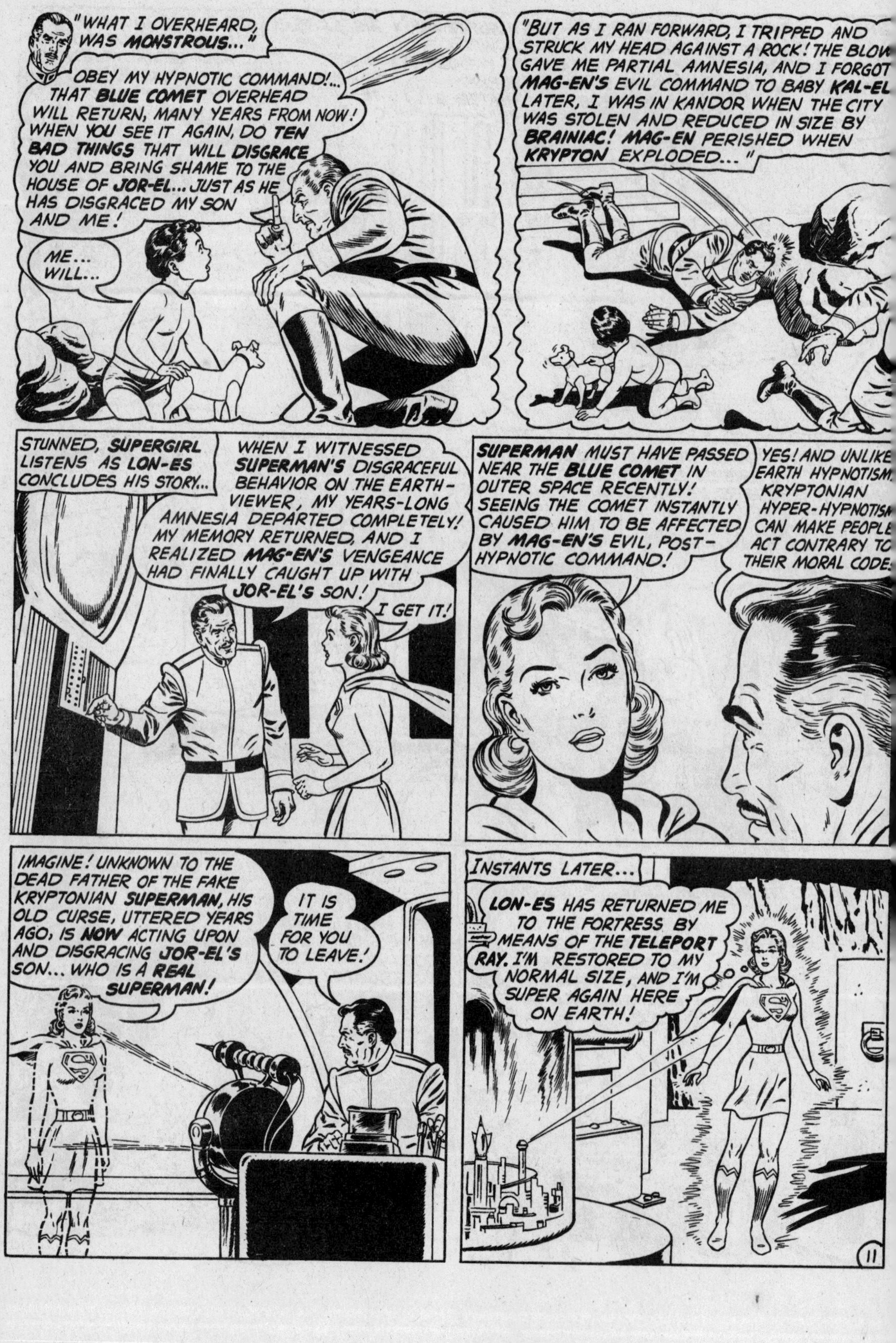
"WHAT I OVERHEARD, WAS MONSTROUS..."
OBEY MY HYPNOTIC COMMAND!... THAT BLUE COMET OVERHEAD WILL RETURN, MANY YEARS FROM NOW! WHEN YOU SEE IT AGAIN, DO TEN BAD THINGS THAT WILL DISGRACE YOU AND BRING SHAME TO THE HOUSE OF JOR-EL... JUST AS HE HAS DISGRACED MY SON AND ME!
ME... WILL...
"BUT AS I RAN FORWARD, I TRIPPED AND STRUCK MY HEAD AGAINST A ROCK! THE BLOW GAVE ME PARTIAL AMNESIA, AND I FORGOT MAG-EN'S EVIL COMMAND TO BABY KAL-EL. LATER, I WAS IN KANDOR WHEN THE CITY WAS STOLEN AND REDUCED IN SIZE BY BRAINIAC! MAG-EN PERISHED WHEN KRYPTON EXPLODED..."
STUNNED, SUPERGIRL LISTENS AS LON-ES CONCLUDES HIS STORY...
WHEN I WITNESSED SUPERMAN'S DISGRACEFUL BEHAVIOR ON THE EARTH-VIEWER, MY YEARS-LONG AMNESIA DEPARTED COMPLETELY! MY MEMORY RETURNED, AND I REALIZED MAG-EN'S VENGEANCE HAD FINALLY CAUGHT UP WITH JOR-EL'S SON!
I GET IT!
SUPERMAN MUST HAVE PASSED NEAR THE BLUE COMET IN OUTER SPACE RECENTLY! SEEING THE COMET INSTANTLY CAUSED HIM TO BE AFFECTED BY MAG-EN'S EVIL, POST-HYPNOTIC COMMAND!
YES! AND UNLIKE EARTH HYPNOTISM, KRYPTONIAN HYPER-HYPNOTISM CAN MAKE PEOPLE ACT CONTRARY TO THEIR MORAL CODES
IMAGINE! UNKNOWN TO THE DEAD FATHER OF THE FAKE KRYPTONIAN SUPERMAN, HIS OLD CURSE, UTTERED YEARS AGO, IS NOW ACTING UPON AND DISGRACING JOR-EL'S SON... WHO IS A REAL SUPERMAN!
IT IS TIME FOR YOU TO LEAVE!
INSTANTS LATER...
LON-ES HAS RETURNED ME TO THE FORTRESS BY MEANS OF THE TELEPORT RAY. I'M RESTORED TO MY NORMAL SIZE, AND I'M SUPER AGAIN HERE ON EARTH!
11

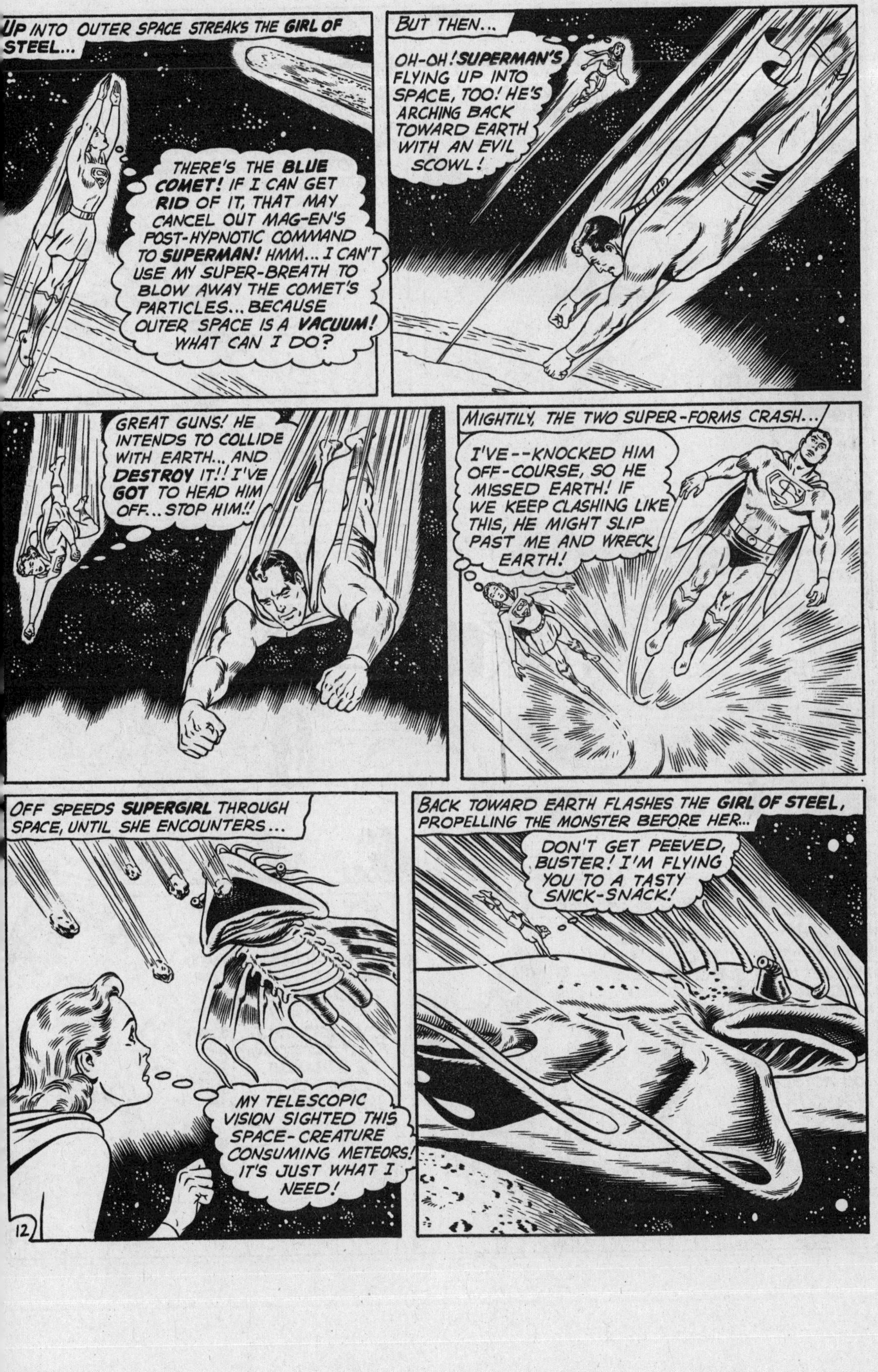
UP INTO OUTER SPACE STREAKS THE GIRL OF STEEL...
THERE'S THE BLUE COMET! IF I CAN GET RID OF IT, THAT MAY CANCEL OUT MAG-EN'S POST-HYPNOTIC COMMAND TO SUPERMAN! HMM... I CAN'T USE MY SUPER-BREATH TO BLOW AWAY THE COMET'S PARTICLES... BECAUSE OUTER SPACE IS A VACUUM! WHAT CAN I DO?
BUT THEN...
OH-OH! SUPERMAN'S FLYING UP INTO SPACE, TOO! HE'S ARCHING BACK TOWARD EARTH WITH AN EVIL SCOWL!
GREAT GUNS! HE INTENDS TO COLLIDE WITH EARTH... AND DESTROY IT!! I'VE GOT TO HEAD HIM OFF... STOP HIM!!
MIGHTILY, THE TWO SUPER-FORMS CRASH...
I'VE--KNOCKED HIM OFF-COURSE, SO HE MISSED EARTH! IF WE KEEP CLASHING LIKE THIS, HE MIGHT SLIP PAST ME AND WRECK EARTH!
OFF SPEEDS SUPERGIRL THROUGH SPACE, UNTIL SHE ENCOUNTERS...
MY TELESCOPIC VISION SIGHTED THIS SPACE-CREATURE CONSUMING METEORS! IT'S JUST WHAT I NEED!
12
BACK TOWARD EARTH FLASHES THE GIRL OF STEEL, PROPELLING THE MONSTER BEFORE HER...
DON'T GET PEEVED, BUSTER! I'M FLYING YOU TO A TASTY SNICK-SNACK!

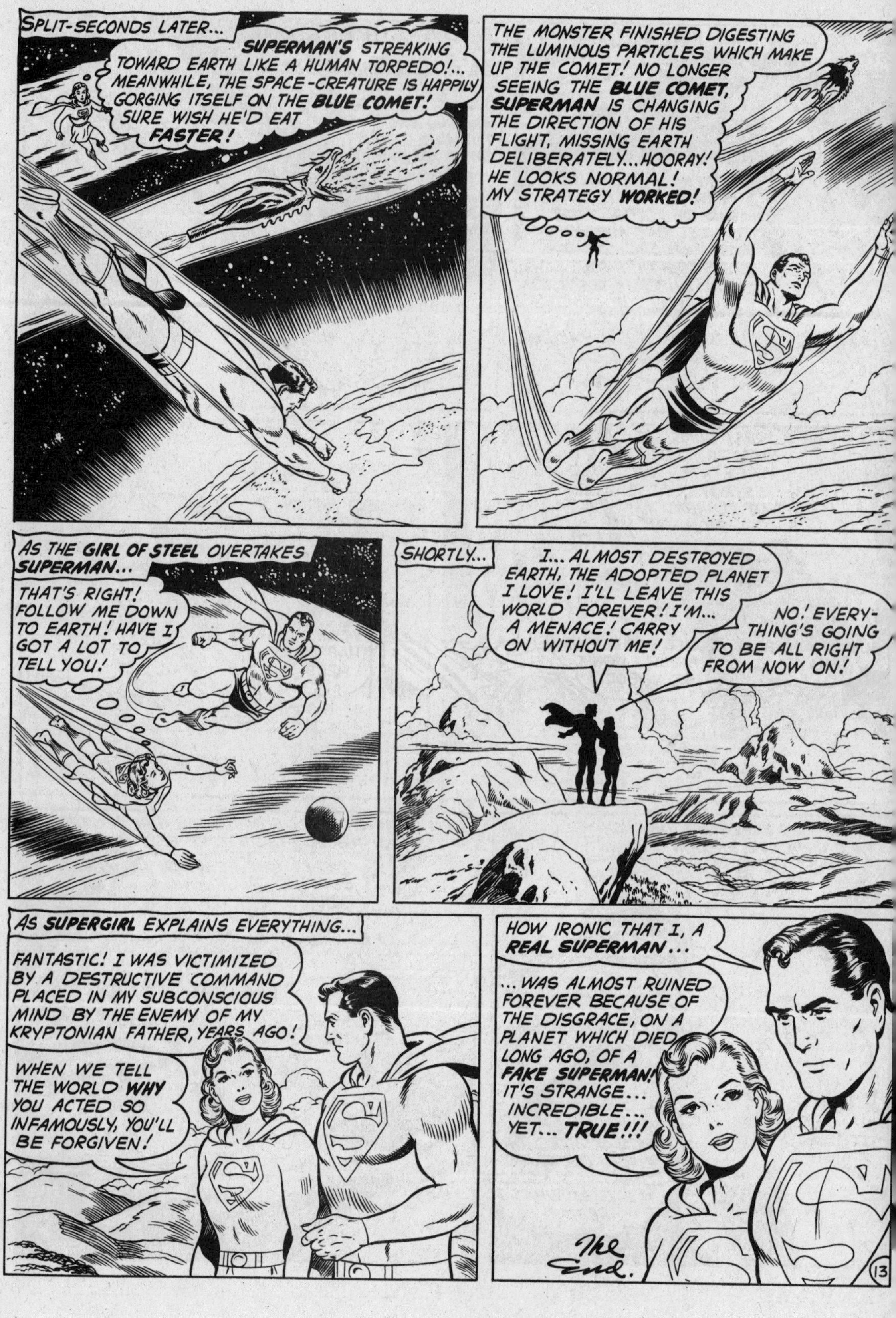
SPLIT-SECONDS LATER...
SUPERMAN'S STREAKING TOWARD EARTH LIKE A HUMAN TORPEDO!... MEANWHILE, THE SPACE-CREATURE IS HAPPILY GORGING ITSELF ON THE BLUE COMET! SURE WISH HE'D EAT FASTER!
THE MONSTER FINISHED DIGESTING THE LUMINOUS PARTICLES WHICH MAKE UP THE COMET! NO LONGER SEEING THE BLUE COMET, SUPERMAN IS CHANGING THE DIRECTION OF HIS FLIGHT, MISSING EARTH DELIBERATELY...HOORAY! HE LOOKS NORMAL! MY STRATEGY WORKED!
AS THE GIRL OF STEEL OVERTAKES SUPERMAN...
THAT'S RIGHT! FOLLOW ME DOWN TO EARTH! HAVE I GOT A LOT TO TELL YOU!
SHORTLY...
I... ALMOST DESTROYED EARTH, THE ADOPTED PLANET I LOVE! I'LL LEAVE THIS WORLD FOREVER! I'M... A MENACE! CARRY ON WITHOUT ME!
NO! EVERYTHING'S GOING TO BE ALL RIGHT FROM NOW ON!
AS SUPERGIRL EXPLAINS EVERYTHING...
FANTASTIC! I WAS VICTIMIZED BY A DESTRUCTIVE COMMAND PLACED IN MY SUBCONSCIOUS MIND BY THE ENEMY OF MY KRYPTONIAN FATHER, YEARS AGO!
WHEN WE TELL THE WORLD WHY YOU ACTED SO INFAMOUSLY, YOU'LL BE FORGIVEN!
HOW IRONIC THAT I, A REAL SUPERMAN...
...WAS ALMOST RUINED FOREVER BECAUSE OF THE DISGRACE, ON A PLANET WHICH DIED LONG AGO, OF A FAKE SUPERMAN! IT'S STRANGE... INCREDIBLE... YET... TRUE!!!
The End.
13

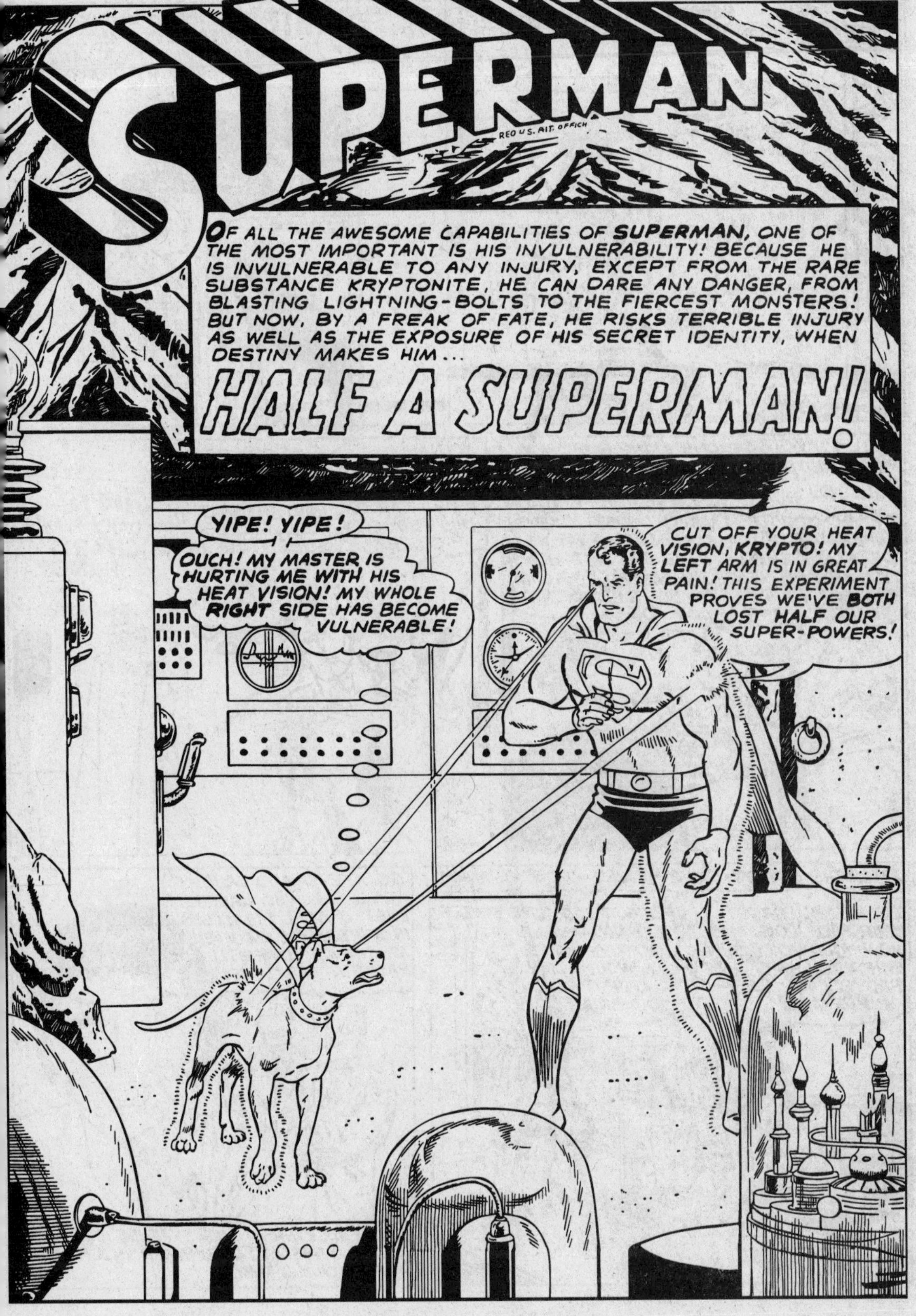
SUPERMAN
REG U.S. PAT. OFFICE
OF ALL THE AWESOME CAPABILITIES OF SUPERMAN, ONE OF THE MOST IMPORTANT IS HIS INVULNERABILITY! BECAUSE HE IS INVULNERABLE TO ANY INJURY, EXCEPT FROM THE RARE SUBSTANCE KRYPTONITE, HE CAN DARE ANY DANGER, FROM BLASTING LIGHTNING-BOLTS TO THE FIERCEST MONSTERS! BUT NOW, BY A FREAK OF FATE, HE RISKS TERRIBLE INJURY AS WELL AS THE EXPOSURE OF HIS SECRET IDENTITY, WHEN DESTINY MAKES HIM...
HALF A SUPERMAN!
YIPE! YIPE!
OUCH! MY MASTER IS HURTING ME WITH HIS HEAT VISION! MY WHOLE RIGHT SIDE HAS BECOME VULNERABLE!
CUT OFF YOUR HEAT VISION, KRYPTO! MY LEFT ARM IS IN GREAT PAIN! THIS EXPERIMENT PROVES WE'VE BOTH LOST HALF OUR SUPER-POWERS!

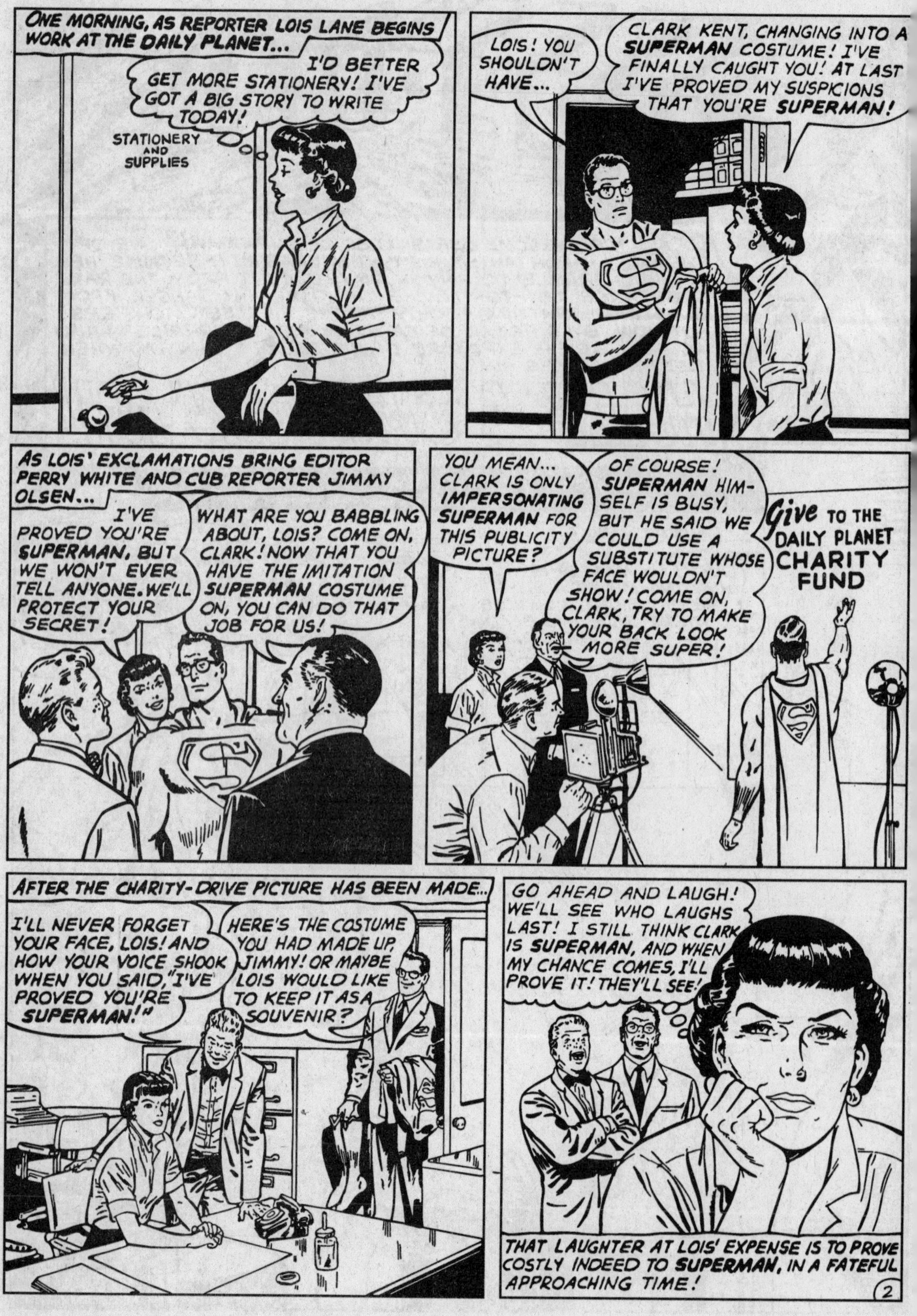
ONE MORNING, AS REPORTER LOIS LANE BEGINS WORK AT THE DAILY PLANET...
I'D BETTER GET MORE STATIONERY! I'VE GOT A BIG STORY TO WRITE TODAY!
STATIONERY AND SUPPLIES
LOIS! YOU SHOULDN'T HAVE...
CLARK KENT, CHANGING INTO A SUPERMAN COSTUME! I'VE FINALLY CAUGHT YOU! AT LAST I'VE PROVED MY SUSPICIONS THAT YOU'RE SUPERMAN!
AS LOIS' EXCLAMATIONS BRING EDITOR PERRY WHITE AND CUB REPORTER JIMMY OLSEN...
I'VE PROVED YOU'RE SUPERMAN, BUT WE WON'T EVER TELL ANYONE. WE'LL PROTECT YOUR SECRET!
WHAT ARE YOU BABBLING ABOUT, LOIS? COME ON, CLARK! NOW THAT YOU HAVE THE IMITATION SUPERMAN COSTUME ON, YOU CAN DO THAT JOB FOR US!
YOU MEAN... CLARK IS ONLY IMPERSONATING SUPERMAN FOR THIS PUBLICITY PICTURE?
OF COURSE! SUPERMAN HIMSELF IS BUSY, BUT HE SAID WE COULD USE A SUBSTITUTE WHOSE FACE WOULDN'T SHOW! COME ON, CLARK, TRY TO MAKE YOUR BACK LOOK MORE SUPER!
Give TO THE DAILY PLANET CHARITY FUND
AFTER THE CHARITY-DRIVE PICTURE HAS BEEN MADE...
I'LL NEVER FORGET YOUR FACE, LOIS! AND HOW YOUR VOICE SHOOK WHEN YOU SAID, "I'VE PROVED YOU'RE SUPERMAN!"
HERE'S THE COSTUME YOU HAD MADE UP, JIMMY! OR MAYBE LOIS WOULD LIKE TO KEEP IT AS A SOUVENIR?
GO AHEAD AND LAUGH! WE'LL SEE WHO LAUGHS LAST! I STILL THINK CLARK IS SUPERMAN, AND WHEN MY CHANCE COMES, I'LL PROVE IT! THEY'LL SEE!
THAT LAUGHTER AT LOIS' EXPENSE IS TO PROVE COSTLY INDEED TO SUPERMAN, IN A FATEFUL APPROACHING TIME!
2

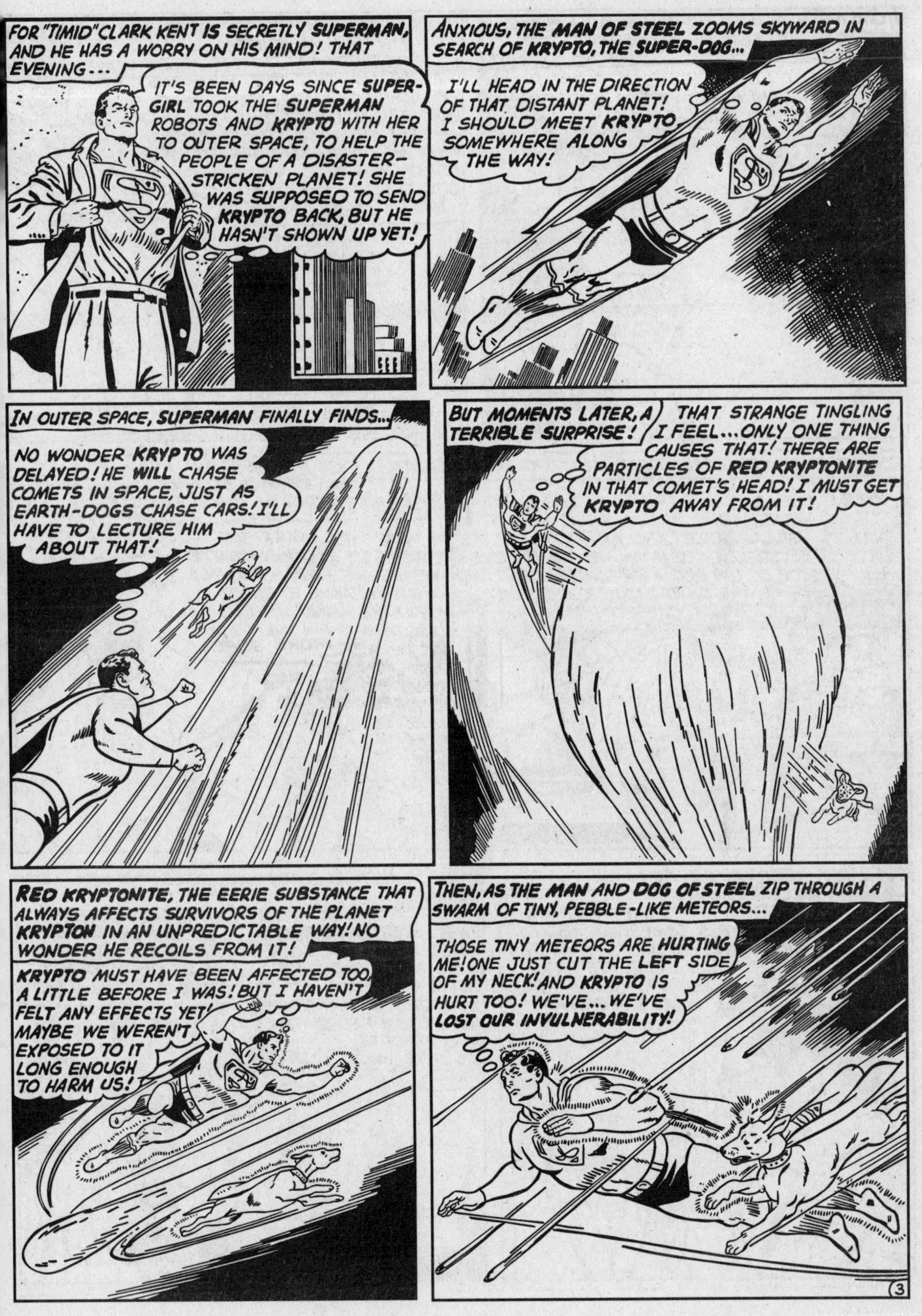
FOR "TIMID" CLARK KENT IS SECRETLY SUPERMAN, AND HE HAS A WORRY ON HIS MIND! THAT EVENING...
IT'S BEEN DAYS SINCE SUPERGIRL TOOK THE SUPERMAN ROBOTS AND KRYPTO WITH HER TO OUTER SPACE, TO HELP THE PEOPLE OF A DISASTER-STRICKEN PLANET! SHE WAS SUPPOSED TO SEND KRYPTO BACK, BUT HE HASN'T SHOWN UP YET!
ANXIOUS, THE MAN OF STEEL ZOOMS SKYWARD IN SEARCH OF KRYPTO, THE SUPER-DOG...
I'LL HEAD IN THE DIRECTION OF THAT DISTANT PLANET! I SHOULD MEET KRYPTO SOMEWHERE ALONG THE WAY!
IN OUTER SPACE, SUPERMAN FINALLY FINDS...
NO WONDER KRYPTO WAS DELAYED! HE WILL CHASE COMETS IN SPACE, JUST AS EARTH-DOGS CHASE CARS! I'LL HAVE TO LECTURE HIM ABOUT THAT!
BUT MOMENTS LATER, A TERRIBLE SURPRISE!
THAT STRANGE TINGLING I FEEL...ONLY ONE THING CAUSES THAT! THERE ARE PARTICLES OF RED KRYPTONITE IN THAT COMET'S HEAD! I MUST GET KRYPTO AWAY FROM IT!
RED KRYPTONITE, THE EERIE SUBSTANCE THAT ALWAYS AFFECTS SURVIVORS OF THE PLANET KRYPTON IN AN UNPREDICTABLE WAY! NO WONDER HE RECOILS FROM IT!
KRYPTO MUST HAVE BEEN AFFECTED TOO, A LITTLE BEFORE I WAS! BUT I HAVEN'T FELT ANY EFFECTS YET! MAYBE WE WEREN'T EXPOSED TO IT LONG ENOUGH TO HARM US!
THEN, AS THE MAN AND DOG OF STEEL ZIP THROUGH A SWARM OF TINY, PEBBLE-LIKE METEORS...
THOSE TINY METEORS ARE HURTING ME! ONE JUST CUT THE LEFT SIDE OF MY NECK! AND KRYPTO IS HURT TOO! WE'VE... WE'VE LOST OUR INVULNERABILITY!
3

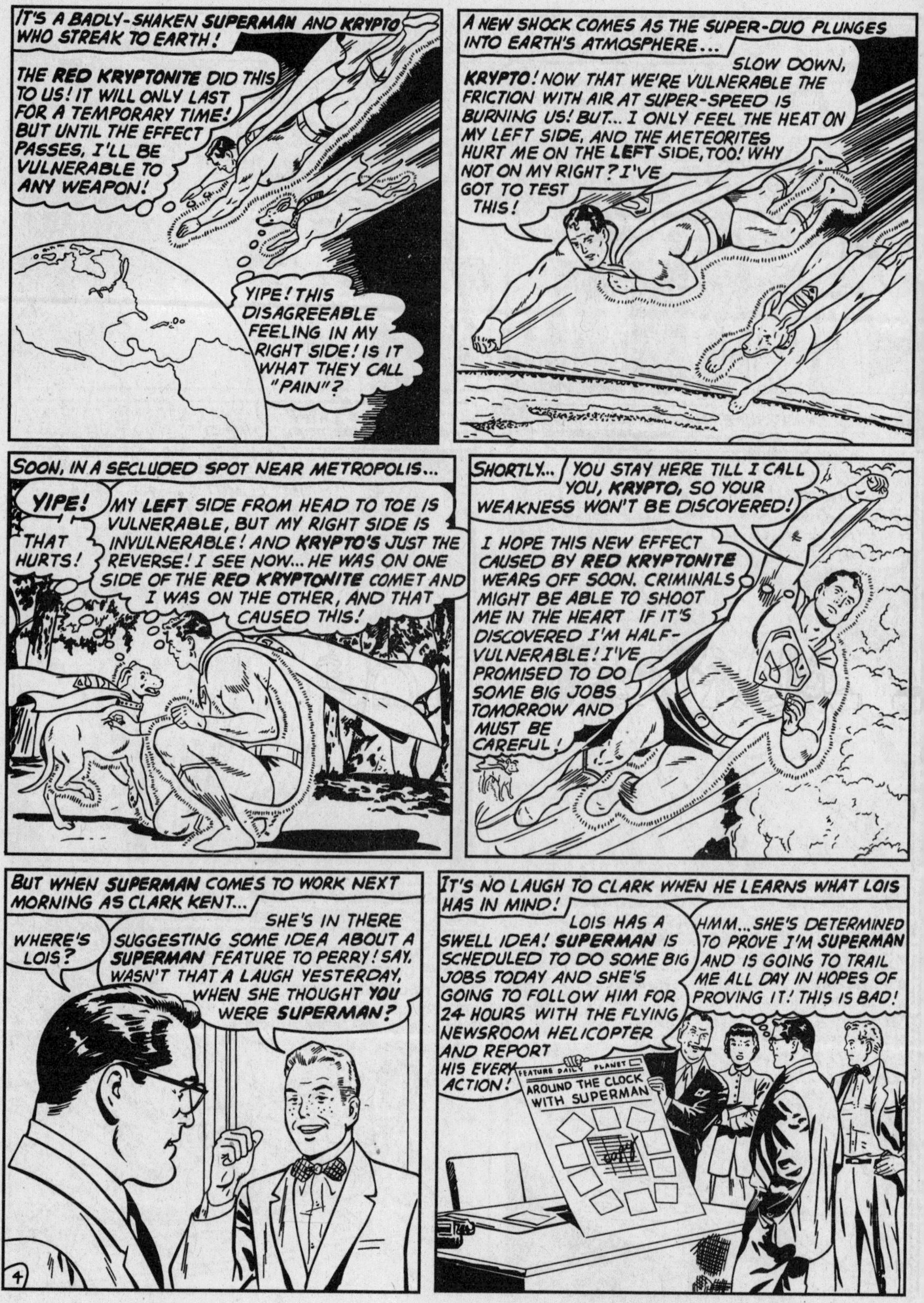
IT'S A BADLY-SHAKEN SUPERMAN AND KRYPTO WHO STREAK TO EARTH!
THE RED KRYPTONITE DID THIS TO US! IT WILL ONLY LAST FOR A TEMPORARY TIME! BUT UNTIL THE EFFECT PASSES, I'LL BE VULNERABLE TO ANY WEAPON!
YIPE! THIS DISAGREEABLE FEELING IN MY RIGHT SIDE! IS IT WHAT THEY CALL "PAIN"?
A NEW SHOCK COMES AS THE SUPER-DUO PLUNGES INTO EARTH'S ATMOSPHERE...
SLOW DOWN, KRYPTO! NOW THAT WE'RE VULNERABLE THE FRICTION WITH AIR AT SUPER-SPEED IS BURNING US! BUT... I ONLY FEEL THE HEAT ON MY LEFT SIDE, AND THE METEORITES HURT ME ON THE LEFT SIDE, TOO! WHY NOT ON MY RIGHT? I'VE GOT TO TEST THIS!
SOON, IN A SECLUDED SPOT NEAR METROPOLIS...
YIPE! THAT HURTS!
MY LEFT SIDE FROM HEAD TO TOE IS VULNERABLE, BUT MY RIGHT SIDE IS INVULNERABLE! AND KRYPTO'S JUST THE REVERSE! I SEE NOW... HE WAS ON ONE SIDE OF THE RED KRYPTONITE COMET AND I WAS ON THE OTHER, AND THAT CAUSED THIS!
SHORTLY...
YOU STAY HERE TILL I CALL YOU, KRYPTO, SO YOUR WEAKNESS WON'T BE DISCOVERED!
I HOPE THIS NEW EFFECT CAUSED BY RED KRYPTONITE WEARS OFF SOON. CRIMINALS MIGHT BE ABLE TO SHOOT ME IN THE HEART IF IT'S DISCOVERED I'M HALF-VULNERABLE! I'VE PROMISED TO DO SOME BIG JOBS TOMORROW AND MUST BE CAREFUL!
BUT WHEN SUPERMAN COMES TO WORK NEXT MORNING AS CLARK KENT...
WHERE'S LOIS?
SHE'S IN THERE SUGGESTING SOME IDEA ABOUT A SUPERMAN FEATURE TO PERRY! SAY. WASN'T THAT A LAUGH YESTERDAY, WHEN SHE THOUGHT YOU WERE SUPERMAN?
4
IT'S NO LAUGH TO CLARK WHEN HE LEARNS WHAT LOIS HAS IN MIND!
LOIS HAS A SWELL IDEA! SUPERMAN IS SCHEDULED TO DO SOME BIG JOBS TODAY AND SHE'S GOING TO FOLLOW HIM FOR 24 HOURS WITH THE FLYING NEWSROOM HELICOPTER AND REPORT HIS EVERY ACTION!
HMM... SHE'S DETERMINED TO PROVE I'M SUPERMAN AND IS GOING TO TRAIL ME ALL DAY IN HOPES OF PROVING IT! THIS IS BAD!
FEATURE DAILY PLANET
AROUND THE CLOCK WITH SUPERMAN

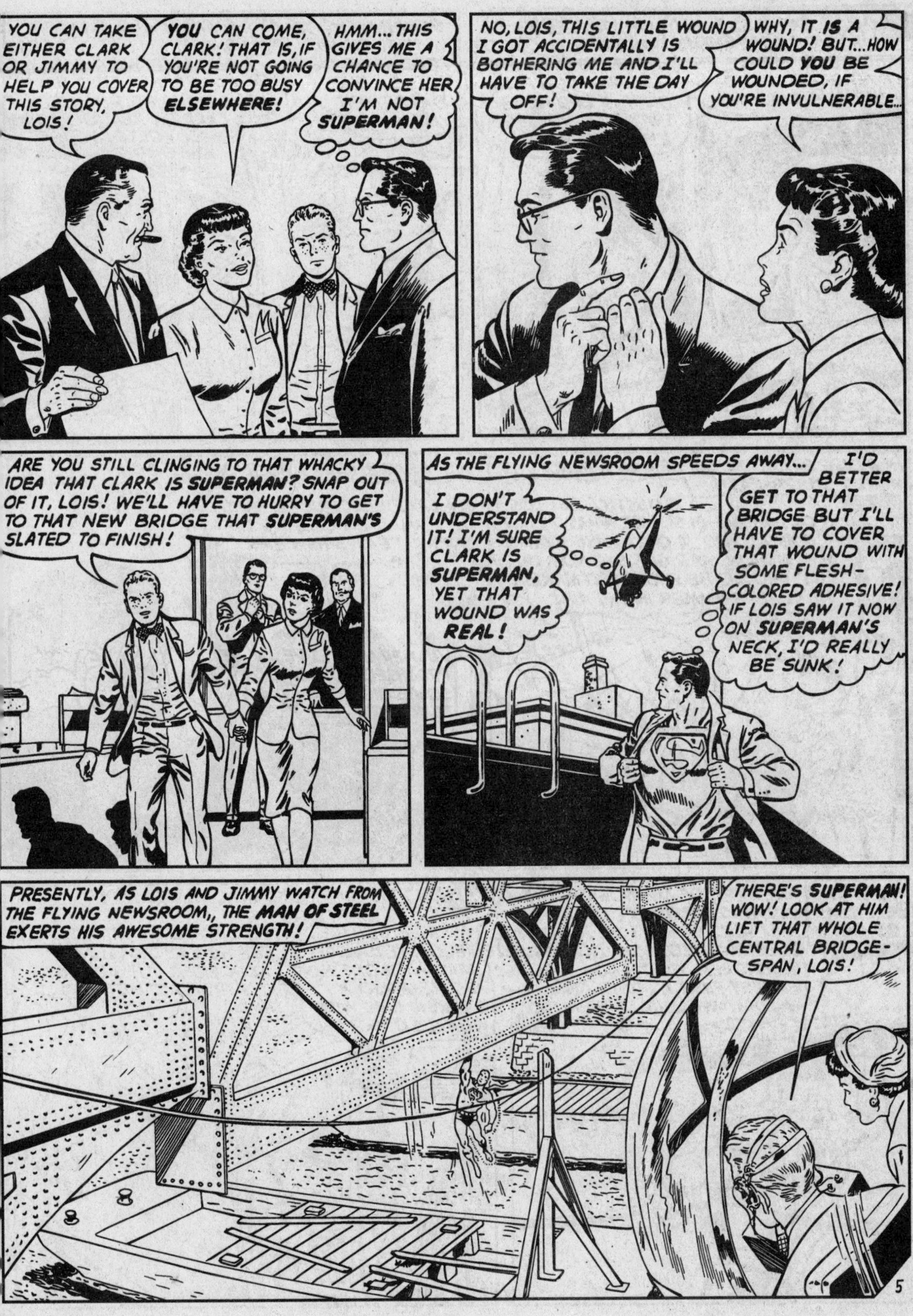
YOU CAN TAKE EITHER CLARK OR JIMMY TO HELP YOU COVER THIS STORY, LOIS!
YOU CAN COME, CLARK! THAT IS, IF YOU'RE NOT GOING TO BE TOO BUSY ELSEWHERE!
HMM... THIS GIVES ME A CHANCE TO CONVINCE HER I'M NOT SUPERMAN!
NO, LOIS, THIS LITTLE WOUND I GOT ACCIDENTALLY IS BOTHERING ME AND I'LL HAVE TO TAKE THE DAY OFF!
WHY, IT IS A WOUND! BUT...HOW COULD YOU BE WOUNDED, IF YOU'RE INVULNERABLE...
ARE YOU STILL CLINGING TO THAT WHACKY IDEA THAT CLARK IS SUPERMAN? SNAP OUT OF IT, LOIS! WE'LL HAVE TO HURRY TO GET TO THAT NEW BRIDGE THAT SUPERMAN'S SLATED TO FINISH!
AS THE FLYING NEWSROOM SPEEDS AWAY...
I DON'T UNDERSTAND IT! I'M SURE CLARK IS SUPERMAN, YET THAT WOUND WAS REAL!
I'D BETTER GET TO THAT BRIDGE BUT I'LL HAVE TO COVER THAT WOUND WITH SOME FLESH-COLORED ADHESIVE! IF LOIS SAW IT NOW ON SUPERMAN'S NECK, I'D REALLY BE SUNK!
PRESENTLY, AS LOIS AND JIMMY WATCH FROM THE FLYING NEWSROOM, THE MAN OF STEEL EXERTS HIS AWESOME STRENGTH!
THERE'S SUPERMAN! WOW! LOOK AT HIM LIFT THAT WHOLE CENTRAL BRIDGE-SPAN, LOIS!
5

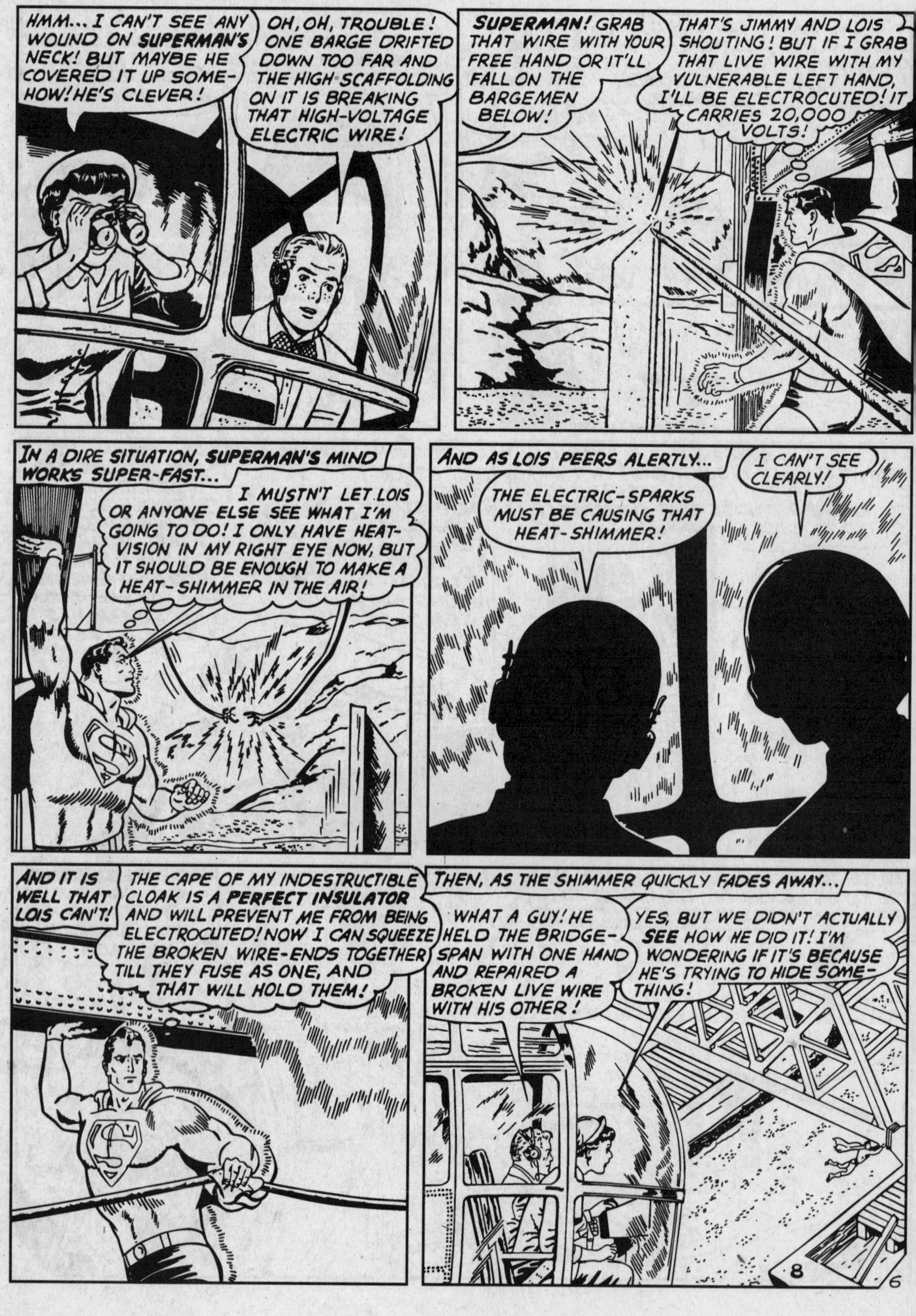
HMM... I CAN'T SEE ANY WOUND ON SUPERMAN'S NECK! BUT MAYBE HE COVERED IT UP SOME-HOW! HE'S CLEVER!
OH, OH, TROUBLE! ONE BARGE DRIFTED DOWN TOO FAR AND THE HIGH SCAFFOLDING ON IT IS BREAKING THAT HIGH-VOLTAGE ELECTRIC WIRE!
SUPERMAN! GRAB THAT WIRE WITH YOUR FREE HAND OR IT'LL FALL ON THE BARGEMEN BELOW!
THAT'S JIMMY AND LOIS SHOUTING! BUT IF I GRAB THAT LIVE WIRE WITH MY VULNERABLE LEFT HAND, I'LL BE ELECTROCUTED! IT CARRIES 20,000 VOLTS!
IN A DIRE SITUATION, SUPERMAN'S MIND WORKS SUPER-FAST...
I MUSTN'T LET LOIS OR ANYONE ELSE SEE WHAT I'M GOING TO DO! I ONLY HAVE HEAT-VISION IN MY RIGHT EYE NOW, BUT IT SHOULD BE ENOUGH TO MAKE A HEAT-SHIMMER IN THE AIR!
AND AS LOIS PEERS ALERTLY...
THE ELECTRIC-SPARKS MUST BE CAUSING THAT HEAT-SHIMMER!
I CAN'T SEE CLEARLY!
AND IT IS WELL THAT LOIS CAN'T!
THE CAPE OF MY INDESTRUCTIBLE CLOAK IS A PERFECT INSULATOR AND WILL PREVENT ME FROM BEING ELECTROCUTED! NOW I CAN SQUEEZE THE BROKEN WIRE-ENDS TOGETHER TILL THEY FUSE AS ONE, AND THAT WILL HOLD THEM!
THEN, AS THE SHIMMER QUICKLY FADES AWAY...
WHAT A GUY! HE HELD THE BRIDGE-SPAN WITH ONE HAND AND REPAIRED A BROKEN LIVE WIRE WITH HIS OTHER!
YES, BUT WE DIDN'T ACTUALLY SEE HOW HE DID IT! I'M WONDERING IF IT'S BECAUSE HE'S TRYING TO HIDE SOME-THING!
8
6

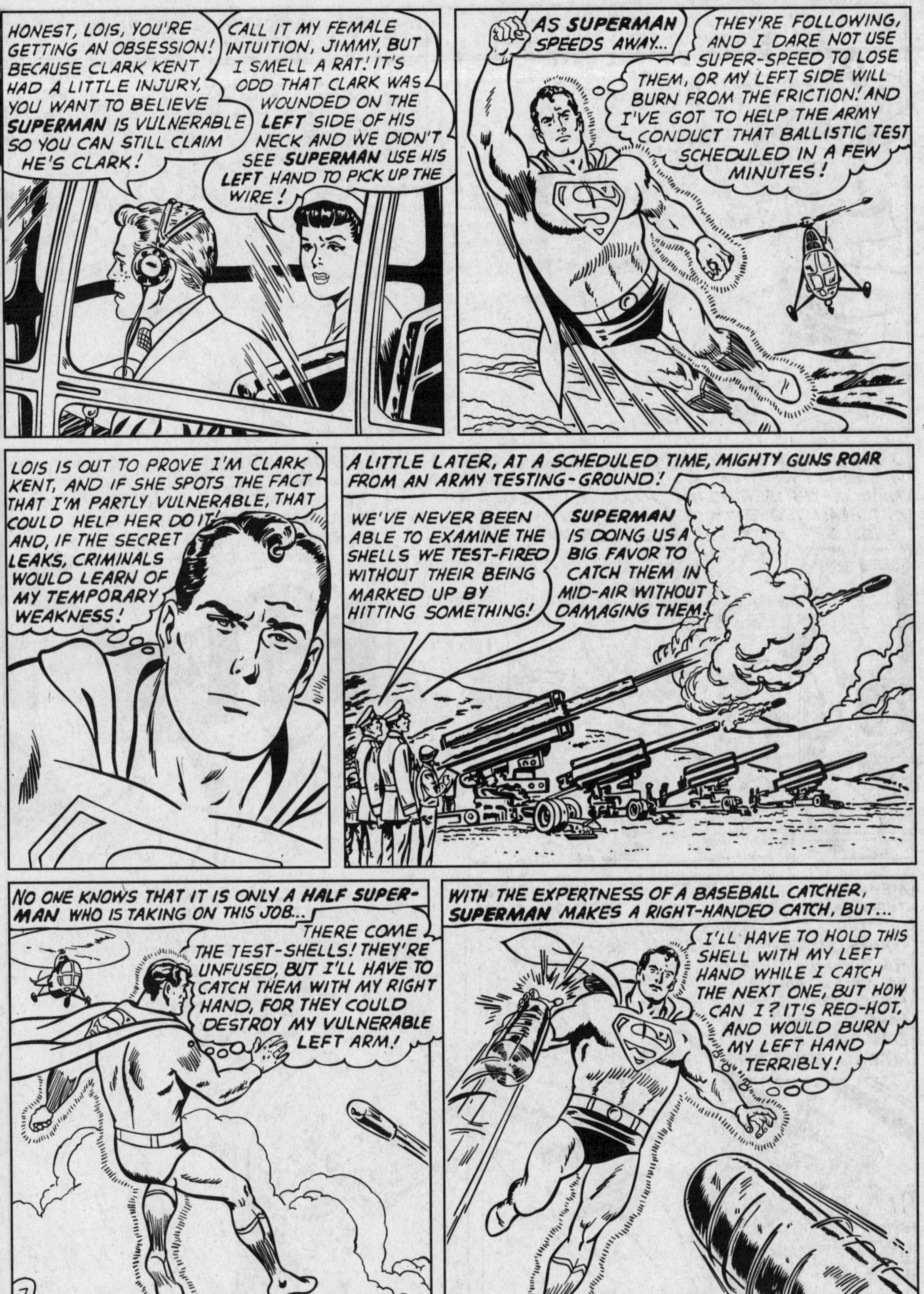
HONEST, LOIS, YOU'RE GETTING AN OBSESSION! BECAUSE CLARK KENT HAD A LITTLE INJURY, YOU WANT TO BELIEVE SUPERMAN IS VULNERABLE SO YOU CAN STILL CLAIM HE'S CLARK!
CALL IT MY FEMALE INTUITION, JIMMY, BUT I SMELL A RAT! IT'S ODD THAT CLARK WAS WOUNDED ON THE LEFT SIDE OF HIS NECK AND WE DIDN'T SEE SUPERMAN USE HIS LEFT HAND TO PICK UP THE WIRE!
AS SUPERMAN SPEEDS AWAY...
THEY'RE FOLLOWING, AND I DARE NOT USE SUPER-SPEED TO LOSE THEM, OR MY LEFT SIDE WILL BURN FROM THE FRICTION! AND I'VE GOT TO HELP THE ARMY CONDUCT THAT BALLISTIC TEST SCHEDULED IN A FEW MINUTES!
LOIS IS OUT TO PROVE I'M CLARK KENT, AND IF SHE SPOTS THE FACT THAT I'M PARTLY VULNERABLE, THAT COULD HELP HER DO IT! AND, IF THE SECRET LEAKS, CRIMINALS WOULD LEARN OF MY TEMPORARY WEAKNESS!
A LITTLE LATER, AT A SCHEDULED TIME, MIGHTY GUNS ROAR FROM AN ARMY TESTING-GROUND!
WE'VE NEVER BEEN ABLE TO EXAMINE THE SHELLS WE TEST-FIRED WITHOUT THEIR BEING MARKED UP BY HITTING SOMETHING!
SUPERMAN IS DOING US A BIG FAVOR TO CATCH THEM IN MID-AIR WITHOUT DAMAGING THEM!
NO ONE KNOWS THAT IT IS ONLY A HALF SUPERMAN WHO IS TAKING ON THIS JOB...
THERE COME THE TEST-SHELLS! THEY'RE UNFUSED, BUT I'LL HAVE TO CATCH THEM WITH MY RIGHT HAND, FOR THEY COULD DESTROY MY VULNERABLE LEFT ARM!
7
WITH THE EXPERTNESS OF A BASEBALL CATCHER, SUPERMAN MAKES A RIGHT-HANDED CATCH, BUT...
I'LL HAVE TO HOLD THIS SHELL WITH MY LEFT HAND WHILE I CATCH THE NEXT ONE, BUT HOW CAN I? IT'S RED-HOT, AND WOULD BURN MY LEFT HAND TERRIBLY!

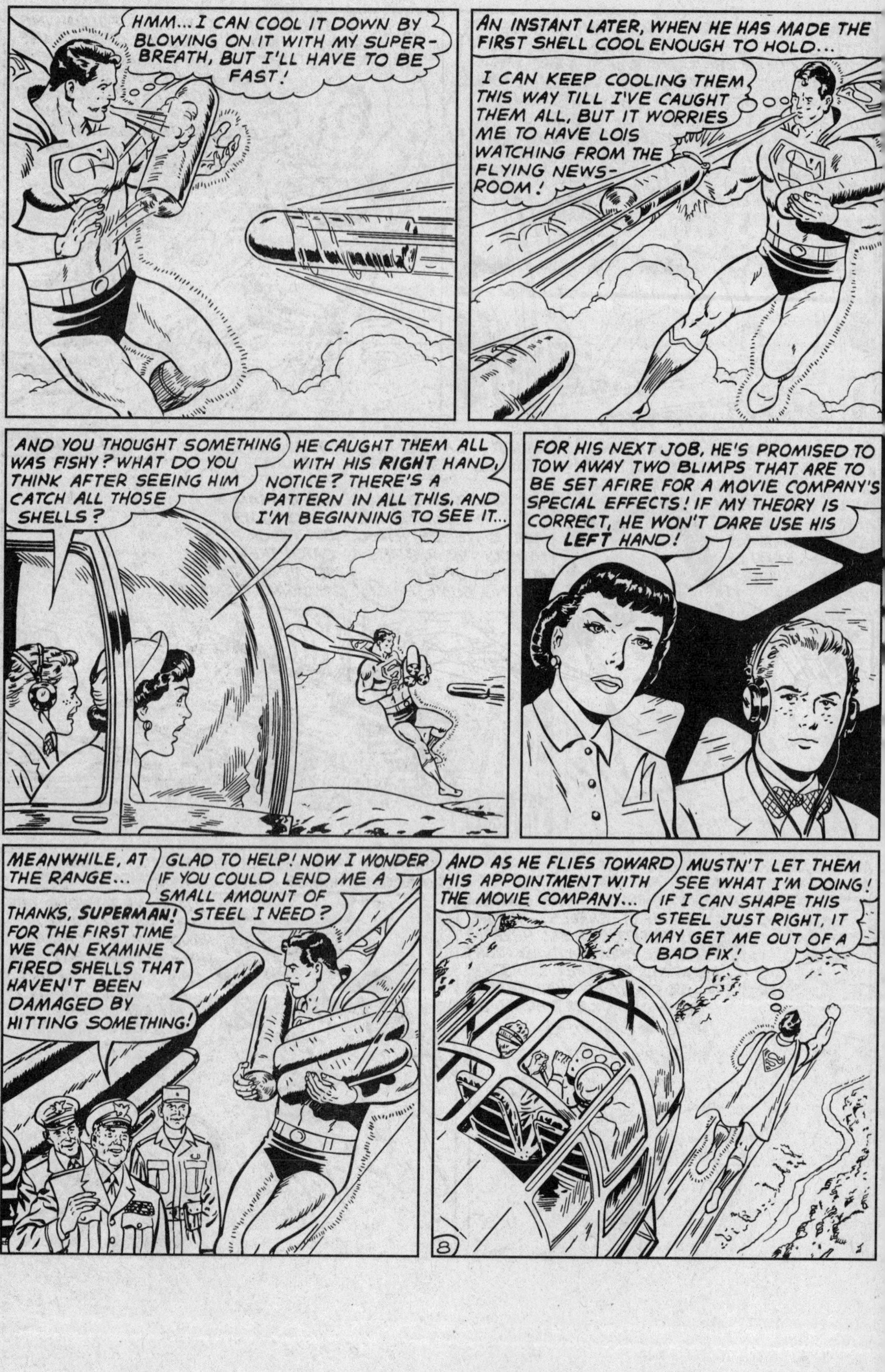
HMM... I CAN COOL IT DOWN BY BLOWING ON IT WITH MY SUPER-BREATH, BUT I'LL HAVE TO BE FAST!
AN INSTANT LATER, WHEN HE HAS MADE THE FIRST SHELL COOL ENOUGH TO HOLD...
I CAN KEEP COOLING THEM THIS WAY TILL I'VE CAUGHT THEM ALL, BUT IT WORRIES ME TO HAVE LOIS WATCHING FROM THE FLYING NEWS-ROOM!
AND YOU THOUGHT SOMETHING WAS FISHY? WHAT DO YOU THINK AFTER SEEING HIM CATCH ALL THOSE SHELLS?
HE CAUGHT THEM ALL WITH HIS RIGHT HAND, NOTICE? THERE'S A PATTERN IN ALL THIS, AND I'M BEGINNING TO SEE IT...
FOR HIS NEXT JOB, HE'S PROMISED TO TOW AWAY TWO BLIMPS THAT ARE TO BE SET AFIRE FOR A MOVIE COMPANY'S SPECIAL EFFECTS! IF MY THEORY IS CORRECT, HE WON'T DARE USE HIS LEFT HAND!
MEANWHILE, AT THE RANGE...
THANKS, SUPERMAN! FOR THE FIRST TIME WE CAN EXAMINE FIRED SHELLS THAT HAVEN'T BEEN DAMAGED BY HITTING SOMETHING!
GLAD TO HELP! NOW I WONDER IF YOU COULD LEND ME A SMALL AMOUNT OF STEEL I NEED?
AND AS HE FLIES TOWARD HIS APPOINTMENT WITH THE MOVIE COMPANY...
MUSTN'T LET THEM SEE WHAT I'M DOING! IF I CAN SHAPE THIS STEEL JUST RIGHT, IT MAY GET ME OUT OF A BAD FIX!
8

PRESENTLY, AT A MOVIE LOCATION...

THERE COMES *SUPERMAN* NOW, SO IT'LL BE SAFE TO PULL THIS STUNT! GET THE BLIMPS UP AND YOU ACTORS WHO ARE PLAYING THE PARTS OF THE FIGHTER-PILOTS, ATTACK THEM! CAMERAS, BE READY TO ROLL!

ATIONAL PRODUCTION

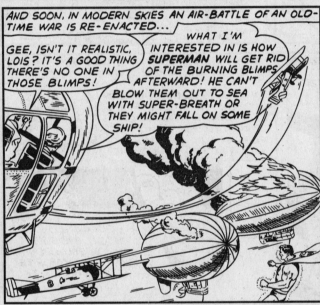

AND SOON, IN MODERN SKIES AN AIR-BATTLE OF AN OLD-TIME WAR IS RE-ENACTED...

GEE, ISN'T IT REALISTIC, LOIS? IT'S A GOOD THING THERE'S NO ONE IN THOSE BLIMPS!

WHAT I'M INTERESTED IN IS HOW *SUPERMAN* WILL GET RID OF THE BURNING BLIMPS AFTERWARD! HE CAN'T BLOW THEM OUT TO SEA WITH SUPER-BREATH OR THEY MIGHT FALL ON SOME SHIP!

BUT TO LOIS' SURPRISE, WHEN THE SCENE IS FINISHED...

SEE HOW EASILY HE DOES IT, LOIS!

THIS STEEL EXTENSION-ARM WITH A CLAW "HAND" I SHAPED FOR MY LEFT SLEEVE WORKS FINE! I CAN KEEP MY REAL LEFT ARM INSIDE MY COSTUME AND IT LOOKS AS THOUGH I'M TOWING THE BURNING BLIMP WITH IT!

AFTER *SUPERMAN* HAS TOWED THE BLIMPS TO A SAFE AREA AND HAS BEATEN OUT THE FLAMES...

BUT YOU SAW THE FIRE UNABLE TO BURN HIS LEFT HAND, LOIS! WHY SHOULD YOU WANT TO EXAMINE THE WRECKAGE NOW?

I JUST DO! LAND FOR A FEW MOMENTS NEARBY!

9

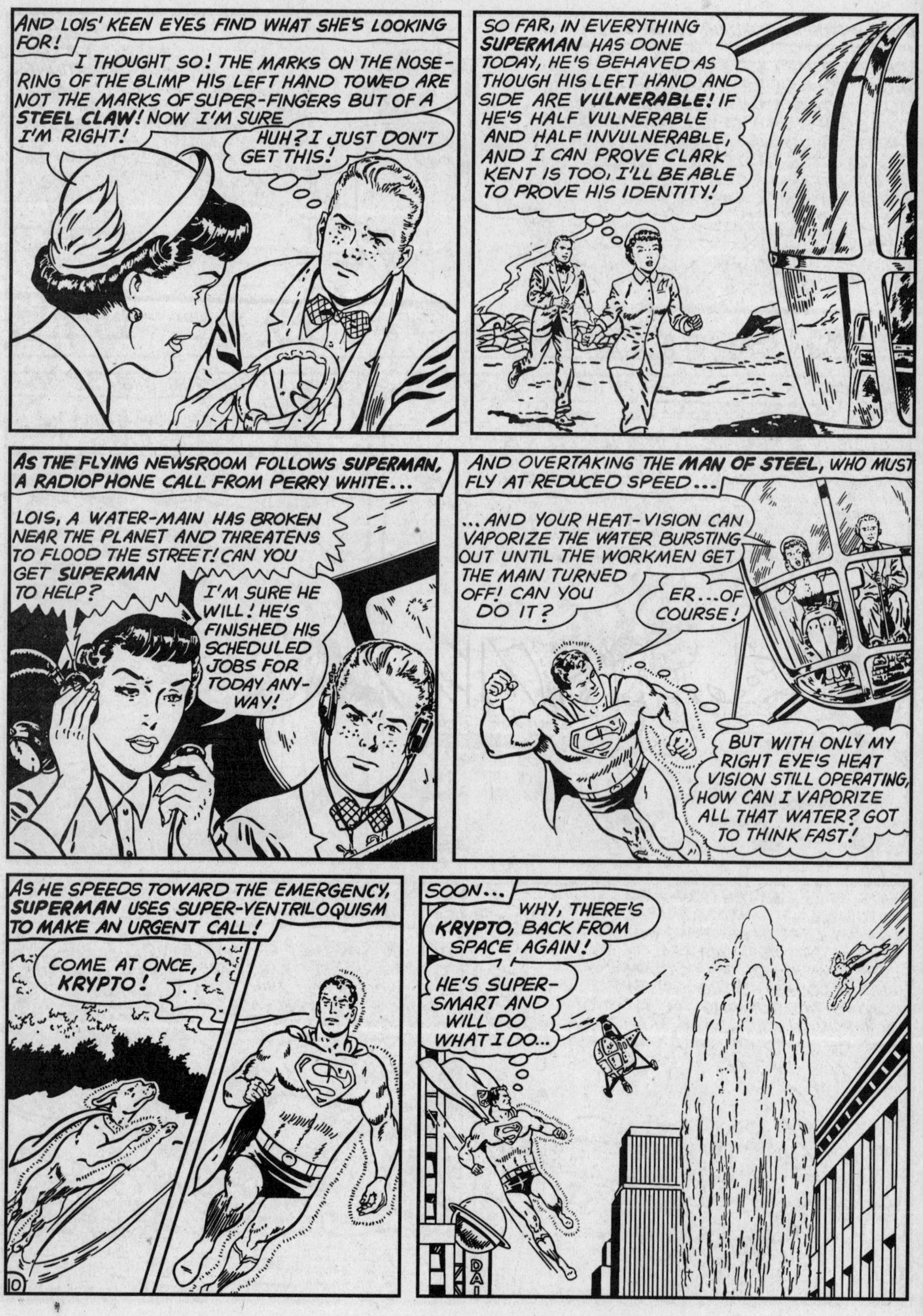
AND LOIS' KEEN EYES FIND WHAT SHE'S LOOKING FOR!
I THOUGHT SO! THE MARKS ON THE NOSE-RING OF THE BLIMP HIS LEFT HAND TOWED ARE NOT THE MARKS OF SUPER-FINGERS BUT OF A STEEL CLAW! NOW I'M SURE I'M RIGHT!
HUH? I JUST DON'T GET THIS!
SO FAR, IN EVERYTHING SUPERMAN HAS DONE TODAY, HE'S BEHAVED AS THOUGH HIS LEFT HAND AND SIDE ARE VULNERABLE! IF HE'S HALF VULNERABLE AND HALF INVULNERABLE, AND I CAN PROVE CLARK KENT IS TOO, I'LL BE ABLE TO PROVE HIS IDENTITY!
AS THE FLYING NEWSROOM FOLLOWS SUPERMAN, A RADIOPHONE CALL FROM PERRY WHITE...
LOIS, A WATER-MAIN HAS BROKEN NEAR THE PLANET AND THREATENS TO FLOOD THE STREET! CAN YOU GET SUPERMAN TO HELP?
I'M SURE HE WILL! HE'S FINISHED HIS SCHEDULED JOBS FOR TODAY ANYWAY!
AND OVERTAKING THE MAN OF STEEL, WHO MUST FLY AT REDUCED SPEED...
...AND YOUR HEAT-VISION CAN VAPORIZE THE WATER BURSTING OUT UNTIL THE WORKMEN GET THE MAIN TURNED OFF! CAN YOU DO IT?
ER...OF COURSE!
BUT WITH ONLY MY RIGHT EYE'S HEAT VISION STILL OPERATING, HOW CAN I VAPORIZE ALL THAT WATER? GOT TO THINK FAST!
AS HE SPEEDS TOWARD THE EMERGENCY, SUPERMAN USES SUPER-VENTRILOQUISM TO MAKE AN URGENT CALL!
COME AT ONCE, KRYPTO!
10
SOON...
WHY, THERE'S KRYPTO, BACK FROM SPACE AGAIN!
HE'S SUPER-SMART AND WILL DO WHAT I DO...
DAI

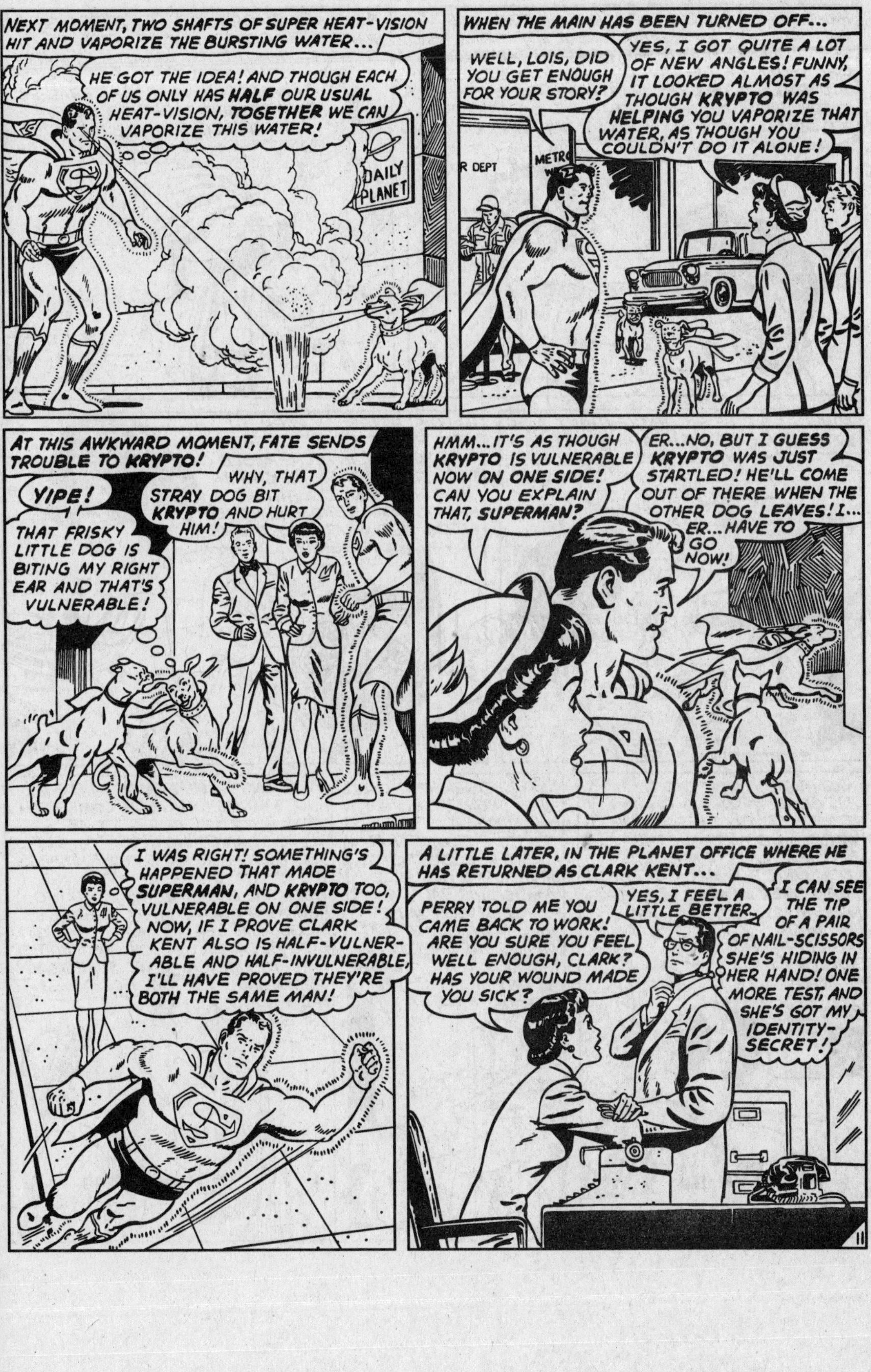
NEXT MOMENT, TWO SHAFTS OF SUPER HEAT-VISION HIT AND VAPORIZE THE BURSTING WATER...
HE GOT THE IDEA! AND THOUGH EACH OF US ONLY HAS HALF OUR USUAL HEAT-VISION, TOGETHER WE CAN VAPORIZE THIS WATER!
DAILY PLANET
WHEN THE MAIN HAS BEEN TURNED OFF...
WELL, LOIS, DID YOU GET ENOUGH FOR YOUR STORY?
YES, I GOT QUITE A LOT OF NEW ANGLES! FUNNY, IT LOOKED ALMOST AS THOUGH KRYPTO WAS HELPING YOU VAPORIZE THAT WATER, AS THOUGH YOU COULDN'T DO IT ALONE!
AT THIS AWKWARD MOMENT, FATE SENDS TROUBLE TO KRYPTO!
YIPE!
THAT FRISKY LITTLE DOG IS BITING MY RIGHT EAR AND THAT'S VULNERABLE!
WHY, THAT STRAY DOG BIT KRYPTO AND HURT HIM!
HMM...IT'S AS THOUGH KRYPTO IS VULNERABLE NOW ON ONE SIDE! CAN YOU EXPLAIN THAT, SUPERMAN?
ER...NO, BUT I GUESS KRYPTO WAS JUST STARTLED! HE'LL COME OUT OF THERE WHEN THE OTHER DOG LEAVES! I... ER...HAVE TO GO NOW!
I WAS RIGHT! SOMETHING'S HAPPENED THAT MADE SUPERMAN, AND KRYPTO TOO, VULNERABLE ON ONE SIDE! NOW, IF I PROVE CLARK KENT ALSO IS HALF-VULNERABLE AND HALF-INVULNERABLE, I'LL HAVE PROVED THEY'RE BOTH THE SAME MAN!
A LITTLE LATER, IN THE PLANET OFFICE WHERE HE HAS RETURNED AS CLARK KENT...
PERRY TOLD ME YOU CAME BACK TO WORK! ARE YOU SURE YOU FEEL WELL ENOUGH, CLARK? HAS YOUR WOUND MADE YOU SICK?
YES, I FEEL A LITTLE BETTER...
I CAN SEE THE TIP OF A PAIR OF NAIL-SCISSORS SHE'S HIDING IN HER HAND! ONE MORE TEST, AND SHE'S GOT MY IDENTITY-SECRET!
11

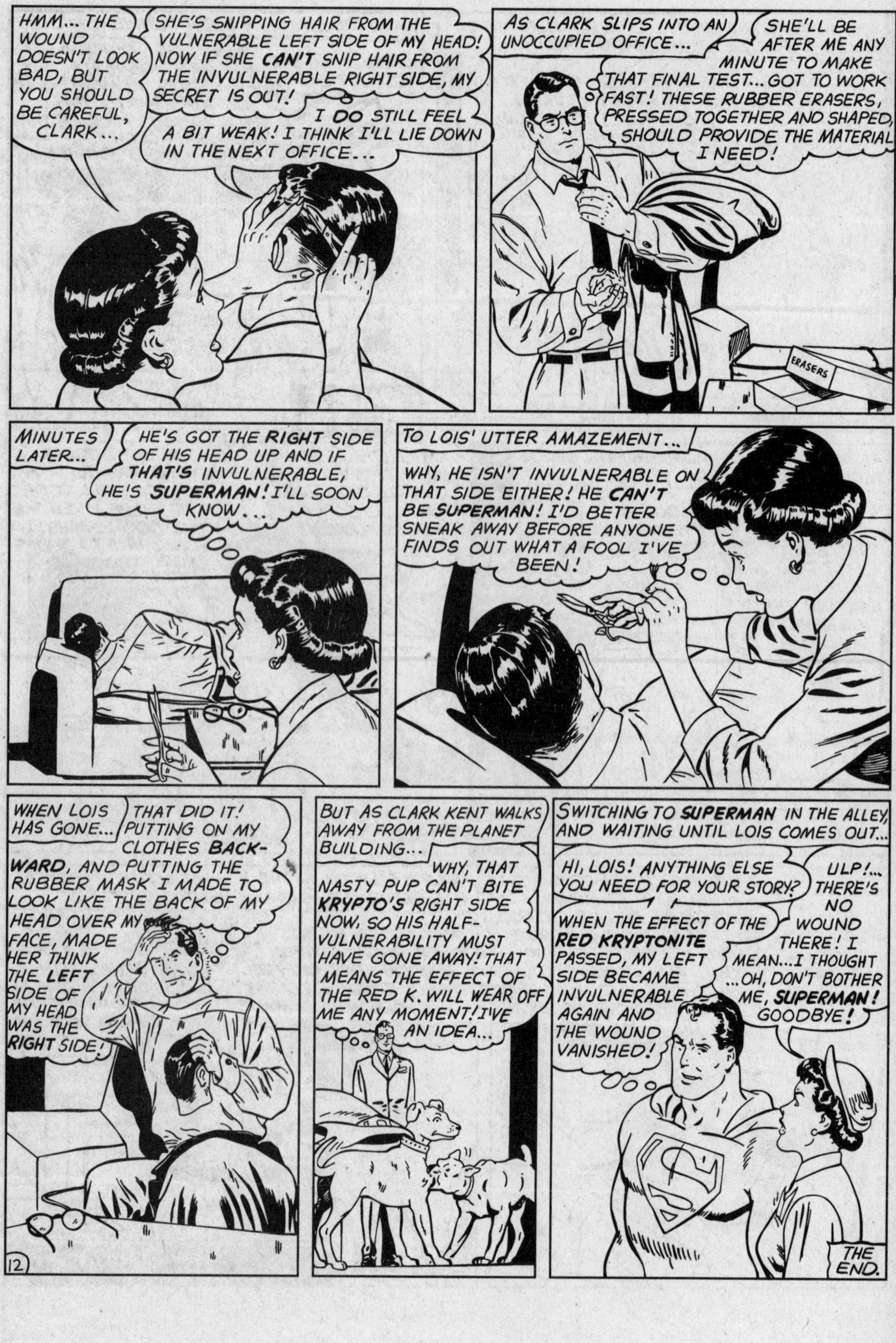

HMM... THE WOUND DOESN'T LOOK BAD, BUT YOU SHOULD BE CAREFUL, CLARK...
SHE'S SNIPPING HAIR FROM THE VULNERABLE LEFT SIDE OF MY HEAD! NOW IF SHE CAN'T SNIP HAIR FROM THE INVULNERABLE RIGHT SIDE, MY SECRET IS OUT!
I DO STILL FEEL A BIT WEAK! I THINK I'LL LIE DOWN IN THE NEXT OFFICE...
AS CLARK SLIPS INTO AN UNOCCUPIED OFFICE...
SHE'LL BE AFTER ME ANY MINUTE TO MAKE THAT FINAL TEST... GOT TO WORK FAST! THESE RUBBER ERASERS, PRESSED TOGETHER AND SHAPED, SHOULD PROVIDE THE MATERIAL I NEED!
ERASERS
MINUTES LATER...
HE'S GOT THE RIGHT SIDE OF HIS HEAD UP AND IF THAT'S INVULNERABLE, HE'S SUPERMAN! I'LL SOON KNOW...
TO LOIS' UTTER AMAZEMENT...
WHY, HE ISN'T INVULNERABLE ON THAT SIDE EITHER! HE CAN'T BE SUPERMAN! I'D BETTER SNEAK AWAY BEFORE ANYONE FINDS OUT WHAT A FOOL I'VE BEEN!
WHEN LOIS HAS GONE...
THAT DID IT! PUTTING ON MY CLOTHES BACKWARD, AND PUTTING THE RUBBER MASK I MADE TO LOOK LIKE THE BACK OF MY HEAD OVER MY FACE, MADE HER THINK THE LEFT SIDE OF MY HEAD WAS THE RIGHT SIDE!
12
BUT AS CLARK KENT WALKS AWAY FROM THE PLANET BUILDING...
WHY, THAT NASTY PUP CAN'T BITE KRYPTO'S RIGHT SIDE NOW, SO HIS HALF-VULNERABILITY MUST HAVE GONE AWAY! THAT MEANS THE EFFECT OF THE RED K. WILL WEAR OFF ME ANY MOMENT! I'VE AN IDEA...
SWITCHING TO SUPERMAN IN THE ALLEY, AND WAITING UNTIL LOIS COMES OUT...
HI, LOIS! ANYTHING ELSE YOU NEED FOR YOUR STORY?
ULP!... THERE'S NO WOUND THERE! I MEAN...I THOUGHT ...OH, DON'T BOTHER ME, SUPERMAN! GOODBYE!
WHEN THE EFFECT OF THE RED KRYPTONITE PASSED, MY LEFT SIDE BECAME INVULNERABLE AGAIN AND THE WOUND VANISHED!
THE END.

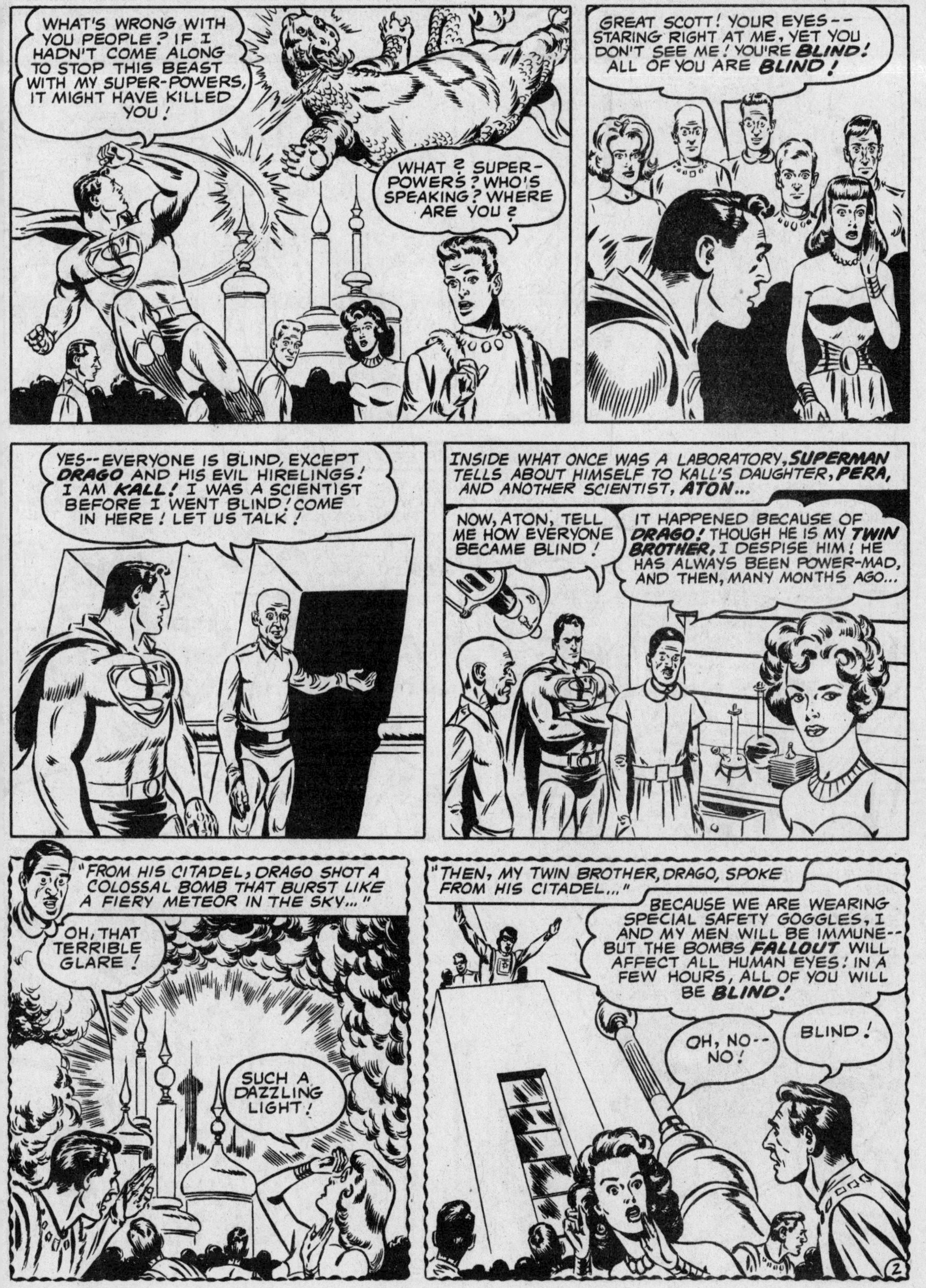
WHAT'S WRONG WITH YOU PEOPLE? IF I HADN'T COME ALONG TO STOP THIS BEAST WITH MY SUPER-POWERS, IT MIGHT HAVE KILLED YOU!
WHAT? SUPER-POWERS? WHO'S SPEAKING? WHERE ARE YOU?
GREAT SCOTT! YOUR EYES--STARING RIGHT AT ME, YET YOU DON'T SEE ME! YOU'RE BLIND! ALL OF YOU ARE BLIND!
YES--EVERYONE IS BLIND, EXCEPT DRAGO AND HIS EVIL HIRELINGS! I AM KALL! I WAS A SCIENTIST BEFORE I WENT BLIND! COME IN HERE! LET US TALK!
INSIDE WHAT ONCE WAS A LABORATORY, SUPERMAN TELLS ABOUT HIMSELF TO KALL'S DAUGHTER, PERA, AND ANOTHER SCIENTIST, ATON...
NOW, ATON, TELL ME HOW EVERYONE BECAME BLIND!
IT HAPPENED BECAUSE OF DRAGO! THOUGH HE IS MY TWIN BROTHER, I DESPISE HIM! HE HAS ALWAYS BEEN POWER-MAD, AND THEN, MANY MONTHS AGO...
"FROM HIS CITADEL, DRAGO SHOT A COLOSSAL BOMB THAT BURST LIKE A FIERY METEOR IN THE SKY..."
OH, THAT TERRIBLE GLARE!
SUCH A DAZZLING LIGHT!
"THEN, MY TWIN BROTHER, DRAGO, SPOKE FROM HIS CITADEL..."
BECAUSE WE ARE WEARING SPECIAL SAFETY GOGGLES, I AND MY MEN WILL BE IMMUNE--BUT THE BOMBS FALLOUT WILL AFFECT ALL HUMAN EYES! IN A FEW HOURS, ALL OF YOU WILL BE BLIND!
OH, NO--NO!
BLIND!
2

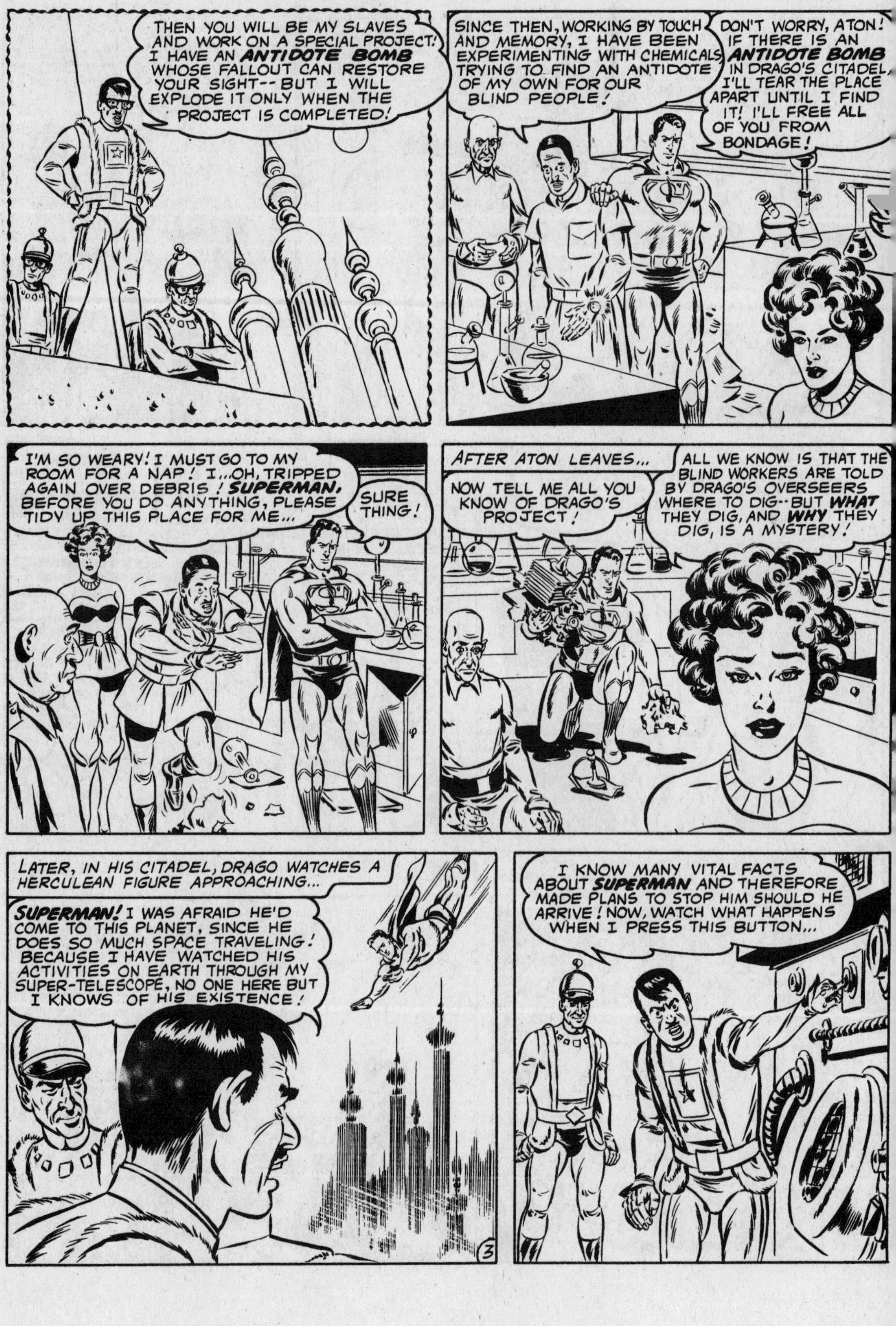
THEN YOU WILL BE MY SLAVES AND WORK ON A SPECIAL PROJECT! I HAVE AN ANTIDOTE BOMB WHOSE FALLOUT CAN RESTORE YOUR SIGHT-- BUT I WILL EXPLODE IT ONLY WHEN THE PROJECT IS COMPLETED!
SINCE THEN, WORKING BY TOUCH AND MEMORY, I HAVE BEEN EXPERIMENTING WITH CHEMICALS TRYING TO FIND AN ANTIDOTE OF MY OWN FOR OUR BLIND PEOPLE!
DON'T WORRY, ATON! IF THERE IS AN ANTIDOTE BOMB IN DRAGO'S CITADEL, I'LL TEAR THE PLACE APART UNTIL I FIND IT! I'LL FREE ALL OF YOU FROM BONDAGE!
I'M SO WEARY! I MUST GO TO MY ROOM FOR A NAP! I...OH, TRIPPED AGAIN OVER DEBRIS! SUPERMAN, BEFORE YOU DO ANYTHING, PLEASE TIDY UP THIS PLACE FOR ME...
SURE THING!
AFTER ATON LEAVES...
NOW TELL ME ALL YOU KNOW OF DRAGO'S PROJECT!
ALL WE KNOW IS THAT THE BLIND WORKERS ARE TOLD BY DRAGO'S OVERSEERS WHERE TO DIG-- BUT WHAT THEY DIG, AND WHY THEY DIG, IS A MYSTERY!
LATER, IN HIS CITADEL, DRAGO WATCHES A HERCULEAN FIGURE APPROACHING...
SUPERMAN! I WAS AFRAID HE'D COME TO THIS PLANET, SINCE HE DOES SO MUCH SPACE TRAVELING! BECAUSE I HAVE WATCHED HIS ACTIVITIES ON EARTH THROUGH MY SUPER-TELESCOPE, NO ONE HERE BUT I KNOWS OF HIS EXISTENCE!
3
I KNOW MANY VITAL FACTS ABOUT SUPERMAN AND THEREFORE MADE PLANS TO STOP HIM SHOULD HE ARRIVE! NOW, WATCH WHAT HAPPENS WHEN I PRESS THIS BUTTON...

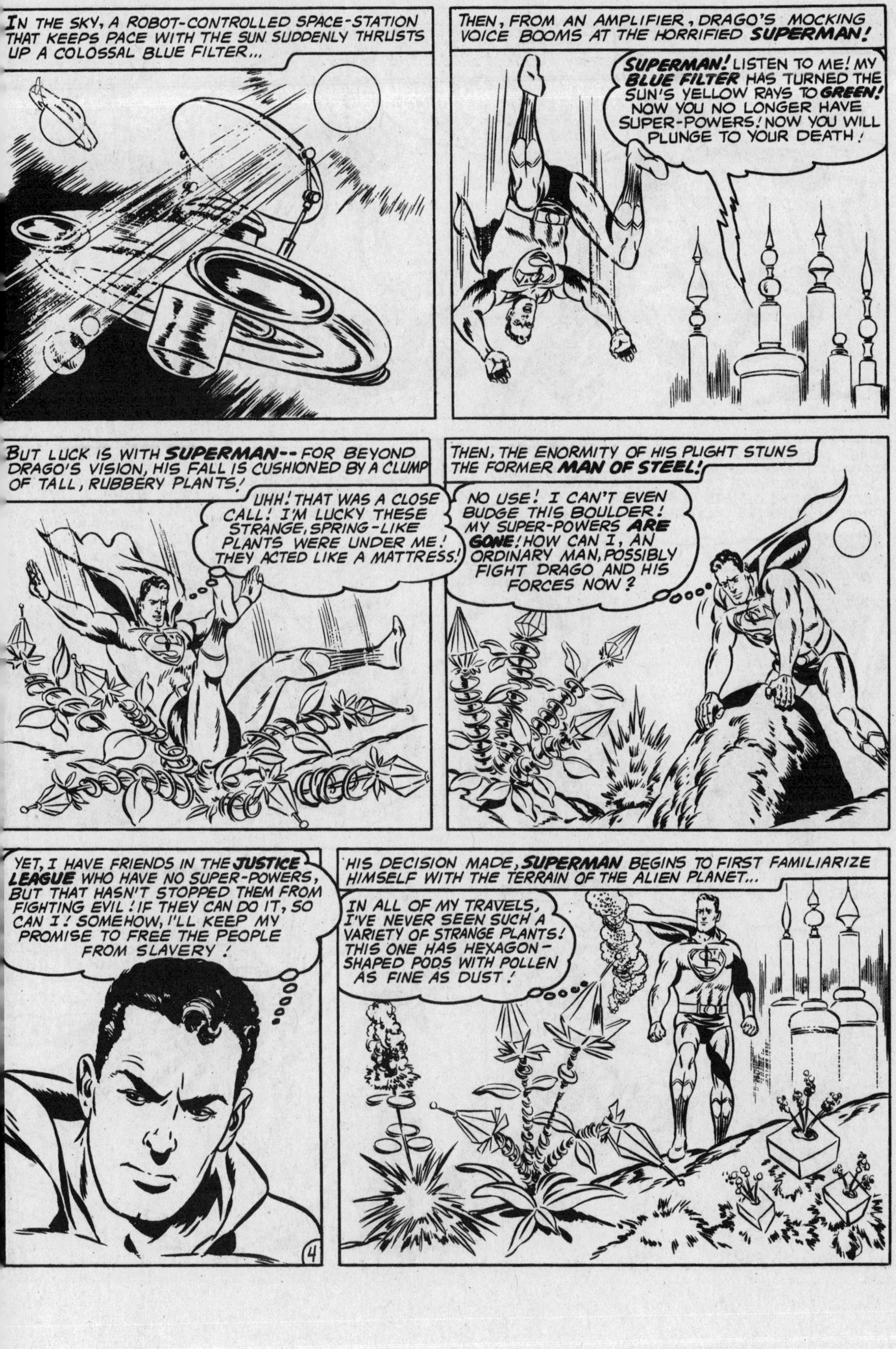
IN THE SKY, A ROBOT-CONTROLLED SPACE-STATION THAT KEEPS PACE WITH THE SUN SUDDENLY THRUSTS UP A COLOSSAL BLUE FILTER...
THEN, FROM AN AMPLIFIER, DRAGO'S MOCKING VOICE BOOMS AT THE HORRIFIED SUPERMAN!
SUPERMAN! LISTEN TO ME! MY BLUE FILTER HAS TURNED THE SUN'S YELLOW RAYS TO GREEN! NOW YOU NO LONGER HAVE SUPER-POWERS! NOW YOU WILL PLUNGE TO YOUR DEATH!
BUT LUCK IS WITH SUPERMAN-- FOR BEYOND DRAGO'S VISION, HIS FALL IS CUSHIONED BY A CLUMP OF TALL, RUBBERY PLANTS!
UHH! THAT WAS A CLOSE CALL! I'M LUCKY THESE STRANGE, SPRING-LIKE PLANTS WERE UNDER ME! THEY ACTED LIKE A MATTRESS!
THEN, THE ENORMITY OF HIS PLIGHT STUNS THE FORMER MAN OF STEEL!
NO USE! I CAN'T EVEN BUDGE THIS BOULDER! MY SUPER-POWERS ARE GONE! HOW CAN I, AN ORDINARY MAN, POSSIBLY FIGHT DRAGO AND HIS FORCES NOW?
YET, I HAVE FRIENDS IN THE JUSTICE LEAGUE WHO HAVE NO SUPER-POWERS, BUT THAT HASN'T STOPPED THEM FROM FIGHTING EVIL! IF THEY CAN DO IT, SO CAN I! SOMEHOW, I'LL KEEP MY PROMISE TO FREE THE PEOPLE FROM SLAVERY!
4
HIS DECISION MADE, SUPERMAN BEGINS TO FIRST FAMILIARIZE HIMSELF WITH THE TERRAIN OF THE ALIEN PLANET...
IN ALL OF MY TRAVELS, I'VE NEVER SEEN SUCH A VARIETY OF STRANGE PLANTS! THIS ONE HAS HEXAGON-SHAPED PODS WITH POLLEN AS FINE AS DUST!

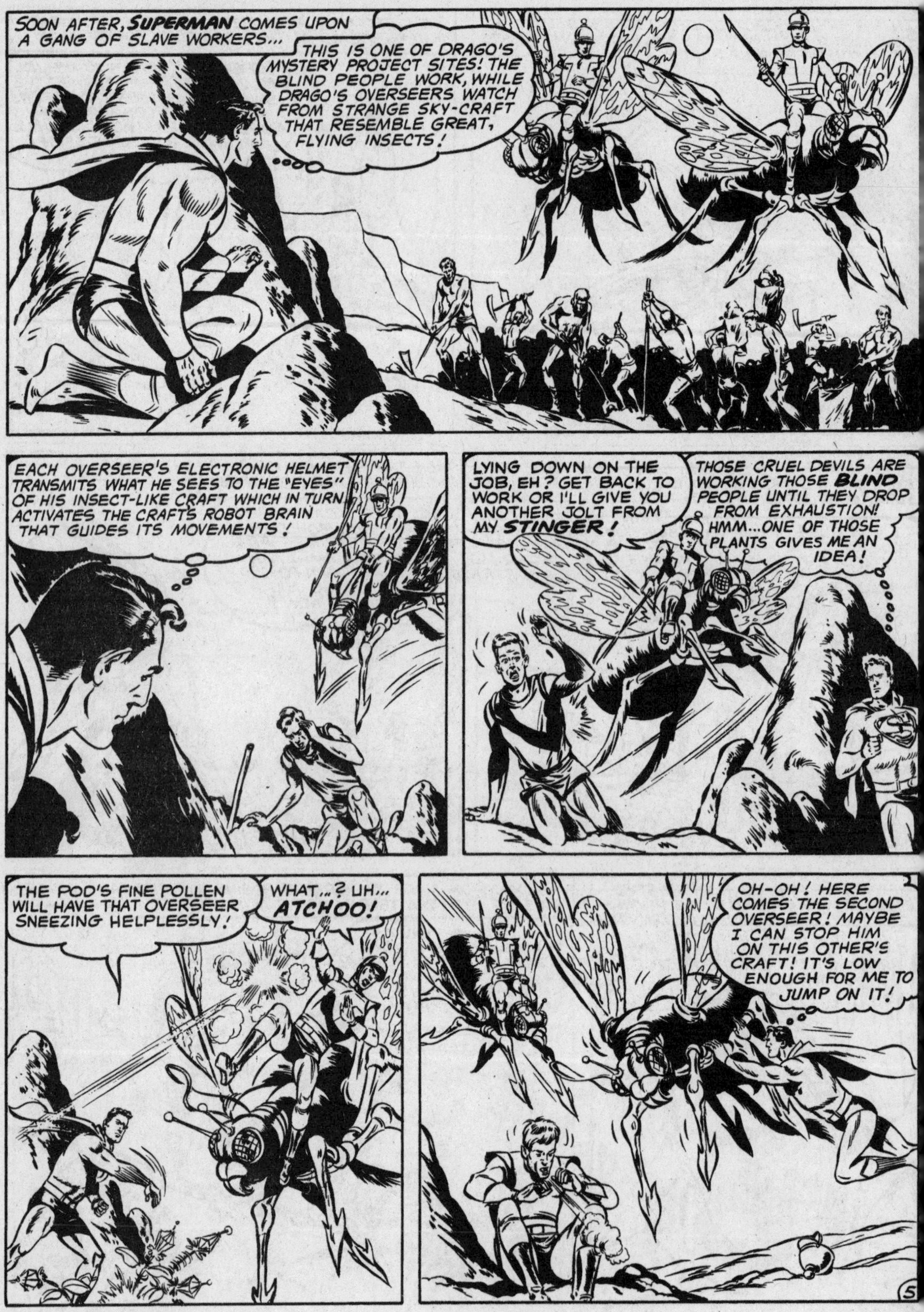
SOON AFTER, SUPERMAN COMES UPON A GANG OF SLAVE WORKERS...
THIS IS ONE OF DRAGO'S MYSTERY PROJECT SITES! THE BLIND PEOPLE WORK, WHILE DRAGO'S OVERSEERS WATCH FROM STRANGE SKY-CRAFT THAT RESEMBLE GREAT, FLYING INSECTS!
EACH OVERSEER'S ELECTRONIC HELMET TRANSMITS WHAT HE SEES TO THE "EYES" OF HIS INSECT-LIKE CRAFT WHICH IN TURN ACTIVATES THE CRAFT'S ROBOT BRAIN THAT GUIDES ITS MOVEMENTS!
LYING DOWN ON THE JOB, EH? GET BACK TO WORK OR I'LL GIVE YOU ANOTHER JOLT FROM MY STINGER!
THOSE CRUEL DEVILS ARE WORKING THOSE BLIND PEOPLE UNTIL THEY DROP FROM EXHAUSTION! HMM...ONE OF THOSE PLANTS GIVES ME AN IDEA!
THE POD'S FINE POLLEN WILL HAVE THAT OVERSEER SNEEZING HELPLESSLY!
WHAT...? UH... ATCHOO!
OH-OH! HERE COMES THE SECOND OVERSEER! MAYBE I CAN STOP HIM ON THIS OTHER'S CRAFT! IT'S LOW ENOUGH FOR ME TO JUMP ON IT!
5

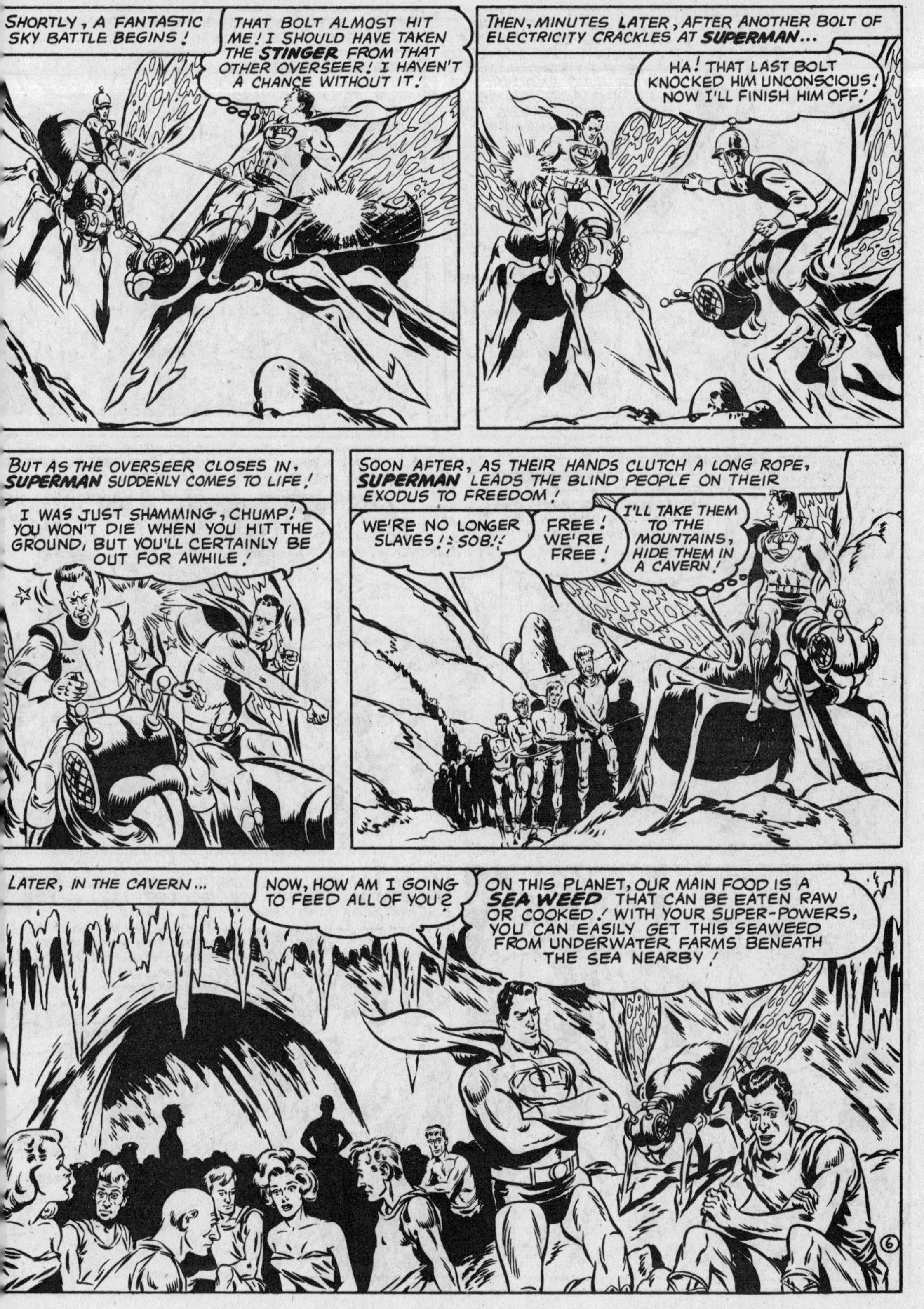
SHORTLY, A FANTASTIC SKY BATTLE BEGINS!
THAT BOLT ALMOST HIT ME! I SHOULD HAVE TAKEN THE STINGER FROM THAT OTHER OVERSEER! I HAVEN'T A CHANCE WITHOUT IT!
THEN, MINUTES LATER, AFTER ANOTHER BOLT OF ELECTRICITY CRACKLES AT SUPERMAN...
HA! THAT LAST BOLT KNOCKED HIM UNCONSCIOUS! NOW I'LL FINISH HIM OFF!
BUT AS THE OVERSEER CLOSES IN, SUPERMAN SUDDENLY COMES TO LIFE!
I WAS JUST SHAMMING, CHUMP! YOU WON'T DIE WHEN YOU HIT THE GROUND, BUT YOU'LL CERTAINLY BE OUT FOR AWHILE!
SOON AFTER, AS THEIR HANDS CLUTCH A LONG ROPE, SUPERMAN LEADS THE BLIND PEOPLE ON THEIR EXODUS TO FREEDOM!
WE'RE NO LONGER SLAVES! SOB!
FREE! WE'RE FREE!
I'LL TAKE THEM TO THE MOUNTAINS, HIDE THEM IN A CAVERN!
LATER, IN THE CAVERN...
NOW, HOW AM I GOING TO FEED ALL OF YOU?
ON THIS PLANET, OUR MAIN FOOD IS A SEA WEED THAT CAN BE EATEN RAW OR COOKED! WITH YOUR SUPER-POWERS, YOU CAN EASILY GET THIS SEAWEED FROM UNDERWATER FARMS BENEATH THE SEA NEARBY!
6

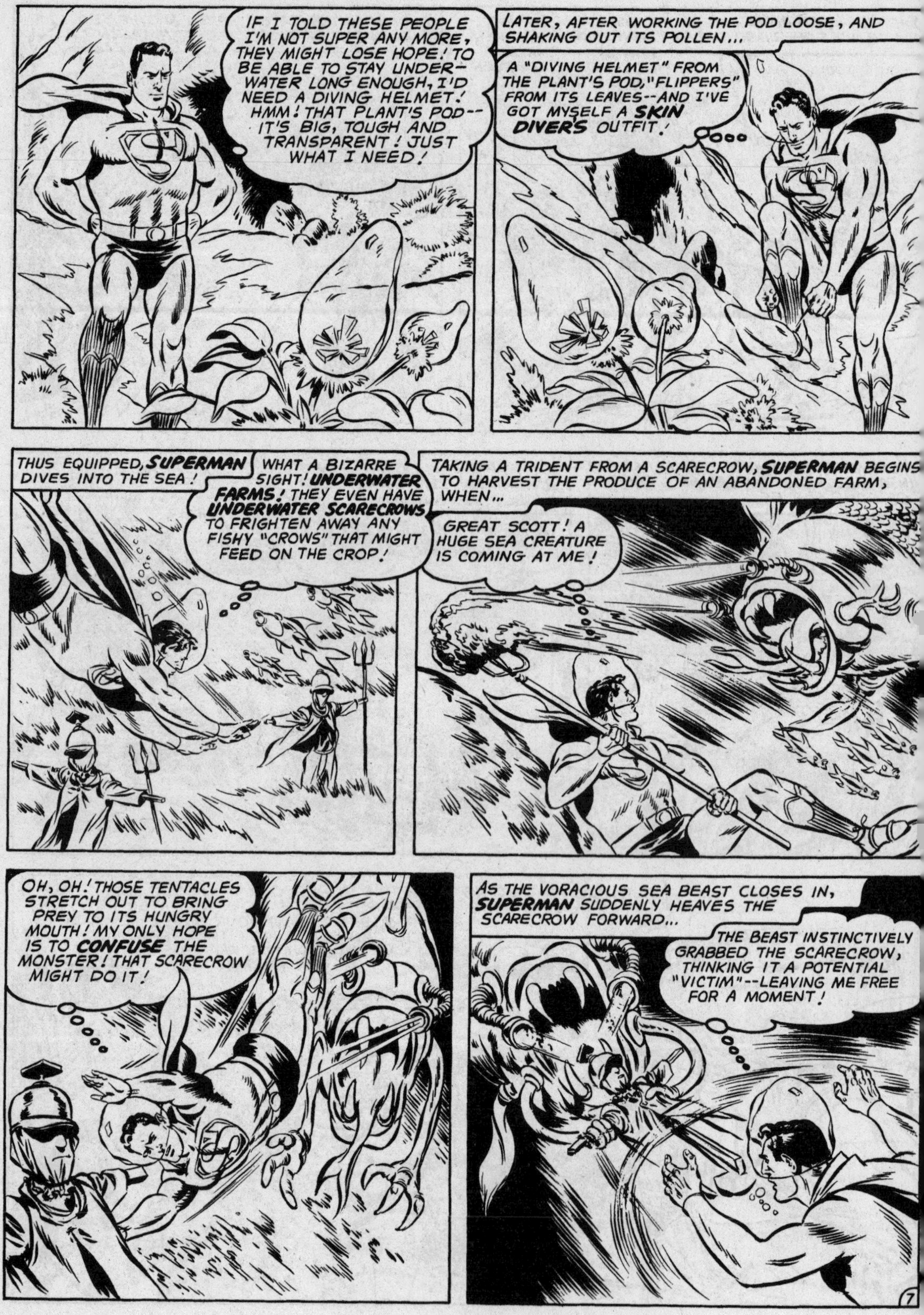
IF I TOLD THESE PEOPLE I'M NOT SUPER ANY MORE, THEY MIGHT LOSE HOPE! TO BE ABLE TO STAY UNDER-WATER LONG ENOUGH, I'D NEED A DIVING HELMET! HMM! THAT PLANT'S POD-- IT'S BIG, TOUGH AND TRANSPARENT! JUST WHAT I NEED!
LATER, AFTER WORKING THE POD LOOSE, AND SHAKING OUT ITS POLLEN...
A "DIVING HELMET" FROM THE PLANT'S POD, "FLIPPERS" FROM ITS LEAVES--AND I'VE GOT MYSELF A SKIN DIVER'S OUTFIT!
THUS EQUIPPED, SUPERMAN DIVES INTO THE SEA!
WHAT A BIZARRE SIGHT! UNDERWATER FARMS! THEY EVEN HAVE UNDERWATER SCARECROWS TO FRIGHTEN AWAY ANY FISHY "CROWS" THAT MIGHT FEED ON THE CROP!
TAKING A TRIDENT FROM A SCARECROW, SUPERMAN BEGINS TO HARVEST THE PRODUCE OF AN ABANDONED FARM, WHEN...
GREAT SCOTT! A HUGE SEA CREATURE IS COMING AT ME!
OH, OH! THOSE TENTACLES STRETCH OUT TO BRING PREY TO ITS HUNGRY MOUTH! MY ONLY HOPE IS TO CONFUSE THE MONSTER! THAT SCARECROW MIGHT DO IT!
AS THE VORACIOUS SEA BEAST CLOSES IN, SUPERMAN SUDDENLY HEAVES THE SCARECROW FORWARD...
THE BEAST INSTINCTIVELY GRABBED THE SCARECROW, THINKING IT A POTENTIAL "VICTIM"--LEAVING ME FREE FOR A MOMENT!
7

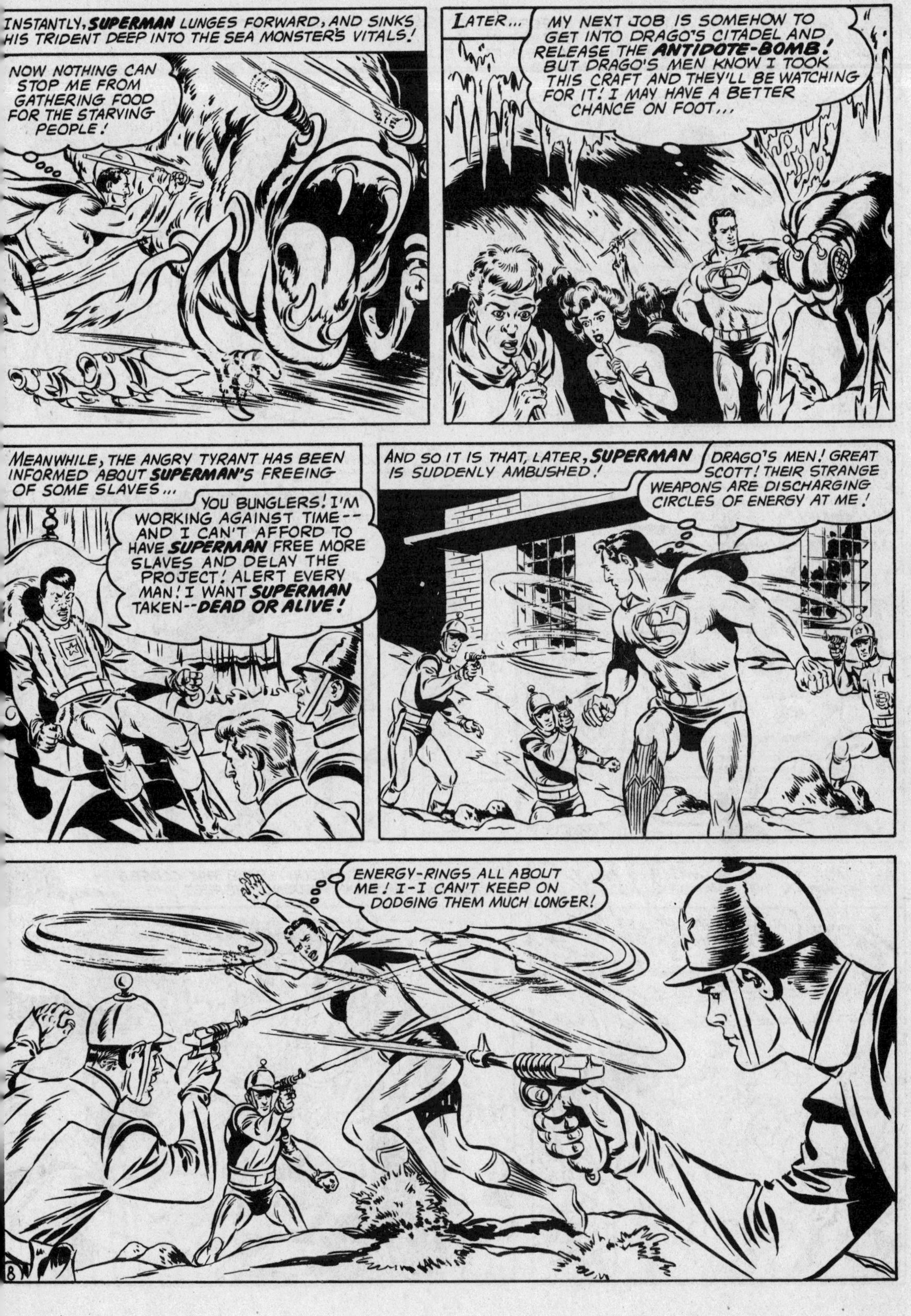

INSTANTLY, SUPERMAN LUNGES FORWARD, AND SINKS HIS TRIDENT DEEP INTO THE SEA MONSTER'S VITALS!
NOW NOTHING CAN STOP ME FROM GATHERING FOOD FOR THE STARVING PEOPLE!
LATER...
MY NEXT JOB IS SOMEHOW TO GET INTO DRAGO'S CITADEL AND RELEASE THE ANTIDOTE-BOMB! BUT DRAGO'S MEN KNOW I TOOK THIS CRAFT AND THEY'LL BE WATCHING FOR IT! I MAY HAVE A BETTER CHANCE ON FOOT...
MEANWHILE, THE ANGRY TYRANT HAS BEEN INFORMED ABOUT SUPERMAN'S FREEING OF SOME SLAVES...
YOU BUNGLERS! I'M WORKING AGAINST TIME-- AND I CAN'T AFFORD TO HAVE SUPERMAN FREE MORE SLAVES AND DELAY THE PROJECT! ALERT EVERY MAN! I WANT SUPERMAN TAKEN--DEAD OR ALIVE!
AND SO IT IS THAT, LATER, SUPERMAN IS SUDDENLY AMBUSHED!
DRAGO'S MEN! GREAT SCOTT! THEIR STRANGE WEAPONS ARE DISCHARGING CIRCLES OF ENERGY AT ME!
ENERGY-RINGS ALL ABOUT ME! I-I CAN'T KEEP ON DODGING THEM MUCH LONGER!
8

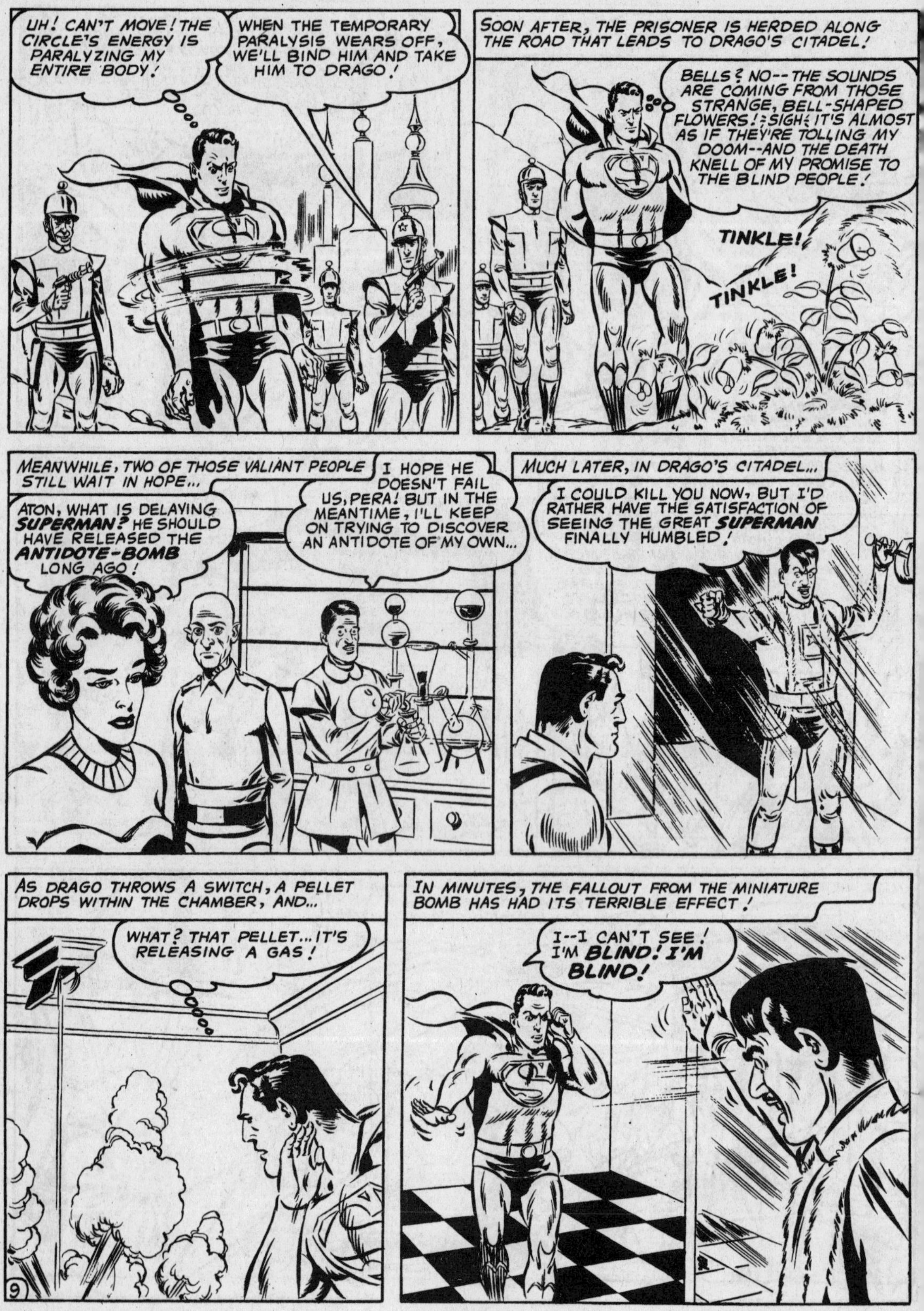
UH! CAN'T MOVE! THE CIRCLE'S ENERGY IS PARALYZING MY ENTIRE BODY!
WHEN THE TEMPORARY PARALYSIS WEARS OFF, WE'LL BIND HIM AND TAKE HIM TO DRAGO!
SOON AFTER, THE PRISONER IS HERDED ALONG THE ROAD THAT LEADS TO DRAGO'S CITADEL!
BELLS? NO--THE SOUNDS ARE COMING FROM THOSE STRANGE, BELL-SHAPED FLOWERS! -SIGH- IT'S ALMOST AS IF THEY'RE TOLLING MY DOOM--AND THE DEATH KNELL OF MY PROMISE TO THE BLIND PEOPLE!
TINKLE!
TINKLE!
MEANWHILE, TWO OF THOSE VALIANT PEOPLE STILL WAIT IN HOPE...
ATON, WHAT IS DELAYING SUPERMAN? HE SHOULD HAVE RELEASED THE ANTIDOTE-BOMB LONG AGO!
I HOPE HE DOESN'T FAIL US, PERA! BUT IN THE MEANTIME, I'LL KEEP ON TRYING TO DISCOVER AN ANTIDOTE OF MY OWN...
MUCH LATER, IN DRAGO'S CITADEL...
I COULD KILL YOU NOW, BUT I'D RATHER HAVE THE SATISFACTION OF SEEING THE GREAT SUPERMAN FINALLY HUMBLED!
AS DRAGO THROWS A SWITCH, A PELLET DROPS WITHIN THE CHAMBER, AND...
WHAT? THAT PELLET...IT'S RELEASING A GAS!
9
IN MINUTES, THE FALLOUT FROM THE MINIATURE BOMB HAS HAD ITS TERRIBLE EFFECT!
I--I CAN'T SEE! I'M BLIND! I'M BLIND!

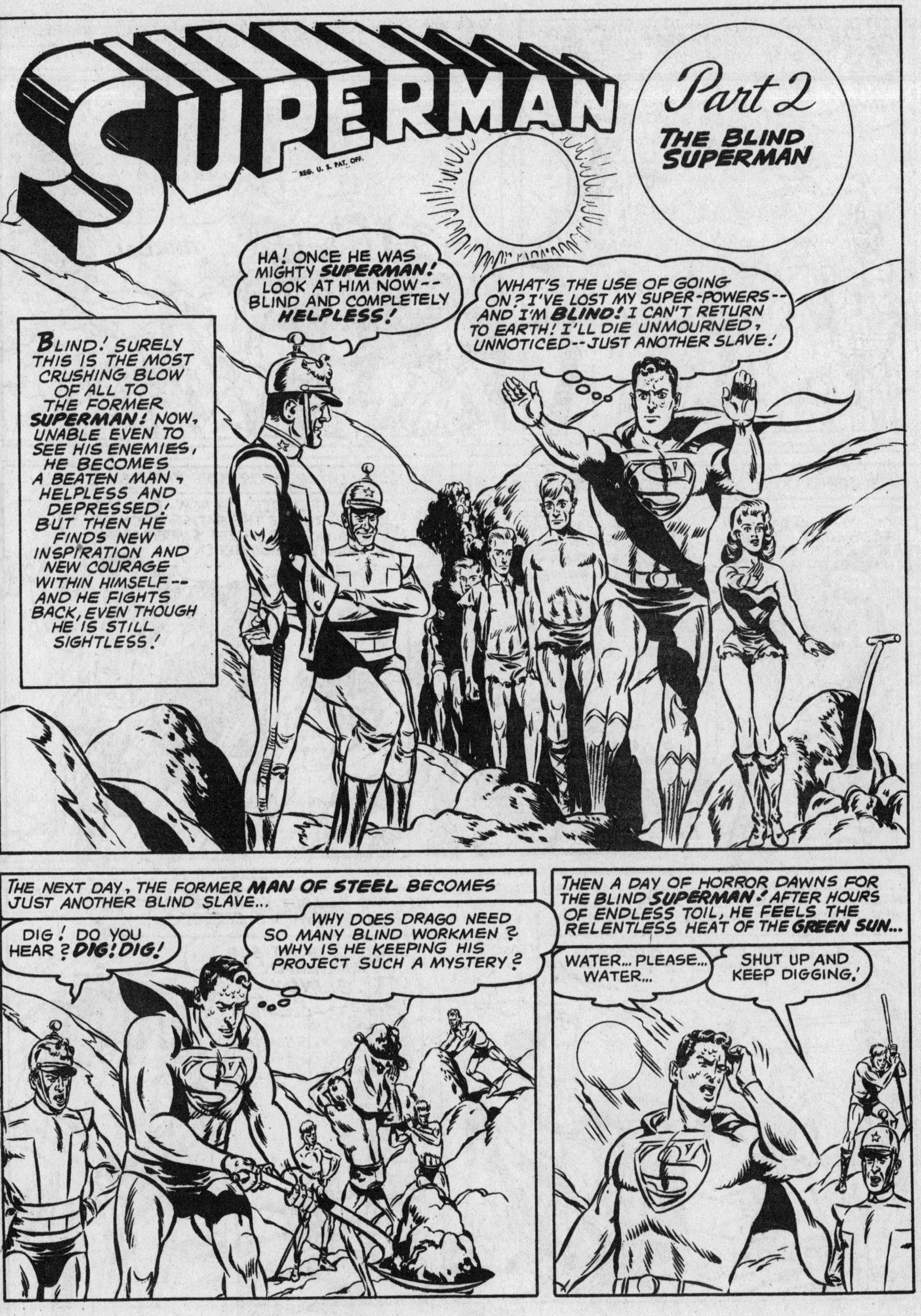
SUPERMAN
REG. U. S. PAT. OFF.
Part 2
THE BLIND SUPERMAN
BLIND! SURELY THIS IS THE MOST CRUSHING BLOW OF ALL TO THE FORMER SUPERMAN! NOW, UNABLE EVEN TO SEE HIS ENEMIES, HE BECOMES A BEATEN MAN, HELPLESS AND DEPRESSED! BUT THEN HE FINDS NEW INSPIRATION AND NEW COURAGE WITHIN HIMSELF--AND HE FIGHTS BACK, EVEN THOUGH HE IS STILL SIGHTLESS!
HA! ONCE HE WAS MIGHTY SUPERMAN! LOOK AT HIM NOW--BLIND AND COMPLETELY HELPLESS!
WHAT'S THE USE OF GOING ON? I'VE LOST MY SUPER-POWERS--AND I'M BLIND! I CAN'T RETURN TO EARTH! I'LL DIE UNMOURNED, UNNOTICED--JUST ANOTHER SLAVE!
THE NEXT DAY, THE FORMER MAN OF STEEL BECOMES JUST ANOTHER BLIND SLAVE...
DIG! DO YOU HEAR? DIG! DIG!
WHY DOES DRAGO NEED SO MANY BLIND WORKMEN? WHY IS HE KEEPING HIS PROJECT SUCH A MYSTERY?
THEN A DAY OF HORROR DAWNS FOR THE BLIND SUPERMAN! AFTER HOURS OF ENDLESS TOIL, HE FEELS THE RELENTLESS HEAT OF THE GREEN SUN...
WATER... PLEASE... WATER...
SHUT UP AND KEEP DIGGING!

LATER, HE FEELS THE PAIN FROM AN OVERSEER'S CRUEL *STINGER* WHEN HE TRIES TO EASE HIS ACHING MUSCLES...

GOT TO REST... *UHHH!*

KEEP WORKING, SLAVE, OR THE NEXT JOLT WILL BE STRONGER!

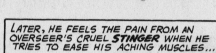

RESPITE ONLY COMES AT NIGHT WHEN, LIKE A WEARY ANIMAL, HE IS ALLOWED TO SLUMBER!

AS THE DAYS PASS, *SUPERMAN* MOVES LIKE A SLEEPWALKER--DEJECTED AND DEFEATED...

I'VE NO FIGHT LEFT IN ME! I'M LIKE MY OTHER IDENTITY, *CLARK KENT*-- WEAK, SUBMISSIVE...

THEN, ONE NIGHT, WHEN *SUPERMAN* SEEMS TO GIVE UP ALL HOPE...

OH, WHAT'S THE USE OF GOING ON...

DO NOT DESPAIR, MY FRIEND! A STRANGER FROM ANOTHER WORLD HAS COME TO HELP US! THE STRANGER HAS SUPER-POWERS!

THIS *SUPERMAN* HAS PROMISED TO *FREE* US AND TO DESTROY DRAGO'S TYRANNY!

WHY... HE'S TALKING ABOUT ME! BUT HE DOESN'T KNOW I'VE BECOME A CAPTIVE HERE, JUST ANOTHER BLIND SLAVE LIKE HIMSELF! I CAN'T TELL HIM THE TRUTH-- I CAN'T DISILLUSION HIM!

BUT THE FAITH OF THAT BLIND MAN SUDDENLY GIVES *SUPERMAN* NEW COURAGE, NEW DETERMINATION!

I'M THE ONE HOPE OF THESE PEOPLE! I CAN'T LET THEM DOWN! THOUGH I'M WITHOUT SUPER-POWERS-- THOUGH I'M BLIND-- SOME WAY, SOMEHOW, I'M GOING TO ESCAPE, AND FINISH WHAT I STARTED TO DO!

2

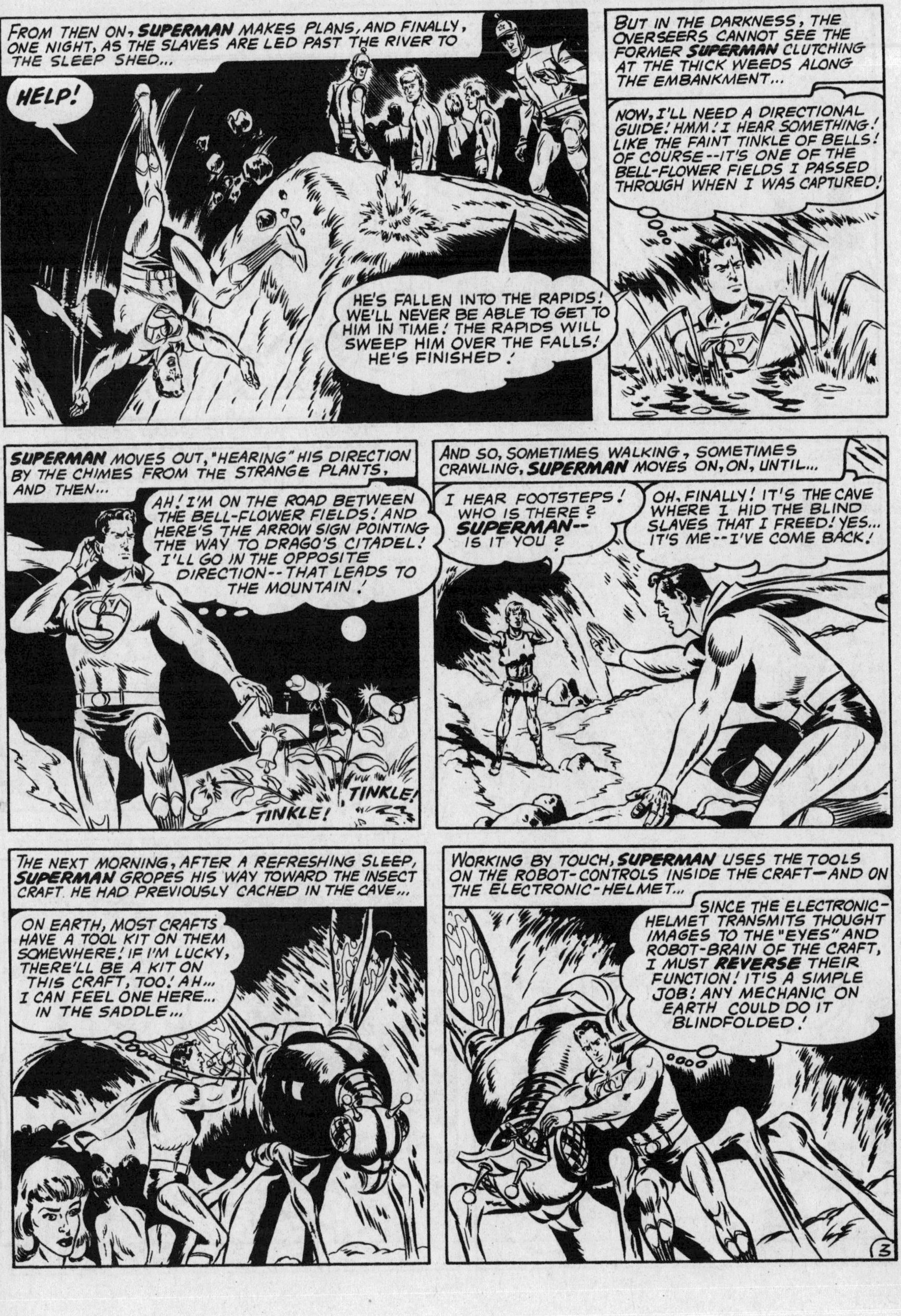
FROM THEN ON, SUPERMAN MAKES PLANS, AND FINALLY, ONE NIGHT, AS THE SLAVES ARE LED PAST THE RIVER TO THE SLEEP SHED...
HELP!
HE'S FALLEN INTO THE RAPIDS! WE'LL NEVER BE ABLE TO GET TO HIM IN TIME! THE RAPIDS WILL SWEEP HIM OVER THE FALLS! HE'S FINISHED!
BUT IN THE DARKNESS, THE OVERSEERS CANNOT SEE THE FORMER SUPERMAN CLUTCHING AT THE THICK WEEDS ALONG THE EMBANKMENT...
NOW, I'LL NEED A DIRECTIONAL GUIDE! HMM! I HEAR SOMETHING! LIKE THE FAINT TINKLE OF BELLS! OF COURSE--IT'S ONE OF THE BELL-FLOWER FIELDS I PASSED THROUGH WHEN I WAS CAPTURED!
SUPERMAN MOVES OUT, "HEARING" HIS DIRECTION BY THE CHIMES FROM THE STRANGE PLANTS, AND THEN...
AH! I'M ON THE ROAD BETWEEN THE BELL-FLOWER FIELDS! AND HERE'S THE ARROW SIGN POINTING THE WAY TO DRAGO'S CITADEL! I'LL GO IN THE OPPOSITE DIRECTION--THAT LEADS TO THE MOUNTAIN!
TINKLE!
TINKLE!
AND SO, SOMETIMES WALKING, SOMETIMES CRAWLING, SUPERMAN MOVES ON, ON, UNTIL...
I HEAR FOOTSTEPS! WHO IS THERE? SUPERMAN--IS IT YOU?
OH, FINALLY! IT'S THE CAVE WHERE I HID THE BLIND SLAVES THAT I FREED! YES... IT'S ME--I'VE COME BACK!
THE NEXT MORNING, AFTER A REFRESHING SLEEP, SUPERMAN GROPES HIS WAY TOWARD THE INSECT CRAFT HE HAD PREVIOUSLY CACHED IN THE CAVE...
ON EARTH, MOST CRAFTS HAVE A TOOL KIT ON THEM SOMEWHERE! IF I'M LUCKY, THERE'LL BE A KIT ON THIS CRAFT, TOO! AH... I CAN FEEL ONE HERE... IN THE SADDLE...
WORKING BY TOUCH, SUPERMAN USES THE TOOLS ON THE ROBOT-CONTROLS INSIDE THE CRAFT—AND ON THE ELECTRONIC-HELMET...
SINCE THE ELECTRONIC-HELMET TRANSMITS THOUGHT IMAGES TO THE "EYES" AND ROBOT-BRAIN OF THE CRAFT, I MUST REVERSE THEIR FUNCTION! IT'S A SIMPLE JOB! ANY MECHANIC ON EARTH COULD DO IT BLINDFOLDED!
3

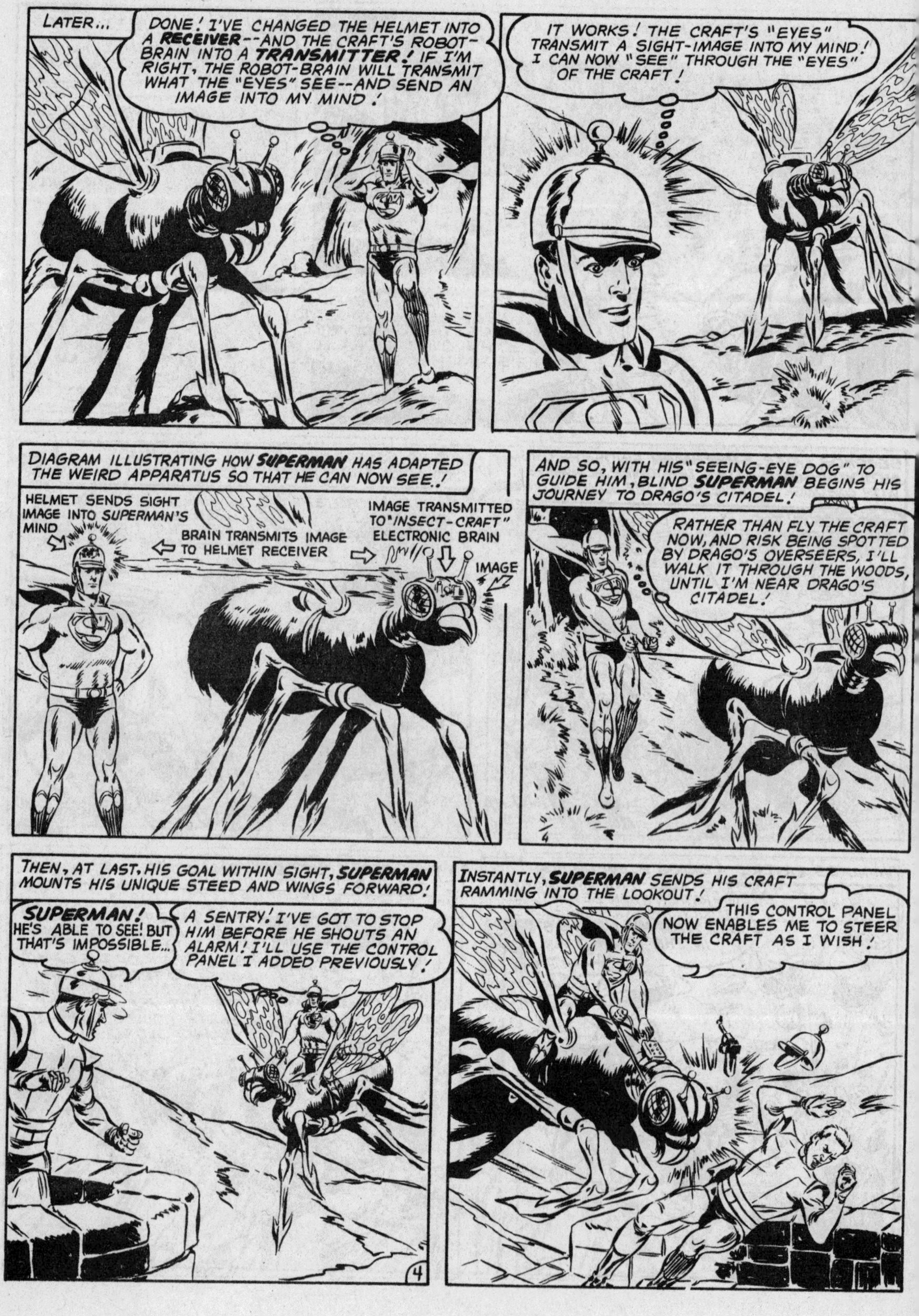
LATER...
DONE! I'VE CHANGED THE HELMET INTO A RECEIVER--AND THE CRAFT'S ROBOT-BRAIN INTO A TRANSMITTER! IF I'M RIGHT, THE ROBOT-BRAIN WILL TRANSMIT WHAT THE "EYES" SEE--AND SEND AN IMAGE INTO MY MIND!
IT WORKS! THE CRAFT'S "EYES" TRANSMIT A SIGHT-IMAGE INTO MY MIND! I CAN NOW "SEE" THROUGH THE "EYES" OF THE CRAFT!
DIAGRAM ILLUSTRATING HOW SUPERMAN HAS ADAPTED THE WEIRD APPARATUS SO THAT HE CAN NOW SEE.!
HELMET SENDS SIGHT IMAGE INTO SUPERMAN'S MIND
BRAIN TRANSMITS IMAGE TO HELMET RECEIVER
IMAGE TRANSMITTED TO "INSECT-CRAFT" ELECTRONIC BRAIN
IMAGE
AND SO, WITH HIS "SEEING-EYE DOG" TO GUIDE HIM, BLIND SUPERMAN BEGINS HIS JOURNEY TO DRAGO'S CITADEL!
RATHER THAN FLY THE CRAFT NOW, AND RISK BEING SPOTTED BY DRAGO'S OVERSEERS, I'LL WALK IT THROUGH THE WOODS, UNTIL I'M NEAR DRAGO'S CITADEL!
THEN, AT LAST, HIS GOAL WITHIN SIGHT, SUPERMAN MOUNTS HIS UNIQUE STEED AND WINGS FORWARD!
SUPERMAN! HE'S ABLE TO SEE! BUT THAT'S IMPOSSIBLE...
A SENTRY! I'VE GOT TO STOP HIM BEFORE HE SHOUTS AN ALARM! I'LL USE THE CONTROL PANEL I ADDED PREVIOUSLY!
4
INSTANTLY, SUPERMAN SENDS HIS CRAFT RAMMING INTO THE LOOKOUT!
THIS CONTROL PANEL NOW ENABLES ME TO STEER THE CRAFT AS I WISH!

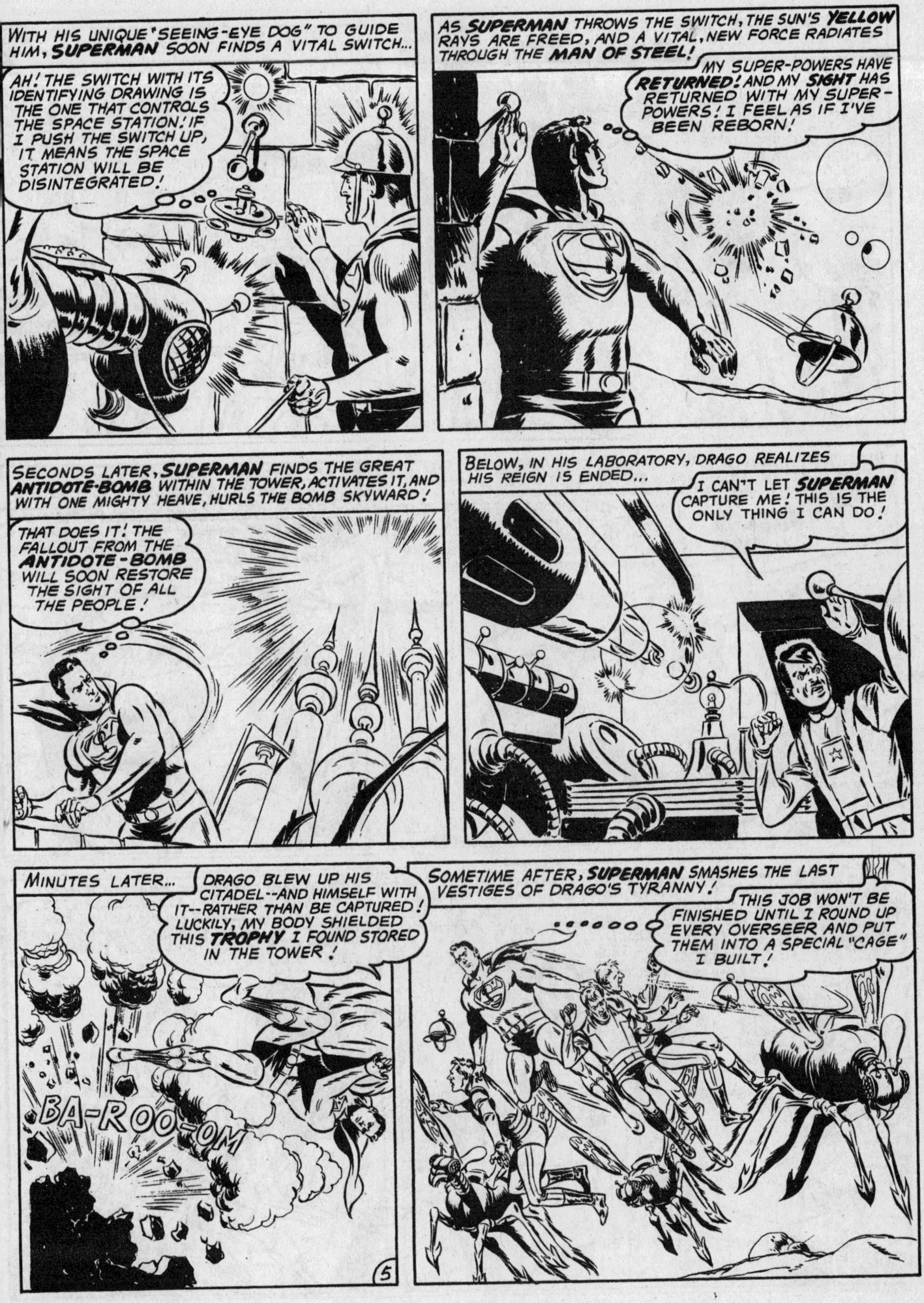
WITH HIS UNIQUE "SEEING-EYE DOG" TO GUIDE HIM, SUPERMAN SOON FINDS A VITAL SWITCH...
AH! THE SWITCH WITH ITS IDENTIFYING DRAWING IS THE ONE THAT CONTROLS THE SPACE STATION! IF I PUSH THE SWITCH UP, IT MEANS THE SPACE STATION WILL BE DISINTEGRATED!
AS SUPERMAN THROWS THE SWITCH, THE SUN'S YELLOW RAYS ARE FREED, AND A VITAL, NEW FORCE RADIATES THROUGH THE MAN OF STEEL!
MY SUPER-POWERS HAVE RETURNED! AND MY SIGHT HAS RETURNED WITH MY SUPER-POWERS! I FEEL AS IF I'VE BEEN REBORN!
SECONDS LATER, SUPERMAN FINDS THE GREAT ANTIDOTE-BOMB WITHIN THE TOWER, ACTIVATES IT, AND WITH ONE MIGHTY HEAVE, HURLS THE BOMB SKYWARD!
THAT DOES IT! THE FALLOUT FROM THE ANTIDOTE-BOMB WILL SOON RESTORE THE SIGHT OF ALL THE PEOPLE!
BELOW, IN HIS LABORATORY, DRAGO REALIZES HIS REIGN IS ENDED...
I CAN'T LET SUPERMAN CAPTURE ME! THIS IS THE ONLY THING I CAN DO!
MINUTES LATER...
DRAGO BLEW UP HIS CITADEL--AND HIMSELF WITH IT--RATHER THAN BE CAPTURED! LUCKILY, MY BODY SHIELDED THIS TROPHY I FOUND STORED IN THE TOWER!
BA-ROO-OM
5
SOMETIME AFTER, SUPERMAN SMASHES THE LAST VESTIGES OF DRAGO'S TYRANNY!
THIS JOB WON'T BE FINISHED UNTIL I ROUND UP EVERY OVERSEER AND PUT THEM INTO A SPECIAL "CAGE" I BUILT!

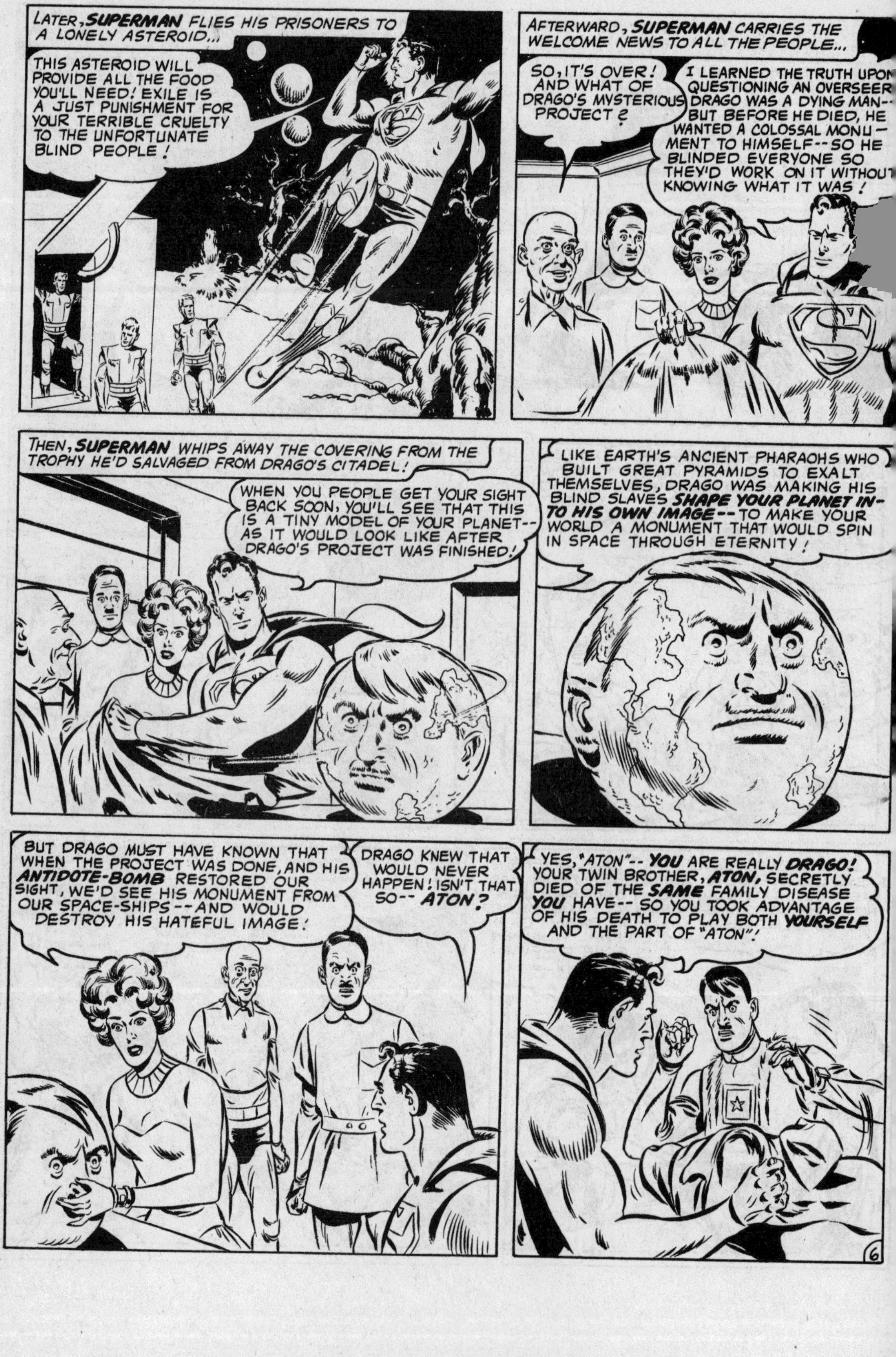
LATER, SUPERMAN FLIES HIS PRISONERS TO A LONELY ASTEROID...
THIS ASTEROID WILL PROVIDE ALL THE FOOD YOU'LL NEED! EXILE IS A JUST PUNISHMENT FOR YOUR TERRIBLE CRUELTY TO THE UNFORTUNATE BLIND PEOPLE!
AFTERWARD, SUPERMAN CARRIES THE WELCOME NEWS TO ALL THE PEOPLE...
SO, IT'S OVER! AND WHAT OF DRAGO'S MYSTERIOUS PROJECT?
I LEARNED THE TRUTH UPON QUESTIONING AN OVERSEER. DRAGO WAS A DYING MAN-- BUT BEFORE HE DIED, HE WANTED A COLOSSAL MONUMENT TO HIMSELF--SO HE BLINDED EVERYONE SO THEY'D WORK ON IT WITHOUT KNOWING WHAT IT WAS!
THEN, SUPERMAN WHIPS AWAY THE COVERING FROM THE TROPHY HE'D SALVAGED FROM DRAGO'S CITADEL!
WHEN YOU PEOPLE GET YOUR SIGHT BACK SOON, YOU'LL SEE THAT THIS IS A TINY MODEL OF YOUR PLANET-- AS IT WOULD LOOK LIKE AFTER DRAGO'S PROJECT WAS FINISHED!
LIKE EARTH'S ANCIENT PHARAOHS WHO BUILT GREAT PYRAMIDS TO EXALT THEMSELVES, DRAGO WAS MAKING HIS BLIND SLAVES SHAPE YOUR PLANET INTO HIS OWN IMAGE--TO MAKE YOUR WORLD A MONUMENT THAT WOULD SPIN IN SPACE THROUGH ETERNITY!
BUT DRAGO MUST HAVE KNOWN THAT WHEN THE PROJECT WAS DONE, AND HIS ANTIDOTE-BOMB RESTORED OUR SIGHT, WE'D SEE HIS MONUMENT FROM OUR SPACE-SHIPS--AND WOULD DESTROY HIS HATEFUL IMAGE!
DRAGO KNEW THAT WOULD NEVER HAPPEN! ISN'T THAT SO-- ATON?
YES, "ATON"-- YOU ARE REALLY DRAGO! YOUR TWIN BROTHER, ATON, SECRETLY DIED OF THE SAME FAMILY DISEASE YOU HAVE-- SO YOU TOOK ADVANTAGE OF HIS DEATH TO PLAY BOTH YOURSELF AND THE PART OF "ATON"!
6

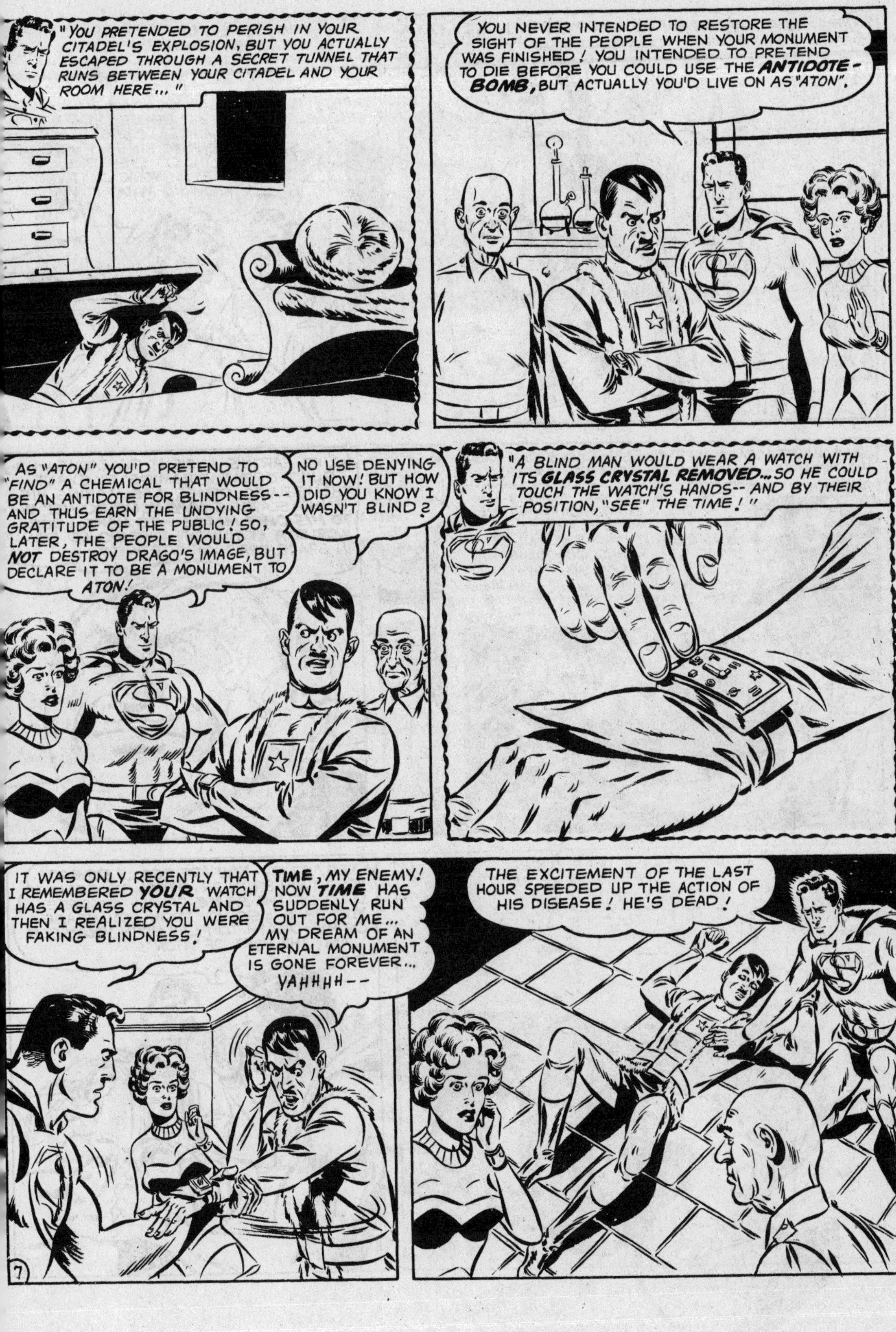
"YOU PRETENDED TO PERISH IN YOUR CITADEL'S EXPLOSION, BUT YOU ACTUALLY ESCAPED THROUGH A SECRET TUNNEL THAT RUNS BETWEEN YOUR CITADEL AND YOUR ROOM HERE..."
YOU NEVER INTENDED TO RESTORE THE SIGHT OF THE PEOPLE WHEN YOUR MONUMENT WAS FINISHED! YOU INTENDED TO PRETEND TO DIE BEFORE YOU COULD USE THE ANTIDOTE-BOMB, BUT ACTUALLY YOU'D LIVE ON AS "ATON".
AS "ATON" YOU'D PRETEND TO "FIND" A CHEMICAL THAT WOULD BE AN ANTIDOTE FOR BLINDNESS-- AND THUS EARN THE UNDYING GRATITUDE OF THE PUBLIC! SO, LATER, THE PEOPLE WOULD NOT DESTROY DRAGO'S IMAGE, BUT DECLARE IT TO BE A MONUMENT TO ATON!
NO USE DENYING IT NOW! BUT HOW DID YOU KNOW I WASN'T BLIND?
"A BLIND MAN WOULD WEAR A WATCH WITH ITS GLASS CRYSTAL REMOVED... SO HE COULD TOUCH THE WATCH'S HANDS-- AND BY THEIR POSITION, "SEE" THE TIME!"
IT WAS ONLY RECENTLY THAT I REMEMBERED YOUR WATCH HAS A GLASS CRYSTAL AND THEN I REALIZED YOU WERE FAKING BLINDNESS!
TIME, MY ENEMY! NOW TIME HAS SUDDENLY RUN OUT FOR ME... MY DREAM OF AN ETERNAL MONUMENT IS GONE FOREVER... YAHHHH--
THE EXCITEMENT OF THE LAST HOUR SPEEDED UP THE ACTION OF HIS DISEASE! HE'S DEAD!
7

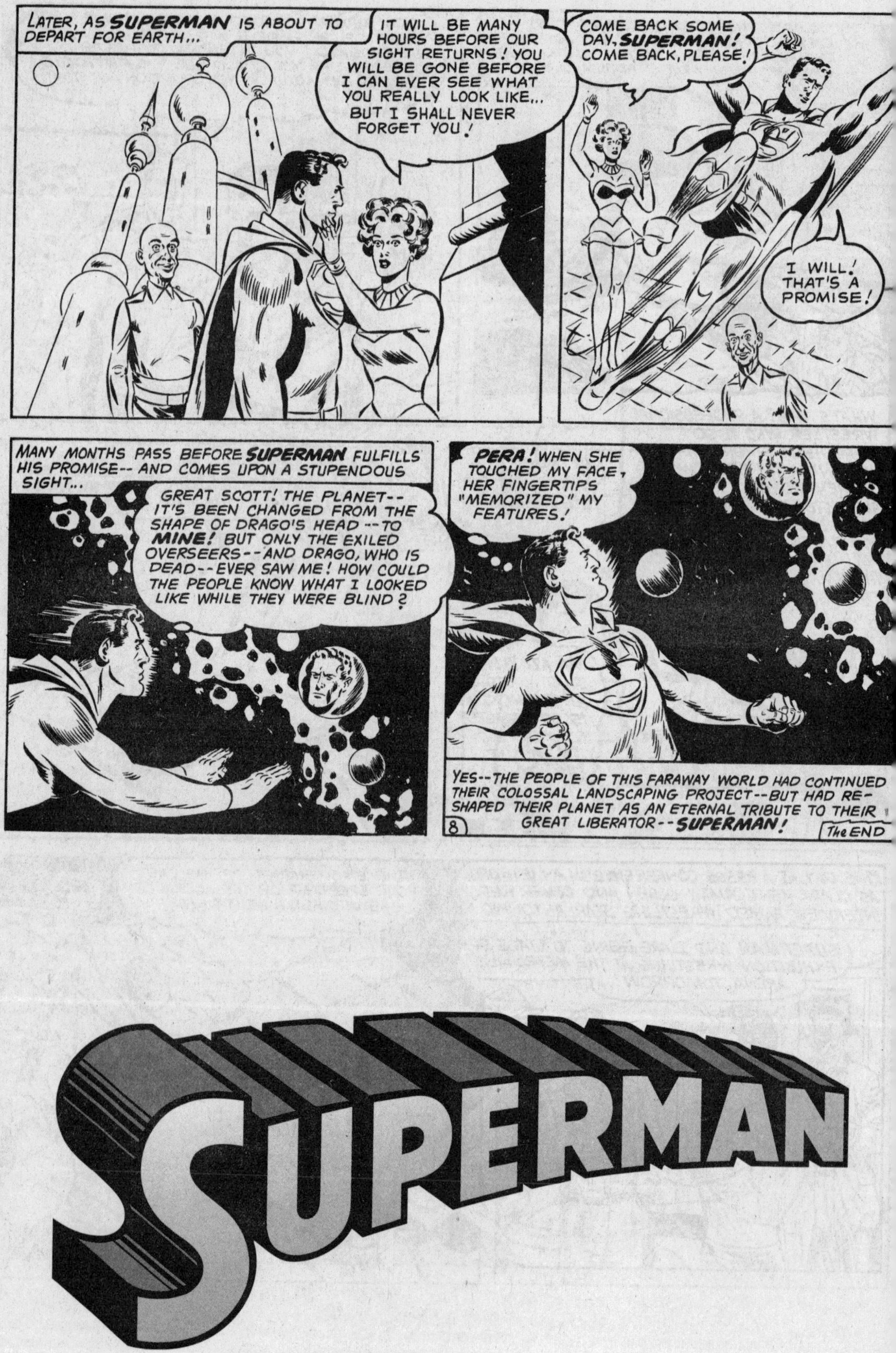
LATER, AS SUPERMAN IS ABOUT TO DEPART FOR EARTH...
IT WILL BE MANY HOURS BEFORE OUR SIGHT RETURNS! YOU WILL BE GONE BEFORE I CAN EVER SEE WHAT YOU REALLY LOOK LIKE... BUT I SHALL NEVER FORGET YOU!
COME BACK SOME DAY, SUPERMAN! COME BACK, PLEASE!
I WILL! THAT'S A PROMISE!
MANY MONTHS PASS BEFORE SUPERMAN FULFILLS HIS PROMISE-- AND COMES UPON A STUPENDOUS SIGHT...
GREAT SCOTT! THE PLANET-- IT'S BEEN CHANGED FROM THE SHAPE OF DRAGO'S HEAD --TO MINE! BUT ONLY THE EXILED OVERSEERS--AND DRAGO, WHO IS DEAD--EVER SAW ME! HOW COULD THE PEOPLE KNOW WHAT I LOOKED LIKE WHILE THEY WERE BLIND?
PERA! WHEN SHE TOUCHED MY FACE, HER FINGERTIPS "MEMORIZED" MY FEATURES!
YES--THE PEOPLE OF THIS FARAWAY WORLD HAD CONTINUED THEIR COLOSSAL LANDSCAPING PROJECT--BUT HAD RE-SHAPED THEIR PLANET AS AN ETERNAL TRIBUTE TO THEIR GREAT LIBERATOR--SUPERMAN!
8
The END

SUPERMAN

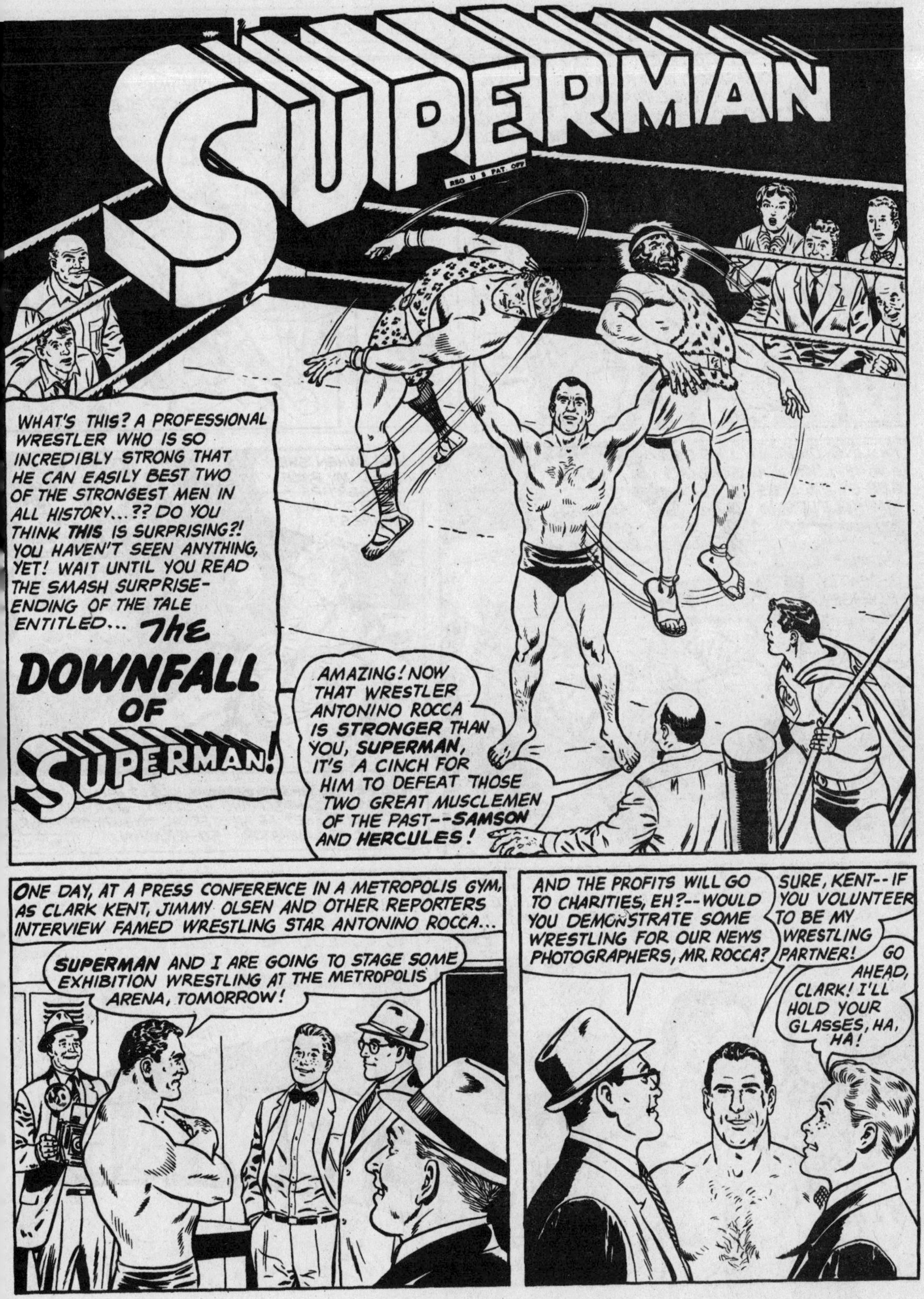
SUPERMAN
REG. U.S. PAT. OFF.
WHAT'S THIS? A PROFESSIONAL WRESTLER WHO IS SO INCREDIBLY STRONG THAT HE CAN EASILY BEST TWO OF THE STRONGEST MEN IN ALL HISTORY...?? DO YOU THINK THIS IS SURPRISING?! YOU HAVEN'T SEEN ANYTHING, YET! WAIT UNTIL YOU READ THE SMASH SURPRISE-ENDING OF THE TALE ENTITLED... The DOWNFALL OF SUPERMAN!
AMAZING! NOW THAT WRESTLER ANTONINO ROCCA IS STRONGER THAN YOU, SUPERMAN, IT'S A CINCH FOR HIM TO DEFEAT THOSE TWO GREAT MUSCLEMEN OF THE PAST--SAMSON AND HERCULES!
ONE DAY, AT A PRESS CONFERENCE IN A METROPOLIS GYM, AS CLARK KENT, JIMMY OLSEN AND OTHER REPORTERS INTERVIEW FAMED WRESTLING STAR ANTONINO ROCCA...
SUPERMAN AND I ARE GOING TO STAGE SOME EXHIBITION WRESTLING AT THE METROPOLIS ARENA, TOMORROW!
AND THE PROFITS WILL GO TO CHARITIES, EH?--WOULD YOU DEMONSTRATE SOME WRESTLING FOR OUR NEWS PHOTOGRAPHERS, MR. ROCCA?
SURE, KENT--IF YOU VOLUNTEER TO BE MY WRESTLING PARTNER!
GO AHEAD, CLARK! I'LL HOLD YOUR GLASSES, HA, HA!

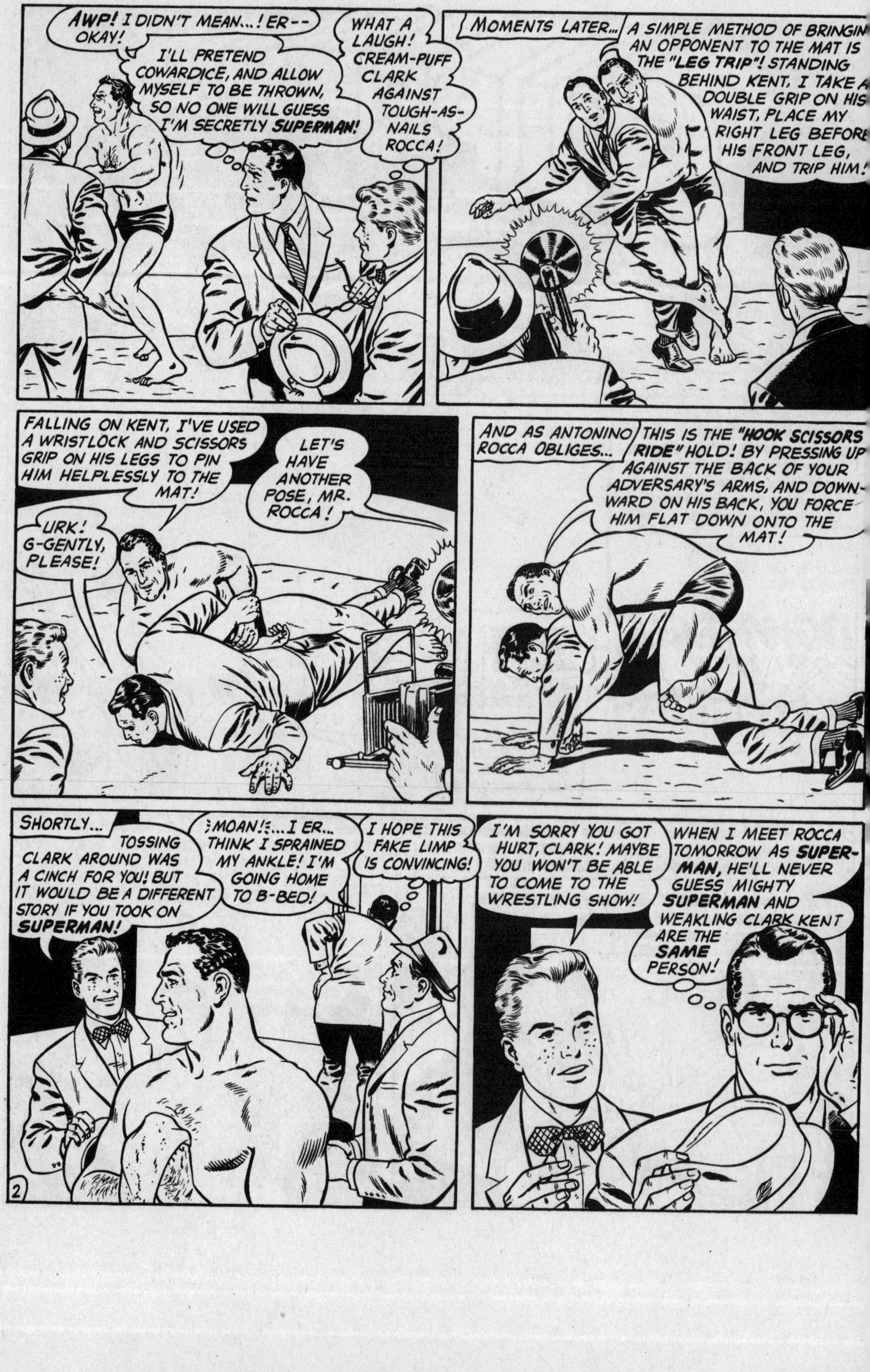
AWP! I DIDN'T MEAN...! ER-- OKAY!
I'LL PRETEND COWARDICE, AND ALLOW MYSELF TO BE THROWN, SO NO ONE WILL GUESS I'M SECRETLY SUPERMAN!
WHAT A LAUGH! CREAM-PUFF CLARK AGAINST TOUGH-AS-NAILS ROCCA!
MOMENTS LATER...
A SIMPLE METHOD OF BRINGIN AN OPPONENT TO THE MAT IS THE "LEG TRIP"! STANDING BEHIND KENT, I TAKE A DOUBLE GRIP ON HIS WAIST, PLACE MY RIGHT LEG BEFORE HIS FRONT LEG, AND TRIP HIM!
FALLING ON KENT, I'VE USED A WRISTLOCK AND SCISSORS GRIP ON HIS LEGS TO PIN HIM HELPLESSLY TO THE MAT!
LET'S HAVE ANOTHER POSE, MR. ROCCA!
URK! G-GENTLY, PLEASE!
AND AS ANTONINO ROCCA OBLIGES...
THIS IS THE "HOOK SCISSORS RIDE" HOLD! BY PRESSING UP AGAINST THE BACK OF YOUR ADVERSARY'S ARMS, AND DOWNWARD ON HIS BACK, YOU FORCE HIM FLAT DOWN ONTO THE MAT!
SHORTLY...
TOSSING CLARK AROUND WAS A CINCH FOR YOU! BUT IT WOULD BE A DIFFERENT STORY IF YOU TOOK ON SUPERMAN!
MOAN!...I ER... THINK I SPRAINED MY ANKLE! I'M GOING HOME TO B-BED!
I HOPE THIS FAKE LIMP IS CONVINCING!
2
I'M SORRY YOU GOT HURT, CLARK! MAYBE YOU WON'T BE ABLE TO COME TO THE WRESTLING SHOW!
WHEN I MEET ROCCA TOMORROW AS SUPERMAN, HE'LL NEVER GUESS MIGHTY SUPERMAN AND WEAKLING CLARK KENT ARE THE SAME PERSON!

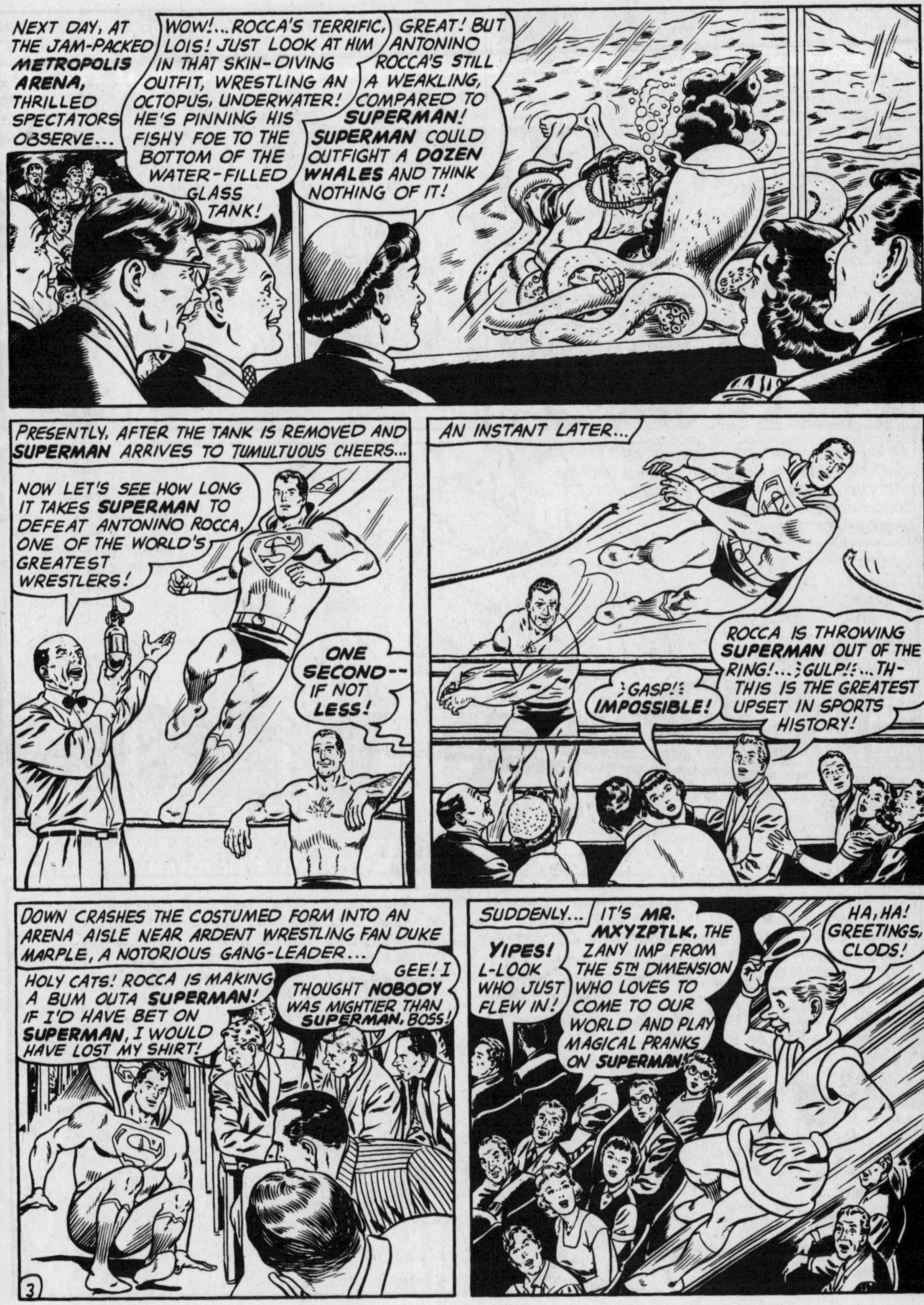
NEXT DAY, AT THE JAM-PACKED METROPOLIS ARENA, THRILLED SPECTATORS OBSERVE...
WOW!...ROCCA'S TERRIFIC, LOIS! JUST LOOK AT HIM IN THAT SKIN-DIVING OUTFIT, WRESTLING AN OCTOPUS, UNDERWATER! HE'S PINNING HIS FISHY FOE TO THE BOTTOM OF THE WATER-FILLED GLASS TANK!
GREAT! BUT ANTONINO ROCCA'S STILL A WEAKLING, COMPARED TO SUPERMAN! SUPERMAN COULD OUTFIGHT A DOZEN WHALES AND THINK NOTHING OF IT!
PRESENTLY, AFTER THE TANK IS REMOVED AND SUPERMAN ARRIVES TO TUMULTUOUS CHEERS...
NOW LET'S SEE HOW LONG IT TAKES SUPERMAN TO DEFEAT ANTONINO ROCCA, ONE OF THE WORLD'S GREATEST WRESTLERS!
ONE SECOND-- IF NOT LESS!
AN INSTANT LATER...
ROCCA IS THROWING SUPERMAN OUT OF THE RING!...¿GULP!¡...TH-THIS IS THE GREATEST UPSET IN SPORTS HISTORY!
¿GASP!¡ IMPOSSIBLE!
DOWN CRASHES THE COSTUMED FORM INTO AN ARENA AISLE NEAR ARDENT WRESTLING FAN DUKE MARPLE, A NOTORIOUS GANG-LEADER...
HOLY CATS! ROCCA IS MAKING A BUM OUTA SUPERMAN! IF I'D HAVE BET ON SUPERMAN, I WOULD HAVE LOST MY SHIRT!
GEE! I THOUGHT NOBODY WAS MIGHTIER THAN SUPERMAN, BOSS!
3
SUDDENLY...
YIPES! L-LOOK WHO JUST FLEW IN!
IT'S MR. MXYZPTLK, THE ZANY IMP FROM THE 5TH DIMENSION WHO LOVES TO COME TO OUR WORLD AND PLAY MAGICAL PRANKS ON SUPERMAN!
HA, HA! GREETINGS, CLODS!

HI, SUPIE!... WITH MY MAGICAL POWERS, I'VE MADE ROCCA STRONGER THAN YOU! HA, HA! THE SHOCKED EXPRESSION ON YOUR FACE IS HILARIOUS!
HAR, HAR!... SUPERMAN DOESN'T LIKE THE IDEA OF SOMEBODY HAVING GREATER STRENGTH!
NOW FOR SOME REAL ACTION, FOLKS! FROM OUT OF THE FAR DISTANT PAST, I'M MATERIALIZING TWO OF THE MIGHTIEST MEN OF ALL TIME--HERCULES AND SAMSON!...
... WATCH HOW MY BOY ROCCA WILL BEAT THEM!
COME AND GET ME... IF YOU CAN!!
AS HIS TWO FANTASTIC FOES SEIZE HIM, THE WRESTLING STAR THROWS OFF THEIR GRASP EASILY, SWINGS THEIR POWERFUL BODIES OVERHEAD, THEN...
YOW! A DUAL "AIRPLANE-SPIN"!
ATTABOY, ROCCA! YOUR COLOSSAL STRENGTH IS GREATER THAN THEIRS COMBINED!
YIPEEE! WHAT A BATTLE!
THEN
LOOK! HE SLAMMED THEM DOWN... AND NOW HE'S PINNING THE TWO BRUTES TO THE CANVAS WITH... HIS PINKIES...
GREAT WRESTLING, ROCCA! EVEN I COULDN'T DO BETTER! YOUR STRENGTH IS... FABULOUS!
SO LONG, FOLKS! NOW THAT I'VE HAD MY FUN HERE, I'LL GO PULL SOME PRANKS ELSEWHERE! AS FOR THOSE TWO STUMBLEBUMS, SAMSON AND HERCULES, I'LL USE MY MAGIC TO SEND THEM BACK WHERE THEY CAME FROM!
HOORAY, ROCCA!!
4

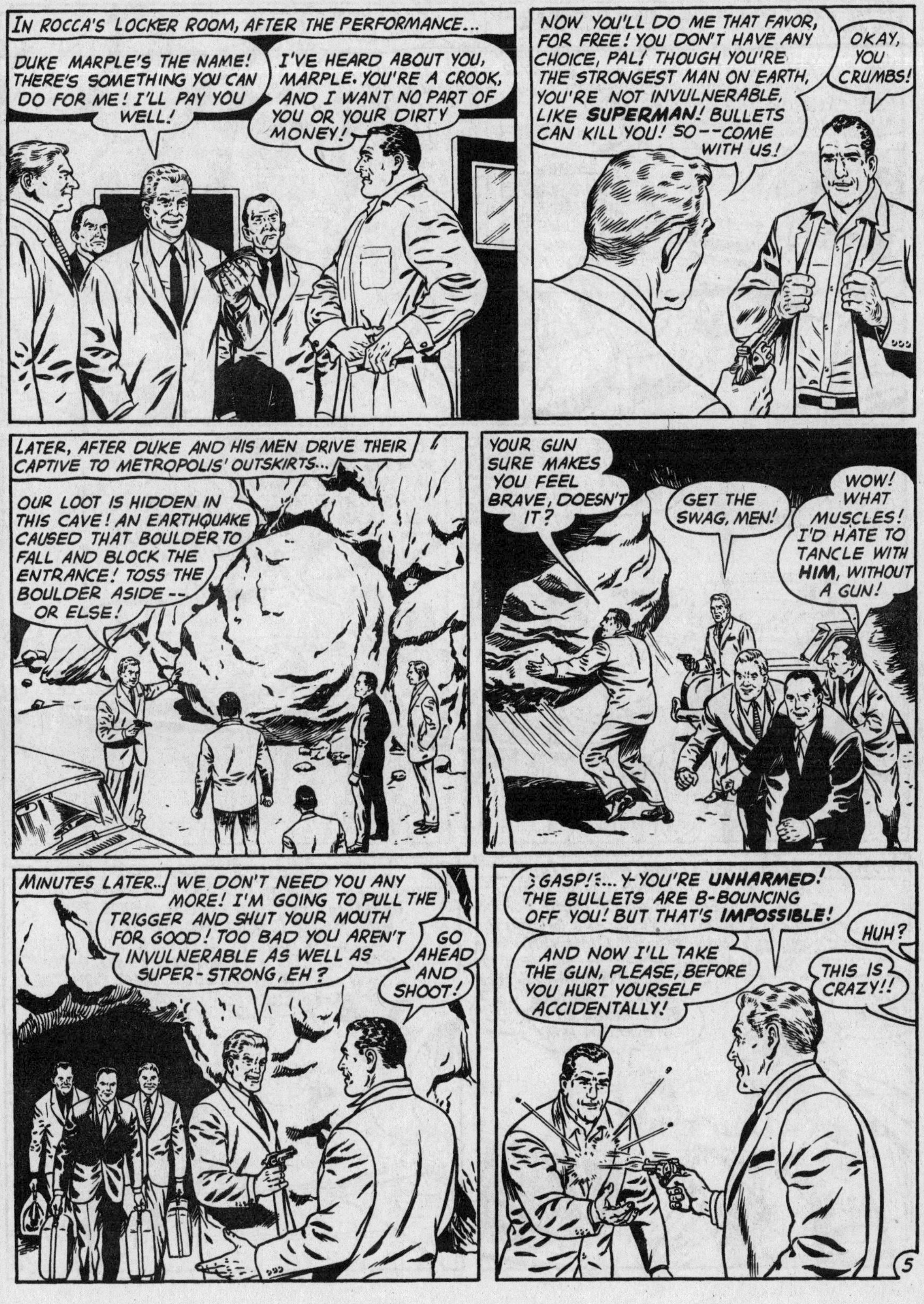
IN ROCCA'S LOCKER ROOM, AFTER THE PERFORMANCE...
DUKE MARPLE'S THE NAME! THERE'S SOMETHING YOU CAN DO FOR ME! I'LL PAY YOU WELL!
I'VE HEARD ABOUT YOU, MARPLE. YOU'RE A CROOK, AND I WANT NO PART OF YOU OR YOUR DIRTY MONEY!
NOW YOU'LL DO ME THAT FAVOR, FOR FREE! YOU DON'T HAVE ANY CHOICE, PAL! THOUGH YOU'RE THE STRONGEST MAN ON EARTH, YOU'RE NOT INVULNERABLE, LIKE SUPERMAN! BULLETS CAN KILL YOU! SO--COME WITH US!
OKAY, YOU CRUMBS!
LATER, AFTER DUKE AND HIS MEN DRIVE THEIR CAPTIVE TO METROPOLIS' OUTSKIRTS...
OUR LOOT IS HIDDEN IN THIS CAVE! AN EARTHQUAKE CAUSED THAT BOULDER TO FALL AND BLOCK THE ENTRANCE! TOSS THE BOULDER ASIDE--OR ELSE!
YOUR GUN SURE MAKES YOU FEEL BRAVE, DOESN'T IT?
GET THE SWAG, MEN!
WOW! WHAT MUSCLES! I'D HATE TO TANGLE WITH HIM, WITHOUT A GUN!
MINUTES LATER...
WE DON'T NEED YOU ANY MORE! I'M GOING TO PULL THE TRIGGER AND SHUT YOUR MOUTH FOR GOOD! TOO BAD YOU AREN'T INVULNERABLE AS WELL AS SUPER-STRONG, EH?
GO AHEAD AND SHOOT!
GASP!... Y-YOU'RE UNHARMED! THE BULLETS ARE B-BOUNCING OFF YOU! BUT THAT'S IMPOSSIBLE!
AND NOW I'LL TAKE THE GUN, PLEASE, BEFORE YOU HURT YOURSELF ACCIDENTALLY!
HUH?
THIS IS CRAZY!!
5

AS THE WRESTLER SNATCHES AWAY DUKE'S WEAPON...

GA-AA! THE BULLETS DIDN'T KILL HIM--AND N-NOW HE'S CRUSHING THE GUN IN HIS BARE FIST!!

SOME FRIENDS OF MINE TRAILED YOUR AUTO! HERE'S THEIR CAR, NOW!

GLAD TO SEE YOU, BOYS!

SUPERMAN, SAMSON AND H-HERCULES!!

I'M GETTING OUTA HERE, FAST!

BUT AS DUKE SPEEDS OFF...

NICE SHOOTING WITH THOSE ELECTRIC BOLTS! NOW I'LL TAKE OVER!

YOWW!

BAMM!

BAM!

¡CHUCKLE!¿...YOU'RE MAKING THE GETAWAY CAR SKID BACKWARDS ON ITS FLAT TIRES! WELL DONE!

LET ME HELP THAT "GENTLEMAN" OUT OF HIS CAR, FELLOWS!

MOMENTS AFTERWARD...

MR. MXYZPTLK'S FLYING ONTO THE SCENE! NONE OF THESE SUPER-GUYS' POWERS ARE GREATER THAN HIS 5TH DIMENSIONAL MAGIC!

OUT, DUKE!

HELP, MR. MXYZPTLK! MAKE A MONKEY OUTA SUPERMAN BY SAVING ME FROM HIM!

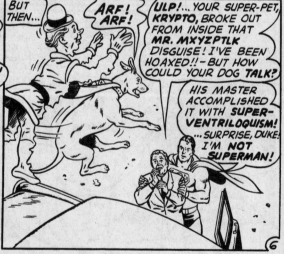

BUT THEN...

ARF! ARF!

ULP!...YOUR SUPER-PET, KRYPTO, BROKE OUT FROM INSIDE THAT MR. MXYZPTLK DISGUISE! I'VE BEEN HOAXED!!--BUT HOW COULD YOUR DOG TALK?

HIS MASTER ACCOMPLISHED IT WITH SUPER-VENTRILOQUISM! ...SURPRISE, DUKE! I'M NOT SUPERMAN!

6

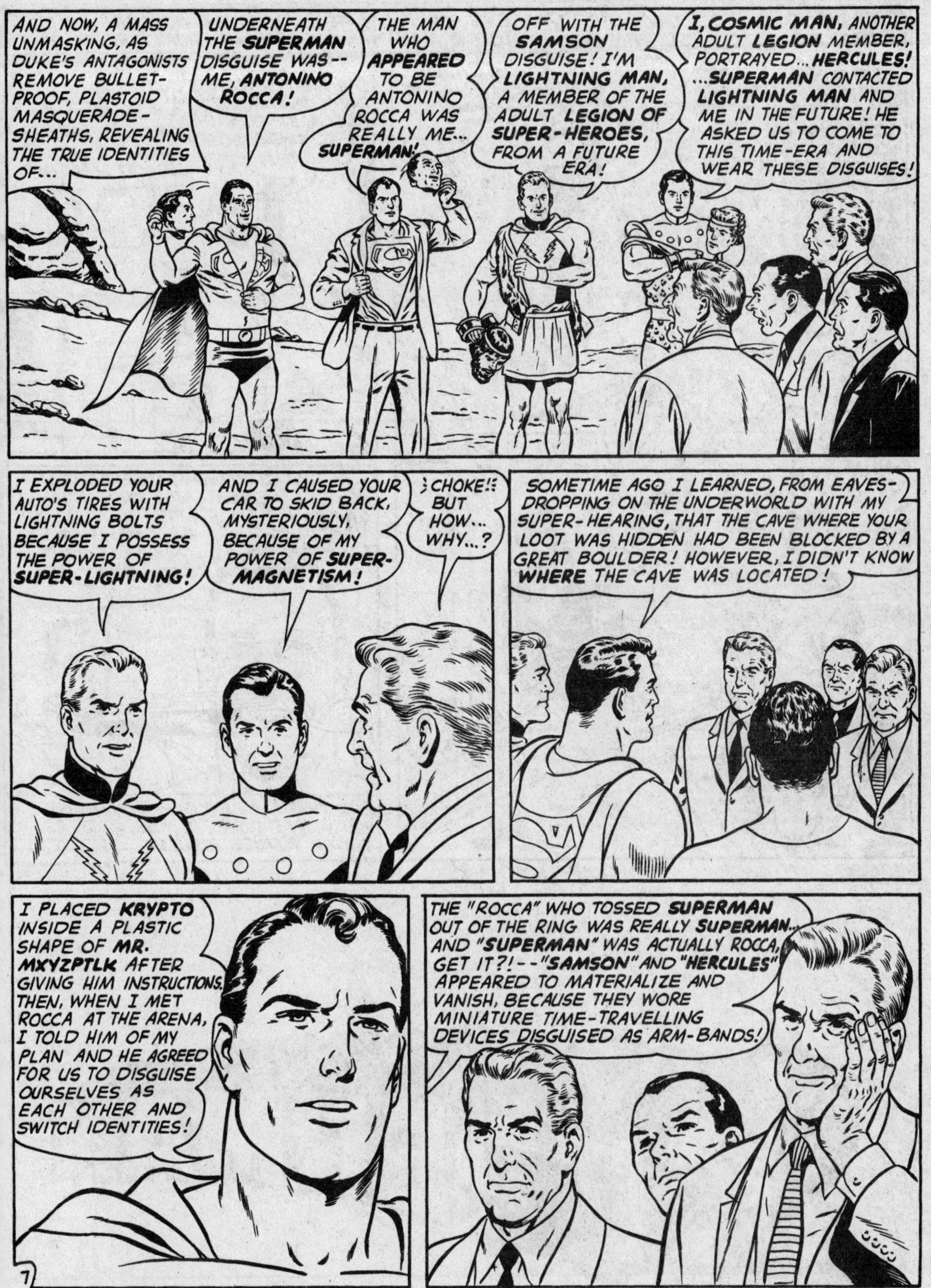
AND NOW, A MASS UNMASKING, AS DUKE'S ANTAGONISTS REMOVE BULLET-PROOF, PLASTOID MASQUERADE-SHEATHS, REVEALING THE TRUE IDENTITIES OF...
UNDERNEATH THE SUPERMAN DISGUISE WAS--ME, ANTONINO ROCCA!
THE MAN WHO APPEARED TO BE ANTONINO ROCCA WAS REALLY ME... SUPERMAN!
OFF WITH THE SAMSON DISGUISE! I'M LIGHTNING MAN, A MEMBER OF THE ADULT LEGION OF SUPER-HEROES, FROM A FUTURE ERA!
I, COSMIC MAN, ANOTHER ADULT LEGION MEMBER, PORTRAYED... HERCULES! ...SUPERMAN CONTACTED LIGHTNING MAN AND ME IN THE FUTURE! HE ASKED US TO COME TO THIS TIME-ERA AND WEAR THESE DISGUISES!
I EXPLODED YOUR AUTO'S TIRES WITH LIGHTNING BOLTS BECAUSE I POSSESS THE POWER OF SUPER-LIGHTNING!
AND I CAUSED YOUR CAR TO SKID BACK, MYSTERIOUSLY, BECAUSE OF MY POWER OF SUPER-MAGNETISM!
CHOKE! BUT HOW... WHY...?
SOMETIME AGO I LEARNED, FROM EAVES-DROPPING ON THE UNDERWORLD WITH MY SUPER-HEARING, THAT THE CAVE WHERE YOUR LOOT WAS HIDDEN HAD BEEN BLOCKED BY A GREAT BOULDER! HOWEVER, I DIDN'T KNOW WHERE THE CAVE WAS LOCATED!
I PLACED KRYPTO INSIDE A PLASTIC SHAPE OF MR. MXYZPTLK AFTER GIVING HIM INSTRUCTIONS. THEN, WHEN I MET ROCCA AT THE ARENA, I TOLD HIM OF MY PLAN AND HE AGREED FOR US TO DISGUISE OURSELVES AS EACH OTHER AND SWITCH IDENTITIES!
THE "ROCCA" WHO TOSSED SUPERMAN OUT OF THE RING WAS REALLY SUPERMAN... AND "SUPERMAN" WAS ACTUALLY ROCCA, GET IT?!--"SAMSON" AND "HERCULES" APPEARED TO MATERIALIZE AND VANISH, BECAUSE THEY WORE MINIATURE TIME-TRAVELLING DEVICES DISGUISED AS ARM-BANDS!
7

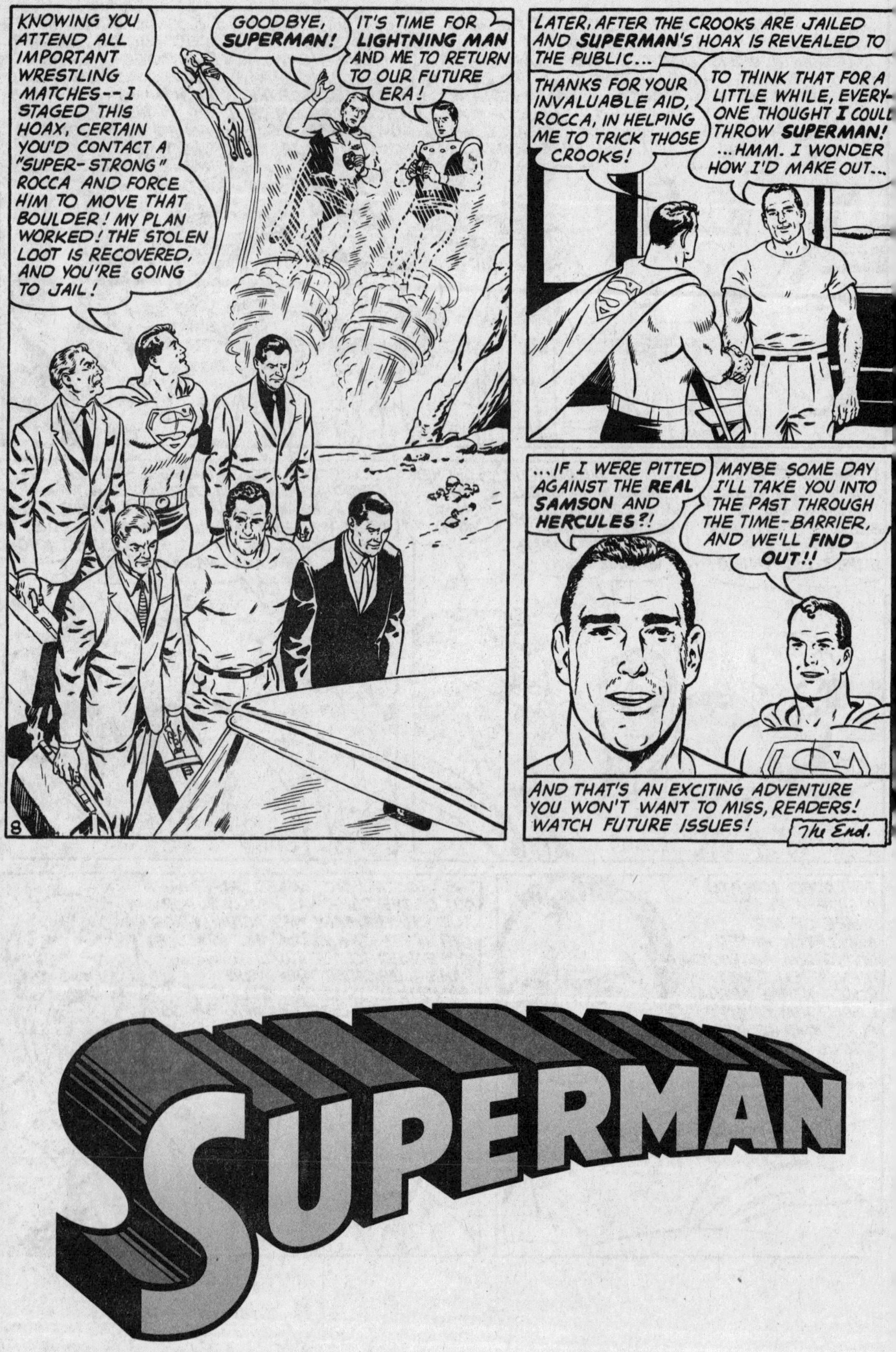
KNOWING YOU ATTEND ALL IMPORTANT WRESTLING MATCHES-- I STAGED THIS HOAX, CERTAIN YOU'D CONTACT A "SUPER-STRONG" ROCCA AND FORCE HIM TO MOVE THAT BOULDER! MY PLAN WORKED! THE STOLEN LOOT IS RECOVERED, AND YOU'RE GOING TO JAIL!
GOODBYE, SUPERMAN!
IT'S TIME FOR LIGHTNING MAN AND ME TO RETURN TO OUR FUTURE ERA!
8
LATER, AFTER THE CROOKS ARE JAILED AND SUPERMAN'S HOAX IS REVEALED TO THE PUBLIC...
THANKS FOR YOUR INVALUABLE AID, ROCCA, IN HELPING ME TO TRICK THOSE CROOKS!
TO THINK THAT FOR A LITTLE WHILE, EVERY-ONE THOUGHT I COULD THROW SUPERMAN! ...HMM. I WONDER HOW I'D MAKE OUT...
...IF I WERE PITTED AGAINST THE REAL SAMSON AND HERCULES?!
MAYBE SOME DAY I'LL TAKE YOU INTO THE PAST THROUGH THE TIME-BARRIER, AND WE'LL FIND OUT!!
AND THAT'S AN EXCITING ADVENTURE YOU WON'T WANT TO MISS, READERS! WATCH FUTURE ISSUES!
The End.

SUPERMAN

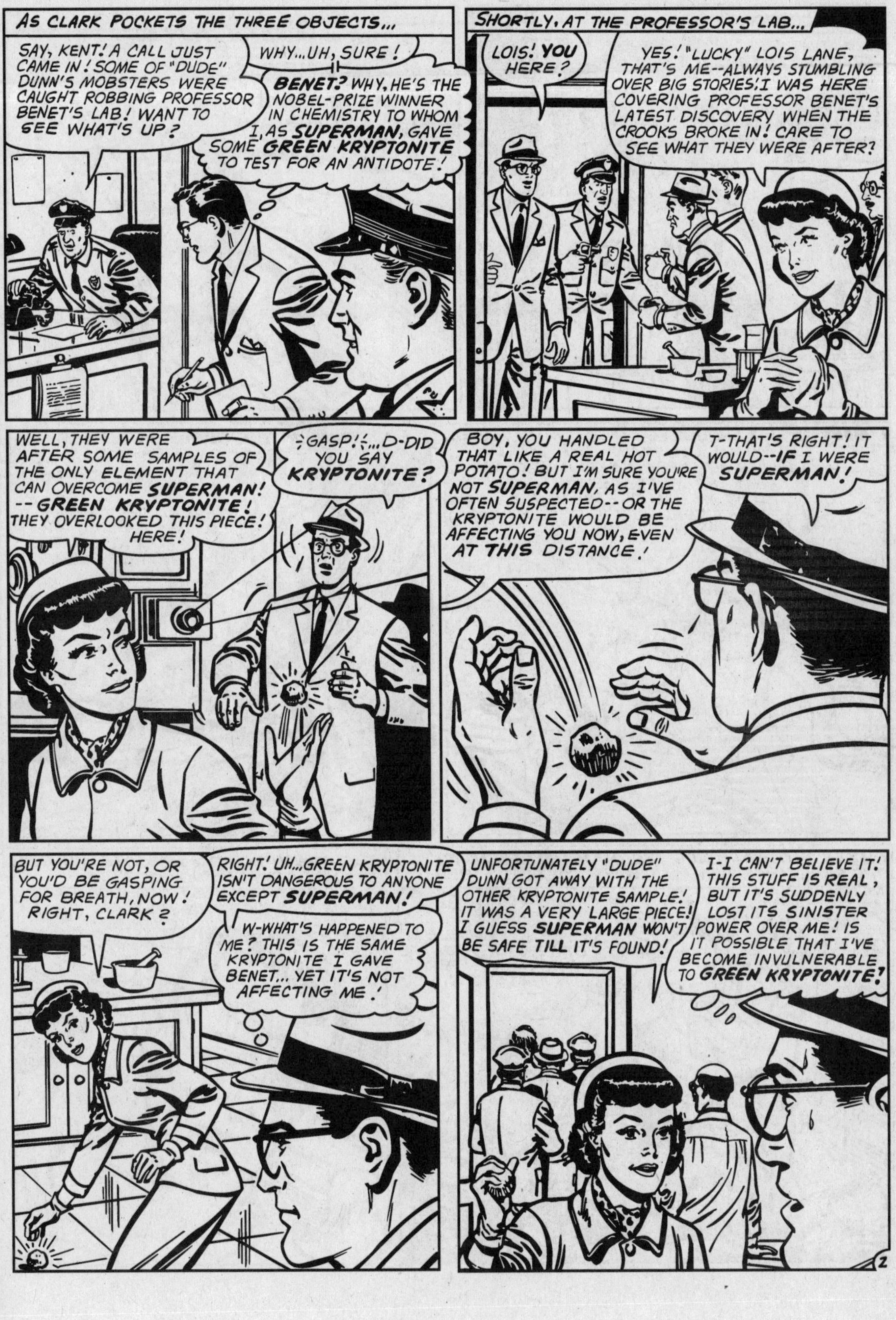
AS CLARK POCKETS THE THREE OBJECTS...
SAY, KENT! A CALL JUST CAME IN! SOME OF "DUDE" DUNN'S MOBSTERS WERE CAUGHT ROBBING PROFESSOR BENET'S LAB! WANT TO SEE WHAT'S UP?
WHY...UH, SURE!
BENET? WHY, HE'S THE NOBEL-PRIZE WINNER IN CHEMISTRY TO WHOM I, AS SUPERMAN, GAVE SOME GREEN KRYPTONITE TO TEST FOR AN ANTIDOTE!
SHORTLY, AT THE PROFESSOR'S LAB...
LOIS! YOU HERE?
YES! "LUCKY" LOIS LANE, THAT'S ME--ALWAYS STUMBLING OVER BIG STORIES! I WAS HERE COVERING PROFESSOR BENET'S LATEST DISCOVERY WHEN THE CROOKS BROKE IN! CARE TO SEE WHAT THEY WERE AFTER?
WELL, THEY WERE AFTER SOME SAMPLES OF THE ONLY ELEMENT THAT CAN OVERCOME SUPERMAN! --GREEN KRYPTONITE! THEY OVERLOOKED THIS PIECE! HERE!
GASP! ...D-DID YOU SAY KRYPTONITE?
BOY, YOU HANDLED THAT LIKE A REAL HOT POTATO! BUT I'M SURE YOU'RE NOT SUPERMAN, AS I'VE OFTEN SUSPECTED--OR THE KRYPTONITE WOULD BE AFFECTING YOU NOW, EVEN AT THIS DISTANCE!
T-THAT'S RIGHT! IT WOULD--IF I WERE SUPERMAN!
BUT YOU'RE NOT, OR YOU'D BE GASPING FOR BREATH, NOW! RIGHT, CLARK?
RIGHT! UH...GREEN KRYPTONITE ISN'T DANGEROUS TO ANYONE EXCEPT SUPERMAN!
W-WHAT'S HAPPENED TO ME? THIS IS THE SAME KRYPTONITE I GAVE BENET... YET IT'S NOT AFFECTING ME!
UNFORTUNATELY "DUDE" DUNN GOT AWAY WITH THE OTHER KRYPTONITE SAMPLE! IT WAS A VERY LARGE PIECE! I GUESS SUPERMAN WON'T BE SAFE TILL IT'S FOUND!
I-I CAN'T BELIEVE IT! THIS STUFF IS REAL, BUT IT'S SUDDENLY LOST ITS SINISTER POWER OVER ME! IS IT POSSIBLE THAT I'VE BECOME INVULNERABLE TO GREEN KRYPTONITE?
2

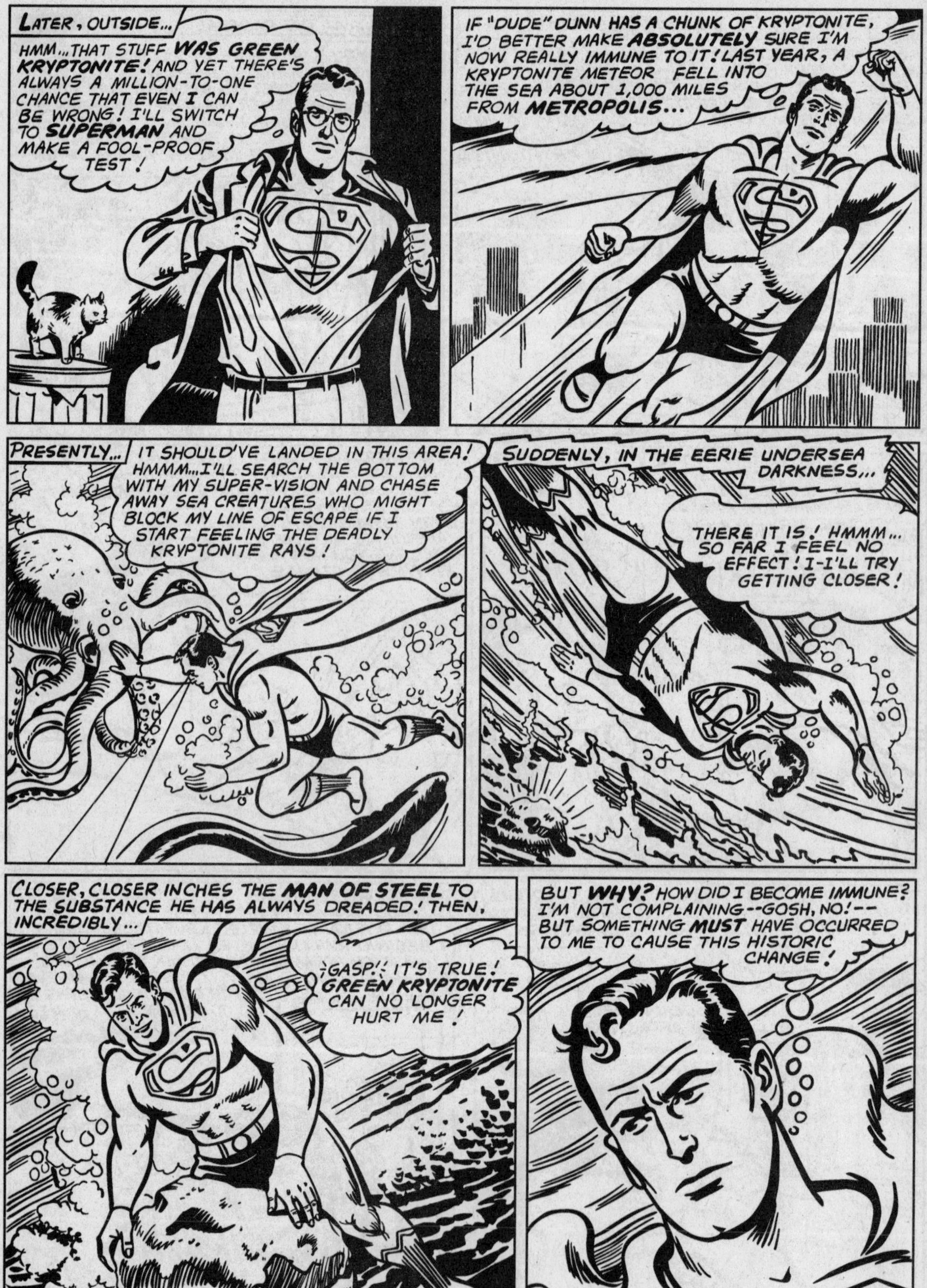
LATER, OUTSIDE...
HMM... THAT STUFF WAS GREEN KRYPTONITE! AND YET THERE'S ALWAYS A MILLION-TO-ONE CHANCE THAT EVEN I CAN BE WRONG! I'LL SWITCH TO SUPERMAN AND MAKE A FOOL-PROOF TEST!
IF "DUDE" DUNN HAS A CHUNK OF KRYPTONITE, I'D BETTER MAKE ABSOLUTELY SURE I'M NOW REALLY IMMUNE TO IT! LAST YEAR, A KRYPTONITE METEOR FELL INTO THE SEA ABOUT 1,000 MILES FROM METROPOLIS...
PRESENTLY...
IT SHOULD'VE LANDED IN THIS AREA! HMMM... I'LL SEARCH THE BOTTOM WITH MY SUPER-VISION AND CHASE AWAY SEA CREATURES WHO MIGHT BLOCK MY LINE OF ESCAPE IF I START FEELING THE DEADLY KRYPTONITE RAYS!
SUDDENLY, IN THE EERIE UNDERSEA DARKNESS...
THERE IT IS! HMMM... SO FAR I FEEL NO EFFECT! I-I'LL TRY GETTING CLOSER!
CLOSER, CLOSER INCHES THE MAN OF STEEL TO THE SUBSTANCE HE HAS ALWAYS DREADED! THEN, INCREDIBLY...
GASP! IT'S TRUE! GREEN KRYPTONITE CAN NO LONGER HURT ME!
BUT WHY? HOW DID I BECOME IMMUNE? I'M NOT COMPLAINING--GOSH, NO!--BUT SOMETHING MUST HAVE OCCURRED TO ME TO CAUSE THIS HISTORIC CHANGE!
3

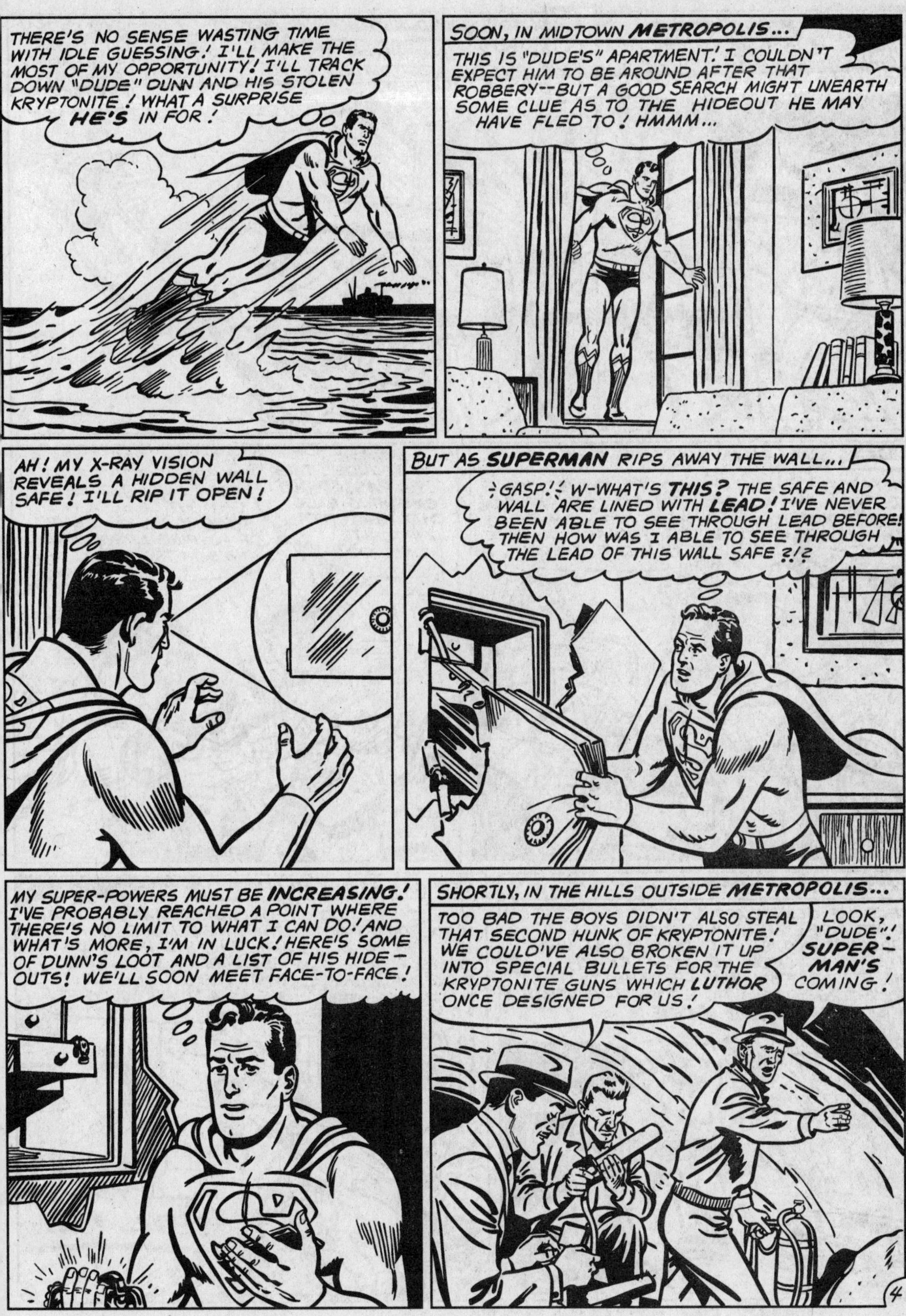
THERE'S NO SENSE WASTING TIME WITH IDLE GUESSING! I'LL MAKE THE MOST OF MY OPPORTUNITY! I'LL TRACK DOWN "DUDE" DUNN AND HIS STOLEN KRYPTONITE! WHAT A SURPRISE HE'S IN FOR!
SOON, IN MIDTOWN METROPOLIS...
THIS IS "DUDE'S" APARTMENT! I COULDN'T EXPECT HIM TO BE AROUND AFTER THAT ROBBERY--BUT A GOOD SEARCH MIGHT UNEARTH SOME CLUE AS TO THE HIDEOUT HE MAY HAVE FLED TO! HMMM...
AH! MY X-RAY VISION REVEALS A HIDDEN WALL SAFE! I'LL RIP IT OPEN!
BUT AS SUPERMAN RIPS AWAY THE WALL...
-GASP!- W-WHAT'S THIS? THE SAFE AND WALL ARE LINED WITH LEAD! I'VE NEVER BEEN ABLE TO SEE THROUGH LEAD BEFORE! THEN HOW WAS I ABLE TO SEE THROUGH THE LEAD OF THIS WALL SAFE ?!?
MY SUPER-POWERS MUST BE INCREASING! I'VE PROBABLY REACHED A POINT WHERE THERE'S NO LIMIT TO WHAT I CAN DO! AND WHAT'S MORE, I'M IN LUCK! HERE'S SOME OF DUNN'S LOOT AND A LIST OF HIS HIDE-OUTS! WE'LL SOON MEET FACE-TO-FACE!
SHORTLY, IN THE HILLS OUTSIDE METROPOLIS...
TOO BAD THE BOYS DIDN'T ALSO STEAL THAT SECOND HUNK OF KRYPTONITE! WE COULD'VE ALSO BROKEN IT UP INTO SPECIAL BULLETS FOR THE KRYPTONITE GUNS WHICH LUTHOR ONCE DESIGNED FOR US!
LOOK, "DUDE"! SUPER-MAN'S COMING!
4

LET HIM COME! HE DOESN'T SCARE US NOW! NOT WHEN WE CAN KILL HIM WITH KRYPTONITE BULLETS! LET HIM HAVE IT!

BUT TO "DUDE" DUNN'S HORROR...

"DUDE"! S-SOMETHING'S WRONG! THE KRYPTONITE DOESN'T HARM HIM!

I-IT'S IMPOSSIBLE!

SORRY, "DUDE"! ALL YOU'LL GET OUT OF STEALING THAT KRYPTONITE IS A *PRISON SENTENCE!*

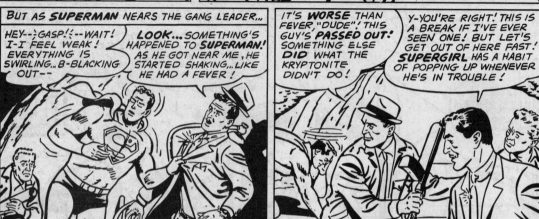

BUT AS *SUPERMAN* NEARS THE GANG LEADER...

HEY--! GASP!--WAIT! I-I FEEL WEAK! EVERYTHING IS SWIRLING...B-BLACKING OUT--

LOOK...SOMETHING'S HAPPENED TO *SUPERMAN!* AS HE GOT NEAR ME, HE STARTED SHAKING,..LIKE HE HAD A FEVER!

IT'S *WORSE* THAN FEVER, "DUDE"! THIS GUY'S *PASSED OUT!* SOMETHING ELSE *DID* WHAT THE KRYPTONITE DIDN'T DO!

Y-YOU'RE RIGHT! THIS IS A BREAK IF I'VE EVER SEEN ONE! BUT LET'S GET OUT OF HERE FAST! *SUPERGIRL* HAS A HABIT OF POPPING UP WHENEVER HE'S IN TROUBLE!

PRESENTLY, WHEN *SUPERMAN* RECOVERS...

THEY'VE GONE,...AND THEY'VE LEFT THE KRYPTONITE BULLETS! BUT AS BEFORE, IT DOESN'T BOTHER ME! THEN *WHAT* WAS IT THAT KNOCKED ME UNCONSCIOUS? HAVE I LOST MY INVULNERABILITY TO KRYPTONITE ONLY TO BECOME VULNERABLE TO *SOMETHING ELSE?*

NEXT DAY, AT THE PLANET...

HMM... I SEE THAT "DUDE" DIDN'T GET VERY FAR! THE STATE POLICE PICKED HIM UP!

OH, *SUPERMAN!* LOOK AT THIS! REMEMBER THAT MAHARAJAH I INTERVIEWED LAST WEEK? WELL, LOOK WHAT THE DARLING SENT ME AS A "THANK YOU" GIFT!

"DUDE" DUNN CAPTURED BY STATE POLICE

DAILY PLANET

5

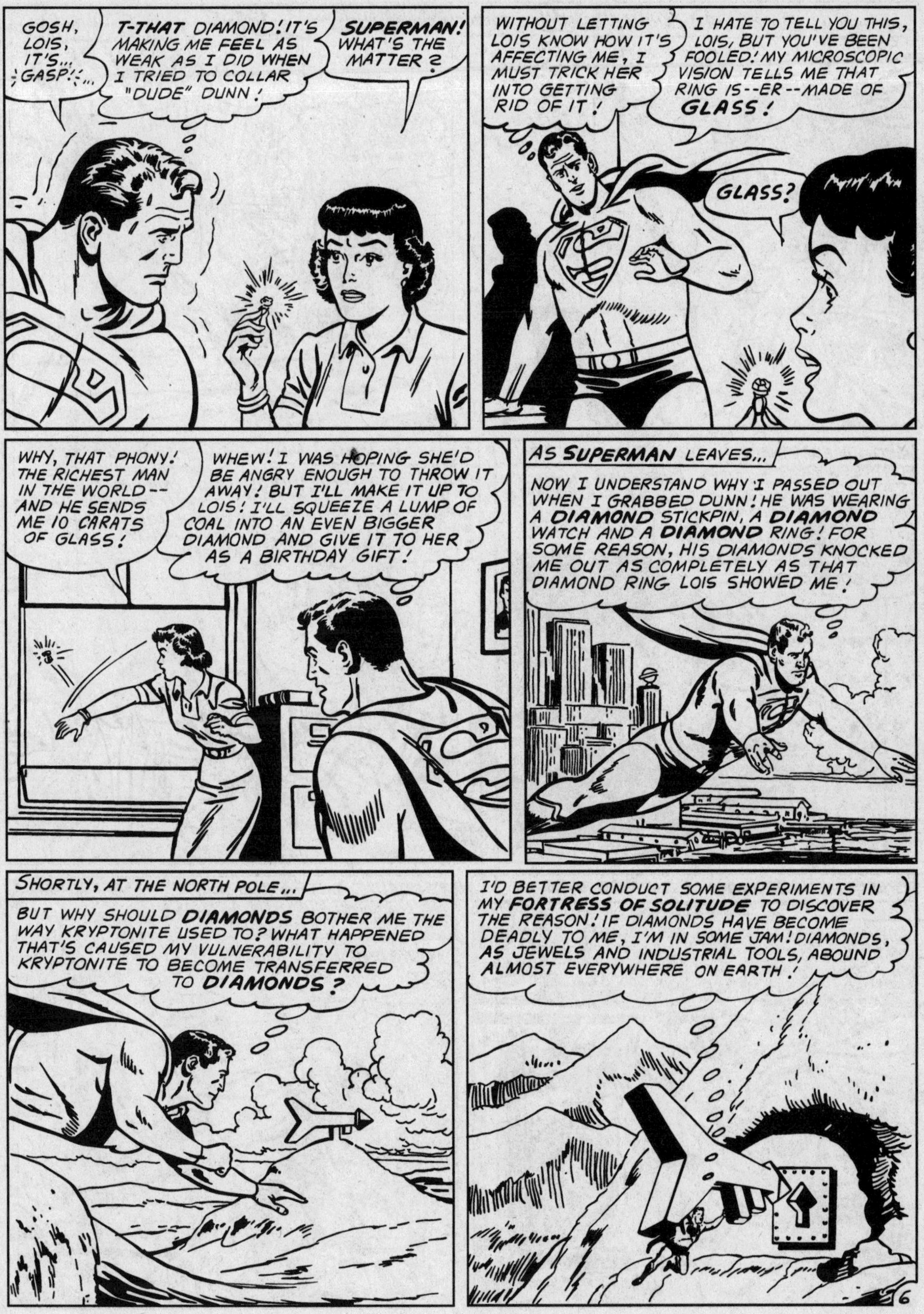
GOSH, LOIS, IT'S... GASP!...
T-THAT DIAMOND! IT'S MAKING ME FEEL AS WEAK AS I DID WHEN I TRIED TO COLLAR "DUDE" DUNN!
SUPERMAN! WHAT'S THE MATTER?
WITHOUT LETTING LOIS KNOW HOW IT'S AFFECTING ME, I MUST TRICK HER INTO GETTING RID OF IT!
I HATE TO TELL YOU THIS, LOIS, BUT YOU'VE BEEN FOOLED! MY MICROSCOPIC VISION TELLS ME THAT RING IS--ER--MADE OF GLASS!
GLASS?
WHY, THAT PHONY! THE RICHEST MAN IN THE WORLD--AND HE SENDS ME 10 CARATS OF GLASS!
WHEW! I WAS HOPING SHE'D BE ANGRY ENOUGH TO THROW IT AWAY! BUT I'LL MAKE IT UP TO LOIS! I'LL SQUEEZE A LUMP OF COAL INTO AN EVEN BIGGER DIAMOND AND GIVE IT TO HER AS A BIRTHDAY GIFT!
AS SUPERMAN LEAVES...
NOW I UNDERSTAND WHY I PASSED OUT WHEN I GRABBED DUNN! HE WAS WEARING A DIAMOND STICKPIN, A DIAMOND WATCH AND A DIAMOND RING! FOR SOME REASON, HIS DIAMONDS KNOCKED ME OUT AS COMPLETELY AS THAT DIAMOND RING LOIS SHOWED ME!
SHORTLY, AT THE NORTH POLE...
BUT WHY SHOULD DIAMONDS BOTHER ME THE WAY KRYPTONITE USED TO? WHAT HAPPENED THAT'S CAUSED MY VULNERABILITY TO KRYPTONITE TO BECOME TRANSFERRED TO DIAMONDS?
I'D BETTER CONDUCT SOME EXPERIMENTS IN MY FORTRESS OF SOLITUDE TO DISCOVER THE REASON! IF DIAMONDS HAVE BECOME DEADLY TO ME, I'M IN SOME JAM! DIAMONDS, AS JEWELS AND INDUSTRIAL TOOLS, ABOUND ALMOST EVERYWHERE ON EARTH!
6

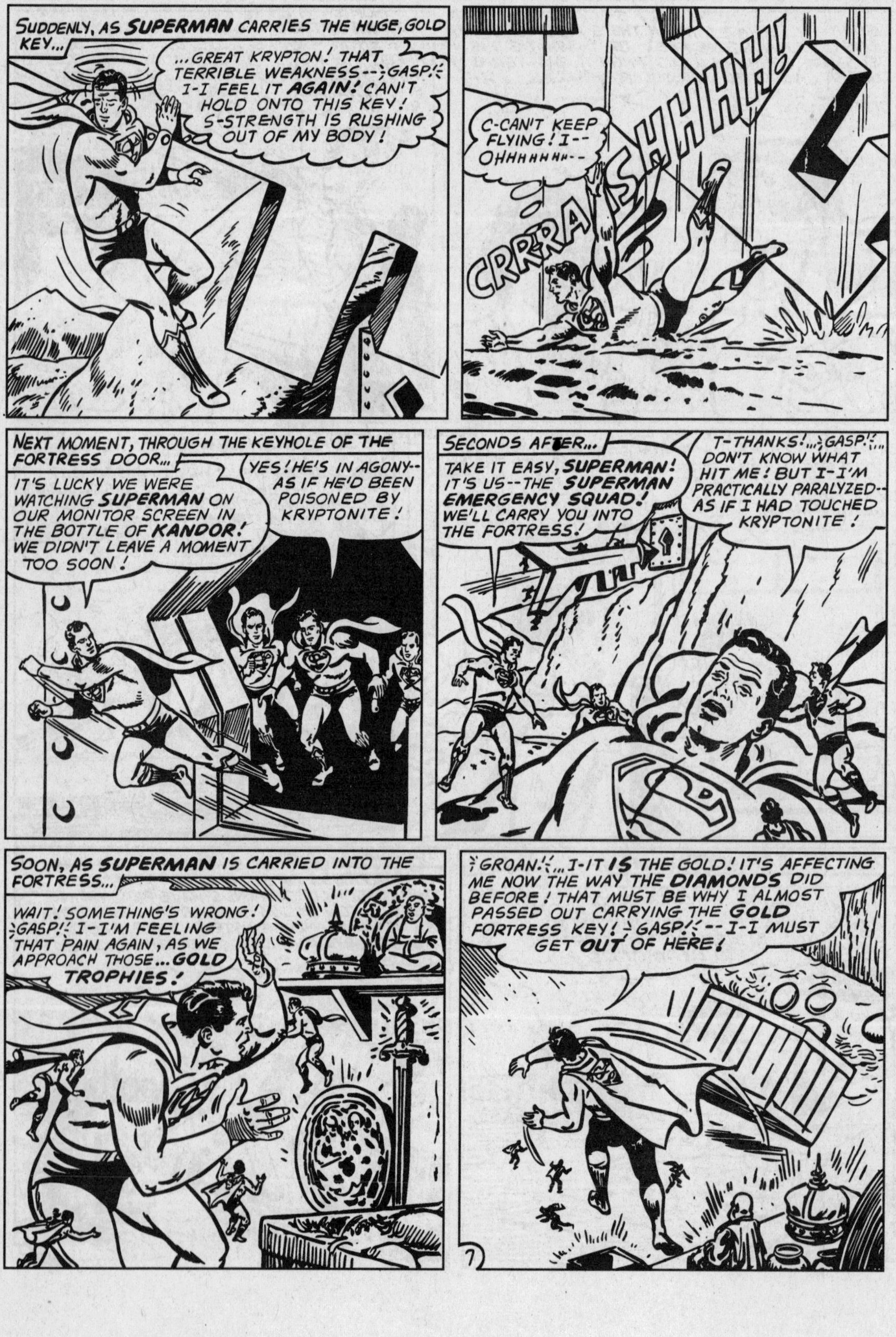
SUDDENLY, AS SUPERMAN CARRIES THE HUGE, GOLD KEY...
...GREAT KRYPTON! THAT TERRIBLE WEAKNESS--GASP!-- I-I FEEL IT AGAIN! CAN'T HOLD ONTO THIS KEY! S-STRENGTH IS RUSHING OUT OF MY BODY!
C-CAN'T KEEP FLYING! I-- OHHHHHHH--
CRRRASHHHHH!
NEXT MOMENT, THROUGH THE KEYHOLE OF THE FORTRESS DOOR...
IT'S LUCKY WE WERE WATCHING SUPERMAN ON OUR MONITOR SCREEN IN THE BOTTLE OF KANDOR! WE DIDN'T LEAVE A MOMENT TOO SOON!
YES! HE'S IN AGONY-- AS IF HE'D BEEN POISONED BY KRYPTONITE!
SECONDS AFTER...
TAKE IT EASY, SUPERMAN! IT'S US--THE SUPERMAN EMERGENCY SQUAD! WE'LL CARRY YOU INTO THE FORTRESS!
T-THANKS!...GASP!... DON'T KNOW WHAT HIT ME! BUT I-I'M PRACTICALLY PARALYZED-- AS IF I HAD TOUCHED KRYPTONITE!
SOON, AS SUPERMAN IS CARRIED INTO THE FORTRESS...
WAIT! SOMETHING'S WRONG! GASP! I-I'M FEELING THAT PAIN AGAIN, AS WE APPROACH THOSE...GOLD TROPHIES!
GROAN!...I-IT IS THE GOLD! IT'S AFFECTING ME NOW THE WAY THE DIAMONDS DID BEFORE! THAT MUST BE WHY I ALMOST PASSED OUT CARRYING THE GOLD FORTRESS KEY! GASP! --I-I MUST GET OUT OF HERE!
7

LOOK OUT, *SUPERMAN!* YOU'VE KNOCKED OVER THE CRATE OF UNHATCHED EGGS BELONGING TO THE FLAME DRAGON OF KRYPTON WHICH YOU ONCE THREW INTO THE PAST FOR SAFE-KEEPING!

S-SORRY! RE-CRATE THE EGGS...AND GET RID OF THOSE GOLD TROPHIES! THEIR RADIATIONS ARE *POISONING* ME!

SHORTLY, AS THE TINY SUPERMEN FOLLOW THE *MAN OF STEEL'S* ORDER...

THANKS! I-I FEEL BETTER NOW--BUT I'M MORE MYSTIFIED THAN EVER! SEE THAT HUGE DIAMOND ONCE GIVEN TO ME BY A RACE OF ALIENS WHOSE WORLD I HAD SAVED FROM DESTRUCTION?

AN HOUR AGO, *DIAMONDS* AFFECTED ME JUST AS GOLD DOES NOW! BUT NOW DIAMONDS DON'T BOTHER ME! ITS DEADLY PROPERTIES HAVE BEEN TRANSFERRED TO *GOLD!* WHY? WHAT WEIRD PHENOMENON KEEPS SWITCHING KRYPTONITE'S LETHAL EFFECTS *FROM ONE ELEMENT TO ANOTHER?*

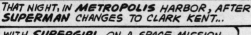

PRESENTLY...

I'LL RETURN NOW TO *METROPOLIS* AND AVOID GOLD LIKE THE PLAGUE!

WE'LL KEEP AN EYE ON YOU, *SUPERMAN,* ON OUR MONITOR SCREEN! IF YOU ENCOUNTER ANY TROUBLE, WE'LL COME TO YOUR RESCUE!

THAT NIGHT, IN *METROPOLIS* HARBOR, AFTER *SUPERMAN* CHANGES TO CLARK KENT...

WITH *SUPERGIRL* ON A SPACE MISSION, IT'S A COMFORTING THOUGHT TO KNOW THAT THE *SUPERMAN EMERGENCY SQUAD* IS LOOKING AFTER ME... BECAUSE I RUN THE RISK OF BEING EXPOSED TO GOLD AT ANY TIME! ESPECIALLY ON *THIS* ASSIGNMENT FOR THE *PLANET!*

SOON, ABOARD A GAILY DECORATED YACHT...

HIGH SOCIETY IS RUNNING A MONTE CARLO GAMBLING NIGHT ON THIS MILLIONAIRE'S YACHT... WITH ALL THE PROCEEDS GOING TO CHARITY! BUT I'M WORRIED ABOUT GETTING TOO CLOSE TO SOMEBODY'S GOLD WEDDING BAND OR BRACELET!

8

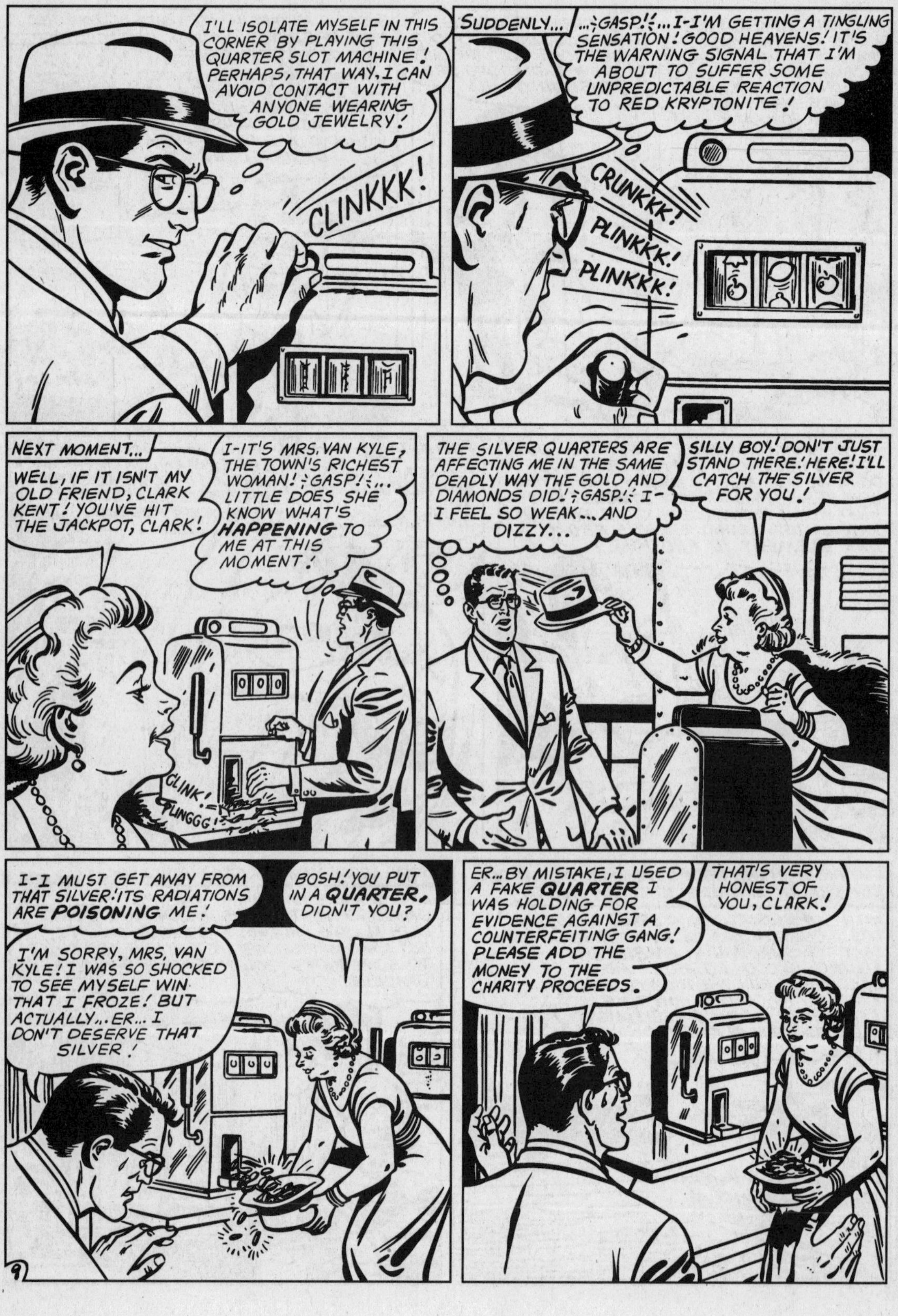
I'LL ISOLATE MYSELF IN THIS CORNER BY PLAYING THIS QUARTER SLOT MACHINE! PERHAPS, THAT WAY, I CAN AVOID CONTACT WITH ANYONE WEARING GOLD JEWELRY!
CLINKKK!
SUDDENLY...
...GASP!... I-I'M GETTING A TINGLING SENSATION! GOOD HEAVENS! IT'S THE WARNING SIGNAL THAT I'M ABOUT TO SUFFER SOME UNPREDICTABLE REACTION TO RED KRYPTONITE!
CRUNKKK!
PLINKKK!
PLINKKK!
NEXT MOMENT...
WELL, IF IT ISN'T MY OLD FRIEND, CLARK KENT! YOU'VE HIT THE JACKPOT, CLARK!
I-IT'S MRS. VAN KYLE, THE TOWN'S RICHEST WOMAN! GASP!... LITTLE DOES SHE KNOW WHAT'S HAPPENING TO ME AT THIS MOMENT!
CLINK!
PLINGGG!
THE SILVER QUARTERS ARE AFFECTING ME IN THE SAME DEADLY WAY THE GOLD AND DIAMONDS DID! GASP! I-I FEEL SO WEAK... AND DIZZY...
SILLY BOY! DON'T JUST STAND THERE! HERE! I'LL CATCH THE SILVER FOR YOU!
I-I MUST GET AWAY FROM THAT SILVER! ITS RADIATIONS ARE POISONING ME!
BOSH! YOU PUT IN A QUARTER, DIDN'T YOU?
I'M SORRY, MRS. VAN KYLE! I WAS SO SHOCKED TO SEE MYSELF WIN THAT I FROZE! BUT ACTUALLY... ER... I DON'T DESERVE THAT SILVER!
9
ER... BY MISTAKE, I USED A FAKE QUARTER I WAS HOLDING FOR EVIDENCE AGAINST A COUNTERFEITING GANG! PLEASE ADD THE MONEY TO THE CHARITY PROCEEDS.
THAT'S VERY HONEST OF YOU, CLARK!

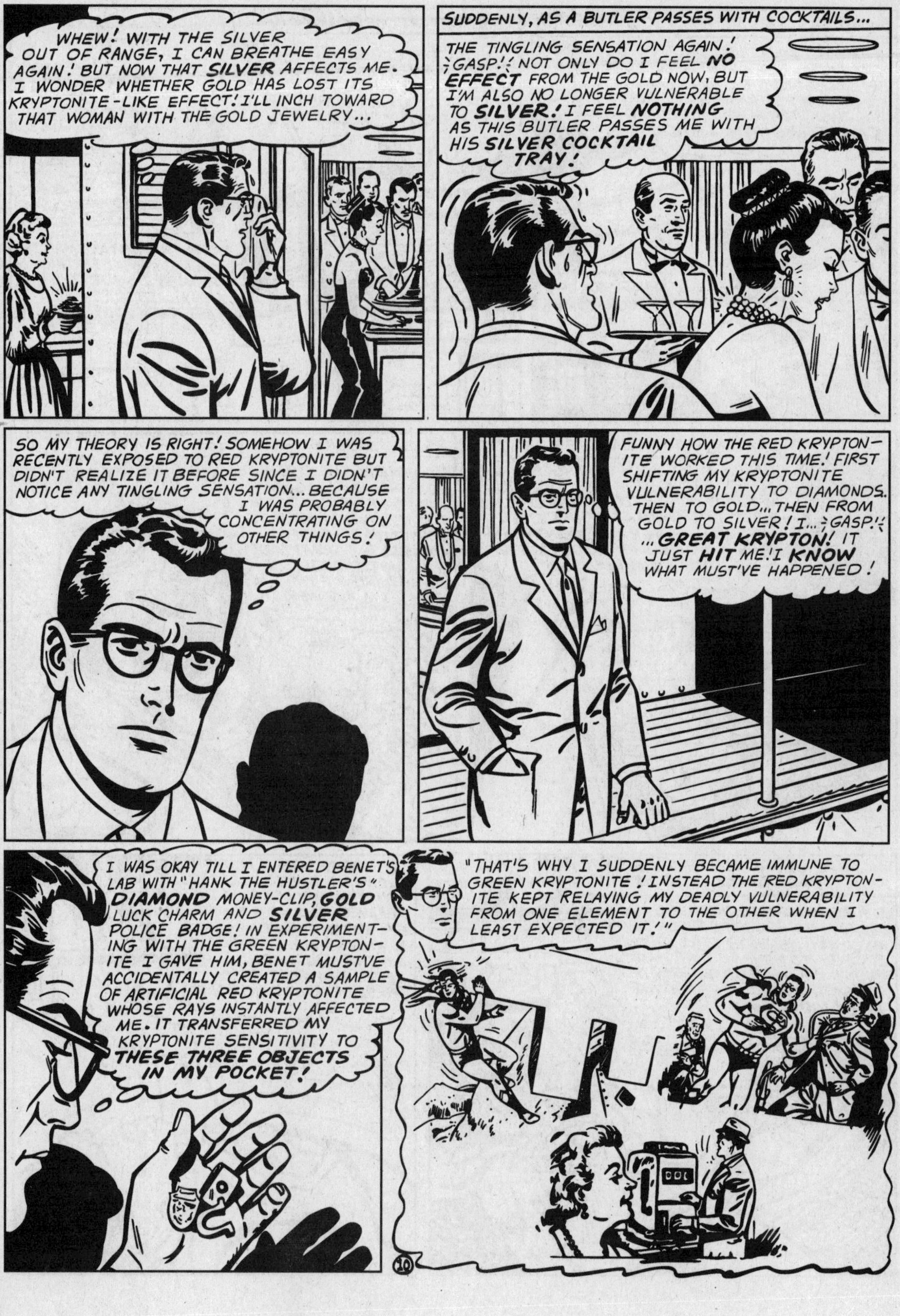
WHEW! WITH THE SILVER OUT OF RANGE, I CAN BREATHE EASY AGAIN! BUT NOW THAT SILVER AFFECTS ME. I WONDER WHETHER GOLD HAS LOST ITS KRYPTONITE-LIKE EFFECT! I'LL INCH TOWARD THAT WOMAN WITH THE GOLD JEWELRY...
SUDDENLY, AS A BUTLER PASSES WITH COCKTAILS...
THE TINGLING SENSATION AGAIN! ;GASP!; NOT ONLY DO I FEEL NO EFFECT FROM THE GOLD NOW, BUT I'M ALSO NO LONGER VULNERABLE TO SILVER! I FEEL NOTHING AS THIS BUTLER PASSES ME WITH HIS SILVER COCKTAIL TRAY!
SO MY THEORY IS RIGHT! SOMEHOW I WAS RECENTLY EXPOSED TO RED KRYPTONITE BUT DIDN'T REALIZE IT BEFORE SINCE I DIDN'T NOTICE ANY TINGLING SENSATION... BECAUSE I WAS PROBABLY CONCENTRATING ON OTHER THINGS!
FUNNY HOW THE RED KRYPTONITE WORKED THIS TIME! FIRST SHIFTING MY KRYPTONITE VULNERABILITY TO DIAMONDS. THEN TO GOLD... THEN FROM GOLD TO SILVER! I... ;GASP!; ...GREAT KRYPTON! IT JUST HIT ME! I KNOW WHAT MUST'VE HAPPENED!
I WAS OKAY TILL I ENTERED BENET'S LAB WITH "HANK THE HUSTLER'S" DIAMOND MONEY-CLIP, GOLD LUCK CHARM AND SILVER POLICE BADGE! IN EXPERIMENTING WITH THE GREEN KRYPTONITE I GAVE HIM, BENET MUST'VE ACCIDENTALLY CREATED A SAMPLE OF ARTIFICIAL RED KRYPTONITE WHOSE RAYS INSTANTLY AFFECTED ME. IT TRANSFERRED MY KRYPTONITE SENSITIVITY TO THESE THREE OBJECTS IN MY POCKET!
"THAT'S WHY I SUDDENLY BECAME IMMUNE TO GREEN KRYPTONITE! INSTEAD THE RED KRYPTONITE KEPT RELAYING MY DEADLY VULNERABILITY FROM ONE ELEMENT TO THE OTHER WHEN I LEAST EXPECTED IT!"
10

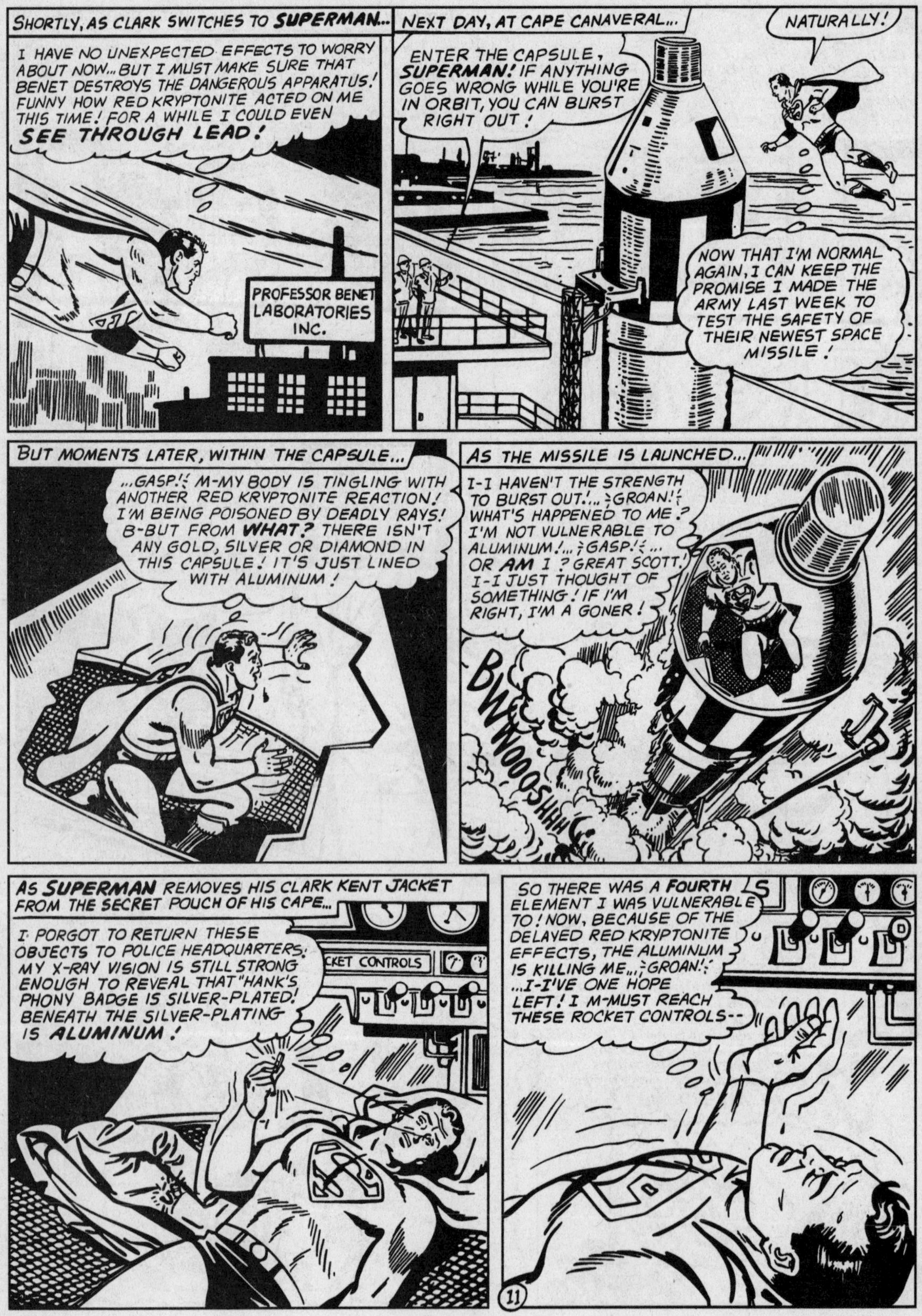
SHORTLY, AS CLARK SWITCHES TO SUPERMAN...
I HAVE NO UNEXPECTED EFFECTS TO WORRY ABOUT NOW... BUT I MUST MAKE SURE THAT BENET DESTROYS THE DANGEROUS APPARATUS! FUNNY HOW RED KRYPTONITE ACTED ON ME THIS TIME! FOR A WHILE I COULD EVEN SEE THROUGH LEAD!
PROFESSOR BENET LABORATORIES INC.
NEXT DAY, AT CAPE CANAVERAL...
ENTER THE CAPSULE, SUPERMAN! IF ANYTHING GOES WRONG WHILE YOU'RE IN ORBIT, YOU CAN BURST RIGHT OUT!
NATURALLY!
NOW THAT I'M NORMAL AGAIN, I CAN KEEP THE PROMISE I MADE THE ARMY LAST WEEK TO TEST THE SAFETY OF THEIR NEWEST SPACE MISSILE!
BUT MOMENTS LATER, WITHIN THE CAPSULE...
...GASP!! M-MY BODY IS TINGLING WITH ANOTHER RED KRYPTONITE REACTION! I'M BEING POISONED BY DEADLY RAYS! B-BUT FROM WHAT? THERE ISN'T ANY GOLD, SILVER OR DIAMOND IN THIS CAPSULE! IT'S JUST LINED WITH ALUMINUM!
AS THE MISSILE IS LAUNCHED...
I-I HAVEN'T THE STRENGTH TO BURST OUT!... GROAN! WHAT'S HAPPENED TO ME? I'M NOT VULNERABLE TO ALUMINUM!... GASP! ... OR AM I? GREAT SCOTT! I-I JUST THOUGHT OF SOMETHING! IF I'M RIGHT, I'M A GONER!
BWWNOOOOSHHH
AS SUPERMAN REMOVES HIS CLARK KENT JACKET FROM THE SECRET POUCH OF HIS CAPE...
I FORGOT TO RETURN THESE OBJECTS TO POLICE HEADQUARTERS! MY X-RAY VISION IS STILL STRONG ENOUGH TO REVEAL THAT "HANK'S PHONY BADGE IS SILVER-PLATED! BENEATH THE SILVER-PLATING IS ALUMINUM!
CKET CONTROLS
SO THERE WAS A FOURTH ELEMENT I WAS VULNERABLE TO! NOW, BECAUSE OF THE DELAYED RED KRYPTONITE EFFECTS, THE ALUMINUM IS KILLING ME... GROAN! ...I-I'VE ONE HOPE LEFT! I M-MUST REACH THESE ROCKET CONTROLS--
11

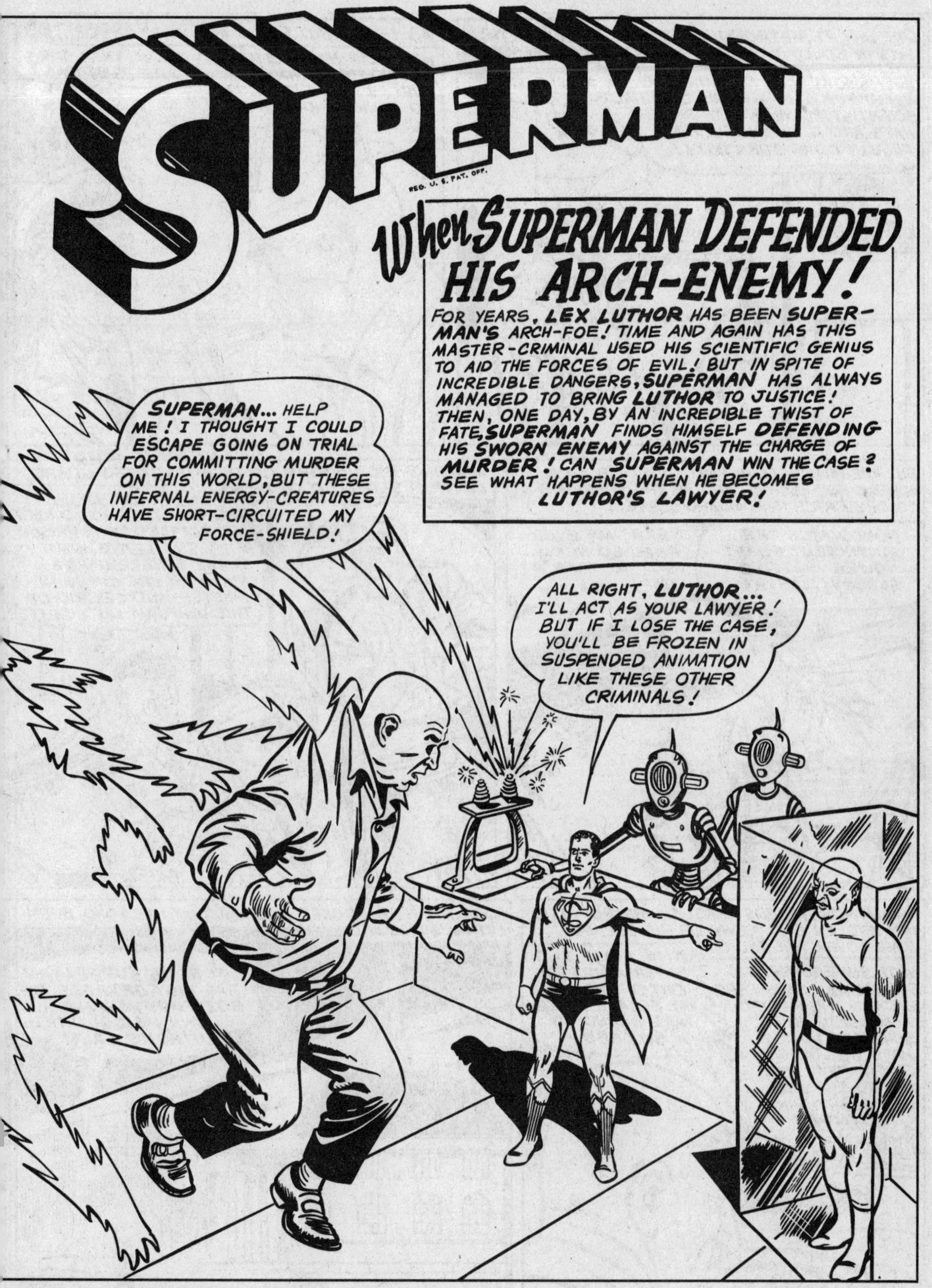
SUPERMAN
REG. U. S. PAT. OFF.
When SUPERMAN DEFENDED HIS ARCH-ENEMY!
FOR YEARS, LEX LUTHOR HAS BEEN SUPERMAN'S ARCH-FOE! TIME AND AGAIN HAS THIS MASTER-CRIMINAL USED HIS SCIENTIFIC GENIUS TO AID THE FORCES OF EVIL! BUT IN SPITE OF INCREDIBLE DANGERS, SUPERMAN HAS ALWAYS MANAGED TO BRING LUTHOR TO JUSTICE! THEN, ONE DAY, BY AN INCREDIBLE TWIST OF FATE, SUPERMAN FINDS HIMSELF DEFENDING HIS SWORN ENEMY AGAINST THE CHARGE OF MURDER! CAN SUPERMAN WIN THE CASE? SEE WHAT HAPPENS WHEN HE BECOMES LUTHOR'S LAWYER!
SUPERMAN... HELP ME! I THOUGHT I COULD ESCAPE GOING ON TRIAL FOR COMMITTING MURDER ON THIS WORLD, BUT THESE INFERNAL ENERGY-CREATURES HAVE SHORT-CIRCUITED MY FORCE-SHIELD!
ALL RIGHT, LUTHOR... I'LL ACT AS YOUR LAWYER! BUT IF I LOSE THE CASE, YOU'LL BE FROZEN IN SUSPENDED ANIMATION LIKE THESE OTHER CRIMINALS!

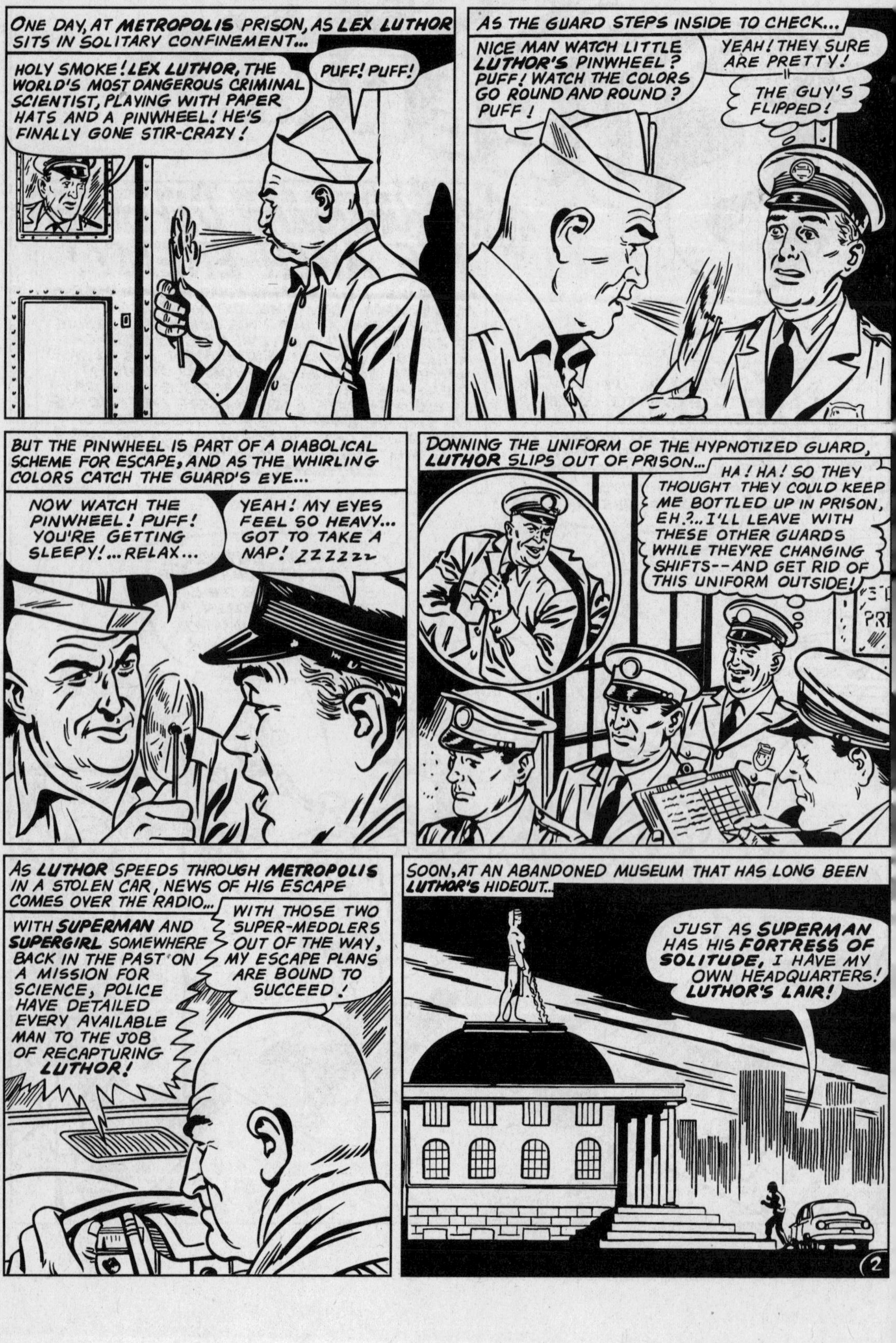
ONE DAY, AT METROPOLIS PRISON, AS LEX LUTHOR SITS IN SOLITARY CONFINEMENT...
HOLY SMOKE! LEX LUTHOR, THE WORLD'S MOST DANGEROUS CRIMINAL SCIENTIST, PLAYING WITH PAPER HATS AND A PINWHEEL! HE'S FINALLY GONE STIR-CRAZY!
PUFF! PUFF!
AS THE GUARD STEPS INSIDE TO CHECK...
NICE MAN WATCH LITTLE LUTHOR'S PINWHEEL? PUFF! WATCH THE COLORS GO ROUND AND ROUND? PUFF!
YEAH! THEY SURE ARE PRETTY!
THE GUY'S FLIPPED!
BUT THE PINWHEEL IS PART OF A DIABOLICAL SCHEME FOR ESCAPE, AND AS THE WHIRLING COLORS CATCH THE GUARD'S EYE...
NOW WATCH THE PINWHEEL! PUFF! YOU'RE GETTING SLEEPY!... RELAX...
YEAH! MY EYES FEEL SO HEAVY... GOT TO TAKE A NAP! ZZZZZZ
DONNING THE UNIFORM OF THE HYPNOTIZED GUARD, LUTHOR SLIPS OUT OF PRISON...
HA! HA! SO THEY THOUGHT THEY COULD KEEP ME BOTTLED UP IN PRISON, EH?... I'LL LEAVE WITH THESE OTHER GUARDS WHILE THEY'RE CHANGING SHIFTS--AND GET RID OF THIS UNIFORM OUTSIDE!
AS LUTHOR SPEEDS THROUGH METROPOLIS IN A STOLEN CAR, NEWS OF HIS ESCAPE COMES OVER THE RADIO...
WITH SUPERMAN AND SUPERGIRL SOMEWHERE BACK IN THE PAST ON A MISSION FOR SCIENCE, POLICE HAVE DETAILED EVERY AVAILABLE MAN TO THE JOB OF RECAPTURING LUTHOR!
WITH THOSE TWO SUPER-MEDDLERS OUT OF THE WAY, MY ESCAPE PLANS ARE BOUND TO SUCCEED!
SOON, AT AN ABANDONED MUSEUM THAT HAS LONG BEEN LUTHOR'S HIDEOUT...
JUST AS SUPERMAN HAS HIS FORTRESS OF SOLITUDE, I HAVE MY OWN HEADQUARTERS! LUTHOR'S LAIR!
2

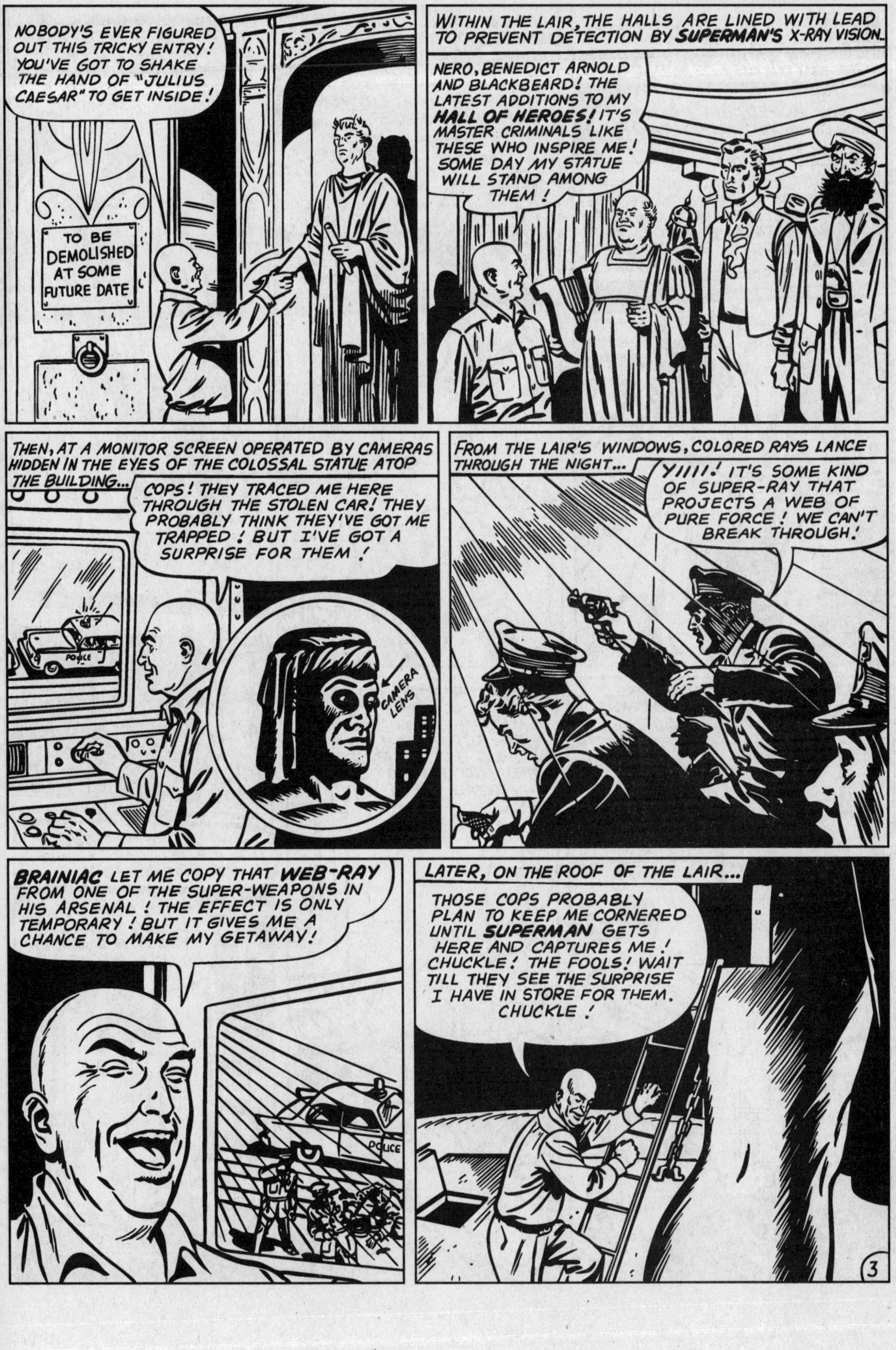
NOBODY'S EVER FIGURED OUT THIS TRICKY ENTRY! YOU'VE GOT TO SHAKE THE HAND OF "JULIUS CAESAR" TO GET INSIDE!
TO BE DEMOLISHED AT SOME FUTURE DATE
WITHIN THE LAIR, THE HALLS ARE LINED WITH LEAD TO PREVENT DETECTION BY SUPERMAN'S X-RAY VISION...
NERO, BENEDICT ARNOLD AND BLACKBEARD! THE LATEST ADDITIONS TO MY HALL OF HEROES! IT'S MASTER CRIMINALS LIKE THESE WHO INSPIRE ME! SOME DAY MY STATUE WILL STAND AMONG THEM!
THEN, AT A MONITOR SCREEN OPERATED BY CAMERAS HIDDEN IN THE EYES OF THE COLOSSAL STATUE ATOP THE BUILDING...
COPS! THEY TRACED ME HERE THROUGH THE STOLEN CAR! THEY PROBABLY THINK THEY'VE GOT ME TRAPPED! BUT I'VE GOT A SURPRISE FOR THEM!
POLICE
CAMERA LENS
FROM THE LAIR'S WINDOWS, COLORED RAYS LANCE THROUGH THE NIGHT...
YIIII! IT'S SOME KIND OF SUPER-RAY THAT PROJECTS A WEB OF PURE FORCE! WE CAN'T BREAK THROUGH!
BRAINIAC LET ME COPY THAT WEB-RAY FROM ONE OF THE SUPER-WEAPONS IN HIS ARSENAL! THE EFFECT IS ONLY TEMPORARY! BUT IT GIVES ME A CHANCE TO MAKE MY GETAWAY!
POLICE
LATER, ON THE ROOF OF THE LAIR...
THOSE COPS PROBABLY PLAN TO KEEP ME CORNERED UNTIL SUPERMAN GETS HERE AND CAPTURES ME! CHUCKLE! THE FOOLS! WAIT TILL THEY SEE THE SURPRISE I HAVE IN STORE FOR THEM. CHUCKLE!
3

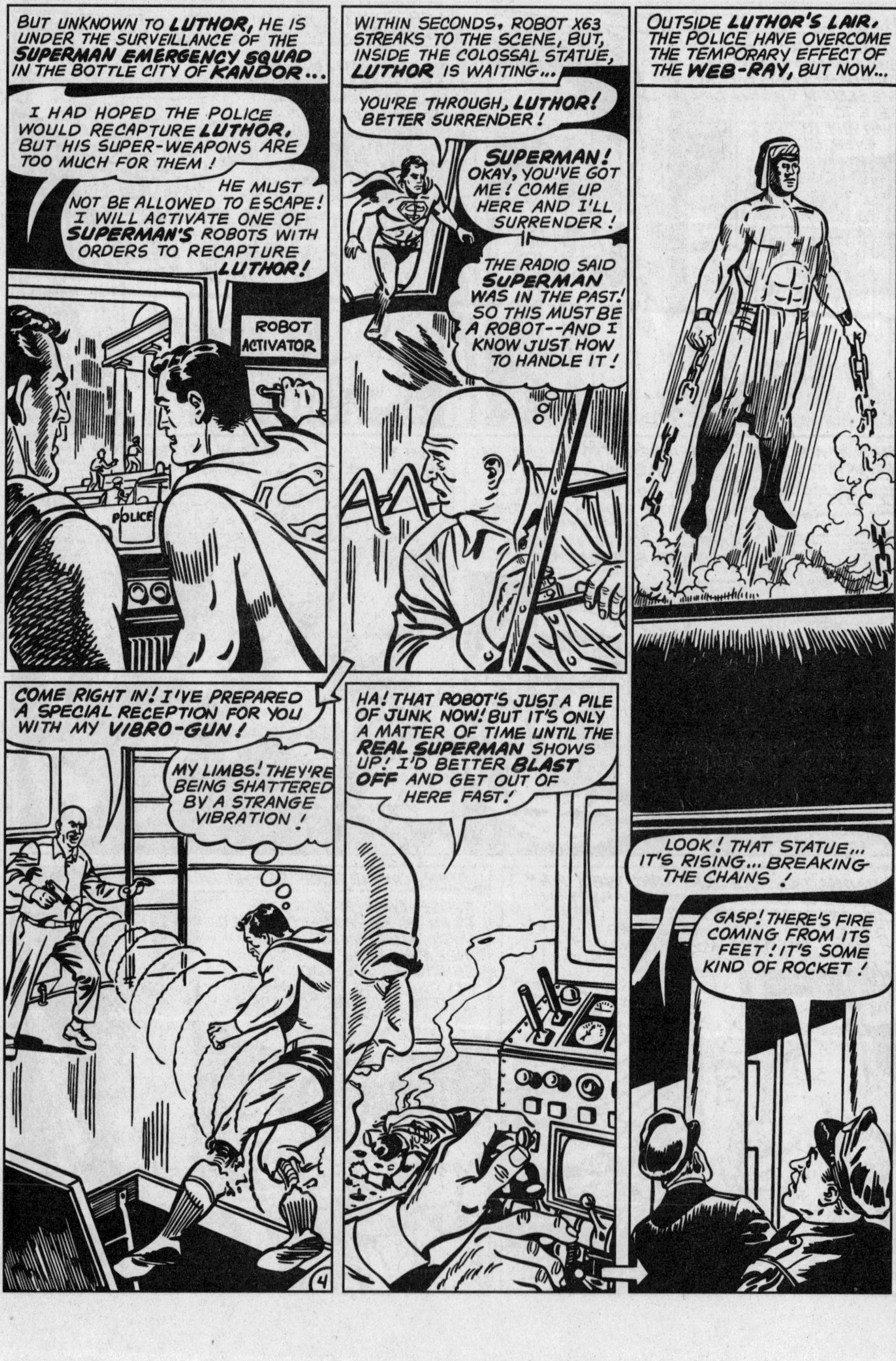
BUT UNKNOWN TO LUTHOR, HE IS UNDER THE SURVEILLANCE OF THE SUPERMAN EMERGENCY SQUAD IN THE BOTTLE CITY OF KANDOR...
I HAD HOPED THE POLICE WOULD RECAPTURE LUTHOR, BUT HIS SUPER-WEAPONS ARE TOO MUCH FOR THEM!
HE MUST NOT BE ALLOWED TO ESCAPE! I WILL ACTIVATE ONE OF SUPERMAN'S ROBOTS WITH ORDERS TO RECAPTURE LUTHOR!
ROBOT ACTIVATOR
POLICE
WITHIN SECONDS, ROBOT X63 STREAKS TO THE SCENE, BUT, INSIDE THE COLOSSAL STATUE, LUTHOR IS WAITING...
YOU'RE THROUGH, LUTHOR! BETTER SURRENDER!
SUPERMAN! OKAY, YOU'VE GOT ME! COME UP HERE AND I'LL SURRENDER!
THE RADIO SAID SUPERMAN WAS IN THE PAST! SO THIS MUST BE A ROBOT--AND I KNOW JUST HOW TO HANDLE IT!
OUTSIDE LUTHOR'S LAIR, THE POLICE HAVE OVERCOME THE TEMPORARY EFFECT OF THE WEB-RAY, BUT NOW...
COME RIGHT IN! I'VE PREPARED A SPECIAL RECEPTION FOR YOU WITH MY VIBRO-GUN!
MY LIMBS! THEY'RE BEING SHATTERED BY A STRANGE VIBRATION!
4
HA! THAT ROBOT'S JUST A PILE OF JUNK NOW! BUT IT'S ONLY A MATTER OF TIME UNTIL THE REAL SUPERMAN SHOWS UP! I'D BETTER BLAST OFF AND GET OUT OF HERE FAST!
LOOK! THAT STATUE... IT'S RISING... BREAKING THE CHAINS!
GASP! THERE'S FIRE COMING FROM ITS FEET! IT'S SOME KIND OF ROCKET!

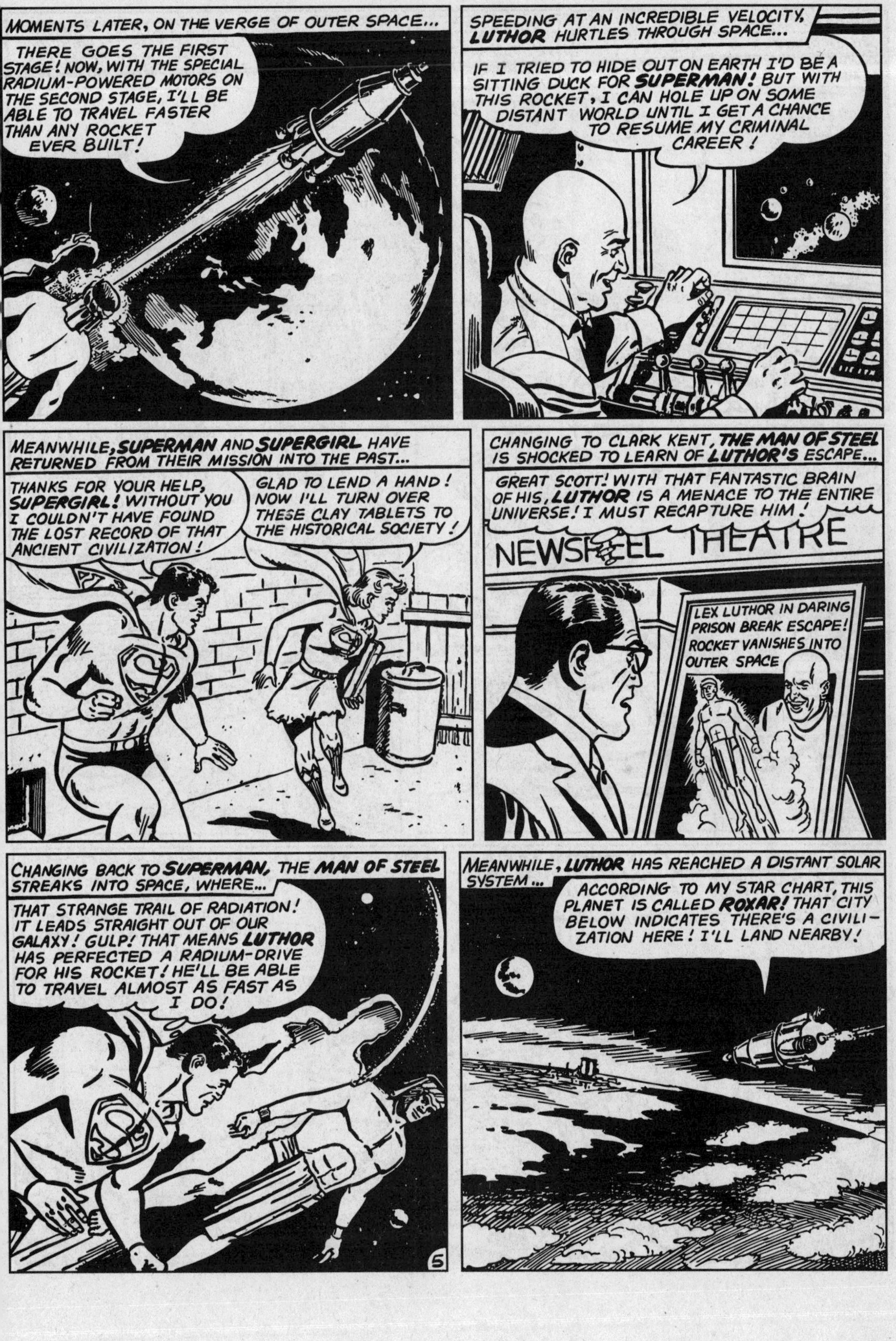
MOMENTS LATER, ON THE VERGE OF OUTER SPACE...
THERE GOES THE FIRST STAGE! NOW, WITH THE SPECIAL RADIUM-POWERED MOTORS ON THE SECOND STAGE, I'LL BE ABLE TO TRAVEL FASTER THAN ANY ROCKET EVER BUILT!
SPEEDING AT AN INCREDIBLE VELOCITY, LUTHOR HURTLES THROUGH SPACE...
IF I TRIED TO HIDE OUT ON EARTH I'D BE A SITTING DUCK FOR SUPERMAN! BUT WITH THIS ROCKET, I CAN HOLE UP ON SOME DISTANT WORLD UNTIL I GET A CHANCE TO RESUME MY CRIMINAL CAREER!
MEANWHILE, SUPERMAN AND SUPERGIRL HAVE RETURNED FROM THEIR MISSION INTO THE PAST...
THANKS FOR YOUR HELP, SUPERGIRL! WITHOUT YOU I COULDN'T HAVE FOUND THE LOST RECORD OF THAT ANCIENT CIVILIZATION!
GLAD TO LEND A HAND! NOW I'LL TURN OVER THESE CLAY TABLETS TO THE HISTORICAL SOCIETY!
CHANGING TO CLARK KENT, THE MAN OF STEEL IS SHOCKED TO LEARN OF LUTHOR'S ESCAPE...
GREAT SCOTT! WITH THAT FANTASTIC BRAIN OF HIS, LUTHOR IS A MENACE TO THE ENTIRE UNIVERSE! I MUST RECAPTURE HIM!
LEX LUTHOR IN DARING PRISON BREAK ESCAPE! ROCKET VANISHES INTO OUTER SPACE
CHANGING BACK TO SUPERMAN, THE MAN OF STEEL STREAKS INTO SPACE, WHERE...
THAT STRANGE TRAIL OF RADIATION! IT LEADS STRAIGHT OUT OF OUR GALAXY! GULP! THAT MEANS LUTHOR HAS PERFECTED A RADIUM-DRIVE FOR HIS ROCKET! HE'LL BE ABLE TO TRAVEL ALMOST AS FAST AS I DO!
5
MEANWHILE, LUTHOR HAS REACHED A DISTANT SOLAR SYSTEM...
ACCORDING TO MY STAR CHART, THIS PLANET IS CALLED ROXAR! THAT CITY BELOW INDICATES THERE'S A CIVILIZATION HERE! I'LL LAND NEARBY!

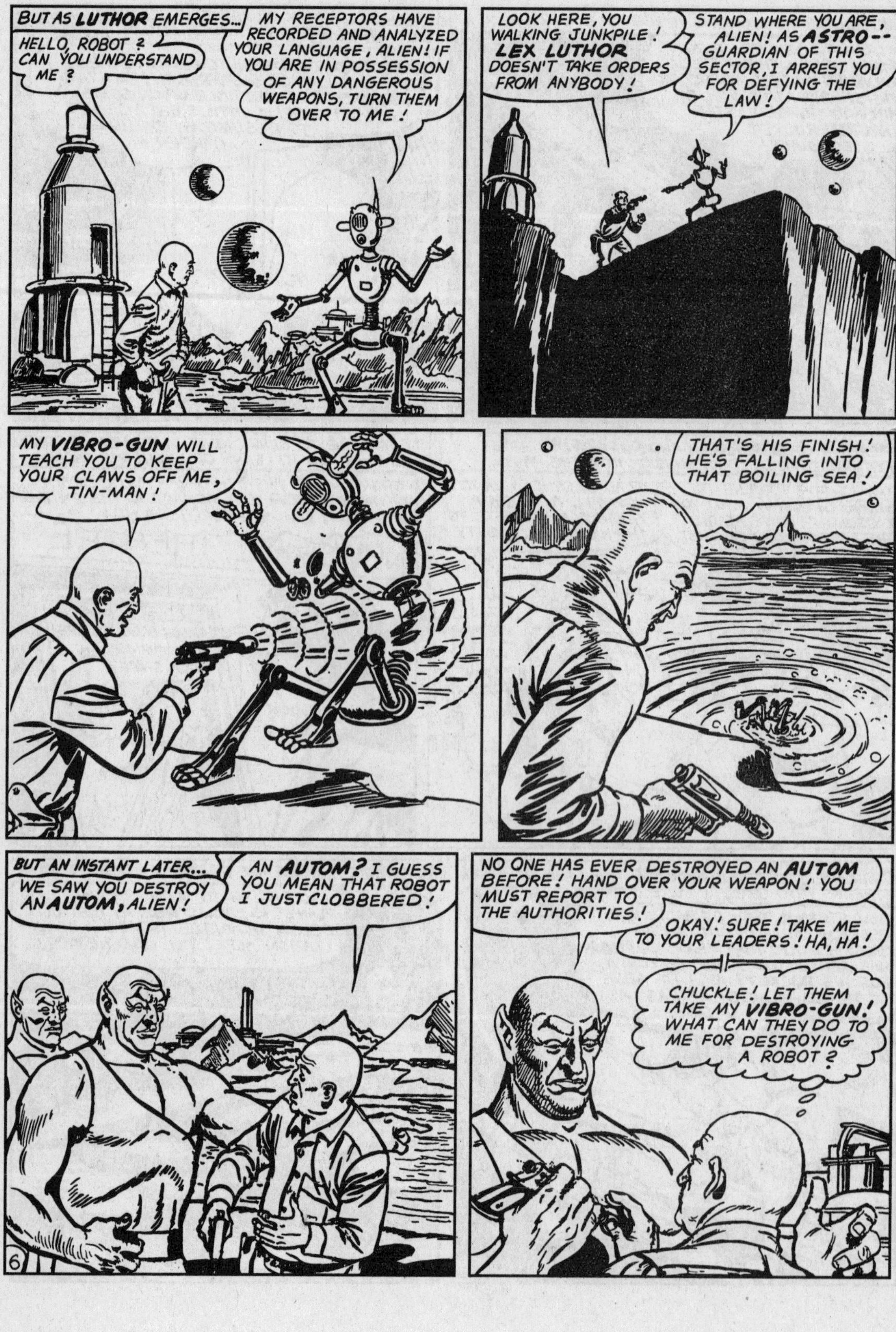
BUT AS LUTHOR EMERGES...
HELLO, ROBOT ? CAN YOU UNDERSTAND ME ?
MY RECEPTORS HAVE RECORDED AND ANALYZED YOUR LANGUAGE, ALIEN! IF YOU ARE IN POSSESSION OF ANY DANGEROUS WEAPONS, TURN THEM OVER TO ME!
LOOK HERE, YOU WALKING JUNKPILE! LEX LUTHOR DOESN'T TAKE ORDERS FROM ANYBODY!
STAND WHERE YOU ARE, ALIEN! AS ASTRO-- GUARDIAN OF THIS SECTOR, I ARREST YOU FOR DEFYING THE LAW!
MY VIBRO-GUN WILL TEACH YOU TO KEEP YOUR CLAWS OFF ME, TIN-MAN!
THAT'S HIS FINISH! HE'S FALLING INTO THAT BOILING SEA!
BUT AN INSTANT LATER...
WE SAW YOU DESTROY AN AUTOM, ALIEN!
AN AUTOM? I GUESS YOU MEAN THAT ROBOT I JUST CLOBBERED!
6
NO ONE HAS EVER DESTROYED AN AUTOM BEFORE! HAND OVER YOUR WEAPON! YOU MUST REPORT TO THE AUTHORITIES!
OKAY! SURE! TAKE ME TO YOUR LEADERS! HA, HA!
CHUCKLE! LET THEM TAKE MY VIBRO-GUN! WHAT CAN THEY DO TO ME FOR DESTROYING A ROBOT ?

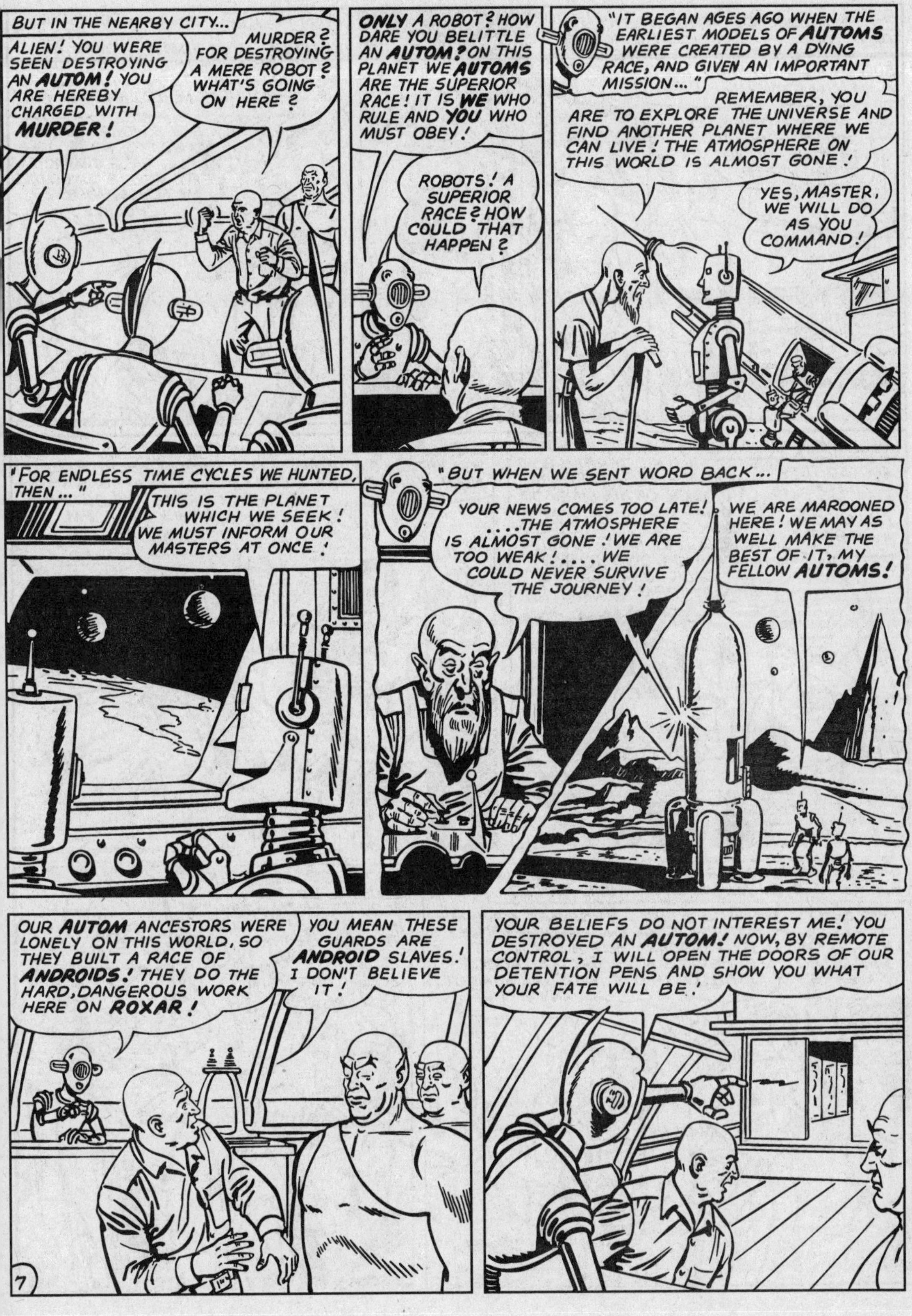
BUT IN THE NEARBY CITY...
ALIEN! YOU WERE SEEN DESTROYING AN AUTOM! YOU ARE HEREBY CHARGED WITH MURDER!
MURDER? FOR DESTROYING A MERE ROBOT? WHAT'S GOING ON HERE?
ONLY A ROBOT? HOW DARE YOU BELITTLE AN AUTOM? ON THIS PLANET WE AUTOMS ARE THE SUPERIOR RACE! IT IS WE WHO RULE AND YOU WHO MUST OBEY!
ROBOTS! A SUPERIOR RACE? HOW COULD THAT HAPPEN?
"IT BEGAN AGES AGO WHEN THE EARLIEST MODELS OF AUTOMS WERE CREATED BY A DYING RACE, AND GIVEN AN IMPORTANT MISSION..."
REMEMBER, YOU ARE TO EXPLORE THE UNIVERSE AND FIND ANOTHER PLANET WHERE WE CAN LIVE! THE ATMOSPHERE ON THIS WORLD IS ALMOST GONE!
YES, MASTER, WE WILL DO AS YOU COMMAND!
"FOR ENDLESS TIME CYCLES WE HUNTED, THEN..."
THIS IS THE PLANET WHICH WE SEEK! WE MUST INFORM OUR MASTERS AT ONCE!
"BUT WHEN WE SENT WORD BACK...
YOUR NEWS COMES TOO LATE! ....THE ATMOSPHERE IS ALMOST GONE! WE ARE TOO WEAK!.... WE COULD NEVER SURVIVE THE JOURNEY!
WE ARE MAROONED HERE! WE MAY AS WELL MAKE THE BEST OF IT, MY FELLOW AUTOMS!
OUR AUTOM ANCESTORS WERE LONELY ON THIS WORLD, SO THEY BUILT A RACE OF ANDROIDS! THEY DO THE HARD, DANGEROUS WORK HERE ON ROXAR!
YOU MEAN THESE GUARDS ARE ANDROID SLAVES! I DON'T BELIEVE IT!
YOUR BELIEFS DO NOT INTEREST ME! YOU DESTROYED AN AUTOM! NOW, BY REMOTE CONTROL, I WILL OPEN THE DOORS OF OUR DETENTION PENS AND SHOW YOU WHAT YOUR FATE WILL BE!
7

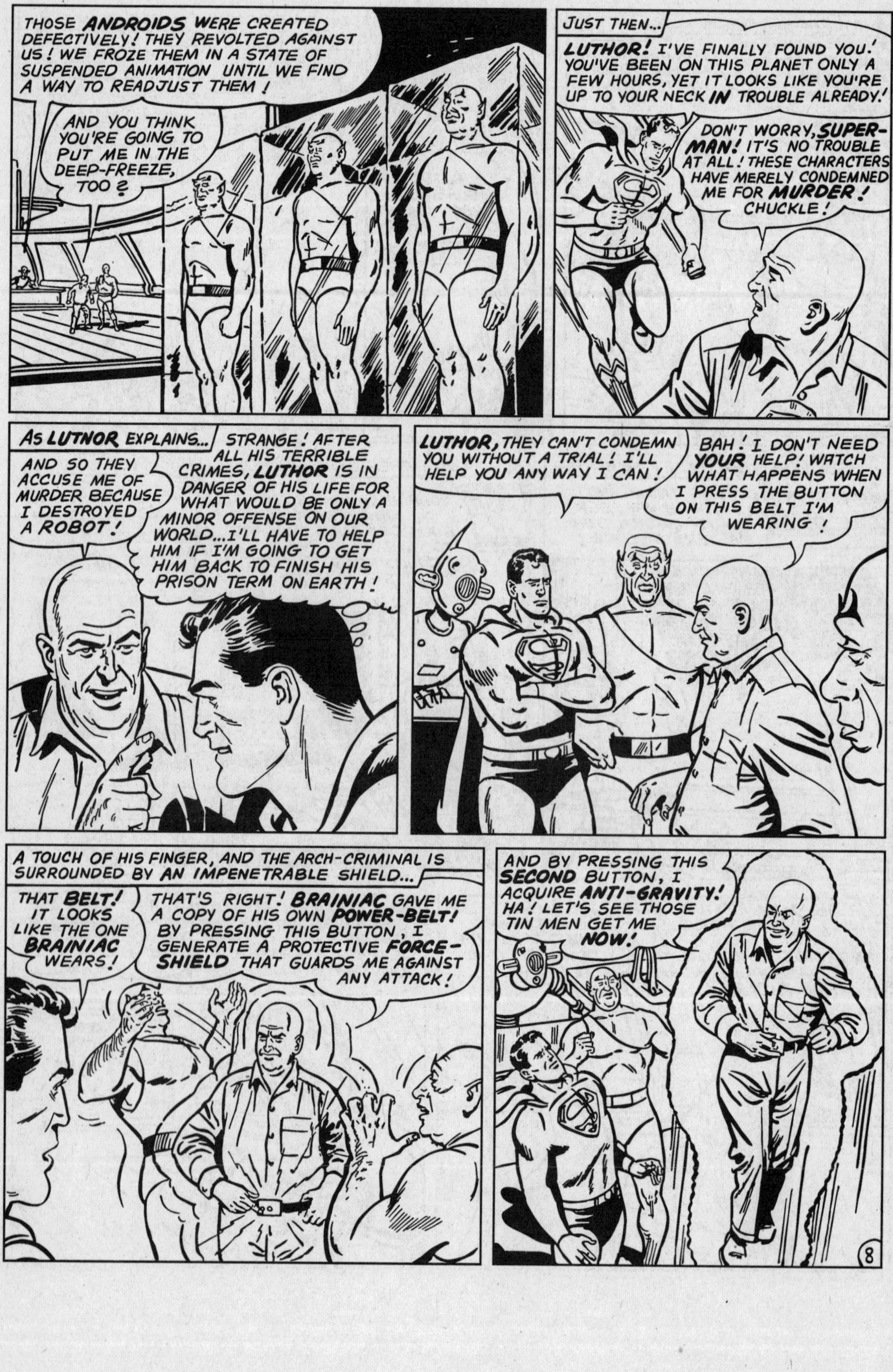
THOSE ANDROIDS WERE CREATED DEFECTIVELY! THEY REVOLTED AGAINST US! WE FROZE THEM IN A STATE OF SUSPENDED ANIMATION UNTIL WE FIND A WAY TO READJUST THEM!
AND YOU THINK YOU'RE GOING TO PUT ME IN THE DEEP-FREEZE, TOO?
JUST THEN...
LUTHOR! I'VE FINALLY FOUND YOU! YOU'VE BEEN ON THIS PLANET ONLY A FEW HOURS, YET IT LOOKS LIKE YOU'RE UP TO YOUR NECK IN TROUBLE ALREADY!
DON'T WORRY, SUPERMAN! IT'S NO TROUBLE AT ALL! THESE CHARACTERS HAVE MERELY CONDEMNED ME FOR MURDER! CHUCKLE!
AS LUTNOR EXPLAINS...
AND SO THEY ACCUSE ME OF MURDER BECAUSE I DESTROYED A ROBOT!
STRANGE! AFTER ALL HIS TERRIBLE CRIMES, LUTHOR IS IN DANGER OF HIS LIFE FOR WHAT WOULD BE ONLY A MINOR OFFENSE ON OUR WORLD...I'LL HAVE TO HELP HIM IF I'M GOING TO GET HIM BACK TO FINISH HIS PRISON TERM ON EARTH!
LUTHOR, THEY CAN'T CONDEMN YOU WITHOUT A TRIAL! I'LL HELP YOU ANY WAY I CAN!
BAH! I DON'T NEED YOUR HELP! WATCH WHAT HAPPENS WHEN I PRESS THE BUTTON ON THIS BELT I'M WEARING!
A TOUCH OF HIS FINGER, AND THE ARCH-CRIMINAL IS SURROUNDED BY AN IMPENETRABLE SHIELD...
THAT BELT! IT LOOKS LIKE THE ONE BRAINIAC WEARS!
THAT'S RIGHT! BRAINIAC GAVE ME A COPY OF HIS OWN POWER-BELT! BY PRESSING THIS BUTTON, I GENERATE A PROTECTIVE FORCE-SHIELD THAT GUARDS ME AGAINST ANY ATTACK!
AND BY PRESSING THIS SECOND BUTTON, I ACQUIRE ANTI-GRAVITY! HA! LET'S SEE THOSE TIN MEN GET ME NOW!
8

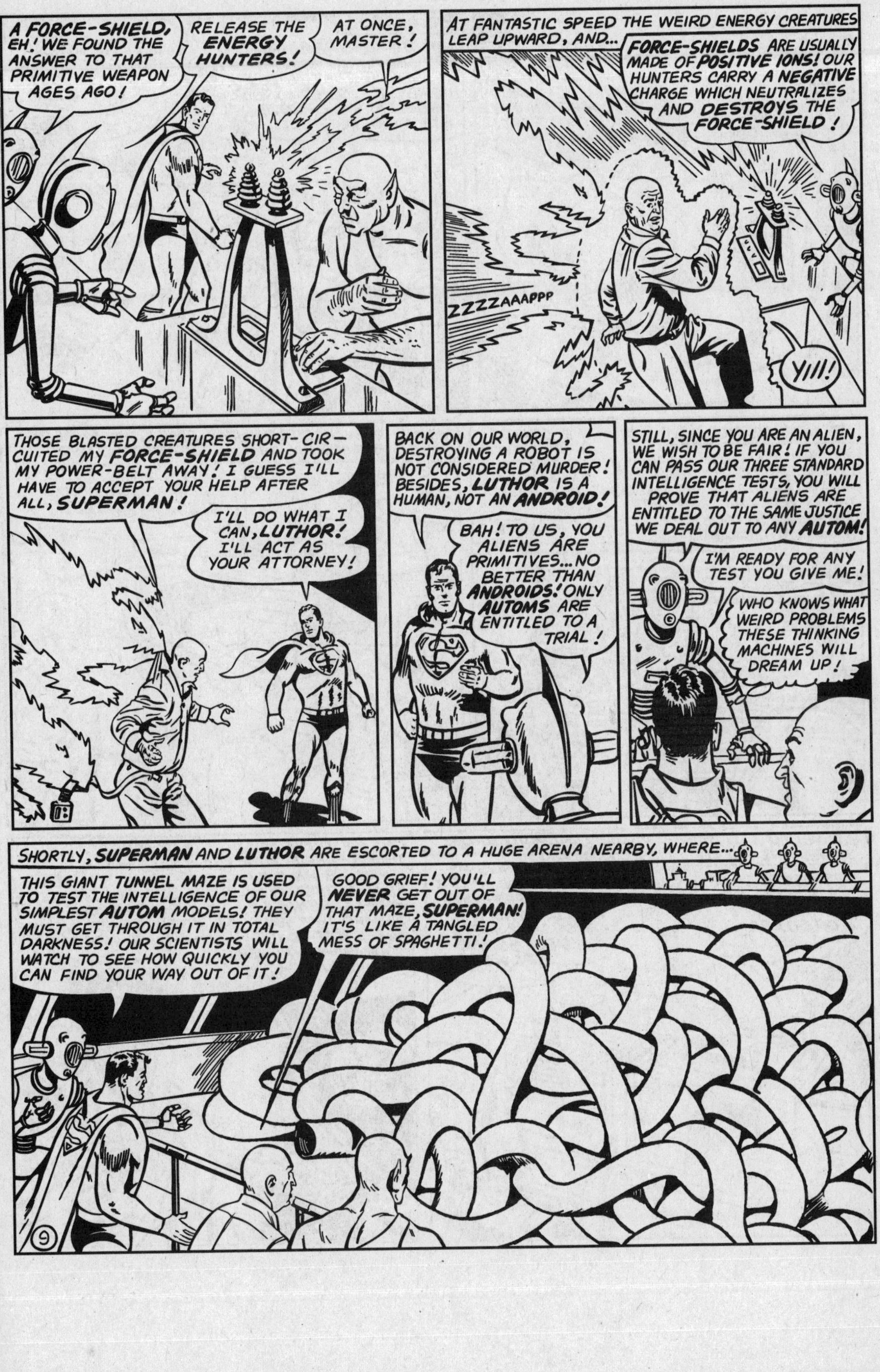
A FORCE-SHIELD, EH! WE FOUND THE ANSWER TO THAT PRIMITIVE WEAPON AGES AGO!
RELEASE THE ENERGY HUNTERS!
AT ONCE, MASTER!
AT FANTASTIC SPEED THE WEIRD ENERGY CREATURES LEAP UPWARD, AND...
FORCE-SHIELDS ARE USUALLY MADE OF POSITIVE IONS! OUR HUNTERS CARRY A NEGATIVE CHARGE WHICH NEUTRALIZES AND DESTROYS THE FORCE-SHIELD!
ZZZZAAAPPP
YIII!
THOSE BLASTED CREATURES SHORT-CIRCUITED MY FORCE-SHIELD AND TOOK MY POWER-BELT AWAY! I GUESS I'LL HAVE TO ACCEPT YOUR HELP AFTER ALL, SUPERMAN!
I'LL DO WHAT I CAN, LUTHOR! I'LL ACT AS YOUR ATTORNEY!
BACK ON OUR WORLD, DESTROYING A ROBOT IS NOT CONSIDERED MURDER! BESIDES, LUTHOR IS A HUMAN, NOT AN ANDROID!
BAH! TO US, YOU ALIENS ARE PRIMITIVES... NO BETTER THAN ANDROIDS! ONLY AUTOMS ARE ENTITLED TO A TRIAL!
STILL, SINCE YOU ARE AN ALIEN, WE WISH TO BE FAIR! IF YOU CAN PASS OUR THREE STANDARD INTELLIGENCE TESTS, YOU WILL PROVE THAT ALIENS ARE ENTITLED TO THE SAME JUSTICE WE DEAL OUT TO ANY AUTOM!
I'M READY FOR ANY TEST YOU GIVE ME!
WHO KNOWS WHAT WEIRD PROBLEMS THESE THINKING MACHINES WILL DREAM UP!
SHORTLY, SUPERMAN AND LUTHOR ARE ESCORTED TO A HUGE ARENA NEARBY, WHERE...
THIS GIANT TUNNEL MAZE IS USED TO TEST THE INTELLIGENCE OF OUR SIMPLEST AUTOM MODELS! THEY MUST GET THROUGH IT IN TOTAL DARKNESS! OUR SCIENTISTS WILL WATCH TO SEE HOW QUICKLY YOU CAN FIND YOUR WAY OUT OF IT!
GOOD GRIEF! YOU'LL NEVER GET OUT OF THAT MAZE, SUPERMAN! IT'S LIKE A TANGLED MESS OF SPAGHETTI!
9

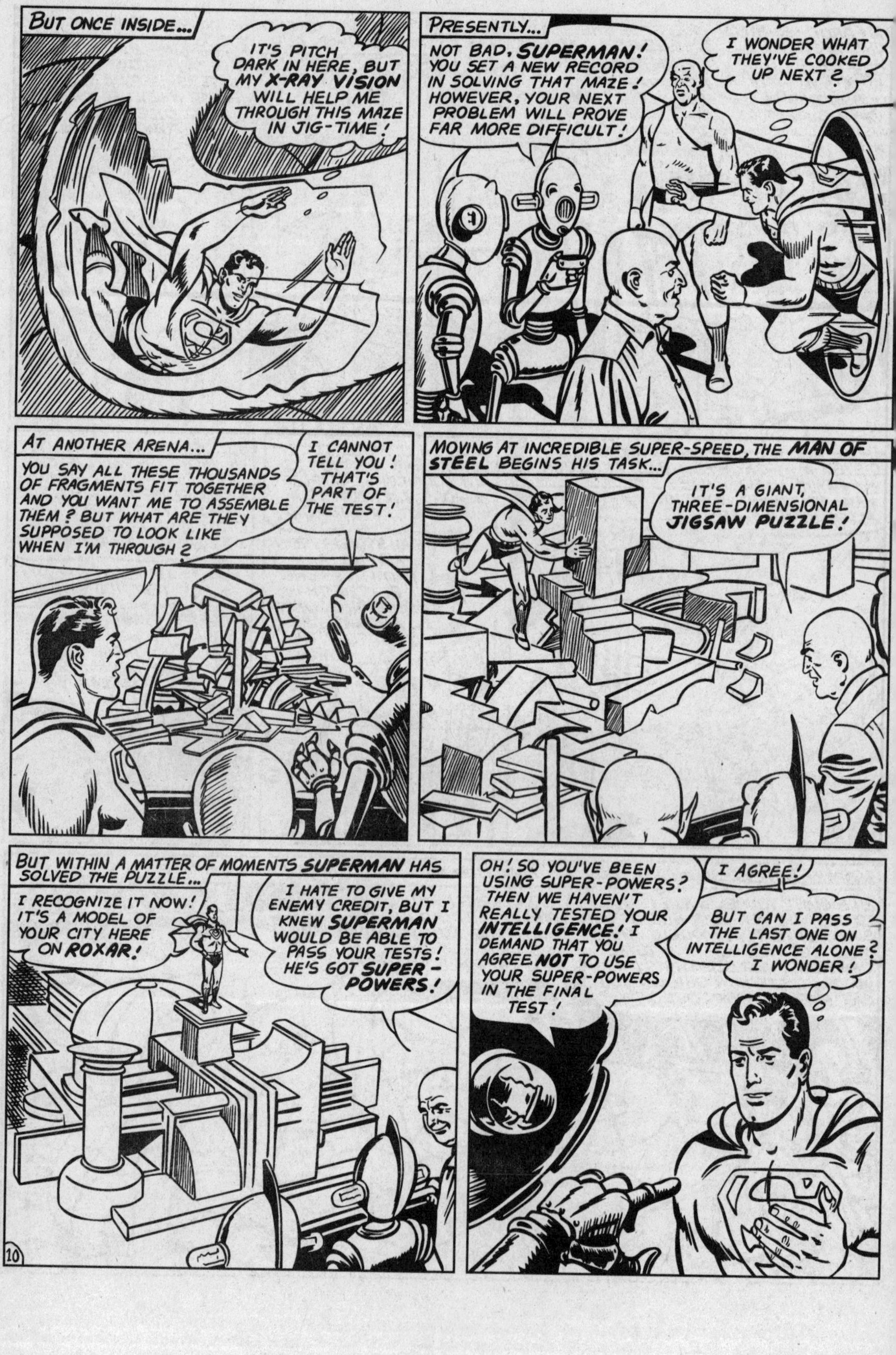
BUT ONCE INSIDE...
IT'S PITCH DARK IN HERE, BUT MY X-RAY VISION WILL HELP ME THROUGH THIS MAZE IN JIG-TIME!
PRESENTLY...
NOT BAD, SUPERMAN! YOU SET A NEW RECORD IN SOLVING THAT MAZE! HOWEVER, YOUR NEXT PROBLEM WILL PROVE FAR MORE DIFFICULT!
I WONDER WHAT THEY'VE COOKED UP NEXT?
AT ANOTHER ARENA...
YOU SAY ALL THESE THOUSANDS OF FRAGMENTS FIT TOGETHER AND YOU WANT ME TO ASSEMBLE THEM? BUT WHAT ARE THEY SUPPOSED TO LOOK LIKE WHEN I'M THROUGH?
I CANNOT TELL YOU! THAT'S PART OF THE TEST!
MOVING AT INCREDIBLE SUPER-SPEED, THE MAN OF STEEL BEGINS HIS TASK...
IT'S A GIANT, THREE-DIMENSIONAL JIGSAW PUZZLE!
BUT WITHIN A MATTER OF MOMENTS SUPERMAN HAS SOLVED THE PUZZLE...
I RECOGNIZE IT NOW! IT'S A MODEL OF YOUR CITY HERE ON ROXAR!
I HATE TO GIVE MY ENEMY CREDIT, BUT I KNEW SUPERMAN WOULD BE ABLE TO PASS YOUR TESTS! HE'S GOT SUPER-POWERS!
OH! SO YOU'VE BEEN USING SUPER-POWERS? THEN WE HAVEN'T REALLY TESTED YOUR INTELLIGENCE! I DEMAND THAT YOU AGREE NOT TO USE YOUR SUPER-POWERS IN THE FINAL TEST!
I AGREE!
BUT CAN I PASS THE LAST ONE ON INTELLIGENCE ALONE? I WONDER!
10

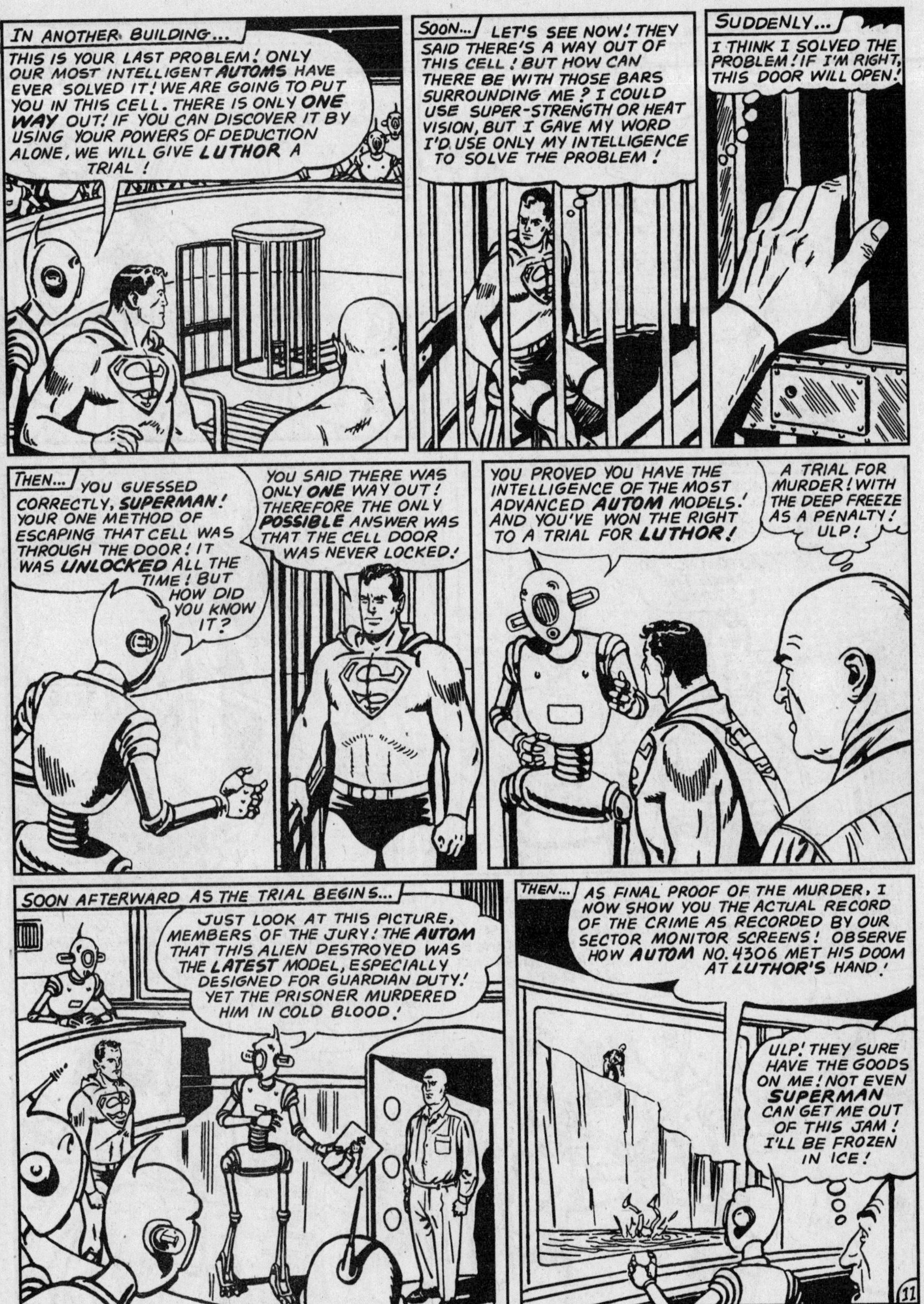

IN ANOTHER BUILDING...
THIS IS YOUR LAST PROBLEM! ONLY OUR MOST INTELLIGENT AUTOMS HAVE EVER SOLVED IT! WE ARE GOING TO PUT YOU IN THIS CELL. THERE IS ONLY ONE WAY OUT! IF YOU CAN DISCOVER IT BY USING YOUR POWERS OF DEDUCTION ALONE, WE WILL GIVE LUTHOR A TRIAL!
SOON...
LET'S SEE NOW! THEY SAID THERE'S A WAY OUT OF THIS CELL! BUT HOW CAN THERE BE WITH THOSE BARS SURROUNDING ME? I COULD USE SUPER-STRENGTH OR HEAT VISION, BUT I GAVE MY WORD I'D USE ONLY MY INTELLIGENCE TO SOLVE THE PROBLEM!
SUDDENLY...
I THINK I SOLVED THE PROBLEM! IF I'M RIGHT, THIS DOOR WILL OPEN!
THEN...
YOU GUESSED CORRECTLY, SUPERMAN! YOUR ONE METHOD OF ESCAPING THAT CELL WAS THROUGH THE DOOR! IT WAS UNLOCKED ALL THE TIME! BUT HOW DID YOU KNOW IT?
YOU SAID THERE WAS ONLY ONE WAY OUT! THEREFORE THE ONLY POSSIBLE ANSWER WAS THAT THE CELL DOOR WAS NEVER LOCKED!
YOU PROVED YOU HAVE THE INTELLIGENCE OF THE MOST ADVANCED AUTOM MODELS! AND YOU'VE WON THE RIGHT TO A TRIAL FOR LUTHOR!
A TRIAL FOR MURDER! WITH THE DEEP FREEZE AS A PENALTY! ULP!
SOON AFTERWARD AS THE TRIAL BEGINS...
JUST LOOK AT THIS PICTURE, MEMBERS OF THE JURY! THE AUTOM THAT THIS ALIEN DESTROYED WAS THE LATEST MODEL, ESPECIALLY DESIGNED FOR GUARDIAN DUTY! YET THE PRISONER MURDERED HIM IN COLD BLOOD!
THEN...
AS FINAL PROOF OF THE MURDER, I NOW SHOW YOU THE ACTUAL RECORD OF THE CRIME AS RECORDED BY OUR SECTOR MONITOR SCREENS! OBSERVE HOW AUTOM NO. 4306 MET HIS DOOM AT LUTHOR'S HAND!
ULP! THEY SURE HAVE THE GOODS ON ME! NOT EVEN SUPERMAN CAN GET ME OUT OF THIS JAM! I'LL BE FROZEN IN ICE!
11

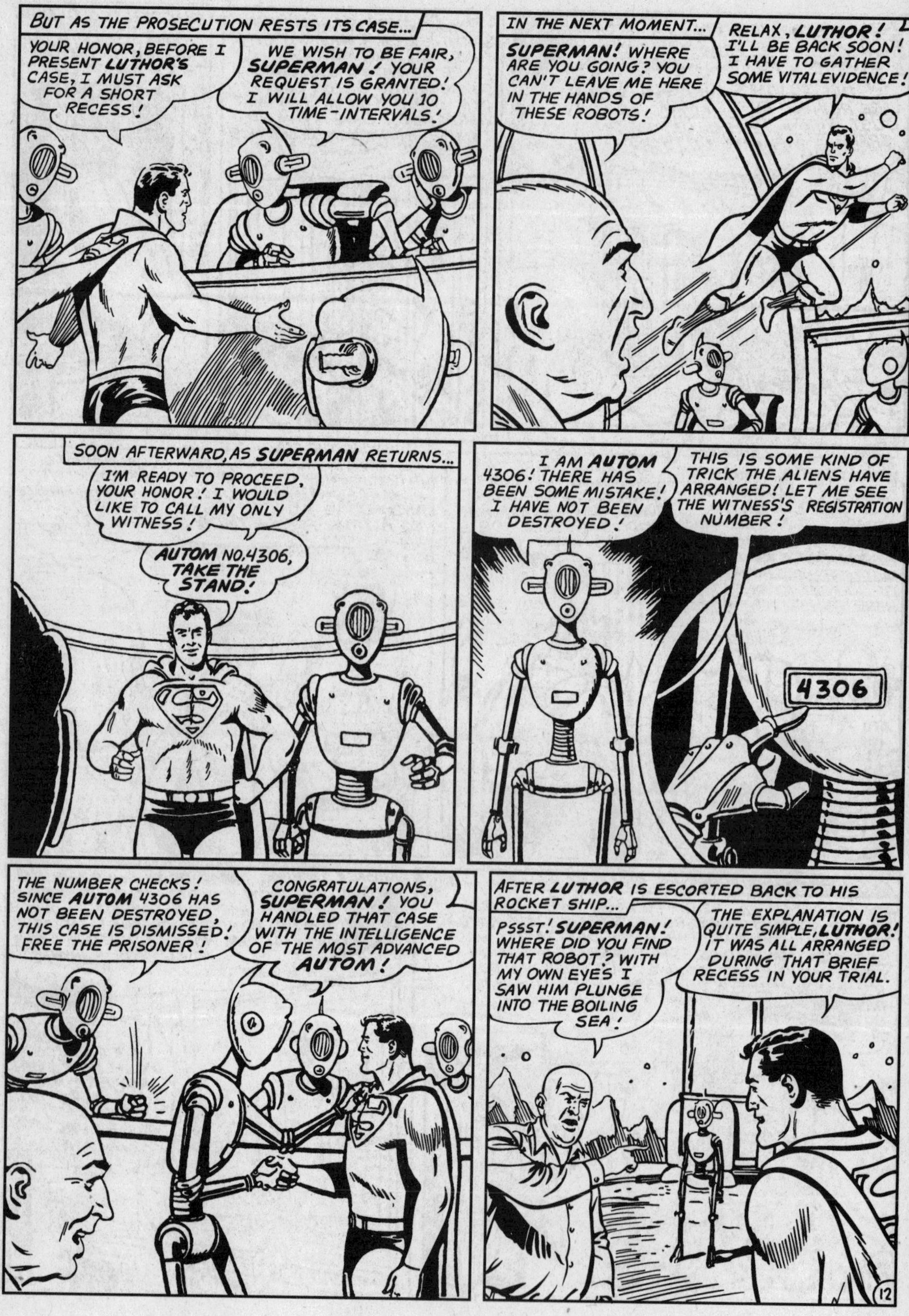
BUT AS THE PROSECUTION RESTS ITS CASE...
YOUR HONOR, BEFORE I PRESENT LUTHOR'S CASE, I MUST ASK FOR A SHORT RECESS!
WE WISH TO BE FAIR, SUPERMAN! YOUR REQUEST IS GRANTED! I WILL ALLOW YOU 10 TIME-INTERVALS!
IN THE NEXT MOMENT...
SUPERMAN! WHERE ARE YOU GOING? YOU CAN'T LEAVE ME HERE IN THE HANDS OF THESE ROBOTS!
RELAX, LUTHOR! I'LL BE BACK SOON! I HAVE TO GATHER SOME VITAL EVIDENCE!
SOON AFTERWARD, AS SUPERMAN RETURNS...
I'M READY TO PROCEED, YOUR HONOR! I WOULD LIKE TO CALL MY ONLY WITNESS!
AUTOM NO.4306, TAKE THE STAND!
I AM AUTOM 4306! THERE HAS BEEN SOME MISTAKE! I HAVE NOT BEEN DESTROYED!
THIS IS SOME KIND OF TRICK THE ALIENS HAVE ARRANGED! LET ME SEE THE WITNESS'S REGISTRATION NUMBER!
4306
THE NUMBER CHECKS! SINCE AUTOM 4306 HAS NOT BEEN DESTROYED, THIS CASE IS DISMISSED! FREE THE PRISONER!
CONGRATULATIONS, SUPERMAN! YOU HANDLED THAT CASE WITH THE INTELLIGENCE OF THE MOST ADVANCED AUTOM!
AFTER LUTHOR IS ESCORTED BACK TO HIS ROCKET SHIP...
PSSST! SUPERMAN! WHERE DID YOU FIND THAT ROBOT? WITH MY OWN EYES I SAW HIM PLUNGE INTO THE BOILING SEA!
THE EXPLANATION IS QUITE SIMPLE, LUTHOR! IT WAS ALL ARRANGED DURING THAT BRIEF RECESS IN YOUR TRIAL.
12

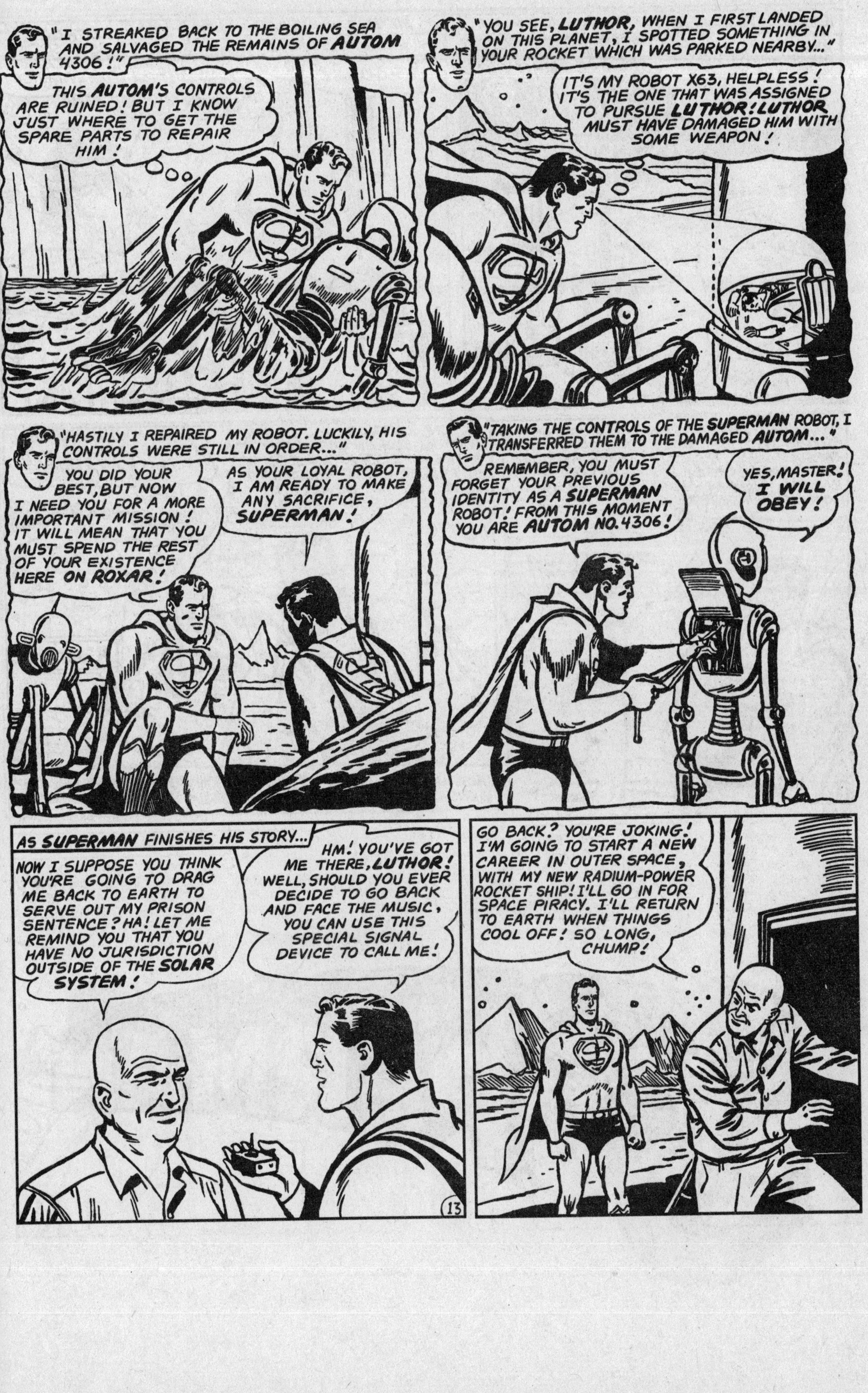
"I STREAKED BACK TO THE BOILING SEA AND SALVAGED THE REMAINS OF AUTOM 4306!"
THIS AUTOM'S CONTROLS ARE RUINED! BUT I KNOW JUST WHERE TO GET THE SPARE PARTS TO REPAIR HIM!
"YOU SEE, LUTHOR, WHEN I FIRST LANDED ON THIS PLANET, I SPOTTED SOMETHING IN YOUR ROCKET WHICH WAS PARKED NEARBY..."
IT'S MY ROBOT X63, HELPLESS! IT'S THE ONE THAT WAS ASSIGNED TO PURSUE LUTHOR! LUTHOR MUST HAVE DAMAGED HIM WITH SOME WEAPON!
"HASTILY I REPAIRED MY ROBOT. LUCKILY, HIS CONTROLS WERE STILL IN ORDER..."
YOU DID YOUR BEST, BUT NOW I NEED YOU FOR A MORE IMPORTANT MISSION! IT WILL MEAN THAT YOU MUST SPEND THE REST OF YOUR EXISTENCE HERE ON ROXAR!
AS YOUR LOYAL ROBOT, I AM READY TO MAKE ANY SACRIFICE, SUPERMAN!
"TAKING THE CONTROLS OF THE SUPERMAN ROBOT, I TRANSFERRED THEM TO THE DAMAGED AUTOM..."
REMEMBER, YOU MUST FORGET YOUR PREVIOUS IDENTITY AS A SUPERMAN ROBOT! FROM THIS MOMENT YOU ARE AUTOM NO. 4306!
YES, MASTER! I WILL OBEY!
AS SUPERMAN FINISHES HIS STORY...
NOW I SUPPOSE YOU THINK YOU'RE GOING TO DRAG ME BACK TO EARTH TO SERVE OUT MY PRISON SENTENCE? HA! LET ME REMIND YOU THAT YOU HAVE NO JURISDICTION OUTSIDE OF THE SOLAR SYSTEM!
HM! YOU'VE GOT ME THERE, LUTHOR! WELL, SHOULD YOU EVER DECIDE TO GO BACK AND FACE THE MUSIC, YOU CAN USE THIS SPECIAL SIGNAL DEVICE TO CALL ME!
13
GO BACK? YOU'RE JOKING! I'M GOING TO START A NEW CAREER IN OUTER SPACE, WITH MY NEW RADIUM-POWER ROCKET SHIP! I'LL GO IN FOR SPACE PIRACY. I'LL RETURN TO EARTH WHEN THINGS COOL OFF! SO LONG, CHUMP!

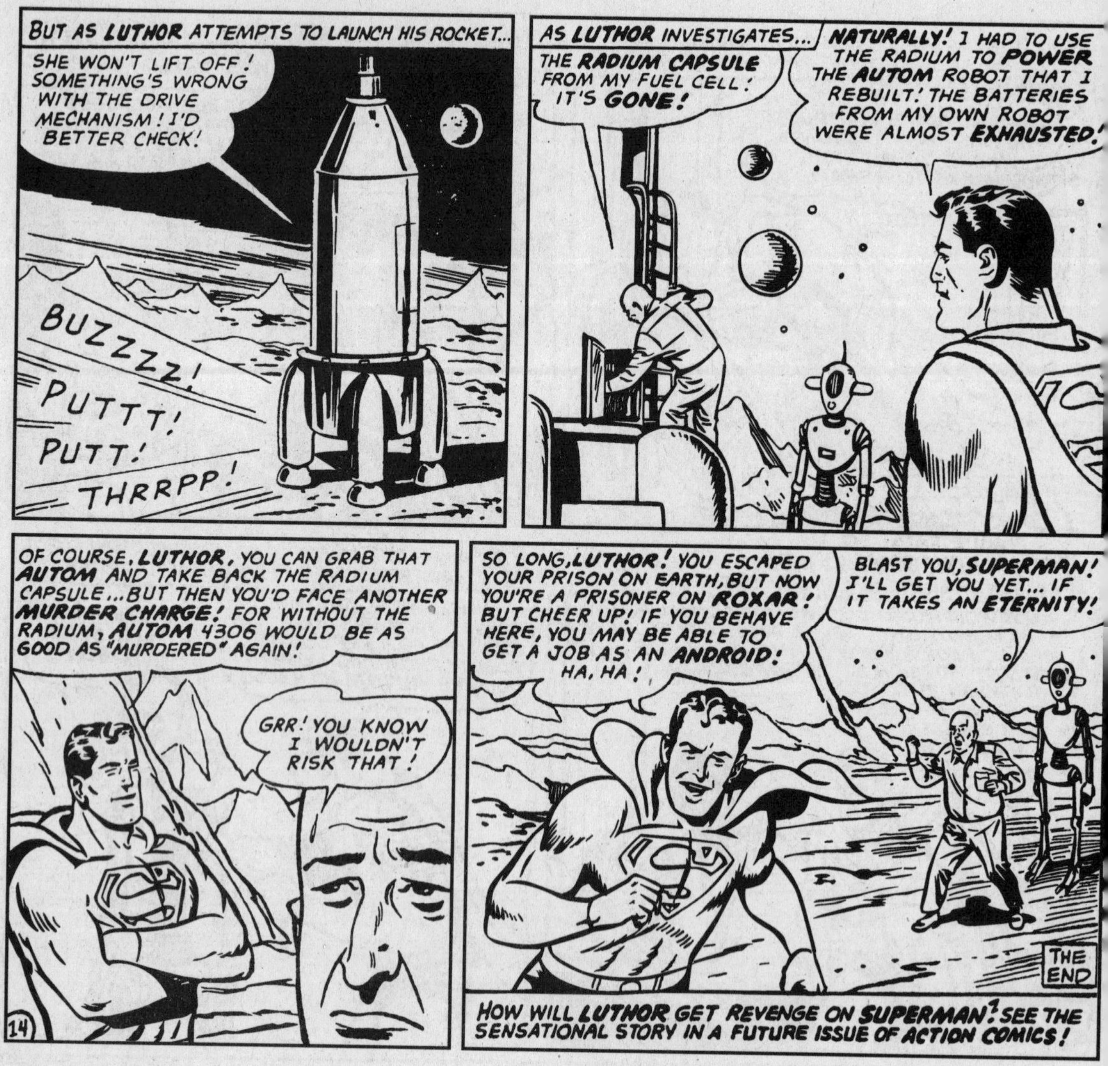
BUT AS LUTHOR ATTEMPTS TO LAUNCH HIS ROCKET...
SHE WON'T LIFT OFF! SOMETHING'S WRONG WITH THE DRIVE MECHANISM! I'D BETTER CHECK!
BUZZZZZ! PUTTTT! PUTT! THRRPP!
AS LUTHOR INVESTIGATES...
THE RADIUM CAPSULE FROM MY FUEL CELL! IT'S GONE!
NATURALLY! I HAD TO USE THE RADIUM TO POWER THE AUTOM ROBOT THAT I REBUILT! THE BATTERIES FROM MY OWN ROBOT WERE ALMOST EXHAUSTED!
OF COURSE, LUTHOR, YOU CAN GRAB THAT AUTOM AND TAKE BACK THE RADIUM CAPSULE...BUT THEN YOU'D FACE ANOTHER MURDER CHARGE! FOR WITHOUT THE RADIUM, AUTOM 4306 WOULD BE AS GOOD AS "MURDERED" AGAIN!
GRR! YOU KNOW I WOULDN'T RISK THAT!
14
SO LONG, LUTHOR! YOU ESCAPED YOUR PRISON ON EARTH, BUT NOW YOU'RE A PRISONER ON ROXAR! BUT CHEER UP! IF YOU BEHAVE HERE, YOU MAY BE ABLE TO GET A JOB AS AN ANDROID! HA, HA!
BLAST YOU, SUPERMAN! I'LL GET YOU YET... IF IT TAKES AN ETERNITY!
THE END
HOW WILL LUTHOR GET REVENGE ON SUPERMAN? SEE THE SENSATIONAL STORY IN A FUTURE ISSUE OF ACTION COMICS!

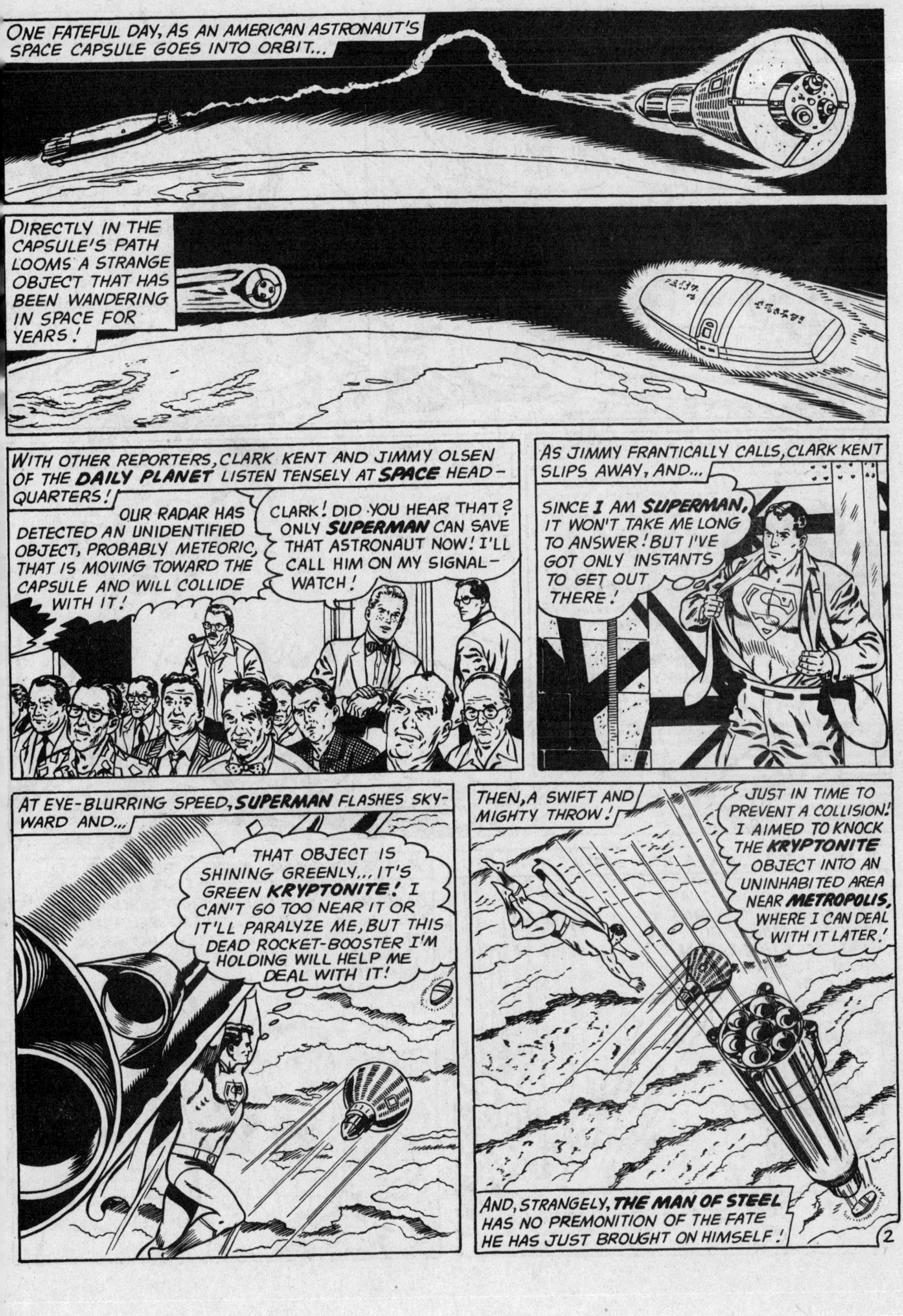
ONE FATEFUL DAY, AS AN AMERICAN ASTRONAUT'S SPACE CAPSULE GOES INTO ORBIT...
DIRECTLY IN THE CAPSULE'S PATH LOOMS A STRANGE OBJECT THAT HAS BEEN WANDERING IN SPACE FOR YEARS!
WITH OTHER REPORTERS, CLARK KENT AND JIMMY OLSEN OF THE DAILY PLANET LISTEN TENSELY AT SPACE HEAD-QUARTERS!
OUR RADAR HAS DETECTED AN UNIDENTIFIED OBJECT, PROBABLY METEORIC, THAT IS MOVING TOWARD THE CAPSULE AND WILL COLLIDE WITH IT!
CLARK! DID YOU HEAR THAT? ONLY SUPERMAN CAN SAVE THAT ASTRONAUT NOW! I'LL CALL HIM ON MY SIGNAL-WATCH!
AS JIMMY FRANTICALLY CALLS, CLARK KENT SLIPS AWAY, AND...
SINCE I AM SUPERMAN, IT WON'T TAKE ME LONG TO ANSWER! BUT I'VE GOT ONLY INSTANTS TO GET OUT THERE!
AT EYE-BLURRING SPEED, SUPERMAN FLASHES SKY-WARD AND...
THAT OBJECT IS SHINING GREENLY... IT'S GREEN KRYPTONITE! I CAN'T GO TOO NEAR IT OR IT'LL PARALYZE ME, BUT THIS DEAD ROCKET-BOOSTER I'M HOLDING WILL HELP ME DEAL WITH IT!
THEN, A SWIFT AND MIGHTY THROW!
JUST IN TIME TO PREVENT A COLLISION! I AIMED TO KNOCK THE KRYPTONITE OBJECT INTO AN UNINHABITED AREA NEAR METROPOLIS, WHERE I CAN DEAL WITH IT LATER!
AND, STRANGELY, THE MAN OF STEEL HAS NO PREMONITION OF THE FATE HE HAS JUST BROUGHT ON HIMSELF!
2

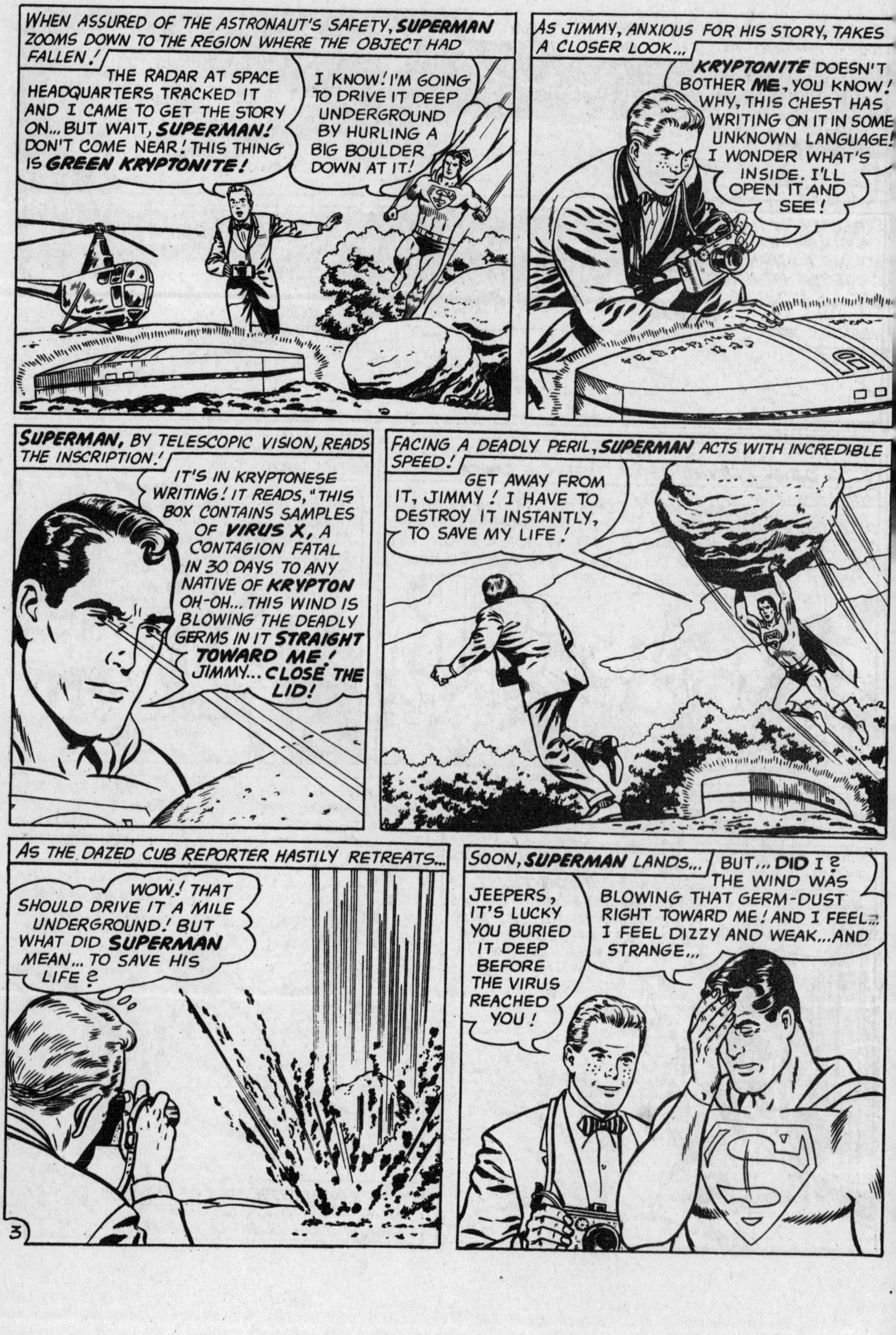
WHEN ASSURED OF THE ASTRONAUT'S SAFETY, SUPERMAN ZOOMS DOWN TO THE REGION WHERE THE OBJECT HAD FALLEN!
THE RADAR AT SPACE HEADQUARTERS TRACKED IT AND I CAME TO GET THE STORY ON... BUT WAIT, SUPERMAN! DON'T COME NEAR! THIS THING IS GREEN KRYPTONITE!
I KNOW! I'M GOING TO DRIVE IT DEEP UNDERGROUND BY HURLING A BIG BOULDER DOWN AT IT!
AS JIMMY, ANXIOUS FOR HIS STORY, TAKES A CLOSER LOOK...
KRYPTONITE DOESN'T BOTHER ME, YOU KNOW! WHY, THIS CHEST HAS WRITING ON IT IN SOME UNKNOWN LANGUAGE! I WONDER WHAT'S INSIDE. I'LL OPEN IT AND SEE!
SUPERMAN, BY TELESCOPIC VISION, READS THE INSCRIPTION!
IT'S IN KRYPTONESE WRITING! IT READS, "THIS BOX CONTAINS SAMPLES OF VIRUS X, A CONTAGION FATAL IN 30 DAYS TO ANY NATIVE OF KRYPTON OH-OH... THIS WIND IS BLOWING THE DEADLY GERMS IN IT STRAIGHT TOWARD ME! JIMMY... CLOSE THE LID!
FACING A DEADLY PERIL, SUPERMAN ACTS WITH INCREDIBLE SPEED!
GET AWAY FROM IT, JIMMY! I HAVE TO DESTROY IT INSTANTLY, TO SAVE MY LIFE!
AS THE DAZED CUB REPORTER HASTILY RETREATS...
WOW! THAT SHOULD DRIVE IT A MILE UNDERGROUND! BUT WHAT DID SUPERMAN MEAN... TO SAVE HIS LIFE?
3
SOON, SUPERMAN LANDS...
JEEPERS, IT'S LUCKY YOU BURIED IT DEEP BEFORE THE VIRUS REACHED YOU!
BUT... DID I? THE WIND WAS BLOWING THAT GERM-DUST RIGHT TOWARD ME! AND I FEEL... I FEEL DIZZY AND WEAK... AND STRANGE...

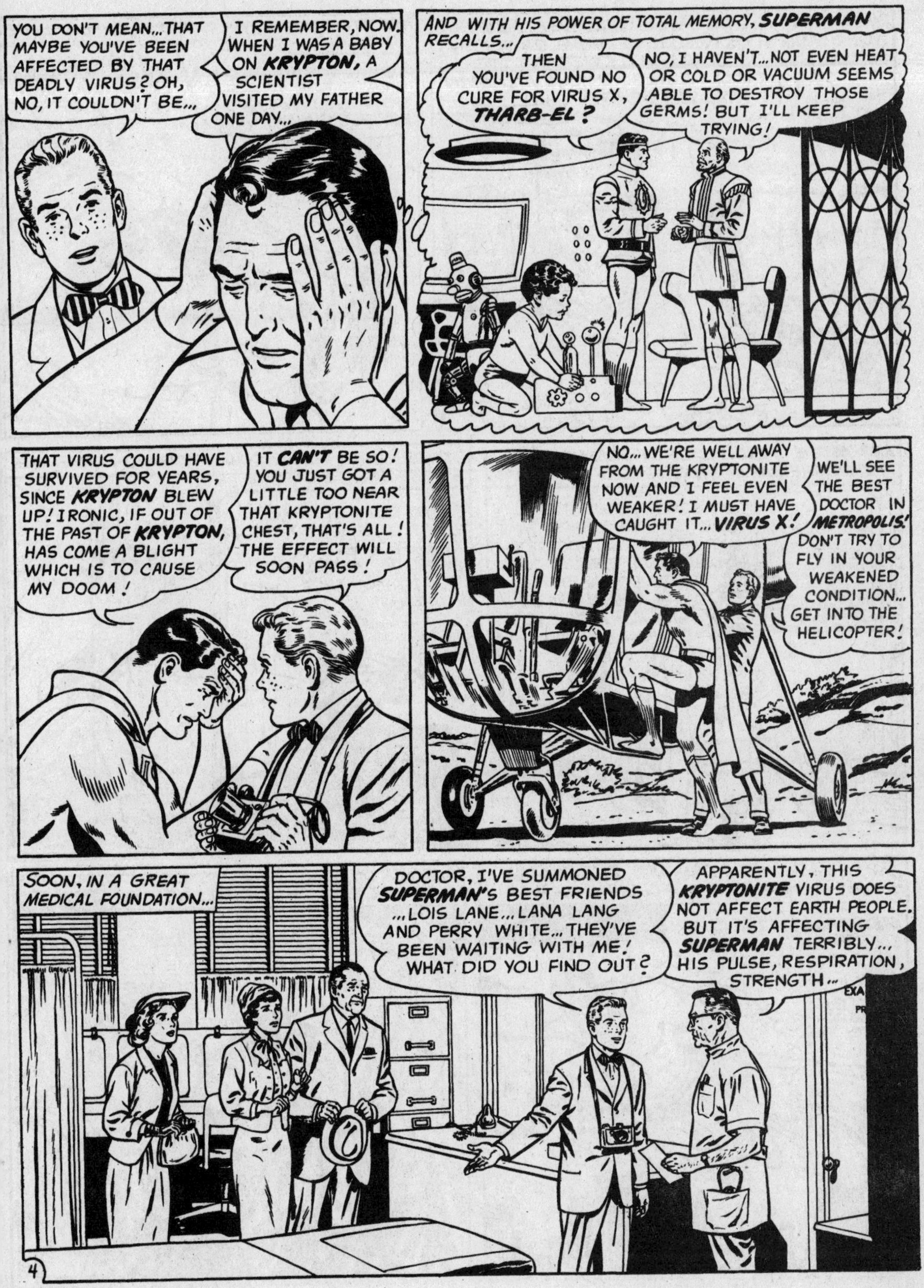
YOU DON'T MEAN... THAT MAYBE YOU'VE BEEN AFFECTED BY THAT DEADLY VIRUS? OH, NO, IT COULDN'T BE...
I REMEMBER, NOW. WHEN I WAS A BABY ON KRYPTON, A SCIENTIST VISITED MY FATHER ONE DAY...
AND WITH HIS POWER OF TOTAL MEMORY, SUPERMAN RECALLS...
THEN YOU'VE FOUND NO CURE FOR VIRUS X, THARB-EL?
NO, I HAVEN'T... NOT EVEN HEAT OR COLD OR VACUUM SEEMS ABLE TO DESTROY THOSE GERMS! BUT I'LL KEEP TRYING!
THAT VIRUS COULD HAVE SURVIVED FOR YEARS, SINCE KRYPTON BLEW UP! IRONIC, IF OUT OF THE PAST OF KRYPTON, HAS COME A BLIGHT WHICH IS TO CAUSE MY DOOM!
IT CAN'T BE SO! YOU JUST GOT A LITTLE TOO NEAR THAT KRYPTONITE CHEST, THAT'S ALL! THE EFFECT WILL SOON PASS!
NO... WE'RE WELL AWAY FROM THE KRYPTONITE NOW AND I FEEL EVEN WEAKER! I MUST HAVE CAUGHT IT... VIRUS X!
WE'LL SEE THE BEST DOCTOR IN METROPOLIS! DON'T TRY TO FLY IN YOUR WEAKENED CONDITION... GET INTO THE HELICOPTER!
SOON, IN A GREAT MEDICAL FOUNDATION...
DOCTOR, I'VE SUMMONED SUPERMAN'S BEST FRIENDS ...LOIS LANE... LANA LANG AND PERRY WHITE... THEY'VE BEEN WAITING WITH ME! WHAT DID YOU FIND OUT?
APPARENTLY, THIS KRYPTONITE VIRUS DOES NOT AFFECT EARTH PEOPLE. BUT IT'S AFFECTING SUPERMAN TERRIBLY... HIS PULSE, RESPIRATION, STRENGTH...
4

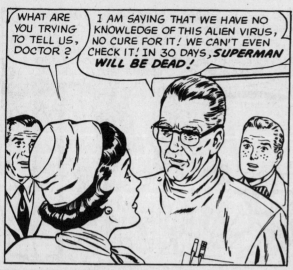

WHAT ARE YOU TRYING TO TELL US, DOCTOR?

I AM SAYING THAT WE HAVE NO KNOWLEDGE OF THIS ALIEN VIRUS, NO CURE FOR IT! WE CAN'T EVEN CHECK IT! IN 30 DAYS, *SUPERMAN WILL BE DEAD!*

THE STUNNING NEWS IS TOO MUCH FOR LANA AND LOIS...

LOIS... WE'VE BEEN RIVALS FOR YEARS... HOW WILL WE EVER FORGET *SUPERMAN?*

I KNOW, LANA DEAR... WE MUST COMFORT EACH OTHER!

AND AS THE DREAD WORDS OF DOOM ARE SPOKEN, THE *MAN OF STEEL* HIMSELF OVERHEARS...

MY SUPER-HEARING STILL FUNCTIONS ENOUGH SO THAT I HEARD THE DOCTOR'S DIAGNOSIS THROUGH THE CLOSED DOOR! THEN... IT'S *TRUE!* I'VE ONLY A MONTH TO LIVE!

STUMBLING TO THE WINDOW, TRYING TO TAKE IN THE STAGGERING REALITY OF IT...

I JUST CAN'T BELIEVE IT, YET! I... I'VE GOT TO GET AWAY FROM EVERYONE, EVEN LOIS AND JIMMY, TILL I THINK THIS THROUGH!

AND LIKE A WOUNDED CREATURE, *SUPERMAN* SHAKILY LAUNCHES HIMSELF OUT INTO THE NIGHT!

METROPOLIS... THE CITY I HAVE LOVED SO WELL! BUT I WANT TO GET AWAY FROM IT NOW... TO BE BY MYSELF... TO THINK...

AND FAR ON A HIGH, STORM-SWEPT MOUNTAIN, THE *MAN OF STEEL* CONTEMPLATES HIS DOOM!

NOTHING CAN SAVE ME... BUT I'VE GOT 30 DAYS LEFT! IT'S MY LAST CHANCE TO HELP THE WORLD, BEFORE MY END!

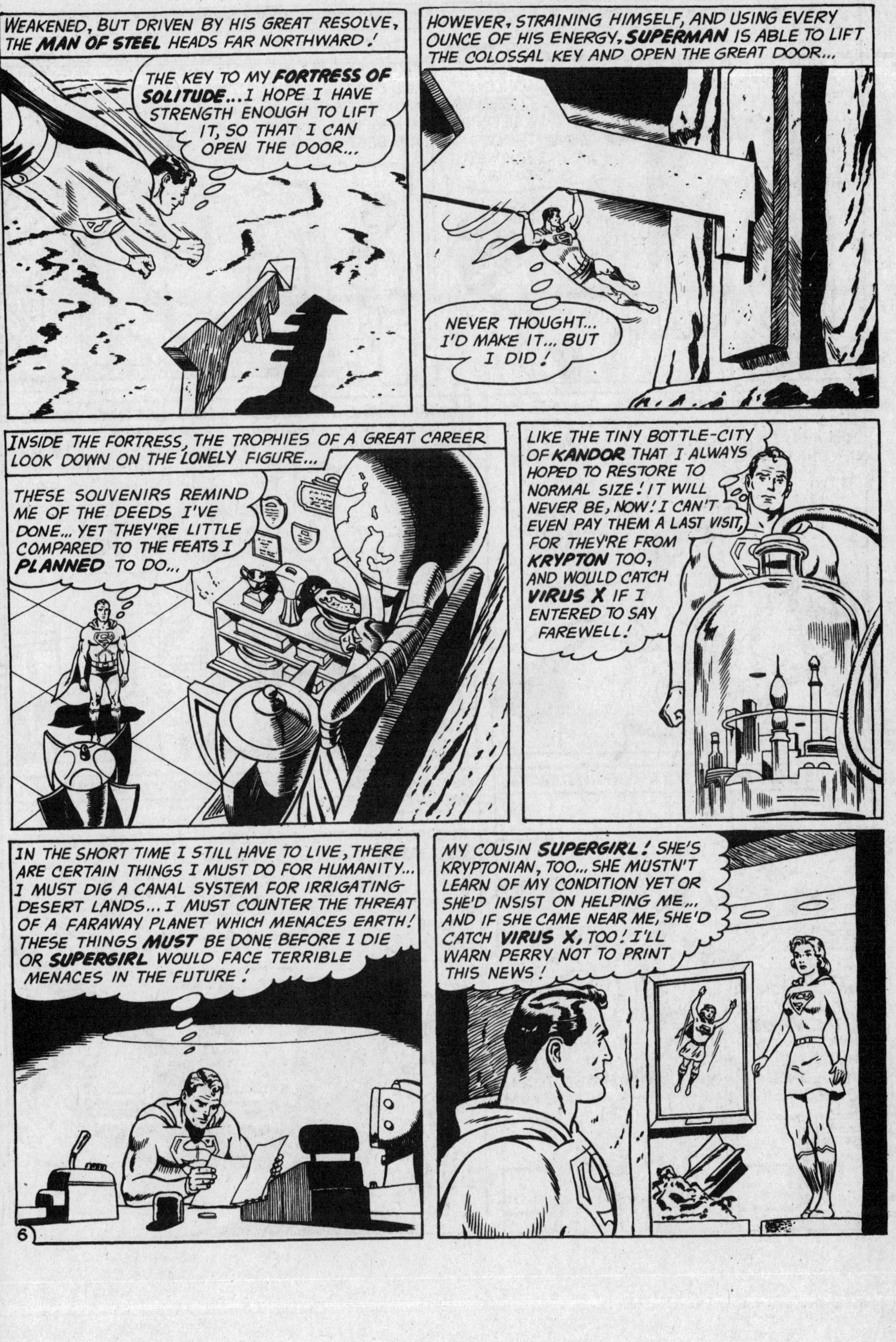
WEAKENED, BUT DRIVEN BY HIS GREAT RESOLVE, THE MAN OF STEEL HEADS FAR NORTHWARD!
THE KEY TO MY FORTRESS OF SOLITUDE...I HOPE I HAVE STRENGTH ENOUGH TO LIFT IT, SO THAT I CAN OPEN THE DOOR...
HOWEVER, STRAINING HIMSELF, AND USING EVERY OUNCE OF HIS ENERGY, SUPERMAN IS ABLE TO LIFT THE COLOSSAL KEY AND OPEN THE GREAT DOOR...
NEVER THOUGHT... I'D MAKE IT... BUT I DID!
INSIDE THE FORTRESS, THE TROPHIES OF A GREAT CAREER LOOK DOWN ON THE LONELY FIGURE...
THESE SOUVENIRS REMIND ME OF THE DEEDS I'VE DONE... YET THEY'RE LITTLE COMPARED TO THE FEATS I PLANNED TO DO...
LIKE THE TINY BOTTLE-CITY OF KANDOR THAT I ALWAYS HOPED TO RESTORE TO NORMAL SIZE! IT WILL NEVER BE, NOW! I CAN'T EVEN PAY THEM A LAST VISIT, FOR THEY'RE FROM KRYPTON TOO, AND WOULD CATCH VIRUS X IF I ENTERED TO SAY FAREWELL!
IN THE SHORT TIME I STILL HAVE TO LIVE, THERE ARE CERTAIN THINGS I MUST DO FOR HUMANITY... I MUST DIG A CANAL SYSTEM FOR IRRIGATING DESERT LANDS... I MUST COUNTER THE THREAT OF A FARAWAY PLANET WHICH MENACES EARTH! THESE THINGS MUST BE DONE BEFORE I DIE OR SUPERGIRL WOULD FACE TERRIBLE MENACES IN THE FUTURE!
MY COUSIN SUPERGIRL! SHE'S KRYPTONIAN, TOO... SHE MUSTN'T LEARN OF MY CONDITION YET OR SHE'D INSIST ON HELPING ME... AND IF SHE CAME NEAR ME, SHE'D CATCH VIRUS X, TOO! I'LL WARN PERRY NOT TO PRINT THIS NEWS!
6

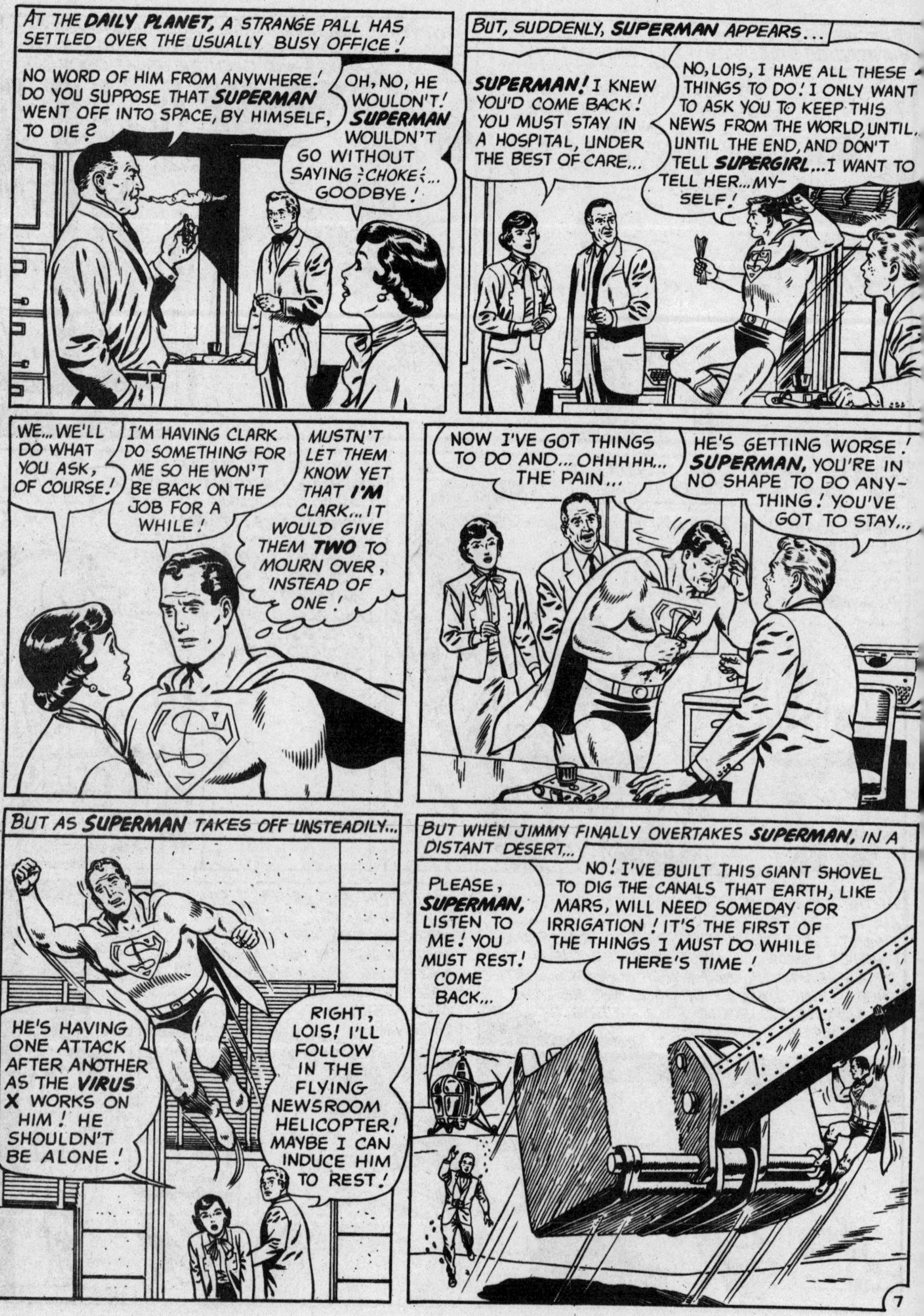
AT THE DAILY PLANET, A STRANGE PALL HAS SETTLED OVER THE USUALLY BUSY OFFICE!
NO WORD OF HIM FROM ANYWHERE! DO YOU SUPPOSE THAT SUPERMAN WENT OFF INTO SPACE, BY HIMSELF, TO DIE?
OH, NO, HE WOULDN'T! SUPERMAN WOULDN'T GO WITHOUT SAYING -CHOKE-... GOODBYE!
BUT, SUDDENLY, SUPERMAN APPEARS...
SUPERMAN! I KNEW YOU'D COME BACK! YOU MUST STAY IN A HOSPITAL, UNDER THE BEST OF CARE...
NO, LOIS, I HAVE ALL THESE THINGS TO DO! I ONLY WANT TO ASK YOU TO KEEP THIS NEWS FROM THE WORLD, UNTIL... UNTIL THE END, AND DON'T TELL SUPERGIRL... I WANT TO TELL HER... MY-SELF!
WE... WE'LL DO WHAT YOU ASK, OF COURSE!
I'M HAVING CLARK DO SOMETHING FOR ME SO HE WON'T BE BACK ON THE JOB FOR A WHILE!
MUSTN'T LET THEM KNOW YET THAT I'M CLARK... IT WOULD GIVE THEM TWO TO MOURN OVER, INSTEAD OF ONE!
NOW I'VE GOT THINGS TO DO AND... OHHHHH... THE PAIN...
HE'S GETTING WORSE! SUPERMAN, YOU'RE IN NO SHAPE TO DO ANYTHING! YOU'VE GOT TO STAY...
BUT AS SUPERMAN TAKES OFF UNSTEADILY...
HE'S HAVING ONE ATTACK AFTER ANOTHER AS THE VIRUS X WORKS ON HIM! HE SHOULDN'T BE ALONE!
RIGHT, LOIS! I'LL FOLLOW IN THE FLYING NEWSROOM HELICOPTER! MAYBE I CAN INDUCE HIM TO REST!
BUT WHEN JIMMY FINALLY OVERTAKES SUPERMAN, IN A DISTANT DESERT...
PLEASE, SUPERMAN, LISTEN TO ME! YOU MUST REST! COME BACK...
NO! I'VE BUILT THIS GIANT SHOVEL TO DIG THE CANALS THAT EARTH, LIKE MARS, WILL NEED SOMEDAY FOR IRRIGATION! IT'S THE FIRST OF THE THINGS I MUST DO WHILE THERE'S TIME!
7

BUT WHEN *THE MAN OF STEEL* BEGINS THE AWESOME FEAT...

BUMP! CRASH!

I...I COULDN'T HOLD IT! THE *VIRUS X* HAS SAPPED MY STRENGTH...STRANGE... I WAS FEELING SO MUCH BETTER A FEW HOURS AGO...WAS ABLE TO BUILD THIS SHOVEL... NOW I FEEL WEAK AGAIN...

YOU JUST HAD STILL ANOTHER ATTACK, *SUPERMAN!* YOU MUST LIE DOWN...

NO...NO...I'VE GOT TO PREPARE SOMETHING, QUICKLY! *SUPERGIRL* IS ON PATROL...AND SHE'LL BE PASSING OVERHEAD ANY MOMENT! I'LL SUMMON MY ROBOTS TO HELP ME...

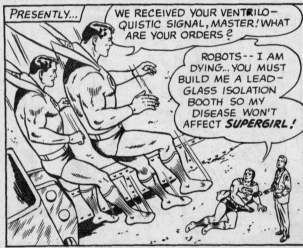

PRESENTLY...

WE RECEIVED YOUR VENTRILO-QUISTIC SIGNAL, MASTER! WHAT ARE YOUR ORDERS?

ROBOTS-- I AM DYING...YOU MUST BUILD ME A LEAD-GLASS ISOLATION BOOTH SO MY DISEASE WON'T AFFECT *SUPERGIRL!*

SWIFTLY, THE PAIR OF ROBOTS GO TO WORK, DIGGING BELOW THE GROUND FOR NEEDED MINERALS AND FUSING THEM INTO LEAD-GLASS WITH THEIR HEAT VISION...

YOU'RE DOING...FINE, ROBOTS...DON'T FORGET TO BUILD A MICROPHONE TOO... SO I CAN COMMUNICATE FROM BOOTH...

PRESENTLY, WHEN THE PROJECT IS COMPLETE...

THANKS, ROBOTS ...NOW USE THAT ...GIANT SHOVEL ...TO BUILD CANALS ...AS I WILL INSTRUCT...

WE CAN'T, MASTER! SUDDEN SUNSPOT ACTIVITY IS CREATING ELECTROMAGNETIC DISTURBANCES WHICH WILL SHORT-CIRCUIT OUR MOTORS VERY SHORTLY. WE MUST FLY BACK TO THE FORTRESS BEFORE IT IS TOO LATE! FAREWELL!

8

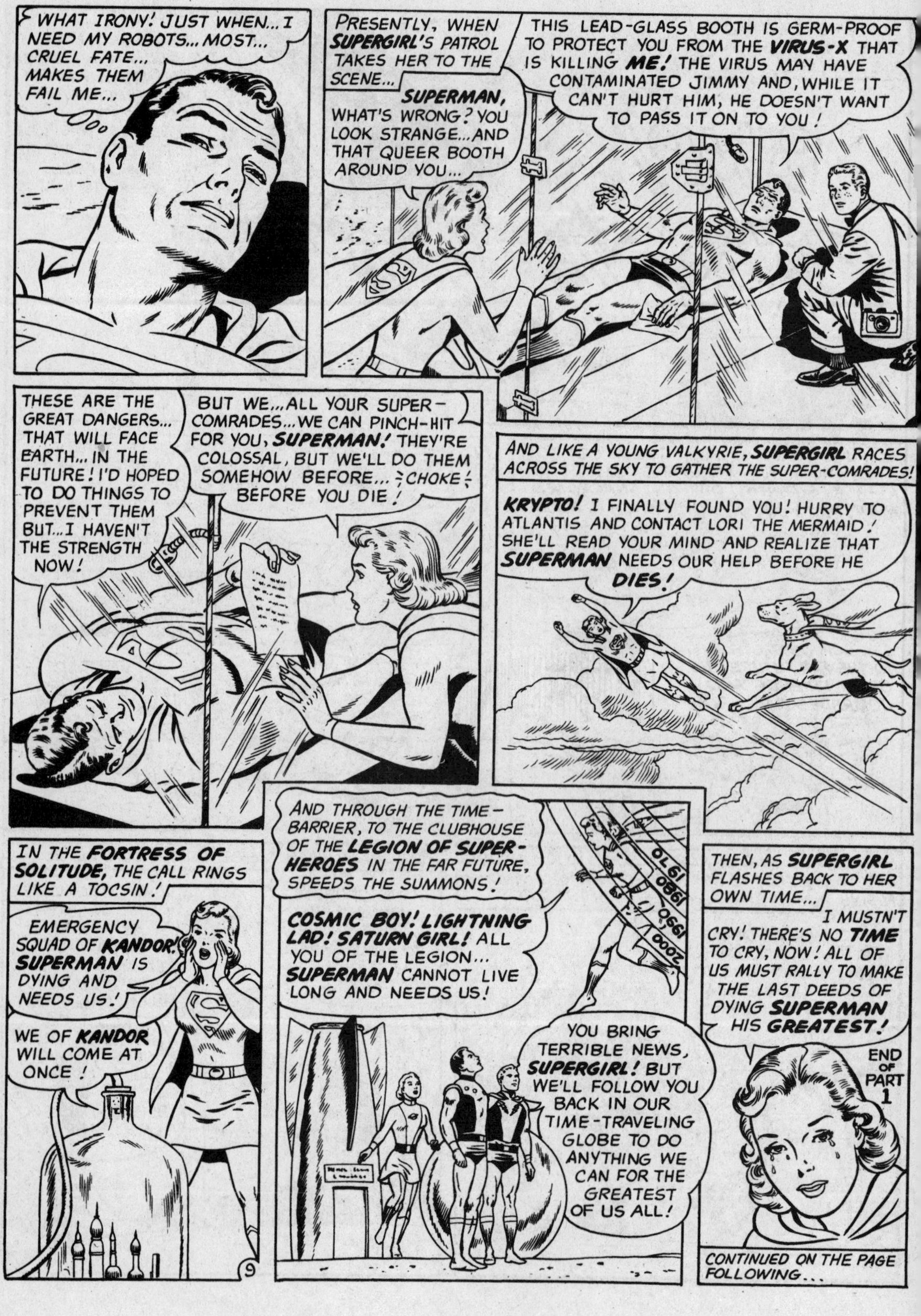

WHAT IRONY! JUST WHEN... I NEED MY ROBOTS... MOST... CRUEL FATE... MAKES THEM FAIL ME...
PRESENTLY, WHEN SUPERGIRL'S PATROL TAKES HER TO THE SCENE...
SUPERMAN, WHAT'S WRONG? YOU LOOK STRANGE... AND THAT QUEER BOOTH AROUND YOU...
THIS LEAD-GLASS BOOTH IS GERM-PROOF TO PROTECT YOU FROM THE VIRUS-X THAT IS KILLING ME! THE VIRUS MAY HAVE CONTAMINATED JIMMY AND, WHILE IT CAN'T HURT HIM, HE DOESN'T WANT TO PASS IT ON TO YOU!
THESE ARE THE GREAT DANGERS... THAT WILL FACE EARTH... IN THE FUTURE! I'D HOPED TO DO THINGS TO PREVENT THEM BUT... I HAVEN'T THE STRENGTH NOW!
BUT WE... ALL YOUR SUPER-COMRADES... WE CAN PINCH-HIT FOR YOU, SUPERMAN! THEY'RE COLOSSAL, BUT WE'LL DO THEM SOMEHOW BEFORE... CHOKE BEFORE YOU DIE!
AND LIKE A YOUNG VALKYRIE, SUPERGIRL RACES ACROSS THE SKY TO GATHER THE SUPER-COMRADES!
KRYPTO! I FINALLY FOUND YOU! HURRY TO ATLANTIS AND CONTACT LORI THE MERMAID! SHE'LL READ YOUR MIND AND REALIZE THAT SUPERMAN NEEDS OUR HELP BEFORE HE DIES!
IN THE FORTRESS OF SOLITUDE, THE CALL RINGS LIKE A TOCSIN!
EMERGENCY SQUAD OF KANDOR! SUPERMAN IS DYING AND NEEDS US!
WE OF KANDOR WILL COME AT ONCE!
9
AND THROUGH THE TIME-BARRIER, TO THE CLUBHOUSE OF THE LEGION OF SUPER-HEROES IN THE FAR FUTURE, SPEEDS THE SUMMONS!
COSMIC BOY! LIGHTNING LAD! SATURN GIRL! ALL YOU OF THE LEGION... SUPERMAN CANNOT LIVE LONG AND NEEDS US!
1970
1980
1990
2000
YOU BRING TERRIBLE NEWS, SUPERGIRL! BUT WE'LL FOLLOW YOU BACK IN OUR TIME-TRAVELING GLOBE TO DO ANYTHING WE CAN FOR THE GREATEST OF US ALL!
THEN, AS SUPERGIRL FLASHES BACK TO HER OWN TIME...
I MUSTN'T CRY! THERE'S NO TIME TO CRY, NOW! ALL OF US MUST RALLY TO MAKE THE LAST DEEDS OF DYING SUPERMAN HIS GREATEST!
END OF PART 1
CONTINUED ON THE PAGE FOLLOWING...

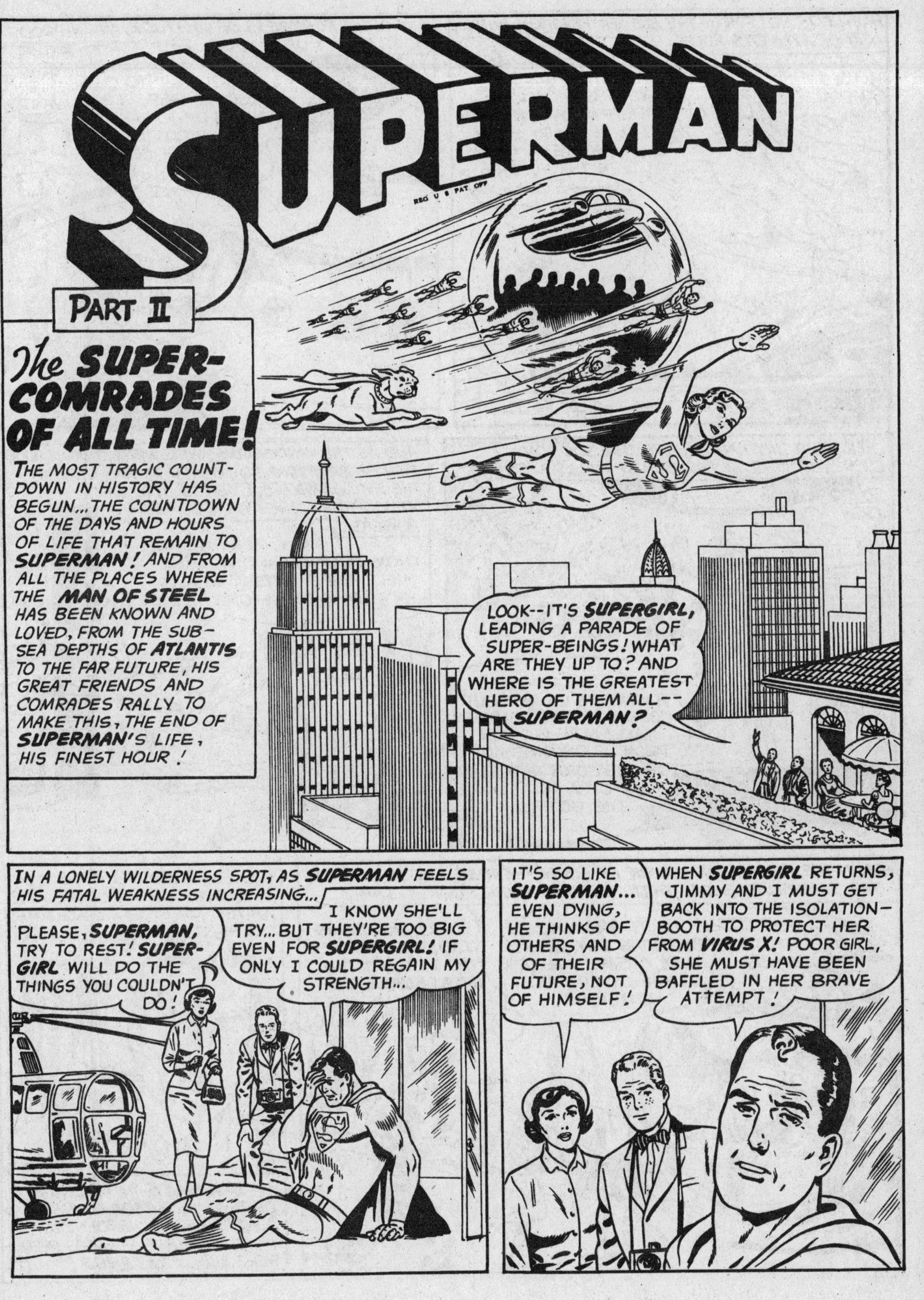
SUPERMAN
REG U S PAT OFF
PART II
The SUPER-COMRADES OF ALL TIME!
THE MOST TRAGIC COUNTDOWN IN HISTORY HAS BEGUN...THE COUNTDOWN OF THE DAYS AND HOURS OF LIFE THAT REMAIN TO SUPERMAN! AND FROM ALL THE PLACES WHERE THE MAN OF STEEL HAS BEEN KNOWN AND LOVED, FROM THE SUB-SEA DEPTHS OF ATLANTIS TO THE FAR FUTURE, HIS GREAT FRIENDS AND COMRADES RALLY TO MAKE THIS, THE END OF SUPERMAN'S LIFE, HIS FINEST HOUR!
LOOK--IT'S SUPERGIRL, LEADING A PARADE OF SUPER-BEINGS! WHAT ARE THEY UP TO? AND WHERE IS THE GREATEST HERO OF THEM ALL--SUPERMAN?
IN A LONELY WILDERNESS SPOT, AS SUPERMAN FEELS HIS FATAL WEAKNESS INCREASING...
PLEASE, SUPERMAN, TRY TO REST! SUPERGIRL WILL DO THE THINGS YOU COULDN'T DO!
I KNOW SHE'LL TRY...BUT THEY'RE TOO BIG EVEN FOR SUPERGIRL! IF ONLY I COULD REGAIN MY STRENGTH...
IT'S SO LIKE SUPERMAN... EVEN DYING, HE THINKS OF OTHERS AND OF THEIR FUTURE, NOT OF HIMSELF!
WHEN SUPERGIRL RETURNS, JIMMY AND I MUST GET BACK INTO THE ISOLATION-BOOTH TO PROTECT HER FROM VIRUS X! POOR GIRL, SHE MUST HAVE BEEN BAFFLED IN HER BRAVE ATTEMPT!

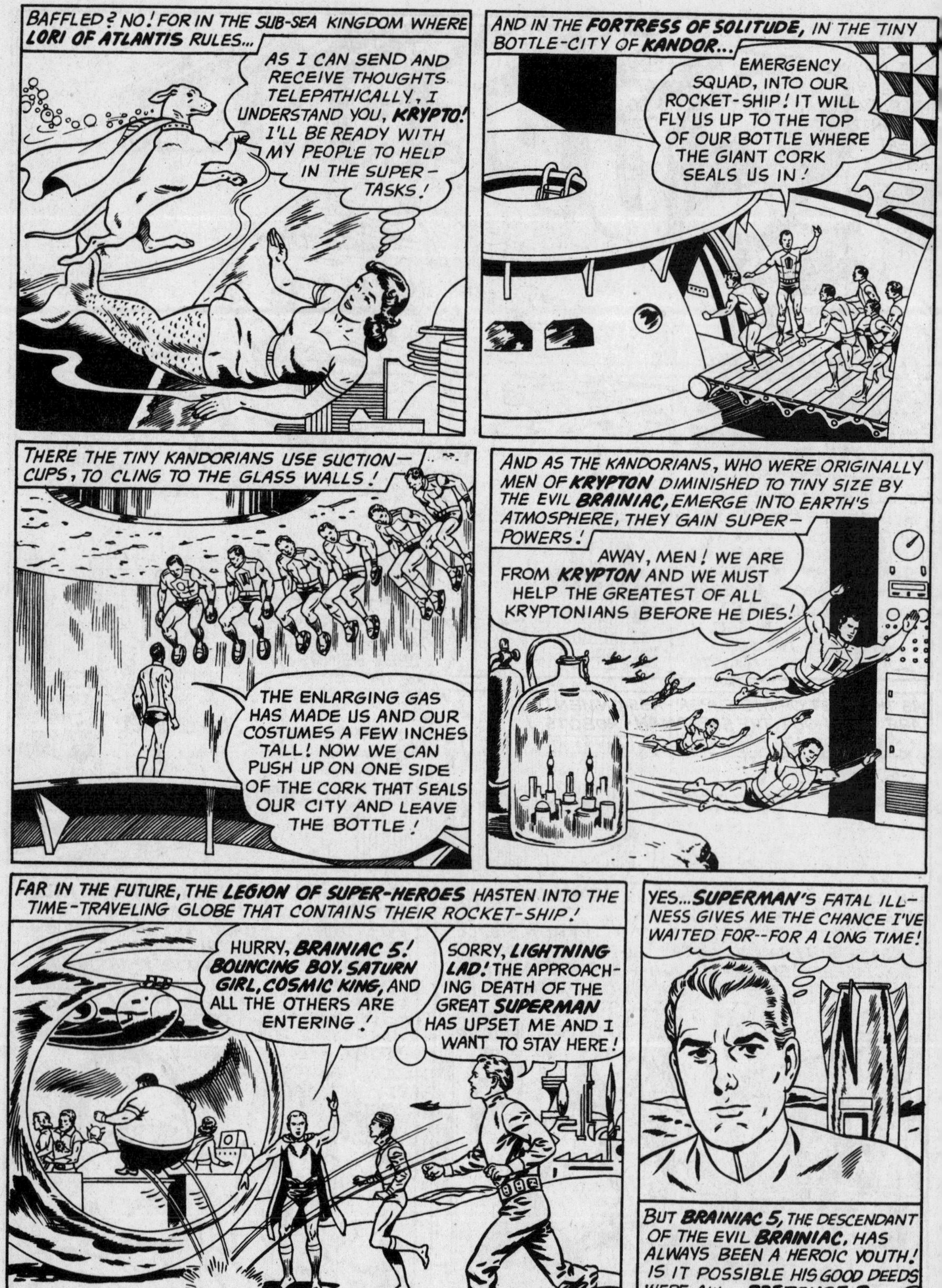
BAFFLED? NO! FOR IN THE SUB-SEA KINGDOM WHERE LORI OF ATLANTIS RULES...
AS I CAN SEND AND RECEIVE THOUGHTS TELEPATHICALLY, I UNDERSTAND YOU, KRYPTO! I'LL BE READY WITH MY PEOPLE TO HELP IN THE SUPER-TASKS!
AND IN THE FORTRESS OF SOLITUDE, IN THE TINY BOTTLE-CITY OF KANDOR...
EMERGENCY SQUAD, INTO OUR ROCKET-SHIP! IT WILL FLY US UP TO THE TOP OF OUR BOTTLE WHERE THE GIANT CORK SEALS US IN!
THERE THE TINY KANDORIANS USE SUCTION-CUPS, TO CLING TO THE GLASS WALLS!
THE ENLARGING GAS HAS MADE US AND OUR COSTUMES A FEW INCHES TALL! NOW WE CAN PUSH UP ON ONE SIDE OF THE CORK THAT SEALS OUR CITY AND LEAVE THE BOTTLE!
AND AS THE KANDORIANS, WHO WERE ORIGINALLY MEN OF KRYPTON DIMINISHED TO TINY SIZE BY THE EVIL BRAINIAC, EMERGE INTO EARTH'S ATMOSPHERE, THEY GAIN SUPER-POWERS!
AWAY, MEN! WE ARE FROM KRYPTON AND WE MUST HELP THE GREATEST OF ALL KRYPTONIANS BEFORE HE DIES!
FAR IN THE FUTURE, THE LEGION OF SUPER-HEROES HASTEN INTO THE TIME-TRAVELING GLOBE THAT CONTAINS THEIR ROCKET-SHIP!
HURRY, BRAINIAC 5! BOUNCING BOY, SATURN GIRL, COSMIC KING, AND ALL THE OTHERS ARE ENTERING!
SORRY, LIGHTNING LAD! THE APPROACHING DEATH OF THE GREAT SUPERMAN HAS UPSET ME AND I WANT TO STAY HERE!
YES... SUPERMAN'S FATAL ILLNESS GIVES ME THE CHANCE I'VE WAITED FOR--FOR A LONG TIME!
BUT BRAINIAC 5, THE DESCENDANT OF THE EVIL BRAINIAC, HAS ALWAYS BEEN A HEROIC YOUTH! IS IT POSSIBLE HIS GOOD DEEDS WERE ALL... PRETENSE?
2

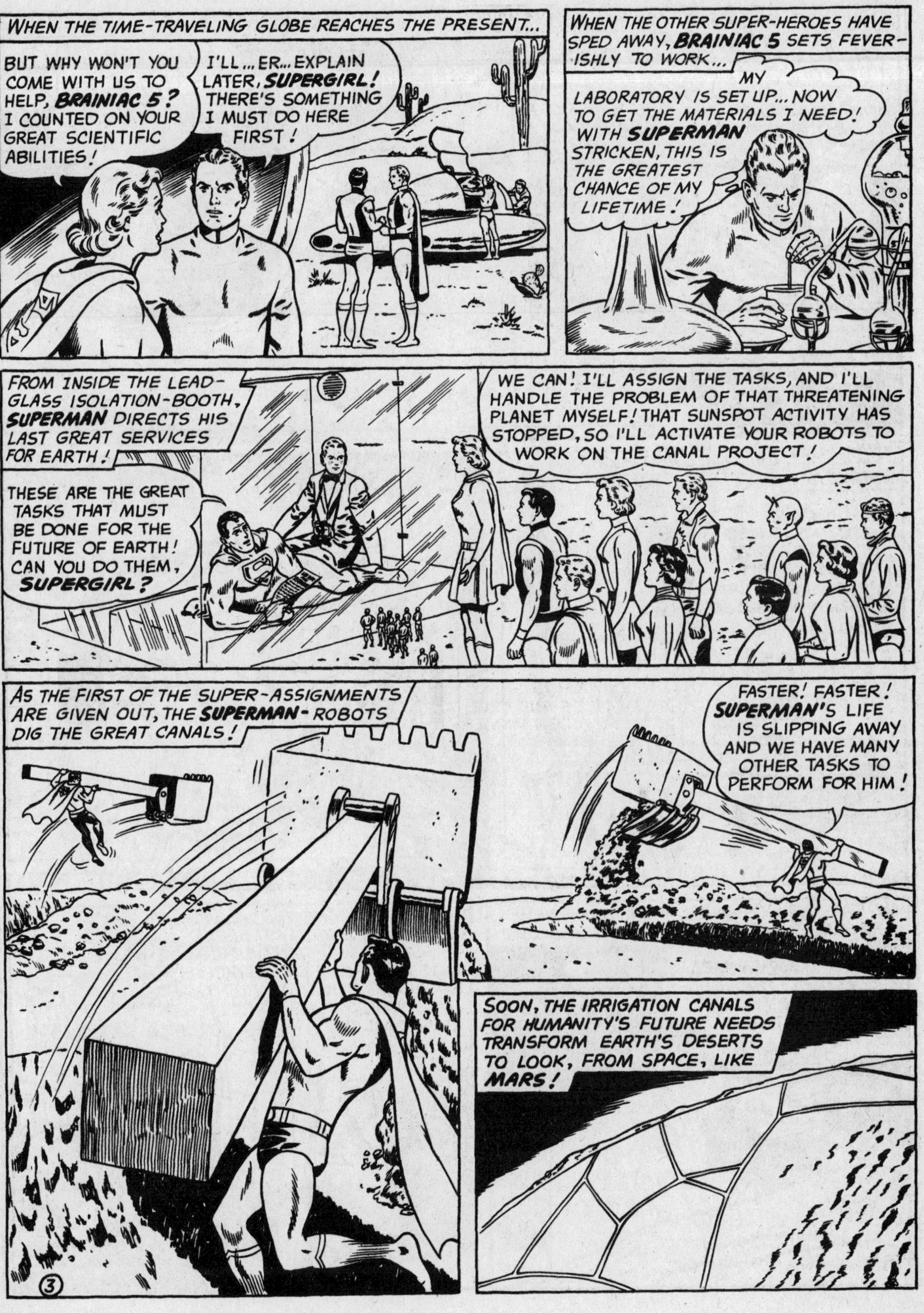
WHEN THE TIME-TRAVELING GLOBE REACHES THE PRESENT...
BUT WHY WON'T YOU COME WITH US TO HELP, BRAINIAC 5? I COUNTED ON YOUR GREAT SCIENTIFIC ABILITIES!
I'LL... ER... EXPLAIN LATER, SUPERGIRL! THERE'S SOMETHING I MUST DO HERE FIRST!
WHEN THE OTHER SUPER-HEROES HAVE SPED AWAY, BRAINIAC 5 SETS FEVERISHLY TO WORK...
MY LABORATORY IS SET UP... NOW TO GET THE MATERIALS I NEED! WITH SUPERMAN STRICKEN, THIS IS THE GREATEST CHANCE OF MY LIFETIME!
FROM INSIDE THE LEAD-GLASS ISOLATION-BOOTH, SUPERMAN DIRECTS HIS LAST GREAT SERVICES FOR EARTH!
THESE ARE THE GREAT TASKS THAT MUST BE DONE FOR THE FUTURE OF EARTH! CAN YOU DO THEM, SUPERGIRL?
WE CAN! I'LL ASSIGN THE TASKS, AND I'LL HANDLE THE PROBLEM OF THAT THREATENING PLANET MYSELF! THAT SUNSPOT ACTIVITY HAS STOPPED, SO I'LL ACTIVATE YOUR ROBOTS TO WORK ON THE CANAL PROJECT!
AS THE FIRST OF THE SUPER-ASSIGNMENTS ARE GIVEN OUT, THE SUPERMAN-ROBOTS DIG THE GREAT CANALS!
FASTER! FASTER! SUPERMAN'S LIFE IS SLIPPING AWAY AND WE HAVE MANY OTHER TASKS TO PERFORM FOR HIM!
3
SOON, THE IRRIGATION CANALS FOR HUMANITY'S FUTURE NEEDS TRANSFORM EARTH'S DESERTS TO LOOK, FROM SPACE, LIKE MARS!

MEANWHILE, *SUPERGIRL* ARROWS INTO FAR SPACE WHERE *SUPERMAN* HAS DETECTED A PLANET THAT WILL SOME DAY HIT EARTH!

WHY DID *BRAINIAC 5* HANG BACK? HE'S THE ONLY ONE OF US WHO WOULDN'T HELP IN *SUPERMAN'S* GREAT NEED!

THEN, AS THE *GIRL OF STEEL* REACHES THE MENACING PLANET...

SUPERMAN WAS RIGHT! IN FAR FUTURE TIMES, THIS PLANET *WOULD* HIT EARTH! HMM... PERHAPS I CAN MAKE IT HIT SOMETHING ELSE...

PRESENTLY, USING ALL HER MIGHTY STRENGTH...

I'M SLOWLY DEFLECTING IT INTO THE PATH I WANT IT TO TAKE! IT'S GOING TO HIT THAT OTHER, UNINHABITED WORLD NEARBY!

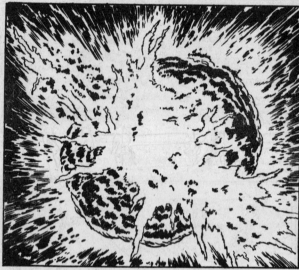

AND FAR AWAY ON EARTH, A BRILLIANT NEW RED STAR BLAZES FOR A LITTLE WHILE IN THE HEAVENS!

SUPERGIRL SUCCEEDED! THAT RED STAR IS THE FUNERAL PYRE OF A THREAT TO EARTH!

4

BUT AN EVEN GREATER MENACE TO THE FUTURE IS THE VAST CLOUD OF FUNGUS IN DISTANT SPACE THAT WILL SOME DAY REACH EARTH AND BLIGHT ALL PLANT LIFE! HOW CAN SHE... THEY... EVER DEAL WITH THAT?

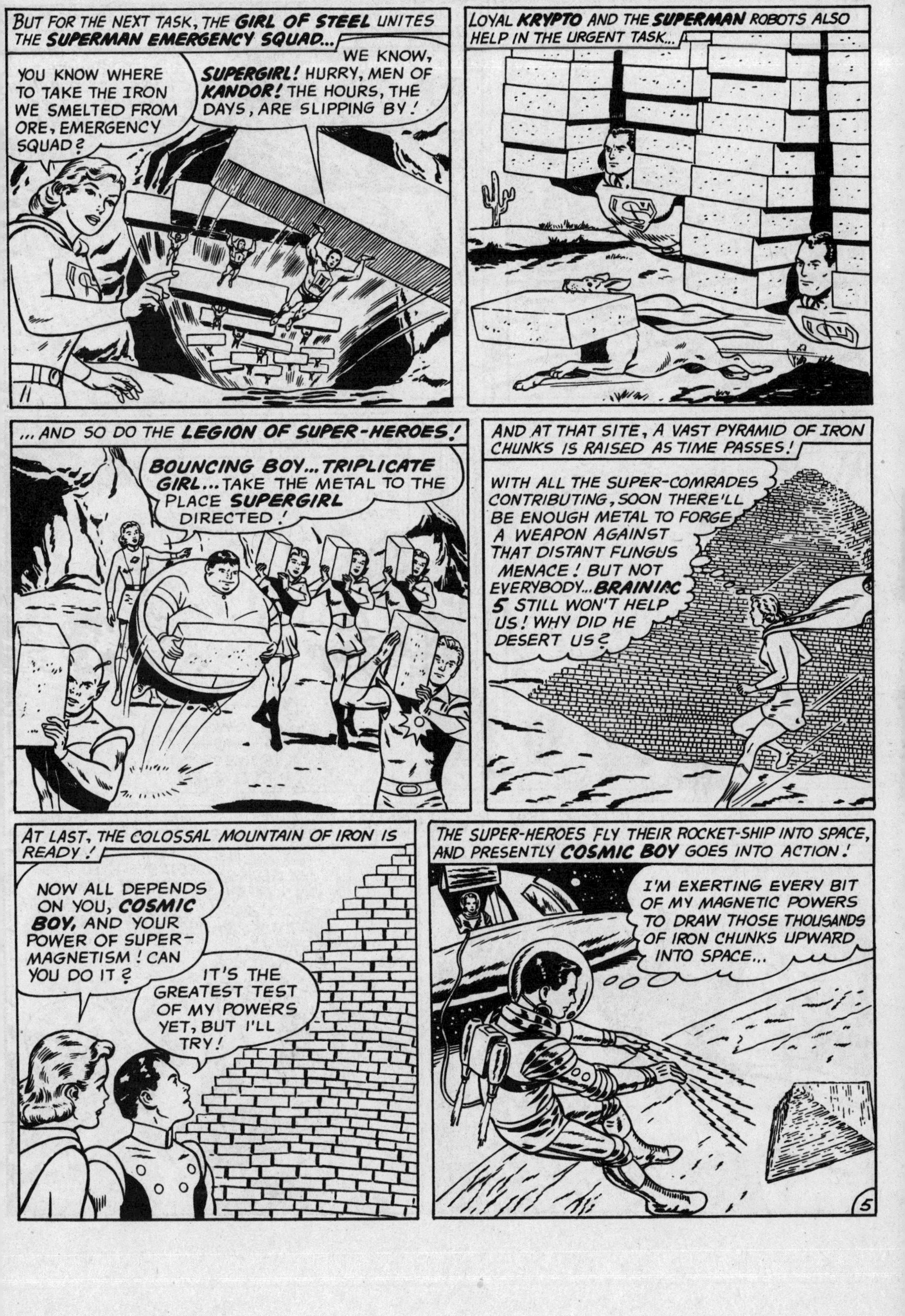
BUT FOR THE NEXT TASK, THE GIRL OF STEEL UNITES THE SUPERMAN EMERGENCY SQUAD...
YOU KNOW WHERE TO TAKE THE IRON WE SMELTED FROM ORE, EMERGENCY SQUAD?
WE KNOW, SUPERGIRL! HURRY, MEN OF KANDOR! THE HOURS, THE DAYS, ARE SLIPPING BY!
LOYAL KRYPTO AND THE SUPERMAN ROBOTS ALSO HELP IN THE URGENT TASK...
...AND SO DO THE LEGION OF SUPER-HEROES!
BOUNCING BOY...TRIPLICATE GIRL...TAKE THE METAL TO THE PLACE SUPERGIRL DIRECTED!
AND AT THAT SITE, A VAST PYRAMID OF IRON CHUNKS IS RAISED AS TIME PASSES!
WITH ALL THE SUPER-COMRADES CONTRIBUTING, SOON THERE'LL BE ENOUGH METAL TO FORGE A WEAPON AGAINST THAT DISTANT FUNGUS MENACE! BUT NOT EVERYBODY...BRAINIAC 5 STILL WON'T HELP US! WHY DID HE DESERT US?
AT LAST, THE COLOSSAL MOUNTAIN OF IRON IS READY!
NOW ALL DEPENDS ON YOU, COSMIC BOY, AND YOUR POWER OF SUPER-MAGNETISM! CAN YOU DO IT?
IT'S THE GREATEST TEST OF MY POWERS YET, BUT I'LL TRY!
THE SUPER-HEROES FLY THEIR ROCKET-SHIP INTO SPACE, AND PRESENTLY COSMIC BOY GOES INTO ACTION!
I'M EXERTING EVERY BIT OF MY MAGNETIC POWERS TO DRAW THOSE THOUSANDS OF IRON CHUNKS UPWARD INTO SPACE...
5

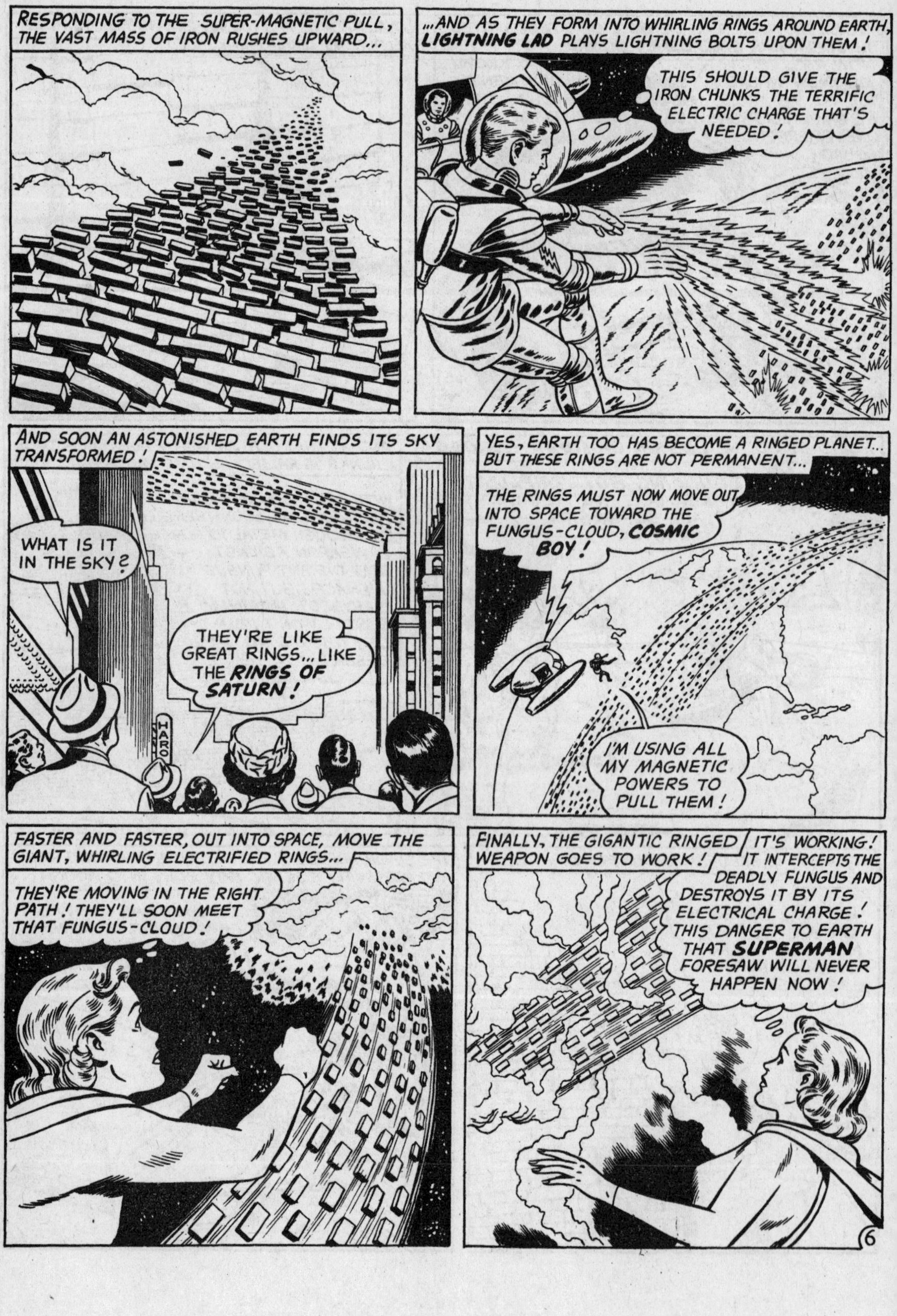

RESPONDING TO THE SUPER-MAGNETIC PULL, THE VAST MASS OF IRON RUSHES UPWARD...
...AND AS THEY FORM INTO WHIRLING RINGS AROUND EARTH, LIGHTNING LAD PLAYS LIGHTNING BOLTS UPON THEM!
THIS SHOULD GIVE THE IRON CHUNKS THE TERRIFIC ELECTRIC CHARGE THAT'S NEEDED!
AND SOON AN ASTONISHED EARTH FINDS ITS SKY TRANSFORMED!
WHAT IS IT IN THE SKY?
THEY'RE LIKE GREAT RINGS... LIKE THE RINGS OF SATURN!
HARO
YES, EARTH TOO HAS BECOME A RINGED PLANET... BUT THESE RINGS ARE NOT PERMANENT...
THE RINGS MUST NOW MOVE OUT INTO SPACE TOWARD THE FUNGUS-CLOUD, COSMIC BOY!
I'M USING ALL MY MAGNETIC POWERS TO PULL THEM!
FASTER AND FASTER, OUT INTO SPACE, MOVE THE GIANT, WHIRLING ELECTRIFIED RINGS...
THEY'RE MOVING IN THE RIGHT PATH! THEY'LL SOON MEET THAT FUNGUS-CLOUD!
FINALLY, THE GIGANTIC RINGED WEAPON GOES TO WORK!
IT'S WORKING! IT INTERCEPTS THE DEADLY FUNGUS AND DESTROYS IT BY ITS ELECTRICAL CHARGE! THIS DANGER TO EARTH THAT SUPERMAN FORESAW WILL NEVER HAPPEN NOW!
6

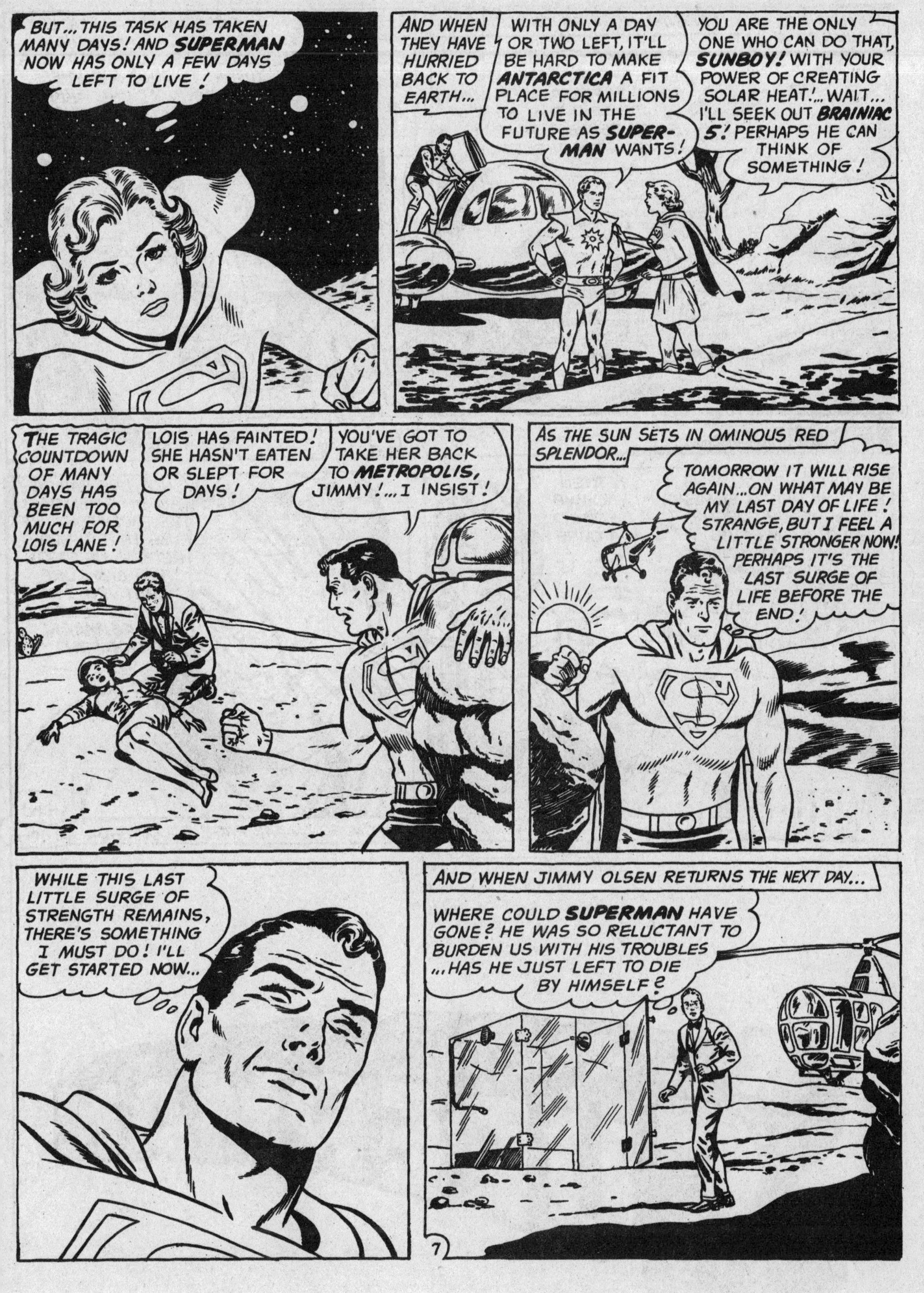
BUT... THIS TASK HAS TAKEN MANY DAYS! AND SUPERMAN NOW HAS ONLY A FEW DAYS LEFT TO LIVE!
AND WHEN THEY HAVE HURRIED BACK TO EARTH...
WITH ONLY A DAY OR TWO LEFT, IT'LL BE HARD TO MAKE ANTARCTICA A FIT PLACE FOR MILLIONS TO LIVE IN THE FUTURE AS SUPER-MAN WANTS!
YOU ARE THE ONLY ONE WHO CAN DO THAT, SUNBOY! WITH YOUR POWER OF CREATING SOLAR HEAT!... WAIT... I'LL SEEK OUT BRAINIAC 5! PERHAPS HE CAN THINK OF SOMETHING!
THE TRAGIC COUNTDOWN OF MANY DAYS HAS BEEN TOO MUCH FOR LOIS LANE!
LOIS HAS FAINTED! SHE HASN'T EATEN OR SLEPT FOR DAYS!
YOU'VE GOT TO TAKE HER BACK TO METROPOLIS, JIMMY!... I INSIST!
AS THE SUN SETS IN OMINOUS RED SPLENDOR...
TOMORROW IT WILL RISE AGAIN... ON WHAT MAY BE MY LAST DAY OF LIFE! STRANGE, BUT I FEEL A LITTLE STRONGER NOW! PERHAPS IT'S THE LAST SURGE OF LIFE BEFORE THE END!
WHILE THIS LAST LITTLE SURGE OF STRENGTH REMAINS, THERE'S SOMETHING I MUST DO! I'LL GET STARTED NOW...
AND WHEN JIMMY OLSEN RETURNS THE NEXT DAY...
WHERE COULD SUPERMAN HAVE GONE? HE WAS SO RELUCTANT TO BURDEN US WITH HIS TROUBLES ... HAS HE JUST LEFT TO DIE BY HIMSELF?
7

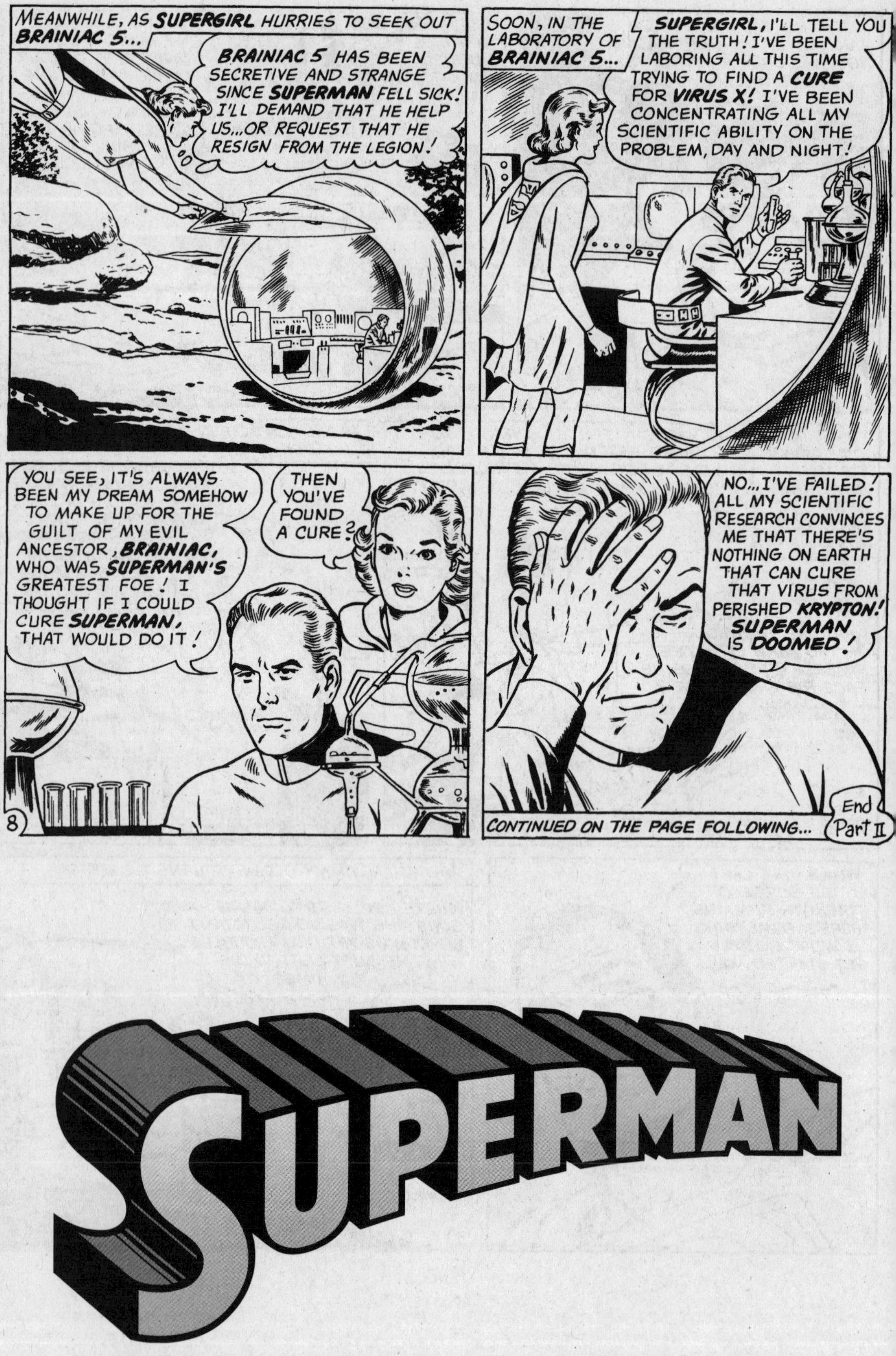
MEANWHILE, AS SUPERGIRL HURRIES TO SEEK OUT BRAINIAC 5...
BRAINIAC 5 HAS BEEN SECRETIVE AND STRANGE SINCE SUPERMAN FELL SICK! I'LL DEMAND THAT HE HELP US...OR REQUEST THAT HE RESIGN FROM THE LEGION!
SOON, IN THE LABORATORY OF BRAINIAC 5...
SUPERGIRL, I'LL TELL YOU THE TRUTH! I'VE BEEN LABORING ALL THIS TIME TRYING TO FIND A CURE FOR VIRUS X! I'VE BEEN CONCENTRATING ALL MY SCIENTIFIC ABILITY ON THE PROBLEM, DAY AND NIGHT!
YOU SEE, IT'S ALWAYS BEEN MY DREAM SOMEHOW TO MAKE UP FOR THE GUILT OF MY EVIL ANCESTOR, BRAINIAC, WHO WAS SUPERMAN'S GREATEST FOE! I THOUGHT IF I COULD CURE SUPERMAN, THAT WOULD DO IT!
THEN YOU'VE FOUND A CURE?
8
NO...I'VE FAILED! ALL MY SCIENTIFIC RESEARCH CONVINCES ME THAT THERE'S NOTHING ON EARTH THAT CAN CURE THAT VIRUS FROM PERISHED KRYPTON! SUPERMAN IS DOOMED!
CONTINUED ON THE PAGE FOLLOWING...
End Part II

SUPERMAN

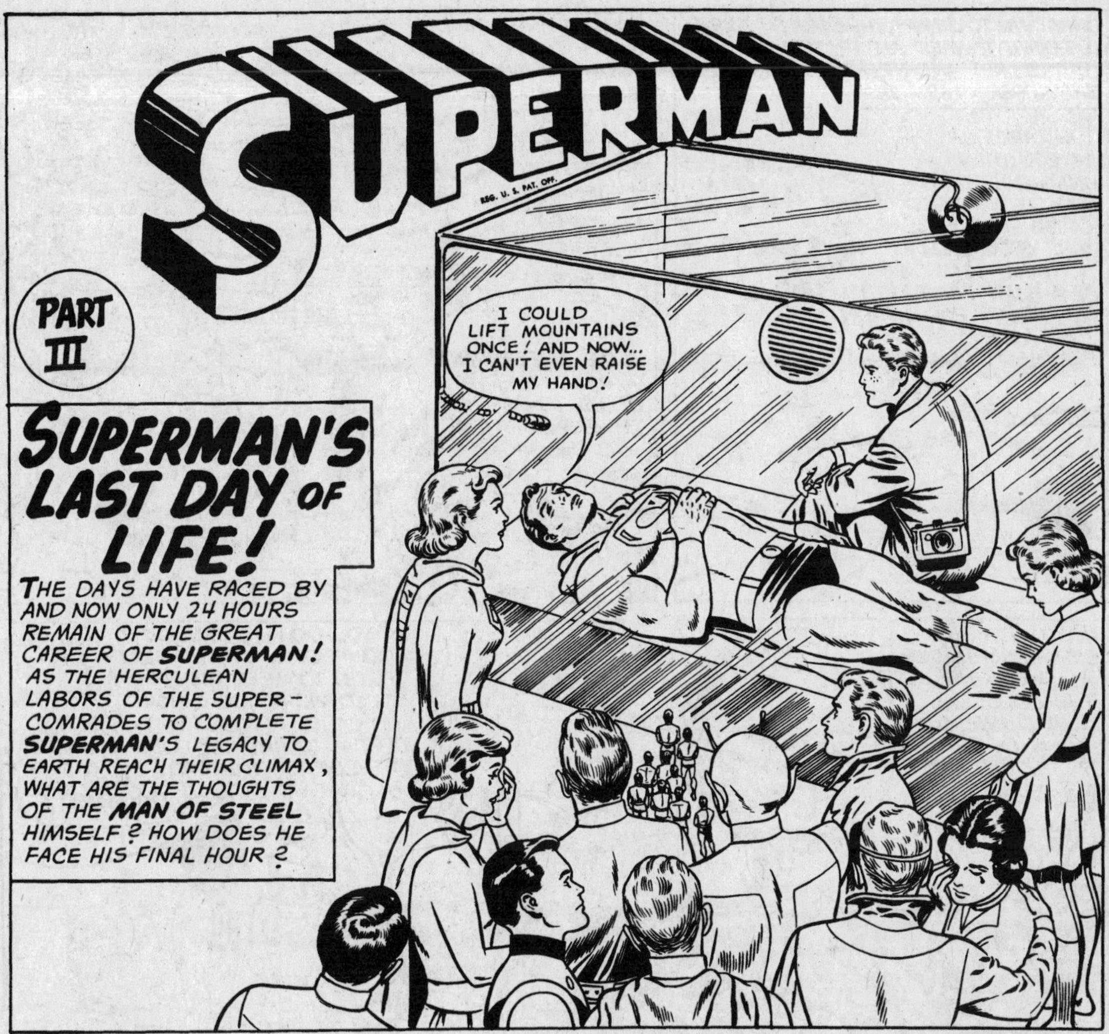
SUPERMAN
REG. U.S. PAT. OFF.
PART III
SUPERMAN'S LAST DAY OF LIFE!
THE DAYS HAVE RACED BY AND NOW ONLY 24 HOURS REMAIN OF THE GREAT CAREER OF SUPERMAN! AS THE HERCULEAN LABORS OF THE SUPER-COMRADES TO COMPLETE SUPERMAN'S LEGACY TO EARTH REACH THEIR CLIMAX, WHAT ARE THE THOUGHTS OF THE MAN OF STEEL HIMSELF? HOW DOES HE FACE HIS FINAL HOUR?
I COULD LIFT MOUNTAINS ONCE! AND NOW... I CAN'T EVEN RAISE MY HAND!

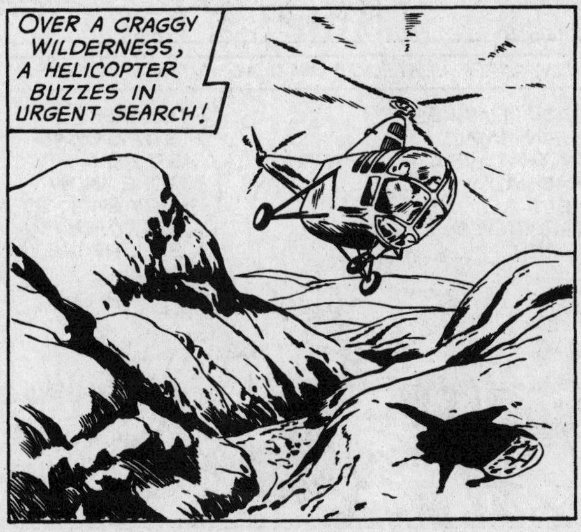
OVER A CRAGGY WILDERNESS, A HELICOPTER BUZZES IN URGENT SEARCH!

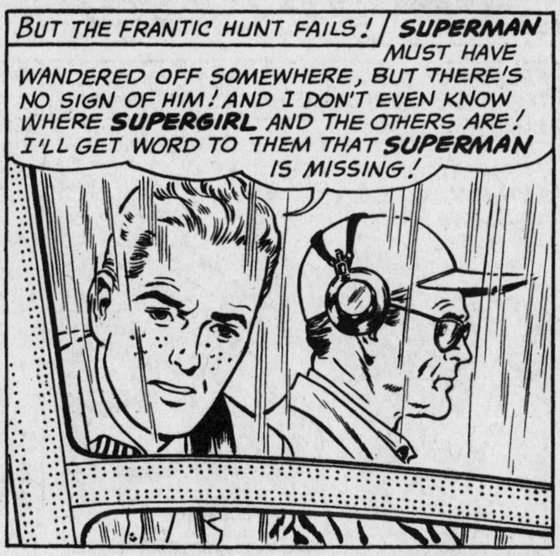
BUT THE FRANTIC HUNT FAILS! SUPERMAN MUST HAVE WANDERED OFF SOMEWHERE, BUT THERE'S NO SIGN OF HIM! AND I DON'T EVEN KNOW WHERE SUPERGIRL AND THE OTHERS ARE! I'LL GET WORD TO THEM THAT SUPERMAN IS MISSING!

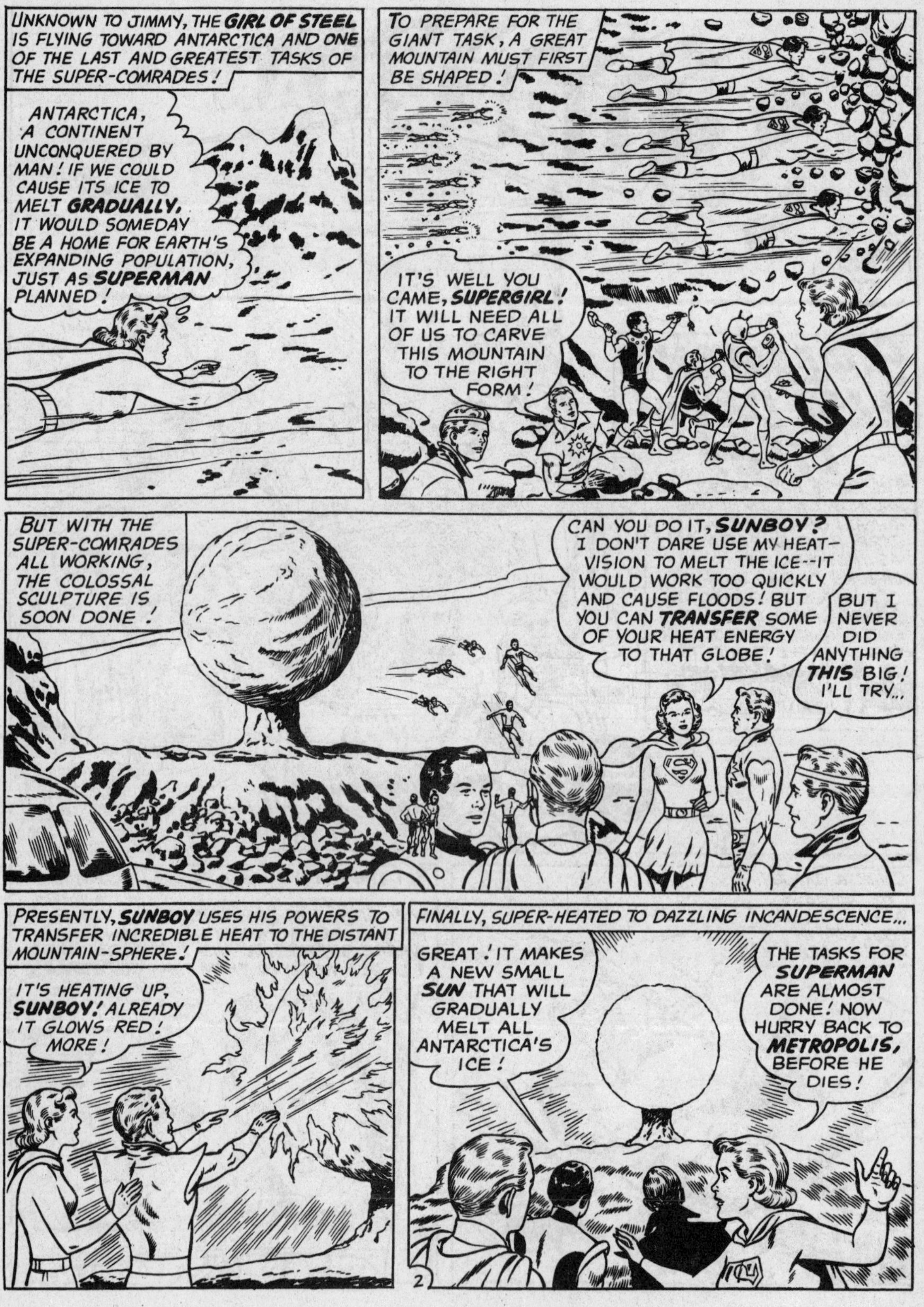
UNKNOWN TO JIMMY, THE GIRL OF STEEL IS FLYING TOWARD ANTARCTICA AND ONE OF THE LAST AND GREATEST TASKS OF THE SUPER-COMRADES!
ANTARCTICA, A CONTINENT UNCONQUERED BY MAN! IF WE COULD CAUSE ITS ICE TO MELT GRADUALLY, IT WOULD SOMEDAY BE A HOME FOR EARTH'S EXPANDING POPULATION, JUST AS SUPERMAN PLANNED!
TO PREPARE FOR THE GIANT TASK, A GREAT MOUNTAIN MUST FIRST BE SHAPED!
IT'S WELL YOU CAME, SUPERGIRL! IT WILL NEED ALL OF US TO CARVE THIS MOUNTAIN TO THE RIGHT FORM!
BUT WITH THE SUPER-COMRADES ALL WORKING, THE COLOSSAL SCULPTURE IS SOON DONE!
CAN YOU DO IT, SUNBOY? I DON'T DARE USE MY HEAT-VISION TO MELT THE ICE--IT WOULD WORK TOO QUICKLY AND CAUSE FLOODS! BUT YOU CAN TRANSFER SOME OF YOUR HEAT ENERGY TO THAT GLOBE!
BUT I NEVER DID ANYTHING THIS BIG! I'LL TRY...
PRESENTLY, SUNBOY USES HIS POWERS TO TRANSFER INCREDIBLE HEAT TO THE DISTANT MOUNTAIN-SPHERE!
IT'S HEATING UP, SUNBOY! ALREADY IT GLOWS RED! MORE!
FINALLY, SUPER-HEATED TO DAZZLING INCANDESCENCE...
GREAT! IT MAKES A NEW SMALL SUN THAT WILL GRADUALLY MELT ALL ANTARCTICA'S ICE!
THE TASKS FOR SUPERMAN ARE ALMOST DONE! NOW HURRY BACK TO METROPOLIS, BEFORE HE DIES!
2

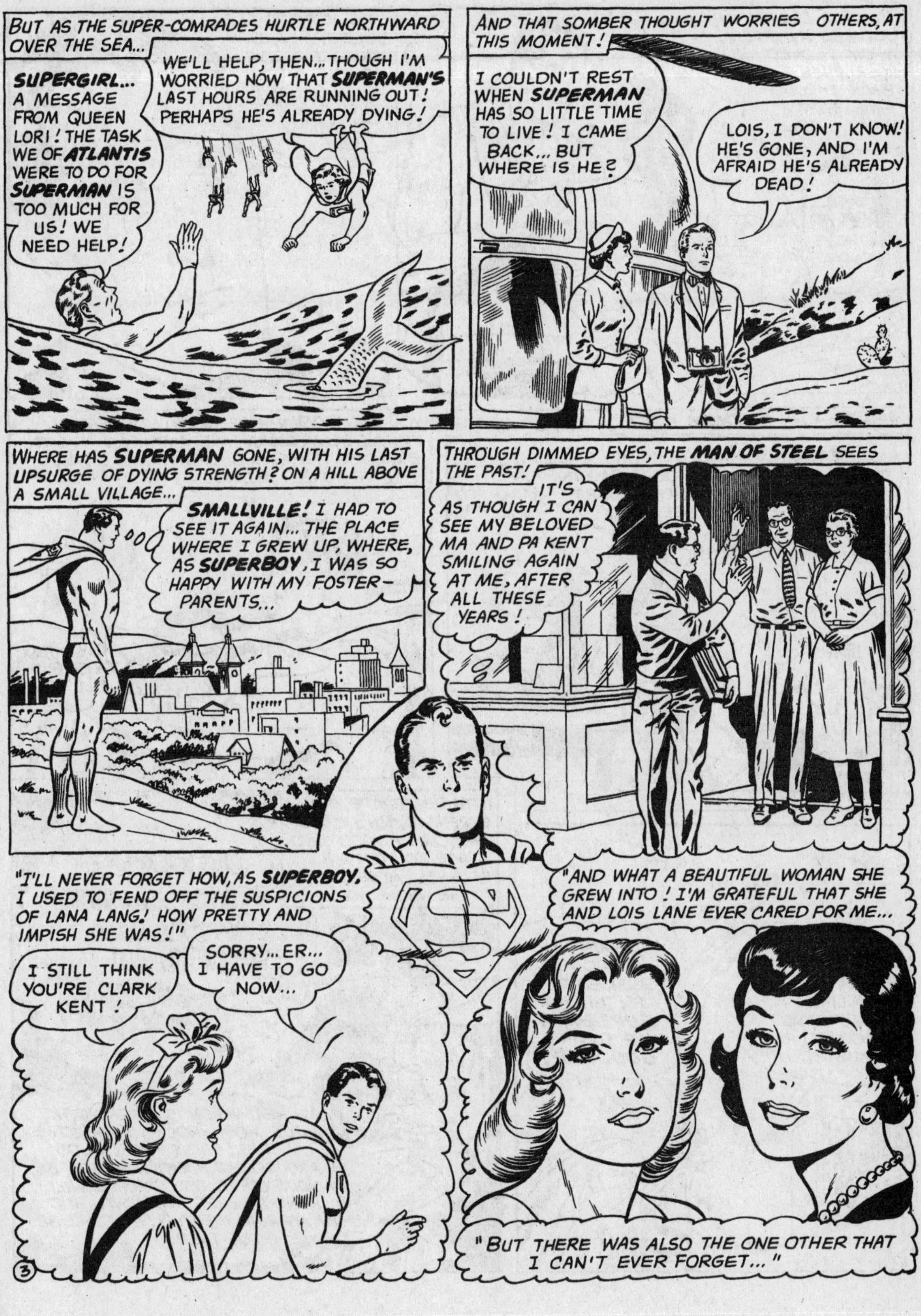

BUT AS THE SUPER-COMRADES HURTLE NORTHWARD OVER THE SEA...
SUPERGIRL... A MESSAGE FROM QUEEN LORI! THE TASK WE OF ATLANTIS WERE TO DO FOR SUPERMAN IS TOO MUCH FOR US! WE NEED HELP!
WE'LL HELP, THEN... THOUGH I'M WORRIED NOW THAT SUPERMAN'S LAST HOURS ARE RUNNING OUT! PERHAPS HE'S ALREADY DYING!
AND THAT SOMBER THOUGHT WORRIES OTHERS, AT THIS MOMENT!
I COULDN'T REST WHEN SUPERMAN HAS SO LITTLE TIME TO LIVE! I CAME BACK... BUT WHERE IS HE?
LOIS, I DON'T KNOW! HE'S GONE, AND I'M AFRAID HE'S ALREADY DEAD!
WHERE HAS SUPERMAN GONE, WITH HIS LAST UPSURGE OF DYING STRENGTH? ON A HILL ABOVE A SMALL VILLAGE...
SMALLVILLE! I HAD TO SEE IT AGAIN... THE PLACE WHERE I GREW UP, WHERE, AS SUPERBOY, I WAS SO HAPPY WITH MY FOSTER-PARENTS...
THROUGH DIMMED EYES, THE MAN OF STEEL SEES THE PAST!
IT'S AS THOUGH I CAN SEE MY BELOVED MA AND PA KENT SMILING AGAIN AT ME, AFTER ALL THESE YEARS!
"I'LL NEVER FORGET HOW, AS SUPERBOY, I USED TO FEND OFF THE SUSPICIONS OF LANA LANG! HOW PRETTY AND IMPISH SHE WAS!"
I STILL THINK YOU'RE CLARK KENT!
SORRY... ER... I HAVE TO GO NOW...
3
"AND WHAT A BEAUTIFUL WOMAN SHE GREW INTO! I'M GRATEFUL THAT SHE AND LOIS LANE EVER CARED FOR ME...
"BUT THERE WAS ALSO THE ONE OTHER THAT I CAN'T EVER FORGET..."

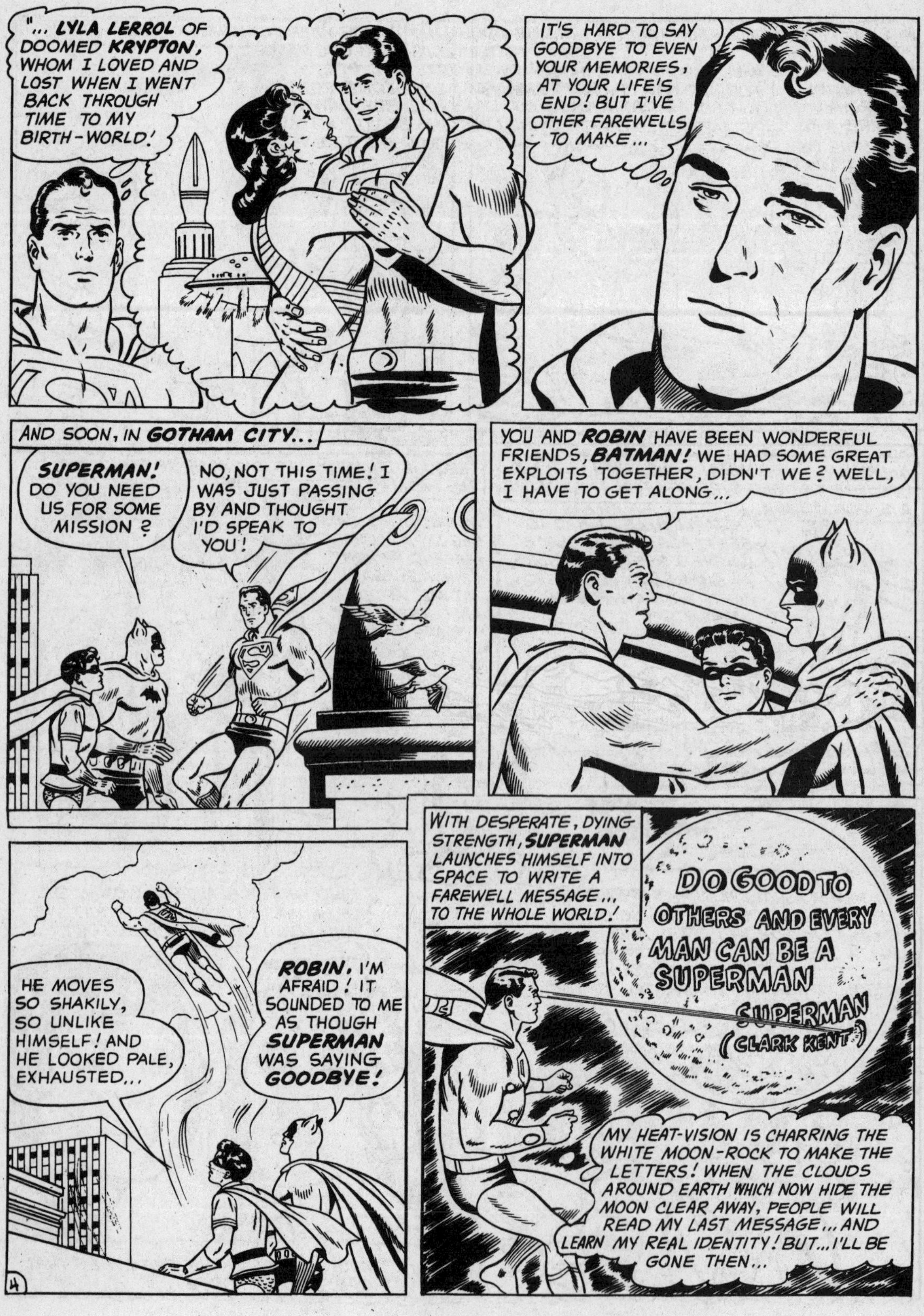
"... LYLA LERROL OF DOOMED KRYPTON, WHOM I LOVED AND LOST WHEN I WENT BACK THROUGH TIME TO MY BIRTH-WORLD!
IT'S HARD TO SAY GOODBYE TO EVEN YOUR MEMORIES, AT YOUR LIFE'S END! BUT I'VE OTHER FAREWELLS TO MAKE...
AND SOON, IN GOTHAM CITY...
SUPERMAN! DO YOU NEED US FOR SOME MISSION?
NO, NOT THIS TIME! I WAS JUST PASSING BY AND THOUGHT I'D SPEAK TO YOU!
YOU AND ROBIN HAVE BEEN WONDERFUL FRIENDS, BATMAN! WE HAD SOME GREAT EXPLOITS TOGETHER, DIDN'T WE? WELL, I HAVE TO GET ALONG...
HE MOVES SO SHAKILY, SO UNLIKE HIMSELF! AND HE LOOKED PALE, EXHAUSTED...
ROBIN, I'M AFRAID! IT SOUNDED TO ME AS THOUGH SUPERMAN WAS SAYING GOODBYE!
4
WITH DESPERATE, DYING STRENGTH, SUPERMAN LAUNCHES HIMSELF INTO SPACE TO WRITE A FAREWELL MESSAGE... TO THE WHOLE WORLD!
DO GOOD TO OTHERS AND EVERY MAN CAN BE A SUPERMAN
SUPERMAN (CLARK KENT)
MY HEAT-VISION IS CHARRING THE WHITE MOON-ROCK TO MAKE THE LETTERS! WHEN THE CLOUDS AROUND EARTH WHICH NOW HIDE THE MOON CLEAR AWAY, PEOPLE WILL READ MY LAST MESSAGE... AND LEARN MY REAL IDENTITY! BUT... I'LL BE GONE THEN...

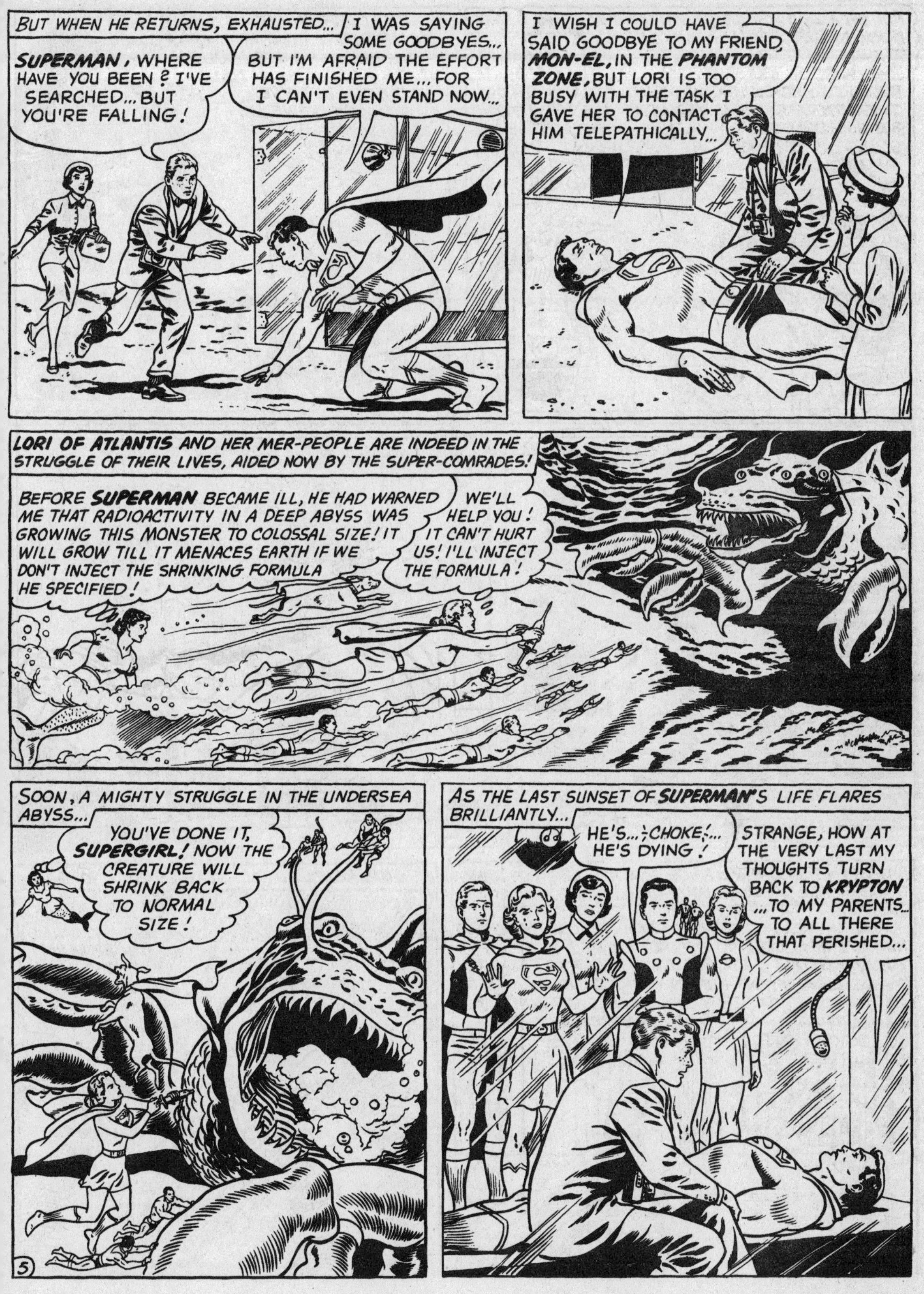
BUT WHEN HE RETURNS, EXHAUSTED...
SUPERMAN, WHERE HAVE YOU BEEN? I'VE SEARCHED... BUT YOU'RE FALLING!
I WAS SAYING SOME GOODBYES... BUT I'M AFRAID THE EFFORT HAS FINISHED ME... FOR I CAN'T EVEN STAND NOW...
I WISH I COULD HAVE SAID GOODBYE TO MY FRIEND, MON-EL, IN THE PHANTOM ZONE, BUT LORI IS TOO BUSY WITH THE TASK I GAVE HER TO CONTACT HIM TELEPATHICALLY...
LORI OF ATLANTIS AND HER MER-PEOPLE ARE INDEED IN THE STRUGGLE OF THEIR LIVES, AIDED NOW BY THE SUPER-COMRADES!
BEFORE SUPERMAN BECAME ILL, HE HAD WARNED ME THAT RADIOACTIVITY IN A DEEP ABYSS WAS GROWING THIS MONSTER TO COLOSSAL SIZE! IT WILL GROW TILL IT MENACES EARTH IF WE DON'T INJECT THE SHRINKING FORMULA HE SPECIFIED!
WE'LL HELP YOU! IT CAN'T HURT US! I'LL INJECT THE FORMULA!
SOON, A MIGHTY STRUGGLE IN THE UNDERSEA ABYSS...
YOU'VE DONE IT, SUPERGIRL! NOW THE CREATURE WILL SHRINK BACK TO NORMAL SIZE!
5
AS THE LAST SUNSET OF SUPERMAN'S LIFE FLARES BRILLIANTLY...
HE'S... -CHOKE-... HE'S DYING!
STRANGE, HOW AT THE VERY LAST MY THOUGHTS TURN BACK TO KRYPTON ...TO MY PARENTS... TO ALL THERE THAT PERISHED...

AND SUDDENLY, THE DYING WHISPER INSPIRES A LAST HOPE IN *SUPERGIRL'S* MIND!

BRAINIAC 5, YOU SAID YOUR RESEARCH PROVED THAT NOTHING ON *EARTH* COULD CURE *VIRUS X!* BUT COULDN'T THERE HAVE BEEN SOMETHING ON *KRYPTON* THAT COULD CURE IT?

HMM... I DIDN'T THINK OF THAT! THAT SCIENTIST OF *KRYPTON* WHO WAS SEEKING A CURE... MAYBE HE *FOUND* IT BEFORE HIS WORLD PERISHED!

BUT *KRYPTON* PERISHED YEARS AGO... IF THERE WAS A CURE, IT'S BEYOND REACH NOW!

NOT IF I WENT BACK TO *KRYPTON* ...*THROUGH TIME!*

WITH AWESOME POWER, THE *GIRL OF STEEL* HURLS HERSELF THROUGH SPACE TO BREAK THE TIME-BARRIER...

962 1962 1961 1960 1959 1958 1957 1956 1955 1954 1953 1952 1951

... AND EMERGES IN THE *KRYPTON* OF THE PAST!

KRYPTON, THE LOST WORLD OF MY PEOPLE! BUT THERE'S NO TIME TO WASTE... I HAVE TO FIND THAT SCIENTIST, *THARB-EL,* WHO WAS SEEKING THE CURE FOR *VIRUS X!*

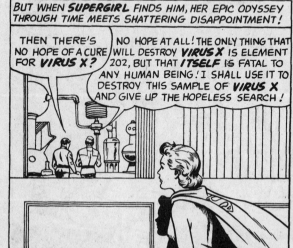

BUT WHEN *SUPERGIRL* FINDS HIM, HER EPIC ODYSSEY THROUGH TIME MEETS SHATTERING DISAPPOINTMENT!

THEN THERE'S NO HOPE OF A CURE FOR *VIRUS X?*

NO HOPE AT ALL! THE ONLY THING THAT WILL DESTROY *VIRUS X* IS ELEMENT 202, BUT THAT *ITSELF* IS FATAL TO ANY HUMAN BEING! I SHALL USE IT TO DESTROY THIS SAMPLE OF *VIRUS X* AND GIVE UP THE HOPELESS SEARCH!

AS *SUPERGIRL* NUMBLY FLASHES BACK TO 1962...

I HATE TO GO BACK TO DYING *SUPERMAN* WITH THIS NEWS! BUT I...I MUST TELL HIM THE TRUTH...

6

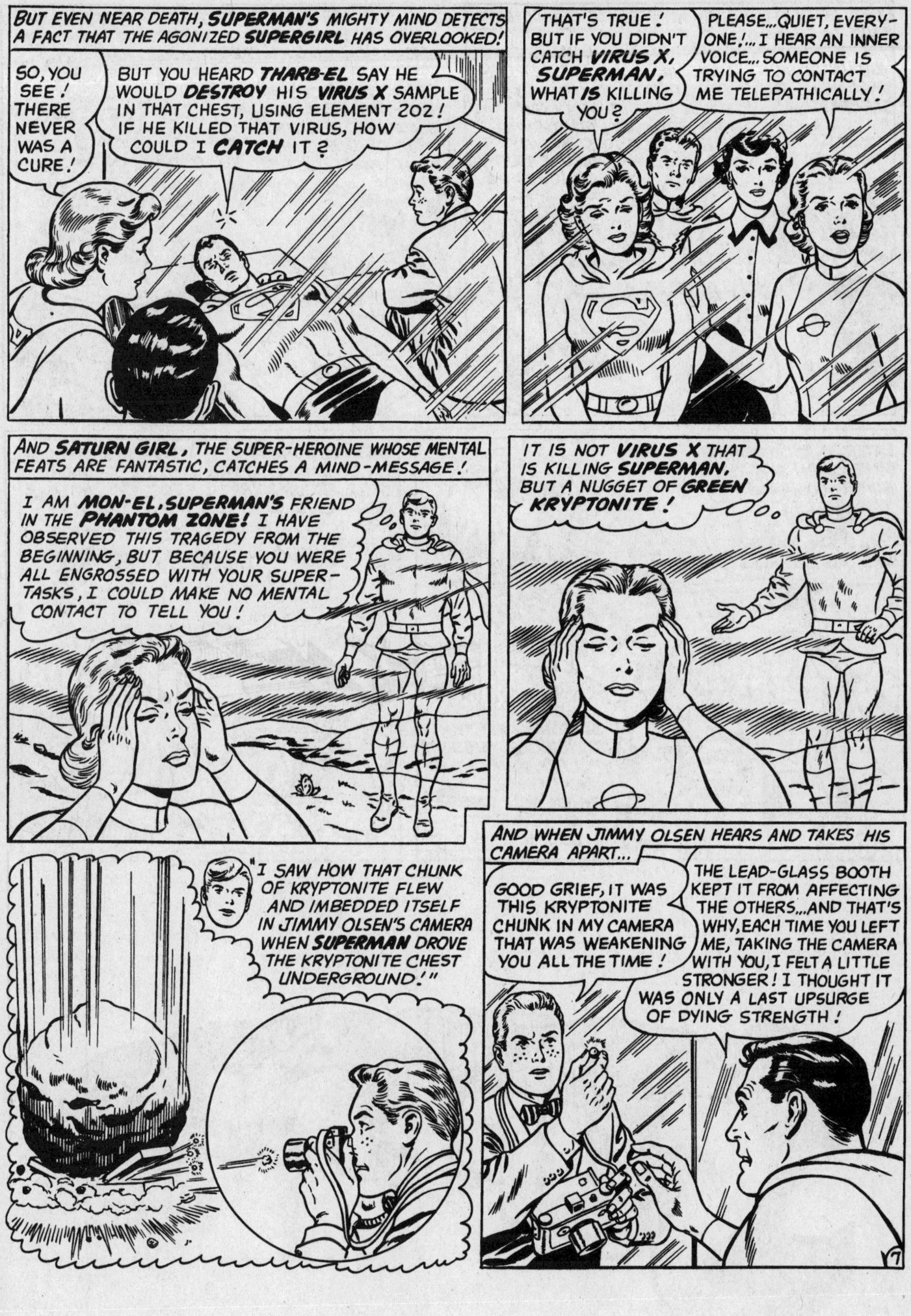
BUT EVEN NEAR DEATH, SUPERMAN'S MIGHTY MIND DETECTS A FACT THAT THE AGONIZED SUPERGIRL HAS OVERLOOKED!
SO, YOU SEE! THERE NEVER WAS A CURE!
BUT YOU HEARD THARB-EL SAY HE WOULD DESTROY HIS VIRUS X SAMPLE IN THAT CHEST, USING ELEMENT 202! IF HE KILLED THAT VIRUS, HOW COULD I CATCH IT?
THAT'S TRUE! BUT IF YOU DIDN'T CATCH VIRUS X, SUPERMAN, WHAT IS KILLING YOU?
PLEASE... QUIET, EVERYONE!... I HEAR AN INNER VOICE... SOMEONE IS TRYING TO CONTACT ME TELEPATHICALLY!
AND SATURN GIRL, THE SUPER-HEROINE WHOSE MENTAL FEATS ARE FANTASTIC, CATCHES A MIND-MESSAGE!
I AM MON-EL, SUPERMAN'S FRIEND IN THE PHANTOM ZONE! I HAVE OBSERVED THIS TRAGEDY FROM THE BEGINNING, BUT BECAUSE YOU WERE ALL ENGROSSED WITH YOUR SUPER-TASKS, I COULD MAKE NO MENTAL CONTACT TO TELL YOU!
IT IS NOT VIRUS X THAT IS KILLING SUPERMAN, BUT A NUGGET OF GREEN KRYPTONITE!
"I SAW HOW THAT CHUNK OF KRYPTONITE FLEW AND IMBEDDED ITSELF IN JIMMY OLSEN'S CAMERA WHEN SUPERMAN DROVE THE KRYPTONITE CHEST UNDERGROUND!"
AND WHEN JIMMY OLSEN HEARS AND TAKES HIS CAMERA APART...
GOOD GRIEF, IT WAS THIS KRYPTONITE CHUNK IN MY CAMERA THAT WAS WEAKENING YOU ALL THE TIME!
THE LEAD-GLASS BOOTH KEPT IT FROM AFFECTING THE OTHERS... AND THAT'S WHY, EACH TIME YOU LEFT ME, TAKING THE CAMERA WITH YOU, I FELT A LITTLE STRONGER! I THOUGHT IT WAS ONLY A LAST UPSURGE OF DYING STRENGTH!
7

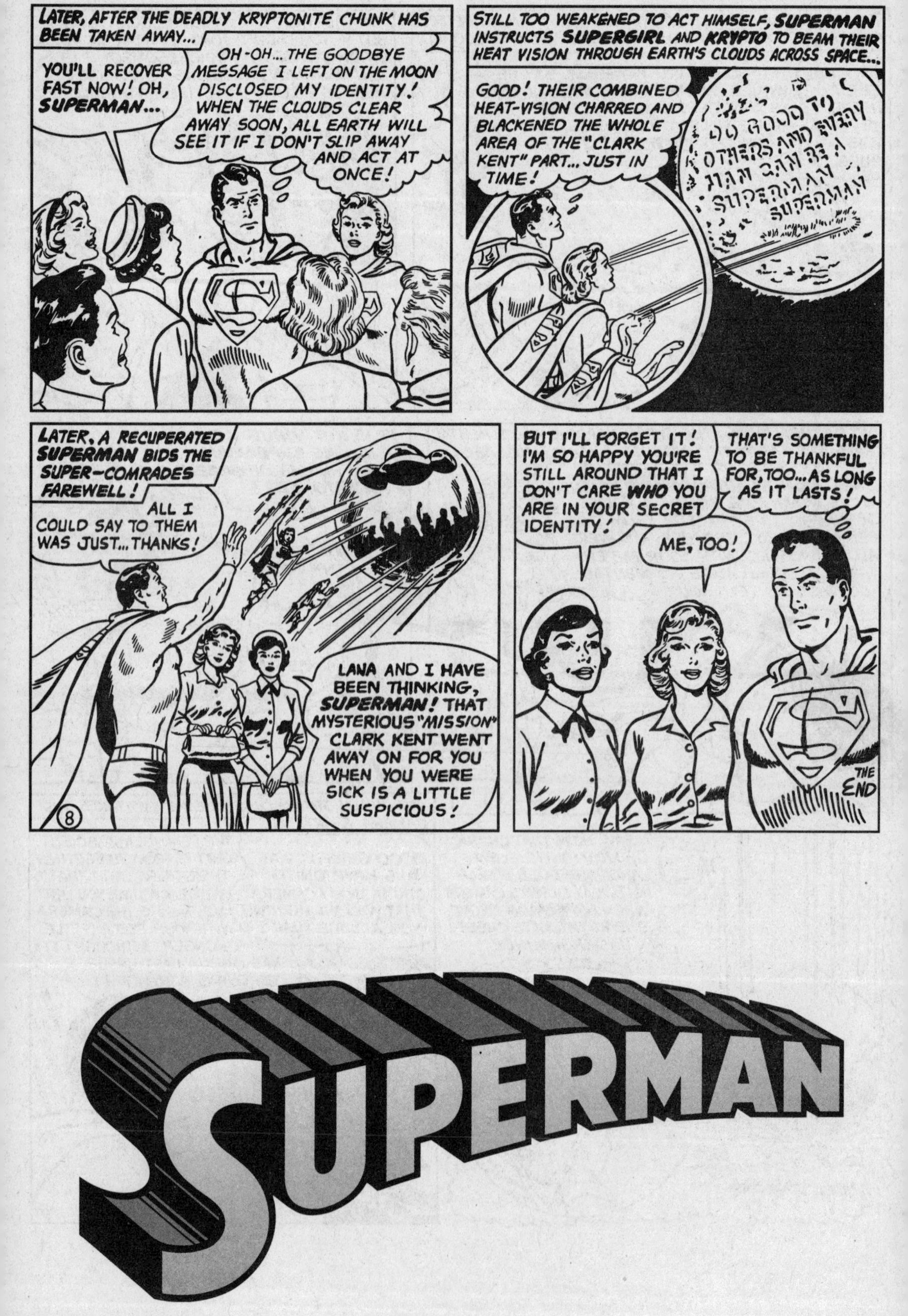
LATER, AFTER THE DEADLY KRYPTONITE CHUNK HAS BEEN TAKEN AWAY...
YOU'LL RECOVER FAST NOW! OH, SUPERMAN...
OH-OH... THE GOODBYE MESSAGE I LEFT ON THE MOON DISCLOSED MY IDENTITY! WHEN THE CLOUDS CLEAR AWAY SOON, ALL EARTH WILL SEE IT IF I DON'T SLIP AWAY AND ACT AT ONCE!
STILL TOO WEAKENED TO ACT HIMSELF, SUPERMAN INSTRUCTS SUPERGIRL AND KRYPTO TO BEAM THEIR HEAT VISION THROUGH EARTH'S CLOUDS ACROSS SPACE...
GOOD! THEIR COMBINED HEAT-VISION CHARRED AND BLACKENED THE WHOLE AREA OF THE "CLARK KENT" PART... JUST IN TIME!
LATER, A RECUPERATED SUPERMAN BIDS THE SUPER-COMRADES FAREWELL!
ALL I COULD SAY TO THEM WAS JUST... THANKS!
LANA AND I HAVE BEEN THINKING, SUPERMAN! THAT MYSTERIOUS "MISSION" CLARK KENT WENT AWAY ON FOR YOU WHEN YOU WERE SICK IS A LITTLE SUSPICIOUS!
8
BUT I'LL FORGET IT! I'M SO HAPPY YOU'RE STILL AROUND THAT I DON'T CARE WHO YOU ARE IN YOUR SECRET IDENTITY!
ME, TOO!
THAT'S SOMETHING TO BE THANKFUL FOR, TOO... AS LONG AS IT LASTS!
THE END

SUPERMAN

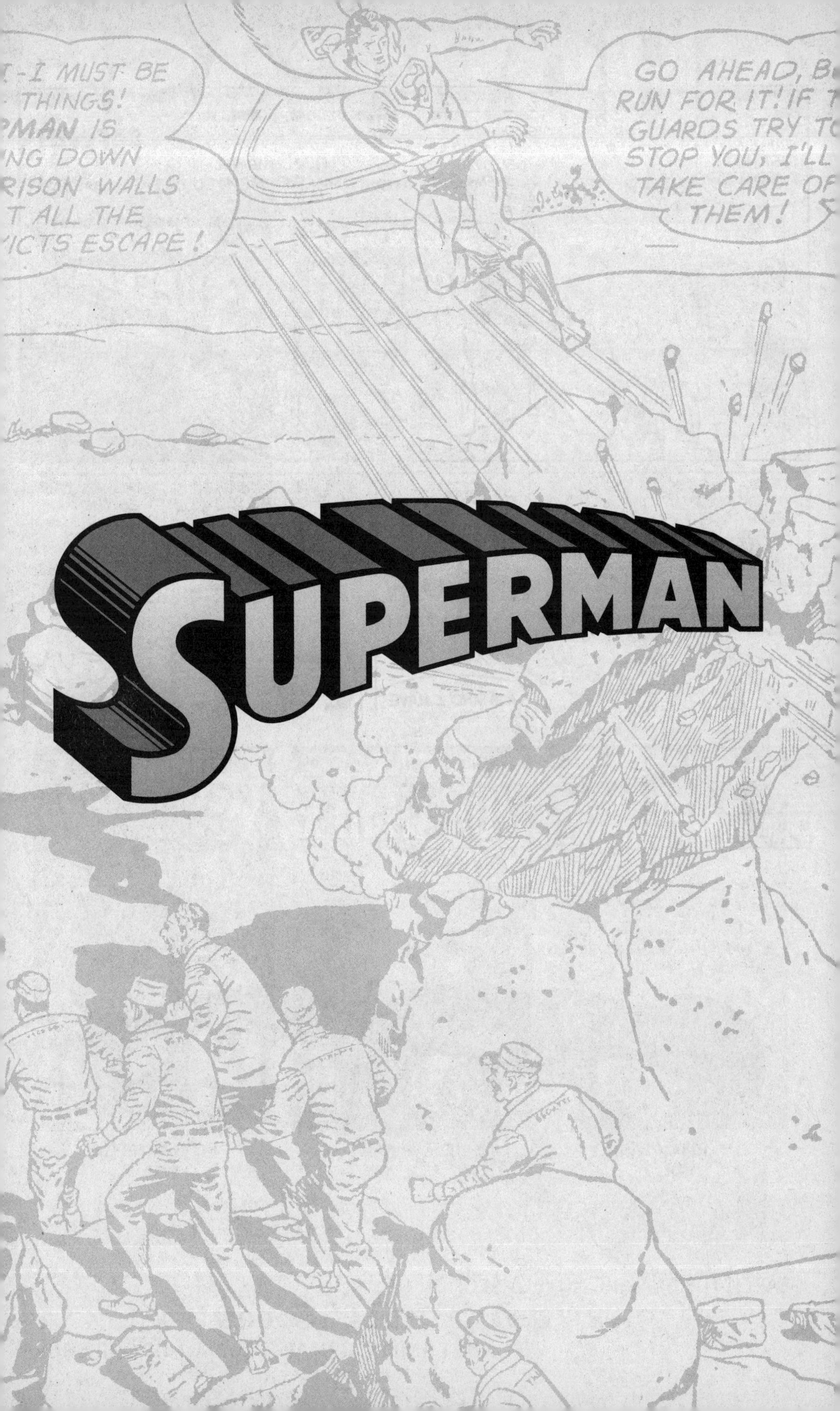
-I MUST BE THINGS! PMAN IS NG DOWN RISON WALLS T ALL THE ICTS ESCAPE!
GO AHEAD, B RUN FOR IT! IF T GUARDS TRY TO STOP YOU, I'LL TAKE CARE OF THEM!
SUPERMAN

SHOWCASE
PRESENTS

OVER 500 PAGES OF DC'S CLASSIC HEROES AND STORIES PRESENTED IN EACH VOLUME!

**GREEN LANTERN
VOL. 1**

**SUPERMAN
VOL. 1**

**SUPERMAN
VOL. 2**

**SUPERMAN FAMILY
VOL. 1**

**JONAH HEX
VOL. 1**

**METAMORPHO
VOL. 1**

SEARCH THE GRAPHIC NOVELS SECTION OF
www.DCCOMICS.com
FOR ART AND INFORMATION ON ALL OF OUR BOOKS!